Baltimore County Families, 1659 – 1759

Baltimore County Families,

1659 – 1759

By Robert W. Barnes

CLEARFIELD

Reprinted for
Clearfield Company, Inc. by
Genealogical Publishing Co., Inc.
Baltimore, Maryland
1996, 1998, 2002

Index by Bill and Martha Reamy

Dedicated To

MARY K. MEYER

CONTENTS

INTRODUCTION

This book is dedicated to Mary K. Meyer, for many years the genealogical librarian at the Maryland Historical Society. During her years of service, Mrs. Meyer gave help and encouragement to countless genealogists, helped formulate plans for the reactivation of the Committee on Genealogy, saw work begin on the Norris Harris Church Register Index, edited the genealogical section of the Maryland Historical Magazine, and finally served as editor of the Maryland Magazine of Genealogy.

She is a Charter Member of the Maryland Genealogical Society, and she helped to start the Genealogical Council of Maryland - an umbrella organization made up of representatives from state and local genealogical societies and libraries in Maryland. One of her ideas, a statewide inventory of Bible records, is being implemented by a number of cooperating societies. As of this writing she is active in the Anne Arundel County Genealogical Society.

Her writings and compilations have been of inestimable help to family historians. Perhaps the most monumental of these has been the three-volume Passenger and Immigration List Index, on which she collaborated with P. William Filby. She has helped to compile Who's Who in Genealogy and Heraldry, and has also compiled Genealogical Research in Maryland: A Guide, and several editions of Meyer's Directory of Genealogical Societies in the U.S.A. and Canada. Of special interest to Marylanders has been Divorces and Names Changed in Maryland by Act of the Legislature, 1634-1854.

For her services to genealogists all over the country, this book is respectfully dedicated to Mary K. Meyer.

Baltimore County Families, 1659 - 1759 is the story of the hundreds of families - and thousands of individuals - who settled along the banks of the Patapsco, Gunpowder, and Susquehanna rivers and their tributaries during the first hundred years of the county's existence. The exact date of the founding of Baltimore County is not known, but the county is mentioned in the records of the Province of Maryland starting in 1659. Originally the county embraced all or parts of present-day Anne Arundel, Carroll, Harford, and Cecil counties. The earliest settlements were along the waterways, but as the seventeenth century gave way to the eighteenth, estates were sited farther inland.

Original settlers came from Southern Maryland - notably Anne Arundel and Calvert counties - and from the Eastern Shore and from Virginia. From the middle third of the eighteenth century a growing stream of settlers also came from Pennsylvania. Other settlers throughout the period under study came directly from the British Isles, often as indentured servants or transported felons. Although it is popularly believed that servants and convicts often ran away and changed their names, or died, a number of Maryland families, such as the Adys, McQueens, Peregoys, Pilgrims, and Shoebridges, trace their origin in Baltimore County to servants, convicts, or Jacobite rebels. Other families such as the Cradocks, Gorsuches, Luxes, Moales, and Thornboroughs, are descended from the yeoman, gentry, or professional classes of seventeenth-century England, while the Buchanans, Dallases, Lyons and Walkers have established Scottish ancestry.

Because of the vast number of families included in this work it has not been possible to carry any one family much later than 1759. Parish registers, administration bonds, administration accounts, inventories and wills have been abstracted and used as the nucleus for each family group. Court records and deeds have been combed (but not completely abstracted) to provide additional insights into activities of the settlers. If there is one serious omission from the sources used, it is that the land records were not completely abstracted.

The family histories have been constructed from a series of family groups starting with the earliest known progenitor, followed by his children, then grandchildren, and in some cases, great-grandchildren. Following the biographical data on the parents, the family group concludes with a list of the known children of those parents. Some of those children are carried forward as heads of their own family groups. Other children, who themselves died childless, are not carried forward. Married daughters are carried forward under their husbands' family groups.

Where there are several family groups, each group, starting with the first progenitor, has been given a number (found in parentheses following the progenitor's name). Subsequent generations have their own numbers and also refer back to the father's number so that a line may be traced back to the original settler quickly.

It has sometimes happened that some surnames (e.g., Smith, Brown, Jones, Taylor, etc.) contain several distinct families. In such cases, all progenitors are successively numbered, but when the account of one family has been completed, the progenitor of the next family will be designated as "no known relation to any of the above."

Documentation is given following each family group, although in cases where published accounts of families have appeared these are mentioned in a short paragraph introducing that family. After the data for each family group the numbered and unnumbered references used in compiling the information are listed. All references are explained more fully in the Bibliography.

Every effort has been made to resolve inconsistencies and variations in spelling of names. An individual's name may be spelled one way in one part of the text and elsewhere have a slightly different spelling (e.g. Johanna and Johannah). Many times variations have been cross-referenced, but users of the book are reminded to look for variations of the name in the index.

As work on the book has progressed a number of ideas for additional research have presented themselves. Now that a "data base" of early Baltimore County families has been created, it would be interesting to investigate how many heads of families came as immigrants paying their own way, how many came as indentured servants, and how many came as involuntary immigrants who came only because the alternative to coming to Maryland was hanging in England.

ACKNOWLEDGMENTS

Many people have helped to make this work possible, and I
am deeply indebted to Bill and Martha Reamy and Marlene Bates
for their many hours of assistance with the Index. Without their
help publication of this book would have been delayed for at least
a year, and more likely for two years.

I am also grateful to my wife, Cathy, and my family for
their patience. Thanks also go to three special friends, Robert
K. Headley, Jr., Edna A. Kanely, and Peggy Keigler, for their
encouragement.

A number of genealogists have made material available over
the years. Some of these people I have never met and with some
I have lost contact. Nevertheless, I am grateful to them for
their help and suggestions with specific families. Many of them
are mentioned in the text or the Bibliography, but I would like
to list those who have been especially helpful here. Their
names are given alphabetically, followed by (in parentheses) the
names of the families with which they have been concerned.
Thanks go to: Mr. and Mrs. H. H. Arnold (Arnold, Wells); Mrs.
Bruce Baher (Treadway); Walter V. Ball (Butterworth, Clark);
Mr. and Mrs. Gerald Barnett (Dallas, Eaglestone); Jean Kolb
Brandau (Eaglestone); Peter S. Craig; Clifford J. Harryman
(Harryman); Mrs. William Hearn (Amos); Edna A. Kanely (Barton,
Galloway); Margaret Smith Keigler (Dallahyde, Freeborne, Miles,
Slade, Tolley); the late Dr. Richard B. Miller (Bosley, Bowen,
Dimmitt); Robert T. Nave (Ford, Tipton); William D. Patrick (Cor-
bin); Shirley Reightler (Corbin, Marsh); Ella Rowe (Ady, Clark);
Edith Ray Saul (Burgain, Gatch); J. Bartley Smith (Thornborough);
Cynthia Snider (Thornborough); and Mrs. Richard Turley (Baker).

I would like to express my appreciation to the staffs of
the following institutions for their help and assistance: the
Baltimore City Archives, Enoch Pratt Free Library (most notably
the microform and Maryland departments), the Maryland Historical
Society, and the George Peabody Library (now part of the Eisen-
hower Library of the Johns Hopkins University), all of Baltimore;
to the staff of the Maryland State Archives (formerly the Hall
of Records) in Annapolis, and to the many helpful staff members
of the Library of Congress and the Library of the Daughters of
the American Revolution, both in Washington, D. C.

Finally, I would like to acknowledge the technical assistance
and support from the Genealogical Publishing Company, especially
Michael Tepper, Eileen Perkins, and Joe Garonzik.

Robert W. Barnes
Perry Hall, Md.
July 1988

ABBREVIATIONS AND SYMBOLS USED

(?), (---)	- used to denote an unknown name
a.	- acre
ackn.	- acknowledged
adm.	- administered, administration
admin., admnx.	- administrator, administratrix
atty.	- attorney
bapt.	- baptized
bast.	- bastard, bastardy
bd.	- bound
cert.	- certificate
ch.	- child, children
conv.	- conveyed (as land)
d.	- died
est.	- estate
exec., extx.	- executor, executrix
f.	- father
ind.	- indicted or individual
inher.	- inheritance, inherited
inv.	- inventory, inventoried
m.	- married
p/a	- power of attorney
pers.	- personalty
pet.	- petition(ed)
res.	- residue, resurveyed
s.	- son
s.-in-law	- son-in-law
surv.	- surveyed, survived
transp.	- transported
val.	- valued

(?), EDWARD, m. 20 Jan. 1703/4 Eliz. Griffith (128).

(?), ELIZABETH, ind. for bast. in June 1731 (29:156).

(?), JOHN, d. by 9 Aug. 1688 when Sarah, now w. of John Hall, adm. the est. (206-10:168).

(?), MARY, serv. to William Few, ind. for bast. in June 1743 (34:185).

(?), MARY, or MARGARET, at William Connell's, ind. for bast. in June 1731 (29:156).

ABBEY, or ABBYSS, EDWARD, d. by 29 Oct. 1748 when admin. bond was posted by Edward Martin with Stephen Onion; est.. admin. by Martin on 15 Sept. 1750; dec. left no relations in Md. (5; 11).

ABBOTT, GEORGE, was transp. to Md. c.1670; in June 1684 surv. 1000 a. Abbott's Forest, which was later held by his heirs (211; 388).

ABELL, JAMES, of Balto. Co., was transp. c.1664 by John Dixon (388).

ABERCROMBIE, ROBERT (1), was in Balto. Co. by 6 Aug. 1756 when he m. Ann Hatton as his 1st w.; m. 2nd by 1772 Salathiel, wid. of Henry Eaglestone and dau. of Jarvis Biddison; his will, 22 Feb. 1784 - 22 May 1784, named w. Salathiel, tract John's Habitation, and ch., John, Mary, Robert, Elizabeth, and Charles; will of wid. Salathiel, 20 May 1802 - 22 Jan. 1803, named dau. Elizabeth Manus and her s. Edward Manus, grandson James Abercrombie, dau. Mary Fauler , s. John, and Otho French with Sarah French as one of the wit.; had iss.: ROBERT; MARY, m. (?) Fauler; JOHN; CHARLES; ELIZABETH, m. by lic. 12 Oct. 1791 Joseph Manus (112; 116; 131; 232).

ABERCROMBIE, ROBERT (2), s. of Robert (1), was in Fairfax Co., Va., by 8 Feb. 1791 when he conv. his portion of John's Habitation to Chainey Hatton and John Hatton of Chainey (231-WG#FF).

ACORNS, JOHN, was fined for getting a bast. ch. on the body of Sarah Buttram in Nov. 1757 (46:74).

ACTON, RICHARD (1), d. by 8 May 1741, having m. Anne Sewell on 11 Dec. 1707 in A. A. Co.; his will, 8 Oct. 1740 - 6 May 1741, named w. Anne, daus. Margaret and Hannah, and grandsons Richard Acton and Richard and Henry Young, with Richard Richson, Edward Norwood, Job Lewis and John Dye as wit.; admin. bond posted 1

Oct. 1747 by extx. Anne, with Henry Lewis; est. admin. 19 Oct.
1748; wid. Ann owned 100 a. Owing's Adventure in 1750; had iss.:
RICHARD, d. c. 1740; MARGARET, m. Sewell Young on 13 Jan. 1736;
HANNAH (4; 11; 110; 133; 153; 263).

ACTON, RICHARD (2), s. of Richard (1) and Anne, d. by 6 Nov.
1740 when admin. bond was posted by George Bailey with William
Hammond and Jno. Stinchcomb; had at least one ch.: RICHARD, who
was alive Oct. 1740 (11; 110).

ADAIR, ROBERT, s. of Dr. Alexander Adair of Kent and Calvert
Cos. by his w. Christiana, only heir of Thomas Sterling of Kent
Co.; he was of age by c.1745; rep. Balto. Co. in the Assembly
in 1768; was in Balto. Co. by 1759 when he purch. 150 a. Selby's
Hope (pt. of a larger tract called Leaf's Cross) from Joshua
Cross; d. c.1768, having m. Martha (?); left sis. Elizabeth,
and Cassandra who m. by 10 June 1778 John Moore of Kent Co.
(79; 80; 81; 231-WG#B; 370).

ADAMS/ADDAMS, RICHARD (1), was in Balto. Co. by Aug. 1666
when he purch. 20 a. on Holman's Creek from John Lee; d. by 20
March 1696 having m. two or three times; m. by 1691 Mary, admnx.
of John Staley; m. by Feb. 1696 Margaret (?); wife in 1697 was
called Mary; in May 1670 purch. 100 a. Phill's Choice from John
and Ann Collier, and in March 1672 purch. 100 a. Neve's Choice
from Philip and Dorothy Macanaday; his will, 9 Feb. 1696 - 20
March 1696, named w. Margaret, s. Charles, granddau. Tamasin
Nowilman, and tract Neve's Choice; est. inv. on 7 May 1697 by
Samuel Sickelmore and Thomas Smith, and val. at £ 163.17.6, with
15,000 lbs. tob. in debts, and filed by execs.; his wid. Mary
and s. Charles; had iss.: RICHARD; CHARLES; poss. a dau. who
was the mother of Tamasin Nowilman (19:146; 94; 96; 98; 121;
138; 206-15:155).

ADAMS, RICHARD (2), s. of Richard (1), was of age in 1692
when listed with his father as a taxable in n. side Gunpowder
Hund.; d. by 8 May 1697 when admin. bond was posted by Charles
Adams with Wm. Lenox and John Boone; est. inv. on 8 May 1697 by
Samuel Sickelmore and Thomas Smith, and val. at £ 42.8.3; m.
by 8 April 1693 Sarah, wid. of John Hall (11; 138; 206-15:155).

ADAMS, CHARLES (3), s. of Richard (1), b. c.1679 as he was not
16 until 1695; admin. est. of his bro. Richard in 1697; came to
possess part of God's Providence and Sarah's Delight (140; 206-
15:155; 211).

ADAMS, DAVID, was transp. to Md. by 1674 and d. by 9 April
1689 when admin. bond was posted by William Cole and Christopher
Gist and Richard Cromwell; est. inv. in 1704 by Jno. Arding and
Edw. Martin and val. at £ 18.11.0 (11; 48:72; 388).

ADAMS, HENRY, in 1742 released to Edward Day 250 a. Taylor's
Mount and Dixon's Choice; in 1750 owned 100 a. Collins Choice
and 50 a. Privilege (77; 153).

ADAMS, MATTHEW, and w. Anne claimed land for service in 1673;
in March 1671/2 he purch. half of Henn's Roost from Thomas and
Margaret Pryor; in June 1673 with w. Anne sold half the lands he
purch. from Pryor to Jonathan Lincoln at Sassafras R. (98; 99;
388).

ADAMS, THOMAS, m. 28 March 1725 Margaret Cambel (133).

ADAMS, WILLIAM, d. by 1699 when his est. was inv. by Francis
Dallahide and Moses Groome and val. at £ 138.8.0, plus 10,000
lbs. tob. in debts (48:19).

ADAMS, WILLIAM, d. by 27 Feb. 1710 when his est. was adm. by admnx. Susanna Adams; adm. on 9 Sept. 1711; and by Susanna Collison on 13 April 1715; Susanna m. as her 2nd husb. William Collison on 3 Dec. 1713 (1; 2; 131).

ADAMS, WILLIAM, was in Md. by 1759 when he was named as a serv. in the inv. of Charles Christie (54:298).

ADKINS, JOHN, d. 1 Oct. 1728 (128:55).

ADKINSON, JOHN, d. 2 March 1728 (128:55).

ADKINSON, JOHN, m. Ann Shepard on 11 Feb. 1734 (128:86).

ADLEMAN, PHILIP, in Balto. Co. by 1750 as owner of 50 a. of Murphy's Retirement; as Philip Edleman, nat. in 1757; m. Margaret (?) by 1761; in 1761 conv. George Meyers 25 a. Idlesburgh and 243 a. Shilling's Folly and Phillipsburgh; conv. 178 a. New Germany to Phillip Baker, and 15 a. Shilling's Folly and part Phillipsburgh to Daniel Adleman (84; 153; 404).

ADY, JOSEPH (1), res. in London and had at least one s.: JOSEPH, bapt. 29 April 1655 (500).

ADY, JOSEPH (2), s. of Joseph (1), was bapt. 29 April 1655 at St. Benet, Paul's Wharf, London, and is prob. the Joseph who m. Mary (?) and had iss.: JOSEPH, bapt. 14 June 1687 at St. Mary Mounthaw, London, and HENRY, bapt. 29 July 1688 at St. Peter's, Paul's Wharf, London (500).

ADY, JOSEPH (3), s. of Joseph (2) and Mary, was bapt. 14 June 1687 at St. Mary Mounthaw, London, and is prob. the Joseph who m. Margaret (?) by whom he had six ch., all bapt. St. Sepulchre, London: OLIVE, bapt. 8 Feb. 1707; HENRY, bapt. 8 May 1709; JOSIAH, bapt. 3 Feb. 1711; WILLIAM, bapt. 11 April 1714; JONATHAN, bapt. 6 Nov. 1715; MARY, bapt. 22 Dec. 1717 (500).

ADY, JONATHAN (4), s. of Joseph (3) and Margaret, bapt. 6 Nov. 1715 in London, is prob. the same Joseph who d. c. Jan. 1800 in Harf. Co., Md.; ind. for theft in 1737, sentenced to death, sentence commuted and transp. to Md., settling in what is now Balto. Co.; m. Rebecca York (dau. of James and Rachel (?) York and gd. of George and Hannah Skelton York) on 4 April 1743; served in Rev. War as a pvt. in Capt. Robert Harris' Co. of the Flying Camp; in 1783 was in Gunpowder Upper and Lower Hundreds, owning 102 a. part Bond's Pleasant Hills; had iss.: RACHEL, b. Dec. 1743, had a s. Thomas Ady b. 23 May 1763; m. Nathan Yearly on 12 Feb. 1767; WILLIAM, b. 23 Aug. 1745; ELIZABETH, b. 23 Aug. 1747; RALPH, b. 14 Dec. 1749; JONATHAN, b. 23 Jan. 1752; MARGARET, b. 16 Aug. 1754, poss. the Margaret who m. John Willson on 22 July 1770; HANNAH, b. 1 Sept. 1756; SARAH, b. 23 Oct. 1758; JAMES, b. 23 Dec. 1760; REBECCA, b. 22 Feb. 1762; JOSHUA, b. 10 April 1767 (131; 243; 296:4; 345:114; 500; 501).

ADY, WILLIAM (5), s. of Jonathan (4) and Rebecca, b. 8 Aug. 1745 or 23 Aug.; living 1793; m. Chloe Standiford on 22 Nov. 1770; in 1783 listed as a cooper in Bush R. Lower Hund , as owner part Friend's Discovery and pt. Colegate's Last Shift, 181 a.; had iss.: CASSANDRA, b. 2 Sept. 1771; m. Humphrey Wilson on 25 Dec. 1791; RALPH, b. 22 Apr. 1773; ANN, b. 25 Aug. 1775; REBECCA, b. 15 Oct. 1779; m. John Preston on 4 Oct. 1804; SOLOMON, b. 27 Jan. 178(?);JONATHAN, b. 27 June 1785, m. Elizabeth McAtee on 4 Aug. 1807;RACHEL, b. 10 Apr. 1787; WILLIAM, b. 26 Dec. 17(?); SAMUEL, b. 24 Oct. 1790; CHLOE, b. 1 Aug. 1793 (131; 353:6; 501).

ADY, JAMES (6), s. of Jonathan (4) and Rebecca (York) Ady,
b. 26 Dec. 1760, d. c.1847, age 87; m. 12 July 1789 Mary Ricketts,
b. 23 Dec. 1767, d. aged 79; served in Rev. War; had iss.: RALPH:
SARAH; HANNAH; MARTHA; THOMAS; JAMES; MARY; WILLIAM H.; AARON;
JOSHUA (354; 501; 502).

ADY, JOSHUA (7), s. of Jonathan (4) and Rebecca (York) Ady,
b. 10 April 1767, may be the Joshua who m. Mary Ford on 6 Nov.
1792 (165).

AIGHFORD, RACHEL, bur. 13 Dec. 1701 at John Kimble's (128:12).

AIKEN (AITKEN), ARCHIBALD, d. test. by 30 May 1768; will dated
11 March 1768 named dau. Ellinor, step-dau. Margaret Kelly; ment.
w., unnamed, to be coexec. with Adam McGaw; had iss.: ELLINOR,
b. 2 Feb. 1756 (112).

ALDER, THOMAS, had iss: THOMAS, b. 13 Feb. 1716; JOSEPH, b.
26 Feb. 1718 (133).

ALEN. See ALLEN.

ALEXANDER, JAMES, m. Lydia Jones 14 Dec. 1757; had iss.:
ELIZABETH, b. 3 Feb. 1759; LYDIA, b. 28 Feb. 1760; RACHEL, b. 27
Nov. 1761 (129).

ALGIRE, JOHN, was in Balto. Co. by 1759 when he was nat. as
John Allgeyer; prob. the Johannes Allgeyer who came from Rothen-
stein, Central Franconia, Bavaria, to Phila. on the ship Fane.
William Hyndman, capt. in 1749; prob. the John Allgeiger who
m. 23 Aug. 1752 Maria Eva Senck in York Co., Penna.; m. 2nd, by
Sept. 1763 Hannah (?); will, 24 Sept. 1763 - 27 May 1764, desc.
himself as a tailor and innholder, named w. Hannah amd ch.: John;
Hannah Peece or Price; Elizabeth; Katherine; Katherine Zimmerman;
Elizabeth Barnet; Margaret Zenk; Mary; Sarah; and Zachariah Zenk;
Hannah stated to have 14 ch. of her own incl. George and John
Zenk; prob. had iss.: JOHN; ELIZABETH; KATHERINE; MARY; and
SARAH (112; 404; 407; 422).

ALGOOD, LYDIA m. William Bashteen; banns pub. March 1699
(129).

ALKEMORE, JOHN, transp. by 1661; in Nov. 1664 agreed to purch.
land from John Collett (93; 388).

ALLBROOK, ROBERT, came to America by 1718 when he was serv.
to Mr. Butterworth; by 1721 was with Robert Clark; by 1723 with
George Rigdon; later went to Cecil Co.; urged to apply for news
of a legacy in Eng., July 1753 (255).

ALLEN, WILLIAM (1), m. Mary (?) by whom he had iss.: SUSANNA,
b. 19 Oct. 1726; WILLIAM, b. 11 March 1728/9; JOHN, b. 21 Jan.
1731; JOSEPH, b. 3 June 1734; d. 3 Sept. 1734; ZACHARIAH, b. 26
Aug. 1735; JOSEPH, b. 11 Aug. 1738; JAMES, b. 1 Feb. 1742; JOSI-
AS, b. 31 Oct. 1745 (128:53, 57, 70, 79, 85, 100; 129:328, 342).

ALLEN, WILLIAM (2), s. of William (1), b. 11 March 1728/9,
prob. the William who m. Elizabeth Jones on 13 Oct. 1752 and had
iss.: ELIZABETH, b. 22 April 1753; JOSEPH, b. 6 July 1755; WILLI-
AM, b. 25 March 1757; ZACHARIAH, b. 18 Dec. 1758 (129:354, 358).

ALLEN, FRANCES, put to care of James Allen in June 1718, may
be same Frances ind. for bast. in Nov. 1730 (22:266; 29:49).

ALLEN, JAMES, d. 22 Jan. 1728 (128:61).

ALLEN, JAMES, m. Jo(?) and had iss.: MARGARET, b. 15 July
1724 (131).

ALLEN, JAMES, m. Mary (?), who d. 11 Aug. 1755; had iss.:
JOHN, b. 23 Oct. 1734; ANN, b. 20 Feb. 1737, d. 1739; JAMES, b.
8 Jan. 1739 (may be the James Allen of Deer Creek named by Rebecca Gladding in Nov. 1756 as the f. of her ch.); REUBEN, b. 7
March 1743; MORDECAI HANBY, b. 9 June 1746; WILLIAM MULLIN, b.
3 May 1748 (41:311; 131).

ALLEN, JOHN, d. by 1683 when his est. adm. by Edward Inglish
(200-70:429).

ALLEN, JOHN, m. Ann Rhodes 24 Nov. 1740; had iss.: RICHARD,
b. 15 Nov. 1741 (prob. the Richard who d. Wilkes Co., N.C., aged
91, whence he imm. from Balto. Co. at an early age, acc. to an
obit in the Wash., D. C. Nat. Intelligencer of 21 Nov. 1832;
m. Nancy Lindsay and was a capt. in the Rev. War) (131; 353).

ALLEN, JOSEPH, d. 8 May 1737 at Swan Cr., having m. Elizabeth
(?); will, 26 Apr. 1737 - 31 May 1737, left entire est. to w.;
had iss.: MARGARET, b. 8 Nov. 1718, d. 20 March 1731 (110; 128:
46, 61).

ALLEN, NATHANIEL, d. 24 Oct. 1733; m. Frances (?) who surv.
him and m. 2nd John Mason; admin. bond posted 12 Nov. 1733 by
admnx. Frances Allen, with Thomas Hatchman and Thomas Sligh,
and admin. on 27 Sept. 1735 and 29 Sept. 1738 by Frances, w. of
John Mason; had iss.: MARY, b. April 1727 (3; 5; 11; 131).

ALLEN, ROBERT, was a taxable in s. side Patapsco Hund. in
1692 (138).

ALLEN, THOMAS, serv., transp. to Balto. Co. by c.1664; claimed
land for service in 1673 (388).

ALLEN, or ALLING, WILLIAM, serv., with three yrs. to serve,
"being much distempered," in inv. of David Hagan's est., made
15 Sept. 1724 (52).

ALLEN, ZACHARIAH, d. 1708 in Balto. Co., having m. Anne (?),
prob. by 25 March 1684 when Zach. and Ann wit. the will of Mar-
garet Tench; d. test. with will, 17 April 1708 - 10 May 1708,
which named s. Joseph and dau. Susanna, with Henry Wriothesley
as exec.; admin. bond posted 3 June 1708 by Wriothesley with
John Ewings and Henry Donahue; est. inv. 13 Nov. 1708 by Francis
Whitehead and Matt. Green and val. at £ .7.7.9; had iss., b. in
St. James and All Hallows Parishes in A. A. Co.: SUSANNA, b. 1
Jan. 1691; JOSEPH, b. 26 Dec. 1692; BENJAMIN, b. 30 Jan. 1695;
MARGARET, b. 15 Oct. 1697 (11; 51; 121; 122; 219-1; 219-3).

ALLENDER, JOSHUA, d. c.1748 in Balto. or Cecil Co., having m.
Mary (?) who m. as her 2nd husb. Bezaleel Foster on 10 Dec. 1749;
will, 6 March 1748 - 15 April 1748 (dated in Cecil, or in Balto.
Co.), named bro.'s s., Joshua, and his own ch.: William (eld. s.).
Mary, Joshua, and Nicholas (ygst. s.); Robert Siars, and exec.
Thomas Ellett; admin. bond posted 15 April 1748 by extx. Mary
Allender, with Thomas and Joseph Allender; est. adm. on 25 March
1749, by which date one of his ch. had d.; bond posted Aug. 1750
by Thomas and Joseph Allender to pay orphans of dec. Joshua: William, Mary, and Nicholas; had iss.: WILLIAM; MARY (poss. the Mary
who m. Peter Body on 25 Aug. 1757); JOSHUA, d. by March 1749;
NICHOLAS, over 14 in Nov. 1759 when he chose Thomas Sligh as his
guardian (5; 11; 37:6,171; 44; 131).

ALLENDER, JOSEPH, poss. bro. of Joshua Allender, above, d. by 5 Jan. 1769 when admin. bond was posted by Corbin Lee (11).

ALLENDER, THOMAS, poss. bro. of Joshua Allender, above, in 1750 owned 50 a. part Freeman's Mount (153).

ALLENDER, JOHN, d. c.1786 in Harf. Co.; m. Lucina Roberts on 27 March 1749 (she was b. 11 March 1725, dau. of John and Mary Roberts); his will, 20 May 1786 - 28 Nov. 1786, named w. Lucina; her will, 27 Oct. 1788 - 17 March 1789, named s. William, dau. Margaret Wane (and her ch. John, Sarah, and Lucina Wane), and her sons John and Nicholas; had iss.: WILLIAM, b. 28 Sept. 1752, d. 6 Oct. 1752; MARGARET, b. 18 Jan. 1753, m. (?) Wane; WILLIAM; JOHN; and NICHOLAS (131; 244-AJ#2).

ALLENDER, JOSHUA, nephew of Joshua, was prob. the Joshua who m. by 6 Aug. 1755 Avarilla, dau. of Edward Day (229:185).

ALLENDER, NICHOLAS, m. by 16 April 1755, Jane, dau. of Edward Day (229:166).

ALLENDER, WILLIAM, m. by 18 June 1766, Ann, dau. of Edward Day (230:93).

ALLERHELLICK, MARY, admin. the est. of John Shaw on 15 Sept. 1723 (50:372-373).

ALLEYN, ZACHARIAH. See ALLEN, ZACHARIAH.

ALLING, ROBERT. See ALLEN, ROBERT.

ALLNUT, WILLIAM, was in Balto. Co. by 19 Sept. 1724 when he bought a tract called Elberton from Ephraim Gover of Calvert Co. (70:83).

ALLOM, NICHOLAS, transp. to Md. by 1667, bought land from William Fisher, chirurgeon, on 1 Sept. 1666 (94; 388).

AMBROSE, ANN, serv. to John Parrish, ind. for bast. in March 1730/1, June 1731, and Nov. 1737, and tried in March 1737/8 (29: 156,166: 31:129, 160).

AMBROSE, JAMES, serv., judged to be age 11 in June 1695 (20: 416).

AMONE, RICHARD, judged to be age 13 in March 1684/5; in 1695 was a taxable in n. side Patapsco Hund. (18:235; 140).

THE AMOS FAMILY has been studied by Hayward, and is the subject of a pamphlet by Schmitz. The compiler is indebted to Mrs. William K. Hearn for invaluable suggestions.

AMOS, WILLIAM (1), d. in Balto. Co. by 1759; m. Ann (?); was a member of the Anglican Ch. and an officer in the militia; acc. to trad. one day in 1738 a conversation with members of the Society of Friends convinced him of their religion, and he helped to establish Little Falls Meeting; in 1750 owned 200 a. Claxon's Purchase, 400 a. Branter's Ridge, and 200 a. Joshua' Ridge; his will, 24 Sept. 1757 - 10 March 1759, named his w. Ann and six sons; had iss.: THOMAS, b. 23 Nov. 1713; ELIZABETH, b. 18 Oct. 1715, may have d. young; WILLIAM, b. 3 March 1718; JAMES, b. 18 Feb. 1721; BENJAMIN, b. 2 Feb. 1724; JOSHUA, b. 25 Oct. 1725; MORDECAI, b. 7 Feb. 1727 (111; 131; 153; 245).

AMOS, THOMAS (2), s. of William (1), b. 23 Nov. 1713, alive in 1745; m. 25 Dec. 1735 Elizabeth, dau. of Nicholas and Eliza-

beth (Cox) Day, b. 17 March 1719; had iss.` WILLIAM, b. 15 Dec.
1736; BETHIA, b. 22 Feb. 1738; THOMAS, b. 1 Aug. 1740; NICHOLAS
DAY, b. 19 Sept. 1742 (served in the Rev. War); ELIZABETH, b. 14
Nov. 1745, m. Charles Baker on 6 March 1764 (131; 353).

AMOS, WILLIAM, (3), s. q : William (1) and Ann, b. 3 March 1718,
d. 26 Feb. 1814; m. 1st in 1739 Hannah McComas, dau. of Wm. McComas; m. 2nd on 4 day, 7, 1765 Martha M. Bull, wid., and dau. of
Luke Wiley; served in the Rev. War as a lieut. in the 6th Co. of
the 92nd Regt. under Col. William Smith, but is said to have left
the army for religious reasons; admitted to membership in Gunpowder Mtg. on 27 day, 9, 1751; his obit. stated he was in his
96th year, and for 76 years a member of the Soc. of Friends, and
that he left 16 ch., 92 grandchildren, 133 great-grandch., and 6
great-great-grandchildren; had iss. (11 ch. by 1st w., and at
least 3 ch. by 2nd w.): ANN, b. 22 day, 12, 1740, m. Thomas James
on 27 day. 8, 1761; NICHOLAS, b. c.1741; MAULDIN. b. 25 Dec. 1747,
d. 23 May 1845, having m. Rachel Bull, and rendered pat. serv. in
the Rev. War; HANNAH, b. 27 day, 10, 1747, m. 1st Peter Perine,
and m. 2nd John Stewart; WILLIAM, b. 26 day, 6, 1749, m. Susannah
Howard in 7 mo.. 1773; ELIZABETH, b. 21 day, 10, 1752, m. Edward
Norris; MARTHA, m. William Norris in 1773; ELEANOR, m. William
Bull in 1774; MARY, b. 10 May 1758, m. Elisha Tyson; PRISCILLA,
m. 1st William Jeffries on 2 day, 12, 1783, and 2nd John Morgan;
JAMES, b. 31 Jan. 1764 at Little Falls, m. Hannah Lee; (by 2nd
w.): LUKE, b. 20 day, 5, 1768; NANCY, b. 12, 4, 1771, m. Thomas
Shepherd; BENJAMIN, b. 29 day, 8, 1773 (136; 261; 353; 354; 425-
vol. 4).

AMOS, JAMES (4), s. of William (1) and Ann, b. 18 Feb. 1721,
d. 1805 in Harf. Co.; m. 29 Jan. 1739 Hannah Clarke, dau. of
Robert Clarke; later m. wid. Elizabeth Standiford; on 15 July
1799 signed a deed naming Benjamin Standiford, s. of his present
w., who m. Rachel, dau. of James' son Mordecai; his will, 3 April
1797 - 10 April 1805, named granddau. Rachel, dau. of Mordecai,
and testator's sons; had iss.: ROBERT, b. 31 May 1741, m. Martha
McComas; ELIZABETH, b. 15 Jan. 1743; WILLIAM, b. 16 Aug. 1745,
m. Elizabeth (?); JAMES, b. 8 Jan. 1746; BENJAMIN, b. 4 Oct. 1748;
m. Sarah Bussey; JOSHUA; MORDECAI, b. 1753, d. 1840 having served
in the Rev. War (128:81; 131; 241-JLG#O; 244-AJ#C; 353; 354).

AMOS, BENJAMIN (4), s. of William (1) and Ann, b. 2 Feb. 1724,
d. 1775; m. Sarah Lyon on 19 Dec. 1752; his will, 11 April 1775 -
May 1775, named w. Sarah and six ch.: BENJAMIN, b. 11 Oct. 1753;
JOHN, b. 16 March 1756; ELIJAH: ANN; SUSANNA: ELIZABETH; and ZACH-
ARIAH (131; 244-AJ#2; 503).

AMOS, JOSHUA (5), s. of William (1) and Ann, b. 25 Oct. 1725,
may be the Joshua who m. Elizabeth Stiles on 17 Sept. 1749; was
enrolled in the Harf. Co. militia by ens. Aquila Amos in 1778;
had iss: WILLIAM, d. c.1783, having m. Mary (?) (131; 503).

AMOS, MORDECAI (6), s. of William (1) and Ann, b. 7 Feb. 1727;
m. Mary Scott on 16 Feb. 1748 (131).

ANDERSON, BENJAMIN (1), was in Balto. Co. by 1720 and was alive
in 1741: m. Sarah (?); had iss.: WILLIAM, b. 30 March 1730; BENJA-
MIN, b. 4 Feb. 1732; MARY, b. 18 Jan. 1738: JOHN, b. 8 May 1741
(131).

ANDERSON, BENJAMIN (2), s. of Benjamin (1) and Sarah, b. 4 Feb.
1732; prob. the Benjamin, age 11, who with Israel Standiford, age
23, and latter's w. Cassandra, age 17, were granted a lease for
three lifetimes by Thomas Brerewood (77).

Unrelated Andersons.

ANDERSON, ANDREW, b. c.1668, was a taxable in the n. side of
Patapsco Hund. in 1692; age 50 in 1718; was conv. 136 a. James'
Pasture by Lewis Barton on 29 Nov, 1709; admin. the est. of Thom-
as Brashar on 14 April 1711 (1; 67; 138; 203-3; 310).

ANDERSON, ANN, age 9 mos. on 13 June 1747, bound to John Morgan on March 1746/7 to age 16 (36:380).

ANDERSON, CHARLES, d. by 23 July 1740 having m. Grace Preston
on 2 Nov. 1726 (dau. of James Preston who d. 1728/9); Charles
named as a son in the will of Margaret, wid. of Obadiah Pritchett;
his will, 2 Jan. 1739 - 23 July 1740, named w. Grace and four ch.
named below; wid. Grace m. as her 2nd husb. Thomas Horner on 27
Oct. 1741; had iss.: SARAH, b. 7 June 1728; MARGARET, b. 22 Feb.
1730, d. 12 March 1730; CHARLES, b. 27 March 1734, bound to
William Bennet in Aug. 1750; DANIEL, b. 4 Feb. (1735?), bound
to William Bennet in Aug. 1750; MARGARET, b. 4 Jan. 1736 (37:
152: 110; 125; 127: 128:55, 56, 67, 80, 95; 129).

ANDERSON, JOHN, in Balto. Co. by 1692 as a taxable in s. side
Gunpowder Hund.; d. by 9 April 1711 when admnx. Jane Anderson
posted bond with William Robinson and William Wright; Jane m. as
her 2nd husb. Edward Buck; will of John Anderson, proved 26 March
1711, named w. Jane and four ch. named below, and with Oliver Harriott, John Kammerenaugh. John Robinson, Susanna Adams and Urith
Adams as witnesses; est. inv. on 10 Apr. 1711 by Daniel Scott and
Thomas Hutchins and val. at £ 44.6.4, with a notation that the
dec. "had no kin in this country," and that his ch. were under
age; est. admin. by Edward Buck and w. Jane on 19 Nov. 1711, 3
Aug. 1713, and 13 Aug. 1714; had iss.: WILLIAM; REBECCA; MARY.
age 9 in April 1714 and bound to John and Susanna Stokes in June
1714 to age 16; JOHN, age 6 on 17 Dec. 1713 and bound to Wm. and
Elizabeth Robinson in June 1714 (1: 2; 11; 21:504: 52; 110; 138).

ANDERSON, JOHN, d. by 1724 when his est. was inv. (51).

ANDERSON, LEONARD, in Sept. 1756 conv. Thomas Broad 49 a. of
a tract called Buffalo (82:585).

ANDERSON, MARTHA, m. Martin Depost in Dec. 1729 (129).

ANDERSON, MOUNTS, a Swede who settled in New Sweden in 1648,
took up land in Balto. Co., was naturalized in 1674, and then
disappeared (379).

ANDERSON, THOMAS, d. by March 1738/9 leaving one son: THOMAS,
age 7 on 1 April 1739 bound to Thomas Wells in March 1738/9 (31:
351).

ANDERSON, WILLIAM, in 1750 owned 100 a. Anderson's Barrens
and 50 a. Sign of the Painter (153:12).

ANDERSON, WILLIAM, m. 21 Aug. 1755 Mary Harrard (Herod or
Harriott), dau. of Susanna Herod whose will, dated 2 Nov. 1764,
named dau. Mary Anderson (112; 131).

ANDREWS, JOSEPH (1), d. by Nov. 1711; m. Sarah (?), whose
sis. m. William Holland; had iss.: WILLIAM, b. c.1709 (21:269;
127:176).

ANDREWS, WILLIAM (2), s. of Joseph (1), b. c.1709; age 3 on
23 Apr. 1712, in Nov. 1711 was bd. to serve William and Elizabeth
Holland to age 16; d. by 17 Aug. 1784 having m. 1st on 14 Feb.

1732 Mary, dau. of William Bond, and 2nd by Aug. 1784 Mary Lynchfield; in 1735 with s. Andrew purch. tract Back Lingan from Bigger
and Martha Head of Calvert County; in 1750 owned 100 a. Beavan's
Adventure, 100 a. Windley's Rest, 207 a. Richardson's Level, 77
a. Smith's Discovery, and other tracts; his will, 21 Dec. 1782 -
17 Aug. 1784, named w. Mary Lynchfield and 8 ch.; had iss.: AN-
DREW, b. by Jan. 1735; BILLY DREW, b. 17 July 1738, m. (?) Bunt-
ing; ABRAHAM; ELIZABETH DURBIN; WILLIAM (a minor in 1783); WILLI-
AM, b. 23 Sept. 1744; SARAH, b. 23 Nov. 1745 (not in his will);
ABARILLA; MARTHA, b. 3 May 1756, m. John Hay on 2 Sept. 1777; MARY
m. (?) Galloway; WILLIAM HOLLAND, b. 8 Oct. 1760 (3; 21:269; 79;
81; 84; 91; 112; 125:39; 131; 153).

ANDREWS, JAMES, d. by 4 June 1764 when his est. was adm. by
Agnes Andrews; left 5 ch., all minors (6).

ANDREWS, NATHANIEL, transp. by 1677, bur. 24 June 1699; his
will, 19 June 1699 - 26 June 1699, named Thomas Greenfield, Thomas Preble and his ch. John and Ann Preble, and Thomas Capel; admin. bond posted by exec. Thomas Capel with James Ives and Samuel
Jackson (11; 120; 128:7; 388).

ANDREWS, WILLIAM, "an old man," ran away from Balto. Town
by Feb. 1759 (307).

ANGLER, MARY, ind. for bast. in June 1756 (36:2).

ANGLING, CORNELIUS, d. by 5 April 1738 when admin. bond was
posted by Thomas Biddison with Thomas Sheredine and Edward Stevenson; m. Barbara (?) by 4 June 1729; in Nov. 1734 was ind. for begetting an illeg. ch. on Jane Hopham; est. admin. 10 Nov. 1738 by
Thomas Biddison; had iss.: CORNELIUS, b. 4 June 1729 (4; 11; 30:
305, 306; 133).

ANGLING, MARY, m. Robert Gardner on 5 Jan. 1728 (133).

ANNIS, SARAH, ind. for bast. in Nov. 1746, and tried in March
1746/7 (36:220, 399).

ANNIS, or ENNIS, SUSANNA, ind. for bast. in Nov. 1750 (38:1).

ANNISEE, SARAH, ind. for bast. in June 1746 and March 1746/7
and tried in the latter month (36:2, 378, 394).

ANNS, WILLIAM, m. Ruth Kerksey on 26 Dec. 1734; d. by 9 Dec.
1743, when admin. bond was posted by John Hall, Sr., admin., with
John Matthews; est. admin. on 14 Nov. 1744; had iss.: JOHN, b.
7 Nov. 1737 (3; 11; 128:83, 104).

ANTER, Capt. JOHN, in 1750 owned 200 a. Brother's Choice as
well as a 1 a. lot in Balto. Town (153).

APPLEBY, NATHANIEL, was in Balto. Co. by 1694 as a taxable
in n. side Patapsco Hund. (139).

APPLEBY, WILLIAM, d. by 16 May 1759 when admin. bond was posted by admin. John Skinner with John Owings and William Williams;
est. admin. on 27 Sept. 1759; may have been the William Appleby
who was comm. for prison to be tried for the murder of his 12 or
13 year old son in March 1748; may have been the William who m.
Mary Jones on 13 Nov. 1750 (4; 11; 131; 262).

THE ARCHER FAMILY has been discussed by Burrage, and is the
subject of a sketch in the Magazine of American Genealogy, no. 7.
(504).

ARCHER, JOHN (1), was b. c.1680 at Rathmelton near Londonderry.
Ireland; settled nr. Brinkley's Mills, Cecil Co., Md.; m. Esther
Irwin, and had iss.: THOMAS, b. 1722; NATHANIEL, b. 1722; ESTHER,
b. 1724, d. 1808, m. John Hays; JAMES, b. 1726 (504).

ARCHER, THOMAS (2), s. of John (1) and Ester, was b. 1720, d.
1772; m. 1738 Elizabeth Stevenson; in 1750 owned 250 a. Uncle's
Goodwill; had at least one s.: JOHN, b. 5 May 1741 (131; 153).

ARCHER, JAMES (3), s. of John (1), b. 1726, m. Katherine Mortimer on 8 Jan. 1752 (131; 504).

ARCHER, JOHN (4), s. of Thomas (2) and Elizabeth, b. 5 May
1741, d. 28 Sept. 1810 in Harf. Co.; m. Catherine Harris; comm.
Maj. in the Continental Army; physician and member of Congress.

ARDEN, JOHN (1), came to Balto. Co. by 1676 and d. c.1694; m.
Sarah (?) by April 1679; left a will, 21 Nov. 1692 - 20 April
1694 naming ch. John, Alice, Samuel, and Richard, tracts 220 a.
Walton's Neck, 50 a. Ardington, and 300 a. Bachelor's Delight;
wife Sarah to have dower rights; est. inv. on 17 Sept. 1696 and
val. at £ 59.5.0 plus 3.0; admin. on 17 Sept. 1696 by extx. Sarah
now w. of Joseph Strawbridge; had iss.: poss. SUSANNA; JOHN; ALICE;
RACHEL; SAMUEL; Mary (in 1714 named as the heir of Joseph Strawbridge), in March 1714/5 and Nov. 1717 she named Thomas Felps as
the f. of her ch. (1; 21:602; 22:204; 102; 121; 206-13A:149; 388;
507).

ARDEN, SAMUEL (2), s. of John (1), d. by 1699 when his est. was
inv. by Benjamin Bowen and Joseph Gostwick and val. at £ 35.8.3;
Benja. Partridge and John Boone signed the inv. (48:218).

ARDEN, SAMUEL, rel. to others not proven; d. by 23 April 1719
when admin. bond was posted by admnx. Honor Arden with Jonas Bowen
and Edmund Mahy; est. was admin. by Honor on 7 Sept. 1720; she m.
as her 2nd husb. Jacob Peacock, 26 Oct. 1720 (1; 11; 133).

ARDY, FRANCIS, m. Margaret Mitchell in Jan. 1733 and had iss.:
WILLIAM, b. 25 May 1735; THOMAS, b. 22 Aug. 1737, and d. same year
(131).

ARMIGER, THOMAS, was transp. to Md. by 1661; d. by 26 Jan. 1676
when est. was inv. by John Hill and William York and val. at 10600
lbs. tob.; will, 4 March 1675 - 22 May 1676, named dau. Sarah, and
dau.-in-law Jane Trippers, with Thomas Preston as exec.; est. admin.
by Preston on 21 June 1677; Preston was summoned to answer charge
of Mistreating Armiger's dau.; had iss.: SARAH, alive in 1684 (2;
18:165; 51:99; 110; 388).

ARMSTRONG, JOHN (1), of A. A. Co., d. by 9 June 1699 in Balto.
Co., when admin. bond was posted by Abraham Taylor and wife Jane,
with Thomas Preston and Thomas Staley; m. Jane (?), who m. as her
second husband Abraham Taylor; est. was inv. by Thomas Preston and
(Jane?) Boone on 11 March 1699/1700, and val. at £ 11.19.3; had
iss. (b. in All Hallow's Par., A. A. Co.): JOHN, b. 4 Aug. 1679;
GEORGE, b. 2 Nov. 1681; MARY, b. 5 Dec. 1682; ROBERT, b. 5 April
1688; SOLOMON, b. 25 June 1692; THOMAS, b. 30 Jan. 1692/2; HENRY,
b. 12 Jan. 1695 (11; 48:95; 219-1).

ARMSTRONG, JOHN (2), s. of John (1) and Jane, b. 4 Aug. 1679
in A. A. Co.; came to Balto. Co.; m. Rebecca Hicks on 26 Aug. 1714;
had iss.: WILLIAM, b. 24 Nov. 1716; HENRY, b. 24 June 1720; SOLO-
MON, b. 15 April 1723; ELIZABETH, b. 7 March 1725/6; NEHEMIAH, b.
25 Feb. 1729; GEORGE, b. 5 May 1732; MARY, b. 26 Feb. 1735 (131).

ARMSTRONG, SOLOMON (3). s. of John (1) and Jane, b. 25 June 1692; m. 1st by Feb. 1729 Mary (?), and 2nd, on 2 Aug. 1744 Sarah Standiford; may have been the Solomon who admitted he was the father of Sarah Deason's child in Aug. 1746; his will, 14 Jan. 1748 - 24 Nov. 1749, named w. Sarah and ch: Joshua, Sarah, and Solomon, with Isaac Cord, Daniel Judd, and Jno. Barnes as witnesses; admin. bond posted 20 Oct. 1749 by exec. Solomon Armstrong, who admin. the est. on 22 June 1751 and 18 Oct. 1751; had iss. (all by 1st w except the last ch.): SOLOMON, old enough to be exec. of his father's est.; MARY, d. 12 Feb. 1729; SARAH, b. 14 Nov. 1729; JOSHUA, b. 16 May 1731; MARY, b. 16 April 1734; MARGARET, b. 16 Jan. 1736 (poss. the Margaret Armstrong fined for bast. in Nov. 1759); KEZIAH, b. 9 Dec. 1745 (5; 11; 36:132; 46:240; 128:61; 131).

ARMSTRONG, THOMAS (4), s. of John (1) and Jane, m. by July 1721 Frances (?) and had iss.: THOMAS, b. 11 July 1721, d. 12 April 1722; FRANCES, b. 13 March 1722; JAMES, b. 2 May 1725 (131).

ARMSTRONG, WILLIAM (5), s. of John (2) and Rebecca, b. 24 Nov. 1716, d. by Jan. 1755; m. Elizabeth Sheppard 1735; she may have m. as her 2nd husb. Archibald Standiford for he and his w. Elizabeth adm. Armstrong's est. on 9 Jan. 1755 and 1 Aug. 1755; had iss.: TEMPERANCE, b. 21 Dec. 1736; m. James Elliott on 8 May 1753; REBECCA, b. 4 Feb. 1742; poss. NATHANIEL SHEPPARD (5; 131).

ARMSTRONG, HENRY (6), s. of John (2) and Rebecca, b. 24 June 1720, m. Mary (?) by whom he had iss.: REBECCA, b. 4 Feb. 1742; HANNAH, b. 28 Jan. 1744; SOPHIA, b. 23 July 1748; ELIZABETH, b. July 1750; TARASHAR, b. 3 March 1753; HENRY, b. 3 March 1756; LYDIA, b. 12 Feb. 1759; ISAAC, twin, b. 26 July 1761; JACOB, twin, b. 26 July 1761; JOHN, b. 4 Feb. 1746 (131).

ARMSTRONG, SOLOMON (7), s. of John (2) and Rebecca, b. 15 Apr. 1723, may be the Solomon who admitted he was the father of Sarah Deason's ch. in Aug. 1746; may be the Solomon who m. Elizabeth Barnes on 25 Feb. 1749 (either of these items could refer to his cousin Solomon (3) above or the latter's son, Solomon (36: 132; 129).

ARMSTRONG, GEORGE (8), s. of John (2) and Rebecca, b. 5 May 1732; m. Mary Grimes on 4 Feb. 1754 (131).

ARMSTRONG, JOSHUA (9), s. of Solomon (3) and Mary, b. 16 May 1731; m. Margaret Barnes on 20 Feb. 1757, and had iss.: SOLOMON, b. 7 May 1758; MARY, b. c.1760; FORD, b. c.1763; MARGARET, b. c. 1767; JOSEPH, b. c. 1769; HANNAH, b. c.1773; ALICIA, b. c.1775 (129; 277:184).

ARMSTRONG, JAMES, d. by 7 April 1691 leaving a w. and one s.; his wid. m. as her 2nd husb. John Bird; had iss.: JAMES, age 12 c.1685 when bound to James Phillips (18:212).

ARMSTRONG, JAMES, m. by 1 June 1769 Martha, dau. of Elizabeth Chapman (210-37:123).

THE ARNOLD FAMILY has been thoroughly researched by Mr. and Mrs. H. H. Arnold who generously made their unpublished material available to the compiler.

ARNOLD, ANTHONY (1), of A. A. Co., d. after 12 Jan. 1689 when his will was dated; m. Johanna (?); his will left 50 a. to his w. and named his ch.: Hester Little, Rachel, Thomas, John, and Anthony Arnold, and Thomas Maddox; had iss.: HESTER, m. (?) Little; RACHEL; THOMAS; JOHN (not yet 18 in 1689); ANTHONY (not yet 18 in 1689); poss. a dau. who m. Thomas Maddox (121).

ARNOLD, ANTHONY (2), s. of Anthony (1), not vet 18 in 1689, d.
by 9 Oct. 1721 in Balto. Co.; m. Sarah (?), bapt. 1706 aged 20 in
St. Ann's Par., A. A. Co.; she m. as her 2nd husb. Charles Wells
by 3 June 1726; will of Anthony, 20 July 1721 - 9 Oct. 1721, nmd.
w. Sarah, ch. William, Joseph, John, and Anthony, all to be of
age at 18, dau. Mary to be of age at 16, and an unborn ch.; admin bond posted 9 Dec. 1721, _ extx. Sarah with Patrick Murphy
and Thomas Taylor; est. admin. by Sarah now w. of Charles Wells
on 3 June 1726; had iss.: WILLIAM; MARY; JOSEPH; HENRY, bapt. 23
(?) 1706 in St. Ann's Par.; JOHN, bapt. 27 March 1709: ANTHONY,
bapt. 1 Oct. 1716; poss. unborn ch. (3; 11; 124:74; 133: 219-2).

ARNOLD, JOSEPH (3), s. of Anthony (2) and Sarah, d. in Fred.
Co., Md., in 1757, having m. Susanna Chapman on 20 July 1736; in
1750 owned 50 a. Pleasant Level; his will, 3 Aug. 1757 - 30 Sept.
1757, named w. Susanna, tract Arnold's Harbor (owned by his bro.
Anthony in 1750) and the following ch.: BENJAMIN, b. 21 Aug.
1736: JOSEPH, b. c.1744; GREENBURY; ELIZABETH: RACHEL; PATIENCE;
and SUSANNA (133; 153; 210-10:377).

ARNOLD, ANTHONY (4), s. of Anthony (2) and Sarah, bapt. 1 Oct.
1716 in St. Ann's Par., A. A. Co.; d. in Fred. Co., by 27 Sept.
1792; m. Margaret (?) by 19 June 1742 when she joined him in conveying 50 a. Arnold's Chance to William Odle; in 1750 owned 20
a. Arnold's Harbour or Arbour; conv. said tract to bro. Joseph in
1752; will of Anthony Arnold, 13 Aug. 1792 - 27 Sept. 1792, named
these ch.: ANN; SAMUEL ARCHIBALD; ANTHONY; JOHN: CATHERINE;
WILLIAM: and JOSEPH (81; 153; Fred. Co. Wills, GM#2, p. 453).

Unrelated Arnolds

ARNOLD, BENJAMIN, m. by 1696 Susanna, wid. of James Phillips;
she d. 21 Feb. 1708, leaving a will, 22 Sept. 1708 - 4 Jan. 1708/9
wh. named gd. Avarilla, dau. of Mary Carvill, gd. Mary , dau. of
Martha Paca, and s.-in-law Aquila Paca (2; 122; 128:25; 206-15:
25).

ARNOLD, HENRY MITCHERLE, serv. to Ulick Burke, d. 21 Dec.
1732 (131).

ARNOLD, JOHN, charged with begetting a ch. on Elizabeth Chapman in Nov. 1733 (30:142); may be the same John Arnold owner of
75 a. part Arthur's Choice in 1750 (153).

ARNOLD, MARY, d. 3 Jan. 1726 (128:53).

ARNOLD, MARY, charged with bast. in March 1728; may be the
same Mary who m. John Cannaday on 2 Dec. 1729; another Mary was
ind. for bast in March 1746/7 (28:95; 36:. 378 ; 129).

ARNOLD, THOMAS, m. Sarah Smith on 15 Sept. 1742 and had iss.:
WILLIAM, b. 13 Sept. 1743 (129).

ARNOLD, WILLIAM, adm. pat. of Mary Tregill's ch. in June 1746
(36:5).

ARNOLD, WILLIAM, m. Sarah (?) and had iss.: WILLIAM, b. 24
March 1746; JOSEPH, b. 3 April 1754 (129).

ARNOLD, WILLIAM, m. Elizabeth Gilbert on 23 Nov. 1722 and had
iss.: THOMAS, b.10 Dec. 1723; WILLIAM, b. 5 July 1726; MARY, b.
Dec. 1730; JOHANNA, b. 22 Dec. 1732; SARAH, b. 20 June 1735;
ELIZABETH, b. 4 March 1737; FANNY, b. 9 April 1740; MARTHA, b.
20 Aug. 1742 (128:45, 47, 68, 89, 100, 113: 129).

ARNOLD, WILLIAM, m. Comfort Courtnev on 10 July 1747; had iss.: EPHRAIM, b. 22 Oct. 1752 (129).

ARNOLD, WILLIAM, in 1750 owned 100 a. part Hammond's Hope; another William in 1750 owned 100 a. Hammond's Richland; another William in 1750 owned 50 a. part The Division (153).

ARPIN, FRANCIS, m. 21 March 1735 Ann Macfarlan (128:91).

ARTHORNE. See ARDEN, JOHN.

ARUNDEL, or ARRINDELE, JOHN, age 6 in March 1724/5 was bound to Thomas Wright by John's father William Ingle, to age 21 (27: 128).

ARUNDEL, WILLIAM, b. 20 June 1719 (no parents named) (133).

ASELWORTHY, CHARLES JOHN, m. Blanche (?) and had iss.: LINNAH, b. 21 Oct. 1757 (129).

ASHBURN, JOHN, serv. of James Todd, assigned to William Wilkinson on 15 June 1703 (66:283).

ASHBY, WILLIAM, was in Balto. Co. by 1692 as a taxable in Spesutia Hund. (138).

ASHEE, JOHN, petitioned the court in March 1721/2 that he had entered Md. in the Cone of Bristol, Capt. Neale commander, as a serv. to sd Neale; was cheated of his indenture, and sold as a serv. in Md. for 5 years (18:11).

ASHER, ANTHONY, was in Balto. Co. by 1727 and d. there by 15 Oct. 1764: m. Susanna (?) who survived him; admin. the est. of Jacob Grove in Feb. 1752; in 1750 owned 220 a. Asher's Purchase; his will, Aug. 1764 - 15 Oct. 1764. named w. Susannah, sons Anthony and Abraham, and tract Asher's Purchase; had iss.: SARAH, b. 6 July 1727, prob. the Sarah who m. Daniel Nusewonden on 4 Nov. 1761; ANTHONY, b. 2 July 1732, m. Sarah Beven on 19 Dec. 1749: ANNE, b. 21 Sept. 1735, m. James Robeson on 7 June 1752: RACHEL, b. 20 Sept. 1737, m. Joseph Beven on 15 Jan. 1754; ELIZABETH. b. 31 Dec. 1742; ABRAHAM, b. 29 Feb. 1744; ANTHONY (3: 111; 131; 153).

ASHER, MARY, m. Samuel Wilkinson on 14 April 1748 (131).

ASHES, JOHN, conv. Shaw's Choice by Christopher and Elizabeth Shaw; d. by 20 Oct. 1692 when admin. bond was posted by Christopher Shaw with Roland Thornbury and Edw'd Baxter (11; 59:211).

ASHFORD, RACHEL, bur. 13 Dec. 1701 at John Kemball's (129).

ASHFORD, THOMAS, m. Mary Cox on 1 June 1735 (128:89).

ASHLE, (?), and his w. were the par. of ELIZABETH, b. 20 June 1693: WILLIAM, b. 27 July 1694; JOHN, b. 25 July 1695 (128:12).

ASHLEY, HENRY, was listed as a servant in the 1759 inv. of David Bissett (54:331).

ASHLEY, SARAH, was ind. for bast. in March 1746/7; as serv. to Darby Lux was tried for bast. in June 1750 (36:378; 37:11).

ASHLY, MARY, serv. of John Smith, confessed to having a bast. in Nov. 1741 (33:178).

THE ASHMAN FAMILY has been discussed by Barnes (259), Johnston (328), Newman (355), and by Lantz. (508)

ASHMAN, GEORGE (1), was transp. to Md. c.1678; d. by 1699 when the State House in Annap. was struck by lightning; m. Elizabeth, wid. of William Cromwell, and prob. the dau. of George Trehearne; delegate to the Assembly from Balto. Co. in 1692; his will, 10 Aug. 1698 - 23 Feb. 1699, named bros. John, and James, and ch.: Charity, Elizabeth, and John, stepsons Thomas, William, and Philip Cromwell; w. to be extx.; admin. bond was posted 27 Feb. 1699 by wid. Elizabeth with William Cromwell and Richard Mose; left est. worth £ 278.8.0, and incl. over 600 a. of land; est. admin. by Thomas Cromwell on 8 Aug. 1706 and 27 May 1712; wid. Elizabeth d. by 24 Feb. 1702/3 when admin. bond was posted by Thomas Cromwell with James Murray and William Cromwell; est. inv. on 24 Feb. 1702/3 by Edward Dorsey and Thomas Hedge and val. at £ 480.18.2; est. admin. by Thos. Cromwell on 15 May 1707 and 27 May 1712; had iss.: JOHN, b. c.1689; CHARITY, b. c.1691; ELIZABETH, b. 1693, d. 1714, m. 25 June 1713 John Gale in St. Margaret's Par., A. A. Co. (1; 2; 11; 48; 110; 219-4; 259; 328; 355; 370).

ASHMAN, JOHN (2), s. of George (1) and Elizabeth, b. 1689, d. 1737 in A. A. Co.; m. by 1714 Constant, dau. of John and Jane Wilmot; in Aug. 1728 was nearly killed by a beating from John Giles; his will, 31 May 1733 - 10 Oct. 1737, named ch.: George, John, William, Elizabeth, Constant, Charity, Ruth, Rachel, and Patience, w. Constant and her bro. John Wilmot; had iss.: GEORGE, b. 8 Nov. 1714; JOHN, b. 1 Sept. 1716; ELIZABETH, b. 17 March 1720, m. Daniel Stansbury on 22 April 1748; CONSTANT, b. 17 March 1720, m. 1st William Cockey and 2nd William Cromwell; RUTH, b. 12 March 1724, m. Hugh Merriken; RACHEL, b. 29 Oct. 1726, d. testate by 24 May 1769; PATIENCE, b. 26 March 1728, m. (?) Jacobs; WILLIAM, b. 8 July 1731, d. unm. and testate in 1762 (1; 28:23; 126; 210-31:328; 210-37:196; 259:4).

ASHMAN, GEORGE (3), s. of John (2) and Constant, b. 8 Nov. 1713, m. 4 Dec. 1725 Jemima, dau. of Josephus and Ruth Murray; moved to the Green Spring Valley area of Balto. Co. and acquired several tracts of land; by 1750 owned 134 a. pt. Counterscarpe, 20 a. Additon to Counterscarpe, and 230 a. Addition to Ashman's Delight; was on the vestry of St. Thomas' Par., and in Nov. 1737 was constable of Upper Patapsco Hund.; no record of his death or settlement of his est. has been found; may have moved away from Balto. Co.; had iss.: GEORGE, b. 20 May 1740; JOSEPHUS, b. 8 May 1745; NANCY, b. 29 Nov. 1747; ELIZABETH, m. Richard Colegate; ELLEN, m. John Colegate on 17 Feb. 1781; SARAH, b. 1765, m. Benjamin Elliott (134:8; 153; 398:26; 259:4).

ASHMAN, JOHN (4), s. of John (2) and Constant, b. 1 Sept. 1718, d. c. 1774 in A. A. Co.; m. Anne Greenbury Hammond, dau. of Nicholas and Mary Hammond; had iss.: WILLIAM, b. 3 March 1760, m. to Rebecca Boyce (259:4).

ASHMORE, WALTER (1), was in Balto. Co. by 1737; in 1750 owned 400 a, part Arabia Petrea; m. Margaret (?), and had iss.: WILLIAM; REBECCA, b. 2 July 1737; poss. ELIZABETH, b. 19 Jan. 1738; MARGARET, b. 13 Dec. 1740; JAMES, b. 4 Nov. 1742 (128:92/b, 102, 114; 129:303, 326).

ASHMORE, WILLIAM (2), s. of Walter (1), m. Susannah, wid. of Daniel O'Neale on 19 July 1756 (as Susana Lacey she m. O'Neale on 12 June 1743); Susanna was a dau. of William and Margaret Lacey; had iss.: WILLIAM, b. 21 May 1759; MARGARET, b. 27 July 1761 (3; 129:365, 367; 131).

ASHMORE, FREDERICK, was the father of Ann McLachlan's ch. in Nov. 1756; m. Bridget Ayres on 8 Feb. 1759; had iss.: JOHN, b. 22 Jan. 1760; ELIZABETH, b. 29 Dec. 1761 (41:312; 129).

ASHMORE, PETER, in Nov. 1745 pet. the court to be levy free (35:743)

ASKLEMAN, DANIEL, in 1750 owned 290 a. Smith's Chance and 81 a. Bedford (153).

ASKEW, RICHARD, was in Balto. Co. by 1690; may have been the Richard Askee transp. c.1674; m. 1690 Mary, extx. of Edward Reeves; with w. Mary conv. one-half of 350 a. United Friendship to Thomas Preston; d. by 20 July 1698 when admin. bond was posted by Simon Person with Samuel Brown (11; 17:128; 18:84; 64:68; 388).

ASKEW, Capt. THOMAS, commander of the Maryland Merchant, d. in Balto. Town; execs. appointed Lancelot Jacques to settle the est, c. Nov. 1754 (255).

ASKEW, WILLIAM, of St. Paul's Par., pet. for the church to be repaired; was named sole heir in the will of Richard Winn on 25 Sept. 1758; as schoolmaster was made exec. of the will of Sarah Boreing in Oct. 1757 (111; 208-1:119; 210-31:997).

ASPEY, THOMAS, m. Martha Morehead on 5 June 1737 (131).

ASSELL, NATHANIEL, m. Sarah Jackson on 18 Sept. 1754; had iss.: MICHAEL, b. 19 Oct. 1755; MARTHA, b. 11 March 1758 (129).

ATBY, STEPHEN, in Balto. Co. by 1692 as a taxable in n. side Patapsco Hund. (138).

ATHERTON, RICHARD, advert. in June 1723 that he would not pay the debts of his wife Susannah (69:143).

ATHOS, JOHN, d. by 26 May 1692 when his est. was inv. by Luke Raven, William Farrar, and Christopher Shaw, and val. at £ 22.0.6 plus 5286 lbs. tob. debts (206-10:493).

ATKINSON, BARTHOLOMEW, m. Sabra (?); sold land Allen's Rest to John Hurd, and left Md. by 1727 (200-38:405).

ATKINSON, ELIZABETH, placed in care of Abraham Johns in Nov. 1730 (19:51).

ATKINSON, JOHN, was involved in several lawsuits betw. 1729 and 1738; in 1750 owned 190 a. Broad Neck and Clement's Den, 99 a. Dogwood Ridge, 214 a. Parker's Folly, 62 a. Landito, 224 a. Parker's Choice; his will, 26 Nov. 1753 - 3 Dec. 1754, named w. Anne and bro. Michael (18:373, 374; 30:210; 31:334; 35:308, 322; 111; 153).

ATTICKS, MARY, fined for bast. in Nov. 1758, had s. WILLIAM (46:163).

AUCHER, LAWRENCE, m. Alce Batts on 1 Sept. 1737 (128:97).

AUGHARD, JOHN, d. in Balto. Co.; his will, 27 Nov. 1746 - 26 May 1748, named Anton Deaver, John Beaver, bro. William Hodworth, sisters Ann Reece, Hannah Goodwin, Elizabeth Hodsworth, and Sarah Hodsworth, bros.-in-law Benjamin Goodwin and William Reece, and 50 a. of land over Deer Creek; admin. bond posted 8 June 1748 by Benjamin Goodwin, acting exec., with N. Ruxton Gay (11; 110:427).

AUSTIN, HENRY, gave age as c.62 in Sept. 1763 (88:90).

AUSTIN, MARY, tried for bast. in March 1754; Edward Bowen was tried as the father of her ch. (39:35).

AVERLY, PASSTOHR, m. Pattey (?), and had iss.: GEORGE, b. 26 May 1736 (133).

AYRES, ABRAHAM, owned 174 a. Arabia Petrea in 1750; m. Bridget (?) and had iss.: BRIDGET, b. 23 Oct. 1738 (131; 153).

AYRES, BENJAMIN, m. Mary (?), and had iss.: THOMAS, b. 1 Oct. 1740 (128:112).

AYRES, EDWARD, imm. by 1666; bought 200 a. Wandsworth from William and Susanna Orchard in March 1666/7; surv. 100 a. Ayres Addition in April 1668; d. by 27 April 1674 when admin. bond was posted by James Collier, with William Osbourne and James Phillips (11:27; 94; 211:33; 388).

AYRES, JEREMIAH, m. Mary Franklin on 2 April 1738 (133).

AYRES, NATHANIEL, was in Balto. Co. by March 1723/4 when he was named father of Lydia Crompton's illeg. ch.; ind. to stand trial Nov. 1724; surv. 28 a. Ayres Desire in 1736; surv. 45 a. Buck's Range in 1745 which he owned in 1750; m. Rhoda (?) and had iss.: RUTH, b. 2 Feb. 1730; JOHN, b. 1 March 1731/2; THOMAS, b. 1 Jan. 1733/4 (26:214; 27:32; 133; 153; 207).

AYLEWARD, WILLIAM, surv. 500 a. Concord on 20 Jan. 1686; later noted as "gone away" (211).

BACON, MARTIN (1), was in Balto. Co. by 1738; m. Mary (poss. Watson); his will, 28 Feb. 1772 - 2 July 1785, named w. and three ch.: WILLIAM, b. 19 July 1738; ELIZABETH, b. 23 Nov. 1741, m. Edward Fugate on 12 Jan. 1758; JOHN, b. 20 Aug. 1743 (113; 131).

BACON, JOHN (2), s. of Martin (1) and Mary. b. 20 Aug. 1743, d. by 7 Dec. 1786; m. Temperance Hunt on 25 Aug. 1771; in 1783 was in Mine Run Hund., owning Smith's Lot, 126 a. Martin's Lot, 6 a. Add'n to Martin's, and 7 a. of Bell's Lot; est. admin. by Temperance Hunt and Daniel Shaw on 7 Dec. 1786 and 13 April 1791; had iss.: MARY, m. Gabriel Holmes on 17 Feb. 1793; ELIZABETH, a minor in 1792 when she chose her mother as guardian; MARTIN, also a minor in 1792 who may be the Martin b. 26 June 1776, d. 5 April 1858 bur. at St. James' Church, My Lady's Manor (8; 10; 131; 240-2:283).

BADHAM RICHARD, m. Sarah (?); had iss.: JOHN, b. 30 March 1724; THOMAS, b. 13 Nov. 1728 (128:72; 131).

BAGFORD, JAMES, was in Balto. Co. and m. to Elizabeth (?) by Aug. 1718 when they were made guardians of Henry Yanston, s. of Laurence; d. by 1720; wid. Elizabeth m. 2nd Samuel Hinton, whose will dated 4 April 1720 named son-in-law James Bagford; she m. 3rd (?) Stone; her will, dated 28 Jan. 1736, named sons James Bagford and John Sampson; had iss.: JAMES, aged 18 or 19 in May 1735 (23:4; 74:237; 124; 126).

THE BAILEY FAMILY OF ST. PAUL'S PARISH has been discussed by Walter D. Barnes in his Barnes-Bailey Gen. (271).

BAILEY, GEORGE (1), d. in Balto. Co. by 29 Aug. 1754, having m. Sarah, dau. of Hector McLane or McClane; in 1750 owned 217 a. Athol, 323 a. Bailey's Inheritance and 100 a. Hopyard; his will,

25 May 1754 - 29 Aug. 1754, named seven sons and two daus.; admin.
bond posted 29 Aug. 1754; est. admin. by McClane and Jabez Bailey, the execs., on 5 Sept. 1755; had iss.: JOHN (called oldest
s. in will); McCLANE; JABEZ; ENOCH; EPHRAIM; KERRENHAPPUCK, b. 3
Oct. 1728, m. (?) Hamilton; SAMUEL; ELIJAH, b. 20 June 1736; and
SARAH (5; 11; 111; 133; 523).

BAILEY, JOHN (2), s. of George (1) and Sarah, was b. c.1713,
gave his age as 54 in 1767, d. c.1789; m. Helen, granddau. of
Thomas Newsom; had iss.: MARY, b. 5 April 1740; SARAH, b. 24 Feb.
1741/2, m. 1765 John Calvert, 1742 - 1790, de jure 8th Lord
Balto.; ELAM, twin of Sarah, b. 24 Feb. 1741/2; HELEN, m. 1772
John Calvert, widower of her sis.: GEORGE; JOHN NEWSOM, d. 1801;
ELIZABETH, m. (?) Parker (4; 84:49; 310; 346-1:148-149).

BAILEY, McCLANE (3), s. of George (1) and Sarah, d. by 23
June 1763 when Jabez Bailey advert. he would settle the est.
(256)

BAILEY, JABEZ (4), s. of George (1) and Sarah, d. by 3 May
1769 when his will, dated 4 Jan. 1768, was proved, naming his
bro. Enoch and Enoch's sons Joseph, William, George, Ephraim, and
Enoch, and sis. Kerrenhappuck Hamilton and her son William Hamilton, as well as tracts 111 a. Maiden's Choice, Athol, Addition
to Athol, and Hopyard (112:107).

BAILEY, ENOCH (5), s. of George (1) and Sarah, d. 1766: m.
Kerrenhappuck, dau. of Josephus Murray; his will, 7 March 1766 -
29 April 1766, named his w., bro. John Murray, 400 a. Butler's
Farm, 84 a. Frederickstadt Enlarged, and 15 a. Small Hopes, and
these ch.: JOSEPHUS; EPHRAIM; WILLIAM, d. by 1806 in Notoway Co.
(sic), Va. leaving a wid. Prudence who sold land in Balto. Co.;
SARAH; ENOCH; and GEORGE (112; 231-WG#89).

BAILEY, SAMUEL (6), s. of George (1) and Sarah, d. 1772: his
will, 21 May 1772 - 2 July 1772, named his mother Sarah, and
exec. Benjamin Wells (112:295).

BAILEY, ELAM (7), s. of John (2) and Helen, b. 24 Feb. 1741/2,
took the Oath of Allegiance in 1778; in 1775 was a First Lieut.
in the 4th Mil. Co. of Balto. Co., and was later a captain of
militia (208-3; 417-1).

THE BAILEY FAMILY OF ST. JOHN'S PARISH.

BAILEY, THOMAS (8), no known rel. to above, d. in Balto. Co.
in 1771; m. Ann (?); in 1750 owned 175 a. Dandy Hills; his will,
13 March 1771 - 16 Dec. 1771, named grandson William Bailey,
tract Dandy Hills, and these ch.: THOMAS, d. 1795; GROOMBRIGHT
m. Mary Moore on 5 Oct. 1757; MARY, m. (?) Green; RUTH, b. 17
June 1740, m. Henry Fitch on 28 Feb. 1758; RACHEL, b. 21 May
1741; CATHERINE, b. 24 April 1743, m. Thomas Hatton on 29 Jan.
1767; KEZIA, b. 1 Nov. 1745, m. Chaney Hatton on 31 Dec. 1761
(.112:183; 131; 153).

BAILEY, THOMAS (9), s. of Thomas (8) and Ann, d. 1795: m.
Rachel, dau. of William Towson, on 26 Dec. 1750; his will, pr.
23 Sept. 1795, named lands James' Park, Dandy Hills, and Carroll's
Scrutiny, and one son and four daus.; had iss.: WILLIAM, b. 10
Sept. 1759; RUTH, b. 16 March 1761; RACHEL, b. 10 Jan. 1763, m.
James Crook on 13 Jan. 1784; THOMAS, b. 7 Nov. 1764; SARAH, m.
George Collins on 26 Dec. 1790; and CATHERINE (114:316; 131;
238-1; 264).

Unrelated Baileys

Unrelated Baileys.

BAILEY, (?) (poss. THOMAS), m. by 12 April 1752 Ann, dau. of John Legatt (111).

BAILEY, or BALY, CHARLES, had dau.: SARAH, she pet. the court in 1694 (20:263).

BAILEY, CHARLES, m. Sarah (?); d. by 16 March 1748 when admin. bond was posted by John Paca with John Hall of Swan Town; est. admin. by Paca on 8 Aug. 1750; had iss.: COTTERAL, b. 10 Nov. 1734; ELIZABETH, b. 10 Jan. 1736; JOHN, b. 6 Oct. 1740; MARGARET, b. 26 Dec. 1742; JOSEPH, b. 18 Oct. 1744 (5; 11; 128:84, 95, 111; 129).

BAILEY, GEORGE, b. c.1676, gave his age as 63 in 1739 (310).

BAILEY, GEORGE, had s. ENOCH who was bur. 2 July 1736 (133).

BAILEY, GEORGE, m. Mary (?); had iss.: GEORGE, b. 12 Oct. 1728; JOHN, b. 2 Sept. 1730; RUTH, b. 8 March 1732; WILLIAM, b. 28 Oct. 1735; BENJAMIN, b. 22 Sept. 1739; MARY, b. 4 April 1741; THOMAS, b. 18 Oct. 1744; SARAH, b. 10 Dec. 1749 (133: 134).

BAILEY, GEORGE, Jr., d. by 2 Oct. 1742, having m. Rachel (Hammond), wid. of John Moale; Rachel was b. 1708, d. by 22 April 1749, when admin. bond was posted by Charles Croxall; Rachel posted admin. bond earlier on the est. of George Bailey, and she admin. the est. of John Moale on 24 Dec. 1743; in 1750 she (or her heirs) owned 50 a. Moale's Improved Purchase, 55 a. Job's Beginnings. 350 a. Moale's Quarter, 202 a. Hampton Court, 3 a. Cedar Isle and other lands (3; 11; 153).

BAILEY, GEORGE, in 1750 owned 50 a. Bailey's Lot (153).

BAILEY, or BAILY, GODFREY, imm. from London c.1659, d. c. 1670/1; m. Rose (?), poss. wid. of John Scotcher; in Dec. 1658 John Bayspole, merch. of London, conv. all his goods to Godfrey Baly, Gent., late of London; rep. Balto. Co. in the Assembly, in 1659/60; on 1 Aug. 1659 surv. 100 a. Hamsted's Marshall in Balto. Co.; his will, 7 Jan. 1669 - 27 Aug. 1670, named Rose Salmon, w. Rose, and daus. Eliza and Rosamond; John Van Heck, Jos. Hopkins and Thos. Salmon were overseers; Van Heck and Salmon posted admin. bond on 15 Dec. 1670 with Nathaniel Stiles and John Gilbert; est. val. at 19,723 lbs. tob.; had iss.: ELIZABETH, m. George Warner; ROSAMUND (11; 94; '120:54; 370).

BAILEY, JOHN, of A. A. Co., d. by 16 July 1719; had 350 a. D Danby Hills due from George Burgess; his sons THOMAS (see Baileys of St. John's Par., above) and JOHN divided the land between them (71:26).

BAILEY, JOHN, d. on 29 Oct. 1732; m. Lucy Ann (?) who posted admin. bond on 7 March 1732 with EdwardCantwell and Thomas Williamson; the latter two admin. the est. on 16 July 1743; had iss.: MARY, b. 2 Jan. 1719/20; JOHN, b. 13 March 1723/4; JOANNA, b. 1 March 1725/6; HENRY, b. 28 Feb. 1727/8; RALPH (in 1750 the heirs of John Bailey owned 50 a. Mould's Success) (3; 11; 31:225; 128: 41, 43, 49, 50, 74; 153).

BAILEY, JOHN, m. Ann Welch on 19 Jan. 1735 (133).

BAILEY, JOHN, m. Mary (?); had iss.: MARY, b. 19 Sept. 175(?); WILLIAM, b. 23 April 1756 (131).

BAILEY, JOSEPH, m. Margaret Osborne on 27 Dec. 1748; may
have been the Joseph Bailey b. c.1720, d. p.1790 and who served
as a pvt. in the Rev. War from Md.; had iss.: JOSIAS, b. 28 Sept.
1749; CHARLES, b. 17 Nov. 1745; AQUILA, b. 7 Nov. 1756; BENEDICT,
b. 15 Jan. 1759; SARAH, b. 8 Oct. 1761 (129; 353).

BAILEY, RICHARD, d. 9 April 1740 (128: 108).

BAILEY, THOMAS, ordered to be levy free in Aug. 1755 (40:219).

BAILEY, WILLIAM, shoemaker, runaway serv. from Thomas Towson
or Thomas Stevens by Aug. 1753 307).

THE BAIN or BAYNE FAMILY has been researched by John W. Bayne,
Jr., in the Bayne Family Newsletter. (509).

BAIN or BAYNE, JOHN, m. 30 Aug. 1753 Mary Webber and had iss.:
WILLIAM, b. 23 April 1756; MARY, b. 19 Sept. 1758 ; CATHERINE, b.
7 Jan. 1761; ANN, b. 3 July 1763; MARY, b. 1 May 1766 (131).

BAIN or BANE, WILLIAM, m. Lydia Johnson on 14 Oct. 1761 (131).

BAKEN, THOMAS, in Balto. Co. as a taxable in n. side Patapsco
Hund. in 1692 (138).

THE BAKER FAMILY has been researched by Mrs. Richard Turley who
has generously shared her material with the compiler. Mrs. Turley
feels that Charles Baker, s. of Maurice who d. 1700, the Charles
who m. Hannah, and the Charles who m. Avarilla were all really the
same person. She bases her conclusions on three reasons: first,
there was only one Charles Baker in the first quarter of the 18th
century; second, the entry in St. John's Parish showing Theophilus, b. 1701, to be a son of Charles and Avarilla may be in
error and that Theophilus was really a son of Charles by his first
wife Hannah; and third, the names Maurice, William, and Indimeon
appear in both families. The author is indebted to Mrs. Turley.
    Family Bible Records of the Charles Baker family are found
at the DAR Library in Washington, D. C.

BAKER, MAURICE (1), progenitor of the family, imm. to Md. by
1675 and settled in A. A. Co., where he d. in 1700; m. Eliza (?)
who d. there in 1703; acquired 50 a. The Range orig. surv. for
Eliza Hill on 20 May 1666, and later sold by John Baker; will
of Maurice Baker, 10 Nov. 1700 - 28 Dec. 1700, named ch. Charles,
William, Morris, Indimeon, Mary Smith (and her s. James Smith),
and John, and w. Eliza, also lands Baker's Choice, Baker's Addition, Charles' Forest, and land on Rock Creek; will of Eliza
Baker, 10 Aug. 1703 - 20 Nov. 1703, named daus. Martha Smith,
Sarah Gosnell, Mary Jones, and sons Charles, Morris, William, and
John (who was not yet of age); had iss.: MAURICE, b. c.1675;
CHARLES; WILLIAM; INDIMEON (d. by Nov. 1703 in A. A. Co., leaving
a will which named bros. Morris, Charles, and William, and leaving Baker's Add'n to bro. John); MARY, m. 1st (?) Smith (by whom
she had a son James), and 2nd by 10 Aug. 1703 (?) Jones; MARTHA,
m. by Aug. 1703 (?) Smith; SARAH, m. (?) Gosnell; JOHN, under
age in 1703 (121; 122; 211).

BAKER, MAURICE (2), s. of Maurice (1) and Eliza, b. c.1675,
d. by 4 June 1762; gave his age as 47 in 1722; m. Sarah Nicholson on 9 Jan. 1704/5 in St. Anne's Par., A. A. Co.; in 1750 owned
50 a. Tanyard conv. him by William and Ann Baker in June 1712;
conv. 295 a. Charles' Forest to Lancelot Todd in Oct. 1720, and
100 a. Scotchman's Desire to Francis Dorsey in Oct. 1732; his
will, 21 Nov. 1761 - 4 June 1762, named s. Nicholas; grandson
Francis Dorsey, lands 50 a. Tanyard and 100 a. Scotchman's
Desire; will was wit. by William Seabrooke, John and Richard

Parrish and Thomas Porter; had iss.: ALEXANDER, d. by 1750; NICH-
OLAS; a dau. (?) who m. (?) Dorsey (67; 68; 73; 111; 153; 219-2;
310; 510).

BAKER, CHARLES (3), s. of Maurice (1) and Eliza, d. by May
1739; m. 1st Hannah, prob. dau. of William Hawkins (whose will
of 25 June 1711 named s.-in-law Charles Baker; and 2nd Avarilla
(?); inher. Baker's Choice, which he and Hannah conv. on 1 June
1703 as Baker's Chance to John Rattenbury; purch. 242 a. Aberly
Lodge, James Isham's dwelling plantation and 150 a. Samuel's
Hills; in July 1738 he and Avarilla conv. parts Preston's Deceit to sons Lemuel and Indimeon; admin. bond posted 11 May 1739
by Maurice Baker and Jacob Bull with William Dallam and Peter
Carroll; had iss.: THEOPHILUS, b. 2 Nov. 1701 (by Hannah); CHARLES,
b. c.1703 (by Hannah); MAURICE; LEMUEL; INDIMEON; SARAH, b. 23 Aug.
1718; ELIZABETH, b. 17 Sept. 1724; BRIDGET, b. 27 July 1727; and
GIDEON (3; 4; 11; 66; 67; 73; 75; 122; 131).

BAKER, WILLIAM (4), s. of Maurice (1) and Eliza; m. Ann (?);
alive in 1743; in Aug. 1711 William and Ann conv. 50 a. Baker's
Chance to James Drane, in June 1712 pt. Tanyard to Maurice Baker,
and in March 1724 conv. tract Overlooked (granted in 1719 to
Maurice Baker) to John Furley; in Feb. 1742 leased 150 a. Food
Plenty to George Buchanan; conveyed residue of Tanyard to Charles
Ridgely in April 1743; had iss.: ZEBEDIAH (67; 69; 77; 231-AL#K).

BAKER, JOHN (5), s. of Maurice (1) and Eliza, was under age
in 1703, and alive in 1752; m. Margaret (?); in June 1714 conv.
The Range to Henry Wright of A. A. Co.; in March 1724 conv. 40
a. Baker's Delight to John Buckingham; in 1750 owned 50 a. Jones
Mistake which he and Margaret conv. to John Hawkins in July 1751
or 1752; in 1737 John Baker was in Soldier's Delight Hund. with
Abner and "Dem'n." Baker; had iss.: CHARLES; ABNER (at least 16
in 1737); INDIMEON (16 in 1737) (61; 69; 77; 81; 149; 153; 217-
IB#2).

BAKER, ALEXANDER (6), s. of Maurice (2) and Sarah; in Balto.
Co. in 1737; d. by 13 July 1750; m. Zipporah (Hillyard), wid. of
Thomas Floyd; she m. 3rd Henry Maynard; with Maurice Baker in
Patapsco Upper Hund. in 1737; in 1750 owned 100 a. Christian's Lot
(mentioned in the 1738/9 will of Thomas Floyd); 50 a. Brother's
Expectation; admin. bond on his est. posted 4 Aug. 1750 by Zipporah Baker with John Robinson and Dorsey Petticoat; est. admin.
on 13 July 1750 and 9 Oct. 1753; Henry and Zipporah Maynard agreed
to the sale of Christian's Lot and Brother's Expectation by John
and Thomas Floyd in June 1756; had iss.: NICHOLSON, b. 23 April
1741; OBED, b. 17 June 1746; MAURICE, b. 8 July 1748 (5; 11; 82:
570; 127; 133; 136; 149; 153).

BAKER, NICHOLAS (7), s. of Maurice (2) and Sarah, d. in Balto.
Co. in 1799; may have m. Mary Stevens on 18 Jan. 1749/50; his
will, 20 Sept. 1795 - 11 Sept. 1799, named these ch.: MARY (b.
12 March 1765); SUSANNAH (b. 5 Aug. 1768), m. (?) Hamilton;
RACHEL, m. (?) Hamilton; SARAH, m. (?) Rowles; REBECCA, m. (?)
Randall; ELIZABETH, m. 4 Jan. 1786 Samuel Hamilton; HELEN; MILCAH,
m. (?) Balderston; NICHOLAS, inher. The Tanyard, which he conv.
in 1807 to his niece Nancy Osler (115; 129; 133; 231-WG#94; 232;
287).

BAKER, THEOPHILUS (8), s. of Charles (3) , prob. by his 1st
w. Hannah although St. John's Par. Reg. gives his mother as Avarilla; b. 2 Nov. 1701; may be the Theophilus Baker who in 1788 ¦
made a deed of trust with sons Gideon, William, and James to maintain him and his w. Elizabeth; may have had iss.: THEOPHILUS, age
46 in 1767; GIDEON; WILLIAM; and JAMES (92; 131; 241-JLG#E).

BAKER, CHARLES (9), s. of Charles (3) and Hannah, b. c.1704, d. 1789; m. Providence Robinson by Nov. 1730; in March 1725 was sold 100 a. Pork Forest by Robert Love; in Nov. 1730 Charles and Providence sold pt. Leaf's Chance to Josias Hendon; in 1750 owned 100 a. Pork Forest; in 1742 he leased 115 a. Baker's Pleasure on Gunpowder Manor for the lifetimes of himself and his ch. Charles and Providence; in Nov. 1751 bought Oblong from John and Aliceanna Bond; in 1767 he was 63 and his s. Charles was 26; his will, 30 March 1787 - 21 Jan. 1790, named grandsons Nathan, Isaac, and Zacheus Baker (all brothers), grandson Charles Waters, dau. Elizabeth Towson, s. James (and James' dau. Providence), s. Charles (and Charles' dau. Ann), great-granddau. Providence Rightly, and John Cox, s. of Winifred Cox; had iss.: ELIZABETH, b. 13 April 1735, m. (?) Towson; PROVIDENCE, b. 4 March 1738; CHARLES, b. 1 Oct. 1741; JAMES, b. 8 Oct. 1744 (70; 73; 81; 113; 153; 389).

BAKER, MAURICE (1), s. of Charles (3), prob. by Avarilla, d. 1774 in Harf. Co.; m. Christian, dau. q : William Grafton; in Nov. 1735 bought Antioch from William and Margaret Grafton; in 1750 he owned 100 a. Antioch, 55 a. Samuel's Hills, and part Preston's Deceit; his will, 15 Feb. 1774 - 19 March 1774, named above three tracts, w. Christian, and these ch.: Charles, Morris, William, Grafton, John, Nathan, Hannah, Mary Garrett, Rhoda Thomas, Margaret Garrett, Martha Whitaker, Rachel, and Ann Baker; will of Christian Baker, 8 Feb. 1792 - 15 Jan. 1793, named dau. Ann w. of Michael Denny, grandson Grafton Baker of Morris, dau. Hannah w. of Samuel Everett, ch. Nathan, John, Grafton, Charles, William, Mary Morrow, Rachel Pendigrass, Martha Whitaker, and Margaret Garrett; had iss.: HANNAH, b. 18 May 1733, m. 1st Stephen White on 1 Jan. 1751, and 2nd Samuel Everett on 9 Dec. 1755; MARY, b. 4 March 1734, m. 1st by 1774 (?) Garrett and 2nd by 1792 (?) Morrow; RHODA, b. 21 March 1738, m. (?) Thomas; WILLIAM, b. 12 Feb. 1749; CHARLES, "of Morris," m. Elizabeth Ditto on 6 March 1764; MORRIS; GRAFTON; JOHN; MARGARET, m. John Garrett on 22 Nov. 1759; RACHEL, m. (?) Simmons, and 2nd, on 26 Jan. 1768 Luke Pendergrass; ANN, m. Michael Denny; NATHAN (74:33; 128:76; 131; 153; 244-AJ#2).

BAKER, LEMUEL (11), s. of Charles (3) and Avarilla, m. Sophia Mead on 5 March 1739; in 1738 was conv. pt. Preston's Deceit by his par., and sold pt. of this land to Thomas Durbin in 1740; had iss.: DORCAS, b. 18 June 1740; m. Samuel Higginson on 29 Jan. 1760; JAMES, b. 25 Aug. 1644; ANN, twin, b. 25 Aug. 1744; MARY, b. 14 June 1741 (75; 131).

BAKER, INDIMEON (12), s. of Charles (3), was living in 1746; m. Sarah Downs on 22 April 1738; in July 1738 was conv. part of Preston's Deceit by his par.; sold 50 a. of this land to Jonathan Hughes; had iss.: CHARLES, b. Aug. 1746 (75; 76; 131).

BAKER, ZEBEDIAH (13), s. of William (4) and Ann, m. by 13 July 1731 Keturah (?), and was still alive in 1773; in Oct. 1745 sold pt. of a tob. crop of Sylvester Baker to John Ridgely; in 1773 conv. 160 a. Food Plenty to Benjamin Wells, Sr.; had iss.: MORRIS, b. 13 July 1731; MESHACK, b. 27 Sept. 1733 (78; 133; 231-AL#K).

BAKER, CHARLES (14), s. of John (5) and Margaret owned 50 a. Charles Delight in 1750 and 1763; prob. the Charles Baker who with his w. Margaret conv. 50 a. Baker's Delight and 29 a. of Baker's Desire to Vachel Dorsey of A. A. Co. (92:213; 153; 159).

BAKER, ABNER (15), s. of John (5) and Margaret, was in the household of John Baker as a taxable in 1737; in 1744 conv. 50 a. Abner's Camp to Thomas Leven; in 1750 owned 12 a. Abner's Delight, which he conv. to Christopher Sewell in 1765 (77:537; 90:179; 149; 153).

BAKER, INDIMEON (16), s. of John (5) and Margaret, was a taxable in his father's household in 1737, and was alive in 1768, having m. Catherine (?); in 1750 owned 50 a. Baker's Chance which he and Catherine sold to Richard Wilmot in Sept. 1753; had iss.: DELILAH, b. 14 Nov. 1738; MOSES, b. 19 March 1740; RACHEL, b. 24 Jan. 1742; SARAH, n. 16 Aug. 1744; MARGARET, b. 13 Dec. 1747; INDIMEON, b. 19 July 1750 (82:135; 133; 134; 149; 153).

BAKER, CHARLES (17), s. of Charles and Providence, b. 1 Oct. 1741; m. Elizabeth Wheeler, dau. of Leonard; had iss.: NATHAN, b. 14 Oct. 1760; ANN (named in her grandfather's will) (131; 210-31).

BAKER, MORRIS (18), s. of Zebediah (13) and Keturah, b. 13 July 1731, d. by 1820 in Tyler Co., (now West) Va.; m. 1st Elizabeth Dorsey, dau. of Francis and Elizabeth (Baker) Dorsey; m. 2nd Ann (?) who d. 1803; may have had iss.: ZABEDIAH, b. c.1755/9, d. by 1830, m. Cassandra (?): JOHN, b. c.1755, d. c.1850 in Tyler Co.; CHARLES, b. c.1760/70, m. Susan (?); ESIAS, b. 1765, d. 1850, m. Mary (?); RUTH, m. (?) Wells, and moved to Washington Co., Penna.; MAURICE, b. 1775, d. 1809, m. Elizabeth Wells (Data from Mrs. Turley).

BAKER, MESHACK (19), s. of Zebediah (13) and Keturah, b. 27 April or Sept. 1733; m. Elizabeth, dau. of William Hamilton, and had iss.: SAMUEL, b. 1764; JACOB, b. 1766; MAURICE, b. 1768; EPHRAIM, b. 1770, m. Stacey Reimy (6; 133; 353; data from Mrs. Turley).

Unrelated Bakers.

BAKER, (?), m. by 3 Feb. 1759 Rachel, dau. of William Gosnell (210-31:714).

BAKER, ABSOLOM, m. Mary (?) by March 1746 when they sold to Peter Gosnell 40 a. Absolom's Place; in 1767 to Vachel Dorsey tracts William's Chance, Dorsey's Goodwill, and Baker's Industry (79:330; 92:216).

BAKER, ANN, Widow, m. by banns pub. June or July 1699 William White (129:187).

BAKER, CATHERINE, imprisoned for debt in June 1734, and her two children to be kept by Benjamin Mead (30:255).   She may be the Mrs. Catherine Baker summoned by the vestry of St. John's Par. in July 1736 for unlawful cohabitation with Edward Mead, after having lived with him for 7 years (132:14).

BAKER, CHARLES, m. 9 Jan. 1749 widow Elizabeth Cockey, wid. of John Cockey, ana dau. of William Slade (131; 200-30; 84:90).

BAKER, ELIZABETH, m. George Coale on 26 Oct. 1735 (133).

BAKER, ELIZABETH or ELIZA, ind. for bast. in March 1745/6; may be the same Elizabeth summoned by the vestry of St. Thomas' Parish for unlawful cohabitation with John Roberts in July 1750 (35:800; 135:123).

BAKER, HENRY, of Cecil Co., in 1750 owned 100 a., part Hall's Plains, and 110 a. Prichard's Security (153:71).

BAKER, ISAAC, in 1702 sold 200 a. Preston's Luck by Thomas Preston and wife (66:199).

BAKER, JAMES, Jr., d. Feb. 1743 (131)

BAKER, JAMES, m. Catherine Smith on 25 Sept. 1742 (131).

BAKER, JOHN, of Hunting Ridge, in 1750 owned 50 a. Parker's Palace (80:175; 153).

BAKER, JOHN, m. Mary Hilliard on 16 Apr. 1734 (133).

BAKER, JOHN, of Absolom, in 1750 owned 40 a. John's Park (153).

BAKER, NICHOLAS, m. 4 Jan. 1741 Martha Wood, named as sis. in the will of Joshua Wood made 21 March 1749; had iss.: PROVI-DENCE, b. 17 Sept. 1743; NICHOLAS, b. 1 Sept. 1748; BENJAMIN, b. 16 March 1750; MARTHA, b. 12 March 1754; JOHN WOOD, b. 2 July 1756; GEORGE, b. 23 Jan. 1759; JOSHUA, b. 1 June 1761 (129; 210-26:99).

BAKER, NORTON GROVES, m. 23 d, 1 mo., 1742 Mary Rawlings (136).

BAKER, SAMUEL, in Balto. Co. by 1692 as a taxable in Spesutia Hund.; d. by 25 May 1699 when admin. bond was posted by Ann Baker with Henry Jackson and Evan Miles (11; 138).

BAKER, SAMUEL, m. Catherine (?) and had iss.: SAMUEL, b. 19 Sept. 1727; MARY, b. 22 Oct. 1730; BETHIA, b. 2 Nov. 1732; HANNAH, b. 26 March 1734; JOHN, b. 10 Oct. 1736; JAMES, b. 5 April 1743 (131).

BAKER, SARAH, ind. for bast. in June 1741 and again in Nov. 1758 (33:56: 46:162)

BAKER, THEO'S, m. Eliz. Beldem on 6 Oct. 1748 (131).

BAKER, THOMAS, m. Mary (?), had iss.: MARY, b. 14 Feb. 1731; ELIZABETH, b. 21 April 1733 (128:87).

BAKER, THOMAS, m. Mary Crawford on 14 April 1734, had iss.: WILLIAM, b. 13 Sept. 1742 (128:77; 129).

BAKER, WILLIAM, m. Elizabeth Cannon on 16 Sept. 1737; had iss.: WILLIAM, b. 20 June 1738 (128:92b).

BAKER, ZEBEDIAH, m. Hannah Baker on 28 Jan. 1749/50 (133).

BAKER, MATTHEW, of Balto. Co., late of New Eng., iron master, on 1 March 1745 conv. William Bond 100 a. Pork Hall (79:129).

THE BALCH FAMILY was the subject of a family genealogy by Thomas Willing Balch, pub. in 1907. (510).

BALCH, JOHN (1), came to Md. by 1658, possibly having m. Catherine Cleland, and had iss.: THOMAS, b. c.1660; ROBERT. (510)

BALCH, THOMAS (2), s. of John (1), was b. c.1660, d. 1730; may have gone back to Eng. and taken part in Monmouth's Rebellion and then ret. to Annapolis, Md., c.1685; m. Agnes Somerville; had iss.: HEZEKIAH. (510).

BALCH, HEZEKIAH (3), s. of Thomas (2), was living in Balto. Co. as late as 1725; admin. the est. of William Jenkins on 7 Aug. 1724; m. 1st, on 30 July 1707 in St. Anne's Par., A. A. Co., Martha Brewenton, and 2nd, by Nov. 1717 Dorothy; had two ch. by 1st w. and three by 2nd: JAMES, b. 5 Dec. 1714; JOHN, b. 23 Jan. 1715/6; (by 2nd w.): THOMAS, b. 15 Nov. 1717; HEZEKIAH, b.

6 March 1721; MARY, b. 2 Oct. 1725 (2; 128:44, 45, 46; 219-2: 372). (510).

BALCH, JAMES (4), s. of Hezekiah (3) and Martha, b. 5 Dec. 1714, d. 1779; in 1769 moved to N. C.; m. in Balto. Co. on 19 Jan. 1737 Ann Goodwin; had iss.: ELIZABETH, b. 7 March 1738; MARY, b. prob. 7 March 1738; MARGARET; RHODA; HEZEKIAH JAMES, b. 1746; STEPHEN BLOOMER, b. 5 April 1747; JAMES, b. 25 Dec. 1750, d. 1821 in Sullivan Co., Ind., a Presbyterian minister; WILLIAM GOODWIN, b.1751, d. 14 Oct. 1822, m. Elizabeth Rodgers, and rendered patriotic service in N. C. during the Rev. War; RACHEL; AMOS, b. 2 July 1758; JOHN, b. 1760 (128:92b, 107; 353).

BALCH, JOHN (5), s. of Hezekiah (3) and Martha, b. 23 Jan. 1715/6; went to N. C. in 1763 where he rendered patriotic service during the Rev. War; m. 1st on 24 March 1735 Mary Cannon, and 2nd Sarah (?); had iss.: HEZEKIAH, b. 1741 Deer Creek, became a Presbyterian minister, m. and had iss. (128:92; 353).

BALCH, HEZEKIAH JAMES (6), s. of James (4) and Ann, b. 1748, d. 1776 in Mecklenburg Co., N. C., bur. Poplar Tent Presbyterian Church; est. granted to wid. Martha (nee Scovell) (353).

BALCH, Rev. JAMES (7), s. of James (4) and Ann, b. 25 Dec. 1750 in Balto. Co., d. 12 Jan. 1821; m. Susanna Lavinia Garrison; served in the Rev. War, and is bur. in Mann Twp., Sullivan Co., Ind. (353; 361:50).

BALCH, AMOS (8), s. of James (4) and Ann, b. 20 July 1758, d. 1835 in Bedford Co., Tenn.; m. Ann Patton; was a pvt. and then a sgt. in the N. C. militia; from Mecklenburg Co.; was blind in the eye; later moved to Christian Co., Ky. (353).

BALCH, HEZEKIAH (9), s. of John (5) and Mary, b. 1741, was a Presbyterian minister, may have m. Martha McKinley on 27 Oct. 1768, and had iss. (131).

THE BALE FAMILY is more fully discussed by Barnes (259)

BALE, (?) (1), prob. lived in Withycombe Rawleigh, Co. Devon, Eng.; m. Urath (?) who was living in 1720; had iss.: THOMAS, b. c.1664: HANNAH, d. by 31 May 1727, m. Thomas Randall by 2 Feb. 1708; MARY, living in Exmouth, Co. Devon in Jan. 1729 as Mary Wooton; ANTHONY, d. by 30 April 1720 in Balto. Co. (259:5-6).

BALE, THOMAS (2), s. of (?) (1) and Urath, b. c.1664, bur. in St. Geo. Par. on 5 Feb. 1708; m. (prob. as 2nd w.) Sarah, dau. of Miles Gibson; she was bur. 18 March 1708; in Balto. Co. by 1702; gave his age as 40 in 1704 and named Robert Gibson as a bro.; bought 100 a. Rich Level in 1702 and surv. 386 a. Green Spring Punch the same year; will, 14 March 1706 - 18 March 1708, named sis. Hannah Bale, sis. Mary Bale, bro. Anthony, dau. Urath, "honored mother Urath Carnall," Mrs. Elizabeth Cromwell, James Phillips, Aquila Paca, Richard Jones, Richard Smithers, Jemmy Hollingsworth, (testator's) w. Sarah; admin. bond posted 31 Jan. 1711 by Anthony Bale with Thomas Cromwell and Roger Matthews so that Anthony could amin. all est. not previously adm. by Thomas' extxs. Sarah and Urath; est. inv. in March 1708 by John Stokes and Richard Smithers and val. at £ 1069.4.10; est. adm. in April 1714 by Anthony Bale; Sarah Gibson Bale d. by 24 March 1710 when her est. was inv. by Lawrence Draper and Roger Matthews and val. at £ 370.6.4; her est. adm. by Anthony Bale on 28 Aug. 1710, 30 Jan. 1711 and 31 Aug. (1715?); Thomas had iss.: URATH, d. leaving a will, 18 June 1708 - 19 Nov. 1708, which named mother-in-law, uncle Anthony Bale and aunt Hannah Randall; her admin. bond was posted 3 Aug. 1709 by Richard Smithers with John Stokes and Roger Matthews (1; 2; 11; 48:9, 296; 51:14; 128:14, 15; 259; 398:26).

BALE, ANTHONY (3), s. of (1) and Urath, d. in April 1720, having m. 15 June 1713 Anne Plummer; his will, 10 April 1720 - 30 April 1720, named w. Anne, sis. Hannah Randall, sis. Mary Wooten now in Eng., and his dear "and antient" mother if still alive, and Roger Matthews; will was wit. by Matthews, Thomas Newsham, and Richard Hardiman; admin. bond posted 2 Oct. 1723 by Michael Taylor with Charles and Daniel Carroll; wid. Ann may have m. 2nd Michael Taylor; poss. iss.: ANTHONY, d. 1742 in Som Co. (111; 128:33).

THE BALL FAMILY has been discussed by Gossett, Johnston, Sweeny, Walne et al. (516; 517; 518; 519; 520).

BALL, Col. WILLIAM (1) of Millenbeck, Lancaster Co., Va., ancestor of Pres. George Washington, had several ch., incl.: RICHARD.

BALL, RICHARD (2), s. of Col. William (1), d. c.1677 in Balto. Co. having imm. by July 1659 and again by 1663; acquired several portions of land, ans was Justice of the Co. Court in July 1665; d. by 27 July 1677 when William Ball came to Md. to settle his son's est.; m. Mary, wid. of Thomas Humphreys and had iss.: HANNAH, m. by 12 May 1681 Thomas Everest of Balto. Co. and moved to Calvert Co. by Feb. 1683 when they sold 60 a. Ball's Additon to John Bennett (10:38, 68, 71; 11:59; 200-3:529; 200-10: 38, 68, 71; 200-67:134; 59:72).

BALL, WILLIAM, imm. by 1662 and in Oct. 1676 was in A. A. Co. when he sold William Cockey 100 a. Ball's Enlargement; his will, 10 April 1684 - 8 May 1686, named w. Mary, Mrs. Eliza Crumwell and her son William; est. inv. in 1686 (101; 110; 206-9:152; 388).

BALTON, CHARLES, in 1750 owned 200 a. part Bond's Gift (See also Charles Bolton) (153).

BANDELL, JOSEPH, pet. to be levy free in Nov. 1756 (41:302).

BANISTER, JAMES, surv. 200 a. Good Hope on the east s. of Bush R., adj. land orig. taken up by Ogburn Banister: d. by 1700 and his heirs were carried out of the Province (211).

BANISTER, WILLIAM, came from Stafford Co., Va., bought 50 a. Royston's Study from John Royston on 6 Aug. 1747 and till owned the land in 1750 (79; 153).

BANKS, WILLIAM (1), in Balto. Co. by 1729; in 1750 owned 77 a. Bank's Delight; m. Mary (?) and had at least two ch.: MARY, b. 18 Sept. 1729; JOHN, b. 22 July 1735 (133; 153).

BANKS, JOHN (2), s. of William (1), b. 22 July 1735, prob. the John who m. Mary Kelley on 18 Sept. 1756 and had: JOHN, b. 7 Oct. 1757; JAMES, b. 5 May 1759; ELIZABETH, b. 8 Feb. 1761; WILLIAM, b. 14 Jan. 1763 (133; 134).

BANKS, NICHOLAS, transp. to Balto. Co. by 1668 and claimed land for service in 1674 (388).

BANKS, THOMAS, in Balto. Co. by 1692 as a taxable in s. side Gunpowder Hund. (138).

BANKSON, JOSEPH (1), d. in Balto. Co. by 14 June 1732 when admin. bond was posted by his w. Hannah with John Parrish and Charles Wells; m. Hannah (?) who m. 2nd William Hughes on 11 Dec. 1735; est. admin. 26 April 1738 by William and Hannah Hughes; had iss.: JOSEPH; REBECCA; ARIANA; SUSANNA (4; 11; 30:91; 32:6; 133).

BANKSON, JOSEPH (2), s. of Joseph (1) and Hannah, was alive in 1761 having m. 16 Jan. 1752 Elizabeth Giles, wid. of James Slemaker who had m. Elizabeth Giles on 15 Sept. 1745; signed a pet. for St. Pauls Par. to hire an organist in 1760; his will. 2 Feb. 1762 - 6 Dec. 1762, named w. Elizabeth and three ch.: MARY, b. 12 July 1754, m. George Daffin on 13 Feb. 1773; JAMES, b. 1 Oct. 1759; JOSEPH, b. 23 March 1761 (6; 111; 133; 200-61:500).

THE BANNEKER FAMILY has been discussed in a magazine article by Henry E. Baker and a book by Sylvio Bedini. (521; 522).

BANNEKER, ESTHER, m. William Black on 22 Sept. 1744 (133).

BANNEKER, KATHERINE, black, m. James Boston, black, on 22 May 1735 (133).

BANNEKER, ROBERT, was in Balto. Co. by 1736 when in March he and his wife were made levy free so long as their crippled mulatto dau. Julian was living; in Nov. 1743 his two daus were made levy free; in 1750 he owned Stout, 100 a., and 25 a. Timber Point (31:2; 35:78; 153).

BARDLEY, ANN, was ind. for bast. in March 1743/4 (35:154).

BARDWELL, JOSEPH, m. Jane (?) and had iss.: JOHN, b. 12 Aug. 1745; JOSEPH, b. 2 Aug. 1748; CHARLES, b. 24 Jan. 1751; in 1783 lived in Delaware Upper Hund. and owned 50 a. Barnes Level (134; 283).

BARHAM, JOHN, m. Sarah Demett in 1753 (131).

BARKALL, SAMUEL, owned 300 a. Bachelor's Choice in 1750 (153).

BARKER, JOHN, cooper, d. after 12 June 1705 when his will was dated, naming bro. Charles and Dr. John Rattenbury, the latter to have 150 a. Barker's Choice (110).

BARKER, WILLIAM, was in Balto. Co. by 1694 as a taxable in the s. side Patapsco Hund.; m. Mary (?), admnx. of Francis Watkins, by 1698; d. after 12 Sept. 1701 when his will was dated naming w. Mary, Philip Cole s. of Philip and Mary, Thomas Lambert s. of John and Sarah, and the two sons of John and Eliza Barker, as well as tracts Stepney and Middlesex; est. inv. 15 Nov. 1701 by John Barrett and Nicholas Rogers and val. at Ł 148.6.0; admin. bond posted 2 Aug. 1703 by John Oldton with Charles Merryman, Sr., and Jonas Bowen (11; 51; 121; 139; 206-16:209).

BARKLEY, GEORGE, Irish tailor, age c.26, ran away from William Thompson, living at Joppa, in Nov. 1743 (384:403).

BARLAR, MARY, was tried for bast. in March 1754 (39:31).

BARLOW, JAMES, d. in Balto. Co. by 2 Dec. 1721, having m. Johannah (?) who m. as her 2nd husb. Charles McDaniel; his will, 8 June 1721 - 2 Dec. 1721, named w. Johanna, John Marsh, Sr., and these ch.: Joab, Zachariah, John, William, James, and Bathsheba; admin. bond was posted 2 Dec. 1721 by Johanna Barlow and Joab Barlow, the execs., with Christopher Randall and Maurice Baker; est. admin. on 2 Nov. 1723 and 2 July 1725 by Johanna, now w. of Charles McDaniel and on 2 Nov. 1728 by Christopher Randall; had

BATHSHEBA, m. by Nov. 1728 James Harris; JOAB; JAMES, d. test., his his will, 16 May 1721 - 2 "8ber" 1721, named bro. Joab as exec., mentioned other bros. and sis., and appointed his father as exec.; JOHN; WILLIAM; ZACHARIAH, in March 1724/5 chose Christopher Randall and Maurice Baker as guardians (1; 2; 3; 11; 27:127; 28:71; 110; 111).

BARLOW, REBECCA, named William Groves as the father of her ch. in June 1722 (24:169).

BARLY, MARY, was ind. for bast. in June 1729 (28:41).

BARNABY, EDWARD, m. Elizabeth Farmer on 22 Sept. 1745 (131).

THE BARNES FAMILY of Harford County has been the subject of a family genealogy pub. by Walter D. Barnes. (271).

BARNES, WILLIAM (1), progenitor, d. in St. Georges Par. 22 May 1720, leaving one s. JOB (128:39).

BARNES, JOB (2), s. of William (1), was b. c.1678, d. c.1703; m. c.1697 Elizabeth, dau. of Thomas Ford; she m. 2nd Mathias Clark (by whom she had a dau. Elizabeth), and 3rd John Norton (by whom she had five ch.); Job d. by 11 Oct. 1703; Elizabeth was alive in Oct. 1735 when she conv. her s. Ford Barnes 200 a. Repulta, which she had inher. from her father; had iss.: FORD, b. 12 April 1698; JOB, b. 20 Dec. 1701; JAMES, b. 26 March 1704 (11; 110; 253).

BARNES, FORD (3), s. of Job (2) and Elizabeth, b. 12 April 1698, d. June 1749; m. 21 Sept..1721 Margaret, dau. of Gregory Farmer; Margaret d. by 30 Aug. 1756; his will, 2 Sept. 1748 - 25 June 1749, named w. Margaret and ch.: James, Elizabeth, Gregory, Ann, Margaret, Martha, Ford, and Hannah Mitchell; admin. bond posted k3 May 1749 by Margaret Barnes with Jonathan Jones and Ford Barnes; in 1750 the heirs of Ford Barnes owned 150 a. Repulta and 60 a. Barnes' Delight; the est. of Margaret was inv. 30 Aug. 1756 by Richard Johns and Philip Gover and val. at ₤ 18.10.4; had iss.: FORD, b. 26 June 1724; JAMES, b. 7 June 1726; d. 27 March 1727; HANNAH, b. 26 Sept. 1728, m. (?) Mitchell; JAMES, b. 5 Jan. 1730; ELIZABETH, b. 26 Jan. 1732; GREGORY FARMER, b. 21 Jan. 1734; ANN, b. 31 March 1737; MARGARET, b. 26 Feb. 1738; MARTHA, b. 8 June 1742, d. 12 Oct. 1742; MARTHA, b. 1 Jan. 1743; JOB, b. 5 March 1747 (11; 50; 128:32, 43, 49, 57, 63, 75, 86,95, 96, 101; 129; 153).

BARNES, JOB (4), s. of Job (2) and Elizabeth, b. 20 Dec. 1701, d. 11 Nov. 1739; m. 11 Oct. 1722 Constant, dau. of Robert West, b. 20 April 1703 and m. as her 2nd husb. Joseph Morgan in Sept. 1740; admin. bond posted 15 Jan. 1739 by Constant Barnes with Jacob Giles and John Cook; est. adm. on 7 July 1741; in March 1745/6 ch. John and Keziah chose Col. Rigbie as their guardian; had iss.: JOB, b. 20 Dec. 1723; MARGARET, b. 30 July 1725; JOHN, b. 2 Feb. 1727; ELIZABETH, b. 2 May 1730, d. 23 Aug. 1734; CASSIAH, or KEZIAH, b. 2 May 1732; ELIZABETH, b. 23 Aug. 1735; THOMAS, b. 27 Sept. 1737; CONSTANCE, b. 30 Sept. 1739 (4; 11; 35:801; 128:32, 42, 44, 63, 84, 89, 98, 104, 114).

BARNES, JAMES (5), s. of Job (2) and Elizabeth, b. 26 March 1704, d. by 22 Aug. 1747; m. Bethiah Loney on 27 May 1726; admin. bond. posted by Bethiah Barnes on 22 Aug. 1747 with John Loney and Amos Garrett; est. adm. 16 May 1754; had iss.: JOHN, b. 24 Nov. 1727; JEMIMAH, b. 5 May 1729; JAMES, b. 4 April 1732; RACHEL, b. 4 June 1734; WILLIAM, b. 17 Nov. 1736; RICHARD, b. 1 June 1740; MARY, twin, b. 1 June 1740; FORD, b. 11 Sept. 1743; BETHIA, b. 11 Feb. 1745/6 (4; 11; 128:32, 67, 79, 94, 116; 129).

BARNES, FORD (6), s. of Ford (3) and Margaret, b. 26 June 1724, d. 8 April 1761; m. Ruth Garrett on 20 Oct. 1743; his will, 24 May 1761 - 31 Dec. 1761, named w. Ruth and ch.: Bennett, Richard, and Amos, bro. Gregory, bro.-in-law Amos Garrett, ment. four ch. in all; had iss.: FORD, b. 7 Sept. 1749, d. 8 April 1761; CASSAN-DRA, b. 17 Feb. 1751; BENNETT, b. 17 Sept. 1753; ARABELLA, b. 17 Jan. 1755; RICHARD, b. 5 Nov. 1757; AMOS, b. 17 Nov. 1759; FORD, b. 24 June 1761, d. 29 June 1761 (111:325; 129).

BARNES, GREGORY FARMER (7), s. of Ford (3) and Margaret, b. 21 Jan. 1734; m. Elizabeth Mitchell on 30 Nov. 1758; had iss.: AVA-RILLA, b. 6 Dec. 1759; FORD, b. 4 April 1761; RICHARD, b. 25 June 1762; RACHEL, b. 23 March 1764 (129).

BARNES, JOB, (8), s. of Job (4) and Constance, b. 20 Dec. 1723; m. Mary Crawford on 2 Feb. 1749; had iss.: JOB, b. 11 June 1752; RACHEL, b. 13 Aug. 1754; EZEKIEL, b. 4 July 1758 (129:353).

THE BARNES FAMILY of Anne Arundel and Baltimore Counties is of no known rel. to the family in Harford County. The Anne Arundel Co. family is discussed in the Dorsey Genealogy, by Dorsey et al.

BARNES, JAMES (9), no known rel. to William (1), was in Balto. Co. by 1701, and d. by 18 June 1726 having m. Keturah, dau. of Adam and Lois Shipley; owned 103 a. Eve's Dowry, pt. of Adam the First, on the s. side of Patapsco Hund.; admin. bond was posted 18 June 1726 by Keturah S. Barnes with Robert Shipley and Robert Barnes: est. inv. 13 July 1726 by Jno. Hammond and (?) Wainwright and val. at £ 85.18.9; Keturah was alive in Aug. 1730; had iss.: RICHARD, alive in 1751; ROBERT, d. 1775 in Fred. Co., having m. 11 Feb. 1728 Lois Porter; ADAM, d. testate in A. A. Co., 1779, hav-ing m. Hannah, dau. of John and Honor Dorsey; JAMES, d. 1740; PETER, d. 1759 in A. A. Co.; JOSHUA, alive 1745, m. Ruth (?); KETURA, m. 22 Oct. 1728 Richard Shipley; SUSANNA, b. 15 May 1715, may have m. Charles Porter; NATHAN, b. 18 June 1757, d. 1760, having m. Ellis (?) (11; 51; 67; 143; 210-30:631; 210-31:88; 31:88; 41:186; 217; 219-2).

BARNES, RICHARD (10), s. of James (9), and Keturah, was in Balto. Co. in 1751, m. 1st on 28 July 1716 Sarah Stevens, and 2nd by 1740 Catherine (?); owned 250 a. Good For Little, 146 a. Ship-ley's Search, 103 a. Eve's Dower, and 200 a. Bold Venture; had iss.: BENJAMIN, b. 3 Oct. 1716; RICHARD, Jr., ind. for breach of peace in A. A. Co. (216; 217; 219-2).

BARNES, JAMES (11), s. of James (9) and Keturah, d. testate in Balto. Co.; his will, 4 June 1740 - 18 April 1740 (sic), named bros. Adam and Peter, tracts 235 a. Day's Discovery and 80 a. of Barnes' Luck, and three sons: RICHARD; JAMES; JOHN (127).

BARNES, BENJAMIN (12), s. of Richard (10) and Sarah, b. 3 Oct. 1716, bapt. 29 July 1717, was alive in Aug. 1764; m. Martha (?); pat. 50 a. Barnes' Level; in 1750 owned 25 a. Absolom's Chance; prob. d. or left the county or March 1769 (79:329; 153; 207; 219-2; 339:134).

BARNES, ISABELLA, age over 14, chose John Patterson as her guardian in Aug. 1757 (46:53).

BARNES, JOHN, m. Elizabeth Scott on 10 Aug. 1749; may be the par. of: ELIZABETH, b. to John and Elizabeth, 4 Dec. 1761 (129: 375; 131:34).

BARNES, MARY, named Dorsey Petticoat as the father of her ch., in March 1746/7 (36:392).

BARNES, PHILEMON, m. by Nov. 1756 a dau. of George Ogg
(229:232).

BARNES, RICHARD, b. 20 Feb. 1763 in Balto. Co., d. 7 Nov.
1845 in Danville, Hendricks Co., Ind.; enl. in the Rev. War from
Henry Co., Va. (361:52).

THE BARNEY FAMILY has been discussed briefly in a biography of
Commodore Joshua Barney by Adams. (523).

BARNEY, WILLIAM (1), progenitor, in Balto. Co. by 1707, d. test.
by 19 March 1746/7, m. 1st Elizabeth, dau. of Edward and Mary (?)
Stevenson, and 2nd Mary (?) who m. as her 2nd husb. Richard Rutter
and d. 1779; Wm. owned 150 a. Morgan's Delight, 100 a. Valiant
Hazard; by 1750 his wid. owned 100 a. Timber Ridge, 100 Valiant
Hazard, and 100 a. Absolom's Chance; William's will, 20 Feb.
1746/7 - 19 March 1746/7, named w. Mary and ch.: William, Martha
wife of Richard Hooker, Absolom, Benjamin, another William, Moses,
Mary, Ruth; admin. bond posted 31 Aug. 1747 by extx. Mary Barney
with Thomas Sheredine and Absolom Barney; est. adm. 25 May 1748
and 31 Aug. 1748 by extx. Mary Barney, and on 9 Nov. 1752 by Mary
now w. of Richard Rutter; will of Mary Rutter, dated 13 Feb. 1779,
named ch.: Absolom, Benjamin, William, Moses, Mary Butler, Ruth
Ford and gch. William Barney of Moses and Absolom and Pearson
Barney; had iss. (2 ch. by 1st w., and 6 ch. by 2nd w.): WILLIAM,
b. 20 March 1718; MARTHA, m. Richard Hooker; ABSOLOM, b. 2 Oct.
1722; BENJAMIN, b. c.1728; MARY, b. 22 Feb. 1730, m. Absolom Butler; RUTH, b. 28 Jan. 1732, m. Mordecai Ford; WILLIAM, b. 6 March
1734/5; MOSES (4; 5; 11; 63:481; 71:100; 110; 112; 133; 153; 200-
44:246).

BARNEY, WILLIAM (2), s. of William (1) and Elizabeth, b. 20
March 1718, d. by 1773; m. Frances Holland Watts on 26 Jan. 1743
(she d. 27 June 1788); gave his age as 54 on 15 May 1772; pet.
the Assembly to record a deed to his mother from her mother; by
1750 owned 214 a. pt. Willim, and 22 a. Morgan's Delight; was
k. when a s. accidentally discharged a gun in Aug. 1773; his wid.
d. June 1788 in her 64th yr. and was bur. in the family burial
ground in Patapsco Neck; had iss.: ELIZABETH, b. 27 April 1745;
MARGARET, b. 2 June 1747, d. 24 Sept. 1748; PEGGY, b. 20 Aug.
1749; JOHN HOLLAND, b. 24 July 1752; WILLIAM STEVENSON, b. 28
Dec. 1754, was a marine officer in the Virginia, captured by the
British in 1778, later kept a hotel in Georgetown; MARY, b. 20
Aug. 1757, d. 29 Aug. 1758; JOSHUA, b. 6 July 1759 hero of the
Rev. War and the War of 1812 (133; 255:4; 257:2).

BARNEY, ABSOLOM (3), s. of William (1) and Mary, b. 2 Oct.
1722, d. by 1 Dec. 1804; m. by 6 Dec. 1752 Mary, dau. of Thomas
and Leah Ford, b. 6 Feb. 1725; in 1750 he owned 150 a. Pearson's
and Benjamin's Lot; in 1773 was a taxable in North Hund., with
Absolom, Jr.; had iss.: RUTH, m. Hugh Brown on 15 Aug. 1771 and by
Dec. 1804 was in Jefferson Co., Ohio; THOMAS, living 1804; MARY,
m. (?) Tracey; ABSOLOM, Jr., alive and a taxable in North Hund.
in 1773; LEAH, m. by lic. 30 Oct. 1781 John Gill; poss. HANNAH, m.
by lic. 9 March 1786 Nathaniel Sheppard by whom she had a s.
Absolom Barney Sheppard; poss. ELEANOR, m. by 26 Sept. 1759 John
Foster and had two sons George and Absolom Foster (5; 131; 133; 153
153; 161; 200-33; 231-WG#53; 232).

BARNEY, BENJAMIN (4), s. of William (1) and Mary, b. c.1728,
living in 1787; m. 23 April 1758 Delilah, dau. of Joseph Bosley;
gave his age as 44 in June 1772; named as the father of Mary
Cross's child in March 1754; prob. had iss.: RUTH; JOSEPH BOSLEY,
d. by 24 May 1790 having m. by lic. 2 Feb. 1788 Rebecca Pickett
who admin. his est. (9; 10; 39:29; 85; 89; 131; 231-AL#I).

BARNEY, WILLIAM (5), the Younger, s. of William (1) and Mary, b. 6 March 1734/5; chose Absolom Barney as guardian in Nov. 1750; was prob. the William named as the father of Elizabeth Marvell's child in Nov. 1759 (38:2; 46:242).

BARNEY, MOSES (6), s. of William (1) and Mary, d. by Nov. 1784, having m. on 5 April 1758 Sarah Bond, who surv. him; he enl. in Capt. Frederick Deem's 7th Regt. on 21 Dec. 1776, was a corporal by 1 Aug. 1778, and disch. 1 Nov. 1780; enl. again by 1 Aug. 1781 when he was disch. as a sergeant; wife Sarah pet. in Aug. 1781 for her husb. to be disch. as he was the only support for her and six ch. and with her eldest son, had been in the service for 6 yrs; d. by 4 Nov. 1784 when letters of admin. were granted to Sarah with Benjamin Bond, Sr., and Thomas Barney; had iss.: THOMAS, b. 19 July 1759 (prob. the same Thomas enl. by Thomas Lansdale and plassed by Maj. Thomas Jones of Balto. Town on 20 July 1776); BENJAMIN, b. 17 Jan. 1761; ANNA, b. 9 Dec. 1762; WILLIAM (named in will of grandmother Mary Barney Rutter); ELIZABETH (named as dau. of Sarah in the will of Joseph Anderson), m. by lic. 25 Jan. 1794 Edward Trippe; prob. two other unknown children (134; 200-18; 208-5; 232; 235).

BARNHARTON, CATHERINE, serv. of George Pickett, fined for bast. in Nov. 1758 (46:161).

BARRETT, DANIEL, in 1750 owned 170 a. pt. Broad's Improvement and 2 lots in Balto. Town with Peter Miner (153).

BARRETT, JOHN, d. by 25 Feb. 1677 when John Stanesby and Miles Gibson were appointed to inquire into what lands he owned at the time of his death (200-51).

BARRETT, JOHN, d. by 24 March 1717/8 having m. Alice, extx. of Nicholas Corbin; his will, 21 June 1717 - 24 March 1717/8 named "grandson" Nicholas Corbin, eld. s. of Edward Corbin, also John Royston, James Wells, and John Keith, s. of Alex., wife Alice to be extx.; she was alive in Nov. 1718 when Zacheus Richards, age 2, was bound to serve her (23:37; 110; 206-20).

BARRETT, JOHN, was found guilty of murdering his w. and was was executed in Dec. 1753 (385).

BARRETT, JOSEPH, in 1750 owned 100 a. The Fancy (153).

BARRINGTON, TOBIAS, was in Balto. Co. by 1695 as a taxable in s. side of Patapsco Hund. (140).

BARROW, RALPH, was in Balto. Co. by 1692 as a taxable in s. side Patapsco Hund. (138).

BARROW, ROBERT, was a taxable in Spesutia Hund. in 1695 (140).

BARTLE, MARY, had iss.: MARGARET, b. 8 Jan. 1735 (128:90).

BARTLEY, ANN, orph. dau. of Ann, was placed with Andrew Scott in Nov. 1744 (35:387).

THE THOMAS BARTON FAMILY

BARTON, THOMAS (1), was a taxable in n. side of Gunpowder Hund. in 1700; m. Abigail (?); d. by 22 May 1730; will, 6 Jan. 1730 - 22 May 1730, named w. Abigail, Thomas and John Barton, son James Barton, and Elizabeth and Ann Barton; admin. bond was posted 22 May 1730 by Abigail Barton with John Norris and James Barton; est. admin. 10 April 1732 by Abigail, who stated that the dec. left 5 children; had iss.: JAMES; THOMAS, b. 27 June 1710; JOHN, b. 28

June 1715; ELIZABETH, b. 28 Jan. 1717; WILLIAM, b. 15 Dec. 1718, prob. d. young; ANN, b. 8 Oct. 1720 (3; 11; 110; 131; 142).

BARTON, JAMES (2), s. of Thomas (1) and Abigail, m. Temperance Rollo on 8 Sept. 1730; d. by 19 Feb. 1734/5 when his will, dated 20 Oct. 1734, was proved, naming s. James, dau. Phillis, bros. Thomas and John, w. Temperance and her father Archibald Rollo, witnesses were sd. Rollo, Hugh Lowe, Daniel McComas, and Peter Carroll; admin. bond posted 27 Feb. 1734/5 by extx. Temperance with Archibald Rollo and Henry Hicks; est. admin. 20 Dec. 1735 and 10 May 1737; had iss.: PHILLIS, b. 5 Jan. 1731/2; JAMES, b. 3 Oct. 1734 (3; 11; 31:43; 111; 131).

BARTON, THOMAS (3), s. of Thomas (1) and Abigail, b. 27 June 1710; m. Elizabeth Ward on 24 Feb. 1733; had iss.: JOSHUA, b. 23 Nov. 1734; THOMAS, b. 6 May 1737; ANN, b. 3 Jan. 1740; ELIZABETH, b. 3 Jan. 1741; MARY, b. 13 March 1742; JOHN, b. 18 Oct. 1747 (131).

BARTON, JOHN (4), s. of Thomas (1) and Abigail, b. 28 June 1715, d. 1777 in Harf. Co.; m. Ann Hitchcock on 23 May 1738; his will, 4 Jan. 1773 - 6 Aug. 1777; had iss.: KEZIA, b. 4 Feb. 1745, m. Robert Clark on 15 Nov. 1759; JOHN, b. 22 Feb. 1749; JEMIMA, m. James Pocock on 20 Sept. 1756; WILLIAM; JAMES; ELIZABETH; ALISANA (131; 244 -AJ#2).

THE LEWIS BARTON FAMILY

BARTON, LEWIS (5), no known rel. to above, was transp. to Md. as a servant by 1674; purch. 136 a. James' Pasture from Thomas James in May 1688 (the tract was later held by William Farfarr for Barton's Orphans); m. Joan (?) who m. as her 2nd husb. William Farfarr; admin. bond posted by Wm. and Joan Farfarr on 4 March 1692/3 with Francis Watkins, John Hayes, Michael Gormacon and Robert Gardner; had iss.: LEWIS (11; 59; 211; 388).

BARTON, LEWIS (6), s. of Lewis (5), was a taxable in n. side Patapsco Hund. by 1700, d. by 13 Nov. 1716; may have m. a dau. of Selah Dorman; inher. James Pasture which he conv. to Andrew Anderson in Nov. 1709; admin. bond posted 13 Nov. 1716 by Selah Dorman with Thomas Cannon and John Fitzredmond; est. inv. 19 Nov. 1716 by sd. Cannon and Fitzredmond and signed by John and Elizabeth Ensor (could she have been a dau. of Lewis?); prob. father of: SELAH (11; 52; 67; 142; 211).

BARTON, SELAH (7), s. of Lewis (6) and definitely grandson of Selah Dorman, d. by 1757; m. 1st on 27 Dec. 1730 Rebecca Biddison and 2nd, on 24 Jan. 1733, Comfort Roberts; admin. bond posted 25 April 1757 by Comfort Barton with John Roberts and Mark Guishard; est. admin. 27 Sept. 1762 by Comfort, who stated that the dec. left 9 children, incl.: LEWIS, b. 24 Feb. 1737; GREENBERRY, b. 6 Nov. 1739; ASAEL, b. 14 April 1741; SELAH, b. 10 Feb. 1743; JOSHUA b. 22 Nov. 1745; prob. 4 others (4; 6; 11; 23:399; 27:40; 133).

BARTON, LEWIS (8), s. of Selah (7) and Comfort, b. 24 Feb. 1737; m. Johanna Simmons on 30 June 1757; had iss.: JAMES, b. 19 Feb. 1758 (129:131).

BARTON, ELIZABETH, m. 7 May 1727 James Wright (131).

BARTON, JAMES, m. 19 Dec. 1756 Sarah Everett (131).

BARTON, JAMES, d. by 4 July 1774; m. Catherine (?); his will, 2 Dec. 1768 - 4 July 1774, named w. Catherine, ygst. s. William to have Robbin's Camp; and other ch.; had iss.: MARY, b. 26 May 1736; SARAH; JAMES; NATHAN; BENJAMIN; CHARLES; MARGARET; CATHERINE; WILLIAM (112; 133).

BARTON, JOHN, m. 20 Dec. 1770 Ruth, dau. of Charles and
Susannah Gorsuch (q.v.) (131).

BARTON, JOHN, d. by 13 April 1784 when admin. bond was posted by extx. Dorothy Barton with Thomas Brown or Drown and James
Pocock (15).

BARTON, JOSHUA, d. by 6 March 1779 when admin. bond was posted by admnx. Sarah Barton with Greenbury Barton and William Pilott
(15).

BARTON, THOMAS, m. 16 April 1761 Phebe Cammell (131).

BASHTEEN, WILLIAM, m. March 1699 Lydia Algood; had iss.: MARY,
b. 29 April 1700 (128; 129).

BASKETT, RICHARD, m. 31 Jan. 1743 Adfire Boyd (131).

BASSE, JOHN, was in Balto. Co. by 1692 as a taxable in s.
side Patapsco Hund. (138).

BASSETT (als. CATCHAM), MARTHA, was sentenced to death in Jan.
1752 for the murder of Mrs. Clark of Balto. Co. (385).

BASTOCK. See BOSTOCK.

BATH, STEPHEN, servant in the 1725 inv. of Samuel Dorsey (52).

BATSON, EDWARD, surv. 150 a. Batson's Fellowship above the
head of Bush River on 6 Jan. 1698; later sold (211:27).

BAUCHAM, NICHOLAS, m. Mary (?), and had iss.: JOHN, b. 1 July
1725 (128).

BAUSLEY. See BOSLEY.

THE BAXTER FAMILY is the subject of a well documented genealogy by Allan Sparrow Humphrey. (527)

BAXTER, EDMUND (1), progenitor, was a taxable in n. side Patapsco Hund. in 1692; m. Mary (?) with whom he wit. the will of Richard Sampson in Feb. 1714; owned 50 a. Corbin's Rest in 1750; his
will, 26 Aug. 1760 - 5 Nov. 1774, named dau. Elizabeth Green, s.-
in-law Abraham Green, grandch. Greenbury and Rachel Green, and s.
Edward Baxter; had iss.: ELIZABETH, b. 16 Nov. 1722, m. Abraham
Green on 28 Jan. 1749/50; PHILIZANNA, b. 19 July 1725; EDMUNDMAH,
b. 23 May 1728; GREENBURY, b. 11 i Feb. 1731; EDWARD (112; 113;
133; 153).

BAXTER, JOHN (2), no known rel. to above, d. 1757, having m.
Mary, the   of George and Mary (Stevenson) Brown; his will,
26 May 1757 - 4 Aug. 1757, named w. Mary and ch.: Mary, Ann,
Elizabeth, Benjamin, Bethuel, William, Greenbury, Edmond, John,
and George, and tracts Baxter's Choice, Baxter's Folly, Battson's
Forest, and Greenbury's Choice; had iss.: GREENBURY, b. 4 Oct.
1735; JOHN, b. 15 April 1739; MARY, b. 17 Nov. 1742; PHILISANNA,
b. 26 Feb. 1743; ELIZABETH, b. 16 July 1745; JOHN, b. 17 Feb.
1746; EDMUND, b. 28 Nov. 1748; GEORGE, b. 31 Jan. 1751; BENJA-
MIN, b. 31 Jan. 1751; BETHUEL, b. 6 March 1755; WILLIAM, b. 18
April 1757 (111; 133; 153).

BAXTER, GREENBURY (3), s. of John (2) and Mary, b. 4 Oct. 1735,
alive on 26 Feb. 1779; m. Charity (poss. Lane), and had iss.:
SAMUEL; b. c.1758; SARAH; MARY; JOHN, b. c.1768; ELIZABETH; DELIA;
and CHARLOTTE (527).

BAXTER, JOHN (4), s. of John (2) and Mary, b. 17 Feb. 1746, d.
by 30 Aug. 1783; m. Elizabeth, dau. of John and Margaret Sapping-
ton, who m. as her 2nd husb., William Tippings; had iss.: BENJA-
MIN, b. c.1770; EDMUND, b. 25 Feb. 1771; GEORGE; GREENBURY, b.
Feb. 1778; PATIENCE, m. 18 Dec. 1799 Martin Runyon in Madison Co.
Ky.; JOSHUA, m. 22 Sept. 1795 Nancy Nicholson (133; 527).

BAXTER, EDMUND (5), s. of John (2) and Mary, b. 28 Nov. 1748;
res. of Youghieghany Co., Va. in Jan. 1779 when he conv. part of
Baxter's Choice (inher. from his father), to Samuel Baxter of
Balto. Co. (133; 231-WG#C).

BAXTER, GEORGE (6), s. of John (2) and Mary, b. 31 Jan. 1751;
was in Fred. Co., Md., in 1781 when he sold Batson's Forest that
he inher. from his father (133; 527).

BAXTER, ELIZABETH, ind. for bast. in June 1743 and again in
Aug. 1746 (34:185; 36:125).

BAXTER, ELIZABETH, in 1750 owned 120 a. part Goose Harbor
(153).

BAY, ANDREW, clergyman, was b. in Ire.; ordained by New
Castle Presbytery in 1748, and settled in York Co., Penna.;
in April 1759 described as Presbyterian minister of St. George's
Par., Balto. Co., when with his trustees he purchased from Elizabeth Keen, spouse of John Keen, part of Good Neighborhood for the
purpose of building a church and establishing a burial ground;
served Deer Creek Church from 1760 to 1768; moved to Albany,
N. Y.; d. 1777 (83:385; 428:33).

BAYES, JOHN, was in Balto. Co. by 1694 as a taxable in the s.
side Patapsco Hund. (139).

BAYLEY. See BAILEY.

BAYLY. See BAILEY.

BAYNE. See BAIN.

BAYNES (or BEANS), CHRISTOPHER, d. by 1700; owned 1000 a.
Christopher's Camp which he surv. in July 1684; land was later
held by his s. Christopher (211:47).

BAYS, JOHN, m. 12 Sept. 1748 Eleanor Harryman (133).

BAYSPOLE, JOHN, merch., late of London, in Dec. 1658 conv. all
his goods to Godfrey Bayley, Gent., late of London (94).

BEACH. See BEECH.

BEAL (or BEEL), SAMUEL, in 1750 owned 100 a. part Austin's
and Deal's Chance (153).

BEAL, THOMAS, in 1750 owned 85 a. part Bale's Enlargement
(153).

BEAMSLEY, THOMAS, age 40 in Feb. 1744, leased from Thomas Brere-
wood, land, the lease to run for the lifetimes of Beasley, his w.
Mary, age 32, and Sarah Deason, age 4, dau. of Samuel Deason;
Thomas may have d. by April 1753, when Mary Beamsley m. James
Kelley (79:365; 131).

BEARD, WILLIAM, d. by 5 June 1723 when Francis and Mary Ogg posted admin. bond with William Bond and William Hunter; est. inv. on 7 Sept. 1723 by Charles Baker and Roland Shepherd and val. at £ 25.0.6; est. admin. by Francis and Mary Ogg on 4 June 1726 and 3 Aug. 1726; dec. left one minor ch., name unknown (2; 3; 11; 52).

BEARDY, CHRISTIANA, m. 29 Oct. 1728 Edward Sanders (129).

BEASLEY, ELIZABETH, m. 20 Feb. 1725 Edmund Lindsay (129).

BEASMAN, JOSEPH (1), progenitor, d. in Balto. Co. in 1738; was there by 1727; may be the Joseph who m. Mary Persias on 13 July 1707 in St. James Par., A. A. Co.; m. by 1726 Elizabeth (?) who surv. him; will, 24 Sept. 1726 - 20 Feb. 1738, named dau. Ruth not yet 16, wife Elizabeth, and tract 100 a. The Content; admin. bond posted 20 Feb. 1738 by wid. with John Hawkins and George Brown; est. adm. by wid. on 3 July 1740, heirs were s., of full age, and dau. Ruth, under age; had iss.: WILLIAM; RUTH, b. 3 July 1727 (3; 4; 11; 110; 133; 219-3).

BEASMAN, WILLIAM (2), s. of Joseph (1), was of full age in 1740 and d. test. in 1769; m. Ruth, b. 22 Jan. 1720, dau. of William and Sarah Hamilton; in 1750 owned William's Lot and William's Defense; will, 10 April 1769 - 4 Sept. 1769, named w. Ruth and ch.: Joseph, John, Thomas, Ann Chenoweth, Sarah Ogg, Catherine, Helen, and Mary, and tracts Beasman's Discovery Corrected, William's Defense, William's Lot Enlarged, and Addition to William's Defense; est. adm. 8 Sept. 1770 and 1 Dec. 1787, and again 1 May 1790; had iss.: ANNE, b. 27 July 1740, m. 1758 Arthur Chenoweth; JOSEPH, b. Nov. 1742, d. 1817, m. Rachel (?); SARAH, b. 2 Jan. 1744, m. (poss. William) Ogg; KATHERINE, b. 22 July 1746; WILLIAM, b. 4 June 1748, d. 1827; Thomas, b. c.1750, d. 1824, m. Sarah Gorsuch; JOHN; MARY, m. Thomas Weir; HELEN (6; 9; 10; 112; 119; 133; 134; 153; 236-11, 12).

BEASON, NICHOLAS, m. by 12 Dec. 1722 Diana, admnx. of Matthew Hale or Hall (26:157).

BEATY, JOHN, in 1750 owned 100 a., part Selsaid (153).

BEAVEN, JOHN, Sr., aged 83 in 1723 (310).

BEAVENS, JOHN, d. by 14 Feb. 1748 when admin. bond was posted by William Bond with Henry James and Nathan Nichols (11).

See also BEVAN, BEVINS.

BEAVER, WILLIAM (1), m. Mary (?) by 1710; in 1750 owned 100 a. part Mary's Delight, 13 a., pt. Neighborhood, and 100 a. Arabia Petrea; had iss.: HENRY, b. 24 March 1710; WILLIAM, b. 29 July 1713; JOHN, b. 14 Aug. 1721; MICHAEL, b. 12 July 1724 (128; 153).

BEAVER, WILLIAM (2), s. of William (1) and Mary, b. 29 July 1713, d. by 20 Dec. 1742; m. Blanche, admnx. of William Duly by Oct. 1740; admin. bond posted 20 Dec. 1742 by William Rhodes with Jacob Giles and Thomas Gash; had iss.: FRANCIS, b. July 1741 (4; 11; 128; 129).

BEAVER, JOHN (3), s. of William (1) and Mary, b. 14 Aug. 1721, m. 19 Sept. 1749 Sarah, dau. of Robert Hawkins (47:98; 128; 131).

BECHLEY, Mrs. FRANCES, m. Josias Middlemore on 9 Oct. 1720 (131).

BECK, MATTHEW (1), d. by 5 April 1748; m. 1st Mary (?) who d.
19 March 1739, and 2nd on 10 Feb. 1740 Ann (?), admnx. of Nicholas Horner; she m. as her 3rd husb. by 11 Aug. 1749 Henry Waters;
admin. bond posted 5 April 1748 by Ann Beck with John White and
Joseph Smith; est. adm. by Ann Beck, and acct. names ch.: Samuel,
Matthew, Elijah, and a dau. who m. Samuel Smith; had iss.: (by
1st w.) CHARLES, b. 23 June 1729; AVARILLA, m. 30 Aug. 1738
Samuel Smith; (by 2nd w.) CLEMENCY, b. April 1742; (maternity
uncertain) SAMUEL: MATTHEW; ELISHA (4; 5; 11; 131).

BECK, CHARLES (2), s. of Matthew (1), b. 23 June 1729, d.
test. Oct. 1770, leaving a will, 6 Oct. 1770 - 29 Oct. 1770,
naming sis. Abarilla Smith (112).

BECK, SAMUEL (3), s. of Matthew (1), m. 5 Dec. 1753 Mary
Groves (6; 131).

BECK, ELISHA (4), s. of Matthew (1), m. 1st on 31 July 1742
Sarah Baker, and m. 2nd (as Elijah Beck) on 19 Nov. 1752 Martha
Greenleaf; in 1750 owned 130 a. part Robinson's Chance and Hog
Neck; had iss. by 1st w.: AVARILLA, b. 30 June 1743; MARY, b. 15
Feb. 1747 (131; 153).

BECKETT, SYMON, in Balto. Co. by 1692 as a taxable in s. side
Gunpowder Hund. (138).

BECKHAM, JNO., taxable in s. side Patapsco Hund. by 1692 (138).

BEDDOE, JOHN, m. Sarah Litten on 3 Dec. 1724; in Nov. 1735
Sarah was summoned by vestry of St. Geo. Par. for unlawful cohab.
with Godfrey Vine (128; 130:280).

BEDFORD, JOHN, in Balto. Co. by 1692 as a taxable in Spesutia
Hund. (138).

BEDFORD, SARAH, m. 27 May 1700 Thomas Gilbert (129).

BEECH/BEACH, HENRY, alias Wiseman, m. Jane Garvin on 29 April
1740; owned 54 a. pt. Maiden's Bower and 13 a. Miller's Delight
in 1750; had iss.: THOMAS, b. 31 Aug. 1741; ELIZABETH, b. 9 April
1744; see also WISEMAN, HENRY (128; 129; 153).

BEECHAM, JOHN, m. 16 Sept. 1735 Ann Burton (128).

BEECHER, JOHN, in Balto. Co. by 1694 as a taxable in s. side
Patapsco Hund.; m. Edith Cromwell, wid. of 1st Christopher Gist
and 2nd Joseph Williams; will of Edith Beecher, dated 23 May
1694, named her s. Richard Gist and her bro. Richard Cromwell
(123; 139; 259).

BEEDLE, EDWARD, in Md. by 1661 and again by 1665; transp. to
Westmoreland Co., Va., in 1654 by Capt. Nicholas Martiau; d. by
30 Dec. 1696; m. Mary (?), wid. of Garrett Rutten; Justice of
Co. Court in 1683 and Co. Comm., 1684 - 1689; took up 100 a.
Beedle's Reserve in Sept. 1680; est. adm. 11 Oct. 1697 by John
Hall who m. Martha Goldsmith, jt. admnx. with Col. Hayes; acct.
named Mary Beedle, w. of George Utie, both dec., and Garrett
"foter" Garrettson, orph. of Richard (?) Rutten(?); had iss.:
MARY, m. George Utie, Jr.; MARTHA, b. c.1678, d. 4 Feb. 1720,
age 52 yrs, 4 mos., 4 days, m. 1st George Goldsmith who d. 1691
and 2nd John Hall, to whom she had been m. 27 yrs, 6 mos., 19
days (2; 60; 61, 63; 93; 121; 129; 200-5; 211; 313; 388; 420-1).

BEESLEY, JOHANNA, dau. of William Beesley and Alce Carrington,
b. 2 Sept. 1731 (128).

BEESLEY, WILLIAM, d. by 11 April 1715 when admin. bond was posted by Dorothy Beesley with William Jenkins (11).

BELCHER, JOHN, m. by pub. of banns Feb. 1706 Mary, wid. of Richard Perkins, whose est. was admin. by John and Mary Belcher on 1 July 1708; Mary d. 20 Feb. 1735; prob. had one dau.: RUTH, b. 6 Oct. 1708 (par. not named) (2; 128; 129).

THE BELL FAMILY is the subject of a genealogy by Edward J. Bell, Jr.

BELL, WILLIAM (1), was in Balto. Co. as a taxable in Patapsco Upper Hund.; d, by 21 Dec. 1781; m. 1st Sarah (?); m. 2nd, by 23 Feb. 1777 Christiana (?); his will, 23 Feb. 1777 - 21 Dec. 1781, named w. Christiana, son-in-law Michael Mason, grandch. Edward and Mary Bell, and these ch.:WILLIAM, b. 6 April 1744; RICHARD, b. 1 Sept. 1746; CATHERINE, m. Michael Mason; JOHN; EDWARD, m. Sarah (?); (by 2nd w.): ELIZABETH; ROSINA (112; 133).

BELL, WILLIAM (2), s. of William (1) and Sarah, b. 6 April 1744, 1744, d. 20 Dec. 1798; m. Eve (?), b. 3 Jan. 1742, d. 7 Oct. 1812; he took the Oath of Allegiance before Richard Cromwell in March 1778; will of Eve, 24 July 1812 - 10 Oct. 1812, named granddau. Ann, dau. of Edward, and sons Richard, George, and William; had iss.: MARY, b. 27 June 1767; EDWARD, b. 26 Oct. 1768, d. 6 July 1802, m. and had a dau. Ann; GEORGE, b. 2 April 1770; WILLIAM, b. 6 March 1772; RICHARD, b. 30 March 1774; REBECCA, b. 26 Oct. 1776; m. John Bailey on 24 Sept. 1794; SARAH, b. 13 March 1779, m. Michael Young on 6 Feb. 1798; ELIZABETH, b. 31 Aug. 1780, d. 4 Oct. 1800 (119; 133; 232; 345; 417-6).

BELL, RICHARD (3), s. of William (1) and Sarah, b. 1 Sept. 1746; m. Elizabeth (?); had iss.: ANN, b. 25 Aug. 1786; MARY, b. 14 Oct. 1790 (Bell).

BELL, JACOB, m. Elizabeth Rowles on 18 Feb. 1727; had iss.: HENRY, b. 8 Sept. 1730; THOMAS, b. 14 July 1732; RACHEL, b. 9 March 1734/5 (133).

BELL, JOHN, m. by 21 Nov. 1739 Susanna, dau. of John Tye; on 29 July 1746 conv. land which Susanna had inher. from her father to Richard Clark; had iss.: JOHN, b. 21 Oct. 1732; FRANCIS, b. by 21 Nov. 1739; ARTHUR, b. by 21 Nov. 1739; WILLIAM, b. 2 March 1744 (79; 127; 131; 133).

BELL, THOMAS, was in Balto. Co. by 1692 as a taxable in n. side of Patapsco Hund. (138).

BELLAMY, MATHEW, was in Balto. Co. by 1694 as a taxable in Patapsco Hund. (139).

BELLAMY, DAVID, d. by 17 Jan. 1753 when Mary Bellamy posted admin. bond.; est. admin. 14 Feb. 1754; Mary d. by 25 March 1754 when William Govane posted admin. bond; her est. admin. 14 Oct. 1754 by Govane who stated the dec. had no rel. in Md. (4; 11).

BELLICON, MICHAEL, was in Balto. Co. by 4 March 1667/8 when he conv. land on Sassafras R. to the est. of Richard Bennett; may have been the Michael "Bellicane" of Cecil Co., b. of Dutch par., who was nat. on 9 May 1700 with Michael, Jr., and the two sons of the latter, Christopher and James; may be the Michael "Bellecan" of Kent Co., whose will, 15 Nov. 1701 - 23 March 1707, named w. Anne, and these ch.: ANNE; MARY; REBECKAH; CHRISTIAN; MICHAEL; CHRISTOPHER; and JAMES (95; 122; 404).

BELLOS, ANN, tried for bast. in Nov. 1737 (31:146).

BELLOW, THOMAS, was in Balto. Co. by 1737 as a taxable in Back River Upper Hund.; d. after 14 April 1744 when his will was dated naming w. Sarah and sons: THOMAS; and JOHN (111; 149).

BELLROES, CHRISTOPHER, m. Anna Thompson on 23 Sept. 1719 (128).

THE BELT FAMILY was the subject of an article by Christopher Johnston, and Belt Bible Records were published in the NEHG Reg.

BELT, JOHN (1), was transp. to Md. c.1663 with Ann, Humphrey, and Sarah Belt; d. in A. A. Co. by 11 Nov. 1698; m. Elizabeth (?) who m. as her 2nd husb. John Lamb on 25 July 1701; in 1685 he purch. 300 a. Belt's Prosperity from Thomas and Rebecca Lightfoot; his will, 13 May 1698 - 11 Nov. 1698, named w. Elizabeth, and these ch.: JOHN; Col. JOSEPH, b. 1680, d. 1761; BENJAMIN, b. 1682, d. 1773; ELIZABETH; CHARITY; SARAH, m. 11 Sept. 1718 Thomas Harwood; JEREMIAH (not in father's will), b. 1698, m. Mary Wight (59; ?88).

BELT, JOHN (2), s. of John (1) and Elizabeth, was alive in 1727; m. 10 Feb. 1701/2 Lucy, dau. of Benj. Lawrence; moved to Balto. Co. in 1726; conv. 112 a. Belt's Point to dau. Mary who was about to marry Greenbury Dorsey in May 1726; in Dec. 1726 Michael Pasquinet and w. Charity conv. power of atty. to their "loving cousin" John Belt of Balto. Co.; had iss.: JOHN, b. 1703; MARY, m. 1726 Greenbury Dorsey; MARGARET, b. 10 June 1719, m. on 1 Dec. 1743 Basil Lucas (71:36; Johnston).

BELT, JOHN (3), s. of John (2) and Lucy, b. c.1703, d. 1 day, 10, 1788 in Balto. Co.; m. Lucy (?); member of Gunpowder Meeting of Soc. of Friends; his will, 24 Sept. 1788 - 17 Feb. 1789, named six ch. and tract: Aquila's Reserve; had iss.: JOHN; NATHAN; LEONARD (not in father's will, but named as s. of John when received into membership of Gunpowder Meeting; disowned for marrying contrary to disc.); SARAH, m. (?) Randall; LUCY, b. 25 day, 9, 1744, m. (?) Malone; MARY, b. 30 day, 4, 1747; JOSEPH, b. 10 day, 4, 1750 (113; 136).

BELT, JOHN (4), s. of John (3) and Lucy, prob. the John who was b. 27 April 1729, d. 23 Dec. 1814; m. Dinah (?), b. 19 Sept. 1739, d. 12 Nov. 1799; had iss.: LUCY, b. 15 Nov. 1767; JOHN, b. 16 Oct. 1759; JEREMIAH, b. 17 March 1772; GREENBURY D., b. 11 Aug. 1774; MARY, b. 2 July 1777 (Belt Bible Records).

BELT, RICHARD, par. unk., but may have been s. of John (3) and Lucy, d. by 19 March 1789; m. 24 day, 1, 1760 Keturah Price, b. 21 day, 2 mo., 1739, dau. of John and Keturah Price; his will, 18 March 1788 - 19 March 1789, named w. Keturah and four sons; had iss.: JOHN; CHARLTON; AQUILA; BENEDICT; MILCAH, b. 12 d, 1, 1765, m. Jesse Matthews; ISABEL, m. William McGaw (113; 136).

BELT, SARAH, par. unk., but poss. dau. of John (2) and Lucy, tried for bast. in June 1728 and in Nov. 1728, when John Belt posted a bond; had iss.: BENONI, b. c.1728 and fined for bast. in Nov. 1758 (28:16; 38; 46:162).

BELT, SARAH, fined for bast. in Nov. 1758 (46:162).

BEMBRIDGE (BUMBRIDGE), CHRISTOPHER, was transp. to Md. by 1664, was a taxable in n. side Patapsco Hund. in 1692; his will, 9 Aug. 1700 - 3 Sept. 1700, named w. Joanna and Catherine Thompson, aged 6 (121; 138; 388).

BENGER (BENJOR), ROBERT, claimed land in St. M. Co. for service in 1667; d. in Baltimore Co. in 1699; m. 1st by 15 April 1677 or 1678 Katherine, widow and admnx. of John Chadwell; m. 2nd Debo-

rah, wid. of John Johnson; purch. 150 a. Oliver's Reserve from
wid. Mary Harmer in June 1674 (with said Johnson);   named as s.-
in-law of Margaret Ferrell or Therrell in her will of 6 March
1676; gave bond for conv. of 150 a. Oliver's Reserve and 30 a.
Benger's Addition to Thomas Harris in May 1681; for "love and
affection" conv. 50 a. Salisbury Plain to Elizabeth, dau. of
Thomas Peart in July 1682; with w. Katherine conv. 150 a. Oliver's
Reserve and Jenifer's Kindness to Daniel Scott in March 1682/3;
will, 6 Aug. 1699 - 9 Nov. 1699, named w. Deborah and numerous
tracts totalling over 500 a.; will of Deborah Benger, pr. 5 Aug.
1700, named s. Benjamin Johnson and dau. Elizabeth Shaw; Robert
prob. d. without iss. (2; 20:261; 100; 103; 104; 105; 110; 120;
121; 341; 388).

   BENISTER, RICHARD, d. by 6 Sept. 1698 when admin. bond was
posted by John Watson with Francis Robinson and John Ewings (11).

   BENNETT FAMILY of Virginia and Maryland has been the subject
of articles by Archibald Bennett and John B. Boddie (531; 532).

   BENNETT, ROBERT (1), whose will was proved in 1603, res. in
par. of Wiveliscombe, Somerset, Eng.; may have been the father
of: EDWARD; ROBERT; RICHARD; and perhaps JOHN .' (531; 532).

   BENNETT, EDWARD (2), poss. s. of Robert (1), and bro. of ROB-
ERT (3), and RICHARD (4), d. by 30 Sept. 1664, having m. Mary,
dau. of Jasper Bourne of Stanmore Magma, Middlesex, Eng.; was
Auditor of the Virginia Company on 22 May 1622, and a Burgess in
Va. in 1627/8; had iss.: ELIZABETH, bapt. 31 May 1629; SILVESTER,
bapt. 25 Oct. 1630, d. 1706, m. Col. Nicholas Hill; JOHN, bapt.
17 Feb. 1632; ANN, b. 13 March 1633/4, bur. 10 May 1634; JASPER,
bapt. 3 July 1635; MARY, m. 1st (?) Day; 2nd by 8 April 1663
Thomas Bland; and 3rd, on 12 Sept. 1668 Luke Cropley (426).
(531).

   BENNETT, ROBERT (3), poss. s. of Robert (1), and bro. of ED-
WARD (2) and RICHARD (4), d. in Va. by 20 Nov. 1623; in June 1623
wrote to his bro. Edward mentioning his own w. and ch. in Eng.;
prob. had iss.: RICHARD, b. c. 1607/8; ROBERT, b. c.1610, age
18 in 1628 (426). (531; 532).

   BENNETT, RICHARD (4), poss. s. of Robert (1), and bro. of
EDWARD (2) and ROBERT (3), d. 1626 in Va.; m. Judith (?), res.
in St. Bart., London; 8 June 1627 admin. granted to his bro. Edward; had iss.: [names of ch. from Reg. of St. Mary Woolchurch
Haw, London): ELIZABETH, bapt. 2 Aug. 1610, bur. 13 Oct. 1615;
ABIGAIL, bapt. 15 Nov. 1612; ANN, bur. 20 April 1615; RICHARD,
bapt. 16 June 1616, bur. 24 Sept. 1618; EDWARD, bapt. 24 June
1618, bur. 14 Nov. 1619 .(531; 532).

   BENNETT, RICHARD (5), poss. s. of Robert (3), and nephew of
Edward (2), b. c.1607, "of Va.," now in London, age 49 in 1656/7,
was b. 'Wilscombe,' Co. Somerset," came to James City Co., Va.,
by 1628, m. Ann, wid. of John Utie, by 1638; came to Md. in
1648 and ret. to Va. in 1652; Comm. of Parliament for Md., after
1651, and Burgess in Va., 1629-1631; Gov. of Va., 1652-1655;
had iss.: RICHARD, b. c.1638/9; ELIZABETH, m. Charles Scarborough;
ANN, m. 1st Theodoric Bland, and 2nd St. Leger Codd (370).

   BENNETT, RICHARD (6), s. of Richard (5) and Ann, b. c.1639,
d. 1667; came to Md. by 1663 and res. in Balto. Co.; m. Henrietta Maria, dau. of James Neale; she was b. 1647, d. 1697, and
m. as her 2nd husb. Philemon Lloyd; rep. Balto. Co. in the Ass.
1663-1664, and was a Justice, 1665 - 1667; will, 29 Jan. 1655/6 -

6 May 1667, named cous. John Langley, w. Henrietta Maria, poss.
unborn ch., f. Richard Bennett, wife's f. Capt. James Neale,
tract 400 a. Folly; in Sept. 1667 his f. Richard Bennett of Nansemond R., Va., renounced his right to execute the will, and named
his widowed dau.-in-law and her dau. Susanna; had iss.; SUSANNA,
b. 1667, d. 1714, m. 1st John Darnall, d. 1684; 2nd c.1686 Henry
Lowe; RICHARD, b. c.1667, d. 1749 (120; 200-57; 370).

The BENNETT FAMILY of Balto. Co., Md., probably descends from:

BENNETT, WILLIAM (7), no known rel. to Bennetts of Va. and
Md., was in Balto. Co. by 1701; may have been the William in
A. A. Co. on Aug. 1709 who wit. the will of Edward Moore, and
who m. Joan Letherwood on 10 Jan. 1709 in St. Ann's Par., and
also may have been the William who m. Mrs. Ann Chintos on 6 Nov.
1713; prob. the f. of: THOMAS (122; 143; 219-2).

BENNETT, THOMAS (8), s. of William (7), named in the will of
Margaret Slatter, wid. of Annap., on 7 Jan. 1721; prob. the same
Thomas whose will in Balto. Co., 19 Feb. 1764 - 16 April 1764,
named w. Mary, exec., and following ch.: SARAH, m. (?) Mackel-
fresh by 19 Feb. 1764; ELISHA; THOMAS; SAMUEL; WILLIAM; JOHN;
BENJAMIN; ANN, m. (?) Teves by 19 Feb. 1764; MARY; ELANOR; and
LYDIA (6; 7; 111; 124).

BENNETT, BENJAMIN, d. by 1 Aug. 1693; m. Sarah (?) who m. as
her 2nd husb. by that date John Beavan; will, 19 March 1691 - 3
Aug. 1692, named w. as extx.; in Nov. 1677 conv. Edward Jackson
50 a. Rascol's Humor (64; 101; 110).

BENNETT, BENJAMIN, was a taxable in s. side Gunpowder Hund.
by 1692 (138).

BENNETT, ANN, ind. for bast., March 1723; charges dropped for
lack of evidence, June 1723 (26:201, 330).

BENNETT, CHARLES, orph. of Mary, age 11 in March 1742; bound
to Samuel Howard in June 1742; prob. the same Charles who m.
Martha Collins on 11 Sept. 1753 and had iss.: PRISCILLA, b. 27
May 1755; ANN, b. 3 March 1756; CATHERINE, b. 5 Nov. 1758 (33:
436; 131).

BENNETT, JOHN, merch. of A. A. Co., in Feb. 1683/4 bought 50
a. Bennett's Range from Thomas Everett of the Cliffs, Cal. Co.,
adj. to Ball's Addition (106).

BENNETT, WILLIAM, living on Deer Creek c.1748; with w. Hannah
on 10 Oct. 1746 conv. to Stephen Onion tract Envell Chase, wh.
Bennett bought from John Norris of Thomas (79:214; 385).

BENNINGTON, HENRY (1), was in Balto. Co. by 1726, prob. d. by
1740; m. on 26 Dec. 1726 Sarah Harris; she d. by 10 Nov. 1740
when her admin. bond was posted by Jacob Giles with Alexander
Hill; had iss.: MOSES, b. 2 Jan. 1722; HENRY, b. 5 May 1727;
WILLIAM, b. 12 June 1729; JOHN, b. 6 Aug. 1732 (11; 128).

BENNINGTON, HENRY (2), s. of Henry (1) and Sarah, b. 5 May
1727, aged 16 yrs, 6 mos., in Aug. 1742 when bound to John West
to age 21; m. Elizabeth (?) and had iss.: CONSTANT, b. 24 Aug.
1755; NEHEMIAH, b. 8 July 1756; JOB, b. 8 Feb. 1758 (33:3; 128;
129).

BENTLEY, STEPHEN in Balto. Co. by 1692 as taxable in n. side
Patapsco Hund.; gave age as c.57 in 1714/5 when he dep. he had
res. in these parts for 30 yrs.; m. by Nov. 1693 Ann, wid. of

William Pearle and of Philip (Piffions?); owned lands, Planter's
Paradise, 829 a. orig. surv. for William Cornwallis, 200 a. John's
Habitation for the orphans of John Linegar, and 50 a. Jones Neglect; purch. 300 a. Bond's Forest from Peter and Eleanor Bond in
Oct. 1708; d. by 16 June 1718 when admir. bond on his est. was
posted by Amy Fenton with William Fenton and Henry Jones (11;
19:300, 307; 67; 138; 203-3:109; 211).

BENTLEY, THOMAS, serv. with 2 years to serve in the 1739 inv.
of Rev. Joseph Hooper; in 1750 a Thomas Bentley owned 50 a. Hill
Spring (52; 153).

BENTLEY, WILLIAM, m. 30 July 1738 Elizabeth Butler (129).

BERRY, ANDREW, sued Annanias Arnold in Nov. 1711; d. by 9 July
1718 when admin. bond was posted by Mary Berry with Martin Taylor and Patrick Wheyland; est. was inv. on 18 Aug. 1718 by John
Downes and Charles (?), and val. at £ 107.18.11, plus 7802 lbs.
tob. in debts (11; 50; 341).

BERRY, JOHN, m. Susanna (?) and had iss.: JOHN, b. 8 May 1732
(133).

BERRY, JOHN, planned to marry an orphan Sarah Catcham, murdered
his stepfather and tried in Dec. 1751; was sentenced to death and
executed for the murder of Mrs. Sarah Clark in March 1752 (385).

BERTON. See BARTON.

BESS, mulatto serv. to the widow Day, named William Bond as
the father of her child, Aug. 1711 (21:247).

BESSON, THOMAS (1), b. c.1606, gave his age as 68 in 1674 as a
capt. in A. A. Co.; imm. with fam. in 1649; m. Hester (?); his
will, 15 Oct. 1677 - 29 April 1679, named w. Hester, sons John,
William, Thomas, dau. Martha, and son-in-law Nicholas Gassaway;
had iss.: THOMAS, Jr.; JOHN; WILLIAM; MARTHA; HESTER, m. Nicholas
Gassaway (120; 310; 346-2; 388).

BESSON, THOMAS, Jr. (2), s. of Thomas (1) and Hester, m., prob.
in Va., Margaret Saughier, b. 1646, dau. of George Saughier who
was b. March 1600 in Newport, came to Va. c.1620; Thomas and Margaret had iss.: THOMAS, b. Dec. 1667; ANN, b. 26 Dec. 1670, m.
on 26 Oct. 1697 Richard Cromwell; MARGARET, b. 31 Jan. 1673/4, m.
30 Dec. 1701 John Rattenbury; NICHOLAS, b. 22 Dec. 1677; ELIZA-
BETH, b. 1683 (346-2).

BESSON, THOMAS (3), s. of Thomas (2) and Margaret, b. Dec.
1667, d. Dec. 1702/3, prob. the Thomas who est. was inv. by William Hawkins, Sr., and William Hawkins, Jr., and val. at £14.9.6
on 12 June 1706 (48; 346-2).

BESSON, NICHOLAS (4), s. of Thomas (2) and Margaret, b. 22 Dec.
1677, gave his age as 55 in 1734 and stated that his father had
been living 30 years earlier (217-IB#I:79; 346-2).

BEVAN/BEVINS, (?), m. by 3 Aug. 1751 Rachel, heir of William
Denton (5).

BEVAN, JOHN, b. c.1640, gave his age as 83 in Nov. 1723; m.
by 1 March 1685/6 Julyan; was a taxable in n. side Gunpowder Hund.;
in May 1682 surv. 100 a. Haphazard; in 1685 or 1695 surv. 100 a.
Limerick; in 1685 he and his wife conv. 100 a. Limerick to Marcus
Lynch; in 1692 conv. 50 a. Haphazard to Joseph Gallion; in 1693
conv. 70 a. of same to John Fuller;; in 1693 had a cert. for 200
a. Midsummer Hill; in 1694 was conv. 150 a. part Leaf's Chance

by John Ramsey; had iss.: JOHN, Jr. (59:173, 361, 372, 395; 69: 305; 108; 139).

BEVANS, JOHN, Jr., poss. s. of John Bevans above, m. Dec. 1723 Rachel (?); in Aug. 1728, Patrick, William, and Mary Lynch, ch. of Robuck Lynch, sold to John Bevan, Jr., 100 a. Limerick which their father Robuck had inher. from his kinsman Marcus Lynch (71:160; 131).

BEVANS, JOHN, and wife Mary had a dau, Martha whose cattle mark was recorded on 10 July 1723 (69:151).

BEVANS, JOSEPH, admin. the est. of George Grover on 19 Aug. 1736; m. 1st Rebecca (?); prob. m. 2nd on 17 Jan. 1754 Rachel Asher; iss. by 1st wife: AVARILLA, b. 11 Nov. 1725, m. 1 May 1755 Nicholas Merryman; PHILLIS, b. 5 March 1731, m. 11 Sept. 1754 Abram Pines; JOSEPH, b. 24 Dec. 1739 (131).

BEVANS/BEVINS, THOMAS, was in Balto. Co. by 1694 as a taxable in Spesutia Hund.; in 1696 was conv. 150 a. Leafe's Chance by Nicholas Day; m. 1st Elizabeth (?) who was bur. 25 June 1698; m. 2nd on 8 July 1700 (?), name not given; iss. by 1st w.: THOMAS, b. 25 Nov. 1691; WILLIAM, b. 18 Nov. 1693; MARY, b. 27 May 1695; JOHN, b. 13 Feb. 1697 (61:120; 128; 129; 139).

BEVINS, JOHN, m. 6 Sept. 1743 Ann Turner (131).

BEVINS, JOHN, m. 2 Jan. 1755 Ruth Jerman (131).

BEVINS, JOHN, m. 5 Oct. 1760 Eliz. Freeman (131).

BEVIS, NATHANIEL, was in Balto. Co. by 1695 as a taxable in n. side Gunpowder Hund. (140).

BIAYS, JOHN, Jr., was in Balto. Co. by Nov. 1742 when he admin. the est. of Christopher Shaw; may be John BAYES or BAYS (3).

BICARD, HENRY, m. Christiana (?), and had iss.: HENRY, b. 7 July 1723; ANNA MARY, b. 15 July 1725; ELIZABETH, b. 6 July 1728 (129).

BIDDER, JOHN, m. Sarah (?), and had iss.: GEORGE, b. 27 Aug. 1727, JOSEPH, b. 10 Nov. 1729 (129).

BIDDISON, THOMAS (1), b. c.1672/4, d. in Balto. Co. by 13 Sept. 1743; gave his age as 40 in 1714/5, age 44 in 1718, age 62 in 1732; had been a res. of Balto. Co. since at least 1681; in 1695 was a taxable in n. side Patapsco Hund.; owned 100 a. Goosebury Neck, orig. surv. in 1673 for William Ebden; admin. the est. of Matthew Gray in Oct. 1714; signed the inv. of Francis Watkins as creditor in May 1713, and wit. the will of James Crooke in Oct. 1727; m. Mary (?); his will, 13 Sept. 1743 - Dec. 1743, named lands Sister's Hope, The Harbour, and Addition, w. Mary, and ch. Jarvis and Thomas Biddison and Mary Brown; had iss.: JARVIS, b. c.1715; MARY, m. by 13 Sept. 1743 (?) Brown; THOMAS, b. 2 Oct. 1721; SUSANNA, b. 13 March 1724, prob. d. young (1:8, 18; 50:285; 110:344; 125:51; 133; 203-3:109, 464; 140; 211; 224:157; 225: 219).

BIDDISON, JARVIS (2), s. of Thomas (1), was b. c.1715, giving his age as 48 in Sept. 1763; d. by 8 Dec. 1773; m. Mary (?) who d. by 12 Aug. 1788; in 1750 owned 200 a. Sister's Hope and 100 a. Goosebury Neck; his will, 4 Dec. 1772 - 8 Dec. 1773, named w. Mary, ch. Salathiel Abercrombie, Elizabeth, Daniel, and Jeremiah Biddison, and Salathiel's ch., Mary and Charity Eagleston;

his est. admin. in 1775; est. of w. Mary admin. on 12 Aug. 1786
when the acct. named three ch. and a share pd. to Samuel Clark,
guardian of Wm. Clark; had iss.: SALATHIEL, m. 1st Henry Eaglestone and 2nd by 4 Dec. 1772 Robert Abercrombie; JEREMIAH;
DANIEL; ELIZABETH (not living in 1786) (6:335; 8:308; 88:91;
112:272; 153).

BIDDISON, THOMAS (3), s. of Thomas (1), b. 2 Oct. 1721, d. c.
1801; m. Ann Burgain on 17 July 1747; in 1750 owned 70 a. The
Harbour and 100 a. Addition to Harbour; conv. pt. of the former
tract to his grandson William Biddison of Thomas; his will, 9
March 1800 - 28 Feb. 1801, named ch. Rebecca Pocock, Thomas (d.
leaving a s. William), Shadrack, and Meshack; had iss.: JARVIS,
b. 14 Sept. 1747; PRESIOCA, b. 22 May 1750, m. Daniel Watkins on
3 May 1770; REBECCA, m. by lic. 4 May 1785 James Pocock; THOMAS,
d. by 1800; SHADRACK, d. by 1800; MESHACK, m. Kerrenhappuck Pocock (115:6; 131; 133; 153; 231-WG#64, p. 233; 232).

BIDDLE, EDWARD, was in Balto. Co. by 1683 when he was given
a letter of atty. by Robert Jones (59:49).

BIDDLE, JOHN, d. in Balto. Co. by 11 Oct. 1758 when the admin.
bond on his est. was posted by Walter Tolly with James Gittings;
est. admin. by sd. Tolley in May 1761 and Feb. 1763 (4; 6; 11).

BIDLEY, JOHN, was a taxable in Back River Upper Hund. in 1737
(149).

BIGNELL(?), REBECCA, was ind. for bast. in June 1731 (29:156).

THE BILLINGSLEY FAMILY is the subject of a genealogy by Harry
Alexander Davis. (533).

BILLINGSLEY, FRANCIS (1), s. of John and Agatha (?), was b. c.
1620 in Shropshire, Eng.; went to Eng. with his par.; was in Va.
by 1649, having m. c.1647 Ann (?) who was alive in Nov. 1668; imm.
to Md. in 1652 with w. Ann and settled in Calvert Co.; transp.
his bro. Thomas; was a delegate to the Lower House from Calvert
Co., 1678 - 1682; d. intestate c.1684; had iss.: JOHN, b. c.1647;
ANN, b. 1650, d. young; FRANCIS, b. 1653; AGATHA, b. c.1656, m.
Thomas Paget; EDWARD, b. c.1658; ANN ELIZABETH, b. c.1666 (370;
388; Davis).

BILLINGSLEY, JOHN (2), s. of Francis (1) and Ann, b. c.1647
perhaps in Holland; came to Calvert Co., Md., c.1652; d. 1693;
m. 1 Jan. 1669 Ann Billingsley, dau. of John's uncle William;
Ann, b. c.1652, m. as her 2nd husb. William Brown and moved to
Richmond Co., Va.; had iss.: Mary, b. Sept. 1669, m. Edward Wood;
WILLIAM, b. Oct. 1670; SARAH AGATHA, b. 1672/3, m. John Stovall;
ELIZABETH, b. 1675, d. 1752, m. William Bowles; JOHN, d. 1686;
SUSANNA, b. 1679/80, d. young; FRANCIS, d. young; WALTER, b.
1685 (Davis).

BILLINGSLEY, WILLIAM (3), s. of John (2) and Ann, was b. c.
1670, d. intestate by July 1716; m. by 1691 Clearanna (Clair Anna?)
Bowles, who surv. him; had iss.: WILLIAM, b. 1691; CLEARANNA, b.
1693, m. Thomas Gilly; BOWLES, b. 1694; SAMUEL, b. 1696; ANN ELIZA-
BETH, b. 1699, m. John Wood (Davis).

BILLINGSLEY, WALTER (4), s. of John (2), and Ann, was b. c.
1685, d. c.1752; m. by 1706 Elizabeth (?); moved to St. M. Co.;
had iss.: JOHN, b. 1706; JAMES, b. 1710; ELIZABETH, d. unm.;
WALTER, b. 1715/6; ANN, d. unm.; MARY, m. John Williams of St. M.
Co., moved to Balto. Co. in the 1760's and then to York Co., Pa.
(Davis).

BILLINGSLEY, WILLIAM (5), s. of William (3) and Clearanna, was b. Nov. 1691 in Calvert Co.; m. c.1716 Mary Sumner who d. in Dec. 1740; his will, 11 Aug. 1745 - 16 Dec. 1745, named daus. Mary Wood and Ann Hardesty, and ch. William, James, Margaret, Clare, Francis, Sias (son), and Elizabeth; had iss.: MARY SUMNER, b. c. 1718, m. John Wood; WILLIAM SUMNER, b. c.1720; ANN, m. 1745 Henry Hardesty, Jr., moved to Balto. Co., and then to Monongalia Co., Va.; JAMES, b. April 1726; MARGARFT, b. c.1728/9; CLEARANNA, b. 1732 (poss. the Clare Billingsley who was tried for bast. in Nov. 1756 naming John Love as the father); FRANCIS, b. c.1734/5; SIAS, b. 1737/8; ELIZABETH, b. Dec. 1740 (41:312; Davis).

BILLINGSLEY, SAMUEL (6), s. of William (3) and Clearanna, b. Jan. 1696, d. c.1751; m. Mary, wid. of (?) Wilmouth, by whom she had a dau. Elizabeth; his est. admin. on 3 March 1752; had iss.: MARTHA, b. June 1740; BASIL, b. June 1742; WALTER, b. April 1744; MARY, b. May 1746 (Davis).

BILLINGSLEY, JAMES (7), of Walter (4) and Elizabeth, b. c.1710; m. by 1731 Elizabeth (?), and moved to Balto. Co. from Calvert Co.; purch. 100 a. William's Lot by 1750, and later 103 a. Miles' Desire; d. by 1772, and had iss.: JAMES, b. 1731; ELIZABETH, b. 1734, m. 30 Oct. 1760 John Holmony and moved to Berkeley Co., Va.; SARAH, m. c.1752 William Grafton; CHARLES, b. 1739; JAMES, d. young (Davis).

BILLINGSLEY, WALTER (8), s. of Walter (4) and Elizabeth, b. 1715/6, moved to Balto. Co.; m. 27 Aug. 1742 Sarah Bond Love, wid. of Robert Love; in Sept. 1742 conv. prop. to the ch. of his wife by her 1st husb., John, Ruth, and Tamar Love, to be free of all charges after the death of the grantor's wife Sarah; by 1750 owned 150 a. part Bond's Lot, 75 a. Bond's Addition, 100 a. Pork Forest, 77 a. Love's Addition, 100 a. Warford, 23 a. Billingsley's Lot, 95 a. Bond's Fortune; d. testate in Harf. Co., in 1803; had iss.: SARAH, b. 1714, m. 16 June 1761 William Bull (77:4, 6, 7; 129; 153; Davis).

BILLINGSLEY, JAMES (9), s. of William (5) and Mary, b. 1728 in St. M. Co.; m. in 1747 Elizabeth Crabtree; moved to Balto. Co. by 1758, then to Guilford Co., N. C., by 1768 where he was killed by Tories in April 1776; had iss.: SAMUEL, b. 1747; JAMES, b. Oct. 1749; ELIZABETH, b. 1751/2, m. Tydings Lane; JOHN, b. 17 Aug. 1754; CLARANNA, b. 1756, m. William Hamer; WILLIAM HENRY, b. 11 Oct. 1758; MARTHA, b. 3 May 1760, m. as 2nd w. William Hamer; WALTER, b. 14 July 1761; BASIL, b. 2 June 1764 (353; Davis).

BILLINGSLEY, FRANCIS (10) s. of William (5) and Mary, was b. 1734/5 in St. M. Co.; moved to Balto. Co.; m. c.1763 Asenath Howell, dau. of Samuel and Avarilla Howell; moved to Wilkes Co., Ga., where he d. 1798/9, having had issue (353; Davis).

BILLINGSLEY, SIAS (11), s. of William (5) and Mary, was b. 1737/8 in St. M. Co.; moved to Balto. Co.; m. by 1762 Hannah Webster; served in the Rev. War from Harf. Co.; later moved to Monongalia Co., Va., and had iss. (353; Davis).

BILLINGSLEY, BASIL (12), s. of Samuel (6) and Mary, b. in St. M. Co., and moved to Balto. Co.; m. on 29 Jan. 1767 Ruth Smithson, later moved to Rowan Co., N. C., by Sept. 1778, where he d. in 1789; had iss. (131; Davis).

BILLINGSLEY, WALTER (13), s. of Samuel (6) and Mary, b. April 1744 in St. M. Co.; moved to Balto. Co.; m. 13 Feb. 1772 Ruth Clarke; served in the Rev. War from Harf. Co., and d. by 6 March 1805, leaving iss. (353; Davis).

BILLINGSLEY, JAMES (14), s. of James (7) and Elizabeth, b. 1731 in Cal. Co.; moved to Balto. Co., where he m. on 16 June 1767 Ruth (?), wid. of Jarvise Gilbert; his will, 2 March 1772 - 31 Aug. 1772, named w. Ruth, three ch., and tracts, part Jenkins' Range, and 153 a. Billingsley's Best Shift; had iss.: JAMES; SARAH; and WILLIAM (112:213; 131; Davis).

BILLINGSLEY, CHARLES (15), s. of James (7) and Elizabeth, b. 1739 in Balto. Co.; m. on 23 Oct. 1760 Ann Barton, who d. c.1781; moved to Berkeley Co., Va., c.1774/5; served in the Rev. War from Berkeley; m. 2nd Rachel (?); d. testate in Berkeley Co., Va., leaving iss. (131; Davis).

BILLOES, ANN, of North Gunpowder Lower Hund., was ind. for bast. in Aug. 1737 (31:97).

BILLUM, CHARLES, was in Balto. Co. by 1692 as a taxable in s. side Patapsco Hund. (138).

BILSON, THOMAS, was in Balto. Co. by 1695 as a taxable in s. side Patapsco Hund.; d. by 14 May 1706 when admin. bond was posted by admnx. Elizabeth Bilson with John Rattenbury (11; 140).

BINGAN, PETER, in 1750 owned 100 a. William and Elizabeth's Fancy (153).

BINGFIELD, or RINGFIELD, JOHN, inf. s. of William and (?) (the mother's name is illegible), in Aug. 1720 was ordered by the court to be raised by Mary, wid. of John Webster (23:360).

BIRCHALL, ADAM, was in Balto. Co. by 1692 as a taxable in Spesutia Hund.; in May 1685 surv. 150 a. Garden of Eden (later held by his orphans); in June 1685 surv. 100 a. Eden's Add'n (also later held by his orphans, and then by Samuel Brown); d. by 28 March 1694 when his est. was inv. by Simon Jackson and George Smith, and val. at £ 8.0.6; his est. was admin. by James Phillips; dec. left a wid. Mary, and two sons: THOMAS, age 12 on 10 Jan. 1694/5, and SAMUEL, age 2 at same time (1; 20:438; 48:92; 138; 211).

BIRCHFIELD. See BURCHFIELD.

BIRD, JOHN, was in Balto. Co. by 1681 when he was conv. 50 a. by Michael Judd and wife; in 1683 he and his w. conv. 50 a. to Benjamin Bennett; in 1686 he was conv. 100 a. Richardson's Prospect by Thomas Richardson; m. by Nov. 1684 the wid. of John Armstrong; d. by 7 April 1691 when his est. was inv. by William Ebden and Lawrence Richardson, and val. at £20.12.8; his est. was admin. 3 May 1684 by James Phillips (18:212; 51:127; 59:44, 137, 179; 206-12:134).

BIRK, EDMUND, serv. to Col. George Wells, was judged to be age 14 in June 1683 (18:39).

BIRNEY, ROBERT, d. 15 Sept. 1757 at the house of Rev. Andrew Lendrum; his will, 15 Sept. 1757 - 26 Oct. 1757, stated he was from New Castle on Delaware, and named ch. Jean Lendrum als. Birney, wife of Andrew Lendrum and her ch.: Robert Birney Lendrum, Lucinda Lendrum, and Mary Lendrum, trustees William Lendrum of James and Robert Birney of Arthur, also mentioned estate in Ireland, land in the Barony of Clogan and Co. Tyrone, and lands of Gortmore; had iss.: JEAN, m. Rev. Andrew Lendrum (111; 128).

BISHOP, JOHN, d. by 3 April 1708 when admin. bond on his est. was posted by Zachariah Allein (11).

BISHOP, JONATHAN, m. Rachel (?) and had iss.: HANNAH, b. 28
May 1752; RACHEL, b. 23 May 1754; PRUDENCE, b. 18 Nov. 1756;
ELIZABETH, b. 15 Nov. 1759 (129).

BISHOP, ROBERT, m. 14 Feb. 1744 Elizabeth, wid. of Nicholas
Day, and dau. of Christopher and Mary Cox; in 1750 he owned 150
a. The Dock (3; 79; 131; 153).

BISHOP, ROGER, m. 9 April 1735 Avis Jenkins; d. by 19 Aug.
1766; in 1750 owned 100 a. Bachelor's Beginnings; his will, 16
June 1766 - 19 Aug. 1766, named eld. s. Roger, and other ch.
Francis, Samuel, and Elizabeth, and w. Avis; his est. was admin.
22 Aug. 1769 by Avis Bishop; had iss.: ROGER, b. 31 Jan. 1736;
SARAH, b. 26 Sept. 1737; FRANCES, b. 18 Oct. 1749; ELIZABETH,
b. 29 Jan. 1751; SAMUEL, b. 1 Feb. 1754 (7; 112; 128; 129; 153).

BISHOP, THOMAS, m. by 23 Aug. 1751 Margaret, extx. of Hugh
Morgan; conv. land to David Morgan on 6 Nov. 1752 (5; 81:487).

BISSE, WILLIAM, d. in Balto. Co.; will, 4 April 1675 - 9 Dec.
1676, named James Phillips as his sole heir; had imm. by 1650 (120;
388).

THE BISSETT FAMILY was the subject of an article by Peter W.
Coldham. (See Bibliography).

BISSETT, THOMAS (1), of Glenalbert, parish of Kunkeld, Perth,
Scotland, d. c.April 1764, leaving a will which named his dec.
s. James, atty., of Balto. Co., Md., and Dr. Alexander Stenhouse
as his atty.; had iss.: DAVID; THOMAS; Dr. CHARLES, living in
Skelton, Yorkshire, in 1756; ROBERT; JAMES (210-32:220; Coldham).

BISSETT, DAVID (2), s. of Thomas (1), came to Balto. Co. by
June 1753; m. on 30 Jan. 1755 Mrs. Ann Adkinson; drowned 6 Aug.
1758 while bathing; kept a store at the head of Bush River; in
1756 wrote to his bro. Dr. Charles stating he had invited his
bro. James to come to Md.; admin. bond posted by James and John
Bissett; his est. was admin. on 11 Jan. 1760 (4; 11; 128; 129;
262; Coldham).

BISSETT, JAMES (3), s. of Thomas (1); attorney; d. in Balto.
Co.; his will, 10 Jan. 1760 - 31 Oct. 1761, named his father Thomas, and bros. Charles, Thomas, and Robert; his est. was admin.
27 Dec. 1769 by Rev. Andrew Lendrum, and by Alexander Stenhouse
on 12 Feb. 1776 and 22 April 1776 (6; 7; 112).

BISSETT, THOMAS, no known rel. to any of the above, age 6 on
29 May 1732; was bound to Henry Sater in June 1732, until he
should be 21 (29:290).

BLACK, BARBARA, serv., with three yrs. to serve, in the 1736
inv. of William Wood (53).

BLACK, MARGARET, had iss.: SAMUEL, b. 28 June 1740 (133).

BLACK, PETER, m. Elizabeth (?) and had s.: PETER BLACK als.
TASSEY, b. 2 March 1724 (128).

BLACK, PETER, m. 20 April 1735 Elizabeth Wilson and had iss.:
JAMES, b. 30 Oct. 1735; THOMAS, b. 7 July 1737 (128; 129).

BLACKBORNE, THOMAS, was transp. to Md. c.1676; was in Balto.
Co. by 1694 as a taxable in n. side Patapsco Hund. (139; 388).

BLACKLEDGE, REBECCA, m. May 1728 John Thrift (131).

THE BLADEN FAMILY is the subject of an article by Christopher
Johnston in 346.

BLADEN, ROBERT (1), of Hemsworth, Yorkshire, m. Elizabeth
Lacy, dau. of John and Alice (Birkhead) Lacy; had iss.: JOHN.

BLADEN, JOHN (2), s. of Robert (1) and Elizabeth, was admitted
to Gray's Inn, London, in March 1624/5 and was alive in 1632; d. by
by 1649; m. a dau. of Nathaniel Birkhead of East Heage, and had
iss.: NATHANIEL.

BLADEN, NATHANIEL (3), s. of John (2), was alive in 1702;
m. Isabella Fairfax, dau. of Sir William Fairfax of Steeton;
Sir William's maternal grandfather was Edmund Sheffield, Earl
of Mulgrave; had iss.: WILLIAM, b. 27 Feb. 1673; MARTIN, b. 1680,
d. 15 Feb. 1745/6; ISABELLA; CATHERINE; FRANCES, m. William Hammond; ELIZABETH, m. Edward Hawke (by whom she was the mother of
the noted Admiral Lord Hawke).

BLADEN, WILLIAM (4), s. of Nathaniel (3) and Isabella, b. 27
Feb. 1673 at Steeton, bur. at Annap., Md., on 9 Aug. 1718; m.
Anne Van Swearingen, dau. of Garrett Van Swearingen; possessed
some land in Balto. Co.: 300 a. Cullen's Lot, 500 a. Cullen's
Addition, and 38¼ a. Hopewell; held a number of offices in the
provincial government incl. Secretary of Maryland and Attorney
General o f Maryland; had iss.: Col. THOMAS; ANNE, m. 31 Aug.
1711 Benjamin Tasker (211; Johnston).

BLADEN, THOMAS (5), s. of William (4),b. 1698, d. 1780 in
Eng.; Governor of Maryland 1742-1747; later member of Parliament
in Eng.; m. Barbara, eld. dau. of Sir Theodore Janssen, Bart.;
in 1750 owned two tracts of land in Balto. Co.: 3500 a. Blathnia
Cambria, and 500 a. Carse's Forest; had iss.: HARRIOT, m. William,
4th Earl of Essex; BARBARA, m. 3 Aug. 1773 Gen. St. John (153;
Johnston).

BLAIN, WILLIAM, m. Lydia, admnx. of Amos Johnston (4).

BLAIR, (?), m. by 3 June 1765, Mary, dau. of Alexander Hannah,
weaver (112).

THE BLAKISTONE FAMILY is the subject of an article by Christo
pher Johnston in 346.

BLAKISTON, EBENEZER, no. 7 in the Johnston article; imm. to
Md. by 1671; purch. 100 a. from Henry and Parnell Eldesley in Jan.
1672/3; m. by 19 Feb. 1676 Eliza, dau. of William and Ann Tolson
of Cecil Co. (99; 120; 388).

BLISSARD, WILLIAM, m. Luranan (?) and had iss.: ISAAC, b. 19
May 1751; JOHN, b. 3 Sept. 1755 (134).

BLOVER, JOHN, gave his age as about 25 in March 1720/1 (23:
492).

BLUNDELL, LAWRENCE, m. Margaret (?) and had iss.: SARAH, b.
10 Nov. 1728 (133).

BLUNDEN, JAMES, m. on 1 Dec. 1759 Sarah Eights (131).

BOARD, (?) (1), m. by 9 Jan. 1723/4 (?), dau. of Anna, relict
of Francis Mead of A. A. Co., who in her will of that date named
her grandsons James and John Board; had iss.: JAMES; JOHN (124).

BOARD, JAMES (2), s. of (?) (1), was living in 1723/4, and was prob. the James Board whose will, 23 Feb. 1762 - 14 Feb. 1763, named sons: JAMES; FRANCIS (6; 111).

BOARD, JOHN (3), s. of (?) (1), was living in 123/4, and m. Jemima Henderson on 13 Jan. 1733; had iss.: ANN, b. 11 Jan. 1732; JOHN, b. 11 Jan. 1732 or 1735; JAMES, b. 5 March 1740; WILLIAM, b. 18 Dec. 1743 (133).

BODKIN, JOHN, taxable in Spesutia Hund. in 1695 (140).

BODY, PETER, transp. by 1672, m. on 28 Dec. 1686 in Som. Co., Frances, dau. of Stephen Cannon (263; 388).

BODY, STEPHEN (1), poss. a desc. of Peter and Frances (Cannon), d. in Balto. Co., by 9 May 1744; m. 1st on 3 April 1722 Susanna Long, and 2nd, on 10 Feb. 1728 Elizabeth (?); adm. est. of William Robinson on 9 Nov. 1731;purch. part Ballestone from John Long on 6 March 1733; will, 1742 - 3 Nov. 1742, named w. Elizabeth, and ch. Alanson, Penelope w. of Dixon Stansbury, Susanna w. of Neal Fall, Ann, Elizabeth w. of (?) Johnson, and Peter, ment. 170 a. Ballston; admin. bond posted by extx. Elizabeth Body with Nicholas Haile and Dixon Stansbury; est. adm. 9 May 1744 and 18 June 1752 by Elizabeth, now w. of (?) Trotten; had iss.: SUSANNA MEAD, b. 27 April 1723, m. by 1742 Neal Fall; PENELOPE MEAD, b. 27 Nov. 1724, m. 4 Jan. 1740/1 Dixon Stansbury; ANN; ELIZABETH, m. by 1742 (?) Johnson; PETER; ALANSON, b. 13 Aug. 1730, chose John Long as his guardian in March 1746, and his est. was taken out of of Luke Trotten's hands (3; 11; 74; 110; 131; 133).

BODY, PETER (2), prob. s. of Stephen (1), m. on 25 Aug. 1757, Mary Allender (131).

BOHON, EDWARD, m. on 19 March 1761 Elizabeth Jones (131).

BOICE, JOHN, d. 28 Jan. 1737 (128).

BOLTON, JOHN, m. by Nov. 1685 Dorothy Crandon (18:358).

BOLTON, CHARLES, m. by March 1739 Ann, admnx. of John Higginson; in 1750 owned 200 a., part Bond's Gift (4; 32:151; 131; 153).

BOND, PETER (1), progenitor of the family, was in Balto. Co. by 1660, d. by 28 April 1705; m. Alice (?), wid. of 1st (?) Gill (by whom she had a s. Stephen), and of 2nd William Drury (whose will dated 22 Aug. 1676 named w. Alice); in June 1678 Peter and Alice Bond sued James Rigby for her share of Drury's est.; will, 23 Aug. 1704 - 28 April 1705, named w. Alice, sons Thomas, William, John, and Peter, land 300 a. at head of Bush R.; Alice Bond posted admin. bond on 25 June 1705 with Isaac Jackson and George Ogg; est. inv. on 27 June 1705 by Christopher Gardner and Jno. Hurst, val. at £ 55.15.0; admin. est. by Alice Bond on 26 July 1706, and by Alice, w. of Philip Washington on 14 May 1707; by 1708 Philip and Alice had agreed to live apart, and Peter Bond posted he would support Alice Washington; had iss.: PETER, b. c.1677; THOMAS, b. c.1679; WILLIAM, under 16 in 1704; JOHN, under 16 in 1704 (2; 11; 48; 67; 122; 200-67; 388 ; 538; 539).

BOND, PETER (2), s. of Peter and Alice, b. c.1676, d. c.1718; m. Eleanor, dau. of Richard Gwynn; she m. 2nd Hill Savage; Peter served as delegate from Balto. Co. to the Assembly, 1716-1717; was a Justice, 1715-1717; will, 28 Feb. 1717/8 - 16 June 1718, named ch. Richard, William, Thomas, Peter, John, and Benjamin, lands on Garrison Ridge, Bond's Pleasant Hills; admin. bond posted

16 June 1718 by extx. Elinor Bond with William Parish and Thomas
Randall; est. inv. on 17 May 1718 by Edward Teal and William Hamilton and val. at ₤ 227.2.9; wid. had m. Hill Savage, and may
have d. by 15 Aug. 1724 when William Parish admin. Peter Bond's
est.; care of Peter Bond's ch. subject of court cases in 1721
and 1724; had iss.: RICHARD, d. 1763; WILLIAM; THOMAS; PETER;
JOHN; and BENJAMIN (1; 2; 3; 11; 23:553, 625; 27:122; 48; 60;
123; 338; 370).

BOND, THOMAS (3), s. of Peter (1) and Alice, b. c.1679, d. c.
1755; m. on 20 Sept. 1700 Ann Robinson in A. A. Co.; owned much
land in Balto. (now Harf.) Co.; by 1750 owned over 15 different
tracts ranging in size from 20 a. Small Quantity to 1000 a. Poplar Neck and 2877 a. Bond's Forest; will, 18 Dec. 1755 - 10 Jan.
1756, named ch. Thomas, Daniel, Peter, Jacob, William, John, and
Joshua, and dau. Sarah w. of Greenbury Dorsey, and grandchildren
Peter Bond of Peter, Anne Bond of Peter, Sarah Hughes, Edward
Fell, Ann Day, Jennett and Catherine Fell, Thomas Bond Dorsey and
Sarah Dorsey; had iss.: THOMAS, b. c.1703, d. 1787; PETER:
WILLIAM; JOHN, b. 10 Nov. 1712; SARAH, m. 1st William Fell, and
2nd Greenbury Dorsey; JOSHUA, b. 8 Oct. 1718, d. 30 March 1720;
ELIZABETH, b. 16 Feb. 1719; ANN, b. and d. 1720; JACOB, b. c.
1725; DANIEL, m. Patience Bosley; JOSHUA (70:75; 111; 129; 131;
153; 219-1:56).

BOND, WILLIAM (4), s. of Peter (1) and Alice, under age in
1704, d. by 23 Aug. 1742; m. 1st Mary Westbury, bur. 17 Oct.
1732, coheiress with Elizabeth w. of John Butteram of Thomas,
Daniel, and William Westbury; m. 2nd Sarah (?) who d. by 14 May
1770; William's admin. bond posted 6 June 1739 by William Bond
of Thomas with Thomas Bond, Sr., and Luke Stanbury; in Nov.
1739 his s. Peter placed in care of William's s.-in-law Robert
Love; est. adm. in 1742 naming heirs: s.-in-law Thomas Johnson;
dau. Sarah Love; dau. Ann Bond; dau. w. of John Rigdon; dau. w.
of William Andrew; in 1750 his heirs owned 50 a. Addition, 148
a. Buck Range, 150 a. Laurence's Pasture, and 196 a. Hannah's
Delight; will of Sarah Bond, 19 April 1770 - 14 May 1770, named
sis. Elizabeth w. of William David; Margaret Tamon; step-dau.
Alice Johnson, Ann Fryer, Elizabeth Rigdon, Elizabeth Leach,
Salloma Durham, Elizabeth Baker, dau. of Theophilus Baker, bro.
Henry Tamon, John Durham, and exec. George Bradford; had iss.:
PETER, b. c.1705, d. by 14 Jan. 1749 naming bro. William and
bro.-in-law William Andrew in his will; WILLIAM, b. 23 Sept. 1709:
BARNETT; JOHN, b. c.1711, d. 11 Sept. 1723; SARAH, b. 13 March
1713, m. 1st on 9 June 1729 Robert Love, and 2nd Walter Billings-
ley; ALICE, m. Thomas Johnson on 17 Oct. 1724; CLARA, m. (?) Rig-
don; ANN, b. c.1719, d. test. by 4 Feb. 1743/4, naming bros.
William and Peter, sis. Mary w. of William Andrew, nephews William
and Billy Drew Andrew, niece Joanna Oakerson, and sis. Eliz.
Rigdon; MARY, m. on 14 Feb. 1732 William Andrew; ELIZABETH, b. 6
Feb. 1719, d. 6 April 1720; ELIZABETH, b. 16 Feb. 1720/1, m. 1st
(?) Oakerson, and 2nd, on 11 March 1740 John Rigdon (3; 11; 32:
79; 59; 67; 73; 110; 112; 127: 128; 131; 153).

BOND, JOHN (5), s. of Peter (1) and Alice, under age in 1704,
bur. 17 April 1720; m. Mary (?), extx. of Samuel Standiford, by
26 Aug. 1711; she m. 3rd, on 20 Oct. 1721 John Wesley or Wisely;
will proved 7 June 1720 named ch. John, Benjamin, Anne, and Robert, tracts 43 a. Chance, 150 a. Abell's Lot, and 100 a. Harris'
Trust; admin. bond posted 3 Aug. 1720 by Mary Bond with William
Bond and Robert Smith; est. inv. on 12 Dec. 1720 and again on
1 April 1721 by Charles Baker and John Crockett and val. at ₤
₤ 203.7.1 and ₤ 46.16.5; had iss.: JOHN: BENJAMIN; ANN (poss.
the Ann who m. James Carroll on 24 Nov. 1736); ROBERT, b. 11 Oct.
1717 (1; 2; 11; 26:87, 89; 51; 52; 110; 131).

BOND, RICHARD (6), s. of Peter (2) and Eleanor, d. 9 Feb.
1763; m. on 5 Aug. 1731 Mary Jones who d. 30 Dec. 1761 in her
46th yr.; in 1750 owned 100 a. part Middle Ridge, 26 a. Gist's
Search, 50 a. Roundabout, and 150 a. part Roundabout Neighbors;
will, 21 Jan. 1763 - 11 April 1763, named ch. Richard, John,
Shadrack, Nicodemus, Ruth Gott, Mary Bond, Jemima Ensor, Phebe
Bond, Sarah Bond, Helen Bond, Margaret Bond, Ann Constantine, and
Elizabeth Cole, and Philip, John, and Elizabeth Pindell, ch. of
John and Eleanor Pindell; est. adm. 29 Oct. 1764 by Nicodemus
Bond and Richard Gott; had iss.: ELEANOR, b. 15 Feb. 1732, d. 17
June 1756, m. John Pindell; RUTH, b. 5 Dec. 1734, m. on 30 Arril
1758 Richard Gott; MARY, b. 25 Dec. 1736; ANN, b. 3 April 1739,
m. on 29 Sept. 1760 Patrick Constantine; JEMIMA, b. 23 April
1741, m. George Ensor; NICODEMUS, b. 25 July 1743; RICHARD, b.
9 Sept. 1745; ELIZABETH, b. 30 Aug. 1747, m. (?) Cole; JOHN, b.
9 Oct. 1749; SHADRACK, b. 28 Oct. 1751; PHEBE, b. 23 Oct. 1753;
SARAH, b. 23 Dec. 1755; HELEN, b. 13 Jan. 1758; MARGARET, b. 2
May 1760 (6; 112; 133; 134; 153).

BOND, WILLIAM (7), s. of Peter (2) and Eleanor, named in his
f.'s will, may be the William who d. by 1750 when his heirs were
the owners of 50 a. Addition, 148 a. Buck Range, 150 a. Lawrence's
Pasture, and 196 a. Hannah's Pasture (153).

BOND, THOMAS (8), s. of Peter (2) and Eleanor, d. by 18 April
1768; m. on 9 May 1736 Phebe Thomas; in 1750 owned 52½ a. of
Logsdon's Addition, 140 a. of Bedford Resurveyed, 27 a. Bond's
Forest, 100 a. Wooley's Range, and 100 a. Bond's Meadows; in
1747, Thomas, tavernkeeper, and w. Phebe conv. two parcels of
Bedford Resurveyed to Benjamin Bond; est. adm. 18 April 1768 and
3 July 1769 by Phebe Bond; had iss.: SARAH, b. 29 Jan. 1738;
WILLIAM, b. 30 Nov. 1741; THOMAS, b. 27 Sept. 1744 (7; 77; 79;
133; 153; 200-63:248).

BOND, PETER (9), s. of Peter (2) and Eleanor, d. 26 Dec. 1762;
m. on 1 Aug. 1735 Susanna Butler, b. 13 Sept. 1717, dau. of Henry
and Susanna Butler; Susanna Butler Bond m. as her 2nd husb, John
Pitts on 6 Feb. 1766; in 1750 owned 70 a. Bond's Inheritance and
100 a. part Middle Range, 50 a. of Gist's Search, and 100 a.
Buck's Park; will, 26 Dec. 1762 - 11 April 1763, named w. Susanna,
bro. Richard, and ch. Samuel, Peter, Amon, Edward, Sophia, Kerrenhappuck, Benjamin, Henry, Elizabeth, Christopher, Joshua, and
Susanna; had iss.: SAMUEL, b. 26 Sept. 1736; KERRENHAPPUCK, b.
26 Feb. 1742/3; PETER, b. 14 April 1744, d. 1769, leaving a will,
6 Nov. 1769 - 6 Dec. 1769, which named his f. Peter, bros. Henry,
Benjamin, Samuel, Christopher, Joshua, and his f.-in-law John
Pitts; AMON, b. 14 July 1746; EDWARD, b. 12 July 1748; BENJAMIN,
b. 22 Sept. 1750; HENRY, b. 22 April 1753; CHRISTOPHER, b. 2 Nov.
1757; JOSHUA, b. 25 Oct. 1759; SUSANNA, b. 1 Aug. 1762; SOPHIA,
living 26 Dec. 1762; ELIZABETH, living 26 Dec. 1762 (81; 111;
112; 133; 134; 153).

BOND, JOHN (10), s. of Peter (2) and Eleanor, d. by 8 Dec.
1792, having m. Keturah (?); in 1750 owned 50 a. part Chestnut
Ridge, 130 a. of Friendship, 100 a. of Roundabout Neighbors, and
50 a. of Brown's Prospect; conv. 40 a. Bond's Industry to William
Tipton c.1760; will, proved 8 Dec. 1792, named ch. John, Mary Tip-
ton, Ruth Gist, Rachel Harryman and Sarah Hall, and ch. of dau.
Eleanor Gorsuch, and grandchildren John, William, and Keturah
Bond; est. adm. 14 March 1795, naming Joseph Peregoy who m. Mary
Gorsuch, Norman Gorsuch who m. Keturah Gorsuch, David Gorsuch who
m. Rebecca Gorsuch, Stephen Cole who m. Rachel Gorsuch, and
Eleanor, Ruth, Charles, Elizabeth, Ann, Achsah, and Belinda Gor-
such, orphan ch. of Charles Gorsuch; Joshua Hall who m. Sarah
Bond; George Harryman who m. Rachel Bond, and Thomas Gist who

m. Ruth Bond; had iss.: RACHEL, m. George Harryman by lic. of
8 Feb. 1788; JOSHUA, b. 3 Dec. 1740, and may have d. young;
JOHN: m. Rachel Cole; RITH, b. 25 Feb. 1744, m. Thomas Gist;
ELEANOR, b. 22 Oct. 1746, m. Charles Gorsuch; MARY, b. 25 June
1749, m. Aquila Tipton; SARAH, m. Joshua Hall (84; 114; 134;
153; 232; 237:11).

BOND, BENJAMIN (11), s. of Peter (2) and Eleanor, d. by 1750,
m. Sophia, dau. of Henry Butler; vestryman of St. Thomas Par.
after 1749; in 1750 heirs owned 62½ a. of Bedford Resurveyed;
had iss.: URATH, b. 10 Aept. 1742 (5; 133; 153; 398).

BOND, THOMAS (12), s. of Thomas (3) and Ann, b. c.1703, living
1781; m. on 3 Feb. 1725 Elizabeth, dau. of Daniel Scott, b. c.
1705, living 1781; prob. the Thomas Bond, Jr., who in 1750 owned
109 a. Bond's Beginnings, 56 a. part Bond's Fortune, 100 a. Tower
Hill, and Miles' Improvement; w. w. Elizabeth conv. dau. Martha
200 a. Bond's Forest in 1778, Zacheus and Hannah Onion 100 a.of
Bond's Forest in 1780, and 96 a. Bond's Forest to William and
Susanna Amos, and 100 a. Tower Hill to dau. Anne Clemens, her
husb. William Clemens and their s. Thomas Bond Clemens, all of
Chas. Co.; d. by April 1791 when his relict Elizabeth, widow
of Thomas Bond, d. 7 March 1791 in her 87th year, having lived
with her husb. for over 63 yrs.; had iss.: ANN, b. 13 April 1726,
m. William Clemens; ELIZABETH, b. 2 Nov. 1727; THOMAS; HANNAH,
m. Zacheus Onion on 2 Dec. 1757; MARTHA, b. c.1747, age 29 in
1776; SUSANNA, m. William Amos, Jr. (131; 153; 241-JLG#A:414;
241-JLG#D:35, 75; 241-JLG#E:451; 258).

BOND, PETER (13), s. of Thomas (3) and Ann, mentioned in his
f.'s will, but d. by 23 Dec. 1738, having m. Hester, dau. of
Isaac Butterworth; she m. 2nd Caleb Hughes; admin. bond posted
23 Dec, 1738 by Hester Bond with Isaac Butterworth, Henry Garrett
and Abraham Boyd; est. adm. 17 Sept. 1740 by Caleb Hughes and w.
Hester; had iss.: SARAH, b. 9 Dec. 1719; ANN, b. 18 June 1729;
PETER, b. 10 June 1738 (4; 11; 33:10; 131; 558).

BOND, WILLIAM (14), s. of Thomas (3) and Ann, d. by 1769,
having m. Elizabeth Stansbury, dau. of Luke Stansbury; par. con-
veyed him 510 a. Bond's Lot in June 1723; conv. 304 a. Bond's
Forest to Josiah Dyer of Bucks Co., Penna. in 1763, conv. 410 a.
Bond's Forest to Luke Stansbury Bond in 1764, and 193 a. Bond's
Water Mills in (?) to John Bond; in 1745 conv. negro to Ruth,
Luke Stansbury Bond , Priscilla, Elizabeth, Thomas, William, and
Tobias Bond; in 1750 owned 50 a. Filial Care, 100 a. Limerick,
246 a. Midsummer Hills, 180 a. Forberry Neck, and 100 a. Pork
Hall; will, 6 Aug. 1767 - 8 April 1769 , named bro. Jacob and w.
Elizabeth as execs.; ch. Luke, Priscilla Worthington, Ruth Nich-
olson, Cassandra, and James; had iss.: LUKE STANSBURY, b. April
1733; PRISCILLA, b. 3 July 1735, m. Vachel Worthington on 17 Nov.
1757; RUTH, m. 16 March 1749, Nathan Nicholson; CASSANDRA; JAMES;
ELIZABETH; THOMAS ; WILLIAM; and TOBIAS. (69; 78; 87; 88; 90; 92;
112; 127; 131; 133; 153).

BOND, JOHN (15), s. of Thomas (3) and Ann, b. 10 Nov. 1712,
d. 1786, m. Aliceanna Webster, dau. of John, on 26 day of May,
1734, at Nottingham Meeting; in 1750 owned 466 a. of James Park,
2 a. lots in Joppa, 84 a. The Oblong, and 33 a. Bond's Tanyard;
known as John Bond, Gent., lived at Fells Point, Balto., in the
winter, Justice of the Peace, Coroner, and Judge of the Orphans'
Court, 1769-1773; private in Capt. William Marbury's Co. of Ar-
tillery, 1775-1783; had iss.: THOMAS; Dr. JOHN, m. Sarah Elliott; PAMELA, m. William Moore; SAMUEL, m. Cynthia Richardson;
WILLIAM, m. on 16 Nov. 1771 Sarah Wrong; SUSAN, m. 1st Phineas
Hunt, and 2nd (?) Johns; ANN, m. 1st (?) Giles; and 2nd Edward

Fell; JANE, m. Samuel Bradford; ABIGAIL, m. (?) Abbott; HANNAH, "marr. out of meeting," husb. not identified (79; 136; 153; 353; 430:930).

BOND, JACOB (16), s. of Thomas (3) and Ann, b. c.1725, d. Nov. 1780; m. on 28 Dec. 1747 Fanny Partridge; 2nd (?); and 3rd Elizabeth (?); member of the Committee in Harf. Co., and a member of Co. No. 11; in 1774 a delegate from Harf. Co. to protest the tax on tea; delegate to Annapolis in 1776 to draw up State Constitution; was conv. ½ of Poplar Neck by his f. in Nov. 1752; in 1776 res. in Bush R. Lower Hund. with his ch.: ELIZABETH, age 28 in 1776; JACOB, Jr., age 26; SARAH, m. Bernard Preston; JOHN, age 23; PRISCILLA, age 17; DENNIS, age 16; RALPH, age 13; MARTHA, age 10; and CHARLOTTE, age 9 (7; 81; 133; 210:31; 285; 354).

BOND, DANIEL (17), s. of Thomas (3) and Ann, m. on 1 Nov. 1759 Patience, dau. of James and Elizabeth (Parrish) Bosley; had iss.: BETSY ANN; ZACHEUS; JOSHUA, and THOMAS (131).

BOND, JOSHUA (18), s. of Thomas (3) and Ann, d. by 8 July 1768, m. Ann Partridge; in 1750 owned 40 a. Joshua's Meadows; will, 28 Dec. 1767 - 8 July 1768, named w. Anne, and bro. Jacob, and ch.: William, Buckler, Thomas, James, Sarah, Ann, Mary, Elizabeth, and Amelia, and tracts Poplar Neck, part Morgan's Lot, Ranger's Range, part Bond's Gift, and part Joshua's Meadows; had iss.: WILLIAM; BUCKLER; THOMAS; JAMES; SARAH; ANN; MARY; ELIZABETH; AMELIA (7; 83:340; 112; 153; 210:31).

BOND, WILLIAM (19), s. of William (4) and Mary, living on 12 March 1754, having m. Anne (?); had iss.: ANN, b. 6 May 1748; WILLIAM, b. 12 Feb. 1749; SARAH, b. 23 June 1752; DREW, b. 12 March 1754 (131).

BOND, BARNET (20), s. of William (4) and Mary, b. c. 1709, d. 1746; m. Alice (?), who m. as her 2nd husb. William Grimes; conv. 381 Foreberies Neck and Midsummer Hill to William Bond in 1741; conv. 460 a. Bond's Lot and Bond's Add'n to Walter Billingsley in 1744, naming in the deed his f. William, and his sis. Alice Johnson; surv. Bond's Care in 1744 (later pat. by his only s. Thomas); will of Barnett Bond, "late of Maryland in America, now of St. Anne's Limehouse, Middlesex, 25 Jan. 1741 - 20 April 1741, named w. Alice, dau. Mary, bros. Peter and William, sis. Ann, and cousin William; may be the Barnett Bond for whom admin. bond was posted 7 Aug. 1746(?) by William Bond, Jr., with Walter Tolley and Amos Garrett; but probate was granted in 1749 to relict Alice, now w. of William Grimes; bro. and heir in 1750 was one William Bond; despite apparent contradictions, Barnett and Alice seem to have had iss.: MARY; THOMAS of Barnett, living in 1772 when he pat. Bond's Care; poss. JOHN DELCHER; poss. PETER (11; 37:121; 75; 77; 207; 231-AL#B:298).

BOND, JOHN (21), s. of John (5) and Mary, d. by 8 June 1739; m. on 21 Feb. 1733 Isabella Robinson, dau. of William and Elizabeth Robinson; Isabella m. as 2nd husb. by 15 Sept. 1740 George Presbury; admin. bond posted 4 April 1739 by admnx. Isabella Bond with Benjamin Bond and Charles Baker; est. inv. on 8 June 1739 by William Dallam and William Bradford, and val. at £ 216. 18.4, plus £ 4.14.2, while Benjamin Bond and Thomas Richardson signed; est. adm. by George and Isabella Presbury on 15 Sept. 1740 and 10 Oct. 1743; had iss.: ELIZABETH, b. 27 Dec. 1735 (3; 4; 11; 36:210; 131).

BOND, BENJAMIN (22), s. of John (5) and Mary, d. by 11 Oct. 1749; m. on 28 May 1737 Clemency Taylor, heir of Robert Robertson;

Clemency m. as her 2nd husb. on 30 March 1749 James Preston; in
Aug. 1746 Benjamin and Clemency conv. Thomas Bond 150 a. Abell's
Lot; his admin. bond posted 21 April 1749 by James Preston with
Daniel Preston and Andrew Thompson; est. adm. on 11 Oct. 1749
and 21 Aug. 1751; in 1750 heirs of Benjamin owned 86 a. part
Whitely, 92 a. of Taylor's Adventure, and 284 a. part Robinson's
Chance and Hog Neck; had iss.: MARY, b. 24 July 1737; JOHN, b. 14
Oct. 1739; BENJAMIN, b. 15 Sept. 1742; CLEMENCY, b. 12 May 1745;
SARAH, b. 13 June 1748 (4; 5; 11; 131; 153).

BOND, NICODEMUS (23), s. of Richard (6) and Mary, b. 25 July
1743, d. c.1804 in Balto. Co.; m. on 1 Jan. 1765 Rachel Stevenson, b. 1 Jan. 1745, d. 1804, dau. of Richard King and Rachel
(?) Stevenson; had iss. (111; 116; 134; 231-AL#B).

BOND, RICHARD (24), s. of Richard (6) and Mary, b. 9 Sept.
1745; inher. 50 a. of land in f.'s will.

BOND, SHADRACK (25), s. of Richard (6) and Mary, b. 28 Oct.
1751; inher. 50 a. Middle Ridge from his f.; went west as a
sgt. with George Rogers Clark, d. St. Clair Co., Ill. (399:100).

BOND, WILLIAM (26), s. of Thomas (8), and Phebe, b. 30 Nov.
1741, d. by 8 May 1769; m. Susanna (?), who m. as her 2nd husb.
by lic. 31 March 1778, Isaac Hammond (7; 8; 232).

BOND, THOMAS (27), s. of Thomas (8) and Phebe, b. 27 Sept.
1744.

BOND, SAMUEL (28), s. of Peter (9) and Susanna, b. 26 Sept.
1736, d. 1796; m. on 9 Feb. 1766 Charity Clark, and had iss.
(8; 10; 114; 134).

BOND, AMON (29), s. of Peter (9) and Susanna, b. 14 July 1746.

BOND, EDWARD (30), s. of Peter (9), and Susanna, b. 12 July
1748; prob. the Edward who died testate by 22 March 1797, having
marr. and had iss. (114).

BOND, BENJAMIN (31), s. of Peter (9), and Susanna, b. 22 Sept.
1750.

BOND, HENRY (32), s. of Peter (9) and Susanna, b. 22 April
1753.

BOND, CHRISTOPHER (33), s. of Peter (9) and Susanna, b. 2 Nov.
1757; said to have migrated to Ohio; m. and had iss.

BOND, JOSHUA (34), s. of Peter (9) and Susanna, b. 25 Oct.
1759.

BOND, JOSHUA (35), s. of John (10) and Ketura, b. 3 Dec. 1740;
may be the Joshua who d. intestate by 22 Feb. 1775 when admin.
was granted to Ann Bond; may have had s. JOHN, living in Va. as
the subject of an advertisement in the Balto. Md. Journal of 20
July 1787 (235).

BOND, JOHN (36), s. of John (10) and Ketura; m. Rachel Cole.

BOND, THOMAS (37), s. of Thomas (12) and Elizabeth, d. c.1800
in Harf. Co.; m. 3 Feb. 1765 Catharine Fell, dau. of William and
Sarah (Bond) Fell (131; 231-WG#94; 244-AJ#C).

BOND, PETER (38), s. of Peter (13) and Hester, b. 10 June
1738; may be the "Peter Bond of Peter" who chose John Deaver as
his guardian in June 1756 (40:2).

BOND, LUKE STANSBURY (39), s. of William (14) and Elizabeth, b. April 1733, d. c.1772; will, 19 April 1772 - 2 Jan. 1773, named four ch.: THOMAS; JOHN; ELIZABETH; WILLIAM (112; 237-11).

BOND, JAMES (40), s. of William (14) and Elizabeth, living June 1786; m. Martha (?) (538).

BOND, THOMAS (41), s. of William (14) and Elizabeth, living 6 Aug. 1767.

BOND, WILLIAM (42), s. of William (14) and Elizabeth, living 1745, but not in 1767.

BOND, TOBIAS (43), s. of William (14) and Elizabeth, living in 1745, but not in 1767.

BOND, THOMAS (44), s. of John (15) and AliceAnna, living as late as 1771; m. 1st in 1771 Rebecca, dau. of Capt. Tobias Stansbury, and 2nd, Sarah Chew; Judge of the Orphan's Court and Justice of the Peace; had iss.: JOHN, an itinerant preacher; THOMAS EMERSON, editor of The Christian Advocate; ANN, m. Rev. John Wood of New York (353; 430:931).

BOND, Dr. JOHN (45), s. of John (15) and AliceAnna, m. Sarah Elliott.

BOND, SAMUEL (46), s. of John (15) and AliceAnna, m. Cynthia Richardson.

BOND, WILLIAM (47), s. of John (15) and AliceAnna, b. 1746, d. after March 1783, rendered Civil Service in Md. during the Rev. War; m. 16 Nov. 1771 Sarah Wrong (131; 353).

BOND, JACOB (48), s. of Jacob (16) and Fanny Partridge Bond, b. c.1750, living in 1776 w. wife Elizabeth in Bush R. Lower Hund. (285).

BOND, DENNIS (49), s. of Jacob (16) and Fanny, b. c.1760, living in 1776; may have m. in 1787 Mary Merryman (346-2:218).

BOND, RALPH (50), s. of Jacob (16) and Fanny, b. c.1763, living in 1776.

BOND, ZACHEUS (51), s. of Daniel (17) and Patience.

BOND, JOSHUA (52), s. of Daniel (17) and Patience.

BOND, THOMAS (53), s. of Daniel (17) and Patience.

BOND, WILLIAM (54), s. of Joshua (18) and Anne, living on 19 Jan. 1774 when as exec. of his f.'s will he conv. 35 a. Poplar Neck and 3 a. Clarkson's Purchase to his bro. Buckler (231-AL#I).

BOND, BUCKLER (55), s. of Joshua (18), and Anne, was conv. land by his bro. William in 1774; m. by 3 Nov. 1779 Mary, dau. of Tobias Stansbury; may have been the Buckler, age 30, living with (a 1st w.?) Charity, age 32, and Martha, 3, and Sarah, 1, in Bush R. Lower Hund. in 1776 (231-AL#I; 231-WG#E: 285).

BOND, THOMAS (56), s. of Joshua (18) and Ann, living 1768.

BOND, JAMES (57), s. of Joshua (18), and Ann, living 1768.

BOND, WILLIAM (58), s. of William (19) and Anne, b. 12 Feb. 1749.

BOND, THOMAS (59), s. of Barnett (20) and Alice, b. c.1739/40, d. March 1795, bur. 30 March 1795, age 56; m. 7 July 1768 Sarah Bond; pat. Bond's Care in 1772 (tract had orig. been surv. for his f.); admin. granted to Sarah Bond 23 May 1795; est. inv. 5 Aug. 1795 by Chaney Hatton and Nicholas Brian, val. at Ł 276.7.0; wid. Sarah m. 2nd James Gregory; had iss. (131; 203:131; 235; 237:13; 238;1).

BOND, JOHN DELCHER (60), poss. s. of Barnett (20) and Alice.

BOND, PETER (61), poss. s. of Barnett (20) and Alice.

BOND, JOHN (62), s. of Benjamin (22) and Clemency, b. 14 Oct. 1739, living in 1751.

BOND, BENJAMIN (63), s. of Benjamin (22) and Clemency, b. 15 Sept. 1742, living 1751.

Unplaced Bonds.

BOND, ANN, d. by 14 June 1744 when admin. bond was posted by William Andrews, with George Presbury and James Tolly (11).

BOND, CHARLES, m. Eleanor (?) and had iss.: SUSANNA, b. 1 Sept. 1737; CHARLES, b. 21 Nov. 1739 (128).

BOND, JAMES, d. by 26 Jan. 1754 when admin. bond was posted by John Bond, with Thomas Bond (11).

BOND, JOHN, m. Eleanor (?) and had iss.: JANE, b. 27 Aug. 1736 (128).

BOND, SARAH, in 1750 owned 100 a. of Harris' Trust, and 150 a. of Abel's Lot (153).

BOND, URIAH, runaway servt. of Joseph England, Nov. 1745 (35: 742).

BOND, URIAH, blacksmith, d. by 31 Jan. 1748 when admin. bond was posted by David McCulloch, with William Dallam and Talbot Risteau (11).

BONE, EDWARD, was in Balto. Co. by 1692 as a taxable in n. side Patapsco Hund. (138).

BONE, ELIZABETH, admitted to bearing a bast. named Nathan, fathered by a black, March 1758 (46:100).

BONE, JOHN, was in Balto. Co. by 1692 as a taxable in s. side Patapsco Hund. (128).

BONE, WILLIAM, age c.19, runaway conv. servt. of William and James Demitt, in the Forks of Gunpowder, Sept..1742 (384).

BONFIELD, FRANCIS, was in Balto. Co. by 1750 when he owned 100 a. of Arabia Petrea (153).

BONFIELD, JAMES VAINE, s. of Orphy Ensor, was b. 27 Dec. 1757 (133).

BONNADAY, ALICE, ind. for bast., named John Hall as the father, June 1712 (21:316).

BONNADAY, JOHN, s. of Alice, was age 2 in June 1809 when he was bound to John Roberts to age 21; may be the John "Bonadee" who d. 10 Oct. 1713 (21:40; 131).

BONNER, HENRY, in Balto. Co. by Oct. 1684 when he surv. 1000
a. Bonner's Camp, d. test. by 21 Oct. 1702 in P. G. Co., leaving
land in Balto. Co. to widow Eliza; may be the Henry Bonner of
Charles Co. who imm. c.1669 (122:13; 211:50; 388).

BONNER, JOHN, m. 28 Feb. 1754 Christian Ingram, had iss.:
WILLIAM, b. 3 March 1755; SARAH, b. 13 Feb. 1757; ARTHUR, b. 14
Jan. 1759; MARTHA, b. 9 May 1769 (129).

BONNEY, PETER, d. 16 Jan. 1719; as Peter Barney his est. was
inv. 16 May 1720 by Thomas Cord and Thomas Shay, and val. at
Ł 56.17.11; admin. bond posted 17 May 1720 by Thomas Moulder of
Chester Co., Penna., with John Hall and Thomas Cord (11; 48; 128).

BOOKER, RICHARD, of Va., acq. title to land in Md. in 1664;
imm. by 1665 and obtained cert. for land in Balto. Co.; may have
transp. Thomas Booker by 1664; in Jan. 1670/1, Elizabeth Booker,
wid. and Richard Booker, Gent., exch.500 a. on the n. side of Bohemia Cr. for 200 land in New Kent Co., Va. (97; 388).

BOOKER, JOHN, m. by Sept. 1694 Edith, extx. of Christopher
Gist (20:289).

BOONE, HUMPHREY, in Md. by 10 May 1672 when he surv. 160 a.
Boone's Adventure; in A. A. Co. by April 1690 when named as overseer in the will of James Orrouck; d. test. in Balto. Co., with
will, 19 Nov. 1709 - 30 Nov. 1709, named s. Robert, dau. Mary
Merryman; est. admin. 4 Aug. 1710 by exec.; had iss.: ROBERT,
living 1710; MARY, m. by 1709 (?) Merryman (2; 121; 122; 211:107).

BOONE, JOHN, was in Balto. Co. by 1694 as a taxable in n. side
Gunpowder Hund.; d. by March 1718; m. by 1695 Jane widow of John
Durham; in March 1705 w. wife conv. to Matthew Green tract Levy's
Tribe which Samuel Durham left to John Boone ; admin. bond posted
17 March 1718 by admnx. Jane Boone with John Taylor and Mathew
Hale; est. inv. April 1719 by Charles Baker and Jno. Rawlings and
val. at Ł 81.8.0; est. admin. by Jane Boone on 8 April 1721, 11
Aug. 1722, 9 Nov. 1723, and 5 June 1724; Jane Boone living 8 March
1732 (1; 2; 11; 51; 64; 139; 341).

BOONE, ROBERT, was in Balto. Co. by 1750 when he owned 225 a.
Young Richard and 200 a. Rockhold's Range (153).

BOORIN. See BORING.

BOOTHBY, EDWARD, d. by 1698/9, having imm. to Balto. Co. by
c.1685; m. c.1693/4 Elizabeth (Carter) Utie Johnson, dau. of John
Carter of Lancaster Co., Va.; she m. 1st Nathaniel Utie, who d.
1675/6, and 2nd Henry Johnson, who d. 1690/1; Boothby rep. Balto.
Co. in the Assembly, 1692-1693, and 1694-1695; acquired many
parcels of land; will, 11 Dec. 1698 - 10 Jan. 1698/9, named w.
Eliza, dau. Frances (not yet 18), s.-in-law Joseph Johnson, and
Francis Whitehead, Simon Wilmer, and Anthony Drew; he d. 12 Dec.
1698 at Spesutia Island, and his wid. Elizabeth was bur. 4 Aug.
1699 at John Hall's; admin. bond posted 14 Feb. 1692 by his execs.;
est. of Edward and Elizabeth Boothby inv. by Roger Matthews and
Henry Jackson and val. at Ł 310.19.0½ plus debts of Ł31.8.6 and
76942 lbs. tob.; est. adm. by James Phillips on 13 April 1711;
had iss.: FRANCES, under 18 on 11 Dec. 1698, m. Josias Middlemore on 9 Oct. 1720 (1; 2; 11; 128; 131; 206; 211; 370).

BORAM, JOSEPH, m. 7 Aug. 1753 Sarah Demmitt (131).

BORCK. See BURKE.

BORDLEY, JOHN, serv., with 18 mos. to serve in 1742 inv. of Jonas Robinson (53).

BORDLEY, MARTHA, ind. for bast., March 1731 (29:225).

BORDSMAN, WILLIAM, orphan, age 13 next Nov., in June 1757 was bound to Robert and Susanna Mills (46:37).

BOREMAN, EDWARD, d. by 30 March 1706 when admin. bond was posted by John Landys and w. Catherine, with John Yates and John Parker (11). See also BOWMAN.

THE BORING FAMILY is the subject of a family genealogy by Edwin G. Hecklinger and Edwin C. Boring. (540).

BORING, JOHN (1), imm. to Md. by 1670 with dau. Ann; d. in Balto Co. in 1690; may have m. three times; 1st to the unknown mother of Ann; 2nd to Margaret, wid. of Roger Sidwell; 3rd to Ann (?); surv. 50 a. Boring's Range in 1679 and 50 a. Boring's Pasture in 1682; his will, 2 May 1690 - 5 Aug. 1690, named "now wife" Ann, sons Thomas, James, and John (latter to be of age at 18); est. inv. Oct. 1690 by Thomas Long and Francis Watkins and val. at £ 332.11.4; est. admin. 16 May 1704 by Charles Merryman as the orig. exec., John Ferry, was dec.; wid. Ann m. 2nd John Ferry; had iss.: ANN, b. by 1670; THOMAS; JAMES; JOHN, b. c.1682/3; MARY (2; 51; 59; 60; 101; 211; 388).

BORING, JAMES (2), s. of John (1), d. c.1738 in Balto. Co.; m. 1st by 4 March 1719 Jane, dau. and coheir of Daniel Welsh, and 2nd Rebecca, wid. of (?) Gain; she m. 3rd John Frazier; in 1719 with Jane conv. Welsh's Adventure to Otho Holland; leased pt. Blathnia Cambria from Thomas Bladen in Dec. 1736, the lease to run for the lifetimes of himself, w. Rebecca, and dau. Ann; d. by 15 April 1738 when admin. bond was posted by Rebecca, with Charles and John Green; est. admin. 18 Oct. 1741 by Rebecca, now w. of J. Frazier; est. admin. again on 17 March 1742; had iss.: ANN, living in 1742 (3; 4; 11; 31; 61; 67; 68; 70).

BORING, THOMAS (3), s. of John (1), d. by 1723; admin. bond posted 6 May 1723 by James Boring; est. admin. 10 Dec. 1736; had iss.: THOMAS; JAMES; and MARY (2; 11; 31:100; 67).

BORING, JOHN (4), s. of John (1), was b. c.1683 and d. c.1750; m. 1st by 10 May 1707 Mary (?); m. 2nd Pretiosa (?) who d. 2 Feb. 1734; and m. 3rd Sarah (?) who d. 1763; in May 1707 he and Mary conv. pt. Jones' Inheritance to John Norton; in Jan. 1718 he and w. Pretiosa conv. 202 a. Selsed to Thomas Ford; gave age as 50 in 1732 and said his stepfather John Ferry was alive in 1693; in Jan. 1741 conv. 100 a. The Landing to son-in-law Dutton Lane; in Oct. 1749 conv. land to son John and grandsons William, Reuben (of Thomas), and John (of John); admin. bond posted 6 Oct. 1750 by admnx Sarah Boring; est. admin. 13 March 1751 and 15 Oct. 1751; in 1750 his heirs owned 100 a. Hail's Folly, 100 a. Hail's Discovery, 85 a. Knight's Addition, and 100 a. John's Favor ; will of Sarah, 4 Oct. 1757 - 12 Sept. 1763, named Rev. Thomas Chase and Wm. Askew; had iss.: DINAH, m. Dutton Lane; JOHN; and THOMAS (5; 11; 59; 63; 67; 68; 70; 73; 74; 75; 76; 77; 78; 111; 153; 163:157).

BORING: THOMAS (5), s. of Thomas (3), d. test. in 1795; m. 1st, 21 Jan. 1730 Mary Haile (who d. 14 April 1734); m. 2nd Philizanna (?) (who d. 1801); had iss.: MARY, b. 4 April 1734, m. (?) Kelly (she may be the Mary Boring ind. for bast. in Nov. 1740); RUTH, b. 15 Dec. 1745; EZEKIEL, b. 1751; MILENDA, m. (?) Tracey (32:351; 114; 131; 133).

BORING,. JAMES (6), s. of Thomas (3), d. c.1819 in Balto. Co. having m. Martha Wheeler on 25 Dec. 1736; Martha was dau. of Wm. Wheeler; in Aug. 1740 James and Martha conv. 100 a. of land to William Merryman; will of James, 15 Sept. 1807 - 29 Dec. 1819, named these ch.: JOSHUA (to have Green's Desire); ABRAHAM (to have Sportsman's Hall): JAMES, and RICHARD (to have jointly Upland and Meadow Ground); MARY, m. (?) Tipton; ELIZABETH, m. (?) Handle; and REBECCA, m. (?) Cullison (4; 133; 236:11).

BORING, JOHN (7), s. of John (4) and Pretiosa, d. by 1763; m. by March 1746 Avarilla (poss. dau. of Charles Robinson); in March John and Avarilla sold Richard Miller Cole part Boring's Gift, and w. Charles Merryman and w. Millicent conv. pt. of same land to Charles Ridgely; in 1750 as John Boreing II owned 50 a. Boreing Gift, 355 a. Boreing's Forest, and 100 a. Boring's Meadow; was d. by March 1763 when Avarilla Boring, wid., sold to Nicholas Britton her right of dower in 1/3 interest of Boring's Forest, Cuckoldmaker's Hazard, and Boring's Gift; Avarilla was alive in 1774; had iss.: JOHN, living Oct. 1748 when his grandfather conv. him land (79; 87; 153; 231:AL#I).

BORING, THOMAS (8), s. of John (4) and Pretiosa, d. by 1761, having m. 3 Feb. 1734 Elizabeth Welsh, who d. c.1785; in July 1736 Thomas and Elizabeth conv. Thomas' Park to Charles Ridgely; in Feb. 1749 with bro. John conv. Sarah Boring (prob. their stepmoth.) lots 17 and 18 in Balto. Town; will, 30 May 1752 - 11 May 1761, named s. James, w. Elizabeth, and s. Reuben; will of wid. Elizabeth, 20 Jan. 1773 - 21 July 1785, named iss.: WILLIAM, b. 19 Feb. 1735, d. 1811; JAMES; REUBEN; and URATH, m. John Frazier. (79; 80; 111; 113).

BORING, EZEKIEL (9), s. of Thomas (5) and Philizanna, was alive in Aug. 1794 when John and Sarah Boring conv. him 2 acres of Green's Chance; by May 1802 was in York Co., Penna. (231-WG#PP: 231-WG#71).

BORING, JOSHUA (10), s. of James (6) and Martha Wheeler, inher. Green's Chance from his father.

BORING, ABRAHAM (11), s. of James (6) and Martha, inher. land Sportsman's Hall from his father.

BORING, JAMES (12), s. of James (6) and Martha, with bro. Richard inher. parts of Upland and Meadow Ground from their father.

BORING, RICHARD (13), s. of James (6) and Martha, with bro. James inher. parts of Upland and Meadow Ground from their father.

BORING, JOHN (14), s. of John (7) and Avarilla, was conv. land by his grandfather John in Oct. 1749; m. Sarah (?), who in Aug. 1794 joined him conv. 2 acres Green's Chance to Ezekiel Boring, and 19¼ a. Green's Chance, 138 a. Green's Meadows, and 13 a. Anything at All to George Keller of York Co., Penna.; may have had at least one son: JOSHUA, d. 1822 in Balto. Co. (80; 231-_ WG#PP).

BORING, WILLIAM (15), s. of Thomas (8) and Eliz., b. 19 Feb. 1735, d. 1811; m. Martha (?) who d. c.1815; both left wills; in June 1765 William and Martha, and bro. Reuben and latter's w. Nancy conv. 10t 17 in Balto. Town to Mark Alexander; had iss.: THOMAS; JOSHUA; ELIZABETH, m. Henry Green; PETER; POLLY; JOSIAS; ANN; and GREENBURY (90; 118; 133; 153).

BORING, JAMES (16), s. of Thomas (8) and Eliz.; not traced.

BORING, REUBEN (17), s. of Thomas (8) and Eliz., in Oct.

1749 was conv. lot 17 in Balto. Town by grandfather John; m. by
17 June 1765 Nancy, poss. dau. of Abraham Vaughan (6; 80; 90).

BORING, or BOORIN, WILLIAM, no known rel. to above fam., was
in Balto. Co. by 1692 as a taxable in Spesutia Hund.; m. Mary (?)
who was bur. 20 May 1699; he was bur. 21 Jan. 1698/9 and admin.
bond was posted 18 Feb. 1698/9 by Mary Boorin with John Shields
and Jno. Kimball; had iss.: SARA, bur. 20 May 1699; MARY, b. 15
June 1695;CHARLES, bur. 7 Jan. 1698/9, and poss. ROBERT, of The
Level, bur. 25 March 1699 (11; 128; 138).

BORNE, PETER, was in Balto. Co. by 1695 as a taxable in Spesutia Hund. (140).

BORWELL, CHARLES, had banns of marr. to Mary Hammond forbidden
in 1750 (131).

BOSLER, JACOB, m. Rachel (?), and had iss.: HONOR, b. 23 Dec.
1759.

BOSLEY, WALTER (1), progenitor, was in Balto. Co. by 1696/7
when he had surv. 200 a. called Bosley's Expectation on s. side
of w. branch of the Gunpowder; d. in Balto. Co. leaving a will,
29 July 1715 - 2 Nov. 1715, naming w. Mary and ch. Joseph, John,
James, Charles, and ygst. s. William, and disposing of tracts
100 a. Bosley's Palace, 199 a. Bosley's Expectation, and 95 a
Arthur's Choice; in Nov. 1719 Mary petitoned that her ch. be
moved from care of Joseph Abingdon and placed with Mr. Welsh and
with Joseph Bosley; in Nov. 1720 she was ind. for bast.; ch. of
Walter: JOSEPH, d. c.1780; JOHN, d. c.1772; JAMES, d. by June
1762; WILLIAM, b. 11 March 1712/3, and CHARLES, b. 13 May 1714
(23:248, 405; 123:79; 131:6, 19/r; 211:64). (541; 542; 543).

BOSLEY, JOSEPH (2), s. of Walter (1), d. leaving a will, 12
April 1772 - 20 March 1780; m. Ann (?); in 1750 owned 30 a.
Ellege's Grove; will named w. Ann, sons Gideon, Thomas, and
Greenbury, and daus. Delilah Barney, Diana Magers, Ann, Mary,
and Johanna; est. admin. 11 April 1787 by Greenbury Bosley
naming ch.: Gideon, Hannah, Mary w. of Benjamin Barney, Ruth
Cox, the wife of Elias Magers, Thomas, and Greenbury; had iss.:
DELILAH, m. Benjamin Barney in 1758; DIANA, m. Elias Magers in
1763; RUTH, m. (?) Cox; ANN; THOMAS; GREENBURY; GIDEON; MARY;
and (JO)HANNAH) (9:35; 112:393; 153:11).

BOSLEY, JOHN (3), s. of Walter (1), d. in Balto. Co. by 20
April 1772 having m. Hannah (?), wid. of (?) Tipton; she d. by
1777; in 1750 he owned 250 a. Miller's Choice, 100 a. Billy's
Adventure (Bosley's Adventure?), 21 a. Bosley's Meadows, 19 a.
Hopyard, 100 a. Gerar, and 60 a. Hooker's Addition; will, 20
Sept. 1767 - 20 April 1772, named w. Hannah and ch.: Walter and
Joseph; will of Hannah Bosley, 30 July 1776 - 16 Jan. 1777, named
sons Samuel and Mordecai Tipton, dau. Sarah w. of Christopher
Cole, and grandch. Joshua, William, Hannah, Ellen, Philip, Eliza-
beth, Rachel, Daniel, Rebecca, and Belinda Bosley ; had iss.:
WALTER; JOSEPH, d. c.1775/6 (112:213, 305; 153:9).

BOSLEY, JAMES (4), s. of Walter (1), d. by 7 June 1762 when
his est. was admin.; m. Elizabeth Parrish on 26 Nov. 1730; in 1750
owned 143 a. of Bosley's Delight; est. admin. by Elizabeth Bosley
and acct. named his issue: the wife of Benjamin Price, the wife
of Daniel Bond, Ezekiel, William, and Prudence, and mentions seven
other children; had iss.: PATIENCE, b. 16 Sept. 1731, m. Daniel
Bond in 1759; dau., m. by 7 June 1762 Benjamin Price; EZEKIEL;
WILLIAM, b. 1 July 1735; PRUDENCE; JAMES, b. after 1741; GIDEON,
m. Sarah Cole; THOMAS, m. Mary Richards; SARAH, m. Daniel ROWAN;

CHARITY, m. Joseph Parrish; HANNAH, b. c.1760, m. 15 June 1780
John Talbot; ELIZABETH, m. Vincent Talbot (6:131; 131; 133;
153:7; 541; 542).

BOSLEY, WILLIAM (5), s. of Walter (1), b. 11 March 1712/3, e.
by 3 April 1754; m. Mary (?); in 1750 owned 100 a. Expectation;
in June 1737 was ind. for incontinently cohabitaing with Mary
Brown, and had been taken before the vestry of St. John's Parish
for same offense; will, proved 3 April 1754, names wife and
these ch.: JAMES, b. c.1744, m. Temperance Marsh; dau., b. c.
1745 (31:14; 111:59; 131:19/r; 132:281; 153:32; 543:17-19).

BOSLEY, CHARLES (6), s. of Walter (1) and Mary, b. 13 May 1714,
d. by 11 Oct. 1762 having m. by 3 Aug. 1736 Elizabeth, dau. of
William Cox, and sis. of Jacob Cox; Elizabeth d. c.1784/5; on 3
Aug. 1736 William Cox conv. to his dau. Elizabeth, w. of Charles
Bosley, 50 a. Bachelor's Refuge; in 1750 Charles owned 50 a.
Bachelor's Refuge, 47 a. Jacob's Struggle, and 50 a. Bachelor's
Choice; his will, 10 July 1759 - 11 Oct. 1762, named w. Elizabeth
her bro. Jacob Cox, and his own ch.: James, Elijah, Caleb, Zebu-
lon, Charles, Malinda, Lydia, Temperance, James, and Elijah; est.
admin. 1 Aug. 1763; had iss.: JAMES, m. c.1760 Rachel Gorsuch;
ELIJAH; CALEB, m. c.1772 Elizabeth Wheeler; ZEBULON; CHARLES;
MALINDA, m. John Gorsuch; LYDIA; ELIZABETH; TEMPERANCE, m. Benjamin Price. (6; 74:418; 79:12; 80:391; 82:655; 111:131; 153:13).

BOSLEY, JOSEPH (7), s. of John (3) and Hannah, d. in Balto.
Co. between 1775 and 1776; m. Mary Spicer Hall, dau. of Joshua
Hall; est. admin. 24 Nov. 1777 and 16 Dec. 1777, and finally by
Joseph Bosley on 15 Feb. 1791 when last six children were made
wards of Amos Ogden; had iss.: MARY; JOHN; WILLIAM; HANNAH, m.
Charles Gorsuch; JOSHUA; ELLEN; PHILIP; ELIZABETH; RACHEL; DANIEL;
REBECCA; and BELINDA (7:359, 354; 10:303; 543: 188-191).

Unplaced Bosleys:

BOSLEY, (?), m. by 9 April 1751 Eliza, dau. of William Demmitt
(112).

BOSLEY, or BAUSLEY, WILLIAM, m. Elizabeth (?) and had iss.:
JOHN, b. 6 Dec. 1734; JESELILA, b. 10 June 1745 (131; 133).

BOSLEY, ELIZABETH, m. Edmund Linzey on 28 Feb. 1725 (129).

BOSMAN, EDWARD, m. 1st Eliza (?) and 2nd, on Feb. 1750 Rose
Lyon; had iss.: MARGARET, b. 13 Nov. 1744 (131).

BOSMAN, JOHN, on 21 Jan. 1722/3 was named as s.-in-law of
Katherine West (124).

BOSS, THOMAS, English, age c.40, ran away from Balto. Ironworks, Aug. 1753 (307:114).

BOSSEY, JANE (?), ind. for bast. in June 1734 (30:253).

BOSTOCK, THOMAS, imm. by 1663; m. by Nov. 1668 Jane (?) who
joined him in conv. land called Banks to James Magregor; was
alive in Sept. 1669 (95; 388).

BOSTOCK, MARTHA, in Nov. 1743 was ind. for cohabiting with
John Chapman and for bast. (35:72, 171).

BOSTON, SAMUEL, was in Balto. Co. by June 1674 when he was
comm. Sheriff of Balto. Co.; d. by 6 March 1677; m. Mary (?),
wid. and extx. of George Goldsmith; posted admin. bond on est.
of dec. w. Mary on 7 May 1675(?) with Nathaniel Stiles; will,

6 Jan. 1676 - 6 March 1677, named s.-in-law George Goldsmith,
dau.-in-law Mary Goldsmith, James Mills, Richard Clarke, and his
kinspeople in the parish of Pinchbeck, Lincolnshire; est. inv.
on 12 March 1676/7 by John Ives and John Ireland, and val. at 40531
lbs. tob.; est. admin. 6 May 1681 by James Mills (2; 11; 51; 120;
200-51:117).

BOSTON, HILLIARD, m. Mary (?), and had iss.: RACHEL, b. 7 Nov.
1726; SARAH, b. 7 Feb. 1729; HILYARD, b. 20 April 1735 (133).

BOSTON, JAMES, was in Balto. Co. by 1750 as the owner of 50
a. Tanner's Yard (153).

BOSWELL, ANN, m. 26 Dec. 1749 David Shadows (131).

BOSWELL, ANN, m. 25 May 1755 Jesper Goodby (131).

BOSWELL, JOHN, m. 17 Nov. 1745, when banns were pub., Mary
Jennings, and prob. d. by Dec. 1754 leaving one s.: JAMES, aged
9 on 28 Dec. 1754, orphan of John, bound to Isham Hendon in Aug.
1754 (39; 131).

BOSWELL, RUTH, d. Nov. 1750 (131).

BOSWELL, SOLVOLITTE, m. 20 Sept. 1749 Samuel Phillips (131).

BOSWELL, THOMAS, m. May 1752 Mary Chanley (131).

BOSWITH, JOHN, d. by 9 Match 1748 when admin. bond on his est.
was posted by Thomas Sligh with Staley Durham; est. admin. Feb.
1749 (5; 11).

BOSWORTH, DANIEL, chirurgeon, d. by 21 March 1714/5 when an
admin. bond was posted by Richard Owings with Nicholas Rogers
and Hugh Jones; est. inv. 21 April 1715 by Jno. Israel and Nicholas Rogers and val. at £ 12.1.6 plus £24.18.4 in debts; est. adm.
by Owings (1; 11; 48).

BOTTS, JOHN, m. 9 Dec. 1730 Sarah Wood, and d. by 1750 when
his heirs owned 50 a. of West Favour and 50 a. of Knight's Increase; had iss.: GEORGE, b. 10 Dec. 1731; JOHN, b. 18 Feb.
1733; ABRAHAM, b. 31 Jan. 1735; ISAAC, b. 30 May 1738; SARAH, b.
2 Feb. 1739; AVARILLA, b. 5 Aug. 1742; MARY, b. 5 Aug. 1742
(128; 153).

BOTT, RICHARD, s. of Richard, m. 24 d, 1 mo. (Feb.) 1760,
Ketura, dau. of John Price (136).

BOUCHER, SUSANNAH, former servt. to Thomas Sellman, ind. in
March 1759 for bearing mulatto bast. named RICHARD BOUCHER (46:
187).

BOULDIN, WILLIAM, came to Bohemia R., then to Balto. Co. from
Gloucester Co., Va.; will, 26 Aug. 1671 - 12 Nov. 1672, named
Mary Thwaite and her ch. William and Thomas Thwaite. who were b.
at testator's house in Abingdon Par., Gloucester Co., Va.; admin.
bond posted 30 Sept. 1672 by admnx. Mary Thwaite with Augustine
Herman and George Brocas (11; 120:70).

BOULSON, JOHN, m. 1750 Elizab. Stewart (131).

BOULTON, CHARLES, m. 4 July 1739 Ann Higginson, admnx. of John
Higginson (34:19; 128).

BOURDILLON, Rev. BENEDICT, native of Geneva, Switz., came to
Balto. Co. to St. John's Par.; resigned 24 July 1739 and was in-

ducted into St. Paul's Par. the same day; m. Johanna Gertrude
Janssen, prob. a relative of Barbara Janssen who m. Thomas Bladen
and of William and Henrietta Janssen;she may have been a dau. of
Sir Theodore Janssen, Bart;,d. by 22 Jan. 1744 when admin. bond
was posted by Janette JanssenBourdillon with John Risteau and
Henry Morgan; est. adv. for sale in the Md. Gaz. of 4 Feb. 1746
included a collection of Hebrew, Greek, Latin, French and English
books "in good condition;" est. admin. 14 June 1751 by the admnx.;
in 1750 his heirs owned 100 a. of Bond's Pleasant Hills; had
iss.: WILLIAM BENEDICT, b. 29 Oct. 1740; THOMAS, b. 3 Oct. 1742
(Sponsors for first son were proxies for his godparents, William
Janssen, Esq., and Mrs. Henrietta Janssen; sponsors for the
second son were David Bourdillon, Thomas Bladen, Mrs. Barbara
Bladen, and Jacob Bourdillon) (5; 11; 133; 153; 255; 303; 330;
439:281; 440).

BOURN, JOHN, m. 11 Oct. 1744 Barbara Burke (131).

BOWDEN, JOHN, in Oct. 1707 surv. 50 a. Bowden's Liberty (438).

THE BOWEN FAMILY was the subject of two articles in the Maryland Magazine of Genealogy by Robert Barnes. (544; 545).

BOWEN, JONAS (1), progenitor, was in Balto. Co. by April 1676,
and d. by April 1699; may have been twice married; 1st to a dau.
of Lewis Bryan (whose will of Jan. 1676 left 100 a. Bryan's
Forest to Eliz., dau. of Jonas "Bowing"), and 2nd to Martha
(poss. Henchman), wid. of Lawrence Wolden; will of Jonas Bowen,
26 March 1699 - 13 April 1699, named ch. Benjamin, John, Onner,
Jonas, and Martha, grandson Jonas Robinson, James Robinson, and
wife's s., Lawrence Woldon; admin. bond posted 26 April 1699 by
Martha Bowen and Jonas Bowen, with John Thomas and Nathaniel
Ruxton; est. inv. on 13 May 1699 by William Wilkinson and George
Ashman; est. admin. 9 May 1700 by Martha Bowen; will of Martha
(Henchman?) (Wolden) Bowen, 12 April 1703 - 5 March 1703/4, named
ch.: Jonas, Benjamin, Martha wife of John Merryman, John (not yet
of age), Onner (not yet of age), grandson Jonas Robinson; admin.
bond posted 17 May 1704 by Jonas Bowen; est. inv. on 20 April
1704 by Col. John Thomas and William Wilson and cal. at £ 131.7.2;
est. admin. on 28 April 1705 25 July 1706; had iss.: ELIZABETH,
m. Jonas Robinson who d. after 28 March 1695; JONAS, the oldest
s.; MARTHA, m. 30 Dec. 1702 John Merryman; BENJAMIN, b. after
1681; JOHN, b. after 1681; HONOR, under age in 1703; m. Tobias
Stansbury (2; 5; 11; 48; 51:125; 66; 121:97; 164: Box 1, folder
68, and Box 2, folder 6; 211).

BOWEN, JONAS (2), s. of Jonas (1) and Martha, d. in Balto. Co.
by 4 Feb. 1728/9; having m. Ann, poss. wid. of Roger Reeves, who
surv. Jonas, and who may have been the Ann Bowen who m. Jonas
Hewling on 20 Dec. 1732; inher. 20 a. Jonas' Chance from his f.,
and was to hold The Hope during minority of his nephew James
Robinson; will, 12 Dec. 1728 - 4 Feb. 1728, named w. Ann, daus.
Martha Lynch and Rebecca Gray, son William Reeves, s.-in-law
Patrick Lynch, granddau. Martha Lynch, cousin (i.e., nephew?)
Jonas Bowen of John; admin. bond posted 16 June 1729 by extx. Ann
Bowen, with Benjamin Bowen and Patrick Lynch; est. adm. 15 Jan.
1729 by extx., the acct. named dau.Martha wife of Patrick Lynch,
and dau. Rebecca wife of Zachariah Gray (2; 11; 111:194; 133;
164:Box 1, folder 68).

BOWEN, BENJAMIN (3), s. of Jonas (1) and Martha, b. after 1681,
d. by 2 Jan. 1742; m. 1st by Nov. 1710 Mary, wid. and admnx. of
Nathaniel Ruxton, and 2nd, Sarah (?) who survived him and who m.
as her 2nd husband, by 1744, Patrick Lynch; in Aug. 1721 pet.
the court to be excused as his brother was dying; owned 130 a.

Jonas' Outlet, Samuel's Hope, and 100 a. Gooseberry, and other
lands from Richard Hooker; will, 4 Jan. 1739 - 2 Jan. 1742, named
w. Sarah, ch.: Benjamin " Cox," Solomon, Nathan, Josiah, Mary,
Tabitha, and Sarah, daus. to be of age at 16; admin. bond posted
2 June 1742 by Sarah Bowen with Tobias Stansbury and Abraham
Eagleston; est. admin. 7 Dec. 1744 by Sarah now w. of Patrick
Lynch; had iss.: BENJAMIN "COX," als. Bowen; MARY, b. 1 March
1722/3, m. Sabrett Sollers; SOLOMON, b. 18 Dec. 1724; JOSIAH
or JOSIAS, b. 22 Dec. 1729 (his will proved 2 March 1793, named
sis. Mary Sollers, bro. Solomon, and nephews Josias Bowen of
Benjamin and Elijah Bowen of Solomon); TABITHA, b. 20 Feb. 1731,
living Aug. 1746; SARAH, d. 26 Jan. 1732; SARAH, b. 19 Feb.
1734/5, living March 1746; NATHAN, d. 1770, m. Mary Sollers;
JONAS, in Aug. 1744 chose bro. Benjamin as his guardian (11; 21:
187; 23:550; 31; 35:294; 36:207, 586; 112:142; 114:89; 131:148;
133; 136; 164: Box 6, folder 47; 231-WG#95:17).

BOWEN, JOHN (4), s. of Jonas (1) and Martha, under age in Ap-
ril 1703, d. in April or May 1742; m. Mary (?), who d. 1762;
owned 100 a. The Range and 50 a. The Addition, and part Corcell
Hill; will, 16 April 1742 - 6 May 1742, named ch.: Jonas, Martha,
Mary, Samuel, Edward, John, and Elizabeth, and lands Bowen's
Purchase, Jonas' Range, The Addition, and Cossell Hill; admin.
bond posted 6 May 1742 by Samuel Bowen with Joseph Peregoy and
John Sergeant; est. admin. Nov. 1742 and 10 Dec. 1742; had iss.:
JONAS, d. 1751; MARTHA, d. by 14 Jan. 1746 when admin. bond was
posted by Samuel Bowen with Jonas Bowen and Peter Dowell (her
est. admin. 24 Jan. 1747 and named bros. and sis.: Edward, Jonas,
Benjamin, Elizabeth, Mary w. of Jonas or Joseph Green; MARY, m.
Joseph Green on 25 Feb. 1745; SAMUEL; EDWARD; ELIZABETH (may be
the Eliza who chose her mother as guardian in Nov. 1742 and who
m. Abraham Green on 29 Jan. 1749/50); JOHN (d. by 11 May 1742
when Rosanna Bowen posted bond; his est. admin. 23 June 1743 by
Rosanna w. of John Ogle; m. by 22 Jan. 1742 Rosanna, wid. of
Jonas Robinson); BENJAMIN, d. by July 1748 (will, 17 Dec. 1745 -
1 July 1748, named Greenbury Bowen Baxter and Benjamin Baxter,
sons of Elizabeth Baxter, and Joshua Smith son of Ann; and
Elizabeth Baxter and bro. Edward Bowen as execs.; admin. bond
posted 1 July 1748 and est. admin. 5 March 1750 by Edward Bowen
and Abraham Green, husb. of Elizabeth Baxter) (3:260, 364; 4:183;
5; 11; 35:79; 37:164; 67:431, 439; 110; 111; 133).

BOWEN, BENJAMIN, alias Cox (5), s. of Benjamin (3), prob. by
1724 since he m. 1744 Mary, dau. of Thomas Carr, on 4 Oct. 1744;
d. 1770; in 1750 owned 400 a. of Samuel's Hope and 110 a. Morgan's
Delight; will dated 9 March 1770 named w. Mary and ch.: Benjamin,
Josias, Elizabeth, Joshua, Aquila, and Thomas; had iss.: BENJAMIN,
b. 28 July 1746; JOSIAS (in 1750 owned 129 a. Jonas' Outlet and
100 a. Kinderton), d. 1805; ELIZABETH, b. 7, 10th mo. (Dec.)
1748; JOSHUA, b. 13, 10th mo. (Dec.) 1750; AQUILA, b. 26, 10th
mo. (Dec.) 1753, may have d. young; THOMAS (67:252; 84:1, 58;
86:105; 90:97; 111; 116; 136; 153; 159:27).

BOWEN, SOLOMON (6), s. of Benjamin (3) and Sarah, b. 18 Dec.
1724, d. June 1804; m. 28 Nov. 1751 Temperance Ensor, b. 19 Sept.
1732, d. 25 May 1811, dau. of John and Elizabeth Ensor; stated in
his obituary that he would have joined the Revolutionary Army
although he was close to 60, but his relatives returned him to
the bosom of his family; his will, 9 April 1804 - 25 June 1804,
named ch.: Elizabeth Coale, Ruth Tipton, Temperance Hetherington,
Solomon, Benjamin, Josias, William, Elijah and Nathan; had iss.:
JOHN, b. 7 Oct. 1752; SOLOMON, b. 22 March 1754, m. 20 June 1786
Jemima Merryman; RUTH, b. 4 Feb. 1756, m. 16 Nov. 1777 Samuel
Tipton; NAOMI, b. 15 March 1758; BENJAMIN, b. 12 March 1760, m.
Jemima, dau. of Daniel Evans; WILLIAM, m. 21 July 1789 Elizabeth

Hetherington; JOSIAS, m. 18 May 1797 Prudence Stansbury; NATHAN,
m. Elizabeth (?); ELIJAH, m. Catherine (?); ELIZABETH, m. William
Cole on 24 April 1794; TEMPERANCE, m. William Hetherington (116:
293; 118:250; 133; 134; 261; 253, 264; 295:304).

BOWEN, NATHAN (7), s. of Benjamin (3) and Sarah, d. 1770 in
Balto. Co., having m. Mary, dau. of Sabrett and Mary Sollers;
dep. he was age 44 in Sept. 1765 and mentioned a sis. Honour
Stansbury who was alive c.1731/2; will, 29 Nov. 1762 - 5 Dec.
1770, named w. Mary, bro. Benjamin, ch. Nathan, John, and Jehu,
and ment. "all his ch.;" will of Mary Bowen, wid. of Nathan, 7
Oct. 1778 - 4 April 1789, named ch. Nathan, Sarah Watts, Eleanor
Waters, Katherine Bowen, James, Jehu, Sabritt, Ann Sweetin, Mary
Stevenson, and Benjamin and Elam Bowen; had iss.: NATHAN; JOHN;
JEHU; SARAH, m. (?) Watts: ELEANOR, m. (?) Waters; KATHERINE, m.
Joshua Bowen; LYDIA, m. Thomas Watts on 4 Sept. 1783; JAMES, d.
1800, m. 1 Jan. 1783 Margaret Robinson; SABRETT, m. Elizabeth
Humphreys; ANN, m. (?) Sweetin; MARY, m. (?) Stevenson; BENJAMIN;
and ELAM or ELI (91:172; 112; 113; 116; 133; 210-30:860; 264).

BOWEN, JONAS (8), s. of John (4) and Mary, d. in Balto. Co.
c. Nov. 1751; m. 1st Mary (?), and 2nd Elizabeth (?); in 1750
owned 91 a. Jonas' Purchase and 40 a. of Little Goose Harbor;
will, 12 Aug. 1751 - 18 Nov. 1751, named bros. and sis. Samuel,
Joseph, Mary Green, and Elizabeth Sollers,, his present w. Elizabeth, and ch. John, Violetta (dau. of 1st w. Mary), Chloe, and
ygst. dau. Mary; admin. bond posted 18 Nov. 1751 by Joseph Green
with Abraham Eagleston and Edward Bowen; had iss.: VIOLETTA (by
1st w.); JOHN (not yet 16); CHLOE; and MARY (ygst. dau.) (11;
112; 153).

BOWEN, SAMUEL (9), s. of John (4) and Mary, living 1764, m.
Sarah (?); in 1750 owned 100 a. of Bowen's Prospect, 50 a. Jones'
Range, and 51 a. Jonas' Addition, and 23 a. Jonas' Range and
Rider's Industry; had iss.: JOHN, b. 18 Oct. 1764 (133; 153).

BOWEN, EDWARD (10), s. of John (4) and Mary, living in 1754;
m. Mary (?); in 1750 owned 100 a. Cassell Hill; may be the Edward
Bowen tried in March 1754 for begetting a ch. on Mary Austin;
had iss.: WILLIAM, b. 13 May 1741 (39:36; 129:341; 153).

Unplaced Bowens:

BOWEN, CHARLES, d. leaving will, 2 Jan. 1738 - 31 Jan. 1738,
naming w. Anne and sons James, Charles, Jacob, and Basil (127).

BOWEN, ELIZABETH, servant of Thomas Allender, in Nov. 1756
tried for bearing a mulatto; dau. SARAH to be sold (41:322).

BOWEN, ELIZABETH, tried for bast., Nov. 1757 (46:74).

BOWEN, HANNAH, servant, sold to George Utie by Thomas Marsh
in Nov. or Dec. 1673, bore a bast. child which at first she said
was ch. of Thomas Marsh, but Marsh said the father was Edward
Winwood (200-51:460-461).

BOWEN, JOHN, d. by 1748, res. at Bush R., owned 100 a. of
Bell's Camp and part Claxon's Purchase; will, 15 Oct. 1748 - 25
Nov. 1748, named s. Claxson Bowen, dau. Eleanor Deal, and grand-
son John Green, as well as land Bell's Camp (110:153).

BOWEN, JONAS, d. by 27 Oct. 1760 when admnx. Mary Green posted
admin. bond with Samuel Bowen and Edward Bowen (11).

BOWEN, RESSE, was in Back River Upper Hund. by 1737; owned 95
a. Tipton's Puzzle in 1750; will, 23 Aug. 1769 - 23 Oct. 1769,

named Jonathan Tipton of Jonathan, and Tabitha Tipton of William (112; 149; 153).

BOWEN, TABITHA, ind. for bast. in June 1750 and tried for same in Nov. 1750 (37:2; 38:25).

BOWLY, DANIEL, progenitor, b. 21 April 1715, d. 17 March 1744/5 in Balto. Co.; m. 1744 Elizabeth Lux, b. 1725, d. Jan. 1793, dau. of Darby and Ann (?) Lux; will, 17 March 1744 - 3 April 1745, named w. Elizabeth and unborn ch.; admin. bond posted 9 April 1745 by extx. Elizabeth Bowly with Darby Lux and Robert Saunders; est. admin. 4 Dec. 1749; w. Elizabeth d. at Furly, the seat of Daniel Bowly in Jan. 1793 in her 68th yr.; had iss.: DANIEL, b. 6 June 1745, d. 12 Nov. 1807; m. Ann Stewart, and rep. Balto. Co. in the Assembly (4; 5; 11; 111; 258; 370; 392).

BOWMAN, EDWARD, was in Balto. Co. by 1704 as a taxable in the upper part of n. side of Patapsco Hund.; d. by 17 June 1712 when est. was adm. by John Landys, tailor (1; 146; 291). (See also Boreman.)

BOWTON, WILLIAM, d. by 22 Jan. 1675 when admin. bond was posted by Capt. Samuel Boston with John Turpin (11).

BOYCE, CORNELIUS, was in Balto. Co. by 1694 as a taxable in n. side Gunpowder Hund.; d. by 7 Oct. 1704 when admin. bond was posted by John Standifer with Israel Skelton; est. inv. 2 Sept. 1704 by Moses Groome and William Hicks, and val. at £ 8.7.0.; est. adm. at least once by Standifer; Boyce prob. d. without heirs (2; 11; 54; 139; 211).

BOYCE, JOHN, m. 30 Nov. 1721 Elizabeth Jephs, and had iss.: MARY, b. 21 Jan. 1722/3; HANNAH, b. 18 Jan. 1724/5; JOHNSON, b. 27 Feb. 1726 (128; 131).

BOYCE, JOHN, servt., age c.25, ran away from Onion's Iron Works in June, 1751 (385).

BOYCE, ROGER, s. of Roger of Calvert Co. (who d. testate by 9 Dec. 1733), was sheriff of Cal. Co. in 1747; came to Balto. Co. where by 1750 he owned 250 a. Bear Neck; m. Rebecca, dau. of Richard and Eleanor (Addison) Smith; d. leaving a will, 19 Sept. 1766 - 30 March 1772, which named ch. Benjamin, Roger, John, Rebecca, Elinor, Elizabeth, Mary, and Ann, wife's bro. John Addison Smith, Corbin Lee, and tracts: Hutchings' Neglect, Hutchins' Lot, Nicholson's Manor, Bear Neck, Quinn, and Hill's Camp; will of Rebecca Boyce, 25 Nov. 1774 - 19 Jan. 1775, named s. John, dau. Ann, grandch. Rebecca Cowen and Roger Boyce Cowen, as well as s.-in-law Alexander Cowen; had iss.: BENJAMIN; ROGER; JOHN; REBECCA; ELEANOR, m. 2 May 1771 Alexander Cowen; ELIZABETH; MARY; and ANN (112; 126; 131; 153; 346-2:380).

BOYD, ABRAHAM, m. 5 Dec. 1737 Hester Butterworth, and in 1743 adv. for sale 630 a. on Deer Creek (128; 384).

BOYER, RICHARD, was in Balto. Co. by June 1671 when with Francis Robinson he purchased pt. Plumb Park on s. side of Sassafras R. from William Palmer (97).

BOYNE. See BOWEN.

BOYTON, JONATHAN, m. 15 July 1740 Elizabeth Genkins (128).

BRADBORNE, THOMAS, was in Balto. Co. by 1692 as a taxable in n. side Patapsco Hund. (140).

BRADFORD, WILLIAM (1), parish officer of St. Ann's Parish, London, had at least three ch.: JOHN; HANNAH; m. Joseph Presbury (and had James Presbury who came to Md.); SAMUEL, Dean of Westminster and Bishop of Rochester (246).

BRADFORD, JOHN (2), s. of William (1), was a merchant of London, and m. Mary, dau. of Dr. Matthew Skinner of London; had iss.: WILLIAM (246).

BRADFORD, WILLIAM (3), s. of John (2) and Mary, may have come to Md. in the early 18th century as a schoolmaster and officer in the colonial army; may be the same William who in 1722 pet. the court that at the time of his levy, 1721, he was servant whose term expired 16 Sept. 1721; William, the progenitor of the Maryland family, was known to have been a married man with a son in 1718; m. 1st Elizabeth (poss. Lightbody), and 2nd, after 4 May 1751 Catherine, the wid. of (?) Osborne, and dau. of Henry Rhodes; in 1742 comm'd coroner of Balto. Co. as "Capt. William Bradford;" by 1750 owned 76 a. of Enlargement, 200 a. Bradford's Barrens, 20 a. of Come By Chance, and 6 a. of Turkey Hills and Strawberry Hills; d. by 21 March 1757 when admin. bond was posted by George Bradford with Alex. and Aaron McComas; est. admin. 3 March 1760; had iss.: JOSEPH, b. 15 Jan. 1718, d. 28 Feb. 1718; SUSANNA, b. 7 June 1724, m. 3 April 1744 John Norris; JOHN GEORGE (later called George), b. 3 Sept. 1720 or 1721; MARY, b. 18 Sept. 1727; MARTHA, b. 13 April 1731, m. 20 Nov. 1750 James Amos; WILLIAM, b. 1739, d. 12 Feb. 1794, aged 55, m. 16 Feb. 1764 Sarah McComas (4; 11; 26:16; 80; 85; 131; 153; 229:37; 246; 303; 310: 113).

BRADFORD, (JOHN) GEORGE (4), s. of William (3) and Elizabeth, b. 3 Sept. 1721, was ind. for bast. in Nov. 1746; m. Margaret Bonfield on 3 Dec. 1746; by 1750 owned 125 a. of Turkey Hills and Strawberry Hills; had iss.: WILLIAM, b. 20 May 1748 (36:220; 131; 153).

Unplaced Bradfords:

BRADFORD, JOHN, s. of Thomas, bapt. 9 Nov. 1628 at Preston and Sutton Points, Somerset, Eng., came to Balto. Co. by 1666 when he purch. land from William Orchard, and d. by June 1672 leaving as his heir a nephew Thomas (s. of John's bro. William), who by Oct. 1674 was in London with w. Mary (94; 100).

BRADLEY, THOMAS, was in Balto. Co. by 1723; owned 96 a. of Arabia Petrea by 1750; m. Ann (?) and had iss.: MARY, b. 24 Nov. 1723; JANE, twin, b. 28 Sept. 1730; ELIZABETH, twin, b. 28 Sept. 1730; ANN, b. 3 Nov. 1733 (128:153).

BRADLEY, HANNAH, in Nov. 1757 tried for bast.; fined for bast. in Nov.1758; had iss.: WILLIAM (36:163; 44).

BRADSHAW, JOHN, d. 14 March 1720/1; m. Mary (?); admin. bond posted 7 June 1721 by Mary Bradshaw with Archibald Rollo and Robert Cutchin;   second admin. bond posted 6 Nov. 1724 by sd. Rollo and Cutchin with John Fuller and James Durham; est. in 1721 and 1722; est. admin. 14 Dec. 1725, 10 May 1726, and 3 Aug. 1726; had iss.: JOHN, b. 27 Nov. 1719/20 (2; 3; 11; 51; 52; 131).

BRADY, TERRANCE, m. Dec. 1740 Sarah Hilliard, d. by 5 Sept. 1745 when admin. bond was posted by Sarah Brady, with Richard Deaver and Ford Barnes (11; 128).

BRADY, (?), was the father of two sons bound to Wm. Jessop in June 1757: JAMES, age 9 on 23 April 1757, and CHARLES, age 8 on 23 April 1757 (46:38).

BRAGBAN, THOMAS, was a taxable on n. side Patapsco Hund. in 1692 (138).

BRAGG, SARAH, ind. for bast., March 1722/3; named Reuben Hassal as the father, June 1724; had iss.: HANNAH, b. 15 Jan. 1723/4 (26:201, 330; 128).

BRAGG, HANNAH, poss. dau. of Sarah, above; ind. for bast. in March 1739/40; tried for bast. June 1740; had iss.: JOHN, b. 31 Dec. 1740 (32:140, 236; 131).

BRAISHER. See BRASHER.

BRAMLEY, ARTHUR, gave age as 34 in March 1720/1 (23:493).

BRAMWELL, GEORGE, in Balto. Co. by 1750, d. by 1770; m. 7 March 1750 Susanna Fortt; as George Bramwell, schoolmaster, purch. 96 a. of Buckingham's Goodwill in July 1758; will, 29 March 1769 - 24 Sept. 1770, named w. Susanna, sons-in-law Richard and Samuel Fortt, dau.-in-law Ruth Ford, and his own two ch.: HENRY, b. 11 July 1751; MARY, b. 3 May 1757 (112; 134:83).

BRAND, SAMUEL, was transp. to Md. by 1678, d. by 18 Feb. 1688 when admin. bond was posted by Richard Askew with Benjamin Arnold and George Smith; on 22 Aug. 1683 surv. 100 a. Contest; est. adm. by Askew at least once (11; 206:10; 211:18; 388).

BRANGWELL, PETER, m. 30 April 1683 Elizabeth Kemb; marr. was perf. by John Yeo (18:94).

BRANNICAN, EDWARD, "Samuel Brown's man," bur. 28 Nov. 1707 (129). (Cf. to Brannum, below).

BRANNICAN, HUGH, d. 1708; admin. bond posted 23 Aug. 1709 by Phillip Brannican with John Stokes and John Gilbert; est. inv. 5 Oct. 1709 by Owen Swillivan and John Clark and val. at £ 8.18.0 with Philip and Susan Brannican signing as kin; est. of "Henry Brannock" admin. 9 Aug. 1711 by Philip "BRannock" (1; 4; 51).

BRANNICAN, PHILIP, poss. s. of Hugh, m. Susanna Thomas, when banns were pub. Feb. 1699/1700; had iss.: WILLIAM, b. 10 Dec. 1699; ELIZABETH, b. 17 Dec. 1701; SUSANNA, b. 27 Aug. 1707; PHILIP, b. 27 Aug. 1707; HUGH, b. 20 Sept. 1711 (128).

BRANNON, JAMES, b. c.1733 in Ireland, in Md. by Oct. 1753 when he ran away from John Hall and Jacob Giles; advert. stated he professed to be a schoolmaster; may be the James Brannon who d. by July 1785 when his est. was admin. by Rachel Brannon, and left 6 ch. who in June 1788 chose Frederick Parks as their guardian: WILLIAM, b. c.1772; CASSANDRA, b. c.1774; ELIZABETH, b. c.1776; THOMAS; AVARILLA; and JAMES, all born post 1774 (8; 240-WB#2; 385).

BRANNON, PATRICK, m. by Oct. 1751 dau. of Jacob and Sarah Hanson; she later m. (?) Tayman (5; 6; 201:31).

BRANNUM, (?), "Samuel Brown's man," bur. 28 Nov. 1707 (128). Cf. to Edward Brannican, above.

BRASHER/BRASHIER, WILLIAM (1), was in Balto. Co. by 1699 as a taxable in n. side Gunpowder Hund.; d. by 6 Nov. 1708 when admin. bond was posted by John Webster with Christopher Cox and Henry Wriothesley; est. inv. 26 Nov. 1708 by Richard Ruff and Jane Freeland val. at £ 1.2.0; had iss.: WILLIAM, b. 6 May 1696; JOHN, b. 13 June 1699; JAMES, age 6 in Nov. 1710 when she was bound to Sarah or Elizabeth Day; THOMAS, age 3 in 1712, when he was bound to John Webster in June 1712 (11; 17:135; 21:182; 54; 128; 141).

BRASHER, WILLIAM (2), s. of William (1), b. 6 May 1696, d. by 18 Jan. 1728, when admin. bond was posted by William Smith with Richard Caswell, and Joseph Ward; m. Jane (?); est. adm. 26 April 1731 by William Smith; had iss.: RICHARD, b. 6 Feb. 1720 (as orphan of William was bound to Richard Caswell in June 1729, and to William Dallam in Nov. 1737); SARAH, b. 26 Jan. 1723; JANE, b. 31 March 1726 (may be the Jane ind. for bast. March 1743/4. tried for bast. in March 1744, and ind. for bast. in Nov. 1746) (3; 11; 28:144; 31:133; 35:154, 480; 36:220; 128).

BRASHER, JOHN (3), s. of William (1), b. 13 June 1699, may be the John who married Sarah (?) and had iss.: JOHN, b. 23 June 1735; MARTHA, b. 4 Nov. 1739 (131).

Unplaced Brashers:

BRASHER, JAMES, age 5 on next 2 July, in Nov. 1737 was bound to William York and wife Elizabeth to age 21 (31:133).

BRASHER (or BRASSHA), JOHN, named as s. of Alice, w. of John Love, in the latter's will, 1708 (122).

BRASHER, KATHERINE, d. by 16 Jan. 1709 when admin. bond was posted by Michael Gormacon with Cornelius Heath and Michael O'Daniell; est. inv. 17 Jan. 1709/10 by Cornelius Keefe and Michael Daniel, and val. at £ 3.7.6; est. admin. by Michael Gormacon on 30 Jan. 1709 (1; 11; 48).

BRASHER (or BRASIOUR), THOMAS, d. by 9 March 1709/10, when admin. bond was posted by Andrew Anderson with William Farfarr and Michael Gormacon; est. admin. by Andrew Anderson on 14 April 1711; had iss.: JOHN, age 1 on 17 Nov. 1709, bound to Robert Gorsuch in March 1709/10 (1; 11; 21:94).

BRASHER, THOMAS, m. 13 Oct. 1726 Sarah Constance and had iss.: WILLIAM, b. 18 Nov. 1727; ELIZABETH, b. 15 May 1729; THOMAS, b. 18 June 1731; ELIZABETH, b. 25 Nov. 1733; AQUILA, b. 28 July 1740; SARAH, b. 12 June 1744 (129).

BRASHER, THOMAS, m. Jane (?) and had iss.: JOHN, b. 23 May 1736 (128).

BRASHER, THOMAS, in 1750 owned 54 a. Frankfort (153).

BRASHER, THOMAS, m. Elizabeth (?) and had iss.: PETER, b. 1753 (129).

BRASHER, THOMAS, d. by 3 April 1755 when admin. bond was posted by John Paca, Jr., with Edward Morgan and William Bennett (11).

BRASHER, WILLIAM, bought 56 a. Margaret's Mount from John and Mary Miles in Aug. 1722 (69:40).

BRASHER, WILLIAM, and w. Ann conv. 100 a. Grafton's Gift to William Grafton on 10 May 1751 (81).

BRAYFOOT, ANTHONY, was in Balto. Co. by 1738 when he signed a petition (150).

BRERETON, THOMAS, d. by 5 April 1751 when admin. bond was posted by Henry Brereton with Chris. Divers and Thomas Ensor; est. admin. 14 May 1752 and 5 March 1753, and left 5 children, all of age (5; 11).

BREREWOOD, Sir ROBERT (1), was Mayor of Chester, married and had at least one son: THOMAS (441).

BREREWOOD, THOMAS (2), s. of Sir Robert (1), was of the City of Chester and Place House, Horton, Colebrook Par., Bucks.; had at least one son: THOMAS (441).

BREREWOOD, THOMAS (3), s. of Thomas (2), d. in Balto. Co. by 10 Feb. 1746; settled there in 1732; served as agent for renting out lots in Lord Baltimore's Gift (or My Lady's Manor); was Clerk of Balto. Co. from 1741 until his death; in March 1739 conv. prop. to William Brerewood of Som. Co., s. of Francis of London; will, 8 Aug. 1741 - 10 Feb. 1746, named dau. Hon. Charlotte Brerewood, grandson William Brerewood, Mrs. Eleanor Turner; admin. bond posted 6 Feb. 1746 by exec. William Dallam with Richard Dallam and Richard Ruff; had iss.: THOMAS, Jr.; CHARLES, bur. 26 Dec. 1718 at Horton, Bucks; FRANCIS (11:146; 75:231; 77: 450, 453; 79:360; 110:379; 441).

BREREWOOD, THOMAS (4), s. of Thomas (3), b. c.1694, was a poet of some note; m. Charlotte Calvert, dau. of Benedict Leonard, 4th Lord Baltimore; she d. by 11 Jan. 1744/5 when admin. was granted to her husb.; no iss.: (441).

BREREWOOD, FRANCIS (5), s. of Thomas (3), of Scotland Yard, Westminster, d. July 1781 aged 82; m. twice, the 2nd time, 31 March 1773 to Mary (?), who surv. him; was an architecht; had iss. by 1st marr. WILLIAM (441).

BREREWOOD, WILLIAM (6), s. of Francis (5), was in Som. Co. by March 1739 and was named in the will of his grandfather (75:231; 110:379; 441).

BRETT, JOHN, d. by 13 April 1667 when his est. was admin. by Augustine Herrman (200-57:181).

BRETT, MARTHA, fined for bast., Nov. 1757 (46:74).

BREWEN, HUBBARD, of Balto. Co., d. leaving a will, 26 Feb. 1756 - 10 March 1756, named sis. Sarah Brewen, sis. Ann Bestland mother Ann Brewen, and exec. Brian Philpot, Jr.; admin. bond posted 10 March 1756 by Philpot with William Lyon (11; 111; 299).

BREWITT, GEORGE, of Nottinghamshire, collarmaker, ran away from Edward Oursler of Diamond Ridge c. Jan. 1757 (307).

BREYNTON, JOHN, of Balto. Co., imm. by 1670 (388).

BRIAN/BRIANT/BRIEN/BRYAN/BRYANT

BRIAN, (?), m. by 14 March 1738 Hannah, dau. of John Simkins of Balto. Co. (127:20).

BRIAN, DANIEL, m. 28 Nov. 1703 Ann Veares (128:17).

BRIAN (O'BRYAN), DANIEL, m. Mary (?) and had iss.: CHARLES, b. 5 May 1708 in Cecil Co. (129:211).

BRIAN, DAVID, son of John and Catherine, age 1 on 4 July 1758, bound to Dorcas Thomas and Christopher Sutton in Nov. 1757 (44; 46:80).

BRIAN, DENNIS, est. admin. by George Presstman on 6 June 1778 (8:42).

BRIAN (BRYAN), DERBY, was transp. c.1668 and by 1695 was a taxable in Spesutia Hund. (140; 388).

BRIAN, JAMES, m. 4 July 1754 Mary Raven, dau. of Luke and Sarah (Crooke) Raven (131:45; 210-31:123).

BRIAN, JOHN, was in Balto. Co. by 1695 as a taxable in s. side Patapsco Hund. (140).

BRIAN (BRYAN), LEWIS, was in Md. by 1676 and acquired at least one tract called Bryen's Forest; admin. bond posted 20 March 1676 by Jonas Bowen and Nicholas Corbin with Richard Ball and John Hardin; will, 31 Jan. 1676 - 5 Feb. 1676, left property to Nicholas Corbin and 100 a. Bryan's Forest to Eliza, dau. of Jonas Bowen, and if said Eliza d. without heirs, land was to go to the children of William and Ellinor Smith of Nansemond R., Jonas Bowen and Nicholas Corbin were overseers (1:81; 11; 110:107).

BRIAN (BRYANT), MARY, ind. for bast., March 1720/1 (23:435)

BRIAN (O'BRYAN), TERRENCE, m. Margaret (?), and had iss.: DANIEL, b. 19 Sept. 1709 in Cecil Co. (129:211).

BRIAN (BRYAN), THURLO, m. Cecilia or Cissill (?) and had iss.: BENJAMIN, b. 17 Sept. 1721; MARY, b. 17 Jan. 1722; JAMES, b. 15 April 1725; ELLINOR, b. 1 Nov. 1727; EDWARD, b. 15 Aug. 1729; PROVIDENCE, b. 27 Aug. 1731 (133:5, 36).

BRIAN, WILLIAM, m. 5 May 1746 Hannah Wallis, and had iss.: ELIZABETH, b. 10 Nov. 1745 (sic) (131:30, 126/r).

BRICE, JAMES (1), d. in Balto. Co. by 1 July 1765; m. 6 Jan. 1742 Mary Johnson, dau. of Thomas Johnson of Deer Creek; will, 21 April 1765 - 1 July 1765, named eld. s. Samuel to have 100 a. Brice's Purchase (which James owned in 1750), 2nd s. Thomas to have the residue of that tract, and a small tract Region Hill, made w. extx., and mentioned "other children;" had iss.: SAMUEL, b. 6 Jan. 1743; THOMAS, b. 15 Aug. 1746; XTIAN, b. 9 Sept. 1749; JAMES, b. 11 Oct. 1751; WILLIAM, b. 20 March 1753; ALI, b. 14 Nov. 1754; BARNET, b. 16 April 1756; MARGARET, b. 15 March 1758; JOHN, b. 6 July 1760; MARY, b. 31 July 1762 (112:63; 129:327, 343, 372; 153).

BRICE, SAMUEL (2), s. of James (1), b. 6 Jan. 1743, d. after 1810 having m. Rachel Boone, and served as a private in the Rev. War from Penna. (353:84).

BRICE, JAMES (3), s. of James (1), b. 11 Oct. 1751, d. 22 Dec. 1832 in Athens, Ohio, having served in the Penna. Militia under Capt. Zadock Wright in 1781 and 1783; m. 1st Alice or Hester Johnson, and 2nd Anne Grant (353:84; 363:51).

Unplaced Brices:

BRICE, SAMUEL m. 24 Jan. 1739 Elizabeth Anhousin and d. 13 May 1740; erroneously called Thomas in 128:112 (129:315).

BRICE, THOMAS, m. 24 Jan. 1739 Elizabeth Anhousin (129:315).

BRIDGE, JOSIAH, was in Balto. Co. by 1694 as a taxable in n. side Patapsco Hund. (139).

BRIDGES, SARAH, in Aug. 1720 named William Duson as the f. of her child (23:365).

BRIERLY, JOHN (1), m. Catherine (?), and may have d. by 1750 when the wid. of John Brierly owned 239 a. of Arabia Petrea; had iss.: MARY, b. 29 Jan. 1732; ROBERT, b. 15 Feb. 1733; JOHN, b. 5 Sept. 1736 (128; 153).

BRIERLY, ROBERT (2), s. of John (1) and Catherine, b. 15 Feb. 1733, may be the Robert whose will, 4 Sept. 1764 - 7 Nov. 1764, named his aunt Anne Dowtha, and two sons: JOHN; and NATHANIEL (111).

Unplaced Brierlys:

BRIERLY, HUGH, m. Rebecca (?) and had iss.: JOHN, b. Feb. 1746; ELEAZER, b. 31 March 1752 (129).

BRIERLY, ROBERT, d. in Balto. Co. by 20 Oct. 1766; m. Margaret (?) who d. in Harf. Co. by 1 Dec. 1781; in 1750 owned 84 a. Emm's Delight, 50 a. Briarly's Addition, 100 a. Southampton, and Rachel's Delight; later conv. 50 a. Brierly's Addition and 168 a. Emm's Delight to Joseph, William, and John Barnes; his will, 21 Sept. 1766 - 20 Oct. 1766, named ch.: John, Thomas, Hugh, Ann, Isabella, and Robert; will of wid. Margaret, 13 Oct. 1781 - 1 Dec. 1781, named dau. Isabella Armstrong, dau. Ann Huggens, son Hugh, grandchildren Thomas of John, Robert of Hugh and Margaret of Hugh; had iss.: JOHN (d. by 1781, left s. Thomas); THOMAS (may be the Thomas Brierly of Va. who in Sept. 1778 conv. 100 a. Minster to Daniel Thompson); ANN, m. (?) Huggins; ISABELLA, b. 17 Feb. 1740, m. David Armstrong 5 Sept. 1765; ROBERT (83; 128; 131; 153; 210-34; 224-AJ#2:45; 241-JLG#C:16).

BRIGHT, RICHARD, was in Balto. Co. by 1692 as a taxable in n. side Patapsco Hund. (138).

BRIGHT, THOMAS, was in Balto. Co. by 1692 as a taxable in Spesutia Hund. (128).

BRINDLEY, NATHANIEL, m. 1 April 1762 Rachel Spencer; had iss.: SARAH, b. 12 Jan. 1755; ELIZABETH, b. 4 April 1757; CONSTANCE, b. 4. Dec. 1759; JANE, b. 23 May 1762 (129).

BRISCOE, NICHOLAS, was a planter in Balto. Co. on 16 July 1722 when he conv. a mare to Rebecca, dau. of Archibald Rollo (69:60).

BRISPO, ANTHONY, imm. by 1659, was in Balto. Co. by June 1673 when he bought 100 a. Mate's Angle from William Osborne and John Lee and 100 a. Crabb Hill from Richard Morgan (99; 100; 388).

BRITAIN, ABRAHAM, m. by 24 July 1770 Hannah, admnx. of William Tolley Towson (6).

BRITAIN, NICHOLAS, m. 28 Nov. 1761, Althea, wid. of Thomas Finley (who m. Althea Kidd on 22 July 1747); purch. from Avarilla Boring, widow, her third interest in Boring's Gift, Boring's Forest, and Cuckoldmaker's Hazard (6; 7; 87; 133)

BROACH, ELIZABETH, charged with bast., Nov. 1722 (25:23).

BROAD, JOHN (1), progenitor, was in Balto. Co. by 1692 as a taxable in n. side of Patapsco Hund.; d. c.1709; m. Barbara (?), wid. of Dennis Garrett (by whom she had two ch.: Joanna, m. John Cole, and Frances, m. Nicholas Haile); she d. by 6 Aug. 1733; surv. 173 a. Broad's Choice in June 1694 and other tracts; his will, 18 Sept. 1702 - 16 Jan. 1709, named ch. Thomas and Jane, also Frances Garrett and Thomas, s. of John and Johanna Cole; admin. bond posted 3 Jan. 1709 by Barbara Broad; est. inv. on 2 Feb. 1708/9 by John Gill and Nicholas Rogers, and val. at Ɫ 44.7.6, with Thomas and Jane Broad signing as kin; est. admin. 26 May 1712 by extx. Barbara; in Aug. 1712 Barbara conv. prop. to her ch. Thomas and Jane, and to her grandson Dennis Garrett Cole; her s. Thomas was not to marry Grace Ramsey or to go away; in Sept. 1730 she and Frances Haile conv. prop. to Nicholas Haile (100 a. Long Island Point); her will, 19 Jan. 1732 - 6 Aug. 1733, named granddau. Sarah w. of Charles Gorsuch, s. Thomas, dau. Frances Haile, and granddau. Barbara, and Ann, w. of her s. Thomas; admin. bond posted 6 Aug. 1733 by Edward Cox with Thomas Broad and William Green; had iss.: THOMAS, b. c.1692; JANE, b. after 1680, m. Edward Cox (1:356; 11; 19:176; 51:25, 32; 67:221; 72:26; 110:27; 111:285; 122:160; 126:29; 138; 133:195; 211:83, 114).

BROAD, THOMAS (2), s. of John (1) and Barbara, b. c.1692, living 1756; m. Ann, heir of Matthew Hawkins; in June 1723 bought 86½ a. of land from Edward and Jane Cox; with w. Anne joined John and Dinah Cole and Thomas and Rebecca Nowland and Rebecca Hawkins in conv. to Lancelot Todd called Best Success, formerly purch. by the late Matthew Hawkins; alive in 1765 when he signed a lease for 33 a. Poverty Parts Good Company; prob. had iss.: BARBARA, m. James Demmitt on 27 March 1733; JANE, m. William Edwards on 17 Sept. 1748; and prob. also JOHN. (69:194, 209; 70:135, 150; 77:66, 162; 83:9, 55, 244; 90:396; 131; 133:151; 153; 164:223).

BROAD, JOHN (3), poss. s. of Thomas (2), living in 1749; m. 13 Jan. 1733 Jemima Henderson, a granddau. of Joseph Peake, in Oct. 1739 deed with other Peake grandch. in selling 575 a. Boughton's Forest to Daniel Dulany; in Feb. 1746 conv. to William Barney 100 a. Timber Ridge to Barney; had iss.: JOHN, b. 11 Jan. 1732; ANN, b. 11 Jan. 1732; JOHN, b. 11 Jan. 1735; JAMES, b. 5 March 1740; WILLIAM, b. 5 March 1740 (75:336; 79:305; 133:46, 72, 151).

BROADWATER, HUGH, was transp. to Westmoreland Co., Va., by Wm. Heaberd and Wm. Norton c.1663, and brought to Md. by John Dixon c.1665; d. by 4 Jan. 1670 when his will was proved, naming John and Michael Shadwell (120; 388; 420).

BROCAR, PENELOPE, ind. for bast. Nov. 1746, tried March 1746/7; servt. of John Campbell; by June 1750 had borne two children (36: 220, 398; 27:4).

BROCK, ELIZABETH, servt. of Lance Todd, named fellow servt. Hugh Durham as the f. of her child, Aug. 1722; servt. of Charles Rockhold, summoned for bast., March 1724/5; had iss.: WILLIAM, age 15 in April 1737 when he was bound to John Wooley, Aug. 1737 (24:306; 27:127; 31:98).

BROGDON, ANNE, charged with bearing two children out of wedlock in Nov. 1722, named John Mahann as the father; ind. again in March 1733/4 for bast., and tried June 1734; in June 1734 was allowed 50 lbs. tobacco a month for support as she was too lame to support herself; ind. for bast. in June 1740, tried Aug. 1740 (25: 21; 30:183, 256, 263; 32:226, 303).

BROGDON, JOHN, servt. to John Mahone, ind. for felony in March 1736/7; d. by 8 Sept. 1749 or 1769 (illegible) when Wm. Hopham posted admin. bond (11; 31:1).

BROMFIELD, JOHN, was in Balto. Co. by 1664 when w. Margaret was transp.; purch. 225 a. Salveton from William Fisher c.1666 (94; 388).

BROOKE, BASIL, of St. M. Co., in 1750 owned 500 a. His Lordship's Gift, which he inherited from his father John Brooke (126: 127; 153; see also Christopher Johnston's "The Brooke Family," in 346-1:91 ff.).

BROOKE, JOHN, late of Bristol, was brought to Md. by Capt. John Borstall and forced to sign an indenture; in 1759 he sued for his freedom (46:215).

BROOKE, SARAH, of Calvert Co., in 1750 owned 1500 a. called Brooke's Cross (153).

BROOKS, JOSEPH, with 1 year to serve, was listed in the 1747 inv. of Edward Day (54:226).

BROOKS, WILLIAM, age 34, was in Balto. Co. by 1692 as a taxable in n. side Patapsco Hund. (138:310).

BROOKE, WILLIAM, d. by 1751, leaving iss.: CHARLES, orphan of William, and age 15 in April 1750/1, was bound to William Stansbury (38:272).

BROOM, JOHN, was in Baltimore Co. by Aug. 1684 when he surv. 1000 a. Broom's Bloom; d. by c.1700 when his orphans held the land (211).

BROOM, MATTHEW, d. by 10 Feb. 1709, when his est. was inv. by William Howard and Jno. Webster, and val. at E 2.7.0; John Deaver was the admin. (48).

BROOMFIELD, JOHN, age c.27, from London, ran away from W. Hammond of Balto. Co., Oct. 1746 (307).

BROTHERS, THOMAS (1), was in Balto. Co. by 1730 and was alive in 1750 when he owned 100 a. Stevenson's Plains; m. Hannah (?); in Nov. 1739 wit. the will of John Tye; in 1745 mortgaged Stevenson's Plains to Thomas Sheredine; in 1748 conv. 141 a. Murray's Desire to Sheredine; had iss.: NATHANIEL, b. 14 Nov. 1730; and poss. FRANCIS (78; 80; 127; 133; 153).

BROTHERS, NATHANIEL (2), s. of Thomas (1), was b. 14 Nov. 1730, purch. 100 a. Stevenson's Plains from Edward Stevenson in 1752; was in Delaware Upper Hund. in 1783 as a pauper with 9 white inhabitants in the family (81; 133; 283).

BROTHERS, FRANCIS (3), poss. s. of Thomas (1), was b. c.1735, age 21 on 13 July 1756 when he enlisted at Balto. in Capt. Christopher Gist's Co. of Va. militia; purch. 50 a. Buck's Forest and 25 a. Nathan's Desire from Nathan and Rebecca Chapman in Aug. 1764 (89; 286).

THE FRANCIS BROWN FAMILY

BROWN, FRANCIS (1), came to Balto. Co. from Warwick Co., Va.; d. test. by 4 May 1741 as a shipwright of Back R.; his will, 25 Aug. 1740 - 4 May 1741, left land on James R., Warwick Co., Va., to his s. Dickson, and also named his ch.: John, Margaret, Sarah, Frances Coleman, Constant, Mary, and Patience, noted that the heir at law was not yet 13; admin. bond was posted 4 May 1741 by Luke Stansbury with Walter Dallas and Walter Tolley; est. adm. by Tobias Stansbury (since the orig. exec. was dec.) on 12 July 1749, with payments to dau. Margaret wife of Charles Smith, dau. Mary, dau. Patience, Dixon Brown, and to Frances and Nicholas Coleman for a daughter's support; est. admin. again on 25 Sept. 1751; had iss.: FRANCES, m. (Nicholas?) Coleman; MARGARET, m. by 12 July 1749 Charles Smith; DIXON; JOHN; MARGARET; SARAH: CONSTANT;

MARY; and PATIENCE (5; 11; 110:384).

BROWN, DIXON (2), s. of Francis (1), age 16 in Feb. 1743,
bound to Tobias Stansbury in June 1743; d. 1774 in Balto. Co.;
m. Elizabeth Trotten on 17 June 1746; his will, 3 Jan. 1774 - 26
Feb. 1774, named sis. Mary Brown, and the following ch.: SARAH,
m. (?) Wooden; LUKE (to have 250 a. Parker's Palace on Hunting
Ridge); ELIZABETH, b. 11 March 1749/50; DIXON; ANN; THOMAS;
CHARLOTTE; JOHN, b. 26 Jan. 1759 (not in father's will); FRANCIS,
b. 11 Jan. 1761 (33:186; 112:281; 133).

THE GEORGE BROWN FAMILY

BROWN, GEORGE (3), no known rel. to above, d. in Fred. Co. by
24 Feb. 1770; m. c.1714 Mary, dau. of Edward Stevenson; in 1727
pet. the Balto. Co. Court that he had not rec'd a share of the
est. of Edward Stevenson; in 1743 pat. two tracts of land in what
is now Carroll Co.: 350 a. Brown's Delight and 50 a. Pleasant
Grove; owned these tracts in 1750; in 1761 pat. 565 a. Brown's
Plague, which was a resurvey on Brown's Delight; his will, 19
Feb. 1767 - 24 Feb. 1770, and named wife Mary, son Henry, son
John, son George, dau. Rachel, son Edward, dau. Mary, son Richard,
dau. Elizabeth, son William, son Hugh, son Joshua; had iss.:
JOHN, d. c.1810 in Balto. Co.; GEORGE, d. c.1812 in Fred. Co.;
EDWARD, b. 16 Sept. 1734, d. 14 Aug. 1823 in Madison Co., Ky.;
RICHARD, b. c.1740, d. 8 Feb. 1811; MARY, m. John Baxter; ELIZA-
BETH; RACHEL; WILLIAM: HENRY, b. c.1741, d. 1827 in Fred. Co.;
HUGH, d. 11 July 1811 having moved to Jefferson Co., Ohio; JOSHUA,
d. in Fred. Co. by 17 Sept. 1832; poss. ANNE, m. Col. Richard
Wells; poss. SARAH (153; 210-37:546; Dr. Arthur Tracey, Notes on
Carroll Land Patents, MF at MHS; see also Robert Barnes, Descen-
dants of Edward and Mary Stevenson (Balto.: 1966) for a fuller
account of the desc. of George and Mary (Stevenson) Brown).

THE SAMUEL BROWN FAMILY

BROWN, SAMUEL (4), no known rel. to above, was in Balto. Co.
by 1692 as a taxable in Spesuita Hund.; d. 5 Oct. 1712; m. 1st
Mary (?), who d. c.1708/9, and 2nd, on 2 Jan. 1709 Mary Skelton;
on 25 May 1699 admin. est. of Thomas Thurston; his will, 24 Oct.
1712 - 2 June 1713, named w. Mary and ch.: Samuel, James, and
Absolom; admin. bond posted 3 June 1713 by Samuel Brown with John
Standifer and Obadiah Pritchard; est. inv. on 27 July 1713 by
Thomas Newsom and David Thomas, and val. at Ł 192.13.1, and was
signed by kinsman Humphrey Jones and creditor John Hall; est.
admin. by Samuel Brown; had iss., all by 1st wife: SAMUEL, b.
17 Aug. 1690; BLANCH. b. 23 April 1695, d. 9 Dec. 1706; JAMES,
b. 22 Dec. 1697; JAMES, b. 22 Dec. 1697; MARY, b. 9 Oct. 1700;
ABSOLOM, b. 22 June 1703; FRANCES, b. 6 June 1705 (1; 2; 11; 50;
110; 128; 138).

BROWN, SAMUEL (5), s. of Samuel (4), and Mary, b. 17 Aug. 1690,
prob. m. Mary (?) who d. 16 Oct. 1729, and had iss.: PEREGRINE,
b. 9 Sept. 1715; JAMES, b. 8 April 1718; SAMUEL, b. 23 Jan. 1720/1,
d. 4 May 1724; SAMUEL, b. 18 March 1723/4; ABSOLOM, b. 12 April
1727 (128).

BROWN, JAMES (6), s. of Samuel (4) and Mary, b. 22 Dec. 1697,
may be the James who d. 24 Dec. 1720 (128:38).

BROWN, ABSOLOM (7), s. of Samuel (4) and Mary, b. 22 June
1703, in March 1719/20 was placed in care of James Phillips with
his sisters Blanch and Frances; was living in 1750 when he owned
16 a. Huntingworth and 66 a. of James Addition; m. 1st on 19 Jan.
1728/9 Sarah Shepherd, who d. 5 Dec. 1732; m. 2nd on 18 Jan. 1734

Mary Cord, and had iss.: GEORGE, b. 9 Nov. 1732, d. 7 Oct. 1733;
HANNAH, b. 15 Nov. 1737; SARAH, b. 14 April 1740 (23:281; 128;
153).

BROWN, ABSOLOM (8), prob. s. of Samuel (5), b. 12 April 1727;
m. on 5 Dec. 1752 Margaret, dau. of Jacob Hanson; had iss.:
SARAH, b. 2 Jan. 1754; REBECCA, b. 11 Dec. 1756; SUSAN, b. 7 Nov.
1758; GEORGE, b. 1 Oct. 1759; MARTHA, b. 20 Feb. 1761 (6; 128;
129).

THE THOMAS BROWN OF OAKINGTON FAMILY

BROWN, THOMAS (9), no known rel. to above, was in Balto. Co.
by 1692 as a taxable in Spesutia Hund.; purch. 500 a. of Oakington
from Martha, wife of John Hall; and Mary Ann Utie, daus. of Edward Bedell, dec.; his will, 24 Jan. 1707 - 9 April 1708, named
w. Margaret, son John (to have Oakington), and Edward Swan Taylor and Bartholomew Welch (who were to have North Yarmouth); admin. bond posted 4 May 1709 by execs. John and Margaret Browne
with John Stokes and Henry Wriothesley; est. inv. by Roger
Matthews, Sr., and Thomas Cord on 11 March 1708/9, and val. at
£ 513.4.5; had iss. by wife Margaret (who m. as her 2nd husb.
Anthony Drew): JOHN, d. by 1719 (11; 51; 61; 110; 128; 138).

BROWN, JOHN (10), s. of Thomas (9) and Margaret, d. c.1716 in
St. Georges Parish having m. Elizabeth Sicklemore on 18 Nov. 1705;
she m. 2nd by March 1716 Richard Burrough; his will, 14 Jan. 1715 -
16 May 1716, named sons Thomas, Augustus, and Gabriel (the latter
two not yet 21), wife Elizabeth as extx., and numerous tracts:
500 a. Chenton, 150 a. Cook's Cover, 118 a. Hopp, and 400 a.
Brown's Entrance; est. inv. 25 Fen. 1719 by Thomas Cord and Samuel
Jackson and val. at £ 467.15.0, and filed by extx. Elizabeth, now
wife of Richard Burrough, and signed by kinsfolk Anthony and Margaret Drew; admin. bond posted 10 Nov. 1722 by Bennett Garrett with
Edward Hall and Francis Holland, admin. by Garrett on 19 Nov. 1726;
had iss.: THOMAS, b. 18 Sept. 1708; a dau., b. 15 Feb. 1714, d. 15
March 1714; AUGUSTUS, b. 25 or 28 Sept. 1710; GABRIEL, b. 1 May
1712 (2; 11; 22:93; 51; 110; 128).

BROWN, THOMAS (11), s. of John (10) and Elizabeth, b. 18
Sept. 1708, d. by 12 April 1766; m. Sarah (?); in June 1721 pet.
the court that his mother had remarried; in March 1721/2 chose
Archibald Buchanan as his guardian; his lands ordered reappraised
in Nov. 1724; in 1750 owned 500 a. Oakington; his will, 16 Jan.
1765 - 12 April 1766, named wife Sarah, s. John (to have 500 a.
Oakington); sons Thomas, Garrett, and Freeborn, and Thomas Brown
of James; had iss.: ELIZABETH, b. 17 Dec. 1728; JOHN, b. 1 April
1731; JAMES, b. 3 July 1734; THOMAS, b. 22 March 1735; AMILLA,
b. 17 March 1737; SARAH, b. 14 Sept. 1740; GARRETT, b. 21 April
1742; FREEBORN, b. Nov. 1743 (23:509; 24:29; 27:34; 53; 112; 128).

BROWN, AUGUSTUS (12), s. of John (10) and Elizabeth, b. 25
Sept. 1710; living in 1739; m. 22 April 1729 Ann Cutchen; had
iss.: AUGUSTUS, b. 12 May 1744; MARGARET, b. 7 Dec. 1736; THOMAS,
b. 1 April 1739 (128).

BROWN, GABRIEL (13), s. of John (10) and Elizabeth, b. 1 May
1712; m. on 10 Feb. 1734 Mary Kean; had iss.: JOHN, b. 20 July
1733; JACOB, b. 11 Dec. 1736 (128).

BROWN, JAMES (14), s. of Thomas (11) and Sarah, b. 22 March
1735; m. 16 Jan. or Feb. 1758 Elizabeth Morgan ; had iss.:
THOMAS, b. 7 Oct. 1761 (129:363, 374).

THE THOMAS AND SUSANNA BROWN FAMILY

BROWN, THOMAS (15), no known rel. to above, d. 5 July 1749 in St. Georges Par., having m. on 19 June 1739 Susanna Higginson (b. 18 Aug. 1723, d. Jan. 1780, dau. of John and Anne Higginson); she m. 2nd on 18 July 1751 Capt. Daniel Robinson, and 3rd Garrett Garrettson; his admin. bond posted 20 Aug. 1749 by admnx. Susanna with Edward Morgan and Joseph Henley; est. admin. Susanna Brown who named four ch. of dec.: William, 10, Thomas, 5, Eliza, 3, and John, 9 mos.; had iss.: WILLIAM, b. 3 April 1740; JOHN, b. 11 May 1742, d. 8 Oct. 1744; THOMAS, b. 25 Dec. 1744; ELIZABETH, b. 18 July 1747, m. James Stewart; JOHN, b. 6 Jan. 1749/50 (5:128; 11; 128; 129).

BROWN, THOMAS (16), s. of Thomas (15) and Susanna, b. 25 Dec. 1744, d. test. in Harf. Co. by Oct. 1785; m. Mary (poss. Stewart), who m. 2nd (?) Everest; had iss.: JACOB, b. 20 Jan. 1770, d. 2 March 1826, m. 17 Jan. 1809 Mary, wid. of Thomas Brown who d. 1808; ELIZABETH, age 3 in 1776, m. (?) Chauncey; MARY, b. c. 1775; WILLIAM; FENTON; ANN (128; 131; 244; 285).

BROWN, JOHN (17), s. of Thomas (15) and Susanna, b. 6 Jan. 1749/50, bur. 8 April 1796; m. 1st Anne (?), and 2nd c.1783/4, Susannah Wood, dau. of John and Sarah, b. 18 April 1764, bur. 12 April 1810; had iss.: JOHN; MARY; MARTHA; WILLIAM; AQUILA; and SUSANNAH (128; 131).

THE ZACHARIAH BROWN FAMILY

BROWN, ZACHARIAH (18), no known rel. to above, d. in Balto. Co. by 9 Aug. 1711 when admin. bond was posted by admnx. Lidia Brown, with John Deaver and Richard Ruff; his est. was inv. 14 Sept. 1711 by Wm. Howard and John Webster, and val. at £ 43.12.6 plus 4217 lbs. tob. in debts, John Deaver signed as kin, and John Whitacre and John Webster signed as creditors; est. admin. 4 June 1714 by Edward Uany and wife Lidia; had iss.: JOHN, b. c. 1707; MARY (1:26; 11; 23:140; 52:130; 128).

BROWN, JOHN (19), s. of Zachariah (18), b. c.1707, age 12 in 1719; in June 1719 was bound to serve Richard Deaver to age 21; d. 27 Feb. 1738/9, having m. Mary (?); had iss.: ZACHARIAH, b. 20 Sept. 1728; JOHN, b. 8 March 1729/30, age 11 in Nov. 1740, bound to Daniel Ruff; ELIZABETH, d. 5 Feb. 1740; SARAH, b. 2 Oct. 1738 (23:140; 28:369; 32:352; 128:104, 112; 129).

Unplaced Browns.

BROWN, (?), m. by 13 Sept. 1743 Mary, dau. of Thomas Biddison of Balto. Co. (127:237).

BROWN, ABEL, in 1750 owned 470 a. Owen's Outland Plains and 400 a. of John's Chance (153:80).

BROWN, ANN, d. 1749 (131).

BROWN, BLANCH, m. 11 Nov. 1729 Francis Bucknal (129).

BROWN, DICKSON, of Richard and Elizabeth, b. 10 Dec. 1757 (133:100).

BROWN, ELIZABETH, of Ratchford and Ann, b. 21 March 1738 (131).

BROWN, FRANCES, m. Peter Whitaker 10 Jan. 1722 (129).

BROWN, GABRIEL, in March 1669/70 conv. 150 a. Homley to Humphrey Nichols (96).

BROWN, GEORGE, res. Joppa in April 1742 and Aug. 1745 (384: 356, 517).

BROWN, GEORGE, m. Mary (?); both rec'd as members of Gunpowder Meeting in 1754; was disowned in 1760; wife Mary was granted certificate to Gunpowder by Nottingham Meeting in 1753, and d. 3rd day, 5, 1769 (136).

BROWN, GEORGE, listed in inv. of David Bissett in 1759 (52: 330).

BROWN, GEORGE, d. leaving a will, 10 Jan. 1758 - 23 July 1764, named wife Mary, children of Eleanor Green (Mary, Susanna, Daniel, and Eleanor Green) and Sarah Wilson, dau. of testator's eld. sis. (111:173).

BROWN, GRACE, ind. for bast. in March 1709; named John Smart as the father in June 1710 (21:94, 136).

BROWN, JAMES, on 10 March 1663/4 conv. 150 a. Orchard's Neck from William Orchard; called merchant of Salem, New Eng., 6 Jan. 1667/8 when he sold the same tract (93; 95).

BROWN, JAMES, in 1750 owned 15½ a., Barton's Mount (153:90).

BROWN, JAMES, m. 2 April 1746 Sarah Johnson and had iss.: MARY, b. 9 Nov. 1747; SUSANNA, b. 25 Nov. 1750; JAMES, b. 8 Jan. 1752; JOHN, b. 31 April 1755; ELIZABETH, b. 28 Oct. 1757; HANNAH, b. 4 Feb. 1759; WILLIAM, b. 25 June 1761; MARTHA, b. 26 April 1763 (129).

BROWN, JAMES, d. 24 Dec. 1720 (128:38).

BROWN, JOHN, of New Eng., claimed land in Md., c.1662; on 12 March 1665/6 conv. 100 a. Hamstead Marsh to Thomas Overton (94).

BROWN, JOHN, was elected to Assembly but did not serve, term of 1671-1674/5 (370:26).

BROWN, JOHN, age 11 next Sept., June 1743 bound to Tobias Stansbury (34:186).

BROWN, Dr. JOHN, ind. for bast., June 1733; tried for begetting a child on Denny Downes in Aug. 1733 (30:2).

BROWN, John, of Ratchford and Ann, b. 6 June 1747 (131).

BROWN, JOHN, d. 13 Feb. 1749 (131).

BROWN, JOHN, d. 21 Feb. 1749 (131).

BROWN, JOHN, in 1750 owned 123 a. Longworth and 125 a. Parker's Palace (153).

BROWN, JOHN, m. by 15 May 1769 Margaret, extx. of Uriah Davis (7).

BROWN, JOHN, m. Katherine, and had iss.: JOHN, b. May 1759 (134:47).

BROWN, JOSHUA, m . by 14 Jan. 1722, Margaret, sis. of William Chew (1:109).

BROWN, JOSHUA, of John and Elizabeth, b. 10 Nov. 1755, d. Nov. 1788 (131).

BROWN, MARGARET, ind. for bast., June 1730 (28:415).

BROWN, MARTIN, bound to Peter Lester at age 13 in June 1732; bound to Ann Lester in Aug. 1733 to age 21; m. Mary (?), and had iss.: ELIZABETH, b. 24 Sept. 1742 (29:294; 30:64; 129).

BROWN, MARY, dau. of Elizabeth Brown and John Steel; bound to serve Henry Donohue and wife Honour in June 1714; Mary Brown als. Steel ind. for bast. Aug. 1735 (21:510; 30:305).

BROWN, MARY, d. 6 March 1712 (129).

BROWN, MARY, dau. of Ratchford and Ann, b. Feb. 1743 (131).

BROWN, MARY, ind. for cohabiting with William Bosley in June 1737 (31:14).

BROWN, MATTHEW, d. by 10 May 1709 when admin. bond was posted by John Deaver, with William Howard and John Webster (11).

BROWN, NICHOLAS, m. by 1686 Ann, admnx. of Dennis English; d. by 30 March 1687 when admin, bond was posted by George Wells with Richard Edmonds and George Goldsmith; est. inv. by Edmonds and Goldsmith in March 1686/7, and val. at Ł 40.16.8 (11; 56: 328; 206-9:427).

BROWN, PEREGRINE, in 1743 named as a son-in-law of Aquila Paca and in 1745 named as son of Rachel Paca whose est. he admin. on 21 21 April 1749 and 9 May 1749 (4:199; 5:72, 92; 127:277).

BROWN, RATCHFORD; m. Anne (?), who d. 1749 (131).

BROWN, RICHARD, m. Mary (?) and had iss.: ELIZABETH, b. 26 July 1708; MARTIN, b. 12 April 1719 (128:23, 53).

BROWN, SAMUEL, of Balto. Co., granted warrant for land in right of wife' s service (388).

BROWN, SAMUEL, m. Mary (?) and had iss.: HESTER, b. 10 April 1737 (128:95).

BROWN, THOMAS, in Nov. 1742 was orphan of John Brown and would be age 7 next New Year's Day, bound to Richard Ruff (34:63).

BROWN, THOMAS, not yet 21 when named as cousin in will of Thomas Treadway in July 1749 (200-27:22).

BROWN, THOMAS, age c.50, bricklayer, conv. serv. who ran away from John Metcalfe in Patapsco, May 1753 (385:231).

BROWN, THOMAS, m. 25 July 1758 Elizabeth Courtney (129:361).

BROWN, WILLIAM, d. by 1 May 1699 when Henry Ridgely, Sr., posted admin. bond with Charles Greenbury and Richard Jones, Jr. (11).

BROWN, WILLIAM, m. 31 Dec. 1740 Margaret Constance (128:111).

BROWN, WILLIAM BISHOP, son of John and Elizabeth, b. 1 Oct. 1758 (131).

BROWNING, THOMAS (1), imm. with wife c.1665; transported Elizabeth and son John in 1678; d. by April 1672, leaving at least one son: JOHN (94; 388).

BROWNING, JOHN (2), s. of Thomas (1), was transp. to Md. by 1678, but was definitely in Balto. Co. by 6 April 1672 when he and his wife Elizabeth conv. Richard Nash 300 a. of Browning's Plantation, originally conv. to Thomas Browning by Abraham Morgan in Nov. 1663 (94; 98; 388).

BROWNING, JACOB, d. by 7 April 1679 when admin. bond was posted by James Phillips with William Osborn and John Walston (11:60).

BROWNLEY, ARTHUR, married Margaret (?) by whom he had iss.: THOMAS, b. 2 March 1742 (129:328).

BRUCEBANKS, EDWARD (1), was in Md. by 12 July 1694 when he wit. the will of Thomas Plummer of A. A. Co.; m. Jane (?). by whom he had iss.: ABRAHAM, b. Jan. 1719; EDWARD, b. 27 Sept. 1721; BENJAMIN, b. 11 Jan. 1722; FRANCIS, b. 4 Dec. 1725; ANNE CANNOCK, b. 5 Aug. 1733; JANE, b. 7 June 1735 (121; 131:58/r).

BRUCEBANKS, ABRAHAM (2), s. of Edward (1), was b. Jan. 1719, and was still alive in 1762; m. 1st by 9 Nov. 1743 Catherine (?), and 2nd on 3 Dec. 1750 Mary Jackson; in June 1744 was tried in a paternity suit when Martha Thomas named him as the father of her child; had at least two children by Catherine, and five by Mary: FRANCIS OGG, b. 9 Nov. 1743; EDWARD, b. 31 May 1749; ABRAHAM, b. 10 Oct. 1753; BLANCH, b. 27 Oct. 1755; MARY, b. 22 Dec. 1757; MARTHA, b. 14 Jan. 1760; JANE, b. 2 March 1762 (35:227, 343; 129: 356, 364, 379; 131:58/r).

BRUCEBANKS, EDWARD (3), s. of Edward (1), b. 27 Sept. 1721; alive in 1749; may be the Edward who in 1750 owned 40 a. part Chance and 100 a. Plum Point; m. Bridget Baker on 23 June 1743 and had iss.: CAZIAH, b. 5 Nov. 1743; MARY, b. 28 Feb. 1746; JANE, b. 13 Aug. 1749 (131:97/r, 119/r, 123/r; 153).

BRUCEBANKS, ANNE CANNOCK (4), dau. of Edward (1), b. 5 Aug. 1733; tried for bast. in Nov. 1756 and named Luke Griffin as the father; had iys.: FRANCES, b. 1 March 1756 (41:313; 129:359; 131:58/r).

BRUER, JOHN, was in Balto. Co. by 11 June 1763 when John and Ann Collier sold him tract Collier (93).

BRUFF, THOMAS (1), d. by 17 April 1702, leaving a will, 2 Jan. 1701 - 17 April 1702, in which he named his wife Rhoda, son Richard (to have dwell. plant. at Doncaster and one-half of Crouch's Island), son Thomas (to have res. of Crouch's Island), dau. Susanna and dau. Rebecca (to share jointly in Knottley's Enjoyment), and dau. Mary wife of Ralph Stevenson; had iss.: RICHARD; THOMAS; SUSANNA; REBECCA; and MARY, m. Ralph Stevenson (121).

BRUFF, THOMAS (2), s. of Thomas (1), is prob. the Thomas who m. by 17 April 1710 the wid. of James Cullen and mother of John Cullen.

BRYAN, BRYANT. See BRIAN.

THE ARCHIBALD BUCHANAN FAMILY

BUCHANAN, ARCHIBALD (1), was in Balto. Co. by 1704 as a taxable in Spesutia Hund.; m. 9 April 1705 Mary Preble, wid. of Thomas Preble, whose est. was admin. by Archibald and Mary on 30 Sept. 1706; he admin. the est. of Margaret Drew on 15 Feb. 1722 and 16 Nov. 1726; d. 2 March 1728/9; his widow Mary left a will, 17 Jan. 1732 - 6 June 1733, named grandsons Perry, James, and Samuel Brown, son John Preble, granddau. Sarah Preble, grandson Thomas

Preble, dau. Elizabeth Simpson, granddau. Hannah Simpson, dau.
Sarah Poloke, grandson Joseph Poloke, dau. Ann Hawkins, granddau.
Elizabeth Hawkins (dau. of Robert), son Archibald, son John Poloke,
son-in-law William Simpson; Archibald and Mary had iss.: ARCHI-
BALD, Jr., b. 12 April 1705 (1:106; 2:233, 321; 126:23; 128:21,
28, 58; 211:21; 291:39).

BUCHANAN, ARCHIBALD (2), s. of Archibald (1), b. 12 April
1705; gave his age as 26 in 1732; m. Ann (?), who d. 29 Oct. 1749
(128:21; 131:74/r; 225:137).

THE GEORGE BUCHANAN FAMILY has been discussed by Bevan et al.

BUCHANAN, MUNGO (3), no known rel. to above, was of Tullie
Chewan, Scotland, and is said to have had iss.: ROBERT*(272;

BUCHANAN, ROBERT (4), s. of Mungo (3), was of Middle Tullie,
Chewan, Scotland, and had iss.: MUNGO, b. 1622 .

BUCHANAN, MUNGO (5), s. of Robert (4), b. 1622, d. 1696; m.
Barbara Leckie, and had iss.: MUNGO, d. 3 April 1710 ·

BUCHANAN, MUNGO (6), s. of Mungo (5), d. 3 April 1710; m. 22
Jan. 1687 Anna Barclay; admitted writer to the signet on 4 Nov.
1695; had iss.: GEORGE, b. 1698.

BUCHANAN, GEORGE(7), s. of Mungo (6), b. 1698, settled in Balto. Co. where he d. 23 April 1750; m. by 10 Nov. 1729 Eleanor
Rogers, b. 1705, d. 26 Aug. 1758; agreed with Balto. Co. Court
concerning treatment of patients, Nov. 1724; was delegate from
Balto. Co. to the Assembly in 1745, 1745/6-1748, and 1749; one
of the Commissioners appointed in 1729 to lay out Balto. Town;
by 1750 owned 12 different tracts totalling 1684 acres, two of
the largest were: Hab Nab at a Venture, 350 a., and Letter Kenny
329 a.; admin. bond posted 22 May 1750 by Eleanor Buchanan; she
d. by 16 Oct. 1758 when Lloyd Buchanan posted admin. bond on her
est.; had iss.: LLOYD, b. 10 Nov. 1729; ELINOR, b. 4 Sept. 1732,
m. 12 Dec. 1748 Richard Croxall; ARCHIBALD, b. 22 Oct. 1734; ARCHI-
BALD, b. 12 May 1737; GEORGE, b. 23 June 1740; ELIZABETH, b. 28
June 1742, d. 24 Aug. 1818, m. James Gittings; JAMES, b. 24 July
1744, d. 1782-3; KATHERINE, b. 4 Aug. 1746; WILLIAM, b. 7 July
1748 (4:72; 11:84, 139; 27:33; 75:95; 77:248; 133:30, 70, 74,
75, 80, 162; 153:3; 370:52, 53, 54).

BUCHANAN, LLOYD (8), s. of George (7), b. 10 Nov. 1729; d.
1761; m. July 1757 Rachel, dau. of Alexander Lawson; delegate to
the Assembly from Balto. Co. 1752-1754 and 1754-1757; at death
owned 1045 acres and at least one lot in Balto.; had iss.: ELEA-
NOR, b. 1 Aug. 1757, m. 1783 Nicholas Rogers (133:30, 102; 262;
370:55, 57, 180).

BUCHANAN, ANDREW (9), s. of George (7), b. 22 Oct. 1734; d.
12 March 1786; m. Susannah Lawson on 20 July 1760; she d. 26 Aug.
1798; member of Balto. Co. Comm. of Observation, 1774-1776;
Brig.-Gen. of Md. Forces; Judge of Orphans Court of Balto. Co.;
with wife is bur. in family ploy in Druid Hill Park, Balto.: had
iss.: DOROTHY, b. 18 Feb. 1762; Dr. GEORGE, b. 19 Sept. 1763,
d. 9 July 1808, m. Laetitia McKean; ALEXANDER PITT, b. 5 June
1765, d. 19 June 1827 at Winchester, Va.; ANDREW, b. 29 July
1766, m. Ann McKean; LLOYD, b. 1768, d. 1769; ELIZABETH, b. 5
Sept. 1770; ARCHIBALD, b. 22 Sept. 1772; LLOYD; SUSANNA; BETSY;
JAMES (115:131; 133:70, 117, 118, 126; 200-21:242; 208-3; 345;).

BUCHANAN, ARCHIBALD (10), s. of George (7), b. 12 May 1737, d.
1785; m. Sarah; left will, 19 Oct. 1773 - 23 Aug. 1785, named

w. Sarah, sis. Eleanor Croxall, bro. James, and the children of his bros. and sis. (113:72; 133:70).

BUCHANAN, WILLIAM (11), s. of George (7), b. 7 July 1748, was alive in Dec. 1801 when he bought 4 acres of Hannah's Lot from John Wooden (of John) and w. Rachel; had iss. (named in will of his sis. Eleanor Croxall): ELEANOR, m. (?) Cosden; ELIZABETH; PRISCILLA; MARY; FRANCES; MARGARET; ANN; EDWARD (116:371; 133: 80; 231-WG#71).

BUCK, (?) (1), d. leaving a wid. Katherine (?) who m. 2nd, by 22 Aug. 1711 Theophilus Kitten, whose est. was inv. on that date, and amin. on 13 April 1713 and 27 July 1713; will of Katherine Kitton of A. A. Co., 18 May 1734 - 12 June 1734, named ch. John Buck, Edward Buck, Catherine Howard, and granddaus. Rachel and Rebecca Gaither; had iss.: JOHN, m. 20 Dec. 1705 Penelope Martin; EDWARD, m. Jane (?), wid. of (?) Anderson; Catherine, m. 22 Jan. 1716 Benjamin Howard; JANE, m. 21 Aug. 1701 John Gaither (1; 52; 126; 219-1:57; 219-4:102).

BUCK, JOHN (2), s. of (?) (1) and Katherine, living in 1718; m. 20 Dec. 1705 Penelope Martin; admin. of est. of John Martin in latter's will of 21 April 1718; had iss.: CATHERINE, b. 12 April 1710; RUTH, b. 2 Nov. 1711; MARY, b. 19 July 1716; JOHN, b. 1 Oct. 1718; BENJAMIN, b. 24 Aug. 1723 (123; 219-4).

BUCK, EDWARD (3), s. of (?) (1) and Katherine, m. by 19 Nov. 1711 Jane, who was admnx. of John Anderson (1; 2; 122).

BUCK, JOHN (4), s. of John (2) and Penelope, b. 1 Oct. 1717; m. 11 Feb. 1742 Susanna Mead Ingram, b. 21 Sept. 1717, d. c. 1793 in Balto. Co.; she was dau. of Benjamin and Elizabeth (Dawdridge) Mead, and wid. of John Ingram; had iss.: ELIZABETH, b. 30 June 1742; BENJAMIN, b. 10 Oct. 1744, d. 24 Dec. 1807, m. 10 Feb. 1763 Dorcas Sutton; JOHN, b. 12 Dec. 1746; JOSHUA, b. 5 April 1756, d. c.1812, m. 11 June 1778 Sarah Crook; SUSANNAH, b. 31 Oct. 1758, m. Asael Barton; MARY, b. 23 March 1762 (127; 131: 18/r, 112/r, 117/r, 141/r; 210-31:1084; 114).

BUCK, JOHN, in 1738 surv. 550 a. Paying Debts as a Resurvey on Pay My Debts; in 1753 his heirs owned 550 a. Pay My Debts (153: 4).

BUCK, JOHN, in 1750 owned 100 a. Michael's Chance (153:84).

THE BUCKINGHAM FAMILY has been discussed by Buckingham et al.

It is possible that there were two John Buckinghams: one who died by 11 Dec. 1720 when Hannah Buckingham posted an admin. bond, and one who d. by 3 Dec. 1741 when Hannah Buckingham admin. the estate. Further research may unravel this knot. (549; 550).

BUCKINGHAM, JOHN (1), was in A. A. Co. by Jan. 1697, and d. in Balto. Co. by 3 Dec. 1741 when his est. was admin.; m. 1st in Jan. 1697 Frances Hooper (d. 5 Oct. 1720), and 2nd on 31 Jan. 1720/1 Hannah Crans or Craws (prob. wid. of Robert Craws who m. Hannah Gosnell on 28 Nov. 1712); admin. bond for John Buckingham posted 11 Dec. 1720 by wid. and admnx. Hannah Buckingham with Robert Cross of Balto. Co. and William Cross of A. A. Co.; on 21 Feb. 1722/3 John and Margaret Baker sold 40 a. Baker's Delight to John Buckingham; est. admin. 3 Dec. 1741 by Hannah Buckingham; had iss. (three by 1st w. and four by 2nd w.): THOMAS, b. 4 July 1698; JOHN, Jr., b. 28 Oct. 1700, d. 13 Feb. 1723; dau., b. 13 Nov. 1703; BENJAMIN, b. 12 March 1721; FRANCES, b. 27 Nov. 1723; LAVINIA, b. 8 Feb. 1728, d. 31 May 1729; JOHN, Jr., b. 24 June 1730 (11:111; 69:165; 140; 219-4).

BUCKINGHAM,THOMAS (2), s. of John (1) and Frances, b. 4 July 1698, d. in Balto. Co. by Nov. 1750; m. by 6 Oct. 1731 Mary (?), perhaps the Mary Buckingham named in will of William Slade on 2 April 1726; wit. the will of Francis Mead on 4 Jan. 1716; est. mentioned in Balto. Co. Court in Nov. 1750; admnx. Mary had m. William Hall (also now dec.); had iss.: LAVINA, m. 20 Feb. 1747 Gilbert Marsh; BEZALEEL (dau.); THOMAS, b. 6 Oct. 1731; WILLIAM, under age in 1750; ANN, under age in 1750 (38:16; 123:123; 125: 202; 133:28, 161).

BUCKINGHAM, BENJAMIN (3), of John (1) and Hannah, b. in A. A. Co. on 12 March 1721, perhaps living in 1801; by 2 Nov. 1740 m. Avarilla, dau. of William Gosnell; may be the Benjamin who pet. the Gen. Assembly in 1805 stating he was over 60 years old with seven children (three of whom were dumb, and eld. was dau. named Emma); Assembly granted him a pension; had iss.: BENJAMIN, m. Rachel Leatherwood; JOHN, b. 6 March 1748; NATHAN; WILLIAM, b. 177; ANN, b. 1750, m. William Abbott; OBADIAH, b. 3 Oct. 1757; EMILY (80:303; 111:143; 134:13; 219-4; 549).

BUCKINGHAM, JOHN (4), s. of John (1) and Hannah, b. 24 June 1730 in A. A. Co., d. in Balto. Co. by 3 Dec. 1800; on 29 July 1758 Benjamin and Avarilla Buckingham conv. to John Buckingham part Buckingham's Good Will; will of John, 13 Nov. 1800 - 3 Dec. 1800, named s. William (to have Buckingham's Good Will), sons Thomas and Bazel, and daus. Apprilla Delphy, Hannah Delphy, and Ann Abbott, and grandson Levin, s. of William; had iss.: THOMAS; WILLIAM, m. by lic. 29 Aug. 1778 Margaret Gladman; BASIL; AVE-RILLA, m. (?) Delphy; HANNAH, m. by lic. 31 March 1790 Richard Delphea; ANN, m. (?) Abbott (83:192; 115:327; 219-4; 232).

BUCKINGHAM, THOMAS, m. by 7 Nov. 1750, wid. of Thomas Gwynn or Owen (201-29:6).

BUCKLEY, JOHN, Irish, age c.24, coachmaker, ran away from Thomas Harvey on Garrison Ridge, June 1756 (307).

BUCKNELL, THOMAS (1), was transp. by 1663, prob. the Thos. Bucknell whose orphans held 50 a. Lusby in A. A. Co.; poss. had iss.: THOMAS (211:236; 388).

BUCKNELL, THOMAS (2), prob. s. of Thomas (1), was in Balto. Co. by 1699 as a taxable in Spesutia Hund.; d. by 29 Aug. 1720 when admin. bond was posted by extx. Mary Bucknell with Francis Holland and John Cottrall; m. 1st Elizabeth Griffiss (banns posted July 1701), and 2nd on 13 Dec. 1704 Elizabeth or Mary Burk; will, 8 Dec. 1713 - 20 Aug. 1720, named ch. Francis, Henry, Marcy and Mary, and w. Mary; est,inv. 30 Aug. 1720 by Thomas Cord and Richard Burrough and val. at £ 51.16.7; had iss.: FRANCIS, b. 25 April 1705; THOMAS, b. 5 March 1707, may be the Thos. who d. 28 June 1719; HENRY, living 1730; MARCY; MARY, poss. the Mary who m. John Savory on 29 Aug. 1734 (11:77; 51:118; 110:162; 128: 12, 22, 53, 67, 82; 141; 163:112).

BUCKNELL, FRANCIS (3), s. of Thomas (2), b. 25 April 1705; m. Blanche Brown on 11 Nov. 1729; had iss.: JUDITH, b. 11 April 1730; JAMES, b. 10 Feb. 1734; WILLIAM, b. 20 Oct. 1740 (128: 23, 68, 86, 111).

BUCKNER, WILLIAM, bro. of Thomas (see below), came to Balto. Co. from Va.; m. 20 Sept. 1724 Patience Colegate, dau. of Richard Colegate; d. by 7 Feb. 1732 when his wid. relinquished her dower on land sold by his bro. Thomas; she m. 2nd on 12 Jan. 1732 George Elliott; purch. 80 a. Swan's Harbour, 50 a. Boring's Range, 50 a. Boring's Passage, and 189 a. Ferry Range on 18 Feb. 1725 from

John and James Boring and their wives; purch. Turkey Range,
Noble's Desire, and Pearson's Enlargement from Simon Pearson on
7 Aug. 1730; 17 March 1731 admin. bond posted by Patience Buckner with Robert Robinson and Richard Colegate; est. admin. by Geo.
and Patience Elliott on 2 Feb. 1733 and 13 Sept. 1739; had iss.:
BETTY, b. 3 Jan. 1725, d. 16 April 1727; BETTY, b. 25 Oct. 1727;
VIOLETTA, b. 15 March 1729 (1:322; 3:150; 4:42; 11:86; 70:218;
73:13; 133:10, 13, 19, 137, 151, 194).

BUCKNER, THOMAS, brother of William (see above), in Va. on 7
Feb. 1732 when he sold to Simon Pearson the three tracts Pearson
had conv. to William Buckner; Patience wife of George Elliott,
and wid. of said William relinquished her dower; in Aug. 1735
Thomas conv. John Boring land sold to   William by Borings (73:
328; 74:294).

BUCKWELL, MARY, dau. of Robert and Mary, age 2 in Sept. 1725,
in Aug. 1725 bound to Peter and Rebecca Potee (27:307).

BUDD, ELIZABETH, ind. for bast. in June 1711; named Christopher Choate as the father in Aug. 1711 (21:210, 251).

BUDD, SAMUEL, m. Milcah Young on 27 Sept. 1747 by Rev. James
Sterling of the Lower Parish, Kent Co.; had iss.: GEORGE, b. 6
Oct. 1750; MILCAH, b. 3 April 1756; SAMUEL, b. 18 June 1757;
SARAH, b. 25 Nov. 1763; MARTHA, b. 5 Jan. 1765 (129:387).

BUDD, WILLIAM, in Balto. Co. by 1692 as a taxable in s. side
Patapsco Hund.; in Oct. 1694 surv. 132 a. Timber Neck (138; 211:
107).

BULL, JACOB (1), progenitor, was in Balto. Co. by 1717 and
d. there by 1756; m. Rachel (?); wit. the will of Thomas Todd
the Younger on 11 Jan. 1714/5; with s. John wit. the will of a
Charles Simmons on 20 June 1736; in 1750 owned 300 a. part Bell's
Camp, 110 a. Jacob's Square, 200 a. Land of Promise, 120 a. part
The Grove, and 50 a. Willson's Choice;   conv. his son-in-law
William Demmitt a negro boy; will, 22 Nov. 1756 - 13 Dec. 1756,
named dau. Catherine Warden Demmitt (wife of William Demmitt),
son John (and his present w. Hannah and his s. Jacob), dau. Sarah
Marshall, sons William, Samuel, Isaac, Edmond, and Jacob, and
daus. Rachel and Hannah, and tracts Agnes' Lot, Cecil's Adventure,
Land of Promise, Water Course; had iss.:CATHERINE WARDEN, b. 1
Jan. 1717/8, m. 13 May 1736 William Demmitt; JOHN, b. 1 Nov.
1719; SARAH, b. 15 Jan. 1722, m. 3 Oct. 1740 Thomas Marshall;
ABRAHAM, b. 6 Jan. 1723; SAMUEL, b. 29 Dec. 1725; ISAAC, b. 3
Feb. 1727/8; EDMUND, b. 13 Jan. 1729/30; JACOB, b. 8 March 1731;
WILLIAM, b. 28 Feb. 1734; RACHEL, b. 28 Feb. 1736; HANNAH (76:
151; 110:477; 123:51; 125:80; 126:246; 131; 153:2).

BULL, JOHN (2), s. of Jacob (1) and Rachel, b. 1 Nov. 1719,
d. 1756; m. 20 Feb. 1739 Hannah Ruff who d. by 31 March 1760;
in 1750 owned 150 a. Ruff's Chance, 125 a. Howard's Harbor, 100
a. Ayres' Lot, and 45 a. Tench Bedford; will, 9 Jan. 1757 - 16
Feb. 1757, named w. Hannah and ch. John and Jacob, with Henry
Thomas, Edmund Bull, and Eleanor Jarrett as witnesses; will of
Hannah Bull, 19 Jan. 1760 - 5 March 1760, named ch. John, Jacob,
Mary, Hannah, Elizabeth, and Rachel; her admin. bond posted 31
March 1760 by Henry Ruff and Edmund Bull with Henry Waters and
Abra. Bull; had iss.: MARY, b. 30 April 1740; JOHN, b. 6 Dec.
1743; HANNAH, b. 10 Feb. 1747; RACHEL, b. 18 Nov. 1753; JACOB,
b. 24 Feb. 1756; ELIZABETH (11:156; 111:243; 131:112/r, 120/r,
131/r, 134/r; 153:16).

BULL, ABRAHAM (3), s. of Jacob (1) and Rachel, b. 6 Jan.
1723, d. by 5 July 1762, having m. Martha (?); his will, 18 May

1762 - 5 July 1762, named his w. Martha and ch. William, Abraham, Hannah, and Rachel; est. admin. on 20 June 1763 and 14 Feb. 1765; had iss.: WILLIAM; ABRAHAM; HANNAH; and RACHEL (4:325; 6:183; 111:154).

BULL, ISAAC (4), s. of Jacob (1) and Rachel, b. 3 Feb. 1727/8 and seems to have been married twice; 1st on 23 June 1749 to Hannah Robertson, dau. of Richard Robertson; and 2nd on May 1761 to Betsy Ann Slade; had iss. (one by 1st w. and two by 2nd w.): RACHEL, b. 5 March 1755; ISAAC, b. 25 May 1766; MARY, b. 11 Jan. 1769 (112:169; 131).

BULL, EDMUND (5), s. of Jacob (1) and Rachel, b. 13 Jan. 1729/30, d. 8 March 1776; m. Susanna Lyon on 19 Nov. 1752; was a private in Capt. John Love's company of Harford Co. Militia on 14 Sept. 1775; had iss.: RACHEL, b. 23 June 1754; JACOB, b. 17 Aug. 1757, m. Sarah Love; ESTHER, b. 17 March 1760; MARY, b. 29 Jan. 1762; JOHN, b. 26 April 1764 (129:389; 345).

BULL, JACOB (6), s. of Jacob (1) and Rachel, b. 8 March 1731, m. 17 Oct. 1752 Ranrice Bussey; had iss.: JACOB, b. 1758; WILLIAM, b. c.1761; MARY, b. c.1763; RANRICE, b. c.1765; BENNETT, b. c. 1769; ELI, b. c.1771; JARRETT, b. c.1776 (131; 285).

Unplaced Bulls

BULL, ABRAHAM, m. 1 June 1749 Mary Wyle (131).

BULL, ELIONER, of William and Martha, b. 6 Jan. 1741 (131: 103/r).

BULL, ELIZABETH, had dau. Elizabeth Carlisle, b. 27 Jan. 1749 (129:365).

BULL, JOHN, m. Elizabeth (?), and had iss.: JOHN, b. 5 Feb. 1754; ANN, b. 25 May 1756; RICHARD, b. 29 April 1758; ISAAC, b. 30 Dec. 1759 (129:365).

BULLOCK, ISAAC, of Chester Co., Penna., m. Margery (?) who in May 1749 joined him in selling part Isaac's Delight to Ralph Pile (80:190).

BULLOCK, JAMES, m. Sarah (?), and had iss.: SARAH, b. 12 Nov. 1726 (128:49).

BULLOCK, JAMES, m. 4 Jan. 1724 Mary Job and had iss.: ELIZA-BETH, b. 23 Dec. 1731; JAMES, b. 17 Aug. 1734 (128:85).

BULSTONE, EDMUND, was in Balto. Co. by 1692 as a taxable in n. side Patapsco Hund. (138).

BUNELS?, ARNEL?, lame, in inv. of William Orrick on 2 Nov. 1720 (51:164).

BUNHILL, GEORGE, on 6 Dec. 1748 conv. Joshua Bond 95 a. of Bunhill's Makeshift (80:148).

BURCHALL. See BIRCHALL.

BURCHFIELD, ADAM (1), m. Mary (?) and had iss.: THOMAS, b. 21 Feb. 1710/11; ELIZABETH, b. 13 May 1714; MARY, b. 26 Oct. 1716; FRANCES, b. 13 March 1723/4; ADAM, b. 26 May 1726 (128: 37, 46, 53, 65).

BURCHFIELD, ADAM (2), s. of Adam (1), b. 26 May 1726; m. Ann Nelson on 2 Oct. 1753; will, 22 March 1766 - 20 June 1766, named

son-in-law Archibald Johnson, and mentioned grandchildren; had
iss.: HANNAH, b. 28 July 1754; MARY, b. 2 Oct. 1756; PRISCILLA,
b. 19 March 1759; ADAM, b. 15 Feb. 1762 (112:42; 128:53, 65; 129:
377).

BURCHFIELD, THOMAS (3), no known rel. to above, m. 1st on last
day of June 1709 Mary Wilson; 2nd, on 4 Aug. 1721 Joanna, extx.
of Edward Cantwell; and 3rd on 21 Feb. 1725 the wid. Elizabeth
Macarley; and 4th, on 10 Aug. 1727 Mary Johnson; Thomas gave his
age as 45 in 1728; had iss. (four by 1st w. and three by his 2nd):
ROBERT, b. 27 Feb. 1710; THOMAS, b. 8 Aug. 1721; MARY, b. 6 July
1716; ADAM, b. 17 Dec. 1719, d. 17 July 1720; JOHN, b. 15 Dec.
1728; JOSEPH, b. 16 April 1731: JAMES, b. 4 March 1733 (128:26,
27, 30, 38, 41, 45, 50, 52, 66, 78; 224:75).

BURCHFIELD, ROBERT (4), s. of Thomas (3) and Mary, b. 27 Feb.
1710; m. Ann Clark on 3 Dec. 1735 (128:27, 90).

BURCHFIELD, THOMAS (5), s. of Thomas (3) and Mary, b. 8 Aug.
1712, m. 13 July 1736 Sarah Gash; had iss.: AQUILA, b. 9 Aug.
1738; THOMAS, b. 13 Jan. 1739, d. 5 April 1740; HANNAH. b. 3 June
1741; MARY, b. 14 July 1743; SARAH, b. 16 Oct. 1746; ELIZABETH,
b. 16 May 1749 (128:30, 93-b, 100, 109; 129:321, 347).

Unplaced Burchfields

BURCHFIELD, ELIAS, in Aug. 1718 admitted he was the father of
a child born to Mary Longman (23:3).

BURCHFIELD, THOMAS, in 1750 owned 37½ a. Daniel's Neglect
(153:97).

BURCHFIELD, THOMAS, m. 20 March 1755 Elizabeth Turner; she d.
6 April 1756 (129:359).

BURDEN, ELEANOR, ind. for bast. in March 1708/9; Hector Mc-
Laine agreed to pay for the child (21:22).

BURDET, BENJAMIN, named as father of Mary Walker's bast. in
Nov. 1739; tried in March 1739/40 (32:72, 159).

BURGAN, LEWIS, was in Balto. Co. by March 1665 when he surv.
150 a. The Hope; land was later held by Jonas Bowen (211:87).

BURGEN, PHILIP, transp. to Md. by 1678 (388).

BURGIN, ROBERT (1), was in Balto. Co. by 1692 as a taxable in
n. side Patapsco Hund.; d. leaving a will, 15 May 1701 - 31 Oct.
1701, naming wife Margaret, sons John and Robert, and land Major's
Choice; had iss.: JOHN; ROBERT (121:228).

BURGIN, ROBERT (2), s. of Robert (1), was living in Balto. Co.
in 1726; m. Anne (?) and had iss.: ROBERT, b. c.1718/9; PHILIP,
b. 16 Dec. 1720, m. 24 Feb. 1746 Rebecca Green; PRESOCIA, b. 27
Oct. 1723; ANN, b. 19 Aug. 1726 (131; 133:5, 21).

BURGIN, ROBERT (3), s. of Robert (2), gave his age as 44 on
1 Sept. 1762 when he said that he had lived on tract Goose Harbour with his father, Robert, for about 20 years (88:92).

Unplaced Burgins.

BURGIN, JOHN, was in Balto. Co. by 1695 as a taxable in n. side
Patapsco Hund. (140).

BURGIN, THOMAS, m. Anne (?) and had iss.: MARY, b. 24 Nov.
1741; DENNIS, b. 23 Nov. 1743; THOMAS, b. 27 June 1747; CATHERINE,
b. 16 July 1752; JOHN, b. 5 April 1755; JAMES, b. 3 Jan. 1758;
ISAAC, b. 3 Nov. 1760 (129:376)

BURKE, ULICK (1), d. in Balto. Co. by 20 April 1762; m. 1st
on 14 May 1732 Mary Leekings and 2nd, by 5 May 1761 Elizabeth
(?); was in Balto. Co. by Nov. 1724 when Edward and Jane Cox conv.
him 100 a. Cox's Forest; in June 1731 was ind. for unlawful cohabitation with Eliz. Leekings; in 1750 owned 200 a. Cox's Forest; his will, made 5 May 1761 named w. Elizabeth, dau. Mary Ryland, grandchildren Ulick and Thomas Burke (who were to have 100
a. Cox's Forest), Elizabeth Taylor (and her mother now w. of
Thomas Miles), and Thomas, Richard, Sarah, and Eliz. Burke;
est. admin. by Thomas Miles, Jr., on 30 Jan. 1764; had iss.:
THOMAS, living 1798; MARY, m. (?) Ryland; (poss.) MARGARET, m.
1st (?) Taylor, and 2nd on 11 Oct. 1744 Thomas Miles, Jr. (6:81;
29:156; 69:298; 131:15/r, 26; 153:37).

BURKE, THOMAS (2), s. of Ulick (1), eld. s. and heir at law
of said Ulick, on 13 Oct. 1798 conv. to Mary Burke part of Bleth-
nia Cambria, which had been conv. to Ulick Burke by Daniel Dulany;
Burke's w. Elizabeth consented; m. 1st on 14 April 1737 Sarah,
dau. of Sutton Sickelmore, and they had iss.; m. 2nd by 1798
Elizabeth (?); had iss.: W. (or U. for Ulick?), b. 30 Jan. 1740;
ELIZ., b. 5 May 1745; THOMAS, b. 17 Nov. 1747 (131:128/r; 231-
WG#71, p. 280).

Unplaced Burkes

BURKE, BARBARA, m. 11 Oct. 1744 John Brown (131:27).

BURKE, HENRY, d. in Balto. Co. by 14 Jan. 1708/9; m. on 6 Jan.
1706/7 Esther Pine; his will, 23 Nov. 1708 - 17 Dec. 1708, left
prop. to Bennett and Sarah Garrett, and res. of his est. to dau.
Mary; admin. bond posted on 14 Jan. 1708/9 by Richard Garrett
with Richard Smithers and John Roberts; est. inv. on 2 April 1711
and val. at £ 20.2.9; est. admin. on same day by Eliza Garrett,
extx. of Richard Garrett; had iss.: MARY (1:235; 11:64; 48:155;
122:114; 128:18).

BURKE, JAMES, m. by 26 Oct. 1741 Ann, extx. of Christopher
Randall; d. by 1750 when his wid. Ann owned 109 a. part Stout
(4:78; 76:30; 153:30).

BURKE, JAMES, Irish carpenter, ran away from Charles Ridgely;
came to these parts 12 or 14 years ago; 14 Nov. 1745 (384:534).

BURKE, JOHN, d. by 16 May 1712, when Francis Dallahide posted
admin. bond with Simon Person (11:410).

BURKE, JOHN, d. by 15 Sept. 1755 when Thomas Jeffreys posted
admin. bond with John Paca; est. admin. by Jeffreys on 12 Aug.
1764 (6:107).

BURKE, MARGARET, d. 13 Oct. 1759 (131:147/r).

BURKE, SARAH, tried for bast., March 1745/6 (35:807).

BURKE, SARAH, m. Thomas Miller on 24 July 1748 (131:32).

BURKE, THOMAS, in June 1733 was named as father of Sarah
Owings' child (30:136).

BURKHOLDER, ABRAHAM, of Lancaster Co., Penna., in June 1734
purch. land in Balto. Co. from John and Margaret Wheeler; in

1750 owned 229 a. James' Park, 71 a. Thomas' Lot, and 110 a. Padanarum (74:59; 153:44).

BURKHOVER, BALCHER, d. by 15 Dec. 1750 when admin. bond was posted by Jasper Hall, Jr., with Benjamin Jones and Jacob Stroup (11:206).

BURKITT, THOMAS, of Balto. Co., imm. by Oct. 1667; his wife Jane was transp. from Va. by 1673 (388).

BURMAN, EDWARD, d. by 25 April 1706 when his est. was inv. by George Yates and Christopher Gardner and val. at Ł 24.12.6 (48: 89).

BURMAN, LEWIS, was in Balto. Co. by 1692 as a taxable in Spesutia Hund. (138).

BURMAN, ROBERT, in Feb. 1685 surv. 350 a. Burman's Forest (211:93).

BURN, PATRICK, Irish, age c.30, ran away from Balto. Ironworks, 11 July 1750 (307).

BURN, WILLIAM, in Aug. 1679 purch. 175 a. part United Friendship from Edward and Ann Reeves (102).

BURNETT, THOMAS, d. 16 Aug. 1736; his will, proved 6 Aug. 1736 (sic), named Absolom Brown, and Daniel Ruff as residuary legatee (110; 128:93-b).

BURNEY, WILLIAM, in Balto. Co. by 4 July 1723 when he conv. all his property to his sons Simon and William, "for love and affection," and mentioned w. Martha; she died March 1727/8 (69: 192; 131).

BURNINGTON, JOHN, was in Balto. Co. by 1694 as a taxable in n. side of Gunpowder Hund. (139).

BURRELL, JOSEPH, alias Harp, d. by 9 June 1752 when admin. bond was posted by Thomas Norris with James Cary (11:165).

BURRMAN, WILLIAM, from west of Eng., ran away from Lyde Goodwin near Balto. Town, March 1750 (385).

BURROW, MARY, ind. for bast., Nov. 1723 (26:75).

BURROUGHS, RICHARD, m. by March 1716/7 Eliz., relict of John Brown; had iss.: ELIZABETH, b. 16 Oct. 1717; SARAH, b. 8 Jan. 1721 (22:93; 128:37, 43).

BURROWS, THOMAS, d. 30 July 1704 (128:21).

BURTICE, SAMUEL. See BARTIS, SAMUEL.

BURTON, JOHN, was in Balto. Co. by 1692 as a taxable in s. side Gunpowder Hund. (138).

BURTON, JOHN, m. 15 Jan. 1743 Mary Hargas (129:333).

BURTON, WILLIAM, was in Balto. Co. by 1735, and d. there by 15 Sept. 1769; m. Jane (?); in 1750 owned 62½ a. Whitaker's Ridge; his will, 26 Aug. 1769 - 15 Sept. 1769, named w. Jane, and dau. Mary; had iss.: FRANCIS, b. 20 Dec. 1735; MARY, b. 29 Jan. 1738 (112; 129; 153).

BURTRAM, SARAH, tried for bast. with John Acorns in Nov. 1757 (44).

BURTRAM, WILLIAM, s. of John, aged 8 last 16 May, in June 1714 was bound to Daniel Scott the Younger and w. Elizabeth, with cons. of his father John (21:506).

BUSBY, GREENBURY, was rec'd in membership in Gunpowder Meeting, 22nd d., 2 mo., 1758 (136).

BUSBY, THOMAS, rec'd in membership in Gunpowder Meeting, 25th d., 8 mo., 1756 (136).

BUSK, JOHN, m. Ruth (?) and had iss.: WILLIAM, b. 17 Dec. 1743; JAMES, b. 10 April 1748; ELIZABETH, b. 2 May 1750 (133).

BUSSEY, GEORGE (1),possible progenitor of the family in Balto. and Harford Counties, d. 1668 in Md.; m. Anne (?) who surv. him; came to Va. in 1635 with Richard Bennett (one of his great-grandsons was Bennett Bussey; as George Bushy, imm. to Md. c.1653 with his wife and sons George and Henry; his will, 17 April 1668 - 19 May 1668, named wife Anne and mentioned ch.; had iss.: GEORGE; HENRY; poss. HEZEKIAH; and poss. PAUL, who was transp. to Md. by 1655 (120:44; 313:105; 322; 388).

BUSSEY, GEORGE (2), s. of George (1) d. in Calvert Co., in 1693; m. Anne (?); his will, 20 Feb. 1692 - 3 April 1693, names w. Anne as extx., his bro. Hezekiah, and the following ch.; GEORGE; EDWARD; JAMES, d. unm.; HENRY; ANNE, m. Hugh Ferguson; MARY (121:62; 322).

BUSSEY, HEZEKIAH (3), s. of George (1), was named as bro. in will of George Bussey on 20 Feb. 1692; on 19 Oct. 1675 Hezekiah and Edward Bussey were named in the will of Edward Keene of Calvert Co. (120:120; 121:64).

BUSSEY, EDWARD (4), s. of George (2), m. Martha Evans on 10 Aug. 1701, and is said to be the father of: EDWARD (322).

BUSSEY, EDWARD (5), s. of Edward (4), settled in Harf. Co., trustee of the Harford Baptist Church, and d. 1786 leaving a wid. Mary (?) and the following ch.: RENNOUS, m. 17 Oct. 1752 Jacob Bull; JESSE, m. 1st Mary Jarrett and 2nd Elizabeth (?); MARTHA, m. Abraham Jarrett; MARY, m. John James (by whom she had John and Walter James); BENNETT, m. 1st Anne Green and 2nd Mrs. Elizabeth Slade; SARAH, b. 1756, m. Benjamin Amos; ESTHER, m. Dixon Stansbury; THOMAS, m. Susannah (?); EDWARD, m. Ruth Colegate (322).

BUTCHER, JAMES, m. 1st Mary (?), who d. 27 Dec. 1739, and 2nd on 15 May 1740 or 1741 Elizabeth Eastwood; by 2nd w. had iss.: MARY, b. 10 Nov. 1741 (128:105; 129:317, 323).

BUTCHER (?), JOHN, m. Widow Perkins; marr. banns pub. 16 March 1706 (128:18).

BUTLER, HENRY (1), progenitor, b. c.1666, gave his age as 56 in 1722 and 60 or 70 in 1738; d. 1746; m. Susanna (?), b. c.1695, d. c.1769; in 1704 surv. 200 a. The Hope; d. by 12 Sept. 1746 when his est. was admin. by Susanna; inventory said to include 17 punch bowls and "plenty to fill them with;" wid. Susanna left a nuncupative will recorded in 1770; had iss.: HENRY, b. 14 June 1715; ELIZABETH, b. 14 June 1715, m. John Robinson c.1735; SUSANNA, b. 13 Sept. 1717, m. Peter Bond 1 Aug. 1735; URITH, b. 13 Aug. 1719 Stephen Gill; SOPHIA, b. 4 Oct. 1721, m. Benjamin

Bond; AMON, b. 22 July 1723; TEMPERANCE, b. 17 June 1726, m. Benjamin Wells; ABSOLOM, b. 28 Jan. 1728, m. Mary (?); (4:136, 180; 5:74; 11:140; 112:367; 133; 138; 153:92).

BUTLER, HENRY (2), s. of Henry (1) and Susannah, b. 14 June 1715; in 1750 owned 30 a. Jacob's Lot, and 25 a. Hall's Neglect (153:32).

BUTLER, AMON (3), s. of Henry (1) and Susannah, b. 22 July 1723, d. 1806 in Balto. Co.; m. 12 May 1745 Elizabeth Hawkins; in 1750 owned Hall's Approach; in 1768 signed pet. for the removal of the Balto. Co. seat to Balto. Town; his will, 8 Sept. 1806 - 25 Oct. 1806; had iss.: HENRY, b. 13 April 1746; NICHOLAS, b. Aug. 1748, moved to Brooke Co., W. Va., then to Ohio; AMON, b. 24 Dec. 1750; RUTH, b. 23 Feb. 1753, m. Nicholas Haile; ABSOLOM, b. 5 Sept. 1758; ELIZABETH, b. 23 Jan. 1760; JOSEPH, b. 14 May 1763; MARY, m. Abraham Lane (115:152; 134:14, 37, 38; 153; 200-61:529).

BUTLER, ABSOLOM (4), s. of Henry (1) and Susannah, b. Jan. 1723, d. 1768 in Balto. Co.; m. c.1751 Mary (?); in Oct. 1737 was left a legacy by Richard Hewett; est. was admin. on 23 Sept. 1770 and 30 March 1775 and in April 1775; had iss.: WILLIAM, b. 3 March 1752; poss. THOMAS; poss. JOHN; poss. ABSOLOM, d. by 1795; poss. SAMUEL, c.1750 - 1780, m. 1772 Alice, wid. of Hugh Burgess; poss. a dau. who m. Richard Ridgely (Note: Absolom Butler was committed to Balto. Co. gaol for murder in March 1754, was tried, and acquitted in May 1754 (3:255; 6:228, 340, 345; 385:275, 282).

BUTLER, JOHN, in Nov. 1746 admitted he was the father of Mary Fourside's child (36:246).

BUTLER, MARY, was ind. for bast. in Aug. 1735 (30:305).

BUTRAM, BUTTERAM. See BUTTRAM.

BUTTERS, THOMAS, m. 23 Jan. 1696 Mary Burthel and had iss.: FRANCES, b. 5 Jan. 1697 (128:3).

THE BUTTERWORTH FAMILY is the subject of a genealogy by Walter V. Ball, cited in the Bibliography, and referred to in this text as # 553).

BUTTERWORTH, (?), (1), was the father of two ch.: ISAAC, b. c.1673; HANNAH, m. John Webster, and had at least two sons, named in the will of her bro. Isaac; i.e., Michael and Isaac (553).

BUTTERWORTH, ISAAC (2), s. of (?) (1), was prob. b. c.1673; came to Md. by 1694, and d. 7 Feb. 1728; m. Hester Clark; took up 562 a., John and Isaac's Enlargement, in 1714 took up 189 a. John and Isaac's Lot, and Roses Green, 1717; his will, 17 May 1728 - 1 April 1729, named w. Hester or Esther, ch.: Sarah, Isaac, Esther, Mary, Hannah, and Isaac, bro.-in-law Robert Clark, nephews Isaac and Michael Webster, and Thomas Shay; admin. bond posted 1 April 1729 by execs. Esther and Isaac Butterworth with Edward Hall, Benjamin Wheeler, and Gregory Farmer; had iss.: ISAAC, b. 4 Nov. 1704; HESTER, b. 20 March 1711, m. Peter Bond; MARY, b. 10 June 1712,m. Henry Garrett on 19 Dec. 1728; HANNAH, b. 27 April 1714; FRANCES, b. 26 Nov. 1716 (not in father's will); SARAH, m. Thomas John Giles on 16 Oct. 1734 (4; 11; 125; 128:19, 36, 54).

BUTTERWORTH, ISAAC (3), s. of Isaac (2) and Esther, b. 4 Nov. 1704, d. by 3 Feb. 1746; m. 18 Dec. 1728 Jane Wheeler; his will pr. 3 Feb. 1746, named w. Jane and ch.: Benjamin, Isaac, Mary, Eliza-

beth, and Charity; admin. bond posted 13 Feb. 1746 by Jane But-
terworth and Ignatius and Leonard Wheeler; est. admin. 17 March
1748 by extx. Jane, now wife of Lawrence Clark, and again on 15
Feb. 1750, 1 Nov. 1751, and 12 Aug. 1752; had iss.: MARY, b. 25
March 1729; ELIZABETH, b. 24 Feb. 1731; ISAAC, b. 11 Dec. 1734;
BENJAMIN, b. 4 Feb. 1736; CHARITY, b. 11 March 1739; JANE, b. 24
June 1742, d. 27 Oct. 1742 (4:202; 5:118, 217, 254; 11; 110;
128:71, 112; 129:340; 553).

BUTTERWORTH, ISAAC (4), s. of Isaac (3) and Jane, b. 11 Dec.
1734, d. 1766 in Bedford Co., Va.; m. Avarilla Gilbert, who d.
1826; had iss.: BENJAMIN, b. 1766, d. 1823, m. 1786 Rachel Morr-
man; MARTHA, d. 1837, m. Isaiah Harris; POLLY (or MARY), m.
John Hays; JANE, m. 1782 William Harris (553).

BUTTERWORTH, BENJAMIN (5), s. of Isaac (3) and Jane, b. 4 Feb
1736, d. 1801 in Campbell Co., Va.; m. 1st Elizabeth Clement; and
2nd Sarah Hoskins; rendered civil service in Va. during the Rev.
War (353; 553).

BUTTONS, THOMAS, was in Balto. Co. by 1695 as a taxable in
Spesutia Hund. (140).

BUTTRAM/BUTRAM/BUTTERAM, ISAAC, m. 26 Dec. 1743 Ann Lyal, and
had iss.: JOHN, b. 13 March 1744 (129:341).

BUTTRAM, JOHN, was in Balto. Co. between 1710 and 1731; m.
1st by 8 March 1710 Elizabeth, heiress of Thomas, Daniel, and
William Westbury, on that day he and his wife and William and
Mary Bond sold to Simon Person, weaver, their interest in any
lands belonging to the Westbury family; wife Elizabeth d. 7 May
1714; m. 2nd on 8 Sept. 1714 Jane Mayer; had iss.: ELIZABETH, b.
6 Sept. 1713; JACOB, b. 7 April 1731 (67:63; 131:6, 7, 19/r;
128:103).

BUTTRAM, MARGARET, m. 28 Oct. 1742 James Freeman (131:95/r).

BUTTRAM, SARAH, in Nov. 1757 was fined for bast., and named
John Acorns as the father (46:74).

BUTWORTH, HENRY, was in Balto. Co. by 1694 as a taxable in n.
side Patapsco Hund. (139).

BYFOOT, WILLIAM (1), was in Balto. Co. by 1721; m. Sarah (?),
who d. 23 Oct. 1728; m. 2nd Sarah (?); in 1734 was exempt from
the levy; had iss.: THOMAS, b. 3 Nov. 1721; MOSES, b. 12 Oct.
1729 (30:353; 128:41; 131:42/r, 43/r).

BYFOOT, MOSES (2), s. of William (1) and Sarah, b. 12 Oct.
1729; m. Sarah Tayman on 5 Sept. 1749, after having been bound
to William McComas in Aug. 1747 for 4 years (31:98; 131).

BYNAM or BYNUM, JAMES, claimed land for service in 1668; in
June 1671 surv. 200 a. Come By Chance; killed by Indians by 20
May 1674; m. Anne (?), and had iss.: ELIZABETH; and a son (211:
60; 341:359 ff.; 388).

BYWORTH, THOMAS, was in Balto. Co. by Nov. 1673 when he
bought 100 a. Horton's Fortune from Edward Horton (99:349).

CADLE, ZACHARIAH (1), progenitor, was transp. to Md. by 1680,
settled in A. A. Co., m. Anne (?) and had iss.: JAMES, b. 14
Oct. 1688; ZACHARIAH, b. 16 Dec. 1690; THOMAS, b. 1 June 16-(?);
SAMUEL, b. 9 April 1695; BENJAMIN, b. 7 March 1697 (219-3; 388).

CADLE, JAMES (2), s. of Zachariah (1) and Anne, b. 14 Oct.
1688; prob. the James who m. Frances Ridgely on 26 Aug. 1726 in
A. A. Co. (219-1:103).

CADLE, ZACHARIAH (3), s. of Zachariah (1) and Anne, b. 16 Dec.
1690; moved to Balto. Co.; m. Jane (?) and had iss.: BENJAMIN, b.
25 Sept. 1730 (131:35/r).

CADLE, BENJAMIN (4), s. of Zachariah (1) and Anne, b. 7 March
1697; d. in Balto. Co. 30 March 1746; m. Anne (?); in 1733 inher.
Waterton from Bethia Calvert; in 1737 named as bro. in will of
Joseph Mead of A. A. Co.; exec. of est. of Joseph Mead on 14 June
1739; by 1750 his heirs owned 71 a. of Waterton; 16 June 1746
admin. bond posted by admnx. Ann Cadle with George and William
York; est. admin. 16 May 1747 by Ann Cadle; had iss.: ELIZABETH,
b. 8 Jan. 1734, prob. d. young; ELIZABETH, b. 19 Jan. 1735, m.
James Stephens on 2 Nov. 1752; MARY, b. 21 March 1738; CAMELIA,
b. 30 May 1742, m. James Hill on 23 Dec. 1762 (4:45, 162; 11:
360; 126:22, 230; 131:65/r, 84/r, 105/r, 112/r; 153:7).

CADLE, ANN; summoned by vestry of St. John's Par. on 20 April
1746 for unlawful cohab. with James Dorney; m. James Dorney on 9
Aug. 1749 (131:34; 132:82).

CAGE, MARTHA, ind. for bast., March 1693/4; William Wilkinson
ind. as the father; she later came to own 150 a. Waterford, pt.
of 200 a. orig. surv. for Jno. Arding on May 1679 (20:175, 176;
211:89).

CAGILL, JOHN, m. by 13 Oct. 1739, Mary, granddau. of Joseph
Peake (75:136).

CAHELL, MARY, m. 27 July 1702 Thomas Russell (129).

CAIN, JAMES, admin. est. of John Martin on 3 March 1743; m.
30 Dec. 1744 Eliz. Doyle; m. 15 April 1746 Ann Spicer (3; 129;
131).

CAINE, WILLIAM, ordered to be levy free in Nov. 1755 (40:396).

CALE, WILLIAM, and wife Susan of Balto. Co. claimed land for
service by 1672 (388).

CALLMACK, MARY, m. 20 June 1719 John Bradshaw (131).

CALVERT, BETHIA, d. leaving a will pr. 6 June 1733; named
sis. Sarah Drew and Margaret Ryan; exec. Benjamin Cadle and his
heirs to have dwell. plant. Waterton left her by her former hus.
William Lenox (126).

CAMERON/CAMORAN/COMORAN, JOHN (1), m. 1st Sarah (?) and 2nd
Esther (:); d. by 1750 leaving his heirs in poss. of 40 a. Hog
Point; in April 1747 Esther Cameron was summoned by the vestry of
St. John's Par. for unlawful cohab. with Joseph Smith; John had
iss.: ABSOLOM, b. Sept. 1737; TASNER, b. 16 July 1738; JOHN MAR-
TIN, b. 16 July 1742 (131: 132:153).

CAMERON, ABSOLOM (2), s. of John (1) and Sarah, b. Sept. 1737;
by 1783 had moved to N. C.; sold Hog Point in Harf. Co. (deed
stated his f. John had purch. it from James Preston); his parentage estab. by deposition of John Day of Edward (241-JLG#E:436,
437).

CAMERON, JOHN, m. 12 Dec. 1716 Margaret Mackelltons; she d.
1 Jan. 1718/9 (131).

CAMMELL. See CAMPBELL.

CAMORAN. See CAMERON.

CAMPBELL/CAMMELL/CAMPBLE, JOHN (1), was in Balto. Co. by 1694 as a taxable in n. side of Gunpowder Hund.; m. Eleanor (?) and had at least two ch.: JAMES, b. 1 Jan. 1703/4; PHILLIS, b. 7 Nov. 1707; prob. JOHN (131; 139).

CAMPBELL, JAMES (2), s. of John (1), b. 1 Jan. 1703/4, was prob. the James who conf. to begetting a bast. on the body of Catherine Carroll in March 1745/6 (35:818).

CAMPBELL, PHILLIS (3), dau. of John (1) and Eleanor, b. 7 Nov. 1707; ind. for bast. in Nov. 1728; in June 1731 her bro. John Roberts alias Campbell pet. the court to let him take her two ch., Aquila and Benjamin; had iss.: AQUILA, b. by June 1731; BENJAMIN, b. by 1731 (28:65; 29:157; 128).

CAMPBELL, JOHN (4), alias John Roberts, s. of John (1), m. Ann Johnson on 1 Jan. 1734; had iss.: JAMES, b. 15 Jan. 1735; PHEBE, d. 15 Feb. 1739; PHEBE, b. 2 Jan. 1740; JOHN, b. 23 Oct. 1734 (119:91, 111; 128:91, 111).

CAMPBELL, FREDERICK ROBERTS, s. of Asael Roberts and Mary, b. 5 Jan. 1744 (131).

CAMPBELL, MARGARET, m. 28 March 1725 Thomas Adams (133).

CAMPBELL, MOSES , m. Rebecca (?), and had iss.: WILLIAM, b. Sept. 1753; JOHN, b. Oct. 1755; MARY, b. Oct. 1757 (131).

CAMPBELL, PETER, b. Ire.; runaway conv. serv. from Balto. Co., 6 Aug. 1752(385:190).

CAMPBELL, RUTH, m. 8 Dec. 1713, Samuel Sickelmore (131).

CAMPE, THOMAS, m. Mary (?) and had iss.: SARAH, b. 24 Dec. 1732 (133).

CAMPE, WILLIAM, m. Susanna (?) and had iss.: MARTHA, b. 5 Sept. 1729 (133).

CANE, MARY, serv., in inv. of Thomas Lightfoot, April 1688 (51:8).

CANNADAY, JOHN, m. Mary Arnold on 2 Dec. 1729, and had iss.: RACHEL, b. 7 March 1727 (sic) (128:68).

CANNADAY, MARGARET, ind. for bast.; named John Quare as the f.; ordered to serve Robert Green an extra 21 mos. for his trouble, June 1719; had iss.: JOHN, b. 23 Dec. 1718 (23:131, 198; 133).

CANNON, THOMAS (1), claimed land in Balto. Co. by 1682; with James Phillips sued George Gunnell in Nov. 1680; m. Henrietta (?), wid. of William Robinson, Edward Swanson, and who m. as her 4th husb., after the death of Cannon, (?) Reeves; d. by 15 March 1681/2 when admin. bond was posted by Henrietta Cannon with Peter Ellis and Edward Reeves; had iss.: THOMAS (11:306; 101:304; 206: 7-c, pp. 184, 191; 388).

CANNON, THOMAS (2), s. of Thomas (1), in Nov. 1694 was living with his bro. William Ebden; prob. the same Thomas who gave his age as 34 in 1718; may be the Thomas whose inv. was filed 1727 (20:336; 51:307; 135; 203-3:464).

CANNON, JAMES, m. Mary Boren on 24 Dec. 1724 and had iss.:
ANN, b. 28 Aug. 1722 (sic); JAMES, b. 8 Dec. 1725; JOHN, b. 16
Feb. 1727; SARAH, b. 25 May 1729 (128:67).

CANNON, RETURN, in Balto. Co. by 1695 as a taxable in Spesutia
Hund. (140).

CANNON, ROBERT, m. Sophia Johnson, dau. of Daniel Johnson, on
8 July 1725; had iss.: RACHEL, b. 1 Nov. 1726, d. 3 Dec. 1726;
SARAH, b. 28 Feb. 1728, d. 13 July 1729; ELIZABETH, b. 22 July
1730 (3:224; 128:67, 258).

CANNON, ROGER, m. Ann (?) and had iss.: MARY, b. 18 March
1736 (131:60/r).

CANNON, SIMON, in 1709 named as son-in-law of Christopher Durbin; m. by 1718 Elizabeth (?) when they were named as son-in-law
and dau.-in-law in will of John Downs (122:160; 123:161).

CANNON, WILLIAM, in Balto. Co. by 1695 as a taxable in Spesutia Hund. (140).

CANNON, WILLIAM, m. Frances, dau. of Daniel Johnson, on 28
Dec. 1721; on 21 Feb. 1745 William and Frances sold 100 a. Bond's
Manor to John Meyer of Lanc. Co., Penna.; had iss.: MARY, b. 22
Dec. 1722; WILLIAM, b. 20 March 1725; HANNAH, b. 5 Nov. 1727, d.
15 Sept. 1731; CHARITY, b. 18 Dec. 1729 (3:224; 79:76; 128:70).

CANTWELL, EDWARD (1), was in Balto. Co. by 1692 as a taxable
in n. side Patapsco; d. 31 March 1721; m. 5 Dec. 1699 Joan
Chattum (prob. the wid. of Francis Chittum or Chattum); she m.
as her 3rd husb. on 4 Aug. 1721 Thomas Burchfield; his will,
29 March 1721 - 2 May 1721, named w. Johanna as extx. and left
100 a. Taylor's Hall to his s. Edward; John Wilson, Elizabeth
Ryley, and Lucy Ann Bayly signed as witnesses; admin. bond was
posted 7 June 1721 by the extx. with Peter Lester and John Bayly;
est. was inv. 9 May by Edgar Tipper and William Osburn and val.
at £ 99.19.8, with Edward Cantwell and John Bailey signing as
kin; children were named in court proc. of Nov. 1723: LUCY, b.
17 Jan. 1700; LUCIAN, bapt. 31 May 1702; EDWARD, b. 11 Jan.
1702/3; SARAH; JOHN, m. 4 Feb. 1732 Mary Burchfield (1:258; 11:
287; 26:84-86; 48:206; 111:6; 128:11, 13, 15, 38, 73; 129:189,
226, 229; 138).

CANTWELL, EDWARD (2), s. of Edward (1), b. 11 Jan. 1702/3,
d. by June 1749; m. 1st Sarah (?), and 2nd on 5 Jan. 1744 Blanch
Jackson , who m. 2nd on 30 Sept. 1750 Joshua Gray; will of Edward
Cantwell, 30 March 1749 - June 1749, left 100 a. Taylor's Hall to
sons John and Edward; also named ch. Mary, Sarah, Hannah, Johanna,
and Ruth; admin. bond posted 17 June 1749 by the extx. with Guy
Little and Jacob Combest; est. admin. on 2 April 1750 and 29
Sept. 1750; had iss.: MARY, b. 18 Feb. 1725/6·; may have m. John
Handland in 1749; SARAH, b. 15 or 16 March 1728; HANNAH, b. 28
Feb. 1729; LUCY, b. 21 March 1731, d. 27 Jan. 1739; JOHN, b. 27
April 1734; JOHANNA, b. 22 Dec. 1735, may have m. William Collins
on 7 Nov. 1751; RUTH, b. 10 Dec. 1737, may have m. Samuel Sutton
on 25 Aug. 1757; EDWARD, b. 28 Feb. 1739 (5:151, 156; 11:363; 37:
164; 128:50, 53, 66, 74, 83, 90, 110; 129:312, 337, 355, 363;
131; 153:26; 210-26:118).

CANTWELL, JOHN (3), s. of Edward (1), b. by 1721, and was
alive in 1740; m. on 4 Feb. 1732 Mary Burchfield, and had iss.:
JOHANNA, b. 6 Nov. 1733; FRANCIS, b. 6 March 1735; EDWARD, b. 2
Sept. 1737; ADAM, b. 6 Jan. 1740 (128:73, 83, 91, 101, 114).

CANTWELL, MARY (4), dau. of Edward (2) and Sarah, b. 18 Feb.
1725/6, and was prob. the Mary tried for bast. in March 1746/7
(36:402).

CANTWELL, SARAH (5), dau. of Edward (2) and Sarah, b. 15 or 16
March 1728, prob. the Sarah tried for bast. in Nov. 1746 (36:247).

CANTWELL, WILLIAM, b. 1750, d. p. 1801; m. Margaret O'Brien;
pvt. in the Rev. War from Md.; had iss.: WILLIAM, b. 22 Nov. 1776
in Balto. Co., d. 18 Feb. 1858 in Mansfield; moved to Brooke Co.,
W. Va., where on 30 Nov. 1797 he m. Nancy Ann Williams; poss.
EDWARD; poss. JOHN (353:113).

CAPHORT, ANDREW, m. Mary (?), and had iss.: EVE, b. 10 March
1750/1 (133).

CAPLES, THOMAS, was in Balto. Co. by 1695 as a taxable in Spesutia Hund.; bur. 27 April 1704; m. Mary (?), who was bur. 24
Oct. 1706; his will, 19 May 1703 - 24 Jan. 1704, left personalty
to his godson Thomas s. of Greenfield, to John Kimball, Sr., and
to Martha w. of John Hall; res. of est. to w. Mary for her life
or widowhood, and then to John Hall, s. of John; est. inv. 25
Jan. 1703/4 by Thomas Cord and James Ives, and val. at Ł 36.16.5;
est. admin. 29 May 1707 by John Hall, Sr. (2; 51:136; 122:38;
128:18, 20; 140).

CARBACK, JOHN VALENTINE (1), was in Balto. Co. by 18 Dec.
1736 when he m. Mary, dau. of John Harryman; by 1750 owned 50 a.
Molly's Garden; est. admin. by John Carback on 11 May 1778 and
11 Feb. 1792; had iss.: HENRY, b. 28 April 1737; THOMAS; VALEN-
TINE, b. c.1751; JOHN, b. c.1755; MARY; ANNE, m. William Rusk
(5:199; 8; 10; 133; 153:68; 200-30).

CARBACK, HENRY (2), s. of John Valentine (1) and Mary, b. 28
April 1737; d. by 1 Nov. 1788 when his est. was admin. by Mary
Carback who spent money on three ch. of the dec. (9; 133).

CARBACK, VALENTINE (3), son of John Valentine (1) and Mary,
b. c.1751; dep. he was age 32 in 1783 and the s. of Valentine
who was alive 7 to 8 years ago (231-WG#T:655).

CARBACK, JOHN (4), s. of John Valentine (1) and Mary, b. c.
1755, dep. he was age 28 in 1783, and s. of Valentine who was
alive 7 or 8 years earlier; admin. the est. of his f. on 11 May
1778 and 11 Feb. 1792 (8; 10; 231-WG#T:655).

CARBACK, JOHN MARTIN, m. on 14 July 1734 Frances Mahone, dau.
of John and Mary Mahone (4; 5; 133).

CARBACK, WILLIAM, alias William Ingle, on 13 Oct. 1736 was
conv. part of Small Valley by his f. William Ingle; on 3 Aug.
1756 with w. Margaret conv. 32½ a. of Small Valley to John Roberts (79:221; 82:576).

CARDUE, CHRISTOPHER, was in Balto. Co. by 1694 as a taxable
on s. side of Patapsco Hund. (139).

CARLETON, ARTHUR, came to Md. by 1668 with Thomas Carleton,
whose est. he admin. on 17 Dec. 1674; was summoned into court
by Charles James in Oct. 1677 to pay debts his bro. Thomas owed
to said Charles James (200-67; 388).

CARLETON, THOMAS, came to Md. by 1668 with w. Eliza and the
child she was carrying and with Arthur Carleton; d. by 17 Dec.
1674; est. admin. by Arthur Carleton; left a wife and two daus.

94   BALTIMORE COUNTY FAMILIES, 1659 - 1759

as coheirs, and owned 250 a. in Cecil Co. called The Folly; had
iss.: MARY, b. by Oct. 1677; ELIZABETH, b. by Oct. 1677 (200-67;
388).

CARLISLE, DAVID, Sr. (1), in March 1736 made oath he had attended court; was exempt from levy in June 1738; by 1750 owned
390 a. Carlisle's Park; prob. was the father of: DAVID; JOHN;
ROBERT; and GEORGE (31:6, 224; 153).

CARLISLE, DAVID (2), prob. s. of David (1), m. Mary (?) by 15
June 1723, and was alive in 1760; served as co-exec. of est. of
John Summer on 7 May 1759 and 3 Nov. 1760; had iss.: PETER, b.
15 June 1723; ANN, b. 2 May 1729; LANCELOT, b. 10 Nov. 1736 (4:
267, 313; 131).

CARLISLE, JOHN (3), prob. s. of David (1), d. by 23 July 1747
when Richard Johns, age 42, Quaker, and Ford Barnes, age 45,
affirmed or swore to his nuncupative will in which he named his
brothers George and Robert Carlisle, and Daniel Deaver, and cousins Nancy Carlisle and Richard Deaver; his est. was admin. by
Daniel Deaver on 24 June 1748 (4; 210-25).

CARLISLE, ROBERT (4), prob. s. of David (1), m. Easter (?);
d. by 7 Aug. 1751 when admin. bond was posted by David Carlisle,
admin., with George Brown and James Billingsley; had iss.: AGNES,
b. 16 March 1745; JANE, b. 6 Feb. 1746; MARY, b. 2 Oct. 1748
(11; 131).

CARLISLE, PETER (5), s. of David (2), dec.; m. by 7 March 1770
Anne (?) (231-AL#B:1).

CARLISLE, DAVID, m. by 12 March 1767 Mary, dau. of Peter Carroll (230:114).

CARLISLE, Mrs. ELEANOR, m. 11 July 1723 Joseph Presbury (131).

CARLISLE, ELIZABETH, dau. of Elizabeth Bull, b. 27 Jan. 1749
(129:365).

CARLISLE, ELIZABETH, m. William Standiford on 16 July 1750
(131).

CARLISLE, ELIZABETH, tried for bast., June 1750; Robert Carlisle posted bond (37:24).

CARLISLE, Rev. HUGH, was at Newtown, Penna., when he had an
unclaimed letter at Phila., March 1738; was inducted into St.
George's Par. on 31 March 1744; d. by 9 Nov. 1749 when admin.
bond was posted by admnx. Mary Carlisle with Edward Wakeman and
Samuel Webb; est. admin. by Mary now w. of John Loney on 15 May
1752, 22 Sept. 1753, and 14 April 1756; left three ch. (5; 11;
303; 384).

CARLISLE, WILLIAM, serv. to William Hollis, bur. 18 June 1700
(128:11).

CARMAN, JOHN, weaver, from Co. Norfolk, Eng., came with bro.
Richard; age 40 in 1759 when he ran away from Benjamin Young of
Hunting Ridge in Aug. 1759 (307-68:299).

CARMAN, JOSHUA, m. by March 1723/4 Ann Brooks, admnx. of John
Brooks (26:300).

THE CARNAN FAMILY has been discussed by this author in
another work, but some additional data has been discovered which
is included here; see Bibliography).

CARNAN, JOHN (1), of Reading, Berks., Eng., m. by 1 Nov. 1697 Frances (?), and had iss.: ANTHONY, b. 1 Nov. 1697; THOMAS, b. 14 May 1699; WILLIAM, b. 25 April 1700; CHARLES, b. 21 March 1700. (559; 560).

CARNAN, THOMAS (2), s. of John (1) and Frances, b. 14 May 1699, may be the Thomas Carnan, printer, of Reading, who d. 26 March 1785 (Musgrave's Obituary).

CARNAN, WILLIAM (3), s. of John (1) and Frances, b. 25 April 1700, may be the William Carnan who printed a folio edition of Ashmole's History and Antiquities of Berkshire in 1736 (Victoria Hist., Berkshire, I, 401).

CARNAN, CHARLES (4), s. of John (1) and Frances, b. 21 March 1701, in Reading, Berks., and d. by 5 May 1753; m. Prudence (?) and had iss.: JOHN, b. c.1727; CHRISTOPHER. b. c.1730; ROWLAND, d. c.1753 (Rowland Carnan, late of Md.,, lost at sea; est. to be settled by execs. D. Chamier and J. Carnan; CECIL, b. 1742, d. 21 July 1770, m. Gen. Mordecai Gist in 1769 (259; 262).

CARNAN, JOHN (5), s. of Charles (4) and Prudence, b. c.1728, d. 1 June 1767; m. Achsah Ridgely, dau. of Col. Charles Ridgely (Achsah m. 1st Dr. Robert Holliday, and 3rd, after Carnan's death Daniel Chamier); had iss.: PRUDENCE, b. 16 Jan. 1755, d. 23 June 1822, m. Harry Dorsey Gough; CHARLES RIDGELY, b. 6 Dec. 1760, m. 17 Oct. 1782 Priscilla Dorsey, and assumed name Ridgely in accordance with his uncle Charles Ridgely's will; ELIZABETH, m. Thomas Bond Onion; REBECCA (259).

CARNAN, CHRISTOPHER (6), s. of Charles (4) and Prudence, b. 1730, d. 30 Dec. 1769; m. 13 June 1751 Elizabeth, dau. of Capt. Robert and Frances (Todd) North; she m. as her 2nd husb. Samuel Johnston; his will, 8 Dec. 1769 - 12 Jan. 1770, named w. Elizabeth and sis. Cecil, w. of Mordecai Gist; had iss.: CHARLES NORTH, b. 23 June 1752; ROBERT NORTH, b. 1756 (112; 133; 259).

CARNEY, EDWARD, d. by 15 Oct. 1720, when his est. was inv. by Thomas Newsom and Jonathan Ward and val. at £ 11.1.8; estate was admin. by Edgar Tripper (51:96).

CARPENTER, JOHN (1), was in Balto. Co. by Dec. 1739 when he sold personal prop. to Joshua Hall; d. by Nov. 1742 leaving two sons: EDWARD, b. c.1728; JOHN, b. c.1736.

CARPENTER, EDWARD (2), s. of John (1), age 14 on 8 April 1743, bound to William Demmitt in Nov. 1742 to age 21 (34:64).

CARPENTER, JOHN (3), s. of John (1), age 6 on 6 March 1743, bound to John Legatt, Jr., in Nov. 1742 to age 21 (34:64).

CARPENTER, Capt. JOHN, in 1750 owned 200 a. Ann's Dower (153).

CARPENTER, JOSEPH HULL, by 1695 was in Balto. Co. as a taxable in Spesutia Hund. (140).

CARPENTER, MARY, in March 1742/3, ind. for bast. (34:121).

CARPENTER, THOMAS, surv. 300 a. Helmore in Aug. 1702, and 178 a. Helmore's Addition in April 1704 (398:12).

CARR, WALTER (1), was in Md. by 1658 when he and Thomas Turner assigned their right to land to Stephen Benson; m. Juliatha (acc. to some sources the dau. of Thomas Daborne who made her his resid. legatee) poss. a dau. of Richard Gott who came into Md. c.1659 bringing his daus. Juliatha and Susan; Walter was named as bro. in the will of James Billingsley in Nov. 1663; Juliatha Carr named as legatee in will of Thomas Daborne in Oct. 1680 (Daborne left land to Walter Carr, and part of Daborne's Inheritance each to John, Richard, and Thomas Carr; Daborne also named Alexander McFarrand and Susan Carr; Walter Carr d. c.Sept. 1699 when his est. was inv. by John Gale and John Wellwood, and val. at £45.3.0 plus 500 lbs. tob.; est. admin. by John Wiley who m. the widow (of Walter Carr, Jr.?); had iss.: WALTER, Jr., d. by 11 Sept. 1699; JOHN; THOMAS, b. after 1663; RICHARD, b. after 1663; poss. SUSAN (120:27; 206-21:98; 388; Orig. Wills, Box D, folder 1; Test. Papers, Box 12, folder 2).

CARR, WALTER (2), s. of Walter (1) and Juliatha, d. in A. A. Co. by 11 Sept. 1699 when his wid. Martha posted admin. bond with John Willoughby and Augustine Hawkins; est. inv. by John Wellwood and John Gale and val. at £ 61.1.6; est. admin. 10 Oct. 1701 by John Willy or Wiley who m. the widow; had iss.: WALTER, alive in May 1716 when as s. of Walter, Jr., and heir at law of his grandfather, he deeded land to John Giles (206-21:36; 217-IB#2: 273; 219-3; Test. Proc., Box 12, folder 2).

CARR, JOHN (3), s. of Walter (1) and Juliatha, b. after 1663 as he was not yet 17 in 1680, alive in 1719; m. Elizabeth (?) and had iss.: ELIZABETH, m. on 24 Dec. 1731 Nicholas Norman (217-CW#1: 195; 219-3:368).

CARR, THOMAS (4), s. of Walter (1) and Juliatha, b. after 1663 as he was not yet 16 in 1680; d. in Balto. Co. by 5 June 1758; m. on 22nd day, 9 mo., 1705 Elizabeth Price, dau. of Mordecai and Mary Price; sold land he inher. from Thomas Daborne in A. A. Co. in 1703 and 1708; in Balto. Co. by 1715 when he sold George Westgarth of London tract Knocker's Hall which Thomas Daborne left to Richard Carr (since dec. without heirs); by 1750 owned 505 a. of Regulation; signed the inv. of Teague O'Tracey as kin in June 1712; will of Thomas Carr, 1 May 1758 - 5 June 1758, named w. Elizabeth, ch.: Mary, w. of Benjamin Bowen, Aquila, Averilla w. of John Wilmot, and granddau. Mary Cotterall; William Lux to be a guardian of Aquila, and Samuel Cole to be guardian of Mary Cotterall; est. admin. by Benjamin Bowen on 18 June 1759 and 12 Nov. 1759; had iss.: MARY, m. Benjamin Bowen; AVARILLA, m. John Wilmot; AQUILA; poss. THOMAS, Jr.; and poss. a dau. who m. (?) Cotteral (4:271, 279; 136; 153; 210-30:501; 217-WT#2:37; 217-PK:76; 217-IB#2:208).

CARR, SUSAN or SUSANNAH (5), dau. of Walter (1) and Juliatha, b. c.1669; m. 1st c.1687 John Sivick; m. 2nd c.1688 Augustine Hawkins; and 3rd, on 15 Jan. 1701 Thomas Tracey (217-IB#2:273).

CARR, AQUILA (6), s. of Thomas (4) and Elizabeth Price, m.1st 21st d, 2 mo., 1745 Susannah Parrish; m. 2nd Susannah Bond; by 1750 owned 200 a. part Price's Good Will, which he sold to Thos. Cole in 1760; had iss. (by 1st w.): ELIZABETH, b. 22nd d., 1 mo. 1745; RACHEL, b. 13th d., 3 mo. 1747; MARY, m. Francis Matthews on 15th d., 10 m. 1777; JAMES, m. Elizabeth Price; WILLIAM, m. 3rd d., 8 mo., 1791 Sarah Herbert (136; 153; 231-B#H:267; 231-B#Q:332).

CARR, BENJAMIN (7), no known rel. to above, in 1716 purch. from Thomas Hooker 100 a. Carr's Pleasure, part of a larger tract called Samuel's Hope; had iss.: THOMAS, called Thomas, Jr. (67:452).

CARR, THOMAS, Jr. (8), s. of Benjamin (7), in 1750 owned part Samuel's Hope; was received into Gunpowder Meeting in 1750, and is prob. the Thomas Carr who moved to the Carolinas c.1752/3 (136; 153).

CARR, Capt. JOHN, of Balto. Co., imm. from Delaware in 1673 with w. Petronella, and ch.: RICHARD; ELIZABETH; MARY; and PETRONELLA (388).

CARR, PRISCILLA, m. 9 Aug. 1725 William Galloway (131).

CARRAWAY, JOHN, d. in Balto. Co. leaving a will, 30 June 1673 - 8 May 1674, named Francis Peteet, Eliza Boulin, and the son of John Boulin; John Boulin to be exec. (120:81).

CARRINGTON, ALCE,. tried for bast. in Aug. 1729; named Thomas Baker as the father; her dau. Mary bound to Hezekiah Balch to age 16; had dau. Johanna Beesley by William Beesley b. 2 Sept. 1731; ind. for bast. Nov. 1733, her s. James Hogg alias Carrington bound to James Lee; had iss.: MARY, b. by Aug. 1729; JOHANNA BEESLEY, b. 2 Sept. 1731; JAMES HOGG, b. by Nov. 1733 (28:274, 277; 30:139; 128:75).

CARRINGTON, JOHN, imm. to Md. by 1665; by 1692 was in Balto. Co. as a taxable in n. side Patapsco Hund.; m. Catherine (?) who m. as her 2nd husb. John Scutt (whose will named w. Catherine and Henry, Margaret, and Catherine, ch. of John Carrington); the will of John Carrington, 22 March 1695 - 9 April 1696, named w. Catherine, and ch. John, George, Mary, Daniel, Henry, Margaret, and Ann, tracts Carrington's Increase and Carrington's Venture, and directing sons to be of age at 21, and daus. at 16; est. inv. 29 April 1696 by John Wilmot and John Broad and val. at Ł 33.9.6; est. admin. 11 May 1697 by Catherine Carrington; later admin. by Catherine wife of Matthew Organ; had iss.: JOHN; GEORGE; MARY; DANIEL; HENRY; MARGARET (may have m. 1st Philip Connor, and 2nd David Hagan); ANN (in Jan. 1693/4 dep. that Robert Parker, ferryman, had gotten her with child) (2:47, 220; 50:230; 110:54; 121:105; 122:14; 138; 388).

THE CARROLL FAMILIES of BROOKLANDWOOD and THE CAVES have been fully treated in Barnes (259).

CARROLL, CHARLES, Esq., by 1750 owned 500 a. Eleanor O'Carroll, 2500 a. Clynmalira, and 282 a. Come By Chance, and 321 a. Howard's Range (153:99).

CARROLL, CHARLES, Esq., and Co., by 1750 owned 100 a. Bond's Improvement, 920 a. Frederickstadt, 1568 a. Georgia, 100 a. of Organ's Fancy, 200 a. New Town, and other tracts (153:101).

CARROLL, CHARLES, Jr. (s. of Dr. Charles Carroll), in 1750 owned 1770 a. Cole's Caves, 170 a. Lisard, 100 a. Choate's Delight, and 100 a. Pleasant Green (153:101).

CARROLL, CHARLES, in 1750 owned 35 a. Rich Neck Park, 800 a. Georgia, 384 a. Carroll's Island, 300 a. Neglect, 47 a. Dettington, and other tracts (153:100).

CARROLL, Dr. CHARLES, in 1750 owned 106 a. Smith's Forest and part Yates' Forbearance (153:96).

CARROLL, DANIEL, in 1750 his heirs owned 500 a. of Eleanor O'Carroll, 200 a. Litterluna, 500 a. Burgess' Camp, 2500 a. of Clynmalira, 625 a. Valley of Jehosophat, and other tracts (153:98).

CARROLL, CATHERINE, in March 1745/6 James Campbell admitted paternity of her child (35:818).

CARROLL, DANIEL, ind. for bast. in June 1744 (35:228).

CARROLL, EDWARD, m. Catherine (?) and had iss.: MARY, b. 30 Jan. 1729; MORDECAI, b. 18 June 1731; CATHERINE, b. 10 June 1734 (128:83).

CARROLL, JAMES, m. 24 Nov.1736 Ann Bond; by 1750 owned part Harris' Trust; had iss.: ELIZABETH, b. 12 May 1738; JAMES BOND, b. 22 Feb. 1739; PETER BOND, b. 6 May 1741; MARY, b. 12 April 1745; ELINOR, b. 20 July 1747; ANN, b. 17 Dec. 1749; JOHN, b. 5 June 1752; SARAH, b. 15 Dec. 1754; HANNAH, b. 26 Aug. 1757; BENJAMIN, b. 25 Aug. 1760 (131; 153).

CARROLL, JOHN, of Balto. Co., Gent., gave his age as 51 in 1741 (310:120).

CARROLL, JOHN, m. 24 Dec. 1760 Cas. Welch (131).

CARROLL, PETER, m. 4 May 1710 Mary Renshaw (128:87).

CARROLL, PETER, m. 8 June 1739 Anne extx. of William Hitchcock; by 1750 he owned 135 a. of Expectation and 15 a. Barton's Chance; had iss.: ELEANOR, b. 23 March 1739/40 (131; 153).

CARROLL, PETER, had antenuptial agreement with Elizabeth Kitely on 2 Oct. 1766 when she conv. all her est. to William Kitely (91: 259).

CARSE, MARY, servant, with 2 years to serve, in inv. of est. of William Robinson, July 1717 (52:123).

CARSEY, THOMAS, in Balto. Co. by 1694 as a taxable in Spesutia Hund. (139).

CARTEE, BRIAN, m. 2 Jan. 1750 Frances LeShordie, and had iss.: MARY, b. 1751; JOHN, b. 1754; HANNAH, b. 14 Nov. 1757; MARGARET, b. 12 Jan. 1760; FRANCIS, b. 14 April 1762 (131:37, 18/r, 66/r, 138/r, 143/r).

CARTEE, DARBY; m. 14 Nov. 1756 Susannah Wooling; had iss.: JOHN, b. 1 April 1758; MARGRETT, b. 10 June 1761 (131:48, 78/r, 143/r).

CARTEE (CARTY), TIMOTHY, ind. for bast. in Nov. 1737; as serv. of George Presbury was tried for getting a bast. on the body of Ann Belloes in March 1737/8 (31:129, 189).

CARTER, JOHN (1), in Balto. Co. by 1718; d. by 23 June 1733; m. Elizabeth (?) who m. 2nd Thomas Green and/or Thomas Gidden; Carter's est. admin. 23 June 1733 by Thomas Green and wife Elizabeth; admin. on 28 July 1736 by Thomas and Elizabeth Gidden; had iss.: RICHARD, b. 17 Oct. 1718; ROBERT, b. 4 Xber (Dec.?) 1721; ABRAHAM, b. 7 June 1728 (prob. d. young); ELIZABETH, alive in March 1736 (3:124, 213; 31:3; 133:4, 21).

CARTER, RICHARD (2), s. of John (1) and Elizabeth, b. 17 Oct. 1718; m. by 16 Feb. 1750 Rebecca (?); in 1750 owned 75 a. Egypt; conv. sons John and Josias parts of Egypt on 6 Dec. 1777 and son Joseph his third part of Stoney Hill in Feb. 1779; had iss.: JOSEPH, b. 16 Feb. 1750; JOHN, alive in Dec. 1777; JOSIAS, alive in Dec. 1777 (133:4, 88; 153:96; 231-WG#A:387, 389; 231-WG#C:300).

CARTER, Col. EDWARD, of Nansemond and Upper Norfolk Co., Va.; in July 1661 surv. 400 a. Carter's Rest, later sold to Edward

Beedle; later was in Nansemond Co., Va., when he bought the res.
of Planter's Delight from Thomas Goldsmith; in Oct. 1662 bought
200 a. of land from John Collett which he assigned to his bro.-
in-law Joseph Hopkins in Feb. 1667/8 (93; 95; 211:4).

CARTER, JAMES, m. Hannah (b. c.1713), dau. of John and Mary
Chenoweth.

CARTER, JOHN, of Lancaster Co., Va., had dau. Elizabeth who
m. Col. Nathaniel Utie of Md., c. Jan. 1667; Utie settled one-
third of Spesutia Manor on her in a marriage settlement (207-
CD:3, 4).

CARTER, JOHN, servant to Garrett Garrettson, judged to be 13
yrs old in June 1714 (21:512).

CARTER, JOHN, m. Frances (---) by July 1748; in Aug. 1751 he
and Frances conv. 50 a. Carter's Choice to William Wright; had
iss.: WILLIAM, b. 2 July 1748; MARY, b. 18 Jan. 1751; SARAH, b.
25 Feb. 1753; ELIZABETH, b. 4 April 1756 (81:227; 134:23, 28).

CARTER, RACHEL, tried for bast. in Nov. 1755, and named Joseph
Merryman as the father of her child (40:400).

CARTER, RICHARD, transp. by 1668; was assigned land in Nov.
1663 by William Lewis; in March 1663/4 Richard and wf. Catherine
authorized John Guyn to obtain from Howell Powell an acknowledgment of conv. for 300 a. that Lewis sold to Carter. (93; 388).

CARTER, WILLIAM, d. by 12 Sept. 1744 when his est. was admin.
by William Carter, admin. with will annexed; one-third est. went
to widow (3:365).

CARTER, WILLIAM, in 1750 owned 105 a. of Merryman's Lot (153).

CARTER, WILLIAM, m. Anne (?), and had three ch., b. in St.
Paul's Par.: JOHN, b. 14 June 1736; RACHEL, b. 11 March 1737/8;
SOLOMON, b. 19 March 1758 (twenty year span!) (133:50, 58, 101).

CARTER, WILLIAM, m. Mary Day on 24 June 1759; had iss.: JOHN,
b. 8 March 1761 (131:54, 141/r).

CARTREELE, PARMELE, in March 1720/1 ind. for bast. (23:435).

CARVER, WILLIAM, d. by 22 April 1699 when his est. was admin.
by Edward Finch and Aug. Morrow and val. at 4100 lbs. tob. plus
£ 68.0.0 (48:88).

CARVILLE, (?) (1), was the father of at least two ch.: ROBERT,
b. c.1636, d. by 1705; THOMAS, d. post 1709 (313:109-110).

CARVILLE, ROBERT (2), s. of (?) (1), and bro. of Thomas (3),
b. c.1636, d. by 1705; imm. to Md. c.1669 with w. Johanna, dau.
of Alexander D'Hinozossa, Dutch Gov. of Del.; held many public
offices incl. that of delegate from St. Mary's City to the Assembly of Md., 1674-1675, 1676-1682, and 1682-1684; never held any
office after 1689 as he was a Catholic; had iss.: MARGARET, d.
by 1721, m. Cecil Butler (313:109-110; 370:202; 388).

CARVILLE, THOMAS (3), s. of (?) (1), and bro. of Robert (2),
d. after 1709; transp. to Md. by 1669; res. in St. Marys and
Calvert Counties until 1682 when he moved to Kent Co.; m. Susannah (?); he and wife were legatees in will of John Eyres of Chas.
Co., Nov. 1702; had iss.: JOHN, d. 1709 (313:110; 388).

CARVILLE, JOHN (4), s. of Thomas (3) and Susannah, d. by 1709; m. Mary Phillips, dau. of James and Susannah (?) (Orchard); Mary m. as her 2nd husb. Richard Smithers; Carville was a delegate to the Assembly from Kent and Cecil Counties; will, 20 May 1709 - 6 Sept. 1709, named w. Mary and ch.: John, and four daus.; also named bros.-in-law James Phillips and Aquila Paca; had iss.: JOHN, alive 1750; AVARILLA, m. 31 Oct, 1717 Edward Hall; SUSANNA, m. (?) Johnson (by whom she had a daughter Mary); PHOEBE, m. Charles Hynson; BLANCHE, m. 1st Parker Hall, and 2nd Luke Griffith (66:57; 122:163; 313:110-112; 370:202).

CARVILLE, JOHN (5), s. of John (4) and Mary, alive 1750 when he owned 255 a. Pool's Island; m. Jane Harris on 25 Nov. 1732, and had iss.: MARY, b. 4 Aug. 1736 (153:59; 313:112).

CARVILLE, MARY, m. 14 Nov. 1710 Roger Matthews (129).

CARY. See CAREY.

CASDROP, JOHN, d. by 20 Dec. 1757 when Thomas Casdrop, admin., posted bond with Joseph Lusby; est. admin. by sd. Thomas on 25 April 1759; had iss.: THOMAS, of age in 1757 (4:278; 11:392).

CASEBOLT, THOMAS, was in Balto. Co. by 1750 as the owner of Casebolt's Delight, 50 a.; on 26 Jan. 1754 conv. the tract to John Gill; m. Sarah (?) who joined him in the sale (82:149; 153: 65).

CASEY, JAMES, age c.23, runaway serv. of Christopher Divers on Gunpowder Neck, April 1748 (385:14).

CASEY, JOHN, in June 1724 conv. cattle to his s. John; had iss.: JOHN, alive 1724 (69:265).

CASH, MARY, servant with 4½ yrs. to serve in the inv. of John Roberts, appraised 20 Sept. 1729 (51:242).

CASSADY, JAMES, m. Mary (?); had iss.: JAMES, b. 4 Dec. 1734 (128:34).

CASSADY, MARGARET, m. Edward Mulain (q.v.).

CASSADAY or CASSATEY, MARY, age 3, in Aug. 1746 ordered to serve Robert Jeffreys to age 16 (36:117).

CASSADY, or CASSADAY, SAMUEL, s. of Mary Murph-(?), b. 6 June 1759 (129:374).

CASSIDY, SIM, m. Elinor (?), and had iss.: CATHERINE, b. 1 March 1756 (129:358).

CASTEPHENS, THOS., had 15 mos. to serve in inv. of John Boring, Oct. 1690 (51:6).

CASTOLO, JOHN, age c. 22, runaway serv. from Samuel Webb, June 1744 (384:450).

CASWELL, RICHARD, b. 1685, London, Eng.; came to Balto. Co. c.1712; d. 1755 in Johnston Co., N.C.; m. 12 Jan. 1723 Christian Dallam, dau. of Richard and Elizabeth Dallam; delegate to Lower House of Assembly from Balto. Co. 1738, 1739-1741; also sheriff, justice, and coroner; admin. est. of Brian Taylor on 11 Dec. 1738 and 31 Oct. 1741, and 17 Aug. 1743; had iss.: ELIZABETH, b. 1724, d. 1725; WILLIAM, b. 8 Dec. 1726, d. 1755 on shipboard on voyage to Md.; RICHARD, b. 3 Aug. 1729, d. 1789, was Gov. of N. C.;

MARY, b. Aug. 1731; MARTIN, b. 15 Feb. 1733, d. 1789; JOSEPH, stillborn 1736; CHRISTIAN, b. 1737, d. 1758; BENJAMIN, b. 1732, d. 1792; JOSEPH WINSTON, b. 1739, d. 1761; SAMUEL, b. 1742, d. 1785; ANN, b. 1742, d. 1784 (4:7, 38, 82, 344; 131; 370).

CATCHAM, JOSEPH, bought 50 a. Come By Chance from John Dorsey (71:43).

CATCHAM, SARAH, orphan whom murderer John Berry planned to marry, Dec. 1751 (385).

CATISAY, JOHN COCK, admin. est. of Emanuel Selah in Aug. 1711 (1:252).

CAUSELL, THOMAS. See CANSELL, THOMAS.

CAVANAGH, JAMES, Irish, runaway conv. serv. from William Bennett, June 1748 (385:20).

CAVE, JAMES, d. by 7 March 1733, when admin. bond was posted by Samuel Webster with Richard and Daniel Ruff; est. admin. on 16 April 1736 (3:215; 11:284).

CAVENAH, PATRICK, m. by 8 Dec. 1752 Mary, extx. of John Renshaw of Balto. Co.; conv. land to Samuel Webb (39:517; 81:480; 201-33:309).

CAWDRICK, JNO., in 1750 owned 103 a. Little Britain (153).

CAWEN. See COWEN.

CAWTHORN/CAWTHRAN, WILLIAM, minister of St. John's Par.; d. having made a will on 11 April 1739, naming as legatees: William Caswell, Rev. Dunbar in Va., Thomas Norris, Sr., Mrs. Mary Crockett, Dr. Josias Middlemore, Dr. Wakeman, Dr. Walker, Maj. Thomas White, Capt. Richard Caswell, Rev. Joseph Hooper, William Dallam, John Lloyd, Walter Tolley, Edward Day, William Bradford, Gilbert Crockett, Thomas Coale, and housekeeper Mary Haycock; est. was admin. by Josias Middlemore (5:31; 127).

CAWTHREY, JOHN, m. 27 Aug. 1731 Isabel Allen (128:61).

CEELEY or SEALAH, EMANUEL, transp. by 1676; was in Balto. Co. by 1694 as a taxable in Spesutia Hund.; d. 14 Jan. 1708; in Nov. 1684 was sued by John Wright for killing a horse; est. inv. in 1709 by John Cottrell and William Loney and val. at £ 4.15.4; est. admin. by John Cock Catisay on 8 Aug. 1711 (1; 48:252; 128; 139; 388). (He m. by Sept. 1698 Sarah; 63:292).

CHADBOURNE, WILLIAM, m. by 28 Nov. 1674 the wid. of Richard Faxon or Fexton of Balto. Co.; Chadbourne had imm. to Cecil Co. c.1669 and was Deputy Surveyor of Balto. and Somerset Counties, Nov. 1675 (2; 388).

CHADWELL or SHADWELL, JOHN (1), was transp. to Westmoreland Co., Va., by Wm. Heaberd and Wm. Horton in 1663; transp. to Md. c.1665; claimed land for service in 1670; in Aug. 1670 bought 100 a. at Hunting Neck from Godfrey and Mary Harmer; d. by 1 Dec. 1676 when wid. Catherine Chadwell posted admin. bond with Robert Benger & David Jones; wid. Catherine m. as her 2nd husb. afsd. Benger by 15 April 1677/8 when she admin. Chadwell's est.; had iss.: JOHN (2:41; 13:449; 96:231; 388; 420:481).

CHADWELL, JOHN (2), s. of John (1), was a taxable in n. side Gunpowder Hund. in 1694; on 6 March 1700 was s. and heir of John

Chadwell, dec., when he sold to Daniel Scott 150 a. Scott's
Lodge: m. by Sept. 1701 Mary (?) who joined him in sale of 190 a.
Stanharket and 100 a. Chestnut Neck to Daniel Scott; d. by 21
July 1724 leaving a dau. Margaret; had iss.: MARGARET, m. by
21 July 1724 John Jones who joined his w. in another deed con-
veying Chestnut Neck, Stanharket, and Harman's Hope to Daniel
Scott the Younger, s. of Daniel Scott the Elder (66:12, 95; 69:
352; 139).

CHAFINCHE, JO'N, admin. the est. of Chris. Green on 9 Nov.
1717 (1:313).

CHALK/CHOCKE, GABRIEL (1), b. c.1650, d. c.1700; transp. to
Md. by James Berry c.1672; m. Anne (?), and was the father of:
JOHN, b. c.1680 (388; 570; 571; 572).

CHALK, JOHN (2), s. of Gabriel (1), b. c.1680, d. 1736 in A.
A. Co., Md.; m. Margaret Tudor on 14 Oct. 1703 in St. James' Par.;
had iss.: JOHN, b. 1704; GEORGE, b. 1706; SARAH, b. 1708; MARY,
b. 1710; MARTHA, b. 1713. (570).

CHALK, JOHN (3), s. of John (2) and Margaret, b. 1704, d. by
24 June 1765; m. Mary (?); was a member of Gunpowder Meeting;
will, 16 day, 2 mo., 1762 - 24 June 1765; named s. George (to
have 24 a. Chock's Addition and 21 a. Ogg King of Bashan); sons
Joshua and John (to share Chock's Reserve and Dulany's Adventure),
son Tudor (to have 100 a.), and daus. Margaret, Mary, Elizabeth,
Sarah, Martha, and Priscilla, and w. Mary; est. admin. 11 Nov.
1766 when acct. stated one dau. had m. Daniel Thompson and one
had m. Thomas James; and dau. Sarah m. (?) Clark; had iss.:
MARGARET, b. 19, 5, 1736; MARY, b. 30, 12 (Feb.) 1737, m. Daniel
Thompson; ELIZABETH, b. 23, 12 (Feb.) 1739, m. Thomas James;
SARAH, b. 10, 1 (March) 1741, m. (?) Clarke; GEORGE, b. 1 Jan.
1744; d. 1828 having m. 1st Elizabeth Hughes and 2nd Hannah (?);
MARTHA, b. 24 March 1747, m. 1st Alexander Smith and 2nd Henry
James; JOSHUA, twin, b. 23 Oct. 1749; JOHN, twin, b. 23 Oct. 1749;
TUDOR, b. 26 Oct. 1752, d. 1815; PRISCILLA, m. Edward Blaney (7;
112; 136).

CHAMBERLAIN, THOMAS (1), was in Balto. Co. by 1708; d. by 20
Dec. 1722 when his wid. Mary m. Henry Weatherall; Thomas admin.
est. of James Gallion on 31 March 1708, and est. of Robert Shaw on
in May 1712; had his serv. Rachel Jones set free in Nov. 1718
for not having taught her to read; owned 160 a. Sarah's Delight
and God's Providence originally both laid out for John Tilyard
in 1676; on 20 Oct. 1703 Thomas Grunwyn of St. Marys Co. left
500 a. to sis. Mary Chamberlain (land was in Balto. Co. and may
have been the 500 a. Cullen's Addition assigned to Thomas Grunin
in 1683); had iss.: JOHN, b. 17 Dec. 1713; THOMAS, b. 7 May 1717;
GEORGE, b. 27 Dec. 1720 (1:362; 2:90; 23:35; 131:5, 9, 24, 25,
2/r, 39/r; 122:36; 211:44, 63).

CHAMBERLAIN, JOHN (2), s. of Thomas (1), was b. 17 Dec. 1713,
and d. 1775 in Balto. Co.; m. 31 Oct. 1737 Margaret Gittings,
dau. of Thomas and Elizabeth (Redgrave) Gittings; on 14 Jan. 1773
leased land from Lord Balto. for the lifetimes of his children,
Thomas, Elizabeth, and Mary; his will, 12 Oct. 1774 - 15 Dec.
1775, named w. Margaret and ch.: Thomas, Philip, Samuel (father
of John Hethcote Chamberlain), James, John, Mary Lucas, Priscilla,
Margaret, Elizabeth, Cassandra, Rachel, and Susanna Standiford;
est. admin. 16 April 1791 with legacies paid to: Philip, Elisha
Green, John, Elizabeth Hathcote, and James (all named Chamberlain); will of Margaret Chamberlain made 6 Aug. 1795, proved 29
April 1801; had iss.: ELIZABETH, b. 12 Oct. 1738, m. Darby Henly,
Jr., on 12 April 1757; THOMAS, b. 19 Feb. 1739, m. Eliz. Wilkin-

son on 9 Dec. 1764; MARY, b. 17 July 1743, m. Thomas Lucas on 2 March 1762; MARGARET, b. 23 Feb. 1744 (sic); PHILIP, b. 12 Dec. 1746; JOHN, d. by 8 Feb. 1792 (est. was admin. by Richardson Stuart, and John Kittleman was paid for boarding a ch. of the dec.); JAMES; PRISCILLA; CASSANDRA; RACHEL; SUSANNA, m. Abraham Standiford on 8 Oct. 1769; SAMUEL, m. Elizabeth Pak't (Hathcote?) on 24 Oct. 1771, and d. by 15 June 1791 (left a s. John Heathcote Chamberlain) (2:49, 61, 66, 92/r; 10:356, 384, 517; 80:487; 115:393; 210-40:631).

CHAMBERS, ANTHONY, was granted a cert. from Gunpowder Mtg. to Monacacy Mtg., 26 d, 6 mo., 1741 (136).

CHAMBERS, JAMES, m. by 13 Nov. 1775 Mary, dau. of John Tipton; sold land of John Tipton in Nov. 1775 and Oct. 1790 (231-AL#M:513; 231-WG#FF:124).

CHAMBERS, SARAH, ind. for bast., June 1734 (30:253).

CHAMBERS, THOMAS, m. 6 Aug. 1748 Mary Fox and had iss.: WILLIAM, b. 1747; ELINOR, b. 1749; poss. THOMAS, b. 1752; poss. JOS., b. 1755; JNO., b. 1 Oct. 1760 (131:64/r, 139/r).

CHAMBLEY, JOHN (1), b. c.1659, alive in 1731; in Nov. 1724 pet. to be levy free and stated he had been a res. of the county for 26 yrs; in March 1731 stated he was 72 yrs, and had had a sore leg for 10 years; prob. had: JOHN (27:37; 29:229).

CHAMBLEY, JOHN (2), prob. s. of John (1), m. Margery Cheek on or after 1 Oct. 1708 when the banns were pub.; alive in Aug. 1723; had iss.: MARY, b. c.1709, in June 1714 was bound to John and Sarah Rawlings; in Aug. 1723 at age 14 was bound to William Bradford and his wife to age 16 (21:508; 25:420; 128:24).

CHAMNESS, ANTHONY, m. 24 Nov. 1735 Sarah Cole, dau. of Joseph; Anthony may have been b. c.1713 in London; Sarah was b. 1 May 1718; they moved to Fred. Co., Md., then to Orange Co., N. C. (112:144; 133; Gen. and Hist., query 4061).

CHAMNEY, MARY, ind. and tried for bast in March 1733/4; see George Edgerton (30:183, 199).

CHAMPION, ISAAC, named as the father of Mary Fitzpatrick's bast. child in June 1731 (29:168).

CHANCE, JEREMIAH, was in Balto. Co. by 25 Nov. 1752 when he m. Wealthy Ann Milldews; had iss.: ANNE, b. 21 March 1754 (poss. m. Jonathan Hunter c.1770); MARY, b. 25 Nov. 1755; ELIZABETH, b. 6 March 1758; JOHN, b. 6 Nov. 1759; SARAH, b. 28 Nov. 1761; WILLIAM, b. 28 Feb. 1764; WEALTHY ANN, b. 14 Jan. 1766 (131:136/r, 141/r, 144/r, 152/r).

CHANCY. See CHAUNCEY.

CHANEY, BENJAMIN, m. June 1719 Ruth Chaney; had iss.: SARAH, b. 25 April 1720, m. James Murphy on 15 Dec. 1746; RUTH, b. 20 June 1722; BENJAMIN, b. 20 June 1722; ELIZABETH, b. 20 Dec. 1726; RICHARD, b. Nov. 1730; JACOB, b. May 1733; ELEANOR, b. 26 Feb. 1738; GREENBERRY, b. Aug. 1740; THOMAS, b. July 1743 (131:31, 85/r, 106/r, 107/r).

CHANEY. See also CHENEY.

CHAPMAN, ROBERT (1), was in Balto. Co. by 1705 as a taxable in Elk Ridge Hund.; d. by 9 Nov. 1749; m. Elizabeth (?); pat. 100 a.

of Betty's Adventure in 1710; he and w. Elizabeth sold this to John Hall in 1720; bought 100 a. Yate's Forbearance from John and Elizabeth Yate; sold same to William Hammond in Oct. 1741; exempt from levy in Nov. 1739; admin. bond posted 9 Nov. 1749 by Robert Chapman with William Macclan and Nathaniel Smith; est. inv. 7 Feb. 1749/50, filed by Robert Chapman and signed by Joseph Arnold and John Chapman as kin; had iss.: ROBERT, b. c.1707/8; SUSANNA, m. Joseph Arnold on 20 July 1736; JOHN; poss. ISAAC who m. Mary Fitzpatrick on 27 Oct. 1734 (11:366; 32:80; 63:473; 68:191; 76:31; 133; 205-41; 207; 291:55 ; 573; 574).

CHAPMAN, ROBERT (2), s. of Robert (1), b. c.1707/8, gave age as 68 on 9 Dec. 1776; may be the Robert who m. Elizabeth Taylor on 30 June 1736; was m. to Margaret (?) by Dec. 1749 when as "wheelwright, son and heir of Robert Chapman, dec." with w. Margaret sold Yate's Forbearance to Daniel Dulany; in 1750 owned 200 a. Buck Forest; in May 1759 with w. Margaret conv. Buck Forest to one Nathan Chapman; elected churchwarden of St. Thomas' Parish; had iss.: ROBERT, d. 1804; LUKE; NATHAN, d. 1807; DANIEL, d. 1753; JAMES, d. 1772; HELEN, b. 18 June 1763, d. 1823, m. Thomas Gorsuch in 1778 (80:385; 83:380; 133; 135; 153:200).

CHAPMAN, JOHN (3), s. of Robert (1), so placed because he signed the inv. of Robert Chapman in 1749/50 as kin; may be the John who was father of Martha Bastock's child in Nov. 1743; prob. the John who m. Mary, wid. of William Hall on 17 July 1746; prob. the John who signed the 1768 petition favoring removal of county seat from Joppa to Balto. Town (5; 35:72, 171; 133; 200-61).

CHAPMAN, LUKE (4), s. of Robert (2), prob. d. by 1790; m. 1754 Sophia, wid. of Charles Conaway and dau. of John and Mary Wooden; in Sept. 1755 bought 132 a. Morgan's Tent Resurveyed from George Ogg; elected to vestry of St. Thomas' Par. in April 1764; living 1779 when he conv. Morgan's Tent Res. to Dorsey Barnes; wife Sophia was b. 29 Sept. 1727; had iss.: CHARLES, b. 20 Oct. 1755 or 1756; MARGARET, b. 5 March 1757; DANIEL, b. 10 Nov. 1758; STEPHEN, b. 19 Jan. 1760; MARY, b. 13 Aug. 1761; SARAH, b. 20 July 1763; LEAH, b. 24 May 1766; EPHRAIM, b. 27 Jan. 1767; SOPHIA, b. 29 Jan. 1769; SAMUEL, b. 9 Nov. 1770 (82:453; 133; 134:44, 45, 293; 135; 231-WG#C:118).

CHAPMAN, NATHAN (5), s. of Robert (2), b. c.1740, d. in 1807; m. Rebecca Griffith in 1760; Rebecca d. 1827; in 1759 bought 50 a. Buck Forest from Robert and Margaret Chapman; in 1763 bought 132 a. White Oak Bottom from Thomas and Martha Askew; with w. Rebecca conv. Francis Brothers 50 a. Buck Forest and 25 a. Nathan's Desire in Aug. 1764; bought 40 a. Parrish's Folly from Richard and Margaret Davis in Sept. 1769; left a will, 19 May 1807 - 8 July 1807; had iss.: JEMIMA, m. by lic. 2 Nov. 1780 William Hudson and by 1827 was in Mo.; ELIZABETH, m. by lic. 20 Feb. 1781 John Dettor, and by 1827 in Va.; WILLIAM, b. 1827 in Va.; REBECCA, m. by lic. of 5 Oct. 1791 Benjamin Gist Vaughan; JAMES, m. by lic. of 15 Feb. 1798 Rachel Merryman; NATHAN, Jr.; JOB, b. 1776; HELEN, b. 1774, d. 2 March 1831, m. John Reister, III, on 20 Dec. 1801; MARY, m. by 1827 Matthias Rider; HANNAH, d. 14 Sept. 1823; JOSHUA, d. 1795 (83:380; 87:470; 89:318; 117:198; 135; 231-AL#A).

CHAPMAN, BENJAMIN, b. c.1760 in Balto. Co., Md., d. in Roane Co., Tenn.; served in the Rev. War from Md.; m. Sarah McCorkle; by 1790 was in Washington Co., Tenn.; had iss.: SAMUEL; MARGARET, m. (?) Ford . (573).

CHAPMAN, ELIZABETH, bore a child and named John Arnold as the father, Nov. 1733 (30:142).

CHAPMAN, JOHN, surv. 150 a. Chapman's Fellowship in Jan. 1698 (211:27).

CHAPMAN, JOHN, married Hannah Markum when banns were pub. in June 1701 (128:11).

CHAPMAN, JOHN, m. Ann (?) and had iss.: JAMES, b. 10 Feb. 1719 (131).

CHAPMAN, NICHOLAS, b. 1758 in Balto. Co., Md., d. 25 July 1851 in Burke Co., N. C.; fought in the Rev. War from Burke Co.; m. and had iss.: GEORGE; JAMES; ROBERT; JOSHUA; JOHN; and MARY, m. (?) Hoil (574).

CHAPMAN, RICHARD, in Balto. Co. by 3 Jan. 1670/1, when he purch. land from Robert Morgan, cooper, and w. Bennett (97:123).

CHAPMAN, ROBERT, in Balto. Co. by 4 Aug. 1668 when he purch. land at Black Wolf Neck from Richard Farendall; but by Oct. 1672 was in Kent Co., Md., when he sold Wolf's Neck to Thomas Phelps of A. A. Co. (95:258; 99:347).

CHAPMAN, WILLIAM, was in Balto. Co. by 13 Jan. 1670/1 when he purch. part Taylor's Mount from John Owen; conv. the land back to Owens in Sept. 1671 (97:125; 98:45).

CHAPPELL, HENRY, in Balto. Co. by 1692 as a taxable in s. side Patapsco Hund. (138).

CHAPPELL, JOHN, merch., b. c.1732, gave his age as 53 in 1785 (310:121).

CHARNOCK, MARGARET, age 12 in Sept. 1737, was bound in the preceding June to William Robinson of Spesutia until she was 16 (31:48).

CHARLETON, HENRY, in Balto. Co. by 1750 as the owner of 210 a. The Grove (153:21).

CHASE, SAMUEL (1), freeman of London, member of the Honorable Company of Tylers and Bricklayers, owned land in Maidenhead Court and Westminster, d. by 1725; m. Henrietta Catherine Davis who d. 1725; had iss.: THOMAS, b. c.1703; RICHARD, d. c.1742; an unnamed son   (575).

CHASE, Rev. THOMAS (2), s. of Samuel (1) and Henrietta, was b. c. 1703; d. in Balto. Co. d. 1779; educ. at Cambridge Univ.; inducted in Stepney Par., Somerset Co., Md.; m. 1st Matilda, dau. of Thomas Walker of Som. Co.; she d. 1741, and he m. 2nd on 19 July 1763 in St. Paul's Par., Balto. Co., Ann Birch, eld. dau. of Thomas Birch, chirurgeon and man-midwife of Warwick, Eng.; was rector of Stepney Par., Som. Co., Md., from 1740, and rector of St. Paul's Par., from 1743 until his death; had iss.: by 1st w.: SAMUEL, b. 1741, Signer of the Declaration of Independence and Justice of the Supreme Court; by 2nd w.: THOMAS, b. 1765, d. 1773; ANN; ELIZABETH; GEORGE RUSSEL BIRCH; RICHARD   (133).

CHASE, RICHARD (3), s. of Samuel (1) and Henrietta, d. 1742; educ. at Cambridge Univ., Eng.; chaplain to Lord Balto.; came to Md., where he was Rector of St. Margaret's Par., Westminster, A. A. Co., and other parishes; m. Margaret Frances, dau. of London merchant Jeremiah Townley; had iss.: RICHARD, d. 1757; JEREMIAH, delegate to the Assembly from St. M. Co., 1754-1755. m. Judith Dent, and d. s. p. 1755; (Judith d. 1790) (370).

CHASE, SAMUEL (4), s. of Rev. Thomas (2) and Matilda, b. 1741, d. 1811, Signer of the Declaration of Independence and Justice of the United States Supreme Court; chose Mayberry Helms as his guardian in June 1759; m. 1st Ann, dau. of Thomas and Agnes Baldwin of A. A. Co., and 2nd, in 1784, Hannah Kitty Giles (44; 370; 575).

CHASE, RICHARD (5), s. of Rev. Richard (3) and Margaret Frances, d. 1757; m. Catherine (?); Balto. lawyer; his will, 3 March 1756 - 23 Dec. 1757, named ch. Jeremiah and Frances Hatton; and also named Samuel Chase, son of Rev. Thomas Chase; admin. bond posted 25 Feb. 1758 by Dr. John Stevenson with Thomas Cockey Deye and William Young; est. admin. 4 May 1759; had iss.: JEREMIAH TOWNLEY, b. 1748, d. 1828 (m. 24 June 1778 Hester Baldwin, dau. of Thomas and Agnes Baldwin of A. A. Co.); FRANCES HATTON, m. Richard Moale (133; 370; 575:10).

CHASE, JOHN, in Balto. Co. by 1692 was a taxable in n. side of Patapsco Hund. (138).

CHASE, JOHN THOMAS, in July 1695 surv. 400 a. called Chevy Chase in Balto. Co. (211:55).

CHATE, or CHASE, HENRY; inv. filed in Balto. Co. (53:242).

CHATHAM/CHEETAM/CHITTUM, FRANCIS, bur. 9 March 1699; m. Joan (?), prob. the Joan Chattum who married Edward Cantwell on 5 Dec. 1699; admin. bond posted 25 May 1699 by Joan Chatham with Henry Jackson; est. inv. 3 June, 1699, by Richard Perkins and William Lofton and val. at £ 3.13.8; had iss.: ELIZABETH, b. 13 Oct. 1693 (11:300; 48:286; 128:6).

CHATHAM, HENRY, m. Mary (?) who d. by March 1740/1; had iss.: FRANCIS, b. 1 Oct. 1726; EDMUND (or EDWARD), b. 23 June 1729, and age 11 in March 1740/1 when his mother died and he was placed in care of Bezaleel Foster (33:7, 8; 128:57, 65).

CHAUNCEY/CHANCY, GEORGE (1), was in Balto. Co. by 1692 as a taxable in n. side Patapsco Hund.; m. 22 June 1706 Sarah Smith (nee Hollis), wid. of Benjamin Smith; on 2 Feb. 1708 he and his wife admin. the estates of William Hollis and Benjamin Smith; his will, 18 March 1715/6 - 5 June 1717, named w. Sarah, and son George (not yet 18, to have Turkey Neck); admin. bond posted 5 June 1717 by Sarah Chancey with John Parker and Joshua Cockey; est. inv. 1 Oct. 1717 by Roger Matthews and David Thomas, and val. at 7643 lbs. tob., plus £ 277.8.7; wid. Sarah m. as her 3rd husb. Benjamin Hanson by March 1722 when they were sued by James Croke or Crooke; had iss. GEORGE, b. 12 May 1708; JAMES, b. 2 April 1712, may have d. young (2:170, 202; 11:281; 25:292; 52:289; 110: 143; 128:18, 22, 27; 138).

CHAUNCEY, GEORGE (2), s. of George (1) and Sarah, b. 12 May 1708; alive in 1776; m. 28 Nov. 1734 Susanna Ogg; in 1750 owned 75 a. Turkey Neck and 118 a. part Hollis' Refuse; admin. est. of his mother Sarah Hanson on 19 Sept. 1744; in Nov. 1767 conv. prop. to his children: James, Benjamin, Susan, and John; in 1776 at age 68 lived in Harford Lower Hundred with Margaret, age 59, Benjamin, age 17, and Jacob Greenfield, 13, and Mary Greenfield, 9; had iss.: SARAH, b. 26 Nov. 1735; GEORGE, b. 12 Nov. 1738; MARY, b. 3 Sept. 1744; JAMES, b. 18 Oct. 1746; poss. SUSAN, alive 1767; poss. JOHN, alive 1767 (3:378; 128:83, 90, 104; 129:333, 334; 153:31; 230: 168 ff.; 285).

CHAUNCEY, GEORGE (3), s. of George (2) and Susanna, b. 12 Nov. 1738; m. Mary (?); in 1776 was living in Harf. Co. with wife Mary, 29, and following (prob. his ch.): SARAH, b. c.1766; GEORGE, b. c. 1768; MARTHA, b. c.1772; WILLIAM, b. c.1771 (128:104; 285).

CHEEK, MARGERY, m. John Chambley on or after 1 Oct. 1708 when banns were pub. (129:207).

CHEETAM. See CHATHAM.

CHENEY, or CHERRY, (?), m. by 9 Sept. 1759, Margaret, dau. of Patrick Montgomery (111).

CHENEY, BENJAMIN BURGESS, m. Margaret (?), and had iss.: ANN, b. 23 Nov. 1756; RUTH, b. 11 April 1758; ADAM, b. 5 Aug. 1759; RACHEL, b. 18 Dec. 1761 (134:33).

CHENEY. See also CHANEY.

CHENOWETH/CHENNIWORTH/CHENOWITH/CHINWORTH, JOHN (1), progenitor, is said to have been born in St. Martin's In Meneage, Cornwall, England, and to have d. in Frederick Co., Va., in 1746; lived for a while in Balto. Co.; m. Mary (?), claimed by some descendants to have been a member of the noble Calvert Family of Maryland (but proof has not been established); with wife were admins. with will annexed of William Wood of Balto. Co. on 29 Oct. 1737; the will of John Chinoweth, blacksmith, 11 April 1746 - 6 May 1746, named ch. John, Richard, Arthur, William, Thomas, Mary Watson, Hannah Carter, and Ruth Pettit, grandson John Watson, Jr., and son-in-law John Pettit; will was witnessed by Joseph Stanley and Mary Stanley, and William Joliffe; had iss.: JOHN, b. c.1706 in Balto. Co.; MARY, b. c.1708, m. John Watson on 24 May 1733; RICHARD, b. c.1710; HANNAH, b. c.1713, m. James Carter; ARTHUR, b. c.1713, m. Saphira Hooker; WILLIAM, b. c.1718; THOMAS, b. c. 1720, m. Mary Prickett; RUTH, m. John Pettit (209-30:360; 576; 577; 578).

CHENOWETH, JOHN (2), son of John (1) and Mary, b. c.1706 in Balto. Co.; d. c.1770/1 in Frederick Co., Va.; m. Mary Smith on 26 Nov. 1730 in Balto. Co.; had iss.: WILLIAM, b. 8 Jan. 1732; RICHARD, b..c.1734; JOHN, b. 13 Nov. 1735; THOMAS, b. c.1737; ARTHUR, b. c.1742; ABSOLOM, b. 1745; MARY, b. c.1748; ELIZABETH, b. c.1750, m. (?) Stuart; RACHEL, b. c.1753 (131:13/r, 14/r; 133: 50).

CHENOWETH, RICHARD (3), s. of John (1) and Mary, b. c.1710 in Balto. Co., and d. there in 1781; m. Kezia; in 1750 owned 100 a. part Merryman's Adventure; his will, 1 Oct. 1781 - 4 Dec. 1781, named w. Kezia and named these children: RICHARD, b. c.1734; ARTHUR, b. c.1737; THOMAS, b. c.1740; JOSEPH, b. c.1743; JOHN, b. 1746; SUSAN, b. c.1749, m. (?) Price; HANNAH, b. 1752, m. (?) Ashton; KEZIA, b. c.1755, m. (?) Murray; WILLIAM, b. 1758 (112: 434; 153:84).

CHENOWETH, ARTHUR (4), s. of John (1) and Mary, b. c.1716 in Balto. Co., where he d. by 7 April 1802; m. Saphira Hooker; in 1750 he owned 49 a. Arthur's Lot and 100 a. Arthur's Addition; was first to spell his name Chinworth; vestryman of St. Thomas' Par., 1749-50; wife Saphira was dau. of Thomas Hooker; in 1761 he made a deed of gift to s. Arthur, Jr., and in 1768 made a deed of gift to his s. John; his will, 4 Dec. 1800 - 7 April 1802, named ch., Richard, Samuel, Thomas, Ruth Butler, and Hannah Ogg, and Richard's dau. Elizabeth; had iss.: ARTHUR, b. 31 March 1740; HANNAH, b. 20 Nov. 1742; m. (?) Ogg; RICHARD, b. c.1744; JOHN, b. July 1745, moved to Berkeley Co., Va., where he d. 1820; SAMUEL, b. 1 Dec. 1747, also moved to Berkeley Co.; WILLIAM, b. 29 July 1750; THOMAS, b. 21 March 1753; RUTH, b. 1756, m. Amon Butler (116:533; 134:22, 23; 153:17).

CHENOWETH, WILLIAM (5), s. of John (1) and Mary, b. c.1718, d. in Berkeley Co., Va., some time before 20 Dec. 1785; m. Anne (?);

on 12 Feb. 1743/4 he bought land on Mill Creek from John Mills, Sr., of P. G. Co., Md.; on 6 Oct. 1788 Absolom and Anne Chenoweth of Berkeley Co., Va., sold to Adam Smith land conveyed to William Chenoweth by John Mills; will of William Chenoweth of Berkeley Co., made 10 Oct. 1785 - 20 Dec. 1785, named w. Anne, and ch., Absolom and William, Mary, Ann, and Hannah, and heirs of dec. son Joseph; had iss.: ABSOLOM; WILLIAM; JOSEPH, d. in Berkeley Co., Va., leaving a wife Sarah and a dau. Newly; MARY; ANNA; and HANNAH. (576; 577).

CHERN. See CHURN.

CHESHIRE, ELIZABETH, tried for bast., June 1734 (30:265).

The CHEW FAMILY was the subject of an article by Francis B. Culver in Maryland Genealogies, and another article by Joseph C. Hopkins in the Maryland Magazine of Genealogy.

CHEW, JOSEPH, son of Samuel and Ann, was in Balto. Co. by 1750 as the owner of 100 a. Bachelor's Good Luck; m. Sarah (?), who took as her second husband William Yates; Samuel Chew's will, 12 Sept. 1750 - 18 Oct. 1750, named w. Sarah and ch., Thomas (not yet 21), and Elizabeth and Susanna (both under 16); est. admin. 9 May 1757 by William and Sarah Yates, naming three children: ELIZA, age 10 in 1757; SUSANNA, age 8 in 1757; and THOMAS, age 5 in 1757 (5; 111; 153).

CHEW, SAMUEL, in 1750 owned 400 a., part Friendship (153).

CHEW, SAMUEL, d. by 1750 leaving heirs who in 1750 owned 609 a. part Margaret's Lot (153).

CHEW, WILLIAM, d. in Balto. Co. by 15 Nov. 1720 when his admin. bond was posted by his sis. and admnx. Sydney, wife of Charles Pierpoint, with William Hamilton and Peter Shipley; est. inv. on 4 June 1721 by John and Benjamin Howard; est. admin. 14 Jan. 1722 and 1 Nov. 1724 naming these bros. and sisters of the dec.: Benjamin, Ann w. of Christopher Randall, Joanna, Sydney w. of Charles Pierpoint, Margaret w. of Joshua Brown, and Eliza (1; 3; 11:294; 51:270; 205-5:87; N.B.: this account does not agree with that in Culver).

CHEYNE, RODERICK, m. Elizabeth (?), and had iss.: FREDERICK, b. 7 Dec. 1741, d. 25 Jan. 1742; PAMELA, b. 6 Feb. 1743 (may have m. John Owen on 12 Nov. 1761); CHLOE, b. 24 Nov. 1745 at the Balto Co. Free School (131:90/r, 98/r, 60).

CHILCOTT, HUMPHREY (1), progenitor, d. in A. A. Co. in 1708, and was bur. in St. James Parish on 22 Jan. 1708; in 1698 he m. Mary Tindall, who may be the Mary Chilcott who m. Jonathan Tipton on 15 Dec. 1709; there was a Mary Chilcott who m. Paulus Rose on 28 July 1698 in St. James Par., who may have been Humphrey's sister, but the relationship has not been proven; issue of Humphrey and Mary: JAMES, b. 24 May 1702; JOHN, b. 13 Aug. 1703, d. 31 March 1704; JOHN, b. 10 April 1706; MARY, b. 22 March 1708(219-3: 295, 322, 329, 337, 339).

CHILCOTT, JAMES (2), s. of Humphrey (1) and Mary, b. 24 May 1702 in St. James Par., A. A. Co.; m. Elizabeth (?); moved to Balto. Co.; on 5 Aug. 1733 Jonathan Tipton conv. James Chilcott 30 a. Addition to Poor Jamaica Man's Plague; on 29 April 1738 James Chilcott and w. Elizabeth conv. Mary Barney 100 a. part Valiant Hazard; may be the James Chilcott who conv. John Stevenson 50 a. Macclan's Friendship; had iss.: HUMPHREY, b. 26 April 1723; ELIZABETH, b. 4 Dec. 1728 (74:103; 75:64; 84:125; 133:1, 23).

CHILCOTT, JOHN (3), s. of Humphrey (1) and Mary, b. 10 April 1706; m. Margaret (?); on 7 Jan. 1744 John Chilcott conv. to John Pindall 90 a. of Friendship and 77 a. Gist's Search; in 1750 he owned 100 a. pt. Merryman's Adventure; had issue: ROBINSON, b. 8 Dec. 1739; JAMES, b. 4 June 1741; JOHN, b. 30 March 1743; poss. JOSHUA, by 1783 was living in North Hundred, Balto. Co.; poss. HUMPHREY, b. 1749, d. 9 Sept. 1804 in Huntington Co., Penna. (78:29; 133:72; 153:83; See Bibliography).

CHILCOTT, HUMPHREY (4), s. of James (2) and Elizabeth, b. 26 April 1723 in Balto. Co.; m. Sarah, and had iss.: MARY, b. 13 Sept. 1745 (133:1, 85).

CHILCOTT, ROBINSON (5), s. of John (3) and Margaret, b. 8 Dec. 1739; moved to Huntington Co., Penna.; served in the Rev. War in N. C., and d. of swamp fever; had iss.: NICODEMUS, d. in Huntington Co., Penna., of paralysis; JOHN, settled in Tenn.; HEATHCOTE, moved to Licking Co.. Ohio: HUMPHREY, d. in Cromwell Twp., Huntington Co., Penna.; BENJAMIN, b. c.1758, d. 31 July 1854 aged 96; m. Comfort McLain; JAMES, d. c.1838 in Cassville, Pa. (Jordan, The Juniata Valley, III, 1157).

CHILCOTT, JAMES (6), s. of John (3) and Margaret, b. 4 June 1741; m. Elizabeth Ensor, b. 1748, d. 8 June 1832 in Perry Co., Ohio, dau. of George and Elizabeth Ensor; had iss.: JAMES, m. Elizabeth (?); ANNA, m. Robert Curran; JOSHUA, m. Sarah (?); ROBINSON, m. Jemima Chilcott; SARAH, m. Joshua Morrison; NATHAN, m. Honor Chilcote; MARGARET, m. PHILIP MILLER.

CHILCOTT, JOHN (7), s. of John (3) and Margaret, b. 30 March 1743, alive in 1783; m. Providence or Prudence, dau. of George and Elizabeth Ensor; in 1783 owned 47 a. of Henry's Folly; had iss.: ELIJAH: JOHN; JOSEPH; MORDECAI; ELISHA; ELIZABETH; MARGARET; ENSOR (283).

CHILCOTT, HUMPHREY (8), s. of John (3) and Margaret, b. c.1749 in Balto. Co.; d. 9 Sept. 1804 in Huntington Co., Penna.; m. 3 March 1771 Sarah, dau. of George and Elizabeth Ensor; in 1783 was living in Middle River and Back River Upper Hundred; had iss.: ELIZABETH, d. young; DARBY, m. Sarah (?); PRUDENCE; JEMIMA, m. Robinson Chilcott; MICAJAH; HONOR, m. Nathan Chilcott; HUMPHREY, m. Nancy (?); JOHN; ELIZABETH, m. Joseph Cornelius; SARAH, m. (?) Drinker; ENSOR, m. Mary Waters (283).

CHILDS, FRANCIS (1), was in Balto. Co. by 4 March 1667/8 when he conv. Richard Leake, tailor, 500 a. The World's End; poss. the Francis Chilice who was transp. by 1663; by Aug. 1698 was in Cecil Co. when he and Grace Childs wit. the will of John James of Cecil Co.; his will, 11 Jan. 1698/9, proved 5 March 1699/1700, named w. Grace and ch., NATHANIEL; SUSANNA; FRANCIS; and GEORGE (95; 122:175, 195; 388).

CHILDS, GEORGE (2), s. of Francis (1), d. testate in Cecil Co.; will, 3 Dec. 1733 - 18 Jan. 1733/4, named w. Margaret, and ch.: BENJAMIN; NATHANIEL; and HENRY (126:58).

CHILDS, BENJAMIN (3), s. of George (2), was in Balto. Co. by 1750 as the owner of 236 a. part Warrington; m. 26 Dec. 1733, Matty Bellows; d. by 29 April 1755 when admin. bond was posted by admnx. Martha Childs with Robert Greenall and Burch Swan; Martha was prob. the Martha Childs fined for bast. in Nov. 1757, naming Cuthbert Greenwell as the father; iss. of George and Martha: GEORGE, b. 1 Oct. 1737; RACHEL, b. 30 Aug. 1739; MARY, b. 15 March 1742; SARAH, b. 4 Oct. 1744; ELIZ., b. 1 Nov. 1745; SUSANNA, b. 11 Jan. 1747; HANNAH, b. 28 Sept. 1748; Martha alone was the mother of: CUTHBERT GREENWELL CHILDS, b. 1 March 1760 (11:368; 46:75; 131:105/r, 111/r, 119/r, 121/r, 143/r; 153).

CHILDS, BENJAMIN, m. Martty Bellows on 26 Dec. 1733 in St. Stephen's Parish, Cecil Co.; by 1750 a Benjamin Childs was listed in the Baltimore County Debt Book as owning 236 acres, part of a tract called Warrington (153:58; 263:33).

CHILDS, GEORGE, m. Nov. 1736 Martha Smithson, dau. of (?) and Sarah (Mounts) Smithson; Sarah was the sis. of Christopher Mounts and the dau. of wid. Martha Mounts, all of Cecil Co.; had iss.: JOHN, b. April 1738; WILLIAM, b. 5 April 1740, d. May 1744; ELINER b. 20 June 1744 (127:12, 13; 131:108/r).

CHILDS, JOHN, m. 1st, on 17 Dec. 1743 Eliza Mead who d. 9 Aug. 1747, and 2nd on 22 July 1752 Sarah Groves or Crones; by 1st w. had iss.: WILLIAM, b. 1 Sept. 1744, d. the same year; RICHARD, b. 27 Sept. 1744 or 1746 (131:40, 105/r, 115/r, 120/r).

CHILDS, MARK, was transp. by 1663/4, and in Nov. 1684 was in Balto. Co. when John Arden conv. him 150 a. of Waterford (59:159; 388).

CHILDS, MARTHA, of Balto. Co., age 36 in 1756, had a dau. Mary, age 16 in 1756.

CHILSON, DAVID, m. by 25 Aug. 1766 Mary, dau. of John York (230:92).

CHINDALL, PHILIP, servant, with four years to serve in the inv. of the est. of Martha Bowen made 24 April 1704 (51:125).

CHINES, ISABELLA, serv. of Richard Taylor, ind. for bast. in June 1711; named William Powers as the father, Aug. 1711 (21:210, 246).

CHISNALL, JOHN, d. by 1699 when his est. was inv. by Anthony Bale and David Thomas, and val. at £ 27.6.3 plus £ 11.9.16 (for 2756 lbs. of tob. debts, totalling £ 38.15.9 (48:142).

CHISNALL, JOHN, d. 1 April 1714; m. Eleanor (?); his est. was admin. 30 Nov. 1716 by Samuel Jackson; had iss.: THOMAS, b. 2 Sept. 1704 (1:206; 128:29; 129:215).

CHITTUM. See CHATHAM.

CHOATE, CHRISTOPHER (1), was in Balto. Co. as a taxable in the upper part of n. side of Patapsco Hund. in 1706; m. Flora (?); in Aug. 1711 Elizabeth Bud named him as the father of her child; in Aug. 1722 Richard and Zipporah Gist conv. him part Street's Adventure and part Green Spring Traverse; in 1750 owned 100 a. Street's Adventure; had iss.: AUSTAIN or AUGUSTINE, b. 6 Nov. 1716; CHRISTOPHER, b. 12 Aug. 1720; RICHARD, b. 8 Nov. 1722; MARY, b. 5 Oct. 1724; ZABRITT, b. 19 March 1730 (21:251; 69:111; 133: 24; 153:94).

CHOATE, AUGUSTINE (2), s. of Christopher (1), b. 6 Nov. 1716; in June 1739 was tried for fathering the ch. of Sarah Savage; d. by 2 April 1740 when Josephus Murray, Jr., posted admin. bond with John Stinchcomb and John Hamilton (15:280; 22:408; 133:24).

CHOATE, EDWARD, was in Balto. Co. by 1706 as a taxable with Christopher Choate on the upper part of n. side of Patapsco Hund. (291:63).

CHOATE, EDWARD, m. Ellinor Savage on 22 May 1735 (133:153).

CHOATE, EDWARD, Jr., m. by 6 Nov. 1752 Elizabeth, dau. of Samuel Underwood; on that day Edward and Elizabeth conv. John Ford 50 a. Friendship; and on 24 Oct. 1753 he and his w. joined Samuel Underwood, Jr., son of Samuel, and Mary, widow of Samuel Underwood, in conveying the land to Ford again (81:451; 82:145).

CHOCKE. See CHALKE.

CHOICE, WILLIAM, d. testate in Balto. Co.; m. Jane (?) who m. as her 2nd husb., by March 1682/3, John Durham; will of William Choice, 28 Oct. 1680 - 1 March 1681, left 82 a. on Bush R., and res. of est. to w. Jane (17:13, 14; 120:104).

CHRISTIAN, JOHN, was in Balto. Co. by 1699 as a taxable in s. side Patapsco Hund.; d. by 30 Jan. 1721 when Lloyd Harris posted admin. bond with Thomas Taylor and Henry Carrington; his est. was inv. 2 Feb. 1721/2 by Henry Sater and Samuel Merryman, and val. at £ 15.16.6; est. admin. by Harris on 23 Feb. 1724 (2:329, 362; 11: 292; 51:208; 141:6).

CHRISTIAN, or CHRISTESON, JOHN, m. Margaret Hamilton on 12 Sept. 1745; on 10 March 1745/6 John Christian leased land from Thomas Brerewood for the lifetimes of himself, his wife Margaret, age c.19, and Thomas Hamilton, age c.16; had iss.: ELIZABETH, b. 7 March 1746 (79:371; 131:28, 127/r).

CHRISTIE, JAMES (1), of Stirling, living 1709; m. 4 May 1694 Margaret, dau. of Thomas Walker of Craigs of Plean, Parish of St. Ninians; James was bro. of Laird of Sheriffmuirlands, and was himself elected a Magistrate and appointed a Town Councillor for Stirling in Sept. 1696; Dean of the Guild in Sept. 1704; elected Provost in Sept. 1709; had iss.: JAMES, b. 14 April 1695; THOMAS; WILLIAM, b. 11 Feb. 1699, m. Margaret Edmonstone; JOHN, b. 15 Sept. 1700; m. Agnes Neilsen; HENRY, b. 15 Nov. 1702, m. Elizabeth Campbell on 29 June 1733; ALEXANDER, b. 9 Jan. 1704; KATHERINE, d. unm.: CHRISTIAN,m. Michael Downie in 1736; JEAN; JANET; ELIZABETH (580 ; see Bibliography).

CHRISTIE, JAMES (2), s. of James (1) and Margaret, b. 14 April 1695, d. 7 Aug. 1745; m. Katherine, dau. of Francis Napier, Provost of Stirling; was a merchant of Stirling, Glasgow, London, and Baltimore in North America; had iss.: JAMES, b. 13 June 1718, d. s.p. 1767; FRANCIS, b. 20 Jan. 1720, d. young; GABRIEL, b. 16 Sept. 1722; ROBERT, b. 1724, drowned in a flood in the River Forth; JOHN, b. 1725, drowned in a flood in the River Forth; WILLIAM, b. 18 July 1730, one of the Founders of the Stirling Bank; CHARLES, b. 21 Nov. 1732 .(580).

CHRISTIE, THOMAS (3), s. of James (1) and Margaret, b. 10 Jan. 1697; on 22 Oct. 1731 m. Mary, dau. of John Watson, merchant of Thirty Acres and Woodend; burgess of Stirling on 22 April 1721; held other offices; had iss.: six daus., all of whom d. s.p., and also had: JAMES, b. 22 Dec. 1738; WILLIAM, b. 1746, d. 1750: ANN, m. Capt. John Bachop of the 54th Regt., and d. 1820.(580).

CHRISTIE, CHARLES (4), s. of James (2) and Katherine, b. 21 Nov. 1732; stated in Burke to have married twice, and to had issue among others Charles, commander of the Belvidere East Indiaman; m. 2nd on 21 July 1754 Cordelia Stokes in Balto. Co.; after he d. she m. 2nd Dr. Alexander Stenhouse; the will of Charles Christie, 17 March 1757 - 15 April 1757, named w. Cordelia, s. Gabriel, mother Katherine Napier in Scotland, brother William, sisters Mrs. Johnson and Elizabeth Christie, sister-in-law Mrs. Francis

Stokes and friend William Young; admin. bond posted 2 May 1757
by Cordelia Christie and David McCulloch with Hugh Deans and John
Hall; est. admin. by wid. on 26 Feb. 1759, 17 May 1760, 8 Nov.
1762 (Cordelia now w. of Dr. Stenhouse), and 24 Oct. 1764; iss.
of Charles: (poss. by 1st wife): CHARLES, commander of the East
Indiaman **Belvidere;** (by 2nd wife): GABRIEL CHARLES, b. 28 Nov.
1756; CHARLES JAMES, b. 2 Dec. 1757 (4:250. 296, 364, 373; 11:
382; 129:351, 370; 131; 210-30:279).

CHRISTIE, JAMES (5), s. of Thomas (3) and Mary, b. 22 Dec.
1738, d. 1803; m. 1st, in 1772 Mary, dau. of George Milligan; she
d. 15 Dec. 1774 having borne one s., and he m. 2nd in 1783 Mary
Turner, eld. dau. of the Hon. Charles Maitland, who was 2nd s. of
Charles, 6th Earl of Lauderdale; James res. on Balto., Md., but
was obliged to leave during the Rev. War because of his royalist
sympathies; purch. est. of Durie in parish of Scoonie, Co. Fife
in 1783; had iss.: (by 1st w.): THOMAS, b. 10 June 1773, d. 1838,
Capt. of the 70th Regt.; (by 2nd w.): CHARLES MAITLAND, b. 31 Dec.
1785; JAMES, b. 21 Feb. 1787, m. Frances Dickinson; GABRIEL, b. 1
July 1791; ROBERT STARK, b. 5 Nov. 1792; WILLIAM, b. 25 Nov. 1793:
PETER, b. 18 Aug. 1796, d. at Balaklava in the Crimean War; NAPIER
TURNER, b. 26 June 1801; MARY, d. Aug. 1841, m. Alexander Smith;
ISOBEL, m. Rev. William Fortescue; MARGARET, m. John Irvine Bos-
well; ERSKINE, m. Matthew Fortescue; ANNE, d. unm. (580).

CHRISTIE, GABRIEL CHARLES (6), s. of Charles (4) and Cordelia,
b. 28 Nov. 1756, and d. 1 April 1808 in his 51st yr; m. 18 Nov.
1779 Priscilla Hall, dau. of John Hall of Cranberry; during the
Rev. War was a private in Capt. Josiah Carville Hall's co. of
Harf. Co. Militia; was later Collector of the Port of Balto., and
at his death (from a pulmonary complaint), vessels in the Harbor
wore their colors at half-mast; had iss.: CHARLES, b. 29 Sept.
1780; CORDELIA, b. 12 Oct. 1782; MARTHA, b. 1783, m. Alexander
Rodgers; NATHAN; ELIZA, b. 1787, d. 20 March 1850 in her 62nd yr.
(129:351, 392, 393; 261; 314; 345).

CHRISUP. See CRESAP.

CHURCH, ELIZABETH, d. 1764 (111:183).

CHURCH, JOHN, conv. prop. to his w. Elizabeth on 13 Feb. 1764
(230:20).

CHURN/CHERN, WILKES, was in Balto. Co. by 1694 as a taxable in
n. side Gunpowder Hund.; his s. JOHN was bur. 18 Feb. 1696/7 (128:
5; 139).

CHURN, WILLIAM, was in Balto. Co. by 1694 as a taxable in n.
side Gunpowder Hund. (139).

CIBBLE, ROBERT, d. by 27 March 1750 when Jacob Starkey admin.
his est.; est. admin. again on 30 July 1751 (5:149, 184).

CLAPHAM, WILLIAM, was transp. to Md. c.1679 and was in Lancaster Co., Va., in 1670 when he conv. 500 a. to Richard Ball (96:
232).

CLAPLATEL, FRANCIS, m. Roseen (?) and had iss.: KATHERINE, b.
11 July 1736 (133).

CLARIDGE, JANE, wid., made an antenuptial agreement with John
Wright (59:136).

CLARISTON, EDMUND, was in Balto. Co. by 1692 as a taxable in
n. side Patapsco Hund. (138).

THE CLARK FAMILY OF ST. MARY'S AND BALTIMORE COUNTIES

CLARK, ROBERT (1), called "Hon. Robert Clarke," because of his many high positions, and progenitor, was b. c.1611, prob. in Eng., and d. 1664 in Md.; m. 1st an unknown wife; m. 2nd by Nov. 1654 Winifred Seyborne, wid. of Nicholas Harvey and of Thomas Greene; m. 3rd in 1656 Jane, wid. of John Cockshutt and Nicholas Causine; a Roman Catholic and a Gentleman, he was appointed to the Council of Maryland, and was present at the Assemblies of 1637/8, 1638/9, and others, was Surveyor General of Md., and was a Justice of the Provincial Court; in 1647 conv. property to his ch. John and Mary; his will, 4 July 1664 - 21 July 1664, named old. s. John, son Robert (now 12), s. Thomas (now 10), and dau. Mary; had iss.: JOHN; MARY; ROBERT, b. c.1652, d. having made a will 14 Dec. 1682 in St. Giles Cripplegate, London, naming his mother Jane, and bro. John; THOMAS, d c.1711 in St. M. Co. (120:25; 122:69; 200-4: 341; 370; 553:132 ff.).

CLARK(E), JOHN (2), s. of Robert (1), b. c.1640, d. 1686 in St. Marys Co.; m. Ann (?); in 1665 was granted Crouch's Gift, Clark's Marsh, Clark's Inheritance, and Clark's Purchase; his will, 28 Nov. 1685 - 6 March 1686, named w. Anne, and ch., John, Robert, Benjamin, Francis, and Ann; had iss.: JOHN; BENJAMIN; ROBERT; FRANCIS; ANN; and poss. ESTHER who was not in her father's will, but who named her bro. Robert Clark when she was w. of Isaac Butterworth (121:1; 553:136-137).

CLARK(E), THOMAS (3), s. of Robert (1), b. c.1654, d. 1711 in St. Marys Co., having m. by 1695 Juliana, dau. of Thomas Mudd; his will, 4 June 1711 - 4 Dec. 1711, named w. Julian, and these ch.: THOMAS; JOHN; ADAM; WILLIAM; BENJAMIN; LUKE (122:221).

CLARK(E), JOHN (4), s. of John (2) and Anne, was in P. G. Co. by 1699 when he and his w. Elizabeth joined his bros. Robert, Benjamin, and Francis in selling Clark's Purchase to William Herbert on 24 Feb. 1699, and Crouch's Gift to John Counts on the same day (553:137).

CLARK(E), BENJAMIN (5), s. of John (2) and Anne, was in P. G. Co. by 1699 when he and w. Judith joined his bros. in the deeds cited above (553:137).

CLARK(E), ROBERT (6), s. of John (2) and Anne, b. c.1668, not yet 16 in 1686; d. by 18 Jan. 1757 in Balto. Co.; m. 17 Feb. 1717 or 1718, Selinah, bapt. 14 July 1700, dau. of George and Hannah (?) Smith; in Chas. Co. by 1694 when he bought Clarkson's Purchase from William Clarkson; in P. G. Co. and a lawyer in 1715 when he sold that tract to John Ridgeway; moved to Balto. Co. by 5 Nov. 1716 when Benj. Wheeler of P. G. Co. sold him 1000 a. called Wheeler's and Clark's Contrivance; patented various lands incl. Robert and John's Lot in 1720; in 1750 owned 120 a. Robert's Garden, 156 a. Robert and John's Lot, part Good Neighborhood, 100 a. Wheeler's Union, and other lands; his will, 22 Dec. 1755 - 18 Jan. 1757, named s. Robert (to have Robert's Garden), s. William (to have Robert and John's Lot), s. George (to have Robert's Chance and Robert's Venture), s. David (to have Good Neighborhood and Wheeler's Union), and daus. Frances Renshaw, Hannah Amos, Sarah, Elizabeth, Ann Clark, Mary Johnson, Hester Johnson, and Selina Clark; admin. bond posted 30 May 1757 by Robert and Selina Clark, with Henry Thomas and Thomas Johnson, Jr.; had iss.: FRANCES, b. 1 April 1719, m. Thomas Renshaw on 29 Jan. 1739; HANNAH, b. 8 June 1721, m. James Amos on 28 Jan. 1739; MARY, b. 25 Oct. 1723, m. Thomas Johnson, Jr., on 29 Nov. 1748; ROBERT, b. 1 May 1726; WILLIAM, b. 18 Jan. 1728; SARAH, b. 30 July 1730; GEORGE, b. 9 Jan. 1732; HESTER, b. 24 Jan. 1734, m. Barnett Johnson; ELIZABETH,

b. 2 June 1736; DAVID, b. 21 March 1737; SELINA; ANNE, b. 29 May 1743 (11:383; 67:443; 111:221; 128:81; 153; 553:137-138).

CLARKE, ROBERT (7), s. of Robert (6) and Selina, b. 1 May 1726, d. 1766 in Balto. Co.; may be the Robert who m. by 4 Sept. 1760 Elizabeth, dau. of William Jenkins; his will, 29 July 1766 - 1 Sept. 1766, named w. Elizabeth, extx. (to have 100 a. Simmons' Exchange), s. Robert (to have 86 a. Stone's or Stokes), and other ch., Aquila, Thomas, Daniel, Elizabeth, and Martha; had iss.: ROBERT; SARAH; AQUILA; DANIEL; ELIZABETH; MARTHA; and THOMAS (6: 24; 112:50; 553).

CLARKE, WILLIAM (8), s. of Robert (6) and Selina, b. 18 Jan. or 18 June 1728; m. 7 Dec. 1749 Tamar Lowe (128:81; 129:251, 274).

CLARK, ABRAHAM, transp. to Md. c.1654 or 1658/9, was in Balto. Co. by March 1662/3 when he assigned 200 , a. called Nashes Creek (that he had from John Collett) to Thomas Muntross; later Walter Dickenson conv. him 450 a. Spring Neck; d. by 7 Dec. 1676 when admin. bond was posted by Miles Gibson with Thomas Long and John Arding; est. inv. on 11 Dec. 1676 by Arding and John Boring, and val. at 26,714 lbs. tob.; est. admin. in 1686 by Miles Gibson who stated that Clark's w. Sarah had also died; had iss.: MARY, m. by 11 June 1694 William Hollis; ELIZABETH, m. by Sept. 1684 William Wilkinson (2:39; 11:413; 18:199; 48:62; 59:301; 93; 388).

CLARK, EDWARD, servant, with 16 mos. to serve, in inv. of John Israel's est., 19 April 1725 (52:184).

CLARK, ELIZABETH, no parents given, b. 15 Nov. 1707 (128:32).

CLARK, ELIZABETH, d. 16 April 1736 near Susquehanna River (128: 91).

CLARK, GEORGE, d. by 5 March 1764 when his est. was admin. by his wid. Mary Clark; est. admin. again on 21 May 1764; left no issue (6:80, 89).

CLARK, JAMES, in Nov. 1755, tried for bast. as the father of Martha West's child (40:399).

CLARK, JOHN, serv. of Johanna Goldsmith, judged to be between 18 and 20 years in March 1685/6; prob. the John Clark who was a taxable in 1692 in s. side of Patapsco Hund. (18:398; 138).

CLARK, JOHN, d. without issue when his est. was admin. by Jeremiah Hacks and w. Mary (2:107).

CLARK, JOHN, d. by 28 July 1703 when his est. was inv. by Nicholas Day and Daniel Scott, Jr., and val. at £ 6.11.0 (48:56).

CLARK, JOHN, d. by 12 March 1711 when his est. was inv. by Jno. Deaver and Richard Ruff and val. at £ 3.6.6 (50:248).

CLARK, JOHN, d. by 7 March 1711/2 when admin. bond was posted by John Webster with Christopher Cox and John Whitticar; est. was admin. on 15 Aug. 1712 by John Webster (1:224; 11:451).

CLARK, JOHN, m. 16 Oct. 1713 Elizabeth Draper; she d. 4 April 1720 (128:30, 33, 37).

CLARK, JOHN, m. Eliza (?), and had iss.: BENJAMIN, b. Oct. 1748; ELIZ., b. Nov. 1761 (131:75/r, 120/r).

CLARK, JOHN, of "The Level," d. in Balto. Co. by 19 Dec. 1754, having m. Hannah (?); in 1750 he owned 50 a. Clark's Meadows, 150

a. Clark's Town, and 362 a. Clark's Rest; his will, 6 Oct. 1754 -
19 Dec. 1754, left all three tracts to his s. John (not yet 21),
and named his w. Hannah and ch., Mary, Hannah, and Annabel; admin.
bond posted 15 April 1755 by extx. Hannah Clark with Jno. Hall and
Andrew Lendrum; had iss.: HANNAH, b. 25 Sept. 1734; MARY, b. 7
Feb. 1735; JOHN, b. 23 Feb. 1737; ANNABEL, b. 27 Dec. 1739; and
SARAH, b. 10 June 1744 (11:396; 111:48; 128:92; 129:342; 153:23).

CLARK, JOHN, cordwainer, and w. Susannah on 31 Oct. 1746 conv.
to William Gist part Wolf's Den orig. surv. for John Berry (79:
232).

CLARK, JOHN, in 1750 owned pt. Ogg King of Basham, and Pearson's
Outlet and Weatherall's Addition, 100 a. (153:53).

CLARK, JOHN, of Patapsco, in 1750 owned 50 a. Hopewell, and 50
a. Clark's Lot (153:63).

CLARK, JOHN, of Balto. Co., was injured and his w. Sarah was
murdered by his son-in-law John Berry, prior to Dec. 1751 (385:
158).

CLARK, JOHN, gardner, runaway conv. serv. of W. Buchanan in
Balto., c. June 1754 (385:290).

CLARK, JOHN, d. by 13 July 1767; est. admin. by John Hammond
Dorsey (7:295).

CLARK, LAWRENCE, m. by 17 March 1748 Jane Wheeler, wid. of
Isaac Butterworth; in 1750 owned 350 a. part Uncle's Goodwill,
180 a. John and Isaac's Lot, and 100 a. The Addition (4:202; 5:
217; 153).

CLARK, MARTHA, d. 15 Oct. 1713 (128:32).

CLARK, alias POLSON, MARY, ind. for bast., June 1750; tried
for bast., March 1750/1 (37:2, 282).

CLARK, MATTHIAS, m. Elizabeth (?), and had: ANN, b. 24 Feb.
1715; MARGARET, b. 16 Feb. 1720 (128:67).

CLARK, RICHARD, servant, with 4 years to serve, in inv. of Aquila Paca, 20 Aug. 1722 (50:142).

CLARK, RICHARD, in July 1746 purchased from John and Susanna
Bell the tract Cloy; in 1750 owned 100 a. Clay, and 50 a. The
Par-(?) (79:119; 153:55).

CLARK, RICHARD, in 1750 owned 97 a. Middle Jenifer (153:94).

CLARK, ROBERT, m. Sarah (?), and had: ROBERT, b. 13 Dec. 1708
(131:20/r).

CLARK, ROBERT, named as the father of Sarah Clark's child in
June 1709 (21:43).

CLARK, ROBERT, m. 5 Dec. 1729 Elizabeth Smithson, and had iss.:
SARAH, b. 3 April 1730; ELIZABETH, b. 5 April 1733 (both in St.
George's Par.), and poss.: AQUILA, b. 24 May 1738 (in St. John's
Par.) (128:79; 131:77/r).

CLARK, ROBERT, of Winter's Run, in 1750 owned 100 a. of Bell's
Camp, and 100 a. Pleasant Hill (153:16).

CLARK, ROBERT STEEL, d. by 15 May 1769 when his est. was admin.
by the extx. Elizabeth Clark (7:17).

CLARK, SAMUEL, b. c.1740, d. 21 April 1798; m. Sophia, dau. of George and Ann (Wilkinson) Harryman; a private in the Balto. Town 8th Co., 1st Batt'n, Md. forces under Capt. Samuel Smith; had iss.: WILLIAM, m. Dorcas Fitz; SAMUEL, m. Mary Lucas; ANN, b. c. 1770, m. Hezekiah Viers; and GEORGE (345; also Wilson M. Cary, chart of Harryman Fam., MHS).

CLARK, SARAH, in June 1709, named Robert Clark as the father of her child (21:43).

CLARKSON, ROBERT (1), d. c.1666; imm. by 1657, settled in A. A. Co., where he rep. that county in the Assembly, 1659/60; m. Milcah (?) who m. as her 2nd husb. Richard Hill; his will, 5 Dec. 1665 - 22 May 1666, named w. Milcah, s. Robert (to have 400 a. Horn Point), dau. Eliza (to have 400 a. South Centre on Patapsco R.), and dau. Mary, to have 200 a. on Todd's Creek; one dau. m. by 1674 John Brown of A. A. Co.; Robert and Milcah had iss.: ROBERT, d. c.1686; ELIZABETH, m. John Brown of A. A. Co.; MARY, m. 1st Thomas Francis, and 2nd Samuel Young (120:33; 206-1:166; 370).

CLARKSON, ROBERT (2), s. of Robert (1), d. c.1686; m. by 1683 Joanna, wid. of John Hillen, and dau. of Thomas Hooker; surv. several tracts of land in Balto. Co., incl. 600 a. Clarkson's Hope and Clarkson's Purchase, also 600 a., both in Sept. 1683; had iss.: MILCAH, m. 7 Oct. 1699 in A. A. Co., John Bowen, Jr.; on 8 June 1711 John and Milcah Bowen sold 200 a. of Clarkson's Purchase to Henry Wright (120:121, 128; 211:44, 45; 219-3).

CLARON, AGNES, serv. of Thomas Hatchman, d. Sept. 1726 (131:43/r).

CLARON, ELIZABETH, in Aug. 1744 bore a child to Charles Mulholland (35:320).

CLARY, JOHN, of Balto. Co., d. by 11 Aug. 1740; m. Mary (?); his will, 25 Feb. 1739/40 - 11 Aug. 1740, named bro. William Devorn, bro. William, w. Mary, and these ch.: VACHEL (to have Clary's Forest), and RUTH (127:93).

CLAWSON, JACOB, in July 1746 sold Thomas Sheredine 50 a. of Pleasant Valley (79:99).

CLAY, ELIZABETH, ind. for bast., in March 1743/4, and tried in June 1744 (35:154, 236).

CLEGATE, THOMAS, had four yrs. to serve, in 1749 inv. of Capt. Robert North (53:374).

CLEGG, JOHN, d. by 8 Nov. 1723 when admnx. Ann Clegg posted admin. bond with Edward Hall and Bennett Garrett; est. inv. in 1725; Ann Clegg d. 24 Feb. 1743 (11:291; 52:169; 129:333).

CLEMENS, WILLIAM, m. by 10 April 1749 Ann, extx. of Leonard Wheeler of Balto. Co. (5:84, 185, 267).

CLEMENTS, (?), m. by 29 Nov. 1769 Martha, dau. of Thomas Wheeler (112:171).

CLIBORN, MARY, ind. for bast., June 1732 (29:289).

CLINCH, THOMAS, in Balto. Co. by 1692 as a taxable in n. side of Patapsco Hund. (138).

CLOSE, GARRETT, ind. as the father of Susanna Simpson's child (21:210).

CLOWDER, JNO., lad, in the inv. of William Orrick, 2 Nov. 1720 (51:164).

COALE. See COLE.

COAN. See COWAN.

COBB, JAMES (1), b. c.1651, was transp. to Md., c.1676, moved from Calvert Co. to Balto. Co. by Nov. 1721, when at age 70 he pet. the court to be levy free; prob. was the father of a son: JAMES, d. 12 March 1718 (13:625; 388; see Bibliography).

COBB, JAMES (2), prob. s. of James (1), d. 12 March 1718; m. 30 Oct. 1709 Rebecca, wid. of Jas. Emson; admin. bond posted 8 Aug. 1722 by John Hawkins with John Hawkins, Jr., and Antil Deaver; est. admin. 12 July 1725, 1 Oct. 1734, and 22 July 1737; wid. Rebecca m. John Hawkins; had iss.: REBECCA, b. 26 March 1710; PRISCILLA, m. John White on 18 May 1726; FRANCES, m. Charles Jones on 26 Dec. 1727; CHARITY, b. 15 April 1712, as Christiana Cobb m. 2 Feb. 1728 Zachariah Spencer; MARGARET, b. 15 May 1714, m. Seaborn Tucker on 2 April 1730; JAMES, b. 16 Sept. 1716 (3:45, 155, 247; 11:297; 128:34, 35, 95; 129:255, 256, 257).

COBB, JAMES (3), son of James (2) and Rebecca, b. 16 Sept. 1718, m. 1st on 21 Jan. 1734 Ruth Elledge, and 2nd, on 18 March 1741 Mary Poge; had iss.: (by 1st w.): JAMES, b. 27 Nov. 1735; JOSEPH, b. 4 Feb. 1737; (by 2nd w.): MARGARET, b. 25 Dec. 1742 (128:95; 129:326, 327; 133:153).

COCHRAN, THOMAS (1), m. Mary, and had iss.: ELLINOR, b. 7 Jan. 1736, and poss. THOMAS (133:53).

COCHRAN, THOMAS (2), s. of Thomas (1), dec., in March 1745/6 was bound to George Jones, joiner, to age 21; in Aug. 1746 was to be kept by Catherine Jones (35:801; 36:118).

COCHRAN, WILLIAM, d. by 20 Sept. 1740 when his est. was admin. by Alexander Black of A. A. Co. (4:62).

COCK, JOHN, was in Balto. Co. by Sept. 1668 when he conv. 200 a. Cock Crow Thrice to Bartlett Hendrickson; in March 1668/9 Hendrickson conv. him None So Good in Finland which he conv. to Edmund Webb in March 1668/9; in Sept. 1669 purch. land from Axell Still, and in Nov. 1669 purch. 100 a. on Back R. from Cornelius Petterson; in Nov. 1671 he and Ann Cock and Andrew Peterson conv. William Ward 300 a. The Leney (95; 96:229; 97:126).

THE COCKEY FAMILY has been the subject of fuller treatments by Barnes and Newman (259:19-26; 358).

COCKEY, WILLIAM (1), progenitor, d. in A. A. Co. in 1697; as "William Cockey of Severn," m. 1st c.1668 in Som. Co., Md., Frances Vincent, and 2nd Sarah (?) who surv. him; in Oct. 1676 bought 100 a. Ball's Enlargement in Balto. Co. from William Ball; in April 1696 surveyed 300 a. Cockey's Trust; his will, 7 May 1698 - 21 May 1698, named daus. Elizabeth Hammond, Mary, Ann, Sarah, and sons Thomas and John; had iss.: THOMAS, b. c.1676, d. c.1737; ELIZABETH, b. c.1678, m. Col. William Hammond; MARY, b. c.1681; Capt. JOHN, b. c.1682/3; Capt. EDWARD, b. c.1685; ANN, b. c.1686; JOSHUA, d. by 8 March 1720; SARAH, b. c.1689; RICHARD, b. c.1691, m. Elizabeth (?); WILLIAM, d. by Oct. 1721 (101:301; 200-54:279; 259:19-20; 358).

COCKEY, THOMAS (2), s. of William (1) and Sarah, b. c.1676, d. c.1737; m. Elizabeth (Hammond) Moss, wid. of Rev. Richard Moss;

in March 1699 bought 200 a. Francis Choice from Francis and Sarah
Dallahide; his will, 10 Dec. 1733 - 22 Oct. 1737, left considerable prop. to Thomas Cockey Deye, Charlotta Cockey Deye, Cassandra
Cockey Deye, and Charcilla Cockey Deye, Penelope Deye, William
and Solomon Turner (bros.), William Eager, bro. John and latter's
s. Thomas, bro. Edward and his s. Charles, and his own dau. Ann
w. of Thomas John Hammond; had iss.: ANN, b. 4 Dec. 1704, m. 21
June 1721 Thomas John Hammond; also alleged to be the father of
four ch. by Penelope Deye (q.v.) (66:10; 126:225-226; 259).

COCKEY, Capt. JOHN (3), s. of William (1) and Sarah, b. c.1681,
d. 15 Aug. 1746; m. Elizabeth Slade, who m. as her 2nd husband
Charles Baker, and d. 5 Aug. 1780, age 85; came from A. A. Co.,
and settled in the Green Spring Valley area of Balto. Co.; a Justice of the Balto. Co. Court in Aug. 1728; his will, 22 May 1740 -
17 April 1747 named ch., William (eldest s.), John, Joshua, Edward,
Peter, Thomas, Sarah, Susanna Gist, Mary w. of Joshua Owings; admin. bond posted 21 Oct. 1749(?) by William Cockey and Joshua Owings; est. admin. 30 Nov. 1747, 8 May 1748, 21 Oct. 1749, 4 July
1751, and 4 Nov. 1751; had iss.: SUSANNA, b. 2 Nov. 1714, m. Thomas Gist; MARY, b. 10 Dec. 1716, m. Joshua Owings; WILLIAM, b. 20
Feb. 1718; SARAH, b. 26 Feb. 1721, m. Thomas Boone; THOMAS, b. 13
Dec. 1724; JOHN, b. 12 March 1726, d. by 16 Feb. 1748 (est. admin.
16 Feb. 1748, 21 Oct. 1749, 3 July 1751, and 26 Sept. 1753, the
admin. bond having been posted 21 Oct. 1749(?) by William Cockey);
JOSHUA, b. 18 May 1729; Col. EDWARD, b. 20 Dec. 1730; PETER, b.
11 March 1734, d. unm. by 20 July 1752 when Thomas Cockey posted
admin. bond, and est. admin. 20 July 1750, 4 Nov. 1751, and 27
Feb. 1752 (4:158, 187, 209; 5:60, 63, 112, 187, 189, 201, 202,
255, 290; 6:4; 15:60, 63, 112, 255; 28:22; 37:155; 110:360; 133:
34, 46; 134:26; 259:20-21).

COCKEY, Capt. EDWARD (4), s. of William (1) and Sarah, b. 1685,
d. 1750 in Q. A. Co., Md.; m. 1st 1 Aug. 1717 widow Rhoda Harris,
and 2nd Mary (?); his will, 5 Nov. 1750 - 23 May 1751, named w.
Mary and these ch.: CHARLES; EDWARD; JOHN; MORDECAI; WILLIAM;
THOMAS; PETER; and ANN (259:20).

COCKEY, JOSHUA (5), s. of William (1) and Sarah, d. by 1 Dec.
1720/1; m. Sarah (?); his will, 15 April 1720 - 8 March 1720/1,
named bro. John and w. Sarah to have tract Jerusalem; admin. bond
posted 8 Sept. 1721 by Sarah Cockey with Benjamin Hanson and Joshua
Merriken; before his death Cockey was accused of damaging the
prop. of Jacob and Thomas Hanson, orphans of Thomas Hanson, and
in June 1719 Anthony Drew and Samuel Jackson were appointed to investigate (11:286; 23:141; 28:38; 110:170).

COCKEY, SARAH (6), dau. of William (1) and Sarah, named Sylvanus Pumphrey as the father of her ch., March 1718/9 (23:62).

COCKEY, RICHARD (7), s. of William (1) and Sarah, b. 1691; m.
Elizabeth (?) (259:20).

COCKEY, WILLIAM (8), s. of William (1) and Sarah, d. by 16 May
1720 when admin. bond was posted by his wid. Mary, now Mary Pumphrey, with Nathan and Walter Pumphrey and Richard Young; m. Mary
(?) who m. as her 2nd husb. Nathan Pumphrey;; est. inv. by Thomas
Randall and Benjamin Howard and val. at £ 189.16.9 (Pumphrey testified he gave Thomas Cockey notice of the time and place of the Ap-
praisal; est. admin. by Nathan and Mary Pumphrey on 2 Oct. 1721;
had iss.: SARAH; MARY; ANN; ZEPHORA; and ELIZABETH, all alive in
March 1722/3 (3:84; 11:303; 48:261; 25:219; 48:216; 259:20).

COCKEY, WILLIAM (9), s. of Capt. John (3) and Elizabeth, b. 20
Feb. 1718, d. 1756; m. Constant, dau. of John Ashman; she m. as
her 2nd husb. William Randall; in 1750 owned 200 a. Cockey's Trust,

66¼ a. Tye's Delight, 118 a. Cockey's Delight, 200 a. Helmore,
119 a. Helmore's Addition, 50 a. Anthony's Delight, 66¼ a. Cow
Hill, and 100 a. Cockey's Folly; his will, 14 Sept. 1756 - 14 Oct.
1756, named w. Constant, and ch., John, Rachel, William, Constant,
Elizabeth, dec. f. John, mother Elizabeth Baker, bro. Edward, and
cousin John, s. of uncle Edward; admin. bond posted 22 Nov. 1756
by Constant Cockey and George Ashman with Samuel Howard and Jabez
Bailey; est. admin. 21 Sept. 1761 by William and Constant Randall
and George Ashman, and named the following ch.: JOHN, b. c.1743,
d. 1808, m. Chloe Cromwell; WILLIAM, b. c.1746, d. 1775, m. Hannah
Owings; CONSTANT, b. c.1748, m. 1st William Corsey(?) and 2nd William Bagford; RACHEL, b. c.1753, m. Richard Cromwell (4:341; 6:6;
11:380; 111:86; 153:84; 259:21).

COCKEY, THOMAS (10), s. of Capt. John (3) and Elizabeth, b. 13
Dec. 1724, d. 1784, m. 15 May 1753 Prudence, dau, of Stephen Gill;
antenuptial contract dated 12 May 1753; in 1750 owned 100 a. of
Gardner's Garden or Farm, 200 a. Addition to Gardner's Garden,
150 a. Sewell's Hope, 100 a. Sewall's Contrivance, 50 a. Land End,
50 a. Maiden's Folly, part Jamaica Man's Plague, Addition to Jamaica Man's Plague, Selside, Port Royal, and Addition to Port
Royal, 600 a.; had iss.: THOMAS, b. 15 April 1754, m. Ruth Brown;
ACHSAH, b. 16 Nov. 1755, m. Thomas Ford; ELIZABETH, b. 18 April
1757, m. Philip or Philemon Coale; JOHN, b. 20 Dec. 1758, d. 1824,
m. Mary Cole; ANN, b. 29 April 1760, m. Elias Brown; CHARLES, b.
14 Feb. 1762, d. 1823; STEPHEN, b. 23 Jan. 1764, d. 1797; CALEB,
d. 1800 (134:26, 30, 38; 153:100; 229:93; 259:21).

COCKEY, JOSHUA (11), s. of Capt. John (3) and Elizabeth, b. 18
May 1729, d. 17 Dec. 1764; m. 27 Aug. 1755 Charcilla Cockey Deye,
dau. of Penelope Deye; in 1750 owned 100 a. Cockey's Trust, 33¼ a.
Tie's Delight, 56¼ a. Cockey's Delight, 100 a. Helmore, and 59 a.
Addition; his will, 3 Dec. 1764 - 23 March 1765, named w. Charcilla, and ch., Thomas Deye, Penelope Deye, Frances Thwaites, and
unborn child, bro.-in-law Thomas Cockey Deye; had iss.: PENELOPE
DEYE, b. 2 April 1757, d. 25 Sept. 1820, m. Thomas Gist; THOMAS
DEYE, b. 9 April 1762, d. 1813; FRANCES THWAITES, b. 8 Sept. 1763,
d. 8 Feb. 1845; JOSHUA FREDERICK, b. 6 July 1765 (112:15; 153:91;
259:21).

COCKEY, EDWARD (12), s. of Capt. John (3) and Elizabeth, b. 20
Dec. 1730, d. 1 Feb. 1795; m. 19 June 1753 Eleanor, dau. of Philip
Pindell; served in the Rev. War, was a magistrate, and was at one
time sheriff of Balto. Co., and a delegate to the Lower House of
the Assembly, 1786-1787, 1787-1788; had iss.: URATH, b. 27 April
1754, m. Charles Cockey; JOSHUA, b. 20 Oct. 1755; WILLIAM, b. 21
May 1758, d. 5 Oct. 1775, unm.; THOMAS, b. 21 March 1762, m. Elizabeth Owings; MORDECAI, d. 1764 (134:27, 297; 259:21-22; 370).

COCKEY, CHRISTOPHER, no known rel. to above, was in Balto. Co.
by 1692 as a taxable in s. side Patapsco Hund. (138 ; he may have
been Christopher Cox).

COCKEY, EDWARD, was in Balto. Co. by 1692 as a taxable in s.
side Patapsco Hund. (138). (See Edward Cox).

COCKIN, JOHN, and wife, in Nov. 1750 were allowed 1000 lbs.
tob. for their maintenance (38:20).

COE, (?), m. by 2 Nov. 1764 Susanna, dau. of Susanna Herod
(112:13).

COE, JOHN, son of Mary Dandy; aged 11 on 5 March 1722/3. when
bound to Lawrence and Agnes Taylor (35:214).

COENS. See COWAN.

COFFIN, ABRAHAM, and w. Joyce were in Balto. Co. by 15 June(?)
1670/1 when they conv. 100 a. Marksfield to John Gilbert; earlier
Abraham conv. 100 a. Tombeye to William Toulson in March 1667
(95; 97:126).

COFILL, PAT., m. Mary (?) and had iss.: JAMES, b. Dec. 1749;
MARGARET, b. 30 June 1752 (131:131/r).

COGELL, JAMES, d. by 14 March 1676 when James Phillips posted
admin. bond with Thomas Long and Richard Ball (11:282).

THE GEORGE COLE FAMILY

COLE, GEORGE (1), was in Balto. Co. by Nov. 1709 when he
purch. from Thomas and Christian Stone 174 a. Stone's Range on w.
side Back R., and d. there by June 1751; m. Elizabeth (poss. Love);
in 1750 owned Stone's Range; his will, 16 June 1749 - 4 June 1751,
named w. Elizabeth and s. George (who was to have afsd. tract);
had iss.: GEORGE (prob. the George was was b. 13 March 1713), and
poss. RICHARD MILLER (67:26; 133:7; 153:61; 210-28:66).

COLE, GEORGE (2), s. of George (1) and Elizabeth, poss. the
George who was b. 13 March 1713 in St. Paul's Par.; d. by 2 Aug.
1762; his will, 5 July 1762 - 2 Aug. 1762, named sons Richard and
William (to have 60 a. Stoney Hill), and sons Nathan and George
(to share Stone's Range); had iss.: RICHARD; WILLIAM; GEORGE;
NATHAN, b. after 1746 (111:134; 133:7).

COLE, RICHARD MILLER (3), poss. s. of George (1) and Elizabeth,
is placed here because his s. George who d. 1766 also owned 194 a.
Stone's Range; prob. the Richard Cole who m. Sabina Haile on 15
May 1735; d. by 1766; in March 1746 John Boring, Jr., and w. Abarilla conv. him part Boring's Goft, and in 1750 he still owned 50
a. of this land; had iss.: GEORGE, b. 18 March 1735/6; SARAH, b.
27 March 1745 (79:478, 481; 133:48, 90, 153; 153:14).

COLE, GEORGE (4), s. of Richard Miller (3) and Sabina, was b.
18 March 1735/6, and d. by 16 June 1767; m. Patience (?); his will,
20 March 1766 - 16 June 1767, named w. Patience, dau. Ruth, land
Stone's Range, 194 a.; in a codicil dated 21 March 1766 he directed that Boring's Gift which had been conv. to his f. by John Boring, should be made over to Capt. Charles Ridgely; had iss.: RUTH
(112:58; 133:48).

THE JOHN COLE FAMILY is the subject of a chart by Johnston.

COLE, JOHN (5), no known rel. to any of the above, was b. c.
1669, and d. in 1746; m. 1st Johanna Garrett (b. c.1675, d. c.
1715, dau. of Dennis and Barbara (?) Garrett), and 2nd Dinah Hawkins, alive in 1747, dau. of Matthew Hawkins; Cole's birth date
determined by depositions giving his age as 38 in 1707, 63 in 1732,
and 67 in 1737; Cole testified at the trial of Capt. John Oldton
for the murder of Cole's father-in-law Dennis Garrett; in Sept.
1702 John Broad (who m. Dennis Garrett's wid. Barbara) made a will
naming Thomas, s. of John and Johanna Cole; in Aug. 1712 Barbara
(?) Garrett Broad conv. prop. to her grandson Dennis Garrett Cole,
s. of John and Hannah Cole; in Nov. 1712 John conv. his s. Joseph
part Daniel's Whimsey, and conv. part of same tract to his son
John in March 1733; with w. Dinah, Thomas Nowland and w., Thomas
Broad and w. Anna, and Rebecca Hawkins, conv. to Lancelot Todd
land of the late Matthew Hawkins; in June 1731 was made exempt
from paying taxes; his will, 12 Nov. 1745 - 5 Nov. 1746, named w.
Dinah and ch., Charles, Joseph, and Matthew; admin. bond posted

23 Nov. 1747 by Joseph Taylor with William Barney and Thomas Williamson; est. admin. by Taylor on 5 Feb. 1747/8 and 7 Nov. 1754; had iss.: ELIZABETH, m. John Ensor; JOSEPH, d. c.1721; JOHN, m. MARY; THOMAS, m. Sarah; SARAH, b. c. 1693, d. 1758, m. Charles Gorsuch; DENNIS GARRETT; WILLIAM, d. c.1770; (by 2nd w.): CHARLES; JOSEPH; MATTHEW (4:177, 244; 11:364; 19:276; 29:161; 66:183, 256; 67:362; 68:18; 69:209; 70:340; 73:121; 74:47; 75:25; 77:485, 686; 78:107; 110:373; 122:160; 310:125).

COLE, JOSEPH (6), s. of John (5) and Johanna, d. in Balto. Co. by 13 March 1720, having m. Susannah (?); his will, 22 Jan. 1720 - 13 March 1720, named w. Susanna, dau. Sarah (not yet 16), and dau. Susanna (begotten of his w. Susanna); Charles Gorsuch and his w. Sarah (formerly Cole), Thomas Cole and his w. Sarah; had iss.: SARAH, b. after 1704, m. 24 Nov. 1735 Anthony Chamness and moved to N. C. by 1764; SUSANNA (90:82; 110:167; 112:133; 133:154).

COLE, JOHN (7), s. of John (5) and Johanna, alive in 1750 when he owned 100 a. Cole's Chance; m. Mary Chaffinch on 25 Dec. 1730; in Oct. 1737 he and his w. joined his f. John in selling part Daniel's Whimsey to John Ensor; in March 1740 he bought part of Spring Garden from Edward and Mary Richards; and in March 1745/6 James Tracey of Craven Co., N. C., appointed John Ensor of Patapsco. his atty. to ackn. sale of James Meadow and Teague's Park to John Cole, Jr.; had iss.: JOSEPH, b. 15 April 1736 (75:25, 472; 79:248; 133:150; 150:6).

COLE, THOMAS (8), s. of John (5) and Johanna, alive in 1781; m. Sarah (?); in 1725 surv. 100 a. Christopher's Lot; between 9 Jan. 1726 and 6 March 1733/4 obtained portions of Levy's Tribe, Addition to Levy's Tribe, and Green's Chance; in 1750 owned 100 a. Christopher's Lot, and 56 a. Thomas Lot; in March 1768 he sold and bought back these two tracts to and from his s. Thomas, Jr.; in 1781 conv. to s. Christopher tracts Christopher's Lot and lease of Mountain; had iss.: CHRISTOPHER, b. by 1718; THOMAS, b. 14 Feb. 1718; JOANNA, b. 28 May 1720; SARAH, b. 15 Aug. 1722; BROAD, b. 12 Aug. 1725; ABRAHAM, b. 10 Jan. 1727/8; MARY, b. 12 May 1730; ELIZABETH, b. 13 Feb. 1733/4 (70:290, 406; 72:21, 193; 74:32; 207-IL#A:557; 207-PL#6:65; 231-WG#G:230, 232).

COLE, DENNIS GARRETT (9), s. of John (5) and Johanna, d. c.1773 in Balto. Co., having m. Rachel, dau. of Mordecai and Mary (Parsons) Price; in 1750 owned 50 a. Price's Favor and 50 a. Maynor's Beginning; his will, Dec. 1772 - 16 June 1773, named grandson Dennis Cole, sic ch. of his dec. dau. Edith Mallonee, grandson Stephen Gill, born of his dau. Cassandra Gill, daus. Urith Price and Rachel Pearce, s. Henry, granddau. Rebecca Pitt, and w. Rachel, sons-in-law John Price, Jr., and Stephen Gill; had iss.: EDITH, b. 28 Aug. 1728, m. 8 Nov. 1748 Edith Mallonee; URITH, b. 25 Nov. 1731, m. John Price, Jr.; DENNIS, b. 9 Dec. 1734, d. 1770; RACHEL, m. (?) Pearce; HENRY; CASSANDRA, b. 1751, d. 1811, m. 1772 Stephen Gill; REBECCA, m. (?) Pitt (112:252; 131:32; 133:50; 153:12).

COLE, WILLIAM (10), s. of John (5) and Johanna, d. in Balto. Co. in 1770; m. Mary Giles; prob. the William Cole of Deer Creek who in 1750 owned 183 a. Arabia Petrea; his will, 18 Jan. 1769 - 25 June 1770, named lands Cross' Park, Cole's Favor, Cole's Manor, Cole's String, Cole's Castle, Cole's Struggle, and Cole's Chance, his f. John, w. Mary, and ch., William, Giles, Vincent, Joseph, Alice, m. Caples, Hannah, Cordelia, Elizabeth, Mary, and Rebecca, Sarah, dau. and heir of testator's bro. Joseph and Sarah's husband Anthony Chamness, kinsman Joseph Ensor; had iss.: WILLIAM; JOHN; GILES; VINCENT; JOSEPH, b. c.1752; ALICE, m. Robert Caples; HANNAH; CORDELIA; ELIZABETH; SYBIL; REBECCA; and MARY (112:144; 153:51).

COLE, CHARLES (11), s. of John (5) by his 2nd w. Dinah, b. c.
1717, alive in May 1744 when he leased from Thomas Brerewood a
lot in Charlotte Town, the lease to run for the life spans of
himself, then age 27, and his bros. Joseph, 18, and Matthew, 12
(79:360).

COLE, MATTHEW (12), s. of Joseph (5) and Dinah, b. c.1736, was
alive in 1744, and d. by 12 Nov. 1754 when admin. bond on his est.
was posted by Charles Cole with Isaac Sampson (11:376; 79:360).

COLE, CHRISTOPHER (13), s. of Thomas (8), b. c.1718, d. by 7
Dec. 1785 when his est. was admin. by Sarah Cole; m. Sarah Tipton,
b. 3 Oct. 1722, dau. of William and Hannah (Price) Tipton; may
have m. 2nd Sarah Hooker; in Jan. 1737 bought 100 a. Panthers
Hills from John Parrish; still owned this land in 1750; in 1781
his f. Thomas, Sr., conv. him Christopher's Lot and the lease of
Mountain; est. admin. 7 Dec. 1785 by Sarah Cole; had iss.: CHRIS-
TOPHER, Jr.; EZEKIEL (75; 153:14; 231-WG#G:230, 232; 231-WG#VV:
592, 594).

COLE, THOMAS (14), s. of Thomas(8), b. 14 Feb. 1718, d. c.
1793; m. 1st Elizabeth (?) who d. by 25 Jan. 1747, and m. 2nd on
that date Sarah, dau. of Mordecai and Elizabeth Price; was disch.
from Gunpowder Meeting on 23 d, 5 mo., 1759 for drinking to excess
and for gaming; bought part Price's Good Will from Aquila Carr in
June 1760; his will, 27 Aug. 1792 - 9 Jan. 1793, named grandch.,
Stephen, Elisha, Micajah, Salathiel, and Aquila Cole, and Thomas
Wheeler, and the following ch. (Thomas is said to have had three
by his 1st w. and seven by his 2nd w.): THOMAS, m. Rebecca; CHRIS-
TOPHER; SALATHIEL; MORDECAI, m. Artridge Price; ELIZABETH, b. 31
Jan. 1747; SOPHIA, b. 8 Nov. 1751, m. William Price; RACHEL, b.
19 Nov. 1753, m. John Bond, Jr.; SARAH, m. Joshua Ford on 10 June
1786; ANNE, m. (?) Bosley; REBECCA; MARY, m. (?) Wheeler (84:267;
112:252; 131:32; 133:50; 136).

COLE, ABRAHAM (15), s. of Thomas (8), b. 10 Jan. 1727/8, d. c.
1822 in Balto. Co.; his will, 12 June 1818 - 20 March 1822; m. and
had iss.: SARAH, m. (?) Bosley; ANN, m. Thomas Donovan; RUTH, d.
by 1 Feb. 1843; EDITH, m. (?) Hall; BELINDA, m. William Stansbury;
ELEANOR; ABRAHAM, b. c.1760; JAMES . (236-11:404).

COLE, JOSEPH (16), s. of William (10) and Mary, b. 1752, d. 21
Oct. 1821, m. Sophia Osborne by lic. 24 Dec. 1788; had iss.: VACHEL,
m. Jemima Ensor; KEZIAH, m. Abraham Cole; URITH, m. (?) Price;
RACHEL, m. (?) Benson; ERNESTUS, m. Mary J. Cole; JOSEPH; RUTH;
SALATHIEL; STEPHEN; SOPHIA; GILES. (Cole notes, MHS).

COLE, GILES (17), s. of William (10) and Mary, d. by 14 March
1828 when his est. was admin. by wid. Sarah; had iss.: HARRIET, m.
Edward Norwood; TALITHA, m. Johnsee Wooden; LUTHER; PENELOPE; MA-
TILDA, m. Patrick Lynch; ABIJAH, under age in 1828; ALFRED, under
age in 1828; WILLIAM; under age; JOHN, under age (237-25:456).

COLE, ANGELICO, in Dec. 1758 was named as dau.-in-law in will
of Alexander Grant of Balto. Co. who also named his w. Elizabeth
(127:13).

COLE, CASSANDRA, d. testate in Balto. Co.; her will, 19 June
1745 - 13 May 1746, named s. Skipwith, s. William (and his ch.);
dau. Cassandra Rigbie, dau. Ann Johns, grandch., Skipwith, Cassandra Johns, Susanna Rigbie, and son-in-law Nathan Rigbie (110:368).

COLE, ELIZABETH, had iss.: COMFORT, b. 7 Feb. 1714; COMFORT,
b. 8 Nov. 1720 (131:5, 38/r).

COLE, GEORGE, m. 2 March 1732 Martha Litton, and had iss.:
HENRY, b. 25 March 1736 (128:70, 92).

COLE, JAMES, d. in Balto. Co. by 1 July 1772; m.
19 July 1748 Jane Poloke; his will, 29 May 1772 - 1 July 1772, named tracts
Monreal, Paradice, and other land, and his ch.; his est. admin. 5
May 1773 by execs. James and Jane Cole; had iss.: JANE, b. 7 July
1749; JAMES, b. 29 July 1751; EPHRAIM, b. 7 April 1754; COMFORT,
b. 14 May 1756; ELIZABETH, b. 2 Sept. 1758; THOMAS; EZEKIEL (6:
317; 112:210; 129:360, 361).

COLE, JOHN, and WILLIAM, were Quakers from A. A. Co., who resided at Bush River c.1700 (433:366).

COLE, JOHN, m. Mary (?), and had iss.: WILLIAM, b. 24 July 1741
(128:116).

COLE, JOHN, d. by 28 Dec. 1745, when admin. bond was posted by
William Fell with Robert North and William Hammond (11:359).

COLE, MARY, m. 21 Jan. 1729 John Miles Youngblood (129:254).

COLE, PHILIP, d. by 26 July 1734, when his estate was admin.
by Cassandra Cole (See Cassandra Cole above); had iss.: SKIPWITH;
CASSANDRA, m. Nathan Rigbie; WILLIAM; MARY (3:172).

COLE, SKIPWITH, prob. s. of Philip above and Cassandra, d. by
11 Oct. 1755 when admin. bond was posted by Margaret Cole with
James Rigbie and Richard Johns; in 1750 owned 352 a. Stone Hill
and 110 a. Arabia Petrea; m. Margaret (poss. Holland), and had
iss.: SKIPWITH, b. 16 March 1736; WILLIAM, b. 5 Aug. 1738; PHILIP,
b. 6 Dec. 1740; CASSANDRA, b. 8 Jan. 1742 (11:388; 128:115; 129:
331; 153:62).

COLE, THOMAS and w. Priscilla imm. to Md. c.1649; he and his
w. and a Sarah Cole were mentioned in the will of John Godfrey,
made 29 May 1672, proved 19 June 1672; in Aug. 1673 Thomas Cole
surv. 450 a. Maiden's Choice which was later held by Charles Gorsuch's son; may have acquired other tracts: Cole's Harbour, 350
a. on which the original 60 acres of Balto. Town were laid out,
and Marybone, 200 a.; these tracts were sold by Charles Gorsuch
and his w. Sarah on 8 Dec. 1679 to David Jones (the deed stated
that the tracts were inherited by Sarah Gorsuch by the will of her
father Thomas Cole, but no such will has been found); had iss.:
SARAH, b. c.1657, m. by 13, 3rd mo., 1677, Charles Gorsuch then
living on the Eastern Shore where the Tred Avon meeting called him
to account for taking a wife contrary "to the truth" (60:46; 120:
69; 211:110; 388).

COLE, THOMAS, m. Elizabeth (?) and had iss.: ZIPPORAH, b. 17
Jan. 1716; JAMES, b. 24 Nov. 1724 (128:84; 131:9).

COLE, THOMAS, d. by 22 May 1745; was in Balto. Co. by 7 June
1727 when he bought part Bond's Last Shift from Thomas and Anne
Bond; m. by 4 Nov. 1741 Mary (?) who joined him in selling Young
Man's Adventure, orig. granted to William Cole, to William Cole;
his will, 25 April 1745 - 22 May 1745, left s. William 420 a. of
Bond's Last Shift, and named dau. Sarah, nephews Aquilla and
Jonathan Collier Massey, and bro.-in-law Samuel Richardson; admin.
bond posted 12 June 1745 by Samuel Richardson of P. G. Co. with
Joseph Richardson and Joseph Richardson, Sr.; had iss.: WILLIAM;
SARAH (11:370; 70:418; 76:22; 111:207; 153:14).

COLE, WILLIAM, in Nov. 1741 purch. from Thomas Cole Young Man's
Adventure, Martinton, and Martin's Addition; in 1750 owned 200 a.

Youngman's Adventure, 100 a. Martinton, 100 a. Martin's Addition, and 97 a. Charles Goodluck or Chance (76:22; 153:101).

COLE, WILLIAM, in 1742 leased 100 a. Gunpowder Manor called Cole's Manor for the lifetimes of his s. William, 45, Mary, 43, and Broad Cole, 34 (ages as of 1767) (389:5).

COLE, WILLIAM, Jr., m. 22, 12 mo., 1756 at Herring Creek Meeting Sarah Robertson of Calvert Co., dau. of Samuel and Elizabeth (Harris) Robertson; she was bur. 28 Jan. 1766 in her 35th yr. at her husband's plantation in Balto. Co.; had iss.: SARAH, b. 21, 3 mo. 1759; SAMUEL ROBERTSON, b. 10 d, 1 mo., 1761; ELIZABETH, b. 5, 6 mo. 1763 (136).

COLEGATE, RICHARD (1), was in Balto. Co. by 1700 as a taxable in n. side of Patapsco Hund.; d. 1721/2; m. Rebecca, dau. of Eleanor Herbert; Rebecca m. 2nd James Powell; Colegate was a factor for the London merchants of Thomas Yoakley and Pettet, admin. the estates of John Leasor and Miles Temple in April 1707, and was a delegate to the Assembly from Balto. Co. at various sessions, 1707 to 1721, and held military ranks of captain, colonel, and major; his will, 8 Aug. 1721 - 16 Feb. 1721/2 named w. Rebecca and seven ch.; est. inv. at £ 3,792.17.8 and held over 5000 acres of land; admin. bond posted 26 April 1722 by extx. Rebecca Colegate with Thomas Hammond and Lance Todd and John Dorsey; est. admin. on 20 Oct. 1724 and 10 June 1731; had iss.: PRUDENCE, m. John Talbott on 10 Jan. 1726/7; PATIENCE, m. 20 Sept. 1724 William Buckner, and m. 2nd by June 1733 George Elliott; RICHARD, b. 10 March 1710; TEMPERANCE, b. 24 Feb. 1712; JOHN, b. 5 March 1713; THOMAS, b. 22 Jan. 1716; BENJAMIN, b. 2 Nov. 1719 (1:322; 2:80, 179, 291; 3:7, 97; 11:295; 27:51; 30:9; 124:104; 133:3; 291; 370: 228; 581; 582).

COLEGATE, RICHARD (2), s. of Richard (1) and Rebecca, b. 10 March 1710, d. 1759; m. Bridget Garrettson, dau. of Henry and Elizabeth (Cantwell) Garrettson; she d. 1778; in Nov. 1724 he chose John Gardner of Clapham's Creek as his guardian; had iss.: MARY, b. 1744, d. 1790, m. 1st Dr. John Dale, and 2nd Dr. Buchanan; JOHN; HENRY; RICHARD (27:32).

COLEGATE, JOHN (3), s. of Richard (1) and Rebecca, b. 5 March 1713, d. c.1782; m. 1st Honour, dau. of Edward Tully, and 2nd Elizabeth Prosser; in 1730 was a ward of John Talbott; in 1750 owned 844 a. John and Thomas' Forest; his will, 6 Dec. 1781 - 7 Jan. 1782, named ch.: ASAPH, b. 1765, went to Huntington Co., Pa.; RICHARD, m. Elizabeth Ashman; JOHN, m. Ellen Ashman; RACHEL, m. James Lytle; ANN, m. Stephen Watters; REBECCA, m. 9 Jan. 1772 John Murray (29:51; 112:464, 470; 136; 153:46).

COLEGATE, THOMAS (4), s. of Richard (1) and Rebecca, b. 22 Jan. 1716, d. 1796; m. by 15 Feb. 1777 Cassandra, dau. of Penelope Deye; in 1730 was a ward of John Talbott; in 1750 owned 844 a. part of John and Thomas Forest; had iss.: COCKEY DEYE, m. John Cockey Owings; JOHN; THOMAS; PRISCILLA; MARY: CHARLOTTE, m. Edward Owings (29:51; 112:562; 153:55; 370:288).

COLEGATE, BENJAMIN (5), s. of Richard (1) and Rebecca, b. 2 Nov. 1719, d. 1762; m. 1739 Charity, dau. of Benjamin Wheeler; she d. 1763; in March 1724/5 was ward of Eleanor Herbert; in 1750 owned 500 a. Friend's Discovery; 163 a. Colegate's Last Shift, 110 a. Maiden's Mistake, 20 a. part St. Omer, 60 a. Turkey Range, 100 a. Colegate's Contrivance, and other land; his will, 27 Oct. 1758 - 28 June 1762, named w. Charity and six ch., and appointed James Scott and William Rogers to see his children were brought up in the Prot. faith; est. admin. 28 Oct. 1768 by Job Key; had iss.:

THOMAS, b. 1740; REBECCA, d. 1800, m. Job Key; ELIZABETH, m. William Downs; MARY, m. Nathan Scott; ANN, m. (?) Thomas; RUTH, m. 1776 Edward Bussey (7:328; 27:126; 111:127; 153:101).

COLEGATE, ASAPH (6), s. of John (3), b. 1765, went to Huntington Co., Penna.; served in the Rev. War, and was pensioned (277:330).

COLEGATE, THOMAS (7), s. of Benjamin (5) and Charity, b. 1740, d. 1795; m. 1st Elizabeth Partridge who d. 23 April 1768, and m. 2nd Elizabeth Clark, b. 1740; his will, 9 Dec. 1794 - 25 March 1795, named w. Elizabeth and four ch.; had one dau. by 1st w., and four ch. by 2nd; had iss.: ELIZABETH PARTRIDGE, b. 22 April 1768, m. (?) Emerson; MARY, b. 1771, d. in inf.; REBECCA, b. 1774; SARAH, b. 1777, d. 1822, m. Josias Stansbury; THOMAS, b. 1780. (115:249).

COLEMAN, DUNCAN, with w. Sarah admin. the est. of Thomas Towson on 16 April 1731 (3:85).

COLEMAN, ELIZABETH, had iss.: MARY, b. 5 July 1699 (128:20).

COLEMAN, RICHARD, d. by 8 June 1767 when his est. was admin. by Mary w. of Jeremiah Croney (7:304).

COLESON, ELIZABETH, ind. for bast., March 1731 (29:224).

COLESPEEGLE, ELIZABETH, ind. for bast. June 1728 (28:31).

COLESPEEGLE, JOHN, d. 23 April 1741; m. 19 May 1735 Deborah Cottrell; est. admin. 11 March 1742 by Joseph Johnson; had iss.: THOMAS, b. 10 Aug. 1736; MARY, b. 1738 (3:254; 128:87, 93B, 113).

COLLETT, JOHN (1), b. 1578, d. 1650; m. Susanna Ferrar, b. 1581, d. 1657, dau. of Nicholas and Mary (Woodnoth) Ferrar; had iss.: THOMAS, d. 1675, m. Martha Sherinton; FERRAR; EDWARD; RICHARD, b. 1602, d. 1668; NICHOLAS, d. 1684; JOHN, b. 1604, d. 1669; MARY, d. 1680; ANN, d. 1638; JUDITH, d. unm.; HESTER, d. unm.; MARGARET, d. unm.; JOYCE, d. unm.; SUSANNA, m. John Mapletoft (her dau. Mary m. 1st Lawrence Ward of Nansemond, Va., and 2nd Nathaniel Utie of Balto. Co., Md. (212-8:203; 583; 584).

COLLETT, RICHARD (2), s. of John (1) and Susanna, b. 1602, d. 1668, imm. to Balto. Co. c.1650, and again in Nov. 1652; m. Emerentiana (?) who imm. c.1651-8; by Jan. 1664 had m. 2nd Elizabeth (?) who joined him in sale of land to his bro. John; his will, 8 Jan. 1667 - 28 April 1668, left w. Eliza his extx. and sole legatee, to have 200 a. Susquehanna Point: his relict Eliza m. by 1677 Christopher Rousby (94; 120:43; 388).

COLLETT, JOHN (3), s. of John (1) and Susanna, b. 1604, d. 1669; m. Ann Goldsmith and imm. to Balto. Co. c.1650 with w. Ann and ch. George and John (s. Samuel had been transp. c.1650); acquired many tracts of land incl. 100 a. Collingham; in June 1661 appointed Clerk to Commissioners of Balto. Co., and in 1662 and 1665 was sheriff of Balto. Co.; his will, 31 Oct. 1669 - 29 Oct. 1670, named bro.-in-law John Goldsmith and three ch.: SAMUEL, eld. s.; JOHN; GEORGE, not yet 21 (93; 94; 95: 97:123, 125; 98:44, 45, 46, 48; 129:55; 200-3; 211:5; 388).

COLLETT, SAMUEL (4), s. of John (3) and Ann, b. c.1640, d. 1706, living 28 Feb. 1668/9 when he sold 250 a. Woodland Neck to John Tarkinton; may have been father of: DAVID (96).

COLLETT, JOHN (5), s. of John (3) and Ann, d. by 21 June 1673; m. Elizabeth (?) who m. as her 2nd husb. Henry Haslewood, and 3rd by 1693/4 Miles Gibson; his will, 26 March 1673 - 21 June 1673, named Peter Ellis, cous. Mary Goldsmith, Henry Haslewood, cous. Matthew Goldsmith (not yet 14), Matthew's sis. Eliza, tracts Turkey Hill, Elk's Neck, Small Hopes, Collett's Point; may have had iss.: HENRY; WILLIAM; JOHN (120:74; 206-7A:361; 206-12:149, 157).

COLLETT, DAVID (6), s. of Samuel (4), according to the Collett Genealogy, was the father of: DANIEL, b. 1701; RUTH, b. 1703; MOSES, b. 1705.

COLLETT, DANIEL (7), poss. s. of David (6), d. 13 Feb. 1725/6; m. Ruth (?); est. admin. by Ralph Lowe on 9 Nov. 1733; had iss.: RACHAEL, alive 1737; DANIEL, b. 15 Feb. 1724; MOSES, b. c.1725; poss. ELIZABETH, b. c.1727, m. on 15 Dec. 1754 Martin Murphy (3: 128; 31:43, 137; 128:48; 131:45).

COLLETT, DANIEL (8), s. of Daniel (7), b. 15 Feb. 1724, d. by 15 June 1784; m. 1 Aug. 1749 Susanna McKenley; his will, 18 Aug. 1783 - 15 June 1784, named w. Susanna and these ch.: RUTH; MOSES; ELIZABETH, m. (?) Sampson; JEMIMA; ABRAHAM; MARY; WILLIAM; RACHEL; STEPHEN (112:555; 128:48; 131:34).

COLLETT, MOSES (9), s. of Daniel (7), b. c.1725, d. 1802; m. 12 Jan. 1743 Elizabeth Wyle; had iss.: STEPHEN, b. 4 May 1746; RACHEL, b. 1748, m. John Kilpatrick; MOSES, b. 1750, d. 1836; ABRAHAM, b. 1752, d. 1790; JOHN, b. 1760, d. 1834; ELIZABETH, b. 1754, m. John Tague or Teague; ISAAC, b. 1762, d. 1780; AARON, b. 1763; SARAH, b. 1765 (131:25, 115/r).

COLLETT, MICHAEL, parentage not given, b. 7 Aug. 1713 (128:31).

COLLETT, SAMUEL, m. Catherine (?), and had: SAMUEL, b. 1 Oct. 1704; ANN, b. 5 March 1706; JOHN, b. 19 July 1709 (128:29).

COLLIER, Mrs. ANN, m. Jonathan Marcy (Massey?) on 25 Nov. 1701 (129:196).

COLLIER, JAMES, with William York admin. the est. of John Warton (2:57).

COLLIER, JOHN, came to Md. by 1659 when he claimed land for service, and d. by 5 July 1676; bought Upper Ollies from Oliver Sprye in March 1661/2; with w. Ann sold tract Collier to John Bruer in June 1663; bought Gunworth from Walter Dickeson in Aug. 1663; sold 100 a. Phills Choice to Richard Adams and William Robinson in May 1670; est. inv. 5 July 1676 by John Hill and James Collier; val. at 7863 lbs. tob., inv. filed 22 Oct. 1676 (48:58; 93; 96; 388).

COLLIER, JOHN, d. by 1688; m. by March 1684/5 Sarah, admnx. of George Hooper; in 1686 John and Sarah Collier were named as bro. and sis. of Abraham Holman in latter's will; d. by 1688 when his est. was admin. by John Hall with payment to a Philip Collier (18:252; 121:6; 206-9:504, and 10:168).

COLLINS, FRANCIS (1), m. Ann, and was alive in 1736; on 10 April 1725 was son-in-law of Matthew Molton of Balto. Co.; had iss.: SILENCE, b. 13 Nov. 1725; MOSES, b. 20 May 1728; SARAH, b. 4 Oct. 1734; HANNAH, b. 24 March 1736 (124:99; 128:45, 73, 83, 96).

COLLINS, SILENCE (2), dau. of Francis (1), b. 13 Nov. 1725; tried for bast. in Nov. 1756; son ISAAC, b. 15 Jan. 1756 (41:312; 128:45; 129:352).

COLLINS, MOSES (3), s. of Francis (1), b. 20 May 1728; m. 6 Jan. 1750 Patience Powell, and had iss.: CASSANDRA, b. 12 March

1751; JACOB, b. 1 Oct. 1754; SAMUEL, b. 15 April 1756; SARAH POWELL, b. 8 April 1759 (129:363).

COLLINS, WILLIAM, m. 7 Nov. 1751 Joanna Cantwell; had iss.: SUSANNA, b. 10 May 1752; SARAH, b. 13 July 1755; JOHN, b. 12 Sept. 1756; EPHRAIM, b. 13 Jan. 1759 (129:363).

COLLISON, WILLIAM, m. 3 Dec. 1713 Susannah, admnx. of William Adams (1:212; 131:4).

COLMORE, THOMAS, m. by Nov. 1723 Anne Milner; perhaps the same Thomas who m. by June 1730 Anne Miller (26:170; 28:425).

COLSON/COLSTON, BENJAMIN, serv. of Thomas Brown, d. 12 Oct. 1702 (128:14).

COLSON, JOHN, m. Rebecca (?), and had iss.: JOHN, b. 3 March 1737; HENRY, b. 10 Nov. 1741 (128:92b; 129:327).

COLSWORTHY, GEORGE, d. by 12 Oct. 1703, when his est. was inv. by Thomas Carpenter, and val. at £ 80.15.4 (51:128).

COLT, DANIEL, servant, with 1 yr. to serve in the 1754 inv. of Stephen Onion (49:221).

COMBEST, JOHN (1), d. by 3 Aug. 1710; was in Balto. Co. by 1692 as a taxable in Spesutia Hund.; admin. bond posted 3 Aug. 1710 by George Wells, with Jonathan Massey and William Lenox; est. was inv. 27 Aug. 1710 by Roger Matthews and Jos'h Johnson, and val. at £ 26.3.11; had iss.: SARAH, b. 17 Jan. 1693, m. William Robinson on 8 Dec. 1713; KETURAH, b. 10 Oct. 1695; MARY, b. 20 April 1698; MARTHA, b. 9 Sept. 1700 (11:452; 48:158; 128:1, 5, 11; 129:213; 138).

COMBEST, KETURAH (2), dau. of John (1), b. 10 Oct. 1695; ind. for bast. in June 1716; had iss.: JOHN, s. of "Anna Jury" Combest, b. 24 Dec. 1715 (22:14; 128:1, 34).

COMBEST, MARTHA (3), dau. of John (1), b. 9 Sept. 1700; fined for bast. in March 1718/9, and would not name the father; had iss.: JACOB, b. 10 Nov. 1718 (23:64; 128:1, 38).

COMBEST, JOHN (4), s. of Keturah (2), was b. 24 Dec. 1715, prob. the John who m. Mary Bowley on 25 Feb. 1741 and had iss.: THOMAS, b. 13 June 1742 (128:34; 129:328).

COMBEST, JACOB (5), s. of Martha (3), b. 10 Nov. 1718, d. by 22 April 1767; m. Mary Solovan or Sullivan on 2 June 1743; in 1750 owned 11 a. George's Hall and 11 a. Smith's Fancy; his will, 11 Jan. 1767 - 29 April 1767, named tract Middleborough, w. Mary, and ch.: Jacob, Israel, Martha, and Cassandra; a codicil of 17 March 1767 named John Hall, Jr., s. of John Hall, as exec. if w. Mary died; est. was admin. 22 Aug. 1769 by John Hall, and had iss.; JACOB, poss. by an earlier marriage; MARTHA, b. 24 May 1744; ISRAEL, b. 24 May 1744; CASSANDRA, b. 15 Nov. 1746 (7:2; 112:67; 129:331, 338, 344; 153:71).

COMBEST, THOMAS, no known rel. to above, m. 20 Nov. 1735 in Penna. Elizabeth Thornbury; had iss.: JOSIAH, b. 10 Dec. 1736; KEZIAH, b. 26 Feb. 1738; JOHN, b. 18 March 1740 (128:95, 103, 111; 130:280).

COMBEST, JOHN, mulatto, age 11½ years, was bound to George Wells in June 1716 (22:12).

COMBO, ELIZA, in March 1739/40 was ind. twice for bast.; and as servant to William Hammond was tried twice on separate charges in June 1740 (32:140, 239, 240).

COME, WILLIAM, in 1750 owned 67 a., part Hunting Quarter (153: 51).

COMINGS, WILLIAM, surgeon, d. by 9 Dec. 1712, when admin. bond was posted by James Gordon with John Willmot, Sr., and John Ashman; est. was inv. 17 March 1714 and val. at £ 20.1.1 plus £18.19.0 with John Rattenbury and Thomas Todd signing; est. was admin. 29 July 1714 by James Gordon (1:5; 11:307; 50:280).

COMLEY, JAMES (1), his wife and ch. were received into membership in Gunpowder Meeting on 28 d, 6, 1751, from Abington Meeting, Pa.; had iss.: JACOB; JAMES; JONATHAN; DAVID; RACHEL; JOHN (136).

COMLEY, JAMES (2), s. of James (1), m. a dau. of Richard Hooker by 24 d, 7, 1765 (136).

COMORAN. See CAMERON.

COMPTON, JOSEPH, was in Balto. Co. by 1694 as a taxable in s. side Patapsco Hund.; d. by March 1718/9 leaving iss.: WILLIAM, b. 15 May 1709; JOSEPH, in March 1718 was bound to serve George Eves to age 21 (23:70; 128:26; 139).

COMPTON, LYDIA, in Nov. 1724 bore a bast. to Nathaniel Ayres (27:32, 41).

COMWORTH/CONEYWORTH/ CORNWORTH, MICHAEL, was in Balto. Co. by 1694 as a taxable in n. side Patapsco; d. by 6 Sept. 1698 when admin. bond was posted by Andrew Anderson with Xpher Bembridge and Xpher Shaw (11:305; 139; 140).

CONAWAY, JOSEPH (1), d. in A. A. Co. by 4 June 1707, when his will, signed 1 May 1705, was proved; m. Jane (---), who joined him in a sale of Davis' Lot to Alexander Lumley in May 1698; purch. 1 parcel of 80 a. of Friendship from Edmund Talbot, and 80 a. of the 160 a. tract from William Travelle; in his will he left the first parcel to son Joseph, and second to sons John and James; had iss.; JOSEPH; JOHN; JAMES; ANNE (63:277; 122:88).

CONAWAY, JOSEPH (2), s. of Joseph (1), m. Rebecca (?) and had moved to Balto. Co. by 1712 when he sold his share of Friendship, and was still there in June 1721 and Dec. 1724 when he wit. the wills of George Hope and Henry Hall (124:60, 199).

CONAWAY, JOHN (3), s. of Joseph (1), d. in A. A. Co., leaving a will, 29 March 1728 - 12 Aug. 1729; m. 1st on 17 Aug. 1714 Ann Aegillston in St. Ann's Par.; m. 2nd on 15 July 1729 Catherine (?); in 1712 he purch. 80 a. of Friendship from Joseph and Rebecca Conaway, and about 1713 he and his w. Ann sold 120 a. of this land to Robert Cross; his will named a cousin Joseph, and these ch.: JOHN (inherited Low Neck from his father); CHARLES, b. 15 April 1722 in St. Margarets Par., A. A. Co.; JANE, m. Benjamin Larkin; SARAH (125:135; 217-1B#2; 219-2; 219-4).

CONAWAY, JAMES (4), s. of Joseph, (1), d. in A. A. Co., by 1 March 1748, having m. on 11 May 1714 Sarah Chappell; had iss.: JOHN (on 10 Feb. 1733/4 John Conaway of James was left prop. by the will of Edward Fuller); ANNA, b. 5 Sept. 1715; JOSEPH, b. 21 April 1718 (mentioned in the will of Edward Fuller); CHARLES, b. 12 Aug. 1723 (inherited Narrows and Roberson's Addition from

his father); JAMES, b. 8 Jan. 1721; GEORGE, b. 6 Aug. 1725 (126:
88; 210-26:30; 219-4).

CONAWAY, JOHN (5), s. of John (3), was alive in 1749; in 1729
he inherited Low Neck from his father; in 1738 he bought 100 a.
Bares Thicket from Benjamin Larkin; in 1740 he sold Low Neck to
Benjamin Fowler, and in 1749 he conv. Luckey Hole to Vachel Oley
(217-RB#1; 217-RB#3).

CONAWAY, GEORGE (6), s. of James (4), d. in A. A. Co., leaving
a will, 19 May 1772- 28 July 1772, in which he named tracts Al-
dridge, Bakers Folly, The Narrow, Point Lookout, and Roberson's
Addition; had iss.: GEORGE; DELILAH, m. (?) Moss; ARA; AMELIA;
and VACHEL (210-38:829).

CONAWAY, JOHN, rel. to above not estab., was in Balto. Co. by
14 May 1744 when he m. Ann Norwood; poss. the John Conaway, "bro.
and heir at law to Miles Love," who sold certain lands in Balto.
Co. in Sept. 1762; had iss.: RACHEL, b. 9 Feb. 1745; CHARLES, b.
25 Aug. 1748, m.Margaret Stocksdale; SARAH, b. 21 Dec. 1750;
RUTH, b. 21 March 1753; ANN, b. 20 March 1755; JOHN, b. 11 July
1757; SUSANNA, b. 12 July 1760 (86:301; 133:78, 105, 166).

CONAWAY, MICHAEL, b. 27 Jan. 1738 near Balto. Md., d. by 1847
in Harrison Co., Ohio; m. 1779 Elizabeth Davis; pvt. in the Ship
Defense during the Rev. War (364:84).

CONGDON, NICHOLAS, was in Balto. Co. by 1692 as a taxable in
n. side Gunpowder Hund. (138).

CONNAY, PHILIP. See CONNER, PHILIP.

CONNELL, WILLIAM (1), d. in Balto. Co. by March 1736; m. Mary
(?), by whom he had iss.: JOHN, b. 2 April 1720 (acc. to court
rec.) or 1730 (acc. to ch. reg.); HESTER, b. 8 April 1725; WILLIAM,
b. 21 June 1727; MARY, b. 1 Jan. 1730; REBEKAH, b. 20 July 1735;
JOSEPH, twin to Mary, b. 20 July 1735 (133:1, 9, 13, 20, 44; 31:2).

CONNELL, JOHN (2), s. of William (1) and Mary, was b. 2 April
1720; as orphan of William, in March 1736 was bound to Redmond
Dearing to age 21, his age given as 15 on 2 April next; m. Mary
(?) by whom he had iss.: ELIZABETH, b. 15 July 1746; ANN, b. 9
Oct. 1748 (31:2; 133:76, 79).

CONNELY. See CONNOLLY.

CONNER/CONNAY/CONNOR, PHILIP, d. leaving a will, 6 May 1710 -
15 July 1710, leaving personalty to Eliza Burk and John Macklove,
and appointing his wife (not named) as extx. and residuary legatee; admin. bond posted 15 July 1710 by extx. Margaret Conner
with Patrick Murphy and Richard King; est. admin. by sd. Margaret on 27 Aug. 17100; m. Margaret (poss. Carrington) who m. 2nd
David Hagan; had iss.: ELEANOR, b. c.1709 (in Aug. 1719
Thomas Taylor pet. the court that 3½ years earlier, David Hagan,
father-in-law to sd. Eleanor, then 7 years old (orphan of Philip
and Margaret Conner, and goddau. to Taylor's wife),requested Taylor to raise the child; shortly after the June Court, Eleanor's
uncle, Henry Carrington took the child; Taylor's petition to have
the child restored to him was rejected (1:373; 11:302; 23:215;
122:182).

CONNER, JOHN, m. Aug. 1744 Susanna Burgess and had iss.: JOHN,
b. 30 July 1746 (131:119/r).

CONNER, JOHN, d. in Balto. Co., leaving a will, 31 Oct. 1757 -

2 Dec. 1757, mentioned est. in Balto. and Cecil Cos.; named servant Thomas McLaughlin and friend William Baxter (111:239).

CONNER, MARGARET, serv. to Luke Trotten, was tried for bast. in March 1740/1 and ind. for bast. again in Nov. 1742 (33:20; 34:59).

CONNER, PHILIP, servant, was listed in the 1749 inv. of James Carroll Croxall (53).

CONNEY, ELIZA, with 5 yrs., 9 mos. to serve, was in the 1749 inv. of Edward Day (54:226).

CONNINGHAM, GEORGE, was in Balto. Co. by Nov. 1684 when Edward Reeves transf. certain property to him (107).

CONNINGTON, WILLIAM, bachelor, d. in Balto. Co. by July 1676 when probate was granted to his bro. Walter Connington (298).

CONNOLLY, BARNABY, m. Mary (?), and had iss.: MARY, b. 12 Oct. 1743; ROSANNAH, b. 11 Sept. 1745; CATHERINE, b. 10 Sept. 1747; ANN, b. 15 Jan. 1752; ELEANOR, b. 15 March 1755; ALICE, b. 10 April 1759; SARAH, b. 1 Sept. 1761 (129:377).

CONNOLLY/CONNELY, MARGARET, admitted bearing an illeg. ch. in June 1737 (See Nicholas Hutchins) (31:57).

CONNY, ELIZABETH, in March 1746/7 was ind. for bast. (36:378).

CONSTABLE, HENRY, was in Balto. Co. by 1695 as a taxable in s. side Patapsco Hund.; may be the Henry who imm. to A. A. Co., by 1673 (140; 388).

CONSTABLE, ROBERT, d. by 14 Dec. 1754 when admnx. Frances Constable posted admin. bond with John Wilmot and Thos. Clendenning; est. was admin. 6 July 1756 by Frances, now w. of Thomas Pert; left a son: JOHN (5:302; 11:378; 82:376).

CONSTANT, JOHN, m. Susannah (?), who d. 22 March 1736; had iss.: MARGARET, b. 30 March 1722; SUSANNAH, b. 3 May 1724; JOHN, b. 14 Aug. 1725; WILLIAM, b. 23 May 1727; ELIZABETH, b. 1 May 1733 (128:72, 85, 98).

CONSTANT, SARAH, m. 13 Oct. 1726 Thomas Brashier (129:262).

CONSTANTINE, CORNELIUS, age 13 in Nov. 1744 was bound to John Ashman (35:383).

CONSTANTINE, PATRICK, m. 29 Sept. 1760 Ann, dau. of Richard Bond (134:72; 210-31:892).

CONVEATHERUM, MARY, servant to Thomas Sligh, was ind. for bast. in Aug. 1739, and tried in Nov. 1739 (32:1).

CONWAY, PHILIP. See CONNER, PHILIP.

THE JOHN COOK FAMILY.

COOK, JOHN (1), earliest known ancestor, was in Balto. Co. by May 1678 when he surv. Cook's Chance in Spesutia Hund.; d. c.1713; est. was inv. on 1 Aug. 1713 by Joseph Johnston and Cadwallader Jones, and val. at £ 19.8.4; est. admin. on 4 Oct. 1714 by William Cook; had iss.: JOHN, b. 21 Dec. 1681; WILLIAM, b. 8 Nov. 1684 (1:15; 50:253; 128:1; 211).

COOK, JOHN (2), s. of John (1), was b. 21 Dec. 1681; may be the John who d. 22 Dec. 1738; m. 30 Dec. 1726 Sarah West; in Aug. 1718 the petition of John Cook to be levy free was granted; had iss.: MARY, b. 13 March 1726/7; PRISCILLA, b. 27 March 1730; ROBERT, b. 15 Aug. 1732; JOHN, b. 8 Dec. 1734 (23:40; 128:50, 64, 75, 86, 93).

COOK, WILLIAM (3), s. of John (1), b. 8 Nov. 1684, d. 26 Sept. 1731; m. Sarah Garrett on 27 Aug. 1713; admin. the estates of John Cook and John Miles on 4 Oct. 1714; his will, 24 Sept. 1731 - 8 March 1731/2, named sons Jeremiah and John, daus. Elizabeth and Sarah, and w. Sarah; may be the William Cook who in 1730 gave his age as 46, and named his father-in-law Emanuel Ceely; had iss.: SARAH, b. 1 March 1720, d. 15 May 1720; RICHARD, b. 21 May 1715, d. 31 March 1722; JEREMIAH, b. 1 Jan. 1717/8; JOHN, b. 28 Feb. 1721/2; ELIZABETH, b. 5 April 1725, prob. the Elizabeth who m. Jacob Cord on 20 June 1750; SARAH, b. 12 March 1727; WILLIAM MINER, b. 25 May 1732 (1:15, 20; 125:217; 128:61, 38, 49, 77; 129:362).

COOK, ROBERT (4), s. of John (2), b. 15 Aug. 1732; in Aug. 1750 chose Ephraim Gover as guardian (37:152).

Unrelated Cooks.

COOK/COOKE, EDWARD, d. by 2 March 1726 when admin. bond of his est. was posted by Hugh Johns, with James Moore and John Royston; a second bond was posted 4 March 1727 or 29 March 1727 by James Moore with John Royston and Edward Evans; est. was admin. 1 Aug. 1729 by James Moore (2:277; 11:289, 298; 133:193).

COOK, ELIZABETH, had iss.: SARAH, b. 7 July 1727 (129:361).

COOK, ELIZABETH, was tried for bast. in March 1744 (35:480).

COOK, JAMES, m. Anne (?), and had iss.: MARTHA, b. 12 Nov. 1737, d. 24 Nov. 1737; MARTHA, b. 7 Nov. 1738 (128:93).

COOK, JEREMIAH, m. 9 Nov. 1758 Ann Brucebanks (129:359).

COOK, JOHN, was in Balto. Co. by 1694 as a taxable in s. side Gunpowder Hund. (139).

COOK, JOHN, in Nov. 1718 pet. that his son should be levy free; d. by March 1719/20, leaving a son William (23:40, 344).

COOK, JOHN, d. by 1750 when his heirs owned 50 a. part Maidens Mount, and 25 a. part Paradice (153:37).

COOK, JOHN, in 1750 owned 200 a. Welshes Adventure (153:79).

COOK, JOHN, d. leaving a will, 18 April 1768 - 31 Aug. 1768, named 162 a. Mount Pleasant, w. Mary, and these ch.: JOSHUA; THOMAS; AMBROSE; JOHN (112:83).

COOK, JOHN, b. c.1723, gave his age as 70 in 1793 (231-WG#NN, p. 410).

COOK, JOHN, m. Mary (?), and had iss.: WILLIAM, b. 1 Sept. 1749 (133:90).

COOK, RICHARD, age 30, English, runaway serv. from Charles Ridgely, Aug. 1747; had formerly served Patrick Lynch (384:649)

COOK, THOMAS, was in Balto. Co. by Jan. 1678/9 when Arthur Taylor conv. him 315 a. Spring Neck; his will, 19 Dec. 1681 - 13

Feb. 1681, named Michael Judd, Jr., Mary Cornelius, and his own dau. Anne Cooke to have plantation (120:103; 206-8:235).

COOK, THOMAS, in 1750 owned 50 a. Cook's Purchase (153:57).

COOK, THOMAS, m. Anne (?); had iss.: MATHEW, b. 3 April 1740; JOHN, b. 15 Aug. 1742; ANNE, b. 2 Jan. 1745; WILLIAM, b. 20 June 1748; MARY, b. 11 Feb. 1750; THOMAS, b. 4 Nov. 1752 (133:97).

COOK, WILLIAM, of Joppa, d. leaving a will, 23 April 1739 - 8 May 1739, naming w. Hannah, cous. Wilhelmina, dau. of his uncle William; in Aug. 1740 his est. was admin. by Hannah, w. of Robert Courtney (32:323; 127:36).

COOLEY, EDWARD, m. Elizabeth (?); had iss.: JOHN, b. 22 Sept. 1729; EDWARD, b. 23 March 1731; ALICE, b. 2 Feb. 1734; WARNER, b. 31 March 1738; RACHEL, b. 20 May 1738 (sic); MARY, b. 25 March 1740 (128:88, 99, 100; 129:337).

COOLEY, ELIZABETH, m. Thomas Cooke on 15 July 1728 (131).

COOLEY, JAMES, left these parts seven months ago leaving the child he had by a servant of Col. Maxwell in the keeping of Jane Harper, in June 1724 (26:320).

COOLEY, JAMES, m. Elizabeth (?), and had iss.: JOSEPH, b. 28 Feb. 1728 (131:8).

COOPER, JOHN (1), was in Balto. Co. by 1694 as a taxable in n. side of Patapsco Hund.; was named as a s. of Jane, w. of Robert Wilmot, in the latter's will, 9 May 1696; Cooper was to inherit the bulk of Wilmot's est. after the death of Cooper's mother; may have had iss.: JOHN (121:110; 139).

COOPER, JOHN (2), poss. s. of John (1), but Gibson's Hist. of York Co., Penna., states he came from Kendal, Eng., c.1720; d. by 8 Nov. 1759 in Balto. Co., Md.; m. Alice Gill on 23 Oct. 1722; by 1722 had the only settlement n. of Maiden's Mount; acquired a small tract orig. surv. for Elijah Perkins in 1719, to which he added Cooper's Range (surv. May 1720), and Deserts of Arabia (surv. July 1721), creating 620 contiguous acres straddling the Md.-Penna. boundary; by 1750 owned 50 a. Elijah's Lot, 350 a. Cooper's Range, 220 a. Deserts of Arabia, 250 a. Cooper's Addition, and Cullins Park, among others; his will, 1 Oct. 1759 - 8 Nov. 1759 , named in order his sons (given below), dau. Elizabeth, and grandchildren Cooper Boyd and John Boyd; had iss.: PRISCILLA, b. 17 Oct. 1724; ALICE, b. 8 July 1726; JOHN, b. 29 Nov. 1728; THOMAS, b. 23 March 1731; STEPHEN, b. 13 May 1733; NICHOLAS, b. c. 1734; ALEXANDER (111:296; 128:41, 43, 80; 153:37; 339:123-124).

COOPER, THOMAS (3), s. of John (2) and Alice, was b. 23 March 1731, d. 18 Sept. 1798 in Peach Bottom Twp., York Co., Penna.; m. 14 Feb. 1764 Mary Abercrombie (poss.); during the Rev. War served in the 6th Batt. of York Co. Militia, organized under Col. William Ross and Capt. Laird; had iss.: JAMES, d. in inf.; ISAAC, d. in inf.; ARMFIELD, m. Robert Morgan; ALICIA, b. 1770, d. 1849, res. in Erie Co., Penna., m. John Grubb (b. 1767, d. 1845, alleged to have been a Capt. during the Whiskey Rebellion); DUCKETT, b. 15 Aug. 1775, m. William Stump; STEPHEN THOMAS, d. 1855, member of the Penna. Legislature, 1826-1828, m. Keziah Bell of Washington Co., Penna. (128:80; 345; 432:765).

COOPER, NICHOLAS (4), s. of John (2) and Alice, b. c.1734, d. 1799; m. 1st Sarah Gill (poss. dau. of John and Mary Rogers Gill), and m. 2nd Elizabeth Gill; private in the 6th Batt. of York Co. Militia during the Rev. War; had iss.: MARY, m. William Chapman; NICHOLAS, m. Sarah Balderstone; ALICE, m. Ezekiel Jones; SARAH, m. William Barclay; STEPHEN, m. Isabella (?); JOSHUA, b. 20 April 1785, m. Margaret (?); ELEANOR, m. Benjamin Brindley; PRISCILLA, m. Thomas Hawkins; HANNAH, b. 31 Aug. 1789, m. Benjamin Lukens (128:80; 345).

COOPER, LYDIA, d. by 16 Feb. 1743 when James Rigbie posted admin. bond with Richard Johns and William Coale (11:358).

COOPER, SAMUEL, d. by 17 April 1747 when his est. was admin. by James Rigbie, Quaker, and leaving a minor heir: LYDIA (4:65).

COOPER, SAMUEL, m. Sarah (?), and had iss.: SAMUEL, b. 1 Feb. 1730 (128:64).

COOPER, THOMAS, in Feb. 1713/4 signed the inv. of Cornelius White (50:207).

COOT, SAMUEL, b. in Eng., age c.25, runaway serv. from David Gorsuch in Balto. Town, Aug. 1759 (307).

COPAS, JOHN, m. by Nov. 1685 Ann, wid. of Matthew Wood, may have been the John Copas who was a taxable in n. side Patapsco Hund. in 1692 (18:356; 138).

COPAS, JOHN, m. by 30 March 1699 Sarah Teale, mother of Ales Teale (63:338).

COPAS, JOHN, m. 24 Jan. 1742 Manaly Wright; had iss.: MARY, b. 25 Dec. 1743 (131:96/r, 101/r).

COPE, ELEANOR, in Aug. 1746 was ind. for bast., and tried in Nov. 1746; John Wilmot admitted paternity; had iss.: ELIZABETH, b. 29 May 1744, bound to Samuel Owings to age 16 (36:116, 232, 241, 248).

COPE, JOHN, m. Mary Bush on 5 Feb. 1748 (131:29).

COPE, JOHN, m. Brigett Teate on 5 Feb. 1753 (131:41).

COPELAND, (?), m. by 17 Sept. 1756 Mary, dau. of George Little (210-20:297).

COPELAND, DAVID, m. Eliz. Duglas on 27 Aug. 1747; was named as bro. in the will of John Copeland on 6 Sept. 1754 (111:52; 131: 31).

COPELAND, ELIZ., m. David Lynn on 24 Aug. 1746 (131:30).

COPELAND, ELIZ., m. Sol. Whealand on 18 Jan. 1761 (131:58).

COPELAND, HUGH, lived in the area of Gunpowder R., June 1748 (385:19).

COPELAND, JOHN, d. by 26 Dec. 1754; m. 1st Mary (?), who d. 30 Nov. 1744; m. 2nd Mary (?), living in 1755; his will, 6 Sept. 1754 - 7 Nov. 1754, naming w. Mary, and ch. Sarah, William, Anne, Elizabeth, Jane (or Jeanne), Hugh, George, and John; admin. bond posted 26 Dec. 1754 by Mary and David Copeland; est. admin. 19 Nov. 1755 by Mary Copeland; had iss.: SUSANNA, b. 14 Jan. 1731; WILLIAM, b. 7 Feb. 1732; JOHN, b. 10 Feb. 1735; ANNE, b. 10 May 1737 (may be the Ann Copeland who m. John Bayley on 23 Dec. 1759); ELIZABETH, b. 10 May 1742; JANE, twin, b. 29 Nov. 1744; MARY, twin, b. 29 Nov. 1744; SARAH; HUGH; GEORGE (5:343; 11:384; 111: 52; 131:55, 58/r, 69/r, 108/r; 153:73).

COPELAND, MARY, m. John Henry on 10 Feb. 1757 (131:49).

COPELAND, SARAH, m. John Timmons on 18 April 1745 (131:28).

COPELAND, WILLIAM TAYLOR, d. by 30 Nov. 1772; nuncupative will, made 29 March 1772, named sis. Lilly Goldsmith; will sworn to by Nicholas Corbley and Anna Goldsmith, dau. of Lilly Goldsmith (112: 209).

COPITON, TOBIAS, and wife, were summoned to appear to answer the complaint of Mrs. Mary Staneby concerning their treatment of an orphan child (18:29).

COPLEY, THOMAS, d. by 26 Jan. 1748 leaving a wid. Abigail Copley (80:212).

COPPER, JOHN, gave his age as 21 in 1728 (71:113).

CORAM, WILLIAM, of Balto. Co. claimed land for service in 1673 (388).

THE CORBIN FAMILY has been the subject of much research by William D. Patrick who has generously shared information with the compiler.

CORBIN, NICHOLAS (1), came to Md. by Nov. 1671, d. by 11 May 1697; in 1667 surv. 100 a. Costrell Hill; in Nov. 1671 claimed land for bringing himself, w. Elizabeth, and daus. Elizabeth and Mary into the Province; m. 1st Elizabeth (?) by 1671; m. 2nd by 30 March 1695 to Alice (?) who m. as her 2nd husb. John Barrett; his will, 30 March 1695 - 11 May 1697, named daus. Eliza Roberts and Mary Gostwick, son Edward, and w. Alice; est. was inv. on 11 May 1697 by Jonas Bowen and John Mounfield, and val. at £32.5.6; wid. Alice m. 2nd John Barrett, and was alive on Nov. 1718 when Zacheus Richards, age 2, was bound to her to age 21; had iss.: ELIZA, came to Md. by 1671, m. by 30 March 1695 (prob. Thomas) Roberts; MARY, came to Md. by 1671, m. Joseph Gostwick; NICHOLAS, Jr.; and EDWARD (23:31; 121:126; 123:146; 138; 206-15:156; 388).

CORBIN, NICHOLAS (2), s. of Nicholas (1), first appeared in the tax lists in 1694, indicating he was b. c.1676-1678; may be the Nicholas "Corver" whose wid. owned 100 a. part Bachelor's Choice in 1750 ; issue not proven (139; 153:91).

CORBIN, EDWARD (3), s. of Nicholas (1), was first listed as a taxable in 1701, placing his birth date as c.1685; alive in 1750; m. Jane, dau. of William Wilkinson some time prior to 1716; Sept. 1716 Edward Corbin and w. Jane sold John Bowen pt. of Corcell Hill and on the same day John and Mary Bowen sold Corbin pt. of Jones' (or Jonas') Range; in March 1722 Edward and Jane conv. widow Tamar Wilkinson 425 a. Land Is All and 50 a. Wilkinson's Spring; in Sept. 1737 they sold Thomas Sligh pt Corbin's Rest, which Edward said he had inher. from his father; in 1750 owned 200 a. Cumberland; in May 1758 Edward and Jane conv. land to Robert Wilkinson previously conv. to his mother in March 1722 (this was done to clear up any question of title; had iss. : NICHOLAS (named in the will of John Barrett in June 1717); poss. EDWARD; poss. WILLIAM WILKINSON; ABRAHAM, b. 7 Sept. 1722; PHYLIS-ANNA, b. 12 May 1725; PROVIDENCE, b. 26 June 1727; UNITY, b. 2 March 1730 (67:431, 439; 69:6; 75:13; 83:157; 133:6, 8, 13, 18; 153:5).

CORBIN, EDWARD (4), s. of Edward (3) and Jane, may be the Edward who d. leaving a will, 14 July 1770 - 30 Nov. 1770, naming a w. Mary and six ch.: EDWARD, b. 11 April 1746; ELIAKIM; MARY; JOHN; RACHEL; and LEAH (112:144; 131).

CORBIN, ABRAHAM (5), s. of Edward (3) and Jane, b. 7 Sept. 1722 in St. Pauls Par., d. c.1798; prob. the Abraham who m. Rachel Marshall on 4 Dec. 1766; had iss.: ABRAHAM; THOMAS; NICHOLAS, by June 1805 was in Bourbon Co., Ky., when as one of the heirs of Abraham Corbin, dec., he sold pt. The Valley of Jehosophat to Joshua Marsh; NATHAN; SARAH, m. Thomas Marsh, Jr.; ELEANOR, m. Beale Marsh (131; 133; 231-WG#56:122; 231-WG#86:252).

CORBIN, PROVIDENCE (6), dau. of Edward (3) and Jane, b. 26 June 1727, m. Henry Peregoy on 14 Jan. 1745 (131).

CORBIN, UNITY (7), dau. of Edward (3) and Jane, b. 2 March 1730, m. Robert Green on 21 or 25 Sept. 1745 (131).

Unrelated Corbins.

CORBIN, BENJAMIN, m. Sarah Lye or Sye on 9 Dec. 1755 (131).

CORBIN, ELIZABETH, m. Edmond Deadman on 30 Jan. 1753 (131).

CORBIN, JOHN, was in Balto. Co. by 30 Aug. 1722 when he bought 100 a. Beal's Camp from Archibald and Jane Edmondston (69:198).

CORBIN, LEAH, m. Laban Welsh on 3 Sept. 1761 (131).

CORBIN, NATHANIEL, m. Sarah James on 16 Oct. 1758 (131).

CORBIN, RACHEL, m. Solomon James on 18 June 1760 (131).

CORBIN, SOPHIA, m. Thomas Marsh on 10 Feb. 1745 (131).

CORBIN, WILLIAM, m. Rachel Wright on 11 Aug. 1745 (131).

CORD, THOMAS (1), d. in May or June 1721; was in Balto. Co. by 1692 when he was High Constable of Spesutia Hund.; m. Hannah Matthews on 4 Aug. 1698; as Thomas Cordey was one of the first vestrymen of St. George's Par.; his will, 7 May 1721 - 7 June 1721, named tract Cook's Plantation, bro.(-in-law) Roger Matthews, and ch. Abraham, Thomas, Roger, Jacob, Isaac, Mary, and Hannah; admin. bond was posted 7 June 1721 by exec. Roger Matthews, with Francis Holland and John Clark; est. admin. 3 April 1722 by Matthews and a legacy to Mary Cord was pd. to Mary Marshall; had iss.: SARAH, b. 1 Sept. 1699; ABRAHAM, b. 3 March 1700; THOMAS, b. 28 July 1703; ROGER, b. 25 Aug. 1707, in June 1722 was bound to Obadiah Pritchard to age 21; ISAAC, b. 15 Sept. 1710; SUSANNA, b. 16 April 1713; d. 4 Aug. 1716; JACOB, b. 13 June 1715; MARY, b. 16 Oct. 1717; HANNAH, named in will (1:88; 11:293; 24:178; 124:60; 128:8, 12, 21, 23, 28, 29; 129:219; 130; 138:8).

CORD, ABRAHAM (2), s. of Thomas (1) and Hannah, was b. 3 March 1700, alive in 1742 when he leased to Abraham Taylor part of French Plantation, Peter's Addition, Cord's Purchase and Ten Pound Pur-(?) m. 1st Rebecca (?), who was the mother of his ch., and on 19 Feb. 1733 Mary, sis. of Joseph Pritchard; in Feb. 1736 he was summoned by the vestry of St. Georges Par. to answer a charge of unlawful cohabitation with Elizabeth Harges; in Aug. 1737 was ind. by the grand jury on the same charge; in Nov. 1742 his sons Jacob James were placed with John Stinchcomb; had iss.: RUTH, b. 11 June 1723, d. Nov. 1724; ISAAC, b. 18 Aug. 1725; STINCHCOMB, b. 14 April 1728; (poss. RUTH, b. 13 Dec. 1730, no parents named); JAMES, b. 25 Oct. 1732; JACOB, alive in 1742 (31:97; 34:68; 77:365; 126: 64; 128:42, 53, 56, 60, 77, 78; 130:277).

CORD, THOMAS (3), s. of Thomas (1) and Hannah, was b. 28 July 1703, and was alive in 1750; m. Mary Williams on 10 Feb. 1730; in

1750 he owned 50 pt. of French Plantation, 50 a. Peter's Plantation, and pt. Halls Purchase; his wife Mary was alive in 1776, age 70 in Spesutia Hund.; had iss.: PHEBE, b. 2 March 1731; LUHANNAH, b. 16 July 1735; AMOS, b. 14 March 1737; ASBURY, b. 2 Dec. 1741 (128:60, 78, 88, 101; 129:322; 153:70; 277:152).

CORD, JACOB (4), s. of Thomas (1) and Hannah, was b. 13 June 1715, prob. d before 1776; m. Elizabeth Cook on 20 June 1750; in 1750 owned 100 a. Cook's Rest; had iss.: HANNAH, b. 11 March 1751; SUSANNA, b. 25 Dec. 1753, unm. in 1776; ROGER, b. 15 May 1756; NAOMI, b. c.1762, at home in 1776, prob. the Naomi who m. James Lee in Feb. 1784; JACOB, b. c.1765 (129:362; 153:50; 277:188).

CORD, MARY (5), dau. of Thomas (1) and Hannah, was b. 16 Oct. 1717; may have been the Mary who was ind. for bast. in Nov. 1734, and who had iss.: MARTHA, b. 7 Aug. 1734 (30:350; 128:46, 83).

CORD, HANNAH (6), dau. of Thomas (1) and Hannah, b. by 7 May 1721, may have been the mother of ISAAC, "son of Hannah," b. 12 Oct. 1736 (128:94).

CORD, AMOS (7), s. of Thomas (3) and Mary, was b. 14 March 1737; m. Susanna Kemble (b. c.1744), on 13 Nov. 1763; had iss.: HANNAH, b. 9 June 1764; GREENBURY, b. 21 Aug. 1766; AQUILA, b. 27 March 1768; SARAH, b. c.1771; AMOS, b. c.1775 (129:302, 387; 285).

CORDEMAN, ANN, ind. for unlawful cohabitation with William Holmes in Aug. 1744 (35:293).

CORDEY. See COWDRY.

CORDU, CHRISTOPHER, was in Balto. Co. by 1695 as a taxable in s. side Patapsco Hund. (140; see also Christopher Cardue).

CORNE, THOMAS, m. by Aug. 1714 Elizabeth, extx. of John Mortimore, dec. (21:566).

CORNELIUS, HENRY, and wife Ann, of Balto. Co., claimed land for service by 1674; Henry was a taxable in s. side Gunpowder Hund. by 1695 (140; 388).

CORNELIUS, JOHN, m. by March 1719 Sarah, admnx. of Stephen White (1:279; 23:342).

CORNELIUS, JOHN, m. Eleanor, and had iss.: JOSEPH, b. 15 Sept. 1752; WILLIAM, b. 15 Feb. 1754; JOHN, b. 25 May 1756; JOSHUA, b. 26 Dec. 1758; SAMUEL, b. 28 May 1761 (134:16, 19, 21).

CORNELIUS, JOSEPH, and wife Elizabeth conv. to Thomas Stocksdale one-half the tract Curgafurgis in May 1741; in May 1744 Joseph, a carpenter, conv. 100 a. of the same tract to Robert Cross (77:539, 673).

CORNELIUSON, MATTHIAS, imm. to Md. by 1658 with his wife Margaret and dau. Alicia; in Nov. 1660 conv. 50 a. to Peter Mounson (94; 379).

THE CORNWALLIS FAMILY has been discussed by Newman in 359, and by George Ely Russell in MMG 4 (1981) 57-60.

CORNWALLIS, THOMAS (1), imm. to Md. in 1634 on the ship Ark with his partner, Mr. John Saunders who d. at sea, and 12 serv.; imm. again in 1660; by July 1669 was back in Stanhow, Co. Norfolk, Eng., with w. Penelope, when they conv. 1000 a. Verina in Balto. Co. to George Wilson; had iss., among others: WILLIAM (96; 359; 388; Russell).

CORNWALLIS, WILLIAM (2), s. of Thomas (1), is mentioned in
Md. Patents 20:147; surv. 829 a. Planter's Paradise in Balto. Co
but died without heirs; some years later an adventurer named William Vanhaesdunk arrived in Md. claiming to be William Cornwallis
s. of Thomas (211; 388; Russell).

CORNWELL, ANN, named as dau.-in-law of Richard Gwinn in the
latter's will in 1692, and was to have Gwin's Farm (121:65).

CORNWORTH. See COMWORTH.

CORUS, THOMAS, was in Balto. Co. by 1694 as a taxable in the
s. side of Patapsco Hund. (139).

CORVER, NICHOLAS, d. by 1750 when his widow is listed as the
owner of 100 a. part Bachelor's Choice (153:91; see also Carver
and Corbin).

COSFORD, THOMAS, d. by 1675; Edward Crockett swore on 15 Feb.
1675 that he was at Henry Exon's house when Exon asked Cosford,
who was very ill at the time if he would like to make a will;
Exon promised to send the rest of Cosford's est., after Exon's
debts were deducted, to Cosford's father if he was still alive
(110:102).

COSTLEY/COSTLY/COSLE, JAMES (1), was b. c.1653, and was alive
in Aug. 1724 when at age 71 he pet. to be levy free; had at least
four ch.: JAMES, b. 8 Sept. 1684; WILLIAM, b. 15 Sept. 1686;
MARGARET, b. 12 April 1691; MARY, b. 20 Feb. 1692/3 (26:437; 128:
4).

COSTLEY, WILLIAM (2), s. of James (1), was b. 15 Sept. 1686,
and d. 12 Dec. 1728; m. Mary Ellis on 26 Dec. 1709; Mary Costley
d. 27 Jan. 1739; had iss.: WILLIAM, b. 29 June 1714; THOMAS, b.
13 March 1715; JAMES, b. 15 Oct. 1720; MARY, b. 15 Oct. 1720; JOHN,
b. 30 May 1720 (sic); SUSANNA, b. 27 Feb. 1724; MARGARET, b. 27
28 Nov. 1727 (128:26, 53, 54, 109).

COSTLEY, MARY (3), dau. of James (1), was b. 20 Feb. 1692/3,
and was prob. the Mary who m. George Eaves on 1 Sept. 1714 (128:
4, 215).

COSTLEY, JAMES (4), s. of William (2) and Mary, was b. 15 Oct.
1720, m. Mary Hill on 3 Jan. 1744; in June 1733 as orphan of Mary
Cosley was bound to Bennett Garrett to age 21 to learn the trade
of cooper; had iss.: WILLIAM, b. 23 June 1745; MARTHA, b. 12 Sept.
1747; THOMAS, b. 6 Nov. 1756 (30:2; 128; 131).

COSTLEY, ALICE, was ind. for bast. in June 1733; had iss.:
WILLIAM, b. 16 Aug. 1727, d. 22 Jan. 1727/8 (30:2; 128:53).

COSTLEY, JAMES, m. Elizabeth (?), who d. 15 April 1714; m.
2nd Elinor Chisnald on 2 Aug. 1714 (128:32).

COSTLEY, MARY, was ind. for bast. in March 1737/8 and again
in June 1738 (31:169, 221).

COSTLEY, OLIVE, was ind. for bast. in June 1733 (30:2).

COSTOS, EASTER, mulatto, aged 1, dau. of Mary Costos, was
sold to William Lewis to age 31, in March 1743/4 (35:155).

COSTOS, MARY, serv. to William Lewis, was ind. for bast. in
June 1743, ind. for bearing a negro bast. in Nov. 1743, tried
that month, and tried again in March 1743/4 (34:185; 35:71, 88;
35:163).

COTTAM, GEORGE, was in Balto. Co. by 1694 as a taxable in n. side Patapsco Hund. (139).

COTTEN, JOHN, of Balto. Co., imm. to Md. by 1671 (388).

COTTINGTON, EDWARD, was in Balto. Co. by 1692 as a taxable in s. side Patapsco Hund. (138).

COTTON, WILLIAM, of Balto. Co., d. by 16 Sept. 1720; est. was inv. by Thomas Cord and John Clark, and val. at £ 67.16.10, with no kinfolk or creditors signing; his will, 15 Sept. 1720 - 8 Dec. 1720, directed he was to be bur. in the Church of St. George, and named Dr. Evan Evans of St. Johns Par., George Read of Balto Co., and William Osborn of St. Par. as his exec. and residuary legatee (51:23; 110:164; 128:40).

COTTRELL, JOHN, was b. c.1658, and in March 1728 pet. the court to be levy free; m. Elizabeth (?); by 1730 she pet. the court saying she was b. c.1667, and mentioning her husband living some 32 years earlier; his will, 22 Jan. 1721 - 8 April 1730, left 100 a. Cottrell's Purchase to w. Elizabeth and dau. Isabella; his will also named other ch. listed below; had iss.: ELIZABETH, b. 8 Aug. 1698, m. William Perkins (and had a dau. Mary); ISABELLA; MARGARET, m. by Jan. 1721 Joseph England; SARAH, b. 6 Feb. 1712 (28: 95; 125:162; 128:5, 39; 163:116).

COTTRELL, JOHN, m. 14 June 1752 Ann Wood, and m. 2nd on 10 March 1763 Sarah Raven, both prob. widows; his will, 26 Nov. 1766 - 9 Dec. 1766, named w. Sarah, dau.-in-law Martha Wood, son-in-law Luke Raven, bro. Thomas, cousin John Cottrell, and John Buck, Sr., as exec. (112:38; 131).

COTTRELL, THOMAS, perhaps bro. of John above, m. Frances Millhuse on 4 Aug. 1743; in 1750 owned 100 a. Tower Hill; had iss.: RACHEL, b. 18 Oct. 1744; JOHN, b. 14 May 1747; WEALTHY ANN, b. 17 Aug. 1749 (131:97/r, 129/r; 153:89).

COULSTON, JOHN, d. by 7 Sept. 1748, when admin. bond was posted by Joseph Hopkins, with Nathan Rigbie (11:369).

COULTER, MATTHEW, surv. 240 a. Bedford Resurveyed in April 1732; d. leaving a will, 22 Nov. 1757 - 4 Nov. 1760 (311; 398: 17-18).

COUNTS, JOHN, was in Balto. Co. by 1750 when he owned 150 a. Digges Choice; as John George Counts of Little Conewago conv. prop. to Philip Morningstar , John Couts, and Adam Hoopard in July 1745; d. by 11 Oct. 1755 when admin. bond was posted by Nicholas and Catherine Hutchins with William Winchester and Woolerick Ercler (11:391; 79:190; 153:91).

COURTENAY, JOHN, m. 16 Aug. 1739 Frances Greenfield; in Aug. 1748 he and (2nd?) w. Usaan conv. to Col. Thomas White the land John had from his father Robert Courtney; had iss.: RACHEL, b. 18 June 1740; WILLIAM, b. 28 Oct. 1742, d. 21 Dec. 1742; ELIZABETH, b. 18 March 1743 (80:27; 128:104; 129:305, 328, 336).

COURTENAY, JONAS, m. 16 Jan. 1738 Comfort Cole; had iss.: ELIZABETH, b. 12 Jan. 1740; THOMAS, b. 15 Jan. 1743 (128:102, 112; 129:361).

COURTENAY, ROBERT, m. Abigail (?), and had iss.: ABIGAIL, d. 30 Dec. 1735 aged about 16; ROWLAND, b. 2 May 1734 (Robert's w. Abigail d. 27 March 1739 and he m. 2nd 2 Oct. 1740 Hannah Cook (128:79, 104, 111).

COVELL, JACOB, tailor, age c.17, ran away from William Thompson in Nov. 1743 (384:430).

COVENTRY, WILLIAM, was a taxable in Balto. Co. by 1694 in s. side Patapsco Hund.; prob. s. of Flora (?) wid. of (?) Coventry and who m. 2nd James Kyle of A. A. Co.; named in the will of James Kyle of A. A. Co.; named as son(in-law?) in the will of Richard Baly of A. A. Co.; d. leaving a will, 20 March 1698 - 24 April 1698, leaving his entire est. to son Charles, naming bro. Ralph Hopkins as exec., and also naming John Downes, husb. of Margaret, as another bro.; admin. bond posted 24 April 1699 by Ralph Hawkins, with John Downes and Charles Turner; had iss.: CHARLES, minor in 1699, not found in Balto. Co. Tax Lists 1699 - 1706 (11:299; 121:46, 116, 169).

COWDRAY, JAMES, was in Balto. Co. by 1699 as a taxable in n. side Gunpowder Hund.; d. Nov. 1720 (131; 142:8).

COWDRAY, JAMES, d. 26 Dec. 1728; m. Ann Green in Sept. 1723, she was dau. and coheir of Matthew Green, and granddau.of Jane Boone; on 4 March 1729/30 Ann Cordey (sic) conv. her interest in Levy's Tribe, Green's Chance, and Joyce Trippas to Thomas Coale; wid. Ann prob. the Ann Cowdrey who m. Thomas Downey in 1730; iss. of James and Ann: JOHN, b. 10 March 1724, d. May 1725; MARY, b. 11 Sept. 1726; SARAH, b. 25 June 1729, d. Oct. 1729 (72:193; 131).

COWDREY, JOHN, d. April 1721 (131).

COWDREY, MARY, m. Joseph Yates on 5 Nov. 1712 (129:244).

COWDREY, THOMAS, m. Ann (?), and had iss.: JOHN, b. Oct. 1736 (131).

COWAN/COWEN/COEN/COWIN, JOHN (1), d. in Balto. Co. by 31 Oct. 1749, having m. Susanna Teague on 25 Sept. 1712; Susanna d. 3 April 1741; in June 1746 was made levy free in 1750 his heirs were listed as owning 100 a. pt. Cawin's Settlement; his admin. bond was posted 3 Nov. 1748 by Edward Cowen, exec., with Jno. Preble and James Pritchard; his est. was admin. on 31 Oct. 1749 and his heirs were named in court in Aug. 1750; had iss.: SARAH, b. 18 July 1713; JOHN, b. 21 May 1715; ELIZABETH, b. 2 Feb. 1715; MARTHA, b. 2 Jan. 1718/9; THOMAS, b. 26 May 1721; WILLIAM, b. 14 April 1723; EDWARD, b. 5 June 1725; ELIAS, b. 14 Feb. 1726/7; SUSANNA, b. 27 March 1735 (5:78; 11:397; 36:3; 37:165; 128:33, 37, 43, 45, 49, 98, 112; 153:8).

COWAN, SARAH (2), dau. of John (1), was b. 18 July 1713, d. 27 April 1739; had a dau. MARY, b. 20 March 1738 (128:109; 129: 312).

COWAN, JOHN (3), s. of John (1), was b. 21 May 1715; m. 1st on 22 April 1743 Elizabeth Bond; m. 2nd on 9 March 1745 Elizabeth Wood; in 1750 owned 76 a. Cowen's Settlement; had iss.: HANNAH, b. 10 Jan. 1746; WILLIAM, b. 19 Feb. 1747 (129:216, 328, 345; 153:21).

COWAN, THOMAS (4), s. of John (1), was b. 26 May 1721; in March 1742 pet. the court concerning the custody of a child born to one of his sisters on her deathbed; at the same time he stated that another one of his sisters married a Papist; in 1750 owned 100 a. Cawin's Addition (34:129; 153:21).

COWAN, RICHARD, age 10, in Aug. 1741 was stated to have been raised by Richard Pinkham since infancy (33:68).

COWAN, SAMUEL, in July 1704, with Henry Jackson appraised the est. of Blanche Wells (54:2).

COWAN, SARAH, ind. for bast. in June 1739 and tried in Nov. 1739 (32:85, 401).

COWAN, THOMAS, was a taxable in Spesutia Hund. between 1704 and 1706 (291:39, 49, 57).

COWAN, THOMAS, age 14 in Aug. 1741, was bound to Richard Pinkham to age 21 (33:68).

COWAN, ZADOCK, age 11 in Aug. 1741, stated to have been raised by Richard Pinkham since infancy (33:68).

COWLEY, JAMES, of St. James, Westminster, Mddx., Eng., coachman, bound himself to Christopher Veale of Shoreditch, woolcomber, to serve him for 4 years in Md., Aug. 1718 (69:25).

COWLING, WILLIAM, from the west of Eng., age c.30, ran away from Balto. Iron Works, Aug. 1755 (307).

THE JACOB COX FAMILY

COX, JACOB (1), was in Balto. Co. by 25 Sept. 1722 when he m. Elizabeth Merryman, dau. of Charles Merryman; she m. 2nd on 3 Sept. 1727 Samuel Smith; he d. 1 Nov. 1724; admin. bond was posted 3 May 1725 by Elizabeth Cox with Jonas Robinson and John Hayes; his est. was inv. in 1725, and admin. on 8 Nov. 1726 by Eliza Cox; the will of Elizabeth Smith, 22 June 1770 - 7 Dec. 1770, named ch.: Merryman Cox, Rachel, Elizabeth (mother of Mary Fowler Smith), John, Charles, Sophia Greenfield, and grandchildren: the son of Jacob Cox, and grandson Thomas Smith; had iss.: MERRYMAN, b. 22 Jan. (1723/4?); JACOB, b. 7 July 1725 (11:301; 112: 175; 124:208; 133:2, 10, 147, 150, 193).

COX, MERRYMAN (2), s. of Jacob (1), was b. 22 Jan. 1723/4, m. 26 Dec. 1745 Honour Hall; on 30 Oct. 1745 he and Honour conv. 40 a. East Humphreys to Tobias Stansbury; on 21 Sept. 1748 Merryman and Jacob Cox and Samuel and Elizabeth Smith conv. 40 a. of East Humphreys to Tobias Stansbury (79:229; 80:93; 133:2, 158).

COX, JACOB (3), s. of Jacob (1), was b. 7 July 1725; d. 1798; m. 1st Elizabeth Gain and 2nd Keziah Peregoy; his will named these ch.: ZEBEDIAH; JACOB; ELIJAH; ELISHA, m. Arabella Wheeler; WILLIAM, m. 1783 Susanna Bosley; DIANA, b. 15 July 1751, m. Capt. John Murray (115:121; 353; see Murray Bible in Bibliography).

THE CHRISTOPHER COX FAMILY

COX, CHRISTOPHER (4), no known rel. to above, d. 15 Nov. 1713; was prob. the Christopher Cox who was transp. by 1675 and who was a taxable in s. side Patapsco Hund.; his will, 10 Nov. 1713 - 3 March 1713/4, named w. Mary, s. Joseph (who was to have the dw. plantation after Mary's death), and dau. Eliza, w. of Nicholas Day; admin. bond was posted 3 March 1713/4 by exec. Nicholas Day with Obadiah Pritchard and William Hicks; est. admin. 9 April 1716 by Day; had iss.: JOSEPH; ELIZABETH, m. Nicholas Day (1: 200; 11:412; 50:189; 110:105; 131:20/r; 139; 388).

COX, JOSEPH (5), s. of Christopher (4) and Mary, d. 20 Nov. 1713; admin. bond was posted 24 May 1714 by George Berry and his w. Mary, admins., with Simon Person and John Standifer (Standiford); no record of any heirs (11:280; 131:20/r).

EDWARD COX AND HIS POSSIBLE BROTHERS.

COX, (?), (6), name unknown, may have been the father of several individuals who were closely associated, and were probably
brothers: EDWARD; WILLIAM; JOSEPH; and RICHARD.

COX, EDWARD (7), s. of (?) (6), and prob. bro. of William,
Joseph, and Richard; was in Balto. Co. by 1717/8 when he took up
Cox's Fancy; m. Jane, dau. of John Broad, and d. by Dec. 1737
when his est. was admin. by Thomas Sligh; in Aug. 1723 pet. the
court that his younger bro. (unnamed), aged 13, be bound to him;
in June 1723 he and Jane conv. to Thomas Broad 86½ a. of land
left to Jane by her father; conv. 100 a. Cox's Fancy to Robert
North of London, mariner, in June 1724; in Nov. 1724 was ind. for
horse stealing, but bill was dropped; in Nov. 1724 he and Jane
conv. 100 a. Cox's Forest to Ulick Burke; in March 1725 conv.
100 a. Cox's Prospect (which he took up in 1724) to James Nicholson; on 12 Dec. 1737 wid. Jane renounced her right of admin. in
favor of Thomas Sligh; est. inv. 22 Dec. 1737 by Sligh with Richard and Joseph Cox signing as next of kin; est. admin. 9 May 1744
by Sligh; had iss.: EDWARD, Jr. (5:5; 25:426; 27:32; 69:194, 263,
298; 70:64, 144; 205-23:142; 206-23:142; 207; 209-30:384).

COX, WILLIAM (8), s. of (?) (6), and prob. bro. of Edward,
Joseph, and Richard, d. in Balto. Co. by July 1737; m. 1st Eliza-
beth (?), and 2nd by March 1727 Mary (?) who survived him; in
March 1727 Wm. and Mary sold John Green 50 a. Green's Palace; sold
Green 50 a. of same tract in March 1731; bought 50 a. Bachelor's
Refuge from William and Sarah Rogers in Sept. 1730, and conv. it
in Aug. 1736 to his dau. Elizabeth, w. of Charles Bosley; est. inv.
in July 1737 by Joseph and Richard Cox; additional inv. filed 12
May 1744 by sd. Taylor; in Nov. 1737 widow Mary was assigned to
Edward Cox for care; had iss.: ELIZABETH, b. 15 March 1721, m. by
Aug. 1736 Charles Bosley; JACOB, b. 11 Feb. 1723, in Nov. 1737
age 14 was bound to Charles Bosley; SUSANNAH, b. 17 July 1726,
bound to Joseph Cox in Nov. 1737; SARAH, b. 17 Nov. 1728, age 9
in Nov. 1737; WILLIAM, b. 14 May 1730, age 7 in Nov. 1737 when
bound to Joseph Cox; MARY, b. 31 March 1734, in Nov. 1737 bound
to Edward and Jane Cox, and in Nov. 1742 bound to Charles Bosley;
PROVIDENCE, b. c. March 1737 (3:374; 31:132-133; 34:61; 70:364;
73:195, 184; 74:418; 133:39; 205-22:327; 205-29:85).

COX, JOSEPH (9), s. of (?) (6), and prob. bro. of Edward,
William, and Richard, d. by May 1738; m. Elizabeth (?) who m.
2nd by March 1740/1 Henry Fuller; d. by May 1738 when widow re-
bounced admin.; in June 1738 his wards William, Providence, and
Susanna Cox (ch. of his dec. bro. William) were bound out to
others; est. inv. in Nov. 1738 by Edmund Hernley with Elizabeth
and Edward Cox signing as kin; est. admin. by Edmund Hernley on
22 Feb. 1739, 3 Nov. 1740, and 28 May 1741, and by Darby Hernley
in March 1742/3; had iss.: SOPHIA, b. 17 Feb. 1736 (4:9, 25; 5;
24; 31:222; 33:8; 34:122; 205-23:449; 209-30:419).

COX, RICHARD (10), s. of (?) (6), and prob. bro. of Edward,
William, and Joseph, in July 1737 signed the inv. of William
Cox as kin, and in Dec. 1737 signed the inv. of Edward Cox as
kin; in 1737 leased 100 a. of Gunpowder Manor called Double
Diligence, for the lifetimes of Ann Cox (age 55 in 1767), and
Elizabeth Cox (age 33 in 1767); moved to Va., then to S. C.
about 1764; prob. m. Ann (?), b. c.1712, and had iss.: ELIZABETH,
b. c.1734 (205-22:327; 205-23:142; 389:6).

COX, EDWARD, Jr. (11), s. of Edward (7), signed the inv. of
his uncle Joseph Cox in Nov. 1738, and in July 1745 with w. Necia
sold John Holloway 30 a. Cox's Hope (78:343; 205-23:449).

COX, JACOB (12), s. of William (8) and Elizabeth, was b. 11
Feb. 1723; m. by 5 March 1745 Elizabeth (?) when he sold Charles
Bosley 47 a. Jacob's Struggle; in July 1759 was named as a bro.
of Charles Bosley's w. Elizabeth (79:112; 111:131).

COX, WILLIAM (13), s. of William (8) and Mary, was b. 14 May
1730, d. by May 1767; m. Ruth (?); gave his age as 31 in May 1764
as bro. of Jacob; est. was inv. by Ruth Cox, admnx., and signed
by Jacob Cox and Elizabeth Bosley; est. admin. on same day; dec.
left 8 children, all minors (89:140; 201-56:299; 205-91:262).

COX, BENJAMIN, "alias Bowen," named as son in the will of Benjamin Bowen of Balto. Co., and inherited Samuel's Hope.

COX, ELIZABETH, was ind. for bast. in March 1746/7 (36:379).

COX, HANNAH, was ind. for bast. in June 1731; tried in June
1733 and named Zachariah Gray as the father; ind. for bast. in
June 1739 and tried in Aug. 1739; ind. again in Nov. 1742 and
tried again in March 1746/7 (29:156; 30:135; 32:10, 401; 34:59;
36:378).

COX, JOHN, in Sept. 1743 was to be examined concerning the con-
cealment of diverse effects of Robert Gott late of Balto. Co., dec.;
testified that Richard Sampson had two rugs; in Feb. 1764 leased
85 a. Cox's Park to George Myers (89:43; 209-31:409, 427).

COX, ROBERT, b. c.1729 in Northants. or Oxfordshire, ran away
from Balto. Ironworks in Sept. 1754, having been transported on
the ship Appolo (307; 385:305).

COX, SARAH, was ind. for bast., June 1719 (23:198).

COXSILL, MARY, alias Mary Hagan, was ind. for bast. in March
1709/10 (21:94).

COYLE, PATRICK, registered his contract with his servant Hugh
Hine, in court, Nov. 1719 (23:241).

CRABTREE, WILLIAM (1), progenitor, was in Balto. Co. by 1706
and d. c.1756; m. Jane (?); in 1728 conv. 100 a. Crabtree's Lot
to Grace Hayes as a gift; in 1747 conv. 300 a. Turkey Forest to
John Crabtree; his will, 4 Nov. 1747 - 9 Oct. 1756, named w. Jane,
ch. William, Thomas, John, James, Samuel; admin. bond was posted
18 June 1756 by James Billingsley, with Robert Brierly; est. inv.
on 3 Nov. 1756 by Daniel Preston and Thomas Johnson, and val. at
£ 62.16.10½, and signed by James and Jno. Crabtree as kin; est.
was admin. in 1758; had iss.: WILLIAM; THOMAS, b. 12 Oct. 1707;
GRACE, b. 29 May 1711; ANNE, b. 15 Jan. 1714; JAMES, b. 20 Feb.
1716; JOHN, b. 5 Sept. 1718; ELIZABETH, b. 13 Dec. 1720; SAMUEL,
b. 25 July 1725 (11:400; 72:20, 22; 75:298; 79:579; 111:112; 131;
Balto. Co. Orig. Inventories, Box 13, folder 54; Orig. Admin.
Accts., 12, folder 5).

CRABTREE, WILLIAM (2), s. of William (1) and Jane, prob. the
William who m. Mary Pike on 17 Feb. 1725; in 1750 owned 100 a.
Begin; had iss.: WILLIAM, b. 22 Dec. 1726; ELIZABETH, b. 5 Nov.
1728 (131; 153:11).

CRABTREE, THOMAS (3), s. of William (1) and Jane, was b. 12
Oct. 1707, m. Mary (?); in 1750 owned 100 a. Minister; had iss.:
THOMAS, b. 7 July 1733 (131; 153:11).

CRABTREE, GRACE (4), dau. of William (1) and Jane, was b. 29
May 1711, and m. John Hays on 31 Oct. 1727 (131).

CRABTREE, ANN (5), dau. of William (1) and Jane, was b. 15 Jan. 1714; m. William Wilborn on 21 Jan. 1731 (131).

CRABTREE, JOHN (6), s. of William (1) and Jane, was b. 5 Sept. 1718; in 1750 owned part Turkey Forest (131; 153:83).

CRABTREE, ELIZABETH, m. John Poteet, 20 Sept. 1748 (131).

CRABTREE, JOHN, m. Hannah Butcher on 22 April 1755 (131).

CRABTREE, THOMAS, m. Elizabeth Barton on 23 Oct. 1760 (131).

CRABTREE, WILLIAM, m. Hannah Whitaker on 27 May 1746 (131).

CRABTREE, WILLIAM, m. Ann Kiley on 25 April 1754 (131).

THE CRADOCK FAMILY has been discussed by Barnes (in 259), and by William Voss Elder. Biographical articles on Rev. Thomas Cradock have been written by David Curtis Skaggs and by Dawn F. Thomas.

CRADOCK, JOHN (1), of Trentham, Staffordshire, Eng., m. 20 Aug. 1673 Elizabeth, dau. of Arthur Taylor, and had iss.: WILLIAM, bapt. 5 Nov. 1674 (father of John Cradock, Archbishop of Dublin); RICHARD, bapt. 12 Jan. 1680/1; and prb. ARTHUR (259:26-27).

CRADOCK, ARTHUR (2), prob. s. of John (1) and Elizabeth, was prob. named for his maternal grandfather Arthur Taylor; m. Ann Marsen on 29 April 1717; she was a half-sister of John Worrell, citizen and bookseller of the Bell Yard, Rolls Liberty, Co. Middlesex, Eng., whose will was dated Feb. 1771; iss. of Arthur and Anne were: Rev. THOMAS, bapt. 8 Nov. 1717; WILLIAM, bapt. 9 Nov. 1718; ESTHER, bapt. 26 March 1722, bur. 12 April 1723; JAMES, bapt. 26 March 1722, d. by Feb. 1771, leaving a widow Sarah and one dau. Anne; and JOHN, bapt. 11 March 1724; and ARTHUR, bapt. 16 Aug. 1726, d. in inf. (259:27).

CRADOCK, Rev. THOMAS (3), s. of Arthur (2) and Anne, was bapt. 8 Nov. 1717 in Trentham, Staffordshire; d. in Balto. Co., Md., 7 May 1770; m. 31 March 1746 Katherine, dau. of John Risteau; she d. 20 Aug. 1795; was made Rector of St. Thomas' Parish in 1743; by 1750 owned 50 a. Rich Level, 70 a. The Addition, and 50 a. of George's Beginning; his will, 20 March 1769 - 21 June 1770, named w. Catherine, dau. of late John Risteau, and ch.: Arthur, dec., Thomas, John, and Ann; had iss.: ARTHUR, b. 19 July 1747, d. unm. 23 Feb. 1769; JOHN, b. 25 Jan. 1749; THOMAS, b. 30 May 1752, d. 19 Oct. 1821; ANN, b. 21 Feb. 1755, m. Charles Walker on 1 Sept. 1772 (112:147; 134:13, 17, 21, 25; 153:82; 259:27-28).

CRADOCK, JOHN (4), s. of Rev. Thomas (3) and Catherine, was b. 25 Jan. 1749, d. Oct. 1794; m. Ann, dau. of John and Mary (Todd) Worthington in 1775; was on the Committee of Observation for Balto Co.; after the male line died out the name Cradock was assumed by Thomas Cradock Walker by Act of the Legislature; had iss.: MARY, b. 27 Feb. 1778, d. 30 May 1870; prob. the Mary Cradock who m. Stephen Cromwell on 10 April 1797; CATHERINE, b. 5 Dec. 1779, m. Thomas Cradock Walker on 17 Feb. 1818; ARTHUR, b. 17 April 1782, d. 5 Oct. 1821; ELIZABETH, b. 9 Oct. 1784; ANN, b. 1786 (134:49, 50; 259:28).

CRAINE, ANN, was ind. for bast. in June 1730, and tried in Aug. 1730 (28:415; 29:8).

CRASHOW, WILLIAM, d. by Aug. 1685; m. Elizabeth Russell who m. 2nd William Harris (18:385).

CRAWFORD, JAMES (1), d. c.1756, having m. 1st Elizabeth (?), and 2nd Sarah (?); in 1719 patented 100 a. The Three Springs in what is now Harf. Co.; in 1743 pat. 50 a. Crawford's Double Purchase; in Nov. 1745 was made levy free; in 1750 owned Crawford's Double Purchase; d. by Sept. 1764 when Sarah Crawford, his widow, with her s. James and the latter's wife Margaret sold 50 a. of the latter tract to Thomas Husband; the will of James Crawford, 16 April 1755 - 3 March 1756, named w. Sarah, and ch.: James, Mordecai, Josias, Rachel, John, Elias, Jennet, Ruth, Sarah, Hannah, and Rebecca; had iss.: ELIAS, b. 8 Nov. 1706; JENNET, b. 27 July 1709; RUTH; JOHN; SARAH, b. 23 Nov. 1724; HANNAH, b. 15 Dec. 1725, prob. d. young; HANNAH, b. 10 Dec. 1726; MORDECAI, b. 24 June 1729; JAMES, b. 20 Dec. 1733; REBECCA, b. 9 March 1735; RACHEL, b. 15 May 1738; JOSIAS, b. 2 Dec. 1742 (35:743; 89:356; 111:107; 128: 44, 49, 59, 77, 97, 102; 129:325; 153:46; 207).

CRAWFORD, MORDECAI (2), s. of James (1) and Sarah, was b. 24 June 1729, d. in Harf. Co. in 1785; m. Susanna Tucker on 16 Sept. 1750; his will, 20 July 1785 - 10 Sept. 1785, and the will of his widow, 16 Oct. 1793 - 9 Jan. 1797, named these ch.: SEABORN; SUSANNA, m. (?) Davis; SARAH, m. (?) Hawkins; MARGARET, m. (?) Williams; JAMES, b. c.1759; HANNAH, b. c.1761, m. (?) Gorrall; MORDECAI, b. c.1766; JOHN, b. c.1771; RUTH, b. c.1773 (128:59; 244-AJ#2:100 and 121).

CRAWFORD, JAMES (3), s. of James (1) was b. 20 Dec. 1733; m. Margaret (?); by 1765 was in Fayette Co., Penna.

CRAWFORD, JOSIAS (4), s. of James (1), was b. 2 Dec. 1742; by 1765 was in Fayette Co., Penna. (129:325).

CRAWFORD, JAMES, m. Frances (?), who d. 23 April 1716, leaving iss.: JOHN, b. 11 March 1703; CATHERINE, b. 15 Feb. 1712 (128:34).

CRAWFORD, SARAH, m. 21 June 1720 John Cameron (131).

CRAWFORD, THOMAS, m. Martha (?), and had iss.: ELIZABETH, b. 16 Feb. 1746 (131:126/r).

CRAYTON. See CREIGHTON.

CREAG, ROBERT, d. 4 Sept. 1739; est. admin. 7 July 1741 by Constant Barnes; dec. left a widow and two sons in Ireland (4:113; 128:114).

CREAGHEAD, ROBERT, age 5, s. of Robert, in June 1738 was bound to Gervase Biddison (31:222).

CREIGHTON/CRAYTON/CRETIN, (?) (1), was the father of at least two sons who lived in Balto. Co.: WILLIAM, d. 1757; and JOHN.

CREIGHTON, WILLIAM (2), s. of (?) (1), d. by 16 March 1757; m. Mary (?); his will, 17 Feb. 1757 - 16 March 1757, named w. Mary, ch. John and William, and bro. John; admin. bond was posted 15 March 1757 by the exec. John Creighton with John Murra and Thos. Archer; had iss.: WILLIAM, b. 25 May 1755; JOHN, alive Feb. 1757 (11:385; 129:375; 210-30:247).

CREIGHTON, JOHN (3), s. of (?) (1), alive in Feb. 1757 when he was named in the will of his bro. William; m. by 1746 Martha (?); bought land from Philip Quinlin in Aug. 1758; in Nov. 1759 may have been the John Cretin named as the father of Ann Cretin's illeg. ch.; had iss.: PATRICK, b. 14 Nov. 1746 (46:241; 83:221; 129:344).

CRETIN, ANN, no known rel. to the above, in Nov. 1759 was fined for having an illeg. ch.; named John Cretin as the father (46 241).

CRESAP, THOMAS, came to Md. c.1717 from Yorkshire to Md.; m. 30 April 1727 as Thomas Crisup to Hannah Johnson, dau. of Daniel Johnson; gave his age as 31 in 1733; by 1748 was in Augusta Co., Va.; organized the Sons of Liberty; had iss. at least one ch.: DANIEL, b. 27 Feb. 1727 (128:54; 290-1:295; 310:130).

CRESWELL/CRISWELL, RICHARD, was in Balto. Co. by 28 May 1746 when he m. Mary Wooden; did not own any land in 1750; had iss.: WILLIAM, b. 19 Jan. 1747; ELEANOR, b. 14 Aug. 1749; poss. RICHARD, b. c.1747/9, served in the Rev. War, d. 25 Jan. 1839 in Ohio Co., W. Va.; poss. BENJAMIN, b. c.1757, took the Oath of Allegiance in Balto. Co., 1778; poss. JAMES, b. c.1757, took the Oath of Allegiance (133:78, 90; 417).

CRETIN. See CREIGHTON.

CRISWELL. See CRESWELL.

CROCKER, THOMAS, was in Balto. Co. by 1695 as a taxable on s. side of Patapsco Hun.; admin. the est. of Richard Horner on 30 Nov. 1711 (2:1; 140).

CROCKETT, ELI (1), trustee of Bush River Meeting Soc. of Friends; had iss.: GILBERT, m. 1727 Mary Chew; JOHN, m. 1727 Mary Richardson (433:366).

CROCKETT, GILBERT (2), s. of Eli (1), m. in 1727 Mary Chew; he d. by 28 Dec. 1744 when his est. was admin. by James Harrison and w. Mary; had iss.: prob. GILBERT (3:346; 263).

CROCKETT, JOHN (3), s. of Eli (1), m. Mary Richardson; d. by 1736 when his inv. listed a number of books; she d. by 11 June 1742 when Nathan Richardson admin. the est.; had iss.: ELIZABETH, m. Nathan Richardson of William and Margaret on 30 d, 8, 1735; MARY, m. 24 Jan. 1744 Elie Dorsey; JOHN, in Nov. 1742 chose Nathaniel Richardson as his guardian; HANNAH, living in March 1742/3, was prob. the Hannah who in 1750 owned 656 a. of Capito (3:284; 34:60, 125; 131; 153:88).

CROCKETT, GILBERT (4), poss. s. of Gilbert (2), d. in Balto. Co. leaving a will, 9 March 1772 - 4 April 1772, in which he named a friend William Webb, and these ch.: GILBERT; SAMUEL; BENJAMIN (112:233).

CROCKETT, JOHN (5), s. of John (3), d. by 2 Dec. 1727, having m. Mary Richardson, dau. of Joseph Richardson, in 1747; his will, 31 Oct. 1747 - 2 Dec. 1747, left sis. Hannah 500 a. Isle of Caprea, w. Mary 500 a. Marino and 300 a. Colerain, res. of Marino to Mary, dau. of his bro.-in-law Eli Dorsey, and res. of his tract Colerain to nephew Nathan Richardson of Nathan; admin. bond was posted 2 Jan. 1747/8 by wid. and extx. Mary Crockett, with Joseph Richardson and Philip Hopkins; Mary was alive in 1750 and was listed as the owner of 712 a. Marino (11:374; 111:12; 153:1).

CROCKETT, Dr. BENJAMIN, m. 30 June 1750 in Cecil Co. Elizabeth Chew; d. by 24 Jan. 1760 when admin. bond was posted by admin. Gilbert Crockett with Samuel and William Webb; had iss.: BENJAMIN, b. 25 May 1751; JOHN, b. 19 April 1754; GILBERT, b. 26 July 1756 (11:441; 129:350).

CROCKETT, EDWARD, d. in Balto. Co. by 1675 (110:102).

CROCKETT, JOHN, d. by 3 Oct. 1730 when Edward Smith renounced as executor (125:172).

CROCKETT, JOHN, m. 25 Dec. 1744 Ann Fixson or Hickson; in Sept. 1746 John, age 30, leased land from Thomas Brerewood, said lease was to run for the lives of Crockett, his wife Ann, age 30, and Ann Row, dau. of William, age c.8 (131; 79:368).

CROCKETT, JOSEPH, m. Jane (?), by whom he had iss.: MARY, b. 2 March 1739; SAMUEL, b. 9 March 1740 (128:108; 129:323).

CROCKETT, MARY, m. Johns Hopkins on 14 d, 9 mo., 1749 (Records of West River Monthly Meeting in 219-6).

CROCKETT, SAMUEL, m. Esther (?), and had iss.: SAMUEL, b. 11 Feb. 1739; JEAN, b. 24 Feb. 1741 (128:109; 129:323).

CROCKLAND, JOHN, from Norfolk, Eng., ran away from William Towson in or before Sept. 1743; age given as 25 years old in an advert. of 11 Oct. 1744 (384:468).

CROFT, ROBERT, in 1750 owned 50 a. Cergafergus (153:63; may be Robert Cross, q.v.)

CROMPTON, JOSEPH, m. Mary Costley on 19 Oct. 1703, and had iss.: DAVID, b. 27 Aug. 1704; LIDDIA, b. 19 March 1706 (128:17, 18, 20).

CROMPTON, MARGARET, m. John Crow on 6 April 1719 (129:227).

THE CROMWELL FAMILY has been discussed by Culver (346-1:339-356) and by Newman (355). To date no proof has been found linking the Maryland Cromwells with the family of Oliver Cromwell, Lord Protector of Great Britain.

CROMWELL, (?), (1), was the father of at least four children, who settled in Md.: WILLIAM; JOHN; RICHARD; and EDITH, b. c.1660, m. 1st c.1682 Christopher Gist, 2nd c.1692 Joseph Williams, and 3rd c.1693 John Beecher (Culver).

CROMWELL, WILLIAM (2), s. of (?) (1), came to Md. in 1667, d. 1684; m. Elizabeth Trehearne, poss. a widow, who m. as her 3rd husb. c.1685 George Ashman; will of William, 19 June 1680 - 1 May 1684, named w. Elizabeth (formerly Trehearne), minor s. William, s. Thomas, and bros. John and Richard; had iss.: WILLIAM, b. c. 1678; THOMAS, b. c.168-(?); PHILIP (named in the will of George Ashman, 1699); poss. JOSHUA (388; Culver).

CROMWELL, JOHN (3), s. of (?) (1), was in Md. by 1670, d. testate by 1714; had iss.: JOSHUA, d. after 1748 having m. Frances Ingram (Culver).

CROMWELL, RICHARD (4), s. of (?) (1), d. by 1717; m. 1st Ann Besson, who d. 29 Aug. 1698, and 2nd Elizabeth (?); used an armorial seal when he signed the will of George Ashman in 1699; on 30 Sept. 1707 admin. the est. of Thomas Edmonds; his will, 12 Aug. 1717 - 23 Sept. 1717, named w. Elizabeth and s. John as execs., eld. s. Richard, cous. Joshua Cromwell, Margaret Rattenbury and her dau. Hannah, Edith Gist, dau. ofRichard and Zipporah, cous. Richard Gist, mother-in-law Besson, bro.-in-law James Phillips, cous. Thomas Cromwell, Isaac Larogne, and Nicholas Besson; admin. bond was posted 18 Oct. 1717 by the execs., with James Phillips and Thomas Cromwell; est. inv. on 13 Sept. 1717 by John Israel and Lance Todd and val. at £1512.13.5, with Thomas and Joshua Cromwell signing as kin; est. admin. on 8 June 1719 by the execs.; had iss.:

NICHOLAS, b. 15 Aug. 1698, d. 10 July 1715 (by 1st w.); RICHARD,
d. unm.; JOHN, d. 1733, m. Hannah Rattenbury (2:145; 4:112; 11:
283; 52:299; 110:144; 346-2:106-109; Newman, Heraldic Marylandi-
ana, p. 51).

CROMWELL, WILLIAM (5), s. of William (2), b. c.1678, gave his
age as 53 in 1731, d. 1735; m. Mary Woolquist, dau. of Arthur and
Margaret (Johnson) Woolquist, and granddau. of Aaron Johnson of
Newcastle, Penna.; Mary was b. c.1674, giving her age as 65 in
1739; by 1695 was a taxable in s. side Patapsco Hund.; had iss.:
WILLIAM, b. 1703; JOSEPH, b. 21 Aug. 1708; ALEXANDER, b. 1715;
WOOLQUIST, b. 1715 (Johnston, Chart of Cromwell Family).

CROMWELL, THOMAS (6), s. of William (2), was b. c.168-(?), d.
by 20 Aug. 1723; m. in 1705 Jemima (Morgan) Murray, wid. of James
Murray, and dau. of Col. Thomas Morgan; was named as son-in-law
of George Ashman in 1699; admin. the estates of Eliza and George
Ashman on 15 May 1707 and 27 May 1712; his will, 17 July 1723 -
12 Aug. 1723, named sons Thomas and Oliver, bros. John Ashman
and William Cromwell, and cousins John Cromwell and George Bailey;
admin. bond was posted 20 Aug. 1723 by Patrick Sympson with George
Bailey and William Cromwell; est. inv. in 1724 and admin. 3 Nov.
1724 by Patrick Simpson; had iss.: THOMAS; OLIVER (1:349, 354;
2:84, 100, 108, 207, 363; 3:17; 11:288; 51:229).

CROMWELL, JOSHUA (7), s. of John (3), d. after 1748, having m.
Frances Ingram, and had iss.: JOHN, b. 1711, d. 1772, m. in 1738
Comfort Robosson; left iss. in A. A. Co. (355).

CROMWELL, JOHN (8), s. of Richard (4), d. in A. A. Co., having
m. Hannah Rattenbury; his will, 16 Dec. 1733 - 9 May 1734, named
w. Hannah (who m. 2nd (?) Worthington), lands in Gunpowder Forest,
Cromwell's Park, Cromwell's Chance, and Cromwell's Addition, and
four children: HANNAH, m. Nicholas Cromwell; MARGARET, d. unm.;
JOHN, m. Elizabeth Todd; and ANN, m. Thomas Sheredine (3:318;
126:74).

CROMWELL, WILLIAM (9), s. of William (5) and Mary, was b. 1703,
d. 1758; m. 1st Constant, heir of John Wilmot of Balto. Co., and
2nd Charity Ashman; Deputy Surveyor of A. A. Co., in 1734; may be
the William who in 1750 owned 50 a. Gist's Search and 50 a. of
Ellege's Addition; his will was proved in A. A. Co. on 7 July 1758;
est. was admin. in Balto. Co. by Joseph Cromwell on 5 Nov. 1759
and on 10 Nov. 1760, naming a son William and a dau. who m. Wm.
Ashman; had iss.: (by 1st w.): PHILEMON, alive 1777 in Balto.
Co.; HANNAH, m. John Chenoweth; PATIENCE, m. Samuel Chenoweth;
RUTH, m. 27 Nov. 1760 William Gill; WILLIAM, m. Chloe (?); (by
2nd w.): DINAH, age 14 in 1759, chose Robert Wilmot as guardian
in Nov. 1759, m. 11 Oct. 1761 John Wells (4:256, 298; 5:146; 44;
153:94; 355).

CROMWELL, JOSEPH (10), s. of William (5) and Mary, b. 21 Aug.
1707, d. 12 Oct. 1769; m. Comfort (?); fought in the French and
Indian Wars; gave £ 4.0.0 for the building of St. Thomas' Church;
purch. Nicholson's Manor from Kensey and Susanna Johns in Jan.
1761; in 1750 owned 220 a. Deer Park, 260 a. Cromwell's Enlargement; in June 1754 was ind. for refusing to act as vestryman or
churchwarden of St. Pauls Parish; in Aug. 1759 purch. 250 a.
Todd's Forest; his will, 14 Sept. 1768 - 8 Nov. 1769 named ch.
Joseph, Stephen, Richard, Ruth Towson (and her dau. Sarah), Chloe
Cockey (and her dau. Rebeckah), and Nathan, and bro. William; had
iss.: NATHAN, b. 1731; RUTH, b. 1738, m. Ezekiel Towson; RICHARD,
b. 1739, d. 1802, m. Rachel Cockey; JOSEPH, b. 1741, d. 1782, m.
Ann Orrick; PHILEMON, b. 1743, d. 1767; Capt. STEPHEN, b. 1747,
d. 1783, m. Elizabeth Murray; CHLOE, b. 1736, d. 1823, m. Capt.

John Cockey(39:184; 83:506; 85:15; 112:101; 126:158; 153:47; 355).

CROMWELL, ALEXANDER (11), s. of William (5) and Mary, b. 1712, age 25 in 1737 when he deposed concerning his father William and his uncle John Ashman; m. 17 April 1733 Sarah, dau. of John and Comfort (Stinson) Dorsey; had iss.: COMFORT, b. 19 May 1738; MARY, b. 1 Sept. 1740; ELISHA, b. 4 Nov. 1742; ALEXANDER,b. 26 Dec. 1744; SARAH, b. 30 Jan. 1746 (217-IB#I:102; 355).

CROMWELL, THOMAS (12), s. of Thomas (6) and Jemima, was alive in Nov. 1727 when he and w. Eleanor conv. Hunting Quarter to Henry Wright, David's Fancy to Capt. John Cromwell, and Maiden's Choice to William Hammond; d. by 1745 (355).

CROMWELL, OLIVER (13), s. of Thomas (6) and Jemima, was b. 15 Oct. 1708, d. 24 June 1786; m. Anna Maria, dau. of John and Sarah (Welsh) Giles; in 1750 owned 225 a. Maiden's Choice and 152½ a. Cromwell's Chance; member of the Balto. Co. Committee of Observation in 1775; had iss.: JOHN GILES, b. 30 June 1737, d. s.p. 1801; JACOB, m. Elizabeth Wooden; ANN, m. (?) Lewis; SARAH, m. William Locke; OLIVER; JAMES OLIVER, m. Elizabeth (?); THOMAS IRETON, m. Hannah Smith; NATHANIEL, m. Lydia (?) (128:99; 153:46; 355).

CROMWELL, JOHN (14), s. of John (8), in 1750 owned Cordwainer's Hall, 200 a. Cromwell's Range, 700 a. Cromwell's Park, 169 a. Cromwell's Addition, 148 a. Maiden's Dairy, 125 a. Gist's Search, and 300 a. Cromwell's Chance (153:82).

CROMWELL, (?), with (?) Stansbury, in 1750 owned 500 a. of Joshua's Lot and 83 a. of Milford (153:85).

CROMWELL, JAMES, orphan age 4 next 1 Dec.; in Nov. 1758 was bound to Thomas Gittings (44).

CROMWELL, JOHN, age c.17; in March 1743/4 chose Philip Jones, Jr., as his guardian (35:155).

CROMWELL, THOMAS, in Aug. 1724 was ind. by the grand jury for begetting an illeg. ch. on the body of Elizabeth Peacock (26:438).

CROMWELL, WILLIAM, age 13, in March 1739/40 was bound to William Rogers (32:147).

CRONEY, JEREMIAH, m. 23 Dec. 1766 Mary, admnx. of Richard Coleman (7:304; 131).

CRONEY, PAUL, m. 12 Aug. 1751 Elizabeth Carson (129:353).

CROOK, JAMES (1), d. by 26 Dec. 1727; on 27 Dec. 1716, m. in St. Anne's Par., A. A. Co., Sarah, wid. of Edward Burgess and Dr. Thomas Majors (the latter her 1st husb.); in Sept. 1706 bought 773 a. Jacob's Choice from Thomas and Susanna Long; his will, 5 Oct. 1727 - 26 Dec. 1727, left Bushey Neck and Hopewell to dau. Chloe and Trident, and a lot in Annapolis to s. Charles; est. admin. on 21 April 1729, 22 Jan. 1730, and 24 Oct. 1732, when dau. Chloe was the wife of Walter Dallas; his widow left a will, 7 Dec. 1737 - 20 Dec. 1737, naming s. Charles, and grandchildren Elizabeth Riddle Dallas and Chloe Dallas (daus. of Walter Dallas), and Sarah, Chloe, Mary, Abarilla, and Luke Raven (ch. of Luke and Sarah Majors Raven); had iss.: CHARLES; CHLOE, m. by 1732 Walter Dallas (2:84, 92, 105, 137, 174, 257, 309; 3:115; 59:544; 125:51; 126: 232).

CROOK, CHARLES (2), s. of James (1), d. by 8 March 1748 when Walter Dallas posted admin. bond with John and Charles Merryman; in 1750 his heirs owned 250 a. Gunner's Range and 108 a. Trident; may have had iss.: JOSEPH, m. 24 April 1757 Priscilla Galloway; ELIZABETH, m. by 29 Dec. 1767 Aquila Hatton (11:365; 131; 153: 47).

CROSBY, JOHN, and Sarah Hodson had iss.: ELIZABETH, b. 18 May 1752 (133:96).

CROSBY, or CROSLEY, RICHARD, serv. to Samuel Stansbury, in Nov. 1757 was tried for begetting a bast. on the body of Elizabeth Sedgehill (44).

CROSHOW, WILLIAM, d. in Balto. Co. by 1684; m. by Nov. 1682 Elizabeth, wid. of Thomas Russell, and admnx. of John Thompson; est. was admin. in 1684 by William and Elizabeth Harris (18:22; 206-8:214, and 206-8C:330).

THE CROSS FAMILY OF CROSS'S PARK AND CROSS'S LOT.

CROSS, (?) (1), is presumed to be the father of at least four sons, two of whom were listed in the 1737 tax list of Back River Hund.: JOHN, d. by 1764; JOSEPH; WILLIAM; and RICHARD (149).

CROSS, JOHN (2), s. of (?) (1), d. by 22 Aug. 1764; m. by 1726 Dinah, admnx. of John Wheeler; surv. 50 a. Cross's Park in 1742, and which he owned in 1750 along with 50 a. Wheeler; in 1751 conv. Cross's Park to his s. John, Jr.; his will, proved 22 Aug. 1764, named w. Dinah, eight ch., and grandson Abraham Cross of William; had iss.: JOHN; SOLOMON, d. 1777; BENJAMIN (prob. the Benj. who m. Elizabeth Cole on 20 Jan. 1754); WILLIAM; ZACHARIAH; RICHARD (poss. the Richard who m. Tabitha Hicks on 1 Jan. 1761); ASAEL, m. Mary Demmett on 24 Aug. 1760; RUTH, m. (?) Cole (3:120; 51:74; 81:407; 131; 153:65; 207; 210-32:227).

CROSS, JOSEPH (3), s. of (?) (1), was listed in 1737 in Back River Hund.; m. 13 Sept. 1730 Elizabeth, dau. of Charles Merryman, and had iss.: MARY, b. 5 Sept. 1732; JOHN, b. 10 Dec. 1733 (4:21; 131; 133:25, 149).

CROSS, WILLIAM (4), s. of (?) (1), was listed in 1737 in Back River Hundred; prob. the same William, who with Richard Cross, orphans, were ordered to be raised by Jonathan Tipton in Aug. 1730; in Aug. 1746 bought 50 a. Level Bottom from William Hall, weaver, and w. Mary; in 1750 owned Level Bottom, and 23 a. Cross's Lot, which he had surv. in 1746; m. Ann (?), who gave consent to sale of both tracts to Samuel Lane in Jan. 1756; d. by 31 Aug. 1761 when Benjamin Cross posted admin. bond with Richard and Jeremiah Belt; had iss.: prob. BENJAMIN (11:444; 27:9; 79:155; 82: 493; 153:74).

CROSS, RICHARD (5), s. of (?) (1), was a minor orphan in Aug. 1730 when he and William Cross were placed with Jonathan Tipton, who was to teach them to read and to follow the trade of a cooper (29:9).

CROSS, JOHN (6), s. of John (2), was named as his father's eldest s. in 1751 when he was conv. 50 a. Cross's Park; prob. the same John who m. Philizanna Hicks on 28 Aug. 1753; John and Philizanna conv. Lowe's Range to George Myers in Oct. 1765; d. by 18 March 1775 when Stephen Price posted admin. bond with John and Henry Stevenson; est. admin. by Price on 6 Feb. 1778 (8:41; 11: 500; 81:407; 90:552).

CROSS, SOLOMON (7), s. of John (2), d. by 1 Aug. 1777; m. Mary
Keith on 8 Feb. 1754; his will, 22 June 1777 - 1 Aug. 1777, left
land Buck Range to sons Israel and Benjamin, and also named ch.:
Solomon, Mary, and John, with Benjamin Cross as a witness; had
iss.: ISRAEL, alive in 1783 in North Hund., owning 50 a. Buck
Range, and with 5 whites; BENJAMIN, living 1783 in North Hund.,
owning 52 a. land with 5 whites; SOLOMON, alive in 1783 in North
Hund., owning 80 a. Buck Range; MARY; JOHN, in 1783 owned 100 a.
Buck Range, and had 8 whites in his household (112:351; 131; 283).

CROSS, BENJAMIN (8), s. of John (2), m. Elizabeth Cole on 20
Jan. 1754; in April 1764 he and w. Elizabeth conv. 50 a. Lowes
Range to William Cross, and 50 a. of same tract to John Cross
(89:47, 50; 131).

CROSS, WILLIAM (9), s. of John (2), d. in 1770; m. Alice Cole
on 24 April 1753; in April 1764 purch. Lowe's Range from Benjamin
and Elizabeth Cross; his nuncupative will, made before he died on
19 Feb. 1770, and proved 7 May 1770, left everything to wife Alice;
his son Abraham, named in the will of John Cross, with Alice Cross
in Aug. 1772 deeded 50 a. Lowe's Range to John Ensor of Abraham;
William's name may have been misread as "Brittain Cross;" had iss.:
ABRAHAM; prob. ELIJAH; prob. WILLIAM; prob. ZACHARIAH (89:50; 112:
148; 231-AL#E :418).

CROSS, JOHN (10), s. of Joseph (3), b. 10 Dec. 1733, and in
Nov. 1760 as "son of Joseph Cross of York Co., dec.," conv. 50
a. John's Adventure to Michael Deeds, with the consent of his
(John's) wife Edith (84:433; 133:149).

CROSS, BENJAMIN (11), s. of William (4), m. by 10 June 1765
Mary (?) who joined him in selling 70 a. Cross's Meadow to Andrew
Bergebile (90:282).

CROSS, ABRAHAM (12), s. of William (9) and Alice, was b. c.
1752, and gave his age as 80 in 1832 in his pension application;
by 1777 was in Sullivan Co., N. C. (now Tenn.), and applied for
a pension there in Sept. 1832 (Rev. War Pension Application No.
S-1900).

CROSS, ELIJAH (13), poss. s. of William (9) and Alice, was b.
c.1758 in Balto. Co., and in Aug. 1832 was in Sullivan Co., N.C.
(now Tenn.), where he applied for a pension for his revolutionary
service; was associated with Aquila, William, Abraham, and Zachariah Cross in various land transactions (Rev. War Pension Application No. S-1947; Land Records of Sullivan Co., Tenn., abstracted
at the DAR Library in Washington, D. C.).

CROSS, WILLIAM (14), poss. s. of William (9) and Alice, was
b. c.1761/2 in Balto. Co., Md., served in the Rev. War from Sullivan Co., Tenn., where he applied for a pension in July 1833 in
Anderson Co., Tenn. (Rev. War Pension Application No. S-3221).

CROSS, ZACHARIAH (15), poss. s. of William (9) and Alice, stated
he was b. 25 March 1761 in Balto. Co., Md.; d. 27 Feb. 1838 in
Wayne Co., Ill.; served in the Rev. War from Sullivan Co.; applied
for a pension on 8 Feb. 1833 in Logan Co., Ky.; m. Easter Johnson
about 15 Aug. 1792, perhaps in Logan Co., Ky.; she d. 21 Dec.
1841; had iss.: RACHEL, m. (?) McDonald; WILLIAM, moved to Ala-
bama; MARY, m. (?) Funkhouser; EDNEY, m. (?) Reeves; JAMES; OLI-
VER V., moved to Missouri Terr.; ROBERT F. (Rev. War Pension Application No. R-2519).

THE CROSS FAMILY OF CERGAFERGUS

CROSS, ROBERT (16), no known rel. to above family, was in St.

Margaret's Par., A. A. Co., where he m. 1st, on 25 July 1709 Ann
Board (poss. the Ann "Craus" who d. 28 July 1712); and m. 2nd
on 28 Nov. 1712 Hannah Gosnell (who may be the Hannah Cross who
m. John Buckingham on 31 Jan. 1720); had iss.: (by 1st w.): HAN-
NAH, b. 28 April 1711; (by 2nd w.): WILLIAM, b. 10 Dec. 1713;
ROBERT, b. 3 Sept. 1719 (219-4:20, 25, 99, 100, 166).

CROSS, WILLIAM (17), s. of Robert (16) and Hannah, b. 10 Dec.
1713, d. by 10 Aug. 1746; m. 24 Dec. 1738 Dorcas Groscumb who m.
2nd on 10 Aug. 1746 Hancelip Nelson; had iss.: OBADIAH BUCKINGHAM,
b. 22 March 1738 (sic); CHARLES, b. 15 Aug. 1743 (219-4:20, 41,48,
105, 108).

CROSS, ROBERT (18), s. of Robert (16) and Hannah, was b. 3 Sept.
1719, moved to St. Thomas' Par., Balto. Co., by 13 March 1744 when
he m. Jemima Gosnell; bought 100 a. Cergafergus from Joseph Cornelius in May 1744; with w. Jemima conv. 50 a. to William Mattox
in Oct. 1759; owned 50 a. in 1750; had iss.: ANN, b. 27 Nov. 1748;
HANNAH, b. 24 March 1754; NICODEMUS, b. 19 July 1759; BENJAMIN, b.
23 April 1760; ANN, b. 13 Jan. 1763 (77:673; 80:317; 134:12, 35,
36, 72; 153:63).

CROSS, NICODEMUS (19), s. of Robert (18) and Jemima, m. Barbara
Gladman and had iss.: MICHAEL, b. 8 Nov. 1794 (134:67).

THE CROSS FAMILY OF CROSS'S FOREST

CROSS, JOHN (20), no known rel. to the above, d. c.1712; m. by
30 Aug. 1688 Elinor, dau. of Edward Selby of A. A. Co.; Elinor d.
by 2 Nov. 1719 in A. A. Co.; on Aug. 1704 John and Elinor conv.
357 a. Cross's Forest to David McElfresh; John d. c.1712 "about
17 years ago" acc. to the 1739 dep. of Thomas Carr; the will of
Elinor, 23 Oct. 1719 - 2 Nov. 1719, named dau. Priscilla Fowler,
Jacob Lusby of John, dau.-in-law Mary Cross, to have Ferry Point,
and sons Joshua and Thomas, to have residue of Beard's Dock; had
iss.: JOSHUA; THOMAS; PRISCILLA (66:346; 121:32; 123:220; 225:60).

CROSS, JOSHUA (21), s. of John (20) and Eleanor, was in Balto.
Co. by July 1750 when he conv. 150 a. Selby's Hope, pt. of Leaf's
Chance, to Robert Adair (81:170).

CROSS, THOMAS (22), s. of John (20) and Eleanor, is prob. the
Thomas who m. June 1727 Sarah, dau. of Joseph Hughes; Thomas and
Sarah conv. 50 a. Chance to James Standiford in April 1728, 140
a. (being one-half of Mathews Double Purchase) to Henry Wetherall
in March 1731, and 10 a. Hughes Chance to William Rhodes in June
1734; Thomas d. April 1741 (73:77, 198; 74:67; 129:324; 225:15).

THE JOHN AND RACHEL CROSS FAMILY

CROSS, JOHN (23), no known rel. to any of the above, m. Rachel
(?), by whom he had a son HENRY, b. c.1717 (25:320).

CROSS, HENRY (24), s. of John (23) and Rachel, was b. c.1717,
was age 6 in June 1723 when bound to Thomas Sheredine; admin. the
est. of John Royston in Dec. 1741; m. Mary, wid. of John Royston;
reg. a stray in Aug. 1759; in Sept. 1763 would not pay the debts
of his w. Mary, who had left him; d. by 20 Nov. 1782 when admin.
bond was posted by Moses Collett and Rebecca Cross with Benjamin
Royston and John Miller, securities; had iss.: HENRY, b. 12 Dec.
1739; SOLOMON, b. 29 May 1745 (4:96; 15:136; 35:320; 47:220; 79:
497; 131:114/r; 133:66).

CROSS, HENRY (25), s. of Henry (24) and Mary, was b. 12 Dec.
1739; m. Margaret Hicks on 19 June 1759; reg. a stray in May 1760
(47; 131:54; 133:66).

Unrelated Crosses.

CROSS, BRITTAIN, alleged to have m. a Miss Cole, moved from Balto. Co. to Sullivan Co., Tenn.; see WILLIAM CROSS, no. 9 above.

CROSS, JOHN, purch. 100 a. Hog's Norton, being part of a larger tract called Roberts' Forest, from Eliza Roberts in March 1711; conv. tract to James Moore in Nov. 1726 (67:179; 70:288).

CROSS, JOHN, m. Sarah (?), and had iss.: SARAH, b. 25 March 1740 (128:110).

CROSS, JOSEPH, m. Rodia (?), and had iss.: ANN, b. 3 May 1739; RACHEL, b. 25 April 1741 (131:88/r).

CROSS, MARY, alias HEETH, was tried for bast. in March 1754 and named Benjamin Barney as the father (39:29).

CROSSWELL, JOHN, was ordered to be levy free for the duration of the lameness of his arm, June 1757 (46:39).

CROUCH, BART, blacksmith with 5 years and 9 mos. to serve in the inv. of Edward Fottrell, 1743 (53:70).

CROUCH, JAMES, m. 22 Sept. 1757 Hannah Starkey, wid. of Joshua Starkey; on 10 Sept. 1759 conv. tract Cullen Burn to Jonathan Starkey (83:497; 131).

CROUCH, JOSEPH, m. 3 Jan. 1719 Mary Lynch; in Aug. 1719 was allowed 400 lbs. tob. for taking care of Ann Dyton; in 1722 Mary Crouch recorded a servant man for her son William Lynch (23:206; 69:36).

CROW, JAMES, b. 11 Nov. 1713, parents not given; m. 16 Nov. 1738 Hannah Sympson; Hannah d. 1 March 1742, and James m. 2nd 7 Feb. 1743 Grace Denson; had iss. by 1st w.: JOHN, b. 1 Jan. 1740; MARY, b. 22 July 1742 (128:31, 103, 112, 329, 330, 333).

CROW, JOHN, m. Margaret Compton on 6 April 1719 (128:39).

CROW, JOHN, m. Judith Magee on the Monday before Ash Wednesday (year not given); had iss.: MARGARET, b. 9 Jan. 1734; JOHN, b. 2? Feb. 1736; JAMES, b. 14 April 1740; THOMAS, b. 14 April 1740; MANSFIELD, b. 23 Nov. 1742 (128:78, 88, 95, 107; 129:340).

CROW, JOHN, d. by 14 Feb. 1745 when his est. was admin. by James Crow; admin. again on 2 June 1747; left heirs: widow and five children, James, Margaret, Thomas, John, and Mansfield (4: 157; 5:49). (This is prob. the John Crow above, and the admin. was in all likelihood James Crow listed first).

CROW, MARY, d. 16 Nov. 1713 (128:30).

CROWLEY, DENNIS (1), was in Balto. Co. by Dec. 1699 when he surv. Crowley's First Venture; in March 1699/1700 surv. 200 a. Crowley's Contrivance; his will, 22 March 1708/9 - 20 April 1709, left his dwelling plant. to Mary Crowley, and named Henry Knowles as exec.; admin. bond posted 20 April 1709 by Knowles with Henry Wriothesley and William Wilkinson; est. inv. 3 Sept. 1709 by Chris. Gardner and Hector McLane and val. at £ 47.1.0, additional inv. of £ 8.3.0, made 19 Oct. 1709; est. admin. by Henry Knowles on 7 June 1711 and 13 May 1719; may have had iss.: DANIEL (1:376; 2: 132; 11:405; 48:322; 51:33; 110:36; 438:1).

CROWLEY, DANIEL (2), s. of Dennis (1), formerly of Balto. Co., by 31 Oct. 1735 was in N. C. when he sold Benjamin Tasker land laid out in March 1699 for Dennis and Daniel Crowley (213-PL#8: 399).

THE CROXALL FAMILY has been discussed by Barnes (259).

CROXALL, RICHARD,(1) first known ancestor of the Maryland Croxalls, was living in 1716 as a farmer in Stoke-Golding, Co. Leicester, Eng., and had at least one son: RICHARD (259).

CROXALL, RICHARD (2), s. of Richard (1), may have been born as early as 1685, was alive in 1690, and d. c.1747 in Balto. Co., Md., having m. Joanna Carroll, who d. 18 March 1756; she was perhaps a dau. of Anthony Carroll of Lisheenboy, Co. Tipperary, Ireland, and a niece of Charles Carroll, the Attorney General; the parentage of Richard is proved by a series of depositions published after his death by his sons Charles, Richard, and James, who denied the reports that their father had lost an ear as punishment for some crime; a memorandum dated 4 Aug. 1716 stated that Richard Croxall, farmer, had come before the Mayor and two justices of the peace of Stoke-Golding, and testified that in 1690 his son and heir Richard had been riding in a cart when he fell off and the cart wheel passed over his ear, cutting it off; the will of Richard's widow, Joanna, proved 20 March 1756, named granddaughters Rachel Croxall of Charles, and Mary and Elizabeth Rumney of Nathaniel, and dau.-in-law Eleanor Croxall; had iss.: RICHARD, d. 11 May 1785, s.p.; CHARLES, b. 27 June 1724; JAMES, d. by 29 Nov. 1748; MARY, m. Nathaniel Rumney; dau., m. (?) Howard (259).

CROXALL, CHARLES (3), s. of Richard (2), b. 27 June 1724, d. 25 June 1782; m. 23 July 1746 Rebecca, dau. of John Moale (she was b. 29 Feb. 1728, d. 21 Nov. 1786); in 1750 owned 199 a. Brother's Inheritance, 100 a. Hammond's Struggle, 198 a. Hammond's Purchase, 81 a. Huckleberry Forest, and 1 lot in Balto. Town; had iss.: ELIZABETH, b. 21 May 1747; RACHEL, b. 6 Jan. 1749, m. Daniel Carroll; JAMES, b. 27 Dec. 1751; REBECCA ELIZABETH, b. 11 March 1754, m. Nicholas Ridgely; CHARLES MOALE, b. 7 Oct. 1756; RICHARD, b. 7 Feb. 1759; JOHN, b. 30 May 1761; THOMAS, b. 2 May 1764; ANASTASIA, b. 28 May 1766, m. Nicholas Orrick Ridgely; SAMUEL MOALE, b. 8 Nov. 1768 (153:81; 259).

CRUTCHINGTON, ROGER, d. by June 1754, leaving execs., Mark and Deborah Guichard, and orphans:GEORGE; and MARY (39:185, 188).

CRUTCHINGTON, GEORGE, s. of above Roger, in March 1754 chose Joseph Hendon as his guardian (39:16).

CRUTE, ROBERT, d. 31 March 1761, having m. on 18 Aug. 1751 Rachel Barnes who m. 2nd on 21 June 1762 William Stevenson; had iss.: REBECCA, b. 24 Nov. 1752; SARAH, b. 17 Feb. 1755; RICHARD, b. 19 March 1757; FRANCIS, b. 15 April 1759; CORDELIA, b. 21 April 1761 (128:382, 383).

CRYDER, FREDERICK, in 1750 owned 100 a. Neighborly Kindness (153:90).

CRYDER, JOHN, in 1750 owned 100 a. Molly's Industry (153:90).

CUFFEE, MATTHEW, age c.16, servant to James Rider, made a deposition in March 1720/1 (23:490).

CULLEN, or CULLING, THOMAS, d. Oct. 1731; m. Catherine (?) who m. 2nd by June 1738 Edward Thorp; his will, 4 Oct. 1731 - 3 Nov. 1731, named w. Catherine, cousin William Jenkins; sister Sarah

and her children, Sarah Gwin, Avis Jenkins, Thomas Jenkins, and
William Jenkins, and godchildren John, Mary, and Elizabeth the
ch. of Robert and Ann Hawkins; est. admin. 1 July 1737 by extx.
Catherine, wife of Edward Thorp (3:324; 31:226; 125:216; 128:65).

CULLINDER, MARY, in Nov. 1724 was buried by Jane Van Diver,
who was allowed 200 lbs. tob. by the Court for her trouble (27:
37).

CULVER, BENJAMIN, in 1750 owned 400 a. Broom's Entrance; in
June 1759 Thomas and Hannah Wilkinson conv. him 25 a. Margaret's
Purchase (83:468; 153:71).

CUMMINGS, WILLIAM, d. leaving an est. inv. by John Rattenbury
and Edward Stevenson and val. at £ 53.0.1½ (50:350).

CUNNINGHAM, HUGH, m. Mary Acre; banns were pub. in March and
April 1749 (131).

CURRIER, THOMAS, d. by 3 Oct. 1716 when his est. was admin. by
William Husbands, admin. of Currier's orig. admnx. Mary Brooke,
dec. (1:207).

CURTIS, BENJAMIN, m. by 12 Nov. 1745 Abarilla; on 28 July
1744 he and his w. Abarilla admin. the est. of Nicholas Gostwick
(who had m. Abarilla Yanston on Dec. 1720); had iss.: JOHN, b. 12
Nov. 1745 (3:360; 133:89, 147).

CURTIS, DANIEL, m. 5 Nov. 1758 Rachel Pearce; had iss.: JOSEPH,
b. 17 Aug. 1759; HANNAH, b. 15 June 1761 (134:33, 72).

CURTIS, MARY, in Aug. 1710 was ind. for bast.; Enoch Spinks
agreed to pay her fine if she could not (21:164).

CURTIS, RICHARD, orphan, age 11, in Nov. 1739 was bound to
Robert Courtney and wife Hannah to age 21 (32:76).

CUSTAVIN, THOMAS, was in Balto. Co. by 1692 as a taxable in n.
side Gunpowder Hund. (138).

CUSTIS, RICHARD, age 11 next 6 Feb., was bound to William Cook
in Nov. 1738 (31:310).

CUTCHIN/GUDGEON, ROBERT (1), m. by 11 Oct. 1702 Dorothy, wid.
of Moses Groome, whose est. they admin. on that date; admin. est.
of Ralph Eaves in Dec. 1706; in April 1709 wit. the will of John
Ewings who left personalty to Robert Cutchin of Robert; in Nov.
1702 bought 158 a. Sicklemore's Dock from Samuel and Sarah Sicklemore; in Nov. 1705 purch.200 a. Holland's Adventure from Francis
Watkins; in March 1716 was reimbursed for caring for Charles Hewitt, during the latter's illness; in Aug. 1719 wife Dorothy was
ordered to examine Kate Kerevan, servant of John Roberts, for
signs of pregnancy; Robert d. 30 March 1718; 6 March 1728 the
est. of Robert was inv. by William Low and Archibald and val.
at £ 114.11.6½, and signed by Robert and Elizabeth; had iss.:
ROBERT, of age in 1728; ELIZABETH, of age in 1728, prob. the Elizabeth who m. Richard Perkins, Jr., on 5 Jan. 1735 (2:83, 100, 220;'
22:91; 23:208; 51:88; 66:181, 215; 64:9; 122:145; 131:9/r).

CUTCHIN, ROBERT (2), s. of Robert (1), of age in 1728, d. by
1740; m. Winiford Breavinton on 20 April 1731 (poss. she was the
Winifred "Cutalerin" named as sis. in the 1743 will of Richard
Brereton of Som. Co.; Brereton also named Bigging Cutchin); est.
of Robert admin. by Winifred on 2 April 1740 and 14 Oct. 1744; had
iss.: BEGGING, b. 22 Jan. 1732; GREENBURY, b. 9 April 1734, d.

Oct. 1734; MARY, b. 14 Oct. 1735 (may be the Mary who m. Benjamin Ricketts on 2 June 1755); PROVIDENCE, b. 19 Feb. 1736 (4:65; 5: 32; 127:146; 131:51, 59/r).

Unplaced Cutchins.

CUTCHIN, ANN, m. 22 April 1729 Augustus Brown (129:269).

CUTCHIN (or GUDGEON), ROBERT, of A. A. Co., claimed land for service in 1675 (388).

CUTCHIN, SARAH, orphan of John, dec., was placed in the care of Abraham Taylor, Jr., in Nov. 1710 (21:184).

CUTCHIN, THOMAS, b. c.1677, age 51 in 1728, was bro.-in-law of Samuel Sicklemore (163:46).

CUTCHIN, THOMAS, m. 28 Oct. 1713 Jane Hicks (21:633; 131).

CUTCHIN, THOMAS, m. 5 Dec. 1743 Mary Gott (131).

CUTCHIN. See also GUDGEON.

CUTLER, FRANCIS, m. 30 Jan. 1745 Eleanor Wooden (133:158).

DA COSTA, MATTHIAS, native of Fayal, Azores, and wife Elizabeth imm. to Md. by 1664 when they bought the Manor of Danby Wiske from Chancellor Philip Calvert; in Sept. 1655 (?), sold 700 a. to Thomas Ireton; Matthias d. by 1703 when w. Elizabeth m. as her 2nd husb. Thomas Williams of St. M. Co. (93; 366:328; 388).

DADD, ANN, m. 27 April 1714 John Whitaker (131).

DALE, GEORGE, Eng., age 22, ran away from Balto. Ironworks in Sept. 1754 (385:305).

DALE, Dr. JOHN, m. by 28 July 1767 Mary, dau. of Richard Colegate (230:148).

DALEY, JAMES, Irish, age c.40, weaver, ran away from Hugh Copeland (385:19).

DALLAHIDE, FRANCIS (1), was in Balto. Co. by 1695 as a taxable in s. side Gunpowder Hund.; d. by May 1721 when admin. bond was posted by admin. Francis Dallahide, with James Maxwell, Sr., and John Roberts; m. 1st Providence (?), and 2nd Sarah (?), who m. as her 2nd husb. William Graves; rep. Balto. Co. in the Assembly in 1704-1707, 1715, 1716-1718, and 1719-1720; was a captain and held other offices; his w. Sarah joined him in deeds between 5 March 1699, 7 July 1702, and 24 Nov. 1713; at the latter date they conv. to Simon Pearson their interest in Waterstowne; at his death owned about 550 a. of land; had iss.: FRANCIS; prob. PROVIDENCE who m. John Frizzell between Nov. 1721 and 25 Oct. 1722; prob. SARAH who m. William Denton on 17 Feb. 1725 (11:526; 51:323; 66:10, 174, 275; 67:253; 131; 140; 370).

DALLAHIDE, FRANCIS (2), s. of Francis (1), was living as late as Nov. 1737 when he pet. the county court for maintenance, being an object of charity; m. Mary (?) by Sept. 1725 when they were debtors of John Bradshaw; in Nov. 1722 was summoned to court as admin. of Francis Dallahide, Sr., to answer a complaint of Lloyd and Eleanor Harris (25:45; 31:143; 51:178).

DALLAHIDE, ELIZABETH, in June 1745 her s. Benjamin Hart was bound to Edward Sprucebanks to age 21 (35:542).

DALLAHIDE, PROVIDENCE, named in the will of John Bennett of
A. A. Co., May 1695 (121:167).

DALLAHIDE, SARAH, m. 28 Dec. 1752 Thomas Armstrong (131).

DALLAHIDE, SARAH, m. 6 Feb. 1754 Henry Dixson (131).

DALLAHIDE, THOMAS, m. by 3 Aug. 1751, a dau. of William Denton;
in Nov. 1750 was tried for cutting wood on an orphan's land (5:55;
5:186; 38:26).

THE DALLAM FAMILY has been the subject of much research by
Mrs William Bain of Seattle, Washington, who has graciously made
the results of her research available to the compiler.

DALLAM, ROBERT (1), of Farnworth, Cheshire, Eng., had at least
one son: THOMAS (Bain).

DALLAM, THOMAS (2), s. of Robert (1), was b. c.1575, d. c.
1630; organ builder who provided an organ for Queen Elizabeth I
to give to the Sultan in 1599; had iss.: ROBERT, b. c.1602, d. c.
1665, bur. at New College, Oxford, m. Isabella Turpin and had iss.;
RALPH, d. c.1672, bur. at St. Alphage, Greenwich, Eng.; GEORGE, d.
c.1685 at Purple Land or Portpool Lane, m. Jane; THOMAS; MAY;
poss. KITTY (Bain material).

DALLAM, THOMAS (3), s. of Thomas (2), b. c.1608, may be the
Thomas who d. 6 April 1699 in St. James Par., A. A. Co., having
been transported to Md. c.1662; had at least one son: WILLIAM
(388; Bain material).

DALLAM, WILLIAM (4), s. of Thomas (3), b. c.1638, was transp.
to Md. by 1678, and had at least one s.: RICHARD (388; Bain material).

DALLAM, RICHARD (5), s. of William (4), b. c.1680 in Calvert
Co., d. there in April 1714; m. c.1702 Elizabeth Martin, b. c.
1674/6, dau. of William Martin; she m. as her 2nd husb. William
Smith; Richard is stated in Burke's Landed Gentry, 1913 ed., p.
2646, to have been a son or nephew of Robert Dallam the organ
builder; held many public offices including the clerkships of
several committees in the Assembly, and in 1704 was granted 20
shillings to buy a ring for   his   services in helping to pre-
serve public records from the State House fire; in Nov. 1709 was
admitted to practice law in A. A. and Calvert Cos.; had iss.:
Maj. WILLIAM; Col. RICHARD; CHRISTIAN, m. Richard Caswell and
moved to N. C.: ELIZABETH, m. 1st Samuel Webster, and 2nd Nathan
G. Smith (Bain material).

DALLAM, WILLIAM (6), s. of Richard (5) and Elizabeth, b. 21
Sept. 1706, d. 21 Sept. 1761; m. 1st on 10 Jan. 1737 Elizabeth
Johnson, dau. of Joseph and Anne (Todd) Johnson; m. 2nd on 23 July
1754 Ann Matthews; in 1750 he owned 329 a. Biter Bit, 640 a. Spruce
Inheritance, 200 a. Mates Infinity (Affinity?), 27 a. part Moores-
field, and 100 a. Eliza Chance, and other lands; had iss.: JOSIAS,
b. 8 Aug. 1739, d. 3 Sept. 1744; WILLIAM, b. 8 Jan. 1741, d. 8
Oct. 1742; RICHARD, b. 24 Sept. 1743; JOSIAS WILLIAM, b. 3 Nov.
1747; by 2nd w.: FRANCIS; ELIZABETH (129:350; 131:76/r, 85/r,
110/r, 120/r, 121/r; 153:34; 414-3).

DALLAM, RICHARD (7), s. of Richard (5) and Elizabeth, b.c.1708,
d. c.1865; m. Frances Wallis, b. c.1710; in 1750 owned 64 a. Arabia Petrea, 100 a. Miles Improvement, and 180 a. pt. Neighborhood;
est. admin 1767 by Richard Dallam; had iss.: RICHARD, d. c.1734;
WILLIAM, b. 13 Nov. 1735; SAMUEL, b. 13 Oct. 1737; ANN, b. 10 Dec.

1739; FRANCES, b. c.1740, m. 29 March 1770 Rev. Joseph Toy; JOHN,
b. c.1744; WINSTON SMITH, b. c.1749; CASSANDRA, m. (?) Johns (6:
182; 128:110; 153:46; Bain material).

DALLAS, WALTER, b. c.1704, d. by Aug. 1758; m. by 24 Oct. 1732
Chloe, dau. of James Crook; wit. a will in P. G. Co. on 9 Jan.
1724; as a merchant in Annap. wit. another will in Aug. 1729;
Sarah Crooke, wid., of Annap., in her will of Dec. 1737 named
her granddaus. Chloe and Elizabeth Riddle; in 1750 he owned ?59
a. Hopewell, 170 a. Outlet to Bushey Neck, and 311 a. Kindness
Resurveyed; d. by Aug. 1748 leaving a 14 yr. old son; had iss.:
ELIZABETH RIDDLE, alive in 1737, prob. d. young; CHLOE, m. 15
Sept. 1734 Thomas Eaglestone; prob. SARAH, m. 1st on 18 Aug. 1764
Benjamin Eaglestone, and 2nd Nathaniel Martin; ELIZABETH RIDDLE,
b. 16 March 1741; WALTER, b. after 1744 (3:115; 44; 125:2; 126:
217, 232; 131; 153:60; 204-2464).

DANDRIDGE. See DAWDRIDGE.

DANDY, RALPH, d. by 2 March 1725 when admin. bond was posted
by James Standiford with Henry Wetherall and Robert Robertson; m.
Mary Fox on 23 Sept. 1714; est. inv. 10 May 1726 by Charles Baker
and William Burney; est. admin. 15 March 1731 by James Standiford;
had iss.: JANE, b. 8 May 1715; RUTH, b. c.1719, age 11 in Jan.
1730, in Aug. 1730 bound to Roger Matthews to age 16; ELIZABETH,
b. 25 June 1720, age 12 in June 1733 when she was bound to Jonathan Hughes and his w. Jane (3:102; 11:522; 29:3; 30:4; 51:60;
128:33; 129:214).

DANIEL, CHARLES, d. by 13 June 1737; his will, 19 Dec. 1736 -
13 June 1737, left prop. to the eldest son of his sis. Mary Dunbar, and left his land in Balto. Co. and his house to his w. Elizabeth; admin. bond posted 13 Oct. 1737 by extx. Rachel, with John
Orrick, Wm. Worthington, Jr., and Thomas Henderson and Josias
Slade; extx. Rachel m. 2nd, on Nov. 1743 Charles Hopkins (3:296;
13:34; 35:79; 126:212).

DANIEL, EDWARD, d. 9 Aug. 1713; admin. bond was posted 27 Aug.
1713 by admin. Thos. Newsom with Peter Lester; est. inv. on 23 Oct.
1713 by William Norris and David Thomas and val. at £ 11.14.6 with
Edward Jackson and Robert Williams as creditors; est. admin. in
1714 by Thomas Nusham (1:38; 11:504; 50:300; 128:30).

DANIEL, or O'DANIEL, THOMAS, was in Balto. Co. by 8 April 1663
when he surv. 150 a. Daniel's Neck; d. by 10 Feb. 1675 when admin.
bond was posted by James Denton with Thomas Richardson; est. was
admin. on 26 April 1678 by Denton, who had m. Thomas' widow;
inv. was 9700 lbs. tob.; had iss.: JANE, m. by 27 July 1686 Thomas
Thurcall; MARY, m. by 5 Nov. 1684 William Horne (2:55; 11:544; 18:
164; 106; 108; 211:36).

DANNELLY, JEREMIAH, m. 24 Oct. 1731 Elizabeth York (131).

DANNEY, DANIEL, was in Balto. Co. by 1692 as a taxable in n.
side Gunpowder Hund.; was in the same hund. in 1695 as Daniel
Darney (138; 140).

DANNOCK, JOHN, m. 16 Jan. 1743 Mary Palmore (131).

DANSCOMB, PATRICK, Irish conv., ran away from Zachariah Maccubbin in Balto. Co. in or before April 1749 (307-68:303).

DANSY, MICHAEL, orphan, 14½ years in June 1716 when he was
bound to William Cook (22:8).

DARBY, LUKE (1), d. leaving a will, 20 Jan. 1742 - 2 March 1742, making his wife extx., naming a son Nathaniel, and leaving 40 a. called Darby to Philip Jones; in 1750 the wid. Darby owned pt. of Todd's Range and pt. Darby; had iss.: NATHANIEL (127:197; 153:36).

DARBY, NATHANIEL (2), s. of Luke (1), is prob. the Nathaniel who m. the widow Elizabeth Demitt on 10 April 1721, was ind. for assault and battery in Nov. 1724, but the bill was marked "Ignoramus;" had iss.: NATHANIEL, b. 16 Feb. 1732 (27:43; 133:2, 146).

DARBY, JOHN, m. 3 Dec. 1733 Alice Gay, and had iss.: DANIEL, b. 4 Aug. 1734; JAMES, b. 28 Jan. 1735/6; JOHN, b. 14 Dec. 1737 (133:17, 51, 57, 131).

DARBY, MARY, was ind. for bast. in Nov. 1745 and tried in March 1745/6; ind. for bast. again in Nov. 1746 (35:734, 809; 36:220).

DARLIN, JOHN, was in Balto. Co. by 1692 as a taxable in s. side Gunpowder Hund. (138:5).

DARLINGTON, WILLIAM, m. 4 June 1745 Ann Hind (133).

DARNAL, FRANCIS, m. 12 Sept. 1756 Margaret Hernley (131).

DARNAL, HENRY, in 1750 owned 2000 a. Land of Promise (153:100).

DARNALL, PHILIP, in 1750 owned 400 a. Hee Convenience, and 100 a. Hee Refuse, as well as 800 a. Rich Level (153:100).

DARTE, or DARFE, WILLIAM, was in Balto. Co. by 1692 as a taxable in s. side Patapsco Hund. (138).

DAUGH, BRIDGET, was the mother of: ELIZABETH, b. 31 March 1701, and OWEN, b. 11 Dec. 1710 (128:29).

DAUGH, WILLIAM, m. Ann (?); had iss.: WILLYALMAH, b. 7 March 1740 (131:88/r).

DAUGHADAY, JOHN, was in Balto. Co. by 25 Feb. 1754 when he bought 50 a. Panther's Ridge from Benjamin and Elizabeth Knight; in Nov. 1757 was tried for begetting a bast. on Sarah Taylor; in Oct. 1761 bought 50 a. Knight's Addition from Benjamin Long, and also bought 201 a. Daughaday's Purchase, being part of Chenoweth's Adventure from Richard and Keziah Chenoweth (44; 82:175; 85:337, 340).

DAUGHADAY, JOSEPH, b. 26. 12 mo., 1738, called bro. of Richard Daughaday, who was a cousin of Richard Taylor (136).

DAUGHADAY, RACHEL, b. 26, 10 mo., 1740, called sis. of Richard Daughaday, who was cousin to Richard Taylor (136).

DAUGHADAY, RICHARD, b. 28, 9 mo., 1736, called bro. of Joseph and Rachel Daughaday, was cousin of Richard Taylor (136).

DAUGHERTY, JOHN, age 15, with the consent of Margaret Wiley was bound to Samuel Collar in Oct. 1745 to learn the trade of Blacksmith in Oct. 1745 (78:331).

DAUGHERTY/DOUGHERTY, NATHANIEL, of Cecil Co., in Nov. 1729 conv. 94 a. Creek Plantation to Gregory Farmer (72:152).

DAUGHERTY/DOCHERTY/DOUGHERTY, WILLIAM, m. 2 Oct. 1737 Mary Bartle; in Nov. 1745 purchased Mary's Repose and Roberts Choice

from Amos Garrett, son and heir of Bennett Garrett; his will, 19
Aug. 1767 - 3 May 1768, named ch. George, Margaret, and Eleanor
(each to have one shilling), William (to have all the land), and
Usen (not yet 21); had iss.: GEORGE, b. 11 Oct. 1737; MARY, b. 28
March 1739; ELEANOR, b. 20 Dec. 1742; WILLIAM, b. 22 April 1745;
UFAN, b. 25 June 1753; MARGARET (78:396; 112:85; 128:105; 129:
328, 342, 365).

DAVICE. See DAVIS.

DAVID, BENJAMIN, age 15 on 11 Nov. 1739, in June 1739 was bound
to Obadiah Pritchard; called s. of Elizabeth Evans (32:402).

DAVID, ELIZABETH, tried for bast. in Aug. 1725 (27:312).

DAVIDGE, HUDSON, m. Susanna (?); in Aug. 1747 conv. prop. to
Jacob Lusby; had iss.: ELIZABETH, b. 29 Aug. (year not given)
(79:530; 128:111).

DAVIDSON, PATRICK, d. by 1705 when his est. was inv. by William
Eden and Jno. Wells and val. at ₤8.2.0 (48:67).

DAVIDSON, ROBERT, d. by 11 April 1763 when his est. was admin.
by James Wood; est. also admin. on 29 July 1765; m. Elizabeth
(?) and had iss.: ELIZABETH KEY, b. 30 Sept. 1760 (6:72, 150;
133:108).

DAVIES. See DAVIS.

DAVIS/DAVICE/DAVIES, ANN, servant to Joshua Merriken, pet. the
court (23:212).

DAVIS, BENJAMIN, in March 1739/40 was exempt from the levy
(32:149).

DAVIS, BENJAMIN, of Augusta Co., Va., in April 1750 conv. John
Risteau 50 a. Benjamin's Prospect; Margaret Davis wit. the sale
(80:424).

DAVIS, BENJAMIN, m. Mary (?) and had iss.: JOHN, b. 28 May
1754, and ELIZABETH, b. 26 May 1757 (129:360).

DAVIS, EDWARD, m. Susanna Cope on 4 June 1735 and had iss.:
ESTHER, b. 25 April 1736 (133:57).

DAVIS, ELIZABETH, ind. for bast. in March 1724; m. Evan Miles
on 24 July 1726; had iss.: BENJAMIN, b. 20 Jan. 1724/5 (27:127;
128:51).

DAVIS, GEORGE, m. Mary (?) and had iss.: BARTHOLOMEW, b. 25
Oct. 1714 (131:7).

DAVIS, HENRY, d. by 31 July 1714, leaving a will, 24 Dec. 1713-
31 July 1714, left entire est. to his wife who was to be extx.,
named s. Henry (not yet 18), dau. (not yet 16); admin. bond was
posted 31 July 1714 by extx. Ann Davis, with Peter Bond and Wm.
Hamilton; est. inv. same day by latter two, and val. at ₤7.4.6;
had iss.: HENRY, b. after 1695; dau., b. after 1697 (11:532; 48:
215; 123:19).

DAVIS, HENRY, m. Sarah (?), and had iss.: DAVID, b. 6 Jan.
1734; HENRY, b. 2 Jan. 1730; JANE, b. 3 June 1733; MARY, b. 13
Oct. 1737; CHARLES, b. 23 Jan. 1739; ELEANOR, b. 5 May 1742 (128:
89, 102, 108; 129:328).

DAVIS, HENRY, of Balto. Co., being sick with small pox, left
a will, 20 Nov. 1769 - 6 April 1770, named par. William and Elizabeth, and sisters Mary Richardson, Elizabeth Norris, Ann Lowe,
Martha Hawkins, and Sarah Richardson, as well as Vincent Richardson of Wm., and Henry Richardson, and named tract Macedon (112:
149).

DAVIS, JACOB, m. Elizabeth (?) and had iss.: SARAH, b. 6 Oct.
1746; ELIZABETH, b. 31 March 1750; MARY, b. 10 July 1755 (131:
154/r).

DAVIS, JOHN, was in Balto. Co. by 1694 as a taxable in s. side
Patapsco Hund.; m. 12 Sept. 1702 Esther Fugat (128:22; 139).

DAVIS, JOHN, m. Ann (?), and had iss.: DANIEL, b. 15 Oct.
1753 (131:161/r).

DAVIS, JOHN, age c.40, b. in Eng., ran away from Thomas Sligh
in Balto. Co., 10 June 1742 (384:364).

DAVIS, JOHN, s. of Walter, in March 1757 conv. William Andrew
tract Bachelor's Mistake; in April 1761 purch. pt. Denton's Hope
from William Denton and w. Mary (83:16; 85:100).

DAVIS, NATHANIEL, was in Balto. Co. by 1729, and was alive in
May 1760; m. Mary (?); in 1750 owned 50 a. Little Mountain and 50
a. Davis' Hope; in May 1760 Edward Stocksdale conv. him 67 a. Stock-
dale's Addition; had iss.: ZEPORAH, b. 16 June 1729; SUSANNA, b.
6 Oct. 1732; RICHARD, b. 1 April 1734; MARGARET, b. 6 July 1736;
ROBERT, b. 7 June 1739 (133:51, 54, 60; 84:184; 153:184).

DAVIS, RICHARD, servant with 3 years to serve, was listed in
the inv. of Robert Hopkins, 24 Dec. 1703 (51:38).

DAVIS, RICHARD, and w. Margaret, in Sept. 1769 conv. 40 a. of
Parrishes Folly to Nathan Chapman (231-AL#A:484).

DAVIS, SUSANNA, being old, pet. the court for maintenance, in
March 1740/1 (33:7).

DAVIS, THOMAS, d. by 4 Nov. 1748 when Thomas Sligh posted admin.
bon with Thomas Sheredine and John Metcalfe; est. admin. by Sligh
on Feb. 1749 and Feb. 1750; in 1750 his heirs owned 80 a. Duke's
Discovery Corrected; had iss.: JUDITH, b. 30 June 1736 (5:70, 117;
13:27; 133:56; 153:80).

DAVIS, THOMAS, m. 31 Jan. 1758 Eliz. Carback (131).

DAVIS, URIAH, in Aug. 1740 tried for begetting a bast. on the
body of Mary Watkins; his will, 31 Oct. 1767 - 1 Feb. 1768, named
w. Margaret, children (listed below), and tracts Uriah's Abode and
Uriah's Addition; est. admin. 12 Oct. 1770 by Margaret, now w. of
John Brown; had iss.: SOLOMON; URIAH; WILLIAM; DIANA; SHADRACK;
RACHEL; MESHACK; ABEDNEGO; MARIA; and TOSKAWAY(?) (6:207; 32:305;
112:97).

DAVIES, VAUGHAN, of the City of New York, m. by 2 Dec. 1723
Catherine, only dau. and heir of Gideon Skaats, dec.; on that day
Vaughan and Catherine conv. John Dorsey tract Swanson (69:283).

DAVIS, WILLIAM, of Balto. Co. claimed land for service in 1678;
gave his age as 42 in 1692/3; was a taxable in n. side Patapsco
Hund. in 1692 (138; 310:133; 388).

DAVIS, WILLIAM, m. Elizabeth (?), and had iss.: WILLIAM, b.
9 Feb. 1727 (131:9/r).

DAVIS, WILLIAM, in 1750 owned 114 a. Antioch, which Thomas Preston conv. to him in May 1737 (75; 153:62).

DAVIS, WILLIAM, m. Elizabeth (?); had iss.: JOHN, b. 16 July 1754; WILLIAM, b.26 Jan. 1756; RICHARD, b. 18 Feb. 1762 (129:377).

DAVISON, PATRICK, d. by 20 Nov. 1698 when admin. bond was posted by admnx. Isabella Davison, with Thomas Preston (11:520).

DAWDRIDGE/DANDRIDGE. See DOTTRIDGE.

DAWINASIN, THOMAS, in 1750 owned 50 a. Narrow Neck (153:60).

DAWKINS, (?), m. by 1693/4 Elizabeth, heir of John Collett, and wid. of (?) Goldsmith (206-12:149).

DAWKINS, RICHARD, m. 10 Feb. 1733 Jane Thornton who d. 6 Oct. 1737; he m. 2nd by 23 April 1742 Mary (?); had iss.: (by 1st w.): ELIZABETH, b. 12 May 1734; RICHARD, b. 23 Oct. 1736, d. 12 March 1737; (by 2nd w.): RICHARD, b. 23 April 1742 (128:77, 86, 99; 129: 327).

DAWKINS (DOCKINGS), SIMON, d. by 21 June 1686 when his est. was inv. by Richard Edmonds and Lawrence Taylor, and val. at Ł 17.10.0 plus 2263 lbs. tob.; est. admin. by Col. George Wells on 13 Sept. 1687 (Wells had posted admin. bond on 1 June 1686 with Lawrence Taylor and Peter Fucate) (11:530; 50:362; 206-9:417).

DAWLEY. See DULEY.

DAWNEY. See DOWNEY.

DAWSEY, JOHN, was in Balto. Co. by 1695 as a taxable in s. side Patapsco Hund. (140).

DAWSON, THOMAS, in Dec. 1734 inherited Constant Friendship from his mother, the widow Mary Dawson of P. G. Co. (126:125).

THE DAY FAMILY has been discussed by Schmitz in her Amos Genealogy.

DAY, NICHOLAS (1), the progenitor, was in Balto. Co. by 1699 as a taxable in n. side Gunpowder Hund.; d. by 4 Feb. 1704/5, having m. Sarah (?) who d. by 28 Dec. 1736; the will of Nicholas Day, 1 Dec. 1704 - 4 Feb. 1704/5, left tract William the Conqueror first to s. Nicholas then to s. Edward, named dau. Sarah, Obadiah Pritchard, daus. Elizabeth and Dinah; admin. bond posted 23 May 1705 by extx. Sarah Day with Thomas Preston and Samuel Brown; est. inv. on 22 Sept. 1705 by John Rollins and Charles Baker; est. admin. on 22 March 1708 by wid. Sarah Day, who d. by 28 Dec. 1736 when admin. bond on her est. was posted by Josias Hendon and Thomas Amos, and her est. was admin. by Nicholas Day on 31 March 1737; had iss.: NICHOLAS, d. 1739; EDWARD, d. 1746; ELIZABETH, m. Alexander McComas on 9 Nov. 1713; SARAH, m. 1st Obadiah Pritchett, and 2nd after 1704 John Greer; DINAH (2:164; 3:243; 11:518; 13: 32; 48:24; 122:46; 141:3).

DAY, NICHOLAS (2), s. of Nicholas (1) and Sarah, d. by 25 May 1739; m. Elizabeth Cox, dau. of Christopher Cox; she m. 2nd Robert Bishop; in 1727 he purch. The Dock from William and Elizabeth Demmett; his will, 31 March 1738 - 25 May 1739, left half of the William the Conqueror to s. Thomas, and the other half to his s. Laban, left three lots in Joppa to s. Samuel, who was also to have 150 a. The Dock, also named ch. Hannah, John, Elizabeth, Mary and Sarah; admin. bond posted 9 Aug. 1739 by extx. Eliza Day with Ed-

ward Hall and Joshua George, and admin. by wid. Elizabeth on 30
Aug. 1742, and after she m. Bishop, on 14 Feb. 1744 and 4 Nov.
1745; had iss.: NICHOLAS, b. 25 Feb. 1710/11, d. 18 June 1733;
MARY, b. 23 Oct. 1713; JOHN, b. 6 Sept. 1716; ELIZABETH, b. 17
March 1719, m. Thomas Amos on 25 Dec. 1735; SARAH, b. 29 Jan. 1720;
THOMAS, b. 5 July 1723; LABAN, b. 2 April 1726, left a nuncupative
will sworn to on 4 Aug. 1750 by Elizabeth Bulkeley and Thomas Tu-
dor, and naming his mother Elizabeth Bishop and bros. Samuel and
John Day, and sis. Hannah Day, as well as Nicholas Day of John;
HANNAH, b. 19 Dec. 1728; SAMUEL, b. 1 March 1730; NICHOLAS, b.
23 April 1734, d. Aug. 1735 (3:292, 366; 5:47; 13:30; 70:3; 79:
63; 127:36; 131).

DAY, EDWARD (3), s. of Nicholas (1) and Sarah, d. by 12 Feb.
1746, m. Avarilla Taylor on 22 May 1722; she was a dau. of John
Taylor, and m. 2nd on 20 April 1747 Patrick Lynch; the will of
Edward Day, 8 Jan. 1746 - 12 Feb. 1746, named ch. John, Nicholas,
Edward, Sarah Dorsey, Avarilla, Jane, and Anne, and son-in-law
Vincent Dorsey; admin. bond posted on Feb. 1746 by exec. John
Day with Park. Hall and William Young; est. admin. 15 June 1748;
the will of Avarilla Lynch, 29 Nov. 1766 - 4 Feb. 1767, named
sons John and Edward, and daus. Avarilla Allender and Jane Allen-
der; had iss.: JOHN, b. 25 April 1723; AVARILLA, b. 23 Oct. 1727,
d/ 6 Jan. 1734; SARAH, b. 11 March 1725, m. Vincent Dorsey; ED-
WARD, b. 20 Feb. 1729; NICHOLAS, b. 19 Jan. 1732, d. 27 Jan.
1748; AVARILLA, b. 16 Jan. 1735; m. (?) Allender; JANE, b. 30
Jan. 1737, d. 5 Nov. 1746; ELIZABETH, b. 13 April 1742, d. Nov.
1746; ANNA, b. 15 Nov. 1744 (4:190; 13:26; 110:315; 112:72; 131).

DAY, JOHN (4), s. of Nicholas (2) and Elizabeth, b. 6 Sept.
1716 in Balto. Co., d. c.1790 in Burke Co., N.C.; m. and had
iss.: NICHOLAS, b. c.1745/50 in Burke Co., d. 1815 in Burke Co.,
N. C.; JOHN, Jr., b. c.1755, m. 1778 Mary Stalling; JAMES, b. c.
1758; LABAN, m. c.1793 in Burke Co., Mary McKinsey; EDWARD, m.
1797 in Burke Co., Susanna Edwards.

DAY, SAMUEL (5), s. of Nicholas (2) and Elizabeth, b. 1 March
1730, m. by 25 Feb. 1752 Sarah, dau. of William Talbott; in Aug.
1757 James Talbot conv. Samuel Day 50 a. Pearsons Outlet and pt.
Weatherall's Last Addition; in April 1762 Samuel and Sarah conv.
this land to Robert Patterson; had iss.: JOHN; ROBERT; poss. a dau.
who m. (?) Bowman (83:45; 86:49; 111:38; 131).

DAY, JOHN (6), s. of Edward (3) and Avarilla, b. 25 April 1723;
d. by 7 Feb. 1784; m. 20 July 1742 Philizanna Maxwell, dau. of
James and Mary Maxwell, b. 3 March 1723, d. 21 March 1759; m. 2nd
on 30 Dec. 1764 Sarah York; in 1750 owned 360 a. pt. Conclusion
and 42 a. Goodwill; on 11 Dec. 1764 conv. prop. to his dau. Avarilla and s. John; his will, 16 Dec. 1782 - 7 Feb. 1784, named
tracts part Maxwell's Conclusion, Day's Double Purchase, Holmwood,
and Gay's Meadows, and ch., John, Nicholas, Edward, Sarah, Charlotte Elizabeth, Mary, w. of (?) Hynson, Avarilla w. of Robert
Cruikshanks, nephew William Allender of Avarilla, and niece Sarah
Allender of Jane; had iss.: MARY, b. 5 Feb. 1743, m. (?) Hynson;
JAMES MAXWELL, b. 29 Oct. 1746, d. 23 Jan. 1747; AVARILLA, b. 16
Sept. 1749, m. Robert Cruikshanks; JAMES, b. 24 March 1753, d. 31
,arch 1753; JOHN, b. 14 Oct. 1755; PHILIZANNA, b. 21 May, d. 22
May 1759; NICHOLAS; EDWARD; SARAH, b. 20 Jan. 1768; CHARLOTTE
ELIZABETH (82:6; 131:29/r, 98/r, 117/r, 121/r, 125/r, 149/r; 153:
80; 230:36; 244-AJ#2 :150).

DAY, EDWARD (7), s. of Edward (3) and Avarilla, b. 20 Feb.
1729, d. by 23 May 1779; m. 1st 8 Feb. 1749 Ann Fell, and 2nd
Rebecca Young, wid. of (?) Clagett; Rebecca m. as her 3rd husb.,
John Weston; Edward advert. his w. Ann had eloped "again" in

July 1757 and also in Aug. 1767; in 1750 he owned 200 a. part
Taylor's Mount, 57 a. Nothingworth, 300 a. Dixon's Chance, 110 a.
Taylor's Enlargement, and 1 lot in Balto. Town; his will, 29 Jan.
1778 - 10 April 1779, named sons John, Lloyd, Edward, and William
Fell, all under 21, daus. Elizabeth, Jennet Reed, and Margaret,
granddau. Anne Taylor, dau. Elizabeth, and sis.-in-law Elizabeth
Young, and named as execs. his wife, bro. John Day, William and
George Young, and Rev. Mr. West; had iss.: SARAH, b. 30 June 1752;
ISHMAEL, b. 30 Sept. 1753; JANET, b. 30 Sept. 1753; ANN, b. 14
Oct. 1755, d. young; EDWARD, b. 7 Nov. 1757, d. young; EDWARD, b.
17 Aug. 1759; WILLIAM FELL, b. 11 July 1765; MARGARET, b. 2 Jan.
1768; by 2nd w.: JOHN YOUNG, b. 7 July 1772; ELIZABETH, b. 24
Oct. 1774; LLOYD, b. 18 Aug. 1776; NICHOLAS, b. 19 Aug. 1779
(10:5, 352; 112:379; 131; 153:97; 255).

DAY, BRYAN, Eng., ran away from Patapsco Ferry by Feb. 1744
(384:436).

DAY, EMMORY, in Nov. 1757 was fined for bast.; named Richard
Moale as the father (46:75).

DAY, HUMPHREY, was in Balto. Co. by 1692 as a taxable in n.
side Patapsco Hund., and d. by 3 Aug. 1698 when admin. bond was
posted by Thomas Smith with John Lakins and Wm. Farfar; est. was
inv. 9 Aug. 1698 by John Terip and Robuck Lynch and val. at
£ 35.0.0 (11:524; 48:70; 138).

DAY, JOHN, age 16 next June, bound to Joshua Starkey to age
21 in March 1733/4 (30:189).

DAY, MARY ELIZABETH, dau. of Bridget Others, b. 31 March 1707
(128:25).

DAY, THOMAS, ran away from Balto. Town in Feb. 1759 (307-68:
303).

DEADMAN, EDM'D., m. Eliz. Corbin on 30 Jan. 1753 (131).

DEADMAN, THOMAS, servant with 4 years to serve, in inv. of
Capt. John Ferry, May 1699; wit. the will of Jane Peacock of Balto.
Co. (122:257).

DEADMAN, THOMAS, m. Sarah (?), and had iss.: AVARILLA, twin, b.
5 March 1728; KERBY, twin, b. 5 March 1728, as "Curl" Deadman, age
16 in March 1745, was bound to Charles Robinson in Nov. 1744 (35:
385; 133:46).

DEADMAN, THOMAS, m. Sarah Griffith on 2 Oct. 1749 (131).

DEANS, Rev, HUGH, resigned as rector of St. Margarets Par.,
A. A. Co., in July 1742 and was inducted into St. John's Par.; in
1750 owned 550 a. Stoxdilemore, and part William The Conqueror;
age 69 in 1773; his will, 9 Dec. 1766 - 24 Feb. 1777, named w.
Christian as extx. (112:326; 153:55; 303).

DEAN, JOHN, in Nov. 1736 was to be levy free (31:302).

DEAN, JOHN, in Sept. 1758 bought 50 a. Frugality from Richard
Richards (83:233).

DEARING, JOHN, d. in Balto. Co., having left a will, 9 Feb.
1670 - 1672/3, named w. Alse, s. John, Charles Gorsuch, and
Thomas Hooucker and Robert Franklin, wit. by John Graw, and Roger
Sedwell; had iss.: JOHN (Balto. Co. Orig. Wills, Box 1, folder 4
at Hall of Records).

DEASON/DESON/DEYSON/DISON/DYSON, WILLIAM (1), was in Balto. Co.
by 1692 as a taxable in n. side Gunpowder Hund.; d. by 27 April
1693 when his est. was inv. by Richard Adams and Robert Dowlas;
his wid. Elizabeth m. as her 2nd husb. John Devega; may have had
one s.: WILLIAM (3:103; 51:1; 138; 206-16A:66).

DEASON, WILLIAM (2), poss. s. of William (1), was in Balto. Co.
by 1699 as a taxable in n. side Gunpowder Hund. in the household
of James Maxwell; in 1720 leased 100 a. of Gunpowder Manor for
the lifetimes of Samuel, William, Jr., and John Deason (ages not
given); d. by 12 May 1730 when wid. Mary ren. admin. in favor of
Luke Stansbury, who posted admin. bond on 27 July 1730 with Thomas Stansbury and Walter James; had iss.: poss. ENOCH, b. by 1721
as he was a taxable in 1737; MARY, m. Abraham Enloes in 1730;
SAMUEL, b. c.1704; WILLIAM, b. c.1707; REBECCA, b. 9 March 1712,
and ind. for bast. in Aug. 1738; JOHN, b. 25 Sept. 1714; BENJAMIN,
b. Sept. 1719; EDMOND, b. 30 March 1721; poss. CATHERINE, who as
Catherine Dawson d. March 1728(13:35; 31:267; 131; 141; 142; 143;
144; 145; 389).

DEASON, SAMUEL (3), s. of William (2), b. c.1704, gave his age
as 63 in 1767; in Upper North Hund. of Gunpowder in 1737; married
Mary Johnson in Sept. 1737; in 1742 leased pt. My Lady's Manor in
1742, the lease to run for the lifetimes of his ch.: William age
5, Jemima age 2, and Mary age 2; had iss.: WILLIAM, b. 24 June
1738; JEMIMA, b. c.1740; MARY, b. c.1740; SAMUEL, b. 19 Nov. 1746
(77:156; 131; 149).

DEASON, WILLIAM (4), s. of William (2), b. c.1707, gave his age
as 60 in 1767; in 1737 was in Upper North Hund. of Gunpowder;
m. Ann Shepperd on 9 Feb. 1739; had iss.: MARY, b. 8 April 1739;
ELISHABEE, b. Dec. 1743; ALIMSWAY, b. 28 Dec. 1747 (131; 149; 389).

DEASON, JOHN (5), s. of William (2), b. 25 Sept. 1714; m. Mary
Hall on 1 May 1749; had iss.: MARY, b. 7 March 1752 (sic); KERREN-
HAPPUCK, b. 17 July 1752 (sic) (131).

DEASON, BENJAMIN (6), s. of William (2), b. Sept. 1719, m. on
9 Dec. 1742 Tarrisha Shepperd; was in Craven Co., S. C., by 5 Dec.
1759 when he sold land in Rowan Co. to John Walker of Rowan; his
w. Terezier gave her consent (131; Rowan Co., N.C., Deed Book 4,
p. 239).

DEASON, EDMUND (7), s. of William (2), b. 30 March 1721, m.
Elizabeth (?), b. c.1725; in 1742 leased part My Lady's Manor,
the lease to run for the lifetimes of the lessee, age 22, his w.
Elizabeth age 17, and their dau. Rebecca then about 2 mos. old;
had iss.: REBECCA, b. 27 Nov. 1743; may be the Reb. Deason who m.
William Standiford, Jr., on 27 May 1767; ELIZA, b. 13 Nov. 1745
(77:154; 131).

DEATH, RANDALL (1), d. by Nov. 1692, when his wid. m. as her
2nd husb. Anthony Demaster; may have had iss.: EDWARD; and RAN-
DALL (19:325).

DEATH, EDWARD (2), poss. s. of Randall (1), is placed here
because in Nov. 1701 Edward Death wit. the will of Thomas Fenick
of Balto. Co. (120:242).

DEATH, RANDALL (3), poss. s. of Randall (1), was old enough
to have a son Edward, bapt. 12 July 1702; may have moved to Cecil
Co., where on 22 day, 1 mo., 1736/7 when Paul Paulson, Randall
Death, and Randall's w. Honor conv. 200 a. of land orig. taken up
by Richard Gray called The Glass House, to Thomas Coulson of West
Nottingham, Chester Co., Penna; d. leaving a will, 3 Nov. 1751 -

23 April 1752, named sons James, John, Asel, George, w. Honour, and a dau. Charity Comegys, son James was to have the 50 a. where Edward Death lived, and son John was to have all the land where the testator was living; had iss.: EDWARD, bapt. 12 July 1702; JAMES, age 56 in 1776; JOHN; ASEL; GEORGE; CHARITY, m. (?) Comegys; poss. JACOB (128:13; 210-28:338; Cecil Co. Land Records, Book 5, p. 296).

DEATH, JAMES (4), s. of Randall (3), b. c.1720, age 56 in 1776; in 1750 owned 10 a. part Daughter's Chance, 54 a. Creek Plantation, and pt. Neighborhood; in 1762 was a surety for Sarah Yates, admnx. of William Yates; in 1768 with James Death, Sr., Edward Death, and James Death signed petition favoring keeping the county seat at Joppa; m. Sophia Simmons, b. 1 Oct. 1716 on 23 Oct. 1746; had iss.: EDWARD, b. 27 April 1748; JAMES, b. 30 Oct. 1752; WILLIAM, b. 30 Oct. 1754; CHARITY, b. 3 April 1758; GEORGE, b. 23 April 1762, and SOPHIA, d. 17 March 1795 (47:25; 153:40; 200-68:579, 580; 209-38:281; Hist. of Fayette Co., Penna., p. 708, states he was the son Sir Thomas Death of Knowlton Court, near London, but this statement needs verification).

DEAVER, JOHN (1), progenitor, was in Balto. Co. by 1703; d. on 4 Jan. 1731; m. Hannah (?); left a will, 3 Jan. 1731/2 - 8 March 1731/2, named w. Hannah and ch. Richard, Samuel, John, Antil, Mary and Elizabeth who m. (?) Preston; est. admin. on 6 Sept. 1733 and 31 May 1735 by the widow and extx.; had iss.: RICHARD; JOHN; ANTIL, b. c.1689; ELIZABETH, b. 1 Aug. 1703, m. Thomas Preston on 9 Dec. 1721; SAMUEL, b. 20 Aug. 1705; MARY, b. 29 March 1708, may be the Mary who was ind. for bast. in March 1730/1; HANNAH, b. 2 July 1710; THOMAS, b. 16 Jan. 1713; KEZIAH, d. 15 Aug. 1716 (3:131, 189; 13:33; 125:215; 128:33, 36; 27:96).

DEAVER, RICHARD (2), s. of John (1), inherited part of Turkey Hills from his father, and d. 30 Nov. 1746; m. Mary (?) who d. leaving a will, 29 July 1749 - 4 Nov. 1749; this couple may be the Richard "Devor" and Mary Shierbott m. 16 Dec. 1711; will of Mary named her sons John, Daniel, and Richard (and Richard's dau. Mary), kinswoman Mary Hollandsworth, Alex Nichols, and his sis. Phebe, and Elizabeth Wood; admin. bond of Richard Deaver was posted 6 May 1747 by Mary Deaver with Pak. Hall and Richard Ruff; had iss.: MARY, b. 23 Feb. 1713; BENJAMIN, b. 25 Oct. 1710, d. leaving a will, 1 Oct. 1738 - 14 March 1739, naming father Richard and bro. John; JOHN; DANIEL; RICHARD (13:22; 127:68; 128:82; 129:343; 210-27:96; 219-2:344).

DEAVER, ANTIL (3), s. of John (1), was b. c.1689, gave his age as 40 in 1720, d. by 6 Dec. 1770; m. Sarah (?) whose will was proved 23 June 1766; his will, 2 July 1762 - 6 Dec. 1770, named ch.: John, Hannah McComas, grandson John Deaver (of John and Ann), granddau. Sarah Morris (dau. of John and Sarah), and Ann Mayes, Ann Saunders, and Ann Yates; will of Sarah Deaver, 6 May 1766-23 June 1766, named ch.: John, Ann w. of George Yates (and their dau. Sarah), Sarah Morris, and her dau. Margaret Morris, tracts Webster's Desire and land on the Eastern Shore; had iss.: HANNAH, b. 27 May 1720, m. John McComas; SARAH, b. 18 Aug. 1725, m. John Morris on 17 May 1748; MARY, b. 3 May 1728; JOHN, b. 1 May 1731; ELIZABETH, b. 29 July 1733; ANN, m. 2 July 1735 George Yates; MARTHA, b. 2 Oct. 1737, d. 13 May 1743 (112:47, 177; 128:39, 47, 54, 60, 72, 88, 98; 129:323; 163:93).

DEAVER, THOMAS (4), s. of John (1), b. 16 Jan. 1713, d. 26 May 1739; m. Deborah Hartley on 9 June 1730; admin. bond posted 17 July 1739 by Deborah Deaver with Richard Deaver and Richard Deaver, Jr.; est. admin. 12 Jan. 1741 by Deborah Deaver and on 27 July 1747 by Deborah, now w. of Alexander McComas; had iss.: '

166   BALTIMORE COUNTY FAMILIES, 1659 - 1759

THOMAS, b. 25 June 1731; STEPHEN, b. 6 Nov. 1733; JOHN, b. 25 Oct.
1735; MARY, b. 21 (?) 1737; THOMAS, b. 28 Dec. 1739 (4:73, 174;
13:30; 128:87, 99, 108).

DEAVER, JOHN (5), s. of Richard (2) and Mary, may be the John
who m. on 21 Oct. 1742 Perine Greenfield, dau. of William Greenfield; est. admin. 24 May 1763 by Richard Deaver; had iss.:
MICAJAH, b. 15 Dec. 1746; JOHN, b. 16 Dec. 1748; JAMES, b. 19
Jan. 1750; UFAN, b. 10 March 1752; THOMAS, b. 2 April 1754; ELIZA-
BETH, b. 11 Dec. 1757; WILLIAM, b. 8 Dec. 1759 (6:44, 99; 129:
325, 355).

DEAVER, DANIEL (6), s. of Richard (2), d. by 14 Feb. 1757 when
admin. bond was posted by Mary Deaver with Jacob Giles and Richard Johns; m. Mary (?); in 1750 owned 169 a. of Strawberry Hills
and Turkey Hills; admin. the est. of John Carlisle on 24 June
1748; his est. was admin. 30 Nov. 1759 by Mary Deaver; had iss.:
RICHARD, b. 30 Jan. 1745; DAVID, b. 30 Oct. 1747; DANIEL, b. 3
Aug. 1749 (4:284; 6:213; 13:19; 129:346; 153:69).

DEAVER, RICHARD (7), s. of Richard (2), alive in Aug. 1739; m.
Sarah Pritchard on 1 March 1732; had iss.: MARY, b. 7 March 1733;
MARGARET, b. 17 Oct. 1736, d. 25 March 1740; SARAH, b. 4 Aug.
1739 (128:77, 93B, 104, 107; 129:263).

DEAVER, JOHN (8), s. of Antil (3), b. 1 May 1731, d. by 26
Nov. 1782; m. 1st on 11 May 1756 Ann Bond, dau. of Thomas Bond,
and 2nd Rebecca (?); his will was made 16 Oct. 1782, and proved
26 Nov. 1782; had iss.: THOMAS, b. 13 Feb. 1757; JOHN, b. 13
April 1759, m. 1st Susanna Talbot, and 2nd Sarah Hunt; MARTHA, m.
Benjamin R. Talbott; ANN (44; 84:275; 112:476; 129:351, 352).

DEAVER, BASIL, m. 25 d, 11, 1748 Chew Pierpoint, with her ch.
was granted a cert. to Gunpowder Meeting from Fairfax Meeting in
Sept. 1771; had iss.: ABRAHAM, b. 13 d, 11, 1749; MISAL, b. 6 d,
6, 1751; MARY, b. 15 d, 9, 1753 (136; Hinshaw, Enc. of Amer. Qu.
Gen., VI, 486).

DEAVER, JNO., m. 19 July 1759 Susanna Rigbie (131).

DEAVER, MARY, had iss.: WILLIAM JOHNS, b. 2 Oct. 1731; MARY,
b. 1 Feb. 1735 (128:75, 99).

DEAVER, WILLIAM, m. 16 Dec. 1754 Susanna Birchfield, and had
iss.: JOHN, b. 11 April 1755; MARY, b. 3 Feb. 1757; NATHAN, b. 11
Oct. 1760; WILLIAM, b. 9 Sept. 1762 (129:372).

DEAVER, WILLIAM, b. c.1741, pvt. in Md. Line; transferred from
Ohio Pension Roll, on Pension Roll from 1819; age 78 in Mason Co.
Ky. (421:118).

DEBARY, HUGHES, m. Catherine (?), and had iss.: MARY, b. 9
Sept. 1742 (133:69).

DEBRULER, JOHN (1), progenitor, was in Balto. Co. by 1692 as
a taxable in n. side Gunpowder Hund.; in 1701, John, and his sons
John and William, and all his sons and daughters born in the Province were naturalized; d. in Kent Co., Md., leaving a will, 23
July 1707 - 24 April 1710; m. Eliza (?), and had iss.: GEORGE;
ELIZABETH, m. (?) Hopkins; JOHN; MARY; ROSAMOND; JANE; PETER, not
yet 1721 in 1707, alive 19 May 1721; WILLIAM; ANTHONY, not yet
21 in 1707 (122:175; 138; 404:9).

DEBRULER, GEORGE (2), s. of John (1), d. in Balto. Co. by 24
Feb. 1734; m. 20 Oct. 1713 Hester Lewis, who d. 23 Dec. 1742 in

Balto. Co.; his will, 13 Jan. 1734 - 24 Feb. 1734 named w. Hester and these ch.: ELIZABETH, m. William York on 1 Jan. 1733; WILLIAM; GEORGE; JAMES; JOHN; BENJAMIN, m. Semelia Jackson; MARTHA, b. 6 or 16 March 1727/8; FRANCIS, b. 20 Sept. 1729 (126:142; 131; 263).

DEBRULER, JOHN (3), s. of John (1), m. Mary Drunkord on 12 April 1704; admin. the est. of James Drunkord on 3 March 1708, and was made levy free in Nov. 1746 (2:167; 36:228, 229; 128:18).

DEBRULER, WILLIAM (4), s. of John (1), d. in Kent Co., leaving a will, 19 May 1721 - 21 Aug. 1722, naming w. Ann, dau. Ann, and bro. Peter, and tract Essex; had iss.: ANN (124:97).

DEBRULER, ANTHONY (5), s. of John (1), m. Elizabeth (?), and had iss.: MARY, b. 28 Jan. 1720; JOHN, b. 25 Jan. 1724 (128:57).

DEBRULER, WILLIAM (6), s. of George (2), d. in Balto. Co. by 10 March 1772; m. Diana Greenfield, dau. of William Greenfield, on 23 March 1743; he m. 2nd, on 7 Feb. 1764 Sarah Watters; in 1750 owned 120 a. part Sally's Delight and God's Providence; his will, 16 Feb. 1772 - 10 March 1772, named w. Sarah, and these ch.: CORDELIA/DELILAH, b. 29 March 1744, d. 7 Nov. 1744; GEORGE, b. 3 Dec. 1745 or 1746; CORDELIA, b. 20 Nov. 1748; WILLIAM, b. 14 Feb. 1750; UFAAN, b. 26 Aug. 1752, d. 6 Feb. 1756; JAMES, twin, b. 30 Dec. 1755; MICAJAH, b. 30 Dec. 1755; IFAAN, b. 27 April 1759 (112:225; 131; 153:32).

DEBRULER, JOHN (7), s. of George (2) and Hester, d. in Balto. Co. by 1 July 1749, when admin. bond was posted by Robert Adair, with W. Dallam and Talbott Risteau; on 14 May 1743 or 1744 m. Frances Buredy or Burridge; est. was inv. 9 June 1752 by James Maxwell and John Hoosh, and val. at £ 45.16.7, with William and John Debruler signing as kin; est. admin. on 18 March 1753 by Robert Adair; had iss.: SARAH, b. 1 Nov. 1746 (5:281; 13:21; 48: 373; 129:337, 345; 131).

DEBRULER, BENJAMIN (8), s. of George (2) and Hester, was alive in 1759; m. Semelia Jackson on 25 Feb. 1756, and had iss.: ELIZABETH, b. 14 Dec. 1756; FRANCIS, b. 6 Oct. 1759 (131).

DEBRULER, ELIZABETH, m. Sept. 1724 Thomas Jackson (129:249).

DEBRULER, JOHN, m. by 5 March 1720 Mary, of Thomas Greenfield.

DEBRULER, JOHN, b. c.1736, pvt. in Md. Line; by 1819, age 83, was a pensioner in Bourbon Co., Ky. (421:41).

DEBRULER, MARY, d. leaving a will, 4 Dec. 1751 - 18 Dec. 1751, in which she left land she lived on in Little Britain to William Dawtredge, and stock to William York, with John and Edward York and James Meades of Edward as witnesses (112:415).

DEBUTTS, ROBERT, m. Mary (?), and had iss.: MARGARET, b. 27 April 1732 (133:27).

DECAUSS, LEONARD, was in Balto. Co. by Jan. 1746 when he conv. Job's Addition to Charles Ridgely (79:293).

DEE, PHILIP, m. Ellinor (?), and had iss.: PHILIP, b. 31 Oct. 1726 (128:49).

DEE, SARAH, ind. for bast., March 1722/3 (15:224).

DEEDS, MICHAEL, was in Balto. Co. by 1760 when John Cross (s. of Joseph of York Co., dec.), and w. Edith conv. him 50 a. of

John's Adventures; in March 1771 Michael and w. Eve conv. part of this tract to Alexis Lemmon, Jr. (84:433; 231-AL#C:196).

DEEL, WILLIAM, m. Eleanor (?), and had iss.: WILLIAM, b. 17 or 25 March 1739 (131).

DEERE, SAMUEL, in Aug. 1719 had his levy remitted as he was leaving the Province (23:215).

DEFORGE , NOVELL, or KNOWELL, was in Balto. Co. by 1692 as a taxable in Spesutia Hund.; had a dau. ELIZABETH, b. 28 Dec. 1691 (128:2; 138).

DEHAY, DAVID, m. Sarah (?), and had iss.: MARY, b. 25 Oct. 1736; MARGARET, b. 12 March 1737/8 (133:62).

DELAP, ABRAHAM (1), was in A. A. Co. by Nov. 1659 when he surv. 300 a. Lapton; surv. 50 a. Delapton in Feb. 1662; d. leaving a will, 15 Feb. 1670 - 14 May 1671, naming w. Anne, extx., and these ch.: ABRAHAM; MATTHEW; SARAH; JOHN; and DEBORAH (120: 60; 211:160, 167).

DELAP, ABRAHAM (2), s. of Abraham (1), d. in Balto. Co. by 16 Aug. 1703; m. 1st Martha (?), and 2nd Juliana (?), who m. as her 2nd husb. James Isham; poss. 200 a. John's Interest orig. surv. for Michael Judd, this land was later held by James "Isum" for Delap's orphans, and later by Jeremiah Downes who m. the heir; will of Abraham Delap, 6 Aug. 1703 - 16 Aug. 1703, left dau. Sarah tract Essex on the Eastern Shore, and dau. Mary; admin. bond posted 16 Aug. 1703 by Juliana Delap with Charles Baker and William Howard; est. inv. in 1703 by Thomas Preston and Israel Skelton, and val. at £ 122.12.9; est. admin. by James Isam who m. the widow; had iss., b. in All Hallows Par., A. A. Co.: SARAH, b. 7 April 168-(?); MARY, b. 5 June 168-(?); ANN, b. 9 March 1689 (1:64; 2:189; 11:512; 48:8; 122:18; 211; 219-1; N.B. dau. Mary m. Jeremiah Downes).

DEMASTERS, ANTHONY, was in Balto. Co. by 1692 as a taxable in Spesutia Hund.; m. 1st by Nov. 1692 Rebecca, wid. of Randall Death, and 2nd, by Nov. 1706 Catherine (?); had iss.: ANTHONY, b. 7 Nov. 1706; JOHN, b. 6 Dec. 1709 (19:325; 128:23, 25; 138).

DEMITT.   See DIMMITT.

DEMMITT.   See DIMMITT.

DEMONDIDIER, ANTHONY (1), was b. in France, and transp. to Md. between 1653 and 1656; wife Katherine and dau. Herkier claimed land for service in 1658; naturalized in 1671; purch. land in 1675 and was a taxable in n. side Patapsco Hund., 1692; Justice of the Balto. Co. Court, 1679/80; his will, 2 Oct. 1693 - 6 Nov. 1693, named w. Martha, s. Anthony, daus. Eliza and and Eliza Horton of London, only sis. of testator's w. Martha; est. inv. was sw. on 2 Dec. 1693 by John Thomas and Nicholas Corbin and val. at £ 77. 16.0; had iss.: HERKIER, b. by 1658; ANTHONY; ELIZABETH (2:282; 15:253, 327; 48:127; 121:70; 200-67:425; 340:112; 388).

DEMONDIDIER, ANTHONY (2), s. of Anthony (1), d. by 19 Feb. 1713; m. Alice (?) who posted admin. bond on that date with Charles Merryman, Sr.; est. inv. 29 April 1713 by John Thomas and Joseph Gostwick, and val. at £ 38.15.5, and signed by Edward Stevenson and Nicholas Fitzsimmons; his will, 21 March 1709 - 27 April 1713, left ent. est. to wife Alice; est. admin. 8 Sept. 1714; Alice d. by 10 Oct. 1715 when admin. bond was posted by Charles Merryman, Sr., and John Gardner, with Richard Owings and George

Cole; est. was inv. 20 Oct. 1715 by Garrett Garrettson and John
Clark, val. at £ 5.5.0, and signed by John and Elizabeth Low as
kin; est. admin. by Merryman and Gardner on 24 April 1716 (1:14,
215; 11:508; 12:120; 50:311; 52:4; 122:252).

DEMONDIDIER, ELIZABETH (3), dau. of Anthony (1), m. by 5 March
1700 (?) Green, when she conv. to Edward Stevenson left her by
her father Anthony in his will of 1693; she d. by 6 April 1703
when her admin. bond was posted by admin. Anthony Demondidier,
with Thomas Smith (13:119; 66:51).

DEMOSS, LEWIS (1), was in Balto. Co. by 1715 and was still
there in 1731; m. Catherine (?); in Aug. 1719 was fined for refusing to repair his road; had iss.: LEWIS, b. 10 Nov. 1715;
WILLIAM, b. 22 Sept. 1716; JOHN, b. 9 Aug. 1718; BENJAMIN, b. 25
Oct.1719; PINE (?), b. 25 Oct. 1723; THOMAS, b. 5 Sept. 1726;
JAMES, b. 8 Sept. 1728; CHARLES, b. 2 Nov. 1731 (23:217; 131:
39/r, 62).

DEMOSS. JOHN (2), s. of Lewis (1) and Catherine, b. 9 Aug.
1718; m. Susanna Ramsey on 2 Feb. 1743 (131).

DENBOE. See DENBOW.

DENBOW/DENBOE, THOMAS, was in Balto. Co. by 1735, and was alive
in 1750 when he owned 100 a. part Paul's Choice; m. Elizabeth (?)
and had iss.: ROBERT THOMAS, b. 27 Aug. 1735; JANE, b. 18 Feb.
1738; JOHN, b. 16 March 1741; ELIZABETH, b. 13 March 1744 (131:
84/r, 92/r, 109/r; 153:11).

DENHAM, EDWARD, d. 16 Jan. 1729/30; m. 1st on 20 April 1726
Middleton Derumple who d. 8 June 1726, and m. 2nd on 28 Feb.
1728/9 Mary Gerish (128:50, 51, 53, 59).

DENNIS, EDWARD, was in Balto. Co. by Sept. 1684 when he surv.
500 a. St. Dennis, d. c.1700, leaving no heirs (211).

DENNIS, JAMES, was in Balto. Co. by 1692 as a taxable in n.
side Gunpowder Hund. (138).

DENNIS, ROZANNA, m. 2 Feb. 1726 John Roach (129:246).

DENNIS, SAMUEL, m. Alice Carragan on 24 Nov. 1734, and had
iss.: ELISHA, b. 25 Feb. 1734/5 (128:86).

DENNY, SIMON, was in Balto. Co. by 1750 when he owned 2 lots
in Joppa Town (153:82).

DENSON, JOHN, d. 2 April 1740; m. Elizabeth Cowen on 22 Dec.
1737 and had iss.: SARAH, b. 16 June 1738 (128:98, 101, 106).

DENSON, WILLIAM, d. 9 April 1740; m. 1st Mary (?); m. 2nd
Margaret (?), who d. 7 April 1740; his admin. bond was posted 4
June 1740 by John Lawrey with Jacob Giles and Augustus Brown;
had iss.: ABIGAIL, dau. by 1st w., d. Oct. 1734; (by 2nd w.):
WILLIAM, d. 7 May 1730; BARTHIA, b. 10 April 1731 (128:67, 84,
106, 108; 13:28).

DENTON, JAMES (1), progenitor, was in Balto. Co. by 1678, and
d. there by Aug. 1684; m. Rebecca, wid. of Thomas O'Daniel, by
1677, and on 26 April 1678 admin. the est. of sd. O'Daniel; had
surv. 40 a. Bachelor's Meadow in March 1678; surv. 300 a. Denton's Hope in May 1679; admin. bond was posted 5 Aug. 1684 by
Charles Pines with Robert Benger and Thomas Richardson; in Aug.
1684 George Ogilvie submitted a bill for tailor's work, and named

Denton's children, James, William, Rebecca, Bridget, and Elizabeth; est. admin. by Pines on 21 Sept. 1687, mentioning an inv.
of 23681 lbs. tobacco, and an entry for funeral charges for burying Denton's wife; had iss.: JAMES; WILLIAM; REBECCA; BRIDGET;
and ELIZABETH (2:55; 11:506; 18:164; 206-5:25, 27; 206-9:434; 211).

DENTON, WILLIAM (2), s. of James (1); was a minor in 1692 and
d. 6 Feb. 1747; m. 1st Sarah who bore him 8 ch. between 1707 and
1720 and d. 26 March 1724; m. 2nd on 17 Feb. 1725 Sarah Dallahide
who d. Nov. 1737; m. 3rd in March 1739 Anne Wooden who d. March
1740; in Sept. 1692 chose Robert Oleff as his guardian; died
leaving a will, 17 Dec. 1744 - 2 March 1747, naming tracts Bachelor's Hope, Bachelor's Meadow, and Salt Peter Neck, named sons
William, and John, William's daughter, John's children John and
Priscilla, grandsons James and William Denton, granddau. Rachel
Bevins, grandson Abraham Andrews, and daughters Jane Dallahyde and
Providence Denton; admin. bond posted 19 March 1747 by William and
John Denton and with Thomas Jarman and John Parks; est. admin. on
8 Aug. 1749 and 3 Aug. 1751; had at least 8 ch. by his 1st w., and
1 by his 2nd; had iss.: JAMES, b. 15 Feb. 1707; REBECCA, b. 14
April 1708; SARAH, b. 1 Oct. 1709; JEANE, b. 10 March 1710, m.
Thomas Dallahide; WILLIAM, b. last day of Jan. 1712; ELIZABETH,
b. 10 July 1716 and d. 1 Oct. 1716; RACHEL, b. (?), bapt. 8 May
1720, d. Feb. 1739; LEAH, b. 24 Oct. 1720; by 2nd w.: PROVIDENCE,
b. Feb. 1725, m. James Arnold on 2 Oct. 1751; JOHN, named in his
father's will(5:55, 186; 13:25; 19:243; 37:158; 131; 210-25:206).

DENTON, WILLIAM (3), s. of William (2) and Sarah, b. last day.
of Jan. 1712; was alive in 1756; in 1735 m. Rosanna Standton; in
Feb. 1744 as William Denton, Jr., m. Elizabeth James, dau. of
Walter; may be the William who m. Mary Roberts on 14 Dec. 1756;
had iss.: JAMES, b. 10 Feb. 1735; WILLIAM, b. 25 Feb. 1740, prob.
d. young; WILLIAM, b. 25 March 1749 (5:243; 131).

DENTON, JOHN (4), s. of William (2), is named in his father's
will, and m. Rachel Downs on 3 Feb. 1739; d. after 1750 when he
owned 50 a. of Saltpeter Neck, 20 a. of Bachelor's Meadows, and
150 a. of Denton's Hope; alive in Aug. 1763 when he and wife Rachel and (son?) John conv. land to William Andrews; est. admin.
(date not given) by Rachel Denton; had iss.: JOHN, b. 31 Oct.
1741; PRISCILLA, b. 4 Sept. 1742; EZANE (dau.), b. 14 Aug. 1748;
CHLOE, b. 30 Jan. 1749 (6:145; 80:510; 87:391; 131; 153).

DENTON, JAMES, was ind. for bast., March 1733/4 (30:188).

DENTON, JOHN, admin. the est. of James Drunkord on 3 March
1708 (2:167).

DEPOST, MARTIN, b. c.1655, age 66 in 1731, was in Balto. Co.
by 1692 as a taxable in Spesutia Hund.; gave his age as 64 in
1729 and 66 in 1731, and age 68 in 1732 when he deposed he had
been in the county some 36 years; m. Tammeson Holt on 16 Jan.
1697 (129:178; 138; 163:74, 164).

DEPOST, MARTIN, m. Dec. 1729 Martha Anderson (128:58).

DEPOST, PRISCILLA, d. 1 Nov. 1729 (128:58).

DE RINGE, HANS JACOB, Dutch, imm. to Md. by 1664 and was nat.
in Balto. Co. in 1671 (388; 404:6).

DERUMPLE, JOHN, of Calvert Co., on 12 Dec. 1749 conv. to John
Bond his claim to land Nova Scotia, orig. surv. for Thomas Sterling, dec., who devised part of the tract to his bro. William who
d. leaving a s. John, who d. testate leaving a s. John, the present
grantor (80:465).

DERUMPLE, ROBERT, d. by 7 Jan. 1721 when his admnx. Middleton
Derumple, with Mary Marshall and Thomas Birchfield; est. was admin. on 8 Aug. 1722 by Middleton and her 2nd husb., Edward Denham, whom she m. 20 April 1726; iss. of Robert and Middleton:
ROBERT, b. 16 Nov. 1721; poss. HENRY, bound to John Swineyard
in Aug. 1722 to age 21; poss. JOHN, bound to John Swineyard in
Aug. 1722 (2:8; 11:505; 14:294; 128:50).

DERYDOR, JOHN JAMES, m. Sarah (?), and had iss.: MARY, b. 8
June 1728, d. 4 April 1729 (133:15).

DESELL, HENRY, upholsterer, age 18, Eng., runaway serv. from
Samuel Forwood at Deer Creek in Aug. 1754 (385:300).

DESJARDINE, JOHN, imm. to Md., c.1668 with wife Hester and
son John; native of France, nat. in June 1674; in June 1672
conv. to Bristol merchant John Rogers a 50 a. tract, Port Royal,
pat. to Desjardine in May 1672 (98; 388; 404).

DESNEY. See DISNEY.

DETTER, WILLIAM, m. 6 Oct. 1736 Jane Quine (131).

DEVANS, JOHN, m. Sarah (?), and had iss.: MARY, b. 9 April
1724 (131:1/r).

DEVEGA, JOHN, was in Balto. Co. by 1694 as a taxable on n. side
Gunpowder Hund.; m. by Sept. 1693 Elizabeth, admnx. of William
Dison; Elizabeth Devegh, in her will made 5 Jan. 1693, left prop.
to her husb. John (20:103; 139; 200-38:241-242).

DEVES. See DIVES.

DEVIS. See DIVES.

DEW, ROBERT, m. 3 Oct. 1754 Easther Raven (131).

DEW, THOMAS, of Balto. Co., d. leaving a will, 11 Dec. 1757 -
12 June 1758, mentioned wife, named bro. Robert, son Robert (in
Fairfax Co., Va.), and s. Thomas; admin. bond posted 10 July 1758
by admnx. Eliza Dew with Robert Dew and Thomas Harryman; est. admin. 24 Sept. 1759 by Elizabeth Dew, and on 2 June 1760 by said
Elizabeth, now w. of John Murray who stated that the dec. had
left five ch.; had iss.: ROBERT, in Fairfax Co., Va., by 1758;
WILLIAM, in Feb. 1762 was conv. lot # 50 in Balto. Town by John
Murray and w. Elizabeth; three others (4:274, 307; 13:18; 86:
126; 111:81).

DEWLEY. See DOOLEY.

DEYE, PENELOPE, was in Balto. Co. by 1750 when she was listed
in the Debt Book as owning 280 a. pt. Gerar, 1022 a. Taylor's
Hall, 750 a. Logsdon's, 600 a. Thomas and John Cockey's Meadow,
and 150 a. Wason's Farm; in June 1733 Thomas Hooker and his w.
conv. her 280 a. Gerar, and in 1733 Thomas Cockey, Gent., left
her Taylor's Hall; her will, 17 Feb. 1777 - 30 Oct. 1784, named
these ch.: THOMAS COCKEY, b. c.1728; CHARLOTTA COCKEY, m. Thomas

Ford; CHARCILLA COCKEY, b. 1731, d. 1806, m. Joshua Cockey; CASSANDRA COCKEY, d. by 1777, having m. Thomas Colegate (72:301; 126:225; 153:36; 370:268).

DE YOUNG, JACOB CLAUSE, of Balto. Co., of Dutch birth, was nat. in 1671 (404).

DEYSON. See DEASON.

DIANS, ROBERT, in Nov. 1685 had surv. 1000 a. called Constant Friendship, which by c.1700 had passed to his orphans (unnamed) (211).

DICKENS, JOHN, d. by 21 June 1763 when his est. was admin. by Thomas Dickens (6:47).

DICKENS, THOMAS, prob. s. of John, above, b. 1747, d. 1838, m. 30 May 1769 Mary Perdue, and later moved to Penna. (131; a query in BMGS 14 (2) 17.

DICKENSON, WALTER. See DIXON, WALTER.

DICKERS, WILLIAM, was in Balto. Co. by 1692 as a taxable in Spesutia Hund. (138).

DICKSON, HENRY, m. 5 Oct. 1758 Eliz. Yate (131).

DICKSON, PETER, m. 24 May 1760 Margaret Peckoo (129:68).

DICKSON, WALTER, was in Balto. Co. by 1695 as a taxable in Spesutia Hund. (140). (See WALTER DIXON).

DIGGS, JOHN, in 1728 leased 150 a. of Gunpowder Manor, which was called Ford's Chance, for the lifetimes of Philip Diggs, b. c.1717, Edward Diggs, b. c.1719, and William Diggs, b. c.1721 (398:8).

DIKES, HENRY, m. 24 Dec. 1756 Ann Alexander (131).

DIMMITT/DEMITT/DEMMITT, WILLIAM (1), was in Balto. Co. by 1692 as a taxable in n. side Patapsco Hund.; d. by 31 March 1711 when admin. bond was posted by Philip Washington with William Wilkinson and Wm. Pearle; est. was inv. 25 April 1711 by said Wilkinson and Edward Sweeting and val. at £ 10.0.10, and signed by George Fitz-Simmons and Susanna Dimmitt; est. admin. by Washington; not known to have had issue (2:6; 11:507; 48:233; 138).

DIMMITT, (?) (2), rel. to above not known, m. Susannah (?) who m. as her 2nd husb. (?) Moorcock; she conv. Cole's Adventure to her s. Thomas; had iss.: THOMAS, d. by 14 May 1759 having m. Sophia (?); RICHARD, living 14 May 1759; poss. WILLIAM (83:414, 422).

DIMMITT, THOMAS (3), s. of (?) (2) and Susannah, d. by 5 May 1748 when extx. Sophia Dimmitt posted admin. bond with Tobias Stansbury and D. B. Partridge; Thomas m. Sophia Stansbury on 26 Dec. 1734; she m. as her 2nd husb. Peter Robinson by March 1754;

on 23 July 1754 Susanna Moorcock conv. all her prop. except 100
a.cole's Adventure, which she had previously conv. to her s.
Richard; est. of Thomas admin. 27 April 1751 by Sophia Dimmitt;
in March 1754 Peter Robinson gave bond he would pay the orphans
of Thomas Dimmitt their share of their father's est.; ch. of
Thomas and Sophia: LETITIA , named in 1754 but not in 1751; ROBERT,
b. c.1736; WILLIAM, b. c.1738; HELLEN, b. c.1741; STANSBURY,
b. 15 April 1744; PRESBURY, b. 15 April 1744; and RUTH (13:24;
39:19; 74:85; 83:414, 422; 133:73, 74, 153).

DIMMITT, RICHARD (4), s. of (?) (1) and Susannah, d. by 1766
in Balto. Co.; m. Rachel (?); signed the inv. of Philip Washington as one of the kin; by 1734 had been conv. 100 a. Cole's Adventure by his mother now Susanna Moorcock; still owned the land
in 1750; his will, 5 Sept. 1763 - 3 Aug. 1766, named his w. Rachel,
ch. John, Elizabeth, Patty Price, his "other ch.," and grandson
Richard Dimmitt of Joshua; had iss.: JOHN, b. 18 Aug. 1728; JOHN,
b. 19 Aug. 1729/30; MATTHEW, b. 20 May 1732; JOSHUA, b. 29 Nov.
1735; PATTY, m. (?) Price (51:138; 74:85; 83:414, 422; 122:6;
133:18, 21, 59; 153:6).

DIMMITT, WILLIAM (5), poss. s. of (?) (1) and Susannah, d. in
Balto. Co. by 1751; m. 1st Eliza (?), and 2nd Sarah Smithers on
3 Oct. 1744; in 1720 leased 100 a. Gunpowder Manor from (?), the
lease to run for the lifetimes of James, b. c.1707, and William
b. c.1711; in 1742 leased part Gunpowder Manor called Guyton's
Chance, for the lifetimes of the same James, William, and of
William, Jr. (b. c.1751); in 1727 conv. Nicholas Day The Dock;
in Oct. 1747 conv. his right to Dimmitt's Delight to William
Dimmitt, Jr.; his will, 9 April 1751 - 27 Oct. 1751, named ch.
James, Sr., Eliza Bosley, William, Jr., w. Sarah. and grandson
James Dimmitt, Jr., son of William; admin. bond posted 27 Oct.
1751 by exec. James Dimmitt, with Thomas Broad and Sutton Sickelmore, the wid. abides by what the law allows her; est. was admin.
23 Sept. and 8 Dec. 1752; had iss.: JAMES, b. c.1707; WILLIAM,
b. 1 June 1715, and ELIZA, m. (?) Bosley (5:230, 251; 70:3;
79:541, 544; 131:8; 389:5, 10).

DIMMITT, WILLIAM (6), s. of Thomas (3), was alive in April
1760 when he conv. William Holmes 50 a. called Jones' Neglect;
Sophia, wid. of Thomas relinquished her dower; in April 1761
conv. part Dividente to Thomas Stansbury (84:160; 85:107).

DIMMITT, JOSHUA (7), s. of Richard (4), was alive in 1763; m.
Ann or Hannah; had iss.: RICHARD, b. 19 Oct.- 1760 (by Ann);
RACHEL, b. 13 Nov. 1763 (by Hannah) (133:107, 131).

DIMMITT, JAMES (8), s. of William (5), was b. c.1707; age 60
in 1767 when he was stated to have gone to Carolina; m. Barbara
Broad on 27 March 1733; in 1742 leased 200 a. of Gunpowder Manor
for the lifetimes of himself, Athaliah, b. c.1738, and Elizabeth, b. c.1740; in July 1761 was conv. the right to 10 a. of
Dimmitt's Delight and 160 a. Addition to Dimmitt's Delight
by William Dimmitt who was a son of William ; by Aug. 1765 he
was in Leesburg, Va., when he and his wife Barbara assigned a
lease to William Lux; had iss.: MARY, b. 29 Dec. 1734, d. Jan.
1743; ATHALIAH, b. 21 Feb. 1738; ELIZABETH ANN, b. 26 Aug. 1740;

MARY, b. Dec. 1744; JAMES, b. 17 Feb. 1748 (13:15; 85:185; 90: 680; 91:265, 267; 131:54/r, 88/r, 105/r, 112/r, 126/r; 389:5, 6).

DIMMITT, WILLIAM (9), s. of William (5), b. 1 June 1715, m. Catherine Warden Bull on 13 May 1736; in June 1742 was conv. some pers. prop. by his father-in-law Jacob Bull; had iss.: JAMES, b. 30 March 1737; WILLIAM, b. 16 Jan. 1740; JOHN, b. 7 Feb. 1742 (76:151; 131:54/r, 55/r).

DIMMITT, ELIZABETH, wid., m. Nathaniel Darby on 10 April 1721 (133:146)

DIMMITT, JAMES, b. 1725 in Md., d. May 1827(?) in Ky.; m. 22 Sept. 1757 Rachel Sinclair (131; 353).

DIMMITT, JOHN, d. by 8 June 1734, when admin. bond was posted by Thomas Demmitt with William Demmitt and Samuel Harryman (13: 33).

DIMMITT, JOHN, m. Frances Watts on 5 Aug. 1759 (131).

DIMMITT, JOHN, m. Rhoda Sinkler on 10 Jan. 1765 (131).

DIMMITT, MARY, m. Zachariah Gray on 19 Dec. 1719 (133:147).

DIMMITT, SUSANNA, ind. for bast. in June 1711; ind. again in March 1715 (21:210, 676).

DIMMITT, THOMAS, in 1750 owned 150 a. Upper Spring Neck and 50 a. Jones Neglect (153:30).

DIMMITT, VIOLA, in Nov. 1759 was fined for bast., and named Job Garrettson as the father (46:242).

DISNEY/DESNEY, WILLIAM, m. Catherine Loge on 20 Nov. 1756; she m. 2nd on 3 Nov. 1756 William Johnson; iss. of William and Catherine: JOHN, b. Oct. 1756; MARGARET, b. 5 March 1758 (131: 18/r, 48, 69).

DITTO, JAMES (1), was in Balto. Co. by 1700 as a taxable in n. side Gunpowder Hund.; prob. m. Christiana (?) who as Christian Ditter m. Thomas Gadd on 22 Jan. 1732/3; had iss.: ABRAHAM, bapt. 14 Sept. 1718 (131; 389).

DITTO, ABRAHAM (2), s. of James (1), was bapt. 14 Sept. 1718 and d. by 7 June 1794 in Washington Co., Md. in 1748 leased 100 a. of Gunpowder Manor which he called Ditto's Delight, for the lifetimes of Abraham (age 50 in 1767), Mary (age 45 in 1767), and Diana (age 27 in 1767); had iss.: prob. DIANA, b. c. 1722, as Dinah Detter m. George Knox on 25 Dec. 1755; ELIZA-BETH, m. Charles Baker on 6 March 1764 (131; 389:6).

DIVERS/DIVES/DEVES/DEVIS, CHRISTOPHER (1), d. 8 Nov. 1766; m. 1st on 10 Dec. 1728 Frances Hill; m. 2nd on Aug. 1736 Sarah Ar-nell, who d. 25 July 1760; m. 3rd on 24 June 1762 Sarah Nixon, poss. wid. of a Thomas Nixon; his will, 7 Nov. 1766 - 11 Dec. 1766, named w. Sarah, her ch. Thomas Nixon, William Nixon, Per melia Nixon, and Zediuah (Zedediah?) Divers; also named son-in-

law Henry Oram, Jr.; had iss.: (by Frances) FRANCIS, b. 5 Nov.
1729 or 1739; (by Sarah Arnell) MARY, b. Oct. 1737; JOHN, b. 17
Jan. 1739; TAMZIN, b. 3 March 1740; ELIZ., b. 17 May 1743; SARAH,
b. 7 May 1746; ANANIAS, b. 7 May 1746; (by Sarah Nixon) TERRUCH
or ZEDUIAH, b. 9 April 1764) (112:33; 131:61, 23/r, 86/r, 113/r,
153/r, 158/r).

DIVERS, FRANCIS (2), s. of Christopher (1) and Frances, b. 5
Nov. 1729 (or 1739), m. 21 Nov. 1753 Mary Watters; had iss.:
WILLIAM, b. 18 Feb. 1758; FRANCES, b. 14 April 1760; JOHN, b. 4
Feb. 1764; FRANCES, b. 18 Sept. 1765 (131:43, 23/r, 81/r, 157/r,
143/r).

DIVERS, JOHN (3), s. of Christopher (1) and Sarah (Arnell),
was b. 17 Jan. 1739; m. Mary Greer on 10 June 1766 (131).

DIXON, HENRY, d. by 3 Dec. 1754 when admin. bond on his est.
was posted by David Bissett with James Phillips (13:20).

DIXON, JOHN, d. c.1670; m. Jane (?), wid. of (?) Waites; she
m. as her 3rd husb. Maj. Thomas Long; John and Jane imm. by 25
Jan. 1665 when he was granted a warrant for 600 acres for trans-
porting himself, w. Jane, and Christian Waites, James Cogell,
Edward Walder, Hugh Broadwater, Miachel Shadwell, John Shadwell,
Edward Horton, Richard Anderson, James Abell and Anne Bohemont;
served as Justice of Balto. Co. Court, 1665; bought 420 a. called
Dickenston (orig. pat. to Walter Dickenson) from Daniel Jones in
Aug. 1664; in March 1668/9 conv. 300 a. Dixon's Chance to Richard
Ellinsworth; his will, 12 Oct. 1669 - 27 Aug. 1670, left pers.
prop. to Christiana Waites and Eliza Southard; left 420 a. of
Dickenson and 450 a. Dixon's Neck to w. Jane for life, latter
plantation to go to dau. Abigail after death of w. Jane, named
Thomas Howell and Nath. Stiles as overseers, and was wit. by
James Cogell, John Stevens, and John Clough; admin. bond was
posted 28 March 1670 by Jane Dixon with James Cogell and Giles
Stephens; had iss.: ABIGAIL, m. 1st Thomas Scudamore, and 2nd
John Hayes (11:515; 93; 95; 120:55; 388; See also J. Hall Pleas-
ants, "Gorsuch Fam.," in Va. Mag. of Hist., 25:92).

DIXON/DICKENSON, WALTER, imm. by July 1659; conv. 450 a. Spring
Neck to Abraham Clark; conv. 420 a. Dickenson to Daniel Jones in
Oct. 1663; in June 1659 conv. 287½ a. Roade River to Thomas Powell of Corotoman, Lancaster Co., Va.; in July 1661 surv. 81 a.
called Gunworth, which he conv, to John Collier in Aug. 1663;
by 1676 was in Talbot Co. with w. Sarah (93; 101:302; 211; 388).

DOBBINGS, JAMES, b. 11 July 1760, s. of James, was impressed
at Balto. in 1774/5, served in the Rev. War, and later lived in
Marion Co., Ind. (400:125).

DOBSON, JAMES, m. Jane Mungumry on 1 July 1745 (131).

DOCE, JOHN, m. Eliz. Taylor on 26 Nov. 1759 (131).

DOCKINGS. See DAWKINS.

DOD, ELIAS, m. Sarah (?), and had: SARAH, b. 1 June 1735
(133:45)

DODD, THOMAS, was in Balto. Co. by 1695 as a taxable in s. side Patapsco Hund. (140).

DODDRIDGE. See DOTTRIDGE.

DOE, SARAH (1), in Aug. 1714 named mariner Robert Edwards of the merchant shop Patapsco as the father of her child; in Aug. 1718 was ind. for bast. again, and because she refused to name the father, she was to receive 25 lashes, and to serve the w. of Charles Merryman for 8 mos.; prob. had one son: JEFFREY (17: 537; 23:3, 4; 26:201).

DOE, JEFFREY (2), s. of Sarah (1), was age 11 in Feb. 1733/4; and in Nov. 1734 was bound to Humphrey Yates to age 21 (30:351).

DOLLESON, JOHN, aged 15 in June 1714; s. of Elizabeth Wood, dec., was bound to serve Rowland and Bridget Shephard in Aug. 1714; in Nov. 1718 was ordered to have ten lashes (21:538; 22:32).

DONAHUE, HENRY (1), d. in Balto. Co. by 9 May 1722 when admnx. Honor Donahue posted admin. bond with John Crockett and Wm. Noble; m. Honor (?), who m. as her 2nd husb. Jeremiah Henley by March 1723/4; in Nov. 1718 Honor swore she was in fear for her life because of a threat made by John Steele; in March 1718/9 she was taken into custody for abusive language and behavior before the Court; in Aug. 1719 Henry was ind. for refusing to repair his road; the will of Henry, 16 Jan. 1720 - 9 May 1722, named w. Honor, eld. s. Henry, youngest s.Roger (who were to divide Emm's Delight), s. John (to have 20 a. Donahue's Shift), and dau. Eleanor; his est. was admin. 14 Oct. 1723 and 8 Nov. 1723; had iss.: HENRY; JOHN; ROGER; and ELEANOR (in March 1721/2 she named William Hunter as the father of her child named William Hunter, who was b. 29 Jan. 1720); she m. by 8 Nov. 1723 John Kinsey (1:129, 176; 11:535; 14:8; 23:32, 65, 217; 26:204; 124:105; 131: 41/r).

DONAHUE, HENRY (2), s. of Henry (1), m. Rachel, dau. of Thomas Smithson by 11 Aug. 1731; in Nov. 1724 he was accused of assault and battery on William Gwin (27:43; 126:253).

DONAHUE, ROGER (3), s. of Henry (1), d. by 31 Jan. 1748 when admin. bond was posted by exec. Samuel Gilbert with Robert Bryarly and Andrew Thompson; m. 16 Jan. 1734 Elizabeth Thompson, mother of James Thompson; in 1750 Roger's heirs owned 125 a. part Southampton and 20 a. Donahue's Strife; his est. was admin. on 13 Jan. 1749, 15 Nov. 1751, and 27 July 1753; had iss.: HANNAH, b. c.1736; ELIZABETH, b. c.1738; GILBERT, b. 29 Feb. 1739; DANIEL, b. c.1742, and SARAH, b. c.1744 (5:71, 219, 338; 13:23; 128:84, 109; 37:169; 153:36).

DONAHUE, WILLIAM, d. by 2 June 1752 when admin. John Kersey posted bond with William Dallam (13:17).

DONAWIN/DUNAVIN, DANIEL, m. Johanna Arnold; had iss.: PHILIP, b. 7 July 1749; DANIEL, b. 19 Sept. 1751 (his mother was named "Hannah"); WILLIAM, b.30 Sept. 1754; JACOB, b. 25 Oct. 1756; THOMAS, b. 25 Oct. 1756; MARGARET, b. 25 March 1758 (129:348, 356, 357).

DONAWIN, CATHERINE, serv. to Robert Clark, was tried for bast. in March 1736 and ind. for the same offense in June 1740 (31:36; 32:226).

DONOVAN, TIMOTHY (1), m. Mary (?), and had iss.: THOMAS, b. 29 June 1706 (128:36).

DONOVAN, THOMAS (2), s. of Timothy (1), b. 29 June 1706, is prob. the Thomas Donawin who m. Frances Hall on 6 March 1731 and had iss.: AMEY, b. 1 Aug. 1733; SARAH, b. 24 June 1738 (128:36, 66, 90, 112).

DONOVAN, LELLEN(?), m. Edmund Gradde on 10 March 1697 (129: 178).

DONSTON, JOHN, alias Nickhoskell, d. by 21 Aug. 1682 when his admin. bond was posted by James Phillips, with Thomas Jones and John Johnson (13:35).

DOOLEY/DULEY, JOHN (1), m. Elizabeth (?), and had iss.: WILLIAM, b. 6 Sept. 1703 (128:35).

DOOLEY, WILLIAM (2), s. of John (1), b. 6 Sept. 1703, d. in 1739; m. Blanche Jones in Oct. 1725; she was b. 28 Jan. 1706, dau. of Cadwallader and Mary (Paywell) Jones; Blanche m. as her 2nd husb. William Deaver, Jr., in Oct. 1740; admin. bond on the est. of William Dooley was posted 4 March 1739 by Blanche Dooley with Richard Dallam and Edward Morgan; William and Blanche had iss.: ELIZABETH, b. 22 Nov. 1726, d. 6 Aug. 1727; ELIZABETH, b. 10 May 1728 (ind. for bast. in June 1750 and tried for bast. in Aug. 1750); RACHEL, b. 7 May 1730; AQUILA, b. 2 Oct. 1735; MARY, b. by March 1743; BLANCH, alive in 1743 (4:110; 13:31; 34: 190; 128:47, 55, 63, 69, 88; 129:237, 248, 259, 284, 320; 37:2, 177).

DORMAN, ROBERT (1), was transp. to Md. by 1663; in Oct. 1670 had surv. 120 a. Selah's Point on n. side of Back River; land was later held by Selah Dorman; may have had at least one s.: SELAH (211; 388).

DORMAN, SELAH (2), s. of Robert, was of age in 1692 to be a taxable in n. side Patapsco Hund.; in June 1710 bought 100 a. Inloes Loine from Thomas and John Boring; d. by 14 Feb. 1717 when admin. bond on his est. was posted by John Ensor with James Durham and Samuel Watkins; est. was inv. on 10 July 1718 by Daniel Scott and Thomas Hutchins, and val. at £ 134.4.5; est. was admin. by James Durham, bondsman for Selah Barton, on 25 May 1724 and 18 May 1727; by Nov. 1724 his heir was his grandson Selah Barton; had iss. at least one ch., a dau., who m. (?) Barton (2:289,, 345; 11:527; 48:277; 67:82; 138).

DORMAN, SARAH (3), poss. dau. of Selah (2) is so placed because in Aug. 1702 Sarah's grandmother, Elizabethe Swindall conv. one half of her est. to Sarah; in Aug. 1706 Selah Dorman admin. the est. of the afsd. Elizabeth Swindall; Sarah may have been the dau. who m. (?) Barton (1:6; 2:4, 238; 66:151).

DORNEY. See DOWNEY.

DORSEY FAMILY. This family has been well researched by Maxwell J. and Jean Muir Dorsey and Nannie Ball Nimmo in The Dorsey
Family (1947). For that reason only the line settled in Baltimore County is traced.

DORSEY, EDWARD (1), the progenitor, was in Lower Norfolk Co.,
Va., by 1645, and came to Anne Arundel Co., Md., by 1650; m. Ann
(?), who may have outlived her husb. and returned to Va.; became
a convert to the Soc. of Friends; drowned off the Isle of Kent
by 2 Aug. 1659; had iss.: EDWARD, d. 1705; JOSHUA, d. 1688; JOHN,
d. 1714; SARAH, d. by 1691 having m. Matthew Howard, Jr. (Dorsey
et al., pp. 1-4).

DORSEY, EDWARD (2), s. of Edward (1), d. c.1705 in Balto. Co.,
having m. 1st, c.1670, Sarah, dau. of Nicholas Wyatt, and 2nd,
c.1693, Margaret Lacon, who m. as her 2nd husb. John Israel and
who d. 1707; he was trans. to Md. by 1661 by Robert Bullen; held
a number of public offices including delegate to the Assembly
from A. A. Co., 1694-7, and from Balto. Co., 1701-4; a firm ad-
herent of Lord Baltimore in 1689; contested the will of his wife's
father, Nicholas Wyatt in 1675; his will, 26 Oct. 1704 - 31 Dec.
1705; admin. bond was posted 28 Feb. 1705/6 by extx. Margaret
Dorsey with Joseph Howard, Andrew Wellpley, John Petticoat, and
Wm. Taylard; a second bond was posted 8 Aug. 1707 by John Israel
with Evan Jones and J. Earnshaw of A. A. Co.; est. inv. 1 April
1706 by Thomas Hammond and William Talbott and val. at £ 528.18.11;
est. was admin. by Margaret on 15 Oct. 1706 and 7 Aug. 1707 and
by John Israel on 24 Oct. 1710; had iss. 8 ch. by 1st w. and 5
by 2nd w.: EDWARD, b. by 1677,d. unm.; SARAH, b. by 1677, m. 1st
John Norwood and 2nd John Petticoat; HANNAH, b. c.1679, m. Joseph
Howard; SAMUEL, b. c.1682, m. Jane (?); JOSHUA, b. 1686, m. Ann
Ridgely; JOHN, b. 1688, m. Honor Sta-(?);   NICHOLAS, b. c.1690,
m. Frances Hughes; BENJAMIN, d. c.1692, d. unm.; LACON, b. c.
1694, d. unm.; FRANCIS, b. c.1696, m. Elizabeth Baker; CHARLES,
b. c.1698; EDWARD, b. c.1700, m. Phebe (?); ANN, b. c.1702, m.
John Hammond (Dorsey et al, pp. 8-25; 2:74, 139, 241; 11:516,
540; 48:43, 370).

DORSEY, JOSHUA (3), s. of Edward (1), d. in A. A. Co. in 1688,
having m. Sarah Richardson, d. 1705/6, who m. 2nd Thomas Blackwell;
his will, 20 Feb. 1687 - 21 June 1688, named w. Sarah, cous. John
Howard, cous. Samuel and cous. Matthew Howard, s. John (not yet
21), and bros. Edward and John; had iss.: JOHN, b. c.1682, m.
Comfort Stimson (Dorsey et al,   pp. 121-123).

DORSEY, Hon. JOHN (4), s. of Edward (1), d. in Balto. Co. in
1714, having m. Pleasance (?), d. by Aug. 1734; she m. as her
2nd husb. Thomas Wainwright; Dorsey held many offices including
that of Member of the Council, 1711-1715; his will made 6 Nov.
1714; admin. bond was posted 22 March 1714 by exec. Caleb Dorsey
with Richard Warfield and Joseph Howard; est. inv. on 25 April
1715 and signed by Richard Clagett, John Dorsey, John Hammond,
and John Israel; est. admin. 11 April 1716 and again on 11 Feb.
1717/8; had iss.: EDWARD, d. 170C/1, m. Ruth (?); CALEB, b. 1685,
m. Elinor Warfield; DEBORAH, m. 1st Charles Ridgely, and 2nd

Richard Clagett (Dorsey et al, pp. 133-139; 1:195, 218; 11:523; 50:193; 370).

DORSEY, SAMUEL (5), s. of Col. Edward (2), d. by 24 Feb. 1724 when admin. bond was posted by Edmund Benson with Thomas Davis and Abraham Woodward of A. A. Co.; m. Jane (?) who d. by 1762 having m. as her 2nd husb. Henry Ayton; his est. was admin. 17 May 1727 by Edmund Benson of A. A. Co.; had iss.: JANE, m. Richard Ayton; SARAH, b. 16 May 1716, d. 7 March 1717; ANN, b. and d. 21 Aug. 1718 (Dorsey et al, pp. 34-36; 11:541; 2:290).

DORSEY, NICHOLAS (6), s. of Col. Edward (2), was b. c.1690, d. 1717 in Balto. Co.; m. Frances Hughes on 20 Dec. 1709; she was b. 18 May 1692, dau. of Thomas Hughes; will of Nicholas Dorsey, 16 Sept. 1717 - 13 Feb. 1717/8; admin. bond was posted 27 Feb. 1717 by extx. Frances Dorsey with Samuel Dorsey and Andrew Norwood; est. inv. 4 July 1718 by John Israel and Edward Norwood and val. at £ 347.15.9 and signed by Joshua and John Dorsey; est. admin. 14 Feb. 1718 and 4 Sept. 1721 by Frances Dorsey; Frances was charged with bast. in Aug. 1721; iss. of Nicholas and Frances: THOMAS, d. by 1732; NICHOLAS, b. c.1712, m. Sarah Griffith; BENJAMIN, b. c.1713, m. Sophia (?); EDWARD, b. 1717, d. by 1732 (Dorsey et al, pp. 63-64; 1:154, 161, 272; 11:537; 23:270; 48: 235).

DORSEY, BENJAMIN (7), s. of Col. Edward (2), b. c.1692, d. by 1717, unm.; admin. bond posted 4 June 1717 by admin. Jno. Dorsey with Thomas Tolly and Jno. Clark (11:536)

DORSEY, LARKIN (8), s. of Col. Edward (2), b. c.1694, d. c. 1712 in Balto. Co.; in June 1710 he chose John Pettigoe as his guardian (21:137).

DORSEY, FRANCIS (9), s. of Col. Edward (2), was b. c.1696, d. 1749 in Balto. Co.; m. c.1724 Elizabeth Baker who in June 1728 joined him and his bro. Edward in selling 150 a. United Friendship to Hyde Hoxton; bought 100 a. Scotchman's Desire from Maurice and Sarah Baker; will of Francis Dorsey, 5 June 1749 - 17 Feb. 1749, names tracts Scotchman's Desire and Dorsey's Addition, child.: Francis,Lacon, Elizabeth and Venetia and son-in-law William Murphy; admin. bond posted 20 July 1749 by exec. William Murphy with John Hurd and Robert Gilcrest; est. admin. by Murphy on 1 Sept. 1750, 17 Jan. 1752, 15 Dec. 1752, and 4 Aug. 1753; iss.: PRISCILLA, b. 22 March 1725/6, m. William Murphy; VENETIA, b. 16 Oct. 1728; SARAH, b. 28 Jan. 1730, m. Charles Wells; ELIZABETH, b. 16 Aug. 1733, m. Morris Baker; KEZIA, b. 25 April 1735, d. by 1752; MARGARET, b. 18 June 1738/9; FRANCIS, b. 23 June 1741, d. 1769, m. Ann (?); LACON, b. 15 Feb. 1747, m. by 1770 Lucy (Dorsey et al, pp. 68-69; 5:132, 244, 247, 293; 13:20; 73:322; 133:65; 134:15).

DORSEY, Col. JOHN (10), s. of Joshua (3), was b. c.1682, d. after 1736; m. Comfort Stimson on 22 Aug. 1702; she was b.1686, d. 1747 in Balto. Co.; was colonel of Balto. Co. militia and a delegate to the Assembly from Balto. Co.; will of Comfort Dorsey, 6 Jan. 1747 - 23 Jan. 1747; est. of Comfort Dorsey was admin. by John Hammond Dorsey on 12 April 1750 and 10 April

1751; iss. of Col. John and Comfort: SARAH, bapt. 29 June 1708, d. young; VENETIA, bapt. 29 June 1708, d. young; GREENBERRY, b. 1710/11, m. Mary Belt; JOSHUA, b. 1712, m. Flora Fitzsimmons; VINCENT, m. Sarah Day; SARAH, m. Alexander Cromwell; VENETIA, m. Woolquist Cromwell; JOHN HAMMOND, b. 1724, m. Frances Watkins (Dorsey et al, pp. 123-126; 5:96, 139; 370).

DORSEY, EDWARD (11), s. of Hon. John (4), d. by 1700; m. Ruth (?) who m. 2nd John Greeniff, and 3rd John Howard; est. of Edward was admin. by Ruth, w. of John Greeniff on 4 Nov. 1703, 11 July 1710, and 30 July 1712; had iss.: JOHN, b. c.1699; EDWARD, b. c.1701, m. Ruth Todd (Dorsey et al, pp. 139-141; 2:30, 228; 4:126).

DORSEY, Col. NICHOLAS (12), s. of Nicholas (6), was b. c. 1712, d. 1780 in Balto. Co.; m. by 1732 Sarah Griffith who was b. 13 May 1718, d. 1 Sept. 1794; Nicholas was on the Comm. of Observation in 1775; was comm'd. ensign in 1776, and later promoted to colonel; his will, 21 March 1769 - 28 March 1780; had iss.: RACHEL, b. 1737, d. 1805, m. Anthony Lindsay, b. 1736, d. 1808 after having moved to Ky.; LYDIA, m. Charles Dorsey of Edward and moved to Nelson Co., Ky.; NICHOLAS, b. 1741, d. 1796, m. Ruth Todd; CHARLES, b. 1744, d. 12 Sept. 1814, m. Nancy Dorsey Elder, wid. of Owen Elder; CATHERINE, m. Robert Wood; SARAH; HENRY; VACHEL; LUCRETIA, b. 4 June 1754; m. John Welsh; FRANCES, m. Eli Warfield; ORLANDO, m. Martha Gaither; ACHSAH, m. Beal Warfield (112:344; Dorsey et al, The Dorsey Family, pp. 64-65).

DORSEY, BENJAMIN (13), s. of Nicholas (6), was b. c.1713, d. 1747 in A. A. Co.; m. 1739/40 Sophia (?) who d. 1788 in Balto. Co., having m. 2nd John Talbott; had iss.: BENJAMIN, d. 1775, unm.; ELISHA, b. c.1743, m. Mary Slade; CASSANDRA, b. by 1747, d. unm. after 1804 (Dorsey et al, The Dorsey Family, p. 65).

DORSEY, FRANCIS (14), s. of Francis (9), was b. 23 June 1741, d. 1769, m. Ann (?); his will, 1 March 1769 - 5 Sept. 1769, named w. Anne and ch. Basil John, Priscilla, and unborn ch., and Patience Davis; had iss.: BASIL JOHN, b. c.1762·, d. 1807; PRISCILLA (Dorsey et al, pp. 69-70; 112:128).

DORSEY, GREENBERRY (15), s. of Col. John (10), was b. 1710/11, and was alive in 1778 in Fairfax Co., Va.; m. 1st on 18 June 1726 Mary Belt, dau. of John Belt; m. 2nd by 1750 Sarah, wid. of William Fell; m. 3rd by 1760 in Fairfax Co., Va., Catherine, wid. of William Grimes; had iss.: JOHN, d. 1785 in Harford Co., Md, having m. Elizabeth Gardiner of John on 9 May 1751; GREEN-BERRY, Jr., b. 29 March 1729/30, d. 1798, m. 1st Frances Frisby and 2nd Sophia, wid. of John Clark; COMFORT, named in will of grandmother (Dorsey et al, pp. 127-128; 5:115; N.B. In 1750 Greenberry Dorsey owned 187½ a. Nanjemy and 100 a. Better Hope: see 153).

DORSEY, JOSHUA (16), s. of Co. John (10), was b. 1712, d. by 1784, m. Flora Fitzsimmons on 3 Nov. 1734; she was a dau. of Nicholas Fitzsimmons; iss. of Joshua and Flora: FREDERICK, b. 1735; PEREGRINE, b. 1737; PROVIDENCE, b. 1739, m. 1st Richard Lane, and 2nd Samuel Maccubbin Lane; GREENBERRY, b. 1741; HAMU-

TEL, b. 12 Jan. 1742; ELIZABETH, b. 9 Oct. 1744; JOSHUA, b. 3
March 1745; JAMES; JOHN; NICHOLAS; REBECCA (Dorsey et al, p.
128; 127:267; 133:152; births of children recorded in St. Margaret's Parish, A. A. Co., 219-4).

DORSEY, VINCENT (17), s. of Col. John (10), d. 1753 in Balto.
Co.; m. Sarah Day on 26 Oct. 1742; his will, 5 Nov. 1752 - 5
Feb. 1753; had iss.: KETURA, b. 27 July 1747, d. 3 Oct. 1747
(Dorsey et al, pp. 130-131; 131:95/r, 86/r, 116/r).

DORSEY, JOHN HAMMOND (18), s. of Col. John (10), was b. 1724
and d. 1774 in Balto. Co.; m. Frances Watkins on 16 Feb. 1743;
in 1744 Comfort, John Hammond and Vincent Dorsey conv. 500 a.
Best Endeavour to John Webster; ch. of John Hammond and Frances:
JOHN HAMMOND, b. 12 Feb. 1744; STEPHEN, b. 29 Nov. 1747, d. 1749;
MARY HAMMOND, b. 21 Feb. 1749, m. John Hammond Cromwell; REBECCA,
b. 22 March 1752, m. John Lane; JOHN HAMMOND, Jr., b. 14 Feb.
1754, m. Anne Maxwell; FRANCES, b. 19 April 1756; STEPHEN, b. 7
March 1758, m. Rachel Ewing (Dorsey et al, p. 131; 77:542;
131:16/r, 136/r, 144/r).

DORSEY, (?), m. by 8 Feb. 1762 Sophia, dau. of John Owings
(112:8).

DORSEY, ANDREW, was exempt from levy in March 1739/40; in
1750 owned 50 a. Dorsey's Prospect (32:149; 153:95).

DORSEY, AQUILLA, in Nov. 1757 was named as the father of Ann
Gardner's child (46:74).

DORSEY, BASIL, and CALEB, held land for the heirs of Thomas
Todd in 1750: 190 a. Denton, 300 a. North Point, 546 a. Old Road,
and 1000 a. Shawan Hunting Ground (153).

DORSEY, CHARLES, in Nov. 1718 chose his bro. John as his
guardian; in 1750 owned 100˜a. Charles' Lot (23:36; 153:87).

DORSEY, GREENBERRY, Jr., m. Frances (?), and had iss.: MARY,
b. 2 Aug. 1756; FRISBY, b. 14 Sept. 1758; BENEDICT, b. 15 Jan.
1761 (129:361, 369).

DORSEY, ELI, in 1750 owned 246 a., part Capria (153:88).

DORSEY, JOHN, of Cecil Co., carpenter, m. by 11 Dec. 1727
Sylvia, wid. of John Heathcote of Cecil Co. (71:82).

DORSEY, JOHN, of Edward, in 1750 owned 800 a. Bell's Hills
and part Taylor's Park (153:99).

DORSEY, JOHN HAMMOND, in 1750 owned 186 a. Wignall's Rest, 15
a. Webit, 6½ a. Waterton's Neglect, 50 a. Fox Hall and 16 a.
part Owner's Landing (153:52).

DORSEY, JOHN, in 1750 owned 109 a. Dear Bitt, alias Beeford
(153:104).

DORSEY, PATRICK, Irish, runaway serv. from James Richard in Balto. Town, July 1750 (307-68:304).

DORTRIDGE. See DOTTRIDGE.

DORUMPLE. See DERUMPLE.

DOTTRIDGE/DAWDRIDGE/DODDRIDGE/DORTRIDGE, WILLIAM (1), d. 15 Jan. 1720/1, m. Lettice Taylor on 18 Sept. 1717; she was dau. of Abraham Taylor; William d. by 7 June 1721 when admin. bond on his est. was posted by George York with John Ellitt and Richard Thrift; est. was admin. 2 Sept. 1724; had iss.: WILLIAM, b. 22 Sept. 1721 (1:285; 2:336; 11:525; 28:152; 123:213; 131).

DOTTRIDGE, WILLIAM (2), s. of William (1) and Lettice, was b. 22 Sept. 1721, and m. Margaret Murphy on 19 Oct. 1749; had iss.: ZELPHA, b. 3 Feb. 1750; LEAH, b. 27 March 1755; RACHEL, b. 2 Nov. 1757; SARAH, d. March 1759; LETTICE, b. 11 Aug. 1761 (131).

DOUBTY, THOMAS, m. Luraner Poulson on 2 Nov. 1760 (131).

DOUGH, BRIDGET, had iss.: ELIZABETH, b. 31 March 1701; OWEN, b. 11 Dec. 1710 (128:29).

DOUGHERTY, WILLIAM, in 1750 owned 100 a. Thomas and Mary Repose and 69 a. Roberts' Choice (153:56).

DOUGLAS/DUGLES, JOHN, m. Mary (?), and had iss.: ALEN'S, b. 9 (?) 1758 (133:101).

DOUSE. See DOWSE.

DOWELL, PHILIP (1), in Oct. 1722 bought part New Year's Purchase from Thomas and Eleanor Hooker and Richard and Zipporah Gist; his will, 26 Jan. 1733 - 22 April 1734, named these ch.: PHILIP (to have afsd. land); PETER; JOHN; ELIZABETH; RICHARD; LUKE; ANN WILSON; MARY BRESHIERS; and CHARITY (69:69; 126:88).

DOWELL, PETER (2), s. of Philip (1), in 1750 owned 150 a. of Corbin's Rest and 75 a. Jones' Range and Ryder's Industry (153: 72).

DOWLEY. See DOOLEY.

DOWLING, DANIEL, serv., was sentenced to serve his master, John Atkinson, four extra mos. for running away in March 1754 (39:17).

DOWNES. See DOWNS.

DOWNEY, JOHN (1), m. Lydia, dau. of Mark Swift in March 1716; in July 1723 he and Lydia released tract Edward's Lot to Abraham Taylor; in 1750 he owned 190 a. York's Hope; d. by 10 April 1754 when admin. bond was posted by James Downey with Jas. Maxwell; had iss.: SARAH, b. 28 May 1718; JAMES, b. 20 June 1720; JOHN, b. 7 Feb. 1722, d. March 1724; ANN, b. 9 Oct. 1727; MARY, b. 12 Oct. 1732 (5: 340; 13:15; 69:205; 131:13, 8/r, 13/r, 35/r; 153:47).

DOWNEY, JAMES (2), s. of John (1), was b. 20 June 1720, and
m. Mary Yeats on 14 Dec. 1743; in April 1746 he and Ann Cadle
were summoned by the vestry of St. Johns Parish for unlawful
cohabitation; m. 2nd on 9 Aug. 1749 Ann Cadle; had iss.: JOHN,
b. 14 Dec. 1744 (131; 132:82).

DOWNEY, DANIEL, m. Hannah (?), and had iss.: ANN, b. 29 Oct.
1732 (131:106/r).

DOWNEY, JOSEPH, age 10 mos. in June 1754, was bound to John
Gregory (39:185).

DOWNEY, MARY, was ind. for bast. in Aug. 1746 (36:116).

DOWNEY, THOMAS m. Ann Coudrey in 1730; in Aug. 1742 purch.
part Warrington from John Baldwin and Sabina Rumsey, wid. of Wm.
Rumsey; owned the land in 1750; on 2 June 1756 purch. 6+3/4 a.
Day's Privilege from John Day; had iss.: FRANCES, b. 21 Feb. 1730;
BEATRIX, b. 1737; THOMAS, b. 1740 (77:322; 82:541; 131:13/r, 91/r).

DOWNEY, WILLIAM, imm. to Md., and had iss.: JOHN, b. 20 Aug.
1753, d. 26 Sept. 1825, m. Ruhama Stocksdale (Scharf, Western
Maryland, I, 609).

DOWNS/DOWNES, HENRY, was in Kent Co. by Jan. 1666/8 when he
and w. Bridget conv. land at Elk River to Obadiah Judkins of Talbot Co. (99:346).

DOWNS, ANN, was ind. for bast. in June 1731 (29:156).

DOWNS,DARBY, d. by Aug. 1728; admnx. m. Ralph Woodall; dec.
left one dau. RACHEL (28:29).

DOWNS, DENNY, was tried for bast. in June 1733 and pleaded
guilty (30:15).

DOWNS, JEREMIAH, m. Mary (?), who d. 1 Feb. 1717/8; had iss.:
MARY, b. 24 Oct. 1714; SARAH, b. 7 Jan. 1716/7 (131:7, 12).

DOWNS, JOHN, was in Balto. Co. by April 1688 as a servant of
Thomas Lightfoot; m. by 16 June 1711, Mary, admnx. of Christopher
Durbin; his will, 1 April 1718 - 3 June 1718, named Rose Trotten,
dau.-in-law and son-in-law Elizabeth and Simon Cannon, sons-in-
law Thomas and Christopher Durbin, and dau. Kedeemoth; admin. bond
was posted 3 June 1718 by John Eager and Luke Trotten, execs.,
with Nathaniel Darby and Abraham Shavers; est. was inv. on 19
June 1718 by S. Hinton and Richard Gott and val. at £ 96.0.0,
and signed by John Eager and Luke Trotten; est. admin. on 29 July
1719, 29 Oct. 1724 and 6 Sept. 1725; dec. left iss.: KEDEMOTH
(1:190; 3:10; 11:518; 50:258).

DOWNS, THOMAS, alive in 1761, m. 15 Aug. 1738 Gulielmus
Gooden; in 1750 owned 100 a. Lowe's Lot and 25 a. Gilbert's Outlet; in March 1761 he and w. Gulielmus sold former tract to Thomas Mitchell; had iss.: MARY, b. 7 June 1740; ELIZABETH, b. 31
Aug. 1742 (85:68; 128:109; 129:330; 153:87).

DOWNS, THOMAS, m. Mary Clark on 5 Feb. 1754 (131).

DOWSE/DOUSE, EDWARD, and w. Elizabeth were transp. with others
by William Wheatley on the Constant Friendship in 1673; by 1683
was in Balto. Co. where he and Emanuel Selye surv. 200 a.
called Mate's Affinity (later held by the heirs of Edward Boothby); in
Nov. 1686 he and Selye surv. 200 a. The Range (later held by Wm.
Dane of Kent Co.); in June 1687 he and w. Elizabeth joined Emanuel Ceely (sic) and w. Sarah in conv. 200 a. The Forest to William
Deane; in Oct. 1687 purch. 200 a. Ogilsby's Chance from George
Ogilsby and w. Johanna; died test. leaving a will, 30 Oct. 1690 -
22 Dec. 1690 leaving 100 a. The Range to son-in-law Oliver Harriot and 100 a. of the same to dau.-in-law Unity Harriot, 200 a.
Ôglesby's Chance to Mary Harrison, prop. to John Anderson; left
iss.: prob. dau.: MARY, m. 1st by Oct. 1690 (---) Harrison; m.
2nd Thomas James by 1696 when Thomas and Mary sold 200 a. Oglesby's
Chance to Francis Whitehead; m. 3rd by Sept. 1707 John Hillen
(19:111; 59:230, 332, 524; 109:219; 211; 388).

DOYLE, DAVID, cooper, age 30, Irish, runaway serv. from Thomas
Sligh was in advert. of Dec. 1743 (384:433).

DRAPER, LAWRENCE (1), of A. A. Co., imm. to Md. by 1679; surv.
128 a. Mayden Croft in 1688 and 117 a. Chelsey in 1695; by 1704
was in Spesutia Hund., Balto. Co., as Captain Lawrence Draper;
d. leaving a will, 8 April 1713 - 5 Aug. 1713, named w. Eliza as
jt. extx. with s. Lawrence, dau. Mary Lissby w. of Robert Lissby
and their dau. Hannah, witnessed by Eliza Cottrell, John Brown,
and Susanna Simpson; actual date of death was April 1713; admin.
bond posted 5 Aug. 1713 by Lawrence and Elizabeth Draper with
John Cottrell and Garrett Garrettson; est. inv. 19 Jan. 1713/4 by
John Stokes and Roger Matthews and val. at £ 335.4.8½, and was
signed by Lawrence Draper and Elizabeth Clark; wid. Elizabeth m.
as 2nd husb. John Clark on 16 Oct. 1713; left iss.: LAWRENCE;
MARY, m. by 8 April 1713 Robert Lissby or Lusby (11:538; 50:216;
122:247; 128:30; 129:213; 211; 388).

DRAPER, LAWRENCE (2), s. of Lawrence (1), m. Mary Drew on 24
Dec. 1713; on 24 Feb. 1720 was named guardian of James Drew, s.
of Anthony Drew, dec.; had iss.: LAWRENCE, b. 6 Sept. 1715; AN-
THONY, twin, b. 29 July 1717; MARY, twin, b. 29 July 1717; DIGBY,
b. 8 Jan. 1719/20; FRANCES, b. 21 Aug. 1723; BETHIA, b. 14 Oct.
1726 (1:151; 128:31, 36, 45, 49).

DRAPER, JOHN (3), no known rel. to above, m. Abigail Simmons
on 17 Nov. 1709 in St. James Par., A. A. Co.; had iss.: JOHN, b.
27 Nov. 1709; SUSANNA, b. 25 Dec. 1713; MARY, b. 6 Oct. 1718;
THOMAS, b. 26 Sept. 1724, prob. d. young; THOMAS, b. 16 Sept.
1725; JONATHAN, b. 29 Nov. 1727, d. 12 March 1728; MARTHA, b. 28
Dec. 1728 (128:35, 43, 69; 219-3).

DRAPER, JOHN (4), s. of John (3), was b. 27 Nov. 1709, m. Mary
Rees on 9 Feb. 1734, and had iss.: RACHEL, b. 16 June 1736; THOMAS
SYMMONS, b. 9 March 1738; WILLIAM, b. 13 Sept. 1740; MARY, b. 26
April 1744 (128:85, 96, 103, 116, 337).

DRAPER, ABIGAIL, was ind. for unlawful cohabitation with Wm.
Wooford in Nov. 1746 (36:220).

DRAPER, JOHN, serv., with 2 yrs, 2 mos. to serve, in 1742 inv. of Jonas Roberson (53:201).

DREW, ANTHONY (1), progenitor, was in Balto. Co. by 1692 as a taxable in Spesutia Hund.; d. by 17 May 1720; m. 1st by 1688 the dau. of Geo. Utie of Balto. Co.; m. 2nd Margaret Brown, on 17 May 1709; Margaret d. 21 Feb. 1721/2;will of Anthony Drew, 9 Apr. 1720 - 17 May 1720, left Gum Neck, Hamstead Marshalls and Overton's Care to s. George, left Rum Key and Utley's Addition to s. James Utely, 250 a. (---) Hall to s. John, named daus. Sarah, Bertha, Fanney and Mary, left 70 a. Dogwood Ridge to John Steward, will was wit. by William Lenox, Benj. Cadle, and Edgar Tipper; after the will was proved, evidence was presented that showed that Edgar Tipper drew the will, that Isabel Steward was present, and that Anthony also had a dau. Susannah; admin. bond was posted 13 Sept. 1720 by exec. George Drew with Francis Dallahyde and Wm. Lenox; two inventories were filed, the second on 16 Oct. 1724 by Roger Matthews and John Clark, and val. at £ 37.13.3; his est. was admin. 24 Feb. 1720, 3 Oct. 1726, and 7 Oct. 1724; will of Margaret Drew, 15 Jan. 1721 - 6 March 1721, named grandson Thomas, s. of John Brown, dau.-in-law Elizabeth, w. of Richard Burrough, and left res. of her est. to her grandch., Thomas, Augustine, and Gambrill Brown; her admin. bond was posted 7 March 1721 by Archibald Buchanan; iss. of Anthony, prob. by his 1st w.; SUSANNA, b. 3 Jan. 1695, m. by Feb. 1720 James Lanham; ANTHONY, b. 26 Dec. 1691, not in father's will; SARAH, b. 30 April 1702; GEORGE, b. 1 April 1700; BETHIA, m. 1st William Lenox, and 2nd (---) Calvert; JOHN; JAMES UTELY; and poss. MARY who m. Lawrence Draper (1:151; 2:337, 357; 11:529, 539; 23:382; 51:198, 284; 124:11, 102; 128: 3, 6, 10, 13, 26, 111; 129:182, 185; 206-10:170).

DREW, GEORGE (2), s. of Anthony (1), was b. 1 April 1700, and d. 9 Jan. 1735; m. poss. 1st Hannah Lusby , and perhaps 2nd Johannah Phillips; will of George Drew, 7 Jan. 1735 - 6 Feb. 1735, named w. Johannah, s. Anthony (to have 888 a. Drew's Enlargement, 150 a. Collett's Meadows, and 100 a. Thomas and Ann Desire), named daus. Frances, Mary Ann, and Priscilla (not yet 16), and an unborn ch.; admin. bond posted by execs. on 19 March 1735; est. was admin. 11 March 1742 and 20 Aug. 1742; had three ch. by 1st w. and one or two by 2nd w.: MARY ANN, b. 21 Nov. 1723; ANTHONY, b. 29 April 1726; FRANCIS, b. 11 Jan. 1727; PRISCILLA (as "Drusilla,"), b. 6 Aug. 1733; SUSANNA, b. 4 July 1736 (3:266, 277; 13:31; 126:159; 128:53, 91, 94).

DREW, ANTHONY (3), s. of George (2), was. b. 29 April 1726; may have been one of the "heirs of George Drew," listed in 1750 as owning 788 a. Drew's Enlargement; m. Ann (---), and had iss.: HANNAH, b. 21 Sept. 1747; ANN, b. 2 Nov. 1749; GEORGE, b. 7 Feb. 1752; JAMES, b. 31 March 1754; HENRY, b. 20 Feb. 1756; MARY, b. 5 May 1758; SARAH, b. 6 Sept. 1762(?); ANTHONY, b. 3 Sept. 1762 (128:53; 129:360, 383; 153:19).

DREW, FRANCES, m. Amos Garrett on 23 Aug. 1744 (129:337).

DREW, MARY, m. Lawrence Draper on 24 Dec. 1713 (129:213).

DREW, ROBERT, m. by 28 July 1755, one of the heirs of Jos'h Ward (5:351).

DREW, SARAH, m. Christopher Sheppard on 5 Sept. 1733 (129: 271).

DRISDALE/DRYSDALE, ROBERT, was transp. to Md. as a servant by 1676; in Sept. 1683 surv. 200 a. Drysdale's Habitation near land of Edward Beedle; by 1692 was a taxable in Spesutia Hund.; d. leaving a will, 3 May 1704 - 19 June 1704 in which he left entire est. to sons-in-law John Fisher and Thomas Jackson, the execs.; witnesses were Thos. Newsom and Thos. Bucknall, and Jno. Kemball; admin. bond posted 12 April 1705 by John Roberts with Samuel Jackson and Thomas Edmonds; est. inv. on 14 May 1705 by John Kimble and Miles Hannis and val. at £ 11.12.0 (11:528; 48:163; 122:38; 138; 211; 388).

DROUGHEDA, AGNES, gave her age as 40 in 1730 (Chancery Depositions IR#I, p. 304).

DRUMPLE. See DERUMPLE.

DRUNKORD, JAMES, was in Balto. Co. by 22 Dec. 1700 when he m. Mary Greenfield; d. 1 Feb. 1704/5 and Mary m. 2nd, on 12 April 1704 John Debruler; admin. bond posted 12 April 1705 by John Debrular, Jr., with Thomas Cord and Samuel Jackson; est. inv. on 12 Nov. 1705 by Thomas Edmunds and Jno. Kimble, and val. at £ 55.9.0; est. admin. 3 March 1708 by John Debruler (2:167; 11: 514; 48:146; 122:53; 128:10, 21; 129:201).

DRURY, RACHEL, was ind. and tried for bast. in March 1745/6 (35:800, 812).

DRURY, THOMAS, runaway serv. from David Gorsuch in Balto. Town was in advert. of Sept. 1757 (307-68:304).

DUCKETT, PATIENCE, living at John Carrington's, was ind. for bast. in Nov. 1685 (18:358).

DUCKEN, JAMES, m. by 2 Oct. 1707 Margaret, extx. of William Galloway (2:182).

DUDNEY, MARY, living at Owen Bright's, had a child born in May 1703 (128:25).

DUDNEY, ROGER, m. Jean Fork or York on 10 Sept. 1708 (128:24).

DUGLES. See DOUGLAS.

DUKEHART, VALERIUS, innholder, was in Balto. Co. by May 1756 when he was killed by a gust of wind which blew a barn down on him; admin. bond was posted May 1756 by Daniel Chamier with J. Carnan, and Christ. Carnan; Chamier warned all persons to be on the lookout for two runaway Dutch servants and some property stolen from the late Dukehart's dwelling; est. admin. 17 June 1757; had at least one s.: VALERIUS, b. 28 d, 2 m., 1744, d. 24 Sept. 1783, having m. Margaret Roberts Humphreys and had iss. (5:329; 13:17; 136; 255:19; 262:53).

DUKES, CHRISTOPHER (1), d. in Balto. Co. by 2 March 1749; admin. bond posted 25 March 1749 by exec. Christopher with John

Long and Isaac Raven; in Oct. 1745 purch. 457 a. Northwick from
John Long, s. and heir of Thomas Long; est. admin. 2 March 1749
by Christopher Duke; left iss.: CHRISTOPHER; SARAH, b. c.1728;
MARCY, b. c.1730; FAMILIAR, b. c.1734; CHARLES, b. c.1738 (5:
86; 13:24; 37:160; 79:8).

DUKES, CHRISTOPHER (2), s. of Christopher (1), was alive in
1758, having m. Judith (---); in 1750 he was listed as owning 100
a. Hab Nab at a Venture, and 300 a. part Norwick; had iss.: WIL-
LIAM, b. 15 Sept. 1757 (133:103; 153:62).

DUKES, WILLIAM, d. in Balto. Co. by 13 Feb. 1709 when admin.
bond was posted by William Holland with Francis Whitehead and
Samuel Merryman; est. admin. 31 July 1710 by William Holland
(2:120; 11:511).

DULANY, DANIEL, in Oct. 1739 purch. 575 a. Boughton's Forest
from John Kemp, Mary w. of John Caggill, and Jemima w. of John
Broad, grandch. of Joseph Peake; poss. the same Daniel Dulany who
in 1750 owned 363 a. Dorsey's Plains, 36 a. Lowlands, and 1000 a.
Charles Bounty; may be the Daniel Dulany who m. 2 Dec. 1754
Elizabeth Bradley (75:336; 129:373; 153:100).

DULANY, DENNIS, age 14 in May 1744, in Nov. 1743 was bound to
Edward Sprusbanks; m. Easter Fugate on 23 Jan. 1749 (35:75; 131).

DULANY, THOMAS, of Balto. Co.., d. leaving a will, 5 March
1738 - 4 April 1739, named s. William (to have 100 a. Wright's
Forest), sons Thomas and Dennis (to have 403 a. Richardson's
Neglect, son Daniel, and a dau. Elizabeth; 4 April 1739 admin.
bond posted by Sarah Dulaney with Stephen Body and Nicholas Haile;
est. admin. 4 Dec. 1741 and 16 Oct. 1747; had iss.: DANIEL;
WILLIAM; THOMAS; DENNIS, b. 28 May 1731; JOHN, b. 11 Feb. 1733;
ELIZABETH (4:84, 161; 13:29; 127:20; 131:13/r, 58/r).

DULANY, THOMAS, m. Ann (---), and had: THOMAS, b. 3 June 1743;
ELIZABETH, b. 17 Aug. 1746 (131:113/r).

DULANY, WALTER, in 1750 owned 1250 a. part Vale of Jehosophat,
2000 a. part No Name, part Enlargement to the Vale of Jehosophat,
part Deer Park, and 1413 a. part Brother's Care (153:104).

DULANY, WILLIAM, m. 1736 Mary Anderson, and had: SABARENT, b.
7 Feb, 1787'; REBECCA, b. 8 Sept. 1742; WILLIAM, b. 1 Jan. 1744
(131:72/r).

DULEY, DULY. See DOOLEY.

DULREPLE, HENRY, m. Mary Smith on 27 Oct. 1757 (131).

DUNAM. See DURHAM.

DUNCAN, JOHN, was in Balto. Co. by 1692 as a taxable in s.
side Gunpowder Hund. (138).

DUNCAN, RICHARD, d. by 20 June 1716 when admin. bond on his
est. was posted by John Brown with Nicholas and John Dorsey;
est. inv. by Ben Johnson and Nicholas Dorsey and val. at £8.11.6;

est. admin. 8 July 1717 by John Brown of A. A. Co. (1:267; 11: 510; 48:222).

DUNKERTON, WILLIAM, imm. to Md. by 1668, and by 1673 was in Balto. Co. when he purch. Two Necks from Robert Hawkins (99:348, 349; 388).

DUNN, ARTHUR, m. Margaret (---), and had iss.: HENRY, b. 20 March 1746 (134:7).

DUNN, CATHERINE, age 20, Irish, runaway serv. from Amos Garrett of Balto. Co., was in advert. of May 1747 (384:626; 385:2).

DUNN, DENNIS, m. Bridget (---), and had two ch.; d. by 8 July 1748 when admin. bond was posted by Dr. Charles Carroll of Annapolis, with Charles Carroll, Jr., and Thomas Williamson; had iss.: ELIZABETH, b. 12 Oct. 1744; DENNIS, b. 13 April 1746 (5:97; 13:26; 129:343).

DUNN, DENNIS, m. Jane Crump on 15 June 1746 (133:159).

DUNN, JOHN, m. Christian (---); in 1750 owned 320 a. part of Arabia Petrea; est. was admin. in 1769 and 1770; had iss.: JENIT, b. 19 Nov. 1729; WILLIAM, b. 27 Dec. 1731; ROBERT, b. 20 June 1734; MARTHA, b. 6 Nov. 1736; MARY, b. 6 May 1739 (6:233; 7:66; 128:70, 87, 108; 153).

DUNN, RICHARD, m. Isabella Dunahue on 6 March 1753; had iss.: JOHN, b. 15 March 1758; WILLIAM, b. 21 Oct. 1758 (sic) (131:18/r).

DUNNAWAY, THOMAS, m. Frances Hall on 6 March 1731 (128:66).

DUNNICK, JOHN, m. Mary Pasmore on Nov. or Dec. 1742 (131).

DUNNIGAN, HUGH, Irish, servant of Col. George Wells, was judged to be 10 years of age in March 1691/2 (19:150).

DUNNIGAN, PHILIP, Irish, serv. of Col. George Wells, was judged to be 13 years of age in March 1691/2 (19:150).

DUNSELL, MARY, servant of Christopher Duke, was ind. for bast. in March 1733/4 and tried in Aug. 1734 (30:188, 308).

DURANT, ANTHONY, was in Balto. Co., where he d. by 16 June 1718 when admin. bond on his est. was posted by admnx. Sabra Durant with Henry Jonas and Will Fenton; est. inv. 26 July 1718 by Jno. Norton and S. Hinton and val. at £ 37.13.0, and signed by Silvia Durant (as kin), Samuel Harryman, Hugh Conn, and Richard Colegate (as creditors); est. admin. by Sabrina Durant on 21 April 1721; Sabrina Durant was tried for bast. in Nov. 1733, ind. for same in June 1734, tried for bast. in Aug. 1734 and Nov. 1734, and ind. again in Nov. 1742 (1:78; 11:533; 30:135, 253, 309, 400; 34:59; 50:278).

THE DURBIN FAMILY has been discussed by Kerry William Bate in "Thomas Durbin of Baltimore County, Maryland," Md. and Del. Gen., 15 (1974) 56).

DURBIN, THOMAS (1), progenitor, was in A. A. Co. by 1676 when he purch. tract Johnston from Walter Dickenson, and d. in Balto. Co. by 1697; by 1692 was a taxable in n. side Patapsco Hund. in Balto. Co.; admin. bond posted by Roger Newman with John Kemball and James Reed; est. was inv. on 3 May 1697 by William Wilkinson and Stephen Johnson, and val. at £ 60.2.8; admin. acct. of his est. showed that Newman paid for two black walnut coffins and paid the funeral charges of Thomas Durbin and his wife's burial; Durbin had surv. 350 a. Hab Nab at a Venture in Balto. Co., and this land was later held by his orphans; left iss.: JOHN, d. 1743; CHRISTOPHER, d. 1709; WILLIAM, alive in 1709 when he wit. the will of Christopher Durbin; ELIZABETH, poss. the Elizabeth "Durdain" who m. Samuel Burgess of Edward in All Hallows Par., A.A. Co.; poss. JAMES; poss. SAMUEL (11:52; 138; 206-14:145; 211; Bate, op. cit., p. 56).

DURBIN, JOHN (2), s. of Thomas (1), was of age to appear in the tax list of 1702, making his date of birth as c.1686; d. in Balto. Co. in 1743, having m. on 20 Dec. 1715 Avarilla, dau. of Daniel and Jane Scott; after Avarilla's death on 1 Dec. 1741, John m. a second wife Elioner Odan; in June 1716 he pet. the Court that his nephews Thomas and "Xpher" Durbin be taken away from their Step-father John Downes; his will, 22 Sept. 1743 - 2 Nov. 1743, named his ch., John, Thomas, Daniel, William, Avarilla, Hannah, Mary, son-in-law James Pritchard, and a poss. unborn child, mentioned tracts Betty's Lot, Imbles Union, and Hughes Choice and Hughes Enlargement; admin. bond posted 26 Nov. 1743 by acting exec. John Durbin with Samuel Hughes and Michael Gilbert; est. admin. 17 May 1746 by John Durbin; in Nov. 1746 the wid. chose her thirds; had iss.: ELIZABETH, b. 25 Oct. 1718, m. James Pritchard on 1 June 1735; JOHN, b. 15 April 1721; THOMAS, b. 18 Dec. 1723; DANIEL, b. 2 July 1725; SARAH, b. 15 April 1728, may be the Sarah who m. Samuel Howell on 11 Sept. 1747; WILLIAM, b. 26 Jan. 1730; AVARILLA, b. 22 Aug. 1733; MARY, b. 22 Feb. 1735; HANNAH, b. 25 Oct. 1735; poss. UNBORN CH. (4:27; 11:28; 22:21; 33:286; 127:238; 128:37, 40, 43, 45, 73, 77, 93-b; 131; 144).

DURBIN, CHRISTOPHER (3), s. of Thomas (1), d. in Balto. Co. in 1709; m. Mary, wid. of (---) Cannon; after Durbin's death she m. as her 3rd husb. John Downs; in March and June 1703 sold portions of Hab Nab at a Venture to John Eaglestone; and in May 1705 Durbin and w. Mary sold part of same tract to John Gardiner; in Nov. 1705 as second s. of Thomas Durbin, dec., sold 38 a. of Westminster to Samuel Greening; d. leaving a will, 23 Oct. 1709 - 28 Nov. 1709, left tract Johnston to old. s. Thomas, and named s. Christopher, w. Mary and children-in-law Simon Cannon and (---) Cannon; admin. bond was posted 28 Nov. 1709 by wid. and extx. Mary Durbin with John Downes and Samuel Merryman; est. was inv. on 9 Dec. 1709 by John Gay and Charles Merryman, and val. at £ 38.17.0, with John Durbin signing as kin; Mary, w. of John Downes, admin. the est. on 16 June 1711; the Downs were wards of Christopher's orphans, whose uncle John wanted to take them away; iss. of Christopher and Mary: THOMAS, m. Ann Cowdry; and CHRISTOPHER (11:513; 48:156; 60:183; 64:12; 66:252, 315; 122: 160; 123:161).

DURBIN, JAMES (4), poss. s. of Thomas (1), m. Margaret (---)

who d. Nov. 1720 in St. John's Par.; had iss.: prob. JOHN, d. by
25 Aug. 1762; ANN, m. William Noble on 21 Feb. 1731 (131; Bate).

DURBIN, SAMUEL (5), poss. s. of Thomas (1), was of age to wit.
the will of William Holland in 1721; d. in Frederick Co., Md. in
1752; his w., Ann Logsdon, whom he married on 4 July 1723, d. in
Fred. Co. in 1770; in 1750 owned Cobb's Choice ; had iss.: SARAH,
b. 19 Sept. 1725, m. (---) McKensey; WILLIAM, b. 4 Jan. 1726;
SAMUEL, b. 29 Jan. 1727; THOMAS, b. 13 July 1732; CHRISTOPHER,
b. 13 July 1741, moved to Madison Co., Ky.; JOHN; NICHOLAS; ED-
WARD; BENJAMIN; MARGARET, m. Edward Brown; MARY, m. (---) Logsdon; HONOUR (133: 23, 57, 66, 146; 153:81; 210-38:134).

DURBIN, ELIZABETH (6), dau. of John (2) and Avarilla, was b.
25 Oct. 1718, and m. James Pritchard on 1 June 1735; she may be
the Elizabeth Durbin who bore a child out of wedlock, and was ind.
for bast. in March 1733/4 and tried in June 1734 (30:264; 128:
37; 129:283).

DURBIN, JOHN (7), s. of John (2) and Avarilla, was b. 15 April
1721, and m. Mary Hawkins on 16 Oct. 1740; in 1750 owned 100 a.
Betty's Lot, 25 a. Triple Union, and 150 a. Durbin's Choice; had
iss.: DANIEL, b. 1 Dec. 1741; JOHN, b. 11 June 1743; WILLIAM, b.
25 Feb. 1747; SAMUEL, b. 11 Feb. 1749; AVARILLA, b. 22 Sept. 1752
(128:111; 129:314, 381; 153:90).

DURBIN, THOMAS (8), s. of John (2) and Avarilla, was b. 18
Dec. 1723 and is prob. the Thomas listed in 1750 as owning 67 a.
part Hughes' Choice and 17 a. part Hughes' Enlargement (128:43;
153:68).

DURBIN, DANIEL (9), s. of John (2) and Avarilla, was b. 2 July
1725, m. Ann Mitchell on 11 Aug. 1746; in 1750 owned 50 a. Durbin's Chance, 38 a. Hughes' Enlargement, 133 a. Hughes' Choice,
and 75 a. Triple Union; had iss.: SCOTT, b. 11 Oct. 1746; JOHN,
b. 11 March 1747 (128:45; 129:346; 153:36).

DURBIN, THOMAS (10), s. of Christopher (3), m. Ann Cowdrey in
Jan. 1737; and in June 1740 purch. from Lemuel and Sophia Baker
tract Preston's Deceit, which he owned in 1750 with 60 a. Chance;
had iss.: DRUSILLA, b. 9 Oct. 1738, m. James Nicholson on 24 Dec.
1757; KETURA, b. 23 March 1741 m. George Williamson on 15 June
1758; THOMAS, b. 8 March 1743; MARY, b. Nov. 1746 (75:386; 131:
50, 52, 68/r, 123/r; 153:53).

DURBIN, CHRISTOPHER (11), s. of Christopher (3), d. in Balto.
Co. by Nov. 1739, leaving at least one ch.; JOHN, b. c.1732, in
Nov. 1739 as "age 7 this Nov.," was bound to Daniel Scott in Nov.
1739 (32:37).

DURBIN, WILLIAM (12), s. of Samuel (5), was b. 4 Jan. 1726;
may be the William Durbin alive in Fred. Co. in 1790 (133:23;
1790 Census of Md.)

DURBIN, CHRISTOPHER (13), s. of Samuel (5), b. 13 July 1741,
d. Dec. 1825, having m. Margaret (---), by 1789 was in Madison
Co., Ky., having m. and had at least one ch.: EDWARD, m. Betty

Porter (133:66; 354:63; "First Census of Kentucky," 1790, p.31).

DURBIN, DANIEL (14), s. of John (7) and Mary, b. 1 Dec. 1741,
d. in Harrison Co., Ky.; m. on 12 Jan. 1764 Mary, dau. of Richard
and Anne Johns; had at least five ch., b. in Md. by 1776; had
iss.: CASSANDRA, b. c.1766, m. Dr. Richard K. Sappington on 8
Oct. 1784; MARY, b. c.1769; SARAH, twin. b. c.1771; REBECCA, twin,
b. c.1771; JOHN, b. c.1776 (129:381; 285:105; Family Records of
Mrs. William B. May, made available to the compiler).

DURBIN, CHRISTOPHER, in 1750 was listed as the owner of 50 a.
Durbin's Venture (153:91).

DURBIN, JOHN, m. Elioner Odan on 13 Dec. 1743, and had iss.:
RALPH, b. 18 Dec. 1743 (129:336).

DURBIN, JOHN, m. Rachel Childs on 16 Sept. 1755, and had iss.:
CORDELIA, b. 8 Sept. 1757 (131:46, 147/r).

DURBIN, JOHN, m. Elizabeth Smithson on 2 Jan. 1759 (131).

DURBIN, JOHN, poss. # 7 above, had two sons: WILLIAM, age 12
on 1 Feb. 1759; bound to Samuel Webb in Aug. 1759, and SAMUEL,
age 10 on 1 Feb. 1759, bound to same Webb in Aug. 1759 (44; 46:
235).

DURBIN, THOMAS, and MARY DURBIN, were named as the ch. of
Christopher Shaw in the latter's admin. acct. (3:279).

DURBIN, THOMAS, m. Margaret Stephens on 4 Oct. 1744 (131).

DURBIN, THOMAS, was in Penna. on 6 Nov. 1784 when he sold 50
a. of Durbin's Beginnings to the heirs of Nicholas Baker of Harford Co., dec. (241-JLG#F:183).

DURHAM, JOHN (1), progenitor, was in Md. by 1673 when he
claimed land for completion of his service; d. in Balto. Co. by
11 June 1695; m. by March 1682/3 Jane, admnx. of William Choice;
she also m. John Boone; by 1692 was a taxable in s. side Gunpowder Hund.; in June 1693/4 bought 250 a. called Chilbury from
James Durham and w. Mary (dau. of John Lee for whom the land was
orig. surv.); in April 1681 had surv. Addition to Levy's Tribe;
d. leaving a will, 20 Feb. 1694 - 30 May 1695, leaving 125 a. to
s. John, Levey's Tribe and Levy's Addition to s. Samuel, land to
s. Francis, and naming daus. Eliza and Mary; wife was to have her
dower rights and she and her two ch. were to be maintained out of
the est.; his est. was inv. by Samuel Maxwell and Moses Groome
and val. at £ 109.0.0, plus 5624 lbs. tob.; had iss.: SAMUEL;
JOHN; FRANCIS, may have d. young as he does not appear in the
tax lists between 1692 and 1706; ELIZA; MARY, prob. m. Matthew
Green; in Nov. 1713 Mary Green pet. that Samuel Durham of John,
from his infancy had been maintained partly by her mother and
partly by her husband, lately dec., and she pet. the court to
have Samuel Durham bound to her (18:13, 14; 21:445; 48:49; 59:
390; 70:406; 121:97; 138; 388).

DURHAM, SAMUEL (2), s. of John (1), d. in Balto. Co. by 8

March 1704/5, leaving a will dated 9 Feb. 1700, left 100 a. of
Levy's Tribe to John Boone, Levy's Addition was to go to his bro.
John, while personalty was left to Mary and Francis Durham; the
will was witnessed by Jno. Taylor, Matthew Green, and Jno. Durham
(122:33).

DURHAM, JOHN (3), s. of John (1), was a taxable in n. side of
Gunpowder Hund. in 1692; d. by 2 Dec. 1709 when admin. bond was
filed by Matthew Green and John Standifer and Charles Baker; est.
was admin. by Green on 28 June 1710; had iss.: SAMUEL (2:128; 11:
543; 138).

DURHAM, SAMUEL (4), s. of John (3), was b. c.1697 in Balto.
Co., where he d. in 1772; m. Eleanor Smithson, b. c.1703 on 15
Jan. 1772; in Nov. 1709 was bound to Matthew Green when Samuel
was almost 12; in Nov. 1713 Matthew Green's wid. Mary pet. that
Samuel be bound to her; in Jan. 1726 Samuel and w. (unnamed)
sold part Addition to Levy's Tribe to John Cole, stating in the
deed that the land had been surveyed in April 1681 by John (#1)
Durham, inherited by John's s. Samuel (# 2), who left it to
his bro. (John (#3), father of said grantor; in 1750 Samuel
owned 100 a. part Edmond's Camp, 189 a. Bilberry Hall, 35 a. Durham's First Addition to Bilbury Hall, 25 a. Durham's Second Addition to Bilbury Hall, 61 a. Durham's Third Addition to Bilbury
Hall, and 400 a. Ewing's Contrivance; left iss.: JOHN, b. 8 Oct.
1723; SARAH , b. 2 June 1725; SAMUEL, b. 18 Feb. 1726/7; JAMES,
b. 1 Jan. 1728; JOSHUA, b. c.1733; MORDECAI, b. 1 Feb. 1734;
DANIEL, b. 26 Jan. 1736; JOHN, b. 22 Feb. 1738; HANNAH, b. 26 Jan.
1740; DAVID; AQUILA (21:69, 445; 70:406; 131; 153:70).

DURHAM, SAMUEL (5), s. of Samuel (4), was b. 18 Feb. 1726/7,
was alive in 1776 in Bush River Lower Hund., having m. Anne (---);
had iss.: MARY, b. c.1756; SUSANNAH, b. c.1759; ELINOR, b. c.
1761; SAMUEL, Jr., b. c.1765; THOMAS, b. c.1768; AQUILA, b. c.
1770; LLOYD, b. c.1772; LEE, b. c.1774 (285).

DURHAM, JOSHUA (6), s. of Samuel (4), was b. c.1733, was alive
in 1776 in Bush River Lower Hund.; m. Sarah, dau. of Andrew Thompson, whose will of 19 Dec. 1760 named dau. Sarah w. of Joshua Durham; had iss.: JOHN, b. c.1755; ELIZABETH, b. c.1757; DANIEL, b.
c.1760; BENJAMIN, b. c.1762; ALICEANNA, b. c.1765; CLEMENCY, b.
c.1769; PRISCILLA, b. c.1771; HANNAH, b. c.1773 (285).

DURHAM, EDWARD, m. Mary Gerish on 28 Feb. 1728/9 (129:246).

DURHAM, ELIZABETH, signed the inv. of Edward Swan as kin on
4 April 1712 (50:357).

DURHAM, HUGH, serv., in Aug. 1722 was named as the father of
Elizabeth Brock's child; ind. by the grand jury for begetting a
child on the body of Elizabeth Brock in June 1725 (24:306; 27:
224).

DURHAM, JAMES, was a taxable in n. side Gunpowder Hund. in
1692; in June 1693/4 he and w. Mary, dau. of John Lee, conv. 250
a. (Chil)bury, formerly laid out by said Lee, to John Durham
(59:390; 138).

DURHAM, JAMES, poss. the same as James above, was named as son-in-law in will of Thomas Staley on 16 Feb. 1696; Staley also named James' ch. Mary (grandau. of said Staley, to have one half of 165 a. Moores Fields) and James (to have the other half; Staley also named his niece Eliza Swift, w. of Mark Swift (121:208).

DURHAM, JAMES, m. by 2 Oct. 1707 Margaret, dau. of Hendrick Enloes, sis. of Abraham Enloes, and wid. of William Galloway; she may be the same Margaret who in Nov. 1712 named John Rattenbury as the father of her child; Margaret d. Nov. 1720, but it would appear that this James may have died earlier (2:7, 182; 21:335; 48:6; 131:71/r).

DURHAM, JAMES, m. Rebecca Anderson on 12 Feb. 1720, and had iss.: JOHN, b. 17 Jan. 1723; SARAH, b. 2 March 1724, d. 23 Oct. 1725 (131:15; 133:7, 8, 193).

DURHAM, JAMES, d. by 29 March 1725 when admin. bond on his est. was posted by John Muckeldory with Archibald Rollo and George Rigdon; est. admin. 30 June 1726 by John McElroy (3:54; 11:534).

DURHAM, JAMES, admin. the est. of Selah Dorman on 25 May 1724 and 18 May 1727 (2:289, 345).

DURHAM, SAMUEL, s. of John Durham Gott; in June 1726 dropped the surname Gott; had a sis. Elizabeth Durham who m. John Stand (30:161).

DURHAM, STALEY, m. Mary Parlett on 18 Feb. 1734/5 and had iss.: ANN, b. 26 Nov. 1737; STALEY, b. 10 April 1740 (133:62, 63, 153).

DURHAM, STALEY, in 1750 owned 100 a. part Smith's Choice (153:8).

DURHAM, THOMAS, m. Alice (---), and had iss.: BENJAMIN, b. 22 March 1722/3 (133:7).

DURICK, MARY, was ind. for bast. in June 1739 (32:401).

DURIN, MARY, was tried for bast. in Aug. 1740 (32:302).

DURRAM. See DURHAM.

DUSKIN, DENNIS (1), m. Mary (---) who m. as her 2nd husb. John Fraser who was dec. by Jan. 1717; iss. of Dennis and Mary: MICHAEL, age 8 on 24 Oct. 1716; DANIEL, age 6 on 7 April 1717 (63:523).

DUSKIN, MICHAEL (2), s. of Dennis (1), was b. c.1708; poss. the same Michael who m. Sarah Johnson on 6 June 1751 and had a son: MICHAEL, b. 27 Oct. 1752 (63:523; 131:131/r).

DUTTON, JOHN (1), was b. c.1647 in Overton, Eng., and was bur. in Phila. on 4 May 1693; m. in Eng. Mary Darlington; came to New Castle by Aug. 1682; had iss.: JOHN, Jr., b. 29 Oct. 1675 in Eng.; EDWARD, b. 18 Jan. 1676/7 in Eng., m. Gwin Williams; THOMAS, b. 3 March 1679, m. Leusy Barnard; ELIZABETH, b. 1681, d. 1682; ROBERT, b. 13 Sept. 1687, d. by 4 April 1737 (528:14).

DUTTON, ROBERT (2), s. of John (1), was b. 13 Sept. 1687 in Delaware Co., Penna., d. in Cecil Co., Md., between 1725 and 4 April 1737; m. 13 Sept. 1707 in Penna., Ann Brown, by whom he had iss.: MARY, b. 15 Aug. 1708, m. (---) Brown, and d. leaving a will made 13 June 1764 in which she named her bro. Robert Dutton; ANN, b. 10 Oct. 1711; ELIZABETH, b. 25 Jan. 1722; ROBERT, b. 26 Aug. 1713(210-37:19; 528:14, 15).

DUTTON, ROBERT (3), s. of Robert (2), was b. 26 Aug. 1713 in Cecil Co., d. 13 Sept. 1770 in Balto. Co.; m. 1st 11 Dec. 1744 Mary Merriken, and 2nd on 24 Feb. 1757 Susannah D. Howard, dau. of Lemuel and Ann Howard; in 1750 owned 559 a. Merriken's Inheritance, 130 a. George's Hill, and 93 a. Merriken's Branch; d. leaving a will, 5 Sept. 1770 - 6 Oct. 1770, which named ch., Robert, Mary, Elizabeth, John, and Anne, and a legacy from Lemuel Howard, family Bibles, and tract America's Inheritance; had iss., 4 by 1st w., and 3 by 2nd w.: MERRIKEN, b. 7 Aug. 1747; MARY, b. 20 March 1749, m. Benjamin Howard; ELIZABETH, b. 13 Nov. 1752; SARAH, b. 16 Nov. 1755; by 2nd w., had: ROBERT, b. 24 d, 12 mo., 1759; ANN, b. 23 day, 12 mo., 1761; JOHN, b. 23 Dec. 1761 (131:27, 119/r, 127/r, 129/r, 136/r; 136: 153:50; 112:150; 528:15).

DYER, DARBY, was in Balto. Co. by 1692 as a taxable in n. side Patapsco Hund. (138).

DYER, MARY, was ind. for bast. in March 1731 (29:225).

EAGAN, JAMES, m. Rachel (---), and had iss.: ELEANOR, b. 22 Feb. 1735 (128:114).

EAGAN, RICHARD, m. Elizabeth (---) and had iss.; JAMES, b. 7 May 1733; MARGARET, b. 18 Aug. 1735 (128:82, 90).

EAGAN, RICHARD, m. Catherine (---) and had iss.: RICHARD, b. 24 Aug. 1736; BARNETT, twin, b. 20 June 1740; HUGH, twin, b. 20 June 1740 (128:93b, 114).

EAGAN, SAMPSON, age 12 last Feb., was bound to James Eagan in June 1754 (39:185).

EAGER, GEORGE (1), progenitor, was in A. A. Co., Md., by 23 Sept. 1684, and d. by 10 July 1710, when his est. was admin.; m. by 1686 Mary (---), wid. of (---) Wheelock, and of Thomas Bucknall, 22 Dec. 1705 - 23 Jan. 1706, named sons Thomas, George, and John, and tracts Johnson's Dock and Luns Lot; his orig. exec., s. Thomas, had died, so est. was admin. 10 July 1710 by John Rattenbury and James Read; had iss.: THOMAS, b. 23 Sept. 1684; GEORGE, b. 20 March 1687; JOHN, b. 23 Feb. 1691 (2:157; 120: 125; 122:82; 206-10:70; 219-4).

EAGER, THOMAS (2), s. of George (1) and Mary, d. in Balto.

Co., leaving a will, 17 April 1708 - 3 May 1708, in which he
named his wife Mary (to have 250 a. Powell's Pumpkin Patch), bro.
John (to have 100 a. Lun's Point), and Dr. John Rattenbury and
James Read to be execs.; admin. bond was posted 3 May 1708; est.
was inv. 28 July 1708 by John Thomas and William Hawkins and val.
at L 457.7.6; and an additional inv. was filed 9 Nov. 1708, val.
at L 44.3.6 by John Thomas and William Wilkinson; est. was admin.
7 Oct. 1712 and in July 1719 (1:352; 2:183; 13:46; 50:331; 54:
25; 122:110).

EAGER, GEORGE (3), s. of George (1), was b. 20 March 1687 in
St. Margaret's Par., A. A. Co., and m. Hannah Pennington on 24
Aug. 1705 (219-2:390; 219-4).

EAGER, JOHN (4), s. of George (1), was b. 23 Feb. 1691 in St.
Margaret's Par., and d. in April 1722 in St. Paul's Par., Balto.
Co., and bur. 11 April; m. Jemima (---) who m. as her 2nd husb.
on 29 May 1723 Philip Jones; left a will, 10 April 1722 - 18 May
1722, which named w. Jemima, and ch. George (to have Powell's
Pumpkin Patch and Lunn's Point) and Ruth; the wid. claimed her
thirds on 18 May 1722 when she posted admin. bond with Thomas
Sheredine and Luke Trotten and Alexander Grant; est. admin. by
Philip and Jemima Jones on 6 Sept. 1725; had iss.: GEORGE, b. 9
Oct. 1718; in 1750 owned 130 a. Jones Chance, 200 a. Lunn's Lot
and Powell's Point; RUTH, b. 23 May 1721, m. Cornelius Howard
(3:43; 13:49; 124:103; 133:2, 146, 193; 153:16).

EAGLESTONE, JOHN (1), progenitor, was b. c.1674, d. by 1750;
gave his age as 60 in 1734; was in Balto. Co. by 1692 as a taxable in the household of Richard Cromwell; in June 1703 purch. part
Hab Nab at a Venture from Christopher Durbin; purch. 33 a. Eaglestone's Addition from Charles Gorsuch; purch. 24 a. Eagleston's
Inlet from Francis J. Holland in 1722; and 150 a. Ogg's Bashan
from George Ogg in Oct. 1736; wife's name is not known; had iss.:
ABRAHAM; poss. ISABELLA, who was ind. for bast. in Nov. 1738
(31:307; 59:551; 61:310; 66:252; 69:97; 138).

EAGLESTONE, ABRAHAM (2), s. of John, d. in Balto. Co. by 25
Oct. 1783; m. Charity Johns, dau. of Hugh and Ann Johns, on 20
Dec. 1730; in 1750 owned part Willin (Eaglestone's Addition which
his father had purch. from Charles Gorsuch was part of a larger
tract named Willin), 210 a. Abingdon's Enlargement, and 78 a. of
Roberts' Choice; left a will, 20 Oct. 1782 - 25 Oct. 1783, named
his s. Jonathan, grandson Abraham of Benjamin, daus. Mary Stans
bury and Elizabeth Green, dau. Ann Davis, dau. Charity w. of Wm.
Slayter, son Henry and his daus. Charity and Mary, son Thomas
and his daus., son Benjamin and his ch., son-in-law Vincent Green;
left iss.: JOHN, b. 4 Oct. 1733, m. by 29 March 1768 one of the
heirs of Tobias Stansbury; ABRAHAM, b. 20 Dec. 1734; HENRY, b. 2
Feb. 1735/6; RICHARD, b. 26 May 1737; BENJAMIN, d. by 1 Sept.
1786 having m. Sarah Dallas; THOMAS, d. by 25 Nov. 1780 having
m. Chloe Dallas; JONATHAN, d. by 11 Feb. 1791, m. Eleanor (---);
MARY, m. George Stansbury; ELIZABETH, m. Vincent Green; ANN, b.
20 April 1749, m. (---) Davis; CHARITY, m. William Slayter (7:
321; 8:164; 9:191; 10:107; 112:494; 133:40, 46, 54, 84; 153:30).

EALES, WILLIAM, was in Balto. Co. by 1692 as a taxable in
s. side Gunpowder Hund. (138).

EARL, ELIZABETH, serv. to Aquila Massey, was tried for bast. in Aug. 1739 (32:13).

EARL, JAMES, servant, with 6 mos. to serve in 1736 inv. of William Wood (53:27).

EARP, JOSHUA, s. of John and Mary (dau. of William Budd of Balto. Co.), was deeded land called Timber Neck in Sept. 1737 (213-PL#8:558).

EASTWOOD/YESTWOOD, MICHAEL, d. 26 May 1739; m. Elizabeth (---) on 30 June 1729; left 25 a. Margaret's Purchase to his heirs; had iss.: JAMES, b. 7 June 1730, was bound to John Graton to age 21; HANNAH, b. 3 Feb. 1732, in Aug. 1745 was bound to Antil and Sarah Deaver; MARY, b. 12 June 1734, d. 1 Oct. 1738; ELIZABETH, b. 2 Dec. 1736, d. 12 Sept. 1738; MICHAEL, b. 18 Jan. 1738, d. 18 Sept. 1738 (35:615; 128:84, 94, 102, 111; 153:47).

EATON, JEREMIAH, Gent., of Kent Co., d. there in 1676; in Aug. 1672 purch. 550 a. Stoakley Manor on Bush River from Vinson Elliott, boatwright (98:48).

EAVES/EVES/EWES, EDWARD, m. Lucy Ann Pine on 17 Feb. 1752 and had iss.: WILLIAM, b. 23 Feb. 1752; ANN, b. March 1754 (131:39, 131/r).

EAVES, GEORGE, was b. c.1668, and gave his age as 75 in 1743; in March 1718/9 the court had Joseph Compton bound to him to age 21; may be the George Eaves who m. Mary Costley on 1 Sept. 1714, and had iss.: ELIZABETH, b. 23 April 1716 (23:70; 128:32, 34; 164:92).

EAVES, RALPH, was in Balto. Co. by 1695 as a taxable in n. side Gunpowder Hund.; d. by 20 Nov. 1703 when his est. was admin. by Robert Cutchin who posted bond with John Low and Richard Perkins (2:220; 13:42; 140:18).

EBDEN, WILLIAM (1), and w. Jane were in Balto. Co. by 1669 when he surv. 100 a. Hockley (later held by Col. Edward Dorsey); surv. 100 a. Gooseberry Neck in May 1673 and conv. it to Jonas Bowen in April 1676; surv. 180 a. Forsebury Neck in July 1676; d. by 8 May 1678 when admin. bond was posted by wid. and admnx. Jane, with Michael Judd, and Symon Dawkins cooper; by March 1691/2 wid. Jane had m. 2nd Michael Judd; had iss.: WILLIAM (13: 43; 19:156; 101:301; 211:35, 87, 101).

EBDEN, WILLIAM (2), s. of William (1) and Jane, was of age by 1692 when he was listed as a taxable in n. side Gunpowder Hund.; in March 1691/2 was ref. to in court as the "natural son" of Jane, now w. of Michael Judd; in Nov. 1694 Thomas Cannon, orph. of Thomas Cannon was living with his bro. William Ebden; in Aug. 1698 Thomas Cannon, s. of Thomas, dec., conv. half of Collett's Neglect to William Ebden; in Sept. 1698 William and his w. Elizabeth conv. 300 a. part Collett's Neglect to John Armstrong of A. A. Co.; later his wid. Elizabeth held 150 a. of tract John's Interest (orig. surv. for Michael Judd) for William's orphans; d. by 1699 when his admnx. Elizabeth posted admin. bond with

James Phillips and John Rallings; his est. was inv. on 6 May 1699 by Israel Skelton and Samuel Sickelmore, and val. at Ł 103.7.10 plus 5074 lbs. tob.; had iss.: WILLIAM, in March 1709 bound to Roger Matthews; JAMES, in Nov. 1709 was bound to John Stokes to age 21 (13:46; 19:165; 20:336; 21:69, 95; 48:83; 63:282, 289; 138:6; 211:42).

ECKLER, ULRICK, d. in Balto. Co. by 27 May 1762; left will, 30 Dec. 1761 - 27 May 1762, named eld. s. Ulrick (to have 150 a. on Pipe Creek), s. Joseph (to have 150 a. on Bar Creek), ment. two daus.; the Great Bible and two Christian books were to remain betw. his two sons; est. was admin. on 5 July 1763 by exec. Ulrick, who named four other ch.; dec. left iss.: ULRICK; JOSEPH; JACOB; ANNE, w. of Henry Buker; and MAGDALENA, w. of Nicholas Holstader (6:62; 111:129).

EDMONDS/EDMUNDS, RICHARD (1), d.Balto. Co. prior to May 1694 when his est. was admin. by Eliza Gibson (late Edmonds); the acct. ment. her late husb. Henry Hazlewood; est. was worth Ł 132. 11.13 plus 27,250 lbs. tob.; on 1 May 1699 Elizabeth Gibson conv. prop. to her son Thomas Edmonds; had iss.: THOMAS (63:347; 206-12:151).

EDMONDS, THOMAS (2), s. of Richard (1) and Eliza, was conv. prop. by his mother in May 1669; d. 23 Dec. 1705; was bur. 29 Dec. 1705; admin. bond posted 27 Jan. 1705/6 by Richard Cromwell with Thomas Bale and Michael Dollison; est. inv. on 1 Feb. 1705/6 by Thomas Cord and Sam. Jackson and val. at Ł 136.17.4; est. was admin. by Richard Cromwell in Sept. 1707 (2:145; 13:44; 48:38; 63:347; 129:203).

EDMONDS, MARY, dau. of Elizabeth Ellis, was b. 16 Feb. 1705 (128:19).

EDMONDS, THOMAS, was in Balto. Co. by June 1665 when he conv. 300 a. The Dividing to William Price (94).

EDNEY, THOMAS, m. Eleanor Thornton on 1 Dec. 1737 (133:160).

EDWARDS, MOSES (1), was in Balto. Co. by 1692 as a taxable in n. side Patapsco Hund., and d. 6 Aug. 1727; in June 1702 conv. 282 a. Come By Chance to John Cole; in June 1705 was conv. 89 a. by William and Tamar Wilkinson; took up Edwards' Lot in Jan. 1701 and Edwards' Enlargement in Oct. 1707 (both in the vicinity of North Ave. and York Road, Balto.); in March 1694/5 was named by Capt. John Oldton to be one of the Rangers of Balto. Co.; may have had at least one s.: JOHN (66:256; 67:284; 133:148; 153:4).

EDWARDS, JOHN (2), poss. s. of Moses (1) above, was in Balto. Co. by 23 Jan. 1727 when he m. Mary Merryman, dau. of John and Martha (Bowen) Merryman; Mary d. 16 April 1791; in 1750 he was listed as the owner of 218 a. Come By Chance; d. leaving a will, 14 Oct. 1769 - 10 July 1770, in which he named his w. Mary and these children (whose births are recorded in St. Paul's Par.): MOSES, b. 27 Jan. 1728; MARY, b. 16 Aug. 1730, m. (---) Tudor; ALICE, b. 18 June 1732, m. (---) Pedigo; EDWARD, b. 1 Jan. 1734; JOHN, b. 19 March 1737; MARTHA, b. 18 Jan. 1739, m. (---) Knight;

CHARLES; JOSEPH; BENJAMIN; TEMPERANCE (112:148; 133:4, 16, 17, 23, 39, 67, 148; 153:4).

EDWARDS, MOSES (3), s. of John (2) and Mary, was b. 27 Jan. 1728; m. Ann Pickett on 1 May 1753 (131; 133).

EDWARDS, EDWARD (4), s. of John (2) and Mary, was b. 1 Jan. 1734; m. Cas. Beard on 1 April 1762 (131; 133).

EDWARDS, JOHN (5), s. of John (2) and Mary, was b. 19 March 173EP' m. Unity Legatt on 23 Nov. 1769 (131; 133).

EDWARDS, JOHN, of Balto. Co., imm. to Md. by c.1678 (388).

EDWARDS, JOHN, Minister of the Gospel, settled in St. John's Par., 1702; may have been the s. of Thomas Edwards of Llanwrthwl whose s. John was b. c.1678 and matric. at Merton Coll., Oxford University in Feb. 1694/5 age 17, took his A.B. in March 1698/9, and took the King's Bounty for Md. in May 1701; Rev. John of St. John's Par.. was in St. Marys Co. on 1 Jan. 1710/11 when he made a will leaving his prop. to his godson John Stokes, s. of John (122:209; 200-38:140-141; 428:209).

EDWARDS, PHILIP, and w. Ann on 28 Aug. 1758 conv. 350 a.Edwards' Discovery to John Brunts (83:236).

EDWARDS, ROBERT, mariner, of merchant ship Patapsco, was named as the father of Sarah Doe's child in Aug. 1714 (21:537).

EDWARDS, THOMAS, d. 23 Dec. 1705 (128:20).

EDWARDS, WILLIAM, m. Jane Broad on 17 Sept. 1748 (131).

EDWARDS, WILLIAM, m. Lusandah (---), and had iss.: ELIZABETH, b. 13 Jan. 1750; THOMAS, b. 11 Nov. 1753; WILLIAM, b. 2 Nov. 1755; JOHN, b. 30 Oct. 1758; CHARLES, b. 26 Dec. 1759; EPHRAIM, b. 25 Nov. 1762 (133:100, 117).

EDWARDS, WILLIAM, m. Mary Manes on 12 April 1760 and had iss.: WILLIAM, b. 16 Sept. 1760 (131:56, 65/r).

EDY. See ADY.

EELES, JOHN, was in Balto. Co. by 1694 as a taxable in n. side of Gunpowder Hund. (139:12).

EGERTON, GEORGE, was tried for begetting an illeg. ch. on the body of Mary Chamney in March 1733/4 (30:199).

ELBERTON, JOHN, d. by 24 Jan. 1708/9 when admin. bond was posted by Thomas Morris with Moses Groome and Samuel Jackson (13:47).

ELDER, DAVID, was in Balto. Co. by 1695 as a taxable on s. side of Patapsco Hund. (140).

ELDESLEY, HENRY, was in Balto. Co. by March 1669/70 when he bought 275 a. from Thomas Howell, Gent., and w. Elizabeth; in March 1670/1 with w. Parnell he conv. 100 a. to James Wrath; he conv. land to Wrath again in Nov. 1673 (96; 97; 99).

ELINGER, CATHERINE, age 10 in June 1754, was bound to Thomas Thornton (39:185).

ELINGER, GEORGE, age 13 in June 1754, was bound to Thomas Thornton (39:185).

ELLARD, DANIEL, was in Balto. Co. by 1695 as a taxable in n. side Patapsco Hund. (138:3).

ELLEDGE, FRANCIS, s. of Joseph, was in Balto. Co. as a minor when he comp. against James Crooke; Francis was comm. to the custody of John Hays until Crooke answered the complaint (21:471, 473).

ELLEDGE, JOSEPH, was living in Balto. Co. in 1730 when he and w. Elizabeth conv. to John Taylor 100 a. Better Hopes; in Oct. 1736 Joseph and Elizabeth conv. Joseph Murray 50 a. Elledges Farm orig. surv. for Joseph Elledge in March 1731 (61:308; 73:59).

ELLEDGE, JOSEPH, m. Mary Rhodes, dau. of Richard and Magdalena, on 4 Sept. 1733; they had iss.: MARY, b. 21 June 1734; ABRAHAM, b. 17 Feb. 1736; ISAAC, b. 20 Aug. 1740 (131:15/r, 46/r, 53/r, 85/r).

ELLLEDGE, THOMAS, and w. Elizabeth, dau. of John Thornbury, dec., were in Bedford Co., Va., when they conv. 100 a. Sellsed to Benjamin Bowen (90:97).

ELLETT. See ELLIOTT.

ELLING, FRANCIS, was in Balto. Co. by 2 Nov. 1665 when he and Christopher Tapley were conv. 100 a. by James Phillips (95).

ELLINGSWORTH, RICHARD, was in Balto. Co. by 1 March 1668/9 when John Dixon conv. him 300 a. Dixon's Chance; d. c.1700 when his orphans held 124 a. Richardson's Reserve (95; 211).

ELLITT. See ELLIOTT.

ELLIOTT/ELLETT/ELLITT, THOMAS (1), m. Sarah (--), and had iss.: JUDITH, b. 19 March 1708; JUDE, b. 29 March 1709, m. Thomas Palmer on 28 Dec. 1732; THOMAS, b. 18 Nov. 1711 (as s. of Thomas and MARY, sic); WILLIAM, b. 18 June 1715 (128:28; 131:10, 53/r).

ELLIOTT, THOMAS (2), s. of Thomas (1), was b. 18 Nov. 1711; m. in Nov. 1736 Elizabeth Barton, b. 28 Jan. 1717, dau. of Thomas and Abigail Barton; m. 2nd by Aug. 1746 Ann (---), when he conv. to William Bennett the tract Expectation formerly belonging to Thomas Barton (79:198).

ELLIOTT, WILLIAM (3), s. of Thomas (1), was b. 18 June 1715; d. by 16 March 1767 when his est. was admin. by John Hammond Dorsey; in 1743 Thomas Johnson conv. him part of Giles and Webster's Discovery, of which William still owned 98 a. in 1750; had iss.: PEARCY, b. b. 12 Feb. 1741/2; WILLIAM, b. 13 Nov. 1743; THOMAS (in 1795 conv. to William Morgan one-half of the tract Giles and Webster's Discovery conv. to William Elliott by

Thomas Johnson); EDWARD (in 1795 was living on part. Giles and
Webster's Discovery); MARY, b. 12 Oct. 1752; SAMUEL, b. 30 Jan.
1755; RACHEL, b. 15 Feb. 1757; ELIZABETH, b. 24 Sept. 1759 (7:
284; 128:114; 129:332, 335, 371; 153:67; 241-JLG#M:507).

ELLIOTT, ANN, d. 15 June 1747 (131:118/r).

ELLIOTT, EDWARD, was in Balto. Co. by 1692 as a taxable in
n. side Gunpowder Hund. (138).

ELLIOTT, GEORGE, m. Patience, wid. of Richard Colegate and
William Buckner, on 12 Jan. 1732; on 5 Nov. 1737 Thomas and Ann
Bond conv. George Elliott 163 a. Colegate's Last Shift; in Nov.
1737 George and Patience conv. 663 a. Friends Discovery and
Colegate's Last Shift to Benjamin Wheeler (3:150; 4:42; 75:35, 54;
133:147, 151).

ELLIOTT, GEORGE, m. by July 1736 Ann (---) when the vestry of
St. John's Par. summoned them both for unlawful cohabitation;
in Aug. 1743 Ann was reported to the vestry for unlawful cohabitation with John Elliott; is is prob. this George Elliott who
in 1736 leased 100 a. Chamberlain's Inheritance, part Gunpowder
Manor, for the lifetimes of Ann Elliott (age c.75 in 1767) and
Susanna Westwood (age c.45 in 1767) (132:14, 64; 389:3).

ELLIOTT, GEORGE, in 1741 purch. 180 a. United Friendship from
James Isham, Jr.; Geo. conv. the 180 a. to Henry Morgan in June
1746 (75:543; 79:259).

ELLIOTT, GEORGE, in 1746 leased 100 a. Elliott's Success from
Benjamin Tasker for a term of 99 years (79:178).

ELLIOTT, GEORGE, d. by 18 June 1748 when admin. bond on his
est. was posted by Darby Henley with James Moore and William
Wright; est. was admin. in July 1751 by Henley who stated that
the dec. had no known rel. in Province; est. was admin. by James
Moore in March 1754 (5:181; 13:51; 37:254; 39:24).

ELLIOTT, JAMES, m. Mary Weecks on 29 Dec. 1736; left a will,
14 Jan. 1785 - 28 Sept. 1786, in which he named w. Mary, and these
ch. (births recorded in St. John's Par.): JEMIMA, b. 30 Nov. 1738,
w. of (---) Enloes; JOHN, b. 6 Jan. 1740; JAMES, b. 29 March 1742;
MARY, b. 24 May 1744, w. of (---) Enloes; MICHAEL, b. 29 Oct.
1747; SARAH, b. 24 Jan. 1749, w. of (---) Robinson; WILLIAM;
SUSANNA, w. of (---) McNeill; KEZIAH, w. of (---) Hooper; ELIZA-
BETH, w. of (---) McBroom; KERRENHAPPUCK, w. of (---) McBroom
(113:173; 131:101/r, 121/r, 123/r).

ELLIOTT, JAMES, in 1750 owned 200 a. Elliott's Risque (153:10).

ELLIOTT, JAMES, m. Temperance Armstrong on 8 May 1753 (131).

ELLIOTT, JAMES, m. Agnes Harris on 29 Dec. 1757; left a will,
4 Nov. 1784 - 16 Nov. 1784, naming sons John in Carolina, grandson James Elliott, wife Agnes (to have all his est. and to be co-
exec. with William Johnson/Johnston); daus. Agnes (w. of William

Johnson) and dau. Sarah (131; Harford Co. Wills, Book AJ#2, p. 190).

ELLIOTT, JOHN, was in Balto. Co. by 1723 when he and others agreed on the boundaries of United Friendship; on 15 Aug. 1730 he and w. Sarah conv. 25 a. Small Hopes to Richard Sampson; on 8 Nov. 1733, John conv. 20 a. United Friendship to James Isham; m. 1st Sarah (---), who was summoned with him in July 1736 by the vestry of St. John's Par. for unlawful cohabitation; in Aug. 1743 his w. Sarah complained that John was unlawfully cohabiting with Ann Elliott, w. of George Elliott; had iss.: RHODA, b. 20 March 1720/1 (69:127; 73:5; 74:2; 131:38/r; 132:14, 64).

ELLIOTT, JOHN, in Oct. 1724 was assigned 200 a. by Skelton Standiford which Elliott had surv. in March 1725 and pat. as Elliott's Risque in Sept. 1728; about 18 years later JAMES ELLIOTT (see above) had a cert. for 104 a. Elliott's Interest, which incl. 33 a. Elliott's Risque (389:7).

ELLIOTT, JOHN, m. Unity (---), and had iss.: FAITHEY, b. 5 Jan. 1739; WILLIAM, b. 9 April 1744 (129:313, 336).

ELLIOTT, MARBERILL, m. Jemima Standiford on 13 Jan. 1756 (131).

ELLIOTT, MARGARET, had iss.: ELIZABETH, b. March 1756 (131: 59/r).

ELLIOTT, MARY, m. 7 Nov. 1707 John Murphew (129:245)

ELLIOTT, PHILIP, m. Sarah Wright on 22 Dec. 1752 (131).

ELLIOTT, THOMAS, in 1742 conv. 360 a. Elliott's Tents to William Dallam (77:360).

ELLIOTT, THOMAS, m. Ann Robinson, sis. of Charles Robinson, on 14 April 1748 (112:233; 131).

ELLIOTT, THOMAS, m. Rebecca Norris (b. 15 Sept. 1729, dau. of John Norris) on 30 Jan. 1753 (131).

ELLIOTT, VINSON, was in Balto. Co. by 6 Aug. 1672 when he conv. 550 a. Stoakley Manor to Jeremiah Eaton; as Vincent Ellet had claimed land for service in 1668 and in Sept. 1669 had surv. 550 a. called "Stocktylemoe" which he gave for the maintenance of a protestant minister (98:48; 211:51; 388).

ELLIS, PETER (1), was transp. to Md. by 1664; was in Balto. Co. by 1680 when he claimed land for service; in June 1676 was conv. 75 a. Beaver Neck by Thomas and Jane Overton; in Aug. 1679 he and w. Elizabeth conv. 70 a. Beaver Neck to Simon Dawkins; in Sept. 1683 surv. 350 a. Expectation which was later held by the heirs of John Ellis; prob. had at least one s.: JOHN (60:41; 63:235; 211:17; 388).

ELLIS, JOHN (2), prob. s. of Peter (1) and Elizabeth, was in Balto. Co. in March 1702 conv. Miles Hannis 50 a. called Bedlam, part of Expectation; in March 1702 conv. Cadwallader Jones

100 a. of Expectation; in March 1704 conv. 100 a. of the same
tract to Samuel Jackson (60:132; 64:7; 66:287).

ELLIS, CHARLES, d. by 12 Jan. 1713/4 when admin. bond was posted by Thomas Todd with Nicholas Rogers; est. inv. 12 Sept. 1713
by Jno. Eager and Jos'h Hood and val. at £ 12.5.10; est. admin.
by Todd on 18 Oct. 1714; dec. left no relations (1:25; 13:45;
48:150).

ELLIS, ELIZABETH, had iss.: MARY EDMUNDS, b. 16 Feb. 1705/6
(129:202).

ELLIS, JAMES, was in Balto. Co. by July 1673 when he surv. 210
a. Chance, or Ellis' Chance, later held by Robert Welsh; in Sept.
1683 surv. 500 a. James Park, which was later held by his orphans
and then by Mary Ellis; d. in A. A. Co., leaving a will, 14 April
1683 - 25 Aug. 1693, which named w. Mary (formerly w. of Maj.
John Welsh), wife's son Robert Welsh, and his own dau. Mary who
was not yet 16; James' Park was to go to dau. Mary, and Ellis'
Chance was to go to Robert Welsh(121:52; 211:48, 49, 111).

ELLIS, JANE, had iss.: SARAH, b. 14 Nov. 1750 (134:19).

ELLIS, MARY, m. Cadwallader Jones on 23 April 1702 and was
bur. 17 June 1703 (128:21; 129:196).

ELLIS, MARY, m. William Costley on 26 Dec. 1709 (129:208).

ELLSOM, ROBERT, m. Jane Taylor on 15 Dec. 1735, and had s.:
THOMAS, b. 20 June 1736 (133).

ELMES, JOHN, was in Balto. Co. by 1692 as a taxable in n.
side Patapsco Hund. (138).

ELSTON, ROBERT, m. Elizabeth Parker on 1 Aug. 1731 (128:62).

ELWIES, LION, serv. with 4 years to serve, was listed in the
1732 inv. of Rowland Shepherd (53:120).

ELWOOD, RICHARD, m. Mary Lindsay on 9 Oct. 1748 (131).

THE EMERSON FAMILY has been discussed by Robert Barnes in
"The Em(er)son-Cobb-Hawkins Connection," Maryland Magazine of
Genealogy, vol. 4, no. 2 (Fall 1981), pp. 67-73.

EMERSON, JAMES (1), also known as James Empson or Emson,
was in Calvert Co., Md., in 1686 as the husb. of Rebecca, wid.
of John Darnall; Emerson was exec. and legatee of William Har-
butt in latter's will of 26 Jan. 1699; moved to Balto. Co. by
Nov. 1703 when Thomas Thurston, s. of late Col. Thomas Thurston,
sold 500 a. Elberton to James "Empson of Cal. Co.;" d/ in St.
George's Par., leaving a will, 5 Jan. 1707/8 - 31 Jan. 1707/8,
named his w. Rebecca as extx., and ch. James (not yet 17), Eliza,
Rebecca, and Anne; his est. was admin. 9 Oct. 1710 by the extx.
Rebecca now w. of James Cobb; Rebecca later m. John Hawkins, Sr.;
dec. left iss.: JAMES, not yet 16 in 1707; ELIZA, m. 1st Mark

Whitaker on 13 Feb. 1717, and 2nd on 6 Oct. 1729 Francis Taylor;
REBECCA, b. 12 March 1701 in Calvert Co., m. John Hawkins, Jr.,
on 23 Dec. 1718; ANNE, m. Cornelius Poulson on 23 Dec. 1720;
RACHEL, b. 7 June 1708 (after her father's death), m. Gregory
Farmer on 14 June 1723 (2:147; 122:104; 128; 129; Barnes, op.
cit., pp. 67-68).

· EMERSON, JAMES (2), s. of James (1) and Rebecca, d. 21 Feb.
1719/20 (128:37).

EMERSON, HENRY, illeg. s. of Mary Emerson (serv. to John Price)
was bound to said Price in June 1732 (29:297).

EMERSON, MARY, serv. of John Price, was tried for bast. in
June 1734; had s. HENRY, b. by June 1732 (29:297; 30:264)

EMERSON, TOBIAS, m. 1st Mary Bur on 10 Dec. 1704, and 2nd
Elizabeth (---); d. by 6 April 1724 when admin. bond was posted
by admnx. Elizabeth Emerson with Thomas Taylor and Charles Wells;
est. inv. in 1724; and admin. by Elizabeth Emerson on 2 April
1725 and 8 June 1731; had dau. (---), b. 29 Dec. 1708 (3:30, 98;
13:41; 26:482; 51:227, 228; 128:22, 25).

EMES, JOHN, m. Elizabeth Stiles on Sept. 1749 (131).

EMMETT, SAMUEL, m. by 4 Sept. 1760 Mary, dau. of William Jenkins (6:24; 210-31:316).

EMMETT, WILLIAM, of Balto. Co., claimed land for service in
1673 (388).

EMORY, ROBERT, m. by 14 March 1722 or 1726 Anne, wid. of Wm.
Hawkins (1:146).

ENGLAND, JOHANNES (1), m. Amice (---) and lived in Burton-
on-Trent, Staffordshire, Eng., and had s.: LUDOVIC (LOUIS),
bapt. 5 Feb. 1677 (Church of Jesus Christ of Latter Day Saints,
International Genealogy Index: Staffordshire, July 1984).

ENGLAND, LOUIS (2), s. of Johannes (John) (1), as Ludovic was
bapt. 5 Feb. 1677 at Burton-on-Trent, m. Sarah (---), and were
prob. the par. of: JOSEPH (136).

ENGLAND, JOSEPH (3), s. of Louis and Sarah, was b. 11 d, 4
mo., 1716 at "Benton-on-Trent," prob. Burton-on-Trent, Staffordshire, Eng.; d. by 8 Aug. 1763 in Balto. Co., Md.; m. 20 d, 2
mo. (April) 1742 Elizabeth Dutton, dau. of Robert Dutton of
Northeast, Cecil Co., Md.; was in Balto. Co. by Oct. 1747 when
he purch. 100 a. Fox Hall from John and Catherine Evans; in 1750
was listed as the owner of Fox Hall; est. admin. by Elizabeth
England and William Amos on 8 Aug. 1763 and 27 Feb. 1764; had
iss.: ROBERT, b. 7 Sept. 1743; WILLIAM, b. and d. 1745; HANNAH,
b. 12 Nov. 1746; JOSEPH, Jr., b. 11 July 1749, moved to London
Grove MM, Pa., in 1765; GEORGE, b. 3 Nov. 1751; JOHN, b. 20 Feb.
1755; SAMUEL, b. 23 July 1757; ELIZABETH, b. 26 June 1760 (6:22,
82; 79:580; 136; 153:83).

ENGLAND, JOSEPH, m. by 22 Jan. 1721 Margaret, dau. of John
Cotterell, and had iss.; JEMIMA, b. 11 Sept. 1723 (125:62; 128:
43).

ENGLISH, DENNIS, may be the Dennis English who was transp. by
1663 or the Dennis English who was an imm. to Md., c.1669; in Nov.
1675 purch. 75 a. Hazle Park from Rutgerston Garrett; d. by 16
Sept. 1687 when his est. was admin. by Col. George Wells, admin.
of Nicholas and Ann Brown who were English's orig. admins. (101:
303; 206-9:427; 388).

ENGLISH, JOHN, was in Balto. Co. by 1694 as a taxable in Spesutia Hund. (139).

ENLOES, HENDRICK (1), progenitor, was in Balto. Co. by 1674
and d. there c.1707/8; m. by 5 Nov. 1679 Christian (---) who surv.
him; as a Dutchman was naturalized by Act of the Legis. of 6 June
1674; took up lands, incl. Dutch Neck in and 100 a. Tryangle Neck
in May 1673, 100 a. Swallow Fork in May 1683, 150 a. The Oblong
in June 1687, and 33 a. Low Lands in March 1687; with w. Christian
conv. 100 a. Inloes Loyne to John Boring in Nov. 1679, and 100 a.
Swallow Fork to John Fuller in Aug. 1682; his will, 10 Dec. 1707 -
18 May 1708, named w. Christian, s. Abraham, the heirs of s. John,
daus. Hester and Margaret, also Christian Wright and Henry Galma;
had iss.: HENRY (not in will); ABRAHAM; JOHN; HESTER; MARGARET,
m. 1st William Galloway and 2nd by 5 Oct. 1709 James Durham (48:
6; 59; 60:44; 122:53; 145; 211:66, 67; 404).

ENLOES, HENRY (2), s. of Hendrick (1), was alive in Kent Co.
in June 1728 when he signed a quitclaim on a deed for Sawyer's
Choice, taken up by his father Hendrick "Inloes" in June 1661;
his w. Mary joined him in the deed (71:219).

ENLOES, ABRAHAM (3), s. of Hendrick (1), d. in Balto. Co. c.
1709; m. Eliza (---) who m. 2nd, by March 1709/10 John Ensor; in
April 1700 he and w. Elizabeth conv. Enloes Cover to William Holland; his will, 24 April 1709 - 20 July 1709, named sons John and
Anthony (to have 100 a. Tryangle Neck), s. William (to have 50 a.
Duck Neck), s. Abraham (to have 50 a.), dau. Margaret, and an unborn ch., with w. Elizabeth as extx.; admin. bond posted 20 July
1709 by extx. Elizabeth Enloes with William Farfarr and William
Wright; est. inv. 5 Oct. 1709 by Luke Raven and Daniel Scott, val.
at £ 96.11.5, signed by extx. Elizabeth Enloes, sis. Margaret
Durham, and cous. Mary Enloes as kin and William Wright and Edward Stevenson as creditors; est. admin. on 6 Oct. 1720; left
iss.: ANTHONY, d. 1750; JOHN; WILLIAM; ABRAHAM; MARGARET; and a
poss. unborn ch. (1:180; 13:43; 21:133; 48:6; 66:27; 122:145).

ENLOES, JOHN (4), s. of Hendrick (1), was alive in 1701; m.
Elizabeth (---), who may have m. as her 2nd husb. John Lorkings
or Leakings who held 100 a. Swallow Fork and 50 a. Salisbury
Plain for the orph. of John Enloes; est. was admin. by Lorkings
and w. Eliza (date not given); had iss.: ABRAHAM, b. c.1701, age
13 on 20 March 1714 and in June bound to serve Charles and Hannah
Simmons; HENRY, in June 1714 bound to William Wright (2:230; 3:
145; 21:406, 505; 211:66).

ENLOES, ANTHONY (5), s. of Abraham (3), d. by 1752; m. Eleanor
(---) who m. 2nd William Grover; in 1750 owned 100 a. Tryangle,
62 a. Inloes Rest, and 33 a. Low Lands and 100 a. Duck Neck; left
a will, 12 Sept. 1750 - 18 Oct. 1750, which named s. Abraham,
daus. Elizabeth and Eleanor, unborn ch., and mentioned his w.;
admin. bond was posted 14 Dec. 1750 by extx. Eleanor, with Moses
Galloway and Abra. Enloes; est. admin. by William Grover and w.
Ellinor on 15 April 1752 and 16 Nov. 1752; left iss.: ABRAHAM;
ELEANOR; ELIZABETH, and poss. unborn ch. (5:262, 263; 13:51; 111:
33; 153:18).

ENLOES, ABRAHAM (6), s. of Abraham (3), was b. c.1705, and d.
1758 in Balto. Co.; m. Mary Deason in 1730; she admin. his est.;
in 1733 he leased 100 a. Gunpowder Manor for the lifetimes of
ary, age 55, and Benjamin, age 28; admin. bond was posted 25
Jan. 1758 by admnx. Mary Enloes with James Elliott and William
Ensor; est. admin. by Mary Enloes who noted that the dec. left
ten ch.; had iss.: ANTHONY, b. Aug. 1731; ABARILLA, b. 1734, m.
Robert Gardner; BENJAMIN, b. 19 Jan. 1738; SARAH, b. 16 Feb.
1740; ENOCH, b. 1741, d. 1799 in York Co., S. C.; ISAAC, b. 13
Feb. 1745, d. 10 June 1819 in York Co., S. C.; ABRAHAM; THOMAS,
m. Sarah James; MARY; DEASON; and CHRISTOPHER (6:17; 13:53; 131:
74/r, 75/r, 87/r; 389:8; see also Thomas A. Enloe Gen. Coll.,
MS # 5099 at MHS).

ENLOES, HENRY (7), s. of John (4), was b. c.1684, and was
the father of: ABRAHAM, b. c.1726/9, d. 1808 in Washington Co.,
Penna.; m. Jemima Elliott. (Thos. A. Enloe Gen. Coll.).

ENLOES, ABRAHAM (8), s. of Henry (7), was b. c.1726/9, d.
1808 in Washington Co., Penna.; m. Jemima Elliott on 28 Nov. 1754
(131; Thos. A. Enloe Gen. Coll.).

ENLOES, ABRAHAM, in June 1759 was fined for bast., having been
named by Rashia Morgan as the father of her child (29:211).

ENLOES, ANTHONY, d. by 5 July 1761, leaving a dau. who m. Joseph Thompson (85:462).

ENLOES, HENRY, m. Mary Elliott on 26 May 1763 (131).

ENLOES, JOHN, and Sarah Leggatt were summoned by the vestry of
St. John's Par. for unlawful cohabitation (131:2).

ENLOES, MARY, m. Thomas Johnson on 3 Sept. 1716 (131).

ENNIS, WILLIAM, m. Ruth (---), and had iss.: JOHN, b. 7 Nov.
1737; See also ANNIS. (128:104).

ENOCH, RICHARD, was in Balto. Co. by June 1684 when he and
Francis Freeman were conv. 111 a. by Thomas Long; was k. by Indians c.Feb. 1687/8; Enoch's w. and Francis Freeman were also woun-
ded; in June 1692 his two orphans were placed in care of Edward
Jones (19:185; 106:289; 200-8:5).

THE ENSOR FAMILY has three separate and so far unrelated progenitors in Baltimore County: John, Thomas, and George. In

addition to three separate families, there were a number of
references to persons named John Ensor in 17th century Anne Arundel and Baltimore Counties. It is difficult to tell whether all
or some of the references refer to the same person or to separate
persons.

JOHN ENSOR was b. c.1665, giving his age as 50 when he made a
deposition in 1715; by 1 Aug. 1691 had m. Jane, with whom he
posted admin. bond on the est. of John Maynard, with Hugh Jones
and William Gaine as securities; Ensor admin. the est. of Maynard on 23 May 1696; Jane may have d. and Ensor felt no more
responsibility for the est. of Maynard for in 1706 Hugh Jones
and William Gaine inv. the est. of Maynard; 3 Nov. 1697 Capt.
John Oldton sold 300 a. Darley Hall to John Ensor; 11 Nov. 1700
John and Jane Ensor wit. the will of Nathaniel Ruxton of Balto.
Co.; 25 June 1709 Ensor gave bond he would conv. to Grace Ramsey 100 a. Bald Friars formerly owned by John Cole; 15 Dec. 1713
Ensor sold Richard Taylor 1 a. of Friendship part of a larger
tract Darley Hall; Ensor's w. Elizabeth joined him in this deed;
on 9 Nov. 1716 John and Elizabeth Ensor signed the inv. of Lewis
Barton; Ensor died by 6 Oct. 1720 when Elizabeth Ensor, extx. of
Abraham Enloes admin. the est. and referred to statements made
earlier by her dec. husb. John Ensor(2:133; 48:172; 64:104; 67:
120, 277; 121:202; 206-38B:158; 209-16:170; 210-12:144).

There was a John Ensor in A. A. Co. who m. the wid. Elizabeth
Hines Evans on 14 May 1700; d. c.1706-7 and his wid. m. Thomas
Crane on 16 Sept. 1707; Crane and his w. filed an admin. acct.
of Ensor's est. on 17 Nov. 1710 (219-1:76).

THE JOHN ENSOR FAMILY

ENSOR, JOHN (1), progenitor, is probably the John Ensor of
the first paragraph above, who was b. c.1665; d. by 6 Oct. 1720;
m. 1st by 1691 Jane, admnx. of John Maynard, and 2nd by 1713
Elizabeth, extx. of Abraham Enloes; had iss., prob. by 1st w.:
JOHN, Jr., b. c.1695; JANE, b. c.1694/8, m. Thomas Gorsuch ;
poss. ABRAHAM; poss. ANN who m. John Stansbury on 12 Feb. 1733/4
(data from Fred Chilcott of San Diego, CA., and Ronald Cofiell
of San Francisco, CA., made available to the author).

ENSOR, JOHN (2), s. of John (1), was b. c.1695, and d. in
Balto. Co. in 1773; m. Elizabeth Cole, dau. of John and Johanna
(Garrett) Cole; on 7 July 1731 John conv. 100 a. Ensor's Choice
to Thomas Gorsuch; in Aug. 1731 William and Martha Maynor conv.
80 a. Maynor's Privilege to John; by 1750 owned 300 a. Darley
Hall, 100 a. Daniel's Whimsey, 200 a. Chevey Chase, 80 a. of
Manor's Privilege, 75 a. of Mount Pleasant, and 80 a. Bold Adventure; in July 1764 gave his age as 70 and stated he was a s. of
John Ensor; his will, 1771 - 1773, named his ch., given below,
and grandch. Luke (of Abraham), Deborah (of John), Jane Bungey,
Mary, Elizabeth, and John Holland (all ch. of dau. Jane Bungey),
and John, Jonathan, and Nathan Markland (ch. of dau. Orpah Mark-
land), John and Elizabeth Bonfield (ch. of dau. Naomi Bonfield),
and Elizabeth, Jane, and Temperance Stansbury (ch. of dau. Ann
Stansbury ; had iss.: poss. JOHN, b. 15 Aug. 1711 in St. John's
Par.; ELIZABETH, b. 12 July 1721, m. William Stansbury on 14
Feb. 1739/40; JOHN A., b. 25 Sept. 1723; JANE, b. 29 Jan. 1725,

not in will; son ABRAHAM, b. 5 Feb. 1727; JOSEPH, b. 11 April 1730; TEMPERANCE, b. 19 Sept. 1732, m. Solomon Bowen on 28 Nov. 1751; NAOMI, b. 22 Sept. 1734, m. (---) Bonfield; LUKE, b. 9 March 1736/7; ANNE, m. (---) Stansbury; RUTH, m. 1st (---) Bungey and 2nd (---) Holland ; ORPHA, fined for bast. in Nov. 1758; m. 1st (---) Edenfield and 2nd on 19 Nov. 1770 William Markland (29:162; 73:145, 152; 89:309; 131; 133; 134; 153:3; 210-39:101).

ENSOR, JOHN (3), s. of John (2) and Elizabeth, was born on 25 Sept. 1723; d. in Balto. Co. by April 1793; on 6 March 1753 m. Eleanor Todd, dau. of Thomas and Eleanor (Dorsey) Todd; in Nov. 1757 he and his w., joined Geo. Risteau and Geo.'s wife Frances in conveying to John Cromwell and w. Elizabeth part of Shawan Hunting Ground which Thomas Todd left to his three daus., the aforesaid Elinor, Elizabeth, and Frances; will of Eleanor (Todd) Ensor, 7 Dec. 1799 - 13 Aug. 1801, named iss.: ELIZABETH, b. 28 April 1734; m. Nathan Griffith; ELEANOR, b. 19 Nov. 1755, m. John Griffith; FRANCES, b. 14 Dec. 1757, m. Elijah Merryman; MARY, b. 20 Nov. 1759, m. Micajah Merryman; DEBORAH, m. Nicholas Merryman (83:91, 93, 95; 115:447; 133:111, 167; 204#1160; 204#2029).

ENSOR, ABRAHAM (4), s. of John (2) and Elizabeth, was b. 5 Feb. 1727, and m. Mary Merryman on 30 Jan. 1750; d. by 12 March 1801 when his ch. conv. to Job Garrettson two parcels called Coles Harbour or Todd's Range, and Mounteny's Neck; had iss.: JOHN; LUKE; WILLIAM; SARAH, m. John Plowman Ensor; ANN, m. John Holland (133; 231-WG#68:467).

ENSOR, JOSEPH (5), s. of John (2) and Elizabeth, was b. 11 April 1730; m. Mary Bouchelle on 7 April 1757; had iss.: dau., m. Maj. Edward Oldham of Cecil Co.; JOSEPH, Jr. (336:221-222).

THE GEORGE ENSOR FAMILY was researched by Fred M. Chilcotte who made his findings available to the compiler.

ENSOR, GEORGE (6), no known rel. to the above, was in Balto. Co. by 24 Dec. 1739 when he m. Elizabeth Reeves; d. leaving a will, 22 May 1771 - 11 Nov. 1771; wid. Elizabeth d. leaving a will, 23 Jan. 1813 - 7 July 1815; left iss.: GEORGE, b. c.1740; RACHEL, b. 14 May 1741; JOHN, b. 29 Oct. 1745; DARBY, d. 1825; NATHAN, d. Oct. 1821; ELIZABETH, may have m. James Chilcoat; PRUDENCE, m. John Chilcoat; SARAH, m. Humphrey Chilcoat (112:197; 119:51: 131).

THE THOMAS ENSOR FAMILY

ENSOR, THOMAS (7), no known rel. to above, was in Balto. Co. by 27 Jan. 1739 when he m. Mary Costley; had iss.: WILLIAM, b. 7 May 1741; THOMAS, b. 5 May 1745, d. Sept. 1745; JAMES, b. 23 Aug. 1746; THOMAS, b. 19 Nov. 1749; ELIZABETH, b. Nov. 1754 (131:94/r, 118/r, 128/r, 134/r).

ENSOR, THOMAS (8), s. of Thomas (7), was b. 19 Nov. 1749, and m. Mary Talbott on 22 Nov. 1770; had iss. at least one dau.: ELENOR, b. 28 Jan. 1772 (131:128/r, 160/r).

ERICKSON, ERIC, was in Balto. Co. by 8 April 1730 when he and

w. Mary sold to Thomas Coale a tract Levy's Tribe wh. Mary had
inher. from her father Robert Smith (72:210; 74:32).

ERICKSON, ERIC (poss. the same one above) d. 1750 having m.
Elizabeth Baker on 27 July 1745; she m. 2nd Nicholas Poor on 6
Jan. 1753; in 1750 he owned 150 a. Erickson's Garrison; d. leav-
ing a will, 2 March 1748/9 - 14 March 1752 which named his w.
Elizabeth as extx., dau. Elisacas, unborn ch., and tract Erick's
Garrison, and neighbor Samuel Smith; admin. bond was posted 24
April 1752 by extx. Eliza Erickson with Morris Baker and Indimeon
Baker; est. admin. 1753 and on 3 Nov. 1755 by Eliza, now w. of
Nicholas Poor; left iss.: FRENATTA, b. 2 June 1746, d. 17 Sept.
1746; ELISACAS, b. 26 Oct. 1747; FANNY ANN, b. 6 July 1759 (in
March 1759 both Nicholas Power and her uncle Charles Baker pet.
to be her guardian (5:285, 342; 13:52; 44; 131:28, 41, 112/r,
128/r, 139/r; 153:33; 210-28:204).

ERRELL, ANN, ind. for bast. in Nov. 1719; William Ingle was
the father; Ann was to serve Joseph Taylor for three extra mos.
(23:246, 249, 284).

ESPLINE, ADAM, d. by 7 June 1733 when admin. bond was posted
by Josias Middlemore with Thomas Bond and William Bond (of Bond's
Forest) as sec. (13:48).

EUSTON, CHRISTOPHER, d. by 9 Aug. 1750 when admin. bond was
posted by Skipwith Coale with James Rigbie and John Henley (13:
63).

EVANS, JOB (1), progenitor, was in Balto. Co. by 1680 when he
wit. the will of William Cromwell; was b. c.1656, giving his age
as 55 in 1711; d. by 7 May 1716; m. 1st, sometime after 1682
Margaret (wid. of John Burridge and Samuel Lane) and sis. of
Francis Mauldin and dau. of Grace (---) Mauldin who m. as her
2nd husb. William Parker and as her 3rd husb. Edward Lloyd; Job
m. 2nd, by 1700, Sarah (---) with whom he admin. the est. of
John Perry; surv. 1000 a. Friend's Discovery in June 1694; may
have been the possessor of Hamcross on behalf of the orphans of
one Drayden of London; in 1713 pet. the court that he "had fallen
into decay," and had a disabled wife with four small ch.; d. by
May 1716 when admin. bond was posted by wid. Sarah with Thomas
Randall and Tobias Emerson; est. inv. on 9 July 1716 by Thomas
Hammond and John Israel and val. at Ł 84.7.2, signed by Charles
Carroll and John Martin; left with four minor ch. alive in 1713,
one known son: JOB, Jr., d. by 1706 (13:45; 21:403; 52:37; 120:
180; 206-19½B:126; 211:81, 82; 310:143; Kendall, "Lane Notes,"
MHS; Slagle, "Samuel Lane, 1628-1681,...," in 346).

EVANS, JOB (2), s. of Job (1), may be the Evans who d. in A.
A. Co. by 1706 leaving three small children who were at John
Ensor's: JOB; JOHN; SAMUEL (390:38).

EVANS, JOB (3), prob. s. of Job (2), was b. 1705, giving his
age as 66 in May 1772; m. 1st Mary (---) who was the mother of
his ch., and 2nd Mary (---), mentioned in his will as his 2nd
w.; bought Fox Hall from John Bond in 1720; in July 1739 sold
part of that to John Evans; by 1750 owned 100 a. Fox Hall and

53 a. Timber Ridge; his will, 10 Jan. 1777 - 10 Jan. 1780 left
land to s. Job (who may have d. in 1775), tract Fox Hall to s.
Daniel, grandson Job Green, 2nd w. Mary, and "all his children;"
had iss.: JOB, twin, b. 18 March 1730; MARY, twin, b. 18 March
1730 (who may have m. as his 2nd wife Joseph Merryman; JEMIMA,
b. 29 March 1734; AMOS, b. 20 Feb. 1735; DANIEL; poss. also
THOMAS, b. 14 Jan. 1741; LEVI, b. 14 April 1743; EZEKIEL, b. 24
Sept. 1745; JOB, b. 8 April 1747; HENRY, b. 30 Sept. 1750 (71:
202; 75:251; 112:400; 133:22, 34, 47; 153:51; "Diary of John
Evans;" letter to the author from Mr. G. Herbert Baxley of Ridge-
wood, N. J.).

EVANS, JOHN (4), s. of Job (2), and bro. of "ancient Job Evans," was b. 1708, d. by 27 Nov. 1758; m. Catherine Cook on 19
Dec. 1731; she m. 2nd by 27 Nov. 1758 Henry Young; bought 100 a.
Evans' Beginning (part of Fox Hall) from Job and Mary Evans in
Oct. 1747; conv. 100 a. Fox Hall to Joseph England; in 1750 he
owned 100 a. Evans' Venture; admin. bond posted 12 March 1757 by
John Evans with Job Evans and John Cook; est. admin by John Evans
who stated he was eld. s. of dec., and that his mother refused to
take out letters of admin.; est. admin. in Nov. 1758, heirs were
the wid., now w. of John Young, dau. w. of Andrew Poulson,
and daus. Sarah and Catherine; dec. left six ch. in all: PRUDENCE,
b. 9 Jan. 1732; JOHN, b. 30 Nov. 1734; SARAH, b. 10 Nov. 1736;
CATHERINE, b. 19 Dec. 1738; and two ch. living in 1758 (5:237;
13:53; 75:251; 29:580; 133:27, 38, 40, 53; 153:87; "Evans Diary,
(See bibliography for full citation)").

EVANS, ALSE, serv. woman in inv. of John Hawkins filed Dec.
1733 (51:485).

EVANS, AMOS, in Balto. Co. by 1695 as a taxable in n. side of
Patapsco Hund. (139).

EVANS, EDWARD, convict, to give security for good behavior;
was put in custody of William Smith, Nov. 1724 (27:31).

EVANS, EDWARD, and Rachel Evans, in June 1725 admin. the est.
of John Hastings; d. by 14 June 1737 when Walter Dallas posted
admin. bond with Christopher Durbin and Jacob Wright (3:45; 13:
49).

EVANS, EDWARD, was in Balto. Co. by 1724 and in Lancaster Co.,
Penna. by March 1746; m. Rachel Johnson in Dec. 1724; bought 200
a. Bond's Manor from Thomas Bond, carpenter; in March 1746 was
in Lancaster Co. when he sold tract Rich Point to William Bennet;
in 1750 still owned 200 a. Bond's Manor; had iss.: HANNAH, b. 17
Sept. 1725; RACHEL, b. 17 Feb. 1729; EDWARD, b. 20 Aug. 1731 (72:
260; 79:474; 128:46, 72; 153:90).

EVANS, ELIZABETH, m. John Gallion on 29 May 1726 (129:239).

EVANS, ELIZABETH, alias Parsons, was ind. for bast. in March
1733/4 and tried in Aug. 1734 (30:188, 308).

EVANS, Rev. EVAN, Rector of St. George's Par., was b. c.1671
in Carnoe, Montgomery, Wales, son of Evan David Evans; took his

A.B. from Brasnose Coll., Oxford, and was made D. D. in 1714;
ordained in 1700; settled in Penna. betw. 1700 and 1718; came
to St. George's Par. in 1718; d. leaving a will, 25 May 1721 -
10 Nov. 1721 w. Alice, dau. Mary w. of Rev. Thomas Lloyd of Den-
bigh, Eng., Rev. Geo. Ross, Charles Read, Edward Hall, and
Roger Matthews, and land in Philadelphia and Eng.; admin. bond
posted 8 Jan. 1721 by Edward Hall and Roger Matthews with Aquila
Hall and Jarvis Gilbert; est. admin. by Matthews and Hall on 8
Oct. 1723 and 4 Aug. 1725; est. mentions Peter Evans of Phila.;
left iss.: MARY, m. Rev. Thomas Lloyd (1:140; 3:33; 13:50; 124:
101; 428:41).

EVANS, EVAN, m. by 23 Oct. 1736 a dau. of Daniel Johnson (3:
224).

EVANS, JOHN, m. 7 Sept. 1755 Mary Forkner (131).

EVANS, MARGARET, serv. of Will Hutchinson, was tried for bast.
in Nov. 1744 (35:391).

EVANS, MARY, had iss.: JOHN, b. 28 Feb. 1725/6, d. 1 July
1726; JAMES, b. 2 Feb. 1726/7 (128:51).

EVANS, MARY, m. Joseph Yates on 30 June 1729 (129:250).

EVANS, SARAH, in Nov. 1723 was ind. for bast., named John
Casey as the father (26:109).

EVANS, THOMAS, m. Christian (---) who in Nov. 1724 was tried
on charge of incontinency with William Teal (27:32, 45).

EVEREN, DAVID, d. after 11 Oct. 1756; will made on that day
named his w. Constant and dau.: JANE (111:117).

EVEREST, THOMAS, was in Balto. Co. by March 1682 when he and
his w. Hannah, dau. and heir of Richard Ball, conv. to Charles
Merryman, wheelwright of Corotoman, Va., 300 a. called East Humphreys; by Feb. 1683/4 had moved to The Cliffs, Calvert Co., when
he and w. Hannah conv. 60 a. Ball's Addition and 50 a. Bennett's
Range to John Bennett (103; 104:224; 106:287).

EVERETT, RICHARD (1), was in A. A. Co. by Dec. 1695 when he
surv. 36 a. Stony Hills, later held by Laurence Gary; in Dec.
1703 Richard and his sis. Sarah were left personalty in the will
of John Howard of A. A. Co.; d. leaving a will, 16 Jan. 1708 - 7
Feb. 1708, which left land bought from Richard Warfield to his
s. John, personalty to grandsons Everett and Edward Gary, and
left pers. est. to daus. Damaris and Hannah Everett; left iss.:
JOHN; SARAH, alive in 1703, may have m. (---) Gary by whom she
had sons Everett and Edward Gary; DAMARIS; HANNAH (122:27, 118;
211:225).

EVERETT, JOHN (2), prob. s. of Richard (1), d. in Balto. Co.
by 25 April 1758; m. 1st, Rebecca Poteet on 31 Oct. 1728, and
2nd, in Aug. 1739 Comfort Pearson; in 1750 owned 104 a. Casken's
Lot, which was (again?) conv. to John Everett in Aug. 1754; his
will, 10 March 1758 - 25 April 1758, named w. Comfort, son John

and Mary, w. of Francis Norrington; dec. left iss.: by 1st w.;
REBECCA, b. 29 Sept. 1729, d. 4 Nov. 1739; JOHN, b. c.1728; MARY,
as dau. of John and Rebecca Everett she was conv. prop. by her
uncle John Poteet in March 1732, later m. Francis Norrington;
by 2nd w.: KEZIA, b. 22 Sept. 1740; JAMES, b. 5 Feb. 1742 (82:
299; 131; 153:46; 210-30:482).

EVERETT, JOHN (3), s. of John (2) and Rebecca, was b. c.1728,
and d. by May 1760; gave his age as 31 in 1759; m. Martha Osborn
who m. as her 2nd husb. on June 1769 Amos Hollis; left a will,
made 1760 and proved 12 May 1760, which named w. Martha and ch.
Ann, James, and John; admin. bond posted 12 May 1760 by extx.
Martha Everett with James and William Osborn; est. admin. by
Martha, w. of Amos Hollis, on 19 June 1769 at which time 2 of
the 3 ch. were dead; left iss.: ANN, b. 30 Aug. 1754, m. John
Hall Hughes; JAMES, b. 3 March 1756; JOHN, b. 5 Sept. 1758 (7:
11; 13:62; 129:372; 131; 210-30:858).

EVERETT, ELIZABETH, was ind. for bast. in June 1746 and was
tried; ind. again for bast. in June 1750 and tried in Nov. 1750
(36:1, 127; 37:2; 38:25).

EVERETT, RICHARD, rec'd in membership at Gunpowder Meeting
on 27 d, 6 mo., 1759, from East Nottingham Meeting; had at least
one son: LIAM (136).

EVERETT, SAMUEL, m. 9 Dec. 1755 Hannah White, admnx. of Steph-
en White (5:315; 131).

EVERETT, THOMAS, m. 20 Dec. 1747 Margaret Price; had iss.:
BENJAMIN, b. 4 Feb. 1750; WILLIAM, b. 19 Aug. 1752; JOHN, b. 9
May 1755; CASSANDRA, b. 1 Feb. 1758 (129:344, 363).

EVERSTON, JONATHAN, Irish servant, ran away from Joseph Lusby
in Balto. Co., May 1751 (385:130).

EVES. See EAVES.

EWES. See EAVES.

EWINGS, JOHN, was in Balto. Co. by 1694 as a taxable in n.
side of Gunpowder Hund.; d. by 25 July 1709 when admin. bond
was posted by admins. James Maxwell and Moses Groome with John
Roberts and William Howard; est. was inv. 8 Aug. 1709 by Jo'n
Boone and William Lenox and val. at £ 87.2.1; est. was admin.
by Maxwell on 13 Oct. 1718; had iss.: DORCAS, in Aug. 1710 chose
Joshua Merriken as her guardian, and in Oct. 1713 m. Edward
Mead (2:31; 13:42; 21:62; 42:280; 131; 139:12).

EWING(S), ARCHIBALD, d. by Aug. 1757 when Gustavus Ewings admin. the est. (42:26).

EWINS, ELIZABETH, m. 16 Feb. 1709/10 Joshua Merriken (prob.
the wid. of John Ewings above) (129:209).

EXON, HENRY, was in Balto. Co. by 1675 (110:102).

EZARD, SARAH, was tried for bast. in June 1750 (37:19).

FALCONER, RALPH, in May 1751 was a partner in an iron works with Edward Neale of Q. A. Co.; sold 366 a. Arabia Petrea to William Bennett, but Falconer absconded before completing the conveyance.

FALL, NEAL, m. by 1742 Susanna, dau. of Stephen Body (127:196).

FALLOCK, JOHN, in Aug. 1670 was conv. 640 a. Sprye's Inheritance by Godfrey and Mary Harmer; on 6 Feb. 1673/4 he and w. Jane conv. tract to Miles Gibson (96:231; 100:116).

FARBEE, BENJAMIN, d. by 23 May 1658 when admin. bond was posted by admnx. Elizabeth Farby with W. Palmer (13:64).

FARFARR, WILLIAM, b. c.1649, d. c.1721/2; gave his age as 69 in 1718; m. by 11 Aug. 1713 Eleanor, wid. of John Harryman; in Nov. 1718 his pet. to be levy free was granted; his will, 26 Dec. 1721 - 27 March 1721/2, named grandsons Alex. and John Keeth (who were to have parts of Shrewsbury or Dear Bit); dau. Christiana Keeth, and son-in-law Samuel Harryman; admin. bond was posted 22 March 1721/2 by Samuel Harryman with Nathaniel Darby and Jacob Peacock; had iss.: CHRISTIANA, m. (---) Keeth (1:24; 13:78; 23:33; 124:105; 203-3:464).

FARLEY, JOHN, m. 29 Oct. 1737 Mary Weeks (128:92b).

FARLOW, THOMAS, d. by 1 Aug. 1747 when admin. bond was posted by Joseph Henly with Edward Morgan and William Rayle; on 8 Nov. 1734 m. Elizabeth, wid. of James Little; had iss.: MARY, b. 24 Oct. 1735 (4:5; 13:79; 128:87, 89).

FARMER, GREGORY (1), was alive in Balto. Co. as late as 1750 when he was listed as owning 60 a. New Westwood and 40 a. of Margaret's Mount; m. Sarah Hughes on 27 Aug. 1703; on 16 Dec. 1709 wit. the will of Edward Swan; on 26 Nov. 1729 bought 94 a. Creek Plantation from Nathaniel Dougherty; had iss.: GREGORY, b. 2 Aug. 1704; MARGARET, b. 2 Sept. 1706, m. Ford Barnes on 21 Sept. 1721; HANNAH, b. 1 March 1707/8, m. Joseph Wilson on 4 Feb. 1729; SARAH, b. 21 April 1710; JOHN, b. 21 Feb. 1712; ELIZABETH, b. 17 Dec. 1714; PETER, b. 8 Feb. 1715/6; MARTHA, b. 7 Jan. 1717/8; THOMAS, b. 18 (---) 1719; SAMUEL, b. 25 April 1721; SARAH, b. 18 March 1723/4 (72:152; 122:220; 128:17, 32, 33, 34, 36, 37, 39, 41, 43; 129:228; 153:35).

FARMER, GREGORY (2), s. of Gregory (1) and Sarah, waa b/ 2 Aug. 1704 and was alive in Sept. 1754; m. Rachel Emson on 14 June 1723; in Sept. 1754 he and w. Rachel conv. part New Westwood to William Cox (82:288; 128:32, 42).

FARMER, JOHN (3), s. of Gregory (1) and Sarah, was b. 21 Feb. 1712, d. 15 Sept. 1742; m. Sophia Jones, dau. of George and Eliza (Chappell) Simmons; on 26 Feb. 1742 admin. bond was posted by Sophia Farmer with James Crawford, Gregory Farmer, Jr., and Thomas Jr.; est. was admin. on 17 Dec. 1743; dec. left iss.: ELIZABETH, b. 4 March 1735; SARAH, b. 12 Dec. 1737; d. 16 Sept. 1742; HAN-

NAH, b. 15 Oct. 1739; GREGORY, b. 29 Sept. 1741; JOHN, b. 10 Nov. 1742 (3:336; 13:89; 128:89, 91, 98, 105, 116; 129:326).

FARMER, PETER (4), s. of Gregory (1) and Sarah, was b. 8 Feb. 1715/6, d. by 23 Oct. 1745 when admin. bond was posted by Richard Dallam and Gregory Farmer; m. Mary Wood on 22 Nov. 1737; she relinquished right of admin. to Dallam as he was the principal creditor; est. was admin. 20 Nov. 1746; had iss.: MARTHA, b. 22 Dec. 1738; MARY, b. 27 Nov. 1740, d. 2 Dec. 1742; GREGORY, b. 12 Sept. 1743 (4:137; 13:88; 128:34, 91; 129:285, 299, 307, 320, 326).

FARMER, THOMAS (5), s. of Gregory (1) and Sarah, was b. 18 (---) 1719; m. Elizabeth Ross on 21 Jan. 1741; in 1750 owned 183 a. part Arabia Petree; had iss.: ELIZABETH, b. 16 (?) 1743 (128: 37; 129:223, 324, 336; 153:51).

FARMER, SAMUEL (6), s. of Gregory (1) and Sarah, was b. 25 April 1721; m. by 18 Jan. 1754 Elizabeth (---) who joined him in conveying part Farmer's Farm to William Cox (82:127; 128:39).

FARMER, SARAH, d. 22 Oct. 1745 (129:345).

FARRELL, ROBERT, had his pet. to be levy free granted by the Court in Aug. 1718 (23:1).

FARROLL, LAURENCE, Irish, age c.23, ran away from the Balto. Iron Works, July 1759 (307).

FARRENDALE, RICHARD, was in Balto. Co. by Aug. 1688 when he conv. to Robert Chapman land at Black Wolf Neck formerly taken up by Capt. Thomas Harwood (95).

FASSITT, WILLIAM, inherited a lot in Balto. Town by the Jan. 1734/5 will of his father William, a merchant of Somerset Co. (126:139).

FATHER, HENRY, was ordered to be levy free in Nov. 1756 (41: 302).

FAULKNER, THOMAS, servant of Charles Ramsey, d. 24 Dec. 1702 (128:14).

FAULKNER, WILLIAM, tailor, age c.24, was b. in Lincolnshire; ran away from William Lux and N. Ridgely, April 1754 (385:280).

FEDERACO, JOHN CASPER,, servant, was listed in the Oct. 1754 inv. of Stephen Onion (49:221).

FEELER, THOMAS, m. Sarah (---), and had iss.: THOMAS, b. 8 Sept. 1733 (128:82).

FELKS, EDWARD, was in Balto. Co. by 1692 as a taxable in s. side Gunpowder Hund.; made a deed of gift to his intended wife Ann, wid. of Stephen Johnson, on 19 Feb. 1701/2; d. by 10 Nov. 1703 when his est. was inv. by Samuel Sicklemore and Francis Dallahide and val. at £ 151.12.6 (2:27; 51:143; 66:119; 138).

THE FELL FAMILY has been researched by Ms. Jennie Weeks of Salt Lake City who sent some of her findings to the author.

FELL, EDWARD (1), of Ulverston, Lancashire, Eng., was b. c. 1657 and was alive in 1702; m. at Ulverston on 25 April 1682 Anne Perry, b. c.1661; had iss.: EDWARD, b. 28 Nov. 1686 at Trinkeld, Lancs., m. Ann Thomas; SARAH, b. 24 March 1689 at Trinkeld; ELIZA-BETH, b. 13 March 1692 at Dragley Beck; JOHN, b. 25 June 1695 at Dragley Beck; WILLIAM, b. 20 May 1697 at Trinkeld; HENRY, b. 21 April 1700; MARGARET, b. 6 Jan. 1702 at Trinkeld, m. (---) Holmes (Weeks data).

FELL, EDWARD (2), s. of Edward (1) and Ann, was b. 28 Nov. 1686 at Trinkeld, and d. in Md., March 1743; m. at West River Meeting Ann Thomas, dau. of Samuel Thomas; acquired vast land-holdings in Balto. Co.; by 1750 his heirs owned 175 a. Fell's Swathmore, 322 a. Lancaster, 496 a. Fell's Dale, 316 a. Darling-ton475 a. Fell's Retirement, 520 a. Cole's Harbor, and 1 lot in Balto. Town; as Edward Fell, Quaker, of Overkillit, Lancashire, he made a will, 2 Feb. 1738 - 6 March 1743, leaving all his land in Md. to his dau. Ann, land in Great Britain to his bro., and left legacies to the ch. of his bro. Henry, ch. of his sis. Marga-ret Holmes, child of his bro. William, and to Richard Wilson, Anne Withers, and Abigail Yeat;admin. bond was posted 28 July1743 by John Galloway and William Fell with William Bond and Samuel Galloway; a second admin. bond was posted 8 Nov. 1753 by Joseph Taylor with Edward Lamb and Thomas Jennings; est. was admin. by Joseph Taylor on 7 Nov. 1754 and 8 May 1755; left iss.: ANN (4: 227; 5:350; 13:74, 91; 127:217; 153:4; 263).

FELL, WILLIAM (3), s. of Edward (1) and Ann, was b. 20 May 1697 at Trinkeld, Lancashire, and d. in Md. by 1748; m. 18 Jan. 1732 Sarah Bond, dau. of Thomas and Ann (Robinson) Bond; Sarah m. as her 2nd husband (Greenbury?) Dorsey; was one of the commis-sioners of Balto. Town; his heirs (listed in 1750 as the heirs of "Thomas Fell") owned 100 a. Cooper's Harbour, 85 a. Island Point, and 18 a. Trinket Fields; his will left Long Island Point to his son Edward, dau. Ann was to have 296 a. Freeborne's Prog-ress in A. A. Co., while daus. Jennett and Margaret were to have Fell's Forest, and dau. Catherine was to have Stone's Adventure; he also named his cous. William Holmes and w. Sarah; admin. bond was posted 13 Feb. 1748 by Sarah Taylor and Joseph Taylor, execs., with Thomas Bond, Jr., John Bond, and Jos. Bond; his est. was admin. 5 Feb. 1747, 20 Feb. 1750, 26 April 1750 9 Nov. 1752, and finally on 17 April 1756; dec. left iss.: ANN, b. 5 Feb. 1733, m. Edward Day on 8 Feb. 1749; EDWARD, b. 3 Feb. 1735/6; JANET, b. 20 Feb. 1736, m. Isaac Few on 15 Aug. 1754; MARGARET; CATHERINE, m. Thomas Bond on 3 Feb. 1765 (4:149; 5:115, 123, 267, 305; 13: 86; 40:397; 131; 133; 153:15; 210-24:544).

FELL, EDWARD (4), s. of William (3) and Sarah, was b. 3 Feb. 1735/6, d. 1766; m. Ann Bond on 2 Nov. 1758; she m. 2nd James Giles by 14 Jan. 1774; left a will, 26 April 1766 - 9 Aug. 1766, naming his w. Ann, s. William, father-in-law John Bond, sisters Jennet Few and Catherine, nephew William Few, and Thomas Edward Dorsey; est. admin. by his wid. and her 2nd husb. on 14 Jan. 1774; left iss.: WILLIAM, b. 29 Aug. 1759 (7:241; 112:29; 131; 133).

FELL, WILLIAM (5), s. of Edward (4) and Ann, was b. 29 Aug. 1759, d. 1786; was a delegate to the Assembly from Balto. Town in 1782; d. unm. (380:203, 207).

FELL, JAMES, a prisoner in Balto. Co. gaol, pet. the Assembly in 1766 (200-61:95).

FELL, WILLIAM, m. Ann (---), and had iss.: LUCY, b. 24 Aug. 1731; CHRISTOPHER, b. 13 Jan. 1733 (133:38).

FELL, WILLIAM, in Nov. 1750 was conv. 50 a. Liverpoole by James Gardner, schoolmaster (81:46).

FELL, WILLIAM, English, conv. serv., ran away from James Dimmitt of Balto. Co., Aug. 1750 (385:93).

FELPS. See PHELPS.

FEMER, NICHOLAS, m. by 5 Nov. 1755 Elizabeth, extx. of Errick Errickson, late of Balto. Co. (200-38:249).

FENDALL, Capt. JAMES, mariner, from Bright Helmstone, Sussex, Eng.; was in Balto. Co. by 13 Dec. 1683 when he purch 600 a. of Delph from Thomas Thurstone; d. by 10 Oct. 1690 when admin. bond was posted by Edward Bedell and John Walston, Gent., admins., with John Hall and William Osborne; a second admin. bond was posted 17 Feb. 1693/4 by Samuel Fendall with Samuel Browne and Thomas Browne; est. was inv. on 1 Sept. 1693 and val. at £ 133.14.8, and inv. a second time on 26 Sept. 1693 by John Kemble and Roger Matthews with an additional val. of £ 13.8.0; est. admin. by Samuel Fendall on 10 Sept. 1694 (13:66, 67; 48:114; 106:296; 206-13A:224).

FENDALL, JAMES, of Balto. Co. advert. he would not pay debts of his w. Ann (255).

FENDALL, JOHN, was in Balto. Co. by c.1700 when he owned 200 a. Drisdale's Habitation (211:18).

FENDALL, SAMUEL, perhaps a rel. to Capt. James Fendall (above); admin. the latter's est.; was in Balto. Co. by 1694 as a taxable in Spesutia Hund. (139; 206-13A:224).

FENICK, THOMAS, was bur. at William Osborne's on 18 Nov. 1701 (128:12).

FENN or FEEN, THOMAS, d. by 20 March 1702/3 when admin. bond was posted by Daniel Johnson or Johnston with William Loftin; had iss.: JANE, b. 2 Feb. 1688/9; HENRY, b. 10 Aug. 1692 (13:71; 128: 12, 13).

FENIX. See PHENIX.

FENLEY. See FINLEY.

FENO, SIMON, servant, was listed in April 1688 inv. of Thomas Lightfoot; by 1692 was a taxable in s. side Patapsco Hund. (51: 8; 138).

FENTON, WILLIAM, was in Balto. Co. by 1692 as a taxable in
n. side Patapsco Hund.; in June 1718 gave security for Amy
Fenton when she posted admin. bond on the est. of Stephen Bentley; gave his age as 70 in 1721 (11:68; 138; 310).

FENWICK, THOMAS, was in Balto. Co. by 1694 as a taxable in
Spesutia Hund.; prob. the Thomas Fenick bur. 18 Nov. 1701 at
William Osborne (128:12; 139).

FERGUSON, ROBERT, was in Balto. Co. by 1692 as a taxable in
s. side Patapsco Hund. (138).

FERGUSON, WILLIAM, m. Ann (---), and had iss.: JAMES, b. 29
May 1743 (133:79).

FERRALL, JAMES, serv. of Robert Freight, was fined for bast.
in Nov. 1757 (44; 46:75).

FERRY, JOHN, imm. to Md. by 1691, and was a taxable in n.
side Patapsco Hund. by 1692; rep. Balto. Co. in the Assembly,
1694-7 and 1697-1700; m. Ann, wid. of John Boring; d. leaving a
will, 1 March 1688/9 - 11 March 1698/9, which named sons-in-
law John, James, and Thomas Boreing, dau.-in-law Mary Boreing,
Sarah Strawbridge, godson John Uawston, and Ann, dau. of James
Todd; admin. bond posted by trustee Charles Merryman with Samuel
Sicklemore and Charles Adams on 7 Sept. 1699; est. inv. 12 May
1699 by John Gay and John Hayes and val. at Ł 368.15.9 plus 9669
lbs. tob. (13:65; 48:1; 121:171; 138; 370:33, 34, 320).

FETCHAM, ANN, runaway serv. from Samuel Hart of Patapsco, Aug.
1746 (384:572).

FETTYPLACE, ELIZABETH, servant, in Nov. 1717 had her indenture
for 4 years assigned to William Douglas (22:193).

THE FEW FAMILY has been the subject of a genealogy by Florence
Fruth, Some Descendants of Richard Few of Chester County, Pennsylvania, and Allied Lines (Parsons: McClain Printing Co., 1977).

FEW, RICHARD (1), progenitor, was b. by 1625; m. 1st Jane or
Joan Whitfield who d. 1674, and m. 2nd Julian (---); came to
America in 1682; d. 1688; left iss.; JOANE, b. 1651; RICHARD,
b. 1653; WALTER, b. 1656; DANIEL, b. 1660; ISAAC, b. 1664; JOSEPH,
b. 1666 (Fruth, pp. 8-10).

FEW, ISAAC (2), s. of Richard (1), was b. in Wiltshire, Eng.,
6, 4 mo., 1664, and came to Penna. with his father; m. Hannah
Stanfield in 1699; d. 1734, leaving issue: RICHARD, b. 1700;
ISAAC, b. 1701; JAMES, b. 1703; ELIZABETH, b. 1705; DANIEL, b.
1706; JOSEPH, b. 1708; WILLIAM, b. 1714; FRANCIS, b. 1719; SAMUEL,
b. 1722 (Fruth, pp. 11-15).

FEW, WILLIAM (3), s. of Isaac (2), was b. 16, 5 mo. 1714, in
Chester Co., Penna., and moved to Baltimore Co., Md.; in 1743 m.
Mary, dau. of Benjamin Wheeler; in 1750 owned 200 a. Three Sisters and 100 a. Harris' Trust; by 1760 was in N. C., when he
and w. Mary conv. to William Perrine 200 a. Bond's Gift;   had

iss.: BENJAMIN, b. 1744, d. 1805; JAMES, b. 1746, d. 1771;
WILLIAM, b. 1748, d. 1828, m. Catherine Nicholson; ELIZABETH,
b. 1755, d. 1829, m. 1st Greenberry Lee, m. 2nd Benjamin Andrew,
and m. 3rd Thomas Bush; HANNAH, m. Rhesa Howard; IGNATIUS (80:
546; 84:388; 153:17; Fruth, pp. 21-27, 30).

FEW, ISAAC, m. 15 Aug. 1754 Jennett Fell, sis. of Edward
Fell who d.1766, and dau. of William Fell; by June 1760 was in
New Castle Co. (84:277; 112:29; 121).

FEW, MARY, age 3 years in Feb. 1757; in Nov. 1756 was bound
to Thomas Richardson (41:303).

FEWGATE/FUGATE, PETER (1), was transp. to Md. by 1662, and
was naturalized in Sept. 1671; in Sept. 1683 surv. 300 a. Fewgate's Fork (the Rent Roll noted that "Fewgate run away into
Virginia, with no heirs"); Dec. 1685 surv. 100 a. Peter's Addition; prob. the Peter Fuckett who surv. French Plantation in
June 1675; in Oct. 1686 Peter Fucall or Fucatt conv. 200 a. of
land to James Walston; in Jan. 1690 Peter and w. Frances conv.
French Plantation to Thomas Cord, and in Aug. 1694 Peter and
Frances conv. Mould's Success to Edward Boothby; was a taxable
in Spesutia Hund. in 1692, 1694, and 1695; prob. had iss.: JAMES;
PETER, remained in Md. in 1694 and 1695, but prob. left Maryland
by 1699 as he is not in the tax lists for that year(59:208, 329,
419; 138; 139; 140; 141; 211; 388; 404).

FEWGATE, JAMES (2), poss. s. of Peter (1) was of age in Sept.
1683 when he surv. 200 a. North Yarmouth; m. by May 1686 Dorothy
(---); in Jan. 1681 was exec. of Anthony Watson; in May 1686 he
and w. Dorothy mortgaged 200 a. North Yarmouth to Miles Gibson;
James was a taxable in Spesutia Hund. 1699; may have had one
son: JAMES (59:186; 120:139; 141; 211).

FEWGATE, JAMES (3), poss. s. of James (2), was an inhab. of
Balto. Co. by 1726; m. Ann (---); in 1742 leased 108 a. of My
Lady's Manor from Thomas Brerewood, the lease to run for the lifetimes of said James, age 66 (placing his birth as c.1676), and
his sons James alias Peter Fewgate age 15, and son James age 13;
had iss.; SARAH, b. 11 Nov. 172-(?); PETER, b. 1 May 1726; EDWARD
b. 14 Sept. 1731, prob. d. young; EDWARD, b. 10 Aug. 1734; JOHN,
b. 15 March 1732; EASTER, b. 15 March 1732; ANNE, b. 23 April
1735, prob. d. young; ANN, b. Feb. 1738 (77:108; 131).

FEWGATE, EDWARD (4), s. of James (3) and Ann, b. 10 Aug. 1734,
m. Elizabeth Bacon on 12 Jan. 1758; d. by 14 March 1787 when his
est. was admin. by Elizabeth Fewgate (9:25; 131).

FEWGATE (FUGATE), JAMES, in Nov. 1737 was made exempt from the
levy (31:134).

FEXTON, RICHARD, d. by 13 Dec. 1674; his wid. m. William
Chadbourne (q.v.).

FIDRACK, JACOB, m. 14 Nov. 1757 Eliz. Blackwalldren (131).

FIELD, EASTER, m. Edward Gwynn on 15 Nov. 1728 (133:149).

FIELD(S), ELIZABETH, d. 28 Oct. 1727 (128:50).

FIELD, JOHN, m. Catherine Hogg on 23 Dec. 1729, and had iss.:
JO., b. 28 Jan. 1732; ANN, b. 12 April 1734 (128:61, 71; 129:
321).

FIELDS(?), SUSANNA, d. 20 Aug. 1727 (128:50).

FILLY. See TILLY.

FINCHAM/FINSHAM/FINTCHAM/FRINSHAM, ELIZABETH, d. by 5 Feb.
1738/9, when her will, made 5 Nov. 1738, was proved; named dau.
Phoebe Ingram, William Grover, Sarah Burket, Francis Whitehead
and ch. Robert and Elizabeth Whitehead; admin. bond posted 5 Feb.
1738 by Thomas Matthews, exec., with Charles Robinson and William
Harvey; est. admin. by Matthews on 23 June 1740; had iss., prob.
by a previous marr.: PHOEBE WHITEHEAD, m. William Ingram on 6
Nov. 1731; FRANCIS WHITEHEAD; ROBERT WHITEHEAD; and ELIZABETH
WHITEHEAD (4:72; 13:77; 32:297, 357; 127:14; 131).

FINLEY, LYDIA, servant of John Miller, was ind. for bast. in
Nov. 1724 (27:32).

FINLEY, PETER, m. Eleanor Murphy on 12 June 1774 (131).

FINLEY, THOMAS, m. Althea Kidd on 22 July 1747; d. by 7 May
1755 when admin. bond was posted by Althea Finley with John Tipton and Angel Isrello; est. admin. by Althea Finley on 19 Oct.
1756 and by Althea w. of Nicholas Brittain on 28 Nov. 1761; left
iss.: AGNES, b. 18 Dec. 1749 (4:351; 5:310; 13:82; 133).

FINN, PETER, was b. 2 July 1751 in Balto. Co., d. 1837 in Marion Co., Ill.; enlisted in Rev. War in 1778 from Md., and in 1779
from N.C.; pensioned in Ky. (399:87).

FISHBOROUGH, HENRY, m. Ann (---), and had iss.: ANN, b. 23
Sept. 1731; SARAH, b. 25 Nov. 1734 (133:42).

FISHER, ANN, servant with 2 years to serve in Oct. 1754 inv.
of Stephen Onion (49:221).

FISHER, ANN MARIA, servant to John Griffith, tried for bast.
in Nov. 1756 (41:313).

FISHER, HANNAH MARIA, serv. to John Griffin, bore an illeg.
child in Nov. 1759 (44).

FISHER, JOHN, was named as a son-in-law in the will, made 3
May 1703, of Robert Drisdell (122:38).

FISHER, MATTHEW, d. by 5 June 1745 when admin. bond was posted
by John Frazier with John Morgan and John Metcalf; est. admin.
24 Aug. 1747 by Frazier (4:184; 13:88).

FISHER, SEMELIA, was bur. 2 July 1696 (128:5).

FISHER, STEPHEN, m. Elizabeth Goodwin on 26 Jan. 1741; had
iss.: ELIZABETH, b. 13 Oct. 1742 (129:330).

FISHER, THOMAS, m. 18 Feb. 1761 Amelia, wid. of Peter Whitacre (129:369).

FISHER, WILLIAM, was in Balto. Co. by 12 Feb. 1663/4 when Axel Stills conv. him 300 a. Oxelle Neck; he conv. 225 a. Salveton to John Bromfield in 1666; by 4 March 1666/7 was a chirurgeon in Va. when he and w. Frances conv. 1400 a. on s. side Elk River to Henry Ward (94).

FISHER, WILLIAM, in 1759 surv. Fisher's Delight in Balto. Co. (207)

FITCH, HENRY, was in Balto. Co. by 3 Feb. 1734 when he conv. 200 a. Chance to his dau. Mary Parlett with reversion to his grandson William Parlett; iss.: MARY, m. (---) Parlett (74:166).

FITCH, HENRY, m. on 28 Feb. 1758 Ruth, dau. of Thomas Bailey (112:183; 131).

FITCH, WILLIAM, in 1750 owned 100 a. part Smith's Chance (153: 47).

FITCH, WILLIAM, formerly in the army, was a runaway conv. serv. of John Metcalfe of Patapsco, May 1751 (385:231).

FITZEDMOND, JOHN, d. by 19 Oct. 1723 when est. was admin. by Barbara Fitzedmond (1:123).

FITZGARRETT, GARRETT. See GARRETTSON, GARRETT.

FITZGERALD, JOHN, runaway serv. from Michael Gormacon who claimed 25 days extra service, June 1719 (23:131).

FITZPATRICK, CHARLES, m. 20 Oct. 1742 Jane Fairbourn (129: 325).

FITZPATRICK, JOHN, in 1750 owned 50 a. Long Point (153:97).

FITZPATRICK, MARY, ind. for bast. in March 1719/20; ind. for same again in June 1731, naming Isaac Champion as the father; as servant of James Dimmitt was tried for bast. in June 1740; ind. for bast. last of March 1741/2; admitted charge of bast. in Aug. 1742; tried for bast. in Nov. 1757; had iss.: MARY, b. 20 Feb. 1720; JOHN, b. 15 July 1726, prob. d. young; NATHAN, b. 5 April 1731; JOHN, b. 16 Jan. 1739 (age 2 in previous Jan., in Aug. 1742 was bound to George and Ann Elliott in Aug. 1742) (23:279; 29:156, 168; 32:368; 33:294; 34:8; 44; 131).

FITZREDMOND, JOHN, d. by 29 April 1721 when admin. bond was posted by John McKenzy with John McCarthy and John Carrington; a second admin. bond was posted 2 Dec. 1721 by admnx. Barbara Fitzredmond with Robert Chapman and Darby Ragan; est. inv. by Luke Stansbury and Thomas Carr and val. at £ 209.17.24; est. inv. again by Christopher Randall and John Whips and val. at £ 23.9.2, and signed by the children of the dec., Alexander Fitzredmond and Barbara Cannon; est. admin. by Barbara Fitzredmond on 19 Oct. 1723; left iss.: ALEXANDER; BARBARA, w. of (---) Cannon (1:123; 13:76; 51:206; 52:12).

FITZSIMMONS, NICHOLAS, was in Balto. Co. by 1694 as a taxable in n. side Patapsco Hund.; in March 1695 surv. 300 a. Cordwainer's Hall; m. by 1694 Martha, wid. of Joseph Heathcote, and dau. of Capt. Thomas Morgan; d. leaving a will, 11 Oct. 1743 - 2 Jan. 1743, which named daus. Flora, w. of Joshua Dorsey (and her eld. dau.), and Mary; had iss.: FLORA, m. by 11 Oct. 1743 Joshua Dorsey; MARY, m. 9 Oct. 1746 Edward Norwood (20:152; 127: 267; 133:160; 139; 206-13A:195).

FLACK, JOHN, listed as a serv. in inv. (53:242).

FLANAGAN/FLANNAGAN/FLANNIGAN, EDWARD (1), was in Balto. Co. by 1726; m. Mary (---); in 1750 owned 200 a. part Outquarter; d. leaving a will, 1 May 1765 - 14 Oct. 1766, which named ch.: James, Charles, Catherina Anderson, Mary Smith, Nelly Beally, and grandch.: Edward of Charles, John Smith of Richard, and Charles Buckingham of William, servant Robert Guttrey, and Ł 5 to the religious society of which the testator was a member for the purpose of building a chapel; had iss.: CARMACK, <u>alias</u> CHARLES, b. 8 Sept. 1726; JOHN, b. April 1731; KATHERINE, b. 13 Nov. 1733, m. (---) Anderson; MARY, b. 11 Jan. 1735, m. Richard Smith; ELEANOR, b. 2 June 1739, m. (---) Beally; JAMES; poss. a dau. who m. (---) Buckingham (112:28; 128:82; 153:62).

FLANAGAN, CHARLES (2), s. of Edward (1), d. leaving a will, 9 Sept. 1759 - 11 Aug. 1766, in which he named his father Edward, and his own two children: EDWARD (to have Caleb's Necessity); MARY (112:24).

FLANAGAN, BARTHOLOMEW, m. Sept. 1750 Eliz. Clavager and had iss.: MARY, b. 2 May 1750 (sic); WILLIAM, b. 25 Dec. 1755; HENRY, b. 17 May 1757 (131:48, 139/r).

FLANAGAN, EDMOND, alias Burgess, in March 1754 was tried for bast. as the father of Mary Barler's child (39:31).

FLANAGAN, TERRENCE, Irish, age c. 24, was a runaway serv. from the Baltimore Iron Works in May 1746 (384:560).

FLANNER, FRANCIS, m. Sarah Whealand on 2 Oct. 1748 (131).

FLEEHARTEE, JOHN, m. Hannah Penick on 7 April 1735 (128:85).

FLEETWOOD, THOMAS, in March 1733/4 pet. for his freedom, having lived with John Giles for 7 years; Giles was ordered to pay him his freedom dues (30:190).

FLEMING, JOHN, in his 75th year, pet. to be levy free in Nov. 1724 (27:38).

FLEMING, WILLIAM, m. Mary Jane (---) on 5 Nov. 1759 (131).

FLETCHER, THOMAS, was in Balto. Co. by 3 Oct. 1701 when he surv. 100 a. Five Mile End (438, app. p. 1).

FLIN, EDWARD, m. Mary Linsey in (Jan.?) 1748 (131).

FLINT, ANN, was ind. for bast. in Aug. 1744 (35:293).

FLOOD, WILLIAM, m. 26 March 1733 Jane French and had iss.:
MARY, b. 3 June 1733 (128:73).

FLOOD/FLUD, WILLIAM, age 12 last 1st of Jan., son of Michael,
was bound to Zachariah Maccubbin in June 1758 (46:123).

FLOWERS, WILLIAM, m. 8 Feb. 1734 Mary Killey (133:153).

FLOYD, THOMAS (1), planter, was in Balto. Co. by 5 Oct.
1738 when William Hamilton and w. Sarah conv. him Christian's
Lot and Brother's Expectation; on 18 Oct. 1738 Thomas Floyd and
w. Zipporah conv. 100 a. Christian's Lot and 50 a. Tucker's
Fountain back to William Hamilton; Floyd m. Zipporah Hillyard
who m. 2nd by 1750 Alexander Baker, and 3rd, by June 1756, Henry
Maynard; Floyd's will, 28 Jan. 1738/9 - 29 Jan. 1739, left 100
a. Christian's Lot to his sons John and Thomas and 50 a. of a
250 a. tract, Hollingsworth, to his sons; pers. to dau. Mary;
had four ch., three of whom joined their mother when she joined
Gunpowder Meeting in 1755; had iss.: THOMAS; JOHN; CALEB; MARY
(5:241, 268; 11:145; 74:191; 75:137; 127:59; 136; 153; Dorman,
"Maynard Family of Frederick County, Maryland," in Nat. Gen. Soc.
Quarterly, 48:177 ff.)

FLOYD, THOMAS (2), s. of Thomas (1) prob. d. by 1773, having
m. on 23, 4 mo., 1755, Rachel Daughaday, sis. of Joseph and
Richard Daughaday, and cousin of Richard Taylor, was b. 26, 10
mo. 1740; in June 1756 Thomas and w. Rachel, and John Floyd conv.
100 a. Christian's Lot and 50 a. Brother's Expectation to William
Jessop, and Henry Maynard and w. Zipporah acknowledged they had
received full satisfaction for her right of dower; Thomas may
have d. by 1773 when Rachel m. as her 2nd husband Frederick
Gatch; poss. iss.: JOSEPH; WILLIAM THOMAS, said to have been k.
by Indians (82:570; 136; fam. records of Laurence Hill).

FLOYD, CALEB (3), s. of Thomas (1), is not mentioned in his
father's will, but is mentioned in the records of Gunpowder
Meeting 1755 and may be the Caleb Floyd who joined Thomas Floyd
in leasing a lot in Bond St., Balto., from Mary Morton (231-WG#
SS: 1).

FLOYD, HENRY, was in Balto. Co. by 1700 as a taxable in n.
side Patapsco (142).

FLOYD, JAMES, was in Balto. Co. by 1700 as a taxable in
n. side of Patapsco Hund. (142).

FLOYD, ROBERT, was in Balto. Co. by 1701 as a taxable in n.
side Patapsco Hund. (142).

FLOYD, SIMON, d. by 3 Oct. 1724 when admin. bond was posted
by Benjamin Bowen with Jonas Robinson and William King; est.
was inv. 29 Dec. 1724 by John Boring and John Eagleston, and
val. at £ 14.18.4; est. was admin. by Bowen on 5 March 1726
(2:95; 13:83; 51:199).

FLOYD, THOMAS, wit. the will of Johanna Goldsmith on 4 Oct. 1684; does not appear in later tax lists so he may have d. or moved out of the county (121:35; 138; 139; 140).

FLYN, EDWARD, in Aug. 1755 was ordered to be levy free (40: 221).

FLYNN, JOHN, age 13, in Aug. 1746 was bound to John Timmons to learn the trade of a weaver (36:121).

FLYNN, JOSEPH, age 14 next Sept., was bound to Joseph England in Aug. 1746, until he was 21 (36:121).

FOARD. See FORD.

FORD/FOARD, THOMAS (1), progenitor, was in Md. by 1679 when he surv. 300 a. Rockford; was in A. A. Co. by 1662 when he surv. Dinah Ford's Beaver Dam; also surv. 600 a. Goury Banks, and 120 a. Fordstone; may be the Thomas Ford, servant, who was transp. to Md. by 1652; in Dec. 1670 was conv. 300 a. Repulta by Henry Stockett; had iss.: ELIZABETH, m. 1st Job Barnes, 2nd Mathias Clark, and 3rd John or William Norton; JOHN, d. 1737; JAMES (98: 44; 211:14, 117, 118, 130, 142; 388).

FORD, JOHN (2), s. of Thomas (1), d. in A. A. Co. by 24 May 1737, when his will (made 24 Dec. 1746) was proved; m. Jane (---) who m. 2nd Gideon Linthicum; by will left his entire est. to w. Jane and her heirs; had iss.: THOMAS, b. 12 Nov. 1696, bur. 16 Dec. 1696; SARAH, b. 4 April 1698 (126:225; 219-1; 219-3; 346-2:160; Focke, "Linthicum Family.").

FORD, JAMES (3), s. of Thomas (1), d. in A. A. Co. in 1702; m. Elizabeth (---) who m. 2nd on 30 March 1703 John Stodgon, and 3rd, on 27 April 1705, Francis Moor; will of James Ford, 28 July 1702 - 16 Dec. 1702, named w. Eliza as extx., sons Thomas, John, and James, daus. Mary and Elizabeth, and bro. John, and sis. Elizabeth Barnes, as well as tract Upper Plantation, Lower Plantation, Rockford, and Repulta; had iss.: THOMAS, b. 28 Feb. 1692; MARY, b. 4 Oct. 1693, may have m. Joseph Chew on 23 Jan. 1710; JOHN, b. 6 July 1695; JAMES, b. 3 March 1696/7; ELIZABETH, b. 15 May 1699 (121:251; 219-3).

FORD, THOMAS (4), s. of James (3) and Elizabeth, was b. 28 Feb. 1692 in A. A. Co., d. in Balto. Co. c.1748; m. 1 Jan. 1711 Leah Price, dau. of Mordecai and Mary (Parsons) Price; acquired several parcels of land in Balto. Co.: 202 a. Selsed (now called Ford's Chance) from John and Pretiosa Boring in Jan. 1718; Nicholas Haile's share of part of Selsed in March 1747; and 50 a. Selsed (now called Jack's Double Purchase) from Ann, Jonathan, and John Plowman in March 1747; by 1750 his heirs owned 202 a. Selsed; his will, 18 Nov. 1748 - 4 Jan. 1748/9, named ch.: Stephen, Mordecai, John, and Thomas Ford, and Mary Barney; admin. bond was posted 4 Jan. 1748/9 by Charles Robinson and D. B. Partridge; est. was admin. 6 Nov. 1752 by Thomas Ford and named as heirs, son Stephen, dau. Mary w. of Absolom Barney, and granddau. Mary Barney; had iss.: THOMAS, b. 15 April 1714; JOHN, b. 5 Nov. 1720;

WILLIAM, b. 28 Feb. 1721; BENJAMIN, b. 18 Dec. 1723; MARY, b. 6 Feb. 1725, m. Absolom Barney; LLOYD, b. 10 Nov. 1727; MORDECAI, b. 19 Dec. 1729; STEPHEN, b. 15 Oct. 1731 (5:527; 13:80; 63:524; 78:298; 29:384, 386; 110:435; 133; 153:15; 219-3).

FORD, JOHN (5), s. of James (3) and Elizabeth, was b. 6 July 1695; in 1720 he and James Ford of P. G. Co. sold Dr. William Lock of A. A. Co. the tract Rockford, which they had inher. from their father (Nimmo, "Ford Notes").

FORD, JAMES (6), s. of James (3) and Elizabeth, was b. 3 March 1696, and may have at least two ch.: JOSHUA, b. 2 March 1721; ELEANOR, b. 2 Oct. 1722 (Unpub. notes comp. by Mark B. Ford).

FORD, THOMAS (7), s. of Thomas (4) and Leah, was b. 15 April 1714, and d. by 1787 when letters of admin. were granted to Charlotte Ford (nee Cockey); in 1750 owned 50 a. part Selsed; had iss.: son, k. in an accident in Feb. 1753, age 12; THOMAS COCKEY DEYE, b. 26 July 1752; CAROLINE, b. 27 June 1759, m. Samuel Hale; poss. FREDERICK, m. by lic. of 4 June 1782 to Margaret Benjamin; poss. a dau. who m. John Ford of William; poss. ANNE who m. James Bond; poss. PRISCILLA who m. by lic. of 3 March 1787 Charles Gill; and poss. PENELOPE who m. Francis Neale (89:111, 129; 133; 153: 106; 231-AL#F:445; AL#G:11ß; WG#FF:238, 239; 235; 385:217; Unpub. notes made available to the compiler by Robert T. Nave).

FORD, JOHN (8), s. of Thomas (4) and Leah, was b. 5 Nov. 1720; d. by 1784; m. Ruth (or Ruhama), dau. of Edmond Howard; in 1750 owned 100 a. Gist's Search and 100 a. part Reserve; his will was made 18 Aug. 1782 and proved 14 Sept. 1782,; est. admin. 10 Nov. 1784 and 11 Dec. 1790; had iss.: THOMAS, b. 20 Feb. 1744; BELINDA, b. 4 Nov. 1748, m. (---) Simmons; REBECCA, b. 6 March 1750; JOHN HOWARD, b. 30 July 1753; JOSHUA, b. 23 Feb. 1756; ELEANOR, b. 13 April 1758, m. by lic. of 10 Dec. 1781 Benjamin Todd; EDMUND, b. 2 Aug. 1760, m. Catherine Bond; CHARLES, b. 2 Aug. 1760 or 1768, by March 1807 was in Bourbon Co., Ky., when he and w. Sarah sold pt. Gist's Search to Rebecca and Lloyd Ford; LLOYD; CASSANDRA, m. by Fred. Co. lic. of 9 Jan. 1786 Elias Harding (8:136; 10:240; 75:511; 77:574, 583; 81:451; 82:145; 90: 166, 517; 92:374; 134:5, 13, 20, 26; 112:456; 231-WG#95:13)

FORD, WILLIAM (9), s. of Thomas (4) and Leah, was b. 28 Feb. 1721; may have had at least two ch. (proof is lacking): JOHN, of William; BENJAMIN, of William.

FORD, LLOYD (10), s. of Thomas (4) and Leah, was b. 10 Nov. 1727 in St. Paul's Par., and d. 1816 in Washington Co., Tenn.; m. Mary, dau. of Alexander Grant; in Feb. 1778 Thomas Ford of Stephen conv. to him 50½ a. Ford's Choice; in Sept. 1782 Lloyd and w. Mary sold Ford's Choice to John Robert Holliday; had iss.: LLOYD, Jr., b. 1748, d. 1843; JAMES, d. 1845; JOHN, d. 1838; THOMAS, m. Nancy Wood; ALEXANDER (213-WG#A:546; WG#K:158; unpub. Ford data of Robert T. Nave).

FORD, MORDECAI (11), s. of Thomas (4) and Leah, was b. 19 Dec. 1729 in St. Paul's Par., and in 1752 m. Ruth Barney, b. 1732, dau.

of William and Mary Barney; gave his age as 52 in Feb. 1781;
had iss.: BARNEY, d. 1807 having m. Mary Cole in 1783; HORATIO,
m. 1787 Elizabeth, dau. of John and Sarah (Gorsuch) Gill; MORDE-
CAI, b. 20 May 1768, m. Mary Price; THOMAS (231-WG#F:238; data
from Robert T. Nave).

FORD, STEPHEN (12), s. of Thomas (4) and Leah, was b. 15 Oct.
1731 in St. Paul's Par.; d. by 15 April 1778; on 24 June 1773
conv. 101 a. Ford's Choice to Archibald Buchanan; had iss.: STE-
PHEN, b. 1 Jan. 1765, m. Ruth Stevenson; JOSEPH, d. 1790; LEAH
(231-AL#H:64; data from Robert T. Nave; also 8:10, 45; 133:36).

FORD, JOHN, m. Sarah Murphy on 2 June 1755; had iss.: BENJA-
MIN, b. 16 Nov. 1755; DORCAS, b. 3 March 1757; DAVID, b. 1 Nov.
1759; RACHEL, b. 16 March 1762 (129:355, 379).

FORD, MARK, on 26 Aug. 1738 stated to the Vestry of St. Geo.
Parish that he had m. Rose (---), wid. of (---) Swift and of
Thomas Phelps (130:292).

FORD, RICHARD, tailor, servant with 2 years, 7 mos., to serve
was listed in the 1759 inv. of Richard Winn; may be the same
Richard Ford, "tailor from London," who advertised he was in
business at New Town, Balto., in June 1759 (54:309; 255).

FORD, SARAH, was ind. for bast. in Aug. 1746 (36:116).

FOREACRES, ANN, age 5 the previous June was bound to Francis
Wharton in Aug. or Nov. 1755 (40:390).

FOREACRES, LAURENCE, m. by 10 March 1730 Rachel, dau. and
heiress of William Hill of Cecil Co. (73:211).

FOREMAN, JOSEPH, m. Anne (---), and had iss.: WILLIAM, b. 16
Dec. 1721 (133:2).

FORESIGHT, JOSEPH, m. 1st on 28 Dec. 1734 Mary Willson, who
d. 8 May 1730; m. 2nd, 19 Aug. 1731, Mary Marshall; had iss.:
MARY, b. 8 Aug. 1727; PRUDENCE, b. 18 April 1734 (128:68, 99;
131).

FORGASON, ROBERT, was in Balto. Co. by 1692 as a taxable in
s. side Patapsco Hund. (138).

FORRISTER, ANNE, orphan, was to ordered by the Court to be
kept by William Jameson, Nov. 1744 (35:354).

FORSIDAL, ELIAS, was indicted for fathering an illeg. child,
March 1724/5 (27:127).

FORSTER, PATIENCE, was ind. and tried for bast. in March 1730
or 1731; had iss.: JOHN, b. 22 Jan. 1730 (29:96, 105; 133:20).

FORSTER, THOMAS. See FOSTER, THOMAS.

FORT(T), SAMUEL, d. Balto. Co. by 4 April 1749 when admin.
bond was posted by extx. Susannah Fort, with Luke Trotten and

Thomas Norris; dec. left a will; wid. Susannh m. 2nd George Bramwell on 7 March 1750; in 1750 his heirs owned 100 a. part Friendship and 26 a. Addition to Friendship; had iss.: RICHARD, b. 14
Aug. 1739; ELIZABETH, b. 2 Oct. 1741; SAMUEL, b. 15 Nov. 1743
(13:80; 134:25, 71; 153:53).

FORTH, HUGH, of Balto. Co., imm. to Md. by 1670 with w. Rosamond Forth and Alice, Angell, Ann, Jane, Mary, and Rosamond Forth
(388).

FOSTER/FORSTER, THOMAS (1), was in Balto. Co. by 1708 when
William Cromwell conv. him 140 a. Bare Neck; in March 1718 he
was ordered to serve Priscilla Freeborne extra time for running
away from her dec. husb. Richard Freeborne; m. by April 1727
Elizabeth (---); in 1719 Thomas Holland w. Margaret conv. to
Elizabeth Foster 120 a. part Holland's Chance; had iss.: SAMUEL,
b. 8 April 1727 (23:67; 59:613; 68:139, 247; 131).

FOSTER, SAMUEL (2), s. of Thomas (1), was b. 8 April 1727; in
Aug. 1734 was bound by his father to John and Isabella Sumner;
m. Margaret Guyton, dau. of Benjamin Guyton on 26 Feb. 1749; no
known issue (30:305; 112:339; 131).

FOSTER, BEZALEEL (3), no known rel. to above, was in Balto.
Co. by 24 Dec. 1734 when he m. as his 1st w. Mary Meed; m. 2nd,
on 10 Dec. 1749 Mary, wid. of Joshua Allender; in March 1740/1 Edward Chattam, s. of Mary Chattam, dec., was committed to Foster's
care; in June 1735 Benjamin and Margaret Hammond conv. 100 a.
Richardson to Bezaleel; in Jan. 1740 William Slade, s. and heir
of William Slade conv. part Windleys to Foster; in 1750 owned
100 a. Windley's Rest; date of death or settlement of est. not
known; had iss.: THOMAS, b. 6 Oct. 1735; JOHN, b. 3 Nov. 1737;
BENJAMIN, b. 23 Aug. 1737 or 1739; BEZALEEL, b. 6 March 1741
(31:460; 37:6; 74:241; 75:460; 131; 153).

FOSTER, JOHN (4), s. of Bezaleel (3), was b. 4 Nov. 1737; in
April 1756 was conv. 53 a. of Murray's Ridge by William and Diana
Murray; in Nov. 1774 he and w. Eleanor conv. Samuel Tipton part
of Foster's Hunting Ground (90:145; 231-AL#M:12).

FOSTER, MARY, was in Balto. Co. by 1723 when she gave a certificate to Abraham Cord; in the same year she conv. to James Taylor 90 a. Carter's Rest and 100 a. Jackson's Outlet (69:165; 74:
241).

FOSTER, RICHARD, d. by 20 March 1702 when his est. was inv.
by Daniel Scott and Francis Wilhide and val. at £ 14.15.6 (48:24).

FOSTER, RICHARD, d. by 27 Dec. 1703 when admin. bond on his
est. was posted by James Crooke, with Francis Dallahide and Walter Bosley; est. admin. by Crooke on 14 May 1707 (2:84; 13:65).

FOSTER, THOMAS, d. by 3 July 1710 when Elizabeth Foster, admnx.,
posted admin. bond with John Rattenbury and John Thomas; est. was
inv. the same day by Nicholas Fitzsimmons and Lance Todd and val.
at £ 30.17.9 and signed by James Carroll and Samuel Young (13:
71; 52:101).

FOSTER, WILLIAM, m. Mary (---), and was in Balto. Co. in 1727 when he signed the inv. of John Thomas; had iss.: ANN, b. 25 Jan. 1723; WILLIAM, b. 28 Feb. 1726; JAMES, b. 20 Oct. 1728 (128:54).

FOTTRELL, EDWARD, d. in Balto. Co. by 22 May 1742 when admin. bond was posted by Levin Gale of Somerset Co., and Wm. Chapman of A. A. Co. with George Steuart and Samuel Chambers; may be the Edward Fottrell who m. by 28 May 1730 the wid. Ann Grundy Lloyd; m. (2nd?) by 10 May 1739 Achsah, wid. and admnx. of Amos Woodward of A. A. Co., and dau. of Caleb Dorsey; in 1750 his heirs owned 23 a. Swede's Folly and 102 a. Welsh's Addition; had iss.: EDWARD, b. 17 June 1739; THOMAS, alive in Nov. 1748; ACH-SAH, by 8 Sept. 1766 had m. Robert Taffe of Ardee, Co. Lowth, Ireland (4:86; 13:81; 35:10; 133:64; 153:92; 213-DD#4:192; 219-2:429; Johnston, "Lloyd Family," in 346-2:169-179).

FOULKES, JOSEPH, of Balto. Co., d. leaving a will, 27 Feb. 1737 - 3 March 1737, left his entire est. to Dr. Buckler Part-ridge and the latter's heirs; admin. bond was posted 5 April 1738 by Buckler Partridge with Samuel Maccubbin and Joseph Thomas (13: 78; 126:236).

FOUNTAIN, MARY, was charged with bast. in March 1723/4 and tried June 1724 (26:201, 332).

FOURSIDES, MARY, was tried for bast. in Nov. 1746; John Butler admitted paternity (36:246).

FOWLER, RICHARD (1), was in Balto. Co. by 1692 as a taxable in s. side Gunpowder Hund.; ; in 1703 bought 400 a. Todd's Range from James Todd (the land was later held by Fowler's Orphans); d. by 24 April 1704 when admin. bond was posted by Eliza Fowler with Thomas Chamberlaine and Thomas Hutchins; est. was admin. by Eliza on 22 Aug. 1707 with the assistance of her atty. Matthew Green; had iss.: at least one dau., MARGARET, b. c.1699, age 12 the last day of May 1711; in June of that year was bound to James Durham to age 16 or marriage (2:79; 13:67; 21:210; 66:280; 138; 211:370).

FOWLER, JOSHUA (2), no known rel. to above, was in Balto. Co. by 1698; m. Mary (---); in Aug. 1718 pet. the court that his lame son be made levy free; pet. was granted in Nov. 1718; in Jan. 1696/7 surv. 98 a. Fowler's Chance; in June 1718 he conv. this land to Samuel Hughes; in March 1720 Samuel Hughes and w. Jane conv. the tract back to Fowler; d. by 12 Feb. 1731 leaving at least two sons: JOSHUA, b. 2 March 1698/9; JAMES, b. 22 July 1702 (23:5, 40; 68:10; 69:10; 128:9, 15; 211:316).

FOWLER, JAMES (3), s. of Joshua (2), was b. 22 July 1702; m. Margaret (---); on 12 Feb. 1731 as second s. of Joshua Fowler, de dec., he and w. Margaret conv. 98 a. Fowler's Chance to Thomas White; left iss.: JOSHUA, b. 20 Oct. 1731; MARY, b. 10 May 1735; WILLIAM, b. 30 Sept. 1737 (73:188; 128:75, 96, 98).

FOWLER, RICHARD, m. Honour Logsdon on 13 Sept. 1730, and had iss.: EDWARD, b. 14 Feb. 1730; MARY, b. 10 Feb. 1732; JOHN, b. 24 April 1735 (133:45, 149).

FOWLER, RICHARD, m. Mary Fitch on 31 Dec. 1754; in May 1763
was conv. 100 a. Bachelor's Ridge and 16 a. Hines' Desire by Edward Fell of William; in April 1733 was conv. 133 a. part Fitch's
Chance by William and Sarah Fitch; had iss.: WILLIAM, b. 26 March
1755; THOMAS, b. 27 Feb. 1761; JOHN, b. 9 July 1761 (sic); RICHARD,
b. 25 March 1762; BENJAMIN, b. 29 Dec. 1775 (87:235; 131; 133;
231-AL#G:159).

FOWLER, SAMUEL, m. Sarah McCarty on 3 June 1736; had iss.
(mother's name given as Mary): SARAH, b. 5 May 1737; SAMUEL, b.
6 June 1739; MARY, b. 24 Oct. 1741 (128:94, 96, 103, 321).

FOWLER, SARAH, no par. given, was b. 31 March 1704, bur. 6
Feb. 1706 (128:20).

FOX, AARON, in Nov. 1737 deserted his w. Sarah (31:143).

FOX, JOHN, serv., was in April 1688 inv. of Thomas Lightfoot
(51:8).

FOX, MARGARET, had iss.: MARY, b. 2 Oct. 1737 (129:322).

FOXON/FOXUM, RICHARD, was in Tal. Co. in Nov. 1666 when he
bought 175 a. Bluntville from William Stanley; d. by 13 Dec.
1674 when his est. was admin. by William Chadbourne who had m.
his widow (2:202; 94).

FOY, (---), m. by 29 May 1742 Rebecca, dau. of Rebecca Potee
(111:80).

FOY, MICHAEL, d. by 16 Dec. 1702 when admin. bond was posted
by Blanch Wells, admnx., with Anthony Drew; est. was inv. 27 Jan.
1702/3 by Thomas Capel and Richard Smithers and val. at £ 3.9.6
(13:6b; 51:107).

FOY, MILES, was in Balto. Co. by Oct. 1728; d. by 27 Dec.
1751; on 4 Oct. 1728 signed an antenuptial contract with Frances,
relict of Hugh Grant; Frances was b. c.1676, giving her age as 60
in 1736 and stating she had been in the county for 36 years or
more; she had m. 1st Daniel Johnson, and 2nd Hugh Grant; in 1750
Miles owned 147 a. Eightrop; his will, 18 Nov. 1751 - 9 Dec. 1751,
directed he was to be buried at the Roman Chapel, named w. Frances
(to have 150 a. Eightrop), sis. Mary Foy, Winifred Sullivan and
Daniel Sullivan; admin. bond was posted 27 Dec. 1751 by Daniel
Sullivan with Robert Briarly and Thomas Hallam (13:91; 71:317;
112:412; 153; 224:238).

FOY, THOMAS, m. Reb(ecca) (---); in Nov. 1748 as Thomas Foy
or Fowey conv. 100 a. Tracey's Park to George Haile; had iss.:
JOHN, b. 18 Jan. 1726 (80:166; 131:3/r).

FRAISHER. See FRAZIER.

FRAME, WILLIAM, was in Balto. Co. by 1692 as a taxable in n.
side Patapsco Hund.; when he d. his est. was admin. by Edward
Stevenson (2:237; 138).

FRANCIS, HENRY, d. by c.1700 when one Harebottle held 200 a.
Felks' Forest for his orphans (211).

FRANCIS, WILLIAM, servant, with 2 years to serve, was listed
in the 1749 inventory of Capt. Robert North (53:377).

FRANKLAND. See FRANKLIN.

FRANKLIN/FRANKLAND, CHA., m. Hannah Harsh on 19 April 1756
(131).

FRANKLIN, JOSEPH, s. of Mary, was b. 22 May 1736; m. Eliz.
Oakley on 15 Jan. 1756 (131; 133:57).

FRANKLIN, THOMAS, was b. c.1706, d. by 27 April 1787; imm. to
Md. c.1728; m. 1st on 26 Oct. 1729 Ruth Wilmot; m. 2nd by 22 May
1744 Ruth, admnx. of Peasley Ingram, and dau. of Charles Hammond;
on 7 June 1732 conv. part Long Crandon to Joseph Peregoy, Jr., s.
of Henry; by 1750 owned 100 a. Leew's Thicket, 100 a. Franklin's
Delight and Ruth's Garden, 150 a. of Headingham in Buckingham,
88 a. Industry, and Ingram's Rush Neck; rep. Balto. Co. in the
General Assembly, 1751 and 1752-53; at his death owned an est.
of over £ 1700.0.0 and over 2000 acres in Balto. Co.; had iss.:
JAMES, b. 16 Jan. 1730; THOMAS HEATH, d. by 1794; BENJAMIN, d. by
1794; SARAH, m. (---) Smith; ELIZABETH, b. 1745, d. 1771, m.
Aquila Paca (5:10; 73:239; 133:18, 149; 153:22; 370:54, 55, 328,
329).

FRANKS, MATHIAS, m. 26 Nov. 1750 Mary Morris (131).

FRAZIER, ALEXANDER, in Nov. 1719 was lic. to keep an ordinary
at Whetstone Point; d. by 16 Aug. 1720 when admin. bond was posted by wid. Elizabeth Frazier, with George Walker and Thomas Taylor; est. inv. 5 Sept. 1720 by Lance Todd and John Ashman and
val. at £ 90.5.2; est. admin. 13 July 1721 by Eliza (1:297; 13:
73; 23:244; 51:156).

FRAZIER, ELIZABETH,chose Benjamin Price as guardian in Nov.
1730 (29:50).

FRAZIER, JAMES, m. Eliza (---), and had iss.: JAMES, b. 17
March 1743 (131:104/r).

FRAZIER, JOHN (poss. s. of Alexander Frazier above), in 1729
was named as son-in-law in will of Richard Hewitt; in Nov. 1730
with cons. of moth. chose Benjamin Price as guardian; in March
1731 with consent of his mother was bound to John Steward; in 1750
owned 250 a. Todd's Forest and 35 a. Elizabeth's Diligence; 1st w.
unknown; m. 2nd Eleanor (---); d. leaving a will, 7 March 1756 -
2 June 1756, which named w. Eleanor and ch.: Mary, Sarah, Alexander, and John and tracts Weston Run, Todd's Forest, Deep Point,
Elizabeth's Diligence and Thompson's Forest; admin. bond posted
by Eleanor Frazier on 14 June 1756 with John Wooden and Solomon
Wooden; est. admin. by Eleanor on 26 July 1756 and 25 Feb. 1757;
had iss.: MARY; SARAH; ALEXANDER; and JOHN (5:309, 324; 13:90;
29:50, 225; 111:94; 125:149; 153:73).

FRAZIER, JOHN, b. c.1713, gave his age as 50 on 29 Aug. 1763 and stated that 24 years previously he had m. Rebecce, wid. of James Boring; moved to the Island of New Providence, where his will, 23 Sept. 1779 - 27 Sept. 1784, proved in New York, named Eleanor and Charlotte Frazier, ch. of testator's dec. bro. Alexander Frazier of New Providence; the est. of his dec. father John Frazier of Md.; Susanna Towson, late wid. of his dec. bro.; mother Eleanor Frazier; Isaac Cox of Phila.; Martha, dau. of John and Susanna Green of New Providence, sis. Sarah w. of Mr. Hall of Md.; Nicholas Garner and Capt. Thomas Towson, both of New Providence, were to admin. the est. of his bro. Alexander; had iss.: RUTH, b. c.1740, m. John Osborn; ELIZABETH, b. c.1742, m. (---) Brown; JOHN, b. c.1744 (89:134; 112:553; Heckinger, Desc. of John Boring, in 540).

FREDERICK, JOHN, d. by 18 Oct. 1746 when admin. bond was posted by T. Sheredine with Parker Hall and John Hatton (13:87).

FREEBORN, RICHARD (1), m. Jane (---); lived at Catherington, Hampshire, Eng., where their ch. were born: THOMAS, bapt. 8 Dec. 1650; RICHARD, bapt. 6 July 1652; GILES, bapt. 23 Oct. 1654; JOHN bapt. 18 Feb. 1655; CLEMENT, bapt. 15 March 1657 (Freeborn entries in International Genealogy Index for Hampshire; Church of Jesus Christ of Latter Day Saints).

FREEBORN, THOMAS (2), s. of Richard (1) and Jane, bapt. 8 Dec. 1650 at Catherington; came to A. A. Co., by 1674; m. 1st Sarah (poss. Howard), and 2nd Rachel, wid. of Richard Kilbourne and dau of Robert Proctor; came to Possess 268 a. Johnston Bed, orig. sur. April 1684 for John Johnston; also owned 150 a. Johnston's Rest; his will, 3 Jan. 1713 - 13 Jan. 1713, named dau. Sarah Samson, son Richard, daus. Jane Thomas and Priscilla and Ann Freeborn, and granddau. Freenater Thomas; had iss.: SARAH, d. 15 Nov. 1716, m. Jeremiah Sampson, shipmaster; RICHARD, d. Jan. 1718; JANE, m. 18 Jan. 1704 Robert Thomas; PRISCILLA, m. 8 Dec. 1720 Samuel Howell; ANN, m. David Thomas; ELIZABETH, m. 5 Dec. 1702 Garrett Garrettson; MARY, m. Thomas Tolley (122:257; 129:196; 200-35:24; 211; 279; 313:119-122).

FREEBORNE, RICHARD (3), s. of Thomas (2), d. in Balto. Co. by 27 Jan. 1718 when admnx. Priscilla Freeborne posted admin. bond with John Cottrell and Thomas Lofton; est. admin. by extx. Priscilla now w. of Samuel Howell; est. inv. in 1719 by Thomas Cord and William Loney and val. at £ 75.4.5; est. admin. 27 June 1721; dec. left no children (1:244, 260; 13:72; 51:148).

FREEBORN, JOHN, was listed in 1759 inv. of Davis Bissett as a servant (52:330).

FREELAND, GEORGE, m. Mary (---), and had iss.: STEPHEN, b. 14 Oct. 1710, d. 20 Dec. 1714; SARAH, age 2 on 15 Aug. 1715; PERDINE, b. 1 March 1715 (128:27, 34).

FREELAND, STEPHEN, was in Balto. Co. by 1659; m. Sarah (---) by whom he had iss.: GEORGE, b. 7 Oct. 1659; SARAH, b. 8 Aug. 1664; JOHN, b. 10 March 1668 (128:13, 15).

FREELAND, STEPHEN, m. Sarah (---), and had iss.: MARY, b. 25 Dec. 1708; may have d. Feb. 1708/9; MARY, b. 25 Dec. 1710 (128:25, 27, 35).

FREELAND, STEPHEN, d. by 10 June 1710; est. was admin. by William Howard; admin. bond was posted 10 May 1709 (2:150; 13:68).

FREEMAN, FRANCIS, was in Balto. Co. by 4 June 1684 when he and Richard Enock purch. 111 a. from Thomas Long and wife Jane (106: 289).

FREEMAN, FRANCIS, m. Elizabeth Pike on 17 June 1724, and had iss.: MARY, b. 5 Jan. 1727; ELIZABETH, b. 9 Feb. 1729; JOHN, b. 20 July 1733 (128:62, 76).

FREEMAN, HANNAH, in March 1710/11 was ind. for bast. (21:205).

FREEMAN, HENDRICK bought 50 a. at Sassafras R. from Philip Holleger on 10 March 1665/6 (95).

FREEMAN, JAMES, m. Margaret Buttram on 28 Oct. 1742 (131:95/r).

FREEMAN, MARY, m. Hugh Lowe on 5 June 1729 (131).

FREEMAN, WILLIAM, was in Balto. Co. by 1692 as a taxable in n. side Patapsco Hund. (139).

FRENCH, JACOB, in 1750 owned 125 a. Fishing Creek (153:105).

FRENCH, JAMES, d. in Balto. Co., leaving a will, 28 Jan. 1760 - 10 March 1760, named w. Areaunagg as extx.; admin. bond was posted 11 March 1760 by Arianna French with Hannah Hughes and Daniel Chamier; est. admin. 24 Feb. 1761; dec. left no issue (4:349; 13: 103; 210-30:835).

FRENCH, MICHAEL, m. Elizabeth (---), and had iss.: NATHANIEL, b. 1 Oct. 1727 (128:52).

FRENCH, MICHAEL, age 20, came from Ireland c.1746, ran away from John Hall and Jacob Giles in Balto. Town in or before Oct. 1753 (385:258).

FRETWELL, JAMES, m. Ann (---) who d. 12 Oct. 1734 (128:85).

FRETWELL, THOMAS, m. 22 Oct. 1727 Ann Palmer (129:258).

FRIEND, JAMES, m. by March 1683/4 Jane, relict of Ambrose Gillett (18:141)..

FRIFOUGH, BOLSHAR, orphan Dutch boy, aged 8 next 1 Dec., in Nov. 1758 was bound to Peter Brawner, a Dutchman at Lawson's Ironworks (44).

FRINCHAM. See FUNCHAM.

THE FRISBY FAMILY has been the subject of an article by Francis B. Culver in <u>Maryland Genealogies</u>, I, 451-467.

FRISBY, JAMES, was in Balto. Co. by 3 Jan. 1670/1 when he bought 100 a. at Sassafras R. from Oliver Mathiason (97:123).

FRISBY, JOHN, of Kent Co., m. Frances, dau. of Col. George Wells; left iss.: PEREGRINE, SARAH; and MARY, m. Thomas Henderson (209-30:135).

FRISBY, MARY, d. by 15 July 1748 when admin. bond was posted by Mary Henderson of A. A. Co., admnx., with John Hall of Swan Town and John Paca; Henrietta Holland renounced admin. of her sister's est.; est. was inv. on 4 March 1748 by James Osborn and Daniel Ruff and val. at £ 584.12.9, and signed by kin: Cordelia Hall, Henrietta Holland, and Susanna Holland, and filed on 24 May 1749 by Mary Henderson; additional inv. worth £ 86.12.7½ was filed 20 March 1754 (13:85; 49:276; 50:170).

FRISBY, Capt. PEREGRINE, m. Mrs. Mary Holland on 26 Jan. 1738 and d. by 25 March 1747 when admin. bond was posted by admnx. Mary Frisby with John Hall and John Hall of Swan Town; on 15 June 1748 Mary Henderson posted admin. bond; est. was inv. on 4 March 1748 by Daniel Ruff and James Osborn and val. at £ 566.8.0, and signed by kin: Cordelia Hall, Sarah Freeland, and Sarah Hughes; est. was admin. on 17 May 1754 by John Hall of Swan Town; in 1750 his heirs owned 280 a. Planter's Delight, 320 a. Collett's Point, and 100 a. Black Island; left iss.: FRANCES, b. 4 Aug. 1741; SARAH, b. 24 July 1744; THOMAS, b. 15 Sept. 1746 (4:200; 13:84, 85; 40:18; 49:229; 128:105, 115; 129:345; 153:16).

FRISBY, WILLIAM, m. by 4 Aug. 1719 a dau. of George Wells, and had iss.: MARY; PEREGRINE (1:54).

FRISBY, WILLIAM, in 1750 owned 500 a. New Stadt (153:103).

FRIZZELL, (---), d. in A. A. Co., leaving a wid. (---) who m. Timothy Shaw (211:163).

FRIZZELL, ABRAHAM, was named as son-in-law in the will of John Gale of A. A. Co., 31 Dec. 1730; prob. the Abraham Frizzell, age 20, named in 1742 lease of part of My Ladys Manor; married Sabra, dau. of John and Mary Rockhold (77:82; 126:42; Dorsey et al, The Dorsey Family).

FRIZZELL, GALE, b. c.1723, s. of John, is prob. the Gale Frizzell named as a grandson in the Dec. 1730 will of John Gale of A. A. Co.; mentioned in 1742 lease of part of My Lady's Manor; m. Susanna (---), and had iss.: BETSEY, b. 4 Feb. 1743; SARAH, b. 25 Jan. 1745; JOHN GALE, b. July 1748; THOMAS, b. 12 Jan. 1750 (77:82; 126:42; 131:115/r, 129/r).

FRIZZELL, ISAAC, m. by 10 Aug. 1734, Sarah, devisee of Ambrose Nelson of Balto. Co., dec. (217-RD#2:190).

FRIZZELL, JACOB, in Dec. 1730 was named as a grandson in the will of John Gale; age given as 21 in Nov. 1742 lease of part of My Lady's Manor; m. Ann (---), and had iss.: ABRAHAM, b. 2 Aug. 1744 (77:82; 126:42; 131:104/r).

FRIZZELL, JAMES, m. Mary (---), mother of William York; by 1692 was a taxable in n. side Gunpowder Hund.; d. by 10 July 1699 when his wid. Mary conv. release of her right of dower for Edward's Lot and Hathaway's Trust to William and Oliver York, sons of William York; had iss., a son born in All Hallows Par. in A. A. Co.: JAMES, b. 1 Jan. 1692 (19:316; 63:391; 138; 219-1).

FRIZZELL, JAMES, prob. the James b. 1 Jan. 1692, s. of James and Mary, was in Balto. Co. by 8 June 1723 when he conv. 331 a. Happy Choice to Henry Wetherall; in May 1726 signed the inv. of James York as kin (51:50; 69:191).

FRIZZELL, JOHN, m. by 2 Oct. 1703 Eliza, sis. of David Stewart; in April 1709 John and Eliza conv. to Patrick Duncan 50 a. Williamson's Purchase; had iss. (named in will of their uncle David Stewart): JOHN; PRISCILLA (67:30; 122:25).

FRIZZELL, JOHN, in Dec. 1730 was named as son-in-law of John Gale of A. A. Co. (126:42).

FRIZZELL, JOHN, m. Nov. 1721 or Oct. 1722 Providence Dallahide who d. 20 Nov. 1727; had iss.: JOHN, b. Aug. 1724; PROVIDENCE, b. Sept. 1726 (131:13, 17).

FRIZZELL, JOHN, d. by 15 Feb. 1725 when William Frizzell posted admin. bond with Charles Rockhold and Thomas Wright; est. inv. in 1726; additional inv. filed 24 Oct. 1726 and val. at L14.15.9; est. admin. by Wm. Frizzell on 11 July 1727 (3:67; 13:75; 51:68, 280).

FRIZZELL, JOHN, age 6 in Oct. 1729; in Aug. 1729 was bound to Bethia Calvert (28:274).

FRIZZELL, JOHN, of A. A. Co., in Nov. 1742 leased part of My Lady's Manor from Thomas Brerewood, the lease to run for the lifetimes of John's children: GALE, b. c.1723; NATHAN, b. c.1730; and SUSANNA, b. c.1727 (80:138).

FRIZZELL, MARY, d. by 10 April 1726 when George York posted admin. bond with John Taylor and John Armstrong; est. was inv. 29 May 1726 by Jos'a Merriken and James Isham and val. at L 37. 16.5, and signed by kin: James and John Frizzell, and filed by George York (13:74; 49:52).

FRIZZELL, NATHAN, b. c.1730, s. of John of A. A. Co.; m. on 18 April 1751 Margaret Deason (131).

FRIZZELL, WILLIAM, was in A. A. Co. by Sept. 1663 when he surv. 50 a. Adventure, in Oct. 1663 surv. 100 a. Chance; in May 1682 surv. 30 a. Friendship which was later held by John Frizzell; d. by June 1684 when his wid. Jane and her 2nd husb. Patrick Duncan, conv. prop. to William's son John; left iss.: JOHN (211:197, 200, 217; 213-WH#4:107).

FRIZZELL, WILLIAM, in March 1722/3 had bros. John, Jr., and Abraham; d. by 15 Feb. 1725 when admin. bond was posted by William Frizzell with Charles Rockhold and Thomas Wright (13:75; 25:220).

FROST, ROBERT, m. Frances Lye in Feb. 1732 (133:150).

FROST, WILLIAM, m. Susanna Robertson on 21 Dec. 1749 (131).

FROST, WILLIAM, d. by 9 July 1755 when admin. bond was posted by William Lux, with John Ensor, Jr.; est. admin. by Lux on 7 Nov. 1757 (5:318; 13:99).

FRY, DAVID, d. leaving a will, 13 Sept. 1680 - 19 Feb. 1680, in which he left 400 a. on Gunpowder River to Matthew Silby and Thomas Pratt; earlier had surv. 400 a. Fry's Plains in Sept. 1678; this tract was later held by the orphans of Edward Fry (120:97; 211:35).

FRYLEY, WILLIAM, was in Balto. Co. by 1695 as a taxable in Spesutia Hund. (140).

FUGATE. See FEWGATE.

FULKS, JOHN, m. Alice Wood on 18 Feb. 1760 (131).

FULLER, JOHN (1), possibly the progenitor, was in Balto. Co. by 11 Jan. 1655 when he surv. 100 a. known as Fuller's Outlet; may be identical to or may be the father of: JOHN (see below) (211:68).

FULLER, JOHN (2), poss. s. of John (1) above, or else identical to him, was in Balto. Co. by 1682 when Hendrick Enlows conv. to him 100 a. Swallow Fork; in Feb. 1687 surv. 148 a. Buck Range (later held by John Anderson); in 1687 he and his w. conv. 100 a. Swallow Fork back to Henry Enlows; in 1688 purch 16 a. The Falls from Michael Judd and wife; in 1688 Fuller and w. conv. 100 a. Fuller's Outlet to Robert Benger; by 1692 was a taxable in n. side Gunpowder; purch. 70 a. Hap Hazard from John Bevan and w. in 1693 and purch. 200 a. Windley's Rest from John Taylor in 1695; d. by 6 March 1700 when his est. was inv. by Francis Dallahide and William Wright and was val. at £ 25.10.0; in March 1700 wid. Hester Fuller conv. cattle and furniture to her sons John and Henry; she m. as her 2nd husb., by Oct. 1701, John Peters, who made his wife Hester and his son-in-law John Fuller his atty.; in Oct. 1701 John and Hester Peters and John Fuller and w. Sarah conv. Waterton's Neglect to William Peckett; had iss.: JOHN; and HENRY (59:19, 234, 258, 276, 335, 345, 372, 461, 493, 496; 66:56, 93, 146; 138; 206-11B:17; 211:70).

FULLER, JOHN (3), s. of John (2) and Hester, may be the John Fuller of St. John's Parish who was age 40 in 1728; m. by Oct. 1701, Sarah (---) who joined him in a deed; in April 1705 John and Sarah conv. 200 a. of land on s. side of Bush R. to Nicholas Herbert ; in 1720 leased 120 a. Gunpowder Manor for the lifetimes of his sons Henry and Behemiah, born c.1717 and 1719; by 1767 both sons were in Carolina; had iss.: HENRY, and NEHEMIAH (64:57; 66: 146; 389:12).

FULLER, HENRY (4), s. of John (2) and Hester, in 1700 was conv. cattle and furniture by his mother, and may be the Henry Fuller who was a taxable in n. side Gunpowder Hund. in 1704 (66:56; 136).

FULLER, HENRY (5), s. of John (3) and Sarah, was b. 2 Feb. 1715 in St. John's Par.; may be the Henry Fuller who m. Elizabeth Cox, wid. of Joseph Cox, on 26 Aug. 1738; by 1767 he had moved to Carolina; had at least one son: WILLIAM, b. 10 Nov. 1745 (33:8; 131:73/r, 114/r; 389:12).

FULLER, JOHN, s. of Mary Stamford, w. of James Stamford, was bound to Nathaniel Shepherd on 15 Nov. 1727 (71:28).

FULLER, JOHN, m. Ruth Danby on 10 Dec. 1736; in April 1743 as John Fuller of Thomas, leased part of My Lady's Manor, the lease to run for the lifetimes of John, age 28, wife Ruth, age 25, and son Thomas, age 3; had iss.: THOMAS, b. 14 Aug. 1739 (77:233; 131).

FULLER, JOHN, Jr., m. Susannah (---) and had iss.: THOMAS, b. 29 July 1734; JEMIMA, b. 9 Oct. 1736; JOHN, b. 3 Jan. 1738 (131).

FULLER, JOHN, in 1750 owned 100 a. Hutchin's Addition (153: 10).

FULLER, JOHN, m. Ruth Gott on 7 Jan. 1755 (131).

FULLER, MORDECAI, m. Mary James on 16 May 1745 (131).

FULLER, WILLIAM, m. Jane Johnson on 3 Feb. 1733 in Cecil Co. (128:79).

FULTON, FRANCIS, m. Ann Matthew on 17 March 1757 (129:353).

FULTON, JOHN, m. Hannah Norris, dau. of Edward, on 4 Aug. 1754 (3:3; 131).

FURAT, PETER, had iss.: JOHN, b. 27 Feb. 1689 at Musketo Creek; ANN, b. 14 March 1692 at Spesutia Creek (128:2). See FUCAT, PETER.

FURLEY, JOHN, was in Balto. Co. by March 1724 when he purch. tract Overlooked from William and Ann Baker (69:251).

FURNESS, JOHN, m. Jane Green on 10 Feb. 1744 (131).

FUSSE, HENRY, was in Balto. Co. by 1692 as a taxable in s. side Patapsco Hund. (138).

GABRIEL, MARGARET, in Nov. 1738 was tried for bast.; stated the father was dead (31:320).

GADD, (---) (1), was prob. the father of two sons: THOMAS; and WILLIAM.

GADD, THOMAS (2), s. of (---) (1) is placed as a brother of William Gadd because the latter was security for admin. bond on Thomas' est.; m. Christian Ditto on 22 Jan. 1732/3; d. 13 Dec. 1738; admin. bond posted 19 Feb. 1738 by Christiana Gadd with William Gadd and William Ditto; est. was admin. on 21 Nov. 1740 by Christiana; had one ch.: MARGARET, b. 28 March 1734(4:56; 13: 141; 33:164; 131).

GADD, WILLIAM (3), s. of (?) (1), is placed as a brother of Thomas because he was security for the latter's admin. bond; m. Mary Standiford on 29 May 1734 and had iss.: ABSOLOM, b. 9 May 1735; THOMAS, b. 27 April 1738 (13:41; 131:58/r, 80/r).

GADD, ABSOLOM (4), s. of William (3), was b. 9 May 1735 and m. Elizabeth Cullison on 19 Oct. 1758; had iss.: WILLIAM, b. 30 June 1759 (131).

GADD, WILLIAM (5), s. of Absolom (4) and Mary, was b. 30 June 1759, and d. 14 Feb. 1835 having m. Nancy Drake and served in the Rev. War from April 1779 to Nov. 1781 from Penna.; later res. in Ohio Co., Va., then Monroe Co., Ohio, where he applied for a pension in Sept. 1832 (353:256; Report of the Ohio Gen. Society, Aug. 1966, p. 3).

GAFF, JOHN, was in Balto. Co. by 1694 as a taxable in n. side Patapsco Hund. (139).

GAGE, JOHN, was in Balto. Co. by 1694 as a taxable in n. side Patapsco Hund. (139).

GAIN, WILLIAM (1), progenitor, was in Balto. Co. by 1682 when he surv. 156 a. called Wallstowne, and d. in Balto. Co. by 1693; died leaving a will, 10 Nov. 1693 - 14 Nov. 1693, in which he left prop. to sons Samuel and John, and w. Mary; est. was inv. on 2 Dec. 1693 by John Ensor and John Broad and val. at £ 34.1.0; had iss.: SAMUEL; JOHN (51:25; 121:81; 211:85).

GAIN, SAMUEL (2), s. of William (1), was b. c.1675, giving his age as 39 in June 1714 when he pet. the court; by 1694 was a taxable in n. side Patapsco (21:503; 139).

GAIN, MARY, m. John Miller on 11 Feb. 1725 (133:150).

GAIN, WILLIAM, m. 1st Catherine (---), and 2nd on 1 Aug. 1727 Rebecca Hawkins who as Rebecka Gain, wid., m. 2nd, on 5 Aug. 1734 James Boreing; had iss., two by his 1st w., and three by his 2nd w.: WILLIAM, b. 5 July 172p; SAMUEL, d. 18 Jan. 1728; by 2nd w.: ELIZABETH, b. 13 Jan. 1728, may have m. Jacob Cox; JOHN, b. 16 Sept. 1730; WILLIAM, b. 26 Sept. 1730 (133:6, 18, 19, 38, 152, 156, 194; 353).

GAIN, WILLIAM, in Aug. 1750 was ind. for bast. (37:151).

GAITHER, JOHN, m. by March 1723/4 Elizabeth, extx. of Benjamin Warfield (26:278).

GALASPIE. See GILLESPIE.

GALE, GEORGE, and JOHN GALE were listed in the Balto. Co. Debt Book for 1750 as owning 200 a. part Chevy Chase (153:93).

GALE, MARGARET, was ind. for bast. in March 1741/2 and again in March 1746/7 (23:294; 26:378).

GALHAMPTON, ELIZABETH, was ind. for bast. in March 1745/6;

Samuel Jarvis was named as the father; in Aug. 1746 as servant to
Mary Keen she was again tried for bast. (35:800, 815; 36:133).

GALHAMPTON/GALLAHAMPTON/GALLYHAMPTON, THOMAS, was in Balto.
Co. by 10 Nov. 1720 when he m. Elizabeth Hill; the births of
their children are given in both St. George's Par. and St. John's
Par.; because of discrepancies, dates from St. George's Par. are
given first, with those from St. John's given in parentheses;
left iss.: ELIZABETH, b. 3 June 1721 (or 3 June 1723): JOHN, b.
26 May 1725 (or 26 Aug. 1725); CATHERINE, b. 15 Oct. 1728 (or 6
Oct. 1727); MARY, b. 17 Aug. 1732; JANE, b. 1 Oct. 1734; SARAH,
b. 28 May 1737; THOMAS, b. 1 Dec. 1741, m. Ann Mary Moore on 22
Oct. 1761 (128:73, 75, 97; 129:321; 131).

GALLAM, THOMAS, m. Elizabeth (---) and had iss.: JOHN, b. 1
June 1734 (131:64/r).

GALLION, JOHN (1), first known ancestor, was prob. b. c.1678
since he became 16 between 1692 and 1694 when he was a taxable
in n. side Gunpowder Hund.; d. 7 Jan. 1730/1; m. Mary (?); in
March 1711 was appointed overseer of the road that leads from
the Rollinghouse of John Hall to the Upper Quarter; d. leaving a
will, 1730 - 10 June 1731, in which he named ch. John, James
(to have 100 a. The Agreement); Sarah, Thomas (to have 100 a.
Gallion's Addition), Solomon (to have 120 a. Gallion's Hazard),
Samuel (to have part Whiteacre's Ridge), son Henry (to have part
of same tract), son Joseph (to have lower part The Agreement),
dau. Ann wife of John Phibble or Preble; left iss.: JOHN; JAMES;
THOMAS, b. 29 May 1709; SOLOMON, b. 6 Feb. 1712; SAMUEL, b. 27
July 1714; HENRY; ANN, m. John Preble; JOSEPH, b. 9 Nov. 1722,
d. 24 Dec. 1733; SARAH, b. 14 March 1725/6 (poss. the Sarah
Gallion who m. William Hollis on 15 March 1748) (125:200; 128:
26, 33, 64, 76; 139).

GALLION, JOHN (2), s. of John (1) and Mary, d. 10 Dec. 1733,
having m. Elizabeth Evans on 29 May 1726; in his father's will
is described as having removed himself and his family from the
dwelling plantation; left iss.: JOHN, b. 9 May 1730, prob. d.
young; JAMES, b. 12 May 1731; JOHN, b. 12 May 1733 (125:200;
128: 47, 64, 76; 129:321).

GALLION, JAMES (3), s. of John (1) and Mary, d. 1774, having
m. Phebe Johnson on 15 Aug. 1731; Phoebe was alive in 1776; in
1750 James owned 100 a. part The Argument; in 1776 wid. Phoebe
age 63, and Nathan, 27, Christian, 27, Martha, 23, and Sarah,
age 3, were living in Lower Harf. Hund.; had iss.: RACHEL, b.
10 Feb. 1734; JAMES, b. 9 May 1736; FANNY, b. 28 Aug. 1738, d.
26 Feb. 1740; MARY, b. 8 April 1739; JACOB, b. 3 April 1742;
WILLIAM, b. 10 Aug. 1744; SAMUEL; JOHN; MARTHA, b. c.1753; and
NATHAN, b. c.1749 (128:64, 80, 93B, 116; 129:324, 338; 153: 19,
90; 285).

GALLION, THOMAS (4), s. of John (1), was b. 29 May 1709, m.
Mary Young on 1 Oct. 1732 in Cecil Co.; had iss.: JACOB, b. 11
Dec. 1733; SINAI (dau.), b. 9 Aug. 1739; MARGARET, b. 15 Aug.
1743 (128:33, 80, 106; 129:332).

GALLION, SOLOMON (5), s. of John (1) and Mary, was b. 6 Feb.
1712; d. by 5 Nov. 1754 when admin. bond was posted by Charles
Gilbert with James Osborn; m. Martha Johnson on 17 April 1733; in
1750 owned 100 a. The Agreement; est. was admin. 2 June 1756 by
Charles Gilbert; left iss.: HANNAH, b. 22 Jan. 1733; KEZIAH, b.
18 June 1736; MARTHA, b. 31 Jan. 1738; SARAH, b. 25 Oct. 1741;
PHOEBE, b. 2 June 1744 (5:307; 13:162; 128:75, 77,98b, 129:
334, 339; 153:47).

GALLION, SAMUEL (6), s. of John (1) and Mary, was b. 27 July
1714, d. by 21 Sept. 1747 when admin. bond was posted by William
Smith with Nich. Ruxton Gay; his heirs were listed in 1750 as
owning 62½ a. Whitaker's Ridge (13:152; 153:86).

GALLION, JAMES (7), s. of James (3) and Phoebe, was b. 9 May
1736, m. Rachel Mariarty on 7 Sept. 1758 and had: PRISCILLA, b.
5 Aug. 1759; SARAH, b. c.1761; AVARILLA, b. c.1764; PHOEBE, b.
c.1766; MARTHA, b. c.1769; GEORGE, b. c.1771; MARY, b. c.1773;
RACHEL, b. c.1775 (129:367; 285).

GALLION, JACOB (8), s. of Thomas (4) and Mary, was b. 11 Dec.
1733, m. Elizabeth Arnold on 24 Feb. 1755, and had iss.: SOPHIA,
b. 10 May 1755; THOMAS, b. 17 March 1758 (129:358).

GALLION, JAMES, was in Balto. Co. by 1694 as a taxable in n.
side Gunpowder Hund.; d. by 27 June 1705 when admin. bond was
posted by Thomas Chamberlain with H. Wriothesley and Edward Smith;
his est. was inv. 23 Jan. 1706 by Sam'l Standifer and Jo'n Gallion and val. at £ 4.8.8; est. was admin. by Thomas Chamberlain
on 31 March 1708 (2:290; 13:46; 48:241; 139).

GALLION, JOSEPH, was in Balto. Co. by March 1665 when he surv.
100 a. Gallier's Bay; may be the Joseph Gallen who imm. to Md.
in by 1664, with w. Alice; in Sept. 1674 purch. 200 a. from John
and Florence Lee; on 6 Feb. 1676/7 Joseph and w. Sarah sold 100
a. Gallier's Bay to Edward Gunnell; in Aug. 1684 Joseph and w.
Sarah sold 200 a. to Philip Greenslade; d. by 4 Aug. 1697 when
admin. bond was posted by William Peckett with Thomas Heath and
Moses Groom (13:126; 100:119; 101:301, 304; 388).

GALLION, JOSEPH, m. Sarah Auchard on 21 Jan. 1753 and had
iss.: GREGORY, b. 19 Dec. 1754; JOHN, b. 12 March 1757; WILLIAM,
b. 24 Oct. 1759 (129:371).

GALLION, KEZIA, was tried for bast. in Nov. 1759 (46:240).

GALLOHONE, CATHERINE, in June 1750 was tried for bast. and
ordered to be sold for 7 years (37:11).

GALLOW, JOHN, admin. the est. of John Wright on 4 Aug. 1702
(2:217).

GALLOWAY, WILLIAM (1), progenitor, was in Balto. Co. by 1705
when he was named in the will of his s. William; may be the
William who wit. the will of John Powell on 27 Dec. 1675; may
have moved from A. A. Co. to Cecil Co., and back to Balto. Co.;
had at least one son: WILLIAM (110:49; 120:167).

GALLOWAY, WILLIAM (2), s. of William (1), was in Balto. Co.
by 1702 when he was a taxable; d. leaving a will, 1 April 1705 -
14 July 1705; m. Margaret, dau. of Hendrick and Christian Enloes,
and sis. of Abraham Enloes who d. 1709; after William's death
Margaret m. 2nd James Durham; William owned 150 a. Oliver's
Reserve which was later held by James Durham for Galloway's orph-
ans; in his will, William named w. Margaret, and ch.: Henry,
William, Mary Garman (or Jarman), Margaret, and Martha, and his
own "dear and ancient" father, William; admin. bond was posted
14 July 1705 by wid. and extx. Margaret with Abraham Enloes and
John Wallis; est. was inv. on 11 Aug. 1705 by J. Whitehead and
Walter Bosley and val. at Ŀ 130.15.9; Margaret, now w. of James
Durham, admin. the est. on 2 Oct. 1707 and 29 Feb. 1711; Margaret
Durham signed the inv. of her dec. bro. Abraham Enloes as one of
the relations on 7 Oct. 1709; William and Margaret had iss.:
MARY, m. (Robert?) Garman (or Jarman); HENRY; WILLIAM; MARGARET;
MARTHA (2:7, 182; 13:110; 21:125; 48:6; 110:49; 211:67).

GALLOWAY, HENRY (3), s. of William (2), d. in Balto. Co. by
3 Dec. 1716 when admin. bond was posted by William Galloway with
Richard Robinson and Michael Rutledge; no known iss. (13:109).

GALLOWAY, WILLIAM (4), s. of William (2), d. in Balto. Co. by
9 June 1743; m. Priscilla Carr on 9 Aug. 1725; in 1750 his heirs
owned 356 part Galloway's Enlargement, 46 a. White Oak Thicket,
and 50 a. Jones' Chance; his will, 24 May 1743 - 9 June 1743,
named s. Moses (to have Mary's Adventure and 87 a. Galloway's Enlargement), son William (to have dwelling plantation and 132 a.
Galloway's Englargement), and left residue of est. to sons Salathiel, Absolom, and Aquila, also mentioned ch. Elizabeth and Mephitica; admin. bond posted 9 June 1743 by extx. Priscilla with
Thomas Carr and Anthony Enloes; est. admin. 27 Aug. 1744 naming
heirs, Moses, William, Salathiel, Absolom, Aquila, Elizabeth and
"Westphalia (sic);" iss. of William and Priscilla: MOSES, b. 2
Sept. 1726; WILLIAM, b. 2 Jan. 1728/9; SALATHIEL, b. 3 Dec. 1730;
ABSOLOM; AQUILA; ELIZABETH; and MEPHITICA (5:16; 13:150; 35:479;
131; 153:40).

GALLOWAY, MOSES (5), s. of William (4), was b. 2 Sept. 1726;
d. by 25 July 1798; m. 1st on 6 April 1750 Mary Nicholson; m. 2nd
on 6 May 1782 Pamelia Owings; in 1750 owned 80 a. Galloway's Enlargement, and 47 a. Mary's Adventure; died leaving a will, 30
April 1798 - 25 July 1798, naming w. Pamela, s. John (dec.
leaving a s. Moses and others), s. William (had a s. Robert
Christie), s. James (dec. leaving a dau. Pamela Cheyne Galloway);
known iss.: WILLIAM, b. 1 Feb. 1751; JOHN NICHOLSON, b. 4 June
1753; JAMES, b. 31 March 1755 (115:122; 131:155; 153:85).

GALLOWAY, WILLIAM (6), s. of William (4), b. 2 Jan. 1728/9,
was alive in Aug. 1744 (5:16; 35:479).

GALLOWAY, SALATHIEL (7), s. of William (4), was b. 3 Dec.
1730 to William and "Catherine" and d. by 19 June 1756; m. on
28 Sept. 1753 Priscilla James; on 3 Dec. 1745 John Jones conv. to
Salathiel, Absolom, and Aquila Galloway, son of William Galloway,
dec., 50 a. Jones' Chance which John's father William Jones had
promised to conv. to the grantees' father; on 19 June 1756 admin.

bond was posted by Priscilla Galloway with Henry James and Benjamin Ingram; est. was admin. 27 May 1757 by wid. Priscilla, now w. of Joseph Crook; no known iss. (6:1; 13:163; 78:381; 131:13/r).

GALLOWAY, (?), m. Susanna, sis. of Aquila Paca who d. in 1743 (127:277).

GALLOWAY, ANN, was charged with bast. in March 1723 (26:201).

GALLOWAY, JOHN, m. Isabella Benn on 27 May 1744 (131).

GALLOWAY, JOHN, d. by 1750 when his heirs owned 1000 a. The Adventure and 1800 a. Taylor's Forest (153:103).

GALLOWAY, JOSEPH, of A. A. Co., m. Mrs. Susanna Paca on 18 Oct. 1722; in 1750 owned 304 a. Paca's Delight and 1500 a. Goodwill Purchase Again; d. 11 Sept. 1752 at his house on West River (131; 153:98; 262).

GALLOWAY, SAMUEL, m. Rebecca (?), and had iss.: ELIZABETH, b. 8 June 1757 (129:355).

GALLYHAMPTON. See GALHAMPTON.

GALOHOWN, JOHN, age c.24, Irish servant, ran away from Richard Wilmot living at the Forks of Gunpowder; had formerly served in Kent Co.; Sept. 1754 (385:305).

GAMBRALL/GAMBALL, GIDEON, was in Balto. Co. by 1692 as a taxable in Spesutia Hund.; had iss.: REBECCA, b. 21 Feb. 1693/4; ABRAHAM, b. 19 March 1694/5 (128:4; 138).

GARDNER, ROBERT (1), was in Balto. Co. by 1692 as a taxable on n. side of Patapsco; d. leaving a will, 22 Sept. 1710 - 13 April 1711, in which he named w. Ann (to have Cherry Garden), dau. Sarah (not yet 16), s. Alexander (to have rest of Cherry Garden, and named w. Ann as extx.; admin. bond was posted 14 April 1711 by extx. Ann with Andrew Anderson and William Wright; est. was inv. on 17 April 1711 by aforesaid Anderson and Thomas Knighton and val, at £ 43.5.0; est. admin. by Ann, now w. of John Maddy on 5 May 1712 and 12 Aug. 1714; known iss.: ALEXANDER; and SARAH (1:12, 364; 13:117; 48:276; 122:206).

GARDNER, ALEXANDER (2), s. of Robert (1), was left part of Cherry Garden by his father; may have had two ch.: RICHARD; JOHN (122:206).

GARDNER, RICHARD (3), s. of Alexander (2), in June 1714 with consent of his father was bound to Joseph Lobb; in Nov. 1724 Simon Ward was ordered to provide sufficient clothing for Richard (21:506; 27:34).

GARDNER, JOHN (4), is placed as a s. of Alexander (2) because in 1750 he owned 50 a. Cherry Garden; also owned this land in 1763 (122:206; 153:89; 159:77).

GARDNER, CHRISTOPHER (5), no known rel. to above, purch. 125
a. from James Murry; m. Sarah (?); d. leaving a will, 17 Nov.
1725 - 22 Dec. 1725., in which he named s. Christopher (to have
Buck Ridge and 100 a. Gardner's Farm near Ben's Branch), dau.
Hannah Thacker (to have Gardner's Farm and Long Discovery), and
serv. Jane Buck (to have freedom and pers. prop.); admin. bond
posted 22 Dec. 1725 by extx. Sarah with Joshua Sewell and Richard Hacker; a second admin. bond was posted 29 April 1727 by
Lloyd Harris with George Buchanan and Charles Wells, the extx.
Sarah having died and son Christopher renouncing admin. of both
parents' estates; est. admin. 15 Oct. 1728 and 30 March 1738;
wid. Sarah may be the Sarah whose admin. bond was posted 9 Nov.
1727 by Edward Fell with Thomas Bond and James Moore; Christopher
and Sarah had iss.: CHRISTOPHER; HANNAH, m. (?) Thacker (2:213;
4:18; 13:127, 128, 130; 67:390; 124:208).

GARDNER, CHRISTOPHER (6), s. of Christopher (5), is prob.
the Christopher who in 1763/4 owned 50 a. Gardner's Delight
(159:92).

GARDNER, JAMES (7), no known rel. to any of the above, was
in Balto. Co. by 1742 when John Hawkins conv. him 100 a. of Hawkins' Desire; as James Gardner, schoolmaster, was sued by Christopher Randall in June 1750; in 1750 owned 100 a. Hawkins' Desire
and 50 a. Liverpoole, which latter tract he sold to William Fell
in Nov. 1750; m. Mary (?), and had iss.: KATHERINE, b. 4 Nov.
1731; ANNA, b. 22 May 1733; JOHN, b. 25 May 1736; JAMES, b. 6
Sept. 1738; PHEBE, b. 26 Aug. 1741; SARAH, b. and d. 1744 (37:
79; 77:242; 81:46; 133:42, 57, 64, 66, 73; 153:43; 159:39).

GARDNER, JOHN (8), s. of James (7) and Mary, was b. 6 Sept.
1738; in March 1796 purch. from Charles Carroll of Carrollton and
others 100 a. Hawkins' Desire which his father had mortgaged to
the said Carroll; m. Margaret (?) and had iss.: CATHERINE, b. 14
May 1760; ELEANOR, b. 3 June 1763; MARY, b. 29 Dec. 1765; MARGA-
RET, b. 22 July 1768 (133:106, 113, 116, 122; 231-WG#VV:472).

GARDNER, (?), m. by 15 Oct. 1759 Katherine, dau. of William
Hamilton (111:315).

GARDNER, (?), m. by 15 Oct. 1759, Sarah, dau. of William Hamilton (111:315).

GARDNER, ANN, was fined for bast. in Nov. 1757, naming Aquila
Massey as the father (46:74).

GARDNER, HANNAH, servant woman with three years to serve was
listed in the 1723 est. of Matthew Hale (52:90).

GARDNER, JOHN, was in Balto. Co. by 6 Nov. 1700 when he purch.
from John Thomas 102 a. of land formerly granted to William Clapham; purch. Hab Nab at a Venture from Christopher Durbin and w.
in May 1705; bought Claybank from John and Mary Boring and Richard Kemp in Sept. 1711; res. at Clapham's Creek when he bought
100 a. Betty's Adventure from Edward and Johanna Reeston in
Aug. 1722; bought 200 a. The Level from William and Mary Jones
and William and Elizabeth Langley in Oct. 1725; res. at Bear

Creek when he purch. part of Happy Be Lucky from John and Dinah
Cole in Jan. 1726; in March 1731 sold or conv. Body's Adventure
and Garden to his dau. Susanna Walker; admin. the est.
of Alice Demondidier in April 1716; in Nov. 1724 was chosen to be the
guardian of Richard Colegate; d. leaving a will, 5 July 1740 - 22
Sept. 1741, in which he named Robert Godwin of Portsmouth, Hampshire (to have entire est.); admin. bond posted 5 Oct. 1741 by
William Hamilton and Luke Trotten with George Buchanan and Luke
Stansbury; est. admin. on 30 June 1744 and 13 Nov. 1744; his
heirs owned Neighbor's Affinity in 1750; had one dau.: SUSANNA,
m. by 16 March 1731 (?) Walker (1:215; 5:12, 28; 13:147; 27:32;
60:183; 66:45; 67:171; 69:30; 70:183, 340; 127:189; 153:93; 213-
PL#8:89).

GARDNER, JOHN, m. Mary Meeds on 25 Dec. 1759; she d. 3 Dec.
1759; had iss.: MARY, b. 19 Nov. 1759 (131:53, 18/r).

GARDNER, JOHN, m. Mary York on 23 Dec. 1761 (131).

GARDNER, NICHOLAS, age 25, German, servant who ran away from
Stephen Onion c.July 1754 (385:293).

GARDNER, RICHARD, s. of Sarah Gardner and Robert Stansbury,
was b. 21 Feb. 1758 (133:102).

GARDNER, ROBERT, m. Mary (?), and had iss.: ROBERT, living
in March 1719 when he chose Henry Shields as his guardian (23:
278).

GARDNER, ROBERT, m. Mary Angling on 5 Jan. 1728; d. by Aug.
1736 when admin. bond was posted by Cornelius Angling with Thomas
Biddison and John Mahorn; est. was admin. by Thomas Biddison (4:
18; 13:140; 133:149).

GARDNER, SARAH, m. 8 June 1723 Richard Hindon (133:148).

GARDNER, SARAH, fined for bast. in Nov. 1758 (46:162).

GARDNER, SUSANNAH, was tried for bast. in June 1746; John Han-
nassea admitted paternity (36:9, 10).

GARDNER, WILLIAM, m. Sarah (?), and had iss.: WILLIAM, b. 8
Jan. 1753 (134:22).

GARGALL, BENJAMIN, was in Balto. Co. by 1692 as a taxable in
s. side of Patapsco Hund. (138).

GARLAND, HENRY, m. Lydia (?); had iss.: SARAH, b. 2 Aug. 1709,
d. Aug. 1714; ELIZABETH, b. 19 Jan. 1710, d. Aug. 1714; WILLIAM,
b. 6 or 21 Jan. 1712 (128:28, 33).

GARLAND, HENRY, m. Sarah Herrington on 27 Jan. 1743 (129:333).

GARLAND, JAMES, m. Jane Gaddis on 3 Feb. 1761; had iss.:
CATHERINE, b. 13 April 1762 (129:362, 368).

GARLAND, NICHOLAS, m. Sarah (?), and had iss.: ELIZABETH, b.
12 Sept. 1717 (131:83).

GARLAND, WILLIAM, m. Bethia Ogg on 10 June 1728; d. by 16
March 1748 when admin. bond was posted by Henry Garland with
Benjamin Hanson and George Hollandsworth; est. admin. on 1 Aug.
1750 by Henry Garland who stated the dec. left four ch.: James
age c.18; Susannah, age c.12; Francis, age c.9; and Catherine
age 3; had iss.: JAMES, b. 6 Nov. 1730; WILLIAM, b. 5 Sept. 1734;
SUSANNA, b. 29 Nov. 1737; FRANCIS, b. 1 Jan. 1741; CATHERINE, b.
c.1747 (4:276; 5:101; 13:156; 128:52, 66, 83, 110; 129:324).

GARMAN. See JARMAN.

GARMER, ROBERT, was in Balto. Co. by 1695 as a taxable in n.
side Patapsco River (140).

GARNER, HENRY, was in Balto. Co. by 1695 as a taxable in Spesutia Hund. (140).

GARRETT, RICHARD (1), d. in Balto. Co. in May 1709; admin. bond
was posted 8 June 1710 by wid. and admnx. Eliza Garrett with John
Hall and John Stokes; est. was inv. on 23 July 1710 by Geo. Wells
and Roger Matthews, and val. at Ł 85.18.0; an additional inv. was
made 13 Aug. 1710 and val. at Ł6.7.10; in Nov. 1708 Henry Borck
left prop. to Richard Garrett in trust for Borck's dau. Mary;
on 2 April 1711 Elizabeth Garrett admnx. of Richard Garrett also
admin. the est. of Henry Burke; Elizabeth d. by 8 Aug. 1717 when
Bennett Garrett posted admin. bond with Richard Smithers and Wm.
Cooke; Richard and Elizabeth had iss.: prob. BENNET, d. 1740; prob.
SARAH who m. William Cooke on 27 Aug. 1713; prob. HENRY (1:235;
13:112, 113; 48:151; 122:114; 128:26).

GARRETT, BENNETT (2), prob. s. of Richard (1), m. 1st Arabella,
admnx. of William Loney; she d. 20 June 1737 and he m. 2nd on 15
Dec. 1737 Martha Presbury; d. d by 23 May 1740 when Martha Garrett posted admin. bond with George Presbury and William Bradford;
est. admin. 10 Sept. 1741 by Martha Garrett and on 23 Dec. 1742
by Martha now Todd; left iss.: AMOS, b. 10 June 1723; RUTH, b. 21
May 1729; by 2nd w.: EDWARD BEDLE, b. 19 Feb. 1738, d. 26 April
1739 (3:274; 4:97; 13:159; 34:125; 128:42, 58, 89, 97, 104; 129:
324).

GARRETT, HENRY (3), prob. s. of Richard (1), was alive in 1743;
m. Mary, dau. of Isaac and Esther (Clark) Butterworth, on 19 Dec.
1728; had iss.: ISAAC, b. 14 Sept. 1729; BENNETT, b. 30 Dec.
1731; JOHN, b. 29 Aug. 1733; HANNAH, b. 15 March 1734; SARAH, b.
9 Aug. 1736; ELIZABETH, b. 20 Sept. 1738; RICHARD, b. 29 March
1740; AMOS, b. 20 June 1741; MARY, b. 11 June 1743 (128:54, 60,
65, 76, 107; 129:340).

GARRETT, AMOS, admin. the est. of Edward Hancock on 10 Feb.
1720 (1:289).

GARRETT, AMOS, in 1750 owned 495 a. Hazard Enlarged, 114 a.
Matthews Chance, 30 a. Watkins' Inlet, and 159 a. Cook's Double
Purchase, and 100 a. Jackson's Hazard (153:76).

GARRETT, AMOS, in 1750 owned 320 a. Land of Goshen, 500 a.
Elford's Fields, 1250 a. part Solitude, and 65 a. part Shepherd's
Chance (153:105).

GARRETT, DENNIS, was in Balto. Co. by 1685 when Edward Mumford conv. to Garrett and to Thomas Stone 100 a. Long Island Point; m. Barbara (poss. a dau. of Thomas Stone); she m. as her 2nd husband John Broad; Garrett was murdered by Captain John Oldton who hit him on the head with a sword worth 20 shillings on 31 July 1691, and Garrett d. on 2 Sept.; Oldton was tried for murder, sentenced to death, pardoned by the King, and later became Commander of the Balto. Co. Rangers; in March 1693 Thomas Stone conv. the tract Long Island Point to Barbara Garrett and her ch. by Dennis Garrett; Barbara (?) Garrett Broad d. leaving a will, 19 Jan. 1732 - 6 Aug. 1733, in which she named her granddau. Sarah w.of Charles Gorsuch, son Thomas Broad and his w. Ann, dau. Frances Haile, and granddau. Barbara; ch. of Dennis and Barbara: JOHANNA, m. John Cole; FRANCES, m. Nicholas Haile (19:276; 108; 126:29; Crowe, Desc. of First Fam. of Va. and Md.).

GARRETT, ELIZABETH, d. c.1713 when her est. was inv. by Thomas Bucknal and Thomas Bond and val. at £ 121.3.7 (50:294).

GARRETT, ELIZABETH, m. Roger Matthews on 23 May 1726 (129:244).

GARRETT, FRANCIS, age 25 in 1635, came to Va. in the Thomas and John which left Gravesend in June 1635 (Hotten, Orig. Lists, p. 83).

GARRETT, JAMES, m. by Aug. 1675 Johanna Peake, dau. of George and Mary Peake of Balto. Co. (206-1:410).

GARRETT, JNO., m. Margaret Baker on 22 Nov. 1759 (131).

GARRETT, ROBERT, was in Balto. Co. by 6 Aug. 1672 when he purch. 450 a. Dixon's Neck from Richard Thurrell (98:46).

THE GARRETTSON FAMILY has been discussed by Helen Davis in Kindred, is the subject of a chart by Mrs. Elizabeth D. Axford, and a typescript by Earl Aquila Garrettson, entitled "The Garrettson Family," at the Md. Hist. Soc.

GARRETT, RUTTEN (1), or possibly Rutten Garrett, was a native of Amersfort, Netherlands, and d. in Balto. Co. by 8 March 1664, leaving a wid. Mary (poss. from Amersfort, or else Mary Utie) who m. as her 2nd husb. Edward Beedle; Garrett and his wife moved from New Amstel to Md. between May 1661 and Sept..1663 when Garrett Rutten, locksmith, was made a freeman of Maryland; d. leaving a will, proved 8 March 1664, leaving his entire est. to w. Mary for her life or widowhood, then to eld. s. Garrett; no evidence has been found to prove that wid. Mary m. Edward Beedle; left iss.: GARRETT; perhaps others as well (120:41; 313:94-95).

GARRETT, GARRETT (or RUTTEN) (2), s. of Garrett (1) and Mary, d. by 9 June 1679 when admin. bond was posted by admnx. Somelia with Edward Bedell and Robert Jones; Rutgertson Garretts, of Dutch nationality, living in Balto. Co., was naturalized in 1671; purch. 300 a. Oakington from Nathaniel Utie in March 1672; purch. 180 a. part Carter's Rest from Nathaniel and Elizabeth Utie in May 1675; est. was admin. by rel. and admnx. Somelia, now w. of Rev.John Yeo; inv. of est. was val. at 26023 lbs. tob.; left iss.: GARRETT

(2:37, 103; 13:122; 60:2; 63:73; 101:300, 301, 303; 404:6; see also 313).

GARRETTSON, GARRETT (3), s. of Rutten (2) and Somelia, was b. c.1672, and gave his age as 58 in 1730; d. by 23 March 1738; m. 15 Dec. 1702 Elizabeth Freeborn who d. 4 Feb. 1748; in June 1692 Garrett Garrettson, orphan of Rutten, formerly under the care of Edward Bedell, chose Lodwick Martin to be his guardian; in Dec. 1683 Rev. John Yeo gave him 150 a. New Parke, which Garrett Garrettson conv. to Anthony Drew in Aug. 1698; signed the inv. of William Lowe as one of the nearest of kin in Aug. 1719; d. by 23 March 1738 when admin. bond was posted by George and Elizabeth Garrettson, with John and James Garrettson; est. was inv. on 16 April 1739 by Bennett Garrettson and Richard Johns and val. at £ 349.13.11; had iss.: GEORGE, b. 26 Nov. 1703; ELIZABETH, b. 30 April 1704; JOHN, b. 17 Feb. 1706; SARAH, b. 30 Dec. 1708; JAMES, b. 15 Oct. 1709; SOPHIA, b. 15 Nov. 1711, d. 1769, leaving a will, 19 Oct. 1767 - 24 Feb. 1769 (naming bro. Richard, and daus. Sophia and Elizabeth, and bro. Edward, and daus. Elizabeth, Sarah, and Cordelia, bro. Garrett and his daus. Elizabeth and Sarah, as well as Thomas Brown); FREEBORN, b. 18 Feb. 1713, d. 6 Feb. 1748; MARY, b. 28 Feb. 1715, d. 19 July 1749, having m. Walter Tolley on 30 Dec. 1735; SOMELIA, b. 1 June 1718, d. 18 Oct. 1760 having m. John Hanson on 4 Aug. 1743; GARRETT, b. 10 Feb. 1720/1; RICHARD, b. c.1721; EDWARD, b. 5 Feb. 1726 (13:42; 19:183; 48:253; 50:68; 128:15, 34, 35, 37, 41, 54, 92B; 129:345).

GARRETTSON, GEORGE (4), s. of Garrett (3) and Elizabeth, was b. 26 Nov. 1706, d. by 31 March 1757; m. Martha Presbury on 1 Nov. 1744; she was b. 27 Oct. 1718, d. 29 Sept. 1767, dau. of James and Martha (Goldsmith) Presbury, and had m. 1st Bennett Garrett, and 2nd (?) Todd, and 3rd Garrett Garrettson; in 1750 George Garrettson owned 300 a. Oakington; his admin. bond was posted 31 March 1757 by Martha Garrettson with George Presbury and Garrett Garrettson; est. admin. 9 Dec. 1758 by Martha, who named six ch.; in Nov. 1759 the ch. were named in court records; Martha Presbury Garrettson d. leaving a will, 25 Sept. 1767 - 5 Nov. 1767, in which she named dau. Freenata w. of Samuel Griffith (to have Tapley Neck Resurveyed), dau. Frances (to have a legacy from Mrs. Frances Middlemore),, son George, son Goldsmith, and her own bro. George Presbury; had iss.: FREENATA, b. 19 Jan. 1746, m. Samuel Griffith; GARRETT, b. 23 March 1746, d. 11 April 1747; GEORGE, b. 11 March 1747; GARRETT, b. 28 July 1749, d. 2 Sept. 1763; MARY GOLDSMITH, b. 4 Nov. 1750; GOLDSMITH, b. 8 Sept. 1753; FRANCES, b. 10 March 1758 (6:12; 13:164; 44; 112:62; 129: 342, 343, 345, 346, 349, 350, 364, 380).

GARRETTSON, JOHN (5), s. of Garrett (3) and Elizabeth, was b. 17 Feb. 1706, and was alive in Dec. 1759; m. on 21 April 1742 Sarah Hanson, wid. of Edward Mariarte; prob. the James Garrison listed in 1750 as owning 75 a. part New Park; had iss.: GEORGE, b. 28 March 1743; SARAH, b. 25 Dec. 1747; ELIZA, b. 20 Dec. 1749; JOHN, b. 16 Oct. 1759; FREEBORN, b. 17 Oct. 1753; RICHARD, b. 5 Dec. 1755; THOMAS, b. 12 Dec. 1759 (129:324, 379; 153:106).

GARRETTSON, JAMES (6), s. of Garrett (3) and Elizabeth, was b. 15 Oct. 1709, d. Feb. 1763; m. Catherine Nelson on 24 April 1746;

in 1750 owned 75 a. part New Park; d. leaving a will, 14 Feb.
1763 - 9 June 1763, in which he named w. and bro. Garrett as
execs., and seven ch.; had iss.: GARRETT, b. 25 May 1747; ELIZA-
BETH, b. 12 Aug. 1749; FRANCES, b. 18 Feb. 1750; MARTHA, b. 3 Aug.
1753; JAMES, b. 9 April 1759; BENNETT, b. 3 March 1762 (129:342,
346, 352, 378; 153:50; 200-31:932).

GARRETTSON, GARRETT (7), s. of Garrett (3) and Elizabeth, was
b. 10 Feb. 1720/1, and was alive in March 1766; m. Susanna, wid.
of Capt. Daniel Robinson on 21 March 1760; she had m. 1st (?)
Brown, and 2nd Daniel Robinson; had iss.: ELIZA, b. 19 Feb. 1761;
SARAH, b. 6 Nov. 1763; GARRETT, b. 16 March 1766 (129:381).

GARRETTSON, RICHARD (8), s. of Garrett (3) and Elizabeth, m.
Priscilla Nelson on 20 Jan. 1756; in 1750 owned 170 a. Dispatch
and 30 a. Timber Swamp; had iss.: FREEBORN, b. 11 Dec. 1756;
SOPHIA, b. 11 May 1758; AQUILA, b. 10 May 1760: ELIZA, b. 19 Feb.
1763 (129:352, 364, 379; 153:89).

GARRETTSON, EDWARD (9), s. of Garrett (3) and Elizabeth, was
b. 5 Feb. 1726; m. Avarilla Hanson on 21 Dec. 1749; in 1750 owned
100 a. Cavan; had iss.: ELIZABETH, b. 30 Nov. 1750; EDWARD, b. 13
April 1752; GARRETT, b. 30 Nov. 1753; SARAH, b. 25 July 1757; COR-
DELIA, b. 2 Oct. 1759; BENJAMIN, b. 7 April 1761; JAMES, b. 3 Feb.
1763 (129:350, 365, 367, 380, 384; 131; 153:96).

GARRETTSON, JOHN, d. by 25 June 1670 when Lodwick Williams
posted admin. bond with John Collier and John Waterton (13:120).

GARRETTSON, JOHN, in Nov. 1759 was named as the father of
Elizabeth Orum's child (46:242).

GARRISON, PAUL (1), was in Balto. Co. by 8 March 1735 when he
m. Elizabeth Frazier; had iss.: JOB, b. 17 Feb. 1741; poss. SHAD-
RACK (131:102/r; 133:155).

GARRISON, JOB (2), s. of Paul (1) and Elizabeth, was b. 17
Feb. 1741; in Nov. 1759 was named as the father of Viola Demmitt's child; in Oct. 1769 had surv. 52 a. Garrettson's Meadows;
d. leaving a will, 18 Sept. 1805 - 24 Aug. 1806, in which he
named w. Mary, and these ch.: HARRIETT; REBECCA, m. (?) Allburger;
JOB; GARRETT, d. by 1804; dau., m. (?) Stansbury (46:242; 117:89;
131:102/r).

GARRISON, SHADRACK (3), poss. s. of Paul (1), m. Mary (?); d.
leaving a will, 10 June 1787 - 1 Oct. 1787, in which he named a
bro. Job, and w. Mary, and these ch.: WILLIAM; ELIZABETH (113:
288).

GARROD, LEONARD, m. Mary (?), and had iss.: HUSTICE, b. 13
Oct. 1746; ELIZABETH, b. 26 May 1748 (133:102).

GARVISE, ANN, was ind. for bast., June 1732 (29:288).

GASCON/GASKIN/GASQUOINE, DANIEL, was in Balto. Co. by 1692
as a taxable in n. side Gunpowder Hund.; d. by 7 March 1701/2
when his est. was inv. by Richard Kirkland and George Yate;
est. was admin. 4 Aug. 1704 by Luke Raven (2:206; 48:124; 138).

GASCON, ROBERT, was in Balto. Co. by 1692 as a taxable in s. side of Gunpowder Hund. (138).

GASEMAN, MARY, was ind. for bast. in March 1724/5 (27:127).

GASH, THOMAS (1), was in Balto. Co. by 17 April 1704 when admon. bond was posted by Richard Perkins with Samuel Jackson and Thomas Greenfield; will of Thomas Gash, 4 April 1704 - 15 April 1704, left s. Thomas in the custody of Lawrence Draper until he should reach age 21, appointed Richard Perkins as exec., and had Daniel and Frances Johnson as witnesses; est. was inv. on 13 July 1704 by Henry Wright and Daniel Johnson; and val. at £ 15. 18.0; est. was admin. on 6 Oct. 1709 by Mary Perkins, since the orig. admin., Richard Perkins, had died; left iss.: THOMAS, b. c. 1691 (2:136; 13:111; 48:42; 122:41).

GASH, THOMAS (2), s. of Thomas (1), was b. 1691, and gave his age as 39 in 1730; m. Hannah or Johanna Gilbert on 22 Dec. 1715; in 1750 owned 100 a. New Westwood; in June 1751 Thomas and Johanna conv. 60 a. New Westwood and Gash's Purchase to Edward Wakeman; in Feb. 1754 he conv. 50 a. Gash's Purchase to Bennett O'Neal, s. of Henry O'Neal, dec.; will of Thomas, 1 April 1758 - 7 June 1759, named w. Hannah and ch. Thomas and Blanch, with William Parry, Michael Gilbert, and Wm. Perry, Jr., as witnesses; Thomas and Johanna had iss.: JOHANNA, b. 8 Nov. 1716; SARAH, b. 16 July 1719; MARY, b. 8 June 1721 or 1722 and d. Nov. 1724; MARY, b. 10 Dec. 1725; BLANCHE, d. 29 Jan. 1724; MICHAEL, b. 19 May 1728; THOMAS, b. 13 Oct. 1730; BLANCH, b. 8 May 1733 (81:245; 82:159; 111:308; 128:35, 37, 41, 44, 45, 46, 68, 78; 153:16; 163:116).

GASH, MICHAEL (3), s. of Thomas (2), b. 19 May 1728, m. by 10 Sept. 1756 Eliza, admnx. of Garvis Gilbert (5:313; 128:68).

GASKIN. See GASCON.

GASLEN, JAMES, was in Balto. Co. by 1692 as a taxable on n. side of Patapsco (138).

GASQUOINE. See GASCON.

GASSAWAY, NICHOLAS, of South R., A. A. Co., conv. 300 a. of Charles' Purchase to Robert Love of Gunpowder on 3 June 1679 (60).

GASSAWAY, NICHOLAS, Jr., came to Gunpowder Meeting from A. A. Co. in Sept. 1747; m. 4 d, 9, 1747 at Elk Ridge Margaret Pierpoint, and was in Balto. Co. by 1750 when he owned 280 a. Gassaway's Addition (evidently the same 280 a. in the Forks of the Gunpowder which Thomas Gassaway of A. A. Co. left to son Nicholas by will of 1739); had iss.: RACHEL, b. 15 d., 12 , 1750 (127:47; 136; 153:99).

GASSAWAY, THOMAS, d. by 1750 leaving heirs who were listed as owning 1250 a. part Solitude (153:104).

GATCH, GODFREY (1), progenitor, was in Md. by 1743 and d. in Balto. Co. leaving a will, 24 Dec. 1758 - 24 Feb. 1759; in 1727 is said to have come from Prussia with w. Maria,; with (son?)

"Conjuist" was nat. in or after Oct. 1743 by producing a cert.
which said he had taken Communion, wit. by John Willmott and
Eleanor King; in 1750 owned Skidmore's Last; in his will named
these ch.: CORNROW (CONRAD?); NICHOLAS; CONDUEL (CONDUCE) (111:
302; 153:12; 404).

GATCH, CORNROW or CONRAD (2), s. of Godfrey (1), was alive in
1758 with at least one s.: WILLIAM, b. 13 Dec. 1747; age 8 when
in March 1756 he was bound to John Hammond Dorsey (40:466).

GATCH, NICHOLAS (3), s. of Godfrey (1), was alive in 1758 when
his father's will was made; may be the Nicholas Gash (sic) who d.
leaving a will, 19 Sept. 1768 - 8 Nov. 1769, in which he named
his "old woman" Hannah Shaw and their ch. Thomas, and Catherine
Matthews; also Hannah's ch., Ann, Rachel, and Rebecca, all named
Shaw, and James and Jane Matthews, ch. of Catherine Matthews;
his will also disposed of Goose's Harbor, Gash's Discovery, and
land in Fell's Point; left iss.: THOMAS; poss. CATHERINE, m.
(?) Matthews (112:102).

GATCH, CONDUCE (4), s. of Godfrey (1), was nat. with his father
in 1743; said to have been born at sea c.1727, and d. after 1790
in Balto. Co.; m. Presocia Burgan (prob. the Presioca Burgan, b.
27 Oct. 1723, dau. of Robert and Ann Burgan); in 1778 took the
Oath of Fidelity to the State of Maryland; left a will, 4 Dec.
1792 - 28 Oct. 1797, naming these ch.; FREDERICK, b. 27 July 1747;
ANN, b. 17 March 1747/8; m. (?) Dew; PHILIP, b. 2 March 1751, d.
28 Dec. 1835; one of the earliest American born Methodist preach-
ers; NICHOLAS, m. Mary Reiss; SARAH, m. Joseph Taylor; ELIZABETH,
m. Jacob Reiss; BENJAMIN, b. 10 Feb. 1758; MARY (115:47; 133:
90, 91, 101; 382-1:514).

GATES, ROBERT, was in Balto. Co. by 20 Feb. 1670/1 when Richard
Winley and w. Mary conv. him 100 a. Fall Hill; in 1692 was a taxable in s. side Gunpowder Hund.; d. leaving a will, 28 April 1695
30 May 1695, in which he left 50 a. to Sarah Spinke and the res.
to Thomas Litton; est. was inv. 8 June 1695 by Moses Groom and
John Webster and val. at £ 3.13.8 plus 884 lbs. tob.; est. admin.
2 Sept. 1696 by Thomas Litton (48:136; 97:124; 121:97; 138; 206-
14:153).

GAY, JOHN (1), m. by 3 Sept. 1701 Frances, possibly heir of
Nathaniel Ruxton; on that date nd w. Frances conv. to Richard
Colegate Ruxton's Range and Howell's Point; d. by 6 June 1717
when admin. bond on his est. was posted by Frances Gay, admnx.
with John Hayes and Thomas Hinde; his wid. m. 2nd by 20 April
1732 James Moore who joined Frances in admin. the estate of
John Gay; because Frances seems to have been a Ruxton and for
other reasons cited below, John and Frances are presumed to have
had at least one s.: NICHOLAS RUXTON, b. c.1716 (2:12; 13:116;
66:90).

GAY, NICHOLAS RUXTON (2), s. of John (1) and Frances, was b.
c.1716 adn d. leaving a will, 2 April 1770 - 2 June 1770; m. Ann
Lux on 21 Sept. 1751; in his will named w. Ann and nephews and
nieces: Nicholas Ruxton Moore, John Gay Moore, James Francis
Moore, John Darby of S. C., Alice Darby of S. C., Mary Jones,

James Darby, Rachel Chenoweth, and Eleanor Moore, as well as his
bro.-in-law Capt. William Lux and George Lux, John Jones, husb.
of Mary Jones, and Daniel Bowly (112:151; 133:165; Prov. Court
Liber D.D.#2, p. 184).

GAY (or GUY), DAVID, d. in Balto. Co. leaving a will, 5 Nov.
1727 - 25 Nov. 1727, in which he named servants John Lawrence
and James Relley, landlord John Wilmot, and gave 150 a. to Ruth
Wilmot, named John Wilmot, Jr.; will wit. by Thomas Elton, Geo.
Walker, and John Lawrence; admin. bond on his est. was posted
on 2 Jan. 1727/8 by John Wilmott with James Moore and Edward
Dorsey; est. was inv. on 26 Jan. 1727/8 by Benjamin Bowen and
John Eaglestone, and val. at £ 73.13.10; John Wilmott said he
knew of no kin in the Province; est. was admin. on 7 April 1729
by John Wilmot who named John Lawson and Ruth Wilmot in the acct.
(2:304; 13:131; 51:95; 125:46).

GAY, SARAH, was allowed 1000 lbs. tob. for maintenance by the
Court in Nov. 1719 (23:242).

GAY, SARAH, m. Edward Turbell on 10 April 1723 (133:148).

GEARTH, RALPH, d. by 22 Sept. 1679 when admin. bond was posted
by Thomas Long, admin., with John Boring and Thomas Pearle (13:
146).

GEBBINS, JOHN, m. Mary (?), and had iss.: JOSEPH, b. 14 July
1749 (131:126/r).

GEBBS. JOHN. See GIBBS, JOHN.

GEER, ABIGAIL, dau. of Catherine, pet. the court in Aug. 1733
that her mother had bound her to Mary Tolly to age 21, and as
she is now 22 she desires her freedom; in Aug. 1733 tried on
charges of having born four bast. ch. (30:68, 76).

GEERE/GEARE, KATHERINE, was tried for bast. in Aug. 1728 (28:
32).

GEFF, WILLIAM, d. by 10 April 1711; wid. Elizabeth m. as her
2nd husb. John Olwell of A. A. Co. (67:162).

GENKINS. See JENKINS.

GEOGHEGAN, AMBROSE, was in Balto. Co. by Jan. 1720 when he
surv. 100 a. Ambrose's Lot; m. by 8 Sept. 1724 Katherine, extx.
of Pierce Welch; in 1750 owned 150 a. Ambrose's Lot; on 20 Feb.
1752 surv. 490 a. Ambrose's Lot Augmented (2:369; 153:79; 438).

GEOGHEGAN, AMBROSE, m. Elizabeth (?), and had iss.: JAMES, b.
19 Dec. 1760 (133:108).

GEORGE, JAMES, d. by 1699; his wid. and admnx. was Dorothy
George (206-19½A:118).

GEORGE, JOHN, was in Balto. Co. by 4 Aug. 1673 when he sold
Thomas Rumsey 200 a. Fareall (99:347).

GEORGE, JOSHUA, of Cecil Co., admin. the est. of Francis Holland on 24 July 1742 (3:283).

GEORGE, THOMAS, runaway, was taken up by the Sheriff of Newcastle Co., Del., and claimed to have served his time with James Powell of Balto. Co. (384:587).

GERISH, MARY, m. Edward Denham on 28 Feb. 1728/9. but had iss. born earlier: STEPHEN, b. 13 April 1727, d. 5 March 1727/8 (128: 51, 53).

GERMAIN, JOHN, orphan of Thomas, in March 1757 chose Capt. William Bond as his guardian (46:18).

GERMAN. See JARMAN.

GERVISS, ANN, in Nov. 1734 was ind. for bast. (30:350).

GESSES, JOHN, was in Balto. Co. by 1692 as a taxable in s. side Patapsco Hund. (138).

GESTWOOD, MICHAEL, m. by 30 June 1729 Elizabeth (?) (129: 279).

GHISELIN, WILLIAM, in March 1742 was co-exec. of G. Drew (3: 266).

GIBBONS, JOHN, in 1690 was listed in the inv. of John Boring with four yrs. to serve; by 1694 was in n. side of Patapsco Hund. (48:6; 139).

GIBBONS, THOMAS, m. Hannah Sharp on 6 April 1735 (133:153).

GIBBONS, THOMAS, m. Mary (?) and had iss.: SARAH, b. 14 March 1735 in St. Paul's Par.; JOHN, b. 7 April 1736 in St. John's Par. (131:94; 133:49).

GIBBONS, THOMAS, m. Mary Buckley on 28 Sept. 1748 (131).

GIBBONS, THOMAS, in 1750 owned Plunder (153:47).

GIBBS, JOHN, son of John, was transported to Balto. Co. by 1667 (388).

GIBBS, JOHN, m. Hannah Palmer on 1 Jan. 1751 (131).

GIBSON, MILES (1), claimed land for service in 1668, and in Aug. 1668 purch. 240 a. from John Lee and Wm. Osbourne; m. 1st by 19 May 1676 Ann, dau. of Thomas Thurston; m. 2nd Ann, dau. of Thomas and Ann (Gorsuch) Todd; m. 3rd Elizabeth, wid. of John Collett, Henry Hazlewood, and Richard Edmunds; purch. Sprye's Inheritance from John and Jane Fallocke in Feb. 1673/4; conv. land to Samuel Hedge in June 1676; in May 1676 mentioned as having m. Ann, dau. of Thomas Thurston; purch. 50 a. Port Royal from John Rogers; d. by 30 June 1692 when admin. bond was posted by wid. and admnx. Elizabeth Gibson with James Phillips and Edward Boothby; est. was inv. 26 May 1692 by Mark Richardson and Anthony

Drew and val. at £ 516.2.1; had iss. (all b. by 3 March 1683 when
they were mentioned in the will of Francis Lovelace): ROBERT;
SARAH, m. Thomas Bale; and ANN. (13:126; 48:26; 95; 100; 101;
206-7A:361; 206-12:149, 157).

GIBSON, ROBERT (2), s. of Miles (1), was in Spesutia Hund. by
1695; in Jan. 1702 conv. all his share of North Yarmouth which
James Fewgate had conv. to Robert's father Miles; m. by 1693
Martha, wid. and extx. of William O'Derry; m. 15 Dec. 1702 Mrs.
Mary Goldsmith; d. 10 June 1704, leaving a will, 4 June 1704 -
12 June 1704, named w. Mary, extx., sis. Sarah Beall, and Joseph Compton and his heirs; est. admin. 6 July 1708 by extx. Mary
who m. as her 2nd husb. George Wells (2:121; 66:136; 122:37;
128:15, 22; 140; 206-10:333).

GIBSON, Mr., was a taxable in Spesutia Hund. in 1692 (138).

GIBSON, ANN, serv. of Thomas Hatchman, was ind. and tried for
bast. in June 1734 (30:253, 267).

GIBSON, FRANCIS, m. (?), and had iss.: JAMES, b. Oct. 1731
(128:63).

GIBSON, MARGARET, in Aug. 1715 named James Richardson as the
father of her child (21:626).

GIBSON, THOMAS, of Charles Co., in June 1682 purch. part of
Northwick from Thomas and Jane Long; d. leaving a will, 7 Sept.
1675 - 30 Jan. 1685, in which he left 300 a. of Northwick in
Balto. Co. to his son Thomas (64:183; 120:165).

THE GILBERT FAMILY has been researched by Mrs. Harold F.
Hannon (of Bloomington, Illinois) who has generously made the
results of her research available to the compiler.

GILBERT, MICHAEL (1), progenitor, was b. c.1605 and d. 10
Dec. 1677 at Aldborough, Yorkshire; matric. at Christ's Coll.,
Cambridge Univ. in 1621; took his B.A. in 1624; was Vicar of
Aldborough from 1629 to 1677, having temporarily been deposed
during the Commonwealth, 1653-1659; had iss.: MICHAEL, Jr., b.
1642; CHARLES, m. Ann Thornton on 26 Jan. 1668; JOSHUA, b. 1648
at Aldborough, and matric. at Christ's Coll., Cambridge (Data
comp. by Mrs. Hannon).

GILBERT, MICHAEL, Jr. (2), s. of Michael (1), was b. 1642 at
Aldborough; matric. 25 May 1658 at Christ Coll., Camb., age 16;
was ordained a deacon and then priest in 1662; was Head Master of
Leeds School from 1662 to 1690; m. Dorothy Hargrave on 1 March
1668; had iss.: MICHAEL, b. 24 Jan. 1669; MARY, b. 6 Feb. 1670;
ROBERT, b. 4 Sept. 1673; THOMAS, b. 12 Aug. 1676; GARVIS, b. 15
April 1680; CHARLES, b. 11 April 1684 (Data comp. by Mrs. Han-
non).

GILBERT, CHARLES (3), prob. s. of Michael (1), m. Ann Thornton
on 26 Jan. 1668; had iss.: ANN, b. 8 March 1669, d. 5 April 1673;
CHARLES, b. 14 Feb. 1672 (Data from Mrs. Hannon).

GILBERT, GARVIS (or JARVIS or GARVASE) (4), s. of Michael (2), was b. 15 April 1680, and d. 5 June 1739; m. 1st Margaret (?) who d. 16 Jan. 1715; m. 2nd Mary (?) who m. as her 2nd husb., by June 1742, Samuel Johnson; will of Garvis Gilbert, 2 June 1739 - 17 June 1739, named s. Samuel (to have Gilbert's Addition and part Gilbert's Outlet), s. Garvas (to have Bow's Lot and res. of Gilbert's Outlet), ch. Charles, Aquila, Benjamin, Daniel, and Hannah, Martha, and Mary, with w. Mary as co-extx. with s. Michael; admin. bond posted 7 Nov. 1739 by the execs. with John Durbin and Samuel Prichard; est. admin. 12 Aug. 1740 by the execs.; had iss.: MICHAEL, b. 15 June 1707; JARVIS, b. 1708; SAMUEL or SOLOMON, b. 22 May 1709; by 2nd w.: CHARLES, b. 29 Sept. 1717, d. 25 March 1720; MARY, b. 14 Dec. 1719, d. 20 May 1720; DANIEL; HANNAH, b. 28 Oct. 1721; AQUILA, b. 23 Feb. 1726/7; BENJAMIN, b. 14 June 1729; MARY, b. 29 Jan. 1733; MARTHA, b. 8 Aug. 1737; ARABELLA, (posthumous), b. 13 Feb. 1739/40(4; 13; 33:442, 443; 127; 128; data from Mrs. Hannon).

GILBERT, MICHAEL (5), s. of Garvis (4), was b. 15 June 1707, d. 1779; m. 1st, 17 Dec. 1728 Sarah Preston; m. 2nd on 23 Nov. 1738 Mary, dau. of Martin Taylor and heir of Robert Robertson; in 1750 owned 145 a. Hall's Pipe, 100 a. Gilbert's Chance, 40 a. of Union, part Clark's Tobacco; rendered patriotic service during the Rev. War; had iss.: (3 ch. by 1st w. and 9 by 2nd w.): MARTHA, b. 20 Nov. 1729; GARVIS, b. 25 Jan. 1731; MICHAEL, b. 17 May 1734; MARTIN TAYLOR, b. 9 Sept. 1739; ELIZABETH, b. 20 March 1744; WILLIAM, b. 20 Nov. 1746; MICHAEL, b. 10 June 1747; HANNAH, b. 15 Jan. 1749; ELIZABETH, b. 5 July 1750; RACHEL, b. 10 June 1755; JAMES, b. 30 Aug. 1757; SUSANNA, b. 16 Feb. 1759 (4; 128; 129; 153; 354).

GILBERT, GARVIS (6), s. of Garvis (4), was b. 1708, d. by 10 Sept. 1756; m. 10 June 1735 Elizabeth, dau. of James Preston; she m. 2nd Michael Gash; on 11 Aug. 1754 admin. bond on est. of Garvis Gilbert was posted by admnx. Elizabeth Gilbert, with Samuel Gilbert and Laurence Clark; est. admin. 10 Sept. 1756 by extx. Eliza, now w. of Michael Gash; Garvis left iss.: MARGARET, b. 13 Sept. 1736; GARVASE, b. 28 Aug. 1738; SARAH, b. 15 May 1741; PRESTON, b. 10 April 1743, moved to Bedford Co., Va., when on 14 June 1783 he sold part of Matthews Neighbors to Joseph Woolsey; HANNAH; ELIZABETH; MICHAEL; SAMUEL; and ANN (5; 13; 44; 128; 129:283; 241:JLG#E:418).

GILBERT, SAMUEL (7), s. of Garvis (4), was b. 22 May 1709, and was alive in 1758 in Bedford Co., Va.; m. Martha Webster, dau. of John Webster, Jr., on 26 April 1733; in 1750 owned 300 a. John and Isaac's Lot; in Jan. 1749 was exec. of est. of Roger Donahue: SAMUEL, b. 7 March 1736, d. 1820 Madison Co., Ohio; JOHN WEBSTER, b. 27 Dec. 1738; MICHAEL, b. 19 April 1741; WILLIAM, b. 20 April 1743 (5; 153; 353).

GILBERT, CHARLES (8), s. of Garvis (4), was b. 1723, d. 1795 in Harford Co.; m. 27 Sept. 1744 Elizabeth Hawkins; in 1750 owned 60 a. part Union, and 40 a. part Clark's Tobacco; had iss.: MARTHA, m. Martin Taylor Gilbert (128; 129:388; 131; 153; 353; data from Mrs. Hannon).

GILBERT, AQUILA (9), s. of Garvis (4), was b. 23 Feb. 1730/7; d. 1806; m. 17 Jan. 1749 Eliza Butler or Butterworth; had iss.: ISAAC; CHARLES; MICHAEL; BENJAMIN (131; 353).

GILBERT, AQUILA, in June 1741 chose Samuel Pritchard as his guardian (33:61).

GILBERT, AQUILA, in 1750 owned 300 a. The Agreement (153).

GILBERT, CHARLES, in June 1741 chose his bro. Garvis to be his guardian; admin. the est. of Solomon Gallion on 2 June 1756 (5:307; 33:61).

GILBERT, ELIZABETH, m. 16 April 1703 John Kembal, Jr. (129).

GILBERT, ELIZABETH, of Thomas and Hannah, b. 22 June 1708 (128).

GILBERT, ELIZABETH, no parents given, b. 12 July 1711 (128).

GILBERT, ELIZABETH, m. William Arnold on 23 Nov. 1722 (129).

GILBERT, ELIZABETH, m. James Thompson on 30 Oct. 1727 (129).

GILBERT, GARVAS, d. by 15 May 1760 when admin. bond was posted by Ruth Gilbert and John Love with Thomas Johnson and Barnet Johnson as securities; est. inv. 5 Aug. 1760 by Ignatius Wheeler and Edmund Bull and val. at £ 126.7.8, signed by Michael and (Mich.?) Gilbert as kin; (13:179; 52).

GILBERT, HANNAH, m. Thomas Gash on 22 Dec. 1712 (129).

GILBERT, JOHN, of Balto. Co., immigrated by 1671; in May 1671 with Abraham Wild purch. 1000 a. called Grove from Richard Love on 15 June 1670 or 1671 bought 100 a. Markefield from William and Joyce Coffen; on 1 June 1670 sold 1600 a. The ? and Haslemore to Abraham Wild (96; 97; 98; 388).

GILBERT, JOHN, m. Rebecca (?); had iss.: ANTHONY, b. 19 May 1723 (128).

GILBERT, JOHN, in Nov. 1734 was made exempt from levy (30:353).

GILBERT, MARY, was ind. in Aug. 1725 for incontinency with John Taylor (27:306).

GILBERT, NEM, twin dau. of Thomas, was b. 6 Feb. 1700; bur. 13 Aug. 1701 (128).

GILBERT, RACHEL, m. Arthur Macurdhon on 29 June 1726 (129).

GILBERT, SARAH, w. of Thomas, was bur. 15 Feb. 1700 (128).

GILBERT, THOMAS, was in Balto. Co. by 1692 as a taxable in Spesutia Hund.; had s. Thomas, Jr., who first appeared as a taxable in 1695 in Spesutia Hund. (138; 140).

GILBERT, THOMAS, Jr., m. 1st on 27 May 1700 Sarah Bedford
who was bur. 15 Feb. 1700; m. 2nd on 1 April 1703 Hannah Ashford, d. 24 Oct. 1713; his will, 24 Oct. 1713 - 2 June 1714,
named ch. Thomas, Michael, and other ch., w. Hannah, tracts
Gilbert's Adventure or Stony Hill; admin. bond posted on 2 June
1714 by Hannah Gilbert; est. admin. on 17 Sept. 1715 by Hannah
Gilbert, sworn to by John Hicks; had iss.: (by 1st w.): THOMAS,
twin, b. 6 Feb. 1700, bur. 20 Feb. 1700; NEM, dau., b. 6 Feb.
1700, bur. 13 Aug. 1701; THOMAS, b. 1 July 1705; ELIZABETH, b.
22 June 1708; MICHAEL, s. of Thomas and "Johannah, d. 3 Sept.
1716 (1; 13; 123; 128; 129).

GILBERT, THOMAS, d. by 22 July 1710 when his est. was inv. by
John Cattall and John Clark, and val. at £ 31.11.8, and Eliz.
Gilbert signed as kin (48).

GILBERT, THOMAS, s. of Thomas and Hannah, was b. 1 July 1705;
m. Elizabeth Cole on 25 Dec. 1727; she d. 7 Feb. 1740; m. 2nd
Mary Fowler on 14 June 1745; had iss. (bu 1st w.): RUTH, b. 13
Oct. 1728; THOMAS, b. 11 June 1732; (by 2nd w.): WILLIAM, b. 20
Nov. 1746; MICHAEL, b. 10 June 1747; HANNAH, b. 15 Jan. 1749;
ELIZABETH, b. 5 July 1750; RACHAEL, b. 10 June 1755; JAMES, b.
30 Aug. 1757; SUSANNA, b. 16 Feb. 1759; FRANCES, b. 10 Nov.
1762; MARTHA, b. 16 Feb. 1764 (128; 129).

GILBOURNE/GILLIBOURNE, THOMAS, was in Balto. Co. by 1692 as
a taxable in n. side Patapsco Hund.; m. by March 1691/2 Mary
Pinder, relict of Timothy Pindar (19:164; 138).

GILCHRIST, ROBERT, was in Balto. Co. by June 1750 when he m.
Helen, admnx. of George Uriel; in 1750 owned 70 a. Ralpo, 391 a.
Cockermouth, and 60 a. Mount Pleasant; d. 17 Oct. 1767, age 60,
and is bur. at Mt. Paran Presbyterian Church; his will, 20 Sept.
1763 - 17 Nov. 1757, name w. Helen, nephews Robert of William
and Robert of James, John Cook's daus. Anastasia, Catherine, and
John Craig; the will of Helen Gilchrest, 24 Dec. 1770 - 5 Aug.
1772, named her bro. John Welch (5:296; 37:70; 153:65; 112:65,
220).

GILCOAT, ALEXANDER, m. Mary (?), and had iss.: ROBERT, b. 7
Sept. 1757 (133:111).

GILES, JOHN (1), progenitor, was in A. A. Co., Md., with his
w. Mary by 1667; may be the John Giles who imm. by 1666; no
record of his death or acct. of his est. has been found; births
of five of his ch. found at West River Monthly Meeting: NATHAN-
IEL, b. 10 d, 1, 1667; ELIZABETH, b. 7 d, 2, 1668; JOHN, b. 7
d., 11, 1670; JACOB, b. 11 d., 4, 1673; ARTRIDGE, b. 4, 6 mo.,
16(?), m. Robert Franklin on 19 d., 8 mo., 1697 (219-6; 388).

GILES, NATHANIEL (2), s. of John (1), was b. 10 d., 1, 1667;
prob. the Nathaniel who d. in Balto. Co. leaving a will, 12 Aug.
1730 - 27 Oct. 1730 in which he named ch. Nathaniel, John, Mary,
and Elizabeth w. of Michael Webster (named in will as son-in-law
Michael Webster); admin. bond posted 24 Oct. 1730 by Michael
Webster with Jacob Giles and Richard Ruff; had iss.: NATHANIEL;

266 BARRISON COUNTY FAMILIES, 1609-1759

JOHN, ELIZABETH, d. Michael Webster; and HANNAH VINES, (d.
1724).

GILES, JOHN (4), s. of John (1) and Mary, was b. 7 d., 11,
1670, and d. ...... Co. by 27 Nov. 1725 when admin. bond was
posted by ...... Sarah, John, Nathaniel, and Jacob Giles, with
Nathaniel Giles and Melchizedek Murray as securities; m. Sarah,
dau. of John Welsh, on 1 Oct. 1695 in A. A. Co.; was on 17
March 1702 John and Sarah Giles joined Daniel and Elizabeth
Richardson in selling part of Three Sisters to James Heath,
Gent.; the will of John Giles, 17 ..... Nov. 1725, left Upton
Court to son John and Jacob Giles 50 a. Newtown to son Nath-
aniel, 200 a. David's Fancy tp s. Jacob, named daus. Betty Lewis,
Sophia Murray, Anna, Mary, and Sarah; his est. was inv. on 19
July 1726 by William Parrish and val. at £ 672,10.8½, and signed
by Nathaniel Giles and Melch'd. Murray as kin; had iss.: JOHN;
JACOB; NATHANIEL; ELIZABETH, m. Richard Lewis on 15, 3 mo. 1723;
SOPHIA, m. Melchizedek Murray on 13, 9 mo., 1723; ANNA; MARY;
...... (2:...; 82: 67:5; 124:202; 219-3.281).

GILES, ... (3), s. of John (1) and ......, was b. 11, 4 mo.,
1673 at We...... ; m. Elizabeth Arnold ..... Richard and
Martha Ar...... on 8, 11 mo., 1701; prob. ..... soon after as Elizabeth m. as her 2nd husb. on 30, 5 mo., 1701 Thomas Hawkins, s.
of John and Mary (Records of West River Meeting in 219-6).

GILES, JOHN (5), s. of Nathaniel (2), is prob. the John who
m. 1st on ..... Oct. 1734 Sarah Butterworth, and 2nd by 1 Sept.1752
Hannah ex...... of Daniel Scott; in Nov. 1736 Nathaniel and John
Giles and ... Sarah sold 390 a. Friend's Discovery to Thomas Tay-
..... in ..... 1752 was summoned before the vestry of St. John's
..... for marrying his deceased wife's sister (Daniel Scott had
m. ..... Butterworth in 1740); John ...... her away; had
iss. by 1st w.: NATHANIEL, b. 29 Aug. 1738, HESTER, b. 9 July
17.. ..... b. 14 Jan. 1740 (5:273, 319; 128:83, 93, 94,
111; ......13; 133:152).

GILES, JOHN (6), s. of John (3) and Sarah, d. in Balto. Co.
by 28 April 1736; m. 8, 11 mo., 1728 Cassandra Smith; in 1750
owned 75 a. Upton Court (owned by John's widow); will of John
Giles, 29 March 1736 - 28 April 1736, left Upton Court to w.
Cassandra, and named daus. Sarah and Elizabeth; will of Cassandra Giles, wid. of John, 3, 12 mo., 1754 - 18 Feb. 1755, named
dau. Sarah w. of Samuel Hopkins, dau. Elizabeth w. of Joseph
Bankson, and grandch. James Slemaker and Gerard Hopkins (under
20); iss. of John and Cassandra: SARAH, m. Samuel Hopkins on 2,
7 mo., 1740; ELIZABETH, m. 1st James Slemaker on 15 Sept. 1745,
and 2nd Joseph Bankson on 16 Jan. 1752 (111:54; 126:169; 153:
19; 219-6).

GILES, JACOB (7), s. of John (3) and Sarah, was alive in Balto.
Co. as late as 1759; m. 1st on 3 Jan. 1728/9 Hannah Webster; 2nd
by 13 July 1739 Johannah Phillips, dau. of Col. James; in 1750
owned 220 a. Johnson's Delay, 570 a. Bourne, 400 a. Elberton, 33
a. Giles' Addition, 100 a. Brotherly Love; had at least three
ch. by 1st w. and eight by his 2nd w.; iss.: JOHN, b. 20 Oct.
1729; JACOB, b. 14 Nov. 1733; NATHANIEL, b. 2 Oct. 1735; SARAH,

m. Nathaniel Rigby; ELIZA, b. 8 Aug. 1747; JAMES, b. 2 Feb.
1749/50; JOHANNAH, b. 29 May 1751; JACOB, b. 15 March 1753; THOM-
AS, b. 25 Dec. 1754; AQUILA, b. 29 Aug. 1757; EDWARD, b. 24 April
1759 (4:31; 128:62, 78, 93; 129:384; 153:38).

GILES (or GILLS), JOHN, d. in Balto. Co. leaving a will, 20
Jan. 1727 - 14 April 1727, in which he named his ch. Samuel,
Rachel, Rebecca, Elizabeth, Mary, and Sarah, and ment. his w.
(125:44).

GILES, JOHN, d. by 9 March 1738 when admin. bond on his est.
was posted by Charles Wells with Ulrick Burk and William Hughes
(13:144).

GILHAMPTON. See GALHAMPTON.

THE GILL FAMILY has been the subject of James D. Gill's The
Gill Family of Maryland; 1642, 1659, and 1950 (1970). Publications of the Surtees Society, vol. 110, has a number of references to Stephen Gill in the Knaresborough area of Yorkshire, England in the early 17th century. Nugent's Pioneers and Cavaliers
vol. 1, contains many references to one or more individuals
named Stephen Gill in Virginia between 1636 and 1657. After a
study of land and probate records in 17th century Anne Arundel
and Baltimore Counties, it is still not possible to reconstruct
the first three generations of the family with any great degree
of certainty (420).

GILL, STEVEN (1), was transported to Md. between 1659 and
1664; may be the Steven Gill whose w. Alice m. as her 2nd husb.
William Drury; Alice (?) Gill Drury m. as her 3rd husb. Peter
Bond (see Bond Family this work); may have been the father of at
least one son: STEVEN (120:179; 388).

GILL, STEVEN (2), prob. s. of Steven (1) and Alice, was b. c.
1673, giving his age as 60 in 1733; was named in the 1676 will
of William Drewry as the s. of the testator's w. Alice; in 1687
was conv. 182 a. Littleton by his friend Thomas Thurston (perhaps he was b. before 1673); in 1704 he and w. Elizabeth were
tried for altering the quality of a hogshead of tobacco in A. A.
Co.; in 1707 held 98 a. Brown's Chance for the orphans of Daniel
McComas; may have been the father of two sons and four daus.:
JOHN, d. by May 1717; STEPHEN, d. 1734; ELIZABETH, m. William Bayley on 21 Oct. 1705 in All Hallows Par., A. A. Co.; MARY, m. John
Wooden on 27 Jan. 1716; JANE, left prop. by the will, made 21
April 1722; ALICE, m. John Cooper on 23 Oct. 1722 (59:226; 120:
179; 124:114; 129:270; 133:148; 219-1:71; 224:171; also 211; and
A. A. Co. Judgments G:492).

GILL, JOHN (3), prob. s. of Steven (2) and def. bro. of Steven
(4) below, d. by 1718; m. Jane Guinn who m. as her 2nd husb. (?)
Vandiver or Vandeaver; purch. 100 a. Walnut Neck from George Valentine in Sept. 1704; at same time John Gill and w. Jane sold
100 a. Grimes Addition in A. A. Co. to said Valentine; surv.
Gill's Outlet and Gill's Fancy in 1714 and 1717; d. by 20 April
1717 when admin. bond was posted by Jane Gill with Thomas Randall and Wm. Hambleton; est. inv. 8 May 1717 by Hector McLane and

Christopher Randall and val. at Ł 108.13.2; later an additional
inv. was filed, worth Ł 1.10.0; est. admin. on 16 Nov. 1719 by
Jane now w. of Jacob Van Deaver; the est. was divided among the
wid., John Gill, and the legal heirs of Steven Gill, Jr., also
mentioned but not named were brothers "of the half blood" of
the dec.; est. was also admin. on 26 Nov. 1718 and 10 Oct. 1719
(when Stephen Gill was named as bro. of the dec.; had iss.:
STEPHEN GILL, "Junior," who d. 1717 (1:338; 2:142; 13:116; 50:
261; 52:134; 60:139; 217-WT#2:232; also James D. Gill, The Gill
Fam.)

GILL, STEPHEN (4), prob. s. of Steven (2), and def. bro. of
John (3) above, d. in Balto. Co. in 1734; m. Elizabeth Hubbert
on 16 Dec. 1708 in St. Anne's Par., A. A. Co.; admin. the est.
of his nephew Stephen Gill on 9 Sept. 1724; in May 1710 with w.
Elizabeth conv. 180 a. Littleton to John McComas of Daniel in
exchange for 98 a. Brown's Chance; Stephen and Elizabeth conv.
100 a. Gill's Fancy to William Parrish in March 1729; in Aug.
1729 they conv. 120 a. part Thomas Choice to John Price; d. in
St. Paul's Par., 17 Feb. 1734; left a will, 16 Feb. 1733 - 4
June 1735 in which he named w. Elizabeth (to have part Parrish
Range), sons John, Stephen, and Edward (latter not yet 18);
as "son?" and heir at law of John Gill, conv. Walnut Neck to
William Puntany in Jan. 1725; est. admin. 13 Aug. 1736; left
iss.: JOHN, b. 12 Oct. 1708; STEPHEN; EDWARD, under 18 in 1734;
ELIZABETH, m. Edward Parrish on 3 May 1735; SARAH m. William
Rogers by 10 May 1728; PRUDENCE, b. 26 Jan. 1727 (3:14; 59:
226; 67:78; 72:69; 122:224; 133:25, 153; 134:16; 213-PL#6:129;
219-2).

GILL, STEPHEN, "Junior," (5), s. of John (3), d. in Balto.
Co. leaving a will, 23 Sept. 1717 - 18 Nov. 1717, in which he
named friend Darby Lane, uncle Peter Bond, mother Jane Gill,
uncle Stephen Gill, and following lands: 100 a. his father
bought from Thomas Randall, 100 a. Millestones, and 100 a. his
father bought from George Valentine (124:121).

GILL, JOHN (6), s. of Stephen (4) and Elizabeth, was b. 12
Oct. 1708; d. 15 Jan. 1797; m. 26 Feb. 1730 Mary Rogers, b. 1712,
d. 21 Jan. 1797, dau. of Nicholas and Eleanor (?) Rogers; by
1750 owned 250 a. Batson's Forest, 100 a. Gill's Range, and 13
a. Parrishes Range; d. leaving a will, 22 May 1793 - 21 Jan.
1797; had iss.: ELIZABETH, b. 4 March 1731, d. Aug. 1752 when
she was struck by lightning; SARAH, b. 15 Jan. 1733, d. 23 April
1744; ELEANOR, b. 15 Jan. 1735, m. John Pindell on 6 Nov. 1757;
JOHN, b. 4 Feb. 1737; WILLIAM, b. 12 May 1739; STEPHEN, b. 1 Jan.
1741; EDWARD, b. 2 July 1744; SARAH, b. 2 Jan. 1747, m. (?)
Cooper; NICHOLAS, b. 25 May 1750, d. May 1793; JOSHUA, b. 7 July
1753; ELIZABETH ROGERS, b. 13 June 1755, m. (?) Barclay (114:
467; 134:16, 17, 22, 24, 71; 153; 385:190).

GILL, STEPHEN (7), s. of Stephen (4) and Elizabeth, was of
age to m. Urith, dau. of Capt. Henry Butler on 27 June 1740; d.
by 8 Sept. 1789; in 1750 owned 125 a. Batson's Forest; his est.
was admin. 8 Sept. 1789, 15 Oct. 1789, and 17 Sept. 1790; the
will of Urith Gill was made 20 April 1800 - 25 Nov. 1800; left
iss.: THOMAS; EDWARD, m. Ruth Richards; JOHN, m. Rachel Gill;

BENJAMIN, m. Jemima Murray; RUTH, b. 26 Feb. 1745; MARY, b. 9
July 1747; STEPHEN, b. 7 Feb. 1748; NICHOLAS, b. 25 May 1750;
PRUDENCE; SUSANNA, m. John Hager; URATH, m. Stephen Garrett
Gill (5:74; 10:51, 65, 189; 115:235; 153:71).

GILLESPIE/GALASPIE, ROBERT, m. Eliz. Maxwell on 6 Nov. 1753
(131).

GILLETT, AMBROSE (1), d. by March 1683/4; m. Jane (?) who m.
as her 2nd husb. James Howard or James Friend; had iss.: THOMAS
(18:141).

GILLETT, THOMAS (2), s. of Ambrose (1), in March 1683/4 was
cause of his stepfather's posting bond he would deliver Thomas'
est. to Maj. Thomas Long (18:141).

GILLHAM/GILLIAN, RALPH, was in Balto. Co. by 1694 as a taxable
in Spesutia Hund.; had iss.: SARAH, b. 27 Feb. 1695 (128:4; 129:
181; 139).

GILLINS, THOMAS, m. Elizabeth (?) and had iss.: MARY, b. May
1725; SUSANNA, b. Nov. 1727 (131:5/r).

GILMORE, ANN, was fined for bast. in Nov. 1759 (46:240).

GINCHARD. See GUISHARD.

GINGLE, ISAAC, b. in west of Eng., ran away from John Metcalfe
of Patapsco Hund. (385:231).

GINKINS. See JENKINS.

THE GIST FAMILY has been the subject of a chapter in vol. 2
of The Green Spring Valley also by this author; an article by
Christopher Johnston, and of a book by Maxwell J. and Jean M.
Dorsey (see Bibliography for full citations; see 259).

GIST, CHRISTOPHER (1), progenitor, was in Balto. Co. by 1682
and d. by 10 March 1690/1; m. Edith, sis. of William, Richard,
and John Cromwell; she m. 2nd Joseph Williams, and 3rd John Beecher; Christopher imm. to Md. by 1679; d. leaving a will, 17 Feb.
1690 - 10 March 1690, in which he named his w. as sole extx.,
mentioned his s., named John Robinson and the child of his bro.
Richard Cromwell; the will of Edith Gist Williams, made 23 May
1694, named their one s.: RICHARD (59:311; 388; Barnes; Dorsey
et al; Johnston).

GIST, RICHARD (2), s. of Christopher (1) and Edith, was b.
1684, and d. 28 Dec. 1740; m. Zipporah, dau. of James and Jemima
(Morgan) Murray on 7 Dec. 1704; in April 1706 surv. 200 a. Turkey
Cock Hall; in Aug. 1722 conv. part of Green Spring Traverse to
Christopher Choate; was one of the Commissioners appointed in
1729 to survey Baltimore Town; admin. the est. of Francis Street
on 3 March 1719 and 17 Sept. 1720, and the est. of David Hagen
on 25 Aug. 1725; d. by 15 Oct. 1741 when admin. bond on his est.
was posted by Christopher Gist with Thomas Sligh and William
Rogers: est. admin. by son Christopher Gist on 23 Oct. 1744 and

13 July 1749; had iss.: CHRISTOPHER, d. 1759; NATHANIEL, b. c.
1707; WILLIAM, b. c.1711; THOMAS, b. c.1713; EDITH; JEMIMA,m.
William Seabrooke (1:326; 2:17; 3:28, 363; 5:79; 13:155; 69:
111; 70:68; 74:26; 259).

GIST, CHRISTOPHER (3), s. of Richard (2) and Zipporah, d.
in 1759, having m. Sarah, dau. of Joshua Howard; was comm. Coroner of Balto. Co. in Dec. 1743; left Balto. Co. with his family
c.1745; by 1750 they were living on the Yadkin R. in N. C.: in
1755 was a lieut. in the Va. forces; by 1756 was capt. of a company of scouts; had iss.: RICHARD, b. 2 Sept. 1729, d. 1780 at
the Battle of King's Mountain; VIOLETTA, b. 4 July 1731, m. William Cromwell; Col. NATHANIEL, b. 15 Oct. 1733, m. Judith Carey
Bell; ANNE, b. c.1734; THOMAS, b. c.1735, d. 1785 (76:132; 133:
28, 34; 303; Barnes; Dorsey; Johnston).

GIST, NATHANIEL (4), s. of Richard (2) and Zipporah, was b.
c.1707, d. after 1787; m. Mary, dau. of Joshua Howard; by 1757
was in Bedford Co., Va.; had iss.: ZIPPORAH, b. 24 Dec. 1732, m.
Benjamin Young; CHRISTOPHER, b. 21 Dec. 1734, d. 1794/5, m. Lucy
(?); NATHANIEL, b. c.1736, m. Dinah (?); JOSHUA, b. c.1740, m.
Elizabeth (?); RICHARD, b. c.1742, d. 1780; JOSEPH, b. c.1748,
m. Ann or Mary McNeill (4:40; 75:511; 133:411; Barnes; Dorsey;
Johnston).

GIST, WILLIAM (5), s. of Richard (2) and Zipporah, was b. c.
1711, d. 16 Nov. 1794; m. Violetta, dau. of Joshua Howard, on
22 Oct. 1737; in 1750 owned 50 a. Wolf Den, 50 a. Gist's Enlargement, and 60 a. The Addition; had iss.: JOSEPH, b. 30 Sept. 1738;
WILLIAM, b. 23 Sept. 1743; m. Sarah Fincher; ANNE, b. 16 Sept.
1745, m. James Calhoun, 1st Mayor of Balto.; SARAH, b. 25 Nov.
1747, m. Andrew McClure; THOMAS, b. 19 May 1750, m. Ruth Bond;
ELIZABETH, b. 19 May 1750, m. Ramsay McGee; JOHN, b. 26 July
1752; VIOLETTA, b. 13 March 1755; ELLEN, b. 26 Sept. 1757 (4:40;
153:75; Barnes, et al).

GIST, THOMAS (6), s. of Richard (2) and Zipporah, was b. c.
1713, d. c.1788, m. Susan, dau. of John Cockey on 2 July 1735;
Susan was b. 2 Nov. 1714, d. c.1803; in 1750 owned 216 a. The
Adventure; had iss.: ELIZABETH, b. 14 Dec. 1736, d. 1826; JOHN,
b. 22 Nov. 1738, d. 1800; Col. THOMAS, b. 30 March 1741; MORDECAI,
b. 22 Feb. 1742; RICHARD, b. 1 Nov. 1745, d. 1746; JOSHUA, b. 16
Oct. 1747; RACHEL, b. 7 Sept. 1750, d. 8 Sept. 1825; DAVID, b. 29
April 1753 (134:6, 9, 10, 21, 22; 153:72; Barnes, et al).

THE GITTINGS FAMILY is the subject of a chart and notes by
Christopher Johnston at the Maryland Historical Society.

GITTINGS, THOMAS (1), progenitor, was b. c.1682 and d. 1760
in Balto. Co.; m. 1st on 3 April 1719 in Shrewsbury Par., Kent
Co., Md., Elizabeth, dau. of Abraham Redgrave of Kent Co. (she
was b. 3 March 1703 in Shrewsbury Par., d. c.1733); m. 2nd, c.
1734, Mary, wid. of James Lynch and dau. of James Lee; by 1750
was in Balto. Co. as the owner of 500 a. Clarke's Forest, 800 a.
part Thompson's Choice, and 100 a. H(?) Beginning; left a will,
30 Nov. 1758 - 19 May 1760, in which he named his ch. and grandchildren; had iss.: MARGARET, m. 31 Oct. 1737 John Chamberlain;

ELIZABETH, m. Ephraim Gover; MARY, b. 1725, m. 22 Dec. 1741 Richard Wilmot; SUSANNA, b. 1728, m. John Wilson, 1747; THOMAS, b. 1731; JAMES, b. 1736; ASAEL, b. 1739 (79:340; 80:489; 111:259; 131; 153:53; Johnston, "Gittings Chart.").

GITTINGS, THOMAS (2), s. of Thomas (1) and Elizabeth, was b. 1731, d. 1784; m. Hannah, dau. of John Clarke; had iss.: ELIZABETH, m. (?) Wilson; JAMES; MARGARET; CLARKE: BENJAMIN; HANNAH; SUSANNA; MARY; SARAH; JESSE: JOHN (Johnston).

GITTINGS, JAMES (3), s. of Thomas (1) and Mary, was b. 1736, d. 15 Feb. 1823; m. Elizabeth, dau. of Dr. George Buchanan (she was b. 28 June 1742); had iss.: JAMES, b. 1769, m. Harriet Sterett; ARCHIBALD, m. Elizabeth Bosley; MARY, m. Thomas Ringgold; ELIZABETH, m. Lambert Smith; ANNE, m. William Patterson, Jr.; THOMAS; RICHARD (Johnston).

GIVES, WILLIAM, of Balto. Co., claimed land for service in 1673 (388).

GLADE, WILLIAM, d. by June 1757; had iss.: WILLIAM, age 6 on 16 Sept. 1757; in June 1757 was bound to Samuel Messersmith to learn trade of gunsmith (46:37).

GLADEN, JACOB, m. Sarah Rice on 31 Jan. 1753 (131).

GLADING, REBECCA, was tried for bast. in Nov. 1756 and named James Allen as the father (41:311).

GLADMAN, (?) (1), had at least two ch.: MICHAEL, b. c.1702; and REBECCA, d. in Anne Arundel Co. leaving a will, 20 June 1763 - 8 July 1765, in which she named her nephews and nieces: Michael, John, Thomas and Rachel Gladman, and Rebecca Godman, all ch. of her bro. Michael; also named other legatees: Mary Goldsmith of Mary, Samuel Sligh of Ann, Mrs. Rebecca Wheeler w. of Basil, Mrs. Sarah Button, Eliz. Adams dau. of Nathaniel, John Beresby, and Sarah Lawrence (210-33:263).

GLADMAN, MICHAEL (2), s. of (?) (1), was b. c.1702, d. 1789 in Balto. Co.; gave his age as 65 in 1767; m. Rachel (?); in 1750 owned 50 a. Harkle Pool; left a will, 21 May 1782 - 19 Sept. 1789, in which he named w. Rachel, sons Michael and John, and daus. Rachel Gladman and Rebecca Cross; had iss.: REBECCA, b. 14 Feb. 1728/9, m. 1st (?) Godman, and 2nd (?) Cross; JOHN, b. 2 Aug. 1732; MICHAEL, b. 3 July 1736; THOMAS, b. 5 Feb. 1738, d. by 1770 leaving a will in which he named father Michael, and bros. John and Michael, sis. Rachel, William Mattocks of William and Rebecca, and Michael Gladman of John; RACHEL, b. 9 Jan. 1744/5 (113:381; 133:28, 60, 61, 73; 153:43; 210-37:452; 213-DD#2:179).

GLADMAN, JOHN (3), s. of Michael (2), b. 2 Aug. 1732, m. and had at least one s.: MICHAEL, b. by 28 April 1769 (210-37:452).

GLADMAN, MICHAEL (4), s. of Michael (2), was b. 3 July 1736, d. c.1818; m. Barbara (?); had iss.: THOMAS; CASSANDRA, m. by lic. 9 June 1792 George Maddox; BARBARA, m. by lic. 7 Jan. 1794 Nicodemus Cross; RACHEL, m. by lic. 14 Jan. 1798 Maurice Baker; NANCY (232:345).

GLARON, AGNES, serv. to Thomas Hatchman, d. Sept. 1726 (131).

GLASPIN, WILLIAM, m. Sarah Lowry on 21 Feb. 1729 (128:71).

GLASSINGTON, JOHN, m. Mary Jordan on 1 Aug. 1734 (133:152).

GLASSON. See GLEASON.

GLEASON, NEHEMIAH, s. of Richard, was age 8 years in March 1725/6; in Aug. 1725 was bound to Samuel and Sarah Hooker (27: 306).

GLEDE, WILLIAM, m. Jane Russell on 15 Nov. 1750 (131).

GLOVER, PETER (1), d. in Balto. Co. leaving a will, 8 Feb. 1722 - 6 March 1722, in which he left his entire est. to his s. Richard, and also named Thomas Treadway and Josias Middlemore; admin. bond was posted 7 March 1722 by Middlemore with Daniel Scott and Benjamin Norris; est. inv. 6 June 1723 by Thomas Bond and Wm. McComas, and val. at Ł 42.19.6, no kin signed; est. admin. 5 Nov. 1724 by Middlemore; had iss.: RICHARD (3:2; 13:114; 52: 35; 124:135).

GLOVER, RICHARD (2), s. of Peter (1), was mentioned in his father's will in Feb. 1722 (124:135).

GLOVER, JOHN, was in Balto. Co. by June 1669 when he purch. 250 a. Crock and Pill from Peter Jones, shopman (95).

GLOVER, THOMAS, d. at Mr. Wells' on 22 Aug. 1702 and was bur. on 23 Aug. 1702 (128:15).

GOATLEY, GEORGES, servant to Jos. Hooper, was ind. for felony in March 1736/7 (31:1).

GODBY, JASPER, s. of Jasper Godby of Old Street Square near St. Luke's Church, London, and sentenced to transportation to the colonies in Jan. 1746 and Sept. 1747; by 1756 was living in Balto. Co. when he wrote a letter to his relatives: m. Ann Bosell on 25 May 1755 (54:267; 131; Coldham, "Gen. Gleanings...," Nat. Gen. Soc. Qtly, 65:267).

GODDARD, JOHN, serv. to Lovelace Gorsuch at Chestnut Ridge, Md., was in jail in Trenton, N. J., in Nov. 1753 (385:259).

GODSGRACE, JOHN. (1), m. Rebecca; had iss.: WILLIAM, b. 9 Jan. 1738; REBECCA, b. 7 Match 1740 (131:127/r).

GODSGRACE, WILLIAM (2), s. of John (1) above, d. in Balto. Co., leaving a will, 16 April 1782 - 20 April 1782, leaving all his est. to a s.: ROBERT (112:480).

GOFFE, JOHN, was in Balto. Co. by 1695 as a taxable in n. side Patapsco Hund. (140).

GOING, ELIZABETH, was ind. for bast. in June 1730; as Elizabeth Going, alias Black, tried for bast. in June 1731 (28:415; 29:165).

GOLDEN/GOLDING, PETER (1), d. by March 1755; m. 15 Nov. 1742 Eliz. Earl and had iss.: JOHN, b. 27 Oct. 1744; STEPHEN, b. 10 Aug. 1746; ELIZABETH, b. 18 Aug. 1749 (40:15; 131:94/r, 113/r, 123/r).

GOLDEN, JOHN (2), s. of Peter (1), was age 11 in March 1755 when he was bound to John Hall of Cranberry; in March 1759 was bound to Roger Boyce (40:16; 44).

GOLDSMITH, Maj. SAMUEL (1), first progenitor, came to Md. with w. Johanna, and daus. Susanna and Blanche in 1658; may have come from Va. where in 1672 John Parker rec. land for having transported a number of people including a Samuel, Johanna and Susanna Goldsmith; rep. Balto. Co. in the Lower House of the Assembly, 1659/60 and 1663/4; in July 1658 surv. 800 a. Goldsmith's Hall which was later held by the orphans of Col. George Wells; d. leaving a will, 12 Oct. 1670 - 6 Oct. 1671, in which he named his w. Johanna, daus. Blanche w. of Col. George Wells and Susanna w. of Mark Richardson; also a godson George Goldsmith; the will of Johanna Goldsmith, 1684 - 1687, named husb. Samuel, dau. Blanch w. of George Wells, and dau. Susanna w. of Mark Richardson; her est. was inv. on 20 May 1687 by James Phillips and George Goldsmith; had iss.: BLANCHE, m. George Wells; SUSANNA, m. 1st George Utie, and 2nd Mark Richardson (120:62; 200-1:382, 460; 206-10:105; 211; 388; Balto. Co. Orig. Wills, Box 1, folder 36; Nugent, Cav. and Pioneers, II, 106).

GOLDSMITH, GEORGE (2), poss. nephew of Samuel (1), came to Md. c.1658 with his bros. Matthew (3) and Thomas (4) Goldsmith, below; in Aug. 1659 surv. 200 a. Proctor's Hall; in July 1659 took up 100 a. Hooper's Island; d. 1666 having m. Mary (poss. Collett) who m. as her 2nd husb. Samuel Boston; served in the Lower House as a delegate from Balto. Co. in 1659/60 and also was sheriff, deputy surveyor, justice, and captain; left a will, April 1666 - 20 July 1666, named w. Mary, s. George, daus. Eliza and Mary, uncle Samuel Goldsmith, bro. Matthew Goldsmith, and bro.-in-law Samuel Collett; admin. bond was posted 21 July 1666 by extx. Mary with Samuel Goldsmith; a 2nd admin. bond was posted on 7 May 1675 by admin. Samuel Boston; had iss.: GEORGE; ELIZABETH; MARY (13: 121, 127; 95; 120:35; 211:6; 370:367; 388).

GOLDSMITH, MATTHEW (3), bro. of George (2) and Thomas (4), and nephew of Samuel (1), came to Md. in 1658; d. 1668 having m. Penelope (?); may be the Matthew not yet 14 named in the will of John Collett as not yet 14, in March 1673 (120:74; 388).

GOLDSMITH, THOMAS (4), bro. of George (2) and Matthew (3), was transported to Md. c.1658; with John Hawkins surv. 600 a. Planter's Delight; by 1660 was in Isle of Wight Co., Va. (211; 388).

GOLDSMITH, GEORGE (5), s. of George (2), was b. in Balto. Co. after 1658, d. there in 1692; m. Martha Beedle, b. 1668, d. 1720; she m. as her 2nd husb. Col. John Hall of Cranberry on 18 July 1693; d. leaving a will, 13 March 1691/2 - 8 April 1692, named bro. -in-law Edward Bedle, dau. Mary, w. Martha, and unborn ch.; est. was inv. 23 July 1694 by Ludwick Martin and Thomas Greenfield

and val. at L 196.3.6; est. was admin. by w. Martha now w. of
John Hall on 11 Oct. 1697; had iss.: MARY; MARTHA, m. James
Presbury in Feb. 1708 (2:48, 196; 48:224; 121:72; 129:178, 207;
206-15:182; 206-19:171).

GOLDSMITH, (?), d. by 1693/4, m. Elizabeth, heir of John
Collett, dec.; she m. 2nd (?) Dawkins (206-12:149).

GOLDSMITH, JOHN, m. Elinor (?); had iss.: MARY, b. 14 Dec.
1728; JOHN, b. 24 April 1734; WILLIAM, b. 21 March 1734/5; ELLIN-
ER, b. 21 Oct. 1736 (133:23, 41, 56).

GOLDSMITH, Mrs. MARY, m. Robert Gibson on 15 Dec. 1702 (129:
197).

GOLDSMITH, THOMAS, m. Lilly (?), and had iss.: SARAH, b. 17
March 1749; ANN, b. 21 Aug. 1751; WILLIAM COPELAND, b. 7 Oct.
1753; THOMAS, b. 16 Sept. 1760 (131:61/r).

GOLELY, GEORGE, servant, with 1½ years to serve. listed in
the 1739 inv. of Rev. Joseph Hooper (52:327).

GOLL, ROBERT, m. Mary (?), and had iss.: ELIZABETH, b. 13 Dec.
1725; MARY, b. 19 July 1729; SARAH, twin, b. 19 Feb. 1732; MARY,
twin, b. 19 Feb. 1732; RICHARD, b. 20 June 1734 (131:50/r).

GOLLOHAN, JOHN, m. Frances Peregoy on 16 Feb. 1723 (133:147).

GOOBY, SUSANNA, m. John Ward on 26 Dec. 1721 (129:231).

GOODERICK, HENRY, of A. A. Co., in Aug. 1666 bought 300 a.
West Humphreys from Roland Hathaway, and 100 a. on w. side of
Welshman's Run on s. side Patapsco (94).

GOODING, JACOB, m. Mary (?); had iss.: HANNAH, b. 10 June
1744 (129:336).

GOODING, SAMUEL, was tried for fathering an illegitimate
child in Nov. 1756 (41:311).

GOODRIDGE, GILBERT, English, runaway convict servant in Nov.
1754 (385:317).

THE GOODWIN FAMILY is based in part on a pedigree of "The
Goodwins of Alkerton, and Epwell, Oxfordshire, of Cambden,
Gloucester'," in Miscellanea Genealogica et Heraldica, 4th ser.,
I, 150-152, 191.

GOODWIN, THOMAS (1), progenitor, was taxed in goods at Alkerton in 15 Henry VIII; d. leaving a will, 19 Dec. 1530 - 8 Oct.
1531, directed that he be bur. at Alkerton Churchyard; m. Elizabeth (?) whose will, 2 March 1543/4 - 16 May 1544, also to be
bur. at Alkerton; had iss.: HENRY (for his descendants in Horley
see Misc. Gen. et Her., 4th ser., II, 32); RICHARD; ANDREW; ANNE;
JOHN (Goodwin article cited above).

GOODWIN, RICHARD (2), s. of Thomas (1), was a residuary legatee in the will of his mother; was taxed for goods at Alkerton
in 34 and 35 Henry VIII, and 1 Edward VI; his undated will was
proved 23 March 1559/60; he asked to be buried at Alkerton; by
his unknown w. he was the father of: THOMAS; JOHN, living 13 Jan.
1590/1; HENRY, bur. at Alkerton on 27 May 1590; RICHARD, bapt. 4
Dec. 1553 at Alkerton, prob. d. young; RICHARD, bapt. 4 March
1556/7 at Alkerton, m. and had iss.; ELLEN; MARGERY; ELIZABETH,
bapt. at Alkerton 2 Aug. 1547; AGNES, bapt. at Alkerton 3 April
1549 ("Goodwin of Alkerton and Epwell, Oxfordshire," Misc.
Gen. et Her., 4th ser., I, 150-152, 191).

GOODWIN, THOMAS (3), s. of Richard (2), was a trustee under
his father's will; was taxed for lands at Alkerton in 8, 9, and
23 Elizabeth; bur. at Alkerton on 14 Jan. 1590/1; left a will,
13 Jan. 1590/1 - 27 Jan. 1590/1, in which he left a legacy to
the poos of Alkerton, Epwell, and Shenington; m. Alice (?); she
was bur. at Alkerton on 6 Dec. 1600 having left a will, 3 Dec.
1600 - 23 April 1601; Thomas and Alice had iss.: WILLIAM; DENES,
bapt. 20 Feb. 1567/8, m. John Bourton on 6 Nov. 1587; JOHN, bapt.
2 March 1570/1; matric. at Brasenose Coll., Oxford, and served
as Rector of Great Rollright, 1598-1667, m. and had iss.: RICHARD,
bapt. 10 April 1574, m. and had iss.; HENRY; THOMAS, bapt. 17 Oct.
1579 at Alkerton (Ibid.).

GOODWIN, WILLIAM (4), s. of Thomas (3) and Alice, was bapt. at
Alkerton on 4 Feb. 1564/5; acquired the manor and lordship of Ep-
well under the will of his mother; m. 1st Alice (?) who was the
mother of his ch. and was bur. at Epwell 4 March 1609/10; m. 2nd
at Epwell on 13 May 1613 Anne Hawten who was bur. at Epwell in
Feb. 1620; William was bur. at Epwell on 2 Sept. 1637, having
left a will, 10 May 1637 - 8 Nov. 1637; ch. of William and Alice:
ALICE, bapt. 15 April 1592, m. by 10 May 1637 Richard Burden or
Burton; THOMAS, bapt. 18 Jan. 1596 at Epwell, m. and had iss.;
WILLIAM, bapt. 22 March 1598/9, bur. 28 Nov. 1688, m. and had
iss.; HANNAH, bapt. 16 Aug. 1601 at Epwell, m. John Hawten at
Horley on 26 Oct. 1618; JOHN, bapt. 22 Jan. 1603/4 at Epwell; he
later moved to Combe, near Campden, Gloucester; ANNE, bapt. 25
March 1606 at Epwell m. by 10 May 1637 Richard Walker; RICHARD,
bapt. 22 June 1608 at Epwell, m. and had iss.; BENJAMIN, bapt.
4 March 1609/10, m. and had iss. (Ibid.).

GOODWIN, JOHN (5), s. of William (4) and Alice, was bapt. 22
Jan. 1603/4 at Epwell, Oxford, and moved to Combe, near Campden,
Gloucestershire; prob. was the father of three sons all of whom
disclaimed the right to bear a coat of arms at the Visitation
of Gloucester in 1682/3; had iss.: JOHN of Berington (Campden);
NATHANIEL, of Saintbury; THOMAS, of Combe; poss. MARTHA, age 41
in 1682/3, m. Thomas Bridges or Bruges of Colesbourne (Ibid.;
Fenwick and Metcalfe, Vis. of the County of Gloucester, 1682/3,
p. 217).

GOODWIN, JOHN (6), s. of John (5), disclaimed in 1682/3, may
be the John who m. Hannah (?), and had iss.: AUSTIN; AUGUSTINE,
bapt. 15 Sept. 1668 at Weston Subedge, Glouc., m. and had at
least two sons; ANN, bapt. 1672, m. Thomas Durham; JOHN, bapt.
1684; MARY, bapt. 1690 ("Goodwin of Alkerton...," p. 191; Latter

Day Saints, International Genealogy Index, Gloucester, 1984 ed.;
research by Louise Hargrave of Dallas, Texas, and made available
to the compiler).

GOODWIN, AUSTIN (7), s. of John (6), d. 1756, having m. 1st
on 28 Feb. 1692 at Chipping Campden, Glouc., Joyce Yate; m. 2nd
Susanna Lyde; 3rd, on 16 Sept. 1733 Anne Mugglesworth at the
Cathedral in Bristol; had iss. (by 1st w.): JANE, bapt. 30 Dec.
1693 at Chipping Campden; HUGH, bapt. 23 March 1694; ROBERT,
bapt. 8 April 1698; JOYCE, bapt. 10 April 1699; (by 2nd w.):
LYDE, bapt. 10 Nov. 1718 (Ibid.).

GOODWIN, LYDE (8), s. of Austin (7), was bapt. 10 Nov. 1718
prob. at the Levins Mead Presbyterian Church in the City of Bristol, Gloucester;   was in Balto. Co., Md., by 1750 when he owned
470 a. Howard's Invitation; m. by 24 April 1753 Pleasance, dau.
of Charles Ridgely; d. by 11 March 1756 when Pleasance Goodwin
posted admin. bond on his est., with Charles and John Ridgely;
Pleasance Ridgely Goodwin d. leaving a will, 31 Dec. 1776 - 4
Dec. 1777, in which she named grandch. Thomas Parkin, Elizabeth
Goodwin Dorsey, and William, Rebecca, and Achsah Goodwin, as
well as these ch.: WILLIAM; LYDE, b. 4 Feb. 1754, d. Aug. 1801,
m. Abigail Levy; SUSANNA; RACHEL LYDE, m. (?) Parkin; PLEASANCE
(Ibid.; 13:186; 112:354; 153:69).

GOODWIN, BENJAMIN, m. Hannah Urquhart on 6 Feb. 1742; had iss.:
WILLIAM, b. 7 Jan. 1744; JOHN, b. 7 Feb. 1746; ELIZABETH, b. 28
April 1749; THOMAS, b. 23 Nov. 1752; BENJAMIN, b. 13 March 1755;
JAMES, b. 16 Oct. 1758; ANN, b. 8 March 1760; HANNAH, b. 1 March
1762 (129:331, 335, 371).

GOODWIN, GEORGE, prob. d. by Aug. 1740; m. 1st Elizabeth (?),
and 2nd on 29 March 1730 Ann Rutter; had iss.: GEORGE, b. 23 Nov.
1729; ANN, b. 20 July 1733 (133:17, 31, 149).

GOODWIN, GEORGE, prob. s. of George above; in Aug. 1740 at
age 11 was bound to Richard Rutter (32:290).

GOODWIN, JOHN, m. Margaret (?), and had iss.: JOHN, b. 17
Sept. 1736; WILLIAM, b. 4 Feb. 1738; ALEXANDER PHILIP, b. 20 Aug.
1740 (129:323; 131:93, 94).

GOODWIN, MOSES, d. when est. was admin. 3 Aug. 1769 by wid.
Rachel who named in the acct. the bros. and sis. of the dec.:
Benjamin, William, Joseph, and the child of a sister (7:37).

GOODWIN, SAMUEL, m. 26 Dec. 1755 Rebecca Breeding, and had
iss.: ISAAC, b. 19 Dec. 1756; JOSEPH, b. 10 Aug. 1759; ELIZABETH,
b. 4 July 1761 (129:371).

GOODWIN, STEPHEN, servant with 2 years 8 mos. to serve, in
the inv. of Stephen Onion, Oct. 1754 (49:222).

GOODWIN, WILLIAM, m. Elizabeth (?), and had iss.: SAMUEL, b.
24 Jan. 1734; ELEANOR, b. 11 Dec. 1737 (128:34, 100).

GORDON, DANIEL, m. 23 Nov. 1729 Mary West, and had iss.: JOHN,
b. 19 May 1746 (128:67; 129:353).

GORDON, EDWARD, d. by 23 Oct. 1710 when his est. was admin. by Lawrence Yanstone (2:155).

GORDON, JOSEPH, m. Ruth Chaney on 15 Feb. 1752; had iss.: MARY, b. 17 March 1752; JAMES, b. 16 Oct. 1758 (129:359).

GORDON, MARY, in Feb. 1747 was the subject of a promise by Thomas Brown, woodcutter, to the vestry of St. John's Vestry, that he would put her away (132:329).

GORDON, RICHARD, m. Mary (?); had iss.: SARAH, b. 5 Dec. 1734 (128:86).

GORDON, ROBERT, was in Balto. Co. by March 1725/6 as the admin. of the est. of a Dr. Alexander Mitchell (2:301).

GORE, ANN, m. Jonathan Hurst on 29 Dec. 1729 (133:149).

GORMACON, MICHAEL, was in Balto. Co. by 1692 as a taxable in n. side Patapsco; on 17 March 1723 conv. land where he was then living to his dau. Mary; d. leaving a will, 28 Feb. 1723/4 - 6 July 1725, in which he named w. Ann, and dau. Mary who was to have the tract Passage after the death of her mother; if Mary d. without heirs, est. was to pass to the Roman Catholic Church; had iss.: MARY (69:245; 123:193; 138).

GORMAN, JOHN, orphan of Thomas, in March 1757 chose Thomas Gorman as his guardian (44).

GORMAN, JUDITH, was named as a dau. in the will of Elizabeth Snowdell on 23 Feb. 1704/5 (122:46).

GORMAN, MARY, was named as a daughter in the will of William Galloway, 1 April 1705 (122:53).

GORMAN, SARAH, was ind. for bast. in March 1729/30 (28:362).

GORSNELL. See GOSNELL.

THE GORSUCH FAMILY was the subject of a lengthy series of articles by J. Hall Pleasants, "The Gorsuch and Lovelace Families," orig. pub. in the Virginia Magazine of History and Biography, and reprinted in Genealogies of Virginia Families (Balto.: Gen. Pub. Co., 1981), III, 232-443. Unless otherwise stated all information is from the late Mr. Pleasants' articles.

GORSUCH, WILLIAM (1), merchant of London, was desc. from the Gorsuch fam. of Ormskirk, Lancashire; m. Avice, niece of Robert Hillson, another merchant; had iss.: DANIEL (Vis. of London, 1633-1635 Harl. Soc. Pubs., XV, 327).

GORSUCH, DANIEL (2), s. of William (1) and Avice, was bur. 16 Oct. 1638 at Walkern, Herts.; m. Alice, dau. of John Hall, d. leaving a will, 6 Oct. 1638 - 24 Nov. 1638, in' which he named his w. Anne, dec. mother(-in-law) Hall, s. John and his w. Anne, and ch. of his s. John (John, Daniel, William, Katherine, Robert and Richard), godson Daniel Haynes, bro.-in-law Jonathan Browne, bro.

Richard Beresford, cosens (sic) Margaret Browne, Barnard and
Edward Gorsuch in Lancashire, and William Gorsuch; the will of
Alice Gorsuch, 7 July 1662 - 3 Feb. 1662/3, named grandch. Robert,
Richard, Lovelace, Charles, Daniel, Johanna, and Frances Gorsuch,
Elizabeth Powell (all ch. of her s. John), great-grandch. Ann
Gorsuch (of Daniel), John Gorsuch (of William), and William and
Elizabeth Whitby (of Katherine Whitby); Rev. JOHN; KATHERINE, m.
Thomas Haynes (Pleasants, op. cit.).

GORSUCH, Rev. JOHN (3), s. of Daniel (2) and Alice, d. c.1647,
or may be Dr. Godsuch, Dr. of Theologie, bur. 24 May 1648 at Wil-
burton, Cambridgeshire; m. Anne Lovelace, dau. of Sir William and
Anne (Barne) Lovelace; became Rector of Walkern, Herts.; rec. his
Doctor of Divinity deg.from Cambridge, University; after John's
death, his wid. Ann left for America about 1651 with ch. Elizabeth,
Charles, and Lovelace; she d. in America c.1652; had iss.: DANIEL,
b.c.1628/9, m. and had iss.; JOHN, b. c.1630; WILLIAM, b. c.1631;
KATHERINE, bapt. 26 Nov. 1633 at Walkern, Herts., m. William Whitby of Warwick Co., Va.; ROBERT, bapt. 19 Nov. 1635 at Walkern;
RICHARD, bapt. 19 April 1637 at Walkern; ANNA, bapt. 13 March
1638/9 at Walkern, came to America and m. 1st Thomas Todd of
Va. and Balto. Co.; 2nd David Jones of Balto. Co.; 3rd Capt. John
Oldton of Balto. Co.; ELIZABETH, bapt. 13 May 1641 at Walkern,
came to Walkern, and m. Howell Powell of Va., Balto. Co. and then
of Talbot Co.; CHARLES, bapt. 25 Aug. 1642 at Walkern; LOVELACE,
came to Talbot and Dor. Co., Md.; FRANCES, b. after 1642 (Ibid.;
Michael Overman, A Gorsuch Pedigree, c.r. 1982).

GORSUCH, WILLIAM (4), s. of Rev. John (4), b. c.1631, m. by
lic. of 12 Oct. 1660 as "William Gorsuch of Weston, Herts., bachelor, age 25" to Catherine Morgan of St. Margaret's, Westminster,
London; had iss.: JOHN; DANIEL (Pleasants, op. cit.)

GORSUCH, ROBERT (5), s. of Rev. John (4), was bapt. 19 Nov.
1635 at Walker, Herts.; came to Md. by 1659; his w. was murdered
by Indians in Balto. Co. c.1661 (Ibid.).

GORSUCH, RICHARD (6), s. of Rev. John (4), was bapt. 19 April
1637 at Walker, Herts.; came to Md. c.1661, and moved to Talbot
Co.; m. Elizabeth (?), who m. as her 2nd husb. Samuel Hatton, and
3rd, Herman ffoakes; in March 1661/2 conv. 300 a. to Thomas Powell; in Feb. 1664/5 conv. 300 a. Walnut Neck to Thomas Powell
(Ibid.; 93; 95; 388).

GORSUCH, CHARLES (7), s. of Rev. John (4), was bapt. 25 Aug.
1642 at Walkern, Herts.; d. in Balto. Co. by 25 June 1716 when
admin. bond on his est. was posted by admin. John Gorsuch with
Nicholas Rogers and John Hurst; was in Talbot Co. by April 1679
when he and w. Sarah conv. The Forest to Thomas James; in Aug.
1707 conv. 33 a. Eaglestone's Addition, part of a larger tract
called Willin, to John Eaglestone; in June 1709 conv. 168 a. of
Willin to Jonas Bowen; gave his age as 60 or more in 1714/5; m.
1st Sarah, dau. of Thomas and Priscilla Cole; m. 2nd on 15 d.,
12 (Feb.) 1690, Ann Hawkins, dau. of John and Mary Hawkins; est.
was inv. 25 July 1716 by Thomas Stone and Nicholas Rogers and
val. at £ 11.7.20; had iss.: JOHN, b. c.1678/9; THOMAS, b. betw.
1678 and 1680; CHARLES, b. c.1686/7; prob. ROBERT (Pleasants,
op. cit.; 13:113; 52:1; 59:551; 60:30; 67:3; 203-3:108).

GORSUCH, JOHN (8), s. of Charles (7) and Sarah, was b. 1678/9, d. 1733 when his bro. Thomas succeeded him as admin. of the est. of Robert Gorsuch; m. Elizabeth (?), by whom he had at least one s.: CHARLES, b. c.1720, d. 1806 (Pleasants).

GORSUCH, THOMAS (9), s. of Charles (7) and Sarah, was b. betw. 1678 and 1680; d. in Balto. Co. leaving a will made 23 Sept. 1774 and pr. 4 Nov. 1774; m. Jane Ensor on 19 Aug. 1714, prob. the sis. of John Ensor of Darley Hall; in 1750 owned 100 a. Loveless' Addition, 100 a. Ensor's Addition, 120 a. part Friendship; on 7 July 1731 Thomas purch. 100 a. Ensor's Choice; had iss.: LOVELACE, b. c.1715, d. 1783; THOMAS, b. c.1720, d. 1777; JOHN, b. c.1730/1, d. 1808; ELIZABETH, m. by 1774 (?) Kelly; MARY, m. by 1774 (?) Simkin (Ibid.; 73:145; 153:43).

GORSUCH, CHARLES (10), s. of Charles (7) and Sarah, was b. c.1687, d. by 16 July 1747 when the admin. bond was posted by admnx. Sarah Gorsuch with John and William Gorsuch; may have m. an unknown 1st w.; m. (2nd?) Sarah Cole, dau. of John Cole; est. was admin. 14 Oct. 1751; had iss.: JOHN, b. c.1712/4; WILLIAM, b. c.1715/8; HANNAH, b. c.1712/9, m. 2 March 1735 Thomas Stansbury; SARAH, b. 21 March 1721; m. by 1751 William Parlett; CHARLES, b. 12 Oct. 1725; BARBARA, b. 20 Dec. 1726; m. George Pickett on 16 Feb. 1750/1, may have m. 2nd to (?) Wilkinson; BENJAMIN, b. 17 Oct. 1730; ELIZABETH, b. 3 Feb. 1732; DAVID, b. 2 March 1734; MARY, b. 1 Nov. 1737; RACHAEL, b. c.1739 (Pleasants; 5:197; 13:155; 133:26, 40, 58).

GORSUCH, ROBERT (11), s. of Charles (7) and Sarah, was in Balto. Co. and d. by 16 June 1720 when admin. bond on his est. was posted by John Gorsuch, admin., with will annexed, with Thomas Gorsuch and Charles Gorsuch; m. Johanna (?), who d. 1728; he left a will, 25 June 1714 - 14 June 1720 in which he named his w. Johanna, and ch.: Daniel, Robert, and Dorothy; est. was inv. on 29 Aug. 1720 by Thomas Randall and Thomas Hughes and val. at £ 107.3.1, and signed by Thomas, John, and Charles Gorsuch; est. was admin. by John Gorsuch on 12 Aug. 1721; in Nov. 1722 his admin., John Gorsuch, was summoned to court; Thomas Gorsuch admin. the est. on 6 March 1734; by 1737 the heirs were all of full age; Johanna Gorsuch d. by 20 May 1728 when admin. bond was posted by William Green with Thomas Broad and John Miller; inv. was filed 1 Aug. 1728 by John Wilmot and John Moore, and val. at £ 40.6.2; had iss.: ROBERT, d. 19 March 1733 (admin. bonds were posted on 21 April 1733 by John Gorsuch and on 30 July 1733 by Thomas Gorsuch; DANIEL, alive in 1714; DOROTHY (Pleasants; 1:294; 3:180; 13:125, 129, 136, 137; 25:73; 31:43, 52; 51:165).

GORSUCH, CHARLES (12), s. of John (8), b. c.1720, d. in Balto. Co. by 30 April 1806; m. 1st Susanna (?), and 2nd Margaret Harvey; in 1750 owned 100 a. Canaan; had iss. (by 1st w.): JOHN, alive in 1796; ELIZABETH, m. by 1796 John Lane; ANNE, d. by 1796 having m. William Jones; RUTH, d. by 1796, having m. John Barton on 20 Dec. 1770; (by 2nd w.): NORMAN, d. 1831; HENRY, d. unm. in 1818; AVARILLA, m. 1st John Worrell, and 2nd Nathaniel Wheeler; MARGARET, m. Thomas Pindell; RACHEL, m. Caleb Worrell (Pleasants; 153:70).

GORSUCH, LOVELACE (13), s. of Thomas (9) and Jane, was b. c.
1715, d. leaving a will, 8 May 1779 - 10 July 1783; took the
Oath of Fidelity   to the State of Maryland; had iss.: THOMAS,
b. 11 April 1752; d. c.1815, m. Helen Chapman; NATHAN, b. c.1760,
d.1788 unm.; JOHN, b. 4 May 1772, d. 1838, m. Nancy Goodwin; JANE,
b. c.1760, m. by 1788 Joseph Hawkins; SARAH, m. by 1788 Thomas
Beasman; NANCY, m. Benjamin Bond; ELIZABETH, m. by lic. of 21
Feb. 1778 Henry Bond; CHARCILLA/CHISCILLA, m. 1st by 1788 (?)
Gorsuch, and 2nd by 26 Aug. 1802 Charles Shipley; CHARITY, m.
by lic. of 20 Jan. 1781 Thomas Kelly; PRUDENCE, m. by lic. of 20
Jan. 1789 Benjamin Williams; RACHAEL, m. by lic. of 16 June 1796
Abednego Griffith; RUTH, m. by lic. of 26 Nov. 1791 John Williams
(Pleasants;   417-6:61).

GORSUCH, THOMAS (14), s. of Thomas (9) and Jane, was b. c.1720,
d. by 24 Nov. 1777; wife's name not known; had iss.: LOVELACE, b.
c.1750, m. Elizabeth; THOMAS, b. c.1755; NATHAN, b. c.1765; JOHN.
b. 1769, d. 1833; URITH, m. by lic. 11 May 1779 John Ensor; RUTH,
m. by 1777 William Welsh; RACHEL, m. by lic. 5 Nov. 1783 James
Hooper (Pleasants).

GORSUCH, JOHN (15), s. of Thomas (9) and Jane, was b. c.1730,
d. 2 Aug. 1808; m. Elizabeth Merryman on 11 March 1755, dau. of
John and Sarah (Rogers) Merryman; Elizabeth d. 2 Sept. 1795, age
63; had iss.: ROBERT, b. 7 Aug. 1757, d. 1828, m. Sarah Donovan;
JOHN, b. 1767, d. 1840; RICHARD, d. 1834; NICHOLAS, bur. 7 May
1796; JOSHUA, d. 9 Aug. 1844; DICKINSON, d. 1815; ELEANOR, b. 30
Jan. 1774, m. Joseph Merryman; DEBORAH, m. Nicholas Bryan on 19
Sept. 1793 (Pleasants).

GORSUCH, JOHN (16), s. of Charles (10), was b. c.1712/4, d.
between 6 Sept. 1788 and 20 April 1796; m. Mary Price on 4 March
1735; in 1750 owned 200 a. part Cole's Chance, and 120 a. Continuance to Cole's Chance; had iss.: CHARLES, b. c.1736/40, m. Eleanor
Bond; JOHN, b. c.1740, m. by 1770 Belinda Bosley; RACHAEL, b. betw.
1735 and 1743, m. James Bosley on 18 Sept. 1760; SARAH, b. c.1740,
m. John Gill on 20 July 1758; MARY, m. James Gittings (Pleasants;
153:11).

GORSUCH, WILLIAM (17), s. of Charles (10), was b. c.1715/8, d.
by 17 June 1797; in 1750 owned 100 a. Matthews' Farms, 50 a. of
Matthews Meadows, and 40 a. part Matthews Addition; had iss.:
JOHN, b. c.1755; WILLIAM; CHARLES; JEMIMA; SARAH (Pleasants; 153:
80).

GORSUCH, CHARLES (18), s. of Charles (10), was b. 12 Oct.
1729, d. by 14 Dec. 1792; m. by 1750 Sarah (?); left a will; had
iss.: THOMAS, b. 5 Jan. 1750/1, m. Keziah Wheeler; CHARLES, b. 1
Feb. 1753/4, m. Hannah Bosley; BENJAMIN, b. 29 April 1755, m.
Mary Holland; ELISHA, b. 21 Jan. 1757, m. Susanna Miller; JOSHUA,
b. 20 April 1759; JOHN, b. after 1760; DAVID, b. c.1760/65; WIL-
LIAM, b. 27 Nov. 1769; NICHOLAS, b. 1774; SARAH, b. c.1764, m.
Abraham Hicks; RUTH, b. c.1766, m. Charles Peregoy; DORCAS, b. 30
June 1752 (Pleasants; 133:95, 96, 97, 98, 103).

GORSUCH, BENJAMIN (19), s. of Charles (10), was b. 17 Oct.
1730, and was alive in 1796; m. 1st (?); m. 2nd on 17 July 1760

Kerrenhappuck Johnson, prob. dau. of Jacob Johnson; had iss.:
CHARLES, b. by 1757, m. Delia Demmitt; NATHAN, b. by 1758, m.
Polatia Pearce; THOMAS, m. Rachael McClung; poss. JACOB, who m.
Elizabeth Hetherton; poss. ROBERT, d. young (Pleasants).

GORSUCH, DAVID (20), s. of Charles (10), was b. 2 March 1734,
d. May 1784; m. c.1760 Elizabeth, dau. of Jonathan and Sarah
(Spicer) Hanson; m. 2nd c.1785 Daniel Weatherby, and poss. 3rd
in 1802 Joseph Gardiner;; left iss.: SARAH, b. c.1760, m. 1779
Elijah Stansbury; ELIZABETH, b. c.1764, m. 1st (?) Gorsuch, and
2nd Elijah Stansbury; MARY, b. 1767, d. 1832, m. 1786 Charles
Jessop; JEMIMA, m. 1st James Stansbury, and 2nd Lavalin Barry;
KESIAH, b. 1772, m. 1790 Christopher Buck; ANNE, d. unm. by 1794
(Ibid.; 89:308; 113:3).

GORSUCH, AQUILA, was age 42 in Nov. 1768 (231-AL#G:443).

GORSUCH, JOSEPH, of Fred. Co., gave his age as 35 in April
1761 (87:198).

GOSNELL, WILLIAM (1), progenitor, d. in A. A. Co. in 1709;
m. Elizabeth (?); wit. the will of Samuel Greeniff of A. A. Co.
on 14 Aug. 1703; by 1707 owned 50 a. Baker's Increase, orig. surv.
in 1667 for Morrice Baker; d. leaving a will, 11 May 1709 - 29
July 1709, in which he named three sons William, Peter, and Maurice, dau. Elizabeth Willson, and w. Elizabeth, as well as dau.
Hannah; had iss.: WILLIAM; PETER; MAURICE; ELIZABETH, m. (?)
Willson; HANNAH, poss. the Hannah Gosnel who m. Robert Crans or
Craus on 28 Nov. 1712 (122:15, 168; 211:245; 219-4:99).

GOSNELL, WILLIAM (2), s. of William (1), d. c.1762 in Balto.
Co.; m. by 1752 Elizabeth (?); by 1737 was a taxable in Soldier's
Delight Hund; in March 1746 purch. 50 a. Barnes' Level from Benjamin and Martha Barnes; in March 1747 purch. Long Valley from
Samuel and Mary Whipps; surv. 100 a. William the Conqueror in
1730, and 81 a. William's Folly in 1732; in 1750 as William Gos-
lin (sic) owned 81 a. William's Fancy, 50 a. Barnes' Level; in
June 1742 pet. the Court that his son Vachel be levy free and the
pet. was granted; d. leaving a will, 3 Feb. 1759 - 28 Aug. 1762,
in which he named ch. Zebediah (to have 81 a. William's Folly),
Sarah Stocksdale, Abarilla w. of Benjamin Buckingham, Rachel
Baker, and John, and a granddau. Rebecca Gosnell; had iss.: ZEBE-
DIAH; SARAH, m. (?) Stocksdale; AVARILLA, ind. for bast. in June
1739 and tried in March 1739/40, m. Benjamin Buckingham; RACHEL,
m. (?) Baker; JOHN; VACHEL, alive 1742 but not mentioned in his
father's will (32:158, 401; 79:328, 670; 111:143; 149; 153; 207).

GOSNELL, PETER (3), s. of William (1), d. c.1787 in Balto.
Co., having m. Anne (?); by 1737 was a taxable in Soldier's De-
light Hund.; in March 1746 purch. 40 a. Absolom's Place from
Absolom and Mary Baker; in 1750 owned 50 a. Goslin's Camp, 40 a.
Absolom's Place, 75 a. Addition to Goslin's Camp, and 10 a. of
Goslin's Purchase; in 1747 pat. 75 a. Addition to Gosnell's
Camp and 10 a. Gosnell's Purchase; d. leaving a will, 9 July
1785 - 17 April 1787, in which he named his children Mordecai,
Charles, Ann w. of Adam Shipley, Sarah Brown, and William; had
iss.; JEMIMA, b. 16 Sept. 1724; WILLIAM, b. 25 May 1727; MORDECAI,

b. 16 Jan. 1729; HANNAH, b. 18 April 1732 (may be the "Ann" who
m. Adam Shipley); PETER, Jr., b. 25 Dec. 1734; CHARLES; SARAH, m.
(---) Brown(79:330; 83:72; 85:37; 91: 482; 113:228; 153:40; 159:
60; 219-4).

GOSNELL, MAURICE (4), s. of William (1), was alive in 1768; m.
Susanna Wright, dau. of Henry Wright, on 29 Nov. 1722 in St. Margaret's Par., A. A. Co.; on 13 Dec. 1729 Maurice and Susanna sold
50 a. Gosnell's Range to Edward Stocksdale; in 1768 he signed the
pet. favoring Balto. Town as the county seat of Balto. Co.; had
iss.: RUTH, b. 22 Oct. 1723 (named as granddau. "Ruth Gosnet" in
the will of Henry Wright made 17 Sept. 1742); (poss.) PETER (72:
220; 127:231; 200-61:558; 207; 219-4).

GOSNELL, ZEBEDIAH (5), s. of William (2), d. by 29 Aug. 1807;
in May 1767 purch. Gosnell's Pleasant Pasture from John Gosnell of
William; left a will proved 29 Aug. 1807, naming these ch.: GREEN-
BURY; JAMES; WILLIAM: RACHEL, m. William Parker by lic. 8 March
1788; ANNE, m. Ely Israel by lic. 5 Feb. 1785; SARAH; HENRIETTA,
d. 1827; LEAH (91:700; 117:217; 200-61:537; 232).

GOSNELL, JOHN (6), s. of William (2), was alive in 1768; m.
Sarah who joined him in selling Gosnell's Pleasant Pasture to Zebediah Gosnell in May 1767; in Aug. 1767 John and Sarah sold 63 a.
called Straight to David Bradford, and in Sept. 1767 James and Ape-
rilla Lowery sold 50 a. Lowery's Lot to John Gosnell; in 1768 he
signed the petition favoring Balto. as the county seat; no record
of any ch. (91:700; 92:23, 26; 200-61:531).

GOSNELL, WILLIAM (7), s. of Peter (3), b. 25 May 1727 in St.
Margaret's Par., A. A. Co.; m. Sarah (---); in March 1747 was in
Balto. Co. when he purch. Long Valley from Samuel and Mary Whipps;
in April 1765 William and Sarah sold 31 a. Good Will to John Ford;
on 30 Dec. 1769 William and Sarah sold 60 a. part· of Goodwill to
John Clark; had iss.: PETER; PHILIP; CHARLES: ANN, b. 8 Feb. 1748
(79:670; 83:280; 90:166; 134:13; 219-4; 231-AL#A:601).

GOSNELL, CHARLES (8), s. of Peter (3), moved to Greenville Co.,
S.C.; was in Balto. Co. in 1761 when he reg. a stray; in 1763 was
a taxable in Soldier's Delight Hundred; and in 1768 signed the pet.
favoring Balto. Town as the new county seat; had iss.: JOSHUA, b.
1757 in Md., m. Judith Belew; NICHOLAS, b. 1761 in Md., m. Keziah
Senter; PETER, b. 1764, m. Nancy Wyett; MORRIS, b. 1768; CHARLES,
b. 1772 in Va., m. 1st Sarah E. Linsay, and 2nd Lucy Pruitt (47;
61:545; 157; 200-61:561).

GOSNELL, DAWSON, reg. a stray in Balto. Co. in July 1758 (47:
33).

GOSNELL, JAMES, was in Balto. Co. by 1694 as a taxable in n.
side Patapsco Hund.; in Nov. 1718 was sentenced to serve Thomas
Randall for running away (23:34; 194).

GOSNELL, JOSEPH, in 1768 signed the pet. favoring Balto. Town
as the county seat (200-61:564).

GOSTWICK, JOSEPH (1), progenitor, was b. c.1653/9, and d. in
Balto. Co. on 30 March 1728; may be the Joseph Gostwick, age 24,
who sailed for "Merriland" in Oct. 1677; gave his age as 55 in
1714; was in Balto. Co. by 1692 as a taxable in n. side of Patapsco Hund.; m. 1st, by 30 March 1695, Mary, dau. of Nicholas Corbin,
and 2nd, by 3 March 1722, Elizabeth (---); left a will, 3 March
1722 - 14 June 1728, naming w. Elizabeth, sons Nicholas and Thomas; admin. bond was posted 1 July 1728 by admnx. Elizabeth Gostwick, with Jonas Bowen and Edmund Baxter; est. admin. by admnx.

on 2 Aug. 1729; left iss.: THOMAS: NICHOLAS (2:269; 13:132; 121:126; 125:71; 138; Coldham, "Gen. Gleanings in Eng.," NGSQ, 300-64:218).

GOSTWICK, THOMAS (2), s. of Joseph (1), was prob. b. no later than 1697 since he m. Elizabeth Yanstone on Sept. 1717; d. by 4 Aug. 1732, and wid. Elizabeth m.as 2nd husb., John Sergeant, on 4 Feb. 1732/3; admin. bond on Thomas' est. was posted 30 April 1733 by John and Elizabeth Sergeant, with Robert Green and Joseph Peregoy; est. admin. on 4 Aug. 1737; Thomas and Elizabeth had iss.: ABARILLA, b. 24 April 1724; AQUILA, b. 3 Dec. 1726; JOHN OYSTON (or YANSTON), b. 10 April 1729 and was alive on 29 May 1750 when he admin. the est. of John Sergeant (3:229, 298; 13: 135; 133:5, 15, 18, 147, 150).

GOSTWICK, NICHOLAS (3), s. of Joseph (1), was prob. b. no later than 1700 since he m. Abarilla Yanston in Dec. 1720; d. in Balto. Co. by 23 July 1740 when admin. bond was posted by Abarilla Gostwick, with John Sergeant and Henry Yanston as sec.; wid. Abarilla m. as 2nd husb. Benjamin Curtis, who joined her in admin. est. of Nicholas on 28 July 1744; Nicholas and Abarilla had iss.: MARY, b. 14 Dec. 1722; ANNE, b. 17 Dec. 1723, d. 26 July 1726; JOSEPH, b. 3 Dec. 1726; BETTY, b. 5 Nov. 1729 (may be the Elizabeth Gostwick who was tried for bast. in Nov. 1754, naming Samuel Sindall as the father); NICHOLAS, b. 9 June 1731; GEORGE, b. 16 June 1735 (3:360; 13:157; 133:1, 5, 44, 45, 147, 193).

GOSTWICK, AQUILLA (4), s. of Thomas (2) and Elizabeth, was b. 3 Dec. 1726; d. by 6 July 1781; m. Elizabeth Stansbury on 1 Jan. 1749/50; she was b. 21 Oct. 1730, dau. of Daniel Stansbury; Aquilla d. leaving a will, 18 April 1781 - 6 July 1781, naming his w. Elizabeth, and two ch.: DANIEL; THOMAS (112:422; 133:163).

GOSTWICK, ANNE, m. Richard Rowles on 30 Jan. 1753 (133:166).

THE GOTT FAMILY was the subject of a chart by Christopher Johnston, filed at the Maryland Historical Society, Baltimore.

GOTT, RICHARD (1), progenitor, his wife Susanna and daus. Juliatha and Sarah imm. to Md. in 1650; in 1658 Gott's son-in-law Alexander Gordon claimed land for his service; Richard d. leaving a will, 28 Nov. 1660 - 20 Feb. 1662/3, naming w. Susan, dau. Susan, and s. Richard, not yet 17; the wid. Susan m. as her 2nd husb. Henry Hooper; Richard and Susan had iss.: JULIATHA, imm. in 1650; SUSAN, imm. in 1660, and was named in 1660; RICHARD, b. after 1650 (120:23; 388).

GOTT, RICHARD (2), s. of Richard (1) and Susan, was prob. b. after his parents came to Md.; d. in A. A. Co., leaving a will, 28 Dec. 1713 - 16 April 1715; m. 1st, in 1685, Hannah. dau. of Thomas Pratt, and 2nd, c.1702, Elizabeth, dau. of Anthony Holland; his will named bro.-in-law John Willoughby, son-in-law John Chesheir, and these ch.: HANNAH, b. 29 June 1686; SUSANNA, b. 29 June 1688, m. Abel Hill on 20 July 1711; RICHARD, b. 2 May 1692; ROBERT, b. 2 May 1693; ANTHONY, b. 15 Sept. 1694; MATTHEW, b. 31 July 1697; JOHN, b. c.1700; (by 2nd w.): SARAH, b. c.1704; SAMUEL, b. 7 March 1706/7; CAPEL, b. 27 Sept. 1709 (123:6; 219-1; Gott chart by Johnston).

GOTT, RICHARD (3), s. of Richard (2) and Hannah, was b. 2 May 1692, and d. in Balto. Co. by 4 June 1751; m. Sarah (---); in 1737 leased 100 a. part Gunpowder Manor called Dublin, the lease to run for the lifetimes of Elizabeth, b. c.1725, and Richard, b c.1736; d. testate; had iss.: RUTH, b. 9 Feb. 1715, m. William Towson; SAMUEL, b. 10 May 1718; SARAH, b. 19 Jan. 1722; ELIZABETH

b. 11 May 1724; RICHARD, b. 15 May 1726; CASSANDRA, b. 1 Aug.
1728; ANTHONY, b. 19 March 1731; HANNAH; SUSANNA; RACHEL (112:
417; 133:32; 389:12; Johnston, "Gott Chart").

GOTT, ROBERT (4), s. of Richard (2) and Hannah, was b. 2 May
1693; d. by Nov. 1742 when admin. bond was posted by James Moore,
with John Holloway and Derby Hernly; est. admin. on 16 Sept. 1755
by admin.; m. Mary (---), and had iss.: ELIZABETH, b. 13 Dec.
1725; MARY, b. 19 July 1729; SARAH, b. 19 Feb. 1732; RICHARD, b.
20 June 1734 (5:346; 13:149; 131; Johnston, "Gott chart").

GOTT, SAMUEL (5), s. of Richard (3) and Sarah, was b. 10 May
1718; d. 1787; m. Rachel (---), who d. by 12 June 1797; his will,
23 Feb. 1787 - 9 April 1787, named w. Rachel, sons Edward and
Richard, daus. Ann Bosley, Rachel Stansbury, Sarah Perine and
Elizabeth Gott, and granddaus. Rachel and Susanna Stansbury;
will of Rachel Gott was signed 6 Sept. 1793, proved 12 June 1797;
had iss.: RICHARD; EDWARD; RUTH, m. William Stansbury; ANN, m.
James Bosley; RACHEL, m. Thomas Stansbury; SARAH, m. (---) Perine;
ELIZABETH; SUSANNA, m. (---) Hunt (113:225; 115:2; 133:32).

GOTT, RICHARD (6), s. of Richard (3) and Sarah, was b. 15 May
1726; d. in Balto. Co.; m. Ruth, dau. of Richard Bond, on 30 Apr.
1758; in 1750 owned 400 a. Gott's Hope, and 100 a. Add'n to Gott's
Hope; his will, 14 June 1793 - 25 Feb. 1793, named w. Ruth and
ch. Richard, Mary, Hannah, and Ruth; had iss.: ELIZABETH, b. 22
Jan. 1759; ELEANOR, b. 21 June 1760; RICHARD, b. 6 Jan. 1761;
MARY, b. 30 March 1764; HANNAH, m. (---) Woods; RUTH; ACHSAH
(134:32, 33, 40, 72; 114:87; 153).

GOTT, RICHARD, m. Elizabeth (---), and had two daus.: SARAH,
b. 30 Dec. 1750; RACHEL, b. 3 May 1754 (134:33).

GOUGH, CHRISTOPHER, d. by 23 Sept. 1755, when admin. bond was
posted by admin. Jacob Collier, with John Markey and Mathias
Ringer (13:163).

GOUGH, THOMAS, was in Md. by 23 Sept. 1746 when he adv. he
would sell all his effects at his dw. plan. about a mile from
Patapsco Ferry; in Jan. 1747 he adv. for any books he had loaned
out to be returned; m. Sophia Dorsey, and had iss.: HARRY DORSEY,
b. 28 Jan. 1745 Annap. Md. Gaz.., 23 Sept. 1746 and 6 Jan. 1747;
"Gough-Carroll Bible Records," 346-2:23).

GOULD, Mr., was in Balto. Co. by 1695 as a taxable in Spesutia
Hund. (140).

GOULD, JOHN, d. by 19 Dec. 1702 when admin. bond was posted by
Jesse Williams, with Emanuel Smith and John Cottrell (13:119).

GOULD, JOSEPH, d. by 11 March 1703, when est. was inv. by
Thomas Cord and Owen Swillivant, and val. at E 17.1.1 (48:135).

GOVEN, WILLIAM, admin. the est. of Edward Mariartee on 16
March 1742 (3:265).

GOVER, ROBERT (1), of A. A. Co., d. leaving a will, 11 Nov.
1699 - 6 May 1700, in which he left his s. Robert 100 a. of
Boughton Ashley and 295 a. Gover's Adventure, his s. Samuel to
have half of Gover's Ferrying and 100 a. Knighton's Purchase;
ygst s. Ephraim at his majority to have the res. of Gover's
Ferrying, and 167 a. Gover's Addition; had iss.: ROBERT; SAMUEL;
and EPHRAIM (121:196).

GOVER, ROBERT (2), s. of Robert (1), d. in A. A. Co. having

m. Eliza Cotton on 5 Dec. 1695; his will, 6 May 1700 - 7 Sept. 1700, named w. Eliza, bros. Ephraim, and Samuel, and one dau.; RACHEL, b. 16 April 1697 (121:201).

GOVER, SAMUEL (3), s. of Robert (1), d. testate in A. A. Co.; m. Elizabeth (---), who joined him in witnessing the will of Richard Hall of Cal. Co. on 7 Aug. 1739; his will, 13 Dec. 1743 - 13 Oct. 1744, named ch.: Samuel (to have 295 a. Gover's Adventures and other land), ygst s. Philip (to have 200 a. Gover's Firing and 150 a. in Balto. Co. called Rapatta), s. Ephraim (to have 250 a. Elberton and 50 a. Elberton, and to pay his cousin Elizabeth Gover of Robert when she becomes 21), s. Richard (to have 263 a. Kenton's Purchase, and Expedition in Cal. Co., and to pay his cousin Priscilla Gover of Robert), his bro. Ephraim to have 50 a. Broughton Ashley, which testator's father bought from Francis Holland, Jr.; all sons to have part of Hall's Hill for a warehouse; named daus. Elizabeth Lee, Cassandra Wilson, Priscilla Wilson, and ch. Robert and Ann; had iss.: SAMUEL; EPHRAIM; RICHARD; Poss. ROBERT (father of above mentioned Elizabeth and Priscilla); PHILIP; ELIZABETH, m. (---) Lee; CASSANDRA, m. (---) Wilson; PRISCILLA, m. (---) Wilson (111:186; 122:198; 127:55, 279, 280).

GOVER, EPHRAIM (4), s. of Robert (1), was alive in Dec. 1743 when he was ment. in bro. Samuel's will; may be the Ephraim who gave his age as 56 in 1738, and 73 in 1756 (127:279, 280; 217-IB#I: 122, 469).

GOVER, SAMUEL (5), s. of Samuel (3), inherited 150 a. Rapatta in Balto. Co.; d. by 11 March 1744/5; m. Hannah, dau. of Isaac Webster; his will, 27 April 1744 - 13 March 1744/5, named w. Hannah, s. Samuel, and appointed John Hanbury and Jacob Giles as execs.; execs. refused to act; on 15 March 1744 admin. bond was posted by Isaac Webster with Michael Webster and John Talbot; on 11 Feb. 1744/5 wid. Hannah turned admin. of est. over to her father; est. was admin. by Isaac Webster on 8 Aug. 1746; had iss.: SAMUEL (4:134; 5:145, 192; 13:153; 36:237; 111:23; 127:253).

GOVER, EPHRAIM (6), s. of Samuel (3), s. in Balto. Co. by 3 March 1770; m. Elizabeth (---); in Sept. 1724 was in Cal. Co. when he sold part of Elberton to William Allnut; in 1750 owned 500 a. part Elberton; his will, 8 Dec. 1769 - 3 March 1770, named w. Elizabeth, and these ch.: SAMUEL; EPHRAIM; GITTINGS; ROBERT; MARY; CASSANDRA; MARGARET; PRISCILLA; RACHEL; and ELIZABETH, b. 4 April 1741(37:455; 70:83; 117:154; 128:316; 153:46).

GOVER, PHILIP (7), s. of Samuel (3), in 1743 inher. part of Rapatta in Balto. Co., from his father; in 1750 owned 150 a. of Repalter (127:279; 153:76).

GOYNE, WILLIAM, servant, with 3 years to serve in 1699 inv. of Capt. John Ferry (48:124).

GRACE, EDWARD, m. Patience Foster on 9 Dec. 1735 (133:154).

GRADY (GRADDE), EDMUND, m. Lellen Dunawin on 10 March 1697 (129:178).

GRAFTON, WILLIAM (1), progenitor, was in Balto. Co. at least as early as Nov. 1735 when he and w. Margaret sold part Antioch to Maurice Baker; in 1750 owned 200 a. Grafton's Lot, 150 a. Bramost, 69 a. part Frenchman's Repose, 100 a. Brayser's Desire, amd part Grafton's Gift; his will, 4 Oct. 1767 - 26 Oct. 1767, named dau. Christian, dau. Ann Preston, dau. Mary Smithson, grandsons William, Samuel, Daniel, Aquila, Nathaniel Grafton, granddau. Priscilla Grafton, s. William, and grandch. born of Phoebe Grafton (i.e., William, Daniel, Samuel, Aquila, Nathaniel, Cassandra, Margaretta, Priscilla, and Mary Waite; had iss.: CHRISTIAN, m. Maurice Baker; ANN, m. Daniel Preston on 5 Jan. 1737; MARY, m. Thomas Smithson; WILLIAM; poss. PHOEBE (74:333; 112:56; 129:290; 153:18).

GRAFTON, WILLIAM (2), s. of William (1), d. in Balto. Co.; left a will, 19 Aug. 1769 - 11 Sept. 1769, naming w. Sarah, and these ch.: WILLIAM; SAMUEL; DANIEL; AQUILA; NATHANIEL; CASSANDRA; MARGARET; and PRISCILLA (112:125).

GRAHAM, CHARLES, m. by Aug. 1754 the extx. of Caesar Grice (39:390).

GRAHAM, JAMES, m. Mary Vine on 25 Dec. 1753 (131).

GRAHAM, RICHARD, d. by 23 Sept. 1760 when admin. bond on his est. was posted by James Townsend with Robert Bryarly and John Macgouvain (13:173).

GRAHAM/GRAYHAM, THOMAS, m. Keziah (---), and had iss.: MORDE-CAI, b. 10 March 1732 (133:29).

GRANGE, JOHN, d. by 14 April 1677 when admin. bond on his est. was posted by Cornelius Howard of A. A. Co., with Charles Stevens and John Foster (13:109).

GRANT, ALEXANDER, d. in Balto. Co. prior to 31 Jan. 1738/9, having m. Elizabeth Cole on 16 Feb. 1730; his w. may have been a wid.; his will, 28 Dec. 1738 - 31 Jan. 1738/9, named his res. as St. Paul's Par., his w. Elizabeth, dau.-in-law Angelica Cole, and daus. Mary and Ann; admin. bond was posted 31 Jan. 1738 by the extx. Elizabeth Grant, with Richard Gott and John Merryman, Jr.; est. admin. 9 April 1741 by the extx.; an entry in the Balto. Co. Court Proc. states that he left orphans Angelica, Mary, and Ann; in 1750 Elizabeth Grant owned 50 a. Grant's Addition and 114 a. Gorsuch Folly; had iss.: MARY, may have m. Lloyd Ford; ANN (4:79; 13:139; 33:163; 127:18; 133:29, 150; 153:6).

GRANT, HUGH, d. by 7 Aug. 1728 when admin. bond was posted by Frances Grant, with William Low and William Cannon; m. Frances, wid. of Daniel Johnson; she m. 3rd Miles Foy; est. was inv. in 1728; in Oct. 1728 wid. Frances entered into an antenuptial contract with Miles Foy (13:132; 51:237; 71:317).

GRANT, JAMES, m. 1 Feb. 1753 Elizabeth Morris, and had iss.: DAVID, b. 31 Jan. 1756 (129:354).

GRANT, SUTTON, late of Rhode Island, d. in Balto. Co. by 24 May 1755 when admin. bond was posted by William Lyon, with John Raitt and Robert Swann of Annap. (13:161).

GRAVES, ALEXANDER, was in Balto. Co. by 1700 when he purch. Hopewell, Salisbury Plains, and Addition to Privilege from John Shaw of Cecil Co. (66:53).

GRAVES, WILLIAM, m. Sarah Bever on 15 June 1735; d. by 18 June 1748 when wid. Sarah ren. right of admin.; admin. bond was posted on 23 June 1748 by Roger Donahue with James Preston, Wm. Clemens, Rich. Ruff, and William Bennett (13:147; 128:87).

GRAVES, WILLIAM, m. Catherine (---), and had iss.: CATHERINE, b. 25 Aug. 1759 (128:73).

GRAY, ZACHARIAH (1), was in Balto. Co. by 19 Dec. 1719 when
he m. as 1st w. Mary Demitt; m. 2nd, by 15 Jan. 1729, Rebecca,
dau. of Jonas Bowen; in March 1733/4 was tried for begetting a
bast. ch. on Hannah Cox; in May 1735 John and Ann Gray of A. A.
Co. conv. him 200 a. Nash's Rest; in Dec. 1745 he and w. Rebecca
conv. 20 a. Jones' Chance to Sabrett Sollers; his will, 29 Oct.
1742 - 18 March 1747, named w. Rebecca, and ch.: Ephraim, Absolom,
Zachariah, Elizabeth, and Ann; admin. bond was posted 5 May 1748
by extx. Rebecca Gray with Thos. Sligh, Zachariah Gray, and Peter
Dowell; in Nov. 1750 the extx. posted bond she would pay the
minor orphans their share of their father's est.; had iss. (by 1st
w.): ANN, b. 27 March 1724, m. (---) Baze; (by 2nd w.): ZACHARIAH,
b. 30 June 1730; ABSOLOM, b. 20 Oct. 1733; EPHRAIM: JOHN (in Nov.
1759 chose Edward Stevenson as his guardian); WILLIAM , b. c.
1747 (in March 1755 was bound to Edward Stevenson and in Nov. 1759
was bound to Edward Stevenson); ELIZABETH (2:267; 13:151; 38:9;
39:345, 349, 350; 40:16; 44; 74:298; 79:16; 133:5, 19, 37, 147).

GRAY, ZACHARIAH (2), s. of Zachariah (1) and Rebecca, was b.
30 June 1740; may be the Zachariah who m. Mary Lynch on 22 Dec.
1748; may have m. 2nd, Comfort (---), who on 13 April 1771 joined
her husb. Zachariah in conv. 80 a. Nash's Rest to William Wilkinson (133:162; 231 -AL#C:545).

GRAY, EPHRAIM (3), s. of Zachariah (1) and Rebecca, may be the
Ephraim who m. Mary (---), and had iss.: ANNE, b. 29 Oct. 1760
(133:106).

GRAY (---), m. by 15 Nov. 1770, Mary, dau. of Patrick Lynch
(6:197).

GRAY, ALLEN, s. of Catherine Noble, was b. 7 Feb. 1739 (129:
340).

GRAY, BARBARA, was ind. for bast. in June 1746 (36:2).

GRAY, CATHERINE, was ind. for bast. in June 1746 (36:116).

GRAY, HENRY, m. Judith (---), and had iss.: JANE, b. 15 April
1725; HENRY, b. 27 Feb. 1729 (128:67).

GRAY, JOHN, d. by 30 July 1682 when Hannah Skelton, alias Gray,
posted admin. bond, with Israel Skelton and Michael Judd (13:121).

GRAY, JOHN, was in Balto. Co. by 1692 as a taxable in n. side
of Gunpowder Hund. (138).

GRAY, JOHN, in 1717 signed the inv. of Stephen White as kin
(48:242).

GRAY, JOHN, d. by 1717 when his est. was inv. by Charles Merryman, Sr., and Moses Edwards, and val. at £ 50.0.10, with Richard
Colegate and John Talbott signing as creditors (51:125).

GRAY, JOHN, m. Blanche, admnx. of Edward Cantwell, on 30 Sept.
1750 (39:24; 131).

GRAY, MATTHIAS, d. by 1 June 1713 when admin. bond was posted
by Mary Gray with Thomas Biddison and John Boring; Mary Gray ran
away, and the two securities posted admin. bond on 26 April 1714
with James Boring and Joseph Peregoy; est. was inv. in 1714 by
Robuck Lynch and John Norton and val. at £ 13.14.0; est. was admin. 10 Oct. 1714 by afsd. Biddison (1:18; 13:114, 115; 50:257).

GRAY, MATTHIAS, was named as grandson in the will of John Mahane or Mahone of Balto. Co. (127:192).

GRAY, PATRICK, was in Balto. Co. by 1750 when he was listed as owning 100 a. Logsdon's Addition; d. leaving a will, 10 Dec. 1754 - 31 March 1755, named w. Ann as extx.; m. Ann (---), whose will, 8 Dec. 1755 - 22 March 1756, left ₤ 10 to Eliz. Connell, dau. of Mary Connell of Balto. Town, and ₤ 5 to Sarah Palmer, dau. of Abraham, and left the bal. of her est. to the exec. William Rogers (110:493; 111:116; 153:83).

GRAY, SAMUEL, was b. 2 April 1695, parents not named (133:50).

GRAYDON, WILLIAM, m. Mary Ayres on 4 Dec. 1739 (131:109).

THE ROBERT GREEN FAMILY

GREEN, ROBERT (1), was in Balto. Co. as early as 1692 as a taxable in n. side Gunpowder Hund.; he is prob. the Robert Green who d. intestate by 2 July 1750 having purch. 67 a. Cole's Addition from John Cole; had iss.: WILLIAM, b. c.1690; prob. ROBERT, b. c. 1690; prob. JOHN, b. c.1699; poss. AMY, who m. Henry Peregoy on 16 Feb. 1716 (on 5 April 1728 Henry and Amy Peregoy conv. 50 a. part of Success, to Robert Green (67:191; 71:128; 133:147; 138).

GREEN, WILLIAM (2), eld. s. and heir of Robert (1), was b. c. 1690, giving his age as 70 in 1760; m. Hannah Haile on 21 Aug. 1729; in 1730 Nicholas Haile left his dau. Hannah part of Mount Pleasant, and in 1750 William Green owned 67 a. Cole's Addition and part of Mount Pleasant; in July 1750 William and Hannah sold Cole's Addition, which William's father Robert had purch., to William Hammond; in 1763 William owned 75 a. Mount Pleasant, and 25 a. Addition to Mount Pleasant; had iss.: HENRY, b. 21 March 1729/ 30 (80:500; 87:196; 133:17, 149; 153:4; 159:3).

GREEN, ROBERT (3), prob. s. of Robert (1), was b. c.1690, giving his age as 35 in 1730, and 78 in Nov. 1768; on 5 April 1728 he was conv. 50 a. part Success from Henry and Amy Peregoy; in 1750 he owned 110 a. Burman's Forest; m. Susanna, dau. of Nicholas Haile, who on 4 March 1745/6 conv. his dau. Susanna Green 100 a. of land; the will of Robert Green, 25 Jan. 1750 - 1 July 1774, named w. Susanna, son Moses (to have Green's Purchase), and sons John and Solomon; had iss.: JOSEPH, b. 9 Jan. 1716; JOHN, b. 16 Aug. 1720; SUSANNA, b. 6 Sept. 1723; ABRAHAM, b. 7 Sept. 1726; BENJAMIN, b. 26 June 1729; RUTH, b. 30 Jan. 1732 (par. reg. names her mother as Mary); MOSES, b. 21 June 1734; NATHAN, b. 7 Dec. 1738; SOLOMON, b. 15 Sept. 1742 (38:70; 71:128; 79:10; 112:296; 133:5, 12, 16, 22, 38, 72; 153:43; 231-AL#G:443).

GREEN, JOHN (4), prob. s. of Robert (1), was b. c.1699, giving his age as c.65 on 28 May 1764; m. Mary Sampson on Dec. 1720; pu purch. 50 a. Green's Palace from William and Mary Cox in March 1727 and March 1731; in 1750 he owned that tract and 70 a. Green's Lot; in March 1763 he conv. 80 a. Green's Lot on Mount Ararat and Green's Palace to Isaac Green; was made exempt from the levy in Nov. 1756; had iss.: ISAAC, b. 1 Sept. 1721; ROBERT, b. 25 March 1723; MARY, b. 2 Aug. 1732 (41:303; 70:304; 73:195; 84:141; 87: 122; 133:5, 22, 147; 153).

GREEN, HENRY (5), s. of William (2), was b. 21 March 1729/30, and gave his age as 31 on 13 April 1761 (87:200; 133:17).

GREEN, JOSEPH (6), s. of Robert (3), was b. 9 Jan. 1716, and d. by 14 Feb. 1801; m. Mary Bowen on 25 Feb. 1744/5; on 14 Feb. 1801 his (2nd w. and) wid. Catherine m. John Buck; in 1750 he owned

part of Bowen's Purchase; had iss.: VINCENT, b. c.1750, d. 1800,
m. Mary Eaglestone; JOSEPH, d. by 1800; BENJAMIN: JOSIAS; NATHAN,
m. Mary Burke by lic. of 27 Nov. 1799; MARY, m. Bernard Todd
(131; 153:67; 231-WG#65:377; 231-WG#69:67; 232).

THE CHARLES GREEN FAMILY

GREEN, CHARLES (7), no known rel. to any of above, was b. c.
1698, giving his age as 61 in March 1757; m. Margaret (---); in
July 1743 was a res. of Gunpowder Forest, and in 1750 owned 100 a.
Pleasant Garden; in Nov. 1750 was made levy free; d. by 15 June
1761 when admin. bond was posted by George Green, with Charles
Green and Charles Stevens; had iss.: CHARLES, ; GEORGE, b. 28
Feb. 1720; AMY, b. 21 7'ber 1722 (13:181; 38:20; 133:3; 138;
153:43; 224:304; 384:414).

GREEN, GEORGE (8), s. of Charles (7), was b. 28 Feb. 1720;
gave his age as 43 on 7 May 1764; on 11 Oct. 1754 conv. 50 a. of
Pleasant Garden to Charles Bosley, George's w. Sarah consenting;
may have m. 2nd Ann (---) who joined him on 2 Aug. 1760 when he
conv. 50 a. Green's Desire to Oliver Matthews (82:325; 84:312;
89:137).

GREEN, CHARLES (9), s. of Charles (7), signed the admin. bond
for his father's est. as sec. for George Green; may be the Charles
who m. Mary Colleton on 5 June 1753 (13:18; 131).

THE THOMAS GREEN FAMILY

The Thomas Green Family is Discussed at great length in Walter
V. Ball's John Wheeler, 1630-1693, of Charles County and Some of
His Desc., and in the Raskob-Green Record Book.

GREEN, THOMAS, Knight (10), no known rel. to any of the above,
is said to have been the great-grandson of a man named Green who
received the Rectory of Bobbing from Henry VIII after the dissolu-
tion of the monasteries; Sir Thomas had at least two sons: THOM-
AS; ROBERT, came to Md. but ret. to Eng. (Newman, To Md. From Over-
seas, p. 81).

GREEN, THOMAS (11),s. of Sir Thomas (10),came to Md. with the
Ark and Dove Expedition in 1634; named his manor in Maryland
Bobbing; m. 1st Ann Cox; m. 2nd Millicent Browne; and m. 3rd Winifred Seyborne, wid. of Nicholas Harvey; Winifred later m. as her
3rd husb. Robert Clarke; Thomas was present at the Assemblies of
1637 and 1640/1, and in 1649 was Acting Gov. of Md.; d. by 23 Jan.
1651, leaving iss.: THOMAS; LEONARD; ROBERT; and FRANCIS (359;
370:173-174; Newman, To Maryland.., and Ball, Wheeler Gen.).

GREEN, FRANCIS (12), s. of Gov. Thomas (11), was b. 1648, and
d. 1707, having m. Elizabeth (---); left a will, 16 Sept. 1707 -
7 May 1707, named w. Elizabeth, and these ch.: LEONARD; FRANCIS;
GILES; and CLARE (122:89; Ball).

GREEN, FRANCIS (13), s. of Francis (12), was b. 1693, and d.
1761; m. Elizabeth, b. 1693, dau. of Thomas Wheeler of Charles
Co.; had iss.: HENRY, m. Elizabeth Wheeler; CLEMENT, m. Hannah
(---); BENJAMIN; LEONARD; TERESA, m. Leonard Wheeler; ELIZABETH,
m. Benjamin Wheeler (Ball, p. 29).

GREEN, HENRY (14), s. of Francis (13), was b. c.1726, d. 1797;
m. Elizabeth, wid. of David Thomas of Balto. Co., and dau. of
Benjamin Wheeler; she d. 1777; had iss.: LEONARD; ANN, m. Bennett
Bussey; WILLIAM, b. 20 April 1750; HENRY, b. 29 Oct. 1751; JOB, b.
31 March 1755; ELIZABETH, b. 19 Oct. 1760 (133:88, 96, 97, 107;
Ball).

GREEN, BENJAMIN (15), s. of Francis (13), was b. 17 Jan. 1730, s. April 1808; m. Elizabeth (---), and in 1763 purch. 100 a. of Francis' Delight, 216 a. Bond's Choice, 109 a. Bond's Beginning, 122 a. part Good Neighborhood, and 56 a. part of Bond's Fortune; had iss.: HENRIETTA; LEONARD, m. Mary Wheeler; ELEANOR: ANN; CLEMENT; SARAH; TERESA, m. Benjamin Wheeler; and BENJAMIN (87: 291; Ball).

GREEN, (---), m. by 5 March 1700 Elizabeth, dau. of Anthony Demondidier, dec.; on that day she sold 100 a. where her bro. Anthony lived; she d. by 6 April 1703 when admin. bond was posted by Anthony Demondidier, with Thomas Smith; in 1704 her est. was inv. by John Thomas and Thomas Roberts, and val. at L 3.5.10 (13: 119; 48:1; 66:51).

GREEN, ABRAHAM, b. c.1727, gave his age as 46 in 1773; may be the Abraham who m. Eliza Baxter on 28 Jan. 1749/50, and had iss.: RACHEL, b. 4 April 1750 (133:88, 163; 231-AL#G:447).

GREEN, ANN, m. Thomas Hall on 23 Sept. 1723 (133:148).

GREEN, ANN, servant of William Demmitt, was ind. for bast. in June 1738, and tried in Aug. 1738; may be the same Ann who was tried for bast. in March 1754 and refused to name the father (31: 221, 274; 39:30).

GREEN, CHARLES, was in Balto. Co. by 1692 as a taxable in n. side Patapsco Hund. (138).

GREEN, CHRISTOPHER, d. by 17 Oct. 1716 when admin. bond was posted by John Chaffinch with Samuel Leatherwood and Peter Over- ard; est. was inv. by John Howard and William Orrick in 1717, and was val. at L 8.18.6, and signed by Samuel Leatherwood as kin; est. was admin. by Chaffinch on 9 Nov. 1717 (1:313; 13:118; 55: 312).

GREEN, ELIZABETH, servant to James Standiford, was tried for bast. in March 1744 (35:496).

GREEN, HENRY, m. Sarah Howard on 10 Dec. 1758 (131).

GREEN, JOHN, m. Anna Hardesty on 8 March 1753 (131).

GREEN, JOHN, m. Catherine Todd on 27 March 1757 (131).

GREEN (or Broon?), MATTHEW, d. by 10 July 1709 when his est. was inv. by William Howard and Jno. Webster and val. at L 2.17.0; est. was admin. by Jno. Deaver (48:165).

GREEN, MATTHEW, drowned by April 1713, having m. Mary Durham, dau. of John; on 1 March 1705 John Boone of Balto. Co. conv. to him the tract Levy's Tribe which had desc. from Samuel Durham to John Durham; in Aug. 1719 Jane Boone, wid., conv. to her grand- daus. Catherine, Anne, and Martha Green, daus. of Matthew and Mary Green, 150 a. Joyce Tripass; had iss.: CATHERINE, m. Lewis Potee, Jr., on 12 June 1722; ANN, m. James Cowdry on Sept. 1734; and MARTHA, m. William Hill in Sept. 1724 (64:60; 68:42; 72:193; 72:326; 131:19, 30).

GREEN, RICHARD, was in Balto. Co. by 1692 as a taxable in Spe- sutia Hund. (138).

GREEN, RICHARD, m. Elizabeth Fluallen in Sept. 1743 (131).

GREEN, SUSANNA, was tried for bast. in Nov. 1750; had dau.: PHILLIS BAXTER, b. 23 March 1750 (38:34).

GREEN, THOMAS, in April 1669, with John Artherne purch. 120
a. Walton, from John Walton (96:229).

GREEN, THOMAS, gave his age as 33 or 38 in Sept. 1737, and
stated that 7 or 8 years earlier he had been at John Carter's'
m. Elizabeth, admnx. of John Carter, on 11 Aug. 1732; in 1750
he owned 125 a. part Dear Bitt, and 65 a. Shrewsbury; had iss.:
REBECCA, b. 9 Jan. 1732 (30:133; 133:28, 150; 153:92; 224:12).

GREEN, WILLIAM, m. Mary Hammond on 17 Feb. 1751 (131).

GREENALL. See GREENWELL.

GREENEFF, JAMES (1), d. c.1686/90 in A. A. Co.; m. Ann (---);
in his will named his bro. John Howard and his own ch., John,
James, Samuel, and Hannah; his orphans held 350 a. Harborow, which
he had purch. in 1687 from Thomas Lightfoot; had iss.: JOHN;
JAMES; SAMUEL; HANNAH (59:227; 121:46; 211).

GREENEFF, JOHN (2), s. of James (1), m. by 4 Nov. 1703 Ruth,
admnx. of Edward Dorsey; d. by 18 Jan. 1708/9, when admin. bond
was posted by extx. Ruth Greeneff with Thomas Cromwell and John
Martin; will of John Greeneff, 39 Oct. 1708 - 18 Jan. 1708/9,
named wife's sons Jno. and Edward Dorsey, his own dau. Katherine,
and an unborn ch.; est. was inv. on 17 Jan. 1708/9 by Thomas Hammond and Theophilus Kitten; est. was admin. by Ruth Greeneff on
11 July 1719; had iss.: KATHERINE (2:124, 228; 13:111; 48:287;
122:118).

GREENFIELD, THOMAS (1), was in Balto. Co. by 10 Dec. 1695 when
he pat. 200 a. Hazard; on 8 Aug. 1701 he purch. Hazlewood's Retirement from James Ives; m. Rachel (---) who was bur. 5 Jan.
1704/5; his will, 8 Jan. 1704/5- 2 April 1705, left 200 a. Hazard
to daus. Mary Drunkord, Sarah, and Jane, and s. Thomas; left his
dw. plant. and 50 a. Hazlewood's Retirement and 100 a. Collin-
ham to s. William, left pers. to Eliz. Lowe as compensation for
caring for testator's ygst s. Micajah; admin. bond posted 2 April
1705 by exec. John Hall with Roger Matthews and Thos. Cord; est.
was inv. on 21 July 1705 by Thos. Cord and Thomas Edmunds, and
val. at ₤ 70.8.8; estate was admin. by John Hall on 13 Feb. 1705
and 18 Feb. 1709/10; had iss.: MARY, b. 25 July 1684, m. 1st by 8
Jan. 1704 (---) Drunkord, and 2nd, by 1728 John Debruler; SARAH,
b. 31 Dec. 1691, d. by Aug. 1724; JOHN, b. 24 Jan. 1695/6, bur. 10
Sept. 1696; JANE, b. 8 Sept. 1697, bapt. 9 June 1700, m. by Oct.
1715 Edward Murphy of Cecil Co.; WILLIAM, b. 3 Dec. 1699, bapt. 9
June 1700; THOMAS, b. 18 Nov. 1701; MICAJAH, b. 23 March 1703/4
(13:145; 2:168, 211; 48:193; 66:281; 67:376; 70:161; 71:266; 110:
141; 128:3, 4, 8, 9, 10, 12, 13, 19).

GREENFIELD, WILLIAM (2), s. of Thomas (1), was b. 5 Dec. 1699,
d. in Balto. Co. leaving a will, 30 May 1763 - 21 June 1763; m.
Elizabeth (---); in Aug. 1724 William and Elizabeth sold Hazard to
Patrick Ruark; in 1750 he owned 105 a. Greenfield's Double Purchase to Joshua Wood; his will named sons Micajah, William, and
James, the wives of John Coatney (Courtney?), William Debruler,
and John Deaver; admin. bond was posted 21 June 1763 by exec. Micajah Greenfield, with Greenbury Dorsey, John Wood, and Samuel
Webster; est. was admin. 14 May 1764; dec. left iss.: WILLIAM, b.
14 Oct. 1730; MICAJAH, b. 24 July 1733; PURITY, b. 12 July 1736;
JAMES; PERMINAH, m. John Deaver; dau., m. William Deaver, and
dau., m. John Watkins(6:99; 13:172; 70:161; 73:119; 112:4; 128:
8, 10, 60, 82, 94).

GREENING, SAMUEL (1), was in Balto. Co. by 7 Nov. 1705 when he

purch. 38 a. Westminster from Christopher Durbin; in April 1707
he conv. this land to Henry Dukes; m. Ann Twine on 1 March 1714;
d. by 8 Sept. 1716 when Ann Greening posted admin. bond with
Samuel Hinton and Joseph Lobb; est. was inv. on 24 Sept. 1716 by
John Israel and John Gostwick, val. at Ł 60.4.4, and signed by
Jonathan Plowman and Charles Dryden; Ann m. as 2nd husb. Edward
Mahan by 1 July 1718 when they admin. Greening's est.; Samuel and
Ann had iss.: SAMUEL (1:276; 13:117; 52:6; 64:12; 69:266; 131).

GREENING, SAMUEL (2), s. of Samuel (1), conv. Hare's Green to
Robuck Lynch (76).

GREENSLADE, PHILIP, of Barnstaple, Devon, Eng., purch. 200 a.
from Joseph and Sarah Gallion in Aug. 1684; d. by 25 Aug. 1720
leaving a s. Philip and a wid. Jean who conv. Winter's Run to
Joseph Farmer of Birmingham, Co. Warwick (59:96, 266).

GREENWELL/GREENALL/GREENWALL/GRINALL, ROBERT (1), bro. of
Cuthbert (2), made a nuncupative will on 8 April 1756, it was
proved 10 April 1756, asking his bro. Cuthbert to take care of
his ch., and leaving all his est. in St. M. Co. to his eldest s.,
and his pers. est. to all his ch.; admin. bond was posted 18 June
1756 by exec. Cuthbert Greenwell, with John Crayton , Isaac Risteau, and John Taylor; est. admin. 26 April 1758 by the exec.;
left iss.: JOSHUA, b. c.1747; ROBERT, b. c.1750; JULIA ANN, b. c.
1752 (6:15; 13:160; 46:199; 110:494).

GREENWELL, CUTHBERT (2), bro. of Robert (1), admin. his bro.'s
est.; in Nov. 1757 was fined for begetting a bast. on the body of
Martha Childs.(6:15; 46:199).

GREENWELL, ANN, and SAMUEL GREENWELL, in 1750 were listed as
joint owners of Greenall's Discovery (153:93).

GREENWOOD, SAMUEL, was in Balto. Co. by 1692 as a taxable in
n. side Patapsco Hund., and d. by 27 June 1696 when admin. bond
was posted by Robuck Lynch with N. Fitzsimmons and William Farfarr; est. admin. 8 June 1696 by Luke Raven and Wm. O'Tarf(?),
and val. at Ł 33.16.11 plus 2416 lbs. tob. debts; est. admin.
26 April 1697 by Lynch; evidently left iss. for Lynch held 35 a.
Hare's Green for them (13:123; 206-14:27; 133; 211).

THE GREER FAMILY is the subject of a typescript at the Maryland Historical Society, and also of an unpublished typescript
of Greer Family Data compiled by Mrs. James H. Mero of Hampton,
Virginia.

GREER, JAMES (1), progenitor, was transp. to Md. c.1674 and
settled in Balto. Co., where he m. Anne, dau. of Arthur Taylor;
on 6 June 1687 Taylor conv. 75 a. Arthur's Choice to James and
Ann Greer; Ann m. 2nd Laurence Richardson who is listed in the
Baltimore County Rent Roll as holding the afsd. 75 a. in trust
for the orphan son of James Greer; Ann m. as her 3rd husb. Oliver Harriott; had iss.: JOHN, b. c.1688; JAMES; poss. JOSEPH,
who went to P. G. Co. (67:333; 68:261; 211; 388).

GREER, JOHN (2), s. of James (1) and Ann, was b. c.1688 and
was alive in 1747; in Aug. 1718 John Taylor and John Rawlins
deposed that John Greer was the reputed and supposed son of Ann
and James Greer, and had been b. in wedlock; various deps. by
Greer state he was age 47 in 1732, 50 in 1739, and 58 in 1747,
and that he was the nephew of John Taylor and James Smithers,
and the son-in-law (i.e., stepson) of Laurence Richardson; he m.
Sarah, dau. of Nicholas and Sarah Day, some time before Oct.
1730, when Sarah, wid. of Nicholas Day made her will, naming

her dau. Sarah, w. of John Greer; Greer surv. 100 a. Greer's
Park in 1718, 58 a. Greer's Improvement in 1720, and 92 a. of
Greer's Discovery also in 1720; left iss.: WILLIAM; MOSES, b.
1716; JOHN, b. 1718; AQUILA, b. 1719; SARAH, twin, b. 15 Feb.
1721; ANN, twin, b. 15 Feb. 1721, m. 10 July 1738 John Starke;
BENJAMIN, b. 6 Jan. 1727/8; JOSEPH, b. c.1728 (23:6; 131:18, 43/r;
163:146; 224:146; 225:48, 148, Greer data by Mero).

GREER, JAMES (3), s. of James (1) and Ann, acc. to Mero data,
but s. of John (2) and Sarah, acc. to other data, is prob. the
James who m. Elizabeth, extx. of William Wright by March 1741/2;
Elizabeth m. as her 3rd husb. Heathcote Pickett; the will of
James Greer, 12 July 1742 - 5 Aug. 1742, named w. Elizabeth, her
ygst s. Jacob Wright, a possible unborn ch., Henry Adams, and
son-in-law Abraham Wright (3:267, 312, 358; 5:45; 23:359, 366;
110:340).

GREER, WILLIAM (4), s. of John (2) and Sarah, was b. 1710 in
Balto. Co., Md., and moved to Franklin Co., Va.; was captain of
militia, justice, and member of the Legislature; m. c.1730 Ann,
dau. of William and Sarah Fitch; had iss.: WILLIAM, b. c.1732,
moved to Bedford and later Franklin Co., Va.; JAMES, b. c.1733,
moved to Franklin Co., Va., and may have m. Elinor Hughes on 24
March 1768 in St. John's Par., Balto. Co.; SHADRACK, moved to
Montgomery Co., Va.; JOHN, moved to Halifax, Bedford, and later
Goochland Co., Va.; AQUILA, moved to Wythe Co., Va.; BENJAMIN,
b. c.1740, moved to Franklin Co., Va.; WALTER; MOSES; REBECCA
typescript at Md. Hist. Soc. ; Greer data by Mero).

GREER, MOSES (5), s. of John (2) and Sarah, was b. c.1716;
moved to Pittsylvania Co., Va.; m. Mary Bayley in Jan. 1737; had
iss.: LAWRENCE, b. 7 June 1757; AQUILA, b. 9 Sept. 1760 (131;
231-WG#A:267).

GREER, JOHN (6), s. of John (2) and Sarah, was b. c.1718;
m. Sarah Elliott; in Nov. 1743 was summoned by the vestry of St.
John's Par. for unlawful cohabitation with Chloe Jones; had iss.:
AQUILA, b. 29 July 1737; JOHN, b. c.1740, m. Elizabeth (---)
(131:80/r; 132:65; Greer data by Mero).

GREER, AQUILA (7), s. of John (2) and Sarah, was b. c.1719;
moved to Pittsylvania Co., Va.; after the Rev. War moved to
Green Co., Georgia; left a will, 8 April 1790 - 30 Oct. 1790,
naming w. Elizabeth, and had iss.: SARAH, b. c.1740; JAMES, m.
wid. Ann Haynes Lowe; AQUILA, b. c.1744; WILLIAM, b. c.1748;
MOSES (typescript at MHS; Greer data by Mero).

GREER, BENJAMIN (8), s. of John (2) and Sarah, was b. 6 Jan.
1727, and m. Rachel Lowe on 2 Jan. 1745 (131).

GREER, JOSEPH (9), s. of John (2) and Sarah, was b. c.1721,
and may have m. Ann Lowe on 18 Aug. 1750; may have poss. moved to
Bedford Co., Va., and had a s.: GREENBURY (moved to Davidson Co.,
Tennessee (typescript at MHS; Greer data by Mero).

GREGORY, SIMON (1), d. in Balto. Co. leaving a will, 21 Sept.
1736 - 30 Sept. 1736; admin. bond posted 13 Oct. 1736 by Caleb
Pennill of Cecil Co., exec., with Isaac Webster and John Roberts;
his will named his father-in-law Thomas Babb of Newcastle Co.,
his mother Rebecca Powell, and these ch.: JOHN (not yet 21);
REBECCA; and LYDIA (13:140; 126:196).

GREGORY, JOHN (2), s. of Simon (1), may have m. twice, and d.
by 14 Feb. 1761; m. 1st Elizabeth (---), and m. 2nd, by Oct.
1747 Mary (---); wid. Mary m. as her 2nd husb. Nathaniel Hill; in

1750 he owned 50 a. part Privilege; admin. bond was posted 25
Feb. 1760 by Mary Gregory with William Fitch; est. admin. 14
Feb. 1761 by Mary, now w. of Nathaniel Hill; she stated that the
dec. left five ch.: had iss.: (by 1st w.): THOMAS HARRIS, b. 10
March 1727; MARY, b. 13 Oct. 1729; JOHN, b. 9 March 1731; JAMES,
b. 9 Sept. 1734; ELIZABETH, b. 26 April 1747; (by 2nd w.): SARAH,
b. 7 Oct. 1747; ANN, b. 28 Feb. 1749/50; WILLIAM, b. 7 July 1752
(4:360; 13:178; 133:18, 26, 40, 55, 88, 89, 96; 153:47).

GREGORY, EDMUND, m. Rachel (---); had iss.: RACHEL, b. 4 Sept.
1736 (128:95).

GREGORY, PATRICK, d. by 9 Feb. 1760, when admin. bond was
posted by William Askew, with Amos Fogg and Thomas Rutter (13:180).

GREGORY, RICHARD, age c.30, joiner, runaway servant belonged
to Nathan Rigbie who advert. for his return on 22 Feb. 1744 (384:
437).

GREIST, AMBROSE, d. by 11 March 1684 when admin. bond was
posted by Maj. Thomas Long with James Phillips (13:123).

GRIFFIN, GEORGE, tailor, of Balto. Co., escaped from Phila.
Co. jail, where he had been imprisoned; charged with passing
counterfeit money; May 1751 (385:131).

GRIFFIN, JOHN, m. Rebecca (---), and had: WILLIAM, b. c.1726,
age 14 in Nov. 1740 when bound to Elisha Reed; JOHN, b. 14 Aug.
1733 (31:352; 133:31).

GRIFFIN, JOHN, m. Ann Harp on 4 March 1753 (131).

GRIFFIN, LUKE, in Nov. 1756 was fined for begetting a baseborn ch. on Ann Brusbanks (41:313).

GRIFFIN, MARY, was ind. for bast. in June 1743 (33:186).

GRIFFIN, RICHARD, m. Ann White on 14 Sept. 1736 (131).

GRIFFIN, THOMAS, m. Esther (---), and had iss.: NANCY, b. 17
Dec. 1748 (133:80).

GRIFFIS, ELIZABETH, m. Thomas Bucknall; banns were pub. in
July 1701 (129:192).

GRIFFITH, SAMUEL (1), was in A. A. Co. by 23 Feb. 1693/4 when
he wit. the will of Faith Gongo of A. A. Co.; d. in Calvert Co.,
leaving a will, 2 Oct. 1741 - 2 Nov. 1741, which named these ch.:
SAMUEL (to have land in Balto. Co.); LEWIS; JOHN; BENJAMIN (to
have land called Clark's Skin, which had belonged to his grandfather); ANN; REBECCA; and BATHSHEBA (121:67; 127:148).

GRIFFITH, SAMUEL (2), s. of Samuel (1), d. in Balto. Co. by
7 Aug. 1746 when admin. bond was posted by Mary Griffith and Solomon Hillen, execs., with Abraham and Isaac Raven; owned land
(which his heirs were listed in 1750 as owning): 168 a. part Leaf
Jenifer, 119½ a. of Refuge, 100 a. Phillips' Swamp, 39 a. of William's Hope, 182 a. Abbott's Forest, and 50 a. Hope's Addition;
his will, 12 March 1744 - 24 June 1745, named w. Mary and Solomon Hillen as execs., and named ch. Luke, Mary, Elizabeth, Sarah
and Samuel, ment. 7 ch. in all; left iss.: LUKE, b. c.1729;
SARAH, b. 11 Sept. 1734; SAMUEL, b. 7 April 1737; MARY, b. 25
Sept. 1739; ELIZABETH; ISAAC, b. 4 Sept. 1743, d. 20 March 1743;
AVARILLA, twin, b. 23 Nov. 1744; PRISCILLA, twin, b. 23 Nov. 1744
(13:148; 111:210; 128:83, 100, 105; 129:333, 339; 153:45).

GRIFFITH, LEWIS (3), s. of Samuel (1), may be the Lewis Griffith who m. 1st Alce (---), who d. 10 March 1733, and m. 2nd, on 5 Aug. 1739, Mary Johnson; iss. by 1st w.: THOMAS, b. Feb. 1731 (128:91, 106).

GRIFFITH, LUKE (4), s. of Samuel (2) and Mary, was b. c.1729; gave his age as 30 in 1759; m. on 13 Jan. 1757 Mrs. Blanche Hall, wid. of Parker Hall; she d. 9 March 1763 (4:354; 129:378; 310: 198).

GRIFFITH, ELIZABETH, m. 24 Jan. 1703/4 Edward Swan (129:200).

GRIFFITH, JAMES, in 1750 owned 50 a. Christmas Eve, and 50 a. Griffith's Mount; d. by 18 July 1778, leaving a will signed on 25 March 1775 in which he named the tract Christmas Eve, his w. Rachel, and these ch.: JOHN; WILLIAM; and KERRENHAPPUCK (112:366; 153:47).

GRIFFITH, JOHN, m. Elizabeth Bond on 7 Dec. 1746 (131).

GRIFFITH, MARY, had iss.: ANN, b. 8 Feb. 1742 (129:329).

GRIFFITH, RICHARD, m. Jane Rees on 22 Nov. 1743; she d. 31 Aug. 1744 (129:333, 338).

GRIFFITH, SAMUEL, m. Elizabeth (---), and had iss.: JOHN, b. 11 Feb. 1741, d. 15 Oct. 1742 (129:325).

GRIFFITH, THOMAS, d. by 28 June 1666, when admin. bond was posted by Henry Haslewood with Francis Wright (13:144).

GRIFFITH, THOMAS, m. Esther (---), and had iss.: REBECCA, b. 12 Jan. 1760 (133:104).

GRIMES, HONOR, in Nov. 1721, was charged with bast. (23:631).

GRIMES, JAMES, d. by 7 March 1750, when admin. bond was posted by John Hall of Swan Town, with Isaac Webster (13:159).

GRIMES, JOHN, in July 1743 leased part of My Lady's Manor, the lease to run for the lifetimes of John himself, age 36, w. Mary, age 35, and dau. Mary, 8; had iss.: MARY, b. 8 Feb. 1737;JOHN, b. 20 Dec. 1739 (77:284; 131).

GRIMES, NICHOLAS, late of Balto. Co., now of Prince William Co., Va., on 15 Nov. 1731 conv. 50 a. Grimes' Chance to Thomas Worthington of A. A. Co. (213 -PL#8:61).

GRIMES, WILLIAM, m. Eleanor (---), and had iss.: RUTH, b. 15 July 1722 (133:2).

GRINDALL, Capt. CHRISTOPHER, d. leaving a will, 29 May 1747 - 18 May 1749, naming w. Ann, dau. Mary Hill, nephew Christopher Grindall and niece Ann Grindall, execs. in Eng. were Robert Stebbing of Cornhill, London, linen draper, and James Walford on Tower Hill, sailmaker, execs. in Md. were George Atkinson and James Slemaker; admin. bond was posted in 1749 by the Md. execs., with Robert Swan, James Lomas, Samuel Briscoe, and Wm. Rogers, Jr.; in Aug. 1749 Atkinson and Slemaker advertised the following lands for for sale in the Md. Gaz.: 100 a. Hale's Forest, 80 a. Taylor's Discovery, 50 a. Smallwood, 300 a. Friend's Discovery, 100 a. Stone's Delight, 50 a. Locust Neck, 100 a. Spring Neck, 200 a. The Vineyard, and other lands (13:157; 110:451; Annap. Md. Gaz., 23 Aug. 1749).

GROCE/GROSS/GROVE, JACOB (1), m. Sarah (---), and was in Balto. Co. by Aug. 1720 when he purch. 150 a. Chestnut Neck from Francis Dallahide; d. on 9 Nov. 1728; admin. bond posted 20 Nov. 1728 by Anthony Asher with William Wood and Ralph Wooden, the wid. Sarah having ren. her right to admin. the est.; est. was inv. on 12 Nov. 1729 by William Galloway and val. at £ 179.10.4, and signed by Sarah Gross and John Groves as kin; est. was admin. by Asher on 14 Feb. 1732, and the acct. named these ch.: Isaac, and Rosanna w. of John Hand or Stand; left iss.: SARAH, b. 15 Feb. 1703; RACHEL, b. 15 Feb. 1708; ISAAC, b. 18 Jan. 1712; ROSANNA, m. by 14 Feb. 1732 John Hand or Stand (3:108; 13:133; 51:234; 68:227; 131).

GROCE, ISAAC (2), s. of Jacob (1), was b. 18 Jan. 1712; in June 1734 he was joined by Anthony Asher in granting a quitclaim on all accounts to Anthony Asher; in Aug. 1734 he conv. 150 a. of Chestnut Neck to John Maccubbin, and in March 1736 he conv. 100 a. to John League (61:354; 72:100, 216; 131).

GROOM, MOSES (1), of Balto. and A. A. Co., b. c.1649, d. by 21 Jan. 1698/9 when admin. bond was posted by the wid. and admnx., Dorothy Groome, with Stephen Johnson and Rich. Isaacke; m. 1st, Amy (---), and 2nd, Dorothy (---); his wid. m. as her 2nd husb. Robert Cutchin; Moses was in Md. by 20 Feb. 1667 when he wit. the will of John Peart of A. A. Co.; he gave his age as 19 in 1668; he was left pers. by the will of David Jones; in April 1687 surv. 300 a. Groom's Chance, and also came to poss. 150 a. of a 300 a. tract Taylor's Choice; his est. was inv. 16 June 1698/9 by Thomas Staley and William Peckett, and val. at £ 185.14.1, plus 1200 lbs. tob. in the house, 27963 lbs. tob. in debts, and another 12681 lbs. tob. in "sperate" debts; on 11 Nov. 1702 Robert and Dorothy Cutchin admin. Groom's est., and admin. it again on 1 Oct. 1707; Moses was the father of (by 1st w.): MOSES; REBECCA, m. on 31 Aug. 1698, Robert Saunders, s. of James; ANN, m. Col. James Maxwell; ELIZABETH, m. 1st John Ewings, and may have m. 2nd Joshua Merriken (1:83; 2:100; 13:111; 48:326; 120:44; 121:11; 211:35, 53; chart of Groom fam. by Christopher Johnston).

GROOM, MOSES (2), s. of Moses (1), in Feb. 1704 was called kinsman of Ann Felkes who conv. him 100 a. Taylor's Choice; was alive on 12 April 1709 when he was named as bro.-in-law in the will of John Ewings, and was prob. still living in 1750 when he was listed as owning 200 a. Groom's Chance (60:171; 68:189; 122:145; 153:94).

GROOME, RICHARD, m. Margaret Norton on 13 Feb. 1739, and had iss.: WILLIAM, b. 31 May 1741 (131).

GROSS, JACOB, m. Mary Richards on 9 Jan. 1745 (133:158).

GROVER, GEORGE (1), progenitor, was in Balto. Co. by 1692 as a taxable in s. side Gunpowder Hund.; m. 1st Rebecca (---), who d. May 1727, and in July 1727 Magdalen Kelly, who bore him a dau. Sarah; his will, 29 Sept. 1729 - 8 Nov. 1729, naming s. George, s. John (by 2nd w.), and w. Magdalen; the wit. were William Wood, Anthony Asher, and Ann Jones; admin. bond was posted 12 Nov. 1729 by George Grover, with John Bevan, Jr., and Anthony Asher; left iss.: GEORGE; (by 2nd w.): JOHN; SARAH, b. and d. Sept. 1727/8 (13:135; 125:130; 131; 138).

GROVER, GEORGE (2), s. of George (1), d. by 3 Oct. 1735 when admin. bond was posted by Joseph Bevans, with Thomas Morris, Jr. and William Matheny; est. was admin. by Bevans on 19 Oct. 1736; Grover m. by 1 May 1724 Jane Russell, who on that date granted power of atty. to Joseph Bevans to sell her inheritance in Va.; on 8 Feb. 1724 George Grover, Sr., conv. 50 a. Daniel's Town to his s. George Grover, Jr.; ; iss. of George, Jr.: GEORGE, b. 3 Nov. 1730 (13:38; 69:312; 70:18; 131).

GROVER, JOHN (3), alias John Kelly, was called s. by George
Grover (1); was called orphan of Magdalen Grover on 7 Dec. 1729,
when he was age 4, and made ward of Ralph Woodall in March 1729/
30 (28:363; 125:130).

GROVER, GEORGE (4), s. of George (2), was b. 3 Nov. 1730, and
is prob. the George Grover who conv. part Old Field Land to Richard Farthing on 27 Nov. 1753; m. Bethia Pines on 17 Oct. 1763
(82:208; 131).

GROVER, ANN, was tried for bast. in Nov. 1754 (39:449).

GROVER, JOSIAS, m. Mary Anderson on 25 Dec. 1754 (131).

GROVER, WILLIAM, m. Elizabeth, dau. of Anthony Enloes on 14
Jan. 1752 (5:262; 131).

GROVES, WILLIAM (1), was b. c.1688, giving hus age as 48 in
1736; m. 1st Dorothy (---), who joined him on 7 July 1720 in sale
of their right, title, and interest in Thompson's Neglect to John
Rawlings; Dorothy d. leaving a will, 12 July 1720 - 6 Aug. 1720,
leaving the aforesaid tract to her uncle John Rawlings; William
m. 2nd , on 1 Jan. 1721, Sarah Dallerhide; on 31 Dec. 1722 William
and Sarah conv. 126 a. Thompson's Neglect to Richard Thrift; he d.
by 6 Nov. 1747 when admin. bond was posted by the admnx. Sarah
Groves with James Maxwell and Henry Brereton; est. was admin. on
23 July 1748; dec. left iss.: WILLIAM, alive 1750; GEORGE, alive
1750; (by 2nd w.): JEMIMA, b. 29 May 1723; MARY, b. 2 Nov. 1723;
FRANCES, b. 2 April 1729 (4:186; 13:152; 38:13; 68:245, 289; 69:
125; 110:165; 131; 224:253).

GROVES, GEORGE (2), poss. bro. of William (1), d. by 4 April
1734 when admin. bond was posted by William Lowe with John Norris and Benjamin Jones; William Groves had ren. right to admin.
in favor of said Lowe, who admin. the est. on 28 Feb. 1736 (4:
33; 13:143).

GROVES, GEORGE (3), s. of William (1), may be the George
Groves who m. Johanna Rigbie on 26 Aug. 1752 (131).

GROVES, ELLINOR, was ind. for bast. in June 1733 (30:2).

GROVES, HENRY, d. by 26 Feb. 1704/5 when admin. bond was posted
by the wid. and admnx. Katherine Scutt, with Henry Knowles and
William Wilkinson; est. was inv. in 1705 by Hector MacLane and
Daniel Crowley, and val. at £ 7.0.0 (13:122; 54:9).

GRUNDY, ROBERT, m. Mary or Margaret, extx. of James Pemberton
(1:288).

GUDGEON, LAURENCE, was in Balto. Co. by 1694 as a taxable in
s. side Gunpowder Hund. (139).

GUDGEON, ROBERT. See CUTCHIN, ROBERT.

GUDGEON, THOMAS, was in Balto. Co. by 1695 as a taxable in n.
side Gunpowder Hund.; may be the same Thomas Gudgeon who on 4
Aug. 1725 conv. 100 a. Mary's Delight to Cadwallader Jones (70:
141; 140).

GUDGEON, WILLIAM, was in Balto. Co. by 1692 as a taxable in
n. side Gunpowder Hund. (138).

GUEST, ISAAC, m. Mary (---), and had iss.: GEORGE GILPIN, b.
28 Aug. 1759 in Cecil Co. (133:128).

GUEST. See also GIST.

GUICHARD. See GUISHARD.

GUIN/GWYNE/GWYNN, RICHARD, was prob. the Richard transp. c.1665;
was in Balto. Co. by April 1672 when he and Edward Halton surv.
300 a. Newtown (later poss. by John Lockett, and later by Peter
Bond); on 21 Feb. 1688 surv. 121 a. Gwin's Farm; constable of s.
side Patapsco Hund. in 1692; his will, 19 Sept. 1692 - 1 Nov.
1692, named s. Thomas (not yet 21, to have 60 a. Brandan),
dau. (---) Lockett (to have res. of Brandan), dau. Elinor (to
have Newtown), dau.-in-law Ann Cornwell, son-in-law John Lockett,
and w. Hannah; est. inv. by Richard Roben and Wm. Hawkins and val.
at £ 66.18.0 plus 4800 lbs. tob. debts; had iss.: THOMAS; dau.,
m. John Lockett; ELINOR, m. 1st Peter Bond, and 2nd Hill Savage
(121:65; 138; 206-10:273; 211:103, 107; 388).

GUISHARD/GUICHARD, SAMUEL (1), was b. c.1664/6, giving his
age as 45 in 1711, and 51 in 1715; was in A. A. Co. on 14 June
1720 when he wit. the will of George Simmons; m. Ann Gongo on
2 Nov. 1704 in A. A. Co., where he d. leaving a will, 12 Oct.
1732 - 22 Oct. 1733, naming w. Ann, s..Anthony, s. Mark (to have
Quicksale), dau. Hannah (to have 225 a. in Balto. Co.); had iss.:
ANTHONY; MARK; HANNAH (124:24; 126:44; 219-3; 310:199).

GUISHARD, MARK (2), s. of Samuel (1), wit. the will of Roger
Crudgenton, planter, of A. A. Co., on 5 Oct. 1739; m. Dinah (---)
by 8 June 1748 when they sold 100 a. Green's Park and 58 a. Greer's
Improvement to Thomas Starkey; Mark and Deborah Guishard were the
execs. of Roger Crutchington in June 1754 (39:185, 188; 80:2).

GUISHARD, ANTHONY, m. Frances Jones in Nov. 1751 (131).

GUNEY, MARY, was tried for bast. in Nov. 1754 (39:451).

GUNDRY, BENJAMIN (1), was in Balto. Co. by 26 Sept. 1671 when
he wit. the will of Daniel Silvaine; he wit. the will of William
Salsbury on 30 March 1680; d. by 7 May 1687 when admin. bond was
posted by admnx. Mary Gundrey with John Thomas and Mary Stansby
as sec.; his est. was admin. on 5 July 1708 by Col. James Maxwell, who stated that the dec. left a son; m. Mary, dau. of Godfrey Harmer; she m. 2nd Col. James Maxwell; left iss.: SPRY GOD-
FREY (2:198; 13:124; 120:63, 98; 121:10).

GUNDRY, SPRY GODFREY (2), s. of Benjamin (1), m. Mary (---),
and had iss.: BENJAMIN, b. 3 March 1732, d. 9 March 1732; MARY,
b. 21 July 1735 (131).

GUNDRY, JOSEPH, merchant, was in Balto. Co. by 14 Aug. 1666,
when he purch. 500 a. Yapp from Nathaniel Stiles, Gent. (60:56).

GUNN, or GREEN, BENJAMIN, d. by 31 May 1687 when his est. was
inv. by Michael Judd and Moses Groom, and counted as being worth
£ 49.13.2 (206-9:315).

GUNN, JOHN, d. by 1 March 1678/9, when admin. bond was posted
by William Osborne, innholder, with James Phillips and John Wallston; est. was inv. 10 Aug. 1679 by James Phillips and Nathan
Hampstead, and val. at 2469 lbs. tob. (13:124; 48:91).

GUNNELL, EDWARD (1), poss. bro. of William (2), imm. to Md.
c.1673; on 6 Feb. 1676/7 purch. 100 a. Gallar's Bay from Joseph
and Sarah Gallion; was summ. to the Prov. Court in June 1677; d.
by 14 Aug. 1680 when his est. was inv. by Edward Reeves and Wil-

liam Osborn, and val. at 17,186 lbs. tob.; est. was admin. 25
Feb. 1680 by George Gunnell, who also had to appear in court for
the debts of his bro. Edward, in Sept. 1682 (51:9; 2:70; 101:
301; 200-67:44; 200-70:215; 388).

GUNNELL, GEORGE (2), bro. of Edward (1), imm. to Md. in 1673;
m. by 1677/8 Jane, widow and admnx. of Thomas Overton; by 1678
was in Cecil Co., but by 1692 was back in Balto. Co. as a taxable
in Spesutia Hund.; on 11 June 1694 admin. the est. of Edward
Gunner (2:70; 138; 200-67:322, 341; 388).

GUNNER, EDWARD, d. by 11 June 1694 when George Gunnell admin.
his est. (2:70).

GUNNERY. See GUNDRY.

GUNT, ANN, on 3 Dec. 1716 signed the inv. of Daniel Johnson
(52:1).

GUSSE, JOHN, was in Balto. Co. by 1692 as a taxable in n. side
Patapsco Hund. (138).

GUTTRIDGE, EDWARD, s. of John Guttridge of Waltham Abbey, Essex, Eng., was in Balto. Co. by 1756; m. Mary Scarf on 24 Oct.
1759 (131; 300-65:267).

GUY, DAVID, d. leaving a will, 5 Nov. 1727 - 25 Nov. 1727,
leaving pers. to John Lawrence and John Wilmot, Jr., land to Ruth
Wilmot, and naming a serv. James Relley; admin. bond was posted
2 Jan. 1727 by exec. John Wilmot with James Moore and Edward Dorsey; est. was admin. by Robert Wilmot on 3 June 1758 (6:14; 13:
131; 110:238).

GUYN, RICHARD. See GUIN, RICHARD.

GUYN, WILLIAM, in Feb. 1663/4 purch. land from Paul and Katherine Kinsey (59:11).

GUYTON, JOHN (1), d. in Harf. Co. by 23 March 1783; m. Mary
(---) living in 1785; had iss.: SAMUEL, b. 6 Nov. 1727; JOSEPH,
b. 17 Sept. 1732; NATHANIEL, b. 29 March 1735; SARAH, b. 3 Jan.
1737; ABRAHAM, b. 8 May 1740; ISAAC, b. 19 Aug. 1742; JACOB, b.
11 Nov. 1744; MARY, b. 4 May 1747, m. (---) Underhill; JOHN, b.
1 Sept. 1750; JOSHUA, b. 18 Aug. 1757 (244 -AJ#2:231; Guyton
data in filing case A at Md. Hist. Soc.).

GUYTON, JOSEPH (2), s. of John (1), was b. 17 Sept. 1732, d.
1818; m. Hannah Whitaker on 12 Dec. 1754 in St. John's Par.;
moved to S. C., where he rendered patriotic service during the
Rev. War (131; 353).

GUYTON,BENJAMIN, d. in Balto. Co., leaving a will 17 April
1774 - 7 July 1776; m. (as 2nd w.) Catherine Adams on 26 Sept.
1756; left iss.: HENRY, m. 17 April 1758 Sarah Holt; BENJAMIN,
m. Amelia Scarff on 13 Dec. 1753; UNDERWOOD, m. 12 Aug. 1762
Priscilla Jackson; MARGARET, m. Samuel Foster in 1750; LYDIA,
m. (---) Fouth; ELIZABETH, m. Alexander Smith on 24 Jan. 1758
(4:243; 7:346; 10:539; 111:83; 112:339, 462; 131).

GWIN/GWINN/GWYN/GWYNN, EDWARD, m. Easter Fields on 15 Nov.
1728 (133:149).

GWIN, EVAN, of Md., and John Gwin of Va., on 26 April 1671
sold 100 a. Spring Point to Charles Gorsuch (97:127).

GWINN, HANNAH, in March 1746/7 was ind. for bast. (36:378).

GWINN, RICHARD, d. by 19 Oct. 1713 when his est. was admin. by Ann Gwinn (1:219).

GWINN, THOMAS, was in Balto. Co. by 1709 when he was sued by William Logsdon in Balto. Co. Court; on 2 May 1711 he conv. 153 a. Cromwell's Island and 60 a. Brandon to Thomas Crocus, on the same day Crocus and his w. Ann conv. land to Gwynn or Gwinn; d. by 18 April 1726 when admin. bond was posted by admnx. Mary Gwinn, with Henry Jones and Joseph Crouch; est. was inv. 23 June 1726 by James Moss and William Roberson and val. at £ 31.14.8, and was signed by Ann Richards and Godfrey Watters as kin; est. was admin. 23 June 1727 by the wid. Mary, now w. of William Hall (3:92; 13:128; 51:45; 67:142, 144).

GWINN, WILLIAM, m. Sarah Jenkins on 28 June 1721; was victim of assault and battery by Henry Donahue in Nov. 1724; had iss.: THOMAS, b. 3 April 1722, d. 13 Feb. 1723; SARAH, b. 25 April 1727; RACHEL, b. 6 Feb. 1729; MARY, b. 27 June 1731; ELIZABETH, b. 25 Nov. 1733; WILLIAM, b. 7 Sept. 1736 (27:43; 128:74, 88, 96).

HACK, ANN, was in Balto. Co. by 1669 when a pet. for naturalization requested denization for Ann Hack, native of Amsterdam, Holland, and her sons (who were born at Accomack Co., Va.): GEORGE; and PETER (196:233).

HACKETT, JAMES, d. c.17441 had iss.: ELIZABETH, m. 1st (---) Meads, and 2nd, by 5 March 1744, George York (78:49).

HACKETT, THEOPHILUS, of A. A. Co., imm. to Md. c.1675; purch. 300 a. Paradice; d. by c.1700 when his heirs sold the land to a Mr. James (211:111; 388).

HACKS, JEREMY. See HAKES, JEREMIAH.

HADAWAY. See HATHAWAY.

HADDINGTON, JAMES, was in Balto. Co. by 1739 when his name appeared on a list of levy papers prepared by John Stokes (208-1).

HADGRACE, ISAAC, was in Balto. Co. by 1695 as a taxable in Spesutia Hund. (140).

HAENZ, CONRAD, age 23, German servant, ran away from Stephen Onion, on Gunpowder R., July 1754 (323:42).

HAGAN, DAVID, was in Balto. Co. by June 1719; m. Margaret, wid. of Philip Connor (she had a dau. Eleanor by her 1st husb.); d. by 5 Sept. 1724 when an admin. bond was posted by Richard Gist with John Giles and Richard Owings; est. was admin. by Gist on 25 Aug. 1725 (3:245; 13:28; 23:133, 215).

HAGAN, WILLIAM, d. by 22 Dec. 1716, when his est. was inv. by Thomas Randall, and Tobias Eminson, and val. at £ 7.3.6 (48:217).

HAGE, JAMES, servant, was listed with 10 mos. to serve in the 1743 inv. of Edward Fottrell (54:70).

HAGGES, THOMAS, was in Balto. Co. by 1692 as a taxable in Spesutia Hund. (138).

HAIGH, JOHN, was in Balto. Co. by 1737 as a taxable in Back River Upper Hund.; m. Susan (---), and had iss.: JOSEPH, b. 17 Sept. 1740; JOHN, b. 24 Feb. 1743; SARAH, b. 30 Sept. 1746 (133: 77; 149:21).

THE HAILE FAMILY is the subject of an article that was first published in the William and Mary Quarterly, 1st ser., XVII, 202-203, and 296-299; the article was later reprinted in Gen. of Virginia Families from the William and Mary College Quarterly Hist. Mag., III, 1-6 (Balto.: Gen. Pub. Co., 1982).

HAILE, NICHOLAS (1), first known ancestor of the family, was in Va. by June 1657 when he pat. 500 a. in Lancaster Co.; he pat. 738 a. in May 1660, and 234 a. in May 1666; had iss.: GEORGE, b. c.1647; NICHOLAS, b. 1657 (Gen. Va. Fam., III, 1).

HAILE, GEORGE (2), s. of Nicholas (1), was b. c.1647, d. in Lancaster Co., Va. in 1698; m. Ellen (---) and had iss.: NICHO-LAS; JOHN, b. c.1678, d. 1737 unm.; JOSEPH, b. c.1681, d. 1741, m. Hannah (---); GEORGE, d. 1737; ELLEN, m. (---) Opie; SARAH, b. 1696, m. Newman Brockenbrough in 1715; ELIZABETH, b. 1698, m. John Sydnor in 1728; HANNAH, m. Capt. William Ball; WILLIAM, d. 1732, having m. 1st Elizabeth (---), and 2nd Priscilla Downman (Ibid.).

HAILE, NICHOLAS (3), s. of Nicholas (1), was b. c.1657, and was age 50 in 1707 and 70 in 1729; on 2 May 1689 surv. 56 a. of Haile's Adventure (later owned by Edward Stevenson); surv. 200 a. Hailes Fellowship on 19 Oct. 1694, 100 a. Haile's Addition in Jan. 1701, and 150 a. Mount Pleasant in Feb. 1704; was alive in 1729; no record of any est. has been found, but he is unlikely to be the Nicholas who d.1730 testate, since that Nicholas had ch. born as late as 1721; prob. was the father of at least one s.: NICHOLAS (Ibid.; 211).

HAILE, NICHOLAS (4), prob. s. of Nicholas (3), d. by 18 April 1730; m. Frances, dau. of Thomas and Barbara (---) Broad; d. having left a will, 27 Feb. 1730 - 18 April 1730, leaving one-half of Haile's Fellowship to eld. s. Nicholas, 150 a. Mount Pleasant to daus. Hannah and Ann, 100 a. Haile's Folly on Stony Run to daus. Millicent and Sabina, and named his w. Frances and ch. George, Neal, and Mary; admin. bond was posted on 3 Sept. 1730 by extx. Frances; on 3 Sept. 1730 Frances Haile and Barbara Broad conv. 100 a. Long Island Point to Nicholas Haile; Frances Haile was alive in 1750 and listed as owning 100 a. Addition.; Nicholas and Frances had iss.: NICHOLAS, b. c.1700; GEORGE; MARY, m. Thomas Boring on 21 Jan. 1730; HANNAH, m. William Green on 21 Aug. 1729; MILLICENT, m. Charles Merryman on 2 Feb. 1730; SABINA, m. 1st, on 15 May 1735 Richard Miller Cole, and 2nd, by 27 Oct. 1770 Philip Deaver; NEAL, b. 21 Dec. 1718; HENRY, b. 25 March 1721, may have d. young as he is not in father's will (3:194, 217; 13:241; 31:43, 139; 125:162; 133; 153).

HAILE, NICHOLAS (5), s. of Nicholas (4) and Frances, was b. c.1700, and d. by 1747; m. Ann Long on 25 Dec. 1723; an Act of the Assembly empowered Haile, William Hamilton, Samuel Owings, and Christopher Randall to purch. land and erect a chapel of ease for the inhabitants of St. Paul's Par., who lived in The Forest; this chapel later became St. Thomas' Church; James Slemaker advert. in the Md. Gaz. of 17 March 1747 that he would sell the land and slaves in Balto. Co. formerly owned by Nicholas Haile; Capt. Christopher Grindall advert. in the Md. Gaz. of 23 Aug. 1749 that he owned Haile's land; Nicholas and Ann had iss.: NICHOLAS, b. 2 Nov. 1724; SUSANNA, b. 26 Dec. 1727, m. Robert Green by March 1745/6; MARY, b. 7 July 1730; ANN, b. 20 Dec. 1732, m. Col. William Mead in 1750; SHADRACK, b. 7 Sept. 1735; MESHACK, b. 19 Aug. 1738, m. Catherine Gibson; ABEDNEGO, b. 12 Aug. 1741, m. Johanna Smith; JOHN, b. 13 Sept. 1743 (79:10; 133; 340:352).

HAILE, GEORGE (6), s. of Nicholas (4) and Frances, d. in Balto. Co. in 1791, having m. Elizabeth Chawfinch on 17 Jan. 1735; in 1750 he owned Teag's Park and 100 a. Haile's Fellowship; his will, 1788 - 21 May 1791, named the latter tract and James' Meadows, grandsons Alexander and Joseph Haile; had iss.: GEORGE, b. 16 Feb. 1735; HENRY: JOSEPH; ELIZABETH; NICHOLAS; ABEDNEGO; MESHACK; FRANCES, m. (---) Chenoweth; SARAH, m. (---) Chase, and JOHN (113: 538; 133:153:69).

HAILE, NEAL (7), s. of Nicholas (4) and Frances, was b. 21 Dec. 1718, d. 1796 in Balto. Co., having m. Sarah, dau. of Charles Robinson; in 1750 he owned 130 a. part The Forrest; in April 1771, Neale Haile of Nicholas conv. Joseph Ensor 105 a. Merryman's Lot and 30 a. Haile's Addition; his will was signed 15 June 1796 and proved 24 Sept. 1796; had iss.: CHARLES; DRUSILLA; CHARCILLA; and NEAL (114:402, 404; 153; 231-AF#L:208; 336:344).

HAILE, HENRY (8), s. of Nicholas (4) and Frances, was b. 5 March 1721; not mentioned in his father's will, so he may have d. young, but he also might be the Henry Haile who moved to St. George's Parish where he m. Mary Bradley on 10 Sept. 1741; had iss.: THOMAS, b. 19 Oct. 1742; ANN, b. 13 Oct. 1744 (128:115; 129: 325, 339; 133).

HAILE, NICHOLAS (9), s. of Nicholas (5) and Ann, was b. 2 Nov. 1724 in St. Paul's Par.; d. post 9 April 1807 in Washington Co., Tenn.; m. Ruth (---); took the Oath of Fidelity to the State of Maryland, and also served as an ensign; had iss.: ELIZABETH, b. 21 Jan. 1746, m. (---) Cage; RICHARD; WILLIAM; AMON, b. 1759; NATHAN; NICHOLAS, b. 1762; JOSHUA; RUTH; SARAH, m. (---) Gray; JOHN (134:14; 353; 417-6:45).

HAILE, MESHACK (10), s. of Nicholas (5) and Ann, was b. 19 Aug. 1738, d. in Bedford Co., Va.; m. Catherine, dau. of James Gibson (query in The North Carolinian, vol. 3, no. 2, p. 319).

HAILE, GEORGE (11), s. of George (6) and Elizabeth, was b. 16 Feb. 1735 in Balto. Co., and d. 1805 in Washington Co., Tenn.; m. Ann, dau. of Alexander Grant; had iss.: SAMUEL, m. Caroline Ford in 1789; GEORGE, m. Eleanor Chamberlin in 1797; ELIZABETH; ANN (133; 231-WG#Q:362; Haile data compiled by Robert T. Nave and made available to the compiler; also 231- AL#L:208).

HAILE, MATTHEW, no known rel. to the above, was in Balto. Co. by March 1720, and d. by 12 Dec. 1722/3; m. Dianah (---) who m. 2nd Nicholas Besson; est. was admin. 12 Dec. 1722 by Besson and wife; wid. Dianah was sued by Thomas Colmore and by John and Elizabeth Gaither (1:73; 25:241, 284).

HAILE, MATTHEW, was in Balto. Co. by 2 April 1750 when he conv. the lease of Haile's Park to Jacob Cox; m. by 17 Oct. 1744 Rebecca, dau. of Charles Robinson (80:399; 231-AL#L:208).

HAILE, PATRICK, m. 17 Dec. 1709 (wife's name not given) (128: 26).

HAILE, RICHARD, m. Ann (---), and had iss.: MARY, b. 13 Jan. 1752 (133:96).

THE HAINES FAMILY has been fully discussed in John Wesley Haines' Richard Haines and His Descendants: A Quaker Family of Burlington County, New Jersey, since 1682.(pub. c.1960).

HAINES, RICHARD (1), progenitor, came from Aynhoe, Northamptonshire, Eng., to New Jersey; d. at sea, having m. Margaret

(---) who survived him and brought their ch. to Burlington Co.,
N.J.; Richard and his w. had become members of the Soc.
of Friends about 1672-6, and left for the New World from Gravesend
on the Amity on 23 April 1682; Richard and Margaret had iss.,
incl. a ygst s. JOSEPH (Haines, pp. 37-38).

HAINES, JOSEPH (2), s. of Richard (1) and Margaret, was b.
1682 at sea; d. 12, 9 mo., 1763, having m. 1st, c.1704 Dorothy
(poss. a dau. of William and Mary Leeds); m. 2nd on 1 March 1721/2
Elizabeth, dau. of James Thomas of Whiteland, Chester Co., Penna.;
she d. by 9 March 1767 when her will was proved; Joseph moved
from Burlington Meeting to West Nottingham c1750, later purch.
land in what is now Carroll Co., Md., where two of his sons moved;
his will, 27, 10 m., 1762 - 7 Oct. 1763; had iss.: (a number of
ch. who are traced in Haines' book), among others: NATHAN, b.
1735, m. Sophia Price; DANIEL, b. 1736, m. Mary Price.(Haines,
pp. 63-70).

HAINES, NATHAN (3), s. of Joseph (2) and Elizabeth, was b. at
West Nottingham Meeting on 28, 2 mo. (April) 1735; d. 1802; m.
on 23 d, 10 m., 1755 at Gunpowder Meeting, Balto. Co., Sophia
Price, dau. of Mordecai and Elizabeth (White) Price; in 1756
Nathan and Sophia were granted a cert. to Fairfax Meeting in Va.;
Nathan and Sophia had iss.: MORDECAI, m. Hannah (---); JOSEPH,
m. 1st Rachel Cookson and 2nd Jane Hibberd; ELIZABETH, b. 1 Jan.
1760, m. John Clemson; WILLIAM, b. 1762, m. Esther Edmundson; R
REUBEN, d. 1833 s.p.; NATHAN; DANIEL, m. Rachel Updegraff; RACHEL,
b. 1775, m. Allen Hibberd; SOPHIA (136; Haines, pp. 146-149).

HAINES, DANIEL (4), s. of Joseph (2) and Elizabeth, was b.
at West Nottingham Meeting on 15, 9 mo. (Nov.) 1736; d. 1770;
m. 25, 3 mo., 1762 at Gunpowder Meeting, Mary Price, b. 9 Dec.
1744, dau. of Mordecai and Elizabeth (White) Price; had iss.:
SAMUEL, b. 1763; JESSE, b. 1765, d. 1769; ISAAC, b. 1767; DEBORAH,
b. 1769 (Haines, p. 149).

HAKES/HACKS, JEREMIAH, was in Balto. Co. by 1692 as a taxable
in n. side Gunpowder Hund.; in 1707 he and w. Mary admin. the
est. of John Clark; in March 1706 he purch. 100 a. Dennis' Choice
from James Dennis; on 11 March 1720 he conv. all his prop. to
James Maxwell, Sr., in exchange for Maxwell's agreeing to provide food, clothing and lodging for the rest of Hakes' natural
life (2:107; 59:572; 68:301; 138).

HAKLY, ROBERT, was in Balto. Co. by 1692 as a taxable in s.
side Gunpowder Hund. (138).

HALCLOKE, WALTER, was in Balto. Co. by 1692 as a taxable in
n. side Gunpowder Hund. (138).

HALEY, EDWARD, was age 37 in April 1744 when he leased part
of My Lady's Manor from Thomas Brerewood, the lease to run for
the lifetimes of Edward, his dau. Mary, age 5, and dau. Ann (age
not given); had iss.: MARY, b. c.1739; ANN (77:505).

THE HALL FAMILY OF CRANBERRY AND SWAN TOWN

HALL, JOHN (1), progenitor, was transp. to Md. by Robert Paca
c.1640, and d. in Balto. Co. in 1660; m. Mary Parker, b. c.
1633, d. 1699, dau. of William Parker, by 1658; after Hall's
death his wid. m. as her 2nd husb. Robert Paca; Hall took up 150
a. in A. A. Co. known as Marshes Seat, and 140 a. Gadd's Hill,
which in 1679 was held by his s. John; his est. was admin. by
Robert Paca; ch. of John and Mary: JOHN, b. c1658, d. 1737
(129:191; 131; 313:149-150).

HALL, JOHN (2), s. of John (1) and Mary, was b. c.1658, d.
1737 age 79; m. Martha (Beedle) Gouldsmith, wid. of George
Gouldsmith , and dau. of Edward and Mary Beedle; she d. 4 Feb.
1720, aged 52 yrs, 4 mos., and 4 days; on 30 Dec. 1696 John and
Martha, and Mary Ann Utie, daus. of Edward Beedle, conv. to Thomas Browne 500 a. part Oakington, which they had inher. from their
father; will of John Hall, 4 Jan. 1728 - 27 Aug. 1737, left Cranberry Hall and 600 a. Hall's Rich Neck to his s. Edward, 200 a.
Harmon's Swan Town to grandson John Hall of Aquila (said John
was also to have Woodpecker's Hall and 600 a. Aquila's Inheritance; to grandson Aquila Hall of Aquila he left the res. of
Aquila's Inheritance, son John to have Hall's Purchase, 50 a. of
Maskall's Humor, part Beaver Neck, 400 a. Taylor's Good Hap, and
70 a. Timber Neck, will also named Aquila's dau. Martha, testator's son Parker, dau. Sophia wife of Thomas White, and dau.-in-
law, Mrs. Mary Marshall; admin. bond was posted 9 Feb. 1737 by
execs. John Hall and Parker Hall, with Aquila Paca and Roger
Matthews; est. admin. 31 Dec. 1743; John Hall (2), who was High
Sheriff of Balto. Co., from 1692 to 1694, and was a member of the
Governor's Council in 1709, left iss.: JOHN, b. 13 Jan. 1694, d.
in inf.; EDWARD, b. 15 July 1697; SARAH, b. 1 May 1698, prob. d.
young; AQUILA, b. 27 June 1699; JOHN, b. 3 Dec. 1701; PARKER, b.
13 Sept. 1707; SOPHIA, b. 4 Feb. 1709, m. Col. Thomas White (2:
48; 3:337; 13:235; 20:205; 126:221; 128:3, 11, 16, 23, 27, 38;
129:180, 198, 342; 313:150-151).

HALL, EDWARD (3), s. of John (2) and Martha, was b. 15 July
1697; d. 1742; m. Avarilla Carvill on 31 Oct. 1717; she d. testate in 1755; Edward Hall was High Sheriff of Balto. Co. in 1719
and 1734, and was presiding justice of the county court in 1732;
in 1750 his heirs were listed as owning 580 a. Betty's Choice,
and 200 a. part Cranberry Hall; his will, 25 March 1738 - 23 Aug.
1742 left Cranberry Hall to s. John, and Betty's Choice to dau.
Martha, also made bequests to the vestry of St. George's Par.,
w. Avarilla, Edward Hall, s. of Parker, and Aquila Hall of
Aquila; admin. bond was posted 13 April 1743 by his wid.; his
est. was inv. by Isaac Webster and William Bradford on 11 April
1745 and val. at £ 1031.2.11; an additional inventory was filed
showing assets of £ 7.9.2; his est. was admin. 10 April 1745 by
the extx.; the will of Avarilla Hall, 30 Jan. 1755 - 15 April
1755, named ch. John and Martha, grandch. Edward Carville Tolley,
Martha Tolley, and Sophia, Richard and Martha Hall; admin. bond
was posted 15 April 1755 by John Hall of Cranberry with Andrew
Lendrum and Aquila Hall; Edward and Avarilla had iss.: JOHN, b.
8 June 1719; MARTHA, b. 5 Jan. 1720, m. Walter Tolley on 22
Dec. 1751 (5:38; 13:252, 263; 49:121, 131; 110:492; 127:212;
128:3, 39; 129:227;; 153:17; 303:10; 313:153-154).

HALL, AQUILA (4), s. of John (2) and Martha, was b. 27 June
1699 at Cranberry Hall; d. 28 Dec. 1728; m. on 17 Dec. 1720
Johanna (---), wid. of (---) Kemp and James Phillips; she d. 14
Oct. 1735; in 1720 Johanna Hall executed deeds of gift to her
sons John and Richard Kemp; admin. bond on the est. of Aquila
Hall was posted 21 March 1728/9 by admnx. Johanna Hall with Wm.
Smith, Michael Webster, and George Drew; est. of Aquila Hall was
inv. on Nov. 1731 by John Stokes and Josias Middlemore, and
val. at £ 2688.9.0, signed by Jno. Hall, Edward Hall, and Johanna
Hall as kin; est. was admin. on 5 July 1734 and 15 June 1735;
the will of Johanna Hall, 5 Oct. 1735 - 15 Dec. 1735, named John
Hall, Jr., former husb. James Phillips, and sons John and Aquila
Hall; admin. bond on her est. was posted by John Hall, Jr., with
Edward Hall and Parker Hall; her est. was inv. 21 Jan. 1736/7 by
Nat. Rigbie and Isaac Webster, and val. at £ 1148.7.3, and signed
by James Phillips and Hannah Drew as kin; est. was admin. 19 July

1739, 27 May 1743, and 2 Nov. 1743; Aquila and Johanna left iss.;
JOHN, b. 9 Oct. 1722; AQUILA, b. 7 Oct. 1724, d. 1 Dec. 1724;
MARTHA, b. 6 July 1725, d. 7 Jan. 1734; AQUILA, b. 1 Sept. 1726,
d. 1727; AQUILA, b. 10 Jan. 1727 (3:71, 163, 305, 313; 4:31, 45;
13:227, 239;; 49:292; 68:87;128:41, 55, 89, 90; 200-37:375).

HALL, JOHN (5), s. of John (2) and Martha, was b. 3 Dec. 1701,
d. 1774; m. Hannah Johns on 26 Nov. 1734; she was the extx. of
Abraham Johns, and also the wid. of Asael Maxwell; as Col. John
Hall he is listed in 1750 as owning 200 a. Ann's Delight, 55 a.
Dismal Swamp, 200 a. Hall and Bond's Discovery, 200 a. Young
Man's Addition, and 260 a. Westminster; ch. of John and Hannah
Hall: MARTHA, b. 21 Sept. 1735; JOHN, b. 8 Oct. 1737; JOSIAH, b.
31 March 1739, d. 3 Oct. 1739; MARY, b. 21 May 1740; AQUILA, b.
17 June 1742, d. 30 Oct. 1743; BENEDICT EDWARD, b. 20 Oct. 1744;
JOSIAS CARVILLE, b. 7 July 1746 (3:214; 4:75; 128:90, 114; 129:
326, 341, 342; 153:24).

HALL, PARKER (6), s. of John (2) and Martha, was b. 4 Feb.
1709; d. by 28 May 1754; m. Blanch Carvill, dau. of John and
Mary (Phillips) Carvill; after Parker's death his wid. m. Luke
Griffith; in 1750 he owned 200 a. Stepney, 100 a. Jerico, 28 a.
Sophia's Dairy, 380 a. part Cranberry Hall, and 26 a. Come By
Chance; admin. bond was posted 28 May 1754; est. was inv. 1 April 1755 by William Dallam and (---) Matthews, and val. at
£ 1124.14.2; est. was admin. 14 Oct. 1756 and 9 June 1761; Parker and Blanch had iss.: EDWARD, b. 17 Feb. 1735; MARY, b. 25
Oct. 1739; BLANCHE, b. 27 Feb. 1743 (4:354; 5:316, 340; 13:274;
50:1; 128:92, 111; 153:23; 313:153).

HALL, JOHN (7), s. of Edward (3), was b. 8 June 1719, d. 30
July 1779, called "John Hall of Cranberry," m. Bethia Stansbury
on 9 Aug. 1743; she was dau. of Luke and Jane (---) Stansbury;
in 1750 he owned 967 a. part Cranberry Hall; had iss.: SOPHIA,
b . 25 Aug. 1744; MARTHA, b. 10 Jan. 1746, m. 1st William Robinson Presbury, m. 2nd (---) Griffith; EDWARD, b. 10 Dec. 1748;
JOHN BEEDLE, b. 6 Oct. 1749; JOSIAS, b. 25 March 1752; ELIZABETH,
b. 4 Feb. 1754; AVARILLA, b. 6 March 1756, m. (---) Patterson;
PRISCILLA, b. 20 March 1758, m. (---) Christie; MARY, b. 30 April 1760; ELIZA, b. 8 Dec. 1762; HANNAH, b. 16 May 1766 (129:
341, 342, 343, 345, 348, 351, 365, 378, 384; 153:25; 313).

HALL, JOHN (8), s. of Aquila (4) and Johanna, was b. 9 Oct.
1722; d. 1768; known as John Hall of Swan Town; m. 1st, on 2 June
1742, Susanna Marshall, dau. of William and Mary (Goldsmith)
Marshall (Susanna d. 26 June 1744, and John m. 2nd, on 2 March
1748 Cordelia Knight, b. c.1721, wid. of Francis Holland, Jr.,
and dau. of Stephen and Mary (Frisby) Knight; in 1750 John Hall
owned 700 a. Aquila's Inheritance, 211 a. Goldsmith's Enlargement
and 886 a. Goldsmith's Rest; his will, 3 April 1767 - 8 Dec. 1768,
named w. Cordelia as extx., his bro. Aquila, son William, other
ch.: Cordelia, Sarah, Parker, Susanna Heath, and Aquila; his est.
was inv. 1 May 1769 and val. at £ 3752.17.3½ plus sperate debts
coming to £ 1027.18.7; his est. was admin. on 3 June 1771 and 13
May 1773; had iss.: (by 1st w.): SUSANNA, b. 16 June 1744, m.
James Heath; (by 2nd w.): WILLIAM, b. 18 Nov. 1749; AQUILA, m.
Ann Tolley; CORDELIA, b. 30 June 1758, m. Edward Carvill Tolley;
SARAH, b. 30 March 1760, m. John Beedle Hall (son of John Hall
of Cranberry); MARTHA, b. 30 March 1760; PARKER, b. 17 March
1765 (6:262; 7:117; 49:169; 112:89; 129:326, 346, 364; 153:58;
313).

HALL, AQUILA (9), s. of Aquila (4) and Johanna, was b. 10 Jan.
1727; d. 1779; m. on 14 Feb. 1750 Sophia White, dau. of Col. Thomas and Sophia (Hall) White; in 1750 owned 665 a. Aquila's Inheri-

tance, and had iss.: THOMAS, b. 27 Dec. 1751; AQUILA, b. 2 Sept. 1753, d. 13 Sept. 1754; JAMES WHITE, b. 8 Dec. 1754; WILLIAM, b. 31 July 1756; CHARLOTTE, b. 11 Feb. 1758; MARY, b. 25 Jan. 1760; JOHN, b. 8 March 1762; EDWARD, b. 30 Dec. 1763; SOPHIA, b. 6 Dec. 1765; MARTHA, b. 8 March 1768; ELIZABETH, b. 5 Feb. 1770, d. 9 May 1771; BENEDICT, b. 11 Dec. 1771 (129:348, 390; 153:85; 313).

HALL, EDWARD (10), s. of Parker (6) and Blanche, was b. 17 Feb. 1735; d. by 27 June 1763; m. Sarah Phillips on 2 Sept. 1756; his will, 4 June 1763 - 27 June 1763, named sis. Mary Lee, sis. Blanche Hall, and w. Sarah, as well as tracts Jericho and Cranberry; wid. Sarah m. 2nd, by 21 Jan. 1764, Daniel Magee; admin. bond was posted 14 Jan. 1764 by Daniel Magee and Sarah Magee, with Andrew Lendrum and James Heath (13:316; 49:204; 129:364; 210-31: 1001).

THE HENRY HALL FAMILY

HALL, HENRY (11), no known rel. to above, was in Balto. Co. by 1692 as a taxable in s. side Patapsco Hund.; m. Eliza (---) who joined him on 11 Oct. 1710 in selling 300 a. Hall's Palace to Amos Garrett (this tract had been surv, 9 April 1695 for Henry Hall); on 10 Sept. 1722 Henry Hall, Sr., and w. Elizabeth conv. 100 a. Hall's Addition to s. Henry; his will, 28 Dec. 1724 - 2 Oct. 1725, left 50 a. Round Hills to s. John, res. of land to sons William and Thomas, pers. to dau. Eliza, and named w. Eliza and s. John as execs.; admin. bond was posted 21 Dec. 1725 by John Hall with Thomas Homewood and John Bucknell; est. was inv. 5 Feb. 1725 by Joseph Conaway and Nathaniel Stinchcomb and val. at £ 103.8.6, and signed by James, Henry, and William Hall as kin; est. was admin. 13 March 1726 and 3 June 1727 by John Hall; had iss.: HENRY; JOHN; WILLIAM; THOMAS; and ELIZA (2:296, 314; 13:244; 51:65; 67:105; 69:86; 124:199; 138).

HALL, HENRY (12), s. of Henry (11), and Eliza, in 10 Sept. 1722 was conv. 100 a. Hall's Addition by his parents (69:86).

HALL, CHARLES, was in Balto. Co. by 1694 as a taxable in Spesutia Hund.; in Feb. 1724 purch. 1/5 of Cockey's Enlargement and Ball's Enlargement from William Farrell and w. Mary (70:32; 139).

HALL, EDWARD, servant to John Hall, was bur. 22 Jan. 1704 (128:18).

HALL, GEORGE, planter, d. by 3 Jan. 1705/6 when admin. bond was posted by admin. Col. James Maxwell with John Ewings and Thos. Chamberlain; est. was inv. on 11 Feb. 1706 by John Boone and Wm. Lenox (13:213; 48:223).

HALL, HENRY, parentage not given, was b. 11 Oct. 1710 (128:31).

HALL, J., servant with 5 years and 3 mos. to serve, in inv. of John Hill taken 28 Aug. 1727 (51:289).

HALL, JASPER, m. Sarah (---); had iss.: JASPER, b. 11 May 1725; ELISHA, b. 3 April 1730; SARAH, b. 28 July 1731; BENJAMIN, b. 11 May 1736; DARCUS, b. 3 Oct. 1738 (133:47, 48).

HALL, JOHN, d. leaving a will, 21 Aug. 1674 - 3 Jan. 1674, naming Bernard Utie as exec. and sole legatee (120:87).

HALL, JOHN, m. by 1688 Sarah, dau. of Abraham Holman; she was wid. and admnx. of John Collier and George Hooper, by each of whom she had a dau.: Isabella Hooper, and Ann Collier (66:38; 206-10:168; 206-12:132).

HALL, JOHN, of Bush R., m. Ann (or Amy) Hollis on 6 May 1697;
on 4 Feb. 1697 William Hollis and w. Mary conv. him 100 a. of
Narrow Neck; he d. by 5 March 1744 leaving two daus. and heirs
at law, Frances w. of Thomas Donavin and Sarah w. of William Byfoot, who sold the above tract; John and Amy had iss.: MARY, b.
21 July 1702; JOHN, b. Aug. 1706; FRANCES, b. 10 June 1711, m.
Thomas Donavin; SARAH, m. by 1744 William Byfoot (61:214; 75:51;
128:14, 19, 27; 129:178).

HALL, JOHN, planter, made a will, 24 Jan. 1717/8 - 7 March 1718
naming his m. Jane Novell and his uncle John Rawlins (110:133).

HALL, JOHN, on 2 Sept. 1741 was conv. prop. by Joshua Hall to
secure the plantation where Joshua was now living (75:567).

HALL, JOHN, s. of Joseph and Sarah (Smith) Hall, on 31 May
1737 was named in the will of his grandfather John Smith of Cal.
Co. as as the one who would inherit Smith's Addition; in 1750
John Hall still owned the land (126:545; 153).

HALL, JOHN, in 1750 owned 200 a. Come By Chance (153:72).

HALL, JOHN, m. Mary Price on 14 Aug. 1757 (131).

HALL, JOSHUA, b. c.1708; d. 28 April 1782; m. 1st Diana Spicer,
and 2nd Ann Spicer; on 21 Sept. 1738 he and w. Diana conv. lot
10 in Balto. Town to William Rogers; in Aug. 1739 he was ind.
and tried for not displaying the court order in his tavern; in
Dec. 1739 he purch. pers. prop. from John Carpenter; in Aug. 1741
he gave bond he and w. Diana would appear in court; in Sept. 1
1741 conv. pers. prop. to John Hall, Gent., to secure the rent
of the plantation where he was living; in 1750 he owned 300 a.
Taylor's String, 125 a. Addition to Taylor's String, 200 a. Hall's
Range, 80 a. Taylor's Discovery, and 50 a. Smallwood, as well as
1 lot in Balto. Town; was a member of the Balto. Town Comm. of
of Observation; his will, 8 April 1782 - 10 April 1782, left 1/3
of his real est. to his friend Mrs. Ann Spicer, friends Edward
and William Spicer who had gone to sea; had iss.: MARY, b. 1731,
m. 1st Joseph Bosley and 2nd Amos Ogden; JOHN, m. 1st Mary Price
on 14 Aug. 1757, and 2nd Elizabeth Williamson; THOMAS, m. Ann
Wheeler; and JOSHUA (32:, 3, 63, 76; 33:86; 75:115, 567; 112:
481; 153; 345).

HALL, SAMUEL, and Ann King had the banns of their marr. pub.
three times by Feb. 1746 (131).

HALL, THOMAS, m. Ann Green on 23 Sept. 1723; she d. by 2 July
1736 when admin. bond was posted by Daniel Shaw with Charles Green
and William Sinclair; William Green was willing to allow Daniel
Shaw to admin. the est.; est. was admin. by Shaw on 3 June 1737;
in June 1738 Ann's sons William and Thomas were mentioned; Thomas and Ann had iss.: LIDIA, b. 16 Jan. 1724; THOMAS, b. 22 Sept.
1726; WILLIAM GREEN, b. 4 March 1728; DEBORAH, alive in 1737
(3:251; 13:227; 31:224; 133:9, 17, 43, 148).

HALL, THOMAS, m. Sarah Marler on 15 June 1736 (133:155).

HALL, WILLIAM, was in Balto. Co. by 1694 as a taxable in
Spesutia Hund. (129).

HALL, WILLIAM, d. by 20 July 1749, having m. Mary, wid. and
admnx. of Thomas Gwin on 7 Feb. 1726 in A. A. Co.; admin. bond
was posted 20 July 1749 by Mary Hall, with Robert and John Chapman; wid. m. as 3rd husb. John Chapman by 7 Nov. 1750; est. of
William Hall was admin. by Mary Hall on 31 Oct. 1750 and 7 Nov.

1750; payments were made to the orphans of Thomas Buckingham
(whose est. had been admin. by the dec.), and to Thomas Gwyn or
Gwin, orphan of Thomas Gwin (whose wid. had m. the dec.), and
to Mary, w. of John Chapman, and to the following ch.: MARY;
HENRY; ANN; MARGARET; REBECCA; THOMAS (a minor), and JOHN (a
minor) (3:92; 5:127, 131; 13:260; 38:16; 219-4:104).

HALL, WILLIAM, m. 17 Dec. 1734, Mary, dau. of Charles Merryman,
Jr.; may be the William Hall, weaver, who with w. Mary, on 4 Aug.
1746 sold William Cross 50 a. Level Bottom; prob. the William who
was listed in 1750 as owning part Pleasant Meadows and 50 a. of
Hall's Range; William and Mary had iss.: JOHN, b. 31 July 1735;
MARY, b. 31 May 1737 (133:44, 57, 152; 153:89).

HALLAM, JOHN, m. Isabella Fell on 18 Dec. 1755 (131).

HALLAM, THOMAS, m. Eliz. Deaton on 10 Sept. 1733 (131).

HALLETT, LANCELOT, d. by 27 May 1672 when Richard Hallett of
Lyme Regis, Dorset, Eng., posted admin. bond with Jacob Young
and William Dunkerton (13:218).

HAMBLETON. See HAMILTON.

HAMBY/HAMPY, FRANCIS (1), m. Elizabeth (---), and had iss.:
WILLIAM, age 12 on 24 Aug. 1715; FRANCIS, age 8 on 1 April 1715;
MARY, age 6 on 2 Aug. 1715; SAMUEL, b. 5 Aug. 1715; ELIZABETH,
b. 10 Sept. 1715 (sic) (128:33).

HAMBY, WILLIAM (2), s. of Francis (1), was b. c.1703 as he
was age 12 on 24 Aug. 1715; m. Martha Simpson on 25 Dec. 1722,
and had iss.: ELIZABETH, b. 21 July 1723; FRANCIS, b. 15 March
1724; WILLIAM, b. 14 Oct. 1727; THOMAS, b. 15 March 1728; FRAN-
CIS, b. 1 Jan. 1732; JEREMIAH, b. 11 Dec. 1736 (128:42, 45, 73,
77, 106).

HAMBY, FRANCIS (3), s. of Francis (1) and Elizabeth, was b.
c.1707 as he was age 8 on 1 April 1715; m. Alse Munday on 20
June 1729; had iss.: MARY, b. 21 Dec. 1730; JANE, b. 20 Jan. 1732;
ALCE, b. 26 Oct. 1736; ABIGAIL, unlike her older bros. and sis.
who were b. in St. George's Par., was born in St. Thomas' Par.
on 12 June 1744 (128:67, 84, 95; 134:1).

HAMBY, SAMUEL (4), s. of Francis (1) and Elizabeth, was b. 5
Aug. 1715; m. Mary Sympson on 18 Aug. 1738; d. by 8 March 1749
when admin. bond was posted by Jacob Giles, who admin. the est.
on 19 July 1753; had iss.: ELIZABETH, b. 20 Aug. 1738; SARAH,
b. 8 Sept. 1739; FRANCES, b. 10 June 1743 (5:284; 13:261; 128:
92B; 129:332 which gives date of marr. as 20 Aug. 1737).

HAMBY ELIZABETH, was ind. for bast. in March 1741/2, again in
March 1742/3, and tried in June 1743 (33:294; 34:121, 196).

HAMILTON/HAMBLETON, WILLIAM (1), d. 17 April 1730 in St.
Paul's Par.; prob. the Wm. "Hambleton" who wit. the wills of
Philip Conway on 6 May 1710, Henry Davis on 24 Dec. 1713, and
Catherine Knowles on 8 June 1717; on 13 Nov. 1715 Thomas Randall
and w. Hannah conv. him 100 a. part Christisn's Lot; may have
been the father of: WILLIAM (67:363; 122:182; 123:19, 71; 133:
194).

HAMILTON, WILLIAM (2), prob. s. of William (1), was b. c.1682;
d. 1759 in Balto. Co.; m. Sarah (---) by 3 Oct. 1716; in 1742 he
gave his age as 60; in 1750 he owned 200 a. Rehoboth, 60 a. of
Littleworth, 100 a. Yates Delight, 160 a. Long Men, and 50 a.

Tucker's Fountain and Bald Hills; his will, 15 Oct. 1759 - 7
Nov. 1759, named w. Sarah, Thomas Norris Bond, John Gardner and
the ch. named below; admin. bond was posted 8 Nov. 1759 by George
Ogg, Sr., and George Sater; the will of Sarah Hamilton, wid. of
William, 29 Sept. 1786 - 11 Aug. 1788, named four daus and grandson James Hamilton; est. of Sarah was admin. on 30 July 1791;
William and Sarah had iss.: WILLIAM, d. 1770; JOHN, b. 3 Oct.
1716; CATHERINE, b. 17 Sept. 1718, m . John Gardner; RUTH, b. 22
Jan. 1720, m. William Beasman; SARAH, m. William Gardner; HELEN,
m. George Ogg, Jr.; ELIZABETH, m. Meshack Baker; RACHEL, m. 1st
George Sater, and 2nd John Daughaday; ANNE, b. 2 May 1738 (6:149;
7:279; 10:414; 13:204; 111:315; 113:304; 133:7, 61; 153:28; 164:
28).

HAMILTON, WILLIAM (3), s. of William (2) and Sarah, d. in
Balto. Co. in 1770; m. Kerrenhappuck (---) who d. 1779; his will,
13 Feb. 1770 - 23 March 1770, named his w. and seven ch.; est.
of Kerrenhappuck Hamilton was admin. on 13 April 1786 by William
Hamilton; ch. of William and Kerrenhappuck: WILLIAM, living 1786;
SAMUEL; GEORGE; JAMES, b. 1747; SARAH; HELEN; ELIZABETH (8:261;
112:160).

HAMILTON, JOHN (4), s. of William (2) and Sarah, was alive in
1759 and m. Sydney Brown on 7 Dec. 1738; he may be the John "Hambleton" who was noted in the 1763 tax list of St. Thomas' Par. as
having run away last Spring; had iss.: JANE, b. 27 Oct. 1739;
CATHERINE, b. 18 April 1741; WILLIAM, b. 27 Jan. 1742/3, d. 1765
(his admin. bond posted 6 March 1765 by Edward Murphy and William
Aisquith; est. admin. 6 Aug. 1766 by Murphy; EDWARD, b. 20 Nov.
1746; RUTH, b. 18 Sept. 1746(?); HELEN, b. 25 Oct. 1748; SYDNEY
ANN, b. 26 Sept. 1750; HANNAH, b. 9 May 1752 (7:188; 13:282;
133:64, 69; 134:1, 6, 10, 18, 21, 70; 157:2).

HAMILTON, ANN, was tried for bast. in Nov. 1758, naming Joseph
Morgan as the father (46:164).

HAMILTON, JOHN, d. by 9 June 1710 when admin. bond was posted
by Daniel McIntosh with Robert Roberts and Simon Person; his est.
was inv. 29 March 1710 by Moses Groom and James Richardson and
val. at £ 3.5.0; est. was admin. on 26 Feb. 1710 (2:131; 13:211;
48:149).

HAMILTON, RICHARD, was in Balto. Co. by 1692 as a taxable in
Spesutia Hund. (138).

HAMILTON, ROBERT, m. Rebecca Bignall on 15 Nov. 1733, and
had iss.: ANN, b. 26 March 1734; ROBERT, b. 3 March 1735; THOMAS,
b. 30 March 1738 (128:89, 92, 100; 129:284).

HAMILTON, THOMAS, was age c.50 on 28 May 1744 when he leased
two lots in Charlotte Town from Thomas Brerewood, the lease to
run for the lifetimes of Hamilton, his s. Thomas, Jr., age c.14,
and dau. Margaret, age c.17; had iss.: MARGARET, b. c.1727; THOM-
AS, b. c.1730 (77:559).

HAMILTON, THOMAS, m. Esther Sampson on 30 Jan. 1753 (131).

THE HAMMOND FAMILY was centered in Anne Arundel County, and
has been fully discussed by Harry Wright Newman in Anne Arundel
Gentry Revised; nevertheless, some members of the family did
settle in Baltimore County, and a bare outline of the Anne
Arundel settlers is included in order to show the relationships more fully.

HAMMOND, JOHN (1), was b. 1643, d. 1707 in A. A. Co.; imm. to
Md. c.1655; m. 1st Mary (d. c.1678), dau. of Matthew and Ann Howard; m. 2nd Mary (---) wid. of (---) Roper; rep. A. A. Co. in
the Assembly, 1692-93, 1697/8-1698, and later; had iss.: JOHN,
b. c.1665; WILLIAM, d. 1711/12; CHARLES, b. c.1670, d. 1713; THOM-
AS; MARY, m. Cornelius Howard, and ELIZABETH (355; 370:393).

HAMMOND, WILLIAM (2), s. of John (1), d. 1711/12; m. and had
iss., among others (BENJAMIN, b. 1706 (355).

HAMMOND, THOMAS (3), s. of John (1), d. 1724/5; m. 1st Rebecca
wid. of Thomas Lightfoot (she may have been a dau. of John Larkin);
m. 2nd, by 1718 Mary Heath; rep. Balto. Co. in the Assembly for
several terms starting in 1701; in Nov. 1718 his. w. Mary was
fined for brach of peace against Mrs. Comfort Dorsey; he d. leaving a will, 20 Dec. 1724 - 2 Feb. 1724.5, naming grandch. William
Worthington, and ch.: John, Thomas, Susanna Orrick, William, Lawrence, Katherine, Henry, Haman, and Charles; admin. bond was posted 10 Nov. 1725 by William Hammond with Christopher Gardner and
George Bailey; est. admin. on 19 Oct. 1726, 12 June 1729, and 17
March 1731; had iss.: WILLIAM; JOHN; THOMAS; SUSANNA, m. (---)
Orrick, LAWRENCE; KATHERINE; HENRY; HAMAN, and CHARLES (2:274,
279, 325; 3:113; 13: 240; 23:35; 124:186; 355; 370:399-400).

HAMMOND, BENJAMIN (4), s. of William (2), was b. 1706, d. 1785;
m. Margaret Talbot, dau. of William and Katherine (Ogg) Talbot, on
6 April 1735; had iss.: in 1750 owned 100 a. The Mountain; had
iss.: ANN, b. 10 Jan. 1735.6; GEORGE, b. 1748 (72:377; 133:46, 153;
153:86).

HAMMOND, JOHN (5), s. of Thomas (3), was b. 1694, d. by 14 July
1739 when admin. bond was posted by extx. Comfort Dorsey with Walter Tolley and Lemuel Howard (Vincent Dorsey was also named
exec., but ren.); the will of John Hammond of Cecil Co. was signed
9 Dec. 1733, proved 7 June 1739, named Comfort Dorsey and her four
ch. Vincent, John Hammond, Sarah, and Venesha Dorsey; the est. of
John Hammond was admin. on 16 Sept. 1740, 13 April 1743, and 3
June 1743 and 15 June 1743 (3:320, 323, 326; 4:22; 13:226; 127:37).

HAMMOND, WILLIAM (6), s. of Thomas (3), was b. 1702, d. by 16
Jan. 1752 of small-pox; m. 1st Eliza Raven on 26 Aug. 1735; m. 2nd
Sarah Sheredine on 9 March 1739; was comm. High Sheriff of Balto.
Co. in Nov. 1735; purch. 100 a. Yates' Contrivance from Robert
Chapman in Oct. 1741; w. Sarah was recipient of a gift from her
father Daniel Sheredine in Oct. 1746; in 1750 William owned 152
a. Cromwell's Chance, 200 a. Plains of Parran, 200 a. Hamilheath,
400 a. Malinda, 100 a. Hammond's Fortune, 70 a. Hammond's Discovery, 2 lots in Balto. Town, and other lands; his will, 1 Dec. 1751,
proved 11 Feb. 1752, named w. Sarah, ch. Mary (dau. of dec. w.
Elizabeth), William, Thomas, Larkin, James, Caroline, Rebecca,
and Sarah, testator's bro. Lawrence, and the latter's w. Abarilla;
admin. bond was posted 15 March 1752 by extx. Sarah; she admin.
the est. on 9 Feb. 1754; wid. Sarah d. by Feb. 1756 when Thomas
Harrison and Brian Philpot, Jr., posted admin. bonds on the estates
of both William and Sarah Hammond; William had iss.: (by 1st w.):
MARY; (by 2nd w.): REBECCA, b. 28 Aug. 1741; SARAH, b. 20 Dec.
1742; WILLIAM, b. 7 March 1743; THOMAS, b. 27 Feb. 1744; LARKIN,
b. 17 May 1746; ELIZABETH, b. 9 Jan. 1747; CAROLINE; and BELINDA
(4:215; 13:265, 272, 273; 79:31, 185; 80:500; 133:74, 77, 154,
156; 153:34; 210-28:240; 262:81; 303:38; 355).

HAMMOND, LAWRENCE (7), s. of Thomas (3), in Aug. 1730 chose
Christopher Randall as his guardian; m. Avarilla Simkins on 21
June 1734; had iss.: RACHEL, b. 31 July 1733; MARY, b. 22 April
1735; THOMAS, b. 12 March 1737; WILLIAM, b. 25 Dec. 1739; ELIZA-
BETH, b. 12 March 1741; KATHERINE, b. 16 Feb. 1744; WILLIAM, b.

1 Aug. 1746; and BETTY, b. 8 Feb. 1748 (133:152; 134:2, 5, 13, 38).

HAMMOND, HAYMON (8), s. of Thomas (3), age 14 or 15 in Sept. 1733, was bound to William Hammond to age 21 in March 1733/4 (30: 188).

HAMMOND, JAMES, was in Balto. Co. by 13 May 1678 when he surv. 300 a. Hammond's Hope; d. by 18 Feb. 1688, when admin. bond was posted by Richard Askew with Benj. Arnold and George Smith; est. was admin. by Askew (13:217; 211:5; 206-10:388).

HAMMOND, JOHN, s. of Charles, in 1750 owned 32 a. Stony Hall (153).

HAMMOND, NATHAN, on 25 Sept. 1740 bought 100 a. Tevis' Adventure from Robert and Margaret Tevis; in 1750 owned 195 a. of Hammond's Pursuit (75:448; 153:102).

HAMPTON, JOHN, in July 1713 was named one of the heirs of Theophilus Kitten; in Nov. 1744 he and Daniel Pologue purch. 50 a. Conquest and 50 a. Hall's Park, from Francis and Blanche Bucknall; in 1750 he is listed in the Debt Book as owning 50 a. of Content and 50 a. Hall's Park (1:27; 77:660; 153:73).

HAMSON, ELIZABETH. See HEMPSTEAD, ELIZABETH.

HANNAP, THOMAS, house carpenter, in Feb. 1737 conv. livestock to William Bradford schoolmaster (75:52).

HANCE, ADAM, m. Ruth Sutton on 25 Oct. 1744 (131).

HANCOCK, EDWARD, wit. the will of Roger Newman on 10 May 1704; wit. the will of Francis Potee on 3 June 1707; d. by 10 Feb. 1720 when his est. was admin. by Amos Garrett (1:289; 122:42, 145).

HANCOCK, GEORGE, was in Balto. Co. by 1692 as a taxable in the household of Richard Adams on n. side Gunpowder Hund.; wit. the will of Richard Adams on Feb. 1696 (121:118; 138).

HANCOCK, THOMAS, was in Balto. Co. by 1692 as a taxable in the household of Andrew Anderson; d. leaving a will, 21 July 1701 - 2 Sept. 170, naming a w. Catherine, and a poss. unb. ch. (121: 226; 138).

HANDLAND, JOHN, m. Mary Cantwell, after the pub. of banns for three times in 1749 (131).

HANDS, THOMAS, was tried in June 1737 for begetting a baseborn ch. on Margaret Conley (31:62).

HANKIN, EDWARD, late of Eng., d. by 14 Sept. 1758 when admin. bond was posted by John Paca, atty. in fact for John Warner and Richard Partridge, admins. (13:267).

HANKIN, THOMAS, m. Sarah Hewett on 9 March 1748 (131).

HANLY, JEREMIAH, advert. he would not pay the debts of his w. Honor, in March 1723 (69:242).

HANNAH, ALEXANDER, weaver, d. leaving a will, 3 June 1765 - 24 June 1765, in which he named his w. Elizabeth, and these ch.: JOHN; DAVID (had two daus. Elizabeth and Susanna); MARY (m. (?) Blair and had Elizabeth and William); ELIZABETH; ALEXANDER; WILLIAM; THOMAS; JAMES; JEAN (the last four all minors) (112:22).

HANNAH, JAMES, m. Hannah Jackson on 29 Aug. 1756, and had iss.:
WILLIAM, b. 9 Oct. 1756; MARGARET, b. 26 Aug. 1758 (129:358).

HANNAH, WILLIAM, serv. with 2 years, 8 mos., to serve in the
inv. of Stephen Onion filed 8 Oct. 1754 (49:222).

HANNAS, MILES, was in Balto. Co. by 1692 as a taxable in
Spesuita Hund.; on 21 March 1702/3 he purch. 50 a. Bedlam from
John Ellis; in Oct. 1716 John and Martha Hall conv. him 150 a.
Robinhood's Forest, and in March 1717 he conveyed two-thirds of
this tract, under the name of William and Sarah's Inheritance,
to William Robinson; in Dec. 1718 he leased land from Samuel
Jackson, the lease to run for the lifetimes of Miles and his w.
Elizabeth; d. 5 Feb. 1720; m. 1st Elizabeth (---) who was bur.
4 Aug. 1697; m. 2nd, on 24 Nov. 1698 Elizabeth Kelley; had iss.:
THOMAS, b. 22 Sept. 1695; MICHAEL, b. 20 Dec. 1696, bur. 28 Dec.
1696 (66:287; 67:450, 522; 63:506; 128:4, 5; 138).

HANNASEE, JOHN, admitted he was the father of Susanna Gardner's
child, June 1746 (36:9).

HANSLEY, EDMUND, was in Balto. Co. by 1692 as a taxable in n.
side Gunpowder Hund.; in May 1692 he and w. Sarah conv. land to
Edward Scott; in June 1698 conv. 100 a. Little Marshes to Michael
Judd; in March 1698 granted pow. of atty. to Francis Dallahide to
conv. 200 a. Edmond's Camp to William Wright; in Aug. 1698 Hensley or Hansley, and w. Sarah conv. 100 a. Essex, formerly belonging to Michael Judd, to William Osborn (59:353; 61:246; 64:1, 72;
138).

HANSMAN, WILLIAM, d. by 11 Feb. 1761, or 1766 when admin. bond
was posted by Maria Sophia Hansman, with Conrad Smith and Jacob
Myer; est. was admin. 19 Sept. 1761 by Sophia, now w. of John Sto-
ver; dec. left 3 ch.(4:339; 13:294).

THE JONATHAN HANSON FAMILY

HANSON, TIMOTHY (1), settled in Philadelphia County, and m.
Barbara (---), by whom he had one s.: JONATHAN.

HANSON, JONATHAN (2), s. of Timothy, was in Balto. Co. by
1710, if not earlier, and d. there prior to 28 May 1727; m. 1st
Keziah, dau. of James Murray who d. 1704; m. 2nd, on 29, 5 mo.,
1718, Mary Price, dau. of Mordecai and Mary Price; admin. bond
was posted 27 May 1727 by wid. Mary, who m. as her 2nd husb., on
14 Nov. 1728, George Walker; est. of Jonathan Hanson was admin.
by George and Mary Walker on 28 May 1730, 21 Oct. 1730, and 24
May 1733; Hanson in 1711 bought 31 a. Cole's Harbor from Charles
Carroll, and built a mill near Bath and Holliday Streets; Jonathan had iss.: (by 1st w.): JONATHAN, b. 10 Sept. 1710; (by 2nd
w.): MARY, left 300 a. by George Walker; in 1750 owned 150 a.
Hanson's Woodlot, and 300 a. Mary's Meadow; d. 1778 (2:255, 259,
303; 3:122; 13:221; 112:373; 127:224; 133:149; 153:48; 380;
Register of West River Monthly Meeting in 219-6).

HANSON, JONATHAN (3), s. of Jonathan (2), was b. 10 Sept.
1710, bapt. 12 June 1733 when he m. as his 1st w. Sarah Spicer;
m. 2nd Mary (---); d. leaving a will, 26 Dec. 1785 - 7 Jan. 1786;
in March 1747 surv. 40 a. Mount Royal; in 1750 owned part of
Mount Royal, 200 a. Hanson's Chance, and 50 a. part Evans Lot;
had iss.: JONATHAN, b. 22 Feb. 1733/4; KEZIAH, b. 4 March 1735;
TIMOTHY, b. 9 Feb. 1737/8; MARY, b. 11 Oct. 1739, m. (---) Rutter; ELIZABETH, b. 12 Aug. 1741, m. (---) Gorsuch; EDWARD SPICER,
b. 21 Feb. 1742/3; JOSHUA, b. 2 Oct. 1745; AMON, b. 13 Feb.
1737/8; and JEMIMA, m. Josiah Pennington on 24 Feb. 1771; HANNAH,

m. 1st (---) Courcey, and 2nd (---) Wilson (133:27, 31, 50, 53, 63, 67, 93, 151, 170; 153:29; 380).

HANSON, JONATHAN (4), s. of Jonathan (3), was b. 22 Feb. 1733/4, may be the Jonathan Hanson tried for bast. in Nov. 1758 (46:162; 133:31).

HANSON, EDWARD SPICER (5), s. of Jonathan (3), was b. 21 Feb. 1742/3, d. leaving a will, 27 July 1777 - 14 Oct. 1785, naming his sis. Keziah Askew, Mary Rutter, Hannah Coursey, Eliza Gorsuch, and also Jemima Pennington (113:107; 133).

THE THOMAS HANSON FAMILY

HANSON, THOMAS (6), no known rel. to any of the above, d. 1 Nov. 1713, having m. Sarah, dau. of John Ray, and had iss.: Jacob and Thomas, living in June 1719 when Anthony Drew and Samuel Jackson were appointed to see what damage Joshua Cockey had done to their lands; ch. of Thomas and Sarah: JACOB; THOMAS, and BENJAMIN; JOHN, d. April 1727 (23:141; 128:29, 30; 393:94-95).

HANSON, BENJAMIN (7), eld. s. of Thomas (6), was chosen guardian by his bros. Thomas and Jacob in June 1716 and Aug. 1720 respectively; d. by 16 Jan. 1736; m. by March 1723/4 Sarah, extx. of George Chauncey; gave his age as 46 in 1736 when he made a dep., mentioning his father Thomas living about 28 yrs. earlier; admin. bond posted 26 June 1737 by admnx. Sarah Hanson with Hollis Hanson and Samuel Griffith; est. admin., 7 Feb. 1738; wid. Sarah made a will 24 Nov. 1742; proved 29 Jan. 1742/3, naming s. George Chauncey and his ch. Sarah and George, sons John, Benjamin, and Hollis Hanson, dau. Avarilla Hanson, dau. Sarah Garrettson, granddau. Rachel Mariarte; admin. bond on her est. posted 9 Jan. 1742/3 by George Chancey and John Hanson with William Hanson and John Hughes; her est. admin. 19 Sept. 1744; ch. of Benjamin and Sarah: SARAH, b. 29 March 1718, m. (---) Garrettson; JOHN, b. 14 Nov. 1720; BENJAMIN, b. 1722; HOLLIS, b. 4 June 1726, d. leaving a will, 14 Feb. 1746/7 - 15 Aug. 1747, naming bro. Benjamin, bro. John Hanson, and Erick Erickson; AVARILLA, b. 21 March 1733 (3:378; 4:2; 13:225, 256; 22:10; 23:364; 26:222; 32:. 230, 233; 128:94; 131; 225:248; 127:196).

HANSON, JACOB (8), s. of Thomas (6), was b. c.1699; in Aug. 1720 chose his bro. Benjamin to be his guardian; m. 1st Rebecca Miles on 8 Jan. 1723; she d. Jan. 1737 and he m. 2nd Margaret Hughes on 23 Jan. 1738; gave his age as 51 in 1750; in 1750 he owned 60 a. Covent Garden, 100 a. Lambert's Marsh, and 300 a. Abbott's Forest; d. leaving a will, 8 March 1765 - 17 March 1766, naming ch.: Edward, Mary, Martha w. of Micajah Greenfield, his w. Margaret, and sons-in-law Absolom Browne, William Pike and Patrick Brannon; had iss.: (by 1st w.): SYBIL, b. 15 Feb. 1723/4; THOMAS, b. 7 Oct. 1725; JACOB, b. 10 Oct. 1727; EDWARD, b. 7 Jan. 1731; MARGARET, b. 21 Jan. 1733, m. Absolom Browne on 5 Dec. 1752; SARAH, b. 11 Oct. 1735; JACOB, b. 7 Feb. (1736?); (by 2nd w.): MARY, b. 7 Dec. 1739; MARTHA, b. 3 Nov. 1741, m. Micajah Greenfield; SARAH, b. 25 Nov. 1742; JACOB, b. 13 March 1744, d. 7 Feb. 1746; SAMUEL, b. 20 Oct. 1746, twin; JACOB, b. 20 Oct. 1746, twin; MARY, b. 26 Sept. 1748? (112:16; 128:50, 61, 83, 89, 106, 107; 129:326, 341, 345, 354, 354).

HANSON, THOMAS (9), s. of Thomas (6), d. 1720 (128:58).

HANSON, JOHN (10), s. of Benjamin (7), was b. 14 Nov. 1720; m. Somelia Garrettson on 4 Aug. 1743, and had iss.: BENJAMIN, b. 11 June 1744; JOHN, b. 20 Aug. 1746; HOLLIS, b. 22 Feb. 1748; SARAH, b. 26 Nov. 1749; SOPHIA, b. 12 July 1752; SOMELIA, b. 10

Feb. 1756; ELIZABETH, b. 11 Jan. 1758 (129:332, 338, 343, 345, 357, 358).

HANSON, BENJAMIN (11), s. of Benjamin (7), was b. 1722, m. Elizabeth (---), and had iss.: HOLLIS, b. 17 Jan. 1750; BENJAMIN, b. 25 Dec. 1752; SAMUEL, b. 13 Sept. 1755; MARY, b. 13 Sept. 1755; JOHN, b. 10 Jan. 1757; SARAH, b. 1 Nov. 1760; AVARILLA, b. 12 March 1763 (129:368, 378).

HANSON, CHRISTOPHER, b. 17 Oct. 1759, parents not named (133: 125).

HANSON, JOHN, in 1750 owned 59 a. Buck Range (153:105).

HANSON, JOHN, "in the Neck," in 1750 owned 50 a. Narrow Neck and 100 a. Hanson's Begrudged Neck (153:26).

HANSON, THOMAS, d. by 9 June 1757 when admin. bond was posted by Alisanna Hanson with Samuel Webster and Richard Dallam (13: 202).

HARBERT. See HERBERT.

HARDEMAN, HANNAH, b. 24 July 1711, parents not named (128:31).

HARDEN, ELIZABETH, was ind. for bast., June 1739 (32:401).

HARDEN, SARAH, was ind. for bast. in March 1738/9, tried in Nov. 1739, and tried again in Nov. 1745, June 1746, and June 1750 (31:351; 32:86; 35:747; 36:6; 37:175).

HARDESTY, JOSHUA, Poss. s. of George who d. 1694 in Calvert Co.; m. Keziah Taylor, wid. and extx. of John Taylor on 6 Oct. 1746; in 1750 owned 235 a. Claxon's Purchase, 31 a. The Swamp, and 100 a. Powell's Choice; had iss.: ELIZABETH, b. 28 Dec. 1748 (4:177; 131:120/r; 153:41).

HARDIN, JOHN, was in Balto. Co. by 1692 as a taxable in the n. side of Patapsco Hund. (138).

HARDING, ISAAC, was in Balto. Co. by 1742 when Jacob Jones conv. to him 74 a. Jones Chance, which Harding still owned in 1750 (77:676; 153:17).

HARDISTY, LEMUEL, in Nov. 1755 was tried for bast. as the father of Sarah Thom's child (40:403).

HARE, JOHN, m. Hannah Lanardy in 7 Aug. 1757 (131).

HARE, WILLIAM, of Patapsco, claimed land for service in 1669 (388).

HARECOCK, JOHN, was named as the father of Ann Martin's child in Aug. 1724 (26:449).

HARGAS. See HARGUES.

HARGLO, EDWARD, of Bush River, d. 20 Jan. 1698/9 (128:6).

HARGRAVE, SOLOMON, conv. prop. to Richard Caswell in Aug. 1743 (77:310).

HARGROVES, GEORGE, lived near Bush R., in Aug. 1752 (385:192).

HARGUES/HARGAS, ELIZABETH, in Nov. 1737 was tried for committing adultery with Abraham Cord, a married man; she had iss.:

RUTH, b. 26 April 1734; AQUILA, b. 24 March 1735; STEPHEN, b.
12 Sept. 1738 (31:146; 128:87, 92, 101; 132:278).

HARGUES, THOMAS, m. Elizabeth (---), and had iss.: THOMAS, b.
30 Oct. 1724; MARY, b. 7 Feb. 1725/6; ELIZABETH, b. 15 Nov. 1726;
WILLIAM, b. 14 June 1728 (128:49, 65).

HARKINS, REBECCA, m. William Gain on 1 Aug. 1727 (133:150).

HARLEM, JAMES, was in Balto. Co. by 1692 as a taxable in s.
side Patapsco Hund. (138).

HARLEY (or FARLEY), JOHN, m. Mary Weeks on 29 Oct. 1737 (128:
92b).

HARMAN, WILLIAM, m. Sarah Powell on 17 or 24 June 1744; in
Sept. 1744 William Harman, aged 36, leased 50 a. from Thomas
Brerewood for his lifetime, that of his w. Sarah, aged 30, and
her s. Edward, aged 3 (77:587; 131).

HARMER, GODEFRID or GODFREY, has been the subject of much
research by Peter S. Craig, who has made his findings available
to the compiler, who acknowledges Mr. Craig's generosity with
gratitude. Harmer was the s. of Hans Willem Harmer of Worms,
and a nephew of Pieter Minuiet with whom he went to Goteborg in
Sweden, from there to South River, and by 1661 imm. to Md.;
m. by 20 June 1663 Mary, dau. of Oliver Sprye; in July 1661 he
was naturalized as a citizen of Md., transferring his allegiance
from the King of Sweden to Lord Baltimore; Harmer d. by 2 June
1674, when his wid. Mary (who later m. Dr. John Stanesby), conv.
150 a. Oliver;s Reserve to John Johnson and Robert Benger; ch.
of Godfrey and Mary: SARAH; ELIZABETH; MARY, m. 1st Benjamin
Gundry, and 2nd James Maxwell (96:231, 232; 160:117; 200-3:430;
388; data from Peter Stebbins Craig, esp. article by C. A. Wes-
lager in Delaware History, 20:80).

HARN, PATRICK, m. Honour (---), and had iss.: ELIZABETH, b. 2
July 1732 (133:24).

HARP, ELIZABETH, was tried for bast. in Nov. 1723 (26:75).

HARP, JOSEPH, and w. Elizabeth, on 4 Dec. 1725 conv. one-third
of Yeat's Contrivance, in all 400 a., to Thomas Cockey (70:215).

HARPER, ANTHONY, blacksmith, ran away from Balto. Town in Aug.
1753 (307-69:56).

HARPER, JOHN, m. Jane (---), and had iss.: SARAH, b. 3 Aug.
1715 (131).

HARPER, JOHN, d. by 3 June 1723 when admin. bond was posted
by Nicholas Ridgely, with Benjamin Howard and Charles Ridgely;
est. was inv. on 8 June 1723 and val. at £ 15.19.10 by Thomas
Sheredine and Thomas Stansbury; dec. left a wid. Ann Harper; est.
was admin. by Nicholas Ridgely on 5 Sept. 1727 (3:74; 13:222; 50:
374).

HARPER, SAMUEL, m. Sarah Maccraree on 27 Dec. 1744 (129:339).

HARPER, THOMAS, m. Mary Shields on 19 June 1759 (131).

HARPLE(Y), EDWARD, was in Balto. Co. by 1692 as a taxable in
Spesutia Hund. (138).

HARRAPP, THOMAS, innholder, in April 1739, left articles to
William Govane and John Roberts (75:200).

HARRINGTON.   See HERRINGTON.

HARRIOTT, AMBROSE (1), was transp. to Md. c.1673; d. c.1690 leaving a wid. and two ch., Oliver and Unity; the wid. m. Edward "Dowel" or Dowse, who in his will, dated 30 Oct. 1690 left 100 a. The Range to his son-in-law Oliver Harriott and another 100 a. to his dau.-in-law Unity; ch. of Ambrose: OLIVER, and UNITY (59: 332; 388).

HARRIOTT, OLIVER (2), s. of Ambrose (1), was b. c.1677, and was alive in 1742; in 1693/4 Thomas Hedge, godfather of Oliver, pet. that "Oliver, a poor orphan, s. of Ambrose...," might be bound as an apprentice; he gave his age as 51 in 1728 and 69 in 1742; in 1742 he declared that some 50 years earlier he had lived with Thomas James; in Nov. 1733 Harriott was declared past his labor and made exempt from the levy; he is prob. the father of: OLIVER. Jr. (20:264; 30:131; 139; 224:38).

HARRIOTT, OLIVER (3), prob. s. of Oliver (2), m. 1st by 13 June 1711, Ann, wid. of Lawrence Richardson; she d. 13 May 1716, and he m. 2nd, on 13 Oct. 1717, Susanna Morrow; on 23 Feb. 1749 he was conv. 50 a. Hunting Quarter by Thomas Carr and w. Elizabeth; Oliver and Susanna later conv. this land to their dau. Susanna; admin. bond on his est. was posted 28 March 1750 by admnx. Susanna Harriott with Benjamin Ingram and William Grover; the admin. acct., filed 12 July 1751, named ch.: Richard, Elizabeth, William, Susanna, and Mary; the will of Susanna "Herod," 2 Nov. 1764 - 14 Feb. 1765, named s. William, dau. Elizabeth Trapnall, dau. Susanna Coe, dau. Mary w. of William Anderson, and grandchildren Catherine and Ann Grover; in 1750 the heirs of Oliver Harriott owned 50 a. Hunting Quarter; ch. of Oliver Harriott: RICHARD; ELIZABETH, m. (---) Trapnall; WILLIAM; SUSANNA, m. William Cock or Coe on 18 June 1752; MARY, m. William Anderson on 21 Aug. 1755; poss. ANN who m. William Grover (2:2, 134; 5: 181, 252; 13:262; 75:349, 350; 112:13; 131; 153:36).

HARRIOTT, RICHARD (4), prob. s. of Oliver (3) by his 1st w.; m. Mary (---) who joined him on 5 June 1745 in sale of 50 a. of Privilege to Henry Adams; in Aug. 1746 he leased 100 a. Gunpowder Manor, called Harriott's Hope, for the lifetimes of Richard, b. c.1707, Ann, b. c.1739, and Mary, b. c.1741; had at least two ch.: ANN, b. c.1741; MARY, b. c.1741 (77:130; 389:11).

HARRIS, (---), m. by 13 Oct. 1759, Mary Ann, mother of William Johnson (47:620).

HARRIS, ANN, at Timothy Keen's, was ind. for bast. in March 1724.5 (27:127).

HARRIS, EDWARD, m. 19 June 1719 Frances Johnson; his will, 15 Feb. 1723 - 8 April 1724, left his dwelling plantation to his w. Frances (124:167; 128:41).

HARRIS, EDWARD, d. by 4 April 1720, when admin. bond was posted by John Newsham, with Thomas Newsham and Peter Lester (13:223).

HARRIS, EDWARD, m. Mary (---), and had iss.: ELIZABETH WALTERS, b. 5 May 1726 (131).

HARRIS, GEORGE, of Kent Co., on 4 Aug. 1673 sold land at Stony Point to Henry Eldesley (99:348).

HARRIS, JAMES, m. by 2 Nov. 1728 Bathsheba, dau. of James Barlow (2:311).

HARRIS, JOHN, was in Balto. Co. by 1692 as a taxable in s. side Patapsco Hund. (140).

HARRIS, JOHN, m. Dorothy Rogers in Dec. 1721; on 4 June 1735 he and w. Dorothy conv. 100 a. Harris' Delight to William Poteet; had iss.: ELIZABETH, b. 22 June 1721; JOHN, b. 30 Sept. 1725; BENJAMIN, b. March 1727, d. same month; MARY, b. March 1727, d. same month (74:224; 131).

HARRIS, KATHERINE, serv. of Ludwick Enloes, in Dec. 1691 was brought to court for bearing thee baseborn ch. begotten by Dennis Bryant (19:131).

HARRIS, LLOYD, m. by 10 Nov. 1724, Eleanor, extx. of Nicholas Rogers, was comm. coroner of Balto. Co. in Nov. 1735, was comm. Ranger in Oct. 1737; d. by 28 June 1743, when admin. bond was posted by George Buchanan, the wid. Eleanor having ren.; had iss.: JAMES LLOYD, b. 17 July 1724 (2:349; 13:253; 133:8; 303:38, 51).

HARRIS, SARAH, was ind. for bast., Aug. 1723; in Aug. 1725 she and John Swynyard were ind. for bast. (26:436; 27:306).

HARRIS, SARAH, m. Henry Bennington on 26 Dec. 1726 (129:248).

HARRIS, SUSANNAH, in Aug. 1710 was ind. for bast.; Thomas Cromwell offered to pay her fine if she could not (21:164).

HARRIS, THOMAS, was on Herring Creek by 31 May 1681 when Robert Benger gave him a bond for the conv. of 150 a. Oliver's Reserve and 30 a. Benger's Addition (103).

HARRIS, THOMAS, in Nov. 1719 purch. 370 a. Mount Hayes from John and Mary Ann Hayes (68:13).

HARRIS, THOMAS, m. Ann (---), and had: MARY, b. 5 Jan. 1726/7 (133:13).

HARRIS, THOMAS, in Aug. 1735 conv. 100 a. Farfar's Favor to his grandson William Johnson of William (74:281).

HARRIS, THOMAS, d. leaving a will, 4 May 1740 - 19 June 1740, leaving his 62 a. dwelling plant. to s. Charles, and mentioning but not naming his w.; admin. bond was posted 19 June 1740 by William Fell, with John Whiley and Robert Whitehead, Harris' wid. Darcas having ren.; his est. was admin. by Fell on 24 Sept. 1741; had iss.: CHARLES (4:111; 13:249; 127:84).

HARRIS, THOMAS, d. leaving a will, 20 Jan. 1740 - Feb. 1748, naming w. Mary Ann as sole extx. (110:440).

HARRIS, WILLIAM, m. by 1684 Elizabeth Russell, wid. of William Hollis (18:240).

HARRIS, WILLIAM, in May 1685 conv. 300 a. Harris' Trust to Thomas Hedge (59:141).

HARRIS, WILLIAM, m. Sarah (---), and had iss.: SARAH, b. 16 Feb. 1714; MARGARET, b. 23 Oct. 1716 (133:6).

HARRIS, WILLIAM, m. Mary Ginn on 13 Jan. 1756 (131).

HARRISON, (---), m. by 30 Oct. 1690, Mary, heir of Edward Douse (59:332).

HARRISON, JOHN, m. by 17 March 1719, Margaret, wid. of Daniel Mackintosh (1:49).

HARRISON, JOHN, m. Johanna Morris on 4 Sept. 1733 (133:151).

HARRISON, JOHN, m. by 28 Dec. 1744, Mary, admnx. of Gilbert Crockett, whose est. they admin. on that day; had iss.: JOHN, b. 10 June 1741 (3:346; 133:66).

HARRISON, THOMAS, merchant, of Balto. Co. went to Eng., and empowered James Walker to collect his debts in April 1748; was elected commissioner of Balto. Town in 1745; in 1750 owned 2 lots in Balto. Town as well as 200 a. Robert's Park, 267 a. Ashman's Hope, 2½ a. Harrison's Dock, 100 a. Harrison's Meadows, and other lands (153:66; 255).

THE HARRYMAN FAMILY is discussed more fully in Ethel I. Harryman's Elijah Harryman: His Descendants and Ancestral Background with Allied Lines, 1661-1977 (Fairfield: Tribune Printing Co., n.d.)

HARRYMAN, JOHN (1), progenitor, d. in Balto. Co. by 15 Feb. 1710/11; m. Eleanor (---), who m. 2nd William Farfarr; became the owner of 50 a. Jones' Venture, and 50 a. Thorrell's Neck; d. leaving a will, 4 Feb. 1710/11 - 15 Feb. 1711, leaving tract Waterford to s. John, Thorrell's Neck to sons Samuel and Thomas, and The Orchard to sons George and Charles, with w. Eleanor serving as extx.; est. inv. on 30 April 1711 by John Vickory and Robuck Lynch, and val. at Ł 52.11.6; admin. bond was posted two mos. earlier, on 15 Feb. 1710/11, by extx. Ellinor Harryman, with William Farfar and Robuck Lynch; est. admin. 11 Aug. 1713 by the extx. Eleanor now w. of William Farfarr; ch. of John and Eleanor: JOHN, d. by 1749; SAMUEL, d. after 1750; THOMAS, d. by 1733; GEORGE, d. c.1774; ROBERT; and CHARLES (1:24; 48:217; 122:184; 124:105; 211:78, 96).

HARRYMAN, JOHN (2), s. of John (1) and Eleanor, d. by 8 March 1749; m. Alice (---); in 1750 his heirs owned 226 a. Richardson's Forest; admin. bond on his est. was posted 8 March 1748 by John Harryman and Charles Harryman, with Walter Dallas, and Valentine Carback; est. was admin. on 5 April 1750 and 8 May 1751; ch. of John and Alice: PRUDENCE, b. c.1715, m. (---) Mitchell; MARY, b. c.1720, m. John Valentine Carback on 19 Dec. 1736; ELIZABETH, b. 11 Sept. 1721, m. Edward Parrish; JEMIMA, b. 19 Oct. 1724; JOHN, b. 14 Dec. 1727; CHARLES, b. 25 Jan. 1730; THOMAS, b. 30 Jan. 1735/6, m. Ann Stansbury on 1 March 1756 (5:152, 199; 13:259; 37:163; 133:4, 9, 20, 47, 56; 153:34).

HARRYMAN, SAMUEL (3), s. of John (1) and Eleanor, m. 1st, on 18 Aug. 1723, Jane Smith; she d. 30 March 1727 and he m. 2nd, on 3 June 1728 Comfort Platt Taylor, dau. of Bray Platt and Elizabeth (---) Taylor; on 28 July 1746 Samuel and Comfort conv. 50 a. Todd's Range to John Shaw; in 1750 he owned 50 a. Sedgewell, 50 a. Samson's Favor, and 50 a. Smith's Addition; had iss., all by 2nd w.: ALLINOR, b. 25 Feb. 1728/9, m. John Bays on 12 Sept. 1748; RUTH, b. 26 March 1731, m. William Shaw on 17 Sept. 1750; ELIZABETH, b. 18 Dec. 1733 or 1734, m. Moses Green on 25 March 1762; and SARAH, b. 12 July 1736, m. Samuel Bone on 25 Sept. 1759 (79:274; 133:10, 25, 54, 147, 161, 164, 167, 193; 153).

HARRYMAN, THOMAS (4), s. of John (1) and Eleanor, d. by 17 July 1733 when admin. bond was posted; he made a will on 11 June 1733 naming George Harryman, his own w. Eleanor, and bro. John, and left Ł 1 for paling in the graveyard where his parents are buried; m. Eleanor by 10 April 1729 Elizabeth, extx. of John Norton (2:281; 13:236; 126:22).

HARRYMAN, GEORGE (5), s. of John (1) and Eleanor, d. in Balto.
Co. by 9 Feb. 1774; m. Ann Wilkinson, dau. of William and Tamar
Wilkinson, on 30 March 1725; on 15 Oct. 1743 purch. from John Ingle
the latter's share of the real est. of Christopher Shaw; in 1750
owned 100 a. part Cumberland, 100 a. Project, 8 a. Harryman's
Hope, 100 a. Harryman's Outlet, 100 a. part Shaw's Fancy, 97 a.
part Shaw's Delight, and 83 a. part Shaw's Privilege; his will,
27 Dec. 1773 - 9 Feb. 1774, named grandsons William, Samuel, and
George Clarke, grandsons Thomas and George Jackson, bro. Robert
Harryman, and granddau. Temperance Harryman, and these ch.: GEORGE
b. 19 April 1728; SOPHIA, m. Samuel Clark; TAMAR; PATIENCE, b. 5
Feb. 1733/4, m. Thomas Jackson on 14 July 1757; GEORGE; WILLIAM,
b. 25 Sept. 1746; ANN, b. 2 June 1742; SAMUEL, d. by 1783, having
m. Sophia (---). (77:382; 112:285; 133:18, 36, 51, 69, 148; 153:
33; 231-AL#A:356).

HARRYMAN, ROBERT (6), s. of John (1) and Eleanor, was alive
in 1750; m. Elizabeth Simkins on 24 Jan. 1733; in 1750 he owned
60 a. Harryman's Delight; on 4 Dec. 1742 Robert and Elizabeth
sold 100 a. Bachelor's Ridge to Thomas Hines; had iss.: AVARILLA,
b. 11 March 1735/6; ROBERT, b. 12 March 1736; PRISCILLA, b. 3
Feb. 1738; RACHEL, b. 26 Jan. 1740 (77:196; 133:44, 54, 67, 151;
153:12).

HARRYMAN, CHARLES (7), s. of John (1) and Eleanor, was alive
on 8 Nov. 1738 when he sold 50 a. Turkey Cock Alley to Thomas
Wright (75:130).

HARRYMAN, PRUDENCE, was tried for bast. in March 1736, naming
Joseph Ward, Jr., as the father; in Nov. 1739 confessed to having
born another bast.; had iss.: ELIZABETH, b. 2 Nov. 1736 (31:90;
32:38; 133:56).

HARRYMAN, GEORGE, m. Sarah (---), and had iss.: RACHEL, b. 13
Aug. 1750 (133:94).

HARSE, TIMOTHY, was in Balto. Co. by 1692 as a taxable in
Spesutia Hund. (138).

HART, STEPHEN, was in Balto. Co. by 1692 as a taxable in s.
side Patapsco Hund.; d. by 27 Feb. 1696/7 when admin. bond was
posted by John Scutt and w. Katherine, with Thomas Hooker and
Robert Parker; est. was inv. 23 Feb. 1696/7 by James Jackson and
Christopher Cox, and val. at £ 16.6--; dec. left two ch., incl.:
SARAH; the other not known (13:216; 122:14; 138; 206-14:149).

HARTEGIN, WILLIAM, m. Mary Sawell on 9 Aug. 1748 (133:161).

HARTGROVE, SOLOMON, serv., in the inv. of Joshua Merriken
filed in June 1727 (51:263).

HARTMANN, GEORGE MICHAEL, purch. land in Balto. Town from
Matthew Coulter, 2 Oct. 1753 (82:138).

HARTS, JOHN, was naturalized in Balto. Town in 1758 (404).

HARTSHORNE, GEORGE, was in Balto. Co. by 1692 as a taxable in
n. side Gunpowder Hund.; had iss.: MARY, b. 13 May 1695 (128:1;
138).

HARTSHORNE, ELIZABETH, dau. of John and Clemency Parker, was
b. 20 Dec. 1698 (128:6).

HARTSHORNE, JONATHAN, in 1750 owned 221 a. Arabia Petrea, and
50 a. Rosemary Ridge (153:67).

HARTWAY, VITUS, m. Elizabeth Parnetson on 27 July 1745; on 12 June 1750 conv. lot 32 in Balto. Town to Edmund Talbot, with consent of w. Elizabeth, left a will, 22 April 1749 - 7 Oct. 1777, left everything to w. Ann Elizabeth (80:496; 112:345; 133: 157).

HARVEY, WILLIAM (1), progenitor, was in Balto. Co. by 1727; m. Margaret Norman on 2 Feb. 1726 in All Hallows Par., A. A. Co.; in 1750 owned 40 a. Port Royal; d. leaving a will, 17 Jan. 1767 - 14 Jan. 1774; left iss.: THOMAS, b. 19 March 1727; ELIZABETH, b. 4 April 1729; MARY, b. 10 Jan. 1731, m. Joshua Jones; MARGARET, b. 11 Dec. 1733, m. Charles Gorsuch; WILLIAM, b. 12 Jan. 1736; JOHN; PRISCILLA, d. by 28 June 1790; RACHEL; AVARILLA; SARAH, m. William Cole (10:158, 167; 112:288; 113:389; 133:35; 153:15; 219-1: 104).

HARVEY, THOMAS (2), s. of William (1) and Margaret, was b. 19 March 1727; m. Cassandra Gott on 16 Jan. 1757; had iss.: NICHOLAS NORMAN, b. 26 Nov. 1757; MARGARET, b. 13 June 1759; SARAH, b. 5 Jan. 1761; THOMAS, b. 24 May 1762; WILLIAM, b. 22 Dec. 1764; CASSANDRA, b. 12 Feb. 1767; RICHARD, b. 24 Sept. 1770; RICHARD, b. 24 Sept. 1770; ELIZABETH, b. 17 March 1772 (133:35; 134:27, 30, 32, 42, 45, 47, 295).

HARWOOD, MARGARET, serv. to John Swynyard, in Aug. 1729 was tried for bast., and again in Aug. 1733 (28:276; 30:71).

HARWOOD, RICHARD, on 6 June 1688 purch. Harwood's Hazard from John and Julian Bevans (59:271).

HARWOOD, Capt. THOMAS, master of the Golden Lyon, in July 1659 brought the Lord Proprietary's assent to 12 Laws of Maryland; in Nov. 1664 surv. 300 a. The Lyon or Harwood's Lyon on Gunpowder R.; this tract was later poss. by Richard Harwood (200-1:384; 211).

HARWOOD, Maj. THOMAS, in 1750 owned 300 a. The Lyon, and 36 a. Hazard (153:89).

HASE. See HAYES.

HASLEWOOD/HAZLEWOOD, HENRY (1), d. in Balto. Co. by 1693, having m. the wid. of John Collett; she later m. Miles Gibson, and then Richard Edmunds; in Nov. 1673, Henry Haslewood, "Gent.," and w. Elizabeth conv. 75 a. Hasle's Park to Rutgertson Garretts, and in Jan. 1676 they conv. 100 a. Collingham and 8 a. Haslewood's Retirement to John Ireland, chirurgeon; left iss.: HENRY; JOHN; and WILLIAM (100:300, 302, 303; 206-12:149).

HASLEWOOD, HENRY (2), s. of Henry (1) and Elizabeth, was bur. on his own plantation on 9 June 1699; admin. bond was posted 26 June 1699 by exec. James Ives, with Thomas Cord and Thomas Greenfield; will of Henry, 31 May 1699 - 19 July 1699, named Thomas Greenwood, Emanuel Seale and w. Sarah, Thomas Morris, Thomas Jackson, and Lodowick, s. of Thomas Martin; est. was inv. on 1 July 1699 by Greenfield and Thos. Cord, and val. at £ 81.19.11 plus 5391 lbs. tob. (13:211; 48:229; 121:179; 128:6).

HASLEWOOD, JOHN (3), s. of Henry (1), was bur. 2 April 1699 at the head of Musketa Creek; in Jan. 1696 he had been deeded prop. by his mother Elizabeth Gibson (20:550; 128:6).

HASLEWOOD, WILLIAM (4), prob. s. of Henry (1), was a taxable in Spesutia Hund. in 1692, and was bur. at Rumley Creek on 15 June 1698 (128:5; 138).

HASSELL, REUBEN, in June 1724 was named as the father of Sarah Bragg's child (26:330).

HASTINGS, JOHN, d. in Balto. Co., leaving a will, 24 Feb. 1723 - 5 May 1723, leaving entire est. to Rachel Johnson incl. personalty due from Isaac Butterworth; admin. bond was posted by Rachel Johnson on 5 June 1724 with William Lowe and John Balshar; est. inv. by Garrett Garrettson and Bennett Garrett and val. at £ 7.1.6 plus debts; est. admin. 2 June 1725 by Edward and Rachel Evans (3:34; 13:225; 51:215; 124:166).

HASTWELL, THOMAS, age 24, bricklayer from Friars, London, on 22 Jan. 1722 agreed to serve Christopher Veale, agent, for 4 yrs. in Md.; recorded in Balto. Co., 27 April 1725 (70:54).

HATCH, JOHN, m. by 3 July 1710 Sarah, admnx. of Edward Jones; on 7 Aug. 1723 John Hatch purch. 75 a. Arthur's Choice from Thomas and Sarah Richardson; had iss.: JAMES, b. 3 May 1716 (2:158; 69:313; 131).

HATCHMAN, THOMAS, innholder, was in Balto. Co. by 16 Sept. 1724 when he purch. Taylor's Mount from William and Martha Trew of Kent Co.; on 1 April 1725 he purch. 418 a. Martin's Choice from Richard Lenox; d. leaving a will, 4 Jan. 1734 - 20 Feb. 1734, naming w. Sarah as extx., dau. Martha (believed to be in Dublin, Ireland), half-bro. John Weasley (to have gold ring and seal); admin. bond was posted 20 Feb. 1734 by Sarah Hatchman with John Scott and John Weasley; had iss.: MARTHA (13:225; 69: 383; 70:77; 111:203).

HATHAWAY/HADAWAY/HADDAWAY, JOHN, Gent., was in Balto. Co. by 9 Feb. 168-(?) when he purch. 200 a. Little Marlow from Michael and Jane Judd; on 6 Aug. 1689 he sold 200 a. Hathaway's Hazard to Humphrey Jones; d. leaving a will, 17 March 1691/2 - 30 Aug. 1692, leaving his entire est. to George Smith; est. was inv. on 30 Dec. 1692 by William Osborn and George Grinnett and val. at £ 0.13.0 plus 9723 lbs. tob. in debts (48:324; 59:137, 298, 355).

HATHAWAY, ROLAND, was in Balto. Co. by Feb. 1664/5 when Richard Ball sold him 300 a. on Humphreys Creek; in Aug. 1666 he acquired 300 a. West Humphreys from Ball and sold it to Henry Goodricke of A. A. Co. on the same day; left a will, proved 6 Oct. 1667, naming w. Ursula, her dau. Margaret, and his sons Peter (to have land in Talbot Co.), and George,(to have land in Balto. Co.); had iss.: PETER; GEORGE (94; 120:45).

HATHERLY, JOHN, on 9 Nov. 1719 purch. 60 a. Vine's Fancy from William Vines (68:128).

HATTENPENNY, THOMAS, d. by 9 Aug. 1722, leaving a s. Thomas, who on that day was conv. tract Friendship by Nehemiah Hicks, who had it from his father William Hicks; had iss.: THOMAS (69:29).

HATTON, JOHN (1), of London, d. by 14 Dec. 1654, leaving iss.: JOHN; SARAH; SUSAN; HANNAH; HENRY, and SAMUEL, and THOMAS (120:72).

HATTON, JOHN (2), s. of John (1), made a will 14 Dec. 1654, naming his father John, bros. Thomas, Samuel, and Henry, and sisters Sarah and Susan; mentioned lands left him by his father John of London; his. bro., Thomas, of Tewkesbury, Glouc., pet. concerning his bro.'s est., which included lands Spry Hill and Mount Harmer; in April 1671 Thomas Howell, and James Frisby were appointed to inquire into what lands or tenements the said John died seised of; Hatton's est. was admin. by Francis Holland and John Brewer;

Samuel Hatton of Tal. Co. was atty. for bro. and heir Thomas of
Tewkesbury, Glouc. (120:72; 200-51:101, 362; 200-65:261).

HATTON, THOMAS (3), of John (1), was living in Tewkesbury,
Gloucestershire, Eng.; prob. not the Secretary of Maryland.

HATTON, SAMUEL (4), s. of John (1), imm. to Talbot Co., Md.,
c.1667; in 1674 was atty. for his bro. Thomas, of Tewkesbury,
Glouc., Eng.; ; was sued by James Stavely and Henry Stockett
c.1677/8 when he and his w. Elizabeth, the admnx. of (---) Gorsuch sued William Hemsley; on 11 March 1678/9 he and w. Elizabeth conv. 400 a. Persimmon Point to Miles Gibson (60:32; 200-
65:264; 200-67:390, 391, 433; 388).

THE JOHN HATTON FAMILY

HATTON, JOHN (5), no known rel. to any of the above, d. in
Balto. Co. in Nov. 1770; m. 1st, on 17 May 1733, Sarah Chaney;
m. 2nd on 16 Nov. 1765 Unity Welcher; she was b. Unity Coffee
and had m. John Welcher on 7 Aug. 1750; d. leaving a will, 14
Nov. 1770 - 29 Nov. 1770; est. admin. on 20 Dec. 1771 by Thomas
Hatton; will of wid. Unity, 21 April 1774 - 15 June 1774, named
ch. Benjamin Wilshire, Unity Wilshire, Nancy League, and Sarah
Hatton; ch. of John (prob. all by 1st w., except Sarah): THOMAS,
b. 11 Oct. 1735; ELIZABETH, m. Daniel Scott Watkins on 29 Dec.
1761; JOHN; ELIZABETH; ANNE, m. Robert Abercrombie; CHANEY;
AQUILA; MARY, m. 1st on 22 Aug. 1765 Richard Coleman, and 2nd
on 23 Dec. 1766 Jeremiah Croney; SARAH   (7:76; 112:159, 296;
131).

HAULAWAY. See HOLLOWAY.

HAULING, or HASLING, JONAS, d. by 4 Aug. 1736 when admin. bond
was posted by Patrick Lynch with Robert North and Thomas Todd
(13:229).

HAVEN, JOHN, schoolmaster, was in Balto. Co. by 1750 when he
owned 50 a. Knight's Increase; in April 1754 he and w. Elizabeth
sold the tract to John Wyatt (82:203; 153:69).

HAW, EDWARD, and JOHN HAW, were in Balto. Town by 11 June 1753
when they purch. 83 a. Milford from Samuel and Catherine Hooke
(82:15).

HAWKER, THOMAS, was in Balto. Co. by Sept. 1671 when he purch.
300 a. from John and Sarah Vanheeck (97).

THE HAWKINS FAMILY OF PLANTER'S DELIGHT

HAWKINS, JOHN (1), formerly of N. Y., was in Balto. Co. by
July 1658 when he and Thomas Goldsmith surv. 600 a. Planter's
Delight; d. by March 1670, evidently murdered, when Charles
James posted bond he would appear before the Lieut.-General in
St. Mary's Co. to prosecute the murderers; admin. bond was posted
10 May 1671 by John Damerell with Henry Ward and John Collier;
John Hawkins is not known to have had any ch., but he did have a
bro. and heir, Robert. (13:214; 94; 200-65:1; 211:5).

HAWKINS, ROBERT (2), bro. and heir of John (1), was a ropemaker
and came from London to settle his bro.'s est., by May 1673 when
he sold William Dunkerton and Thomas Overton 700 a. Colleton and
150 a. Tryangle, assigned by Richard and John Collett to the
said John Hawkins; on 6 Nov. 1672 purch. 500 a. Tryumph from John
Collett (63:26, 138; 96:348; Peter Wilson Coldham, Lord Mayor's
Court of London: Depositions Relating to Americans, 1641-1736
(Washington: National Genealogical Society, 1980).

THE HAWKINS FAMILY OF HAWKINS' HILLS AND HAWKINS' DESIRE

HAWKINS, JOHN (3), no known rel. to above, d. in A. A. Co. by
17 March 1676, having m. Mary (---); his will, 3 Feb. 1670 - 17
March 1676, named w. Mary, and these ch.: JOHN; JOSEPH, d. 1726;
ANNE, m. Charles Gorsuch on 15 d, 12, 1690; MATTHEW, d. 1705; and
THOMAS, d. 1715 (120:167; Reg. of West River Monthly Meeting, Soc.
of Friends : see 219-6).

HAWKINS, JOHN (4), s. of John (3), was a res. of A. A. Co.
on 9 Aug. 1684 when as "eld. son of John Hawkins of A. A. Co.,
dec.," he stated his father took up , (or purch.), Pole Almanack
Neck, which the younger Hawkins now sold to Henry Constable (59:
103).

HAWKINS, JOSEPH (5), s. of John (3), d. by 1726; m. by 1699
Elizabeth, wid. of Christopher Rowles of A. A. Co.; on 14 April
1705 was conv. 90 a. Brother's Kindness by his bro. Matthew; in
1723 he surv. 100 a. Hawkins Desire; d. leaving will, 7 Dec. 1725
proved 13 Jan. 1726/7 leaving 100 a. Hawkins' Desire to sons John
and Augustine (both under 18), son-in-law Josephus Murray and
the latter's daus. Ruth and Sarah Murray, children Jemima and
Elizabeth, and w. to have 90 a. Brother's Kindness; admin. bond
posted 8 Nov. 1726 by Joseph Beasman with Edward Roberts and John
Tye; est. admin. 12 Feb. 1732; Joseph and Elizabeth left iss.:
RUTH, m. Josephus Murray; SARAH, m. Morgan Murray; JEMIMA;
ELIZABETH, may have m. Joseph Beasman, since in 1740 as wid. Eliz.
Beasman she sold 90 a. Brother's Kindness; JOHN, b. 23 Dec. 1713,
and AUGUSTINE, b. 15 April 1721 (3:107; 13:218; 30:193, 194; 64:
12; 124:209; 134:19; 206-18:194; 207).

HAWKINS, MATTHEW (6), s. of John (3), d. c.1705 in Balto. Co.;
his will, 14 April 1705 - 24 April 1705, named bros. Joseph and
Thomas, his own sons Matthew and Augustine, daus. Mary, Anne,
Dinah, Anne and Rebecca, tracts 130 a. Hawkins' Hills and 160 a.
Greater Success; admin. bond was posted 31 May 1705 by exec. Jos-
eph Hawkins with John Landis and John Yates; est. inv. June 1705
by Jno. Israel and Edward Burman and val. at £ 46.9.10; est. ad-
min. 2 Dec. 1706 and 31 July 1708, and mentioned a claim from
Eng. against the est.; had iss.: MATTHEW, d. 1762; AUGUSTINE;
MARY, m. by 23 Sept. 1723 Thomas Noland; DINAH, m. by Sept. 1723
John Cole; ANNA, m. by Sept. 1723 Thomas Broad; REBECCA, d. unm.
in 1723 (2:119, 140; 13:212; 49:96; 69:209; 122:48).

HAWKINS, THOMAS (7), s. of John (3), was alive in 1713/4; m.
Elizabeth, dau. of Richard and Margaret Giles; d. leaving a will,
7 Aug. 1715 - 26 Nov. 1715, naming w. Elizabeth and three ch.:
Aaron, Joseph, and Ruth; admin. bond was posted 24 March 1715 by
Thomas Worthington, with Henry Hawkins, the wid. Elizabeth having
ren. the right to admin.; est. was inv. on 28 March 1716 by Richard Warfield and William Mackne, and val. at £ 21.8.2, and signed
by Eliza and Joseph Hawkins with Lance Todd and Sarah Brice; Thomas and Elizabeth had iss.: AARON, b. 11 March 1706; JOSEPH, b. 19
June 1708; RUTH, b. 7 Jan. 1713/4 (13:201; 52:3; 123:84).

HAWKINS, JOHN (8), s. of Joseph (5), was b. 23 Dec. 1713; m.
Mary, dau. of John Simkins by 2 Jan. 1733; in 1750 owned 160 a.
Mount Organ and Simkins Addition and 114 a. Isingley's Glade; had
iss.: PRISCILLA, b. 2 Jan. 1733; JOHN, b. 14 Feb. 1736; ELIZA-
BETH, b. 1 June 1738; JOSEPH, b. 11 Jan. 1739; MOSES, b. 10 Oct.
1742; REZIN, b. 21 Nov. 1743; RUTH, b. 6 June 1746; THOMAS, b. 8
June 1748; WILLIAM, b. 5 Oct. 1750; NICHOLAS, b. 28 March 1753
(127:224; 134:10, 11, 18, 22; 153:48).

HAWKINS, MATTHEW (9), s. of Matthew (6), d. in Balto. Co. by

11 Oct. 1762; m. Elizabeth, sis. of Thomas Francis Roberts, who
in Oct. 1745 conv. his 83 a. Roberts' Park to sis. Elizabeth Hawkins; in 1750 owned 150 a. Hawkins' Fancy; d. leaving a will, 26
Nov. 1760 - 11 Oct. 1762, naming w. Elizabeth, and these ch., all
b. in St. Pauls' Par.: ANNE, b. 14 April 1720, m. 1736 Thomas
Wheeler; ELIZABETH, b. 16 Aug. 1721; MARY, b. 15 Jan. 1723, m.
Leonard Pecaussi on 31 March 1746; ALLERIDGE, b. 15 March 1724;
SOPHIA, b. 9 March 1726/7; MATTHEW, b. 21 Aug. 1729; BENJAMIN, b.
17 Aug. 1731; WILLIAM, b. 17 Nov. 1733; ELIZABETH, b. 15 Feb.
1735/6; ABRAHAM; RUTH (87:196; 91:122; 111:146; 133:5, 6, 8, 13,
16, 31, 70; 153:95).

THE JOHN AND REBECCA HAWKINS FAMILY

HAWKINS, JOHN (10), no known rel. to above, d. 22 July 17133;
m. twice, the 2nd time to Rebecca, wid. of James Emison and of
James Cobb; d. leaving a will, 19 Nov. 1732 - 8 Aug. 1733, naming
s. John, dau. Ann Litton, w. Rebecca, and son-in-law James Cobb;
admin. bond was posted 13 Oct. 1733 by extx. Rebecca with Gregory
Farmer and Cornelius Paulson; est. admin. 1 Oct. 1734 and 22 July
1737; left iss.: JOHN; ANN, m. Thomas Litton (3:174, 246, 247;
13:234; 126:33; 128:75).

HAWKINS, JOHN (11), s. of John (10) by his unknown 1st w.;
m. 28 Dec. 1718 Rebecca Emison, dau. of James and Rebecca (---)
Emison; her mother m. 2nd James Cobb, and 3rd, John Hawkins (10
above); John, Jr., and Rebecca had: JOHN, b. 16 July 1721, prob.
d. young; ANN, b. 29 March 1724; JOHN, b. 13 May 1726; JOSEPH,
b. 23 April 1728; REBECCA, b. 23 Feb. 1729; JAMES, b. 31 July
1733; ELIZABETH, b. 6 Feb. 1735 (128:40, 48, 66, 75, 91).

THE HAWKINS FAMILY OF MARGARET'S MOUNT

HAWKINS, ROBERT (12), no known rel. to any of the above, d. in
Balto. Co. in 1761; m. Ann Preble on 15 Nov. 1709; m. 2nd Sarah
(---); 1st w. Ann was b. 8 Nov. 1689, dau. of Thomas and Mary
Preble; Mary, wid. of Thomas Preble, m. 2nd Archibald Buchanan;
in her will dated 17 Jan. 1732 she named her dau. Ann Hawkins
and granddau. Elizabeth Hawkins; Thos. Cullen of Balto. Co., in
his will of 4 Oct. 1731, named his godchildren, John, Mary, and
Elizabeth Hawkins, the children of Robert and Anne; in 1750 Robert
Hawkins owned 160 a. Margaret's Mount; his will of 1761 left 50
a. to w. Sarah, 50 a. to s. Robert, and named ch. John, William,
Thomas, Ann Renshaw, Elizabeth Gilbert, and Sarah Beaver; est.
of Robert Hawkins was admin. 30 Dec. 1762; ch. of Robert and
Anne: THOMAS, b. 25 Nov. 1712;: JOHN, b. 25 Feb. 1715, m. by
1733 Rebecca (---); ROBERT, twin, b. 27 Sept. 1717; ANN, twin, b.
27 Sept. 1717, m. Abraham Renshaw on 15 June 1738; MARY, b. Nov.
1721; ELIZABETH, b. 19 April 1724, m. Charles Gilbert on 27 Sept.
1744; WILLIAM, b. 20 Jan. 1726 (twin); SARAH, twin, b. 20 Jan.
1726, m. John Beaver on 19 Sept. 1749 (2:233; 4:370; 125:216;
126:32; 128:33, 34, 43,; 129:176, 269, 290, 338; 153; 210-31:417).

HAWKINS, THOMAS (13), s. of Robert (12), was b. 25 Nov. 1712;
m. Elizabeth Farmer on 24 Jan. 1731, and had iss.: SARAH, b. 10
Jan. 1732; GREGORY FARMER, b. 11 Jan. 1734; MARY, b. 14 Jan. 1736;
THOMAS, b. 27 Jan. 1740, d. 15 Feb. 1746; ROBERT, b. 16 Feb. 1742;
SAMUEL, b. 1 June 1745; THOMAS, b. 3 May 1747; MARTHA, b. 29 Jan.
1748 (128:74, 85, 98, 116; 129:325, 344, 346).

HAWKINS, ROBERT (14), s. of Robert (12), was b. 27 Sept. 1717,
d. 5 Nov. 1801; m. Lydia Crutchley on 13 Jan. 1742; rendered
patriotic service to Md. during the Rev.; had iss.: THOMAS, b.
1745; WILLIAM, b. 1749; ROBERT, b. 1751; RICHARD, b. 1753 (129:
269, 326; 277:180; 353).

THE RALPH HAWKINS FAMILY

HAWKINS, RALPH (15), no known rel. to any of the above, d. in
A. A. Co. after 10 Sept. 1699; m. Margaret (---) who may have m.
as her 2nd husb. James Kyle; surv. several tracts in A. A. Co.
which were later held by his s. William Hawkins of Patapsco in
Balto. Co.; these incl. 600 a. Hawkins, surv. Sept. 1652; 150 a.
Little Hawkins, surv. Sept. 1652, 100 a. Ralph's Neck surv. Feb.
1663; 100 a. Hawkins' Habitation, surv. Feb. 1653; Hawkins' will
named w. Margaret, and sons: WILLIAM; RALPH (poss. the Ralph
Hawkins named in the 1688 will of James Kyle) (120:49; 121:46;
211:231, 239).

HAWKINS, WILLIAM (16), prob. s. of Ralph (15), was in Balto.
Co. by 1679, and d. there by 18 July 1711; m. after 1676 Ann,
wid. of Stephen White, and sis. of John Rockhold; he surv. 100
a. Hawkins' Range in July 1679, 134 a. Hawkins' Choice in May
1680, and 203 a. Hawkins' Addition surv. Oct. 1695; William also
held 100 a. White's Addition for the orphans of Stephen White;
John Rockhold, of A. A. Co., in his will of 17 Feb. 1698 left
pers. prop. to his "cousins," (i.e., nephews) Stephen White and
William Hawkins, Jr.; admin. bond posted 18 July 1711 by admins.
Ann and William Hawkins, with Lancelot Todd and Stephen White; est.
was inv. on 11 Aug. 1711 by John Giles and Luke Reed and val. at
£ 169.6.7 and signed by Thomas Hawkins and Elizabeth Slade as kin
and by John Brice and John Rattenbury as creditors; est. admin.
on 1 Aug. 1712; William and Ann had iss.: WILLIAM, Jr.; poss.
THOMAS, fl.1711; poss. ELIZABETH, m. (---) Slade; poss. dau. m.
Edward Smith; poss. dau. m. Charles Baker, and poss. dau. m.
(---) White (1:357; 13:202, 302; 121:313; 122:195; 211:106; 346-
2:313; study of Hawkins fam. in William N. Wilkins Gen. Coll. at
Md. Hist. Soc.).

HAWKINS, WILLIAM (17), s. of William (16) and Ann; d. in
Balto. Co. by 5 April 1722; m. Ann (---) who m. 2nd Robert Emory;
in 1698 was left prop. by his uncle John Rockhold; admin. bond
posted 5 April 1722 with James Moss and Robert Marshall; William's
est. was admin. by said Moss and Marshall on 2 Nov. 1723; wid. Ann
was stated to have m. 2nd Robert Emory (1:100, 146; 13:245; 122:
185).

THE REBECCA HAWKINS FAMILY

HAWKINS, REBECCA (18), no known rel. to any of the above, had
iss.: NATHAN, b. 16 Nov. 1722 (133:18).

HAWKINS, NATHAN (19), s. of Rebecca (18), was b. 16 Nov. 1722;
m. Ruth Cole on 14 Feb. 1744; gave his age as 40 on 7 May 1764
when he mentioned his father-in-law James Boring, whose wid. m.
James Frazier (89:139; 131; 133:18).

HAWKINS, JANE, was ind. for bast. in Aug. 1715 (21:624).

HAWKINS, JOHN, serv. to John Thomas, in June 1695 was judged
to be age 16 (20:416).

HAWKINS, JOHN, m. Sarah (---), and had dau.: RACHEL, b. 21
March 1737 (129:301).

HAWKINS, JOHN, bapt. 12 June 1733, parents not named (133:28).

HAWKINS, JOHN, m. Mary Wells on 1 March 1741 (129:327).

HAWKINS, JOHN, in 1750 owned 100 a. Arabia Petrea (153:2).

HAWKINS, JOHN, d. by 21 May 1751, when admin. bond was posted by William Cox with N. Ruxton Gay (13:270).

HAWKINS, JOHN, in July 1752 purch. pt. Jones' Mistake from John and Margaret Baker (81:371).

HAWKINS, JOHN, alias "Hawksford" or "Oxford," age c.28, Irish, has been some time in the country; ran away from Amos Garrett of Balto. Co.; advert. in May 1747 (384:626).

HAWKINS, JOSEPH, in Aug. 1671 purch. 450 a. Dixon's Neck from Jane Dixon; in March 1671/2 appointed his kinsman Richard Therrell his atty. to conv. the said land to Thomas Long (97:126; 98:46).

HAWKINS, JOSEPH, m. Sarah McDaniel on 19 May 1744 (131).

HAWKINS, MARY, was named as a sis. of Joshua Wood of Balto. Co. in the latter's will, March 1749 (210-26:99).

HAWKINS, THOMAS, in 1750 owned 309 a. Bachelor's Good Luck (153:21).

HAWKINS, WILLIAM, m. by 18 Nov. 1722 Judith, extx. of George Hope (1:178).

HAYES, EDMUND (1), was m. to Mary Mencham by Nov. 1710; she was a minor in June 1699 when she was bound to Nathaniel Ruxton; in Sept. 1729 Edmund and Mary sold 100 a. Edmond's Camp to Thomas Pycraft; in June 1732 Edmund, Jr., and w. Mary conv. 100 a. of Abraham's Delight to Abraham Jarrett; in March 1741/2 Edmund Hayes pet. to be levy free; Edmund and Mary had iss.: MARY, b. 12 Jan. 1704; JOHN, b. 5 April 1708; EDMOND, b. 9 Sept. 1710; THOMAS, b. 16 Oct. 1712; ISAAC, b. 13 Oct. 1714; WILLIAM, b. 26 Aug. 1715; MARY, b. 2 Oct. 1718; ELEANOR, b. 9 May 1719; JAMES, b. 10 May 1721; ABRAHAM, b. 20 May 1722; JACOB, b. 2 April 1724; ELIZABETH, b. 14 Feb. 1726 (21:187; 33:304; 61:97; 73:247; 131:10/r, 38/r, and 40/r).

HAYES, EDMUND (2), s. of Edmund (1) and Mary, was b. 9 Sept. 1710; m. Elizabeth (---) by whom he had iss.: JOHN, b. 18 June 1731; MARY, b. 5 April 1733; ELIZABETH, b. 18 June 1735; MARTHA, b. 9 Dec. 1737; HANNAH, b. 23 July 1744 (128:99; 131:109/r).

HAYES, THOMAS (3), s. of Edmund (1) and Mary, was b. 4 Oct. 1712; prob. the Thomas Hayes who m. Mary Norrington on 11 Aug. 1735, and had iss.: JAMES, b. 21 Oct. 1738; EDMUND, b. 21 or 22 Nov. 1739; ELIZABETH, b. 12 Feb. 1745; MARY, b. 15 July 1747 (131:116/r, 117/r, 120/r).

HAYES, ABRAHAM (4), s. of Edmund (1) and Mary, was b. 20 May 1722; m. Fanny Lyttle after banns were pub., 21 Oct. 1744; she may be the Frances Little (sic), dau. of James and Elizabeth Little, b. 18 Sept. 1725 (128:57).

HAYES, EDMUND, m. Mary Smith in Nov. 1731 (131).

HAYES, EDMUND, m. Mary Bunnell on 8 Aug. 1751 (131).

HAYES, JOHN, was b. c.1663, giving his age as 60 in 1723; was in Balto. Co. by 4 Sept. 1686 when he purch. 100 a. Richardson's from Thomas Richardson; m. 1st by 28 May 1689 Abigail, wid. of Thomas Scudamor and dau. of John Dixon; on that day John Hayes and w. Abigail conv. 136 a., part of 420 a. Dickinson to Thomas Long, Gent.; on 2 July 1694 he surv. 317 a. Mount Hayes; on 6 Jan. 1699 Hayes conv. Dickinson to James Todd(who m. Penelope Scudamore, dau. of Hayes' w. Abigail by her 1st husb.); the deed

ment. Hayes' own dau. Jane; on 10 Oct. 1704 John Hayes was granted 130 a. Scudamore's Last, orig. surv. May 1687 for Thomas Scudamore; Hayes m. 2nd by 3 Aug. 1705 Elizabeth (---) who joined him
in conv. prop. to Richard Longland; the deed also ment. Hayes'
four daus., Jane, Avarilla, Elizabeth, and Jemima; on 5 Sept. 1705
Hayes and w. Elizabeth conv. 100 a. Longland's Purchase , part of
Privilege, to the same Richard Longland; Hayes admin. the est. of
John Oldton on 27 Feb. 1710 and 4 March 1712; in March 1716/7 was
prob. the John Hayes named by Dorothy Richards as the father of
her child, and in Aug. 1717 he was granted a license to keep an
ordinary; may have m. 3rd, by 10 June 1717, Mary, admnx. of Philip Johnson; on 11 Nov. 1719 Hayes conv. Mount Hayes, part of Privilege to Thomas Harris, agreeing that the dower rights of his
(3rd?) w. Mary Ann, would be excepted; on 1 Dec. 1719 Hayes gave
power of atty. to Mary Ann to ackn. sale of 370 a.; the will of
John Hayes, 9 Jan. 1726/7 - 30 Jan. 1726/7, left real est. to his
son (?)   John Stansbury, and pers. est. and 50 a. to his dau.
Elizabeth Lenox; admin. bond was posted 4 Dec. 1730 by Thomas
Stansbury with Thomas Harris, John Gregory, Mary Fitzpatrick and
Thomas Sheredine; dec. left iss.: JANE, b. c.1688, m. Thomas Stansbury; ELIZABETH, m. 1st John Lenox, and 2nd Luke Trotten; AVARIL-
LA; and JEMIMA (1:30; 2:126; 13:241, 368; 22:95, 130; 59:201, 296;
60:187; 63:418; 64:15; 68:12, 13; 69:305; 110:235; 211).

HAYES, JOHN, m. 31 Oct. 1727 Mary Crabtree, dau. of William
Crabtree, who on 4 June 1728 conv. his dau. Hayes 100 a. Crabtree's
Lot; had iss.: MARY, b. 7 Dec. 1728; ELIZABETH, b. 30 April 1731;
ANN, b. 12 Sept. 1733; JOHN, b. 19 Feb. 1735 (72:30; 128:61, 80,
91; 129:253).

HAYES, JOHN, in 1750 owned 125 a., part Uncle's Good Will (153:
87).

HAYES, JOHN, Irish, c. 26, servant, ran away from William Dallam, who advert. for his return in May 1741 (384:313).

HAYES, MARY ANN, in Aug. 1718 was allowed to have a bed, gun,
pot, laborer's tools, and such household equipment as necessary
for subsistence (23:3).

HAYES, THOMAS, m. Anne (---), and had iss.: SARAH, b. 2 March
1744 (135:1).

HAYWARD, JOSEPH, m. Rebecca, dau. of Jacob and Hannah Scott,
on 9 d, 6, 1757; d. by May 1779 when his est. was admin. by Rebecca Hayward; his will, 1 Feb. 1777 - 11 Aug. 1777, named w.
Rebecca, and ch.: WILLIAM; RACHEL; HANNAH; and SARAH (8:50; 112:
345; 136).

HAYWARD, WILLIAM, of A. A. Co., m. Sydney Pierpoint, dau. of
Charles and Sydney, on 29 d, 11m 1757 (136).

HAZLEWOOD. See HASLEWOOD.

HEAD, BIGGER, of Cal. Co., and w. Martha, dau. of Edward Butler of said co., conv. to William Andrew of Balto. Co., and his
s. Andrew Andrew, the land Back Lingan (79:1).

HEAP, SAMUEL, alias John Fisher, carpenter, age c.25, was a
runaway serv. from Stephen Onion, who advert. for his ret. in
March 1752 (385:169).

HEART, JOSEPH, m. Elizabeth (---), and had iss.: JOSEPH, in
Nov. 1754 bound to Thomas Griffin (39:442).

HEATH, JAMES (1), was in A. A. Co. by 5 March 1707 when he purch tract St. George from George Thompson of St. M. Co.; prob. the James Heath who d. in Cecil Co. leaving a will, 6 May 1731 - 31 Jan. 1731/2, in which he left w. Mary part The Holt and Tode's Purchase, also ment. nephew Charles Heath, dau.-in-law Mary Chetham, s.-in-law Edward Chetham, and s.: JAMES PAUL (59:655; 125: 212).

HEATH, JAMES PAUL (2), s. of James (1), d. in Cecil Co. having m. Rebecca (---); his will, 5 Sept. 1745 - 3 July 1746, named w. Rebecca, s. James (not yet 21), s. Daniel, poss. unborn ch., cous. Charles Heath, niece Mary Grafton, neph. John Ward, James Heath of Charles, nephs and nieces James and Susanna Chetham, and James and Mary Ward, directed his sons to be raised in the Roman Catholic faith; had iss.: JAMES (not yet 21); DANIEL (not yet 21); poss. unborn ch. (210-25:63).

HEATH, JAMES (3), s. of James Paul (2) is prob. the James Paul Heath listed in the 1750 Debt Book as owning 400 a. St. Georges; m. Susanna Hall on 25 Oct. 1759; d. in Balto. Co. leaving a will, 23 Nov. 1766 - 1 Dec. 1766, naming w. Susanna, uncle Daniel Dulany's s. Benjamin, uncle Walter Dulant's s. Daniel, Ann Dulany, dau. of uncle Daniel, tracts Holt and Joe's Purchase; admin. bond posted 9 June 1767 by Susanna Heath, with John Hall of Swan Town, Francis Holland, John Hall, Jr., and William Hall (13:282; 112:32; 129:369; 153:102).

HEATH, JAMES, age c.27, from Derbyshire, Eng., ran away from Balto. Co., and was advert. for in April 1759 (307:69:57).

HEATH, THOMAS, was in Balto. Co. by 1692 as a taxable in n. side of Gunpowder; on 3 Aug. 1697 Thomas and w. Sarah conv. 50 a. Hughes Island, 50 a. Blocksedge, and 115 a. Heath's Addition to Henry Matthews; d. leaving a will, 13 May 1698 - 8 June 1698, naming dau. Sarah as extx. and s. Titus, with Edm. Hensley, William Hortina, Catherine Lomax, Susanna Richardson, and Ann Richardson as witnesses; admin. bond was posted 10 July 1698 by Sarah Heath, with Francis Dallahide; est. was inv. on 18 June 1698 by said Dallahide and William Horne; had iss.: SARAH; TITUS (13:214; 48:59; 59:496; 61:154; 121:153; 138).

HEATHCOTE, NATHANIEL (1), came to Md. c.1670, with w. Elizabeth and six other persons whom he transp.; was in A. A. Co. by Oct. 1664 when Philip Allenby made him exec. of his will; in March 1678 surv. 500 a. Heathcoat Cottage in Balto. Co., which was later held by the orphans of Joseph Heathcote and especially by William Pickett who m. the heiress of Joseph; d. before 21 Feb. 1683 when his wid. Elizabeth made a will, proved 21 Feb. 1683, naming John and William Brewer, John Gresham and his s. John, Samuel Heathcote of Derby, Eng., and John, Barbara, Ruth, and Margaret Heathcote, as well as sis. Martha Willis and Capt. Thomas Francier (120:36; 121:152; 311; 388).

HEATHCOTE, JOSEPH (2), heir of Nathaniel (1), but rel. is not clear, inherited Heathcote's Cottage; was in Balto. Co. by 1692 as a taxable in n. side Patapsco Hund.; m. Martha, dau. of Thomas Morgan; she m. 2nd Nicholas Fitzsimmons; he d. by 3 April 1693 when admin. bond was posted by admnx Martha Heathcote alias Fitzsimmons, with William Wilkinson and Nicholas Corbin; est. was inv. on 8 April 1793 by said Wilkinson and Corbin and val. at £ 187.7.0; est. was admin. by Fitzsimmons on 30 July 1694 and 6 Nov. 1694; his orphans owned 500 a. Heathcote's Cottage, orig. surv. in March 1678 for Nathaniel Heathcote, and Nicholas Fitzsimmons held 15 a. Hopewell for Joseph's orphans; had iss.: dau., m. William Pickett; poss. SAMUEL; RUTH, m. by Jan. 1752 Luke Trotten (13:208; 20:116,

152; 138; 206-10:301; 206-13A:195, 196; 211; 210-28:237).

HEATHCOTE, SAMUEL (3), poss. s. of Joseph (2), d. by 3 June 1718 when admin. bond was posted by Luke Trotten with John Eager and Edward Mahy; est. was inv. by Trotten and val. at £ 18.0.0; est. was admin. 29 July 1718 (2:17; 13:224; 50:263).

HEATHCOTE, JOHN (4), called "the true and legal heir of Nathaniel Heathcote of A. A. Co.," d. leaving a will, 19 Feb. 1722/3 - 6 April 1723, in Cecil Co., leaving 500 a. Heathcote Cottage to his w. Sylvia; on 11 Dec. 1727, wid. Sylvia, now w. of John Dorsey of Cecil Co., conv. Heathcote's Cottage to John Baldwin and John Rumsey (71:82; 124:143).

HEATON, JOHN, was b. c.1743, and was alive in 1776 in Deer Creek Lower Hund., with w. Rebecca (---), b. c.1743, and ch.: MARGARET, b. c.1765; SARAH, b. c.1767; THOMAS, b. c.1769; JOHN, b. c.1772; JAMES, b. c.1775 (285:95).

HEDENTON, JAMES, was in Balto. Co. by 1692 as a taxable in Spesutia Hund. (138).

HEDGE, THOMAS (1), poss. bro. of Samuel, Mary, and Henry Hedge, was transp. with them c.1673; by Sept. 1683 was in Balto. Co. when he surv. 254 a. Benjamin's Choice (later held by his heirs); was clerk of Balto. Co., and in 1696 was accused by Col. Thomas Richardson of having one w. in Eng. and another one in Md,; in March 1682 conv. Roger Matthews 100 a. Miles' End, which Hedge had purch. from Miles Gibson; in Nov. 1686 conv. 100 a. Common Garden to Wm. Osborne; on 1 Nov. 1692 he conv. 140 a. Prosperity to Peter Bond; in Aug. 1694 with w. Ann he conv. 140 a. Prosperity to John Hall, and on 6 Nov. 1694 conv. to his s. Henry Hedge these tracts: 100 a. Mate's Neck, 140 a. part Common Garden, 46 a. Broad Street, and two parcels in Rumley Creek; d. by 7 July 1698 when admin. bond was posted by admin. Thomas Hedge with Samuel Sickelmore and Thomas Smith, who inv. the est. on 16 May 1698, and val. it at £ 40. 13.6½, plus £ 689.12.8; an additional inv. was filed 1698; est. was admin. by Thomas Hedge in Jan. 1699; left iss.: THOMAS; HENRY; poss. SAMUEL (2:49; 13:212; 50:231, 233, 240, 349; 59:31, 195, 296, 353, 414, 435; 200-20:507; 211; 388).

HEDGE, HENRY (2), poss. bro. of Thomas (1) and Mary and Samuel Hedge, with whom he was transp. by 1673 (388).

HEDGE, MARY (3), poss. sis. of Thomas (1), Henry (2), and of Samuel Hedge; transp. c.1673 (388).

HEDGE, SAMUEL (4), poss. bro. of Thomas (1), Henry (2), and Mary (3); was in Md. c.1675 in A. A. Co.; in June 1676 purch. 640 a. Sprye's Inheritance from Miles Gibson; by Aug. 1682 was in Fenwick Colony, West New Jersey, when he and w. Ann, by virtue of a power of atty. to Thomas Hedge, conv. 640 a. Sprye's Inheritance to Henry Johnson (59:16; 62:312; 388).

HEDGE, THOMAS (5), s. of Thomas (1), d. by 27 Feb. 1708; on 1 May 1703 purch. 100 a. Copus' Harbor from Thomas Copus, s. and and heir of John, and Thos. Copus' wife Jane; in Feb. 1704 purch. 50 a. Long Island Point from Richard Owens; admin. bond was posted Feb. 1708 by admin. John Ensor with William Tibbitt and Hugh Jones (13:219; 60:135, 168).

HEDGE, HENRY (6), s. of Henry (1), was conv. 100 a. Mates' Neck, 140 a. Common Garden, and other land by his father Thomas; m. Mary Parker after the banns were pub. on Whitsunday 1700; she m. 2nd John Smith, on 2 Feb. 1709/10; Henry d. 25 Feb. 1708/9;

admin. bond was posted 23 July 1709 by Mary Hedge with Martin
Taylor and John Parker; est. was inv. 15 Aug. 1709 by Thomas
Busham and David Thomas and val. at £ 90.17.7; est. was admin.
25 Oct. 1711 by Mary now w. of John Smith; dec. left iss.:
CLEMENCY, b. 14 Aug. 1704 ; MARY, b. 3 Nov. 1706, d. 1720;
HENRY, b. 18 Jan. 1708, d. 1720 (1:378; 13:206; 21:403; 48:107;
59:435; 128:19, 25, 26, 58; 129:191, 208; 138).

HEDGE, SAMUEL (7), prob. s. of Thomas (1), was in Salem Co.,
West Jersey by June 1724 when he sold 180 a. Mate's Neck, Broad
Street, and Common Garden to Roger Matthews; on 31 May 1728, still
in Salem Co., he sold 254 a. Benjamin's Choice to Roger Matthews;
placed as a s. of Thomas (1) because of the above deeds, but could
poss. have been a s. of Samuel (4), since both moved to New Jersey (69:358; 71:169).

HEDGE, BARTHOLOMEW, was in Balto. Co. by 1692 as a taxable in
Spesutia Hund. (138).

HEEL, JONATHAN, was in Balto. Co. by 1692 as a taxable in s.
side Patapsco Hund. (138).

HEIGHE, SAMUEL, m. Sarah, relict of John Israel by 27 July
1727 (2:258; 3:40; 23:29; 71:29).

HELDEBROAD, DEOWALD, m. Mary Pickett on 18 July 1753 (131).

HELEMS, WILLIAM, was in Balto. Co. by 1750 when he owned 100
a. Ardington Adventure (153:30).

THE HELM FAMILY has been discussed in: Robert L. Brownfield
and Rex Newlon Brownfield, "Helm Family of Lancaster County,
Pennsylvania," typescript at the Maryland Historical Society in
Baltimore.

HELM, LEONARD (1), progenitor, d. in Frederick Co., Va., having made a will, probated 5 Dec. 1745, naming these ch.: MEREDITH,
d. 1768 near Winchester, Va., having m. and had iss.: LEONARD;
MAYBERRY; JOSEPH; CHRISTOPHER, and BRIDGET (Brownfield).

HELM(S), MAYBERRY (or ABRAHAM) (2), s. of Leonard (1), was in
Balto. Co. by 1735; d. there by 10 Aug. 1790; m. by 1735 Ann, wid.
of (---) Puntany and dau. of Edward Parrish; in 1750 he owned 263
a. Parrish's Fear; Anne d. leaving a will, 8 March 1776 - 3 May
1776, naming her f. Edward Parrish, her s. Edward Puntany, grandson Edward Puntany of William, granddau. Ann Puntany, granddau.
Ann Helms of John, dau. Mary w. of John McClellan, and the latter's
s. William; Mayberry Helm died leaving a will, 7 Sept. 1789 - 10
Aug. 1790, naming dau. Mary, w. of John McClennan, grandson John
Helms of John, granddau. Mary w. of Lewis Lubies, granddau. Ann
Helm, s. Mayberry and his sons Mayberry and John, granddau. Eliza-
beth w. of George Litzinger, grands. John McClennan, Jr., s. Leon-
ard and his sons James and Joseph, granddau. Ann Ernest, w. of
Caleb Ernest, grandson John Helm of John, grandson William Helm
of Leonard, granddaus. Ann and Elizabeth McClennan, daus. of John
McClennan, Sr., granddaus. Mary Helm of Leonard and Mary Helm of
Mayberry, grandsons Thomas and Stephen Helms, granddaus. Sarah,
Mary, Pleasant, and Rebecca Helm of Mayberry, and John Howard Puntany, s. of Mary Howard and John Puntany; Mayberry and Ann had
iss.: MAYBERRY, b. 12 Aug. 1735, m. and had iss.; LEONARD, b. c.
1738; JOHN, b. c.1736, m. and had iss.; MARY, m. John McClennan
or McClellan (112:324; 113:487; 133:58; 153:61).

HEMPY. See HAMBY.

HEMSLEY, SAMUEL, d. by 19 July 1753 when his est. was admin.
by Jacob Giles (5:284).

HEMSTEAD, NICHOLAS, d. in Balto. Co. leaving a will, 15 Nov.
1690 - 2 Dec. 1690, directing his w. (unnamed) to proceed in
law w. Thomas Thurston; his wid. Elizabeth was grandmother of
Enoch Spinke and d. leaving a will made 9 Dec. 1690, naming
Enoch Spink and his sis. Sarah, the unborn ch. of Eliz. Waly, Mary
Sims, and Thomas Thurston, father of aforesaid Eliz. Waly; admin.
bond was posted 3 Feb. 1691/2 by Robert Love with Samuel Sickelmore, John Fuller, Thomas Smith, and John Hathaway; her est. was
inv. in 1691 by Moses Groome and Samuel Sickelmore and val. at
Ł 25.10.7 (13:205; 59:332; 66:159; 206-10:494; 123:238; 110:137;
12:305).

HENCHMAN, NATHANIEL, was transp. to Md. c.1665; m. by 1677/8
Ann (---); m. 2nd Margaret (---); his will, 20 Oct. 1694 - 17
Dec. 1695, named Benjamin Bowen as exec., and also named Benjamin
Bowen of Jonas the iss. of his w. Margaret, Lawrence Wolden,
Samuel Evans, s. of Amos Evans, friend Mary Green, wid., Rebecca
Bowen of Jonas; Jonas Bowen was to be overseer for the exec., who
was not yet 18; est. was inv. on 8 Feb. 1695 by John Thomas and
Charles Merryman and val. at Ł 46.13.11; est. was admin. by Jonas
Bowen in Sept. 1696; payments were made to Rebecca Bowen, Law-
rence Walden, Amos Evans, and Mary Green (200-67:425; 206-14:
29, 151; 210-7:204; 388).

HENDERSON, THOMAS (1), m. Mary Frisby on 14 Aug. 1729 in A.
A. Co.; they had at least one s.: THOMAS FRISBY (219-4:103).

HENDERSON, THOMAS FRISBY (2), s. of Thomas (1) and Mary, m.
Hannah, wid. of George Hollandsworth, on 19 Sept. 1757; they had
at least two ch.: FRANCIS, b. 17 March 1759; CORDELIA, b. 16 Jan.
1761 (129:380).

HENDERSON, JOHN, d. by 14 Dec. 1720 when his est. was inv.
by Benjamin Bowen and John Hillen, val. at Ł 35.17.0, and approved
by Thomas Long, George Newport, and Thomas Sheredine; est. was admin. by Charles Merryman, Jr., on 5 Feb. 1721, and by Merryman's
extx. Jane, now w. of Benjamin Knight on 12 or 22 Aug. 1729 (1:
70; 2:272; 51:341).

HENDERSON, MARY, d. by March 1755 with Greenbury Dorsey as
her admin.; est. was admin. by Dorsey on 27 Sept. 1759 (4:263;
40:165).

THE HENDON FAMILY is discussed more fully in: George H. Chancey, "The Hendons from Gunpowder River," typescript at the Maryland Historical Society, Baltimore.

HENDON, JOSIAS (1), bro. of Richard, was in Balto. Co. by 8
Feb. 1719 when he was named in the will of Nicholas Rogers; in
1722 he was granted 100 a. called Hab Nab at a Venture; m. c.
1723 Hannah, dau. of William and Elizabeth Robinson; on 15 Feb.
1730 Simon Pierson, "for love, good will, and affection," conv.
to Josias Hendon the land he had purch. from Thomas Ramsey; Josias
d. leaving a will, 1 May 1738 - 7 June 1738, naming his w. and
"all his ch." incl. sons Isham and William; admin. bond was posted by extx. Hannah Hendon on 26 June 1738 with John Elliott and
Thomas Hutchings; est. admin. 22 July 1740 by Hannah Hendon; her
will, 29 Jan. 1748 - 8 March 1748; ch. of Josias and Hannah:
WILLIAM, b. 1 Dec. 1723; ELIZABETH, m. Jacob Johnson on 25 Feb.
1749; ISHAM, b. 1725; HANNAH, b. 31 Oct. 1727; JAMES, d. 1791 in
Wake Co., N.C., having m. Hannah Norris on 7 Feb. 1754; JOSIAS,
m. in Balto. Co. and then moved to Anson Co., N.C. (4:31; 13:231;
73:95; 110:442; 126:252; 131).

HENDON, RICHARD (2), bro. of Josias (1), m. Sarah, dau. of
Robert Gardner on 8 June 1723; in Aug. 1740 was ind. for begetting

a child on the body of Ann Brogden; in 1750 owned 50 a. Cherry
Garden and 100 a. Avarilla's Garden; in 1766 he sold the land his
w. had inher. from her father to Edmund Stansbury; his will, 25
April 1768 - 6 June 1768, named w. Sarah, dau. Lydia, sons Richard and Henry, two ch. (Benjamin and Dinah) of s. Joseph; admin.
bond was posted 6 June 1768 by Richard and Henry Hendon, with
George Crudgington and Geo. Counselman; est. was admin. on 5 April 1769; Richard and Sarah had iss.: LYDIA, b. 7 Aug. 1725, m.
her cousin William Hendon on 11 Nov. 1749; JOSEPH, b. 7 March
1728; SARAH, b. 27 May 1730, m. Mark Guishard; PRUDENCE, b. 27
Oct. 1732, m. Sutton Sickelmore on 29 July 1762; RICHARD, b. 30
Nov. 1734; JOSIAS, b. 7 June 1739; HENRY, m. Mary Westfield on
1 Aug. 1773; JEMIMA, m. John Wright on 4 May 1762 (13:280; 32:
290, 366; 112:86; 131; 133:153:31).

HENDON, WILLIAM (3), s. of Josias (1), was b. 1 Dec. 1723, m.
Lydia Hendon, dau. of Richard, on 11 Nov. 1749; in 1750 owned 170
a. Isham's Garden; in 1757 moved to Bladen Co., N.C., where he d.
(153:7; Chancey).

HENDON, ISHAM (4), s. of Josias (1), was b. c.1725, m. Keziah
Johnson on 27 Feb. 1749; on 7 June 1753 Isham and Keziah conv.
his interest in Leafe's Chance and William the Conqueror to Steph-
en Onion; moved to Bladen Co., and then to Wake Co., N.C., where
he d. 1804 (82:8; Chancey).

HENDON, JOSEPH (5), s. of Richard (2), was b. 7 March 1728; d.
by 10 March 1760 having m. Mary Crudgents. or Crudgenton on 31
July 1753; his will, 31 Jan. 1760 - 10 March 1760. named w. Mary
and ch. Benjamin and Dinah; admin. bond was posted 28 April 1760
by Mary Hendon with Henry Bennett Darnall and Thomas Gittings;
est. was admin. 8 June 1761 by w. Mary, now m. to William Lynch;
had iss.: DINAH, b. c.1754; PENJAMIN, b. c.1756 (4:346; 13:307;
111:280; 131. Chancey).

HENDRESS, ADAM, m. Ruth Sutton after the banns were pub. in
Sept. and Oct. 1744 (131).

HENDRICKSON, HENRY (1), was in Balto. Co. by 4 April 1741
when he purch. 70 a. Duke's Palace from Christopher Duke; on 6
March 1743 he purch. 200 a., one-half of Richardson's Neglect,
from William and Mary Andrew; may have been the f. of: ADAM (75:
470; 77:424).

HENDRICKSON, ADAM (2), poss. s. of Henry (1), in 1750 owned 70
a. of Duke's Palace (153:54).

HENDRICKSON, BARTHOLOMEW, or BARTLETT, Swedish, from New Amstel, was granted denization in Md. in 1661, and claimed land
for bringing himself, Sindrick Hendrickson, Andreas Mullika and
John Jorgenson into Md. in the same year; in 1664 brought his w.
Margaret Anguette and her mother Angueth Poulson into Md.; in
1668 bought Cock Crow Thrice on the n. side of Sassafras R.; later
moved to Cecil Co. (379).

HENDRICKSON, GARRETT, m. by 26 Feb. 1759 Mary Jackson (131).

HENDRICKSON, HENDRICK, was granted denization in Md. in 1661;
in 1662 he and w. Juniber conv. land to William Howard, 50 a.
Hendrick and 50 a. Hendrickson; later he was in Cecil Co. (379).

HENDRICKSON, JNO., m. Ruth Sing on 16 Oct. 1748 (131).

HENESSLY, JOHN, servant, with 22 mos. to serve in the 1721
inv. of John Webster, Jr. (51:334).

HENLY, EDWARD, m. Mary (---), and had iss.: JAMES, b. 3 Dec. 1716 (131).

HENLEY, JEREMIAH, m. by March 1723/4 Honour, relict of Henry Donahue (26:204).

HENLEY, JOSEPH, in 1750 owned 34 a. Henley's Enlargement, and 92 a. Bachelor's Good Luck (153:75).

HENLEY, PETER, m. Mary Wild on 7 June 1761 (129:371).

HENRY, JOHN, m. Mary Copeland on 10 Feb. 1757; d. in Balto. Co., leaving a will, 4 June 1767 - 17 Dec. 1770, naming his sisters Gennet, Margaret, Mary, and Frances, his w. Mary, and cous. Archibald Beatty; his wid. Mary's will, 21 Nov. 1773 - 6 Dec. 1773, named her sons George and John Copeland (112:157, 239; 131).

HENSHAW, (---), in 1756 was mentioned as a neighbor of Robert Wilkinson of Patapsco R., as having a bro. Thomas at the White Horse in the Mincrel, London (300-65:261).

HENSWORTH, RICHARD, was in Balto. Co. by July 1664 when Philip Stevenson assigned his interest in a patent to him (93).

HENTHORN, JAMES, and w. Mary were in Balto. Co. by April 1745 when they conv. 100 a. Providence to Jacob Hoak, weaver (79:49).

HENTHORN, JOHN, and w. Margaret, conv. 100 a. Providence to James Henthorn, and 272 a. of the same tract to Mathias Smyser on 3 May 1745 (77:688, 690).

HENTS, CONRAD, runaway Dutch serv. from Stephen Onion, was advert. for in July 1754 (385:293).

HEPBOURNE, JAMES, was in Balto. Co. by March 1672/3 when Thomas Howell conv. him 200 a. of land (98).

HERBERT, ELEANOR, was in Balto. Co. by Oct. 1694 when she surv. 146 a. Herbert's Care; in May 1703 she surv. 50 a. Addition to Herbert's Care (207; 211).

HERBERT, NICHOLAS, was in Balto. Co. by April 1705 when John and Sarah Fuller conv. 200 a. of land to him; in Dec. 1705 Nicholas and w. conv. John's Interest to James Isham; d. by April 1713 and admin. bond was posted 7 May 1713 by John Fuller with William Wright and James Durham; est. was inv. on 12 Jan. 1713/4 by Archibald Rowles and James Isum and val. at £ 43.11.0½ (13:200; 50:254; 64:57; 67:1; 131).

HERBERT, WILLIAM, and w. Mary were in Balto. Co. by 13 May 1699 when they conv. 210 a. incl. Ball's Addition, Bennett's Addition, and Thomas' Range, to Nicholas Fitzsimmons (66:21).

HERBERT, WILLIAM, m. Eliz. Inchmore on 28 Nov. 1756 (131).

HERIN, JOHN, was in Balto. Co. by 1692 as a taxable in s. side of Patapsco Hund. (138).

HERLY, EDWARD, m. Mary (---), and had iss.: JAMES, b. 3 Dec. 1716 (see also HENLEY) (131).

HERMAN, AUGUSTINE. See HERRMAN, AUGUSTINE.

HERNLEY, DARBY (1), leased part of Gunpowder Manor in 1728, and had iss.: DARBY (389).

HERNLEY, DARBY (2), s. of Darby (1), in 1736 leased 100 a.
of Gunpowder Manor for the lifetimes of three of his ch., all
of whom had gone to Carolina by 1763; in Oct. 1742 John Holloway
conv. him prop. "for love and affection;" had iss.: DARBY, b. 4
May 1733; EDMUND, b. 20 March 1735, m. Lettice Wetherall on 17
Sept. 1759; ELIZABETH, b. 12 July 1737; JOHN, b. 20 July 1739; W
WILLIAM, b. 2 Feb. 1741(77:31; 131; 389).

HEROD, SUSANNA. See HARRIOTT.

HERRINGTON/HARRINGTON, CORNELIUS (1), was in Balto. Co. by
1695 as a taxable in n. side Gunpowder Hund.; surv. 50 a. Seneca
Ridge; surv. 50 a. Rosindale or Robindale on 22 March 1697;
surv. 50 a. Herrington's Inheritance on 9 April 1715; m. Rachel.
dau. of Thomas Jones on 25 April 1701; m. 2nd, by 7 Nov. 1718
Elizabeth (---) who joined him in the sale of Herrington's Inheritance to Jeremiah Downes; on 7 Aug. 1717 conv. 50 a. Seneca Ridge
to James Isam; had iss.: JACOB; KATHERINE, m. Samuel Sickelmore
on 12 Sept. 1716; ISAAC, b. 5 May 1701; WEALTHY, b. 17 Aug. 1718
(63:509; 66:105; 78:90; 131; 140; 207).

HERRINGTON, JACOB (2), s. of Cornelius (1) and Elizabeth; m.
Hannah, dau. of Daniel and Frances Johnson on 26 Oct. 1720;
on 18 July 1727 was conv. all the prop. of Cadwallader Jones with
the understanding that he would support Jones, and the latter's
ch. Frances and Avarilla; on 12 March 1744/5 as s. and heir of
Cornelius, gave quitclaim on Seneca Ridge to James Isham; moved
to York Co., Penna., where he seems to have d. by 1761; had iss.:
HANNAH, b. 31 March 1723, m. William Morton of York Co., Va.;
MARY, b. 30 Nov. 1725; ABRAHAM, b. 7 April 1726; ISAAC, b. 30
Nov. 1727; ANN, b. 13 May 1729, m. Thomas Lawson on 20 July 1749;
JACOB, b. 20 Aug. 1730; THOMAS, b. 18 Feb. 1732; SARAH, b. 2 Ap-
ril 1735 (71:1; 78:90; 128:46, 59, 85).

HERRINGTON, ISAAC (3), s. of Jacob (2) and Hannah, was b. 30
Nov. 1727; moved to York Co., Penna., where he was living in
1761; on 18 June 1761 Isaac and w. Jane conv. to Aquila Duly, s.
and heir of William Duly, 100 a. Mary's Delight in Balto. Co.;
on 30 June 1761 Herrington and w. Jane conv. 81 a. Bulford, orig.
granted to Jacob Herrington, to Daniel Eshelman (85:179, 362).

HERRINGTON, CHARLES, was in Balto. Co. by 1694 as a taxable in
n. side of Gunpowder Hund. (139).

HERRINGTON, JAMES, was in Balto. Co. by 1694 as a taxable in
s. side Patapsco Hund. (139).

HERRINGTON, JOHN, was in Balto. Co. by 1692 as a taxable in
s. side Patapsco Hund. (138).

HERRINGTON, SARAH, was ind. for bast. in June 1734, and tried
in Nov. 1734, naming Thomas Little as the father; was ind. again
in June 1743 and tried in Aug. 1743; had iss.: HANNAH, b. 17 Oct.
1735; SARAH, b. 15 April 1739 (30:253, 365; 34:186; 35:15; 128:
90, 116).

HERRINSHAW, RUTH, was ind. for bast. in Nov. 1733 and tried in
March 1733/4 (30:124, 198).

HERRMAN, AUGUSTINE, merchant, late of Manhattan, in Jan. 1660/1
was granted a patent of denization with rights of residence and
trade; his first will, made 24 May 1661, named ch. Ephraim Georgius and Casparus, to have land incl. Bohemia Manor; his second
will, made 8 Nov. 1665, named ch. Ephraim Georgius, Casparus,

Anna Margarita, Judith, and Francina, w. Johanna Varlett and bro.-
in-law Nicholas Varlett, sis.-in-law Judith Varlett, and Nicholas
Varlett's son-in-law Nicholas Bayard; dec. m. 1st Johanna Varlett
who was ment. in will as dec. w.; m. 2nd Mary (---) who was transported c.1671; had iss.: CASPAR; EPHRAIM GEORGE; FRANCES (or
FRANCINA), m. Joseph Wood; ANNA MARGARITA, m. 1st Henry Ward,
and 2nd Matthias Vanderheyden; and JUDITH, m. John Thompson (94;
120:17; 370; 388; 404).

HERSEY, ANDREW, was in Balto. Co. by 1750 when he owned 600
a. The Golden Grove (153:91).

HERSEY, CHRISTIAN, was in Balto. Co. by 1750 when he owned
400 a. Hersey's Mount (153:92).

HESSY. See HISSEY.

HEVES. See HUGHES.

HEWES. See HUGHES.

HEWETT/HUETT, (---), m. by Nov. 1721, Mary, dau. of Thomas
Williamson (23:626).

HEWETT, CHARLES, was in Balto. Co. by 1694 as a taxable in n.
side Gunpowder Hund.; was described by Edward Boothby in 1697 as
an elderly man familiar with Indian ways who had given Boothby
some valuable information on Indian activities; he was still living in March 1716/ when he was treated for distemper at the county's charge; his w. Anne is also ment. in court records (22:91,
92; 134; 340:115-118).

HEWETT, RICHARD, was in Balto. Co. by June 1727 when William
and Elizabeth Lyall conv. him 100 a. Stone's Delight; d. by 8
Feb. 1729 having m. Elizabeth, wid. of (---) Frazier; she m. 3rd
Benjamin Price; will of Richard Hewett, 3 Nov. 1729 - 28 Feb.
1729/30, named dau. Mary, w. Elizabeth, son-in-law and dau.-in-
law John and Eliz. Frazer, Charles Ridgely, John Flaman, goddau.
Eleanor Powel, John Ridgely and John's sis. Pleasance, Henry
Butler's son, and his own mother Elizabeth Hewett; admin. bond
was posted 8 Feb. 1729/30 by Elizabeth Hewett and Charles Ridgely with Joseph Thurman and Robert Ridgely; a second bond was
posted 7 Sept. 1732 by Charles Ridgely; est. was admin. by Ridgely on 17 Feb. 1737 and 17 Oct. 1737; payments were made to Elizabeth, wid. of Robert Hewett; dec.'s wid. Elizabeth now w. of Benjamin Price, dau. Eleanor w. of James Powell, Adam Butler s. of
Henry; dec. had iss.: ELEANOR, m. James Powell; MARY, b. 9 Sept.
1724, m. Samuel Tipton (3:141, 225, 250, 252; 13:238, 242; 71:9;
125:149; 133:9; 231-WG#65:161).

HEWETT, ROBERT, d. by 1729 when his est. was inv. (51:233).

HEWLING, JONAS; m. 20 Dec. 1732 Ann Bowen; d. by 12 July
1736 when his wid. Ann conv. prop. to her s. Patrick Lynch;
his est. was admin. by Patrick Lynch (3:248; 74:417; 133:150).

HEYBORN, JAMES, of Balto. Co., imm. c.1668 (388).

HICKMAN, SUSANNAH, in Aug. 1709 was ind. for bast. (21:50).

HICKS, WILLIAM (1), d. in Balto. Co. in 1710; was in Balto.
Co. by 6 June 1693 when he purch. 200 a. part Friendship from
Michael and Jane Judd; on 24 April 1706, Wm., Jane, and James
Hicks wit. the will of Israel Skelton; he admin. the est. of
Thomas Smith on 5 July 1708, and the est. of John Parker on

the same day; d. leaving a will, 11 Nov. 1710 - 30 Dec. 1710, naming w. Jane as extx., and leaving land equally to sons William, James, Nehemiah, and Henry; admin. bond was posted 30 Dec. 1710 by Jane Hicks, with Jere. Downes and Wm. Hicks; est. was admin. by Jane Hicks on 1 Aug. 1712; she is prob. the Jane Hicks who m. Thomas Cutchin on 28 Oct. 1713; William and Jane had iss.: WILLIAM; JAMES; NEHEMIAH; and HENRY (2:21, 87, 21; 3:185; 13:210; 59:373; 122:74, 185, 187; 131).

HICKS, WILLIAM (2), s. of William (1) and Jane; m. Ann (---); on 14 May 1730 as eld. s. and heir of William Hicks, dec., he was living in Kent Co., Del., when he sold 400 a. to Erick Erickson; had at least one s.: WILLIAM, b. 10 March 1714 (72:296; 131).

HICKS, JAMES (3), s. of William (1), d. by 4 April 1732, having m. Margaret, wid. of (---) Standifer; admin. bond on his est. was posted on above date by William Standifer, admin. (the wid. Margaret having ren. the right to admin. in favor of her s., William Standifer), with Samuel Deeson and Thomas Johnson; est. was admin. by William Standiford (sic), on 16 Aug. 1734 (3:176; 13:232).

HICKS, NEHEMIAH (4), s. of William (1), d.1769; m. on 12 June 1725 Philizanna Hitchcock, dau. of William; in 1750 he owned 100 a. Timber Hall and 100 a. Haile's Forest; d. leaving a will, 7 Sept. 1769 - 2 Oct. 1769, named w. Philizanna and ch.: Abraham, Jacob, Mary, William, Isaac, Rebecca, Nehemiah, Philizanna, John, Margaret, and Sarah, as well as two servants John Mayes and Thos. Lacey; had iss.: MARY, b. 13 Dec. 1726 or 1727; WILLIAM, b. 14 Jan. or June 1728; ISAAC, b. 3 or 5 Jan. 1729/30; PHILIZANNA, b. 23 May 1737, m. John Cross on 28 Jan. 1753; REBECCA, b. 4 April 1731, m. Stephen Price on 20 April 1749; ELIZABETH, b. 20 Nov. 1733; NEHEMIAH, b. 30 Sept. 1735, m. by 17 Oct. 1774 Elizabeth, dau. of Charles Robinson,; JOHN, b. 8 April 1740; JACOB, b. 25 June 1742; MARGARET, b. 22 July 1743; SARAH, b. 8 Jan. 1744; and ABRAHAM (112:115; 131; 153:41).

HICKS, HENRY (5), s. of William (1), in 1750 owned 100 a. of Hicks' Adventure, and 82 a. Bond's Forest; d. leaving a will, 25 Aug. 1751 - 20 Sept. 1751, naming William Roberson, Laban Hogg, s. James, w. Mary, and mentioning "other children;" admin. bond was posted 12 Oct. 1751 by Mary Hicks and Laban Ogg, with Greenbury Dorsey; had issue, among others: JAMES (13:270; 112:415; 153:45).

HICKS, JAMES (6), s. of Henry (5), in 1755 conv. 52 a. Rolls' Adventure to Charles Baker; may be the James Hix who m. Mary Motherby on 23 April 1761 (82:637; 131).

HICKS, ISAAC, m. 24 Nov. 1748 Eliz. Miller (131).

HICKS, JOHN, in Sept. 1715 took the oath when Hannah Gilbert ad,in. the est. of Thomas Gilbert (1:209).

HICKS, REBECCA, m. John Armstrong on 26 Aug. 1714 (131).

HICKS, WILLIAM, m. Tabitha Stansbury on 24 Dec. 1747 (131).

HICKS, WILLIAM, m. Flora Cole on 12 Jan. 1748 (131).

HICKSON, JOSEPH, m. Jane Wilson by whom he was the father of: HESTER, b. Aug. 1727; HANNAH, b. 2 Sept. 1729 (128:83).

HIGGINBOTHOM, ANN, m. John Hopkins on 27 Dec. 1713 (131).

HIGGINS, JOHN, m. Sarah (---) and had iss.: ANNE, b. 2 Oct. 1725 (131).

HIGGINSON, JOHN (1), m. Anne (---), by 18 Aug. 1723, and d. by 18 Oct. 1736; admin. bond was posted 22 Nov. 1738 by admnx. Ann Higginson, admnx., with Samuel Hughes and Nicholas Baucum; est. was admin. by Ann, now w. of Charles Bolton, on 11 Oct. 1739, 8 Dec. 1740, and 1 July 1741; had iss.: SUSANNAH, b. 18 Aug. 1723, m. Thomas Brown on 19 June 1739; JOHN, b. 19 Feb. 1730; SAMUEL, b. 23 Feb. 1733 (4:26, 119, 126; 13:237; 32:151; 128:106; 129:308; 131:72/r).

HIGGINSON, SAMUEL (2), s. of John (1), was b. 23 Feb. 1733; m. Dorcas Barker on 29 Jan. 1760; in March 1759 Joshua Bond sold Samuel Higginson, brass founder, 167 a. Bond's Forest (83:340; 131).

HIGHLAND, JOHN, of Balto. Co., m. Mary Dorrington, wid., by Dec. 1665 (388).

HIKE, ANDREW, d. by 14 Sept. 1692 when his est. was inv. by Thomas Greenfield and Henry Haslewood and val. at ₤ 1.1.0 plus 1015 lbs. tobacco; prob. the Andrew Highca (sic) who was a taxable in Spesutia Hund. in 1692 (48:295; 138).

THE JOHN HILL FAMILY

HILL, JOHN (1), was in Balto. Co. by c.1676 when he purch. 600 a. Warrington from the trustees of Nathaniel Stiles; d. leaving a will, 17 March 1691 - 6 May 1692, in which he named s. John, dau. Rebecca Osborne, s. William; est. was inv. on 22 April 1695 by Richard Adams and Michael Gund(?), and val. at ₤ 1222.15.0; est. was admin. 2 Sept. 1696 by exec. William Hill; had iss.: WILLIAM; REBECCA, m. (---) Osborne by 17 March 1691; JOHN (48:37; 70:374; 121:97; 206-16:153).

HILL, WILLIAM (2), s. of John (1), on 10 March 1691/2 made all his prop. over to his friend Mary Love on condition that she come to the house where his dec. f. John lived, to be a housekeeper; d. leaving a will, 24 Sept. 1703 - 12 Jan. 1703/4, naming w. Mary, lands Warrington and The Point, bro. John Hill, orph. William Cockerham, and ch. John and Frances; admin. bond was posted 24 July 1704 by Benjamin Lego with Frances Dallahide and Edward Smith; est. was inv. on 14 Dec. 1704 by Thomas Preston, Sr., and Samuel Standiford and val. at ₤ 61.8.1; est. was admin. by extx. Mary, now w. of Benjamin Lego, on 25 Sept. 1707; left iss.: JOHN; FRANCES; WILLIAM (2:169; 13:208; 50:351; 59:383; 122:34).

HILL, JOHN (3), s. of John (1), d. by 14 Feb. 1726, having m. Martha (---), who on 31 May 1695 joined him in sale of 50 a. of Long Looked For (being part of a larger tract called Warrington), to James Cowdrey; had at least one ch.: JOHN (59:464; 70:374).

HILL, WILLIAM (4), s. of William (2), m. Martha Green, dau. of Matthew Green, on Sept. 1727; on 8 March 1732 William and Martha, who was the granddau. of Jane Boone, sold parts of Levy's Tribe, Green's Chance, and Choice Trippas to Thomas Cole; d. leaving a will, March 1765 - 18 May 1765, naming w. Martha, the tracts Warrington and 58 a. Davies' Chance, and these ch.: William, Richard, James, Moses, Thomas, Aaron, Sarah, and Martha, wid. of Aaron Tunis; William and Martha left iss.: JOHN, b. 8 Sept. 1727, d. Sept. 1728; MARY, b. 13 Aug. 1728; RICHARD, b. 22 May 1732; MARY, b. 3 Oct. 1729; ANNE, b. 18 Oct. 1734; WILLIAM, b. 3 Jan. 1736; THOMAS, b. 10 April 1743; MOSES, b. 4 Dec. 1748; AARON, b. 29 Nov. 1751; JOHN, b. 25 April 1756; prob. MARTHA, m. John Tunis on 21 Aug. 1755 (73:326; 112:24; 131).

THE SAMUEL HILL FAMILY

HILL, SAMUEL (5), no known rel. to above, was in Balto. Co. by 3 July 1672 when he surv. 150 a. Samuel's Hills; said to have d. without heirs, but prob. had at least one son: WILLIAM (71:211; 211:34).

HILL, WILLIAM (6), s. of Samuel (5), moved to Cecil Co., where he d. by 10 March 1730, leaving at least one dau.: RACHEL (71: 211).

HILL, RACHEL (7), dau. of William (6), m. by 10 March 1730 Laurence Fouracres, whom she joined in a deed on that date, selling 150 a. Samuel's Hills to Charles Baker (71:211).

HILL, ALEXANDER, was in Balto. Co. by 1743 when he purch. 67 a. Arabia Petrea from Francis and Mary Jenkins; in 1750 he owned 303 a. Arabia Petrea; m. Mary Redman on 15 July 1731, and had iss.: WILLIAM, b. 20 March 1734; ANN, b. 15 Oct. 1738; and MARY, b. 16 Feb. 1740 (77:343; 128:62, 88, 109; 129:327; 153:52).

HILL, ELINOR, was ind. for bast. in March 1739/40, and tried in June 1740, again in Aug. 1740; in June 1743 she admitted she had borne a ch. out of wedlock; had iss.: JAMES, twin, b. 1 May 1743; SARAH, twin, b. 1 May 1743 (32:140, 247, 299; 34:199; 131).

HILL, ELIZABETH, m. Thomas Galhampton on 10 Nov. 1720 (129: 264).

HILL, ELIZABETH, had at least two ch.: THOMAS, b. 1 Sept. 1754; CASSANDRA, b. May 1760 (131).

HILL, FRANCES, m. Christopher Davis or Divers on 10 Dec. 1728 (131).

HILL, JAMES, s. of Elinor King, was bound out as an apprentice in March 1744/5 (35:471).

HILL, JOHN, d. in Balto. Co. leaving a will, 21 June 1755 - 19 Sept. 1768, naming his friend Hugh Whiteford, w. Jeanet, and ch., John, Joseph, and Mary; prob. the John Hill who was made levy free in Nov. 1745; had iss.: JOHN; JOSEPH; MARY, ordered to marry Hugh Calley in her father's will (35:743; 112:92).

HILL, JOSEPH, in 1750 owned 1000 a. Hill's Forest (153:100).

HILL, NATHANIEL, m. by 14 Feb. 1761 Mary, admnx. of John Gregory (4:360).

HILL, RICHARD, surv. 1000 a. Hill's Forest on 4 Sept. 1683; as Capt. Richard Hill came to possess 104 a. orig. laid out for Michael Cusack; former tract later owned by Joseph Hill; latter tract later owned by Richard Hill's heirs (211:43, 76).

HILL, ROGER, was in Balto. Co. by 16 March 1675/6 when admin. bond was posted on his est. by Richard Sims, admin., with Richard Windley; his will, signed 22 Dec. 1675, named Arthur Taylor, Robert Gates, and William Simes (13:197; 164:Box 1, folder 9).

HILL, SARAH, in 1750 owned 550 a. Sparrow's Nest (153:100).

HILL, SARAH, dau. of Eleanor King, was bound out in March 1744/5 (35:471).

HILL, WILLIAM, d. leaving a will, 17 March 1681/2 - 27 Nov. 1682, making James Phillips his exec. and sole legatee; the will was wit. by John Wolston, Robert Ball, Lewis Barton, and Roger Symons (110:60).

THE HILLEN FAMILY was discussed by Emily Emerson Lantz, in "Maryland Heraldry: the Lineage of the Hillens, Baltimore Sun, 6 August and 13 August 1905.

HILLEN, JOHN (1), progenitor, was in Md. by 1679 when he m. Johanna Hooker, b. 15 d, 1 mo., 1660/1 at West River, dau. of Thomas and Johanna Hooker; Hillen d. leaving a will, 5 July 1682 - 6 Feb. 1682/3, naming s. Johannes (not yet 18; to have 300 a. Heydown in Cecil Co.), dau. Deborah (to have pers. prop. at age 16), father-in-law Thomas Hooker, Benjamin and Damaris Hooker, and Thomas Hooker, Jr.; w. Johanna was to be extx.; had iss.: JOHANNES, or JOHN, b. 1 d, 11 mo., 1679/80; DEBORAH, b. 26 d, 12 mo., 1681/2 (120:121; Lantz; Reg. of West River Monthly Meeting, Soc. of Friends in 219-6).

HILLEN, JOHN (2), s. of John (1) and Johanna, was b. 1 d, 11 mo., 1679/80 in A. A. Co.,; d. 2 April 1727 in Balto. Co.; m. Mary, wid. of Thomas James, by 25 Sept. 1707; d. leaving a will, 19 March 1726 - 22 April 1727, naming s. Solomon as exec., and leaving him his entire est.; also named w. Mary; if Solomon d. without heirs, the land was to be divided among the testator's godson Daniel Sheredine (to have Shoemaker Hall), goddau. Elizabeth Harrett (to have 51 a. Addition to Shoemaker's Hall), bro.-in-law Thomas Hines (to have dwell. plantation after death of testator's w. Mary), and three sons-in-law Walter, William, and Watkins James; admin. bond was posted 5 Aug. 1727 by Solomon Hillen, with Oliver Harriott and Walter James; est. was admin. by Solomon Hillen on May 1729; had iss.: SOLOMON, b.c.1708 (2: 283; 13:220; 125:27; 141:5; Lantz; 219-6).

HILLEN, SOLOMON (3), s. of John (2) and Mary, was b. c.1708, and d. by 1748; m. Elizabeth Raven, dau. of Luke and Esther Raven, on 7 Oct. 1729; his wid. m. Thomas Wheeler on 21 Dec. 1748; in 1750 the heirs of Solomon Hillen owned 200 a. Hogyard, 119½ a. Hillen's Refuse, 150 a. Shoemaker's Hall, 300 a. Paradise, and Disappointment; est. of Solomon Hillen was admin. by Thomas and Eliza Wheeler; dec. left iss.: MARY, b. 2 Aug. 1730; ELIZABETH, b. 6 Nov. 1732; JOHN, b. 14 July 1734, d. 11 Oct. 1736; SOLOMON, b. 22 Oct. 1737; NATHANIEL, b. 12 March 1739/40; JOHANNA, b. 2 Oct. 1742, m. (---) Wells; ELIZABETH, b. c.1744, m. James McComas on 15 Nov. 1761 (5:260; 133:19, 32, 43, 66, 71, 149, 162, 196; 153:34).

HILLIARD, HENRY (1), bro. of Daniel (2), on 22 Feb. 1717 purch. 463 a. Timber Neck from William Bladen; on 11 Oct. 1719 Henry and w. Elizabeth conv. that tract to Daniel Hilliard; d. leaving a will, 12 Feb. 1718/9 - 17 May 1720, naming w. Elizabeth and the children named below; wid. Elizabeth claimed her thirds of Timber Neck, at that time held by testator's bro. Daniel, in exch. for his share of Hopkins' Chance; wid. Elizabeth m. 2nd John Fuller who d. by 22 April 1734; Henry and Elizabeth had iss.: DANIEL; JACOB; HENRY; CALEB; ANN; RUTH; RACHEL; and ZIPPORAH (63:420; 68:42; 124:9; 126:88).

HILLIARD, DANIEL (2), bro. of Henry (1), m. Elizabeth Worrell in 1703 in St. Margaret's Parish, A. A. Co.; d. by 4 Nov. 1726 in Balto. Co. when wid. Elizabeth posted admin. bond with Joseph Conaway and John Conaway; Eliz. Hilliard admin. the est. on 13 Nov. 1727 (3:94; 13:220; 219-4:99).

HILLIARD, CALEB, in 1733 was named as son-in-law in the will
of Edward Fuller of A. A. Co. (126:88).

HILLIARD, MARY, serv. to John Townsen, was ind. for bast. in
March 1729/30 (29:96).

HILLIARD, SARAH, servant to Thomas Warren, was ind. for bast.
in June 1733 (30:15).

HILLIARD, THOMAS, m. Susanna West on 7 Feb. 1737; they had:
SUSANNA, b. 14 Oct. 1740 (128:99, 112).

HILLING. See HILLEN.

HILTON, JOHN, m. Sarah (---) by whom he had at least three
ch.: SARAH, b. 25 March 1740; MARY, b. 13 March 1741; and ELIZA-
BETH, b. 9 Aug. 1743 (131:101/r, 104/r).

HILTON, MARY, was ind. for bast. (13:245).

HINCHMAN, NATHANIEL. See HENCHMAN, NATHANIEL.

HINCKLEY, FRANCIS, by 1737 was in Back R. Upper Hund.; on 9
May 1738 conv. 60 a. Litchfield City to William Worthington (75:
65; 149:21).

HINDON. See HENDON.

HINDS, THOMAS, English, runaway convict serv. from Deer Creek,
was advertised for in Nov. 1754 (385:317).

HINES, FRANCIS, b. c.1705, m. by 2 Oct. 1739 Frances, b. c.
1711, dau. of John Roberts, and had iss.: SAMUEL, b. 15 Nov.
1740; ELIZABETH, b. 5 Aug. 1742 (75:285; 77:27, 556; 131).

HINES, HUGH, servant of Patrick Coyle (q.v.).

HINES, PETER, in Jan. 1746 eloped with the w. of Worten Rutlis of Balto. Co. (Annap., Md. Gaz., 21 Jan. 1746).

HINES, THOMAS, of Balto. Co., d. by 23 Dec. 1755; m. Elizabeth
who d. by 5 Jan. 1756; in 1726 he was named as a bro.-in-law in
the will of John Hillen; purch. 257 a. Come By Chance from John
and Presiota Boring in May 1732; purch. 100 a. Bachelor's Ridge
from Robert and Elizabeth Harryman in Dec. 1742; in 1750 owned
8 a. Hines' Industry, 261 a. Hines' Purchase, 50 a. part Hogyard,
16 a. Hines' Desire, and 100 a. Bachelor's Ridge; d. leaving a
will, 28 Nov. 1755 - 23 Dec. 1755, named w. Elizabeth, Mary w.
of William Sinkler, Robert Maxwell, Thomas Franklin, Nicholas
Rogers, Staley Durham, and Thomas Franklin, Jr.; admin. bond was
posted 23 Jan. 1756 by Thomas Franklin and Nicholas Rogers, with
William Rogers; Elizabeth Hines d. leaving a will, 4 Jan. 1756 -
5 Jan. 1756, naming sis. Ann, wid. of Peter Mills of Som. Co.,
niece Mary w. of Moses Galloway, and cousins James and Nathan
Nicholson; admin. bond was posted 27 Jan. 1756 by Nathan Nicholson with Walter Hall and John Hall; iss. of Thomas: THOMAS, b.
c.1748, age 9 on 1 June 1757, in Aug. 1757 was bound to Thomas
Potts (13:263, 266; 44; 46:58; 73:236; 77:196; 111:103; 125:27;
153:16; 210-30:55).

HINKES, THOMAS, m. Sarah Hewett after the banns were pub. in
July 1746 (131).

HINTON, MARY, m. Silvestine Jones in Nov. 1719, after the
death of her dau.: MARGARET HINTON (131).

HINTON, SAMUEL, was in Balto. Co. by 4 Nov. 1710 when he purch.
260 a. Bachelor's Delight from Samuel Arden; d. leaving a will,
4 April 1720 - 15 Dec. 1720, leaving above tract to w. Elizabeth
for life, naming s. Thomas, and dau. Sarah Hinton Olive, son-in-
law James Bagford, Constant Sampson, poss. w. of John Sampson,
and Richard Sampson of Richard; est. was inv. on 27 March 1721
by John Eager and John Eaglestone and val. at £ 67.15.2½; wid.
Elizabeth m. as (3rd?) husb. Thomas Stone; Samuel and Elizabeth
had iss.: THOMAS; SARAH, m. (---) Olive or Iliff (51:63; 67:122;
110:159).

HISER, JOHN, m. Mary (---) and had iss.: SAMUEL, b. 12 Sept.
1742; JOHN, b. 4 Feb. 1744/5; SARAH, b. 3 Sept. 1758 (131; 133)

HISSEY/HESSY, CHARLES, was b. c.1702, and gave his age as 52
in Feb. 1754; m. Jane (---); prob. the Charles Hizzey (sic) listed
in 1750 as owning 18 a. Youngs Chance; had iss.: ELIZABETH, b. 10
June 1731; SARAH, b. 13 Oct. 1734; CHARLES, b. 6 Jan. 1736; HENRY,
b. 24 April 1739; KETURAH, b. 11 Oct. 1742; MARY, b. 4 June 1745
(133:82; 153:65; 224:243).

HISSEY, ELIZABETH, in Nov. 1754 and again in Nov. 1758 was
tried for bast. (39:451; 46:162).

HITCHCOCK, WILLIAM (1), progenitor, was in Balto. Co. by 1703;
d. by 31 Jan. 1738; m. 1st Mary (---); m. 2nd, on 7 Sept. 1716,
Anne Jones, b. c.1700, dau. of Richard and Anne (Gassaway) Jones;
after Hitchcock's death Ann m. as her 2nd husb. Peter Carroll;
William d. leaving a will, 12 Dec. 1729 - 31 Jan. 1738, naming
his ch. William, John, Phillis, Mary, Ashael, Elizabeth, Ann,
Emilia, and Jemima, and tracts Bednal Green, Timber Hall, and
Richardson's Reserve; admin. bond was posted 8 March 1738 by Ann
Hitchcock with Joseph Norris and William Hitchcock; est. was ad-
min. by Ann, w. of Peter Carroll on 8 Oct. 1739 and 16 Oct. 1741;
dec. left iss. (by 1st w.): PHILIZANNA, b. c.1708, m. Nehemiah
Hicks on 12 June 1725; WILLIAM, b. c.1710; JOHN, b. 30 Aug. 1712;
MARY, b. c.1714; (by 2nd w.): ASHAEL, b. 26 April 1719; ELIZA-
BETH, b. c.1721, m. Samuel Talbee on 1 Dec. 1738; ANN, b. c.1722,
d. c.1792, m. John Barton on 23 May 1738; EMILIA, b. c.1724, m.
1st Peter Whitaker on 12 Feb. 1744, and 2nd, John Fisher, on 18
Feb. 1761; JEMIMA, b. c.1726, m. Peircey Poteet on 12 Oct. 1743
(4:19, 71; 13:230; 127:14; 131; 145).

HITCHCOCK, WILLIAM (2), s. of William (1) and Mary, was b. c.
1710, and d. c.1772; m. Susanna Slade on 8 Nov. 1729; in 1750 he
owned 100 a. Bednal Green; d. by 14 Sept. 1773 when his est. was
admin., stating he left a wid. and seven ch.; had iss.: ISAAC,
b. 6 Nov. 1731; WILLIAM, b. Dec. 1733, d. 1733; WILLIAM, b. 26
July 1735; JOSIAH, b. c.1738, m. Susanna Garland, on 10 July
1755; JOHN, b. 15 Oct. 1746; and two children whose names are
not known (6:302; 131; 153:36).

HITCHCOCK, ASAEL (3), s. of William (1) and Anne, was b. 26
April 1719; d. c.1791/2 in Harford Co.; m. Sarah Norris on 8 Oct.
1741 or 1742; she was b. 22 April 1719, and d. by 27 June 1814;
Asael rendered patriotic service in the Rev. War; left iss.:
ANN, b. 11 Dec. 1741 or 1742, m. Jacob Hicks on 2 March 1767;
ASAEL, b. c.1743, m. Sarah (---); WILLIAM, b. 30 Oct. 1744, m.
Cordelia (---); MARY, b. 27 Dec. 1748, m. Isaac Truelock; JOHN,
m. Esther (---); ISAAC, m. Susanna (---); and JOSIAS (131; 244-
AJ#2:314; 244-SR#1:330; 353; Harford Co. Equity Case # 1050).

HITCHCOCK, GEORGE, no known rel. to above, m. by 29 July 1713
Mary, wid. of Teague Tracey; in Feb. 1736 conv. 100 a. Tracey's

Park (which he purch. in Nov. 1724 from James Tracey), to dau. Persosha, w. of John Tye; d. leaving a will, 23, 8 mo., 1747 - 4 Nov. 1747, naming s. and dau. John and Presiota Tye and grandch., George, Ellinor, and Susanna Tye; admin. bond was posted 11 Nov. 1747 by John Tye (Mary Hitchcock having ren. in favor of John Tye), with Henry Sater, John Cooke, John Metcalfe, and James Sage; left iss.: PRETIOSA, m. John Tye on 11 Dec. 1735 (1:4, 37; 13:249; 61:356; 110:400; 153:154).

HITCHCOCK, ISAAC, m. Elizabeth (---) and had iss.:. ISAAC, b. 14 Aug. 1730 (131).

HITES(?), JOHN, servant, with 5 years to serve, was listed in the 1717 inv. of Katherine Knowles (52:317).

HIX. See HICKS.

HOARD, JOSEPH, was in Balto. Co. by July 1713 when he purch. 109 a. Boring's Passage from James Boring and w. Jane and John Boring and w. Mary; d. by 14 Jan. 1718 when admin. bond was posted by Edmund Baxter with Joseph and Thomas Gostwick; est. was inv. on 28 Jan. 1718 by Benjamin Bowen and John Bowen and val. at ₤ 30.16.8, and signed by John Boring and Thomas Sheredine (13:199; 48:292; 67:233).

HOARD, JOSHUA, was in Balto. Co. by 1694 as a taxable in n. side Patapsco Hund. (139).

HOBBS, JOHN, m. Susanna (---), and in March 1725 advert. he would not be responsible for debts of w. Susanna who had deserted him; had iss.: JONAS, b. Dec. 1724 (70:225; 131).

HOCKINGS. See HAWKINS.

HODGE, THOMAS, in Nov. 1692 was in Balto. Co. when he conv. part Harris' Trust to Peter Bond; in 1694 was a taxable in Spesuita Hund. (64:360; 139).

HODGESON, JOHN, of Balto. Co., imm. by 1668, transporting his w. Elizabeth, and in 1671 his ch.: JOB; JOHN; and JOSHUA (388).

HODGKEN, JOSEPH, m. Catherine Carroll on 17 Oct. 1738 (128:103).

HODGKISS, MICHAEL, was in Balto. Co. by 9 Dec. 1743 when he purch. 100 a. Hawkins' Chance from John and Rebecca Hawkins; in 1750 owned 100 a. Hawkins, or Hodskins' Chance; m. Sarah (---), and had iss.: WILLIAM, b. 30 Dec. 1734 (77:399; 133:41; 153:64).

HOFF, or HUFF, MICHAEL, in 1750 owned 90 a. Hickory Bottom (153:87).

HOGAN, DOMINICK, runaway Irish convict serv. from Patapsco Ironworks, was advert. for in July 1745 (384).

HOGAN, JACOB, m. Ann (---), and had iss.: JNO., b. 28 Aug. 1749 (131).

HOGG, (---), dau. of Mary, in Nov. 1721 was bound to Richard Ruff (23:16).

HOGG, AMBROSE, in 1692 was a taxable in n. side of Patapsco Hund. (138).

HOGG, CATHERINE, m. John Field on 23 Dec. 1729 (129:252).

HOGG, MARY, in June 1710 named Daniel Kelly as the father of her child (21:135).

HOGG, MARY, in March 1730/1 was ind. for bast., and tried in June 1731 (29:96, 167).

HOLBROOK, AMOS, m. Hannah (---), and had iss.: JANE, b. 14 Dec. 1747; SARAH, b. 13 May 1749; JOHN, b. 1 April 1756; EDWARD, b. 4 Aug. 1757; JANE, b. 2 May 1761 (133:93, 98, 108).

HOLBROOK, ROGER, m. Mary (---), and had iss.: JOHN, b. 11 July 1745; ROGER, b. 10 July 1748 (133:86, 87).

HOLDMAN.   See HOLMAN.

HOLESTOCK.   See WHOLESTOCK.

HOLLAND, WILLIAM (1), was in Md. by 1692 and d. by 25 Oct. 1732; m. 1st Margaret, dau. of Francis Holland of York Co., Va., and of A. A. Co.; m. 2nd Elizabeth Woolford Makey Ennalls; was capt. of foot, 1693-1696; delegate to the Assembly, 1701; Member of the Council, 1701-1732, and President of the Council, 1721 and 1724-1727; d. leaving a will, 17 Aug. 1724 - 25 Oct. 1732, naming w. Elizabeth, sons Francis, William, and Thomas, grandchildren Francis Utie and Mary Holland, William Thomas, sis. Mary Haskins, neph. Thomas Haskins and kinsman Thomas Haskins; had iss.: FRANCIS, b. 25 Sept. 1691; WILLIAM, Jr., b. 2 June 1695; MARGARET, b. 25 Oct. 1697, d. 15 Aug. 1701; THOMAS, b. 14 Oct. 1700; FRANCES, b. 7 Feb. 1703, d. c.1723, having m. Philip Thomas; MARGARET, b. 21 March 1705, d. 1708; MARY, b. 10 Nov. 1708, d. 1709; JOHN, b. 5 Nov. 1710; SUSANNA, b. 12 Oct. 1712 (219-4; 313:177, 179, 180; chart of Holland Family by Christopher Johnston at the Md. Hist. Soc.).

HOLLAND, FRANCIS (2), s. of William (1), was b. 25 Sept. 1691; d. 7 April 1738; m. c. 1712, Susanna, b. 24 Sept. 1695, d. by 15 March 1744, dau. of George Utie of Balto. Co.; Justice of the Peace in A. A. Co., 1714-1716, and in Balto. Co., 1718-1721; High Sheriff, 1721-1725; admin. bond was posted 17 May 1739 by Joshua George with William Rumsey and John Baldwin; est. was inv. 23 Oct. 1739 by John Clark and Jacob Giles, and val. at £ 712.16.32 (?), and signed by kinsfolk Susanna Holland and Peregrine Frisby; est. was admin. by Joshua George on 30 Aug. 1740 and 24 July 1742; admin. bond for est. of Susanna Holland was posted 15 March 1744 by Francis Holland, with John Matthews and James Phillips; a 2nd admin. bond was posted 4 April 1747 by Cordelia Holland with James Phillips and Talbot Risteau; est. of Susanna Holland was admin. 3 Nov. 1745 by Francis Holland and on 22 Feb. 1748 by Cordelia Holland; Francis and Susanna Holland had iss.: UTIE, d. 14 Nov. 1734; FRANCIS, b. 13 Aug. 1719; MARY, b. 18 June 1721, m. Capt. Peregrine Frisby; HENRIETTA; SUSANNA; FRANCES UTIE, b. 1735, d. 1740 (3:283; 4:67, 206; 5:29; 13:234, 250, 252; 49:143; 128: 37, 40, 90, 92, 115; 313:182-183; chart of Holland Family by Johnston).

HOLLAND, WILLIAM (3), s. of William (1) and Margaret, was b. 2 June 1695; d. 1755 in Calvert Co.; m. Anne (---) and had iss.: WILHELMINA; MARY; MARGARET, m. Skipwith Coale; SARAH, m. (---) Young (313; Holland chart by Johnston).

HOLLAND, THOMAS (4), s. of William (1), was b. 14 Oct. 1700, d. 1742; m. Sarah, dau. of Thomas and Frances (Wells) Frisby; Sarah m. as her 2nd husb. Robert Freeland; in 1750 the heirs of Thomas Holland owned two-thirds of Miner's Adventure; Thomas and Sarah had iss.: FRANCES, m. (---) Reynolds; SARAH; ARIANA;

MARGARET; MARY; and THOMAS (153:97; Holland chart by Johnston).

HOLLAND, FRANCIS (5), s. of Francis (2) and Susanna, was b. 13 Aug. 1719, d. 17 Dec. 1746; m. on 7 June 1744 Cordelia Knight, dau. of Stephen and Sarah (Frisby) Knight; Cordelia, b. c.1721, d. 1782, m. as her 2nd husb. John Hall of Swan Town; in 1750 the heirs of Francis Holland owned 2300 a. Spesutia, and 67 a. Miner's Adventure; inv. was filed by extx. Cordelia Holland on 20 Feb. 1748; est. was val. at £ 1823.6.4, having been appraised by John Paca and William Smith, and the inv. was signed by kin Henella(?) Holland and Susanna Holland; est. was admin. 22 Feb. 1748; dec. left iss.: FRANCIS, b. 1 Aug. 1745; FRANCES, b. 9 May 1747, d. 11 Nov. 1814, m. Thomas Gassaway Howard (4:195; 13:251; 38:8, 9; 49: 251; 313; Holland chart by Johnston).

HOLLAND, FRANCIS (6), s. of Francis (5) and Cordelia, was b. 1 Aug. 1745, d. by 30 July 1795; m. Hannah (---); as orphan of Francis Holland had bond placed by John and Cordelia Hall that they would pay him the balance of his father's est.; had iss.: FRANCIS UTIE, b. 1771; JOHN, b. 1773 (38:8; Holland chart by Johnston).

HOLLAND, GABRIEL, m. Mary (---), and had iss.: THOMAS, b. 10 Aug. 1734 (at age 6 in Aug. 1740 was bound to Juliatha Spicer); CASSIAH, b. 15 Feb. 1735/6 (32:291; 133:37, 50).

HOLLAND, JOHN, m. Sarah Willabee on 8 June 1740; in 1750 owned 141 a. Bond's Forest; had iss.: JOHN, b. 24 Nov. 1740 (128:103, 111; 153:67).

HOLLAND, JOHN FRANCIS, was born in Germany and nat. in Balto. Co. by Act of the Assembly in April 1707; on 4 Nov. 1701 John Francis Holland and w. Jane conv. land to Sarah Steers; in March 1709 conv. to John Eaglestone the tract Eaglestone's Inlet, part of Willin formerly taken up by Charles Gorsuch; d. leaving a will, 23 Feb. 1731 - 28 Oct. 1732, naming John Copper, John Eaglestone, and Edward Sweeting, leaving entire est. to Frances Holland Watts (not yet of age, dau. of Edward and Mary Watts); admin. bond was posted 30 Jan. 1732 by exec. Robert North with Benjamin Bowen and Thomas Sheredine, John Eaglestone having ren. his right to admin.; est. was admin. on 13 March 1734 (3:200; 13:238; 66:96; 69:97; 125:253).

HOLLAND, JOSEPH, English, runaway servant from Baltimore Iron works, was advert. for in Oct. 1760 (307-69:58).

HOLLAND, OTHO, of A. A. Co., in Nov. 1683 was conv. 97 a. of Middle Jenifer; in March 1719 was conv. Welsh's Adventure by James Boring and his w. Jane, dau. and coheir of Daniel Welsh (68:196; 106:286).

HOLLAND, WILLIAM, d. in Balto. Co., leaving a will, 16 June 1721 - 19 Sept. 1727, naming w. Elizabeth, William Andrew (s. of wife's sis., Sarah), Ann Hackman, Thomas Durbin and Elizabeth Shaw (not yet 16) (125:39).

HOLLANDSWORTH. See HOLLINGSWORTH.

HOLLEGER, PHILIP, in March 1665/6 conv. 50 a. at Sassafras River (part of 100 a. Holleger bought from William Fisher) to Hendrick Freeman; in March 1667/8 bought 350 a. on the Sassafras R. from Godfrey Harmer; m. by Aug. 1688, Mary (---) (95).

HOLLEY, THOMAS, orphan of Thomas; age 9 in Aug. 1750 when he was bound to John Ridgely (37:150).

HOLLIDAY, JAMES (1), progenitor, m. Sarah Molton on 30 Oct. 1721; d. 19 Jan. 1722/3; admin. bond was posted 2 April 1723 by Sarah Holliday with Matthew Molton and Joseph Eng(land?); wid. Sarah m. 2nd, by 31 March 1725, Abraham Lake; dec. left iss.: ROBERT, b. 6 Jan. 1721/2; JAMES (3:13; 13:243; 128:40, 41).

HOLLIDAY, ROBERT (2), s. of James (1) and Sarah, was b. 6 Jan. 1721/2, and d. c.1747 in Balto. Co.; m. Achsah Ridgely, dau. of Col. Charles Ridgely, and b. 22 April 1729, d. 12 March 1785; Achsah m. 2nd John Carnan and 3rd Daniel Chamier; the will of Robert Holliday, surgeon, made 2 Dec. 1745 - 2 Oct. 1747, named w., bro. James (not identified), unborn ch., and tract Goshen Resurveyed; admin. bond was posted 3 Oct. 1747; est. was admin. by Col. Charles Ridgely in 1756; in 1750 the heirs of Dr. Robert Holliday owned 400 a. Goshen Resurveyed and 3 lots in Balto. Town; a survey of the twenty-five largest book collections owned by Marylanders between 1700 and 1776 reveals that Dr. Robert Holliday owned 24 books, including a number of histories, a Bible and a prayer book, a Latin testament, 12 volumes of Steele's works incl. The Tatler and The Spectator, but no medical books; Robert and Achsah had iss.: JOHN ROBERT, b. c.1745 (5:289; 13:247; 153: 73; 210-25:163; 259:7; Joseph Towne Wheeler, "Reading Interests of the Professional Classes," Md. Hist. Mag., XXXVI (1941), 299-300).

HOLLIDAY, (---), in 1750 was joint owner with one Stoddart of 417 a. Part Trueman's Acquaintance (153:94).

HOLLINGSWORTH/HOLLANDWORTH, GEORGE (1), d. in Balto. Co. leaving a will, Jan. 1702 - 25 March 1703, naming his ch. George, Otho, Charles, James, and Hannah, all of whom were to share equally in tract Brother's Unity, John and Francis, s. James to live with his mother-in-law (i.e., the testator's w.); admin. bond was posted 25 May 1703 by Margaret Hollingsworth, extx., with Isaac Jackson and Thomas Bale; a second admin. bond was posted by Cornelius Harrington, Matthew Green, and James Isom; est. of George Hollingsworth was inv. 25 March 1703 by Isaac Jackson and Peter Bond and val. at £ 24.14.10; an additional inv. was filed by Thomas Preston, Sr., and William Hicks, and val. at £ 7.1.0; ch. of George Hollingsworth: GEORGE (prob. the George Hollingsworth the Younger whose est. was inv. by Thomas Preston and William Hicks on 23 May 1705 and val. at £ 6.11.3); OTHO; CHARLES; JAMES; HANNAH; JOHN, and FRANCIS (13:205, 207; 48:102, 229; 51:130; 122:6).

HOLLINGSWORTH, JAMES (2), s. of George, d. 14 Nov. 1721 in St. George's Par.; m. Ann Chitching (or Cutching) on 27 Feb. 1714; she may be the Ann Hollingsworth who m. John Welch on 4 July 1724; James and Ann had iss.: GEORGE, b. 17 Nov. 1715; JAMES, b. 28 Feb. 1718; THOMAS, b. 3 Dec. 1721 (128:32, 34, 37, 47; 129:244).

HOLLINGSWORTH, JOHN (3), s. of George (1), is prob. the John who m. Mary Deaver on Aug. 1741; d. in Balto. Co. by 10 June 1758 when admin. bond was posted by Jacob Giles and D. Chamier; Mary Hollingsworth was named as kinswoman in the will of Mary Daver made 29 July 1749; dec. left iss.: ENOCH, b. 9 June 1742 (13:265; 129:323, 331; 210-27:96).

HOLLINGSWORTH, JAMES (4), s. of James (2) and Ann, was b. 28 Feb. 1718, and is prob. the James who d. 30 April 1740 (128:111).

HOLLINGSWORTH, THOMAS (5), s. of James (2) and Ann, was b. 3 Dec. 1721; m. Keziah Hollis on 14 Jan. 1741; may be the Thomas Hollingsworth who d. by 24 March 1763 when admin. bond was posted by admin. John Hanson with James Osborn and Samuel Howard (13: 289; 128:116).

HOLLINGSWORTH, CATHERINE, spinster, on 27 Feb. 1730/1 conv.
lot 29 in Joppa to Stephen Hollingsworth (73:66).

HOLLINGSWORTH, STEPHEN; on 25 Nov. 1731 conv. lot 29 in Joppa
to John Higginson (73:179).

HOLLINS, JONATHAN, serv. to Thomas Greenfield, was bur. 2 July
1700 (128:10).

THE HOLLIS FAMILY was the subject of a chart by Christopher
Johnston at the Maryland Historical Society).

HOLLIS, WILLIAM (1), came to Balto. Co. c.1659, and d. c.1680;
m. Elizabeth (---) who m. as her 2nd husb. (---) Russell, and 3rd
husb., by March 1684/5 William Harris; Hollis surv. Hunting Neck
for 300 a. with Thomas Cole; in Aug. 1679 joined Charles Gorsuch
in conv. Hunting Neck to Miles Gibson; also surv. 45 a. Hollis'
Chance and 22 a. Islington; was Justice of the Peace for Balto.
Co. in 1674; d. leaving a will, 4 Sept. 1675 - 14 July 1680,
leaving Swampy Point to w. Elizabeth, 100 a. Broad Neck to dau.
Elizabeth, 100 a. Holly Hill, 50 a. Howlett's Nest, 100 a. Narrow
Neck to s. William; Miles Gibson testified he had been sent for
to make Hollis' will and found him speechless and senseless;
Hollis' wife told Gibson she knew what her husb. wanted done, persuaded Gibson to draw up a will and guide Hollis' hand to make a
a mark; Hollis later recovered and repudiated the will; dec. left
iss.: WILLIAM; ANNE, may have m. John Hall; and ELIZABETH (38:
280, 284; 60:40; 110:174; 206-7b:168; 211; 429:219; Hollis chart
by Johnston).

HOLLIS, WILLIAM (2), s. of William (1), d. by 8 Feb. 1704; m.
by 1690 Mary, dau. of Abraham and Sarah Clarke; was Justice of
the Peace for Balto. Co., 1694; in 1690 William and Mary conv.
100 a. Broad Neck to William Pritchett; on 11 June 1694 Hollis and
w. conv. Landisell to William Wilkinson; on 4 Feb. 1697 conv.
100 a. Narrow Neck to John Hall; d. leaving a will, 4 Jan. 1704 -
8 Feb. 1704, naming ch. William, Clark, Sarah, Everla; admin.
bond was posted 8 Feb. 1704 by Benjamin Smith with Samuel Brown
and Thomas Newsham; est. was admin. 2 Feb. 1707/8 by George Chancey, admin. of Benjamin Smith the orig. admin.; William and Mary
had iss.: SARAH, b. 1 March 1704, m. George Chancey; AVARILLA,
b. 20 Sept. 1693, m. William Osborne; WILLIAM, b. 10 March 1696/7;
CLARK, b. 16 Jan. 1699; MARY, b. 20 Feb. 1703, d. 9 July 1703;
EVERLA (2:206; 13:197; 19:310; 59:324, 401; 61:214; 122:50;
128:5, 9, 16, 17, 21; 200-20:109; 211).

HOLLIS, WILLIAM (3), s. of William (2), was b. 10 March 1696/7,
d. by 11 April 1763; m. 13 March 1720 Ann Rhodes; on 5 Nov. 1724
conv. 150 a. Hollis' Desire to his neph. William Osborne, s. of
William (dec.) and Avarilla (dec.); on 27 Feb. 1750 gave his age
as c.54; d. leaving a will, 28 Dec. 1753 - 11 April 1763, naming
sons William, Clark, Amos, and daus. Catherine, Anne, and Mary,
and one other dau.; admin. bond posted 10 June 1763 by exec. Wm.
Hollis with John Paca and Daniel Maccomas of Wm.; William and
Ann had iss.: KEZIA, b. 17 Aug. 1723; WILLIAM, b. 10 Oct. 1726;
CLARK, b. 6 June 1729; CATHERINE, b. 30 Dec. 1731; AMOS, b. 15
Nov. 1735; ANN, b. 22 April 1739; MARY, b. 26 Nov. 1741 (13:290;
70:28; 112:2; 128:40, 49, 60, 93b, 112; 129:324; 153:27; Land
Comm., Liber HWS#BB, 188).

HOLLIS, CLARK (4), s. of William (2), was b. 16 Jan. 1699, and
d. 15 Nov. 1721; his inv. was filed in 1721 (51:308; 128:40).

HOLLIS, WILLIAM (5), s. of William (3) and Ann, was b. 10 Oct.
1726; m. Sarah Gallion on 15 March 1748, and had iss.: WILLIAM,

b. 21 Aug. 1749; FRANCES, b. 21 April 1754; JAMES, b. 21 Aug.
1757; CLARK, b. 12 Aug. 1760 (129:359, 360).

HOLLIS, CLARK (6), s. of William (3) and Ann, was b. 6 June
1729; m. Hannah (---) and had iss.: MARY, b. 13 Dec. 1752; HAN-
NAH, b. 27 Jan. 1754; ANN, b. 27 Jan. 1754; RACHEL, b. 17 Aug.
1756; CATHERINE, b. 2 Oct. 1758 (129:339).

HOLLIS, AMOS (7), s. of William (3) and Ann, was b. 15 Nov.
1735 and d. c.May 1789, having m. Martha Osborn, wid. of John
Everett; Martha was b. 11 July 1737, and was dau. of William
and Catherine (Rhodes) Osborn (129).

HOLLIS, ANN, m. 6 May 1697 John Hall of Bush River (129:178).

HOLLIS, JOHN, m. Mary Groom on 12 Aug. 1749 (131).

HOLLOWAY/HAULAWAY, JOHN, m. Elizabeth (---); in May 1728 he
conv. 100 a. Standiford's Hope to Skelton Standiford; on 5 Sept.
1738 John and Elizabeth conv. 150 a. part World's End to Abraham
Vaughan; on 20 Oct. 1742 as John Holloway, Jr., conv. prop. to
Darby Hernly "for love and affection;" in July 1745 he purch. 30
a. Cox's Hope from Edward and Necia Cox; had iss.: SARAH, b. 23
Nov. 1725; ELIZ., b. 26 Nov. 1727; ANNE, b. 28 Dec. 1729; ISA-
BELLA, b. 22 Dec. 1731; MARY, b. 11 Nov. 1733; JOHN, b. 14 Sept.
1735; THOMAS, b. 24 Dec. 1737; WILLIAM, b. 10 May 1740 (71:208;
75:100; 77:31; 78:343; 131:50/r, 89/r).

HOLLOWAY, RICHARD, m. Elizabeth George on 26 Dec. 1760 (131).

HOLMAN, ABRAHAM (1), imm. to Md. c.1650; on 18 Aug. 1663 he
surv. 50 a. Woodham (later held by Joshua Merriken); d. leaving
a will dated 28 Dec. 1663, naming w. Isabell as extx., s. Abraham
(to have Bushwood and Holmwood at age 18), bro.-in-law Robert
Burly; admin. bond posted 22 Nov. 1666 by Edward Ayres who m.
the wid. Isabella, with John Collett and Charles Calvert; est.
was inv. on 4 Jan. 1666 by Wm. Hollis and Jos'h Tallur, and val.
at £ 332.11.4 plus £ 53.17.0; had iss.: ABRAHAM; SARAH, m. 1st
(---) Collier, and 2nd John Hall (13:216; 48:2, 4; 120:29; 121:
6; 211; 388).

HOLMAN, ABRAHAM (2), s. of Abraham (1) and Isabella, d. leaving
a will proved 1 June 1686 naming sis. Sarah Collier, bro. John
Collier, Isabella Hopper and Elizabeth Taylor and Daniel Wine;
admin. bond was posted 23 July 1686 by Sarah Collier with John
Hall, William York, Thomas Jones, and Thomas Preston; est. was
admin. 9 Aug. 1688 by extx. Sarah Collier, now Sarah Hall, with
legacies to Daniel Wind (sic), Elizabeth Taylor, the est. of
John Collier, and Isabella Hopper (13:215; 121:6; 206-10:169).

HOLMONEY, JNO., m. Eliz. Billingsley on 30 Oct. 1760 (131).

HOLMS, ANN, dau. of Easter Holms, was bound to John Cameron
and w. Sarah to age 16 in June 1731; age 2 on last St. Valentine's
Day she was given by John and Ann Cameron to Henry Wetherall
(29:156, 291).

HOLMES, JOHN, orphan, was to be kept by Thomas Presbury, Nov.
1750 (38:6).

HOLMES, MARY, serv. of James Presbury, was ind. for bearing
a mulatto bast. in Nov. 1743; was tried in March 1743/4, and ind.
again for bast. in June 1750 (35:72, 170; 37:2).

HOLMES, WILLIAM, was ind. for unlawful cohab. with Ann Cordeman in Aug. 1744; in 1760 he purch. 50 a. Jones' Neglect from
William Demmitt of Thos. (35:293; 84:160).

HOLSTOCK, THOMAS, d. by 20 Jan. 1742 when admin. bond was
posted by Joseph Johnson, with Thomas Johnson and Ferdoragh
O'Neal (13:258). See also WHOLESTOCK.

HOLT, ARNOLD, m. Martha Boarding on 11 Feb. 1744 (131).

HOLT, JOHN, d. in Balto. Co. by 9 Feb. 1758; m. Sarah (---),
d. leaving a will, 22 June 1757 - 9 Feb. 1758, naming w. as
extx., and ch.: Sarah, Anne, Mary, Elizabeth, Fanny and Clowey;
admin. bond was posted 9 Feb. 1758 by extx. Sarah Holt with John
Young and Benjamin Guyton; est. was admin. 14 Oct. 1758, the
acct. stating that the dec. left five ch., all minors; dec. left
iss.: SARAH; ANNE, b. 12 June 1744; MARY, b. 12 Dec. 1746; ELIZA-
BETH; FANNY; and CHLOE (6:7; 13:272; 111:83; 131:116/r).

HOLT, TAMESON, m. Martin Depost on 16 Jan. 1697 (129:178).

HOMEWOOD, THOMAS, was in Balto. Co. by 1692 as a taxable in
s. side Patapsco Hund. (138).

HOOD, JAMES, in July 1758 purch. 40 a. Baker's Delight from
Benjamin and Avarilla Buckingham (83:209).

HOOD, JOHN, in 1750 owned 50 a. John's Lot (153:103).

HOOD, RICHARD, m. Mary Orford on 5 Feb. 1748 (133:163).

HOOD, ROBERT, was in Balto. Co. by 1692 as a taxable in n.
side Patapsco Hund. (138).

HOOK/HOAK, JACOB, in 1750 owned 100 a. Providence (153:91).

HOOKE, EDWARD, was in Balto. Co. by 1694 as a taxable in s.
side Gunpowder Hund.; in May 1709 Edward and w. Jane conv. 100
a. The Campe to James Crooke (67:66; 139).

HOOKE, SAMUEL, of Balto. Town, on 11 June 1752 deeded 83 a.
Milford to Edward and Jane Haw or How; Samuel's w. Catherine
consented (82:15).

THE HOOKER FAMILY is the subject of a chart by Wilson Miles
Cary at the Maryland Historical Society.

HOOKER, THOMAS (1), progenitor, came to Md. c.1649, and d. c.
1684 in A. A. Co., having m. Joane (---) who d. 12, 12 mo., 1675/6
at West River Meeting; Hooker, an early convert to Quakerism,
surv. 300 a. Hooker's Purchase in A. A. Co., March 1661, 31 a.
The Courant in June 1677, and in July 1678 had 154 a. Hooker's
Chance surv.; in July 1682 was named in the will of his son-
inlaw John Hillen; d. leaving a will, 8 Nov. 1683 - 9 May 1684,
naming s. Thomas, s. Benjamin, s. Jacob, dau. Damaris Hooker and
dau. Joanna Clarkson; had iss.: THOMAS, b. 13, 5 mo., 1660;
JOANNA, b. 15 March 1660/1, m. 1st John Hillen and 2nd John
Clarkson; JACOB, b. 12 d, 6 mo. 1665 (by 1694 was a taxable in s.
side Patapsco Hund.); DAMARIS, b. 1 or 9 d, 11 mo., 1670; BENJAMIN,
b. 15 d, 11 mo. 1670; MARY ANN, b. 31 d, 6 mo., (?), d. 2 d, 6
mo., 1678 (20:121, 128; 139; 211; 388; Hooker chart by Cary, and
Reg. of West River Meeting in 219-6).

HOOKER, THOMAS (2), s. of Thomas (1) and Joane, was b. 13,
6 mo., 1660, and was living 1701; m. Sarah (---); by 1692 was a

taxable in s. side Patapsco Hund.; in Aug. 1692 was appointed
Ranger of Balto. Co. from the Falls of Back River downward to the
extent of the county; in July 1689 purch. 230 a. Mascall's Rest
from George and Mary Yate; in June 1694 surv. 500 a. Samuel's
Hope and in Feb. 1695 surv. 248 a. Maiden's Dairy which he and
w. Sarah conv. to John Yeakley in May 1701; had iss.: THOMAS, d.
c.1744 (59:310; 66:66; 139; 211; 338:106; Hooker chart by Cary).

HOOKER, BENJAMIN (3), s. of Thomas (1) and Joane, was
b. 15 d, 11 mo., 1670, and is prob. the Benjamin Hooker who in
March 1702/3 and was assigned 114 a. of land by Dutton Lane, and
in May 1704 was assigned all of Lane's personal est. (66:340).

HOOKER, THOMAS (4), s. of Thomas (2) and Sarah, d. in Balto.
Co. c.1744; m. Eleanor (---) who survived him; in Jan. 1708/9
Dutton Lane conv. Hooker and Richard Guest their moiety of New
Year's Purchase, 250 a. out of 500 a.; in Nov. 1716 Thomas conv.
100 a. of Carr's Pleasure (part of a larger tract called Samuel's
Hope) to Benjamin Carr; in Sept. 1720 he and w. Eleanor conv. 500
a. Samuel's Hope to Benjamin Bowen, except 150 a. Hooker had made
over to his s. Samuel, and 100 a. conv. to Benjamin Carr; in
Oct. 1722 Hooker and w. Eleanor and Richard Gist (Guest) and w.
Zipporah conv. 250 a. New Year's Purchase to Philip Dowell; in
Nov. 1726 Hooker and w. Eleanor conv. part of Gerar called Hooker's
Farm to s. Samuel; in March 1733 he petitioned the court to be
levy free as he was "very antient and past his labors;" in 1750
his heirs owned 200 a. Jericho and 100 a. Bethel; d. leaving a
will, 14 Dec. 1743 - 7 Nov. 1744, naming w. Eleanor (to have
Eleanor's lookout), the ch. of Benjamin Carr (to have 1 shilling
each), and the following ch.: SAMUEL, d. 1773; RICHARD; BENJAMIN;
JOHN; RUTH; EDITH, b. 24 April 1734 (30:140; 59:634; 67:452; 68:
277; 69:69; 70:287; 72:301; 73:301; 133:71; 153:94; 210-23:656).

HOOKER, SAMUEL (5), s. of Thomas (4) and Eleanor, d. in Balto.
Co. in 1773; m. Sarah (---); on 2 Nov. 1726 Thomas and Eleanor
conv. him part of Gerar; in 1750 he owned 200 a. Lasting Pasture,
100 a. William, 150 a. Point Lookout, 100 a. Addition to William,
and other land; in May 1755 he bought 66 a. Addition to Ellege's
Farm from Josephus Murray; in April 1756 he and w. Sarah sold 307
a., part Come By Chance, to Jonathan Hanson; d. leaving a will,
11 d, 8 mo., 1767 - 4 March 1773, named these ch., whose births
were recoeded in Gunpowder Meeting: SAMUEL, b. 8 April 1724, d.
1756 s.p.; LOVELY, b. 27 March 1727; RICHARD, b. 3 Oct. 1730;
THOMAS, b. 17 April 1733, disowned from meeting; SARAH, b. 15
Aug. 1733, m. Richard Richards on 14 July 1754; SOPHIA, m. Arthur
Chenoweth (70:287; 82:57, 536; 86:236; 112:239; 136; 153:5).

HOOKER, RICHARD (6), s. of Thomas (4) and Eleanor, d. in Balto.
Co. in 1781; m. Martha Barney, dau. of William Barney; applied
for a certificate of Education and Unity with Friends on 28 d, 9
mo., 1739; on 23, 7 mo., Richard and Thomas Hooker were granted
a cert. excusing them from bearing arms; on 27, 9 mo., 1759 was
in trouble with meeting for engaging in sports and neglecting his
attendance at meeting; in Aug. 1734 he bought 70 a. Tipton's Adventure from Jonathan Tipton; in March 1748 he and w. Martha
conv. 100 a. Hooker's Ridge and 70 a. Tipton's Adventure to Wm.
Wheeler; on 12 Aug. 1756 as son of Samuel and bro. and heir at
law of Samuel, dec., conv. 100 a. The Addition to John Ensor;
d. leaving a will, 28 June 1781 - 19 Sept. 1781, naming w. Martha
and these ch.: MARGARET, b. 15 Nov. 1732, m. Dutton Lane, Jr. (on
25, 11 mo., 1749 reported for having been married by a priest;
BARNEY, b. 28 Nov. 1734; in 1759 was disowned by Friends for engaging in sports, m. Kerrenhappuck, and moved to Bedford Co.,
Penna.; URATH, b. 6 Dec. 1736, in trouble in 1763 with meeting
for having been dancing; CHARITY, b. 11 March 1738; AQUILA, b. 22

Feb. 1741; SARAH, b. 28, May 1742, m. (---) Cole; MARY, b. 1 d,
11 mo., 1745, m. Benjamin Ogg; RICHARD, b. 20 Oct. 1745, d. 5
Aug. 1823 in Fairfield Co., Ohio; RUTH, b. 27, 7 mo. 1751, m.
(---) Treacle; SUSANNA, b. 17 March 1753, m. Joshua Hutson; SAMU-
EL, b. 16 Nov. 1757; JACOB, d. 1816 (74:102; 80:163; 82:580; 87:
275; 112:428; 136; 201-33:161).

HOOPER, GEORGE, of Balto. Co., d. by 1683 having m. Sarah,
wid. of (---) Collier, and dau. of Abraham Holman; she later m.
John Hall; admin. bond on his est. was posted 30 March 1683 by
the admnx. Sarah Hooper; on 9 Aug. 1688 and 4 May 1694 by Sarah, now
w. of John Hall; on 1 April 1693 Sarah w. of John Hall conv.
100 a. Holmwood to her dau. Isabella Hooper, and if she d. under
age the land was to go to the grantor's dau. Ann Collier, and
then to John Burley; on the same day John Hall conv. his "dau.-
in-law" (i.e., step-dau.), Isabella Hooper a parcel of Hooper's
Ridge; ch. of George and Sarah: ISABEL, m. 24 Aug. 1699 Robert
Jackson (13:246; 66:38, 122; 129:188; 206-10:169; 206-12:132;
206-13a:185).

HOOPER, JOHN, b. c.1699, in Dec. 1743 leased 50 a. My Lady's
Manor from Thomas Brerewood, the lease to run for the lifetimes
of Hooper, age c.44, Mary Fugate now Mary Knowles, age c. 20, and
Ann Fugate, dau. of James, age c.7 (77:440).

HOOPER, Rev. JOSEPH, Rector of St. Paul's Par., d. in Balto.
Co. leaving a will, 8 July 1739 - 8 Aug. 1739, leaving 390 a.
Bedford to his s. Joseph, and 200 a. Brother's Choice to his dau.
Mary, and naming his sis. Sarah Shorter and his mother Sarah
Hooper; on 29 Oct. 1739 George Walker ren. right of admin., and
on 2 Nov. 1739 Robert Dudley, carp., of A. A. Co., posted admin.
bond with Mord'a Hammond and William Govane; Dudley admin. the
est. on 7 Feb. 1739/40; by his w. Elizabeth, Joseph Hooper had
iss.: JOSEPH, b. 5 Dec. 1733; MARY (4:36; 13:230, 256; 127:48;
133:34).

HOOPER, ROBERT, was in Balto. Co. by 24 Jan. 1680/1 when he
purch. from George Yate 480 a. Bettie's Choice; by 10 June 1683
he was in A. A. Co., when as a cooper he sold the land to Col.
William Burgess(106:287-288).

HOPE, GEORGE, was in Balto. Co. by 9 Aug. 1695 when he surv.
200 a. Hope's Lot; had been in A. A. Co. on Feb. 1682 when he
purch. 250 a. Denchworth from George and Mary Yate; m. Judith
Clark on 27 May 1706 in All Hallow's Par., A. A. Co.; d. leaving
a will, 7 June 1721 - 22 July 1721, naming w. as extx., and ch.:
George, Anne, and Mary, and also naming Samuel Maxfield; admin.
bond was posted 22 July 1721 by extx. Judith Hope with William
Slade and Thomas Taylor; est. was admin. by William Hutchings
or Hawkins, and his w. Judith, on 10 July 1722 and 13 Nov. 1722;
left iss.: GEORGE; MARY; and ANNE (1:69, 78; 3:81; 13:223; 59:
36; 124:60; 207; 219-1).

HOPE, JAMES, was in Balto. Co. by 1695 as a taxable in s. side
Patapsco Hund. (140).

HOPHAM, GEORGE (1), progenitor, was in Balto. Co. by 1692 as
a taxable in n. side Patapsco Hund.; by 1 April 1710; owned
65 a. The Wedge orig. surv. 24 Nov. 1673 for Giles Stevens; admin.
bond was posted by George Newport with John Gay and William
Wright; est. was inv. by John Gay and William Wright and val. at
£ 18.18.0, and signed by Jean Hoppam and William Hoppum (sic) as
kin; est. was admin. 14 May 1711 by George Newport; dec. left
iss.: WILLIAM; JANE (1:246; 13:189; 21:571; 51:26; 211).

HOPHAM, WILLIAM (2), s. of George (1), d. in Balto. Co. by
2 Dec. 1752; m. by June 1724 Jane, admnx. of George Newport; admin. bond was posted 27 April 1751 by John Morgan and Jacob Sindall; est. admin. on 2 Dec. 1752 and again on 6 Aug. 1753 by Francis Rider, who m. Frances Hopham on 7 Aug. 1750, dec. might be a
fifth ch. of William, or a second w.; dec. left iss.: GEORGE, b.
c.1734; WILLIAM, b. c.1737; JANE, b. c.1740; RUTH, b. c.1742 (5:
231, 293; 13:269; 26:356; 131).

HOPHAM, JANE (3), dau. of George (1), is prob. the Jane Hopham ind. for bast. in March 1719/20 again in June 1729, and ind.
again and tried in Aug. 1734 (23:279, 405; 30:305, 309).

HOPHAM, WILLIAM (4), s. of William (2) was living in Balto. Co.
on 30 Nov. 1767 when William purch. Parrishes Range from Stephen
and Sarah Wooden (92:223).

HOPKINS, GERARD (1), progenitor, d. in A. A. Co. in 1692; m.
Thomasine (---); in 14 July 1687 Robert Smith of A. A. Co. left
prop. to Anne and Gerard, ch. of Gerard Hopkins; d. leaving a
will, dated 12 Oct. 1691, naming w. Thomasine and ch.: George,
Ann, Thomsen (sic), and Mary; dec. left iss.: GERARD, d. 1743;
ANN, m. Henry Roberts on 10 Dec. 1699; THOMASINE, m. John Welch
on 13 March 1700; MARY, m. Thomas Wells on 9 Aug. 1705 (121:49;
122:182; 123:17; 219-1; 219-2).

HOPKINS, GERARD (2), s. of Gerard (1) and Thomasine, d. in A.
A. Co. by 1743; m. Margaret Johns, dau. of Richard and Margaret
(Kinsey) Johns; d. leaving a will, 1 Jan. 1741/2 - 2 Feb. 1743/4.
naming w. Margaret and ch.: Joseph, Johns, Gerard, Philip,Samuel,
Richard and William, and granddaus. Priscilla and Mary Hill;
births of the ch. were recorded in West River Meeting, Soc. of
Friends: ELIZABETH, b. 16, 1 mo., 1703; m. (---) Hall; JOSEPH,
b. 2, 9 mo., 1706, m. Anne Chew on 17, 6 mo., 1727; GERARD, b.
7, 1 mo. 1709; PHILIP, b. 9, 1, 1711; SAMUEL, b. 16, 11, 1713;
RICHARD, b. 15, 10, 1715; WILLIAM, b. 8, 6 mo. 1718, m. Rachel
Orrick; JOHNS, b. 30, 8, 1720 (123:143; 127:239; Reg. of West
River 219-6; Kelly, Quakers in the Founding of A. A. Co., p.
96).

HOPKINS, GERARD (3), s. of Gerard (2), was b. 7 day, 1, 1709;
d. 3, 7, 1777, aged 68; m. Mary Hall, dau. of Richard Hall on 7,
3 mo., 1730; may be the Gerard Hopkins listed in 1750 as owning
630 a. Friends' Discovery and 382 a. part Bachelor's Good Luck
(153:98; Reg. of West River Meeting in 219-6).

HOPKINS, SAMUEL (4), s. of Gerard (2), was b. 16, 11 mo.
1713, and d. by 1767; m. Sarah Giles, dau. of John and Cassandra
Giles, on 2, 7, 1740; d. leaving a will, 31, 10, 1765 - 9 May
1767; births of all ch. except James and Johns were reorded in
Gunpowder Meeting; left iss.: GERARD, b. 26 April 1742; SAMUEL,
b. 9 Dec. 1743, m. Hannah Wilson; JOHN, b. 4 Jan. 1746,m. Eliza
beth Chew; MARGARET, b. 2 Sept. 1747, m. Job Hunt; PHILIP, b. 30
Sept. 1749; ELIZABETH, b. 17 Aug. 1751,m. Isaac Webster; poss.
JAMES; CASSANDRA, b. 17 Jan. 1755; RICHARD, b. 31 Aug. 1756;
JOSEPH, b. 2 Sept. 1758; WILLIAM, b. 23 June 1760; NICHOLAS, d.
young; JOHNS, b. 6 June 1764 (112:58; 115:260; 136; 137; Reg. of
Deer Creek Meeting, and Reg. of West River Meeting:see 219-6; 372).

HOPKINS, RICHARD (5), s. of Gerard (2), was b. 15, 10, 1715;
m. Katherine Todd; d. leaving a will, 1780 - 1785; had iss. (b.
in Gunpowder Meeting): NICHOLAS, b. 12 May 1747; RACHEL, b. 31
Jan. 1749; RICHARD, b. 17 Feb. 1750; SARAH, b. 20 Sept. 1751;
KATHARINE, b. 20 Jan. 1753, d. 1763; GARRARD, b. 21 Feb. 1754;

SAMUEL, b. 25, 9 mo., 1756, d. 1757; ELIZABETH, b. 17 d, 9, 1758; JOSEPH, b. 9, 4, 1761 (113:49; 136).

HOPKINS, JOHN, m. Ann Hickinbotham on 27 Dec. 1713 (131).

HOPKINS, JOHN, d. by 10 Aug. 1719 when admin. bond was posted by Francis Dallahide with Matthew Hale and Joseph Presbury; est. was inv. on 3 Oct. 1719 by George York and John Elliott and val. at £ 8.0.0, and signed by Francis Dallahide as admin., notation that one heir was in Eng. and one heir was dead (13:198; 48:262).

HOPKINS, JOSEPH, of Balto. Co., imm. c.1664; on 26 March 1667 Edward Carter assigned his int. in some land to his bro.-in-law Joseph Hopkins; purch. 200 a. part The Folly from Joseph Langley in April 1670, 200 a. Colleton from John Collet in July 1670, and 200 a. Chenyche from John Willis in June 1674 (61:31; 96:230; 100:117).

HOPKINS, JOSEPH, purch. 100 a. Hawkins' Choice from John and Rebecca Hawkins in March 1731; in 1750 he owned 600 a. Phillips' Purchase (61:395; 153:59).

HOPKINS, MARGARET, had a bast. ch., in the care of Elizabeth Jones in Aug. 1724 (26:437).

HOPKINS, ROBERT, was in Balto. Co. by 1694 as a taxable in s. side of Patapsco Hund.; d. by 1 Dec. 1703 when admin. bond was posted by extx. Sarah Hopkins with John Martin and William Mead; est. was inv. on 23 Dec. 1703 by John Grunest and John Gardiner and val. at £ 52.19.6; Hopkins had left a will, 8 Sept. 1703 - 27 Nov. 1703, naming w. Sarah, and leaving 81 a. Hopkins' Lot to dau.: ANN (13:204; 51:38; 122:39; 139).

HOPKINS, WILLIAM, m. Rachel (---) by 2 Nov. 1742 when they admin. the est. of Charles Daniel; on 2 Aug. 1743 William and Rachel conv. 600 a. Hector's Fancy to William Jenkins; had s.: CHARLES, b. 1 Aug. 1741 (3:296; 35:79; 77:296; 129:327).

HORN, WILLIAM, m. by 8 Nov. 1743 a dau. of Abigail Barton and had a dau.: ALICE (77:363).

HORNE, WILLIAM, was in Balto. Co. by March 1681 when he and w. Mary conv. 64 a. Horne's Point to George Oglesby; in Nov. 1684 he and Mary conv. 50 a. Daniel's Nest or Neck (taken up by Thomas O'Daniel, and one part of which desc. to Horne's w. Mary) to John Hall; in Aug. 1695 took up 50 a. William which was later held by Horne's orphans; in 1694 was a taxable in s. side Gunpowder Hund.; d. leaving a will, 27 April 1705 - 9 June 1705, naming s. Francis as exec. and sole legatee; admin. bond was posted 9 June 1705 by Francis Horne with Edward Smith and Alexander Gray; a second admin. bond was posted 20 Sept. 1705 by William Denton with Edward Smith and Henry Wriothesley; est. was inv. by John Rallings and Matthew Groom and val. at £ 11.5.0; est. was admin. by Denton on 19 Sept. 1707; had iss.: FRANCIS (13:207, 209; 48:294; 59:101; 64:159; 122:46; 139; 211).

HORNER, RICHARD (1), d. in Balto. Co. by 17 April 1710 when admin. bond was posted by Thomas Croker and William Slade; est. was inv. by Luke Reed and William Reed; est. was admin. by Thomas Croker on 30 Nov. 1711; had iss.: NICHOLAS, b. c.1698 (2:1; 13: 210; 21:136; 48:102, 162).

HORNER, NICHOLAS (2), s. of Richard (1), was age 12 in May 1710; in June 1710 after his father's death was bound to Stephen White until age 21; m. by 1729 Ann (---) who m. as her 2nd husb. Matthew Beck; d. by 2 April 1740 when admin. bond was posted by

Ann Horner, with Isaac and Jacob Jackson; est. was admin. by Ann,
w. of Matthew Beck, on 13 Nov. 1741 and 4 April 1745; had iss.:
NATHAN, b. 25 March 1729; SARAH, b. 30 June 1731; REASON, b.
1734; RACHAEL, b. 1 June 1737; MARY; and poss. THOMAS (4:112;
5:51; 13:247; 21:136; 35:474-476; 131:76/r).

HORNER, THOMAS (3), poss. s. of Nicholas (1), m. Grace Anderson on 27 Oct. 1741; she was wid. of Charles Anderson, by whom
she had at least two ch., Sarah _ and Daniel; in 1750 Thomas Horner owned 100 a. Carpenter's Plains and 50 a. Woods' Habitation;
d. leaving a will, 16 June 1756 - 2 Oct. 1756, naming w. Grace,
ch. James and William, dau.-in-law Sarah Anderson and son-in-law
Daniel Anderson, and lands Chance and William's Chance; had
iss.: SARAH, b. 26 Dec. 1741; CASSANDRA, b. 21 March 1743; JAMES;
WILLIAM (128:116; 129:324, 333; 153:18; 210-30:150).

HORNER, NATHAN (4), s. of Nicholas (2), was b. 25 March 1729;
in 1750 he owned 200 a. William's Ridge (153:94).

HORNER, JAMES, m. Tam'r Cameron on 25 Dec. 1760, and had:
ESTHER, b. 18 Feb. 1761; MARGARET, b. 26 Dec. 1762 (131:57,
156/r).

HORNER, NATHANIEL, m. Jane Wigglefield on 26 April 1764
(131).

HORNER, WILLIAM, was in Balto. Co. by 1694 as a taxable in n.
side Patapsco Hund. (139).

HORSEMAN, (---), female child, d. 1720 (128:58).

HORSMAN, MARGARET, orphan of Samuel Horsman (who has left the
county), to be kept by William Robinson until next Nov.; Aug.
1714 was the date of the order (21:539).

HORTON, ANN, was ind. for bast. in Aug. 1717 (22:152).

HORTON, EDWARD, in Nov. 1673 sold 100 a. Horton's Fortune to
Thomas Byworth (99:349).

HORTON, JOHN, m. Priscilla (---), and had: WILLIAM, b. March
1743, bound to Samuel Webb in Nov. 1757 (46:81; 131:105).

HORTON, RICHARD, m. Eliz. Davice on 21 Aug. 1755 (131).

HORTON, WILLIAM, m. Elizabeth Wakeman or Pritchard on 21 March
1759; in Jan. 1768 William leased Hall's Plains to Nicholas Baker;
had iss.: EDWARD WAKEMAN PRITCHARD, b. 22 Feb. 1760; WILLIAM, b.
22 Jan. 1762 (92:488; 129:367).

HOSSEY, ISAAC, m. Elizabeth (---) and had iss.: DANIEL, b. 27
Oct. 1732; RACHEL, b. 15 July 1734 (128:84).

HOUCHINS, WILLIAM, m. by 9 Dec. 1724 Judith, extx. of George
Hope, and conv. Westwood to Samuel Westwood (70:89).

HOUCHINS, WILLIAM, d. leaving a will, 26 Feb. 1748 - 8 July
1748, leaving land to w. Hannah for her life and then to Charles
Conaway (210-26:120).

HOUGATE, JONATHAN, m. Elizabeth, and had: WILLIAM, b. 16 Sept.
1722 (131).

HOUSE, JOHN, m. Penelope Bond in 1750 (131).

HOUSMAN, WILLIAM, "history painter," in June 1733 pet. the
court that he came into the country as an indented serv. in the
ship Neptune, Capt. Jerningham Bigg, and asked to have three
months taken off his time (30:8).

HOUSTON, ALEXANDER, d. 18 Nov. 1719 (128:37).

HOUTON, EDWARD, age c.35, was transp. for 7 years from London
in the ship Barwick, John Malger, commander, owned by Norton
Groves Baker, Richard Deaver, wid. Mary Deaver, Michael Webster
and most recently by Jacob Giles, in March 1750; d. by Nov.
1758 leaving iss.; EDWARD, b. c.1751, bound out in Nov. 1758
(44; 385:74).

HOVER, CHRISTIAN, in 1750 owned 100 a. part Digges' Choice
(153:97).

HOW/HOWE, CHRISTOPHER, m. Rebecca (---) who m. as her 2nd
husb. (---) Gilbert; had iss.: SARAH, b. 15 July 1716 (in March
1721/2 as dau. of Rebecca Gilbert was bound to John and Mary
Debruler to age 16 (24:16; 128:36).

HOWACRES, MARY, was ind. for bast. in Nov. 1742 (34:59).

THE HOWARD FAMILY OF ANDERSON'S LOT

HOWARD, LEMUEL (1), d. in Balto. Co. by 6 June 1739; m. Mrs.
Ann Ward on 11 Jan. 1730; she d. by 10 Aug. 1772; in 1750 he
owned 400 a. Anderson's Lot and 262 a. To Luck; d. leaving a will,
2 May 1758 - 6 June 1759, naming w. Ann and ch.: John Greeniff
Howard, Benjamin Howard, Lemuel Howard, and Susanna Dutton; the
est. of Ann Howard was admin. 10 Aug. 1772 by Benjamin Howard;
had iss.: BENJAMIN, b. 12 Sept. 1731; SUSANNAH, b. 18 Sept. 1735,
m. Robert Dutton; LEMUEL, b. 24 Dec. 1736; JOHN GREENIFF (7:133;
111:306; 131:68/r; 153:23).

HOWARD, BENJAMIN (2), s. of Lemuel (1) and Ann, was b. 12
Sept. 1731, was alive in 1776; m. 1st, on 7 Oct. 1755, Sarah
Bond; m. 2nd, on 4 d, 12, 1766 Mary, dau. of Robert Dutton; was
received into membership at Gunpowder Meeting; had iss.: (by 1st
w.): SUSANNAH, b. 1, 7 mo., 1756; ANNE, b. 7, 6 mo., 1758, m.
John Mason; BENJAMIN, Jr., b. 8, 9 mo. 1759; (by 2nd w.): ELIZA-
BETH, b. 13, 12 mo., 1767; LEMUEL, b. 7, 9 mo. 1769; MARY, b. 1,
2 mo. 1772; SARAH, b. 10, 3 mo. 1774 (131; 136).

HOWARD, LEMUEL (3), s. of Lemuel (1) and Anne, was b. 24 Dec.
1736; m. by 11 Aug. 1762 one of the daus. of Aquila Scott;
in 1776 lived in Bush River Lower Hundred, Harford Co.; had iss.:
RUTH, b. c.1762; ELIZABETH, b. c.1764; AQUILA, b. c.1766; ANNE,
b. c.1768; MARTHA, b. c.1770; SARAH, b. c.1772; SUSANNA, b. c.
1772; DORSEY, b. c.1774 (4:375; 285).

THE HOWARD FAMILY OF HOWARD'S SQUARE AND GREY ROCK is more
fully discussed in Vol. II of The Green Spring Valley, its History and Heritage (259).

HOWARD, JOSHUA (4), no knwon rel. to any of the above, poss.
a native of Manchester, Eng., came to Md. c.1685; d. 1738; in
1698 surv. Howard's Square; m. Joanna O'Carroll who d. by 12
Aug. 1765; d. leaving a will, 3 July 1738 - 14 Sept. 1738,
naming s. Francis (to have 100 a. Howard's Inheritance), ch.:
Cornelius, Edmund, Sarah Gist, Mary Gist, Elizabeth Wells, and
Violetta Gist; admin. bond was posted 14 Sept. 1738 by Cornelius
Howard with Josephus Murray and Edmond Howard; est. was admin.
on 8 Jan. 1739 and 20 April 1741; had iss.: FRANCIS; CORNELIUS,

b. c.1706; EDMUND; SARAH, m. (---) Gist; MARY, m. Nathaniel
Gist; ELIZABETH, m. Thomas Wells, and VIOLETTA, m. William Gist
(4:40, 80; 13:228; 112:7; 126:256; 211).

HOWARD, CORNELIUS (5), s. of Joshua (4) and Joanna, was b. c.
1706/7, d. 14 June 1777; m. Ruth, dau. of John Eager on 24 Jan.
1738; she was b. 23 May 1721, d. 17 Nov. 1796; in 1750 Cornelius
owned 100 a. Cornelius and Mary's Lot, 57 a. Joshua's Gift, 150
a. Howard's Square, 50 a. Security, 100 a. Hurd's Camp, and other
lands; had iss.: GEORGE, b. 12 March 1740, m. Mrs. Hannah Edwards
(nee Jones); may be the George whose est. was admin. by Cornelius
Howard on 1 Feb. 1769; RACHEL, b. 5 May 1743; JOSHUA, b. 29 Sept.
1745; RUTH, b. 13 Sept. 1747; RACHEL, b. 14 Oct. 1749; JOHN EAGER,
b. 4 June 1752; CORNELIUS, b. 2 Dec. 1754; VIOLETTA, b. 22 Sept.
1759; ANNE, b. 10 July 1765 (134:5, 7, 14, 21, 24, 25, 30, 295;
153:41).

HOWARD, EDMUND (6), s. of Joshua (4) and Ruth, d. by 4 March
1745; on 30 Aug. 1735 conv. 40 a. part Tanyard with Emanuel Teal;
d. leaving a will, 19 April 1745 - 7 Aug. 1745, naming w. Ruth,
and ch.: Joshua, Ruhammah, Charles, Rebecca, Mary, and Johanna;
admin. bond was posted 4 March 1745 by extx. Ruth Howard, with
John Metcalfe and Emanuel Teale; est. was admin. on 10 Nov. 1755
by admnx. Ruth, w. of William Lewis; had iss.: REBECCA, b. 2 May
1733; JOSHUA, b. 26 Nov. 1735; EDMUND, b. 11 Sept. 1745; RUHAMMAH;
CHARLES; MARY; and JOHANNAH (34:6; 74:285; 111:215; 133:28, 47).

HOWARD, FRANCIS, in 1750 owned 22 a. Howard's Adventure (153:
93).

HOWARD, GEORGE, in 1750 owned 200 a. part Friendship (153:
105).

HOWARD, GIDEON, m. Hannah, admnx. of William Orrick by 23
Oct. 1723 (1:116).

HOWARD, GREENIFF, in 1750 owned 410 a. part Caprio (153:88).

HOWARD, HANNAH, was ind. for bast. in Aug. 1742, and tried for
bast. that November; ind. for bast. again in Aug. 1744 (34:1, 74;
35:293).

HOWARD, JAMES, m. by March 1683/4 Jane, relict of Ambrose Gillett (18:141).

HOWARD, JOHN, was in Balto. by 1692 as a taxable in Spesutia
Hund.; had iss.: THOMAS, b. 7 Oct. 1683; JOHN, b. 6 July 1696
(128:1, 4; 138).

HOWARD, JOHN, of West River, in 1750 owned 250 a. James Forest
and 100 a. John's Delight (153:102).

HOWARD, JOHN GREENIFF, in Aug. 1752 lived in the Forks of
Gunpowder (385:190).

HOWARD, RICHARD, m. Margaret (---), and had: JOHN, b. 28 Feb.
1738 (131:113/r).

HOWARD, SAMUEL, in 1750 owned 250 a. Lucky Adventure (153:
103).

HOWARD, SAMUEL, in 1756 lived at Col. John Hall's, Balto.
Co., and wrote to bro. and sis. Timothy Brent, Jr., at the Office
of Chelsea Water Works, Abingdon Buildings, Westminster, and
referred to bro. Matthew; was a tutor to Col. John Hall's children (300-65:260).

HOWARD, THOMAS, m. Katherine, wid. and extx. of Anthony
Johnson, by 15 April 1724 (2:344; 69:273).

HOWARD, WILLIAM, was in Balto. Co. by Aug. 1688 when he purch.
50 a. Hendrick and 50 a. Hendrickson from Hendrick and Juniber
Hendrickson; may be the William Howard who with w. Martha joined
John and Hannah Webster in Nov. 1704, in selling Cow Pasture to
Christopher Cox in Nov. 1704; d. leaving a will, 8 Jan. 1710 -
5 March 1717, leaving 100 a. Howard's Forest to Henry Munday,
and pers. prop. to Samuel Webster of John, and the res. of his
est. to his wid. and extx. Martha; Martha m. 2nd, by 4 Nov. 1719
William Burney (64:3; 68:60; 95; 110:47).

HOWARD, WILLIAM, d. 29 Jan. 1718 (131:12).

HOWE, SARAH, dau. of Rebecca Gilbert, in March 1721/2, was
bound to John and Mary Debrular to age 16 (24:16).

HOWELL, SAMUEL, (1) in Balto. Co. by Dec. 1720 when he m.
Priscilla Freeborne; was alive in March 1733; had iss.: DANIEL,
b. 15 Sept. 1721; SAMUEL, b. 11 Jan. 1732 (prob. 1722); MORDECAI,
b. 10 June 1725; PHEBE, b. 3 Nov. 1726; AQUILA, b. 3 Sept. 1728;
FRENELLA, date of birth not given; JOB, b. 10 March 1733 (128:
85).

HOWELL, SAMUEL (2), s. of Samuel (1), was b. 11 Jan. 1722(?),
d. by 1769; m. Sarah Durbin on 11 Sept. 1747, with whom he entered into an antenuptial contract on 10 Sept. 1746; his est.
was admin. in 1769 by Sarah, w. of William Virchworth; in 1750
owned 100 a. North Yarmouth; had iss.: ASENATH, b. 31 Jan. 1748;
MORDECAI, b. 18 Jan. 1750; SAMUEL, b. 11 Sept. 1753; AVARILLA, b.
1 Feb. 1756, m. Francis Billingsley (6:305; 7:65; 79:177; 129:
370; 153:98).

HOWELL, THOMAS, was in Balto. Co. with w. Elizabeth by 20
Oct. 1662 when he conv. all but 50 a. of Sutton Underhill to
Nathaniel Stiles; in Sept. 1669, bought 275 a. on s. side of
Sassafras River, from Henry and Ann Jones; in March 1669/70 sold
275 a. to Henry Heldesley; in March 1672/3 sold James Hepbourne
200 a. of land; s. in Cecil Co., leaving a will, 5 Oct. 1675 -
28 Nov. 1675, naming w. Eliza, sons John and Nathaniel, and
dau. Sarah w. of John Vanheck; left iss.; JOHN; NATHANIEL; and
SARAH, m. John Van Heck (93; 95; 86; 99; 110:112; 200-67:281).

HOWGATE, JONATHAN, serv., with 2 mos. to serve in 1722 inv. of
Aquila Paca (50:142).

HOWLAND, JOHN, age c.19, from London, runaway serv., who was
advert. for in April 1759 (307-69:125).

HOWLES, ANN, m. William Wright, Jr., on 4 Sept. 1721 (131).

HOWLETT, ROBERT, req. to pub. the banns of marr. with Elizabeth Boone (131).

HOWS, JOHN, m. Penelope Bond on 22 July 1750 (131).

HOXTON, HYDE, in 1750 owned 100 a. Friends' Adventure (153:
92).

HUBBARD, ADAM, in 1750 owned 150 a. part Brotherly Love (153:
91).

HUBBARD, ED., carpenter, was listed in the 1747 inv. of William Fell (54:204).

HUBBARD, EDWARD, m. Mary (---), and had: SUSANNAH, b. 19 Oct. 1737; ANN, b. 20 Aug. 1742 (133:76, 77).

HUBBARD, JOHN, m. by 1680 Margaret, relict and admnx. of Jno. Leakins (2:45).

HUDGE, JOHN, was in Balto. Co. by Jan. 1756 when he purch. 50 a. Stocksdale's Abode from Thomas and Sarah Stocksdale (82: 492).

HUDGELL, THOMAS, m. Alice (---), and had iss.: JOSEPH, b. 22 May 1746; ELIZABETH, b. 12 Aug. 1748; ANN, b. 9 Dec. 1750; THOMAS, b. 16 July 1752; HENRY, b. 29 Jan. 1755; ROSANNAH, b. 29 July 1758 (134:29).

HUDSON, MATTHEW, was in Balto. Co. by 3 May 1686 when he was granted a power of atty. by Robert Burman; in May 1687 he purch. 350 a. part Burman's Forest from Robert and Ann Burman; d. leaving a will dated 27 Dec. 1688, leaving Burman's Forest to w. Jane for life and then to (---) Black, and reserving 100 a. Jonas' Range to Joseph Perrigo (59:123, 271, 345).

HUDSON, THOMAS, was in Balto. Co. by Jan. 1744 when he purch. 62½ a. Batson's Forest from John and Mary Baxter; still owned the land in 1750; had iss.: WILLIAM, b. 8 Oct. 1746; MARY, b. 9 Sept. 1748; SARAH, b. 24 Dec. 1750; THOMAS, b. 15 March 1752; JOSHUA, b. 16 Sept. 1756; MARGARET, b. 10 May 1759; DANIEL, b. 30 May 1761; ELIZABETH, b. 25 July 1766 (78:27; 134:40, 296; 153:71).

HUDSON, WILLIAM, m. Sarah Deason on 30 Jan. 1749 (131).

HUETT. See HEWETT.

HUFF, or HOUGH, MICHAEL (1), brought a cert. for himself and family from Nottingham Meeting to Gunpowder; d. by 24, 6 mo., 1748, leaving a wid. Janet, and at least two ch.: MICHAEL; JENNET who ret. to Nottingham Meeting in 1753 (136).

HUFF, MICHAEL (2), s. of Michael (1), in 1750 owned 50 a. of Hickory Bottom; ret. to Nottingham Meeting in Dec. 1762 (136; 153:87).

HUGGINS, JOHN (1), was b. c.1700, leased several portions of My Lady's Manor; d. by 6 June 1746 when admin. bond on his est. was posted by Charles Ridgely with John Stinchcomb and Nicholas Gay; m. 1st Sarah (---): JOHN, b. c.1722; ANN, b. 2 Oct. 1725; WILLIAM, b. 11 Oct. 1730; DANIEL, b. 11 Aug. 1733; JAMES, b. 20 July 1736; JACOB, b. 20 July 1739 (13:257; 77:115, 235).

HUGGINS, JOHN (2), s. of John (1), was b. c.1722; m. Mary Downs on 7 Oct. 1742; in Nov. 1742 leased part My Lady's Manor for his lifetime, that of his wife, age 17, and his bro. Daniel, age 9 (77:115; 131).

HUGGINS, JAMES (3), s. of John (1), was b. 20 July 1736; age 13 in March 1746/7 when he was bound to John Chalk (36:379; 131).

HUGGINS, JACOB (4), s. of John (1), was b. 20 July 1739, age 13 in June 1750 (sic) when, as orphan of John, was bound to Thomas Hallam (37:2; 131).

HUGHES, MATTHIAS (1), was a res. of St. James' Par., in A. A. Co., where he d. leaving a will dated 21 Jan. 1702, leaving the tract Paw Paw Ridge to his sons Samuel and John (on their major-

ity), naming daus. Sarah and Margaret, with Sarah Little as the
extx.; dec. left iss.: SAMUEL, b. c.1685; JOHN, under age in 1702;
SARAH, m. Gregory Farmer on 27 Aug. 1703; MARGARET (122:12; 129:
199).

HUGHES, SAMUEL (2), s. of Matthias (1), was b. c.1785, and d.
in Balto. Co., in 1771; m. Jane Scott, wid. of Francis Watkins and
dau. of Daniel and Jane (Johnson) Scott, on 4 Nov. 1714; in April
1746 Samuel Hughes and Hannah Litton, alias Jones were summoned
before the vestry of St. John's Parish for unlawful cohabitation;
in Sept. 1757 Jane Hughes reported her husb. to the vestry for unlawful cohabitation with Henrietta Jones; in 1750 Jane Hughes was
listed in the Debt Book as owning 26 a. part Hathaway's Hazard and
112 a. part Sophia's Dairy; on 19 June 1736 Samuel and Jane conv.
100 a. King's Increase to Gregory Farmer who sold it back to Samuel
Hughes on 28 July 1739; on 3 Aug. 1743 Samuel conveyed to his son
John 174 a. part Hathaway's Hazard; on 13 July 1743 Samuel conv.
livestock to his dau. Sarah, son John, and dau. Margaret or Mary
w. of Jacob Hanson; in 1757 Walter Ashmore conv. 62 a. Beautiful
Island to Samuel Hughes, who conv. 62 a. Addition to Beautiful
Island to his s. Aaron; Jane Hughes, d. leaving a will, 14 April
1762 - 31 Oct. 1765,naming grandson Thomas Hughes, dau. Margaret
Hanson, Jane Osborn, grandsons Thomas Little and John Hall Hughes
son of dau. Sarah Little, dec., also grandchildren Daniel, Francis,
Jane, Elizabeth, Nathaniel, and Daniel Scott Watkins who were ch.
of the testatrix' s. Francis Watkins; Samuel Hughes m. as his 2nd
w. Hannah (---), and d. leaving a will, 5 Jan. 1771 - 11 Feb. 1771,
naming w. Hannah and ch.: John, Margaret, Jane, and Sarah (and her
heirs by Thomas Little); ch. of Samuel Hughes (by 1st w.): MARGAR-
ET, b. 18 Oct. 1716, m. Jacob Hanson on 23 Jan. 1738; JOHN, b. 15
March 1719; JANE, b. 30 May 1721, m. James Osborn on 17 Sept. 1743;
SARAH, b. 15 Oct. 1723; MARY, b. 4 July 1725; (by an unknown w.,
or by Hannah): AARON, of age to be conv. 62 a. land by his father
(74:412; 75:267; 77:291, 378, 379, 380; 128:32, 37, 40, 43, 45;
129:309, 332; 83:109; 91:675; 112:27, 185; 132; 153:26).

HUGHES, JOHN (3), s. of Samuel (2) and Jane, was b. 15 March
1719; prob. the John who m. Elizabeth, dau. of Benjamin Norris, on
11 Sept. 1740; d. leaving a will, 25 Aug. 1785 - 5 March 1791,
naming ch.; had iss.: THOMAS, b. 10 June 1741; JOHN, b. 29 Dec.
1742; MARY, b. 25 July 1745, m. (---) Bond; BENJAMIN; SUSANNAH;
JAMES; ELIJAH; HORATION (poss. the Samuel, age 15 last
17 March who was bound to Robert Brierly in Aug. 1757); ELIZABETH,
m. (---) Brady; MARTHA, m. (---) Wheeler (46:58; 113:526; 129:
330, 331, 342).

HUGHES, SARAH (4), dau. of Samuel (2) and Jane, was b. 15 Oct.
1723; was ind. for bast. in Aug. 1742 and tried in March 1742/3;
later m. Thomas Little; had iss.: JOHN HALL HUGHES, b. 10 July
1742 (34:1, 130; 129:338).

HUGHES, AARON (5), s. of Samuel (2), m. Elizabeth Taylor on
22 Nov. 1764, and was conv. 62 a. Addition to Beautiful Island in
Aug. 1767 (91:675; 131).

HUGHES, CALEB, m. by 17 Sept. 1740 Hester, wid. of Peter Bond
(4:61).

HUGHES, DAVID, m. by 7 Nov. 1730 Mary, wid. and extx. of John
Roberts (2:249; 75:140, 141).

HUGHES, FELIX, m. Catherine Noble on 1 Oct. 1743, and had
iss.: THOMAS, b. 7 July 1744 (129:339).

HUGHES, JOHN, d. by 28 Nov. 1755 when est. was admin. by James
McCabe; dec. left four children (5:341).

HUGHES, JONATHAN, m. Jane, wid. of Rowland Shepherd and dau. of Martin Taylor, Jr., on 10 Dec. 1728; on 29 June 1732 he purch. 36 a. Thompson's Fortune and 150 a. William's Fortune from Robert Robertson and w. Sarah; in 1750 he owned the latter tract as well as 36 a. part Roberts Chance, 50 a. Preston's Devresh(?), and 81 a. Hughes' Fortune; d. by 6 Jan. 1755 when admin. bond was posted by William Scott with James Maxwell and Christ'r Divers; est. was admin. by Scott on 5 March 1757; dec. had iss.: SARAH, b. 14 Sept. 1730; CLEMENCY, b. 25 Sept. 1739; ELIZABETH, b. 4 Aug. 1747 (in Nov. 1757 was made a ward of William Presbury) (4:53; 5:321; 13:268; 44; 46:79; 73:311; 77:114; 128:66; 129:244; 153:26).

HUGHES, JOSEPH, was in Balto. Co. by April 1671 when he sold Thomas Heath 100 a. Red Budd Point; surv. 150 a. Chance in Aug. 1669; d. by 1700 leaving an heiress who was m. to Thomas Preston (in June 1727 Thomas Cross held this land in right of his w. Sarah); had iss.: dau., m. Thomas Preston (97:126; 211; 225:15).

HUGHES, MARY, was ind. for bast. in March 1746/7 (36:478).

HUGHES, ROBERT, of Balto. Co. claimed land for service in 1674 (388).

HUGHES, SAMUEL, of Balto. Co., m. Ann (---) who claimed land for her service in 1673 (388).

HUGHES, THOMAS, was in Balto. Co. by March 1719 when he surv. 50 a. Stony Run Hills; in Nov. 1719 was granted a lic. to keep the Patapsco Ferry; on 15 May 1725 as Thomas Hughes, carp., sold 50 a. Stony Run Hills to Benjamin Belt of P. G. Co.; in Nov. 1725 bought part Duck Cove from Melchizedek and Sophia Murray; his house burned in Nov. 1735; had iss.: MARY, spinster to whom he conv. prop. in March 1724; ELIZABETH, m. by 13 March 1724/5 Luke Raven (23:242; 70:30, 89, 138, 206; 384:120).

HUGHES, THOMAS, poss. an orphan, in May 1740 bound himself as an apprentice with the consent of his uncle Jonathan Hughes (75: 384).

HUGHES, WILLIAM, m. Elizabeth, dau. of John Crowley, on 25 Nov. 1716 in St. Anne's Par., A. A. Co.; he may have been a s. of Thomas who d. 1736/7 in A. A. Co.; had iss.: ESTHER, b. 21 April 1717; JOHN, b. 20 Sept. 1719; ROWLAND, b. 6 Feb. 1721/2; ELIZABETH, b. 12 Feb. 1723; ELEANOR, b. 8 Aug. 1726; GRACE, b. 3 Sept. 1729; GAWAIN, b. 3 Sept. 1732 (128:38, 41, 46, 49, 82; 219-1:398).

HUGHES, WILLIAM, was in Balto. Co. by April 1733 when he purch. part Triple Union from Thomas and Sophia White; in July 1733 purch. 50 a. of the same tract from the same couple; in 1750 he owned 100 a. part Triple Union and 50 a. Hughes' Hogyard; in Nov. 1758 conv. 50 a. Triple Union to John Hughes (61:487; 73:383; 83:268; 153:10).

HUGHES, WILLIAM, m. Hannah, admnx. of Joseph Bankson on 11 Dec. 1735; d. leaving a will, 12 March 1743 - 3 Jan. 1748, naming w. Hannah, and dau.-in-law Hannah Bankson; admin. bond was posted 3 Jan. 1748 by Hannah Hughes with Robert North and Greenbury Dorsey (4:15; 13:261; 110:436; 133:154).

HULL, JOSEPH, m. and had iss.: DAVID, b. 27 March 1696 (128:4).

HUMBLES, THOMAS, was in Balto. Co. by 1694 as a taxable in s. side Gunpowder (139).

HUMPHREYS, FRANCES, serv. to William Hamilton, was ind. for
bast. in Nov. 1743 and tried in March 1743/4; tried for having
borne a mulatto ch. in March 1744; had: ABIGAIL, sold to William
Hamilton in March 1744 (35:71, 168, 471, 481).

HUMPHREYS, RICHARD, and w. Eliza admin. the est. of Henry Jones
on 12 July 1715 (1:336).

HUMPHREYS, THOMAS, d. by 1 March 1661/2; m. Mary (---) who m.
as her 2nd husb. Richard Ball; will of Thomas Humphreys, dated
1660, left 300 a. East Humphreys to w. Mary; wid. Mary had surv.
300 a. East Humphreys in Oct. 1679 which was later held by Charles
Merryman; posthumuous dau. of Thomas and Mary: MARY (200-67:134;
211).

HUMPHREYS, THOMAS, was in Balto. Co. by 26 Aug. 1730 when John
Roberts conv. him 11 a. Red Monk; d. leaving a will, 8 Feb. 1734/5-
19 Feb. 1734/5, naming s. John and friend Catherine Priests; had
at least one s.: JOHN (73:14; 111:204).

HUNN, FRANCIS, m. Margaret James on 17 July 1754; she was wid.
of Nicholas James; Francis and Margaret had iss.: MARY, b. Oct.
1756 (82:203; 131:45, 21/r).

HUNT, JAMES, m. Mary Murrin after pub. of the banns for three
times in Aug. 1742 (131).

HUNT, JOHN, saddler, left Eng., and settled in St. Paul's Par.
also known as Wetstone Parish; later went to Georgia by Feb. 1765;
he was advert. for in Feb. 1765 and urged to contact John Merryman for news of something to his advantage; on 10 Nov. 1742 purch.
100 a. Broad's Improvement from Thomas and Ann Broad; had iss.:
PRISCILLA, b. 20 Oct. 1734; SENECA, b. 31 July 1756; EPICTETUS, b.
8 March 1738/9; ONESIPHORUS, b. 19 Feb. 1740; CHRISTINA EBERHAR-
DINE, b. 20 Feb. 1742 (77:66; 133:60, 79; Annap., Md. Gaz., 21
Feb. 1765).

HUNT, WILLIAM, b. c.1710; m. Elizabeth (---), b. c.1719; had
iss.: SARAH, b. c.1739; TEMPERANCE, b. 14 Nov. 1741; JOHN, b. 27
March 1744 (77:231; 131).

HUNTER, JOHN, d. by 23 Dec. 1756 when admin. bond was posted
for his est. by Isaac Webster, Jr., with Thomas Treadway; m. Margarett (---) by whom he had: ESTHER, b. 17 June 1739 (13:274;
131:78/r).

HUNTER, WILLIAM, m. by 20 April 1722, Mary, extx. of John Webster; in March 1721/2, Eleanor Donahue named William as the father of her baseborn ch.; on 4 March 1724 William and Mary conv.
100 a. Wexford to William Bond; ch. of William: (by Elinor):
WILLIAM, b. 29 Jan. 1720; (by Mary): JOSEPH, b. 25 Feb. 1722;
WILLIAM, b. 2 Dec. 1723; BRADBURY, b. 17 Feb. 1723; JAMES, b. 6
March 1729; OWEN, b. 11 Aug. 1732 (1:66; 24:8; 77:62; 128:41, 42,
53, 59, 70; 131).

HURD, ANDREW, d. in Balto. Co. by 20 Nov. 1713 when admin.
bond on his est. was posted by Elizabeth Hurd, with Christopher
Randall and Thomas Randall; est. was inv. on Jan. 1713/4 by Joseph Johnston and Thomas Newsom and val. at £ 59.4.6, signed by
Anthony Bale as creditor, and filed 11 March 1713/4. (13:200;
50:307).

HURD, JACOB, b. c.1704, gave his age as c. 26 in a deposition
dated Oct. 1730 (Land Comm. HWS # 1, 107).

HURD, JOHN, was b. c.1706, giving his age as c. 24 in Oct.
1730; m. Ruth Norwood on 18 June 1739; in Oct. 1737 purch. 150
a. Rowles' Chance from Charles Carroll of Annap.; in 1750 he was
listed as owning that tract plus 50 a. Minto; in Aug. 1733 he was
charged with begetting the ch. of Mary Barness; d. leaving a will.
26 April 1778 - 11 June 1778, naming w. Ruth, grandson John Hurd
(to have the large Church Bible), grandson Joshua Howard, James
Barnett, the lawfully begotten ch. of his s. Joshua, and the ch.
of his dec. dau. Sarah Howard; had iss.: JOSHUA, b. 22 June 1740;
SARAH, b. 11 June 1742, m. (---) Howard (30:71; 75:22; 112:460;
134:9, 70; 153:31; Land Comm. HWS#1, 107).

HURLEY, TIMOTHY, m. Katherine Gayer on 16 Feb. 1734 (133:153).

HURST, JOHN (1), was in A. A. Co. in April 1695 when he purch.
100 a. part Wansworth from John Devegh; was an innholder in Balto. Co. in March 1701 when he purch. land from James and Penelope Todd; on 13 Oct. 1702 with w. Hannah conv. 135½ a. Cole's Harbor and 164½ a. formerly belonging to Alexander Mountenay; had
iss.: JOHN (in May 1705 was conv. a cow by William Clark);
ALEXANDER, in 1710 was conv. a heifer by Henry Knowles) (59:456;
66:123, 196; 67:70, 81).

HURST, BENNETT, in Oct. 1753 conv. Hurst's Marsh to William
Rogers (82:94).

HURST, JONATHAN, m. Anne Gore on 29 Dec. 1729 (133:149).

HURST, TIMOTHY, was in Balto. Co. by 1694 as a taxable in
Spesutia Hund. (139).

HUSBAND, HERMAN, was a trustee of Bush River Meeting, Soc.
of Friends, c.1750 (433:366).

HUSON, MARY, servant to Stephen Gill, was charged with bast.
in Nov. 1722 (25:22).

HUST, JOHN, in Nov. 1757 was ordered to be levy free (46:39).

HUST, JONATHAN, m. Anne (---) and had iss.: RUTH, b. 4 June
1730 (133:19).

THE HUTCHINS FAMILY has been fully discussed in Elmore Hutchins' Nicholas Hutchins of My Lady's Manor (S.1., n.d.).

HUTCHINS, THOMAS (1), progenitor, was in Balto. Co. by 1702
as a taxable in n. side Gunpowder Hund.; m. by March 1709 Susanna, extx. of Thomas Richardson; purch. Betty's Inheritance from
James Richardson in Aug. 1714; d. leaving a will, 1 March
1731/2 - 4 April 1732, leaving Boon's Delight to his old. s.
John as well as part Leaf's Chance and part Hutchins' Neglect.
to sons Thomas and Nicholas he left part Hutchins' Neglect, to
daus. Elizabeth, Ann, and Susanna he left Hutchins' Addition;
admin. bond was posted 4 April 1732 by Thomas and Nicholas
Hutchins; on 7 May 1732 the four oldest children confirmed to
their sis. Susanna the prop. left her by their dec. father; on
7 Aug. 1745 Thomas and Nicholas conv. 70 a. Hutchins' Beginnings
to Thomas Franklin; Thomas and Susanna had iss.: JOHN; THOMAS;
NICHOLAS; ELIZABETH; ANNE (may be the Ann who m. William Standiford on 28 May 1731); and SUSANNA (13:233; 21:120; 73:254; 78:
405; 131; 144).

HUTCHINGS, JOHN (2), s. of Thomas (1) and Susanna, m. Elizabeth
Wright on 9 May 1726, and had iss.: ELIZABETH, b. 4 July 1727;
d. 25 March 1728/9; JOHN, b. 1 March 1729/30; ANN, b. 7 June
1732; ELIZABETH, b. 30 Sept. 1734 (131:13/r, 44/r, 76/r).

HUTCHINS, or HUTCHINGS, THOMAS (3), s. of Thomas (1) and Susanna, m. Hannah Seemons on 12 May 1736; in 1750 he owned 16 and
3/4 a. part Hutchins' Neglect and 150 a. Hutchins' Lot; d. by 30
Nov. 1758 when admin. bond was posted by Hannah Hutchins with
James Elliott and Thomas Meredith; est. was admin. by Hannah
Hutchins who stated the dec. left four ch.; left iss.: KEZIAH, b.
21 Jan. 1737; ANNE, b. 6 Feb. 1741; THOMAS, b. 5 Dec. 1745;
JAMES, b. 14 Jan. 1747 (4:278; 13:268; 131:73/r, 102/r, 114/r,
127/r, 153:35).

HUTCHINS, NICHOLAS (4), s. of Thomas (1) and Susanna, was b.
c.1711, giving his age as 60 in 1771; m. Elizabeth (---), and d.
by 1794; he was ind. for bast. in June 1734 and tried for begetting the ch. of Elizabeth Cheshire; in June 1737 was tried for
begetting the ch. of Sarah Owens; m. Elizabeth (---), who joined
him on 9 Aug. 1750 in selling 1/3 of a 100 a. tract Norwich to
Isaac Raven; on 8 June 1757 Nicholas sold 166 a. Hutchins' Lot
and Hutchins' Neglect to Roger Boyce; d. leaving a will proved
25 Nov. 1794; had iss.: NICHOLAS; RICHARD; WILLIAM, b. 31 March
1754; JACOB; JOSHUA; ANN, b. 25 March 1745, m. (---) Amos; ELIZA-
BETH (30:253, 309; 31:57; 81:85; 83:86; 114:210; 131; 231_AL#C:
608).

HUTCHINS, ELIZABETH, was charged with bast. in June 1733
and pleaded guilty (30:15).

HUTCHINS, NICHOLAS, and Catherine Hutchins posted admin. bond
for John Counts on 11 Oct. 1755 (11:391).

HUTCHINS, WILLIAM, d. by 12 Dec. 1722 when his est. was admin. by Diana, w. of Nicholas Besson (1:73).

HUTCHINSON, RICHARD, m. Margaret (---), and had iss.: MARTHA,
b. 8 June 1738 (133:68).

HUTTON, JANE, age 13, last 4 May in Aug. 1756 was bound to
William Bennett (41:223).

HUTTS, JOHN, was in Balto. Co. by 1695 as a taxable in s.
side Gunpowder Hund. (140).

HYATT, CHRISTOPHER, m. Elizabeth Taylor on 22 Feb. 1759
(131).

HYDE, SAMUEL, of London, had heirs in 1750 who owned 1000
a. Price's Encouragement, 350 a. part United Friendship, 1000
a. Darnall's Camp, 1500 a. Affinity, and other lands (153:85).

IAMP, BENJAMIN, d. by 9 June 1752 when admin. bond was posted
by James Carey with Thomas Norris; his est. was admin. on 18
Sept. 1754 (4:243; 13:396).

IERDMAN, THOMAS, servant to John Perry, was judges to be 13
years old in June 1695 (20:416).

IGO(U) or IGON, LEWIS (1), progenitor, was in Balto. Co. by
1722; d. by 14 April 1760; m. Mary (---); wit. the will of John
Newman of Balto. Co. on 19 March 1732; in 1735 acq. 100 a. of
land from Walter Dallas which he pat. in 1737 as Friend's Discovery, which he owned in 1750; d. leaving a will, 2 March 1760 -
14 April 1760, naming w. Mary, s. Daniel, s. Peter and other
ch.: Margaret, Elizabeth, William, Mary, and Esther; Louis and
Mary had iss.: MARGARET, b. 25 July 1722; ELIZABETH, b. 20 Feb.
1724; WILLIAM, b. 22 Aug. 1729; MARY, b. 30 Sept. 1731; PETER;
DANIEL:; ESTHER (126:56; 133:11, 24; 153:44; 207; 210-30:87).

IGO, WILLIAM (2), s. of Lewis (1), was b. 22 Aug. 1729; d. by
1798; m. Elizabeth (---); in June 1758 purch. 100 a. Cornelius'
and Mary's Lot from Charles Howard; had iss.: MARY, b.
by 1765; ELIZABETH, alive April 1821; RACHEL, alive April 1821; JOSHUA,
b. 1760, served in Rev. War from Penna.; EPHRAIM, b. 1768; PETER,
d. by by 18 Aug. 1810; JACOB; THOMAS; SUSANNAH (83:202; 231:
WG#MM, 508; 231-WG#86, 371; 335:129, 130).

IGO, PETER (3), s. of Lewis (1), m. by 7 Feb. 1770 Ruth (---);
in 1768 signed a pet. in favor of Balto. as the county seat; in
1769 pat. 300 a. Petersborough, and in Feb. 1770 he and w. Ruth
sold the land to Thomas Cockey Deye (200-61:531; 207; 231-AL#A:
709).

IGO, DANIEL (4), s. of Lewis (1), was a taxable in Soldier's
Delight Hund. in 1763; in Oct. 1765 sold 100 a. Friend's Discovery to Dr. William Lyon; had at least one ch.: LEWIS, b. 1767
(90:706; 134:2; 157; 335:130).

IJAMS, WILLIAM, m. by June 1750, Margaret, admnx. of Jno.
Williams (201-38:47).

IMPEY/EMPEY, JOHANNA, on 9 Feb. 1746 conv. all her prop. to
John Shaw if he would maintain her for the rest of her life; the
deed mentioned Elizabeth Sampson, not yet 16, granddau. of the
said Johanna Empey (79:277).

INCH, JOHN, was in Balto. Co. by 1750 when he owned 100 a.
Strawberry Plains (153:103).

INDRELL, JOHN, was in Balto. Co. by Nov. 1695 when he deposed
that he lived with Thomas Litton at the head of Gunpowder, and
being a fugitive from justice, was hidden by Litton for eight
days, later decided to give himself up rather than stay in the
woods and face starvation (20:605-ff.).

INGLE, JOHN, conv. his share of the est. of Christopher Shaw
to George Harryman on 15 Oct. 1743 (77:382).

INGLE, WILLIAM, was in Balto. Co. by Nov. 1719 when he was
ind. for begetting the ch. of Ann Erroll; in March 1724 bound his
sons, John Arrindale, 6, and Samuel Ingle, 1, to Thomas Wright
until they were 21; on 13 Oct. 1746 conv. 32½ a. Small Valley
to son William Carback alias William Ingle; in 1750 owned 32½ a.
Small Valley; had iss.: JOHN ARRINDELE (poss. the nat. s. born
to Ann Erroll), b. c.1718; SIMON, b. c.1723; SAMUEL, b. 25 Jan.
1724; WILLIAM CARBACK, alias INGLE (23:246; 24:128; 78:271; 79:
221; 133:7; 153:48).

INGRAM, JOHN (1), was in Balto. Co. by 10 Sept. 1698 when he
wit. the will of Joseph Pettibone; m. Mary (---), wid. of (---)
Homewood, and dau. of John Peasley of A. A. Co., on 3 Sept. 1705
in St. Margaret's Parish, A. A. Co.; on 1 Jan. 1708/9 John Peasley named his grandch. Sarah and Thomas Homewood, son-in-law
John Ingram, and grandson Peasley Ingram (who on 17 April 1719
was named as grandson in the will of Hannah Goodhand of Kent Co.);
d. leaving a will, 31 March 1733 - 8 June 1733, leaving Michael's
Chance and Addition to his s. John, then to his s. Benjamin, then
to sons James and William, and dau. Dorcas Tudor, wife to be
extx.; admin. bond was posted 8 Aug. 1733 by extx. Mary Ingram
with Thomas Giddens and Walter James; est. was admin. on 21 May
1735 by Mary Ingram; wid. Mary d. by 7 June 1748, when admin.
bond on her est. was posted by Benjamin Ingram with John Buck
and Abraham Wright; her est. was admin. on 24 July 1749 by Benjamin Ingram who stated she left 8 ch.; ch. of John and Mary:
PEASLEY; JOHN; BENJAMIN; JAMES; WILLIAM; DORCAS, m. (---) Tudor

(3:193; 5:58; 13:378, 389; 37:158; 113:118; 121:172; 124:41;
126:23; 219-4:97).

INGRAM, PEASLEY (2), s. of John (1) and Mary, named in the
will of his grandfather John Peasley on 1 Jan. 1708/9; d. by 9
April 1740 when admin. bond was posted by the wid. and admnx.
Ruth, with Luke Stansbury and John Hammond of Charles; m. 25
June 1730 Ruth, dau. of Maj. Charles Hammond; Ruth m. 2nd Thomas
Franklin, with whom she admin. the est. of Peasley Ingram on 22
May 1744 and 23 June 1752; had iss.: RUTH, d. 1794 (5:10, 238;
13:390; 219-2:432; 370).

INGRAM, JOHN (3), s. of John (1) and Mary, d. by 2 April
1740; m. Susanna, dau. of Benjamin Mead; d. leaving a will, 21
Feb. 1738 - 2 April 1740, naming sis. Dorcas Tudor, bro.-in-law
Humphrey Tudor, bros. Benjamin and James, as well as w. Susanna
and father-in-law Benjamin Mead; had iss.: JOHN, b. 5 Oct. 1740
(127:75; 131:91/r).

INGRAM, BENJAMIN (4), s. of John (1) and Mary, in 1750 owned
100 a. Michael's Addition; m. Susanna Coin on 5 Jan. 1743 (131;
153:37).

INGRAM, JAMES (5), s. of John (1) and Mary, may be the James
who m. Catherine Young on 25 Aug. 1752 (131).

INGRAM, WILLIAM (6), s. of John (1) and Mary, d. by 24 Nov.
1739 when admin. bond was posted by Elizabeth Whitehead with Wm.
Andrews and Thomas Johnson of John; m. Phebe Whitehead on 6 Nov.
1731; in 1738 she was named as a dau.in the will of Eliz. Fisham
of Balto. Co.; she d. within a week of her husb.; his est. was
admin. by Elizabeth Whitehead on 12 Aug. 1743; left iss.: FRANCIS
WHITEHEAD, b. 3 Jan. 1732, in Nov. 1739 was bound to Edward Day;
WILLIAM, b. 6 May 1734, d. 5 Sept. 1734; LEVIN, b. 3 Nov. 1735
(3:343; 13:383; 32:81; 127:14; 131:51/r).

INGRAM, FRANCIS WHITEHEAD (7), s. of William (6) and Phebe,
was b. 3 Jan. 1732; m. Sarah White on 8 Jan. 1756; d. by 16 May
1763 when admin. bond was posted by Sarah Ingram with Chris. Divers and William Bond Whitehead; est. was admin. by Sarah Ingram
on 26 Sept. 1763; William and Sarah had iss.: LEVIN, b. c.1756
WILLIAM, b. c.1759 (6:35, 73; 13:380; 131).

INGRAM, LEVIN (8), s. of William (6) and Phebe, was b. 3 Nov.
1735; m. Hannah Lego on 3 Feb. 1761 (131).

INGRAM, ARTHUR, m. Ann (---) by whom he had iss.: SARAH, b.
15 March 1739; MARY, b. 18 Oct. 1742; ARTHUR, b. 13 May 1749;
WILLIAM, b. 13 Feb. 1752; HANNAH, b. 13 Feb. 1755; WILLIAM, b.
13 Feb. 1758 (128:112; 129:328, 362).

INLOES. See ENLOES.

INSULL, GEORGE, and w. Alice were in Balto. Co. by 1 Aug.
1728 when they conv. 100 a. Wells Angle to Joseph Fuller; on
25 Feb. 1728/9 they conv. 100 a. Longland's Purchase to Thomas
Sheredine (71:249, 251).

IRELAND, JOHN, chirurgeon, was in Balto. Co. by Jan. 1676
when Henry Haslewood and w. Elizabeth conv. him 100 a. Collingham and 8 a. Haslewood's Retirement (101:301).

IRELAND, NATHAN, was fined for bast. in Nov. 1757 (46:74).

IRELAND, WILLIAM, m. by 3 Feb. 1736/7, Mary, dau. of William

Hickman of Calvert County, who left his daughter 300 a. of Clarkson's Hope (126:206).

IRETON, THOMAS, was transp. by 1662; was in Balto. Co. by Sept. 1665 when Mathias da Costa and w. Elizabeth conv. him 700 a. of Manor Wiske (94; 388).

ISAAC, RICHARD, was in Balto. Co. by 1692 as a taxable in n. side of Gunpowder Hund.; d. by 24 May 1700 when his est. was inv. by William Peckett and Henry Wriothesley, and val. at Ł 28.0.0 (138; 206-11b:14).

THE ISGRIG FAMILY has been the subject of a great deal of study by the late Ben Isgrig, who died before his findings could be published, and by Dr. Richard B. Miller, of Pasadena, California, who has generously made his papers available to the compiler. The Society of Genealogists in London has supplied information from its Great Card Index and the List of Apprentices.

ISGRIG, WILLIAM (1), of St. Luke, Middlesex, d. 1755; m. Abigail (---) who d. 1750 and was bur. at St. Luke Old Street, London, and had iss.;   WILLIAM; MARGARET, b. c.1709, m. 18 Jan. 1741 at St. Giles Cripplegate, to George Boxwell, glover, of St. Leonard, Shoreditch, Middlesex. (notes from Dr. Miller).

ISGRIG, WILLIAM (2), s. of William (1) and Abigail,was b. c. 1700; in 1716 was apprenticed to John Wilkerson of St. Katherine, sailmaker; m. Ann (---), and d. Feb. 1740 in St. Luke's, Middlesex; Ann d. 1742; ch. of William and Ann: WILLIAM, b. 9 Sept. 1721; MICHAEL CARTER, b. 1727, in 1742 was apprenticed by his grandfather to Josiah Langton, cooper (notes from Dr. Miller).

ISGRIG, WILLIAM (3), s. of William (2), was b. 9 Sept. 1721, and in 1737 was apprenticed by his father to William Gould, goldsmith; shortly after his father's death, William stole an assortment of silver buckles from his master, was caught, tried, and sentenced to be transported; on 31 May 1740 was removed from Newgate Prison and taken to the ship Essex, Ambrose Cooke, commander,; arrived in Md., and after completing his time of service, m. Hannah (poss. Wooley); acquired some land, and d. in the 1780's in Balto. Co.; had iss.: MICHAEL NICHOLSON, b. 1751, d. 1831 in Hamilton Co., Ohio; JOHN, d. in Penna., having m. Helen or Ellinor Dimmitt; DANIEL, b. 20 Dec. 1756, d. 1849 in Bourbon Co., Ky.; WILLIAM, d. 1802, m. Ann; TEMPERANCE, m. William Pocock on 6 Nov. 1788 (notes from Dr. Miller).

ISHAM/HYSON/ISHUM, JAMES, was in Balto. Co. by 1695 as a taxable in s. side Patapsco; m. 1st, c.1703, Juliana, wid. and admnx. of Abraham Delap; on 30 Dec. 1709 James and Juliana agreed with Charles Baker that they would deliver certain items to Baker's plantation; James m. 2nd, by June 1719, Elizabeth, admnx. of William Robinson; she d. Oct. 1737; and James m. as his 3rd w., Mrs. Mary Warren on 1 June 1738; she d. Aug. 1743; he m. 4th, on 13 Oct. 1743 Jane Johnstone; Isham was granted a lic. to keep an ordinary in Aug. 1719; he d. 1753 in Bladen Co., N.C., leaving iss.: MARGARET; JAMES, twin, b. 25 June 1720; CHARLES, b. 25 June 1720, also a twin (2:28, 189; 23:162, 212; 67:44; 131; 140).

ISOU, JANE, was living at George Goldsmith's when she was ind. for bast. in Nov. 1685 (18:358).

ISRAEL, JOHN (1), merchant of London, was in Md. by 1698; m. 1st, by Aug. 1707, Margaret Larkin, wid. and extx. of Edward Dorsey; m. 2nd Barbara (---); m. 3rd Sarah (---), who m. as her 2nd husb. Samuel Heighe; d. leaving a will, 13 Jan. 1723 - 11 March

1723, naming w. Sarah, sons John Lacon, Gilbert Talbott, and Robert Israel, daus. Sarah and Mary, 35 a. bought of George Yate, and 182 a. Yates' Forbearance; admin. bond was posted 15 March 1724 by execs. Sarah, now w. of Samuel Heighe, Sr., of Calvert Co.; John Lacon Israel, s. of the dec., ren. his right to admin.; est. was admin. 6 Sept. 1725 and 18 April 1726; wid. Sarah d. by 4 June 1730; dec. had iss.: JOHN LACON; GILBERT TALBOTT; ROBERT; SARAH; and MARY (2:74, 258, 323; 13:373; 71:29; 124:167).

ISRAEL, ROBERT (2), s. of John (1) and Sarah, m. Priscilla Baker c.1743, and had iss.: JOHN, b.1749 in Balto. Co. and d. 1823 in Belmont Co., Ohio; BEALE, b. 24 Dec. 1759, m. Elizabeth Burgess (Parran, Reg. of Md. Her. Fam., II, 182, 186, 187).

ISRELLO, ANGEL, was in Balto. Co., by c.1739; m. 1st Sarah (---); m. 2nd Ann (---); naturalized in 1751; d. by 2 Jan. 1759 when admin. bond was posted by Ann Isrello with Renaldo Monk and Nathan Bowen; had iss.: EDWARD, b. 6 April 1739; ISAAC, b. 25 Dec. 1740; JACOB, b. 14 Feb. 1746 (4:268; 13:386; 133:77; 404).

ISWECKS, FRANCIS, d. by 7 Oct. 1748 when admin. bond was posted by James Walker, with James Perkins, Abr. Eaglestone, and Samuel Hart (13:388).

IVES, JAMES (1), was in Balto. Co. by March 1671, when Rowland Williams conv. him 100 a. of Tronolwyn; in   March 1671/2 John Collett conv. him 150 a. at Foster's Neck; Rowland Williams conv. him 300 a. Overton in Nov. 1673; m. by March 1674/5 Martha (---), who joined him in sale of 100 a. Iventon to William Palmer; est. was inv. 26 Nov. 1679 by William Hollis and Peter Ellis and val. at 44253 lbs. tob.; left iss.: JAMES; SUSANNA, m. (---) Wells (18:90; 51:103; 97:126; 98:48; 100:117; 101:300).

IVES, JAMES (2), s. of James (1), was in Balto. Co. and of age to be a taxable in 1692 in Spesutia Hund.; d. leaving a will, 4 March 1703/4 - 13 March 1703/4, naming sis. Susanna Wells and her heirs to have Beaver Neck, Thomas Frisby, Thomas Greenfield and his heirs, John and Thomas, sons of Thomas Preble, Miles Hannas, William Perkins, Thomas Edwards, the two ch. of Mary Cannon, and John Kimble and Richard Smithers; admin. bond was posted 22 March 1703/4 by Richard Smithers with Robert Gibson and Thomas Edmonds; est. was inv. 24 March 1703/4 by Thomas Cord and Thomas Newsome and val. at £ 62.14.6; his est. was admin. 5 July 1706 (2:95; 13: 358; 51:341; 122:30).

IVES, ELIZABETH, was charged with bast. in Aug. 1721 (23:570).

JACKS, THOMAS (1), prob. d. by 7 Nov. 1715; m. 9 Nov. 1704 in A. A. Co., Elizabeth (---) Powell Walters, wid. of John Powell and mother of John Powell, Jr., who d. April 1716, leaving a will, naming bros. Richard and Thomas Jacks (heirs of Thomas Jacks), sisters Eliza and Barbara Jacks, as well as bro. Joseph Powell and Christopher Walters; Thomas Jacks left iss.: THOMAS; RICHARD; ELIZABETH; BARBARA, m. Luke Mercer on 1 Aug. 1738 in Christ Ch., Q. Caroline Par., A. A. Co. (70:276; 123:71; 263).

JACKS, THOMAS (2), s. of Thomas (1), was in Balto. Co. by 3 Feb. 1724/5 when he and w. Mary conv. Jack's Peacock to John Taylor (70:276).

JACKS, RICHARD (3), s. of Thomas (1); m. Ann (---), and in July 1749 purch. Fountain of Friendship from George and Grace Turnbull; in 1750 owned that tract and 249 a. Jack's Delight; had iss.: ANN (or NANCY), b. 15 Oct. 1747 (80:248; 134:9; 153:58).

THE EDWARD JACKSON FAMILY

JACKSON, EDWARD (1), was in Balto. Co. by Nov. 1677 when he
purch. 50 a. Mascall's Humor from Benjamin Bennett (the Rent Roll
states this tract was surv. for Bennett in Nov. 1673 and was later
held by Thomas Jackson and still later by John Hall); had iss.:
THOMAS (101:302; 211).

JACKSON, THOMAS (2), s. of Edward (1); m. Mary, sis. of William Kimball; she m. 2nd, by April 1705, John Roberts; Thomas may
have been a son-in-law Robert Drysdale, whose will dated 3 May
1704 left 200 a. Drysdale's Habitation to Jackson, and later John
and Mary Roberts sold the land to Henry Wriothesley; d. leaving
a will, 17 Dec. 1704 - 1 March 1704/5, leaving his est. to his
w. Mary; admin. bond was posted 12 April 1705 by Mary, now w. of
John Roberts; est. was inv. on 4 July 1705 by Lawrence Draper,
and Roger Matthews, and val. at Ł 18.6.5; est. was admin. by John
and Mary Roberts on 15 April 1706 (2:239; 13:357; 59:655; 64:23;
110:95; 122:45; 128:17; 139).

THE HENRY JACKSON FAMILY

JACKSON, HENRY (3), no known rel. to any of the above, was
bur. in Balto. Co. on 19 Sept. 1705; acquired 40 a. Covent Garden
in June 1687; d. leaving a will, 24 Jan. 1704 - 7 March 1704/5,
naming sons Edward (to have the dwelling plant. of 50 a.), and
Robert; admin. bond was posted 7 March 1704/5 by Edward and Robert Jackson, with John Hall and James Phillips; his est. was inv.
on 6 March 1705 and val. at Ł 48.16.4; est. was admin. on 5 July
1708; dec. left iss.: EDWARD; ROBERT (2:214; 13:366; 48:210; 122:
46; 128:18; 211:24).

JACKSON, ROBERT (4), s. of Henry (3), d. by 8 June 1721 when
admin. bond on his est. was posted by the admnx. Elinor Jackson;
m. Isabella Hooper on 24 Aug. 1699; m. 2nd Eleanor (---), who m.
as her 2nd husb. John O'Bryan on 24 Sept. 1721; Robert and Isabella (whose sis. m. Jonathan Massey) had iss.: ABRAHAM; ISAAC; and
JACOB(13:364; 128:10; 129:188; 229:7-ff.).

JACKSON, ISAAC (5), s. of Robert (4), d. 25 Jan. 1748 in St.
John's Par.; m. Mary Hollingsworth on 17 July 1733; on 1 April
1749 Isaac Jackson conv. 50 a. Hall's Ridge to Benjamin Lego;
d. by 10 March 1748/9 when admin. bond was posted by Mary Jackson, with James Maxwell and Henry Hill; she admin. the est. at
least twice, once on 1 Nov. 1750; in 1750 his heirs owned 100 a.
Holmond, and 168 a. part Hall's Ridge; on 27 Nov. 1752 John Day
(of Edward) and w. Philizanna conv. 42 a. Good Will to Mary Jackson and her daus. Mary, Jr., and Elizabeth; Isaac and Mary had
iss.: ROBERT, b. 31 Aug. 1735; MARY, b. 3 April 1737; ISABELLA,
b. 20 Jan. 1740; ELIZABETH, b. 29 Jan. 1745; in March 1759 as
orphan of Isaac Jackson was bound to George Presbury (5:218, 287;
13:382; 39:25; 46:198; 79:704; 81:509; 128:10; 131; 153:86).

JACKSON, JACOB (6), s. of Robert (4), d. 24 May 1747; m. 1st,
on 4 Oct. 1731 Frances Dallahide, who d. in Nov. 1741; m. 2nd
Jemima (---) who surv. him; in April 1744 he was summoned by the
vestry of St. John's Parish because his second w. was the niece
of his first w.; admin. bond on his est. was posted 2 June 1747
by admnx. Jemima Jackson, with James Maxwell and Benjamin Childs;
she admin. the est. on 9 July 1748; dec. left iss.: ANNE, b. 4
March 1732; PHEBE, b. 19 May 1734, m. Capt. James Maxwell the
Younger; CEMALIA, b. 10 April 1737; ROBERT, b. Nov. 1741 and d.
Dec. 1743; EDWARD, b. Nov. 1741 (4:205; 13:383; 131; 132:67).

THE JAMES JACKSON FAMILY

JACKSON, JAMES (7), no known rel. to above, was in Balto. Co.
by 1692 as a taxable in s. side Patapsco Hund.; acquired 100 a.
Bear's Thicket later held by William Cromwell for Jackson's orphans; d. leaving a will proved 21 May 1696 which left Jackson's
Chance to sons James and John, Vast Thicket to his dau. Eliza,
and pers. prop. to w. Martha and ch., with William Slade and Wm.
Cromwell as execs. and guardians of ch.; admin. bond was posted
25 May 1696 by Slade and Cromwell with Thomas and Philip Cromwell;
dec. left iss.: JAMES; JOHN; and ELIZABETH (13:371; 122:141; 138;
211).

JACKSON, JAMES (8), s. of James (7), is prob. the James Jackson who d. leaving a will, 26 Aug. 1717 - 31 Oct. 1718, naming w.
Sarah, James Wood, and leaving prop. to Thomas Prestwood at 18;
admin. bond was posted 31 Oct. 1718 by admnx. Sarah Jackson with
John Risteau, and John Wood; est. was inv. by Henry Hall and
Joseph Coney on 10 Dec. 1718 and val. at £ 50.0.10; est. was admin. by Sarah Jackson on Aug. 172-(?) (2:15; 13:367; 51:150; 124:
185).

THE SAMUEL JACKSON FAMILY

JACKSON, SAMUEL (9), no known rel. to any of the above, was
in Balto. Co. by 1692 as a taxable in Spesutia Hund.; m. Sarah
Matthews on 11 Dec. 1698 and d. by 6 April 1720; admin. the est.
of Jno. Chisnal on 30 Nov. 1716; acquired 200 a. Expectation (out
of 350 a. surv. for Peter Ellis), 90 a. Carter's Rest (purch. from
Robert Jones), and 100 a. Jackson's Outlet; in Dec. 1718 leased
Jackson's Adventure to Miles Hannahs and wife; d. leaving a will,
12 Nov. 1719 - 6 April 1720, naming dau. Hannah Kimble (to have
200 a. Expectation), dau. Mary (to have 90 a. Carter's Rest and
100 a. Jackson's Outlet), dau. Sarah (to have Jackson's Hazard),
son-in-law Rowland Kimble and bro.-in-law Roger Matthews as the
execs.; admin. bond was posted by said Kimble with Thomas Cord
and William Cook on 5 April 1720; est. was inv. on 12 April 1720
by Jo'n Clark and Thomas Cord and val. at £ 127.13.11; est. was
admin. by Kimble at least once; Samuel and w. had iss.: HANNAH,
b. 7 Sept. 1701, m. Rowland Kimble; MARY, b. 28 April 1704, m.
1st John Thomas, 2nd (---) Foster, and 3rd, on 26 Nov. 1731,
James Taylor; SARAH, b. 30 June 1707 (1:136, 206; 13:360; 48:181;
63:506;124:2; 128:12, 21, 24, 65; 129:185; 211:12, 17).

THE SIMEON JACKSON FAMILY

JACKSON, SIMEON (10), no known rel. to any of the above, was
in Balto. Co. by 1692 as a taxable in Spesutia Hund.; d. 20 Feb.
1695/6 at The Level; m. Elizabeth (---) who m. 2nd, on 14 July
1698, Thomas Morris; his est. was inv. on 18 April 1696 by Ludo-
wick Martin and Daniel Palmer and val. at £ 32.6.4 plus 14,434
lbs. tob.; Simeon and Elizabeth had iss.: JOHN, b. 10 Dec. 1689;
SIMEON, b. 9 Sept. 1691, bapt. 4 July 1699; JUDITH, b. 19 Dec.
1693, d. 4 Sept. 1695; THOMAS, b. 10 Oct. 1695, bapt. 4 July
1699 (21:210; 128:1, 5, 7; 129:178, 183; 138; 206-14:23).

JACKSON, JOHN (11), s. of Simeon (10), and Elizabeth, was b.
10 Dec. 1689 and bapt. 4 July 1699; prob. the John who m. Katherine (---), and d. Nov. 1740 leaving iss.: JOHN, b. last Aug.
1710; SAMUEL, b. 13 Jan. 1713; MARGARET, b. 21 Feb. 1719, d. 12
July 1720; JULIAN, b. 24 Aug. 1720, d. 10 May 1731; JAMES, b. 31
Jan. 17--(?); MARY, b. 14 Nov. 1723; MARGARET, b. 17 Sept. 1726;
d. May 1740; SARAH, b. 3 April 1731; HANNAH, b. 14 March 1733;
JAMES, b. 18 Aug. 1737 (128:33, 38, 42, 50, 58, 66, 91, 97; 129:
323).

JACKSON, SIMEON (12), s. of Simeon (10) and Elizabeth, was b.
9 Sept. 1691, and was alive in 1734; in Sept. 1721 he purch. 50
a. of Division from William Wood; in Nov. 1724 he pet. to be levy
free since he had lost the use of one arm and hand "in a fit;" in
Nov. 1728 Edward Parks recorded a bond that he would conv. Simeon
Jackson 100 a. part of Expectation; had iss.: SIMEON, b. 18 June
1721; BLANCH, b. 26 July 1723; JOSEPH, b. 13 Sept. 1726; SIMEON,
b. 24 Aug. 1729; MOSES, b. 26 Dec. 1731; and MARY, b. 3 July 1734
(27:38; 69:61; 75:9; 128:40, 47, 49, 58, 65, 83).

JACKSON, THOMAS (13), s. of Simeon (10) and Elizabeth, was b.
10 Oct. 1695; m. Elizabeth Debruler on Sept. 17241 had iss.: SIME-
ON, b. 18 Nov. 1727; HANNAH, b. 29 Nov. 1726; d. 26 Dec. 1727;
SAMUEL, b. 8 Nov. 1726(?); SARAH, b. 15 Dec. 1731; WILLIAM, b. 17
June 1733; ELIZABETH, b. 17 July 1735 (128:57, 65, 71, 89).

JACKSON, MOSES (14), s. of Simeon (12), was b. 26 Dec. 1731;
m. Margaret Sutton on 20 Aug. 1756; had iss.: SIMEON, b. 20 Aug.
1759 (129:365).

JACKSON, (---), servant, with 3 years to serve, was listed in
the 1706 inv. of Col. Edward Dorsey (48:46).

JACKSON, HENRY, d. and was bur. 19 Sept. 1705 (128:18).

JACKSON, HENRY, d. by Aug. 1730, leaving Jacob and Isaac Jackson as his execs.

JACKSON, ISAAC, was in Balto. Co. by 1692 as a taxable in s.
side Patapsco Hund. (128).

JACKSON, ISAIAH, s. of Phoebe, age 9 in March 1756; in Aug.
1756 was bound to James Yeo (41:225).

JACKSON, JEMIMA, was ind. for bast. in June 1750, tried in
Aug. 1750, and was tried again in Nov. 1754 (37:2, 176; 39:450).

JACKSON, JOHN, was age 60 in 1743 (164:93).

JACKSON, JOHN, in 1750 owned 10 a. Addition to Jackson's
Chance (153:93).

JACKSON, JOHN, m. Hannah (---) and had iss.: JOHN, b. 14 July
1747; EPHRAIM, b. 31 Oct. 1749; CATHERINE, b. 24 Aug. 1754 (129:
360).

JACKSON, JOSEPH, was in Balto. Co. by 1692 as a taxable in Spesutia Hund. (138).

JACKSON, JOSIAH, was in Balto. Co. by 1694 as a taxable in n.
side Patapsco Hund. (129).

JACKSON, MARY, was tried for bast. in Aug. 1742 and again in
March 1745/6; had iss.: WILLIAM, b. 2 June 1742 (34:8; 35:800,
818; 129:327).

JACKSON, MARY, d. by 27 Feb. 1759 when admin. bond was posted
by Aquila Massey and George Presbury, admins., with William Hill
and Jonathan Massey (13:395).

JACKSON, ROBERT, d. by 1721 when his est. was inv. (51:319).

JACKSON, THOMAS, in Aug. 1720 was named by Elizabeth Jenkins
as the father of her child (23:366).

JACKSON, THOMAS, m. Patience Harryman on 14 July 1757; she d.

leaving a will, 16 April 1763 - 23 June 1763 naming her sons
(along with Samuel Clark): WILLIAM, b. 19 June 1758; GEORGE, b.
2 Jan. 1760; THOMAS; and poss. HENRY (131; 133:109; 210-31:931).

JACKSON, WILLIAM, m. Mary Griffin on 12 Nov. 1730; had iss.:
ELIZABETH, b. 27 Feb. 1730; MARY, b. 20 Feb. 1732 (131:58/r).

JACKSON, WILLIAM, servant, with four years to serve, was listed in the 1737 inv. of Benjamin Hanson (53:92).

JAMERSON, JOHN, was in Balto. Co. by 11 Feb. 1733/4 when he
purch. 100 a. London and 100 a. Pitchcraft and Polecat Ridge from
William Burney (74:21).

THE CHARLES AND JOHN JAMES FAMILY

JAMES, JOHN (1), bro. of Charles (2), was in Balto. Co. by 29
June 1672 when he surv. 200 a. Turkey Hill; on 3 Aug. 1688 he
conv. The Last; on 28 Feb. 1669 he conv. Charles a tract called
Bair's Grime; in Aug. 1672 John granted power of atty. to his
bro. Charles to conv. 100 a. of land to William Pate; on 1 Nov.
1673 John conv. 200 a. Turkey Hill to Thomas Thurston (60:68, 71;
63:56, 161; 211).

JAMES, CHARLES (2), bro. of John (1), was in Balto. Co. by 3
Aug. 1668 when John conv. him The Last; on 28 Feb. 1669 John
conv. him the tract Baire's Grime; on 5 March 1671, Charles Nicholetts, minister of the Gospel, conv. 150 a. Lym to Charles James;
on 3 Sept. 1672 Charles conv. Little Drayton to Thomas Middlefield
(60:68, 71; 63:6, 49).

THE THOMAS JAMES FAMILY

JAMES, THOMAS (3), progenitor of this line, was in Balto. Co.
by 1678 and d. by 1705; m. 1st Sarah (---), wid. and admnx. of
Giles Stevens, by 20 Feb. 1682 when Thomas and Sarah admin. Stevens' est.; m. 2nd by 1696 Mary (---), wid. of one Harrison, and
legatee (and poss. dau.) of Edward Dowse; Thomas James took up
200 a. James Park on 30 May 1678, 50 a. James Forecast on 19 Nov.
1686, and 136 a. James Pasture in Aug. 1687; in July 1687 Thomas
and Sarah sold 100 a. The Forest to Richard Sampson; on 11 May
1686 Thomas and Sarah sold 136 a. James Pasture to Lewis Barton,
by 1696 James was living in Concord, Chester Co., Penna., when he
appointed his 2nd w. Mary his atty. to collect debts and sell his
land; in June 1696, still in Chester Co., he conv. his son-in-law
Giles Stevens 64 a. Horne's Point and 50 a. James Forecast; the
same year Thomas and Mary sold 200 a. Oglesby's Chance (which Edward Dowse had left to Mary as Mary Harrison) to Francis Whitehead;
in Nov. 1699 James, now living in New Castle Co., Penna., conv.
George Grover 200 a. James Park, w. cons. of w. Mary; James d. by
6 June 1705 when admin. bond was posted by wid. and admnx. Mary
James with John Boring and John Hillen and James Presbury; his
est. was inv. 29 July 1705 by John Oldton and Jno. Gay and val.
at £ 19.3.0; est. was admin. 25 Sept. 1707 by Mary, now w. of
John Hillen; iss. of Thomas James (in 1726 they were called sons-
in-law in the will of John Hillen): WALTER: WILLIAM; and WATKINS
(2:35, 170; 13:373; 48:56; 59:277, 498, 524, 529; 60:30; 63:403;
211).

JAMES, WALTER (4), s. of Thomas (3) and Mary, d. in Balto. Co.
by 1 June 1751; in June 1740 he was conv. Felk's Range and Black
Wolf Neck by Samuel and Jane Maxwell; in Jan. 1742 he and his w.
Elizabeth conv. 200 a. James' Park to Thomas Sligh; in 1750 he
owned 50 a. James' Beginnings, 50 a. Mount James, 100 a. of Collins Chance, 150 a. Black Wolf Neck, and 200 a. Felk's Range; d.

leaving a will, 2 April 1751 - 18 May 1751, naming Ruth Sutton w. of Joseph Sutton (to have 100 a. Collason's Choice) Elizabeth w. of William Denton (to have 100 a. Collason's Choice and 50 a. James Beginning), Henry Quine (to have 100 a. Felk's Range and Black Wolf Neck), dau. Priscilla (to have 100 a. of same two parcels), and s. Walter; admin. bond was posted 1 June 1751 by Henry Quine, who as Henry Quine or James admin. the est. on 17 Jan. 1752; est. admin. again on 22 Aug. 1752; Walter James had iss.: HENRY QUINE (or JAMES); ELIZABETH, m. William Denton; PRISCILLA, m. 1st, on 28 Sept. 1753 Salathiel Galloway, and 2nd, on 24 April 1757, Joseph Crook; and WALTER (5:243, 265; 13:397; 33:183; 75:396; 77:100; 112:418; 131; 153:57; 164:226).

JAMES, WILLIAM (5), s. of Thomas (3) and Mary, d. 1738; m. Frances (---) and had iss.: THOMAS, b. 21 Aug. 1724; MARY, b. 5 March 1727; ELIZABETH, b. 24 May 1730; SARAH, b. 15 Feb. 1733; and ANN, b. April 1737 (131:50/r, 108/r).

JAMES, WATKINS (6), s. of Thomas (3),and Mary, d. c.1754; m. Mary (---); d. leaving a will, 24 Sept. 1753 - 15 June 1754, naming w. Mary and these ch.: WATKINS; SOLOMON, b. 6 March 1734; WILLIAM, b. 6 March 1734 (twins); JOHN; MARY; WALTER; BENJAMIN; and DANIEL (111:64; 133).

JAMES, HENRY (QUINE) (7), s. of Walter (4), was b. c.1722, giving his age as 30 in 1752; in Nov. 1741 confessed he was the father of Kedemoth Merryman's child; m. Mary Hernly on 26 June 1745; had iss.: ELIZABETH, b. 3 Aug. 1747; HILLEN, b. 5 Nov. 1747; NATHAN, b. 12 April 1754; JOHN, b. 30 Sept. 1759; HENRY, b. 9 April 1763 (33:183; 131:28/r, 151/r; 164:226).

JAMES, JOHN, d. July 1740 (128:110).

JAMES, JOHN, on 5 March 1741, was named as grandson in the will of John Mahone of Balto. Co. (127:192).

JAMES, MARGARET, in 1750 owned 64½ a. Claxon's Purchase; on 15 July 1754 she purch. 64 a. of the same tract from Josias Simmons (82:272; 153:97).

JAMES, MARGARET, w. of William James, admin. the est. of John Williams on 1 June 1750 (5:210).

JAMES, MARY, dau. of Sarah James, in March 1728/9 was bound to John and Elizabeth Lowe to age 16 (28:92).

JAMES, MICHAEL, was in Balto. Co. by March 1721/2, when he admitted paternity of Elizabeth Joy's child; m. 1st Elizabeth (---), who d. 11 Aug. 1732; m. 2nd, on 26 Aug. 1736 Constant Sheppard; had iss. (by 1st w.): WILLIAM, b. 18 March 1725/6; (by 2nd w.): MICHAEL, b.3 April 1737; EDWARD, b. 8 June 1739; Michael d. by 10 April 1740 when adm. bond was posted 16 June 1740 by Constant James, with John Webster and Henry Stone (13:391; 24:7; 128:50, 103, 107; 131:14/r, 51/r).

JAMES, NICHOLAS, d. by 17 July 1754 when his wid. Margaret m. Francis Hunn (82:203, 333).

JAMES, RICHARD, on 12 Feb. 1669 conv. 200 a. Jones' Adventure to his master John Browning, if Richard's bro. William did not come into the country to settle (200-51:287).

JAMES, ROBERT, was in Balto. Co. by 1692 as a taxable in n. side Gunpowder (138).

JAMES, SARAH, was age c.64 on 26 May 1735 (74:237).

JAMES, WILLIAM, of Balto. Co. leased James Lot, part of Land of Promise, from Henry Darnall on 29 Oct. 1739; d. 26 June 1740 (75:363; 129:110).

JAMES, WILLIAM, m. by 1 June 1750 Margaret, admnx. of John Williams (5:172).

JAMESON, MARTHA, servant of John Watkins, was tried for bast. in Nov. 1739 (32:87).

JAMESON, WILLIAM, was exempt from the levy, Nov. 1738 (31: 309).

JARBO, JOHN, b. at Dijon, France, was naturalized in Nov. 1669 (96:233).

JARMAN, ROBERT (1), was made levy free by the Balto. Co. Court in 1719; m. Mary, poss. the dau. of William Galloway whose will of 1 April 1705 named a dau. Mary Jarman or Gorman; d. leaving a will, 16 Dec. 1722 - 7 March 1722/3, naming w. Mary, sons Thomas and William (to have Come By Chance), ment. six children; admin. bond was posted 7 March 1722 by Mary Jarman with James Durham and Anthony Enloes; est. was admin. 6 Nov. 1723; on 7 Aug. 1741 the wid. Mary conv. 47 a. Mary's Adventure to William Galloway; had iss., with four other ch.: THOMAS; and WILLIAM (1:119; 13:361; 23:130; 75:540; 122:53; 124:13).

JARMAN, THOMAS (2), prob. s. of Robert (1), m. Mary (---); in 1750 owned 100 a. Violin; d. by 11 Feb. 1754 when admin. bond was posted by admnx. Mary Jarman with Nathan Nicholson and Joseph Crook; had iss.: ROBERT, b. 11 Feb. 1734; JOHN, b. 19 Aug. 1735; JOHN, b. Sept. 1737 (in March 1757 chose Capt. William Bond as his guardian); RACHEL, b. 15 Nov. 1739 (13:392; 46:18; 131:78/r, 83/r; 153:89).

JARMAN, WILLIAM (3), prob. s. of Robert (1), m. Sarah (---); on 2 June 1741 William, s. of Robert, and w. Sarah conv. 100 a. Come By Chance to Robert Parks; had iss.: HENRY, b. 1 May 1741; ROBERT, b. 24 May 1743 (75:507; 131:107/r).

JARMAN, BENJAMIN, m. Elizabeth Rutledge on 28 Nov. 1753 (131: 209, 242).

JARMAN, LEWIS, was in Balto. Co. by 1694 as a taxable in Spesutia Hund.; bur. 1 Aug. 1698; admin. bond was posted 29 Aug. 1698 by admnx. Elizabeth Gibson with James Phillips and Garrett Garrettson; est. was inv. on 7 Sept. 1698 by Roger Matthews and Henry Jackson and val. at 1719 lbs, tob., and 4490 lbs. tob. in debts (13:372; 48:61; 128:5; 139).

JARMAN, MARGARET, was charged with bast, in June 1724 (26:309).

JARRETT, ABRAHAM, was in Balto. Co. by June 1732 when he purch. 100 a. Mary's Delight from Edmund Hays, Jr.; in March 1741 Abraham and w. Eleanor and Francis Freeman conv. 50 a. Rachel's Delight to Patrick Vance; on 1 Sept. 1741 purch. 150 a. on s. side Gunpowder R.; in 1750 owned 100 a. Mary's Delight and 76 a. Hopewell; d. leaving a will, 2 Aug. 1747 - 13 Dec. 1757, naming w. Eleanor and ch. Abraham and Mary; admin. bond was posted 9 Jan. 1758 by admnx. Eleanor, with William Grafton and Michael Collins; est. was admin. 3 July 1759 by Eleanor, now w. of Michael McGuire, and again on 31 March 1761; left iss.: ABRAHAM; MARY, m. Jesse Bussey (4:254, 302; 13:385; 73:247; 75:560; 76:113; 153:10; 210-30:402).

JARRETT, HENRY, m. a dau. of Isaac Butterworth, by 8 March 1730 (4:12).

JARTOR, PETER, m. Jane (---), and had iss.: JOHN, b. 20 April 1734 (133:42).

JARVIS/JERVIS, BENJAMIN, m. Elizabeth (---) and had iss.: MARY, b. 16 March 1755; BENJAMIN, b. 24 March 1758 (133:100, 125).

JARVIS, JOHN, m. Sarah Wright on 20 July 1761 (131:59).

JARVIS, JOHN, m. Mary Freeman on 29 Dec. 1761 (133:60).

JARVIS, MARGARET, m. Robert Maxfield on 1 Feb. 1728 (133:149).

JARVIS, MARY, m. Charles Prosser on 20 Nov.1738 (131:75/r).

JARVIS, PHILIP, m. Mary (---), who m. 2nd John Robinson; Philip d. by 27 April 1738 when admin. bond was posted by admnx. Mary Robinson, formerly Jarvis, now w. of John Robinson; est. was admin. 8 May 1744; Philip and Mary had iss.: MARY, b. 23 April 1737 (3: 380; 13:374; 133:62).

JARVIS, SAMUEL, in March 1745/6 was ind. and tried for begetting Elizabeth Gallhampton's child (35:800, 815).

JASON, JAMES, was in Balto. Co. by 1692 as a taxable in n. side of Patapsco (138).

JAY, THOMAS, d. in Balto. Co. by 6 Oct. 1756 when admin. bond was posted by admnx. Jemima Jay with Jacob Giles and Amos Garrett; est. was admin. on 12 Nov. 1759 and 13 Dec. 1759 (4:280, 286; 13:394).

JEBB, JOHN, age c.30, b. Shropshire, Eng., shoemaker, was a runaway serv.; advert for in Aug. 1752 (385).

JEFF, JOHN, servant of Mark Richardson, was judged to be 15 years old in March 1685/6; by 1695 was a taxable in n. side of Patapsco (18:398; 140).

JEFF, WILLIAM, bapt. last day of June 1700, m. Elizabeth Aishley or Cushley; had iss.: MARGARET, b. 6 Jan. 1701/2 (128:10, 11, 12).

JEFFERY, RICHARD, servant, with four years to serve, in the 1690 inv. of John Boring; in 1692 was a taxable in n. side of Patapsco Hund. (51:6; 138).

JEFFERY, JOHN, by 1694 was a taxable in s. side of Patapsco Hund. (139).

JEFFERS, JOHN, age 5 last Feb., was bound to Daniel Stansbury in March 1759 (44).

JEFFREYS, JOHN, orphan, age 5 in Feb. 1759, was bound to Edmund Stansbury in March 1759 (46:197).

JENIFER, JACOB, was in Balto. Co. on 3 Nov. 1683 when for love and affection he conv. 97 a. Middle Jenifer to Otho Holland of A. A. Co.; in May 1684 conv. 733 a. Jacob's Chase to Thomas Long (59:62; 106:286, 287).

JENKINS, WILLIAM (1), progenitor, was in Balto. Co. by 2 Aug. 1715 when he purch. 50 a. Freeland's Mount from George and Mary

Freeland; m. Sarah, sis. of Thomas Cullen of Balto. Co.; Cullen, in his will dated 4 Oct. 1731, named a "cousin" William Jenkins, Joseph Jenkins of Joseph, and the three ch. of Cullen's sis. Sarah Jenkins (Sarah Gwin, Avis Jenkins, and Thomas Jenkins); William d. leaving a will, 22 Nov. 1720 - 2 May 1721, naming w. Sarah, s. William (to have 50 a. Freeland's Mount), sons Francis and Thomas, daus. Sarah and Alie (or Avice), and an unborn ch.; admin. bond for the est. of William Jenkins, Jr. (sic) was posted 2 May 1721 by the extx. Sarah Jenkins with Jere. Downs and Cadwallader Jones; est. was inv. on 14 Jan. 1720 by John McComas and Thomas Ramsey and val. at Ł 8.0.1, and signed by Sarah and William Jenkins as kin; Hezekiah Balch admin. the est. on 7 Aug. 1724; and Sarah Lowry, the extx., admin. the est. on 2 Dec. 1724; Sarah Cullen Jenkins, wid., m. Edward Lowry on 16 Aug. 1722; William and Sarah had iss.: WILLIAM, d. by 1760; FRANCIS; THOMAS; SARAH, m. William Gwin on 28 June 1721; AVICE, m. Roger Bishop; and a poss. unborn child (2:355; 3:362; 52:171; 63:343; 124:48; 125:216; 129:262, 265).

JENKINS, WILLIAM (2), s. of William (1) and Sarah, m. Rachel Balls on 14 Aug. 1726; inherited Freeland's Mount from his father and New Design from his uncle Thomas Cullen; in 1750 he owned 50 a. The Mountain, 167 a. part Arabia Petrea, and 31 a. Bond's Hope; d. leaving a will, 4 Sept. 1760 - 12 Dec., 1760, naming s. Rachel as extx., s. William (to have 50 a. Freeland's Mount), s. Francis (to have 100 a. in The Barrens and James' Place), s. Samuel (to have the dwell. plant. of 166 a. Arabia Petrea), and daus. Rachel, Martha, Sarah w. of (---) Wells, Elizabeth w. of (---) Clark, and Mary w. of (---) Emmett; est. admin. 1 Sept. 1763 by extx. Rachel; dec. had iss.: ELIZABETH, b. 11 Nov. 1727, m. Robert Clark; RACHEL, b. 13 Oct. 1729; WILLIAM, b. 4 March 1732; MARY, b. 27 Feb. 1734, m. (Samuel Elliott) or Emmett; SARAH, b. 25 Oct. 1737, m. (---) Wells; MATTHEW, b. 3 Aug. 1740 (could this be Martha?); MARGARET, b. 4 Aug. 1744; FRANCIS; SAMUEL(6:24; 128:64, 75, 86, 100, 110; 129:336; 153:26; 200-31:316).

JENKINS, FRANCIS (3), s. of William (1), m. Mary Downs on 15 June 1732; owned 247 a. Jenkins' Range in 1750; on 4 Nov. 1743 Francis and Mary sold 67 a. Arabia Petrea to Alex. Hill; on 17 Nov. 1750 Francis deeded 247 a. Jenkins Range to Jacob Giles; had iss.: SARAH, b. 27 Sept. 1732; FRANCIS, b. 1 Feb. 1734; WILLIAM, b. 27 Jan. 1737; MARY, b. 31 Aug. 1739 (77:343; 81:112; 128:85, 100, 115; 153:52).

JENKINS, WILLIAM (4), s. of William (2) and Rachel, was b. 4 March 1732; prob. the William who m. Mary Clark on 25 March 1758; had iss.: HANNAH, b. 1 April 1759; JOHN, b. 22 Jan. 1762; MARY, b. 1 Oct. 1763 (129:363, 379, 380).

JENKINS, ANDREW, m. Eliz. Boyd on 12 Jan. 1743 (131).

JENKINS, ELIZABETH, was ind. for bast. in March 1719/20; in Aug. 1720 she named Thomas Jackson as the father (13:279, 366).

JENKINS, ELIZABETH, was tried for bast. in Nov. 1757 (40).

JENKINS, HENRY, m. Elizabeth Boyd on 25 Dec. 1743 (131).

JENKINS, MARGARET, m. Abraham Watson on 14 Feb. 1705 (129:201).

JENKINS, RICHARD, on 2 June 1725 purch. 100 a. Woods Venture, 145 a. part Drisdale's Habitation, and 40 a. The Division from Joshua and Martha Wood; d. leaving a will, 17 Nov. 1734 - 20 Jan. 1734/5, naming bro. John (living in Derbyshire, near Yorkshire, in Eng.), bro. Thomas, sis. Mary; Isabella Cotterill, and Amos

Pilgrim; admin. bond was posted 7 May 1735 by Josias Middlemore, the exec., with Richard Ruff and Samuel Hughes; est. was admin. on 22 Sept. 1737 and 28 Oct. 1737, and est. was dist. to Richard's bros. and sis., Thomas, John, and Mary, in Aug. 1739 (3:231; 4:4; 32:6; 70:105; 125:126; 128:84).

JENKINS, THOMAS COURTNEY, d. in Balto. Co. leaving a will, 30 Sept. 1757 - 1 Nov. 1757, naming bros. Michael, Joseph, William, Henry, and Ignatius, and sis. Mary Hagar and Jane Fenwick, and nephews and nieces Mary Ann Hagar and Jenkins Hagar; admin. bond was posted 9 Nov. 1757 by Michael Jenkins with William Standiford and Cornelius Brady; est. was admin. by Michael Jenkins on 20 Aug. 1761 (4:334; 13:415; 210-30:368).

JENKINS, WILLIAM, of Patapsco, purch. 60 a. Hector's Fancy, which he still owned in 1750 (77:296; 153:69).

JENNINGS, HENRY, admitted paternity of a child born to an unidentified woman, Nov. 1744 (35:390).

JENNINGS, WILLIAM, Jr., m. Mary (---) and had iss.: WILLIAM, b. 22 April 1738 (131:88/r).

JEPHS, ELIZABETH, m. John Boice on 30 Nov. 1721 (131).

JERVIS. See JARVIS.

JESSOP, WILLIAM, came to Md. by 1748; m. Margaret Walker on 25 June 1748; and became manager of the Baltimore Company; had iss.: ELIZABETH, b. 17 Sept. 1750, d. 12 Sept. 1814 in Tenn., having m. George Teal in 1770; WILLIAM, b. 28 July 1755; NICHOLAS, b. 5 July 1757; CHARLES, b. 6 Nov. 1759; ESTHER, b. 21 May 1762; ABRAHAM, b. 18 March 1766 (133).

JESSOPS, EDWARD, was in Balto. Co. by 1695 as a taxable in n. side Gunpowder (140).

JEWEKS, FRANCIS, d. leaving a will, 14 Sept. 1748 - 7 Oct. 1748, leaving entire est. to bo. Lancelot Jeweks; admin. bond was posted 7 Oct. 1748 by James Walker of A. A. Co., with James Perkins and Abraham Eaglestone (13:388; 110:448).

JEWELL, MATTHIAS, was in Balto. Co. by 1692 as a taxable in n. side Gunpowder Hund. (138).

JIBBUCKER, JOHN, d. 2 Nov. 1713 (128:31).

JOB, MARY, m. James Bullock on 4 Jan. 1724 (129:238).

JOHNS, ABRAHAM, chirurgeon, m. Hannah, dau. of Roger Matthews and sis. of John Matthews; d. leaving a will, 10 Oct. 1731 - 15 Feb. 1731/2, naming father-in-law Roger Matthews, w. Hannah and her bro. John Matthews; admin. bond was posted 6 Sept. 1732 by extx. Hannah Johns, with Roger Matthews, Tho. Sheredine, Edw. Hall, and Brian Taylor; est. was admin. by Hannah Johns on 22 Aug. 1734, and by Hannah, now w. of John Hall, on 27 Oct. 1735 (3:159, 214; 13:377; 110:268; 125:217).

JOHNS, ABRAHAM, was in Balto. Co. by 1750 when he owned 250 a. Christopher's Camp, which he inherited from his father, Isaac Johns, of Cal. Co. (126:72; 153:104).

JOHNS, AQUILA, m. Hannah Bond on 27 Jan. 1757 (131).

JOHNS, HUGH, was b. c.1657/60, giving his age as 21 in 1681 and 50 in 1707 (310).

JOHNS, or JONES, HUGH, was in Balto. Co. by 1692 as a taxable in n. side Patapsco Hund. (138).

JOHNS, HUGH, was in Balto. Co. at least by 1724, but may be the same individual mentioned in either or both of the preceding entries; m. Anne (---) who d. 1 March 1727; acquired Horton's Fortune an' Hobson's Choice; d. 22 March 1726/7 leaving a will, 22 March 1726/7 - 1 April 1727, naming s. Hugh (to have Horton's Fortune), s. Benjamin (to have Hobson's Choice), and other ch. Charity, Clary, Chloe, and Ann, with Benjamin Bowen as exec.; Bowen ren. his right to admin., and on 3 April 1727 James Moore posted admin. bond with Philip Sindall and John Royston; Moore admin. the est. in 1727, showing an inv. worth Ł 76.3.11, but after all debts were paid, there was only Ł 11.3.11 left to dist. among the heirs; left iss.: HUGH; BENJAMIN (alive in 1750 as the owner of 100 a. Hobson's Choice); CHARITY, m. Abraham Eaglestone on 20 Dec. 1730; MARY; CLARY, or CHLOE, b. 25 Aug. 1724; ANNE (2:186; 3:93; 13:362; 110:233; 133:7, 150, 193; 153:59; 211:85).

JOHNS, Capt. ISAAC, in 1750 owned 250 a. Christopher's Camp, which he inher. from his father Isaac of Cal. Co. (126:72; 153:104).

JOHNS, Capt. KENSEY, in 1750 owned 500 a. Christopher's Camp, which he inher. from his father Kensey Johns of Cal. Co. (125:128; 153:104).

JOHNS, RICHARD, was b. c.1705, acc. to a deposition made in 1747; m. Ann (---); in 1750 owned 334 a. Rich Bottom Corrected; d. leaving a will, 18 Aug. 1757 - 28 Oct. 1757, naming w. Ann, tracts Loftin's Run, Chawney's Run, Darnall's Convenience, and the west end of Rich Bottom Corrected, and the ch. named below; admin. bond was posted 28 Oct. 1757 by extx. Ann Johns, with James Rigbie and Aquila Johns; a second admin. bond was posted 8 Dec. 1761 by Richard Johns, after the death of the wid. Ann; dec. had iss.: RICHARD; AQUILA; HOSIER; CASSANDRA, m. (---) Chew; NATHAN; MARY; ANN; PHILIP; SKIPWITH: and HENRY (13:393, 405; 30:367; 153:36; 210-25:113).

JOHNS, RICHARD, fuller, of Cal. Co., d. in Balto. Co., by 14 May 1761 when est. was admin. by the admin. de bonis non, Kinsey Johns (4:350).

THE ANTHONY JOHNSON FAMILY is more fully discussed in vol. II of The Green Spring Valley, Its History and Heritage (259)

JOHNSON, ANTHONY (1), was in Balto. Co. by 1692 as a taxable in n. side Patapsco Hund.; d. 1721, having m. 3 March 1699 Catherine Smith, who m. as her 2nd husb. on 4 July 1726 Thomas Howard; in Nov. 1692 Catherine pet. to be the guardian of Susannah Poteet, orphan of Francis Poteet, dec.; in March 1692/3 Catherine was tried for the murder of Susannah Poteet and evidently acquitted; Anthony d. leaving a will, 30 March 1718 - 5 Feb. 1721, naming ch. Anthony, Benjamin, Thomas, William, John, Mary, and Catherine and w. Catherine; admin. bond was posted 5 Feb. 1721 by extx. Catherine, with Patrick Murphy and John Buck; est. was admin. by Catherine, now w. of Thomas Howard on 15 April 1724 and in 1725; Catherine and her 2nd husb. sold land in April 1724 which had orig. been left to Catherine's son William Johnson, by one Edward Boarman in his will of 10 Feb. 1704; Anthony and Catherine had iss.: ANTHONY, b. 15 Dec. 1700; JOHN, b. 3 April 1704; WILLIAM, b. by 10 Feb. 1704; THOMAS, b. c.1706; BENJAMIN, b. 8 Oct. 1708, d. 1738; CATHERINE, m. Emanuel Teale on 24 Dec. 1734; MARY, m. (---) Williams (2:344; 4:81; 13:363; 19:304, 347; 69:273; 1:282; 124:80; 133:146; 138; Stephenson, "Extracts from Maryland Court Records", NGSQ 53 (3) 201-202).

JOHNSON, WILLIAM (2), s. of Anthony (1) and Catherine, was b. c.1704, and d. leaving a will, 12 Jan. 1721/2 - 3 Dec. 1741, naming bros. Thomas and Benjamin, and sis. Mary and Catherine (127: 150).

JOHNSON, THOMAS (3), s. of Anthony (1) and Catherine, was b. c.1706, and d. 1791; m. 1752 Anne, dau. of Edward Riston; in 1750 owned 97 a. Logsdon's Addition, and 200 a. Turner's Hall; had iss.: RINALDO, b. 1753; HORATIO, b. 1755; RACHEL, m. John Woodward; MARY, b. 8 Sept. 1763, d. 8 Sept. 1821, m. 1st, Lieut. Adam Jamison, and 2nd, Samuel Goldthwaite; ELIZABETH, m. Johns Hopkins Fox; THOMAS, b. c.1764; WILLIAM, unm., lived at Pleasant Green; Capt. CECILIUS, b. c.1771, d. unm. 26 Sept. 1797 age 26; ANNE, m. 11 Aug. 1803 John Beale Owings; JOHN W. (153:48; 259: 49-51).

THE HENRY JOHNSON FAMILY

JOHNSON, HENRY (4), no known rel. to above, d. c.1690/1; m. by 1676 Elizabeth (nee Carter), admnx. of Nathaniel Utie; she m. 3rd Edward Boothby; Elizabeth, dau. of John Carter, and Nathaniel Utie made an antenuptial settlement on 18 Jan. 1667; on 1 Aug. 1682 Henry Johnson purch. 640 a. Spry's Inheritance from Samuel Hedge and wife Ann; Johnson d. leaving a will, made 13 June 1689, naming w. Elizabeth, and sons Henry and Joseph; his est. was inv. 18 Jan. 1690 by Thomas Walston and Edward Bedell and val. at £ 249.10.0; est. was admin. on 11 June 1694 by Edward Boothby who m. the wid., and again in 1708 by Boothby's wid. Elizabeth; dec. left iss.: JOSEPH; and HENRY (2:118; 51:10; 59:16; 200-66: 364; 200-67:49, 190-191; 206-12:147; "Capt. John Utie of Utimara," in 415-5:298-304).

JOHNSON, JOSEPH (5), prob. old. s. of Henry (4), d. by 28 July 1731; m. 5 July 1713 Ann Todd, who d. Feb. 1719, dau. of James Todd, and granddau. of Thomas and Anna (Gorsuch) Todd; may be the Joseph Johnson named as the father of Elizabeth Seamore alias Smither's child; in March 1721 purch. 50 a. Bond's Adventure from William and Mary Bond; d. leaving a will, 15 March 1730 - 28 July 1731, naming dau. Elizabeth and bro.-in-law Josias Middlemore; admin. bond was posted 28 July 1731 by exec. Josias Middlemore with John Scott and William Grafton; est. was admin. by Middlemore on 3 July 1735; left iss.: HENRY, b. 22 March 1715/6, prob. d. young as he is not mentioned in his father's will; ELIZABETH, b. Oct. 1719, m. William Dallam on 10 Jan. 1737; ANN, b. and d. 1728 (prob. by a 2nd w.) (3:182; 13:375; 26:213; 59:676; 125: 192; 128:30, 58; "Gorsuch and Lovelace Families," in 414-3:360).

JOHNSON, HENRY (6), s. of Henry (4), was not yet 16 when his father made his will; may be the Henry who m. Jane (---) and had: MARY, b. 15 Jan. 1733 (128:91).

THE STEPHEN JOHNSON FAMILY

JOHNSON, STEPHEN (7), no known rel. to any of the above, was in Balto. Co. by 1699; in Sept. 1699 he conv. prop. to his w. Ann, and in Jan. 1699 he and w. Ann conv. 250 a. Johnson's Dock to son Robert; d. leaving a will, 20 Sept. 1700 - 3 Feb. 1701/2, naming w. Ann, s. Robert, and granddau. Mary, dau. of Robert Lusby; est. was inv. 13 June 1702 by John Ewings and John Rallings and val. at £ 116.3.8; est. was admin. on 8 Dec. 1703 and 10 Dec. 1707 by wid. Ann who m. 2nd Edward Felkes; Stephen had iss.: ROBERT; dau., m. Robert Lusby (2:27, 201; 51:113; 63:403, 416; 121:228).

JOHNSON, ROBERT (8), s. of Stephen, m. by 29 April 1703 Hannah (---) who joined him in the sale of 250 a. Johnson's Dock to Geo. Eager (66:251).

THE FAMILY OF THOMAS JOHNSON OF GUNPOWDER MANOR has been discussed in Elmore Hutchins' Nicholas Hutchins of My Lady's Manor.

JOHNSON, THOMAS (9), m. Mary Enlows on 3 Sept. 1716; on 4
Nov. 1734 he purch. 43 a. Johnson's Addition, part of 150 a. from
Robert Love; Johnson already owned Jacob's Lot; on 2 Nov. 1743
Thomas and Mary conv. 98 a. of Giles and Webster's Discovery to
Joseph Johnson, and 98 a. to William Ellett's; in 1750 he owned
47 a. of Jamaica, 50 a. Jacob's Lot, and 100 a. Hutchins' Addi-
tion; left iss.: JACOB, b. 15 March 1717/8; TABITHA, b. 11 Sept.
1720; ISRAEL, b. 20 Dec. 1722; JEMIMA, b. 1724; NATHAN, b. 1727;
KEZIA, b. 1729, m. Isham Hendon in 1749; MOSES, b. 1731; and
LUKE, b. 1733 (73:69; 77:345, 375; 131; 153; Hutchins).

JOHNSON, JACOB (10), s. of Thomas (9) and Mary, was b. 15
March 1717/8; m. 1st Hannah Baker, who d. 26 Aug. 1744; m. 2nd,
on 25 Feb. 1749, Elizabeth Hendon; on 16 Nov. 1743 Jacob Johnson
of Thomas leased 100 a. Clynmalira from Charles Carroll of Annap.,
the lease to run for the lifetimes of Jacob, Aaron, and Luke
Johnson; had iss., by 2nd w.: JEMIMA, b. last of Feb. 1752, m.
1773 Thomas Hutchins; HANNAH, b. 13 June 1754; MARY, b. 31 Aug.
1756 (77:418; 131:25, 36, 107/r, 130/r, 131/r, 134/r).

JOHNSON, ISRAEL (11), s. of Thomas (9) and Mary, was b. 20 Dec.
1722; d. 1751 in Balto. Co.; m. Sarah Hutchins on 12 Jan. 1742; d.
leaving a will, 12 Dec. 1750 - 28 Jan. 1750/1; had iss.: THOMAS,
b. 1 Feb. 1745; JOHN HUTCHINS; MARY; SARAH (111:35; 131:96/r,
113/r).

JOHNSON, NATHAN (12), s. of Thomas (9) and Mary, was b. 1727;
m. Elizabeth Wright on 11 Feb. 1755; had iss.: WILLIAM, b. 22
Feb. 1755; MARY, b. 8 March 1757; CHRISTINA, d. 21 May 1759;
CHRISTINA, b. 14 March 1760; THOMAS, b. 22 July 1762 (131:45,
146/r, 147/r, 153/r).

JOHNSON, MOSES (13), s. of Thomas (9) and Mary, was b. 1731;
m. Priscilla Standiford on 1 Feb. 1757 (131).

JOHNSON, LUKE (14), s. of Thomas (9) and Mary, was b. 1733; m.
in 1760 Rachel (---); had nine ch., incl.: MARY, m. John Anderson
Pearce.

THE THOMAS JOHNSON (OF BOND'S LOT) FAMILY

JOHNSON, THOMAS (15), no known rel. to any of the above, d. by
31 Aug. 1767; m. Alice, dau. of William Bond, on 17 Oct. 1724;
she d. 1775 in Harford Co.; in 1750 he owned 355 a. Bond's Lot
and 300 a. part Turkey Forest; d. leaving a will, 1 May 1767 - 31
Aug. 1767, naming w. Alice (to have 150 a. Turkey Forest and 50
a. Noble's Wonder, dau. Mary Brice and her s. James Brice, and
sons William, Barnett, and John; had iss.: MARY, m. James Brice
on 6 Jan. 1742; THOMAS, b. 14 Nov. 1726; WILLIAM, b. 9 Sept. 1729;
BARNETT, b. 5 Nov. 1732; SARAH, b. 1 June 1735, prob. d. young;
JOHN, b. 5 Nov. 1738; SARAH, d. 22 Dec. 1739 (3:271; 112:63; 128:
6, 7, 89, 103; 129:327).

JOHNSON, THOMAS (16), s. of Thomas (15) and Alice, was b. 14
Nov. 1726; may be the Thomas Johnson, Jr., who m. Mary Clark on
29 Nov. 1748 (129:346).

JOHNSON, BARNETT (17), s. of Thomas (15) and Alice, was b. 5
Nov. 1732; m. Hester, dau. of Robert Clark; d. leaving a will, 19
Feb. 1771 - 24 June 1771, naming tracts Turkey Forest and Noble's
Wonder, w. Hester, and these ch.: BARNETT; THOMAS; ROBERT; MARY;
SARAH (may have m. William Clark and had a son Barnett Johnson
Clark); ALICE; and ANN (112:195).

THE WILLIAM JOHNSON FAMILY

JOHNSON, WILLIAM (18), no known rel. to any of the above, m.
Sarah (---), and had iss.: WILLIAM, b. 18 Dec. 1733; RUTH, b. 26
Feb. 1736; PHILIP, b. 29 Dec. 1737; JOHN, b. 29 July 1740; THOM-
AS, b. 25 Sept. 1742; JOSEPH, b. 18 Jan. 1745; SARAH, b. 17 May
1747; BENJAMIN, b. 18 Oct. 1749; MARY ANN, b. 14 July 1752 (133:
40, 85, 96).

JOHNSON, WILLIAM (19), s. of William (18) and Sarah, was b. 18
Dec. 1733; m. Eleanor (---), and had iss.: ABSOLOM, b. 21 Aug.
1757; ELIZABETH, b. 2 Jan. 1760; WILLIAM, b. 29 Jan. 1762; ELANOR,
b. 2 Feb. 1764; GREENBURY, b. 14 Feb. 1766; THOMAS, b. 26 March
1768 (131:121, 122).

JOHNSON, (---), m. by 15 Aug. 1717 Sarah, dau. of Ambrose Nelson, by whom he had at least two ch., named in the will of their
grandfather: AMBROSE; RUTH (125:112).

JOHNSON, ABRAHAM, m. Lydia (---), and had iss.: MARGARET, b.
28 Oct. 1741; MARY, b. 16 Aug. 1744 (129:332, 337).

JOHNSON, ALEXANDER, m. Jane (---), and had iss.: ELIZABETH, b.
27 Jan. 1736 (128:98).

JOHNSON, AMOS, d. by 17 Feb. 1761 when admin. bond was posted
by Lydia Johnson with Peter Miles, with Richard Williams, William
Bull, and Joseph Smith; est. was admin. 8 Nov. 1762 by admnx. Lydia, now w. of William Bain and by Peter Miles; dec. left six ch.,
one of whom was: WILLIAM, by Jan. 1773 was in Colleton Co., S. C.
when he sold Robinson's Outlet to William Bull (4:367; 6:139;
13:389; 231-AL#G:306).

JOHNSON, BENJAMIN, was named in the will of Deborah Benger
(will proved 1700), as a son (121:197).

JOHNSON, CHARITY, was tried for bast. in Nov. 1730 (29:61).

JOHNSON, DANIEL, d. in Balto. Co. on 14 Sept. 1715; m. Frances
(---), who m. 2nd Hugh Grant, and 3rd Miles Foy; on 16 Aug. 1701
Daniel purch. 200 a. Eightropp from William Lofton; d. leaving a
will, 12 Sept. 1715 - 30 Jan. 1715/6, naming w. Frances, unborn
ch., John Low, "all ch. of testator and his w."; admin. bond was
posted 19 Nov. 1716 by extx. Frances Johnson with John Lowe and
George Emery; est. was inv. on 3 Dec. 1716 by Thomas Smith and S.
Hinton, and val. at £ 24.3.10; est. was admin. 10 April 1718 and
11 April 1718 by the extx., and by Frances (now Foy) on 23 Oct.
1736 when these daus. of the dec. were named: the w. of Evan
Evans, the w. of Richard Touchstone, Charity w. of Robert Cannon,
the w. of Thomas Cresap and the w. of William Cannon; Daniel and
Frances had iss.: prob. ELIZABETH, m. John Low; DANIEL, b. 28
Feb. 1699/1700, bur. 29 Aug. 1700; SARAH, b. 18 Sept. 1701, m.
Richard Touchstone on 25 Feb. 1717; FRANCES, b. 1 Nov. 1703, m.
William Cannon on 28 Dec. 1721; HANNAH, b. 6 June 1705, m. Thomas
Cresap on 30 April 1727; RACHEl, b. 5 June 1707; SOPHIA, b. 22
Nov. 1709; CHARITY, b. 17 Feb. 1712, tried for bast. in Nov. 1730;
DANIEL, b. 2 Oct. 1715 (1:265, 270; 3:224; 13:365; 29:61; 52:1;
59:661; 123:65; 128:9, 10, 12, 34; 129:219, 247, 256, 260).

JOHNSON, DANIEL, of Newcastle Co., Del., purch. 100 a. Hammond's
Hope from Robert Courtney in June 1743; on 11 Aug. 1748 Daniel and
w. Levina conv. the tract to Thomas White; ch. of Daniel and Levina: SAMUEL, b. 29 March 1742; MARY, b. 23 Feb. 1743; JAMES, b.
10 Jan. 1743/4 (77:293; 80:32; 129:336).

JOHNSON, FRANCES, was m. to Edward Harris on 19 June 1719 (129:230).

JOHNSON, FRANCIS, of A. A. Co., in Feb. 1669/70 conv. 200 a. Ludlow's Lot to John Larkin (96).

JOHNSON, HANNAH, m. Jacob Herrington on 26 Oct. 1720 (129: 237).

JOHNSON, HENRY, m. Anne Bone on 24 Sept. 1747 (133:160).

JOHNSON, HENRY, d. by 29 March 1751 when admin. bond was posted by Patrick Gray and w., who testified they knew of no kin; James Welsh and John Cook were securities (13:395).

JOHNSON, ISAAC, was in Balto. Co. by 1692 as a taxable in Spesutia Hund. (138).

JOHNSON, ISAAC, d. 20 April 1729 (128:59).

JOHNSON, ISAAC, d. 19 April 1730 (128:70).

JOHNSON, ISABEL, d. 14 June 1728 (128:54).

JOHNSON, JACOB, was in Balto. Co. by 1692 as a taxable in n. side of Patapsco Hund. (138).

JOHNSON, JACOB, m. Alice Moore on 11 Jan. 1704 (128:22).

JOHNSON, JACOB, d. 23 Feb. 1739 (128:106).

JOHNSON, JOHN, was in Balto. Co. by June 1674 when Mary Harmer, wid., conv. 150 a. Oliver's Reserve to him and Robert Benger; m. Deborah (---) who m. 2nd Robert Benger; Deborah d. by 5 Aug. 1700 when her will was proved, naming s. Benjamin (to have 50 a. on Back Creek), dau. Elizabeth Shaw (to have Benger's Privilege and Addition to Privilege and 100 a. at head of Gunpowder); John and Deborah had iss.: BENJAMIN; ELIZA, m. John Shaw of Cecil Co.; and JANE, m. 1st Daniel Scott, and 2nd (---) Watson (77:471; 100; 121:197).

JOHNSON, JOHN, was in Balto. Co. by 1694 as a taxable in Spesutia Hund.; had iss.: JACOB, b. 23 April 1682; AARON, b. 15 July 1684; MOSES, b. 19 March 1692/3; RUTH, b. 16 Sept. 1695 (128:1, 2, 3; 139).

JOHNSON, JOHN, and w. Ann were in Balto. Co. by 30 Aug. 1697 when they conv. 168 a. Johnson's Bed and 150 a. part Johnson's Rest to Thomas Freeborn (61:177).

JOHNSON, JOHN, m. Hannah Mitchell on 1 Jan. 1733; may be the John who d. 18 Sept. 1739; had iss.: JOHN, b. 23 June 1737 (128: 78, 97, 106).

JOHNSON, JOHN, m. Rachel (---), and had: THOMAS, b. 15 Sept. 1734 (128:84).

JOHNSON, JOSEPH, on 2 Nov. 1743 purch. 98 a. Giles and Webster's Discovery from Thomas and Mary Johnson; in 1750 he owned 100 a. of that tract plus 190 a. Mountain; m. Martha (---), and had iss.: THOMAS, b. 12 June 1723; HANNAH, b. 3 Oct. 1725; JEREMIAH, b. 1 May 1728, d. 6 May 1740; JOSEPH, b. 17 Nov. 1730; WILLIAM, b. 31 Dec. 1731; MARY, b. 13 Dec. 1734; JOHN, d. 7 Nov. 1735; JAMES ISHAM, b. 14 March 1736; SARAH, b. 10 Jan. 1739, d. 12 June 1740; MARTHA, b. 6 May 1741 (128:42, 46, 70, 75, 86, 90, 96, 108, 112; 129:324; 153:60).

JOHNSON, MARY, m. Thomas Burchfield on 10 Aug. 1727 (129:343).

JOHNSON, MATTHEW, and w. Sarah of A. A. Co., on 22 June 1750 conv. 100 a. Johnson's Range to Emanuel Teal (80:513).

JOHNSON, PETER, on 8 July 1730 purch. Bond's Pleasant Hills from Peter Bond; on 17 March 1742 he admin. the est. of John Taylor; he may be the Peter Johnson who m. Mary Mayo on 30 Nov. 1731 in All Hallows Par., A. A. Co.; had iss.: ELIZABETH, b. 9 April 1735 (3:257; 73:24; 133:44; 263).

JOHNSON, PHILIP, d. by 10 June 1717 when admin. bond was posted by admnx. Mary Hayes, with John Hayes and Richard Lenox; est. was inv. in 1718 by William Collison and Thomas Biddison and val. at ₤ 11.10.6, plus 3200 lbs. tob. in debts, with Mary Johnson and Elizabeth Ward signing as kin, with John Hillen and James Crooke signing as creditors (13:368; 52:102).

JOHNSON, RACHEL, m. Edward Evans on 3 Dec. 1724 (129:236).

JOHNSON, RAIL, d. 23 April 1734, aged about 20 years (128:77).

JOHNSON, ROBERT, m. Elizabeth (---), and had iss.: MARY, b. 25 Jan. 1743 (129:334).

JOHNSON, SAMUEL, age 9 next Nov., in June 1730 was bound to William Robinson; may be the same Samuel Johnson who m. by 9 June 1742 Mary, admnx. of Garvis Gilbert (28:416; 33:442).

JOHNSON, SARAH, m. Richard Touchstone on 25 Feb. 1717 (129: 256).

JOHNSON, SOPHIA, m. 8 July 1725 Robert Cannon (129:258).

JOHNSON, THOMAS, of St. George's Par., m. Mary (---), by whom he had iss.: THOMAS, d. 30 April 1714; RACHEL, b. 20 July 1714; THOMAS, b. 22 March 1716/7; KEREN(HAPPUCK?), b. 5 Nov. 1724 (128: 33, 44).

JOHNSON, THOMAS, d. 12 Oct. 1730 (128:70).

JOHNSON, THOMAS, m. Mary (---) and had iss.: JOHN, b. 26 Oct. 1736 (128:94).

JOHNSON, THOMAS, d. by 3 Nov. 1744 when admin. bond was posted by John Hall, with James Taylor, and Gabriel Brown; est. was admin. by John Hall on 17 July 1746 (4:128:13:386).

JOHNSON, THOMAS, was made levy free in March 1745/6 (35:802).

JOHNSON, THOMAS, m. Elizabeth Hutchins on 7 Feb. 1743, and had iss.: DAVID, b. 4 Dec. 1744 (131:25, 107/r).

JOHNSON, THOMAS, m. Sarah (---) and had iss.: JOHN, b. 25 Jan. 1743 (129:338).

JOHNSON, THOMAS, b. in Eng., age c.30, run away serv. from Nottingham Ironworks, was advert. for in April 1749 (385:46).

JOHNSON, THOMAS, m. Ann Bradley on 14 Feb. 1751, and had: JOSEPH, b. 2 July 1755; MARTHA, b. 16 June 1757; ELIJAH, b. 29 Dec. 1759; EPHRAIM, b. 24 Aug. 1762 (129:373).

JOHNSON, WALTER, was in Balto. Co. by 1692 as a taxable in Spesutia Hund. (138).

JOHNSON, WILLIAM, m. Mary Ann Poaling on 22 Sept. 1733 (133:
151).

JOHNSON, WILLIAM, s. of William, was conv. 100 a. of Farfar's
Favor, by his grandfather Thomas Harris; William still owned the
land in 1750 (74:28]; 153:151).

JOHNSON, WILLIAM, age c.15, b. in Eng., alias Thomas Martin,
ran away from Thomas Harvey of Garrison Ridge; was advert. for
in June 1756 (307-69:127).

JOHNSTON, SAMUEL, m. Catherine (---), and had iss.: ANN, b. 10
July 1750; MARY, b. 3 March 1753; SARAH, b. 4 March 1755; JEAN,
b. 4 March 1757; CATHERINE, b. 20 Feb. 1759 (129:363).

JOLLY, JAMES, and w. Rachel conv. John Harryman part of Waterford on 21 Dec. 1709 (67:87).

JOLLY, MATTHEW, Irish, age c. 22, runaway conv. serv. from
Patapsco Ironworks; was advert. for in July 1745 (384:511).

JOLLEY, WALTER. See TOLLEY, WALTER.

THE BENJAMIN JONES FAMILY

JONES, BENJAMIN (1), m. Anne (---) who d. 6 May 1737; they had
iss.: BENJAMIN, b. 7 Dec. 1735; ANNE, b. 21 Sept. 1736 (131:51/r).

JONES, BENJAMIN (2), s. of Benjamin (1) and Ann, was b. 7 Dec.
1735; was age 3 in Dec. 1737 and in March 1737/8 was bound to
Samuel Talby and w. Elizabeth (31:352).

THE FAMILY OF BENJAMIN JONES OF FOX HALL

JONES, BENJAMIN (3), no known rel. to any of the above, m.
Elizabeth, dau. of William Pickett, whose inv. Elizabeth signed
on 2 July 1721; on 8 Sept. 1724 Benj. Jones admin. Pickett's est.;
in April 1728 Benj. purch. 50 a. Fox Hall and 6¼ a. of Waterton's
Neglect from Heathcote Pickett, his wife's bro.; on 6 March 1735
Benjamin Jones conv. these tracts to Thomas Franklin; ch. of Benjamin and Elizabeth: JOHN, b. 17 April 1721; PECKETT, b. 24 June
1722; ELIZABETH, b. 24 June 1722 (3:15; 52:31; 74:409; 71:64;
131:40/r, 51/r).

JONES, PECKETT (4), s. of Benjamin (3) and Elizabeth, was b.
24 June 1722, m. Elizabeth James on 16 Dec. 1746, and had iss.:
ANN, b. 17 Feb. 1747 (131:31, 127/r).

THE EDWARD JONES FAMILY

JONES, EDWARD (5), no known rel. to any of the above, was in
Balto. Co. by 1692 as a taxable in n. side of Gunpowder Hund.;
in March 1693/4 agreed to finish the court house and to find timber, boards, and all other conveniences; in March 1693/4 purch.
70 a. Haphazard from John and Hester Fuller; in April 1696 purch.
100 a. Leafe's Chance from Charles Ramsey; in June 1696 with the
cons. of w. Sarah sold the latter tract to John Campbell; d. by 6
Nov. 1706 when admin. bond was posted by the wid. and admnx. Sarah
Jones, with John Boone and Matthew Green; est. was admin. by Sarah
and her 2nd husb. John Hatch, on 3 July 1710, and 26 Feb. 1710
(1710/11?); prob. was the father of: SYLVESTER or SYLVANUS (2:
158, 188; 13:368; 20:28; 59:513, 518; 66:373; 138).

JONES, SYLVESTER, or SYLVANUS (6), s. of Edward (5), may be
the Sylvester Jones who m. Mary Hinton in Nov. 1719; in May 1721

sold 75 a. of Haphazard to Anthony Asher, and in Sept. 1732 sold
100 a. Hall's Plains to John Risteau (68:316; 73:283).

THE JOHN JONES FAMILY

JONES, JOHN (7), no known rel. to any of the above, was b. in
1711; d. 1790; m. Hannah Wooley in Dec. 1732; in Aug. 1736 he
purch. 100 a. Wooley's Range from John and Ann Wooley; had iss.:
JOHN, b. 9 April 1737 in St. John's Par.; BENJAMIN, b. 25 May
1739 in St. Paul's Par.; ELISHA, b. 18 Jan. 1741 in St. Paul's
Par.; JOSHUA (61:329; 131:59/r; 133:67).

JONES, JOHN (8), s. of John (7) and Hannah, was b. 9 April
1737; d. 1785; m. Esther (---); served in the Third Regt. of the
Balto. Co. Militia in 1775; d. leaving a will, 20 Sept. 1785 - 21
Oct. 1785; est. was admin. on 11 April 1790 by John Walton;
Esther Jones d. leaving a will, 3 May 1787 - 5 July 1787; ch. of
John and Esther: ANN, b. 1758, m. John Walton in 1775; JOHN, b.
15 Dec. 1760; SOPHIA, m. Joseph Hook; ELEANOR, m. Benjamin Parks;
ELISHA; JOSHUA; CALEB; and ENOCH (11:24; 113:91, 254; 133:114;
353; DAR Lineage Book, 102:216).

THE JONATHAN JONES FAMILY

JONES, JONATHAN (9), of A. A. Co., no known rel. to any of
the above; m. Mary (---) who m. 2nd Thomas Warren who d. by May
1738; Jonathan Jones d. leaving a will, 2 Oct. 1719 - 5 Nov.
1719, leaving part Paschall's Purchase to s. Thomas, and naming
dau. Mary, s. John, s. Lewis, s. Jonathan (to have 100 a. Quick
Sale); in May 1738 wid. Mary Warren conv. 1/3 part of Rochford
to s. Thomas, and livestock to sons Jonathan and Lewis; wid. Mary
m. as 3rd husb. James Isom (Isham) on 1 June 1738; ch. of Jonathan and Mary: THOMAS; JOHN (may have d. by 1738); LEWIS; JONA-
THAN; MARY (not yet 16 in 1719) (75:69, 70, 71; 123:214; 131).

JONES, THOMAS (10), s. of Jonathan (9) and Mary, d. Jan. 1742;
m. Mary (---) who m. as her 2nd husb. Isaac Litton by 12 May 1746;
d. leaving a will, 29 Dec. 1742 - 7 Feb. 1742/3, naming s. Thomas
(to have 125 a. Neighborhood), s. John (to have residue of that
tract and part Arabia Petrea), and other ch.: Jonathan, Mary,
Cassandra, Eleanor, and Sarah, with w. Mary as extx.; admin. bond
was posted 7 Feb. 1742 by extx. Mary Jones, with William Coale
and Jonathan Jones; in Aug. 1750 his orphans John and Jonathan
were made wards of Jonathan Jones who took the est. from Litton;
Thomas and Mary had iss.: MARY, b. 17 Feb. 1728; CASSANDRA, b. 9
May 1732; THOMAS, b. 27 April 1735; JONATHAN, b. 16 Feb. 1739;
JOHN; ELEANOR (4:132; 13:387; 37:156, 173; 39:187; 127:196; 128:
59, 75, 88, 109; 129:331).

JONES, JONATHAN (11), s. of Jonathan (9) and Mary, orphan in
1730 and was made ward of Benjamin Wheeler; in 1750 owned 99 a.
part Eightrupp; m. Martha Farmer on 10 Nov. 1736 and had iss.:
MARY, b. 26 Sept. 1737; MARGARET, twin, b. 10 Jan. 1738; HANNAH,
twin, b. 10 Jan. 1738; THOMAS, b. 4 Nov. 1740; MARTHA, b. 25 Aug.
1742; SARAH, b. 1 Jan. 1752; CASSANDRA, b. 3 March 1754; ELIZA-
BETH, b. 23 Dec. 1756; PRISCILLA, b. 7 Feb. 1758 (29:3; 128:95,
99, 102, 115; 129:326, 362; 153:62).

JONES, THOMAS (12), s. of Thomas (10), was b. 27 April 1735;
in 31 May 1759 as s. and heir of Thomas Jones, dec., conv. 100 a.
Phillips Purchase to Charles Worthington, with cons. of his w.
Mary; m. 20 June 1757 Mary Dooley; had iss.: SARAH, b. 23 March
1758 (83:450; 129:362).

THE PHILIP JONES FAMILY is the subject of research by Christopher Johnston, whose notes are at the Maryland Historical Society, Baltimore.

JONES, PHILIP (13), of A. A. Co., no known rel. to any of the above, was b. 29 Sept. 1679, and d. 10 March 1753 at his plantation on the n. side of Severn R.; m. 1st, on 3 Jan. 1700, Mary Rowles, who d. 28 Jan. 1716/7; m. 2nd, on 18 Sept. 1719, Hannah Rattenbury, who d. 1721; in 1750 Philip Jones owned 160 a. part Johnson, 18 a. Thomas' Addition, 38 a. Westminster, 105½ a. part Pasture Ground, 88 a. part Triple Union, 100 a. Dickinson, 40 a. part Darby, and 10 a. part Sewall's Relief, as well as other land; had iss.: (by 1st w.): PHILIP, b. 16 Oct. 1701; HANNAH, b. 1705; (by 2nd w.): JOHN, b. 2 Nov. 1721, d. 12 March 1742 (153:55; 262; 263; Johnston, chart of Jones Family).

JONES, PHILIP (14), s. of Philip (13) and Mary, was b. 16 Oct. 1701, d. 1761; m. 1st, on 29 May 1723, Jemima, wid. of John Eager and dau. of James Murray; m. 2nd, on 2 Oct. 1727, Ann Rattenbury; may be the Maj. Philip Jones who in 1750 was listed as the owner of: 250 a. Jones' Contrivance, 400 a. St. John's Park, 400 a. The Eagle's Nest, 155 a. The Folly, 115 a. Jones Preservation, 156 a. Jones' Lot, and other lands; had iss.: (by 1st w.): MARGARET, b. 1724; (by 2nd w.): HENRIETTA MARIA; PHILIP; RACHEL; RATTENBURY; Judge THOMAS; NICHOLAS; HANNAH; ANNE; JOHN (Johnston, chart of Jones Family; 153).

THE RICHARD JONES FAMILY

JONES, RICHARD (15), no known rel. to any of the above, was in Balto. Co. by 2 Nov. 1715 when he surv. Elizabeth's Fancy; d. leaving a will, 18 Nov. 1735 - 13 June 1737, naming w. as extx., and ch.: Richard, Mary, Margaret, Elizabeth, and Ann; had iss.: RICHARD; MARY; MARGARET; ELIZABETH; and ANN (126:212; 398:8, 9).

JONES, RICHARD (16), s. of Richard (15), m. Hannah or Johannah, who joined him in July 1749 in conveying 100 a. Elizabeth's Fancy to Samuel Owings; had iss.: SARAH, b. 18 Oct. 1737; RICHARD, b. 24 May 1739; ANN, b. 9 July 1741 (80:238; 134:8, 9).

THE SOLOMON JONES FAMILY

JONES, SOLOMON (17), surv. 100 a. The Level, in July 1688; was prob. the Solomon who d. in St. Mary's Co. leaving a will, 11 May 1710 - 24 June 1710, naming sons William and Solomon, daus. Katherine and Ellinor, and tracts Scotland, and the Folly; had iss.: WILLIAM; SOLOMON; KATHERINE; ELLINOR; poss. ELIZABETH, m. William Langley (122:177; 211:75).

JONES, WILLIAM (18), s. of Solomon (17), was in St. Marys Co. by 2 Oct. 1725 when he and w. Mary, and William Langley and w. Elizabeth (dau. of Solomon Jones), conv. 200 a. The Level to John Gardner (70:183).

THE THOMAS JONES FAMILY

JONES, THOMAS (19), no known rel. to any of the above, was in Balto. Co. by 2 Sept. 1671 when he purch. 200 a. Swan Harbour from John Towers; m. by 1696 Mary, prob. the Mary Harrison ment. in the will of Edward Dowse on 30 Oct. 1690; in 1696 Thomas and Mary sold Oglesby's Chance to Francis Whitehead (these refs. may pertain to Thomas James); Thomas Jones' wid. Mary m. 2nd (--- Staly), and as Mrs. Mary Staley, on 25 April 1701 paid Bridget, Cadwallader, and Rathvael (now w. of Cornelius Herrington) Jones, each £ 11.4.5 as their share of the est. of Thomas Jones;

Thomas and Mary (---) Jones had iss.: CHARLES, d. by 1700;
CADWALLADER; RATHVALE, m. Cornelius Herrington (59:524; 62:44;
63:33; 66:105).

JONES, CHARLES (20), s. of Thomas (19), was in Balto. Co. by
1692 as a taxable in n. side Gunpowder Hund.; d. leaving a will,
proved 2 June 1701, naming w. Bridget as extx., sons Thomas and
Theophilus, and dau.-in-law Eveula; admin. bond was posted by
Bridget Jones on 14 June 1701, with William Howard and John Webster; Bridget m. 2nd Edward Smith who held 200 a. Swan Harbour
for Charles Jones' orphans; Charles and Bridget had iss.: THOMAS,
minor in 1700; THEOPHILUS (13:370; 121:218; 211:38).

JONES, CADWALLADER (21), s. of Thomas (19), was of age to be
a taxable in 1694 on the n. side of Gunpowder Hund.; gave his age
as 59 in 1729; m. 1st on 23 April 1702, Mary Ellis, who d. 25
June 1703; m. 2nd, on 30 April 1704, Mary Paywell, or Poel; on
18 July 1727 conv. prop. to Jacob Herrington prov. Jacob would
maintain Jones and his two daus. Avarilla and Frances; had iss.:
(by 1st w.): CHARLES, b. 25 June 1703; (by 2nd w.): BLANCH, b.
28 Jan. 1706, m. William Dooley on 15 or 21 Oct. 1725; THOMAS, b.
14 Feb. 1708; AP'A (AVARILLA?), b. 22 April 1710; MARY, b. 13 Jan
1716, d. 7 June 1720; AQUILA, b. 7 June 1721; FRANCES, b. 7 May
1722 (71:1; 128:14, 69; 129:199, 237, 259; 225:88).

JONES, THEOPHILUS (22), s. of Charles (20) and Bridget, d. by
3 March 1735; on 8 Aug. 1734 he and w. Elizabeth purch. 60 a. of
Hughes' Chance from William and Mary Rhodes; d. leaving a will,
15 Feb. 1728/9 - 3 March 1735, naming w. Elizabeth (to care for
his mother Bridget Smith); will was wit. by Thomas Cottrell, Wm.
Andrews, Thomas Coale, T. Crockett, Jos. Middlemore, and William
Jackson; m. Elizabeth (---) who m. 2nd, by 29 Sept. 1737, John
Loyd with whom she posted admin. bond for the est. of Theophilus
Jones, with Thomas Coale and William Dallam; no known ch. of
Theophilus and Elizabeth (13:377; 74:90; 126:169).

JONES, CHARLES (23), s. of Cadwallader (21) and Mary, was b. 25
June 1703, and was alive in 1741; m. Frances, dau. of James Cobb.
on 26 Feb. 1727; had iss.: BENJAMIN, b. 4 Oct. 1728; CHARLES, b.
12 Nov. 1731; CADWALLADER, b. 11 May 1734; ELIZABETH, twin, b. 15
Jan. 1736; THEOPHILUS, twin, b. 15 Jan. 1736; FRANCES, b. 17 July
1739; REBECCA, b. 7 Feb. 1741 (128:66, 96; 129:257, 330, and 331).

JONES, AQUILA (24), s. of Cadwallader (21), and Mary, was b. 7
June 1721, and m. Elizabeth Brice on 7 May 1741; had iss.: MARY,
b. 13 April 174-(?); CHARLES, b. 13 April 1744; ELIZABETH, b. 3
May 1746 (129:322, 341).

THE WILLIAM JONES FAMILY

JONES, WILLIAM (25), of Cal. Co., no known rel. to any of the
above; d. leaving a will made 15 March 1699, naming his sons (not
yet 21): WILLIAM; DAVID; BENJAMIN; JACOB (121:200).

JONES, WILLIAM (26), s. of William (25), and bro. of Benjamin,
was living in the Upper End of the Cliffs, Cal. Co., when he
purch. Neighbor's Affinity from Samuel Sickelmore; no other record; prob. d. s.p. (66:302).

JONES, BENJAMIN (27), s. of William (25), and bro. of William
(26), d. by May 1751, leaving at least one s.: JACOB (81:136).

JONES, JACOB (28), s. of Benjamin (27) was in Balto. Co. by 4
May 1751 when he and w. Rachel conv. tract Neighbor's Affinity
to Thomas Harrison; may be the Jacob who d. by 18 June 1771 when

admin. bond was posted by admnx. Rachel Jones with Moses and Daniel Collett; Jacob Jones and Rachel Cottrell were m. 10 Feb. 1742 (13:410; 81:136; 131).

JONES, AARON, baseborn ch., was formerly bound to Aaron Fox, in June 1732 was placed with Thomas Broad; ordered to be kept by Elizabeth Goodwin in March 1733/4 (29:294; 30:189).

JONES, AMOS, was b. 23 July 1754, d. 12 Sept. 1827; m. by lic. of 26 Aug. 1783, Anne Lewis; was a private in the Rev. War from Md. (232; 353).

JONES, ANN, m. William Hitchcock on 7 Sept. 1716 (131).

JONES, ANN, was b. c.1683, giving her age as 40 in Aug. 1723 (25:443).

JONES, ANN, servant to William Petticoat, was ind. for bast. in June 1743, and tried in Aug. 1743 (34:185; 35:14).

JONES, ANNE, b. in Dublin, runaway servant from William Jenkins, was advert. for in Oct. 1754 (385:310).

JONES, ANN, d. leaving a will, 18 Sept. 1748 - 26 Nov. 1759, mentioning prop. in Prince William Co., Va., leaving est. to Thomas Sligh (111:308).

JONES, BENJAMIN, m. and had at least one s.: WILLIAM, b. 11 May 1715 (131).

JONES, BENJAMIN, formerly of A. A. Co., now of Balto. Co., on 1 May 1724 purch. 400 a. Friendship from George Buchanan, and on 3 Aug. 1726 purch. another 200 a. from Eleanor Buchanan (69: 309; 70:277).

JONES, BENJAMIN, on 4 Aug. 1730 conv. 100 a. Brown's Lot to John Brown; on the same day John Brown and w. Mary conv. 81 a. The Division to Benjamin Jones, the tract being part of Turkey Hills and Strawberry Hills; Jones d. leaving a will, 20 April 1739 - 22 May 1739, leaving entire est. to w. Diana, who is to conv. Turkey Hill and Strawberry Hill to William Bradford; admin. bond was posted 7 Nov. 1739 by Diana Jones with Samuel Pritchard and William Dallam (13:176; 73:1, 3; 127:36).

JONES, BENJAMIN, in 1750 owned 100 a. Hobson's Choice (153: 59).

JONES, BENJAMIN, m. Deborah (---), and had: CHLOE, b. 6 July 1750 (133:93).

JONES, CHARITY, was ind. for bast. in Aug. 1728 and tried in Nov. 1728 (28:22, 74).

JONES, CHARLES, d. by 23 Oct. 1711, when est. was admin. by Edward Smith and w. Margaret (1:297). (Cf. to Charles Jones, #20, in the Thomas Jones Family).

JONES, CLOE, was summoned by the vestry of St. John's Par. for unlawful cohabitation with John Greer in Nov. 1743, and tried for bast. in Aug. 1745 (35:631; 132:65).

JONES, DANIEL, was in Balto. Co. by Oct. 1663 when he bought 420 a. Dickenston from Walter Dickenston; in Aug. 1664 he sold the same tract to John Dickenson (61; 93; 94).

JONES, DANIEL, was in Balto. Co. by 1692 as a taxable in s. side Gunpowder (138).

JONES, DAVID, d. in Balto. Co. by March 1686/7; m. Anne, wid. of Thomas Todd, and dau. of Rev, John and Anne (Lovelace) Gorsuch; gave his name to Jones' Falls; d. leaving a will, 3 Feb. 1686 - 14 March 1686/7, naming John and Thomas Gorsuch (to have 450 a. Maiden's Choice), James Todd (to have 8 a. Black Walnut Neck), Robert Gibson (to have 200 a. Morrayland), sis. Elizabeth Jones (to have plantation after death of testator's w.); if sis. Elizabeth dies s.p., est. to pass to Francis and Aberell Todd; also named Edw. Norish, Sarah Garnet, Moyiss Groome, Daniel Welch, Robt. Jopson, Miles Gibson, and John Williams; w. Ann was made extx. and residuary legatee; est. was inv. 4 April 1687 by Anthony Demondidier and John Carrington, and val. at Ŀ 322.13.6 (121:11; 206-9:259).

JONES, ELIZABETH, was ind. for bast. in March 1733/4 (30:188).

JONES, EVAN, laborer, d. leaving a will, 2 Jan. 1761 - 5 Aug. 1765, naming w. Dorothy, George Bramwell, and George's s. Henry; admin. bond was posted 5 Aug. 1765 by Geo. Bramwell with Nicholas Orrick and Edw. Oursler (13:402; 112:20).

JONES, GEORGE, purch. 110 a. of Arabia Petrea from Henry Jones and w.; m. Elizabeth Linley on 3 Dec. 1740; on 16 Aug. 1749 George and Elizabeth conv. 110 a. Arabia Petrea to Skipwith Coale (77: 306; 78:4; 128:‌113).

JONES, GEORGE, d. by 20 May 1749 when admin. bond was posted by John Casdrop, shipwright, the admin., with Talbot Risteau (13: 381).

JONES, HENRIETTA, was reported by Jane Hughes to the vestry of St. John's Parish for unlawful cohabitation with Jane's husband Samuel Hughes (132:138).

JONES, HENRY, was in Balto. Co. by Sept. 1669 when he and w. Anne conv. to Thomas Howell, Gent., 275 a. on s. side of Sassafras R.; may be the Henry Jones who d. by 6 Feb. 1671 when admin. bond was posted by admin. John West with Francis Child (13:371; 95).

JONES, HENRY, d. by 15 March 1713 when his admin. bond was posted by admnx. Elizabeth Jones, with John Nicholson and Henry Waters; est. was inv. on 6 April 1714 by Charles Bevens and William Anderson and val. at Ŀ 64.2.6; est. was admin. on 12 July 1715 by admnx. Elizabeth, now w. of Richard Humphrey; dec. left three children (1:336; 13:365; 50:265).

JONES, HENRY, in Aug. 1724 pet. that his s. John, who was subject to falling fits, be made levy free (26:442).

JONES, HENRY, was b. c.1666, giving his age as 61 in 1727 (224:33).

JONES, HENRY, m. Eleanor (---) who joined him on 5 Jan. 1739 in cinv. 60 a. part Arabia Petrea to John Wooley, and on 27 Jan. 1714 in conv. 110 a. of same tract to George Jones; in 1750 Henry still owned 202 a. Arabia Petrea (75:345; 78:4; 153:9).

JONES, HENRY, sadler, conv. to Francis Jones 204 a. of the 372 a. tract which Henry had purch. from Michael Webster (81: 134).

JONES, HUGH, was b. c.1657/60, giving his age as 21 in 1681
and 50 in 1707; by 1692 was in Balto. Co. as a taxable in n. side
Patapsco; on 5 March 1715, for "kindness received" conv. 5 unnamed
acres to John Wilmot. (67:382; 138). See also HUGH JOHNS.

JONES, HUGH, m. Sarah (---), and had iss.: MARY, b. 11 March
1735 (133:55).

JONES, HUMPHREY, was in Balto. Co. by Aug. 1689 when he purch.
200 a. Hathaway's Hazard from John Hathaway; by 1692 was a taxable
in Spesutia Hund.; in July 1696 surv. 100 a. Jones' Addition; in
Jan. 1716 conv. Hathaway's Hazard to Samuel Brown after the death
of Jones' w. Mary, provided that Brown should seat himself on the
plantation within the year; in March 1716 conv. 100 a. Jones' Addition to his grandch. William Kimble and w. Mary; in July 1713
he signed the inv. of Samuel Brown as kin; his w. Mary d. 7 Dec.
1725; he had iss.: poss. a dau. (unnamed) who m. (---) Kemble
(50:274; 59:298; 67:389, 435; 128:48; 138; 211).

JONES, IMMANUEL, m. Sarah Leek, poss. wid. of Abraham Leeke;
had iss.: IMMANUEL, b. 13 March 1727; CORDELIA, b. 7 Nov. 1728;
ANNE, b. 30 Jan. 1734 (128:84, 86).

JONES, JACOB, d. 28 April 1729; m. Elizabeth (---), who m. 2nd
John Wallox on 5 Aug. 1731; admin. bond was posted 5 Nov. 1730 by
Elizabeth Jones, with Benjamin Jones and William Maner; est. was
admin. by John and Elizabeth Wallox on 4 Sept. 1742; had iss.:
JACOB, b. 20 July 1720; WILLIAM, b. 10 Jan. 1723; STEPHEN, b. 11
Dec. 1726; BENJAMIN, b. 27 March 1728 (13:379; 128:72).

JONES, JACOB, and w. Elizabeth were in Balto. Co. by 4 Nov.
1744 when they conv. 74 a. Jones' Chance to Isaac Hardin (77:676).

JONES, JAMES, was b. c.1699/1700, giving his age as 23 in Mar.
1722/3 (25:227).

JONES, JOHN, was in Balto. Co. by 1695 as a taxable in Spesutia
Hund. (138).

JONES, JOHN, d. by 3 July 1716 when admin. bond was posted by
the admnx. Eliza Jones with Jeremiah Sampson and John Dodd; est.
was inv. 26 Oct. 1716 by (---) Dorsey and Henry Ridgely, and was
val. at £ 83.0.0; est. was admin. on 27 Feb. 1717, 6 June 1718,
1 Dec. 1718, and 31 May 1723; dec. left seven children, names not
known (1:64, 312; 2:77, 135; 13:366; 26:203).

JONES, JOHN, Sr., was made levy free by the Baltimore County
Court in June 1724 (26:235).

JONES, JOHN, in Nov. 1724 advert. he would not be responsible
for the debts of his wife Johanna, who had eloped with another
man (70:111).

JONES, JOHN, on 26 Jan. 1724/5 conv. 50 a. (formerly taken up
by Emanuel Cely and Edward Dowse) to bro. William Jones (70:88).

JONES, JOHN, m. by 21 July 1724, Margaret, dau. and sole heir
of John Chadwell, the younger; on that day conv. tracts Chestnut
Neck, Stanharket, and Harman's Hope to Daniel Scott of Daniel; on
10 March 1731 they conv. Ebenezer's Park to Bartholomew Milhouse
(which Ebenezer Blakiston and w. Sarah had earlier conv. to John
Jones of Kent Co.); on 10 March 1731 John and Margaret conv. part
Ebenezer's Park to Ralph Woodall (67:538; 69:352; 73:287, 288).

JONES, JOHN, on 10 Oct. 1730 purch. 100 a. Jackson's Chance
from James Jackson (73:27).

JONES, JOHN, on 7 Nov. 1739 conv. 50 a. Jones' Farm to Sarah Dowsett (75:307).

JONES, JOHN, on 3 Feb. 1745 conv. to Salathiel, Absolom, and Aquila Galloway, orphans of William Galloway, 50 a. of Jones' Chance, which William Jones, father of the said John, had promised to conv. to the Galloways' father, William (78:381).

JONES, JOHN, d. by 3 Aug. 1748 when admin. bond was posted by Samuel Jones with William Lyon and John Hunt; est. was admin. by Samuel Jones on 13 Feb. 1748/9 (4:210; 13:358).

JONES, JOHN, d. by 20 July 1749, when admin. bond was posted by William Isgrig, admin., with John Metcalf and Daniel Dumbrain (13:384).

JONES, JOHN, in 1750 he owned 50 a. Rutledge's Delight, which he purch. in Sept. 1745 from William Rutledge; on 11 Jan. 1771 John and w. Sarah conv. the tract to William Andrew, provided that Andrew would promise to find a home for said John and Sarah (78:399; 153; 231-AL#C).

JONES, JOHN, was made levy free in Nov. 1756 (41:302).

JONES, JOHN, m. Mary (---), and had iss.: SOLOMON, b. 2 June 1753; MARY, b. 13 July 1755; GAY, b. 5 July 1758; MARGARET, b. 11 Nov. 1764; CLOE, b. 9 March 1766; COMFORT, b. 10 Feb. 1768 (131:159/r).

JONES, JOHN, Irish, runaway conv. serv. from William Jenkins, was advert. for in Oct. 1754 (385:310).

JONES, JONATHAN, was in Chester Co. by Aug. 1741 when he conv. Jonathan's Inheritance, on Deer Creek, to William Smith of Lancaster Co., Penna.; Gwin Carmack relinq. her right of dower (75:522).

JONES, JOSEPH, on 20 Oct. 1737 purch. 166 a. Arabia Petrea from Isaac Webster and Jacob Giles; on 12 May 1746 he and his w. Patience conv. 58 a. of the tract to Joseph Rogers; in 1750 he still owned 58 a. of the land; on 23 April 1762 he and w. Patience conv. 50 a. of the tract to John Jones (75:18; 79:56; 86:102; 153:48).

JONES, MARGARET, m. Thomas Masters after the pub. of banns on 28 April 1706 (129:201).

JONES, MARY, servant, was listed in the inv. of Capt. John Ferry, May 1699 (48:124).

JONES, MARY, was ind. for bast. in March 1723/4; her mulatto ch. was to be raised by Thomas Hughes in Aug. 1724; she was ind. for bast. again in Nov. 1734 (26:201, 438; 30:350).

JONES, MARY, had iss.: SARAH, b. 29 Nov. 1728; WILLIAM, b. 27 March 1735 (131).

JONES, MARY, in May 1756 was summoned by the vestry of St. John's Par. for unlawful cohabitation with Thomas Hawkins (132:364).

JONES, MARY, was fined for bast. in Nov. 1758; had iss.: AQUILA, b. 12 March 1758 (46:164; 129:353).

JONES, MOSES, Eng., age c.25, wood collier, runaway conv. serv. from Lancashire Ironworks; was advert. for in Aug. 1757 (307-69:127).

JONES, NATHAN, s. of Elizabeth, who in March 1725/6 conv. him all her goods and chattels (70:230).

JONES, PETER, shopman, was in Balto. Co. by June 1669 when he conv. 250 a. Crock and Pill to John Glover (95).

JONES, PHILIP, and Lawrence Porter, in Dec. 1663 purch. from Thomas Powell the 287½ a. that Walter Dickenson conv. to Powell in 1659 (93).

JONES, RACHEL, was ind. for bast. in March 1750/1 (38:270).

JONES, RANDALL, was in Balto. Co. by 1692 as a taxable in s. side Patapsco Hund. (138).

JONES, RICHARD, was in Balto. Co. by 1694 as a taxable in s. side Patapsco Hund. (139).

JONES, RICHARD, was b. c.1677/9, giving his age as 44 in Aug. 1723, and as 50 in 1727 (25:443; 224:10).

JONES, RICHARD, was made levy free in Aug. 1719 and was allowed 1200 lbs. tobacco for his maintenance in Nov. 1719 (23:207, 407).

JONES, RICHARD, in May 1711 purch. 100 a. The Level from Henry Butler, and in Oct. 1717 he and his w. Ann conv. the land back to Butler (67:193, 532).

JONES, ROBERT, was in Balto. Co. by May 1675 when he purch. 90 a. of Carter's Rest from Col. Nathaniel Utie; as the heir of one Thomas Jones, dec., on 4 April 1673 he conv. 73 a. Jones' Addition and 200 a. York's Hope to John Yeo, Gent.; he may be the same Robert Jones who in Sept. 1683 surv. 150 a. Robin Hoods Forest, later held by John Hall; d. leaving a will, 8 Nov. 1685 - 6 Jan. 1693, leaving all his worldly possessions to his landlord George Goldsmith (59:53, 351; 101:301; 211:18).

JONES, ROBERT, sailor, ran away from Balto. Town in Feb. 1759 (307-69:127).

JONES, SARAH, was ind. for bast. in March 1729/30 (28:362).

JONES, THOMAS, of Va. settled in Balto. Co. by 1667 (388).

JONES, THOMAS, in May 1674 purch. 200 a. Nash's Rest from Nicholas and Alice Ruxton; in the deed Jones was described as a boatwright; since this tract was later sold by John Gray and w. Ann of A. A. Co., Thomas prob. d. in A. A. Co. leaving a will, 4 Aug. 1675 - 22 Nov. 1675, leaving his 200 a. on Patapsco R. to Sarah Gray, sis. of Jane and Zachariah Gray(63:219; 74:298; 110: 111; 211:93).

JONES, THOMAS, in July 1676 surv. 79 a. Jones Addition, later held by John Yeo, who purch. the tract, plus 200 a. York's Hope from Thomas Jones' heir Robert Jones (59:53; 211).

JONES, THOMAS, d. by March 1701; est. admin. by the w. of Charles Simmons; dec. left a wid. and orphans (2:238).

JONES, THOMAS, m. in 1736 Mary (b. 19 Feb. 1705), dau. of Geo. and Eliza (Chappel) Simmons.

JONES, WILLIAM, in 1699 was named as a bro. of Richard Jones of Balto. Co. (200-51:287).

JONES, WILLIAM, in March 1740/1 was stated to have been cared for by William Roe since infancy (33:8).

JONES, WILLIAM, in June 1741 sold to Thomas Sligh his claim to one-half the est. of Samuel McCubbin, formerly the right of his wife Ann Jones; on 29 June 1741 William and Ann conv. to their godson William Sligh, son of Thomas and Sophia, 640 a. Tibbs United Inheritance; m. Ann Maccubbin on 30 March 1741; may be the William Jones who d. by 30 Nov. 1748 when admin. bond was posted by Thomas Sligh with Samuel Harryman; est. was admin. by Thomas Sligh on 13 Feb. 1750 (6:116; 13:390; 75:513, 530; 129:106).

JONES, WILLIAM, m. Catherine Brokley on 23 Dec. 1744 (131).

JONES, WILLIAM, m. Ann Higgins on 2 May 1745 (131).

JONES, WILLIAM, m. Elizabeth Williams on 22 Jan. 1751, and had iss.: GILBERT, b. 13 May 1751; ELIZABETH, b. 17 Jan. 1754; MAGDALEN, b. 7 April 1756; WILLIAM, b. 6 June 1758; JACOB, b. 17 June 1760; ISAAC, b. 1 June 1762; CASSANDRA, b. 21 Aug. 1765; STEPHEN, b. 28 Oct. 1767; BENJAMIN GEORGE, b. 10 Nov. 1769 (131).

JONES, WILLS, servant, listed in the inv. of Charles Daniel, in 1737/8 (53:87).

JONES, WINIFRED, servant to Thomas Sheredine, was charged with bearing a mulatto bast. in Aug. 1725, June 1728, and Nov. 1733; the child born in the latter case, James, was bound to Thomas Sheredine (26:313; 28:16; 30:142, 143).

JORDAN/JURDIN, EDWARD, servant to Thomas Long, was judged to be between 15 and 18 years old in March 1685/6; in June 1685 was bound by the churchwardens of the par. of Rock, Worcestershire, Eng., to Francis Carpenter, husbandman of the same county; by 1694 was of age to be a taxable in n. side Patapsco; d. leaving a will, 3 Dec. 1709 - 10 Feb. 1709/10, leaving his entire est. to Lawrence Yanston, who posted admin. bond on 10 Feb. 1710; est. was inv. 10 March 1709/10 by James Read and Robuck Lynch and val. at £ 19.7.5 and signed by Edward Ristone and Edward Stevenson, creditors (13:360; 18:397, 411; 54:20; 122:160; 139).

JORDAN, GEORGE, m. Dinah (---) and had iss.: GEORGE, b. 12 April 1727 (131:3/r).

JORDAN, ROBERT, m. Ann (---); in 1750 he owned 25 a. Jordan's Delight; had iss.: WILLIAM, b. 11 April 1750; THOMAS, b. 20 Oct. 1752; ELIZABETH, b. 7 Jan. 1755; RICHARD NEW, b. 19 Feb. 1757; JOHN, b. 20 Jan. 1759; RUTH, b. 22 May 1761 (134:19, 31; 153:87).

JOY, ELIZABETH, servant of William Holland, named Michael James as the father of her child, in Nov. 1721 (23:619).

JOY. See also FOY.

JOYCE, THOMAS, m. Eleanor Thornton on 1 Dec. 1747 (133:160).

JOYCE, WILLIAM, m. Sarah Lee on 25 May 1760 (133:167).

JUDD, MICHAEL (1), imm. c.1676; settled Balto. Co.; m. Jane (---), former w. of William Ebden; on 2 Aug. 1683 Michael and Jane sold 200 a. at Bow Creek, formerly owned by William Orchard, to John Nicholls; in April 1681 surv. 65 a. Oxford; the rent roll stated Judd had run away and his s. would not claim it; had iss.: MICHAEL (19:165; 106:287; 211; 388).

JUDD, MICHAEL (2), s. of Michael (1), was in Balto. Co. by 1692 as a taxable in n. side Gunpowder Hund.; in April 1700 he and w. Mary conv. to John Hall et al, the land where the Balto. Co. Court House stood (138; 381).

JUDD, DANIEL, m. Sarah Fowler on 19 Nov. 1736; had iss.: WILLIAM, b. 27 Dec. 1737; DANIEL, b. 15 Sept. 1739; JOSHUA, b. 21 Aug. 1741 (128:94, 99, 105, 115).

JUDGE, MARY, dau. of Judy, in March 1755 was bound to Edmund Talbot (40:14).

JUMP, BENJAMIN, d. by by 9 June 1752 when admin. bond was posted by James Carey with Thomas Norris (13:396).

JURDIN. See JORDAN.

JUSHMAN, THOMAS, was in Balto. Co. by 1692 as a taxable in n. side Patapsco Hund. (138).

KANASBEY, ABRAHAM. See KENNEDY, ABRAHAM.

KEASEY, JOHN, Sr., mortgaged land to William Dallam on 9 Aug. 1751; conv. tract Three Brothers to William Dallam (81:174, 410).

KEAT, JOHN, ran away from Charles Motherby on Garrison Ridge and was advert. for in Aug. 1750 (307-69:128).

KECEY, JOHN, m. the dau. of Henry Donahue by 10 Nov. 1722 (205-9:132).

KEENE, HENRY (1), of Worplesdon, Surrey, Eng., m. Anne Halle on 30 Nov. 1623; had iss.: HENRY, bapt. 12 Sept. 1624 and came to Md.; CALIPE, bapt. 21 May 1626; GEORGE, bapt. 19 Nov. 1627; RICHARD, bapt. 7 Dec. 1628, and came to Md.; EDWARD, bapt. 10 Jan. 1629/30, and came to Md.; ANNE, bapt. 2 Sept. 1632; WILLIAM, bapt. 1 Feb. 1634/5 (406:474).

KEENE, RICHARD (2), s. of Henry (1) and Anne (Halle), was bapt. 7 Dec. 1628 in Surrey, Eng.; came to Md., and m. Mary, poss. wid. of (---) Hodgkin; she m. 3rd John Griggs; Richard d. leaving a will in Calvert Co., made 1 April 1672, proved 7 Feb. 1675, naming w. Mary (to be extx.), father Henry Keene of Wadsworth, Surrey, niece Mary (dau. of Henry Keene, dec.), and these ch.: RICHARD; and JOHN (120:115; 200-68:20; 406).

KEENE, JOHN (3), s. of Richard (2) and Mary, was b. in Md.; d. 1723, having m. Mary Hopewell; inher. land from his father in Dor. Co.; d. Dor. Co. leaving a will, 1722/3 - 14 Nov. 1723, naming these ch.: SARAH, b. c.1688, m. Matthew Travers; HENRY, b. 1692, m. Mary Robson; BENJAMIN, b. 1694, m. Mary Stevens; RICHARD, b. 1696, m. Susanna Pollard; JOHN; EDWARD; ZEBULON; and EZEKIEL (124:150; 406:482).

KEENE, RICHARD (4), s. of John (3) and Mary, was b. 1696; m. on 4 Nov. 1714 Susanna, dau. of John (or William) and Sarah Billingsley Pollard; had iss.: Rev. JOHN, b. 1720, m. Sarah Young; VACHEL, b. 1733; Rev. SAMUEL, b. 11 May 1734, d. 8 May 1810 in Tal. Co.; THOMAS BILLINGSLEY, b. 1737, m. Mary Tubman; Rev. WILLIAM; POLLARD; poss. others (406:483).

KEENE, JOHN (5), s. of Richard (4) and Susannah (Pollard), was b. 1720, m. by 19 June 1750 Elizabeth, youngest dau. of John Young, Gent., late of St. Marys Co., dec., who was a son of Samuel Young of A. A. Co.; in 1750 with Pollard Keene owned 904 a. Good Neighborhood; on 19 June 1750 conv. that tract to Mary, eld.

dau. of said John Young, now w. of Pollard Keene; John moved
to Ky.; had iss.: SUSANNA, b. 12 July 1748; ELIZABETH, b. 4 Feb.
1750; REBECCA, b. 22 Aug. 1751; SARAH, b. 2 Aug. 1753; SAMUEL
YOUNG, b. 17 Dec. 1755; ANNA, b. 19 Nov. 1757; LATITIA, b. 11 Feb.
1760 (80:469; 81:42; 129:364; 153:52).

KEENE, POLLARD (6), poss. s. of Richard (4) and Susanna, m.
Mary, eld. dau. of John Young; in 1750 with John Keene, owned
904 a. part Good Neighborhood; had iss.: YOUNG, b. 25 April 1745;
MARY, b. 24 Aug. 1748; AMELIA, b. 26 June 1750; VIOLETTA, b. 1
April 1752; CHARLES, b. 24 Dec. 1755; EDMUND LAKE, b. 21 Jan.
1758; PARTHENIA, b. 8 Jan. 1760 (80:469; 129:365; 153:52).

KEENE, TIMOTHY (7), no known rel. to any of the above, may
have been born 9 Oct. 1685 in St. James Par., s. of Timothy Keene
and begotten on Hostee Marium(?); m. Mary Moon on 14 May 1709; on
3 June 1723 purch. 100 a. Little Scotland from James Durham; d.
leaving a will, 24 Jan. 1732/3 - 20 April 1733, naming w. Mary,
and ch. Aquila, Mary Brown, Ann (to have Little Scotland); admin.
bond was posted by admnx. Mary Keene with William Bradford and
Timothy Jones; est. was admin. by Mary Keene on 9 May 1735 and
by Mary, now w. of Richard Smith, in March 1736; had iss.: MARY,
b. 5 May 1710, m. (---) Brown; ANN, b. 23 Jan. 1714; HANNAH, b.
12 June 1721; AQUILA, living 1737; TIMOTHY, b. 15 April 1733 (3:
190; 12:21; 31:43, 53, 138, 139; 69:323; 126:29; 128:31, 33, 40,
75).

KEENE, TIMOTHY (8), s. of Timothy (7), and w. Ann conv. 108
a. Stoney Ridge to James Armstrong on 26 Sept. 1756 (82:673).

KEENE, HENRY, m. Amelia (---) and had iss.: HENRY WILLIAM, b.
18 Feb. 1735; HENRY, b. 4 July 1740 (128:103, 110).

KEENE, JAMES, in 1750 owned 100 a. Little Scotland, 590 a.
part Out Quarter, and 420 a. Rough Stone (153:64).

KEENE, PENELOPE, d. by 2 Nov. 1759 when admin. bond was posted
by Vachel Keene (12:17).

KEENE, RICHARD, of P. G. Co., was listed as the owner of 200 a.
part Clagett's Forest in 1750 (153:61).

KEEPERS, WILLIAM, was in Balto. Co. by May 1751; d. leaving a
will, 7 Dec. 1756 - 24 Jan. 1757, naming w. Clara, s. Joseph (and
his s. Joseph), dau. Susanna Kempson, dau. Mary Pierce, s. William
and tract Holland; had iss.: JOSEPH; SUSANNA, m. (---) Kempson;
MARY, m. (---) Pierce; WILLIAM (210-30:246; 385:129).

KEEPORTS, JACOB, was b. 1718; d. 8 March 1792; and was nat.
in Balto. Co. in 1758; later served in the Rev. War (353; 404:20).

KEITH, ALEXANDER (1), was b. c.1681, and was age 37 in 1718; d.
by March 1721/2; m. Christianne, dau. of William Farfarr; on 21
June 1717 he and s. John were named in the will of John Barrett;
William Farfarr in his will left his dau. Christianne Keith and
his Keith grandchildren to the care of Alexander Grant; admin.
bond on the est. of Alexander Keith was posted 20 Aug. 1722 by
John Lancaster with Thomas Wicks and Philip Sindall; had iss.:
JOHN, b. by 1718; ALEXANDER, b. by 1721 (12:23; 24:13; 28:70;
123:416; 124:105; 203-3:464).

KEITH, JOHN (2), s. of Alexander (1), was b. c.1710 in Balto.
Co.; m. Katherine (---) who joined him on 9 April 1743 in selling
parts Dear Bit and Shrewsbury to Francis Rider; John later moved
to Hampshire Co., W. Va., and then to Washington Co., Pa., and
had iss.: JOHN; HENRY; WILLIAM; and ALEXANDER (77:241; query #
614 in Genealogy and History, 4 April 1940).

KEITH, DANIEL, orph. of Florance Keith, age 15 on 1 Jan. 1758; in Aug. 1757 was bound to Thomas Reeves (46:58).

KEITH, DAVID, m. Sarah Kitely on 12 Jan. 1743 and had iss.: ELIZABETH, b. 27 May 1756; MARY, b. 14 Nov. 1759 (131:25, 23/r, 139/r).

KELLY, BENJAMIN, m. Sarah (---) and had: PATRICK, b. 21 March 1749/50 (133:87).

KELLY, CHARLES, was in Balto. Co. by 1742 when James Weeding conv. to him 50 a. Weeding's Choice; in 1750 he owned 50 a. of that tract, 10 a. Addition to Narrow Bottom, and 100 a. Mallow; in 1768 he signed the pet. in favor of Balto. Town as the county seat; m. Priscilla (---), and had iss.: CHARLES, b. 22 Nov. 1750; SARAH, b. 20 March 1756; RACHEL, b. 31 Oct. 1758 (77:520; 129: 352; 153:65; 200-61:533).

KELLY, CORNELIUS, m. Alice Lowe on 7 July 1741 (129:322).

KELLY, ELIZABETH, m. Miles Hannas on 24 Nov. 1698 (129:186).

KELLY, JAMES, was in Balto. Co. by 1737, and d. there c.1779/ 1780; m. Prudence, dau. of William and Honour (---) Logsdon; in Sept. 1744 purch. part Gist's Search from John Ford; in 1746 purch. part Friendship from Edward and Susanna Stevenson and John Osbourne; in 1750 he owned both of these tracts; may have been the James Kelly made levy free in June 1757; d. testate; had iss.: MARY, b. 16 Dec. 1736, m. John Banks on 18 Sept. 1756; PATIENCE, b. 7 June 1738 (may be the "Prudence" Reeves, wid., mentioned in James' will); NATHAN, b. 4 July 1740; HONOR, b. 18 Dec. 1742; JAMES, b. 11 Feb. 1744; JOHN, b. 10 April 1750; ELEANOR, b. 4 July 1752; CHARLES, b. 4 Aug. 1754; SUSANNA, b. 19 June 1756; ANN, b. 5 May 1758; THOMAS DEYE, b. 13 July 1760 (46:39; 77:574; 79:208; 112:397; 134:3, 43; 153:52).

KELLY, JAMES, m. Mary Beamsley on 28 April 1753 (131).

KELLY, JAMES, m. Elizabeth (---), and had iss.: ELEANOR, b. 22 Nov. 1745 (129:342).

KELLY, MAGDALEN, m. George Grover in July 1727 (131).

KELLY, MARY, was ind. for bast. in June 1731 (29:156).

KELLY, MORDECAI, m. Mary Hines on 6 Jan. 1757 and had iss.: JOHN, b. 19 Nov. 1757; DELILA, b. 14 Dec. 1760 (131:140/r).

KELLY, PATRICK, m. Mary Mash or Marsh and had iss.: BENJAMIN, b. 8 May 1731; RUTH, b. 10 Sept. 1732; MORDECAI, b. 20 July 1734; WILLIAM, b. 17 July 1738; ELIZABETH, b. 2 Feb. 1739; MARY, b. 13 Dec. 1740; PATRICK, b. 14 Dec. 1742; EMANUEL, b. 29 May 1745; GILBERT, b. 1 March 1746; ANN, b. 1 Nov. 1748 (133:81, 82, 149).

KELLY, RUTH, was tried for bast. in Nov. 1757 (46:74).

KELLY, THOMAS, m. Mary Mushgrove on 4 June 1736 and d. leaving a will, 10 Dec. 1772 - 16 March 1773, naming w. Mary, dau. Martha, daus. Elizabeth, Martha, Mary, Janet (wid. of John Jolly), Sarah (w. of ((---)) Stevenson), son Thomas, and granddau. Nancy Stevenson; had iss.: THOMAS; MARTHA, m. by 4 May 1774 (---) Martin; ELIZABETH; MARY; JANET, m. John Jolly; SARAH, m. (---) Stevenson (7:250; 112:249; 133:155).

KELLY (or KELLEY), WILLIAM, was b. 12 April 1715; d. 10 Oct. 1796; m. 1st Elizabeth, dau. of Thomas and Jane (Ensor) Gorsuch;

m. 2nd Eleanor (---); m. 3rd Mary Miller (antenuptial contract
made 10 Dec. 1779); in 1750 owned 100 a. part Green Spring Traverse; d. testate; had iss.: CHLOE, b. 12 Aug. 1741, m. William
Cromwell on 10 Sept. 1761; URATH, b. 20 Feb. 1744, m. Nathaniel
Owings on 7 Jan. 1763; RACHEL, b. 2 March 1746, d. 2 March 1775;
WILLIAM, b. 7 Feb. 1748, d. 29 Aug. 1749; WILLIAM, b. 10 April
1750; JOSHUA, b. 10 April 1752; NICHOLAS, b. 30 Jan. 1756;
TEMPERANCE, b. 3 Nov. 1756; ZACHARIAH, b. 30 Dec. 1760, d. 12 Oct.
1782; JOSEPH, b. 7 April 1767   (113:425; 134:13, 14; 153:74;
259:53).

KELSEY, WILLIAM, m. Ann Hutchins on 8 Dec. 1761 (131).

KEMP, JOHN (1), was in Balto. Co. by June 1669 when he surv.
100 a. Parker's Haven; in Sept. 1663 surv. 100 a. Kemp's Addition
(both tracts later held by John Thomas for Kemp's orphans); in
May 1672 was left personalty in the will of John Godfrey; d. leaving a will, 1 Dec. 1686 - 15 March 1686/7, naming w. Sarah (nee
Wichell, to have 100 a. Parker's Haven), and dau. Mary (to have
Kemp's Addition), and dau. Mary (to have 100 a. Claybanke); his
est. was inv. 4 April 1687 by Anthony Demondidier and John Carrington and val. at £ 63.12.3 ; had iss.: RICHARD; and MARY, m.
John Boring (120:69; 121:11; 206-9:227; 211).

KEMP, RICHARD (2), s. of John (1), was left 100 a. Parker's
Haven in his father's will; on 10 May 1708 Richard and his sis.
Mary, w. of John Boring conv. 100 a. Kemp's Addition and 100 a.
Parker's Haven to Nicholas Rogers; on 15 Sept. 1711 Richard and
his sis. Mary and her husb. John Boring conv. Claybank to John
Gardner (59:587; 67:171).

KEMP, (---), m. Johanna (---), who m. 2nd James Phillips in
1716, and 3rd, on 17 Dec. 1720, Aquila Hall; on that day Johanna
conv. prop. to her sons: JOHN; and RICHARD (68:287; 131).

KEMP, JOHN, d. by 27 Nov. 1759 when admin. bond was posted by
James Phillips with William Dallam; Capt. James Phillips admin.
his est. on 27 Nov. 1759 (4:275; 11:30).

KEMP, RICHARD, m. Susanna (---); d. leaving a will, 26 Nov.
1725 - 1 Feb.1725/6 , naming w. Susanna and three ch. (named below), all under 18; admin. bond was posted 1 Feb. 1725 by Jonathan Tipton with Thomas Tipton and Thomas Ford (11:24; 124:209).

KEMP, RICHARD, d. 13 Jan. 1735/6, leaving a will, 16 Jan.
1736 - 11 June 1736, leaving a ring to his bro. John (126:74).

KENDALL, DANIEL, was in Balto. Co. by 13 Jan. 1702 when he and
w. Johanna conv. 500 a. Kendall's Delight to John Brice (66:203).

KENDALL, ISAAC, m. Mary (---), and had iss.: MARY, b. 14 July
1746; ELIZABETH, b. 30 Oct. 1747; MARTHA, b. 4 Feb. 1753; Isaac
d. by 5 March 1759 when admin. bond was posted by John Hall of
Swan Town (11:291; 129:356).

KENHAM, COLEWORTH, m. Mary Tridge on 7 July 1744 (131).

KENLY, DANIEL, m. Frances Wells on 6 Nov. 1739; wit. a deed
on 20 Aug. 1748; had iss.: WILLIAM, b. 17 March 1741 (80:63;
129:330).

KENNEDY/KANASBEY/KENNISBY, ABRAHAM, s. of Elizabeth Wood, was
b. 10 May 1711; in June 1714 was bound to serve Henry Matthews
and w. Sarah to age 21 (21:503; 131:7).

KENNINGTON, THOMAS, was in Balto. Co. by 1695 as a taxable in Spesutia Hund. (140).

KENTEN, PETER, was in Balto. Co. by 1695 as a taxable in Spesutia Hund. (140).

KEON, HANNAH, in June 1711 was named by William Lenox, Sr., as the reputed w. of Lodowick Williams, dec. (21:211).

KEREVAN, KATE, serv. to John Roberts, claimed her mistress kicked and beat her; in Aug. 1719 Dorothy w. of Robert Cutchin was ordered to examine her (23:208).

KEREVAN, WILLIAM, age 18, runaway serv. from William Huse of Balto. Co., was advert. for in Sept. 1752 (385:195).

KERKSEY, THOMAS, was in Balto. Co. by 1692 as a taxable in Spesutia Hund.; on 1 Aug. 1693 Thomas purch. 133½ a. Mould's Success from Barbara Mould; on 3 June 1696 Thomas and w. Sarah conv. the tract to Edward Boothby (59:420; 64:99; 139).

KERKSICK, JOHN, of Balto. Co., imm. by 1669; m. 1st Martha (---); m. 2nd Susan (---) (388).

KERSEY, JOHN (1), was in Balto. Co. by 1723; m. 1st Eleanor (---) who d. 1751; m. 2nd on 18 April 1752 Katherine Martin; had iss.: JOHN, b. May 1723; HENRY, b. Nov. 1726; ELEANOR, b. 1 April 1729 (131:4/r, 128/r).

KERSEY, JOHN (2), s. of John (1), was b. May 1723; m. Susanna Shaw on 27 Feb. 1749 (131).

KERSEY, HENRY (3), s. of John (1), was b. Nov. 1726; m. Eliz. Whealand on 21 July 1746; in Jan. 1755 conv. 100 a. Shaw's Privilege to Thomas Sharpe (82:376; 131).

KETTNATT, WILLIAM, was in Balto. Co. by 1692 as a taxable in Spesutia Hund. (138).

KEYS, FRANCIS, d. by 10 April 1722 when Tamar Wilkinson posted admin. bond on his est. with Robert Montgomery and Samuel Harryman; est. was inv. by Benjamin Bowen and John Norton and val. at ₤ 8.10.6, dec. stated to have no known relations; est. was admin. by Tamar Wilkinson on 18 May 1723, and by Richard and Tamar Lenox on 27 Jan. 1724 (1:94; 2:335; 11:20; 52:22).

KEYS, JOHN, was in Balto. Co. by 1750 when he owned 50 a. Keys' Industry; he conv. this land to Stephen Onion in Oct. 1753 (82:80; 153:77).

KIBBLE, ROBERT, d. by 29 March 1749 when admin. bond was posted by Jacob Starkey with Jona'n Starkey (11:18).

KIBBLE, WILLIAM, m. Mary Plowright in March 1734 (133:152).

KIBREN, CATHERINE, was tried for bast. in Nov. 1755, naming Michael Sharpner, servant to Edward Puntney (40:401).

KIEEN. See KEEN.

KIMBLE/KEMBALL/ KEMBOL, ROBERT (1), poss. progenitor of the Kimble family, was in Cecil Co. when he purch. 300 a. Langley's Habitation from John Langley, s. and heir of Thomas Langley; d. by 16 July 1691 when admin. bond was posted by admin. John Kimble with Casparus Herman and Richard Askew; may have been the father of: JOHN (11:29; 59:252).

KIMBLE, JOHN (2), poss. s. of Robert (1), was in Balto. Co. by 1692 as a taxable in Spesutia Hund.; in 1702 John and Rowland were in Spesutia Hund.; in 1703 John, John, Jr., Rowland, and William Kimble were in Spesutia; John, Sr., d. leaving a will, 21 Feb. 1704/5 - 12 April 1705, naming Mary Jackson, Obediah Pritchard, Jane Ashford, and Mary Capell, his s. John, and pers. prop. to Rowland and William; John, Sr., died and was bur. 4 April 1705; admin. bond was posted 12 April 1705 by John Kimble the Younger, with Samuel Jackson and Samuel Brown; dec. had iss.: JOHN; poss. ROLAND (or ROWLAND), poss. WILLIAM; and MARY who m. Henry (or Thomas) Jackson on 25 July 1703   (11:28; 122:56; 128:22; 129:199; 138; 144; 145; and also 122:45).

KIMBLE, JOHN (3), s. of John (2), m. Elizabeth Gilbert on 16 April 1703(?), and had iss.: GILES (128:17, 21).

KIMBLE, ROLAND (or ROWLAND) (4), poss. s. of John (2), d. c. 1754 in Balto. Co., having m. on 15 May (---) Hannah, dau. of Samuel Jackson, who d. 1719 naming his "son and dau. Rowland and Hannah Kimble;" signed the inv. of John Thomas as one of the kin; in 1742 Rowland and Hannah conv. 50 a. of Expectation to Samuel Kimble and 50 a. of the same tract to John Kimble; in 1750 he owned 2000 a. part Expectation, 31 a. Moore's Lot, 110 a. Parkinson, 30 a. of Jackson's Outlet, 20 a. Kimble's Hoe Yard, and 60 a. No Name; d. leaving a will, 31 Dec. 1752 - 11 Nov. 1754, naming s. Robert (to have 40 a. Kimble's Chance), sons William and James (to have parts of Parkinson), sons John and Stephen (to have parts Expectation and Jackson's Outlet), dau. Sarah Taylor, and w. Hannah; Hannah d. leaving a will, 6 March 1764 - 19 March 1764, naming ch. Robert, James, Stephen, and Sarah, and grandch. Roland and Stephen Kimble and Susanna Cord; Roland and Hannah had iss.: ROBERT, b. 16 Jan. 1717; SARAH, b. 7 Dec. 1722, m. James Taylor on 9 May 1747; SAMUEL, b. 27 June 1725; WILLIAM, b. 24 June 1729; JAMES, b. 24 June 1729; JOHN, b. 12 April 1732, d. testate 1757; STEPHEN, b. 15 Aug. 1734, d. 11 July 1737; STEPHEN, b. 13 Sept. 1738 (77:172, 186; 111:45, 241; 124:2; 128:37, 49, 58, 64, 83, 101; 153:1; 210-31: 1086).

KIMBLE, WILLIAM (5), poss. s. of John (2), was named in the latter's will, 21 Feb. 1704/5; named as bro. of testator's wife Mary in the will of Henry Jackson, and is prob. the William who d. 5 Dec. 1717 (122:45, 56; 128:36).

KIMBLE, ROBERT (6), s. of Rowland (4) and Hannah, was b. 16 Jan. 1717, and d. 21 Nov. 1769; m. Sarah Taylor on 12 Oct. 1738; d. leaving a will, 1 Dec. 1767 - 21 Nov. 1769, naming tract Kimble Double Purchase (originally called Expectation) and ch.: Josias, Giles, John, Sophia, Hannah, Mary, Sarah, and Susanna, and had iss.: HANNAH, b. 22 Dec. 1738, d. 28 Aug. 1740; SOPHIA, b. 22 Sept. 1740; JOSIAH, b. 17 Feb. 1742; HANNAH, b. 15 Aug. 1745; MARY, b. 23 July 1747; GILES, b. 1 Jan. 1750; JOHN, b. 5 May 1753; SARAH, b. 13 Feb. 1755; SUSANNA, b. 24 Feb. 1758 (112:129; 128:92/b, 114; 129:329, 344, 356).

KIMBLE, SAMUEL (7), s. of Rowland (4) and Hannah, was b. 27 June 1725, and was alive in 1776; m. Jemima Barnes on 19 Feb. 1747; she was b. 5 May 1729, dau. of James and Bethia Barnes; in 1750 he owned 50 a. Expectation; in 1776 was living in Spesutia Hund.; had iss.: ANN, b. 1 Oct. 1747; RACHEL, b. 9 Jan. 1749; JAMES, b. 22 March 1751; BETHIA, b. 4 May 1753; HANNAH, b. 11 Dec. 1755; JEMIMA, b. 9 Aug. 1756; poss. SUSANNA, b. c.1767; and poss. ZACHARIAH, b. c.1773 (129:352; 153:19; 277:153).

KIMBLE, WILLIAM (8), s. of Rowland (4) and Hannah, was b. 24 June 1729, and d. by 2 March 1761; m. Sarah Hanson on 1 Jan. 1754; she m. 2nd, by 9 Aug. 1765 William Pike; William d. leaving a will,

3 Jan. 1761 - 2 March 1761, naming w. as extx., ch. Roland, Martha, and Frances, and unborn ch., as well as land he inher. from his father Roland; est. was admin. by Sarah, now w. of William Pike, on 9 Aug. 1765; had iss.: MARTHA, b. 5 June 1755; FRANCES, b. 5 June 1756; ROLAND, b. 6 Nov. 1757; poss. unborn ch. (6:186; 111:34; 129:354).

KIMBLE, JAMES (9), s. of Rowland (4), was b. 24 June 1729, and was living in Spesutia Lower Hund., Harford Co.; age 49; on 26 Sept. 1771 admin. the est. of William Pike and mentioned payment for burying Pike's wife; prob. had iss.: FRANCES, b. c.1756; and SARAH, b. c.1774 (7:107; 277:146).

KIMBLE, JOHN (10), s. of Rowland (4) and Hannah, was b. 12 April 132; in 1750 owned 50 a. of Expectation; d. leaving a will, 15 Aug. 1757 - 19 Nov. 1757, naming mother Hannah, and bros. William, Robert, Samuel, James, and Stephen (153:19; 210-30:403).

KIMBLE, STEPHEN (11), s. of Rowland (4) and Hannah, was b. 13 Sept. 1738, and was alive in 1776; m. Margaret Daugherty, alias Barkey, on 22 March 1758; in 1776 was living in Spesutia Hund., with w. and ch.: MARY, b. 22 Jan. 1759; GEORGE, b. 27 Aug. 1760; JAMES, b. c.1762; JAMES, b. c.1769; FRANCES, b. c.1772; and ELEANOR, b. c.1775 (129:360, 366; 277).

KIMBLE, JOHN, d. by 1699 when est. was inv. by Thomas Cord and val. at £ 169.2.9, and was signed by Robert and John Kimble (48: 203).

KIMBLE, MARY, m. Charles Whitaker on 30 Jan. 1717/8 (129:221).

KIMBLE, SARAH, was tried for bast. in March 1739/40, was ind. for the same in March 1743/4, and ind. and tried in March 1745/6; had iss.: SUSANNAH, b. 8 June 1743; SABRA, b. 9 Aug. 1745 (32: 163; 35:1, 154, 167, 800, 816; 129:332, 357).

KIMBRIN, MARY ANN, had iss.: JOHN, b. and d. Dec. 1759 (131: 18/r).

THE HENRY KING FAMILY

KING, HENRY (1), was in Balto. Co. by 1692 as a taxable in s. side Patapsco Hund.; in March 1693/4 was named as one of the Balto. Co. Rangers; came to possess 187 a. Plains, orig. surv. for James Todd; d. leaving a will, 18 Jan. 1717 - 30 April 1718, naming s. William (to have Todd's Plains) and dau. Mary (to have Kingsbury and Addition to Kingsbury), ch. were not to move or sell the "great still," and were to be wards of William Tibbs and Jno. Wilmot during their minority; admin. bond was posted 30 April 1718 by extx. Mary King, and est. was inv. in 1718 by Charles Merryman and Benjamin Bowen, and val. at £ 243.19.5; est. was admin. by dau. Mary, now w. of Samuel Maxwell, on 29 Sept. 1720; dec. left iss.: WILLIAM and MARY, m. by Sept. 1720 Samuel Maxwell (2:15; 12:26; 52:138; 123:161; 138; 211; 338).

KING, WILLIAM, (2), s. of Henry (1), in Nov. 1718 chose Thomas Sheredine as his guardian; m. by 10 Nov. 1724 Susanna (---), who joined him in selling 124 a. Kingsbury and 500 a. Maiden's Hill to Thomas Sheredine; in Aug. 1726 he conv. 187 a. The Plains to Thomas Sheredine; d. by 1750 when his heirs owned 100 a. King's Adventure (23:4; 70:14, 279; 153).

KING, (---), m. by 24 June 1702 Galvilla, dau. of Jane Long (2: 216).

KING, ANN, was ind. for bast. in June 1724 (30:253).

KING, CHARLES, m. Ann Green on 29 March 1741, and had iss.:
EDWARD, b. 25 July 1741; and MARY, b. 25 July 1741 (131:82/r,
90/r).

KING, CHARLES, age c.30, b. in Eng., runaway conv. serv. of
George Brown, was advert. for in Aug. 1745 (384:517).

KING, ELEANOR, in March 1744/5 bound her two ch., James and
Sarah Hill, as apprentices (as Eleanor Hill she had been indicted
for bast. on several occasions) (35:471).

KING, JOHN, age c.25, runaway conv. serv. from Robert North
and Alexander Lawson, and was advert. for in April 1746; may be
the same John King, serv., with two yrs. to serve in the 1749
inv. of Capt. Robert North (50:378; 384:551).

KING, JOHN, b. Eng., age c. 40, weaver, runaway serv. from
Thomas Hallam near Joppa; was advert. for in Nov. 1751 (385:155).

KING, RICHARD, was b. c.1655, and was over 60 in 1715 when he
pet. the court; d. by 4 Aug. 1720; was in Balto. Co. by 1701 as
a taxable in n. side Patapsco Hund; by 1704 was in Elk Ridge
Hund.; on 24 Jan. 1707/8 he wit. the will of Thomas Brown; on 1
Jan. 1710 was conv. 400 a. Stopp by Anthony and Margaret Drew;
on 9 Aug. 1716 was conv. God's Providence by Thomas Chamberlain;
on 3 Oct. 1716 King conv. John March, surgeon of Kent Co.,
various movable prop.; was alive on 1 May 1719 acc. to a statement made by Thomas Knight; d. by 4 Aug. 1720 when admin. bond
was posted by John Hall and Thomas Randall, with Roger Matthews
and Christopher Randall; his est. was inv. on 6 March 1720/1 by
Roger Matthews and John Clark, and val. at Ł 235.11.9; est. was
admin. by John Hall on 11 Aug. 1722; no known ch., but may have
been rel. to the Richard King who d. by 27 April 1754 (see below)
(1:82; 12:22; 21:624; 25:126; 51:56; 67:103, 104, 402; 68:240;
122:14; 141; 146).

KING, RICHARD, was in Balto. Co. by 14 Oct. 1727 when he
conv. 50 a. White Hall to his dau. Ann Marsh; on 10 June 1728
Richard and w. Mary conv. 100 a. White Hall to Hyde Hoxton and
Lloyd Harris; had iss.: ANN, m. by 14 Oct. 1727 (---) Marsh (71:
20, 137).

KING, RICHARD, poss. rel. to the first Richard King ment.
above, d. by 27 April 1754 when his heirs, Thomas Phillibrown,
Jr., of Devonshire St., London, cooper, and Thomas Wright and
w. Elizabeth, of Cullum St., London, woolen draper, conv. God's
Providence to William York (82:295).

KING, THEOPHILUS, was in Balto. Co. by 1694 as a taxable in
n. side Patapsco Hund. (139).

KING, THOMAS, of Balto. Co., imm. by 1664 and m. Joan Strand
between 1669 and 1673; may be the same Thomas King in Balto. Co.
in 1669 when he was conv. 200 a. None So Good in Finland by Edmund Webb of A. A. Co. (96:230; 338).

KING, THOMAS, m. Eleanor Hill on 23 Oct. 1743 oe 23 Oct.
1744 (131).

KINSEY, HUGH (1), imm. to Md. c.1659; in 1662 he transp. his
ch. Daniel and Sarah; in Aug. 1663 he surv. 100 a. Walnut Neck
which was later held by Isaac Jackson (45 a.), and John Wilmot
(55 a.); d. leaving a will made in A. A. Co., 6 May 1667, naming

Sara Clark and Charles Gorsuch, w. Margaret, dau. Eliza Kinsey,
Mary Humphreys, and grandch. Paul and Margaret Kinsey and Hancock Ball; had iss.: DANIEL, transp. in 1662; SARA, transp. in
1662, m. by 1667 (Abraham) Clark; PAUL; and ELIZA (120:40; 211:
82; 388).

KINSEY, PAUL (2), s. or grandson of Hugh (1), was named as a
s. of Margaret Kinsey in 1661; on 31 March 1662 surv. 100 a.
Spring Point, which Paul and Elizabeth Kinsey conv. to William
Gwynn on 5 Feb. 1663; on 2 April 1662 he surv. 200 a. Curtis'
Neck and on 18 Aug. 1663 he surv. 350 a. Harborough; alive on
10 April 1672 when he surv. 200 a. Paul's Neck, later held by
John Lockett for the orphans of Richard Gwynn (59:32; 211; 388).

KINSEY, or KINSBEY, ABRAHAM, orphan, was named in the 1720
will of Henry Matthews (124:222).

KINSEY, or KINSBY, HENRY, m. Mary Wood on 1 Aug. 1710 (128:
27).

KIRK, HENRY, age c.22, butcher, runaway Irish conv. serv.
from Patapsco Iron Works, was advert. for in July 1745 (384:511).

KIRKLAND, RICHARD, in May 1714 conv. 200 a. Brown's Survey to
Alexander Delmeyossa (66:342).

KIRKLAND, ROBERT, was in Balto. Co. by Dec. 1701 when he
surv. 969 a. Chance (207).

KIRKSEY. See KERKESEY.

KITCHIN, ELIZABETH, was ind. for bast. in June 1719, naming
Stephen Yoakley as the father; admitted having an illegit. ch. in
March 1720/1 (23:198, 437).

KITELY, FRANCIS, m. Mary (or Martha) Thomas on 12 May 1751
(131).

KITELY, SARAH, m. David Keith on 25 Dec. or 12 Jan. 1743 (131).

KITTEN, THEOPHILUS, of Balto. Co., in Nov. 1699 bought 361 a.
Gray's Luck from John Gray; m. Katherine, wid. of (---) Buck; d.
by 9 Aug. 1711 when admin. bond was posted by Katherine Kitten,
wid. and admnx, with John Buck and Edward Kitten; est. was inv.
22 Aug. 1711 by Thomas Hammond and Richard Warfield and val. at
£ 99.5.5 and signed by Edward Kitten as kin and John Buck as
creditor; est. was admin. on 13 April 1713 and 27 July 1713 by
Catherine Kitten, who d. in A. A. Co., leaving a will, 18 May
1734 - 12 June 1734, naming sons John Buck, Edward Kitten, dau.
Catherine Howard, and grandch. Rachel and Rebecca Gaither; had
iss.: EDWARD (1:27, 34; 11:25; 52:131; 126:85; 200-38:408).

KNAPP, JNO., m. Ann Miller on 17 Jan. 1756 (131).

THE THOMAS KNIGHT FAMILY

KNIGHT, THOMAS (1), m. Susanna Simpson on 28 Nov. 1718; in
Feb. 1727/8 as Thomas Knight, schoolmaster, he and w. Susanna
conv. 100 a. Knight's Increase to Isaac Butterworth; had iss.:
LIGHT, b. 8 June 1719; ELIZABETH, b. 23 Feb. 1720; THOMAS, b. 12
Sept. 1723; and DAVID, b. 6 May 1726 (71:133; 128:37, 42, 46,
48).

KNIGHT, LIGHT (2), s. of Thomas (1), was b. 8 June 1719; m.
Rachel Ruse on 12 Oct. 1743; had iss.: THOMAS, b. 9 Feb. 1746;

MARY, b. 10 Feb. 1748; ELIZABETH, b. 12 July 1751; ANN, b. 7 Jan.
1753; WILLIAM, b. 29 July 1756; SARAH, b. 8 April 1758; RACHEL,
b. 28 Jan. 1760 (129:382).

THE WILLIAM KNIGHT FAMILY

KNIGHT, WILLIAM (3), no known rel. to any of the above, m. Mary
(---); in 1750 owned 50 a. Panther's Ridge which he conv. in Jan.
1752 to his s. Benjamin; had iss.: MARY, b. Nov. 1719; SARAH, b.
Jan. 1720; WILLIAM, b. Feb. 1722; ELIZABETH, b. Feb. 1723; BEN-
JAMIN, b. April 1725; RACHEL, b. Aug. 1728; HANNAH, b. Jan. 1731;
KETURA, b. Oct. 1732 (81:277; 133:49; 153:42).

KNIGHT, BENJAMIN (4), s. of William (3), was b. in April 1725;
on 27 Jan. 1752 was conv. part Panther's Ridge by his father; on
25 Feb. 1754 Benjamin, his w. Elizabeth, and Jabez Murray conv.
to John Daughaday their right, title, and interest in Panther's
Ridge (81:277; 82:175).

KNIGHT, BENJAMIN, m. Jane, wid. of Charles Merryman on 6 Aug.
1723; Benjamin and Jane admin. Merryman's est. on 22 Aug. 1729
(2:272, 374; 133:146).

KNIGHT, BENJAMIN, m. Sarah (wid. of Morgan Murray); Benjamin
d. leaving a will, 19 Nov. 1742 - 5 April 1743, leaving 100 a.
Hail's Discovery and 35 a. Knight's Addition to his w. Sarah;
as Sarah Knight, wid., she conv. these two tracts to Sarah Boring on 17 June 1745; Sarah Knight d. leaving a will, 4 Aug. 1748 -
20 Jan. 1748(/9) naming Murray ch.: Joseph, Thomas, James, Morgan,
and Sarah Murray, and granddau. Elizabeth Murray, dau. of Thomas
(11:15; 77:253; 110:428; 127:223).

KNIGHT, RICHARD, was in Balto. Co. by 1694 as a taxable in n.
side Patapsco Hund. (139).

KNIGHT, ROBERT, m. Ann Limb on 15 Dec. 1760 (131).

KNIGHT, WILLIAM, m. Sarah Cox on 7 Feb. 1752 (131).

KNIGHTON, THOMAS (1), on 25 Sept. 1716 admin. the est. of Samuel Taylor; had s.: KEYSOR (1:197).

KNIGHTON, KEYSOR (2), s. of Thomas (1), in June 1710 was ret.
to his father, having formerly been bound to John Hall (21:137).

KNIGHTSMITH, THOMAS, was b. c.1662, poss. in London; d. by 30
Jan. 1707/8 in Balto. Co.; in Sept. 1683 signed an indenture to
serve Capt. James Conaway for four years in Md.; sailed on Conaway's ship Baltimore; by 1692 was in Balto. Co. as a taxable in
Spesutia Hund.; in July 1695 surv. Knightsmith's Folly; m. Katherine (---) who m. 2nd Dennis Newman; Thomas d. leaving a will, 10
Dec. 1707 - 30 Jan. 1707/8, naming w. Katherine, dau. Bridget, and
an unnamed son; admin. bond was posted 25 Feb. 1707 by the extx.
Katherine, with William Forman and John Wood; est. was admin.
by extx. Katherine, w. of Dennis Newman on 19 Sept. 1709 and 27
Feb. 1712; had iss.: BRIDGET; and a s., unnamed (1:348; 2:104;
12:30; 122:99; 138; 211:108; 397-1:338).

KNIVINGTON, MATTHEW, was in Balto. Co. by 1671 when John Collett sold him 100 a. part Beaver Neck; on 2 Aug. 1673 Knivington
joined John and Jane Mascord in selling 200 a. Beaver Neck to
Bernard Utie (97:123-124; 99:347-348).

KNIVINGTON, THOMAS, m. Hannah Trego on 15 June 1695 (129:177).

KNOWLAND. See NOLAN.

KNOWLES, HENRY, m. by c.1700 Catherine, wid. of John Scutt;
on 11 Aug. 1707 purch. part Andover, now called Knowles' Purchase,from John Greeneff; d. by 12 June 1714 when admin. bond was
posted by the extx.; his will, 4 Jan. 1713 - 15 May 1714,
naming dau.-in-law Sarah Owings and dau.-in-law Mary Scutt, w.
Catherine (extx.) and tracts Knowles' Purchase, Combes' Adventure, and Margaret's Delight; when wid. Katherine posted the admin. bond she was joined by Robert Parker and Richard Owings, Jr.;
est. was inv. 19 July 1714 by Thomas Randall and Peter Bond, and
val. at £ 441.7.2, and signed by Charles Carroll and Richard Owings; Catherine Knowles d. by 20 May 1717 when admin. bond was
posted by the exec.; her will, 8 June 1716 - 15 June 1716/7,
named daus. Mary Douglass and Sarah Owens (Owings) and the latter's three ch., Richard, Ruth, and Stephen Owens (Owings); sec.
for the bond was provided by Pierce Welsh and Edward Tully; her
est. was inv. on 22 Aug. 1717 by Hector Maclane and George Bailey and val. at £ 240.17.5 plus £ 37.6.8, and signed by Richard
and Sarah Owings as kin, and by Charles Carroll; no known iss.
(12:16, 27; 50:209; 52:71; 59:567; 123:14, 71; 211).

KNOWLES, JOHN, m. Rebecca Blake on 23 July 1748 (131).

KNOWLES, LEWIS, was in Balto. Co. by 1694 as a taxable in n.
side Patapsco (139).

KNOWLES, PETER, was b. c.1716; m. Mary (---) who was b. c.1723;
in 1742 he leased part of My Lady's Manor, the lease to run for
the lifetimes of himself and his s., and s.: PETER, b. 30 Dec.
1741; ANN, b. 12 May 1744 (77:130; 131:102/r, 104/r).

KNOX, GEORGE, m. Dinah Detter on 25 Dec. 1735 (131).

KOBELL, ROBERT, m. Elizabeth Bradgield on 23 March 1746 (131).

LACEY, WILLIAM, d. in Balto. Co. by 3 March 1743 when admin.
bond was posted by Margaret Lacey with George Rigdon and Thomas
Baker Rigdon; est. was admin. on 3 Nov. 1744; Margaret Lacey or
Leslie d. leaving a will, 9 July 1757 - 2 Nov. 1757, naming serv.
William Smith, tract Partner's Trouble on Deer Creek, grandson
Alexander Rigdon, and these children: WILLIAM; ANN, m. (---)
Rigdon; SUSANNA, m. (---) Ashmore (3:371; 12:83; 210-30:401).

LACEY, JOHN, m. Mathew (or Martha) (---), and had iss.: ELIZA-
BETH, b. 18 Sept. 1724 (133:9).

LADD, RICHARD, was in Balto. Co. by 1692 as a taxable in n.
side Patapsco Hund (also given as Richard Sadd or Said) (138).

LAFEE, LEWIS, m. by 2 April 1745 Sarah extx. of William Love
(5:35).

LAKE/LEAK/LEEK, ABRAHAM, m. Sarah, admnx. of James Holliday,
by 31 Jan. 1725; Sarah Leak was ind. for bast. in June 1731;
Sarah later m. Immanuel Jones; ch. of Abraham and Sarah: MARY,
b. 31 Jan. 1725; GRACE, b. April 1731 (3:31; 29:156; 128:82, 83;
133:31).

LAKE, (or LACK), THOMAS, was in Balto. Co. by 1692 as a taxable in n. side Patapsco Hund. (138).

LAMB, JAMES (or JOHN), d. in Balto. Co. by 22 April 1710 when
admin. bond for James Lambe was posted by Nicholas Beason with
John Rattenbury; the est. of John Lamb was inv. on 24 April 1710

by William Hack and Lance Todd and val. at Ŀ 12.15.11; the est. was admin. by Beason on 4 Dec. 1710 (2:154; 12:307; 48:156).

LAMON, JOHN, born in High Germany, was a planter of Baltimore County by 4 June 1738 when he and his ch. were naturalized; had iss.: JOHN; GEORGE; LOUISA; LEONORA; CATHERINE; and MARGARET (303).

LAMON, PETER, in 1750 owned 50 a. part Great Meadow (153:80).

LAMPREY, ARTHUR, of Biddeford, Co. Devon, m. by 1702 Elizabeth, late w. of Joseph Yeo of Md. who d. there leaving a son Joseph; Joseph, Sr., was a bro. of Rev. John Yeo, clerk; Lamprey and w. and stepson appointed William Pauley their atty. to sell any land left by John Yeo or his bro. Joseph (66:242).

LANDERS, EDWARD, s. of Elizabeth, age 9 last 10 Oct., was bound in June 1713 to serve Francis and Catherine Ogg until he was wl (21:379)

LANDIS, JOHN, tailor, admin. the est. of Edward Bowman on 17 June 1712 (1:372).

THE LANE FAMILY and its origins have been the subject of two studies: one set forth by Mrs. F. C. Montgomery in her typescript "Wells of Baltimore County, Maryland," (at the Md. Hist. Soc.), and the other proposed by A. Russell Slagle, in "Major Samuel Lane (1628-1681): His Ancestry and Some American Descendants," in Maryland Genealogies (346-2:128 ff.) Montgomery states that Samuel Lane the Maryland Settler may be descended as follows:

LANE, JOHN (A), of Hammersmith, d. leaving a will dated 1674, having m. on 5 June 1609, Margery, dau. of George Wells, Alderman of Wycombe, Berks.; John and Margery had one son: SAMUEL, bapt. 29 March 1625 at Hughenden.

Slagle proposes the following line of descent; his theory is supported by abstracts of a number of legal and business proceedings with other early settlers of Maryland and Virginia:
LANE, ROGER (B), apothecary of Hereford, married Beatrix (---) and was bur. on 30 April 1603 leaving a wid. and eight living ch. (ten were born to the couple), baptized between Jan. 1590 and Jan. 1602; one of the sons was: RICHARD, bapt. 27 Aug. 1596.

LANE, RICHARD (C), s. of Roger (B), was bapt. 27 Aug. 1596 and on 14 Dec. 1613 was apprenticed to Nathaniel Thornhull , merchant taylor of London; Richard was admitted a freeman of the Merchant Taylor's Company on 26 Feb. 1620; on 7 Oct. 1623 he married Alice, dau. of Humphrey Carter, at St. Mildred Poultry, London; Alice was bapt. 24 Aug. 1603; her father was a citizen and ironmonger of London; in 1635 Richard and Alice went to the Island of Providence with their three children; Richard and one of the sons were drowned by Aug. 1657, and Alice and son Samuel ret. to Eng., where Alice d. by 22 Oct. 1678; Richard and Alice were the parents of: SAMUEL, b. 1628; JOHN, b. 1631; OZIELL, b. 1632; and MARY, m. William Denne.

LANE, SAMUEL (1), progenitor of the Maryland Lanes, may have been a s. of John (A) (acc. to Montgomery) or a son of Richard (C) (acc. to Slagle); was b. c.1628, and d. in Md. c.1682; m. Margaret, wid. of John Burridge; after Lane's death she m. 3rd, Job Evans; Margaret was a sis. of Francis Mauldin, and a dau. of Grace (---) who m. 1st (---) Mauldin, 2nd William Parker, and 3rd Edward Lloyd; the 1669 will of John Burrage named his w. Margaret and dau. Elizabeth w. of Francis Hutchings; the 1684

will of Nathan Smith mentioned land that his w. Margaret had inher. as heir of John Burridge; Grace Lloyd of St. Mary's White(-
chapel, Middlesex, in her will named dau. Margaret Evans, dau.
Grace Mitchell, son Francis Maulden, and dau. Elizabeth Bicker-
field; Samuel Lane d. leaving a will made 18 Jan. 1681, naming
s. Samuel (to have Browsley Hall), s. Dutton (to have res. of
Browsley Hall), dau. Sarah, nephew Thomas Lane, dau. Grace Burridge, and sons-in-law Samuel Smith and Francis Hutchins; Samuel
and Margaret had iss.: SAMUEL; DUTTON; SARAH (120:104, 133; 206-
8:267; Slagle article; James L. Kendall, "Lane Notes," unpub.
ms. at Md. Hist. Soc.).

LANE, SAMUEL (2), s. of Samuel (1), d. in A. A. Co., c.1715,
having m. Sarah, dau. of Richard Harrison; Sarah m. 2nd Dr. Wm.
Locke; Lane d. leaving a will, 13 May 1715 - 19 Aug. 1715, naming w. Sarah, dau. Elizabeth, unborn ch., father-in-law Richard
Harrison, Richard Galloway, and William Harrison; ch. of Samuel
and Sarah: ELIZABETH; RICHARD; HARRISON, m. Sarah Wells; SAMUEL,
d. unm. and intestate in 1741; JOSEPH; BENJAMIN; SARAH; NATHAN,
who d. leaving a will, 22 Jan. 1742/3 - 9 March 1742/3, naming
his bro. Benjamin, bro. Joseph (father of Nathan), bro. Richard
(and his ch. Francis, Benjamin, Toogood, and Mary), bro. Harrison, and bro.-in-law D. Weems   (123:33; 127:198; Christopher
Johnston, "Lane Notes," at Md. Hist. Soc.).

LANE, DUTTON (3), s. of Samuel (1), was b. c.1665; d. by 8
Oct. 1726; m. c.1693 Pretiotia, dau. of Richard Tydings and b. c.
1676; on 2 May 1704 Lane sold all his pers. est. to Benjamin
Hooker; on 15 Jan. 1708/9 Lane and w. Pretiosa sold Thomas Hooker and Richard Gist their share of New Year's Purchase; Dutton
d. leaving a will, 31 May 1716 - 8 Oct. 1716, naming a. Pretiosa
as extx., sons Dutton, Richard, and Samuel (to have Lane's Triangle), and daus. Margaret and Sarah (to have Hampton Court);
ch. of Dutton and Pretiosa: DUTTON, d. c.1783; RICHARD, m. Sarah
Fuller; SAMUEL, d. by 1779; MARGARET, m. William Merryman; SARAH,
m. Robert Sweeting; poss. JOHN, m. Avarilla Bosley in 1754 (59:
634; 66:340; 69:69; 124:231).

LANE, JOSEPH (4), s. of Samuel (2) and Sarah, d. 1751, having
m. Rachel, dau. of Samuel Maccubbin; Lane admin. the est. of
Samuel Maccubbin, Jr., several times before 16 Dec. 1740 and 12
Aug. 1748; d. in A. A. Co., leaving a will proved 1 April 1751;
had iss.: SAMUEL; JOHN; NATHAN; SARAH; RACHEL; and ELIZABETH
(4:60, 72, 156, 208; 5:48; 210-28:108).

LANE, DUTTON (5), s. of Dutton (3), d. in Balto. Co. c.1783;
m. by 1732 Diana Boring, dau. of John Boring; on 2 July 1737 Lane
purch. 100 a. Come By Chance from James Boring; in Jan. 1741 John
Boring, for love he bore his son-in-law Dutton Lane, conv. him 100
a. The Landing; in 1750 Lane owned 50 a. Beef Hall, 100 a. Good
Will, 100 a. Pork Hall, 100 a. Hall's or Hale's Adventure, 141 a.
Spring Garden, and 50 a. Copper Ridge; Dutton and Diana had iss.:
DANIEL, b. 9 Feb. 1732; WILLIAM; THOMAS; DUTTON, Jr.; MARY, m.
by June 1759 James Murray, and DIANA, m. by March 1759 (---)
Gosnell (5:191; 61:476, 477; 76:66; 83:401, 484; 153:3; Johnston,
"Lane Notes").

LANE, RICHARD (6), s. of Dutton (3), was b. c.1696, and was
still living in 1735; m. Sarah, dau. of John Fuller; had iss.:
RICHARD; TIDINGS, b. 30 Aug. 17(-?); DUTTON, b. 15 July 1730; JOHN
FULLER; SAMUEL, b. 4 Oct. 1732; JEMIMA, b. 7 March 1735 (133:29,
37, 39, 48; Kendall, "Lane Notes").

LANE, SAMUEL (7), s. of Dutton (3), d. by 1779 in Bedford Co.,
Penna.; m. Jane (poss. Corbin); on 10 Jan. 1756 William Cross conv.

Samuel Lane 50 a. Level Bottom and Cross's Lot; Lane had Level
Bottom and 120 a. vacant land resurv. as Lane's Bottoms and Hills,
and on 27 Feb. 1757 he sold Capt. William Rogers 82 a. of the
latter tract; Samuel and Jane had iss.: SAMUEL, b. 8 Feb. 1736;
LAMBERT; RICHARD; CHARITY, m. Greenbury Baxter; WILKINSON, b. 21
April 1743; SARAH, b. 8 Nov. 1746, may have m. Joseph Hays; COR-
BIN; DUTTON; ABRAHAM; and JOHN (82:493; 131; 133; 340:346).

LANE, JOHN (8), s. of Dutton (3), d. by 1769; m. Avarilla
Bosley on 18 Sept. 1754; she m. 2nd John Wells; in 1731 Lane
surv. Good Will; d. leaving a will, 3 March 1769 - 5 May 1769,
naming tracts William Forest, Good Will, Henry's Hope, Peasler
Choice, and Peagler Meadows, bro. Dutton Lane, and his own ch.:
William, Elizabeth, Dinah, and John Boring Lane; on 26 Sept.
1787 Elizabeth Baker of Hopewell Twp., Washington Co., Penna.,
sold to Amon Butler part of Good Will and part of William Resurveyed which she had inher. from her father John, and by the death
of her bro. John Boring Lane; on 1 Nov. 1800 as Elizabeth Chainey
heir at law of father John and her bros. John Boring and William
Lane, she sold part I Will and I Will Not which Dutton Lane had
conv. to his grandson William Lane; John and Avarilla had iss.:
WILLIAM, d. by 1 Nov. 1800; ELIZABETH, m. by 26 Sept. 1787 (---)
Baker, and 2nd, by 1 Nov. 1800 (---) Chainey; DINAH; and JOHN
BORING (231-WG#AA:549; 231-WG#64:333; 210-37:89; F. C. Montgomery, "Wells of Balto. Co.," unpub. typescript at Md. Hist. Soc.).

LANE, DARBY, d. in Balto. Co. leaving a will, 21 April 1722 -
14 May 1722, naming John, Robert, Samuel, and Joshua Owings,
Jane Gill, Charles Wells, Sarah and Mary Arnold, John Parish,
Bryant Duff and Robert Stockshill, with John Giles as exec.; admin. bond was posted 18 June 1722 by John Giles with Richard
Gist and Thomas Taylor; est. was inv. in 1722; est. was admin.
in Nov. 1724 and May 1725 (2:353; 3:22; 12:89; 52:34; 124:114).

LANE, MARY, in April 1688 was listed as a serv. in the inv.
of Thomas Lightfoot (51:6).

LANG, JOHN, d. in Cecil Co., leaving a will, 14 March 1740 -
22 May 1741, appointing his w. as extx., naming Randall Death,
and the tract John's Beginning (which he purch. in Sept. 1732
from John Muckeldory of Balto. Co.), to s. John; had iss.: JOHN;
and DANIEL (73:280; 127:129).

LANGLEY, ROBERT (1), was transp. to Md. c.1672; in March 1683
surv. 356 a. Langley's Forest and in April 1684 he surv. 640 a.
Langley's Tents; d. by April 1687 and had at least one s.: JOHN
(211; 388).

LANGLEY, JOHN (2), s. of Robert (1), in April 1687 conv. 300 a.
Langley's Habitation to Robert Kembell of Cecil Co.; may have
d. s.p. as the Baltimore County Rent Roll states that Robert
Langley had died without any (living) heirs (59:252; 211).

LANGLEY, JOSEPH, was in Balto. Co. by 13 April 1670 when he
conv. 250 a. at Turner's Creek to Joseph Hopkins (96:230).

LANGLEY, JOSEPH, was b. 10 Dec. 1753, parents not given (133:
97).

LANGLEY, MARY, was ind. for bast. in March 1746/7 (36:378).

LANGLEY, RICHARD, was in Balto. Co. by 1690 as a serv. with 2
years to serve in the inv. of John Boring; in 1692 was a taxable
in n. side of Patapsco Hund. (51:6; 138:3).

LANGLEY, WILLIAM, m. Elizabeth, dau. of Solomon Jones, on 2 Oct. 1725; he and his w. and William Jones and his w. Mary of St. Marys Co. conv. 200 a. The Level to John Gardner (70:183).

LANGSWORTH, PETER, was in Balto. Co. by 1750 when he owned 50 a. Peter's Second Chance; on 17 Sept. 1755 he and w. Mary conv. Peter Bardell 50 a. Peter's Second Adventure (82:450; 153:70).

LANHAM, JOSIAS, m. by 24 Feb. 1720, Susanna, dau. of Anthony Drew (1:151).

LARMAN, ANN, m. Robert Nairne on 29 Oct. 1724 (131).

LARRISEY, MARY, age 12 next Aug., with the cnsent of her mother was bound to Charles and Grace Anderson in Nov. 1733 (30:125).

LASCELLES, GERVASE, d. in Balto. Co. by 7 Aug. 1683 when Thomas Heath posted admin. bond with James Mills and John Purnell (12:114).

LASHLEY, ELIZABETH, was ind. for bast. in Nov. 1758; had a dau. named JEMIMA (46:163).

LASHLEY, PETER, farmer, and w. Susannah conv. 50 a. Abraham's Garden to Jacob Crouse c.1757 (83:50).

LASTIN, WILLIAM, was in Balto. Co. by 1692 as a taxable in Spesutia Hund. (138).

LATHORN or LATHAIN, CHRISTOPHER, was in Balto. Co. by 1692 as a taxable in Spesutia Hund. (138).

LAUGHLEN, PHILIP, Irish, runaway serv., age c. 25; advert. for by James Martin of Balto. Co. in March 1751 (385:111).

LAURACY, JOHN, m. Mary Denson on 26 Nov. 1738 (128:92/b)

LAWLER, HENRY, was in Balto. Co. by 1692 as a taxable in n. side Patapsco Hund. (138).

LAWRASSEY, MARY, was ind. for bast. in March 1729/30, and tried in Aug. 1730; had iss.: SARAH, b. 13 Aug. 1728 (28:362; 29:7; 128:65). See also LARRISEY, LAURACY above).

LAWRENCE, BENJAMIN, imm. c.1670 from Accomack Co., Va., with w. Ann and ch. Benjamin and Nehemiah (388).

LAWRENCE, BENJAMIN, d. in Balto. Co. by 27 March 1721 when admin. bond was posted by admnx. Rachel Lawrence, with John Dorsey and John Howard; est. was inv. 4 April 1721 by Richard Shipley and Jos'h Dorsey and val. at £ 76.14.3 with Nicholas Gassaway and John Dorsey signing as kin; est. was admin. 13 Sept. 1726 by admnx. Rachel, now w. of John Norwood, one of the people called Quakers (3:57; 12:90; 51:30).

LAWRENCE, DANIEL, was in Balto. Co. by 28 Oct. 1685 when as Daniel Lawrence, tailor, he conv. 100 a. Daniel's Hope to Thomas Lightfoot; d. by 8 Dec. 1690 when admin. bond was posted by Francis Smith and w. Elizabeth; est. was inv. by Robert Drisdale and Richard Perkins and val. at £ 8.1.2 (12:113; 48:164; 59:182).

LAWRENCE, HENRY, was in Balto. Co. by 2 Aug. 1681 when he purch. 65 a. from Michael and Jane Judd; on 6 June 1683 Henry and his w. Elizabeth conv. to Cornelius Boyce 65 a. formerly laid out for John Vaughn (59:47; 64:155).

LAWRENCE, WILLIAM, serv., was named in the inv. of the est. of Nicholas Haile on 13 Oct. 1730 (52:203).

LAWS, or LOW, JAMES, d. by 12 July 1758 when his est. was admin. by Cornelius Stevens; dec. left as heirs: REBECCA; MARY; and a dau. who m. John Pribble (6:2½).

THE ALEXANDER LAWSON FAMILY

LAWSON, JAMES (1), of Banff, Scotland, had iss.: ALEXANDER, b. c.1710; JAMES; and a dau. who m. (---) Logan, and a dau. who m. (---) Robinson (111:337; 343:26).

LAWSON, ALEXANDER (2), s. of James (1), was b. c.1710; d. by 5 March 1761 in Balto. Co.; m. Dorothy, dau. of Walter Smith of Cal. Co., on 13 Nov. 1735; purch. several tracts from John Boring: 80 a. Swan Harbour, 50 a. Boring's Range, 50 a. Boring's Passage, and 189 a. Ferry Range; in 1750 he owned many additional properties; three of his daus. drowned on Christmas Eve, 1752, when the ice gave way; d. leaving a will, 5 Sept. 1760 - 5 March 1761, naming Andrew Buchanan and w. Susanna, daus. Isabella and Rebecca; sisters Mrs. Logan and Mrs. Robinson; granddau. Eleanor Buchanan; bro. James; Henry Shields; w. Dorothy and s. Alexander; had iss.: ALEXANDER; ISABELLA; REBECCA: and SUSANNA, b. 12 Jan. 1743, m. Andrew Buchanan (75:48; 111:337; 153:45; 343: 26; 385:212).

THE JOHN LAWSON FAMILY

LAWSON, JOHN (3), no known rel. to any of the above, m. Frances (---); in April 1729 was named in the admin. acct. of David Guy; d. by 15 March 1769 when est. was admin. by John Lawson; est. admin. again 18 June 1770; had iss.: ANNE, b. 9 Nov. 1730; ELIZABETH, b. 29 Sept. 1733; and MOSES, b. 10 May 1736; JOHN (2:304; 6:192; 7:9; 131:50/r).

LAWSON, MOSES (4), s. of John (3) and Frances, was b. 10 May 1736 in Balto. Co.; d. 1776 in Codorus Twp., York Co.; m. Mary Taylor on 26 Jan. 1763 in the Lutheran Church of York Co., Penna.; had iss.: BENJAMIN, b. Dec. 1763; JOSEPH, b. 16 Feb. 1765; FRANCIS, b. 1767; RICHARD, b. 1769; MOSES, b. 1770; and EDWARD, b. 1772 (131; Lawson records at the York Co. Hist. Soc., York, PA).

LAYCOCK, WALTER, in March 1682/3 sued David Jones for his freedom (18:5).

LEA. See LEE.

LEAGO. See LEGO.

LEAGUE, JAMES, m. Eleanor, dau. of Anthony Enloes on 2 May 1759 (131).

LEAGUE, JOHN, was b. 1703, acc. to a dep. in April 1752; on 3 June 1734 conv. Cross's Outlet to Anthony Asher for love and affection; in March 1741 he and w. Mary conv. 100 a. to Anthony Asher (74:66; 75:459; 224:218).

LEAKE, RICHARD, tailor, was in Balto. Co. by May 1666 when he conv. 100 a. St. Clement's Dane to William Orchard; in Aug. 1668 conv. a life interest in his plant. to Welthen Suthard who "had been a good housekeeper," and had been left poor and homeless by the death of her husb.; m. her by 19 Feb. 1669/70 when he and w. Gwelthian conv. Thomas Howell tract Land's End; on 5 Aug. 1671 Richard and Gwelthin conv. 400 a. Happy Harbour to Henry Pennington (63:65; 94; 95; 96:231; 98:48; 100:117).

LEAKE. See also LAKE.

LEAKINS, ELIZABETH, had dau. born 6 May 1729; m. Ulick Burke on 14 May 1732; iss.: ELIZABETH, b. 6 May 1729 (29:156; 131).

LEAKINS, JOHN, d. by 1680 when his est. was admin. by his wid. Margaret, now w. of John Hubbard; est.was inv. and val. at 14,440 lbs. tob. (2:45; 101:299).

LEAKINS, JOHN, was in Balto. Co. by 1692 as a taxable in n. side Patapsco Hund.; m. by 1708 Elizabeth, admnx. of John Enlows; d. by 5 Nov. 1719 when admin. bond was posted by Stephen Gill, admin., with Eliz. McComas and William McComas; est. was inv. on 6 Sept 1720 by Thomas and Christopher Randall, and val. at £ 14.18.10, and signed by Thomas Hutchings, Edmund Baxter and Richard Gist; est. was admin. on 14 March 1722 (1:103; 2: 230; 12:106; 51:164; 138).

LEASIE, MARGARET; d. in Balto. Co. leaving a will, 29 July 1757 - 2 Nov. 1757, naming 100 a. Partner's Trouble, servant Wm. Smith, grandson Alexander Rigdon, and these ch.: WILLIAM; ANN, m. (---) Rigdon; and SUSANNA, m. (---) Ashmore. (111:240) (See also William LACEY).

LEASOR, JOHN, d. by 8 Jan. 1704/5 when admin. bond was posted by Richard Colegate with Henry Wriothesley; est. was inv. on 2 July 1705 by Charles Merryman, Sr., and Nicholas Rogers, and val. at £ 4.18.9; est. was admin. by Colegate on 3 April 1707 (2:179; 11:107; 51:106).

LEASOR, JOHN, m. Elizabeth (---) and had iss.: JOHN, b. 5 Aug. 1711 (131).

LEATHERWOOD/LETHERWOOD, JOHN (1), was b. c.1645 and settled in Balto. Co. c.1660; in Aug. 1715 he gave his age and length of res. in Balto. Co., and asked to be made levy free; he had been granted 100 a. Old Man's Folly in May 1709; may have had iss.: SAMUEL (21:623; 67:547).

LEATHERWOOD, SAMUEL (2), heir, and prob. s., of John (1); m. Johanna (---) who joined him in sale of 100 a. Old Man's Folly to Pleasance Dorsey, on 16 Jan. 1717 (67:547).

LEAVEN, THOMAS, on 11 March 1744 purch. 50 a. Abner's Camp from Abner Baker (77:537). (See also THOMAS HEAVEN).

THE JAMES LEE FAMILY is the subject of an unpublished typescript by Christopher Johnston at the Maryland Historical Society, Baltimore.

LEE, JAMES (1), progenitor, settled in A. A. Co.; m. c.1703/4 Margaret, wid. of John Wilson of that county; in 1718 purch. 300 a. Friendship from his step-son William Wilson; the tract was in Balto. Co.; d. leaving a will, 29 Jan. 1732 - 7 March 1732, naming ch. James, Margaret Webster, Mary w. of James Lynch, and the latter's dau. Mary; admin. bond was posted 8 March 1732 by execs. James Lee and Isaac Webster with Jacob Giles and Thomas Johnson, and had iss.: JAMES, b. c.1707; MARGARET, m. Isaac Webster on 2 Sept. 1722; MARY, m. 1st, on 23 Nov. 1728, James Lynch, and 2nd, Thomas Gittings (12:93; 125:253; 129:260; Johnston typescript).

LEE, JAMES (2), s. of James (1), was b. 1707, d. 1778; m. on 17 Aug. 1730 Elizabeth Gover, b. 16 June 1710, dau. of Samuel and Elizabeth Gover; in 1750 he owned 100 a. part Simmon's

Choice, 254 a. Planter's Paradice, 50 a. Duly's Mistake, and
50 a. New Westwood, and 50 a. West Beginning; d. leaving a will,
26 Aug. 1776 - 1 Dec. 1778, proved in Harf. Co.; had iss.: MAR-
GARET, m. 6 Feb. 1752 John Paca, Jr.; JAMES, b. 1 March 1733,
prob. d. young; JAMES, twin, b. 16 Oct. 1735; SAMUEL, twin, b.
16 Oct. 1735; MARY, b. 13 Nov. 1739, m. Samuel Wilson; ELIZABETH,
m. William Webb on 12 July 1758; CASSANDRA, m. William Morgan;
JOSIAH, m. Sarah Chew Worthington; RACHEL, m. 1766 Dr. Gideon
Vancleave (128:88, 89, 108; 153:48; 244-AJ#2:384; Johnston typescript).

LEE, JAMES (3), s. of James (2), was b. 16 Oct. 1735, m. as
his 2nd w., in 1779, Sarah Elliott; had iss.: JAMES, b. 31 Aug.
1756; RICHARD; CORBIN (129:373; Johnston typescript).

LEE, SAMUEL (4), s. of James (2), was b. 16 Oct. 1735; m. Mary
dau. of Parker Hall, and had iss.: PARKER HALL, b. 14 Jan. 1759,
d. 1829; Dr. JAMES, b. 10 Dec. 1760, d. 1786 having m. Milcah
(---); PRISCILLA, b. 3 Sept. 1762, m. George Presbury; MARY, m.
John Moores; BLANCH, m. William Welch; ELIZABETH, m. Robert Gover;
CASSANDRA, m. Robert Gover; MARGARET, m. William Smithson (129:
374; Johnston typescript).

LEE, ANN, serv. of Richard Jones, was tried for bast. in Aug.
1745 (25:629).

LEE, EDWARD, in 1750 owned 100 a. Gardner's Farm (153:80).

LEE, ELIZABETH, in March 1731, was ind. for bast.; had iss.:
MARY, b. 8 Nov. 1732 (29:225; 128:73).

LEE, ELIZABETH, servant to Robert West, was ind. for bast.
in March 1736 and in June 1737 was summoned again to answer the
same charge; had iss.: MARGARET, b. 27 May 1726 (31:1, 56; 128:
96).

LEE, FRANCIS, was in Balto. Co. by Feb. 1713 when he surv.
90 a. Lee's Range (207).

LEE, JOHN, was in Balto. Co. by June 1668 when he surv. 250
a. Chilberry Hall; in Nov. 1668 with William Osborn surv. 100 a.
Mate's Angle; also surv. 100 a. Crab Hill in March 1665, 100 a.
Mate's Neck with William Osborn in June 1667, 450 a. Common Garden in June 1667, 150 a. The Island in Nov. 1664, and 200 a. Winter's Run; in March 1670/1 conv. one-half of Chilberry Hall to
Richard Collins; with Osborn conv. Mate's Angle to Anthony Brispo in June 1673, and conv. Crab Hill to Oliver Spry in March
1667/8; had iss.: MARY, m. by 5 June 1693/4 James Durham who
joined her in sale of Chilberry to John Durham (59:390; 60:67;
63:112; 211).

LEE, JOHN, m. Alce, dau. of William Norris on 4 April 1733;
she was b. 16 April 1713, and m. 2nd by 29 Aug. 1741 George Lester; admin. bond on Lee's est. was posted 4 May 1736 by admnx.
Alice Lee with Henry Millan and Samuel Griffith; est. was admin.
by Alice now w. of George Lester on 29 Aug. 1741; dec. left no
legal reps. (4:118; 12:102; 128:75; Myers, The Norris Family).

LEE, JOHN, of St. George's Parish, m. Jane Hickson on 10 June
1735 and had iss.: JOHANNA, b. 7 Feb. 1735/6; MARY, b. 28 Nov.
1738 (128:89, 91, 101).

LEE, JOHN, of St. John's Par., had iss.: MARY, b. 4 Jan. 1730;
JAMES, b. 14 Feb. 1732; AQUILA, b. 23 June 1735; JOSIAH, b. 15
Oct. 1737; PRISCILLA, b. 30 Aug. 1740 (131).

LEE, JOSEPH, was in Balto. Co. by 1692 as a taxable in Spesutia Hund. (138).

LEE, JOSEPH, was b. c.1705, giving his age as 55 in 1760; m. Elizabeth Ashmore on 12 June 1733; in 1750 owned 102 a. part Arabia Petrea (128:73; 153:71; 225:295).

LEE, MARY, was ind. for bast. in Nov. 1750, and tried in Nov. 1756 when she named John Prebble; had iss.: SARAH, b. 4 Dec. 1750; JOHN, b. 26 Oct. 1756; SEABORN, b. 31 Oct. 1759 (38:1; 41: 312; 129:377).

LEE, SHERWOOD, m. Elinor Temple on 3 Nov. 1729; on 30 Nov. 1737 Sherwood and Elinor conv. 70 a. Jones' Addition to Josias Middlemore; had iss.: JOHN, b. 6 or 16 June 1731; SHERWOOD, d. 28 Sept. 1734; SHERWOOD, b. 14 July 1735; ELIZABETH, b. 14 July 1735; ELIZABETH, b. 3 Aug. 1737 (75:39; 128:62, 77, 82, 88; 129:332).

LEE, SUSANNAH, was ind. for bast. in June 1750 (37:2).

LEE, THOMAS, was in Balto. Co. by 1692 as a taxable in Spesutia Hund. (138).

LEE, THOMAS, m. Elizabeth Shields on 8 May 1701 (128:11).

LEE, WILLIAM, m. Elizabeth (---) and had: JAMES, b. 27 Feb. 1741 (129:340).

LEE, WILLIAM, age 7 last 31 March, and son of Ann Lee, in Nov. 1754 was bound to John Bond of Patapsco (39:442).

LEEK. See LAKE.

LEET. See LETT.

LEFF, WILLIAM, m. Ruth Matthews on 12 Aug. 1697 and had iss.: MARGARET, b. 6 Jan. 1701/2 (129:178, 194).

LEGANS, JOHN; had iss.: THOMAS, age 12 last May, was bound to John Gorsuch in Aug. 1722 (25:297).

LEGATT/LEGETT, BRIDGET, was ind. for bast. in March 1736 and tried in June 1737 (31:1, 56).

LEGATT, JOHN, m. Unity (---) and had iss.: SARAH, b. 30 Nov. 1713; he was exempt from the levy in Nov. 1735 (33:39; 131:5).

LEGATT, JOHN, Jr., m. Tamar (---) and had: JOSHUA, b. 10 Dec. 1740 (131).

LEGATT, JOHN, d. 1756 in Balto. Co., leaving a will, 12 April 1752 - 31 March 1756, naming w. Sarah and these ch.: JOHN; UNITY; (w. of Richardson); ANN w. of (---) Bailey; SARAH, m. (---) Wright (111:111).

LEGATT, SARAH. See John Enloes (132:2).

LEGATT, WILLIAM, was made levy free in Nov. 1756 (41:303).

LEGO, BENJAMIN (1), was b. c.1673, and was age 25 on 24 Oct. 1698 when as Benjamin Lego of St. Giles, Cripplegate, London, horn turner, he apprenticed himself to Richard Kitchener of Stepney, Middlesex, to serve him for 4 years in Virginia or beyond the seas; the indenture was recorded in the Balto. Co. Court Proceedings so Lego eventually landed in Md.; by 1699 was a taxable; m. by 25 Sept. 1707 Mary, wid. of William Hill whose est. they admin. on that date; in June 1737 was made levy free; in March 1733/4 agreed to be financially responsible for the illegit. ch. of Mary Lego; Benjamin m. as his second w. on 4 Nov. or 11 Dec. 1723, Jean Taylor, wid.; in 1750 at age 76 made a deposition concerning the births of Robert Jackson's children; had iss. (by 1st or 2nd w., not determined): THOMAS, d. by 1744; BENJAMIN; MARY, tried for bast. in March 1733/4; RUTH, ind. for bast. in Nov. 1733 (2:169; 30:197; 31:49; 63:35; 131; 229:7).

LEGO, THOMAS (2), s. of Benjamin, m. Sarah Clark on 19 Dec. 1728, and d. 20 April 1742; admin. bond was posted 15 Aug. 1743 by admnx. Sarah Lego with Benjamin Lego and William Hill; est. was inv. on 14 Nov. 1743 and val. at £ 64.7.2½, and signed by Benjamin Lego, Sr., and Benjamin, Jr.; est. was admin. on 21 Aug. 1744; had iss.: REUBEN, b. 5 Sept. 1729, prob. d. young; JOHN, b. May 1732, d. June 1742; THOMAS, b. July 1735; HANNAH, b. 25 May 1740; REUBEN, b. 11 Jan. 1742 (5:17; 12:80; 35:479; 52:470; 131).

LEGO, BENJAMIN (3), s. of Benjamin (1), m. Judeax Bruceton on 25 Oct. 1740; in 1750 he owned 150 a. Warrington, 50 a. Lego's Chance, 50 a. Lego's Trouble, and 50 a. part Hall's Ridge; d. leaving a will, 10 June 1759 - 16 July 1759, naming ch. Spencer, Benedict, and Cordelia, and appointing his w. and Benjamin Ricketts as execs.; admin. bond was posted 21 Aug. 1759 by Judea Lego with William Hill and Thomas Presbury; est. was admin. 14 June 1762 by Judea Lego who stated that the dec. left seven ch.; Judith Lego d. in Harford Co., leaving a will, 9 Feb. 1777 - 28 Feb. 1777; dec. left iss.: SPENCER; BENEDICT; CORDELIA, may have been the Cordelia who m. Walter James on 23 Dec. 1762; MARY; REBEC BECCA; poss. two others (6:137; 12:76; 79:704; 111:312; 131; 153:44; 210-41:412).

LEGO, SPENCER (4), s. of Benjamin (3), was b. 25 Oct. 1741; m. Eliza Jackson on 16 Nov. 1762; m. 2nd, on 26 May 1768, Eliz. Hicks; had iss.: ALICE, b. 15 June 1769 (131).

LEGO, MARY, m. William Whaland in Nov. 1751 (131).

LEGO, SARAH, m, John White on 23 Sept. or 4 Oct. 1744 John White (131).

LEMMON, ALEXIS (1), progenitor, was b. c.1718; d. by 28 July 1786; m. 1st Martha (poss. Merryman); m. 2nd Rachel (poss. Cottrell), wid. of Jacob Jones; in 1750 he owned 100 a. Lemmon's Lot; on 7 April 1759 purch. part Teague's Pleasant Ridge from Benjamin Tracey; d. leaving a will, 30 May 1786 - 26 July 1786, naming his w. Rachel, Laban and Ruth, ch. of Laban Headington, and his own ch.; est. was admin. 19 July 1788; had iss.: JOHN, b. 6 Nov. 1740; RUTH, b. 22 Jan. 1742, m. Thomas Stansbury; MARY, m. Ulick Burke on 8 Nov. 1764; ALEXIS, Jr., b. 12 March 1746; HANNAH, b. c.1751; REBECCA, b. 1753, m. Jabez Murray Tipton on 16 Jan. 1781; ELEANOR, b. 1757, m. Zebulon Headington in 1771; MOSES, b. 1759, m. Sarah Jones (9:223; 83:389; 113:151; 131; 133:71; 153:17).

LEMMON, JOHN (2), s. of Alexis (1), was b. 6 Nov. 1740; d. in Balto. Co. in 1811; m. Sarah Stansbury on 6 March 1760; was a seaman and rendered patriotic service in Md. during the Rev. War; d. leaving a will, 11 April 1803 - 13 April 1811; had iss.: ELEANOR, m. Luke Ensor; CHARLES; LEMUEL; HANNAH, m. (---) Corcoran; MARTHA, m. by lic. 20 Jan. 1784 Joshua Price;ALEXIS; THOMAS; JOHN; and BENJAMIN (113; 118; 232; 236-16:376; 353).

LEMMON, ALEXIS (3), s. of Alexis (1), was b. 12 March 1746 in Balto. Co.; d. 21 June 1826 in Morrow Co., Ohio; m. Rachel Stansbury on 29 Nov. 1771; was capt. of militia co. in the Rev. War; had iss.: SARAH; RUTH; ELIZABETH; MARY; REBECCA; JAMES; and TEMPERANCE (353; 364:225).

LEMMON, MOSES (4), s. of Alexis (1), was b. c.1759; d. 29 Aug. 1852 in Union Co., Ind.; m. Sarah, dau. of Jacob Jones; enlisted in the 5th Regt., Md. Militia in the Rev. War; had at least one s.: JOSHUA(9:223, 239; 400:65; Pens. Application R-6283).

LEMMON, ELIZABETH, m. Richard Manning on 7 April 1733 (129: 266).

LEMMON, JOHANNA, was ind. for bast. and tried in March 1733/4; named Thomas Whitehead as the father; had iss.: FLORIA, b. 15 May 1733 (30:198; 134:8).

LEMMON, NEIL, d. by 7 March 1747when admin. bond was posted by William Dobbins with Robert Dobbins and Robert Stephenson (11: 85).

LEMMON, PETER, was in Balto. Co. by Aug. 1746 when John and Christian Piggsler conv. him part The Great Meadow (79:121).

LENDRUM, Rev. ALEXANDER, Rector of St. George's Par. from 1749; m. Jane Burney on 18 Oct. 1749 in Newcastle, Delaware; by 1750 had acquired 200 a. Riley and 10 a. Motson's Lot; d. by 27 April 1775 when his est. was admin. by Robert Burney Lendrum and John Lee Webster; had iss.: ROBERT BURNEY, b. 27 Aug. 1750; LUCINDA, b. 22 June 1752; JAMES, b. 30 Jan. 1754, d. 8 Feb. 1754; MARY, b. 24 Jan. 1755 (6:366; 129:366, 367; 153:23).

LENOX, WILLIAM (1), was in Balto. Co. by 1692 as a taxable in n. side Gunpowder; by 1700 Richard Lenox was with him and by 1703 William Lenox, Jr., was old enough to be a taxable; prob. the Wm. Lenox who with w. Anne conv. 170 a. Leafe's Chance and William the Conqueror to William Robinson; had iss.: RICHARD, b. by 1684; WILLIAM, b. by 1687 (59:606; 138; 142; 145).

LENOX, RICHARD (2), s. of William (1), was b. c.c.1684 or 1680, giving his age as c.52 in July 1732; m. 1st by 6 March 1706 Mary Richardson, who joined him in selling Maiden's Choice to Nicholas Fitzsimmons, the tract had been granted to Mary when she was Mary Richardson; she was sis. of James Richardson, and dau. of Col. Thomas Richardson; Lenox m. 2nd, by 27 Jan. 1724 Tamar, admnx. of Francis Keys and William Wilkinson; d. by 9 Aug. 1733 when admin. bond was posted by Tamar Lenox with John Crockett and John Rogers; est. was admin. by Tamar Lenox on 16 Jan. 1733; had iss.: JOHN; JAMES; RICHARD; and THOMAS (2:330, 335, 360; 3:135; 12:95; 64:40; 68:212; 224:158).

LENOX, WILLIAM (3), s. of William (1), was b. by 1786; on 24 Sept. 1714 purch. Watertown from Simon Pearson; m. by 24 Feb. 1720 Bethia, dau. of Anthony Drew; d. leaving a will, 21 March 1724 - 4 May 1724, left all prop. to w. Bethia; she posted admin. bond on 4 June 1724 with Thomas Tolley; she m. 2nd (---) Calvert, and d. leaving a will proved 6 June 1733, naming her sis. Sarah Drew and her late husb. William Lenox (1:151; 12:241; 51:224; 69: 63; 124:166; 126:22).

LENOX, JOHN (4), s. of Richard (2), with his bros. James, Richard, and Thomas, were conv. prop. by James Richardson; m. by 1726 Elizabeth, dau. of John Hayes, who joined him in Aug. 1730 in selling 268 a. Kindness to Edward Evans; d. by 8 March 1732 when admin. bond was posted by Eliza Lenox with John Scott and Thomas Tolley; est. was admin. by Elizabeth Lenox on 10 June 1735 (3: 198; 12:92; 67:320; 73:12; 125:11).

LENOX, JAMES (5), s. of Richard (2), was b. c.1705, giving his age as 48 in June 1753; m. 1st, by 22 Jan. 1735, Mary, dau. of Robuck Lynch; on the aforesaid date James and Mary conv. to Patrick and William Lynch all land devised to Mary by the will of her father, Robuck Lynch; on 22 Jan. 1735 purch. Wright's Forest from Patrick and Martha Lynch; on 3 Aug. 1727 conv. 38 a. Westminster to Philip Jones; m. 2nd, by March 1743/4 Honor, wid. of Jacob Peacock; a legacy left by James Lenox to Ruth Peacock was mentioned in the admin. acct. of Thomas Todd; had iss.: (all by 1st w.): ANN, b. 15 Jan. 1730; JOHN, b. 8 Oct. 1732; RICHARD LYNCH, b. 8 Jan. 1738; NATHAN, b. 31 Aug. 1740; RICHARDSON, b. 21 Sept. 1743 (3:375; 35:161; 61:513; 74:368, 371; 131:127/r; 133: 20, 37; 224:224).

LENOX, JANE, on 6 July 1728 deposed that Jacob Peacock had no kin (51:86).

LENTALL, MARY, in Aug. 1721 pet. the court about the est. of her father Thomas Williamson who had left two daus. and a wid., since remarried (23:556).

LEONARD, JOHN, d. by 1 March 1678/9 when John Walston, innholder, posted admin. bond with James Phillips and William Osborn; the est. was inv. on the same date by Robert Jones and James Phillips and val. at Ł 4247 lbs. tob. (12:115; 48:41).

LERRISEY. See LARISEY.

LESOURD, or LESHODY, FRANCIS, m. Susannah (---), and had iss.: MYHANNAH, b. 30 Sept. 1757; MARY, b. 9 Oct. 1760 (129:360, 366).

LESTER, (---) (1), prob. m. Ann (---) who d. 17 Aug. 1716, leaving two sons: GEORGE; and PETER (128:35).

LESTER, GEORGE (2), s. of (---) (1) and Ann, was in the household of Edward Boothby in 1695 in Spesutia Hund. (140).

LESTER, PETER (3), s. of (---) (1) and Ann, was a taxable in the household of Edward Boothby; m. (prob. Ann) (---) by 8 May 1713; admin. est. of Thomas Newsham on 8 Oct. 1723; Newsom had made a will on 25 Jan. 1720 naming Peter Lester and Peter's s. George; Ann Lester wit. Newsom's will; Lester d. 4 May 1723; his est. was admin. on 5 June 1735 by Ann Lester who stated that the dec. had two ch.: George and Mary; Ann Lester d. leaving a will, 14 May 1749 - 14 Aug. 1749, naming s. Henry Hail, s. George, granddaus. Sarah and Martha, dau. Mary w. of James Sinclair and Mary's ch. Ann and Lester Sinkler; Peter and Ann had iss.: (poss. MARTHA, b. 30 June 1713; GEORGE, b. 25 Dec. 1717; ANN, b. 5 Sept. 1720, d. 14 Sept. 1720; MARY, b. 19 May 1722, m. James Sinclair (1:120, 17; 12:96; 13:196; 31:43; 124:59; 128:31, 35, 38, 41; 140; 210-27:84).

LESTER, GEORGE (4), s. of Peter (3), was b. 25 Dec. 1717; d. by 22 May 1760; m. Alice Lee on 8 Dec. 1737; she was the admnx. of John Lee, and d. by 12 Sept. 1763; in 1737 Henry Millain named Alice Millain as his sis.-in-law; George Lester admin. Millain's est.; in 1750 he owned 100 a. Eden's Addition, 150 a. Garden of Eden, and 127 a. Spring Garden; est. of George Lester was admin. 22 May 1760; est. of Alice Lester was admin. by Robert Magaw on 11 Oct. 1762, and 12 Sept. 1763; George and Alice had iss.: SARAH, b. 10 Sept. 1739; MARTHA PAIN NORRIS, b. 25 April 1742; MARY, b.

3 Sept. 1743; CHARLOTTE, b. 30 Jan. 1744; SOPHIA, b. 20 July 1748; NORRIS, b. 28 Dec. 1751; WILLIAM, b. 8 Aug. 1756 (4:115, 118, 310; 6:59, 126; 12:74; 126:235; 128:99, 105; 129:326, 335, 360; 360; 153:48).

LESTER, ELIZA, in June 1721 named John Hollandsworth as the father of her child; later recanted the accusation and named an Indian called Sackelah as the father (23:498, 507).

LETHERLAND, GEORGE, m. Margaret Thomas on 24 Dec. 1748 (133: 162).

LETT, JANE, in March 1717/8 named James Ketcham as the father of her child (22:237-238).

LETT, MARY, in Aug. 1728 was ind. for bast., tried in Nov. 1728; in March 1730/1 her two mulatto ch., Sarah and Zachariah Lett, were bound to William Rogers; had iss.: SARAH; and ZACHA-RIAH (28:22, 74; 29:97).

LETT, SABRA, in June 1732 was ind. for bast.; tried in March 1736 (29:289; 31:19).

LETT, ZACHARIAH, m. Margaret (---), and had iss.: LURARIA, b. 27 April 1741; VASHTI, b. 1 Jan. 1743; and DANIEL, b. 29 Oct. 1745 (133:75).

LETTICK. See LITTIG.

LEVENS, THOMAS, was in Balto. Co. by 1750 as the owner of 100 a. Bachelor's Choice (153:162).

LEVERLY, THOMAS, m. Elizabeth Henderson on 7 June 1736 (133: 155).

LEVINS, THOMAS, on 11 May 1744 purch. 50 a. Abner's Camp from Abner Baker; on 18 Aug. 1746 with w. Ann sold that tract to Wm. Hammond; in 1746 surv. 50 a. Thomas' Choice which he still owned in 1750; on 11 Oct. 1746 Thomas and Ann sold 100 a. Bachelor's Choice to James Richards (77:537; 79:219, 242; 153:65; 207). See also Thomas Heaven.

LEWIN, MARY, was ind. for bast. in Aug. 1738 (31:267).

LEWIS, HUMPHREY (1), came to possess 100 a. Brother's Expecta-tion, part of a 250 a. tract orig. laid out for George Hollings-worth in 1695; in May 1709 surv. 40 a. Weaver's Providence; d. by 4 June 1717 when admin. bond was posted by admnx. Susan Lewis with John Israel and Christopher Randall; est. was inv. on 21 June 1717 by Hector Maclane and William Hamilton and val. at £ 6.15.4; dec. left iss.: HENRY (12:105; 48:293; 81:288; 207; 211).

LEWIS, HENRY (2), s. of Humphrey (1), was living on 18 Jan. 1752 when he and w. Keturah conv. 40 a. Weaver's Providence to Daniel Dulany and Co.; m. by 21 Nov. 1730 Keturah, dau. of Robert Parker; in Nov. 1730 Henry and Keturah conv. 250 a. Parker's Pal-ace to George Buchanan; in 1750 owned 40 a. Weaver's Providence; had iss.: EDWARD, b. 5 Aug. 1730; URATH, b. 14 Feb. 1732; ELISHA, b. 27 Oct. 1735; PLEASANCE, b. 3 Jan. 1737; HENRY, b. 27 Jan. 1739; JOHN (mother named as Comfort), b. 8 Dec. 1743; CHARLES, b. 27 Sept. 1746; NICHOLAS, b. 5 Aug. 1750 (73:50; 81:288; 133:82, 83; 153:79).

LEWIS, (---), m. by 1725 Betty, dau. of John Giles (q.v.).

LEWIS, CATHERINE, was charged with bast. in June 1723 (25:331).

LEWIS, EDWARD, m. Sarah (---), and had iss.: JOHN, b. 23 June 1731; EDWARD, b. 6 May 1734; HEZEKIAH, b. 7 Nov. 1736; NATHAN, b. 4 May 1740 or 1744; SAMUEL, b. 10 July 1747; JACOB HURD, b. 15 Nov. 1748 (133:23, 36, 59, 87, 99).

LEWIS, ELIZA, had a dau. Joan Stuart who was made a legatee in the will of Anthony Drew on 24 Feb. 1720 (1:151).

LEWIS, JOHN, m. Margaret Dewley on 18 Dec. 1733; had iss.: JAMES, b. 13 Dec. 1736 (128:82, 94).

LEWIS, JOHN, m. Ann (---), and had: ANN, b. 18 Aug. 1742 (129:334).

LEWIS, JOHN, m. Catherine (---), and had iss.: SARAH, b. 11 July 1755; CATHERINE, b. 24 Sspt. 1758 (133:99, 106).

LEWIS, MARY, was ind. for bast. in March 1746/7 (36:378).

LEWIS, RICHARD, was in Balto. Co. by 1692 as a taxable in Spesutia Hund. (138).

LEWIS, SAMUEL, m. Sarah Marshall on 19 Dec. 1737 and had: MARGARET, b. 15 Sept. 1738 (128:99, 103).

LEWIS, SAMUEL, m. Margaret Hughes on 29 Aug. 1745 (129:341).

LEWIS, WILLIAM, was in Balto. Co. by Aug. 1662 when Howell Powell assigned land to him; on 24 March 1663/4 Lewis and w. Constant authorized John Guyn to obtain acknowledgment of conv. from Howell Powell (93).

LEWIS, WILLIAM, m. Ann, extx. of Nathaniel Stinchcomb by 21 Aug. 1730 (209-29:14).

LEWIS, WILLIAM, m. by 30 Oct. 1742 Ruth, admnx. of Edmond Howard, when they conv. 100 a. to Thomas Norris; in 1750 William owned 100 a. part Cornelius' and Mary's Lot, 200 a. Howard's Fancy, 100 a. The Reserve, and 100 a. The Friendship (5:358; 77:93; 153:32).

LIGHTFOOT, JOHN   d. by 1683, having m. Elizabeth (---), who also d. by 1683 when their orphans were bound to Christopher Gist; had iss.: THOMAS; and ANN (18:28, 49).

LIGHTFOOT, THOMAS, poss. a relative to the above mentioned John Lightfoot;m. by 9 April 1685 Rebecca (---) who in 1691 conv. 140 a. Prosperity to Peter Bond; Thomas was Surveyor of Balto. Co., and on 12 April 1683 was appointed Chief Ranger of Balto. Co.; d. leaving a will, 23 March 1686/7 - 17 June 1687, naming w. Rebecca, cousin John Holland, the boy Thomas Lytfoot (sic) at Christ. Gist's, and sis.-in-law Eliza Larkin, Thomas Larkin, and Thomas Taylor; est. was admin. 2 May 1696 by relict and extx. Rebecca, now w. of Thomas Hammond; mentions payments to Col. Thomas Taylor and s. John (6:111; 20:195; 51:6; 59:351; 111:19).

LIGHTFOOT, THOMAS, age c.30, runaway conv. serv. from Zacha riah and Richard Maccubbin, and was advert. for in May 1750 (307-69:129).

LINCH. See LYNCH.

LINCOLN, JONATHAN, was in Balto. Co. (later Cecil Co.) by June 1673 when he purch. 50 a. at Sassafras R. from Matthew Adams and wife (99).

LINDSAY, ALEXANDER, m. Rebecca (---) and had iss.: REBECCA, b. 12 July 1702 (129:195).

LINDSAY, ALEXANDER, m. Katherine (---), and had iss.: ANN, b. 18 Jan. 1729 (133:32).

LINDSAY, EDMUND, m. Elizabeth Beasley on 20 Feb. 1725 and had iss.: JOHN, b. 28 Jan. 17-(?) (128:45, 70).

LINEGAR, JOHN (1), was in Balto. Co. by 24 Sept. 1683 when he surv. 200 a. John's Habitation; the tract was later held by Stephen Bentley for Linegar's orphans; had iss.: GEORGE; one s. who went to remote parts and was unheard of; also two daus. who d. in Md. (79:537; 211:70).

LINEGAR, GEORGE (2), s. of John (1), res. in Kent Co., Md., and had at least one dau.: SARAH, m. by 24 March 1746 James Power of Cecil Co. (79:537).

LINTALL, MARY. See LENTALL, MARY.

LINTHICUM, GIDEON, was in Balto. Co. by 1750 as the owner of 150 a. Holland's Park (153:102).

LISBEY, LISBY. See LUSBY.

LISTON, JNO., servant, was listed in the inv. of Samuel Noden, Jan. 1722 (52:19).

LITTIG, PETER, d. by 16 May 1763 when est. was admin. by John Siegler and w. Elizabeth; dec. left four ch. (6:43).

THE LITTLE/LYTLE FAMILY has been the subject of study by Kenneth Cameron, whose charts are deposited at the Maryland Historical Society.

LITTLE, GEORGE (1), d. in Balto. Co. leaving a will, 17 Sept. 1756 - 8 June 1757, naming these ch.: THOMAS; JEAN or JANE w. of (---) Patterson; GUY, d. 1764; and MARY, m. 1st (---) Copeland, and 2nd, on 10 Feb. 1757, John Henry (111:245; 131).

LITTLE THOMAS (2), s. of George (1), d. by June 1764; m. Avarilla Osborn on 28 Feb. 1737; she was a dau. of William Osborn and d. 19 March 1740; in March 1745/6 George admitted he was the father of an illeg. ch.; m. 2nd Sarah Hughes; d. leaving a will, 23 March 1764 - 6 June 1764, naming three sons and a dau. Mary, born to Sarah Hughes before he married her; est. was admin. by George Little, admin. de bonis non, on 1 Nov. 1770; ch. of George: WILLIAM, b. 8 Sept. 1737; ANN, b. 15 March 1738; GEORGE, b. 15 March 1740; MARY (by Sarah Hughes); and THOMAS (by Sarah) (5:102; 6:239; 35:811; 111:165; 128:95, 98, 107, 114; 129:318).

LITTLE GUY (3), s. of George (1), d. 20 March 1764; m. on 25 March 1751, Eliza, sis. of John Henry, and extx. of Michael Webster and Daniel Ruff; in 1750 Guy owned 319 a. Ogilvey; d. leaving a will, 24 Nov. 1763 - 10 May 1764, naming bro.-in-law John Henry, w. Elizabeth, and these ch.: JAMES, b. 20 Jan. 1752; ANN, b. 20 Oct. 1754, m. William Osborne on 16 Dec. 1780 or 1781; NATHAN, b. 17 June 1757; GEORGE, b. 22 Oct. 1759; HANNAH, b. 4 May 1763; and JACOB, living in 1784 (5:269; 111:182; 131; 153:67; 201-30:158; 201-33:429).

LITTLE, GEORGE, m. Catherine Roberts on 3 July 1763 (129:380).

LITTLE, HENRY; his marr. to Mary Simm, dau. of William and

Mary Simm, was ren. on 26 Oct. 1763 as the bride was only 12 yrs.
old (230:1).

LITTLE, JAMES, m. Elizabeth (---), and d. by 9 Nov. 1733 when
admin. bond was posted by Elizabeth Little, with Thomas Little
and William Robinson; by Nov. 1737 his wid. had m. Thomas Farlow;
est. was admin. on 18 Nov. 1738; had iss.: FRANCES, b. 18 Sept.
1725; ROSANNA, b. 2 Feb. 1727; ELIZABETH; and JEMIMA (4:5; 12:
94; 31:143; 32:83; 128:57).

LITTLE, JANE, was ind. for bast. in March 1738/9 and tried in
March 1739/40 (31:351; 32:157).

LITTLE, THOMAS, m. 27 June 1731, Mary Shepherd, dau. of Rowland Shepherd of Balto. Co. (125:215; 129:257).

LITTLE, THOMAS, in Nov. 1734 was ind. for bast.; see Sarah
Herrington (30:350).

LITTLE, THOMAS, d. by 10 Aug. 1764 when his est. was admin.
by Eleanor Little; had iss.: JAMES, b. c.1745; GEORGE, b. c.1748;
ELIZABETH, b. c.1750; HENRIETTA, b. c.1752; MARGARET, b. c. 1755;
THOMAS, b. c.1757; MARY, b. c.1759 (6:111).

LITTLE, WILLIAM, m. Elizabeth (---) and had: SARAH, b. 24 Jan.
1728; MARY, b. 7 Dec. 1730; ELLENOR, b. 15 Dec. 1733 (133:32).

LITTON, THOMAS (1), was in Balto. Co. by 1694 as a taxable in
s. side Gunpowder; d. by 7 Nov. 1700; m. Mary (poss. sis. of John
Webster); she may have m. 2nd (---) Miles; is ment. in a deposition as having helped John Indrell hide in the woods c.1697; d.
leaving a will, 29 Oct. 1700 - 7 Nov. 1700, naming w. Mary, bro.
John Webster, and ch. Thomas and Sarah; his wid. Mary held 100 a.
Tall Hill for his orphans; had iss.: THOMAS, minor in 1700; SARAH,
minor in 1700 (21:445; 121:201; 139; 340:117n).

LITTON, THOMAS (2), s. of Thomas (1) and Mary, was a minor in
1700 when his father made his will; m. by 1732 Ann, dau. of John
Hawkins of Balto. Co.; on 15 Sept. 1716 Litton purch. 62 a. of
Father-in-Law's Bounty (being one-half of Margaret's Mount), from
John and Mary Miles; on 28 Jan. 1741 Litton and w. Ann conv. 100
a. Bare Hills to James Rowland; in 1750 owned 123 a. part Marga-
ret's Mount, 80 a. Litton's Fancy, 50 a. Aim's Delight, and 100
a. Arabia Petrea; d. leaving a will, 29 Jan. 1756 - 21 April
1761, naming w. Ann, grandchildren Samuel and Ann Pritchard, and 6
ch.; had.: ELIZABETH, b. 6 April 1715; MARY, b. 1 April 1717;
HANNAH, b. 10 March 1719; THOMAS, b. 30 Jan. 1721; JOHN, b. 10
March 1722/3; ISAAC, b. 13 Feb. 1724/5; MICHAEL, b. 14 April 1730;
ELIZABETH, b. 4 Dec. 1732; SAMUEL, b. 10 Aug. 1735; ANN, b. 25
April 1740; JAMES, b. 5 Feb. 1740(1741?) (67:409; 76:97; 111:342;
126:33; 128:33, 42, 45, 65, 75, 89, 107, 111; 153:33).

LITTON, SARAH (3), dau. of Thomas (1), in Nov. 1718 named
Thomas Miles as the father of her ch.; may be the Sarah Miles
who m. John Beddoe on 3 Dec. 1724; had iss.: MARTHA, b. 27 April
1718 (23:31; 128:36; 129:238).

LITTON, HANNAH (4), dau. of Thomas (2), b. 10 March 1719; may
be the Hannah Litton tried for bast. in Aug. 1742; ind. again in
March 1743/4; also the Hannah Litton alias Jones who was charged
by the vestry of St. John's Parish in April 1746 for unlawful cohabitation with Samuel Hughes; ind. for bast. again in Nov. 1746
(34:8; 35:154; 36:220; 132:82).

LITTON, THOMAS (5), s. of Thomas (2), was b. 30 Jan. 1721; d.

by 15 Feb. 1745; m. by Nov. 1743 Margaret, admnx. of Seaborn Tucker; admin. bond was posted 15 Feb. 1745 by Jacob Giles with Jonathan Jones and John Kemp, the wid. Margaret Litton having renounced; had iss.: ANN (named in the will of her grandfather Thomas) (3:294; 12:82; 35:80; 111:342).

LITTON, ISAAC (6), s. of Thomas (2), was b. 13 Feb. 1724/5; m. by 12 May 1746 Mary, extx. of Thomas Jones; in 1750 owned 50 a. Arabia Petrea and part Neighborhood (4:132; 153:69).

LLOYD, JOHN, m. by 3 Oct. 1737 Elizabeth, extx. of Theophilus Jones; d. leaving a will, 24 Feb. 1742 - 25 March 1743, naming w. Elizabeth and ch. Thomas and Isaac; admin. bond was posted 18 June 1743 by extx. Elizabeth Lloyd with William Dallam and William Andrew; Elizabeth Lloyd d. leaving a will, 19 Nov. 1748 - 17 Dec. 1748, naming Dr. Josias Middlemore and his s. Francis, Thomas Durbin, Mary Andrew w. of William Andrew and their dau. Billy Drew Andrew; ; ch. of John: THOMAS; and ISAAC (5:26; 12:77; 110:420; 127:223; 209-30:354).

LLOYD, PETER, shipwright, runaway conv. serv. from Brian Philpot and Thomas Ward, who came last year with Capt. Dobbins, was advert. for in June 1752 (307-69:130).

LLOYD, SARAH, servant to Samuel Cooper, was charged with bast. in March 1736 and tried in June 1737 (31:1, 56).

LOADER, RICHARD, m. Sarah Elliott on 2 Feb. 1733 (128:77).

LOBB, JOSEPH, of Balto. Co., d. leaving a will, 26 Jan. 1723/4 23 May 1724, naming w. Margaret as extx. and Richard Gardiner; d. 14 Feb. 1723; wid. Margaret m. 2nd, on 3 Sept. 1723, Simon Ward (124:166; 133:149, 193).

LOCHMAN, JACOB, was b. in Germany; was res. in Balto. Co. when he was naturalized on 20 May 1736 (303:43).

LOCK, WILLIAM, m. Jane (---), and had iss.: SUSANNAH, b. 2 May 1755; JANE, b. 30 April 1760 (133:98, 104).

LOCKARD, JOHN, m. Christiana Tippins on 24 Oct. 1739 (128:106).

LOCKERD, ANN, m. Mark Swift on 26 Dec. 1725 (131).

LOCKETT/LORKET, JOHN (1), was in Balto. Co. by 1692 as a taxable in s. side Patapsco Hund.; in 1692 as John Lorkett was named as a son-in-law in will of Richard Green or Guyn; d. leaving a will, 23 Jan. 1704/5 - 6 Feb. 1704/5, naming tracts Rockwell's Range, Brandan, and Chinckapin Forest, his est. in Eng., and ch. John (a minor), Robert, and Joane; admin. bond was posted 6 Feb. 1704/5 by John Rattenbury with Sebastian Oley and Ch. Kilbourne; est. was admin. by Dr. John Rattenbury on 2 Aug. 1706 and 30 Sept. 1706; dec. left iss.: ROBERT; JOHN; and JOANE (2:152, 234; 12:293; 121:65; 122:47; 150).

LOCKETT, ROBERT (2), s. of John (1), may be the Robert who in March 1721/2 chose William Frizzell to be his guardian (24:29).

LOCKETT, JOHN (3), s. of John (1), d. by 19 Aug. 1720 when admin. bond was posted by Lancelott Todd with Morris Baker and Chas. Rockhold; est. was inv. by Benj'n Howard and Jno. Ashman on 14 Sept. 1720 and val. at £ 4.7.0 and est. was admin. by Lancelott Todd on 12 Sept. 1721 and 15 Nov. 1722 (1:169, 202; 12:91; 48:148).

LOCKEY, JOHN, s. of John Lockey at Childrey near Wantage, Berks.,

Eng., was an indentured serv. with one more year to serve; in Balto Co. by 1756 (300-65:259).

LOCKWOOD, JOHN, was in Balto. Co. by 1694 as a taxable in s. side Patapsco Hund. (139).

LOCKYEAR, JOHN, of Balto. Co., yeoman, gave his age as 24 in 1759 (310:226).

LOCOCK/LOWCOCK, THOMAS, d. leaving a will, 15 Oct. 1756 - 12 Nov. 1756, naming John White; admin. bond was posted 26 Nov. 1756 by John White of Fork of Gunpowder, with John Fuller (12:73; 111:115).

LOE, JOSEPH, was in Balto. Co. by 1692 as a taxable in n. side Gunpowder (138).

LOFFERD, JNO., m. Isabella Ray on 14 April 1761 (131).

LOFTIN/LOFTON, WILLIAM (1) was in Balto. Co. by 1691; d. and was bur. on 13 April 1704; m. Elizabeth (---) who d. 20 Dec. 1703/4; on 26 Aug. 1697 he surv. 100 a. Brotherly Love with Richard Perkins on s. side Susquehanna; Loftin and Perkins also came to possess 100 a. of a 150 a. tract Johnson's Rest, which was later held by Loftin's orphans; on 16 Aug. 1701 William Loftin sold 200 a. Eightrupp to Daniel Johnson; William Lofton and his heirs were named in the 4 March 1703/4 will of James Ives; admin. bond on the est. of William Loftin was posted 22 June 1704 by John Hall, with James Phillips and Samuel Brown; est. was inv. on 3 July 1704 by Henry Jackson and Samuel Bond and val. at £ 42.7.0 plus 9853 lbs. tobacco; est. was admin. by Hall on 13 Feb. 1706; William and Elizabeth had iss.: THOMAS, b. 25 Nov. 1691; ISABELLA, b. 19 Dec. 1693; ANN, b. 10 Aug. 1696; WILLIAM, b. 12 Dec. 1699; ELIZABETH, b. 12 July 1702 (2:176, 218; 12:110; 54:27; 59:661; 122:30; 128:4, 8, 13, 18; 211).

LOFTIN, THOMAS (2), s. of William (1), was b. 25 Nov. 1691, and m. Eleanor (---) by whom he had iss.: ELIZABETH, b. 1 Jan. 1714; SARAH, b. 31 Oct. 1716; MARY, b. 10 Nov. 1718; RACHEL, b. 1 Oct. 1720 (128:39).

LOFTIN, ELIZABETH, was ind. for bast. in March 1731 (29:225).

THE LOGSDON FAMILY is the subject of a typescript by Edwin C. Welch entitled "The Maryland Logsdon Family," compiled in 1940 and deposited at the Maryland Historical Society; the typescript is hereinafter cited as Welch.

LOGSDON, WILLIAM (1), progenitor, may have come to Md. c.1674 as Welch suggests but he does not appear in the tax lists for 1692, 1694, 1695 or 1699 through 1703; first appears in 1704 as a taxable in the upper part of the n. side of Patapsco as William "Lodsdean;" Welch also suggests that William Logsdon may have been referred to in early records as William "Loftin," because of the similarity of the names, and because both Loftin and Logsdon owned tracts called Brotherly Love; Logsdon surv. 100 a. Bedford in May 1707 and Logsdon's Addition in Jan. 1719/20; in Sept. 1726 Logsdon and w. conv. a portion of the latter tract, now called Pleasant Green, to their dau. Ann w. of Samuel Durbin; in 1709 Logsdon sued Thomas Gwynn for breach of contract because Gwynn had not finished building a 40 foot tobacco shed on The Island; served on the Baltimore County Grand Jury in 1729; d. by March 1742 when his sons William, John, and Edward, and their respective spouses Ann, Sarah, and Margaret, all of P. G. (now Fred.) Co., sold Brotherly Love to George Couts; this tract had been surveyed on 22 May 1730; at the sale of this tract, Honour, wid. of William Logsdon, Sr., released her right of dower; William and w. Honour were the par. of: PRUDENCE, by 1735 James Kelly; ANN, m. by 1723 Samuel Durbin; WILLIAM, m. Ann Davis; JOHN, m. Margaret Wooley; EDWARD, m. Sarah; THOMAS; m. Mary; and HONOR, m. Richard Fowler in 1730 (146; 398:39; Welch, pp. 5-6).

LOGSDON, WILLIAM (2), s. of William (1), m. Ann, dau. of Henry Davis; in 1750 owned 100 a. Bonner's Delight; on 16 May 1758 with w. Anne conv. Edward Norwood 100 a. Nancy's Fancy; had iss.: COMFORT, b. 27 Feb. 1731; ANN, b. 13 Feb. 1733; prob. WILLIAM (83: 237; 133:28, 37; 153:57; Welch).

LOGSDON, JOHN (3), s. of William (1), m. 1st, on 9 Oct. 1735, Margaret, dau. of John Wooley; and 2nd, by 1743, Sarah (---); gave his age as 78 in 1793 (133:154; 231-WG#NN:406; Welch)

LOGSDON, EDWARD (4), s. of William (1), m. Sarah (---), who in March 1742 joined him in selling Brotherly Love to George Couts (Welch).

LOGSDON, THOMAS (5), s. of William (1), m. by 18 July 1747 Mary (---) who joined him in selling Molly's Industry to John Cryder; on 18 June 1752 Logsdon and w. Mary and Thomas Bond conv. 100 a. Wooley's Range to John Jackson; had iss.: MALINDA, m. c.1772 James Welch; JOSEPH, served as Guide to Gen. Washington; THOMAS, d. after May 1818 in Barren Co., Ky.; WILLIAM, d. c.1808/10; JOHN; and a dau., m. c.1772 John Durbin (79:462; 81:426; Welch).

LOGUE, JAMES, serv. with 3 years and 9 mos. to serve, listed in the 1747 inv. of Edward Day (54:226).

LOMAX, THOMAS (1), m. Ann Hakman in Jan. 1726; d. by 4 June 1740 when William Dallam posted admin. bond with John Paca and James Phillips; had iss.: THOMAS, b. 22 Feb. 1731; THEOPHILUS, b. 25 Dec. 1737 (12:99; 32:266; 131:65/r).

LOMAX, THOMAS (2), s. of Thomas (1), was b. 22 Feb. 1731; would be age 9 in Feb. 1740/1 when in Nov. 1740 he was bound to Charles Baker; m. Sarah Downey on 11 Feb. 1755 (32:353; 131).

LOMAX, THEOPHILUS (3), s. of Thomas (1), was b. 25 Dec. 1737; bound to John Morris in Nov. 1740; and was age 7 in Nov. 1745 when bound to Capt. William Young (32:351; 35:740).

LONEY, WILLIAM (1), progenitor, was in Balto. Co. by 1694 as a taxable in Spesutia Hund.; m. 1st, by 22 April 1700, Jane, dau. an and sole heir of Thomas Overton; m. 2nd on 27 April 1706 Arabella dau. of John Walston; d. by 8 Sept. 1720 when admin. bond was posted by Arabella Loney, with Francis Holland, William Cook, and Benjamin Osborne; est. was inv. on 8 Sept. 1720 by Thomas Cord (or Carr) and Jno. Clark and val. at £ 98.2.9; wid. Arabella m. 2nd Bennett Garrett, who d. by Sept. 1741; William had iss.: (by 1st w.): BETHIA, m. James Barnes of Harford Co.; (by 2nd w.): MARGARET, b. 15 July 1708, m. John Watkins; WILLIAM, d. young; JOHN; BENJAMIN (3:274; 4:97; 12:290; 48:173; 66:54, 81; 128:28; 129:16; 139).

LONEY, JOHN (2), s. of William (1) and Arabella, was b. 22 April 1711, and m. 1st, on 22 Dec. 1737, Sarah Denson; m. 2nd, by 11 Sept. 1751, Mary, admnx. of Hugh Carlisle whose est. Mary Loney on 15 May 1752, 22 Sept. 1753, and 14 April 1756; John Loney d. leaving a will, 25 May 1764 - 27 May 1766; admin. bond was posted 3 Sept. 1766 by admnx. Mary Loney, with Andrew Lendrum and John Henry; est. was admin. 7 Sept. 1767; dec. left iss.: WILLIAM, b. 20 May 1738; JOHN, b. 19 Feb. 1739; STEPHEN, b. 25 June 1742; AMOS and one other child, unnamed (5:232, 289, 295; 7:347; 12:68; 112: 35; 128:101, 106; 129:299, 331; 209-35:79).

LONEY, BENJAMIN (3), s. of William (1), m. Ann Norris on 7 May 1745; on 1 Feb. 1742 he admin. the est. of his sis. Margaret Watkins; on 9 Nov. 1742 he admin. est. of her husb. John Watkins; named as a son of William Loney in the admin. acct. of the est. of Benjamin Garrett (3:263, 264, 274; 131).

THE LONG FAMILY is discussed in Helen E. Davis' Kindred, but this compiler has drawn some different conclusions, based on his examination of the data.

LONG, THOMAS (1), progenitor was in Balto. Co. as early as 19 May 1672, and d. by Nov. 1692; he m. (perhaps as a second w.) Jane (---), wid. of 1st (---) Waites, and 2nd John Dixon; was named as one of the Commissioners of Balto. Co.; in April 1676 was summoned as sheriff of Balto. Co.; and in Sept. 1686 was named as one of the officers of "Middle Town in Middle River;" his public career can be traced in the published Archives of Maryland; in Nov. 1673 he surv. 75 a. Turkey Neck and an unnamed 475 a.; in June 1681 he conv. 100 a. Hopewell to his wife's son-in-law Francis Watkins; in June 1682 Thomas Scudamore and w. Abigail sold Thomas Long, now called Thomas Long, Gent., 136 a. out of a 420 a. tract called Dickenson, being the plantation where Long now lived in right of his wife, and which was formerly the plantation of John Dickson; the same month Long and w. Jane sold to Thomas Peart 100 a. of the 457 a. tract Northwick which had been taken up by Long; he also surv. 185 a. Hopewell in June 1676 and 111 a. Long Port in June 1683; Davis, in Kindred, stated that Long was dead by 1686, leaving a will which named sons John, Robert, George, and Thomas, but this must be a different Thomas Long since the one in question was alive in May 1687 when he was again named Sheriff of Balto. Co.; d. by Nov. 1692 when his wid. Jane Long instituted legal action against John Hayes; his est. was admin. in Oct. 1694; est. was val. at £ 104.10.0 and after debts were paid there was a balance of £ 33.10.5; Jane Long d. leaving a will, 19 May 1696 - 3 June 1696, naming dau. Jane Peake, s. Thomas, dau. Tabitha (not to marry George Chancey), granddau. Penelope Scudamore, grandson George Peake, and also Lettice Robinson, Joseph Peake, Susanna Robinson, and John Wilkinson; her est. was admin. on 6 March 1697 by Joseph Peake and w. Jane, and again on 24 June 1702 by Jane, now w. of Charles Merryman; Thomas and Jane had iss.: THOMAS; JANE, m. 1st Joseph Peake, and 2nd Charles Merryman, Jr,, and 3rd Benjamin Knight; TABITHA, may have m. Thomas Sheredine who had a w. Tabitha and who admin. the est. of Thomas Long, Jr.; and poss. GALVILLA, m. by June 1702 (---) King; Thomas may have also had a s. JOHN, by an earlier marr. (2:34, 52, 216; 4:2; 64:121, 170, 183; 106:289; 121:100; 200-5:503; 200-51: 74, 79; 200-65; 200-67; 200-69; 206-13A:226; 211).

LONG, JOHN (2), poss. s. of Thomas (1), may be the John Long, "son and heir of Thomas Long of Baltimore County, deceased," who on 29 Oct. 1745 sold 457 a. Northwick (assigned to Thomas Long, and part of which descended to the said John by the death of Thomas), to Christopher Duke (79:8).

LONG, THOMAS (3), s. of Thomas (1) and Jane, d. in Balto. Co. by 1721; having m. Susanna Mead, who m. as her 2nd husband Stephen Body on 3 April 1722; in June 1693 was ind.by the Grand Jury for threatening to burn down the Court House; on 5 Sept. 1706 Thomas and Susanna deeded 733 a. Jacob's Choice to James Crooke; est. of Thomas Long was inv. in 1721, and in 1722 Thomas Sheredine, Long's admin., was summoned to answer a complaint of John Gorsuch;

est. was admin. by Thomas Sheredine on 3 Dec. 1724; Susanna Long
had relinquished her right to administer the est. on 13 Jan.
1720/1; dec. left iss.: JOHN; poss. ANN, m. Nicholas Hale, Jr.,
on 25 Dec. 1723 (2:372; 19:428; 24:63; 25:73; 59:544; 133:147,
148).

LONG, JOHN (4), s. of Thomas (3) and Susanna, d. in Balto. Co.
in 1759 having m. Eleanor Owings on 8 March 1735; she was a dau.
of Lewis and Elizabeth (Gurney) Owings; Eleanor's mother m. 1st
Lewis Owings, 2nd, on 10 Feb. 1723 Stephen Body, and 3rd, Luke
Trotten; on 6 March 1733 Long sold part of Ballstone to Stephen
Body; on 6 June 1733 he sold part of the same tract to Joseph Ward;
on 25 Sept. 1740 he and Eleanor sold part of Ballstone to Buckler
Partridge, and on 8 Jan. 1743 John and Eleanor sold 450 a., part
Dixon's Neck, to Thomas Stansbury, Jr.; in 1750 Long owned 136 a.
part Dickinson, 11½ a. Rocky Point, and 250 a. Privilege; he d.
leaving a will, 30 May 1759 - 25 July 1759, naming sons John and
Joshua (to have all lands), w. Eleanor, dau. Susanna Trotten,
and mentioned his "five youngest children;" est. was admin. by
Eleanor Long who named dec.'s dau. Susanna Trotten, a dau. who
m. John Murray, and the dec.'s six children in all; known iss.:
SUSANNA, b. c.1736/7, m. Luke Trotten on 10 Feb. 1754; RUTH, m.
John Murray; ELEANOR, b. 15 Sept. 1749; JOHN, b. 13 Jan. 1753;
JEANE, b. 6 Oct. 1756; JOSHUA, b. 13 May 1759 (4:342; 73:378;
74:29; 75:449; 79:8; 111:311; 133:88, 97, 100, 107, 155, 166;
313:102).

LONG, (---), m. by 6 July 1723, Jane, extx. of John Teal (1:
92).

LONG, BENJAMIN, in March 1740 conv. to Joseph Taylor and Sarah
Fell part of The Forest, orig. granted to Long and Neal Haile;
in 1750 owned 50 a. Addition to Painter's Den; on 2 Oct. 1761 he
conv. 50 a. Knight's Addition to John Daughaday (79:410; 85:340;
153:88).

LONG, JOHN, d. at William Bond's, 15 Nov. 1720 (131).

LONG, JOHN, of Cecil Co., on 5 Sept. 1732 was sold part of
John's Beginning by John Muckeldory (73:280).

LONG, JOHN, m. Blanch Whitaker on 31 Jan. 1748 (131).

LONG, JOHN, in 1750 owned 234 a. Proctor's Hall and the Enlargement (153:56).

LONG, JOHN, on 3 Oct. 1760 conv. 113 a. Lewis' Refuse to John
Struthers (84:373).

LONG, JOHN, m. by 22 Sept. 1753 Mary, admnx. of Rev. Hugh
Carlisle (201-35:174)

LONG, JOSIAS, of Balto. Co., imm. c.1672 (388).

LONG, MARY, unmarried, in March 1721/2 named Jonathan Newgate
as the father of her child (24:9).

LONG, MOSES, runaway serv. from Samuel Hart of Patapsco, talked
"broad Yorkshire," was advert. for in Aug. 1746; m. Margaret Grace
Worbleton on 30 March 1752 (131; 384:572).

LONG, SUSANNA, m. Edward Riston on 3 April 1722 (133:147).

LONG, WILLIAM, was in Balto. Co. by 1692 as a taxable in Spesutia Hund. (138).

LONGLAND, RICHARD, was in Balto. Co. as a servant of John Boring in March 1683/4 when he was judged to be 13 years old; was a
taxable in n. side Patapsco Hund. in 1694; on 22 April 1702 purch.
100 a. Wells Angles from Joseph and Katherine Wells; 3 Aug. 1705
was mentioned when John Hayes directed his w. Elizabeth to make
205 a. of land over to Longland; on 5 Sept. 1705 John Hayes and
w. Elizabeth conv. 100 a. Longland's Purchase (part of Privilege)
to Richard Longland; d. leaving a will, 15 Oct. 1709 - 27 Feb.
1709/10, naming dau. Alice and poss. unborn ch.; admin. bond was
posted 5 Dec. 1709 by Selah Dorman with Benj. Bowen and John Boring; est. was inv. by said Bowen and Boring in 1710, and val. at
£ 42.9.0; est. was admin. by Dorman on 13 July 1713 and 1 Nov.
1714; had dau.; ALICE (1:16; 2:4; 12:40; 18:128; 54:1; 60:187;
64:15; 66:142; 122:160; 139).

LONGMAN, JOHN, son of Mary, was b. 21 Feb. 1728 (131:11/r).

LONGMAN, MARY, in June 1718 named Elias Burchfield as the father of her child; Burchfield admitted paternity in Aug. 1718; she
bore another ch. in June 1722 (22:270; 23:3; 24:179).

LORAH, HENRY, was in Balto. Co. by 1694 as a taxable in n. side
Patapsco Hund. (139).

LORKITT.   See LOCKETT.

LORKINGS, JOHN, m. Eliza who joined in admin. est. of Jno.
Enlows (2:230).

LORRESON, ELEANOR, m. Thomas Temple on 17 April 1699 (129:186).

LOTTEN/LOTON, JACOB, was in Balto. Co. by 1692 as a taxable in
Spesutia Hund.; d. leaving a will, 20 March 1693 - 16 April 1694,
naming w. Eliza as extx. and ment. three ch.; est. was inv. on 9
April 1694 by George Oldfield and Francis Smith, and val. at £178.
11.10; est. was admin. on 20 May 1695 by extx. Elizabeth who m.
by Sept. 1695 William York; had iss.: three children, unnamed
(20:490; 48:196; 121:81; 138; 206-13A:313).

LOUCHLY, SELINA, was fined for bast. in Nov. 1758 and had iss.:
ELIZABETH (46:162).

LOUGH.   See LOWE.

LOVE, ROBERT (1), progenitor, was in Balto. Co., where he d.
1692; may be the Robert who was transp. c.1652; on 3 June 1697
purch. 300 a. Charles' Purchase from Nicholas Gassaway; d. leaving a will, 26 March 1692 - 7 June 1692, naming sons John and
Robert, and mentioning other children; had iss.: JOHN; ROBERT;
TAMAR, m. William Wilkinson; poss. WILLIAM; poss. MARY (60; 121:
51; 388).

LOVE, JOHN (2), s. of Robert (1), d. c.1708/9 in Balto. Co.;
m. Alice (---), wid. of (---) Brashar, by whom she had a s. John;
in June 1692 pet. the court for admin. of the est. of his father
Robert Love, dec.; d. leaving a will, 2 March 1708 - 2 April 1709,
naming s. Robert, wife's s. John Brasher, daus. Constant and Tamar
Love, w. Alice, and bro.-in-law William Wilkinson; admin. bond
was posted 2 April 1709 by extx. Alice Love, with William Wilkinson and Moses Groome; est. was admin. by extx. Alice Love on 19
Aug. 1711; had iss.: ROBERT; CONSTANT, m. Sutton Sickelmore; TAMAR
m. Thomas Lowe on Feb. 1728/9; and ANNE (1:249; 12:42; 19:184;
122:131).

LOVE, ROBERT (3), s. of Robert (1), d. by 1704, having m. 1st,

c.1693 Sarah, dau. of Thomas Thurston, and 2nd Elizabeth (---)
who m. as her second husband Daniel Scott; surv. Lovely Hill on
18 June 1695, surv. Forest of Bucks on 25 Aug. 1699; came to
poss. 600 a. Littleton and 200 a. Come By Chance, both of which
were formerly owned by Thomas Thurston; on 6 June 1693 Love gave
bond to w. Sarah for legacies she had been left by her father
Thomas Thurston; on 7 Dec. 1697 Robert and Sarah conv. 150 a.
Whitticar's Ridge to John Whitticar; d. by 25 March 1704 when adm
admin. bond was posted by Eliza Love with John Whitticar and Wm.
Howard; est. was inv. in 1704 by Nicholas Day and John Deaver
and val. at ℓ 85.2.9; est. was admin. by Eliza, now w. of Daniel
Scott on 15 Sept. 1707 and 14 March 1709; dec. left iss.: MARY,
in Aug. 1709 was bound to Rev. John Edwards, minister of St.
George's Par., to age 16 or until she married (2:109, 180; 12:
111; 19:415, 489; 21:50; 50:142; 61:182; 211; 340:139).

LOVE, WILLIAM (4), poss. s. of Robert (1), d. in Balto. Co.
by 2 March 1708/9; m. Ann (---) who m. as her 2nd husb. John
McComas; may have m. 1st Arabella Walston on 27 April 1706; d.
leaving a will, 23 Feb. 1708 - 2 March 1708/9, naming w. Ann,
kinswoman Mary Love, and ordering his dau. to be christened Juliana, with William Howard as exec.; also mentioned tracts 200 a.
Come By Chance, one-half of Salisbury Plains and the land where
his wife's father lived; admin. bond was posted 10 May 1709 by
exec. William Howard with John Edwards and John Deaver; est. of
William Love was admin. on 10 June 1710; by March 1719/20 his wid.
Ann had m. John McComas; had iss.: JULIANA, in March 1719/20
was taken from William and Martha Burney and placed with her
mother and her stepfather (2:160, 163; 12:108; 23:280; 122:117;
129:201).

LOVE, MARY (5), poss. dau. of Robert (1), in March 1692/3
was left all the testator's property in the will of William Hill,
if Mary would be his housekeeper and repair to the house where
William's father John Hill, now dec., used to live; Mary, wid.
of William Hill married 2nd Benjamin Lego(59:383).

LOVE, ROBERT (6), s. of John (2) and Alice, d. c.1739; on 9
June 1729 he m. Sarah Bond, dau. of William and Mary Bond; after
Love's death she m. Walter Billingsley; on 3 March 1725 Robert
conv. 100 a. part of Pork Forest, to Charles Baker, Jr.; in Nov.
1739 was referred to as son-in-law of William Bond; d. by 8 Aug.
1739 when admin. bond was posted by admnx. Sarah Love with Thomas
Johnson and Abraham Jarrard; est. admin. by Sarah Love, one of
the people called Quakers, on 20 July 1741; Sarah m. William Billingsley by March 1743/4 when her 2nd husb. posted bond he would
pay John, Tamar, and Ruth Love their share of their father's est.;
had iss.; JOHN; WILLIAM, b. 22 Dec. 1731, may have d. by 1742;
TAMAR, b. 10 Nov. 1732; SARAH, b. 5 March 1734; RUTH, b. 11 May
1739 (4:121; 12:98; 32:79, 162; 70:231; 77:5, 6, 7; 128:71, 89,
103).

LOVE, JOHN (7), s. of Robert (6), was prob. the John Love
who conv. 100 a. Pork Forest to Charles Baker in 1755; also may
be the John Love who was named by Clara Billingsley in Nov. 1756
as the father of her child (41:312; 85:438).

LOVE, JEAN LAND(?), poss. w. of William, d. 12 March 1704/5
(128:21).

LOVE, MILES, was b. c.1720, in 1749 was a serv. in the inv.
of James Carroll Croxall; in March 1775 advert. he would not pay
debts of his w. Rachel (58; 255:37).

LOVEALL, HENRY, preacher, was in Balto. Co. by 1742 when Henry
Sater conv. him and some others 1 a. of Sater's Addition on which
to build a meeting house and 50 a. Addition to Budd's Progress; at
the same time John Sumner conv. him 1 a. of land; m. Martha (---)
who in April 1749 joined him in sale of 50 a. Addition to Budd's
Prospect to Thomas Sligh (77:238, 240, 482; 80:215).

LOVEALL, ZEBULON, purch. 50 a. Chestnut Level from Richard
Richards in March 1754 (82:174).

LOVELL, JOHN, was in Balto. Co. by 1692 as a taxable in n.
side of Patapsco; d. by 1699 when his est. was inv. by John Rouse
and Nicholas Fitzsimmons and val. at E 9.3.0 plus 1200 lbs. tobacco in debts (48:120; 138).

LOVELL, MARTHA, m. John Jones on 8 July 1695 (129:177).

LOVEPITSTOW, ROBERT, m. Ann (---) and had iss.: MARY, b. 20
May 1737 (133:57).

LOVETT, RICHARD, was in Balto. Co. by 1692 as a taxable in
Spesutia Hund. (138).

LOVINGTON, RICHARD, m. Martha Warren on 14 June 1736 (133:155).

LOWCOCK. See LOCOCK.

LOWE, WILLIAM (1), progenitor, was in Balto. Co. by 1702; surv.
100 a. Lough's (Lowe's) Lot in Nov. 1705; m. Rebecca (---) and d.
by 15 June 1719 when admin. bond was posted by John Lowe, with
William Lowe and Thomas Norris, William Lowe having ren. right to
admin. his father's est.; est. was inv. 23 June 1719 by Garrett
Garrettson and Richard Burrough; had iss.: WILLIAM; JOHN; JAMES,
b. 29 June 1702; THOMAS, b. 5 Feb. 1706; SAMUEL, b. 16 Jan. 1707/8
and ABRAHAM, b. 19 Jan. 1709/10 (12:104; 48:253; 128:35; 207).

LOWE, WILLIAM (2), s. of William (1), was made guardian of his
younger bro. Thomas in Aug. 1719; m. 1st, on 6 July 1710, Temperance, dau. of William Pickett (and is mentioned in the admin. of
the latter's est. in Sept. 1724 and Oct. 1726); m. 2nd, on 28 Feb.
1736, Sarah, admnx. of George Graves; d. leaving a will, 21 April
1743 - 6 March 1743/4, naming w. Sarah and ch.: William, John,
Thomas, Samuel, Elizabeth, Mary, Sarah, Rachel, and Ann; admin.
bond was posted 6 March 1743 by the extx. Sarah Lowe with George
Elliott and Sarah Mortimore; est. admin. 2 April 1745 by Sarah.
Sarah, now w. of Lewis Lafue or Lafee; had iss. (one def. by 1st
w., and last two def. by 2nd w.): SARAH, b. 22 March 1714; JOHN;
THOMAS; MARY; RACHEL; ELIZABETH, b. 3 June 1721; WILLIAM, b. 6
Aug. 1727; ANN, b. 5 Feb. 1735; SAMUEL, b. 18 Dec. 1739 (2:318;
3:15; 4:33; 5:35; 12:94, 104; 23:209; 129:209; 131).

LOWE, JOHN (3), s. of William (1), gave his age as 46 in 1733;
m. Elizabeth (---) who joined him in Oct. 1715 signing the inv.
of Alice Demondidier as kin; on 12 Sept. 1715 Daniel Johnson left
a watermill to John Lowe and heirs, but John Lowe's w. was not to
share with the other ch. of Johnson in the residue of Johnson's
est.; on 6 June 1734 John and Elizabeth conv. 50 a. Paradice to
John White; had iss.: SARAH, b. 23 Jan. 1714; prob. DANIEL JOHN-
SON LOWE, who in Jan. 1743 was a res. of Prince William Co., Va.,
when he conv. 200 a. Chevy Chase to Edward Evans (52:4; 74:71;
80:385; 123:65; 131).

LOWE, JAMES (4), s. of William (1), was b. 29 June 1702; d.
by 5 March 1747 when admin. bond was posted by Cornelius Steward
with John Murra and Arthur Brownley; m. by 5 Aug. 1735 Mary (---)

who joined him in conv. 50 a. Lowe's Range, now called Whitehead's Folly, to Robert Whitehead; his est. was admin. 26 and 28 May 1750 by Cornelius Howard or Steward; left iss.: REBECCA, b. c. 1732, m. William Perdue; MARY, b. c.1734; JAMES, b. c.1737; ISA-BELLA, b. c.1739; HANNAH, b. c.1742 (4:321; 5:165; 12:86; 74:278).

LOWE, THOMAS (5), s. of William (1), was b. 5 Feb. 1706; was age 14 in Aug. 1719 when he bound himself to his bro. William to age 21 to learn trade of carpenter; m. Thamar Love in 1728/9; was ind. for bast. in June 1734; prob. had dau.: TAMAR, m. William Clark on 7 Dec. 1749 (23:209; 30:253; 131).

LOWE, SAMUEL (6), s. of William (1), was b. 16 Jan. 1707/8; d. by 3 July 1736 when admin. bond was posted by John Grimes, admin., with Thomas Smithson and John Huggins (12:101).

LOWE, ELIZABETH, serv. to Richard Deaver, who agreed to keep her and her s. John Lowe in June 1725; had s. JOHN (27:244).

LOWE, ELIZABETH, had dau.: KEZIAH, b. 4 Jan. 1749 (129:359).

LOWE, HUGH, m. Mary Freeman on 5 June 1729, and had: HUGH, b. 18 Jan. 1732 (131:12/r, 47/r).

LOWE, HUGH, m. Penelope Marsh on 18 Sept. 1755 (131).

LOWE, ISAAC, m. Sarah Mitchell on 5 Nov. 1761 (131).

LOWE, JOHN, m. Susanna Cox in March 1744; had iss.: JOHN, b. 27 Jan. 1745 (131:26, 113/r).

LOWE, JOHN, m. c.1750 Flora Dorsey, and had iss.: NICHOLAS, b. c.1763 (381).

LOWE, JOSEPH, was in Balto. Co. by 1694 as a taxable in Spesutia Hund. (139).

LOWE, JOSEPH, nailor, ran away from John Harris, III, at Ellicott's Lower Mill; had a wife near Upper Cross Roads, Balto. Co. (307-69:130).

LOWE, RALPH, m. Ruth (---); admin. the est. of Daniel Collett on 9 Nov. 1733; had iss.: JOHN, b. 14 Dec. 1723; ABRAHAM, b. 26 Jan. 1725 (3:128; 128:98).

LOWE, THOMAS, was in Balto. Co. by 1694 as a taxable in Spesutia Hund. (139).

LOWE, THOMAS, m. by 24 April 1704, Elizabeth, admnx. of John Shields (1:346).

LOWE, THOMAS, m. Sarah Mainer in Jan. 1754 (131).

LOWE, WILLIAM, m. Mary (---), and had iss.: ANN, b. 8 Oct. 1742; CHARLES, b. 27 Jan. 1745; and ALEXANDER, b. 7 Feb. 1747 (133:78, 84).

LOWE, WILLIAM, m. Ann Davis, dau. of William, and sis. of Henry Davis, on 30 Jan. 1746 (131; 210-37:585).

LOWLER, HENRY, was in Balto. Co. by 1695 as a taxable in n. side Patapsco Hund. (140).

LOWRY, EDWARD, d. 28 April 1723; m. Ann Jenkins on 16 Aug. 1722; she m. William Glaspin on 21 Feb. 1729; Sarah was extx. of William Jenkins (2:355; 128:71).

LOYALL, JOHN, was made levy free in March 1745/6 (35:802).

LUCAS, RACHEL, orphan serv. of Thomas Chamberlain, was to be set free as he had not taught her to read, Nov. 1718 (23:35).

LUMBARD, GEORGE, d. 17 Jan. 1738 (128:92/b).

LUMBER, JOSHUA, was in Balto. Co. by 1692 as a taxable in n. s. side Patapsco Hund. (138).

LUMLEY, ALEXANDER, was in Balto. Co. by 9 May 1688 when he purch. 200 a. Davis' Lot from Joseph and Jane Conaway; d. by 16 Dec. 1699 when admin. bond was posted by Charles Carroll of Annap., with William Bladen; est. was inv. on 29 Jan. 1699 by Thomas Hammond and Nathaniel Stinchcomb and val. at £ 101.7.2; the inv. mentions a servant sent by Madam Lumley's mother to Madam Lumley's dau. (12:112; 48:52; 63:279).

LUSBY/LISBY, ROBERT (1), imm. to Md. c.1662 with w. Dorothy and ch.: Elizabeth, Jacob, and Sarah; surv. 50 a. in A. A. Co. called Lusby; d. leaving a will, 26 Feb. 1674 - 19 May 1674, naming w. Dorothy (to have Georgetown), and ch. Jacob, Zachariah, Robert, and Sarah; had iss.: ELIZABETH; JACOB; SARAH; ROBERT; and ZACHARIAH (120:89; 211; 388).

LUSBY, JACOB (2), s. of Robert (1), was b. by 1662; d. in A. A. Co. leaving a will, 12 March 1708/9 - 19 July 1709, naming bro. Robert, and these ch.: JOHN (eld. son); ROBERT; THOMAS; HANNAH, m. (---) Johnson; MARY; and RUTH (122:142).

LUSBY, ROBERT (3), s. of Robert (1), is prob. the Robert Lusby, planter, who d. in A. A. Co. in 1733; m. 1st, by 20 Sept. 1700, Mary, granddau. of Stephen Johnson; m. 2nd, on 21 Aug. 1707, Mary Baldwin; d. leaving a will, 2 June 1733 - 25 Aug. 1733, naming tracts Chilberry Hall (in Balto. Co.) and Georgetown (in A. A. Co.), and these ch.: ROBERT; JACOB; MARY, m. (---) Turpine; HANNAH, m. George Drew on 26 July 1722; NAOMI, m. William Ghiselin on 29 June 1726; SUSANNA; MILCAH; ZACHARY; DRAPER; HENRY; and JOSEPH (121:288; 126:44; 129:246; 219-2:372).

LUSBY, JACOB (4), s. of Jacob (2); m. Ellenor (---) and had iss., named in his will, 28 July 1730 - 7 Dec. 1732: JACOB; JOHN; AARON; THOMAS; SAMUEL; RACHEL; MARY; and ELLENOR (125:239).

LUSBY, ROBERT (5), s. of Robert (3), on 8 June 1733 inherited part of Chilberry Hall from his father; on 11 March 1742 was co-admin. of the est. of George Drew (3:266, 267; 126:44).

LUSBY, JACOB (6), s. of Robert (3), on 8 June 1733 inher. part of Chilberry Hall from his father; d. by Sept. 1763; m. Elizabeth who admin. his est. on 11 Sept. 1763 and 11 Sept. 1765; in 1750 owned 125 a. part Chilberry Hall, and 111 a. Ditto Resurveyed; had iss.: ANN, b. 3 Nov. 1730; MARY, b. 2 Oct. 1732; SARAH, b. 21 Oct. 1735, prob. d. young; ROBERT, b. 6 March 1737; ELIZABETH, b. 26 Feb. 1739; JOHN, b. 27 June 1742; JOSEPH, b. 28 Aug. 1744; SUSANNA, b. c.1746; MILCAH, b. c.1748; SARAH, b. c. 1751 (6:62, 173; 131:46/r, 110/r; 153:61).

LUSBY, DANIEL, age 14, in March 1740/1 was bound to Christopher Gist (33:3).

LUSBY, JOSEPH, was a res. of Balto. Co. on 23 May 1751 (385: 130).

LUSBY, THOMAS, in 1750 owned 60 a. Lusby's Advantage and 52 a. Fain's Forest (153:102).

LUSBY, ZACHARIAH, d. by 26 March 1739 when admin. bond was
posted by Vachel Denton with John Brice and Edward Fottrell;
est. was admin. by Denton on 24 March 1743 (3:335; 12:88).

THE LUX FAMILY and its English origins were discussed in
"Lux Family Records," in "Maryland Genealogical Records Committee,
vol. VII," pp. 341 ff., at the NSDAR Library in Washington.

LUX, WILLIAM (1), was a res. of Ippleden, Co. Devon, England;
m. Wilmot (---), who survived him; she d. leaving a will, 30
Sept. 1703 - 12 June 1704 (found in the Probate Division of H. M.
Court of Justice at Exeter), naming grandch. William, Darby,
Richard, John, Elizabeth, and Frances (ch. of her s. William),
three daus. of her s. Richard, and these ch.: WILLIAM; RICHARD;
WILMOT; JOHN; ELIZABETH, m. (---) Bowden; and MARY ("Lux Family
Records").

LUX, WILLIAM (2), s. of William (1), was b. c.1657, and at age
18 matric. at Baliol College, Oxford, stating he was a s. of Wm.
of Ippleden, Co. Devon; received his BA in 1678 and MA in 1682;
served as Vicar of Kenton, Devonshire; d. leaving a will, 16 Feb.
1714/5 - 23 March 1714/5, naming s. Darby (to have his est. after
the death of testator's w. Elizabeth), sons William and Richard
(to pursue bachelor's degrees); m. Elizabeth (---) and had iss.
(baptisms of children found in Kenton Parish, Devonshire): WILLIAM
bapt. 11 April 1695; DARBY, bapt. 30 June 1696; MARY, bapt. 23
Feb. 1697 (may have d. young); RICHARD, bapt. 30 June 1697; JOHN,
bapt. 19 May 1698; ELIZABETH, bapt. 14 March or 30 Sept. 1699;
FRANCIS, bapt. 7 May 1702; THOMAS, bapt. 6 June 1704; BENJAMIN,
bapt. 14 March 1705; MARY, bapt. 28 Nov. 1707; JANE, bapt. 15 May
1709 ("Lux Family Records;" Foster, Alumni Oxoniensis; Records
of Kenton Parish, Devonshire entered in the International Genealogy Index of the LDS).

LUX, DARBY (3), s. of William (2), was b. 15 June 1695, bapt.
30 June 1696 at Kenton Par., Devonshire, Eng.; d. 14 Oct. 1750
in Balto. Co.; m. 16 May 1722 in All Hallows Par., A. A. Co.,
Md., Ann Saunders, b. 16 May 1700, d. c.1785, dau. of Robert and
Rebecca Saunders; sea captain and one of the Baltimore Town Commissioners; in 1750 owned 2 lots in Balto. Town, 10 a. Mactington,
450 a. Darbyshire, 100 a. part Groome's Chance, and Lux's Conveni-
ency; his obit. stated he d. of pleurisy in his 53rd year having
served as a magistrate and representative of Balto. Co.; d. leaving a will, 9 Oct. 1750 - 2 Nov. 1750, naming w. Ann, s. William,
daus. Mary, Sarah, Jane, and Elizabeth Bowly; admin. bond was
posted by Ann and William Lux, execs., with Alexander Lawson ;
est. was admin. 10 April 1751; had iss.: WILLIAM; ELIZABETH, b.
1725, d. Jan. 1793, m. Daniel Bowly; MARY; SARAH JANE, b. 1738,
d. 5 Aug. 1817, m. Alexander Stewart on 12 Sept. 1757; ROBERT;
JANE; DARBY; ANN, m. 21 Sept. 1751 Nicholas Ruxton Gay; REBECCA
w. of (---) Hughes; and FRANCES, b. 1747, m. William Russell
(5:279; 12:81; 153:67; 210-27:403; 219-1:90; 262; 392:129).

LYAL, THOMAS, d. 27 Dec. 1726 (128:67).

LYAL, WILLIAM, in 1721 was conv. 100 a. Stone's Delight by
Richard Taylor; m. by 8 June 1727 Elizabeth (---) who in June
1727 joined him in selling the above tract to Richard Huett (69:
402; 71:9).

LYALL, JOHN, m. Ann Muture on 2 Feb. 1717; made levy free in
March 1745/6; his w. Ann d. May 1736; had iss.: THOMAS, b. 13
April 1721; ANN, b. 22 May 1724; John m. 2nd, on 16 Aug. 1736,
Elizabeth Farmer, and had iss.: ELIZABETH, b. 23 Aug. 1741 (128:
48, 98; 129:324).

LYLES, ELIZABETH, was ind. for bast. in Aug. 1728 (28:22).

LYLEY, JAMES, m. Margaret Painter on 14 Aug. 1738 (128:92b).

LYNCH, MARCUS (1), d. in Balto. Co. leaving 100 a. Limbrick (Limerick?) to his kinsman Robuck Lynch, whose ch., Patrick, William, and Mary, on 6 Aug. 1728 conv. the said tract to John Bevan (71:160).

LYNCH, ROBUCK (2), kinsman of Marcus (1), was in Balto. Co. by 1694 as a taxable in n. side Patapsco Hund.; m. (poss. as 2nd w.) Mary (---); d. leaving a will, 16 June 1714 - 12 Nov. 1716, naming ch. Patrick (a minor, to live with his mother-in-law), Anne, William, and Mary, w. Mary; admin. bond was posted 12 Nov. 1716 by extx. Mary Lynch with Samuel Hinton and Henry Jonas; est. was admin. on 7 May 1717 and 11 Oct. 1717; on 1 Oct. 1719 Abraham Shavers and w. Susannah conv. 38 a. Westminster to Mary Lynch; wid. Mary m. as 2nd husb., Joseph Crouch, on 3 Jan. 1719; in 1722 Mary recorded servant man Thomas Camp for her s. William Lynch; dec. left iss.: PATRICK; ANNE, may be the Anne who m. Jacob Rowles on 27 Jan. 1723; WILLIAM, b. c.1707; MARY, m. by 22 Jan. 1735 James Lenox(1:266, 268; 11:103; 13:424; 68:171; 69: 361; 74:371; 123:49; 133:146, 147; 139).

LYNCH, PATRICK (3), s. of Robuck (2), d. by 25 Aug. 1766; m. 1st, in 1722, to Martha Bowen, dau. of Jonas Bowen; m. 2nd, on 20 April 1747, Avarilla Taylor Day, wid. of Edward Day; she d. by 14 Nov. 1769; in March 1723 Patrick was charged with fathering a child; in June 1724 he was named as the father of Ann Galloway's child; in 1750 owned 90 a. part Willen, 133 a. part Bachelor's Delight, 300 a. The Plains, 50 a. part Taylor's Mount, and 72 a. Arthur's Lot; d. leaving a will, 17 June 1766 - 25 August 1766; est. was admin. 15 May 1770 and 15 Nov. 1770; Avarilla Taylor Day Lynch d. leaving a will, 29 Nov. 1766 - 4 Feb. 1767; Patrick had iss. (all by 1st w.): MARTHA, b. 28 Jan. 1725, m. 1st, by 17 June 1766 (---) Acton, and 2nd, by 15 May 1770, (---) Cretin; ROBUCK, b. 23 July 1728; ANN, b. 18 March 1729, m. (---) Flanagan; FLORA, b. 11 Feb. 1732, m. Daniel Smith; and MARY, m. Zachariah Gray on 22 Dec. 1748 (5:197; 6:197; 7:45; 26:201, 330; 112:52, 72; 131; 133:15, 17, 26, 148, 162; 153:25).

LYNCH, WILLIAM (4), s. of Robuck (2), d. in Balto. Co. in 1752; m., on 6 Sept. 1740, m. Elinor Dorsey Todd, wid. of Thomas Todd and dau. of Caleb and Eleanor (Warfield) Dorsey; in 1722 his mother, Mary, recorded a servant, one Thomas Camp for her son; in 1750 he owned 29½ a. part Lydicam, 75 a. Jones' Inheritance, 19 a. Hair's Green, 80 a. Bagford's Fortune, and 80 a. Watkins' Neck; gave his age as 26 in 1733 and 43 in 1750; d. by 12 Oct. 1751 when admin. bond was posted by Eleanor Lynch with Patrick Lynch and John Cromwell; Eleanor Lynch d. leaving a will, 23 July 1760 - 16 Oct. 1760; had iss.: SARAH, b. 5 Nov. 1741; WILLIAM, b. 18 Feb. 1742; JOSHUA, b. 25 April 1745; DEBORAH, b. 26 Oct. 1746; NELLY, b. 25 Feb. 1747; and ANN, b. 14 Jan. 1749 (3:375; 12:78; 133:91; 153:43; 210-31:26; 392:73).

LYNCH, ROBUCK (5), s. of Patrick (3), was b. 23 July 1728, d. b by 25 March 1797; m. Jemima, dau. of Thomas Stansbury, on 16 Aug. 1747; d. leaving a will, 8 Nov. 1796 - 25 March 1797; had iss.: MARTHA, b. 15 June 1748; PATRICK, b. 17 May 1750; ELIZABETH, b. 14 Jan. 1752; WILLIAM, b. by 17 June 1766 (when he was named in the will of his grandfather Patrick Lynch); ROBUCK (also named in the will of his grandfather); JANE, m. (---) Brown (36:221; 112:52; 115:504; 133:91, 97, 160; 210-34:24).

LYNCH, JAMES, m. Mary Lee on 23 Nov. 1728, and d. 5 Feb. 1732;

admin. bond was posted 19 Jan. 1733 by Thomas Bradley, with Jacob Giles and John Roberts; had iss.: MARGARET, b. 10 March 1732; MARY, b. 27 June 1732(sic) (12:97; 128:69, 71, 76).

LYNCH, JOHN, in 1750 owned 200 a. part Cub Hill; d. by 31 Dec. 1753 when admin. bond was posted by Thomas Sligh with John Starkey and Samuel Sindall; est. was admin. 13 Nov. 1754 by Sligh, with payments to Jonathan Lynch, s. of William, of Calvert Co., for his father's est., and to dec.'s wid. Mary for maintaining herself and ch. (4:236; 12:79; 153:89).

LYNCH, MARY, servant of Nathan Bowen, was fined for bast. in Nov. 1756 and fined again in Nov. 1757 when as serv. of Robert Freight she was tried for the same offence (41:313; 44; 46:75).

LYNCH, PATRICK, m. by 7 Dec. 1744 Sarah, wid. and extx. of Benjamin Bowen (3:344).

LYNCH, ROBERT, was in Balto. Co. by 1692 as a taxable in s. side Gunpowder (138).

LYNCH, ROBERT, in 1750 owned 29½ a. part Lydicam, 75 a. Jones' Inheritance, 19 a. Hair's Green, and 50 a. part Poplar (153:88).

LYNCH, WILLIAM, m. 3 Feb. 1749 Margaret Lynch (131).

LYNCHFIELD, WILLIAM, m. Sarah Parks on 26 March 1749 (131).

LYNN, DAVID, m. Eliz. Copeland on 24 Aug. 1746 (131).

THE LYON FAMILY of Wester Ogle, Baltimore County, descends from the Lyon Family of Wester Ogle, Scotland. The following descent is found in the Christopher Johnston papers at the Maryland Historical Society. The same descent is found in Andrew Ross (Marchmont Herald), The Lyons of Cossins and Wester Ogil, Cadets of Glamis (Edinburgh: George Waterston and Sons, 1901).

LYON, JOHN (1), feudal Baron of Forteviot, was the father of: Sir JOHN. (Ross, 4-8).

LYON, Sir JOHN (2), 1st of Glamis, son of John (1), d. 1383, having m. in 1379 Jean or Johanna, daughter of Robert II, K. of Scotland, by his 1st w. Elizabeth Mure; Jean m. as her 2nd husband James Sandilands of Calder; Sir John and Jean had: Sir JOHN. (Ross, 4-8).

LYON, Sir JOHN (3), 2nd of Glamis, s. of Sir John (2), d. in 1435 having m. Elizabeth Grahame, dau. of Sir Patrick Grahame, founder of the House of Montrose, by his wife Elizabeth, Countess Palatine of Strathearn (dau. of David Earl of Strathearn, and granddau. of Robert II, King of Scotland); had iss.: Sir PATRICK. (Ross, 9-11).

LYON, Sir PATRICK (4), 1st Lord Glamis, son of Sir John (3), d. 1459; having m. Issobel Ogilvy, dau. of Sir Walter Ogilvy of Lintrathem; had iss.: ALEXANDER, 3rd Lord Glamis; JOHN, 3rd Lord Glamis; WILLIAM, ancestor of the Lyons of Eatser Ogil; and ELIZABETH, m. Alexander Robertson of Strowan. (Ross, 12).

LYON, JOHN (5), 3rd Lord Glamis, s. of Sir Patrick (4), d. 1497; m. Elizabeth, dau. of Sir John Scrimgeouer of Dudhope; they had iss.: JOHN, 4th Lord Glamis, m. and had iss.: DAVID. (Ross, 19-22).

LYON, DAVID (6), s. of John (5), was of Cossens; was killed

at Flodden, 1513; m. Elizabeth, dau. of David Lindsay, 5th Earl of Crawford, and Duke of Montrose; had iss.: JOHN, 1st of Cossens; GEORGE, d. s.p. (Ross, 24-28).

LYON, JOHN (7), 1st of Cossens, son of David (6), was living in 1513 and 1567; m. Marjory, dau. of James, Lord Ogilvy of Airlie; had iss.: JOHN; PATRICK, had charter, 1553, d. s.p. (Ross, 29-32).

LYON, JOHN (8), 2nd of Cossens, son of John (7), m. Margaret, dau. of William Drummond of Ballock; had iss.: JOHN, 3rd of Cossens, m. Jean Campbell; GEORGE, of Balmuckety. (Ross, 33-37).

LYON, GEORGE (9), of Balmuckety, s. of John (8), was b. 1597 and d. 1640; m. Catherine Wishart of Balgarrock; had a tail of lands of Balmuckety from his father, and was styled George Lyon the younger of Cossens; had iss.: JOHN; THOMAS; and GEORGE. (Ross, 45-47).

LYON, JOHN(10), of Balmuckety, s. of George (9), m. Catherine Ogilvy of Balgour, prob. dau. of Sir John Ogilvy of Innerquharity; John purchased Wester Ogle in 1652, and had: GEORGE; JAMES; SYLVESTER; and JOHN. (Ross, 48 ff.).

LYON, GEORGE (11), s. of John (10), m. Jean Nisbet of Craigentinnie, dau. of Sir William Nisbet of Dean; had 8 sons and 4 daus., incl.: JOHN, d. v.p.; WILLIAM, of Wester Ogle, minister of Airlie; and ROBERT. (Ross, 55 ff.).

LYON, ROBERT (12), s. of George (11), was minister of Kinfauns; m. Jean Dalgliesh; had iss.: Dr. WILLIAM. (Ross, 55 ff.).

LYON, Dr. WILLIAM (13), s. of Robert (12), b. c.1715, imm. to Balto. Co., Md., c.1750; m. Miss Grahame; in 1750 owned 70 a. of Robinson's Park in Balto. Co.; for a fuller account of his life and activities, see the two-volume Hist. of the Green Spring Valley; d. 1794; had one s.: ROBERT (153:50; 259; 398; chart of Lyon Family by Johnston).

LYON, JOHN, in June 1743 was made levy free; in 1750 owned 537 a. Father's Request (34:190; 153:22).

LYTEFOOT. See LIGHTFOOT.

MACANADAY, PHILIP, and w. Dorothy were in Balto. Co. by March 1672 when they conv. 100 a. Neve's Choice to Richard Adams (63: 35).

MACHANELLIN, JOHN, was in Balto. Co. by April 1665 when he conv. 100 a. at Plumb Point to William Orchard (61:17).

MACKAINE, ANGUISH, was in Balto. Co. by 1695 as a taxable in n. side Patapsco Hund. (140).

MACKENALL, WALTER, was in Balto. Co. by July 1669 when he and w. Jane purch. 200 a. York's Hope from William and Elizabeth York (60:73).

MACKINY, JANE, serv. to James Moore, was ind. for bast. in Aug. 1737 (31:97).

MACLOUR, JNO., m. Anne (---), and had iss.: SARAH, b. 20 Dec. 1756 (133:99).

MACURAHON, ARTHUR, m. Rachel Gilbert on 29 June 1726 (128:48).

MADCALF. See METCALF.

MADDOCK, ROBERT, d. by 9 April 1677 when admin. bond was posted by James Mills with John Ireland (12:128).

MADDY, JOHN, m. by 5 May 1712 Ann, admnx. of Robert Gardner
(1:12, 364).

MADEWELL, JAMES, b. c.1714; m. Elizabeth (---); on 10 Feb.
1743 leased part My Lady's Manor, the lease to run for the lifetimes of Madewell, Eliz. Ady Garrison, b. c.1721, and her son
Job Garrison, b. c.1741; had iss.: ALEXANDER, b. 11 March 1745
(77:450; 131:114/r).

MAGILL, ANDREW, m. Mary (---); d. 1764 in Balto. Co.; m.
Mary (---); was in Balto. Co. by 1742 when he conv. Andrew Pigs-
lar and w. part of Great Meadows; on 16 April 1742 purch. 150 a.
Steven's Hope from Samuel and Martha Stevens; in 1750 owned that
land as well as 50 a. Magill's Choice; d. leaving a will, 24 Feb.
1764 - 13 Oct. 1764; had iss.: MARY, m. John McHorge (76:158;
77:334; 153:51; 210-32:300).

MAGILL, Dr. JAMES, d. by 28 Oct. 1756 when admin. bond was
posted by admin. James Magill (12:362).

MAGO, JAMES, was in Balto. Co. by 1692 as a taxable in Spesutia Hund. (138).

MAGREEGORY, JAMES, was in Balto. Co. by Nov. 1672 when he
conv. 250 a. at Onley's Creek in Bohemia R. to Hugh Fouch as well
as 200 a. on the west side of Bohemia River; prob. the James Magriges who was conv. 200 a. Mulberry Mould by Bryant O'Malley in
June 1666 (93; 98:46).

MAHAN, EDWARD, b. c.1684, gave his age as 46 in June 1730; m.
by July 1718 Ann, admnx. of Samuel Greening; d. leaving a will,
7 July 1733 - 19 July 1733, naming Ann Roberts, his brother's son
Edward, his five cousins, Anthony, Patrick, Edward, Mary, and Kat-
rine, who were to inherit his entire est. if his dau. Elinor died;
admin. bond was posted 19 July 1733 by William Rogers with Thomas
Broad and Thomas Sligh; had iss.: ELINOR, alive in Nov. 1734 (1:
276; 12:51; 30:356; 126:22; 163:107; 224:104).

MAHAN, JOHN, of Co. Wicklow, Ireland, bound himself to John
Smith of Biddeford, merchant, for 7 years service in Va. or Md.,
Nov. 1698 (63:354).

MAHANN, JOHN, in Nov. 1722 was named by Ann Brogden as the
father of her two children (25:21).

MAHONE, JOHN, d. in Balto. Co. leaving a will, 5 March 1741 -
23 Oct. 1742, naming w. Mary, youngest dau. Isabel, grandsons
Mathias Gray and John James, and dau. Frances Carback, as well as
John Brogden; admin. bond was posted 5 March 1741(?) by Mary Ma-
hone with Thomas Sligh and Christopher Duke; est. was admin. 18
July 1746 by wid. Mary; had iss.: FRANCES, m. 14 July 1734 John
Martin Carback; poss. others (4:138; 12:180; 127:92; 133:152).

MAINER. See MAYNARD

MAJOR, PETER (1), was in Balto. Co. by July 1723 when he wit.
the will of Thomas Criswell; c.1738 he pet. to have the Old Indian Road cleared; in Sept. 1739 with Edward Roberts was indebted to
to Richard Gist; d. by March 1750/1; m. Mary Slider on 27 Oct.
1730; had iss.: ESTHER, b. 3 April 1729; PETER, b. 5 Feb. 1732;
RACHEL, b. 29 Oct. 1735; ELIAS, b. c.1738 (38:271; 75; 124:153;
133:45, 149; 340:221).

MAJORS, ESTHER (2), dau. of Peter (1), was b. 3 April 1729; m. William Organ on 20 April 1752 after having born a son: JAMES MAJOR, b. 9 April 1752 (133:45; 134:31, 72).

MAJORS, PETER (3), s. of Peter (1) and Mary, was b. 5 Feb. 1732; was deeded a gray horse by Edward Roberts in Aug. 1739; in 1756 pat. 25 a. Peter's Home, and in 1760 pat. 12 a. also called Peter's Home (75:265; 133:45; 207).

MAJORS, ELIAS (4), s. of Peter (1), was b. c.1738; age 12 in March 1750/1 when as "orphan of Peter Majors," he was bound to John Simkins; m. Diana Bosley on 3 Sept. 1763 (38:271; 131).

MAJORS/MAJERD, ISAAC, was in Balto. Co. by 1692 as a taxable in Spesutia Hund. in the household of Thomas Hammond (138).

MAJORS/MAYJORS, JOHN, m. by 26 May 1756 Rebecca, dau. of John Pollard; in March 1761 John and Rebecca conv. Broom's Bloom to Moses Ruth (87:103; 131).

MALLONEE, PETER (1), d. by 5 Dec. 1749; was in Balto. Co. by Aug. 1724 when as "late servant to John Rallings, dec.," he was ordered to receive his freedom dues ; in Nov. 1724 he pet. the court for freedom from Eleanor Presbury but his pet. was denied; again in March 1724/5 he pet. to have his freedom from the est. of Joseph Presbury; on 5 Dec. 1749 admin. bond on his est. was posted by Talbot Risteau with John Roberts; est. was admin. by Risteau on 16 Feb. 1750; may have had one s.: JOHN (5:171; 12: 205; 26:441; 27:34, 129).

MALLONEE, JOHN (2), poss. s. of Peter (1), was b. c.1728; d. 2 Aug. 1783 in Balto. Co.; m. 1st Edith Cole in Nov. 1748; m. 2nd Rebecca (---); in 1750 owned 50 a. Timber Ridge; was a private in the Rev. War; d. leaving a will, 19 Feb. 1780 - 5 June 1783; had iss.: THOMAS; JAMES; RACHEL, b. 14 Feb. 1754, m. Mordecai Parrish on 28 d, 9, 1775; WILLIAM, b. c.1760; LEONARD, b. c.1760; DENNIS; poss. JOHN; poss. PETER (112:252, 536; 136; 153:95; 200-61:526; 353:434; Mallonee notes compiled by Fred. M. Chilcott who made them available to the compiler).

MALLONEE, EMANUEL, m. Margaret Reeves on 11 or 13 Feb. 1749/50 (131).

MALLONY, JOHN, was in Balto. Co. by 1692 as a taxable in n. side Patapsco (138).

MALSTER, SARAH, had iss.: GARRETT, b. 28 Oct. 1744 (134:1).

MANGROLL, MARY, was ind. for bast. in June 1740 and again in June 1744 (32:226; 35:227).

MANNAN, DOROTHY, was tried for bast. in Aug. 1744 (35:307).

MANNING, JOHN, ditcher, runaway serv. from William Mattingly of Patapsco River in Oct. 1740 (384:283).

MANNING, RICHARD, m. Elizabeth Lemmon or Smith on 7 April 1733 (129:366).

MAPOWDER, ANTHONY, of Balto. Co., claimed land for service in 1680 (388).

MARCEY, JONATHAN, was in Balto. Co. by 1695 as a taxable in n. side Patapsco Patapsco Hund. (140). See also MASSEY.

MARCH, GEORGE HENRY, d. by 20 Dec. 1746 when admin. bond was posted by John Combest with Jacob Combest (12:190).

MARCHANT, RICHARD, was in Balto. Co. by 28 July 1723 when he m. Mary Sweeting; on 3 Aug. 1725 he and w. Mary conv. 50 a. John's Interest to Samuel Harryman; had iss.: WILLIAM, b. 15 Sept. 1725; ELLINOR, b. 12 March 1727/8; MARY, b. 27 July 1734 (70:150; 133: 14, 37, 146).

MARCHMONT, PHILIP, miller, servant was in the 1747 inv. of William Fell (54:204).

MARCY. See MASSEY.

MARIARTE, EDWARD, m. Sarah Hanson on 17 Feb. 1736; d. by 23 April 1741 when admin. bond was posted by William Govane with John Lloyd and John Roberts; est. was admin. 16 March 1742; had iss.: RACHEL, b. 25 March 1739 (3:265; 12:181; 128:94; 131).

MARK, JOHN, was in Balto. Co. by 1692 as a taxable in n. side Gunpowder Hund.; on 2 June 1696 conv. 100 a. Thompson's Neglect to Thomas Preston and w. Mary; d. by 16 Dec. 1697 when his est. was inv. by Samuel Sickelmore and Abraham Taylor and val. at £ 58.17.4 (12:131; 51:105; 59:522; 138).

MARK, WILLIAM, was in Balto. Co. by 1695 as a taxable in s. side Gunpowder (140).

MARKHAM, JAMES, d. by 19 March 1740 when Alex. Lawson posted admin. bond with Benjamin Tasker and Charles Carroll (12:172).

MARLEY, THOMAS, was in Balto. Co. by March 1671/2 when he purch. Taylor's Mount from John Owen (98:47).

MARLING, alias MALLEN, JOHN, age 22, from Norfolk, Eng., farmer, runaway from Balto. Ironworks, was advert. for in Sept. 1755 (307-69:131).

MARRIAN, RICHARD, servant, was listed in the 1737 inv. of Briant Taylor (53:66).

MARRINER, MARTIN, d. in Balto. Co. by 24 Oct. 1713 when admin. bond was posted by Nicholas Rogers with John Hurst and Josias Stevens; est. was inv. on 11 Jan. 1713 by Jno. Hurst and Josias Stevens, and val. at £ 4.7.8; est. was admin. by Rogers on 8 April 1714 (1:2; 12:118; 50:289).

THE MARSH FAMILY was the subject of a genealogy by Edward E. Marsh, entitled "Genealogy of the Marsh Family," and hereinafter cited as Marsh.

MARSH, GILBERT (1), poss. progenitor of the family, was in Md. by 1 Aug. 1694 when he leased 400 a. on the e. side of the Potomac River from Edward Turner of Charles Co. for 11 years; d. in P. G. Co. leaving a will, 11 Feb. 1724/5 - 19 Feb. 1724/5, naming Alice Page, John Tolson s. of Francis, Margaret Gunn, servant Catherine McClannon, and a grandson John March; may have had one s. JOHN (124:124; P. G. Co. Deeds, Book A:69, HR).

MARSH, JOHN (2), poss. s. of Gilbert (1), was b. c.1667, and was living in March 1727 when he gave his age as 60 and said that 50 years earlier he had seen a bounded tree and was informed it was the boundary line of Mascall's Hope; by 1692 he was a taxable in the house of Richard Cromwell in s. side of Patapsco Hund.; in June 1721 John Marsh, Sr., was ment. in the will of John Barlow

of Balto. Co., and John Marsh, Sr., and John Marsh, Jr., were
witnesses; may have had s. JOHN (124:74; 138; 355).

MARSH, JOHN (3), first known anc. of the fam., and poss. s.
of John (2), was b. c.1685, and d. c.1750; m. Ann, dau. of Richard and Mary King; in Oct. 1716 Richard King conv. movable prop.
to John Marsh of Kent Co., chirurgeon; in Oct. 1727 King conv.
his dau. Ann Marsh 50 a. part of White Hall; may be the John
Marsh who surv. 200 a. Marsh's Victory; had iss.: RICHARD, b. c.
1715; poss. JOHN, b. c.1718; GILBERT, b. c.1722/3; AQUILA, b. c.
1724; THOMAS, b. c.1726; WILLIAM, b. c.1730; poss. PRUDENCE (68:
240; 70:20; 207; Marsh).

MARSH, RICHARD (4), s. of John (3) and Ann, was b. c.1715;
gave his age as 24 in 1739; in Nov. 1736 was ind. for unlawful
cohabitation with Ann Roberts; in 1750 owned 200 a. Marsh's Victory; in May 1751 conv. that tract, orig. granted to his father
John to Charles Carroll; d. c.1782; had at least one s.: RICHARD
(36:220; 81:165; 153:70; Marsh).

MARSH, JOHN (5), poss. s. of John (3), was born c.1718, and
was alive in 1743; m. Comfort (---), and had iss.: ELIZABETH, b.
12 Feb. 1738; JOHN, b. 15 Aug. 1743 (133).

MARSH, GILBERT (6), s. of John (3), was b. c.1722/3, was age
11 on 16 Feb. 1733/4; in March 1733/4 was bound to William Hammond to age 21; m. Lavina Bucknam (Buckingham?) on 20 Feb. 1747
(30:189; 133:31, 161).

MARSH, AQUILA (7), s. of John (3), was b. c.1724; age 9 in
March 1733/4 when he was bound to Christopher Randall to age 21
(30:189).

MARSH, THOMAS (8), s. of John (3), was b. c.1726, and was
bur. 7 Aug. 1801; age 8 in June 1734 when he was bound to Benjamin Knight to age 21; m. Sophia Corbin 10 March 1745; in 1750
owned 171½ a. part Valley of Jehosophat, 43¼ a. Marsh's Ridge,
112 a. Eagle's Nest and 300 a. Charles' Neighbor; bur. at St.
James' Par., 7 Aug. 1801; had iss.: JOHN; JOSHUA; THOMAS;
DAVID; BENEDICT; CLEMENT; TEMPERANCE; ACHSAH; BEALE; PRUDENCE;
SOPHIA; ELIZABETH (30:254; 131; 204; 244-AJ#C:311; St. James'
Parish Reg., Balto. Co., MHS).

MARSH, WILLIAM (9), s. of John (3), was b. c.1730/5, may
have been the orphan Mash (no first name given) who was bound to
Andrew Kelley in March 1733/4; may have m. Patience Lemon and
moved to Bracken Co., Ky. and had iss. (30:189; query in DAR
Magazine, Feb. 1932, p. 121).

MARSH, PRUDENCE (10), poss. dau. of John (3), in Aug. 1746
was ind. for bast., and tried in March 1746/7; m. Edward Wann on
23 July 1747; Edward d. testate leaving a will dated 29 July
1782, and wit. by Nath. Marsh; his inv. was signed by Thomas
Marsh (36:116, 395; 204).

MARSH, ELIZABETH, m. Richard Dean on 3 Jan. 1739 (133:156).

MARSH, JAMES, in 1742 leased part My Lady's Manor; m. Margaret (---), and had iss.: JOHN, b. 5 June 1744 (77:149; 131).

MARSH, JAMES, Jr., m. Sarah Taylor on 11 Aug. 1756, and had
iss.: ALICE, b. 5 March 1757 (131).

MARSH, JOSIAH, m. Sarah Breeset on 17 Nov. 1745 (133:158).

MARSH, PROVIDENCE was ind. for bast., Nov. 1740 (32:351).

MARSHALL, (---), (1), d. by 31 July 1722, leaving a wid. Ann, a res. of Newry, Co. Devon, Eng., and ch.: WILLIAM; CHARLES; JOSEPH; and ANN (69:254).

MARSHALL, WILLIAM (2), s. of (---) (1) and Ann, was in Balto. Co. by 19 June 1718 when he m. Mary, dau. of George and Martha (Beedle) Gouldsmith; Mary had m. 1st Robert Gibson; 2nd George Wells, and 3rd William Marshall: Marshall d. leaving a will, 23 Nov. 1720 - 15 Dec. 1720, leaving one-half his est. to w. Mary and the res. of his pers. est. to his mother Anne, sis. Anne and bro. Joseph, and appointing his w. Mary, & bro. Charles as his execs.; admin. bond was posted 7 June 1721 by extx. Mary Marshall with John and Edward Hall; est. was inv. in 1722; est. was admin. 27 Oct. 1725 by Mrs. Marshall; wid. Mary Marshall and her sis. Martha, w. of James Presbury, were coheirs of 400 a. Colletts Point; Mary d. leaving a will, 23 Dec. 1746 - 8 April 1749, naming granddau. Susanna, dau. of John Hall, son-in-law John Hall, George Goldsmith Presbury (son of her nephew George Presbury), Aquila Hall of Aquila, Martha w. of George Garrettson, and the bros. of John Hall; admin. bond was posted 8 July 1749 by John Hall of Swan Town; her est. was inv. in 1749 and val. at £ 1354. 19.7 and signed by Edward Wakeman and Charles Mullikin as creditors and John Hall and Parker Hall as kin; had iss.: SUSANNA; poss. ELIZABETH(5:66, 178; 12:137, 203; 49:196; 52:49; 71:43; 110:365; 124:60; 313:97).

MARSHALL, CHARLES (3), s. of (---) (1) and Ann, on 31 July 1722 was given power of atty. by his mother Ann, bro. Joseph, and sis. Anne of Newry, Co. Devon, to recover from the execs. of William Marshall the sums due them by his last will and testament (69:254).

MARSHALL, SUSANNA (4), dau. of William (2) and Mary, is stated to have been born 25 Nov. 1726, but this is prob. an error in the transcription; m. as 1st w. John Hall of Swan Town on 2 June 1742; she d. 26 June 1744 having had one dau.: SUSANNA HALL, b. 16 June 1744 (128:56; 129:326, 336).

MARSHALL, ELIZABETH (5), dau. of William (2) and Mary, is mentioned in a court record of Aug. 1750 (37:169).

MARSHALL, ISAAC, servant of Thomas Long, was judged to be 18 or 20 in March 1685/6; was a taxable in n. side of Patapsco in 1692; d. by 2 Aug. 1699 when admnx. Joyce Marshall posted admin. bond with Edward Stevenson and William Farfarr; est. was admin. 2 Aug. 1699 with an inv. totalling £ 117.10.6 (2:45; 18:397; 138).

MARSHALL, JOANNA, was ind. for bast. in Nov. 1710; John Rattenbury agreed to pay the fine if she did not (21:186).

MARSHALL, RICHARD, d. by Nov. 1730, leaving at least one dau. MARY, age about 9 in Nov. 1730 when she was bound to John Debruler to age 16 (29:50).

MARSHALL, ROBERT, in March 1722 was sec. for admin. of the est. of William Hawkins (1:100, 146).

MARSHALL, THOMAS, was b. c.1708; m. Sarah Bull on 3 Oct. 1740; in Oct. 1742 leased 150 a. The Manor from Thomas Brerewood, the lease to run for the lifetimes of said Thomas, age 34, w. Sarah age 22, and son John age 1; had iss.: JOHN, b. c.1741 (77:52; 131).

MARSHALL, WILLIAM, was. b. c.1725, was age 7 next 7 June when he was bound to Abraham Jarrett, shoemaker, c.1732-6 (30:125).

MARTHAM, LYDIA, serv. with 10 mos. to serve was listed in the 1743 inv. of Edward Fottrell (53:70).

MARTIN, ANN, was ind. for bast. in Aug. 1724 and given 15 stripes for bearing the illeg. ch. of John Harecock or Hancock; ind. for bast. in June 1732 and tried for bast. in March 1736 (26:438; 27:32, 42; 31:10).

MARTIN, BENJAMIN, in 1720 sold Richard Wheeler the tract Benjamin's Beginnings; d. by 6 June 1722 when admin. bond was posted by John Risteau with John Hall and John Stokes (12:142; 59: 667).

MARTIN, JAMES, lived near Deer Creek Meeting in March 1751 (385:118).

MARTIN, JOHN, on 17 Nov. 1670 claimed land for immigrating with w. Ann and his ch.; assigned land to Edmond Beetenson; had iss.: JOHN; MARY; HANNAH; and ELIZABETH (388).

MARTIN, JOHN, of Talbot Co., in Dec. 1684 conv. to John Boring 100 a. on s. side of Back River as formerly granted to his father John Martin (59:115).

MARTIN, JOHN, d. by 12 May 1718 when admin. bond was posted by John Buck with Benjamin Howard and Thomas Fairbrother; m. Eleanor (---) and d. leaving a will, 21 April 1718 - 12 May 1718, appointing w. Eleanor to admin. his pers. est.; est. was inv. in June 1718 by John Gardner and Thomas Hughes and val. at £ 59.5.10½, and signed by Lance Todd, Eleanor Martin, John Martin, and Thos. Worthington; est. was admin. by John Buck on 28 July 1718 and 31 July 1719 (1:192, 275; 12:119; 52:136; 123:135).

MARTIN, JOHN, d. by 4 Sept. 1742 when James Caine posted admin. bond with John Caine; est. was admin. in March 1743 by James Caine; prob. the John Martin of Tal. and Balto. Cos., who d. leaving a s. JOHN, of P. G. Co. (3:335; 12:193; 80:43).

MARTIN, LEURANAH, age 6 next 9 Feb., was bound to Thomas Hutchins in Nov. 1737 (31:133).

MARTIN, LUDOWIC, was in Balto. Co. by 1695 as a taxable in Spesutia Hund.; on 15 Nov. 1696 Lodowick and w. Mary conv. 90 a. part of 400 a. Carter's Rest, to Samuel Jackson; had iss.: LUDO-WICK, b. 30 Dec. 1695 at the Level (61:62; 128:3; 140).

MARTIN, MICHAEL, d. April 1749; m. Mary Fling in March 1736; in 1750 owned 170 a. part Polecat Neck; had iss.: ARAMINTA, b. 31 March 1738; JULI ANN, b. 3 March 1739; SAMUEL, b. 3 Aug. 1742 (131; 153:25).

MARTIN, ROBERT, d. by 9 March 1752 when admin. bond was posted by James Martin and Andrew Martin; est was admin. by James Martin in Dec. 1753 (5:272; 12:224).

MARTIN, THOMAS; had iss.: LUDOWICK, b. by May 1699, mentioned in the will of Henry Haslewood of Balto. Co. (121:179).

MARTIN, WILLIAM, s. of Francis and bro. of Lodowick, d. testate by 21 Jan. 1662 leaving a wid. Patience, mother Margaret, Martha, and Dorothy Needham (200-49:30).

MARVELL, ELIZABETH, was fined for bast. in Nov. 1759; William Barney was the father of her s.: WILLIAM (46:242).

MARYFIELD, ELIZABETH, m. Thomas Sky on 23 July 1706 (129:201).

MASCALL, RICHARD, imm. to A. A. Co. by 1671; in June 1669 had
surv. 100 a. Mascoll's Hope; on 11 Oct. 1670 surv. 100 a. Mascall's Haven; d. by 1 Oct. 1679 when admin. bond was posted by
William Cromwell with Thomas Long and William Ball (12:277; 211;
388).

MASCORD, JOHN, perhaps the one who was transp. by 1664, was
in Balto. Co. by Nov. 1670 when John Tilliard sold him one-half
of Beaver Neck, 100 a.; in Aug. 1673 Mascord and Matthew Knivington sold the tract to Bernard Utie, with Jane Mascord also signing (97:125; 99:347).

MASH, JAMES, m. Margaret Harris in Sept. 1737 (133:156).

MASON, EDWARD, m. Sarah (---) and had iss.: CAROLINE, b. 25
July 1746; CHARLES, b. 10 Dec. 1743; and EDWARD, b. 1 Dec. 1748
(134:3, 9, 11).

MASON, JOHN, m. Elizabeth (---), and had iss.: JOHN, b. 12 Dec.
1732 (128:71).

MASON, JOHN, m. Frances, admnx. of Nathaniel Allen, on 20 Dec.
1733; d. leaving a will, 2 April 1736 - 11 May 1736, naming w.
Frances and s. John; admin. bond was posted 7 Jan. 1736 by Frances Allen; had iss.: JOHN (3:178; 5:145; 126:171; 131; 209-30:
228).

MASON, JOSEPH, m. Maria Grover on 10 April 1757; had iss.:
ELIZABETH, b. 31 July 1758 (129:356).

MASON, THOMAS, servant, was transp. to Balto. Co. by 1664 (388)

MASSARD, JAMES, was in Balto. Co. by 1692 as a taxable in n.
side of Gunpowder Hund. (138).

MASSEY/MARCEY/MARCY, JONATHAN (1), progenitor, m. Ann Collier
on 25 Feb. 1701; on 27 Sept. 1709 Jonathan and Ann conv. 150 a.
to Francis Barney; . d. leaving a will, 26 Feb. 1723/4 - 10 Nov.
1732, naming s. Aquila; had iss.: AQUILA (67:28; 126:28; 128:
14; 143).

MASSEY, AQUILA (2), s. of Jonathan (1), d. in Balto. Co. by 8
March 1739; m. Sarah Coale, dau. of William Coale on 7 Jan.
1724/5; in 1736 gave his age as 33; d. leaving a will, 19 Jan.
1739 - 8 March 1739, naming ch.: Aquila, Jonathan Collier, Ann,
Mary, and Elizabeth, and brother-in-law Thomas Coale; in June
1745 his orphans Aquila and Jonathan were made wards of Richard
Richardson; his admin. bond was posted 1 April 1740 by Thomas
Coale, with William Dallam and John Paca, and his est. was admin.
by Coale on 31 May 1744; Aquila and Sarah had iss.: ANN, b. 1 Feb.
1725/6, prob. the Ann who m. Jno. Rich on 2 Oct. 1759; MARY, b.
10 March 1727; ELIZABETH, b. 25 Feb. 1731; AQUILA, b. 27 July
1733; JONATHAN COLLIER, b. 9 April 1736 (5:21; 35:478, 542;
127:68; 131; 210-24:85; 224:253; 263).

MASSEY, AQUILA (3), s. of Aquila (2), was b. 27 July 1733, and
d. by 10 May 1759; m. Sarah (---); in 1750 was one of the heirs
of Aquila Massey listed as owning 500 a. Massey's Addition and
100 a. Addition to Privilege; d. leaving a will, 18 d, 5, 1756 -
10 May 1759, naming w. Sarah, bro. Jonathan Collier Massey; admin. bond was posted 10 May 1759 by Sarah Massey with William
Cox and Jonathan Massey; est. admin. on 5 Aug. 1760 by Sarah
Massey (4:315; 12:217; 111:310; 153:11).

MASSEY, JONATHAN COLLIER (4), s. of Aquila (2), was b. 9 April 1736; in March 1755 chose Aquila Massey as his guardian; on 6, 7 mo., 1763 he m. Cassandra, dau. of Isaac Webster (40; Reg. of Deer Creek Meeting, Soc. of Friends in 372).

MASSEY, EDWARD, m. by March 1717/8 Ann, admnx. of Samuel Greening (22:253).

MASTERS, JOHN, was in Balto. Co. by Oct. 1670 when Richard Whitton conv. him 50 a. Fox Hall; he conv. the same land to John Watertown, Gent., in Feb. 1673/4 (96:232; 100:116).

MASTERS, MARY, m. William Stigings on 13 July 1721 (129:228).

MASTERS, THOMAS, m. after banns were posted three times, 8 April 1706, Margaret Jones (128:18).

MATHESON, ALEXANDER, m. Sarah Morris on 2 Aug. 1758, and had iss.: JOHN, b. 2 Feb. 1758 (129:355).

MATIN, WILLIAM, d. by 28 June 1751 when est. was admin. by Nicholas Gay, admin. with will annexed (5:184).

MATLANNAN, JOHN, d. by 18 Dec. 1713 when his est. was admin. by James Matlannan (1:221).

MATTHAU, WILLIAM, d. by 17 Oct. 1754 when his est. was admin. by extx. Mary Matthau, now w. of William Williams (4:232).

THE ROGER MATTHEWS FAMILY

MATTHEWS, ROGER (1), progenitor, was b. c.1651; d. in Balto. Co. in Dec. 1709; m. Hannah (---) who was bur. 6 Feb. 1706/7; Roger was transp. by 1668; in March 1682/3 was conv. 100 a. Miles End by Thomas Hedge; in 1701 purch. 100 a. Bratty's Island from Robert Gibson; in 1692 was a taxable in Spesutia Hund.; in 1692 was chosen one of the first seven members of St. George's Par.; d. leaving a will, 11 Nov. 1700 - 7 March 1709/10, naming w. Hannah, s. Roger (to have all land), daus. Hannah and Sarah, and granddau. Sarah; had iss.: HANNAH, m. Thomas Cord on 14 Aug. 1698; SARAH, m. Samuel Jackson on 11 Dec. 1698; ROGER (59; 66: 81; 122:193; 128:20, 26; 129:178, 185; 138; 200-23:20; 388).

MATTHEWS, ROGER (2), s. of Roger (1), d. 20 Oct. 1740; m. 1st, on 14 Nov. 1710 Mary Carvill who d. 4 Aug. 1714; m. 2nd, on 13 May 1726 Elizabeth Garrett; in May 1721 was named "bro." in the will of Thomas Cord, whose est. he admin. on 3 April 1722; d. leaving a will, 13 Oct. 1740 - 9 May 1741, naming s. James, sons Aquila, Bennett, and Levin; daus. Ann and Amelia; admin. bon was posted 9 May 1741 by extx. Elizabeth Matthews with John Matthews and Henry Garrett, since Roger's son John ren. right of admin.; est. of Roger Matthews was admin. 4 July 1752 by Elizabeth Matthews, and on 1 July 1752 by John Matthews; in 1750 wid. Elizabeth Matthews was listed as owning 100 a. of Edwards' Lot, 100 a. Matthews ' Addition, and 100 a. Penny Come Quick and 50 a. United Lot; Elizabeth actually d. by 18 May 1749 when admin. bond was posted by John Matthews with John Hall of Cranberry and James Maxwell; her est. was admin. by John Matthews on 31 July 1752; dec. left iss.: HANNAH, b. 24 Sept. 1711; m. 1st Asael Maxwell, 2nd, Abraham Johns, who d. s. p. 1731; 3rd, on 26 Nov. 1734, Col. John Hall; JOHN, b. 26 June 1714; ROGER, b. 26 April 1718; (by 2nd 2nd w.): JAMES, b. 7 Sept. 1727; AMELIA, b. 7 Sept. 1729, m. Charles Hynson; ANNE, b. 27 July 1731, m. Maj. William Dallam on 23 July 1754; AQUILA, b. 26 Feb. 1733, d. 15 Aug. 1642; LEVIN, b. 10 Sept. 1736; BENNET, b. 10 March 1739 (1:88; 3:353; 5:248, 249;

(12:183, 209; 34:68; 124:60; 127:138; 128:36, 37, 51, 59, 77, 78, 96, 116; 129:216, 325; 153:23).

MATTHEWS, Capt. JOHN (3), s. of Roger (2) and Mary, was b. 26 June 1714; m. 1st, 18 April 1737 Anne Maxwell, dau. of Col. James Maxwell; she d. 30 Oct. 1744, and he m. 2nd Milcah Lusby, on 23 Feb. 1749; in 1750 he owned 533 a. Major's Choice, 627 a. Major's Enlargement, and 22 a. Shipper's Dock; he was alive in 1776, and had iss.: (by 1st w.): JAMES MAXWELL, b. 18 Jan. 1737/8; CASSANDRA, b. 8 Oct. 1739; JOHN, b. 31 July 1741; REBEC-CA, b. 10 March 1742 (by 2nd w.): MARY, b. 26 Dec. 1749; HANNAH, b. 26 Oct. 1751; ROGER, b. 4 Nov. 1653; AQUILA, b. 1 Jan. 1756; JOHN, b. 20 Nov. 1757; MILCAH, b. 14 June 1759; BENNETT, b. 30 Oct. 1761; NAOMI, b. c.1763; FRANCES, b. 1765; JOSIAS, b. 1767; and CARVILL, b. 1769 (128:95, 105; 129:324, 327, 338, 350, 378; 153).

MATTHEWS, JAMES (4), s. of Roger (2), was b. 7 Sept. 1727; in 1750 owned 200 a. part Edwards' Lot, 300 a. Pearson's Park, and part Bonner's Purchase; d. leaving a will made 13 May 1759 in which he named a no. of siblings and nephews and nieces; in May 1759, having occasion to travel, he appointed his bro. John Matthews and kinsman Amos Garrett as his attorneys (153: 23; 210-30:825; Balto. Co. Court Proc., BB#F, f. 49, MHS).

THE THOMAS MATTHEWS FAMILY

MATTHEWS, THOMAS (5), no known rel. to any of the above, came from the north of Britain with his s. Oliver to Newcastle Co., Del.; had iss.: OLIVER (136).

MATTHEWS, OLIVER (6), s. of Thomas (5), was b. in North of Eng.; came with his father to Newcastle Co.; was a Public Friend; m. Elizabeth (---) and had iss.: THOMAS, b. 29 d, 3, 1693; JOHN, b. 8 d, (?), 1694; WILLIAM, b. 5 d, 7, 1697; and poss. GEORGE (136).

MATTHEWS, THOMAS (7), s. of Oliver (6), was b. 29 d, 3, 1693; d. 19 d, 11, 1766; m. by Nov. 1718, Sarah, extx. of John Thomas; on 3 Dec. 1725 Thomas and Sarah conv. 165 a. Thomas' Adventure now called Partridge's Chance to Buckler Partridge of Bristol, merchant; in Nov. 1742 purch. White Oak Bottom from John and Sarah Thomas; in 1750 owned 150 a. White Oak Bottom, 10 a. part of Matthews' Addition, and 50 a. Matthews' Fancy; had iss.: ELIZA-BETH, b. 1 July 1719; OLIVER, b. 28 d, 11, 1721; DANIEL, b. 4 d, 11, 1723; THOMAS, b. 16 d, 6, 1725; GEORGE, b. 19 d, 9, 1729; and SARAH, b. 18 d, 8, 1731 (22:55; 70:208; 77:70; 136; 153: 26).

MATTHEWS, GEORGE (8), s. of Oliver (6), as "George, s. of Oliver of the Potomac," m. Elizabeth, dau. of James and Mary Wright, on 4 d, 6, 1731, at Nottingham Monthly Meeting (136).

MATTHEWS, OLIVER (9), s. of Thomas (7), was b. 28 d, 11, 1721; d. 17 d, 1, 1824 in his 103rd year; rem. to Fairfax Meeting in Va., in 1742; m. Hannah Johns (b. 1728, d. 1791), on 30 d, 6, 1746; had iss.: MARY, d. 1781, m. John Cornthwait; THOMAS, d. 1792, m. Ann Humphreys; WILLIAM, b. 3 mo., 1755, m. Ann Price; DANIEL, b. 5 d, 7, 1763; HANNAH, b. 7 d, 7, 1767 (136).

MATTHEWS, THOMAS (10), s. of Thomas (7), was b. 16 d, 6, 1725; d. leaving a will, 1 Aug. 1774 - 5 Dec. 1774; m. 26 d, 10 or 12 mo., 1751, Rachel Price (b. 1730, d. 1813, dau. of Mordecai and Elizabeth (White) Price; had iss.: SARAH, b. 12 d, 10, 1752, m. Thomas Owens; MORDECAI, b. 12 d, 9, 1755, m. Ruth (---); DANIEL, b. 8 d, 2, 1758, d. 1795; JOHN, b. 22 d, 2, 1760; JESSE,

b. 17, 10, 1762, m. Milcah Belt; RACHEL, b. 19 d, 4, 1765, m.
Isaac Kinsey; ELI, b. 21 d, 2, 1767, m. Mary Cooper; ELIZABETH,
b. 3 d, 4, 1769, m. Thomas Scott; THOMAS, b. 1771; WILLIAM, b.
26, 1, 1774 (112:290; 136).

MATTHEWS, GEORGE (11), s. of Thomas (7), was b. 19 d, 9,
1729; m. 1st, Dorothy Miller, dau. of Robert and Ruth Haines
Miller; m. 2nd, on 3 d, 12, 1771, Sarah Nailor; had iss.: WIL-
LIAM, b. 6 d, 3, 1753; ELIZABETH, b. 11 d, 3, 1755; SAMUEL, b.
14 d, 11, 1756, d. 1842; GEORGE, Jr., b. 14 d, 6, 1762; MARY,
b. 30 d, 4, 1764; DOROTHY, b. 19 d, 10, 1769, m. Jesse Brown;
(by 2nd w.): ANN, b. 26 d, 9, 1778 (136).

MATTHEWS, HENRY, was in Balto. Co. by 3 Aug. 1697 when Thomas
Heath and w. Sarah conv. him 50 a. Hughs' Island, 50 a. Black
Ledge, 115 a. Keith's Addition, (61:154).

MATTHEWS, HENRY, m. Sarah (---); d. by 14 June 1726; left a
will, 6 June 1720 - 5 April 1726, naming tracts Hews' Chance and
Matthews' Double Purchase, orphan boy Abraham Kinsbie, and ch.
Sarah, Mary, Elizabeth, and Catherine Wheland; admin. bond was
posted 14 June 1726 when admin. bond was posted by extx. Sarah
Matthews with Patrick Wheland and William Roles; est. was inv.
2 Nov. 1726 by Robert Robeson and William Matthews, and val. at
£ 52.16.2, and signed by Patrick Whaland and William Rhoads who
m. daus. of the dec.; est. was admin. by Sarah Matthews on 5
Sept. 1727; in Nov. 1728 Sarah Matthews was allowed 1200 lbs.
tobacco for maintaining her dau. next year; she d. by 6 Aug.
1730 when admin. bond was posted by Thomas Cross with Robert Robertson and James Standford; had iss.: CATHERINE, m. Patrick Wayland; MARY, m. by 1721 William Rhodes; SARAH, b. 25 April 1702,
may have m. Thomas Cross; ELIZABETH, b. 10 July 1708 (3:78; 12:
143, 148; 28:66; 51:66; 124:222; 131:7).

MATTHEWS, JAMES, in March 1733/4, being "ancient and past his
labor," was made levy free (30:190).

MATTHEWS, RICHARD, m. Margaret King on 17 Aug. 1758 (131).

MATTHEWS, RUTH, m. William Leff on 12 Aug. 1697 (129:178).

MATTHEWS, THOMAS, m. Elizabeth Matthews on 7 Nov. 1736 (133:
156).

MATTINGLY, WILLIAM, was in Balto. Co. by Aug. 1740 when he
purch. Turner's Hall from Joseph and Sarah Thomas; d. leaving a
will, 11 Feb. 1745 - 25 Aug. 1746, naming Constant Pelly (who
was to have 97½ a. Pleasant Green (formerly called Logsdon's
Addition), 200 a. Turner's Hall, and other est. in Eng. or Md.;
admin. bond was posted 25 Aug. 1746 by wid. Constant Pilley
or Pebley of A. A. Co., with William Mills, John Abercrombie,
and Barton Rodget; est. was admin. by wid. on 14 July 1747 (4:
173; 12:184; 75:458; 384:283).

MATTOCKS, MARY, was ind. for bast. in June 1711; as Mary Mattocks, alias Shorter, named William Winespear as the father of
her child in Aug. 1711 (21:210, 251).

MATTOX, WILLIAM, was in Balto. Co. by Oct. 1749 when he purch.
51 a. part Carryfurgus from Robert and Jemima Cross; in 1750 he
owned 50 a. Carraghferghus; d. by 1773 when his est. was admin.
by John Cross; left six ch. (6:302; 80:317; 153:96).

MATTSON, ANDREW (1), claimed land for service in 1673; may
be the Andrew Mattson who was naturalized 16 Nov. 1683 with John

Cosins and Peter Maide de Moise; was in Balto. Co. by April 1682 when he surv. 10 a. Matson's Lot; in Sept. 1683 he surv. 780 a. Andrew's Conquest; in March 1683 he purch. 200 a. Bailey from Elias Robertson of Cecil Co.; in May 1688 conv. 268 a. (unnamed) to Samuel Underwood; in Feb. 1688/9 conv. 200 a. Bayly or Rayly and 10 a. Matson's Lot to Mark Richardson; m. by March 1686 Jane (---) who joined him in sale of Sister's Dowry to Gideon Gamble (59:87, 267, 315, 318; 211; 388; 404).

MATTSON, MATTHIAS (2), of Penna., blacksmith, in May 1706 was reported that for 40 years he had been known as the brother of Matthias Devoss, late of Balto. Co., dec., and that Matthias Devoss was a bro. of Andrew Mattson (69:58).

(MATTSON?), DEVOSS, MATTHIAS (3), of Balto. Co., d. by 1 May 1706, was said to be a brother of Andrew Mattson and Matthias Mattson (69:58).

MATTSON, JOHN, alias DEFOSS (4), of Newcastle Co., Penna., eld. s. of Matthias Mattson or Matthiason, late of Cecil Co., blacksmith, dec., conv. 480 a. Andrew's Conquest to Edward Hall (68: 76).

MAULAN, JOHN, was in Balto. Co. by 5 Oct. 1753 when he and his w. Margaret conv. 74 a. Addition to Maulan's Hill to Solomon Stocksdale (82:139).

MAXFIELD, ROBERT, m. Margaret Jarvis on 1 Feb. 1728 and had iss.: MOSES, b. 4 Oct. 1729; RACHEL, b. 30 Dec. 1732; MARY, b. 4 June 1736 (133:17, 26, 57, 149).

MAXFIELD, SAMUEL, was in Balto. Co. by 1692 as a taxable in s. side Gunpowder Hund. (138).

MAXFIELD, SAMUEL, m. Hannah (---), and had iss.: JAMES, b. 22 Nov. 1724; SAMUEL, b. 7 Sept. 1727; JOSEPH, b. 26 July 1730 (133: 29, 30).

THE JAMES MAXWELL FAMILY

MAXWELL, JAMES (1), progenitor, d. 1669; m. Mary (---) who m. as her 2nd husband Patrick Hall of A. A. Co., d. 1678; and 3rd John Sperner, f. after 1683; James imm. c.1658 and brought his w. Mary into Md. c.1659; had iss.: JAMES; poss. PHILIZANNA, placed as a dau. of James because she m. Richard Smithers on 18 Aug. 1709 (388; Johnston, Chart of Maxwell Family at Md. Hist. Soc.).

MAXWELL, JAMES (2), s. of James (1), d. 5 Jan. 1728; m. 1st (---), wid. of (Benjamin?) Gundry , and dau. of Godfrey and Mary Harmer; m. 2nd, Ann, sis. of Moses Groome and kinswoman of Ann Johnson, widow, who m. c.1701/2 Edward Felkes; appointed Ranger of Balto. Co. by the Council of Md. in Oct. 1692; admin. the est. of Benjamin Gundry on 5 July 1708; in 1709 was named as bro.-in-law in the will of John Ewings, and admin. Ewings' est. on 13 Oct. 1718; in Aug. 1719 was reimbursed by the County Court for having cared for the child of Elizabeth Kitchin; on 30 Sept. 1712 conv. 50 a. part Galleon Bay to his son-in-law Spry Godfrey Gundry; d. leaving a will, 4 Jan. 1727 - 8 March 1727, naming his sons James and Ashael, and dau. Ann; admin. bond was posted 25 Jan. 1728/9 by the admin. James Maxwell, with Roger Matthews and Nicholas Day, and John Crockett; a second admin. bond was posted 6 June 1733 by William Savory, Jr., with Roger Matthews and Edward Hall; Savory admin. the est. on 17 Nov. 1733; James left iss. (by 1st w.): JAMES, d. by 1733 (by 2nd w.): ASAEL; Capt. JAMES; ROBERT, b. 12 Jan. 1718/9; ELIZABETH; ANN, d. 20 Oct. 1744 having m. Capt. John Matthews on 18 April 1737 (2:31, 198; 3:

137; 12:147, 152; 23:213; 67:207; 125:64; 131; 200-80:398; Chart
of Maxwell Family by Johnston).

MAXWELL, JAMES (3), s. of Col. James (2) and his 1st w., d.
20 May 1734 when admin. bond was posted by William Savory; m.
Mary, poss. dau. of John Marsh; William Savory posted admin. bond
with J. Crockett and Thomas Coale; Savory admin. the est. on 17
Dec. 1744 and mentioned legacies left by one John Marsh to his
granddau. Philizanna Maxwell, and also to the only ch. of Johannah Dehaws; dec. left iss.: ELEANOR, b.12 Feb. 1719, may have d.
young; PHILIZANNA, b. 3 March 1723, m. John Day on 20 July 1742;
MARY, b. 6 April 1724; ELIZABETH, b. 3 June 1727, m. Thomas Walton on 21 June 1750; ELEANOR, b. 12 Feb. 1729, m. Benjamin Ricketts on 18 Oct. 1746 (5:19; 12:154; 131).

MAXWELL, ASAEL (4), s. of Col. James (2) by his 2nd w., d.
1729 having m. Hannah, dau. of Roger Matthews; d. leaving a will,
2 April 1729 - 16 May 1729, naming w. Hannah, sis. Ann and bro.
James; Hannah Matthews Maxwell m. 2nd Dr. Abraham Johns and 3rd,
on 26 Nov. 1734 Col. John Hall (125:120; Johnston chart).

MAXWELL, Capt. JAMES (5), s. of Col. James (2), was b. c.1711
and d. by 25 Feb. 1777; m. Phebe Jackson on 7 Sept. 1755, dau. of
Jacob and Frances (Dallahide) Jackson; in 1750 owned 150 a. Bushwood, 100 a. Gather's Bay, 200 a. Wansworth, 50 a. Daniel's Neglect, 129 a. part Waterton and 50 a. Hamersham; d. leaving a
will, 3 March 1774 - 25 Feb. 1777; had iss.: JAMES, d. 1780;
MOSES; JACOB, d. 1798; ANN, m. 20 June 1772 John Hammond Dorsey;
ELIZABETH, m. Roger Matthews; PHOEBE, m. James Hambleton (210-
41:414; 244-AJ#2:426, 474; Johnston Chart).

THE SAMUEL MAXWELL FAMILY

MAXWELL, SAMUEL (6), no known rel. to any of the above, m. by
29 Sept. 1720, dau. of Henry King; in Nov. 1719 he was licensed
to keep an ordinary at his house; on 9 Dec. 1724 bought Westwood
from William and Judith Houchings; d. by 28 April 1744 by admnx.
Jane Maxwell with Joseph Thomas and Nicholas Day; another admin.
bond was posted 13 Dec. 1744 by Nicholas Day with George Brown and
Robert Dutton; est. was admin. 20 Oct. 1745 by Nicholas Day; in
Aug. 1746 Joseph Thomas was chosen as guardian for Samuel's two
sons: SAMUEL; JAMES (5:44; 12:189, 192; 23:240; 36:120; 70:89).

MAXWELL, JAMES (7), s. of Samuel (6), d. by 4 Aug. 1748 when
admin. bond was posted by Nicholas Ruxton Gay with John Paca and
Isaac Risteau; est. was admin. 9 Nov. 1750 by Nicholas Ruxton
Gay (5:108, 12:196).

MAXWELL, (---), m. by 9 Sept. 1759 Rebecca, dau. of Patrick
Montgomery (112:213).

MAXWELL, DAVID, m. Margaret (---); in 1750 owned 150 a. Jones'
Gift, 100 a. part Brother's Discovery, 100 a. part Giles and Webster's Discovery; d, leaving a will, 18 July 1756 - 4 Aug. 1756,
naming w. Margaret, tract Dunmorrow, and these ch.: JAMES; THOM-
AS; DAVID; and ELIZABETH, m. Robert Gillespie (12:227; 111:101;
153:83).

MAXWELL, ELIZABETH, in 1750 owned 360 a. part Conclusion (153:
69).

MAXWELL, JAMES, was summoned by St. John's Vestry for unlawful cohabitation with Johanna Rigbie in April 1747 and for unlawful cohabitation with Susannah Rigbie in July 1749 (132:68,
82, 97).

MAXWELL, JOSEPH, b. c.1729; in June 1744 was bd. to Joseph Thomas; may be the Joseph Maxwell who owned 100 a. Spring Neck and 100 a. Maxwell's Hope in 1750 (35:229; 153:80).

MAXWELL, ROBERT, was bur. 12 Jan. 1718/9 (131).

MAXWELL, SAMUEL, was in Balto. Co. by 1694 as a taxable in n. side Patapsco Hund. (139).

MAY, THOMAS, was in Balto. Co. by 1695 as a taxable in n. side of Patapsco Hund. (140).

MAYER, JANE, m. John Butteram on 8 Sept. 1714 (131).

MAYES, JAMES, m. Mary (---), and had iss.: ANN, b. 26 Nov. 1747 (131).

MAYES, JAMES, conv. prop. to John Roberts on 4 Nov. 1756 (229:226).

MAYES, JOHN, servant, was named in the will of Nehemiah Hicks on 9 Sept. 1769 (112:115).

MAYJORS. See MAJORS.

MAYNARD/MAINERD/MAYNER, HENRY, m. Susanna (---); on 19 d, 8, 1744, Henry and w. Susanna conv. Mayner's Beginning to Dennis Garrett Cole; had iss.: SARAH, b. 19 Nov. 1733 (77:651; 133:37).

MAYNARD, JOHN, d. by 1 Aug. 1691 when admin. bond was posted by John Ensor and w. Jane, with Houge Jons and William Gaine; his est. was inv. by Hugh Jones with William Gaine, and val. at £38.8.6 (12:133; 48:172).

MAYNARD, JOHN, m. Mary Lawson on 8 Jan. 1756 (131).

MAYNARD, WILLIAM, m. Martha Tucker on 14 Dec. 1729; on 8 Aug. 1731 William and Martha conv. 80 a. Maynor's Privilege to John Ensor; William d. by 9 March 1743 when admin. bond was posted by Tobias Stansbury with William Bond and Charles Crooke, the widow Martha having relinquished the right to admin.; est. was admin. by Stansbury on 4 Sept. 1746 (4:140; 12:195; 73:152; 133:148).

MAYO, JAMES, was in Balto. Co. by 1694 as a taxable in Spesutia Hund. (139).

MAYO, JOSEPH, was in Balto. Co. by 1750 when he owned 2 lots in Balto. Town (153:83).

McCABE, JAMES, was in Balto. Co. by 28 Nov. 1755 when he admin. the est. of John Hughes (5:341).

McCABE, JOHN, m. Eleanor Goodwin on 14 June 1758; had iss.: CATHERINE, b. 8 April 1759; ELIZABETH, b. 25 Sept. 1760; BARNETT, b. 10 March 1762 (129:370).

McCALL, JOHN, of Cumberland Co., Penna., d. leaving a will signed and proved in March 1761; est. was admin. in Balto. Co. on 2 Sept. 1761 by William McCall; had iss.: WILLIAM; JOHN (4: 361; 111:340).

McCAMIS, JAMES, was in Balto. Co. by Oct. 1758 when he bought 25 a. Tipton's Lot from Edward Tipton; moved to Cumberland Co., Penna. by 3 April 1762 when he sold the land to Benjamin Bowen (83:239; 86:105).

MACANADY, PHILIP, was in Balto. Co. by Nov. 1670 when he
purch. 100 a. Neve's Choice from William Pearce (96·233).

McCANN, TIMOTHY (1), d. in Balto. Co. by 10 Sept. 1757 when
his will was proved; m. and had at least one s.; his will, 2 Aug.
1757 - 10 Sept. 1757, appointed John Creton as exec., and guardian of testator's grandchildren Patrick and Ann, ch. of Timothy's s. Daniel; admin. bond was posted by John Craton on 10
Sept. 1757; est. was admin. on 5 Sept. 1757 and 30 May 1759;
had iss.: DANIEL (4:264, 281; 12:229; 210-30:373).

McCANN, DANIEL (2), s. of Timothy (1), m. Ann (---), and d.
by Nov. 1757 when his orphans were made wards of his wid. Ann;
had iss.: PATRICK; ANNE (46·79).

McCANN, OWEN, m. Elizabeth Cullen on 25 April 1735 (128:90).

MACCANALLIS, WALTER. See MACKENALL, WALTER.

McCARTY, DANIEL (1), m. Sarah Norris on 20 Jan. 1714; d. by
10 May 1722 when admin. bond was posted by Bennett Garrett with
John Stokes and Joseph Presbury; est. was admin. by Garrett on
7 Sept. 1724; had iss.: SAMUEL, b. 20 Aug. 1716; MARY, b. 6 Jan.
1718/9; DANIEL, b. 18 March 1720/1 (3:13; 12:141; 128:33, 39).

McCARTY, SAMUEL (2), s. of Daniel (1), was b. 20 Aug. 1716;
m. Sarah Robinson on 16 Nov. 1739; in 1750 owned 50 a. part of
Whitaker's Ridge, which he sold to James Taylor in Sept. 1757;
d. leaving a will, 20 Dec. 1772 - 8 Feb. 1773, leaving 39 a. of
Jackson's Hazard to son William, and parts of the same tract to
dau. Sarah, w. of Samuel Cimble, and s. Jacob Giles McCarty; he
also named his w. Sarah; dec. left iss.: WILLIAM, b. 6 March
(---); SARAH, b. 24 April 1743, m. Samuel Cimble (or Kimble), and
JACOB GILES (83:116; 112:271; 128·107, 113; 129:329).

McCARTY, AQUILA, d. by 26 March 1712 when Edward Reyston posted admin. bond with James Read and William Wilkinson; est. was
inv. 9 June 1712 by William Wilkinson and Samuel Hinton and val.
at £ 24.19.6, and signed by Edward Stevenson and Robuck Lynch as
creditors; est. admin. by Reeston on 7 Oct. 1712 (1·370; 12:295;
50·354).

McCARTY, CHARLES, servant of Thomas Rowles, in Nov. 1716 was
judged to be 15 years of age; may be the Charles Mackarty of
A. A. Co. who sold 100 a. Lucky Hole to John Conaway of Balto.
Co. in Jan. 1723 (22:61; 69:248).

McCARTY/MAKARTE, DANIEL, m. Ann Woolsher on 23 Jan. 1703/4
(128:17).

McCARTY, DENNIS, d. by 19 Nov. 1703 when admin. bond was posted by Owen Swillivant with Thomas Greenfield and Thomas Cord
(2:224, 226; 12:129).

McCARTY, JOHN, of Balto. Co., stated he was aged 35 in 1714/5
and had been a res. of the co. for 14 years; on 23 Feb. 1715
purch. 44 a. Murray's Nest from Josephus Murray, d. by 8
1732 when admin. bond was posted by Josias Middlemore with Thomas
Hatchman and Peter Carroll (12:149; 67:887; 203-3:109).

McCARTY, PHILEMON, was in Balto. Co. by 1695 as a taxable in
s. side Patapsco Hund. (140).

McCARTY, SARAH, m. William Perry on 12 Dec. 1726 (129:258).

McCARTY, WILLIAM, d. by 12 July 1709 when admin. bond was posted by admnx. Elizabeth McCarty with John Rattenbury; a second admin. bond was posted on 3 March 1709/10 by William Robinson with Peter Bond and Hugh Jones; est. was inv. by Luke Reed and Thomas Croker and val. at L 30.19.0; est. was admin. by said Robinson on 19 April 1711 and 2 Oct. 1712 (1:233, 371; 12:126, 295; 48:101).

McCARTY, WILLIAM, m. Jane Smith on 23 March 1739 (128:109).

MACKLAN, PETER, was in Balto. Co. by 1695 as a taxable in s. side Patapsco Hund. (140).

McCLANE. See McLANE.

MACCLANAN, JOHN, d. by 15 Aug. 1711 when admin. bond was posted by James McClannan with Thomas Dowcra of A. A. Co., and Samuel Guichard (12:122).

McCLOUD, WILLIAM, m. Ruth Crawford on 18 Sept. 1737 and had iss.: ANN, b. 28 Aug. 1738; William d. 2 April 1740 (128:97, 101, 111).

McCLOUGHON, THOMAS, m. Deb. King on 10 July 1761 (131).

McCOLLUM, ALEXANDER, m. Elizabeth Beeston on 12 Nov. 1745 (133:158).

McCOMAS, DANIEL (1), progenitor, was in A. A. Co. by 1687; d. by 1699; by 1707 Stephen Gill held 98 a. Brown's Chance for Daniel McComas; his inv. was filed 9 April 1700; his est. was inv. by Nicholas Sheppard and John Marriott, and val. at L 22.9.4; had iss.: JOHN, b. c.1687; WILLIAM, b. c.1689; ALEXANDER, b. c. 1695; DANIEL, b. c.1597 (206-19½B:128; 211).

McCOMAS, JOHN (2), s. of Daniel (1), was b. c.1687; d. c. 1739; m. Ann (---); admin. bond was posted 22 May 1739 by admnx. Ann McComas with Isaac Webster and Richard Ruff; m. by June 1713 Ann, extx. of John Edwards; m. by March 1719/20 Ann, mother of Julian Love; est. was inv. 10 Aug. 1739 by William Bradford and Thomas Tredway, val. at L 100.7.0, and signed by William McComas and William McComas, Jr.; wid. Ann d. Dec. 1741; dec. left iss.. MARY, b. 4 Feb. 1713; JOHN, b. 2 Nov. 1715 (may be the John, Jr., who d. 20 Nov. 1726); ALEXANDER, b. 27 Aug. 1721; MARY, b. 2 April 1724; ANN, b. 6 July 1730 (4:69; 12:165; 21:383; 23:280; 50:49; 128:34, 44, 59, 97, 105; 129:324; 131:20/r).

McCOMAS, WILLIAM (3), s. of Daniel (1), was b. c.1689; d. c. 1749; m. Hannah (---); in June 1729 he purch. part Gresham's College from Solomon and Sarah Wooden; d. leaving a will, 21 Sept. 1747 - 30 Jan. 1748, leaving 50 a. Gresham's College to each of four sons, Daniel, Solomon, Moses, and Aaron, half his dwell. plant. to sons William and John; named daus. Elizabeth Tredway and Hannah Amos and Eleanor Miles; admin. bond was posted 27 Feb. 1748 by Hannah and Daniel McComas, execs., with Thomas Tredway and William Amos, Jr.; est. was inv. on 12 May 1749 by William Bradford and Benj. Norris and val. at L 607.4.7½ and signed by William McComas and Elizabeth Tredway as kin; est. was admin. 24 March 1749 and 19 Oct. 1750 by the execs.; in 1750 his heirs owned 195 a. part Gresham's College and 90 a. part Littleton; had iss.: ELIZABETH, b. 4 Nov. 1728, m. Thomas Tredway; HANNAH, b. 6 April 1723, m. William Amos, Jr.; ELEANOR, b. 2 April 1725, m. Peter Miles; DANIEL, b. 8 Feb. 1721; WILLIAM, b. 24 Nov. 1727; SOLOMON, b. 21 Sept. 1729; MOSES, b. 15 May 1732; AARON, b. 3 July 1734; JOHN, b. 15 Sept. 1736 (5·135, 252, 273; 12:201; 49:366; 72:31; 131; 153:33).

McCOMAS, ALEXANDER (4), s. of Daniel (1), was b. c.1695; d. by 4 Feb. 1761; m. 1st, on 19 Nov. 1713, Elizabeth, dau. of Nicholas and Sarah Day; m. 2nd, on 23 Aug. 1728 Hannah Whitaker sho m. as her 2nd husb. Thomas Miles by 26 Sept. 1762; on 5 May 1724 with w. Elizabeth sold tract Macedon to John Norris; his will was dated 8 Oct. 1760, proved 4 Feb. 1761; wid. Hannah Mc-Comas conv. prop. to ch. Aquila, Hannah w. of Jacob Miles, and Priscilla w. of Thomas Simmons, on 18 Aug. 1761; est. admin. 26 Sept. 1762 by extx. Hannah, now w. of Thomas Miles; had iss.: SARAH, b. 5 Nov. 1714, m. Richard Rhodes; MARY, b. 8 May 1726, m. John Whitaker; HANNAH, b. 25 March 1730, m. Jacob Miles; AQUILA, b. 15 March 1753 (m. Sarah Preston on 2 Jan. 1752); ALEXANDER; DANIEL; ELIZABETH, m. (---) Norris, PRISCILLA, m. Thomas Simmons; DAVID(4:365; 128; 210-31:179; Myers, Norris Fam., p. 73).

McCOMAS, DANIEL (5), s. of Daniel (1), was b. c.1697; d. by 2 Sept. 1765; m. Martha Scott on 26 Dec. 1734 (she was b. 1716, d. 1786); in 1750 he owned 305½ a. Gresham College and 100 a. of Walnut Neck; d. leaving a will, 15 June 1765 - 2 Sept. 1765; left iss.: JAMES, b. 13 Sept. 1735; ELIZABETH, b. 1 July 1737; WILLIAM, b. 17 May 1739; JOHN, b. 20 Oct. 1741; MARTHA, b. 7 June 1749, DANIEL; AQUILA; MARY; SARAH, m. (---) Bradford; and HANNAH (112: 19; 131; 153:8).

McCOMAS, ALEXANDER (6), s. of John (2), was b. 27 Aug. 1721 and was living in 1750 when as Alexander McComas of John he owned 18 a. part of Strawberry Hills and Deaver's Addition (153:70).

McCOMAS, DANIEL (7), s. of William (3), was b. 8 Feb. 1721; he inherited 50 a. Gresham's College; was living in Gunpowder Upper and Lower Hundred in 1783, owning 100 a. Gresham's College and 200 a. part Clagett's Forest (283).

McCOMAS, WILLIAM (8), s. of William (3), was b. 24 Nov. 1727; d. by 7 April 1757; inherited one-half of his father's dwelling plantation; m. Hannah Deaver on 27 July 1742; admin. bond was posted 10 Jan. 1757 by Daniel McComas of William with Solomon and Moses McComas; est. was inv. on 7 April 1757 by Thomas Bond and Geo. Bradford, val. at £ 20.1.1, signed by Solomon and Moses McComas as kin, and by Aaron McComas and David McCulloch as creditors, his est. was admin. by his bro. Daniel McComas of Wm. on 5 June 1758; had iss.: JOHN, b. 7 Oct. 1744 (6:13; 12:198; 50:37; 129:324, 339).

McCOMAS, SOLOMON (9), s. of William (3), was b. 21 Sept. 1729; inherited 50 a. Gresham's College; in 1776 lived with w. Ann (b. c.1736) in Bush R. Lower Hund., with their ch.: WILLIAM, b. c. 1757; AARON, b. c.1760; MARY, b. c.1762; HANNAH, b. c.1764 (277: 137).

McCOMAS, MOSES (10), s. of William (3), was b. 15 May 1732; inherited 50 a. Gresham's College; m. a dau. of Daniel McComas (# 5 above) (7:192).

McCOMAS, JOHN (11), s. of William (3), was b. 15 Sept. 1736; m. Salina (---) (b. c.1741), inherited one-half of his father's dwelling plantation; in 1776 was living in Bush R. Lower Hund. with his w. and three known ch.: HANNAH, b. c.1764; ELIZABETH, b. c.1772; WILLIAM JOSHUA, b. c.1774 (277.133-134).

McCOMAS, AQUILA (12), s. of Alexander (4), was b. 5 May 1731; d. by 21 Oct. 1771; m. 2 Jan. 1752, Sarah, dau. of James Preston; in Aug. 1761 was conv. prop. by his mother; d. leaving a will, 17 Sept. 1771 - 21 Oct. 1771; est. was admin. by extx. Sarah

McComas on 7 April 1773; had iss. (named in will): JOHN; ALEX-
ANDER; MARY; PRISCILLA; ELIZABETH; HANNAH; and SARAH (6:264;
57:111; 112:48, 178; 131).

McCOMAS, ALEXANDER (13), s. of Alexander (4), m. by 27 July
1747 Deborah, admnx. of Thomas Beaver; in 1750 owned 200 a.
Horse Range; had issue: EDWARD DAY; ALEXANDER; NICHOLAS DAY;
ELIZABETH LYTLE; MARY; GEORGE (153:31; McComas and McComas, The
McComas Saga)

McCOMAS, DANIEL (14), s. of Alexander (4), may have m. 1st,
on 15 March 1753 Hannah Taylor; may have m. 2nd on 10 Oct. 1758,
Ann, dau. of Thomas Miles; d. by 25 May 1761 when his est. was
inv. by Joshua Amos and John (Poteet?), val. at L 144.1.3½,
signed by Robert Craige and Aquila Hall as creditors; est. was
admin. by Ann, now w. of John Poteet, on 27 June 1763; left
two ch., unnamed (6:55, 70; 47:55; 49:258, 262).

McCOMAS , JAMES (15), s. of Daniel (5), was b. 13 Sept. 1735;
m. Elizabeth Hillen on 15 Nov. 1761; in Aug. 1762 he purch. part
Littleton from Thomas White formerly of Balto. Co. and now of
Phila.; in 1776 lived with w. and ch. in Bush River Lower Hundred of Harf. Co.; had iss.: WILLIAM, b. c.1762; JAMES, Jr., c.
c.1764; JOSIAH, b. c.1766; MARTHA, b. c.1770; ELIZABETH, b. c.
1772, SUSANNA, b. c.1774; NATHANIEL, b. c.1776 (86:271; 277:136).

McCOMAS, WILLIAM (16), s. of Daniel (5), was b. 17 May 1739,
d. 1815; m. Hannah Bond, and had at least one s.: FREDERICK, m.
1789 Susanna Onion.

McCOMAS, JOHN (17), s. of Daniel (5), was b. 20 Oct. 1741;
may be the John, age 33 in 1776, living with w. Mary, b. c. 1751,
in Bush River Lower Hund., Harf. Co., with one s.: AQUILA, b. c.
1774 (277:130).

McCOMAS, DANIEL, Jr., m. Tabitha Johnson on 26 Jan. 1743 (131).

McCOMAS, Mrs. ELEANOR, d. 4 Aug. 1727 (131).

McCOMAS, MARY, m. 22 Jan. 1742 Samuel Whips (131).

McCONNIKIN, JOHN, was b. c.1716; m. 1st, on 26 Feb. 1653,
Mary Darby, and 2nd, on 20 Sept. 1762 Eleanor Long; gave his
age as c.47 on 1 Sept. 1763 (89:92; 133:168).

McCORMICK, GEORGE, age 3 last 20 May, in June 1757 was bound
to Thomas Miller, Jr. (56:38).

MacCROY, THOMAS, d. by 14 April 1747 when admin. bond was
posted by Avarilla Hall, with Parker Hall (12:118).

MacCUBBIN, SAMUEL, d. in Balto. Co. leaving a will, 29 Sept.
1739 - 11 Dec. 1739, naming his bro.-in-law Joseph Lane, his
father Samuel, and mentioning his w. and two sisters; admin.
bond was posted 11 Dec. 1739 by exec. Joseph Lane, with Buckler
Partridge, Michael Rutledge, and Thomas Dulany; est. was admin.
by Joseph Lane on 16 Dec. 1740, 15 May 1741, 15 Jan. 1745, 18
June 1747, and 12 Aug. 1748, when one of the heirs was named as
Elizabeth, w. of John West (4:60, 72, 156, 208; 5:48; 12:163;
127:67).

MacCUBBIN, WILLIAM, m. Clara Whips on 11 Aug. 1735; in 1750
he owned 240 a. Maxwell's Habitation; admin. bond was posted 20
June 1753 by Clara MacCubbin with Mayberry Helm and Edward Puntany; est. was admin. 16 March 1754 by Clara, who stated that

the dec. left one ch., aged 13; had iss.: WILLIAM, b. c.1741; in
Nov. 1755 William chose Anthony Rhodes his guardian (4:230; 12:
211; 40:398; 133:154; 153:83).

MacCUBBIN, ZACHARIAH, m. Sarah Norwood on 7 Nov. 1745; with
Edward Norwood surv. 256 a. Bachelor's Fear and 44 a. Partnership;
in 1750 owned 245 a. part Ashman's Hope, 200 a. Turkey Island, 22
a. Partnership, and 128 a. part Bachelor's Fear (133:158; 153:68;
207).

McCULLEN, PHILIP, d. by 10 March 1755 when admin. bond was
posted by Andrew Stewart with Andrew Thompson (12:234).

McCULLISTER, EDWARD, m. Mary Ryley on 21 Oct. 1754 (131).

McCULLOCH, DAVID, was in Balto. Co. by 1756 when he wrote to
his bro. Henry McCulloch of Torhouse near Wigtown, Galloway, mentioning his mother and sisters still living; was 2nd s. of John
McCulloch of Torhousekey; m. Mary Dick, dau. of James Dick, on 4
July 1759, in All Hallows Par., A. A. Co.; d. 17 Sept. 1766, aged
48, and was bur. at Joppa Town; d. leaving a will, 28 Aug. 1766 -
6 Oct. 1766, appointing w. as extx., and naming three ch., and
mentioning an unborn ch.; had iss.: JAMES; MARGARET; and ELIZA-
BETH (112:34; 219-1; 300-65:262).

McCULLOCH, JOHN, m. Jane (---), and had iss.: WILLIAM, b. 1
April 1760; and JANET, b. 7 April 1762 (129:376).

McCULLOM, ALEXANDER, d. by 1 May 1750 when admin. bond was posted by Elizabeth McCullom, admnx., of A. A. Co., with John Cromwell and John Cromwell of Joshua; est. was admin. by the admnx.
on 2 May 1751 (5:229; 12:221).

MACURAHOM, ARTHUR, m. Rachel Gilbert on 29 June 1726 (129:340).

McDANIEL, CHARLES, m. Joanna, wid. of James Barlow by 2 Nov.
1723 (1:328; 2:311; 3·21).

McDANIEL, DENNIS, d. by 27 Sept. 1702 when admin. bond was posted by John Jones with John Selby; est. was admin. by John Jones
on 14 Oct. 1704 (2:223, 238B; 12:309).

McDANIEL, ELEANOR, had iss.: JOHN, b. 28 May 1724 (128:98).

McDANIEL, HUGH, of P. G. Co., m. by 13 March 1737, Elizabeth,
relict of John Yates of Balto. Co. (75·61).

McDANIEL, JAMES, m. Sarah Jones on 1 June 1739, and had iss..
ANN, b. 20 Aug. 1739 (128:104).

McDANIEL, JOHN, aged 16 next May, in March 1742/3 was bound to
Samuel Gilbert (34·122).

McDANIEL, MARY, m. John Whitaker on 28 Feb. 1714 (129:215).

McDONALD, DANIEL, d. by 19 Sept. 1757 when admin. bond was posted by Thomas Head, with Richard Cross (12:231).

McDONALD, EVAN, in 1750 owned 50 a. Water Oak Level (153:80).

McDONALD, JANE, in Aug. 1720 named Thomas Chilcoat as the
father of her child (23:367).

McDOWELL, MORTO (1), was in Balto. Co. by July 1722 when he
surv. 100 a. Pleasant Green, on 26 Sept. 1730 he and w. Eleanor
conv. 100 a. to Richard Gist; in 1750 as Murto Mackdaniel he owned

100 a. Bring Me Home; prob. d. by 1752 leaving a s.: MICHAEL (73:38; 153:93; 207).

McDOWELL, MICHAEL (2), heir and poss. s. of Morto (1), was in Halifax Co., Va., by 19 Sept. 1752 when he conv. his share of 100 a. Bring Me Home to Joseph Murray; in Sept. 1755 he gave p/a to John Hawkins to sell the afsd. tract (78:507; 82:407).

McDUGGLE, JOHN, m. Elinor Harmon on 28 June 1747 (131).

McELROY/MACKELDORY, JOHN, m. Frances (---); in Nov. 1716 he surv. 100 a. Francis' Delight; in Aug. 1725 John and Frances conv. his part of 156 a. Robert and John's Lot to Robert Clark who had joined McElroy in taking up the tract; admin. the est. of James Durham on 30 June 1726; had iss.: RACHEL, b. 7 Aug. 1713, m. Avington Phelps on 23 April 1730; JOHN, b. 7 Dec. 1715; WILLIAM, b. 23 Dec. 1718; ARCHIBALD, b. 13 Feb. 1719, prob. d. 1760 in Johnston Co., N.C. (3:54; 70:147; 207).

McEWEN, CHRISTOPHER, m. Ann Walker on 6 Sept. 1747 (133:60).

McFADDEN, ANANIAS, d. by 29 March 1746 when admin. bond was posted by Amos Garret with Vincent Dorsey and William Copeland; est. was admin. by Garret on 29 Oct. 1757; left one s.: JOHN (5: 238; 12:185).

McFADDEN, JOHN, blacksmith, d. by 28 March 1765 when his est. was admin. by David McCulloch; may be the same John who m. Margaret (---), and had iss.: JOHN, b. 16 May 1743; DEBORAH, b. June 1745; RANDALL, b. Sept. 1747; MARY, b. July 1749; THOMAS, b. Sept. 1757 (6:185; 131:146/r).

MacGALL, JOHN, m. Jane Martin on 2 Dec. 1756 (131:214).

McGAY, ROBERT, m. Sarah Lester on 2 Feb. 1758, and had iss.: GEORGE, b. 28 Jan. 1759; JOHN, b. 7 Aug. 1761; ROBERT, b. 2 March 1763; WILLIAM, b. 20 June 1765; HUGH, b. 21 Feb. 1767; and JAMES, b. 11 Feb. 1770 (129:359, 380, 386).

MacGEE, JNO., m. Margaret Little on 15 July 1751 (131).

MacGOMERY, WILLIAM, m. Mary Brierly on 7 Nov. 1738, and had iss.: ELIZABETH, b. 31 Aug. 1739 (129:322).

MackGUGIN, PATRICK, m. Elizabeth MackDaniel on 21 Sept. 1735 (133:154).

McGUIRE, MICHAEL, was in Balto. Co. by 1750 when he owned 100 a. Patience Care; m. by 3 July 1759 Eleanor, admnx. of Abraham Jarrett (4:253, 302; 153:70).

McILVAINE, DAVID, was tried for bast. as the father of Mary Murphy's ch., in March 1754 (39:27).

McILVAINE, ROBERT, d. by 27 July 1751 when admin. bond was posted by James Preston with James Mattingly; was in Balto. Co. by 14 May 1745 when he mortgaged 100 a. Bond's Gift to Joshua Bond; his est. was admin. by James and Mary Preston on 9 May 1752 and 10 Aug. 1752 (5:234, 261; 12:218; 77:102).

McINTOSH, DANIEL, d. by Dec. 1716; was in Balto. Co. by Feb. 1710 when he admin. the est. of John Hamilton; 1st admin. bond was posted 4 Dec. 1716 by admnx. Margaret McIntosh with John Cameron and John Frazier; Margaret m. as her 2nd husb. John Cameron on 12 Dec. 1716, and a 2nd admin. bond was posted 19 April

1717 by Margaret Cameron with Simon Pierson and John Gross; est. was admin. 17 March 1719 by John Harrison who had m. the wid. of the dec. (1:49; 2:131; 12:117, 121; 48:318; 131).

McINTOSH, PETER, Scottish, age c.28, ran away from John Stansbury in Patapsco Forest in Aug. 1734 (307-69:130).

MacKARNY, ANN, was ind. for bast. in Nov. 1710, and named John Carrington as the father (21:187).

MACKELDORY. See McELROY.

MACKELFRESH, DAVID, purch. part of Cross' Forest, 357 a., from John and Elinor Cross on 9 Aug. 1704; surv. 100 a. Pork Hall in Dec. 1705 (66:346; 207).

MACKENALL, WALTER, and w. Jane were in Balto. Co. by July 1669 when they purch. 200 a. York's Hope from William and Elizabeth York; d. by 1 June 1676 when admin. bond was posted by Thomas Jones with Thomas Preston (12:308; 95).

MACKENLEY, ALEXANDER, was in Balto. Co. by 1750 as the owner of 100 a. Michael's Hazard (153:39).

MacKENLEY, ALLEN, m. Susanna Freziel on 23 April 1745 (131).

McKENLEY, ROGER, m. Mary Kelley on 1 June 1760 (131).

McKENNEY, JANE, serv. to James Moore, was ind. for bast. in Aug. 1737; had iss.:MARTHA, b. 25 Aug. 1738 (prob. the Martha who d. 30 Sept. 1741) (31:97; 128:92B; 129:322).

MacKENZIE, GABRIEL, was in Balto. Co. by 1750 as the owner of Gabriel's Choice (153:64).

McKENZIE, JOHN, is found in the 1698/9 inv. of Moses Groome as a servt. man with 3 years and 2 mos. to serve; may be the same John McKenzie who had surv. 100 a. Hopford Choice (48:326; 207).

McKIM, WILLIAM, Irishman, employed as a skipper on a sloop in Back River; abandoned the sloop in April 1744 (384:442).

McKINNEY, CHRISTIAN, was fined for bast. in Nov. 1759 (46: 241-242).

McKINNEY, SAMUEL, m. Rebecca (---), and had iss.: JOHN, b. 24 March 1745 (131:113/r).

McKINNIE, DONALD, overseer for Mr. Diggs, was murdered by Daniel Sullivan, who was convicted of the crime in April or May of 1751 (385:126).

McKINY, JANE. See McKENNEY, JANE.

MacKLEDAY, JOHN, m. by March 1719/20, Ann, extx. of Robert Gardner (23:342).

McKUNE, CHRISTOPHER, m. Ann (---), and had iss.: MARGARET, b. 14 Nov. 1749 (133:88).

McLACHLAN, ANN, was tried for bast. in Nov. 1756, named as the father Frederick Ashmore (41:312).

McLANE/McCLANE/McCLEAN/McLEAN, HECTOR (1), was in Balto. Co. by 1692 as a taxable in n. side Patapsco Hund.; surv. 300 a. of

Hector's Hopyard on 25 July 1694, and 100 a. Hector's Fancy on 20 Feb. 1695; wit. the will of John Carrington of Balto. Co. on 22 March 1695; m. by 9 June 1697 Sarah, dau. of Thomas Morgan, and had iss.: HECTOR (131:105, 140; 138; 211).

McLANE, HECTOR (2), s. of Hector (1), d. in Balto. Co. by 1 Oct. 1722; m. 1st, Ann (---), and 2nd, Amy, dau. of George Norman; she m. as her 2nd husb. John Townsend; in April 1719 surv. 300 a. Hector's Chance and 50 a. Maclane's Friendship; d. leaving a will, 2 July 1722 - 1 Oct. 1722, in which he left 1 shilling to each of his ch. by former w. Ann, wife Amy, and ch. Sarah Bailey, John, William, and Nathaniel; admin. bond was posted 1 Oct. 1722 by extx. Amy with Thomas Cromwell and George Bailey; est. was inv. 22 March 1723 by Christopher Randall and Richard Owen and val. at £ 261.2.3, and signed by John McLane and George Bailey as kin; est. admin. by Amy, w. of John Townsend, on 26 May 1733; left iss.: JOHN; WILLIAM; NATHANIEL; SARAH, m. George Bailey; MARY; and CATHERINE, m. John Stinchcomb (3:12, 126; 12: 144; 30:133;; 52:16;; 124:126; 207).

McLANE, JOHN (3), s. of Hector (2), m. Margaret Taylor on 14 Jan. 1733; in 1750 owned 25 a. MacLaine's Hills, and 50 a. Folly; in Aug. 1752 John and Margaret conv. pt. Addition to McLaine's Hills (orig. granted to said John in Aug. 1752) to Solomon Stocksdale; had iss.: SARAH, b. 16 Nov. 1734; HECTOR, b. 14 Sept. 1736; JOHN, b. 4 Feb. 1738/9 (82:139; 133:42, 55, 62, 151; 153:74; 207).

McLANE, WILLIAM (4), s. of Hector (2), d. by 18 Jan. 1752; m. Mary (---); in 1750 owned 40 a. Bought Well, 40 a. Hector's Fancy and 20 a. part Athol; d. leaving a will, 26 Jan. 1749/50 - 18 Jan. 1752, naming w. Mary and sis. Catherine Stinchcomb; admin. bond was posted 8 Jan. 1752 by extx. Mary McLane with Thomas Johnson and Emanuel Teal (12:219; 111:44; 153:29).

McLANE, JAMES, aged 23, d. leaving a will, 28 March 1724 - 27 May 1724, naming father-in-law Matthew Organ (124:198).

McLECHLIN, HUGH, was fined for bast. in Nov. 1758 (46:162).

McLOUGHLIN, HUGH, servant, was listed in the 1749 inv. of James Carroll (53).

McMAH, JANE, aged 9 last March, dau. of William McMah, was bd. to Thomas Brierly in June 1758 (44).

McMAHAN, BENJAMIN, m. Lucretia, and had iss.: BENJAMIN, b. 25 Jan. 1758; THOMAS, b. 17 Oct. 1760 (129:367).

McMILLON, ALEXANDER, m. Phoebe (---), and had iss.: MATTHEW, b. 13 June 1728; SUSANNA, b. 25 Feb. 1734; and URATH, b. 23 March 1735/6 (133:15, 47).

McNAMARA, MICHAEL, was in Balto. Co. by 1750 as the owner of 800 a. Pimlico (153:103).

McNAMARA, THOMAS, in May 1706 surv. Gunner's Range; d. by 26 Sept. 1719 when his est. was inv. by John Israel and Thomas Randall and val. at £ 341.5.0; an additional inv. was filed 24 Aug. 1720 for £ 5.0.0, and was signed by James McNamara (48:215, 323; 207).

McQUEEN, DUGAL, progenitor, was b. in Scotland, and d. in Balto. Co. c.1746; m. Grace (---) who may have been the wid. of one (---) Brown; was captured after the Jacobite uprising

of 1715, and was taken prisoner at Preston, Lancs., Eng., in Nov.
1716; shipped to Maryland on the Friendship, Michael Mankin,
capt.; in Md. was purchased for 7 years by William Holland; by
1732 was a taxable in Upper Hund. of the Cliffs, Calvert Co.; on
1 March 1739/40 while living in P. G. Co., surv. Cranberry Plains,
near Cranberry Glade; d. leaving a will dated 26 March 1746 and
proved the same year, in which he named w. Grace, son-in-law John
Brown, and ch.: WILLIAM; FRANCIS; and THOMAS (Smith, "Transported
Jacobite Rebels, 1716," in NGSQ, 64:31; Stein, Hist. of Calvert
Co., p. 375; 207; 210-25:10-11).

McQUEEN, WILLIAM (2), s. of Dugal (1), was in Balto. Co. by
March 1761 when he surv. 35½ a. McQueen's Choice; by 1796 was in
Washington Co., Penna. (207; 231-WG#VV:460).

McQUEEN, FRANCIS (3), s. of Dugal (1), was b. 1 Aug. 1741 in
St. Paul's Par., Balto. Co. (133:66).

McQUEEN, THOMAS (4), s. of Dugal (1), was in Balto. Co. by 22
Jan. 1760 when he pat. 29 a. Foxes Thicket (207).

McSHAINE or McSWAINE, ELIZABETH (1), was in Balto. Co. by Sept.
1741 when she had iss.: DAVID (76:29).

McSWAINE, DAVID (2), s. of Elizabeth (1), was aged 7 years, 6
mos. on 26 Sept. 1741 when he was bd. by his mother to Thomas and
Anne Phelps; m. Hannah (---), and had iss.: THOMAS, b. 12 Aug.
1756; JONATHAN, b. 26 March 1758 (76:29; 129:362).

McTAVISH, DANIEL, and w. Margaret were in Balto. Co. by 3 Nov.
1714 when they conv. 100 a. Tower Hill to John Durbin (67:316).

McVEY, OWEN, laborer, age c.25, runaway conv. serv. of Hugh
Copeland, Balto. Co., (385:19).

MEACHAM, EDWARD, m. Anne (---); may be the Edward Meachem,
age c.40 pretending to be a schoolmaster, who ran away from John
Metcalfe at Patapsco R., Balto. Co., in April 1753; had iss. by
Ann: THOMAS, b. 15 May 1743 (133:73; 307-69:132).

MEACK, MORRICK, m. Eleanor Warin on 7 Aug. 1726 (133:148).

THE FRANCIS MEAD FAMILY

MEAD, FRANCIS (1), progenitor of this branch, was in A. A.
Co., where he d. betw. 4 Jan. 1716 and 6 Aug. 1717; m. as his
2nd w. Anne (---) who d. in Balto. Co. in 1725 (Francis' 1st w.
has not been identified); d. leaving a will, 4 Jan. 1716 - 6 Aug.
1717, naming sons William, John, and Benjamin, Susanna Long, son-
in-law Thomas Dawson, granddau. Hannah Crans, dau.-in-law Mary
Wright, and John and James Beard; will of Anna, relict of Francis
Mead, 9 Jan. 1723 - 10 Nov. 1725, naming s. Benjamin, his dau.
Nanney, Anna's dau. Mary Wright and her sons John and William,
and grandch. John and James Boards; admin. bond posted 5 Jan.
1737 by Benjamin Cadle; iss. of Francis: SUSANNA, m. 1st Thomas
Long, and 2nd, on 3 April 1722, Stephen Body; BENJAMIN, d. 1764;
JOHN; WILLIAM (12:157; 123:122; 114:202; 313:101).

MEAD, BENJAMIN (2), s. of Francis (1), d. in Balto. Co. by 20
Feb. 1764; m. Elizabeth Dawdridge on 17 Nov. 1708 in St. Margaret's Par., A. A. Co.; she d. 6 Oct. 1740 in Balto. Co.; was in
Balto. Co. by 1750 as the owner of 200 a. Francis' Chance; d.
leaving a will, 15 April 1761 - 20 Feb. 1764; had iss.: MARY,
b. 27 Aug. 1709 in A. A. Co.; not in father's will; WILLIAM, b.
27 Feb. 1711 in St. Marg.'s Par., not in father's will; ANN, b.

28 May 1714, m. (---) Dulany; ELIZABETH, b. 27 Sept. 1716, not
in father's will; SUSANNA, b. 21 Sept. 1717; m. 1st John Ingram,
and 2nd, on 11 Feb. 1742 John Buck; HANNAH, b. 25 April 1725; m.
1st, on 29 Sept. 1743 Joshua Starkey, and 2nd, on 22 Sept. 1757
James Crouch; BENJAMIN, d. 1774; RUTH, b. 13 March 1729 in St.
John's Par., may have d. young; RUTH, b. 1731 (131; 153:7; 210-
2:364; 219-4).

THE EDWARD MEAD FAMILY

MEAD, EDWARD (3), no known rel. to any of the above, and progenitor of this line, d. in Balto. Co. by 31 March 1763; m. Dorcas "Eums" or Ewens on 13 Oct. 1713; she d. 5 Jan. 1727, and he
m. 2nd Catherine (---); in July 1736 was summoned by the vestry
of St. John's Par., to answer charges of unlawful cohabitation
with Catherine Baker; in 1750 owned 50 a. part Bridal Dock; d.
leaving a will, 5 April 1760 - 31 March 1763; admin. bond was
posted 31 March 1763, and his est. was admin. 18 April 1767 by
Samuel Ricketts; est. of Catherine Mead was admin. by Benjamin
Mead on 3 June 1769 after he posted admin. bond on 3 June 1765;
Edward had six ch. by 1st w., and eight by his 2nd: JOHN EWINGS,
b. 13 Dec. 1714; ZEPHIA, b. March 1717, m. Lemuel Baker on 5
March 1739; JAMES, b. 29 Feb. 1719, m. Anne Forrest on 21 Dec.
1747; ELIZABETH, b. 17 Sept. 1721; ANN, b. 7 April 1724, prob.
d. young; ANN, b. 18 April 1725 (by 2nd w.): ANN, b. 29 April
1728, d. Aug. 1728; MARY, b. 22 Oct. 1730; HANNAH, b. 26 March
1733, m. Samuel Ricketts on 24 Dec. 1733; EDWARD, b. 26 Jan.
1735; JOHN, b. 10 Oct. 1736, d. Aug. 1737; BENJAMIN, b. 26 March
1739; BETHIAH, b. 6 Oct. 1732, d. Aug. 1740; WILLIAM, b. 22 April 1740 (7:34, 301; 12:245, 254; 131; 132:14; 153:1; 210-31:
839).

MEAD, EDWARD (4), s. of Edward (3), was b. 26 Jan. 1735; m.
Ann (---), and had iss.: JAMES, twin, b. 26 Dec. 1752; MORDECAI,
twin, b. 26 Dec. 1752 (131).

THE JOSEPH MEAD FAMILY

MEAD, JOSEPH (5), progenitor, d. in Balto. Co. by 23 Nov.
1737; m. Elizabeth or Eleanor, dau. of John Hackett, on 14 Dec.
1711 in All Hallow's Par., A. A. Co.; d. leaving a will, 17 Sept.
1737 - 23 Nov. 1737, naming bro. Benjamin Cadle, and his own ch.:
Joseph, James, and Elizabeth; admin. bond posted 5 Jan. 1737 by
Benjamin Cadle with James Maxwell and Jacob Jackson; est. was admin. 14 June 1739 by Cadle; the wid. of Joseph Mead m. as her 2nd
husb., by 5 March 1744, George York; Joseph left iss.: JOSEPH, b.
May 1717; JAMES, b. 6 Jan. 1719; ELIZABETH, b. 31 Dec. 1723; SEL-
BY, b. 4 April 1726; son, b. April 1728 (4:45; 12:157; 32:151;
78:49; 126:230; 131; 219-1:78).

MEAD, JOSEPH (6), s. of Joseph (5), was b. May 1717, and on
10 Jan. 1737 he m. Mary Legoe; in 1750 owned 100 a. Cabin Neck;
d. by 8 Aug. 1751 when admin. bond was posted by Robert Adair
with Roger Boyce and John Paca, Jr.; had iss.: ELIZABETH, b. 26
Jan. 1742; ANN, b. 29 April 1741; JOSEPH, b. 11 Jan. 1747 (12:
232; 131; 153:48).

MEAD, ANN, was ind. for bast. in March 1736 (31:1).

MEAD, JOHN, was exempt from levy in Nov. 1738 (31:310).

MEAD, MARY, was summoned by the vestry of St. John's Par. for
unlawful cohabitation with William Savory in March 1753; Savory
promised not to live with her any more (132:117).

MEAD, JAMES, m. Elizabeth James after the banns were pub. three
times in Dec. 1742· (131).

MEAD, THOMAS, m. Mary Rowings on 12 Jan. 1756 (131).

MEADAHOAN, BENJAMIN, in 1738 was named as the father-in-law
of John Ingram of Balto. Co. (127:75).

MEALE, WILLIAM, m. Sarah Hill on 7 Oct. 1759 (131).

MEARS, ABRAHAM, m. Jane Slaughter on 31 Dec. 1752; had iss.:
ELIZABETH, b. 1 March 1753; ABRAHAM, b. 6 Dec. 1754 (131:134/r).

MEDCALFE. See METCALFE.

MEGAY, ROBERT, m. Sarah Lester on 2 Feb. 1758 (129:359).

MEGUMMERY. See MONTGOMERY.

MEKIN, HANGOS, was in Balto. Co. by 1694 as a taxable in n.
side Patapsco Hund. (139).

MELLOR, JOHN, was in Balto. Co. by 23 June 1726 when he conv.
200 a. Scott's Folly to Nehemiah Mellor (70:251).

MELTON, SARAH, had iss.: LEANA (base-born dau.), b. 10 April
1720 and left with John Harper (131).

MERCER, LUKE, in 1750 owned 50 a. Mercer's Lot and 10 a. Raw-
ley's Neck; m. Barbara Jacks on 1 Aug. 1738 in Christ Ch., Q.
Caroline Par., A. A. (now Howard) Co.; d. leaving a will, 22
Sept. 1775 - 14 Nov. 1775, naming w. Barbara and these ch.: FRAN-
CIS; RICHARD; ANDREW; WELDON; ELIZABETH, m. Henry Poole; ANN, w.
of William Wagers (112:305; 153:57; 263).

MERCER, WILLIAM, d. leaving a will, 9 Oct. 1759 - 4 Dec. 1759,
naming bro. John as heir and exec.; admin. bond was posted 4 Dec.
1759 by John Mercer with William Andrew and Christopher Duke (12:
225; 111:303).

MEREDITH, SAMUEL, was b. c.1713, and gave his age as 40 in
March 1753; m. Elizabeth Cook on 3 Feb. 1735, and Jemima Taylor
on 2 Feb. 1748; had iss. (by 1st w.): SARAH, b. 20 June 1736;
ACTIA, b. 20 July 1740; RACHEL, b. 8 May 1743 (133:50, 63, 73;
225:231).

MEREDITH, THOMAS, m. Susanna Cox on 22 May 1755; had iss.:
ANN, b. 7 March 1756; HENRY, b. 4 Aug. 1757 (131:46, 131/r).

MERRICA. See MERRIKEN.

MERRIKEN/MERRICA, HUGH, m. by 23 Dec. 1719 Ann, wid. and extx.
of George Westall (1:46, 47).

MERRIKEN, JOSHUA, d. 8 Nov. 1725; m. 1st, on 16 Feb. 1709/10.
Elizabeth Ewins; she d. 17 Dec. 1716, and he m. 2nd, on 24 June
1718, Dinah Day; d. leaving a will, 6 Nov. 1726 - 8 March 1726/7,
naming w. Diana, unborn ch. to be named Joshua or Diana, ch.
Hugh, Anne, and Mary; admin. bond was posted 5 April 1727 by the
extx. Diana Merriken with Luke Stansbury and Edward Day; Diana
m. as her 2nd husb. , on 5 Jan. 1737, Benjamin Jones; had iss.:
MARY, b. 24 April 171(?), m. Robert Dutton on 11 Dec. 1744; HUGH,
b. 17 Sept. 1721, bapt. 8 April 1722, d 9 March 1738; ANN, d. 4
May 1730 (11:135; 125:11; 128:26; 131:9, 11, 27, 1/r, 40/r, 44/r,
70/r, 76/r).

MERRITT, GEORGE, was in Balto. Co. by 1692 as a taxable in
Spesutia Hund. (128).

THE MERRYMAN FAMILY was discussed by Francis B. Culver in his article of that name first published in the Maryland Historical Magazine, X, 176-185, 286-299, and 398; and XI, 85, and repr. in Maryland Genealogies (364-2:208-232).

MERRYMAN, JOHN (1), progenitor, d. in Lancaster Co., Va., by 10 Nov. 1680, leaving a wid. Audrey (---), who m. as her 2nd husb. Edward Carter of Lancaster Co.; was in York Co., Va. by 1645; transported his w. by 1649; was Constable in 1664 and one of the Justices of Lancaster Co., as well as church warden of St. Mary's Parish; had iss.: WILLIAM, alive in 1677; ELIZABETH, b. by 1652 , and ment. in wills of Gyles Taverner in 1655 and John Bonny in 1666; CHARLES, b. by 1660 (364-2:209-210).

MERRYMAN, CHARLES (2), s. of John(1) and Audrey, was b. in Va. by 1660, and came to Balto. Co., where he d. on 22 Dec. 1725; m. Mary (---); was in Balto. Co. by 1682 when he purch. 300 a. East Humphreys from Thomas and Hannah (Ball) Everest; in 1696 was a capt. of militia; may be the Charles Merryman who m. by Nov. 1693 the admnx. of Andrew Matson or Watson; d. leaving a will, 16 Jan. 1724 - 14 Jan. 1725, naming w. Mary, dau. Elizabeth Cox, grandson Merryman Cox, eld. s. John, ygst s. Samuel; admin. bond was posted 11 Feb. 1725 by Mary Merryman with James Moore and George Cole; est. was inv. on 5 Feb. 1725/6 by John Eaglestone and Luke Trotten, and signed by John Merryman and the admnx. Mary Merryman; est. was admin. on 8 Nov. 1726; had iss.: CHARLES, Jr.,; JOHN, d. c.1749; SAMUEL, d. 1754; ELIZABETH, m. 1st on 25 Sept. 1722 Jacob Cox who d. 1 Nov. 1724, and 2nd, on 3 Sept. 1727 Samuel Smith (3:81; 12:139; 19:425; 51:61; 64:176; 133:150, 193; 200-20:544; 364).

MERRYMAN, CHARLES (3), s. of Charles (2), d. in Balto. Co. on 17 May 1722; m. by 24 June 1702, Jane, wid. of Joseph Peake and dau. of Jane Long (prob. by her 2nd husb. Maj. Thomas Long); Jane m. as her 3rd husb. Benjamin Knight on 6 Aug. 1723; Jane Peake, named in the will of her mother on 19 May 1696, admin. the est. of Jane Long on 24 June 1702 and the est. of Joseph Peake on 14 Jan. 1709 and 13 May 1718; Charles Merryman d. leaving a will, 25 Dec. 1720 - 23 June 1722, naming w. Jane and sons William and Charles; admin. bond was posted 23 June 1722 by extx. Jane Merryman with John Merryman and William Barney; est. was admin. by Jane, w. of Benjamin Knight, on 9 Sept. 1724, 12 Aug. 1729, and 3 Aug. 1739; Charles and Jane had iss.: WILLIAM ; (JOHN) CHARLES; ANN, m. Benjamin Richards; ELIZABETH, m. Joseph Cross on 13 Sept. 1730; JEMIMA, m. Henry Stevenson; KEDEMOTH , b. 23 March 1717 (ind. for bast. in June 1741; Henry Quine alias James admitted paternity); MARY, b. 27 March 1719, m. William Hall on 17 Dec. 1734 (2:19, 100, 212, 216, 275, 374; 12:138; 33:56, 81; 121: 100; 124:115; 133:6, 146, 149, 152, 153, 193; 364).

MERRYMAN, JOHN (4), s. of Charles (2), d. in Balto. Co. by 6 June 1749; m. by 12 April 1702, Martha, dau. of Jonas and Martha Bowen; in 1714 was conv. part Merryman's Addition and part Merryman's Lot by his father; he lived on an estate called Clover Hill, the entrance road to which was formerly called Merryman's Lane, now University Parkway; d. leaving a will, 18 Jan. 1746 - 6 June 1749, naming w. Martha and ch. John, Jr., Moses, Joseph, Johanna, and Mary Edwards; had iss.: JOHN, b. 1703, d. 15 Aug. 1777; MOSES, d. by 31 Jan. 1764; JOANNA, d. by 27 Oct. 1790, m. John Clossey; REBECCA, d. by 4 Feb. 1792, m. Thomas Spicer on 23 Jan. 1727; TEMPERANCE, b. 13 Sept. 1720, d. 5 Jan. 1813, m. Edward Talbott on 28 May 1745; dau., d. in inf.; CHARLES, b. 1723, d. 1729; JOSEPH, b. 14 April 1726, d. 1799 (67:320; 70:159; 77:32 122: 30; 133:4, 148, 154; 210-26:102; 364).

MERRYMAN, SAMUEL (5),.s. of Charles (2), d. by 23 March 1754;
m. Mary, wid. of Thomas Eager, some time after 1708; she d. 26
March 1728, and may have been the dau. of Humphrey Boone who d.
Nov. 1709; in Aug. 1719 Samuel was ind. by the Grand Jury for
drunkenness in court; in 1750 he owned 200 a. Merryman's Pasture;
d. leaving a will, 16 Jan. 1754 - 23 March 1754, naming s. Samuel
(to have Drunkord's Hall), Nicholas (to have Merryman's Pasture),
and daus. Rebecca Price and Keturah Parrish; had iss.: KETURAH,
b. 1717, d. 22 Feb. 1789, m. 1st, on 1 July 1732, Thomas Price
(d. 1741), and 2nd, on 25 Feb. 1743 William Parrish (she may be
the Keturah Merryman ind. for bast. in March 1740/1); SAMUEL,
Jr., b. 12 Nov. 1721, d. 25 Sept. 1809; REBECCA, m. John Price;
NICHOLAS, b. 8 Feb. 1727, d. 1770 (23:211; 33:2;,111:55; 133;
153:27; 364).

MERRYMAN, WILLIAM (6), s. of Charles (3), was alive in 1750
and prob. later; m. Margaret, dau. of Dutton Lane who left part
of Hampton Court in his will made 1713 to his dau. Margaret; on
30 Aug. 1740 William and w. Margaret sold part of Hampton Court
to Charles Ridgely; on 5 May 1750 William and Margaret sold 50 a.
Merryman's Grotto to Jabez Murray; had iss.: JEMIMA, b. 24 Nov.
1726, d. 13 Aug. 1736; MARGARET, b. 24 Feb. 1727; WILLIAM, b.
24 Feb. 1727; GEORGE, b. 25 Oct. 1734; JOANNA, b. 15 Oct. 1736,
and CHLOE, b. 28 Feb. 1741 (75:462; 79:166; 81:14; 124:231; 133:
25, 43, 52, 67; 364).

MERRYMAN, (JOHN) CHARLES (7), s. of Charles (3), was alive as
late as 1746; m. Millicent Haile on 20 Feb. 1730; on 28 Aug. 1742
Charles and Millicent and Richard Miller Cole and his w. Sabina
conv. 100 a. Haile's Folly (in exch. for 100 a. Boring's Gift) to
John Boring, Jr., for the lifetimes of John Boring, Sr., his w.
Sarah, and John Boring, Jr.; had iss.: CHARLES, b. 22 May 1733;
MARY, b. 28 Jan. 1734; MILLICENT, b. 7 Dec. 1736 (77:18, 29;
133:29, 43, 53, 150; 364).

MERRYMAN, JOHN (8), s. of John (4), was b. 1703, and d. 13
Aug. 1777; m. Sarah, dau. of Nicholas Rogers, on 30 Dec. 1725;
she was b. 1708, and d. 3 March 1775 in her 67th year; in 1750
he owned 105 a. part Merryman's Lot, and 100 a. Merryman's Addition, and may be the "John Merryman, Jr.," who owned 102 a. of
Broad's Improvement, 50 a. Ellege's Grove, and 50 a. Merryman's
Chance; d. leaving a will, 4 Feb. 1774 - 11 Nov. 1777; had iss.:
NICHOLAS, b. 11 Dec. 1726, d. 1808; SARAH, b. 12 May 1729, m.
Robert Wilmot on 15 Dec. 1748; MARY, m. Abraham Ensor on 30 Jan.
1750; ELIZABETH, b. 13 June 1734, m. John Gorsuch on 11 March
1755; JOHN, b. 16 Feb. 1726/7; BENJAMIN, b. 1739, d. 30 May 1814
(112:341; 133:12, 20, 37, 162, 164; 153:5, 11; 364).

MERRYMAN, MOSES (9). s. of John (4), d. by 31 Jan. 1764, having m. c.1750 Sarah Glenn, b. 1720, d. Nov. 1799; in 1750 he
owned 150 a. part Merryman's Delight; had iss.: MICAJAH, b. 1750,
d. 1842 (153:73; 364).

MERRYMAN, JOSEPH (10, s. of John (4), was b. 14 April 1726,
and d. 1799; m. 1st Elizabeth (---), and 2nd Mary (---); in Nov.
1757 was named as the_father of Rachel Carter's child; d. leaving
a will, 19 March 1797 - 13 Feb. 1799; had iss.: (by 1st w.): JOHN,
b. 6 March 1749; (by 2nd w.): MOSES, b. 13 Jan. 1758; JOSEPH, b.
15 March 1760; REBECCAm n, Richard Demmitt on 9 Dec. 1783; JEMIMA,
m. Solomon Bowen; ELIZABETH, m. Benjamin Bowen; MARY, m. George
Baxley, and JOB (40:400; 112:159; 133:94, 105; 364).

MERRYMAN, SAMUEL, Jr., (11), s. of Samuel (5), was b. 12 Nov.
1721; d. 25 Sept. 1809; m. Jane Price, who d. 28 April 1771; gave
his age as 40 in April 1761; d. leaving a will, 8 June 1799 - 13

Jan. 1810; had iss.: RACHEL, b. 11 Dec. 1742, m. Charles Stewart; SAMUEL, b. 17 June 1745; MARY, b. 13 June 1749, m. Benjamin Wells; ACTION (or ACHSAH), b. 26 Dec. 1751, m. McLain Stinchcomb; MARICE (or MORDECAI), b. 29 March 1754; CALEB, b. 12 March 1758, d. 21 Nov. 1824; JOHN, b. Jan. 1763; NICHOLAS; and a dau., m. (---) Parks (87:201; 117:468; 133:4, 72, 98; 364).

MERRYMAN, NICHOLAS (12), s. of Samuel (5), was b. 8 Feb. 1727, d. 1770; m. Avarilla Raven, dau. of Luke Raven, on 1 May 1755; d. leaving a will, 7 Nov. 1768 - 18 July 1770; his wife d. leaving a will, 13 Nov. 1784 - 26 Feb. 1785; Nicholas and Avarilla had iss.: SAMUEL, d. s.p., 1787; NICHOLAS, d. s.p., 1787; SARAH, m. William Scott; MARY, b. 9 March 1765, d. 1809, m. Caleb Merryman; KETURAH, m. (---) Hooper; LUKE, d. 1813 (112:152; 113:60; 364).

MERRYMAN, NICHOLAS, m. Jane (---), and had iss.: ELIZABETH, b. 28 Aug. 1750 (133:94).

MERSER. See MERCER.

MESSERSMITH, SAMUEL, had William Glade, s. of William, apprenticed to him in June 1757 to learn the trade of gunsmith (46:37).

METCALFE/MEDCALFE, JOHN (1), d. in A. A. Co., leaving a will, 11 Jan. 1727/8 - 13 March 1727/8, naming sons Thomas and John (to have Balding's Addition and Jonas' Chance and Range), granddau. Larda Holland, dau. Margaret Holland, and mentioning w.; m. Lydia (---) by 20 May 1711; her will, 31 March 1740 - 3 June 1740, was also proved in A. A. Co.; had iss.: THOMAS; JOHN; LYDIA, m. (---) Wells; and MARGARET, m. (---) Holland (122:215; 125:81; 127:109).

METCALFE, JOHN (2), s. of John (1), d. in Balto. Co. by 21 Feb. 1739 when admin. bond was posted by Vachel Denton with John Brice and Thomas Baldwin; est. was admin. by Denton on 10 Nov. 1741; on 10 June 1740 John Norris of West R., A. A. Co., conv. prop. to his granddau. Mary, dau.of John Medcalfe; in March 1746/7 Metcalfe's orphans Thomas and Mary inher. a legacy from Lydia Metcalfe; John had iss. by w. Mary Norris, whom he m. on 6 Aug. 1735 in St. James' Par., A. A. Co.: THOMAS; MARY (4:116; 12: 170; 36:390; 75:397; 219-3).

METCALFE, JOHN (3), no known rel. to any of the above, in Feb. 1746 mortgaged Spring Garden to Rachel Bailey; in 1750 owned 150 a. Metcalfe's Spring Garden, 100 a. Metcalfe's Addition, 100 a. Murray's Meadows, 50 a. Rich Level,70 a. Addition, and 50 a. George's Beginnings; in Oct. 1752 was living at Patapsco; had iss.: JOHN, b. 27 Feb. 1742/3; WILLIAM, b. 6 Jan. 1745; JAMES, b. 19 Nov. 1746; and THOMAS (79:313; 133:71; 134:7; 153:51; 385: 198).

METCALFE, THOMAS (4), s. of John (3), in March 1754 chose John Metcalfe as his guardian; in Aug. 1768 was in Fred. Co., when he sold 100 a. Metcalfe's Addition to Dr. William Lyon (39:17; 92: 643).

METCALFE, PETER, in 1750, owned 100 a. Wells' Forest (153:87).

METCALFE, RICHARD, was in Balto. Co. by 1695 as a taxable in s. side Patapsco River Hundred (140).

METHENY, WILLIAM, m. Eliz. Banberry on 12 Jan. 1735, and had iss.: DANIEL, b. 7 Sept. 1737 (131).

MEYER, JOHN, of Lancaster Co., Penna., in Feb. 1745 bought
100 a. Bond's Manor from William Cannon and w. Frances (79:76).

MEYER, PETER, imm. to New Sweden from Gothenburg in 1643,
came to Md. in c.1661, and was appointed a Commissioner of Balto Co., in 1661; later left Md. (379).

MICHAEL, GEORGE, m. Barbara Rissard on 2 Aug. 1755 (129:354).

MIDDLEFIELD, THOMAS, was in Balto. Co. by c.1672 when he purch.
100 a. from Charles Jones (63:1).

MIDDLEMORE, Dr. JOSIAS, surgeon, of London, was in Balto. Co.
by June 1718 when he purch. 100 a. Webster's Enlargement from
Peter and Mary Overard; d. in Balto. Co. on 27 Feb. 1754, aged
73; m. Mrs. Frances Beckley on 9 Oct. 1720; she was a dau. of
Edward and Elizabeth (Goldsmith Utie) Johnson; ; he was exec. of
the estates of Peter Glover (in Nov. 1724), and of William Caw-
thion; in 1730 he was named as a bro.-in-law in the will of Joseph Johnson; he was exec. of Johnson's est., and Richard Jenkins;
in 1750 he owned over 3000 acres of land incl. 600 a. Palmer's
Forest, 893 a. Fanny's Inheritance. 685 a. Swan Harbour, and other
tracts; he d. Feb. 1755; his wid. d. leaving a will, 11 Aug. 1755
- 17 May 1759; admin. bond was posted 17 May 1759 by exec. John
Paca with Col. John Hall and Robert Adair; had iss.: JOSIAS, b.
1 or 31 Oct. 1726; EDWARD, b. 23 March 1731; FRANCIS, b. 21 March
1733; d. by 24 Nov. 1760 when his est. was inv., signed by George
Presbury and Martha Garrettson as kin, and val. at £ 1430.6.5
(3:2, 182, 231; 4:327; 6:114; 12:215; 48:345, 365; 63:441; 210-
30:681; 341:348).

MIDDLETON, THOMAS, m. Jane Perry on 7 June 1743 (129:329).

MIER, JOHN HENRY, m. Elizabeth (---), and had iss.: ANNE, b.
16 Oct. 1759; GEORGE HENRY, b. 20 March 1761 (133:106).

MILLAM, WILLIAM, d. by 21 Jan. 1730 when admin. bond was posted by Mordecai Hammond with John Merriken and Richard Moss, the
wid. Elizabeth Millam having renounced (12:167).

THE EVAN MILES FAMILY

MILES, EVAN (1), was in Balto. Co. by 1692 as a taxable in
Spesutia Hund.; d. by 5 June 1706; m. Rebecca (---); admin. bond
was posted on latter date by admnx. Rebecca with Cornelius Harrington and Edward Jackson; est. was inv. on 7 Dec. 1706 by Chas.
Baker and Matt. Given or Green, and val. at £ 52.4.11; Evan and
Rebecca had iss.: CHARLES, b. 21 March 1694; MARGARET, b. 21 Dec.
1696; EVAN, b. 7 Oct. 1698; REBECCA, b. 1 March 1699/1700;
WILLIAM, b. 16 Sept. 1702; EDWARD, b. c.1706, age 4 in March 1710
when he was bd. to Matthew Green to age 21, and he pet. the court
in June 1714 (12:127; 21:24, 137, 508; 48:135; 128:2, 4, 5, 9,
13; 138).

MILES, CHARLES (2), s. of Evan (1), was b. 21 March 1694; m.
by Oct. 1726, Mary, dau. of William Peckett (2:318; 122:180).

MILES, EVAN (3), s. of Evan (1), was b. 7 Oct. 1698; d. by 26
June 1737; m. Elizabeth Davis on 24 July 1726; she m. as her 2nd
husb. Robert Price, on 18 Sept. 1739; in March 1708/9 he was bd.
to serve Robert and Mary Smith to age 21; admin. bond was posted
26 June 1737 by admnx. Elizabeth Miles, with Henry Rhodes and
Thomas Donavin; est. was admin. by Elizabeth Miles on 28 Feb.
1738 and by Elizabeth w. of Robert Price on 9 Nov. 1739; had iss.:
CHARLES, b. 8 Nov. 1728; EVAN, b. 14 Dec. 1731; EDWARD, b. 24

June 1734; and THOMAS, b. 18 Dec. 1734 (sic); (4:1, 26; 12:161; 21:24; 128:54, 56, 66, 83, 94).

THE JOHN MILES FAMILY

MILES, JOHN (4), progenitor of this line, no known rel. to any of the above, was in Balto. Co. by 1680 when he appraised the est. of George Gunnell; in Oct. 1683 he surv. 200 a. Stepney; in Oct. 1695 he surv. 200 a. Addition; in 1692 was a taxable in Spesutia Hund.; in March 1709 he conv. 50 a. Farmer's Farm and Margaret's Mount to Gregory Farmer; d. 5 Feb. 1712; admin. bond was posted 1 Aug. 1713 by William Cook with John Stokes and Lawrence Taylor; est. was inv. the same day by Joseph Johnston and Cadwallader Jones, and val. at £ 21.19.0; est. was admin. by sd. Cook on 4 Oct. 1714; had iss.: JOHN, of age to be a taxable in 1695 (1:20; 12:116, 155; 50:356; 59:545, 647; 128:30; 138; 200-69:417; 211).

MILES, JOHN (5), prob. s. of John (4), was a taxable in Spe sutia Hund. in 1695 as John Miles, Jr.; 1st w. not identified; m. 2nd, by Aug. 1715, Mary, wid. of Thomas Litton; at that time John and Mary conv. 100 a. Margaret's Mount to Robert Hawkins; on 3 March 1713 sold 100 a. to Thomas Cullin; on 15 Sept. 1716 conv. 62 a. Father-in-Law's Bounty, being one-half of Margaret's Mount, to Thomas Litton; in April 1722 appointed w. Mary admnx. over his est. for life, mentioned Martha Litton, and "son" (step-son?) John Miles Youngblood; d. 14 March 1731; admin. bond was posted 6 May 1732 by admnx. Mary, with Thomas Litton and John Miles Youngblood; on 17 Jan. 1733/4 Mary Miles conv. all her personal est. to her s. John Miles Youngblood; had iss.: (by 1st w.): THOMAS, b. c.1696; also   JOHN, b. 16 March 1696, bur. 3 May 1697; also (step-son?) JOHN MILES YOUNGBLOOD (12:155; 67:265, 354, 449; 69:136; 74:16; 128:4, 5; 140).

MILES, THOMAS (6), s. of John (5), was b. c.1696; in March 1718 purch. 200 a. Tower Hill from Charles Simmons and w. Hannah; in Nov. 1718 was named by Sarah Litton as the father of her ch.; in Aug. 1733 as son and devisee of John Miles of Balto. Co., dec., he conv. prop. to John Miles' wid. Mary, and then to John Miles Youngblood, mentioning a tract Miles which the late John Miles had given to Mary; Thomas' w. Catherine signed the deed; in Aug. 1734 he and Catherine conv. 100 a. Tower Hill and 40 a. Miles' Enlargement to William Bond; had iss.: (by Sarah Litton): prob. MARTHA LITTON, b. 27 April 1718; (by Catherine who may have been a dau. of Rebecca Poteet): JOHN, b. 9 Feb. 1717/8; THOMAS, b. 18 Aug. 1719; PETER, b. 28 Feb. 1721/2; ISAAC, b. 14 Feb. 1723/4 (23:31; 46:420; 63:530; 73:419; 74:136; 131:20, 38/r, 40/r).

MILES, THOMAS, Jr. (7), s. of Thomas (6), was b. 18 Aug. 1719; prob. the Thomas Miles, Jr., who m. Margaret, mother of Elizabeth Taylor, and herself a dau. of Ulick Burke, on 11 Oct. 1744; may be the same Thomas Miles, Jr., ind. for bast. in June 1744; d. by 11 April 1769 when admin. bond was posted by admnx. Margaret Miles with Aquila Thompson and Wm. Robinson; est. was admin. by Margaret Miles on 28 June 1770; he left 8 ch., unidentified (6:190; 12:256; 35:228; 131:26).

MILES, PETER (8), s. of Thomas (6), was b. 28 Feb. 1721/2; m. Elinor, dau. of William McComas by 19 Oct. 1750 (5:135; 131).

MILES, ISAAC (9), s. of Thomas (6), was b. 14 Feb. 1723/4; m. Ann Preston on 28 Oct. 1742; d. by 2 Nov. 1754 when admin. bond was posted by Ann Miles with James Preston and est. was admin. by Ann Miles on 25 July 1758 (6:11; 12:214; 131:95/r).

MILES, ANN, was fined for bast. in Nov. 1759 (46:240).

MILES, JACOB, m. Hannah, dau. of Alexander McComas, on 10 Nov. 1748 (131:32; 47:111).

MILES, MARTHA, m. William Perkins on 3 Feb. 1703/4 (129:200).

MILES, MARY, m. Lawrence Taylor on 5 Feb. 1699/1700 (129:100).

MILES, MARY, d. 16 March 1733 (128:77).

MILES, REBECCA, m. Jacob Hanson on 8 Jan. 1723/4 (129:243).

MILES, THOMAS, m. Alice (---), and had iss.: MARY, b. 4 June 1728 (133:17).

MILES, THOMAS, in Aug. 1759 conv. a slave to his dau. Ann, w. of Daniel McComas (Balto. Co. Court Records, BB#F, p. 55, MHS).

MILHAM, JOSEPH, m. Jane Candle on 28 Nov. 1756 (129:214).

MILLEN, HENRY, m. Mary Norris on 5 July 1720; admin. the est. of William Norris on 9 May 1722; d. leaving a will, 4 Feb. 1737 - 9 Feb. 1737, naming bro. in Eng., sis.-in-law Alice w. of George Lester, Thomas Williamson, Edward Cantwell, and Ann Arnold; admin. bond was posted 21 March 1737 by George Lester with Henry Rhodes and Adam Burchfield; Lester admin. the est. and his w. claimed her balance as residuary legatee (4:115; 12:168; 126: 235; 128:38, 99; also 3:89).

THE JOHN MILLER FAMILY

MILLER, JOHN (1), m. Mary Gain on 11 Feb. 1725; on 2 Sept. 1729 was conv. 50 a. Success, now Miller's Purchase, by Henry Peregoy; on 1 June 1731 John and Mary Miller conv. part Success (orig. held by Henry Peregoy), and now known as With's Adventure, to George With; d. by 2 Oct. 1742 when admin. bond was posted by Thomas Sligh with Thomas Sheredine and Henry Comming; est. was admin. by Sligh; John and Mary had iss.: ELIZABETH, b. 9 Aug. 1726; RICHARD, b. 27 July 1728; JOHN, b. 4 April 1730; MARY, b. 24 July 1732; JEMIMA, b. 4 Jan. 1734 (5:117; 12:206; 72:174-6; 77:162; 133:20, 22, 41, 150).

MILLER, RICHARD (2), s. of John (1), in 1742 was conv. tract Broad's Improvement by Thomas Broad; still owned the land in 1750; m. Elizabeth Hicks on 4 June 1752; prob. the Richard who d. by 1778 and whose est. was admin. by Elizabeth Miller (7:356; 77: 162; 153:89; 131).

THE JOSEPH AND WILLIAM MILLER FAMILY

MILLER, JOSEPH (3), no known rel. to any of the above, but poss. bro. of William (see below), in 1750 owned 134 a. called George's Park; in May 1747 he and w. Comfort and William and Johannah Miller conv. part George's Park to Christopher Randall (79:396; 153:29).

MILLER, WILLIAM (4), poss. bro. of Joseph (above, # 3); m. by May 1747 Johannah (---) who joined him and Joseph and Comfort Miller in mortgaging George's Park; in 1750 still owned 134 a. George's Park; on 24 March 1750 mortgaged 50 a. George's Park (76:396; 81:155; 153:29).

MILLER, ANN, was ind. for bast. in Nov. 1758 (46:163).

MILLER, JANE, dau. of Jane, dec., in June 1714 was bd. to Aquila and Martha (illegible) (21:510).

MILLER, JOHN, m. Eleanor Smith on 14 Dec. 1745 (133:158).

MILLER, JOHN, m. Eliz. Harris on 9 Oct. 1760 (131).

MILLER, JOSEPH, m. Mary Oursler on 11 Sept. 1759, and had
iss.: ELY, b. 27 Oct. 1760; RACHEL, b. 5 Aug. 1762; GEORGE, b. 25
Sept. 1764; RUTH, b. last day Aug. 1765; ELIJAH, b. 7 April 1768
(133:47, 295; 134:73).

MILLER, MICHAEL, was in Balto. Co. by 7 Feb. 1744 when he purch.
150 a. Bachelor's Choice from John Stinchcomb (78:57).

MILLER, RICHARD, was in Balto. Co. by 1694 as a taxable in
s. side Gunpowder Hund.; gave his age as 41 in 1707; in Sept.
1695 bd. his 6 yr. old dau. Elizabeth to Thomas Richardson; on
28 Sept. 1703 purch. 178 a. Wells' Angles from Joseph Wells; d.
by 22 Feb. 1709 when admin. bind was posted by wid. Eliz. Miller
with John Barnet and Isaac Sampson (12:124; 17:475; 66:330; 139).

MILLER, SOLOMON, from the west of England, ran away from Balto. Town on or about 30 Aug. 1753 (307-69:132).

MILLER, THEOPHILUS, m. Sarah Burk after pub. of banns in July
and Aug. 1748 (131). (Elsewhere in 131 his name is given as Thomas Miller).

MILLER, WILLIAM, m. Hannah (---), who d. 15 April 1734; they
had iss.: HANNAH, b. 8 Sept. 1731; ADAM, b. 13 March 1732 (128:
70, 74).

MILLER, WILLIAM, m. Catherine (---), and had iss.: CATHERINE,
b. 6 April 1753; ANNE, b. 20 June 1755; JOHN, b. 14 Dec. 1758;
SARAH, b. 10 Jan. 1760 (133:107).

MILLES, THOMAS, m. Alice (---), and had iss.; MARY, b. 4 June
1728 (133:17).

MILLEVER, ANN, m. Owen Swillivain on 30 Nov. 1723 (129:252).

MILLHOUSE, BARTHOLOMEW, d. in Balto. Co. by 7 May 1743; m.
Bridget (---), who m. as her 2nd husb. John Parks on 29 Oct. 1743;
in Balto. Co. by 24 March 1733/4 when he wit. the will of Ralph
Woodall; d. leaving a will, 28 March 1743 - 7 May 1743, naming
s. Charles, and sons Miles and Aquila, granddau. Seaborah (or
Deborah?), and w. Bridget ; admin. bond posted 9 June 1743 by
the extx. with John Holloway and Walter James; est. admin. by
Bridget w. of John Parks, on 21 July 1744; had iss.: CHARLES:
MILES; AQUILA, m. Elizabeth Parks on 17 Dec. 1749; (poss.):ELIZA-
BETH, m. John Rutledge on 10 Dec. 1742; (poss.) FRANCES, m.
Thomas Cotterall on 4 Aug. 1743 (3:361; 12:187; 73:287; 126:86,
223; 131).

MILLINER. See MILNER.

MILLS, JAMES, was b. c.1634, prob. in Eng.; imm. by 1669; was
a delegate from Balto. Co. to the Lower House in 1681 and 1682;
purch. 100 a. in Balto. Co., which he sold in 1687; admin. the
est. of Samuel Boston in May 1681 (2:190; 200-67:329, 300; 371).

MILLS, WILLIAM, m. Mary (---), and had iss.: ANN, b. 13 Oct.
1735 (133:48).

MILNER/MILLINER, ANN, was ind. for bast. in Nov. 1711, again
in June 1712, and again in March 1719/20; in Aug. 1720 she admitted she had born an illeg. ch. in Cecil Co. (21:266,   314;
23:279, 365).

MILNER, ISAAC,   purch. 200 a.Westwood and 100 a. Addition
to Westwood from Joseph Strawbridge on 20 March 1696/7; d. by
6 April 1745 when admin. bond was posted by Thomas White with
Alexander Lawson and Thomas Franklin (12:175; 66:25).

MILNER, RICHARD, was in Balto. Co. by 1692 as a taxable in n.
side Patapsco Hund. (138).

MINCHIN, THOMAS, was in Balto. Co. by 1692 as a taxable in n.
side Patapsco; gave his age as 26 in March 1714/5 when he pet.
the court (21:604; 138).

MINER, PETER, in 1750 owned, with Daniel Barrett, 170 a. of
Broad's Improvement and 2 lots in Balto. Town (153:64).

MIRRITT. See MERRITT.

MISER, WILLIAM, m. Ruth Meeds on 4 Nov. 1758 (131).

MITCHELL, THOMAS (1), was in Balto. Co. by 1703 as a taxable
in Spesutia Hund.; was b. c.1684, giving his age as 46 in 1730,
when he stated he had been living in the county for about 30 yrs.;
d. by 11 March 1747 when admin. bond was posted by Thomas Sligh
with Isaac Risteau and Nathan Nicholson; est. was admin. by Sligh
on 14 Feb. 1749; by w. Ann (or Susanna) had iss.: RICHARD; HAN-
NAH, b. 2 Sept. 1713; SUSANNAH, b. Easter Monday, 1716, d. 30
Aug. 1725; THOMAS, b. 7 Feb. 1719/20; m. and had iss.; KENT, b.
2 Jan. 1724/5; EDWARD, b. 21 April 1727; WILLIAM, b. 10 Aug. 1730
(5:67; 12:117, 177; 128:30, 35, 40, 46, 50, 68; 145).

MITCHELL, RICHARD (2), prob. s. of Thomas (1), was b. 26 Aug.
1710 (no parents named in church reg.); d. by 3 June 1749 when
his admnx. Elizabeth Mitchell posted bond, with Thomas Mitchell
and Daniel Durbin; m. Elizabeth Williams on 1 Jan. 1733; in 1750
owned 100 a. St. Martin's Ludgate; est. was admin. by Elizabeth
Mitchell on 5 May 1750, when she named his ch. and their ages:
Mary (15), Anne (12); Elizabeth (10), Richard (8), Thomas (6),
John (5), and Avarilla (3); dec. had iss.: MARY, b. 4 Feb. 1734;
ANNE, b. 14 Oct. 1736; ELIZABETH, b. 10 June 1739; RICHARD, b.
7 Oct. 1740; THOMAS, b. 8 June 1743; JOHN, b. 6 Jan. 1744, and
AVARILLA, b. 2 April 1747 (5:167; 12:208; 128:78, 86, 98, 112;
129:328, 344; 153:13).

MITCHELL, THOMAS (3), s. of Thomas (1), was b. 7 Feb. 1719/20,
and was living in 1750 when he was listed as owning 50 a. part
Gilbert's Outlet and 75 a. Gilbert's Addition; m. Hannah Osborne
on 24 Dec. 1742; had iss.: KENT, b. 8 May 1743 (129:329; 153:
84).

MITCHELL, KENT (4), s. of Thomas (1), was b. 2 Jan. 1724/5,
d. in Harf. Co., in 1793; m. Hannah Barnes, b. 26 Sept. 1728, dau.
of Ford and Margaret Barnes; in 1750 owned 100 a. The Division;
d. leaving a will, 6 July 1793 - 27 Sept. 1793; had iss.: WILLIAM,
b. 12 Aug. 1747; SARAH, b. 5 March 1749; JAMES, b. 5 June 1752;
SUSANNA, b. 12 Aug. 1754; SOPHIA, b. 20 Feb. 1758 (129:361; 153:
31; 200-61:569, 574; 244-AJ#2:458; 271).

MITCHELL, WILLIAM (5), s. of Thomas (1), was b. 10 Aug. 1730;
m. Sophia Osborn on 11 June 1751; she was a dau. of Benjamin Osborne William and Sophia had iss.: MARTHA, b. 22 March 1755; MARY,
b. 6 Dec. 1757; EDWARD, b. 6 Jan. 1759; ELIZABETH, b. 17 March
1761; ANN, b. 16 March 1763 (129:381).

MITCHELL, (---), m. by 3 May 1751 Prudence, dau. of John Harryman, dec. (5:199).

MITCHELL, ALEXANDER, d. by 10 March 1724 when admin. bond was posted by Robert Gordon with Alexander Frazier and William Cumming; est. was inv. in 1725, and admin. by Gordon on March 1725/6 (2:301; 12:145; 52:156).

MITCHELL, ELIZABETH, had iss.: JAMES, b. 14 Sept. 1753; GABRIEL, b. 10 Aug. 1757 (129:361).

MITCHELL, ELIZABETH, was fined for bast. in Nov. 1759 (46:240)

MITCHELL, WILLIAM, m. Elizabeth Elliott on 30 Sept. 1736 (elsewhere in St. John's Par., the date is given as 31 May 1741); had iss.: JOHN, b. 6 Nov. 1737; JOHN, b. 5 Nov. 1739; SARAH, b. 5 Feb. 1740; WILLIAM, b. 23 July 1742 (131:83, 101, 121, 60/r, 76/r, and 93/r).

MITCHELL, WILLIAM, in 1750 owned 200 a. part Bale's Enlargement (153:93).

MITCHENER, JOHN, m. Mary Chanlor on 8 Feb. 1729 (133:149).

MIVER, WILLIAM, m. Eliz. Finer on 10 Oct. 1748 (131).

THE MOALE FAMILY has been fully discussed by the author in 259:62-68 .

MOALE, RICHARD (1), shipmaster of Kenton, Devonshire, m. 1st Elizabeth (---), and 2nd Mary (---); had iss.: JOHN, bapt. 20 Nov. 1695 (by 2nd w.): JAMES, bapt. 25 April 1699; DAMARIS, bapt. 29 Sept. 1700; MARY, m. by 14 Jan. 1739/40 Daniel Russell; ELIZABETH, living Jan. 1739/40 (Extracts from Kenton Parish Register, in Moale folder at Md. Hist. Soc.; 259).

MOALE, JOHN (2), s. of Richard (1), was bapt. 20 Nov. 1695 in Kenton, Devonshire; d. 10 March 1740 in Balto. Co.; m. on 17 April 1723, Rachel, dau. of John and Hannah (Greenberry) Hammond; she m. 2nd George Bailey, and d. in May 1749; Moale was a delegate from Balto. Co. to the General Assembly, and lived at Moale's Point, near what later became Balto. Town; d. leaving a will, 14 Jan. 1739/40 - 9 Sept. 1740, naming sis. and bro.-in-law Mary and Daniel Russell, kinswoman Ann Tomson, sis. Elizabeth, bro. James, w. Rachel, and ch. Rebecca, John, Richard, and Rachel; admin. bond was posted 9 Sept. 1740 by extx. Rachel Moale; his 1742 inv. listed 37 books with books on religion, philosophy, science, law and the arts; in March 1744 Rachel Bailey, executrix, paid legacies to James Moale, Elizabeth Moale, Mary Russell, Ann Thompson, and the four ch. of the dec.; est. admin. 24 Dec. 1743; John Moale had iss.: REBECCA, b. 20 Feb. 1728, m. Charles Croxall on 23 July 1746; JOHN, b. 2 Jan. 1730/1; RACHEL, b. 17 July 1737, d. in her 4th yr.; RICHARD, b. 11 Jan. 1739, d. 1786 s.p. (3:327; 12:171; 35:341, 478; 133:19, 63; 259).

MOALE, JOHN (3), s. of John (2), was b. 2 Jan. 1730/1; d. 6 July 1798 in Balto. Co.; m. Ellen North, dau. of Capt. Robert and Frances (Todd) North, on 25 May 1758; was burgess from Balto. Co. in 1767; member of the Convention, 1774-1775, and member of the Committee of Observation, 1775; lieut.-col. of Balto. Town Battalion in 1776; had iss.: ELIZABETH, b. 8 Sept. 1759, m. Richard Curzon; JOHN, b. 17 May 1761; REBECCA, b. 15 March 1763, m. Thomas Russell; RICHARD HALTON, b. 25 Jan. 1765; THOMAS, b. 22 Sept. 1766; WILLIAM NORTH, b. 1768, d. 1769; ROBERT, b. and d. in 1769; ROBERT NORTH, b. 22 Jan. 1771; SAMUEL, b. 4 Jan. 1773; RACHEL, b. 1775, d. 1776; FRANCES, b. 1777, d. 1781; WILLIAM, b. and d. 1779; GEORGE WASHINGTON, b. 1780, d. young; RANDLE HULSE, b. 26 Jan. 1782; MARY NORTH, b. 1783, d. 1787 (133:107, 114, 143, 144, 272; 259).

MOALE, RICHARD (4), s. of John (2), was b. 11 Jan. 1759, and
d. 1786, s.p.; in Nov. 1757 was fined for bast. as the father of
Emmory Day's ch. (46:75).

MODDEY, JOHN, servant, with 2 years to serve in 1704 inv. of
Martha Bowen (51:125).

MOHARGO, JOHN, was in Balto. Co. by Nov. 1758 when Richard
Richards sold him 50 a. Richards' Chance (83:291).

MOLL, JOHN, age c .30, b. in Staffordshire, ran away from Wm.
Lux and N. Ridgely by 18 April 1754 (385:280).

MOLTON, MATTHEW, was in Balto. Co. by 1705; d. there 15 April
1725; m. Ann (---) who may have been the wid. of (---) Collins;
in 1705 was a taxable in Spesutia Hund.; in May 1720 purch. 100
a. Wood's Close from Thomas and Martha Mitchell; d. leaving a
will, 10 April 1725 - 20 July 1725, leaving 10 a. Wood's Close
to his son-in-law Francis Collins, naming dau. Sarah Lake and
her son Robert Hollyday, s. of James Hollyday, as well as his
own sons Matthew and John; in March 1736 Ann Molton was ind. for
bringing up Robert Holliday in a bad manner; in 1750 she was listed as the owner of 100 a. Wood's Close; left iss.: SARAH, b. 3
May 1705, m. 1st, on 30 Oct. 1721, James Holliday, and 2nd, by
10 April 1725, (---) Lake; MATTHEW, b. 24 Aug. 1709; JOHN, b. 19
Feb. 1715 (31:1; 68:175; 124:199; 128:21, 26, 41, 45; 129: 204,
209, 229, 230; 147; 153:42).

MONDAY. See MUNDAY.

MONK, RENALDO, was in Balto. Co. by July 1748 when he advert.
for William Camm who ran away from the Balto. Iron Works; came
from London; m. by 28 July 1755 Rachel, extx. of Edward Riston
of Balto. Co.; d. leaving a will, 20 Sept. 1768 - 14 Aug. 1768;
had iss.: RENALDO; WILLIAM; SARAH, m. (---) Carrick; MARY, m.
William Jacob on 19 July 1772 (5:348; 112:123; 133:174; Md. Gaz.,
of July 1748).

MONK, RICHARD, m. Agnes Taylor on 26 June 1756; had iss.:
WILLIAM, b. 8 Aug. 1756; MARY, b. 5 Sept. 1758 (129:355).

MONK, WILLIAM, m. Eliz. Fuller on 3 Dec. 1736; may be the Wm.
who d. by 27 May 1738 when William Dallam posted admin. bond with
Samuel Webster and John Taylor (12:158; 131).

MONTAGUE, AGNES, m. Lawrence Taylor on 7 Feb. 1703/4 (129:300).

MONTEDIRE, ALCE. See DEMONDIDIER, ALICE.

MONTGOMERY, JOHN, of Penna., and William Montgomery purch.
150 a. Jones' Gift from Nathaniel and Sarah Porter, on 25 Jan.
1744; on 19 June 1747 John Montgomery and William (and William's
w. Fortune), all of New London Twp., Penna., sold 80 a. to David
Maxfield; also on same day they sold Maxfield 100 a. Brother's
Discovery and 150 a. James' Gift (78:14; 79:455, 457, 459).

MONTGOMERY, MICHAEL, of Chester Co., Penna., in Nov. 1747
with consent of w. Ann sold 100 a. Arabia Petrea to William Deaver (79:607).

MONTGOMERY, PATRICK, d. leaving a will, 9 Sept. 1759 - 17 Oct.
1759, in which he named tracts Patrick's Purchase and St. Patrick,
w. Rebecca, and these ch.: JOHN; WILLIAM; JAMES; AGNES; MARTHA;
REBECCA, m. (---) Maxwell; MARGARET, m. (---) Cheney (111:313).

MONTGOMERY, ROBERT, d. on 21 March 1726; m. Alice Smith on 12 Aug. 1718; she d. 22 March 1726; w. Elizabeth admin. the est. of Thomas Smith on 27 June 1726; admin. bond was posted on 6 April 1727 by Thomas Sheredine with James Moore and Thomas Broad; est. was inv. 25 April 1727 by Philip Jones, Jr., and Wm. Buckner and val. at £ 50.7.2 (3:55; 12:136; 51:97; 133:147, 194).

MONTGOMERY, THOMAS, purch. 200 a. Brice's Endeavor from Samuel Brice on 5 Aug. 1741; owned the land in 1750 (75:523; 153:22).

MONTGOMERY, WILLIAM, m. Anne (---) and had iss.: ANNE, b. 15 Feb. 1745 (131:114/r).

MONTROSS, THOMAS, was assigned 200 a. by Abraham Clarke in March 1662/3; in April 1664 conv. land to John Robinson of Mockjack Bay, Balto. Co. (93).

MONTS, CHRISTISON, m. Margaretta Mujon on 30 March 1755 (131).

MOONE, AUGUST, was in Balto. Co. by 1692 as a taxable in n. side of Patapsco Hund. (138).

MOORCOCK, (---), m. by 23 July 1734 Susanna (---), mother of Thomas and Richard Demett, whom she mentioned in a deed (74:85).

THE JAMES MOORE FAMILY

MOORE, JAMES (1), was b. c.1681, giving his age as 67 in May 1748; was in Balto. Co. by Nov. 1726 when he purch. part of Hogs Norton from John Cross; admin. the est. of Hugh Johns on 12 Feb. 1727 and 23 May 1728; admin. the est. of Edward Cooke on 1 Aug. 1729; m. by 20 April 1732 Frances (---), with whom he admin. the est. of John Gay; was living in the Forks of Gunpowder in Aug. 1748 when he advert. for the return of a runaway conv. serv. by the name of Edward Rose; in 1750 owned 100 a. Wheeler's Mill; may have had iss.: JAMES, Jr. (2:12, 277, 286; 3:93; 70:288; 153: 72; 224:164; Annap. Md. Gaz., 17 Aug. 1748).

MOORE, JAMES (2), poss. s. of James (1), was b. c.1719, giving his age as c.45 in May 1764; in April 1749 leased land from Lord Baltimore, with the lease to run for the lifetimes of Moore's ch. Rezin and Mary; in 1756 he leased 200 a. Gunpowder Manor, called Hunter's Park, for the lifetimes of his ch.: Rezin, b. c.1745, James Francis, b. c.1752, and Nicholas Ruxton, b. c.1755; two letters he wrote to relatives were pub. in the Nat. Gen. Soc. Qtly., 65:260; while living at the Forks of Gunpowder he wrote to his cousin Mrs. Margaret Palman at Mr. Cunningham's in Nassau St., London, referring to the recent death of his father's wife, descr. his father and his own family as being in good health, and mentioning his uncle Beger; in Oct. 1756 he wrote to his cousin Mrs. Eleanor Dioluigarde, at HRH The Princess Caroline's Apartments in St. James' Palace, London, naming his s. Rezin and his uncle Beger; was twice married; 1st w. has not been identified; m. 2nd, on 28 Aug. 1744 Hannah, dau. of John Wilmot; had iss.: (by 1st w.): MARY, b. 11 May 1742; REZIN, b. 16 Aug. 1744; (by 2nd wife): ELIZA, b. 9 Aug. 1746; RACHEL, b. 8 Jan. 1748/9; JAMES FRANCIS, b. 12 Aug. 1751; NICHOLAS RUXTON, b. 21 July 1756; ELEANOR, b. 14 May 1759; JOHN GAY, b. 8 March 1761 (5:146; 80: 411; 89:143; 131; 300-65:260; 389:11).

MOORE, ANN, w. of Walter Moore, and her ch. were rec'd on certificate from Abingdon Meeting, Penna., into Gunpowder Meeting on 23 d, 1 m., 1754; she was admitted in 8 m., 1756, was granted a cert. to visit many meetings; iss. of Ann and Walter: ELIZABETH, b. 19 Dec. 1738; RACHEL, b. 17 July 1741; ANN, b. 16 April

1744, m. Samuel Price; JOHN, b. 21 Oct. 1746, and MARY, b. 28 Sept. 1754 (136).

MOORE, EDWARD, s. of Edmund, was in Balto. Co. by 1692 as a taxable in n. side Patapsco Hund. (138).

MOORE, ELIZABETH, d. 3 Sept. 1721 (128:65).

MOORE, HENRY, m. Agnes Taylor on 20 Oct. 1733; she gave her age as 69 in 27 Feb. 1750; in June 1744 he was made levy free; d. by 1750 when his heirs were listed as owning 66 a. part of Good Speed; on 31 March 1756 Agnes conv. prop. to her son James Taylor (35:230; 128:76; 153:19; 224:188; 229:193).

MOORE, JAMES, d. by 11 Dec. 1769 when admin. bond was posted by James Moore, with James Baker and Thomas Cheneworth (12:261).

MOORE, JOHN, was in Balto. Co. by 1750 when he owned 100 a. part of Cumberland (153:73).

MOORE, JOHN, Irish, was a runaway serv. from Zachariah MacCubbin in Balto. Co. in July 1750 (307-69:132).

MOORE, MARY, m. Timothy Keen on 14 May 1709 (129:208).

MOORE, MICHAEL, m. Keziah Shipton on 20 April 1758 (131).

MOORE, RICHARD, was a res. of Balto. Co. in Aug. 1739 (384:235).

MOORE, SAMUEL, m. Senea Futt on 12 April 1762 (129:372).

MOORE, WILLIAM, m. Martha Mortimer on 16 Dec. 1760 (131).

THE DAVID, HUGH, AND JOSEPH MORGAN FAMILY

MORGAN, HUGH (1), d. by 2 Aug. 1749 when admin. bond was posted by Margaret and David Morgan; d. leaving a will, 1 May 1749, naming w. **Margaret** son John (to have Brother's Discovery), son Moses, with testator's bro. David as co-exec.; est. admin. by David and Margaret Morgan on 27 July 1750 and by David Morgan and Margaret now w. of Thomas Bishop on 23 Aug. 1751; left iss.: JOHN, b. c.1745; MOSES, b. c.1748 (5:103, 195; 12:199; 210-27:21).

MORGAN, DAVID (2), bro. of David (1), and Joseph (3), m. Lydia Cooper on 17 May 1744; in 1750 owned 150 a. part Paradice; d. leaving a will, 14 April 1767 - 24 April 1771, naming tracts Paradice, Morgan's Desire and Morgan's Addition, wife Lydia, and these ch.: ROBERT; MARY; SUSANNA; RUTH; SARAH; and MARGARET (112:182; 131; 153:87).

MORGAN, JOSEPH (3), bro. of Hugh (1) and David (2), in 1750 he was the owner of 50 a. Maiden's Mount, 50 a. part Brother's Discovery, 75 a. part Paradice, 90 a. Favour, and 25 a. Dear Bought and Nothing Got; in Nov. 1758 was named as the father of Ann Hamilton's child (46:164; 153).

THE GEORGE MORGAN FAMILY

MORGAN, GEORGE (4), progenitor, no known rel. to any of the above, m. Johanna (---), and had iss.: RACHEL, b. 10 Dec. 1719, and CHARLES, b. 2 Feb. 1721/2 (128:50).

MORGAN, CHARLES (5), s. of George (4), was b. 2 Feb. 1721/2, was age 12 in June 1734 when he was bd. to Thomas Mitchell; m.

Margaret Pogue on 6 Jan. 1746, and had iss.: GEORGE, b. 29 Oct. 1747; SARAH, b. 2 April 1749; HANNAH, b. 9 Feb. 1751; JOSEPH, b. 20 May 1754; CHARLES, b. 18 Dec. 1757; RACHEL, b. 2 March 1759; EDWARD, b. 10 July 1761 (30:253; 128:50; 129:376).

MORGAN, ABRAHAM, was in Balto. Co. by 3 Nov. 1663 when he and w. Ann sold 300 a. on s. side Bohemia R. to Thomas Browning; d. by May 1665; wid. Ann m. by March 1667/8 Bryan O'Malley (94; 95).

MORGAN, EDWARD, was in Balto. Co. by 1735; m. Sarah, dau. of Abraham and Martha Simmons; in 1750 owned 100 a. part of Simmons Choice; d. by 24 June 1765 when his est. was admin. by Mary Morgan; had iss.: MARTHA, b. 20 April 1735; SAMUEL, b. 8 March 1737; ELIZABETH, b. 18 Sept. 1740; EDWARD, b. 28 Nov. 1742; WILLIAM, b. 14 March 1744; MARY, b. 18 June 1747; SARAH, b. 29 May 1750; JAMES, b. 28 Nov. 1752; ROBERT, b. 24 May 1755; ABRAHAM, b. 27 May 1758 (6:181; 128:86, 100; 129:332, 364; 153:21).

MORGAN, GEORGE, b. c.1654, gave his age as over 70 in March 1724 when he was made levy free; may have been the George Morgan who was a taxable in Spesutia Hund. in 1692 (24:123; 27:123; 138).

MORGAN, GEORGE, m. Elizabeth Smith on 10 Feb. 1699/1700 (129: 190).

MORGAN, HENRY, of Bristol, mariner, was b. c.1699, giving his age as 46 in 1745; m. Sarah Pike on 14 May 1744; in July 1745 bought 270 a. Taylor's Discovery from Thomas Taylor; in 1750 he owned 390 a. First Discovery, 100 a. Spring Garden, 50 a. Knave's Inspection, 100 a. Stone's Delight, and 100 a. Molly and Sally's Delight (75:20, 374; 78:246; 131; 153:15; 310:237).

MORGAN, JAMES, m. Jane Brashier on 13 Dec. 1728 (128:63).

MORGAN, JAMES, m. Elizabeth Walker on 8 July 1737; had iss.: JOHN PERMENTA., b. 12 Feb. 1738 (128:92B, 108).

MORGAN, JAMES, m. Mary Davis on 18 July 1745, and had iss.: PREMENTER, b. 29 Aug. 1755; SARAH, b. 7 Dec. 1757; and JAMES, b. 26 April 1760 (129:372).

MORGAN, JAMES, m. Mary Green on 12 Nov. 1749 (131).

MORGAN, JAMES, perhaps one of the above, on 7 Dec. 1749 purch. 45 a. Shephard's Paradice from Edward Shepherd (80:348).

MORGAN, JOHN, was in Balto. Co. by 1692 as a taxable in Spesutia Hund.; m. and had iss.: SARAH, b. 20 March 1689; MARY, b. 20 Feb. 1691 (128:3; 138).

MORGAN, JOHN, m. by 9 Dec. 1745 Flora, wid. of Joseph Peregoy; may be the John in 1750 who owned 100 a. part Burman's Forest; had iss.: FLORA, b. 26 June 1752; LYDIA, b. 23 April 1754; SARAH, b. 2 Feb. 1757; JOHN, b. 5 Oct. 1758 (5:37, 38; 133:97, 102; 153: 43).

MORGAN, JOSEPH, m. Constance Barnes on Sept. 1740, and had iss.: JOSEPH, b. 3 Feb. 1745 (129:327).

MORGAN, MARY, wid., m. Edward Watts on 18 Sept. 1721 (133: 146).

MORGAN, RICHARD, was in Balto. Co. by Oct. 1670 when he and John Hall purch. 100 a. Crab Hill from Godfrey and Mary Harmer; in Aug. 1671 he purch. Hall's share of the land, and in Feb. 1673/4 sold the land to Anthony Brispo (96:232; 97:126; 100:116).

MORGAN, ROBERT, was in Balto. Co. by Oct. 1668 when he purch.
150 a. Horner from John Collett and Mary Goldsmith; m. by 3 Jan.
1670/1 Bennet (---) (97:123).

MORGAN, THOMAS, Capt. of Militia; d. in Balto. Co. leaving a
will, 9 June 1697 - 1 March 1697/8, naming daus. Jemima Murray,
Sarah McLane, and Martha, w. of Nicholas Fitzsimmons (the latter
to be the extx.); admin. bond was posted 25 May 1698 by Nicholas
Fitzsimmons with John Hays and John Barrett; est. was inv. on 25
May 1698 by sd. Hayes and Barrett and val. at £ 58.3.0; left
iss.: JEMIMA, m. James Murray; SARAH, m. Hector McLane; and MAR-
THA, m. Nicholas Fitzsimmons (6:187; 13:69; 54:10; 111:140).

MORGAN, WILLIAM, was in Balto. Co. by Aug. 1673 when he and
William Welch bought 200 a. Falmouth from William Salsbury (99:
347).

MORLEY, THOMAS, was in Balto. Co. by March 1671 when he purch.
Taylor's Mount from John Owen (63:44).

MORNINGSTAR, JOHN (1), planter, of Balto. Co., was from "High
Germany;" naturalized on 4 June 1738 with three of his ch.: PHIL-
IP; ELIZABETH; and JOHANNA (303:57).

MORNINGSTAR, PHILIP (2), s. of John (1), was naturalized with
his father and two sisters in June 1738; in July 1745 he purch.
150 a. Brotherly Love from John George Courts; still owned the
land in 1750 (79:190; 153:91; 303:57).

MORON, EDWARD, m. Elizabeth Lambeth on 1 May 1736 (129:296).

THE ROBERT MORRIS FAMILY

MORRIS, ROBERT (1), of London, mariner, in 1659 was granted
200 a. Pool's Island (acc. to the Rent Roll his name was Thomas);
d. leaving a wid. Martha who was still alive in 1706, and two
sons: ROBERT, d. by 14 March 1706; and JOHN (67:166; 211:51).

MORRIS, JOHN (2), s. of Robert (1) or Thomas, was a merchant
in London in March 1706 when he sold Pool's Island to John Carvill; no w. signed the deed (67:166).

THE THOMAS MORRIS FAMILY

MORRIS, THOMAS (3), progenitor, no known rel. to any of the
above; was b. c.1670, giving his age as 60 in 1730 and stating
that 40 yrs ago he was a serv. to Lodowick Martin; m. 1st, on
14 July 1699 Elizabeth, wid. of Simeon Jackson; m. 2nd, by 1708,
Mary (---); in Oct. 1703 purch. 100 a. Perkinton from Thomas Edmund; on 10 March 1704 with w. Elizabeth conv. 100 a. Expectation (now called Morris' Folly) to William Stevens; on 3 Jan.
1708 Thomas and Mary conv. 100 a. Perkinton to Rowland Kemble;
in Nov. 1713 conv. 31 a. Morris' Lot to Rowland Kemble;
on 2 March 1720 Thomas and Mary conv. 100 a. Expectation (formerly held by William Stevens of Kent Co.) to Edward Parks; was alive
on 2 Sept. 1721 when he bd. his s. Richard, aged 11, to Rowland
Kemble; had iss.: SARAH, b. 12 Jan. 1698/9, bapt. 2 July 1699;
ELIZABETH, b. 1 Oct. 1701; MARY, b. 10 July 1702; SUSANNA, b. 2
April 1705/6; THOMAS,, b. 1 Aug. 1707;. RICHARD, b. 1 Feb. 1709;
HENRY, b. 20 Oct. 1713 (21:210; 59:627, 678, 679; 60:146; 66:
293; 67:256; 68:315; 128:6, 7, 23, 36, 37; 224:102).

MORRIS, RICHARD (4), s. of Thomas (3), was b. 1 Feb. 1709;
m. Mary Murphy on 25 Dec. 1734; in 1776 lived in Spesutia Lower
Hund.; had iss.: ELIZABETH, b. 6 Aug. 1736; JOHN, b. 28 May

1738; SARAH, b. 3 Jan. 1740; MARY, b. 3 March 1742; THOMAS, b.
15 Jan. 1745; RICHARD, b. 1 March 1749; EDWARD, b. 1 March 1753;
MICHAEL, b. 1 Feb. 1755; JOHN, b. 3 June 1758 (129).

THE JACOB MORRIS FAMILY

MORRIS, JACOB (5), no known rel. to any of the above, was in
Balto. Co. by 1702 as a taxable in s. side Patapsco Hund.; m.
Elizabeth (---) who d. 14 Feb. 1732; as Jacob Morris, cooper, on
23 Aug. 1707 he bought Major's Choice from Robert Burgen; d. having made a will, 30 Nov. 1734 - 17 July 1735, naming ch. Comfort,
John, Jeremiah, Jacob, Rebecca, and Elizabeth, as well as Joseph
Cromwell (to have a writing table and a grindstone if he would
make Morris' coffin); left iss.: COMFORT, of age in 1734, may
have m. Joseph Cromwell ; REBECCA, b. 13 Feb. 1717; ELIZABETH,
b. 29 Aug. 1720; JACOB, b. 2 Dec. 1722 (prob. the Jacob Morris
boatwright who sold 30 a. Jacob's Lot to Thomas Rutter on 7 March
1742); RUTH, b. 15 March 1724, d. 23 Feb. 1728; JOHN, b. 18 April
1728; JEREMIAH, b. 31 July 1730 (59:608; 77:428; 111:200; 133).

MORRIS, EDMUND, m. Mary Debruler on 15 Oct. 1736, and had iss.:
ELIZABETH, b. 4 May 1740; MARY, b. 13 Aug. 1742 (128:93B; 129:
331).

MORRIS, EDMUND, d. by 3 March 1757 when admin. bond was posted
by James Lee, Jr., with John Paca, Jr. (12:228).

MORRIS, JAMES, of Ed'd, age 13 last Oct., in March 1757 was bd.
to Henry Ruff(46).

MORRIS, JOHN, m. Sarah Gilbert on 28 Aug. 1743 (131:97/r).

MORRIS, JOHN, m. Sarah Deaver, dau. of Antil Deaver, on 17
May 1748 (131:32; 210-38:107).

MORRIS, JOHN, m. Mary Plummer on 25 May 1760 (131:56).

MORRIS, MARY, was ind. for bast. in March 1723/4, tried in
June 1724, ind. again in March 1730/1, ind. in June 1731, and
again in June 1732; had iss.: WILBORN WILLIAM, b. 24 March 1727/8;
and SARAH, b. Nov. 1730 (26:201, 331; 29:96, 156, 288; 129: £50;
131:108/r).

MORRIS, ROBERT, surv. 30 a. Hickory Ridge in June 1707; in
1750 a Robert Morris held 50 a. of this tract (153:93; 207).

MORRIS, SARAH, m. Dennis or Daniel McCarty on 20 Jan. 1714
(129:217).

MORRIS, THOMAS, was in Balto. Co. by 1692 as a taxable in n.
side Patapsco Hund.; another Thomas was in Spesutia Hund. in 1692
(138).

MORRIS, THOMAS, d. by 6 Feb. 1695 when his est. was inv. by
Jonas Bowen and John Ensiver, and val. at £ 20.19.0; prob. the
same Thomas whose wid. Ann m. by 18 June 1698 John Mountfield
(61:251; 206-14:20).

MORRIS, THOMAS, m. Mary Murphy on 19 Jan. 1731 (128:68).

MORRIS, THOMAS, m. Frances Shaw on 10 Oct. 1749 (131).

MORRIS, WILLIAM, age 6 next March, was bd. to Peter Cooper in
June 1733 (30:4).

MORRISON, ALICE, was ind. for bast. in March 1741 (33:294).

MORROW, WALTER (1), was in Balto. Co. by Oct. 1700 when he wit. the will of Thomas Litten of Balto. Co.; d. by 31 March 1709; m. Johanna (---) who d. betw. 23 April 1709 and 22 Nov. 1709; came to poss. 50 a. Tall (or Fall) Hill; d. leaving a will, 21 March 1708 - 31 March 1709, leaving 50 a. to his w., 100 a. Fall Hill jointly to sons Samuel and John, and pers. prop. to his son-in-law William (no surname given); admin. bond was posted 23 April 1709 by Johanna "Murrough," with Walter Bosley and Michael Rutledge; a second bond was posted 22 Nov. 1709 by John Morrow and William Picketts with Col. John Thomas; est. was inv. on 5 Dec. 1709 and val. at £ 37.10.3, plus 3044 lbs. tobacco, Thomas Hutchins and Oliver Harriott appraised the est., and Morrow was descr. as an innkeeper; had iss.: SAMUEL; JOHN; (poss.) SUSANNA, who m. Oliver Harriott on 13 Oct. 1717 (12:125, 134; 54:17; 121:201; 122:130; 211).

MORROW, JOHN (2), s. of Walter (1), on 2 Dec. 1709 sold 50 a. Inheritance (being part of a larger tract called Fall Hill, where John's father Walter Morrow had lived) to William Peckett; on 5 Nov. 1716 John and w. Susanna conv. 100 a. Walter's Hope to Thomas Tolley of Kent Co. (67:41, 467).

MORTIMER, EDWARD, was b. c.1704, and on 7 Aug. 1741 leased pt. My Lady's Manor for his lifetime and the lifetimes of his w. Eleanor, b. c.1703, and Eleanor's dau., Hester Bray; in Nov. 1742 he leased another pt. of the Manor for the same three lives; in March 1745 he conv. property to Capt. Henry Morgan and James Richard; in July 1745 he advert. for the return of runaway serv. Thomas King (75:536; 77:206; Md. Gaz., July 1745).

MORTIMER, JOHN, of A. A. Co., in Nov. 1702 purch. 200 a. of Strawberry Hill from Thomas Thurston (66:207).

MORTON, WILLIAM, moved from York Co., Va., to Balto. Co.; he d. leaving a will, 2 April 1750 - 28 March 1751, naming his w. Hannah, Jacob Herrington as the grandfather of his ch., and the four ch. named below; admin. bond was posted 28 May 1750 by Nicholas Ruxton Gay with Talbot Risteau and James Moore, Jr.; had iss.: WILLIAM; ELIZABETH; RICHARD; and MARY (12:235; 112:416).

MORVING, JANE,was ind. for bast. in March 1683/4 (18:131).

MOSS, JAMES, was in Balto. Co. by March 1722 when he admin. the est. of William Hawkins (1:100, 146).

MOTHERBY, CHARLES, m. 1st Rebeckah, wid. of John Newman, on 14 Dec. 1736; m. 2nd, by 20 May 1742, Priscilla, extx. of John Simpson, and 3rd, by 5 Aug. 1747, Ann (---); in 1750 he owned 250 a. part Mount Organ and 50 a. Motherby's Adventure; in Aug. 1749 he was summoned by the vestry of St. Thomas' Parish for unlawful cohabitation with Ann Strang; in Aug. 1750 he was ind. by the Grand Jury on the same charge; had iss. (by Ann)· JOHN, b. 5 Aug. 1747; ELIZABETH, b. 23 May 1749 (3:282; 37:150; 133:156; 134:24; 135:113, 116; 153:32).

MOTTS, MARGARET, parents not named, was b. 27 Aug. 1702 (128:17).

MOULD, JOHN, d. by 6 Sept. 1688 (?), when admin. bond was posted by James Phillips with Edward Douce and Nicholas Rogers; est. was inv. on 2 July 1687 by John Walston and Geo. Goldsmith, and val. at £ 18.15.6; had iss.: FRANCES, m. by 1684 Peter Fucatt; BARBARA, unm. in 1694; and ANN, m. by 1694 John Duncan (12:276; 59:419, 420, 422; 206-10:108).

MOULTON. See MOLTON.

MOUNSEN, PETER, planter, was in Balto. Co. by Aug. 1667 when
he conv. 100 a. at Sassafras R. to Olleof Matthias (95).

MOUNSEUER, ELIZABETH, was ind. for bast. in March 1738/9; as
serv. to Charles Ridgely she was tried again for bast. in Aug.
1739 (31:351; 32:11).

MOUNTENAY, ALEXANDER, in Feb. 1661 obtained a warrant for 200
a. called Mountenay's Neck, located on the e. side of what was
later called Harford Run (341).

MOUNTFIELD, JOHN, was in Balto. Co. by 1695 as a taxable in
n. side of Patapsco Hund.; m. by 18 June 1698 Ann, wid. of Thomas
Morris (61:251; 140).

MOUNTFIELD. See also MUNFIELD.

MOURN, EDWARD, m. Elizabeth Lambeth on 1 May 1736; d. by 27
Aug. 1754 when admin. bond was posted by Samuel Webster with Lemuel Howard and Samuel Gilbert; had iss.: CATHERINE, b. 1 Jan. 1745
(12:212; 129:343).

MOUTRAY, ANN, was ind. for bast. in Nov. 1717 (22:204).

MUCKELDORY, JOHN. See McELROY, JOHN.

MULAIN, EDWARD, m. Margaret Cassady, and had iss.: MARY, b. 18
April 1743 (129:337).

MULHOLLAND, CHARLES, was tried for begetting a child on Elizabeth Claron (35:320).

MULLEHALL, PATRICK, of Queens Co., Ireland, in Nov. 1698 was
bd. to John Smith of Biddiford for 6 years' service in Md. (63:
377).

MULLEN, JOHN, m. Sarah Brown on 16 Jan. 1743 (131).

MULTSHAIR, SARAH, serv. of William Murphy, was ind. for bast.
in Nov. 1743, and was tried in March 1743/4 (35:71, 168).

MUMFORD, EDWARD, was in Balto. Co. by March 1675 when he surv.
50 a. Jones' Neglect (later held by Joseph Perregwa); on 2 March
1685/6 he conv. 100 a. Long Island Point to Thomas Stone and to
Dennis Garrett; on 5 Nov. 1690/1 he and w. Ann conv. 35 a. of
Hart's Green and 15 a. of other land to Samuel Greenwood; d. by
1692/3 when his est. was inv. by Robert Lockwood and John (name
illegible), and val. at £ 515.10.10; had iss.: SARAH, b. c.1671,
m. c.1692 Joseph Peregoe (or Peregoy) (59:320; 208; 206-10:273;
211).

THE ARTHUR MUNDAY FAMILY

MUNDAY/MONDAY, ARTHUR (1), d. in Cecil Co. by 9 June 1713; m.
Catherine (---) who d. there by June 1724; his will, 3 April
1713 - 9 June 1713, named daus. Mary and Alice, and only s. Arthur,
not yet 17; will of his wid. Catherine, 10 Oct. 1718 - 10 June
1724, named dau. Alice and s. Arthur; had iss.: MARY; ALICE, m.
Francis Hamby; and ARTHUR, m. Elizabeth Hamby (122:244; 124:167;
129:258).

MUNDAY, ARTHUR (2), s. of Arthur (1) and Catherine, m. Elizabeth
Hamby on 26 Dec. 1730; they were the par. of: CATHERINE, b. 4 Jan.

1731; CHRISTOPHER, b. 14 Dec. 1736; ARTHUR, b. 22 Sept. 1738
(128:87, 92B; 129:257).

THE HENRY MUNDAY FAMILY

MUNDAY, HENRY (3), no known rel. to any of the above, was in
Balto. Co. by 8 Jan. 1710 when William Howard left him 100 a.
Howard's Forest; m. Susanna Temple on 25 Nov. 1725; d. by 2 July
1740 when Jacob Bull posted admin. bond with Maurice Baker and
Humphrey Wells Stokes; had iss.: JOHN, b. 25 Oct. 1726, d. 29
Sept. 1734; HENRY, b. 28 April 1729 and bd. to Jacob Bull in
June 1740; THOMAS, b. 7 Oct. 1730 and bd. to George Hollingsworth in Nov. 1740; SARAH, b. 2 May 1735, prob. d. young; SARAH,
b. 26 March 1735; JAMES, b. 2 March 1738 and bound to Jacob Bull
in June 1740 (3:307; 12:174; 32:227, 351; 123:146; 128:68, 69,
78, 82, 86, 104).

MUNDAY, HENRY (4), s. of Henry (3), was b. 28 April 1729, and
in 1750 owned 100 a. part Howard's Forest (153:70).

MUNDAY, AVARILLA, dau. of Charles and Bridget Jones, was conv.
a heifer in 1699 by Thomas and Mary Staley (63:377).

MUNDAY, EDWARD, m. Hannah, wid. of Abraham Taylor; d. in
Sept. 1757 leaving a will, 30 Aug. 1757 - 26 Oct. 1757, directing
he be bur. near Francis Hamby on Henry Stump's plantation, ment.
stock bought of John Wood to go to his mother, naming w. Hannah
and unborn ch.; Hannah Munday also d. Sept. 1757 (both she and
her husb. had smallpox); d. leaving a will, 9 Aug. 1757 - 26 Oct.
1757, naming former husb. Abraham Taylor, ch. Francis, Thomas,
and Sarah Taylor, and ch. Isaiah Cord, as well as Mary, dau. of
James Taylor; admin. bond on her est. was posted 29 Oct. 1757 by
Amos Garrett and James Taylor, with Jacob Combest and Isaac Webster; her est. was admin. 29 Jan. 1761 (4:233; 12:222; 129:357;
210-30:371).

MUNFIELD, JNO., was in Balto. Co. by 1692 as a taxable in s.
side Patapsco (138).

MUNGER, EDWARD, m. Mary Singdall on 28 July 1730 (133:149).

MUNGRIL. See MANGRIL.

MUNGRUM, PATIENCE, had iss.: MARY, b. 1 Jan. 1743 (131).

MUNROE, MARGARET, was ind. for bast. in Nov. 1750 and tried
in March 1730/1 (38:1, 283).

MURDAGH, DANIEL, m. Martha Cowen on 23 Oct. 1740; may be the
Daniel Murdock who sold 100 a. Murdock's Chance to Henry O'Neale
on 3 Dec. 1748; had iss.: JAMES, b. 23 July 1741; SARAH, b. 28
March 1743; DANIEL, b. 24 Nov. 1744; SUSANNA, b. 16 April 1747
(80:134; 128:115; 129:329, 342, 343).

MURDOCK, JAMES, m. Christian (---), and had iss.: WILLIAM, b.
29 Oct. 1756; JAMES, b. 17 March 1759; and MARY, b. 10 May 1761
(129:377).

MURFYE, MURPHEW. See MURPHY.

THE JOHN MURPHY FAMILY

MURPHY/MURFYE/MURPHEW/MURPHEY, JOHN (1), was in Balto. Co. by
1692 as a taxable in n. side Gunpowder Hund.; m. Mary Elliott
on 7 March 1707; d. 1 April 1729; left a will, 30 March 1729 -

5 Aug. 1729, mentioning tract Murphy's Hazard, and naming w. Mary, and ch. John and Edward; in Aug. 1730 wid. Mary Murphy had s. Timothy bd. to Henry Millain to age 21; John and Mary had iss.: DARCAS, b. 20 Jan. 1709, d. 15 Feb. 1711; JOHN, b. 11 March 1710; EDWARD, b. 20 Dec. 1712; CATHERINE, b. 28 Sept. 1719; TIMOTHY, b. 17 June 1721; RACHEL, b. 27 Dec. 1723, d. 3 Jan. 1723/4: WILLIAM, b. 16 Aug. 1725; HONOUR, b. 13 Sept. 1728 (73:14, 18; 125: 131; 128:52, 55; 129:214; 138).

MURPHY, JOHN (2), s. of John (1), was b. 11 March 1710, and was in Balto. Co. in Jan. 1732 when he conv. 100 a. Murphy's Hazard to John Thomas (73:320).

MURPHY, TIMOTHY (3), s. of John (1), was b. 17 June 1721 and bd. to Henry Millain by his mother, Mary Murphy, in Aug. 1730; in 1750 owned 100 a. Murphy's Hazard, which he and w. Elizabeth later conv. to Aquila Hall; by w. Elizabeth had iss.: JOHN, b. 2 March 1747; MARY, b. 24 Nov. 1745; WILLIAM, b. 3 Aug. 1749; DIANA b. 17 Dec. 1753 (sic); TIMOTHY, b. 15 Oct. 1753 (sic); USAN, b. 22 Dec. 1756,; JOSEPH, b. 2 Oct. 1759; and MARTHA, b. 10 March 1763 (73:14, 18; 84:85; 129:344; 153:63).

MURPHY, WILLIAM (4), s. of John (1), was b. 16 Aug. 1725, and is prob. the William who m. Sarah Gissard on 2 Aug. 1751, leaving iss.: WILLIAM, b. 12 Sept. 1752; and JOAB, b. 3 Nov. 1755 (129: 354).

MURPHY, BENJAMIN, d. 5 May 1739 (128:206).

MURPHY, BENJAMIN, age 2 last 10 July, in Aug. 1754 was bd. to Thomas Archer (39:345).

MURPHY, BRYAN, was in Balto. Co. by 1695 as a taxable in Spesutia Hund. (140).

MURPHY, DORCAS, was ind. for bast. in March 1739/40; had iss.: SARAH, b. 26 Feb. 1736 (32:140; 128:101).

MURPHY, EDWARD, m. by 2 Oct. 1715, Jane, dau. of Thomas Greenfield; in May 1722 purch, 114 a. Muza's Hazard from Jonathan and Mary Tipton (67:376; 69:46).

MURPHY, JAMES, m. Sarah Chainy on 15 Dec. 1746; she d. 1750 (131:31, 152/r).

MURPHY, JAMES, m. Phebe Skerer on 17 Sept. 1753; had iss.: MARGARET, b. 19 Aug. 1756; ELIZA, b. 3 April 1759 (131:23/r).

MURPHY, JAMES, m. by 18 d, 3, 1758, Hannah, dau. of William Coles (111:72).

MURPHY,, MARGARET, has been kept by John Debruler for 3 years as of June 1737 (31:51).

MURPHY, MARTIN, m. Eliz. Collett on 15 Dec. 1754 (131:211).

MURPHY, MARY, serv., was listed in the 1747/8 inv. of Leonard Wheeler (53:354).

MURPHY, MARY, confessed to having had a ch. out of wedlock, in March 1754, and named David Musselman as the father (39:27).

MURPHY, MARY, had iss.: SAMUEL CASSADY, b. 16 June 1759 (129; 374).

MURPHY, PATRICK, was b. c.1660, giving his age as 47 in

1707 and as 73 in 1730; in March 1699 he surv. 100 a. Cuckoldmaker's Palace. and in Feb. 1702 surv. Murphy's Delight; on 4
May 1726 he and w. Sarah conv. 250 a. Murphy's Delight and Murphy's Addition to George Buchanan (30:64; 70:237; 207).

MURPHY, PATRICK, m. Eliz. Dunahue on 2 Sept. 1755 (131).

MURPHY, RACHEL, was ind. for bast. in Aug. 1750 (37:150).

MURPHY, WILLIAM, in March 1706 surv. 250 a. Murphy's Adventure (207).

MURPHY, WILLIAM, was in Balto. Co. by 1 Aug. 1727 when he and
w. Elizabeth conv. 200 a. Martin's Rest, res. for Benjamin Martin, dec., to George Buchanan (71:15).

MURPHY, WILLIAM, m. Priscilla, dau. of Francis and Elizabeth
(Baker) Dorsey; in 1750 owned 75 a. Roborarum, 100 a. Scotchman's
Desire, 55 a. White Oak Bottom, and 100 a. Dorsey's Addition;
admin. the est. of Francis Dorsey on 1 Sept. 1750, 17 Jan. 1752,
15 Dec. 1752, and 4 Aug. 1753; had iss.. by Priscilla: ELIZABETH,
b. 25 Sept. 1743; PRISCILLA, b. 5 June 1746; WILLIAM, b. 28 April
1748; and BENJAMIN, b. 16 July 1750 (5:132, 244, 247, 293; 134:
1, 61 13; 153:62; Dorsey et al, The Dorsey Family).

MURPHY, WILLIAM, m. Mary (---) and had two ch.: SAMUEL CASSA-
DY, b. 6 June 1759; CATHERINE, b. 27 Jan. 1762 (129:374).

THE JAMES MURRAY FAMILY has been the subject of two other
articles by this author: one was The Descendants of James and
Jemima (Morgan) Murray, pub. c .1964, and the other was the
article in vol. II of the Green Spring Valley, Its History and
Heritage (259).

MURRAY, JAMES (1), progenitor, d. in Balto. Co., c.1704, having m. Jemima, dau. of Capt. Thos. Morgan; Jemima m. as her 2nd
husb., prior to 11 Oct. 1709 Thomas Cromwell; Murray may be the
individual of that name transported by 1676 by Nathaniel Heathcote; by 1692 he was a taxable in the s. side of Patapsco Hund.;
acquired by survey or purchase: 500 a. Morgan's Delight surv.
in 1694, 617 a. Athol surv. Nov. 1694, 89 a. Murray's Addition
surv. in Oct. 1695, with Thomas Cromwell 346 a. Oldton's Garrison, 350 a. Duck Cove and 100 a. Maclane's Hopyard; in June 1702
was named as guardian of the ch. of George Hollingsworth; d. leaving a will, 9 May - 17 July 1704, naming eld. s. Josephus (not
yet 21), and ch. Morgan, Jabez, and Melchizedek; admin. bond was
posted 21 July 1794 by wid. Jemima Murray with Nicholas Fitzsimmons and Thomas Cromwell; est. was inv. 29 July 1704 and val.
at £ 267.2.3, with debts totalling £ 8.2.8 and 7968 lbs. tobacco;
est. was admin. 11 Oct. 1709 by Thomas Cromwell who m. the widow;
left iss.: JOSEPHUS, b. c.1687/9; MORGAN; MELCHIZEDEK; JABEZ, b.
c.1699; ZIPPORAH, m. Richard Gist; JEMIMA, m. 1st John Eager, and
2nd Philip Jones; and KEZIA, m. John Hanson (2:108; 19:225; 21:
286; 63:365; 67:390; 110:91; 121:140; 122:6; 207; 211; 259).

MURRAY, JOSEPHUS (2), s. of James (1), was b. c.1687/8, and d.
1772, having m. Ruth, dau. of Joseph Hawkins. she d. 1782; on 31
Oct. 1724 Josephus and Ruth Murray conv. to Richard Gist all that
land called Addition to Brother's Good Will, being part of Coun-
ter scarpe, which Josephus had already conv. to his sister Zipporah Gist; in Oct. 1736 purch. 50 a. Ellege's Farm from Joseph and
Elizabeth Elledge; in 1750 owned 50 a. of the latter tract, 100
a. Murray's Farm, and 300 a. Murray's Plains; left a will, 12
June 1772 - 13 July 1772; had iss.: JEMIMA, m. George Ashman on

4 Dec. 1736; JOSEPHUS; JAMES: ELIZABETH, b. 8 Sept. 1729; SHAD-
RACK, b. 7 Sept. 1731; WILLIAM, b. 11 Oct. 1732; JOHN, d. 1785;
CHRISTOPHER, d. 1828; KERRENHAPPUCK, b. 9 Aug. 1736, m. (---)
Bailey (47:164; 61:308; 70:69; 71:43; 82:275, 395; 92:174; 112:
216; 153:61; 259).

MURRAY, MORGAN (3), s. of James (1), d. by 24 May 1741; m.
Sarah Hawkins, who m. her 2nd husb. Benjamin Knight and d. leaving a will, 4 Aug. 1748 - 20 Jan. 1748/9, in which she named her
ch. by Murray: JOSEPH; THOMAS; JAMES; MORGAN; SARAH (75:502; 110:
502).

MURRAY, MELCHIZEDEK (4), s. of James (1), d. by 1 Jan. 1748
in A. A. Co.; m. Sophia, dau. of John and Sarah (---) Giles, on
13 Sept. 1723; no known iss. (210-26:42; 259).

MURRAY, JABEZ (5), s. of James (1), was b. c.1699, and d. by
23 May 1761; m. Mary, dau. of William and Martha (West) Wheeler;
Martha was bapt. 29 March 1711; had iss.: MARTHA, b. 26 Nov.
1726, m. John Tipton on 18 Feb. 1747; KEZIAH, b. 10 April 1729,
may have m. Benjamin Wheeler; MARY, b. 14 Feb. 1730/1; JEMIMA, b.
19 March 1743/4; WILLIAM, m. by 23 June 1764 Diana (---) and
moved to Cumberland Co., Penna.: JOHN, b. c.1748, d. 1833 (85:
171, 243; 133:35; 153:60; 219-1; 259).

MURRAY, (---), m. by 27 June 1759 Mary, dau. of Dutton Lane
(83:484).

MURRAY, BENJAMIN, aged 2 on 10 July 1754 (39:345).

MURRAY, FRANCIS, from the N. of England, ran away from Nicholas Dorsey of Balto. Co., about June 1746 (307-69:205).

MURRAY, GEORGE, m. Mary (---), and d. by June 1733 when Samuel
Brown was ind. for not taking care of Murray's Orphans; had iss.:
ELIZABETH, b. 4 Oct. 1720; JAMES, b. 11 Feb. 1722/3; RACHEL, b.
11 April 1725; GEORGE, b. 29 July 1727 (30:2; 128:51).

MURRAY, JAMES, orphan of Cassandra Murray, aged 7 next 1 Dec.,
was bd. to Samuel Owings in Nov. 1758 (44).

MURRAY, LAWRENCE, was in Balto. Co. by 19 March 1733 when he
and w. Sarah conv. a serv. woman to Christopher Randall, and livestock to Daniel Ragan (74:40).

MURRAY, LUCY, m. John Robeson on 10 April 1748 (133).

MURRAY, NATHANIEL, m. Rachel Bailey on 24 Jan. 1760 (131).

MURRAY, THOMAS, was in Balto. Co. by May 1749 when he pat.
43½ a. Hunter's Forest, which he still owned in 1750 (153:95;
207).

MURROW. See MORROW.

MUSCHETT, JOHN, was in Balto. Co. by 22 Sept. 1750 when he and
w. Penelope sold to Hugh Mitchell and Daniel of St. Thomas Jenifer
lot # 46 in Portobacco (Charles Co. Land Records, Liber Z#2, f.
348).

MUSCORD, JOHN, was in Balto. Co. by Aug. 1673 when he and John
Knivington conv. 300 a. Beaver Neck to Bernard Utie (63:126).

MUSGROVE, ANTHONY, m. by 7 Aug. 1758 Margaret (---), wnen they
joined Robert and Mary Teves in selling Addition to Treadway's
Quarter to Abel Browne (83:207).

MUSSE, PATRICK, was in Balto. Co. by 1694 as a taxable in s. side Patapsco Hund. (139).

MUTRAM, ANN, had iss.: JOHN, b. 13 Dec. 1716 (128:53).

MYERS, JOHN, was in Balto. Co. by 1750 when he owned 150 a. Pleasant Garden and 265 a. part Bond's Manor (153:90).

NAIRN. See NEARN.

NANCE, ROWLAND, was in Balto. Co. by 6 May 1681 when he purch. 300 a. United Friendship from Thomas Lightfoot; was naturalized in 1692; d. by 8 Dec. 1688 when his est. was admin. by Henry Constable (64; 206-10:185; 404).

NASH, ELIZABETH, was ind. and tried for bast. in Aug. 1742 (34:1, 9).

NASH, JOHN, was b. c.1658, giving his age as 64 in. 1722 (310).

NAVELL, JOHN, d. by 6 Aug. 1741 when admin. bond on his est. was posted by Alexander Lawson with John Carroll, Patrick Lynch Samuel Gilbert, and Robert Courteney (12:344).

NEAL, Rev. BENNETT, was in Balto. Co. by 1750 when he owned 50 a. Thomas' Beginnings and 65 a. Addition to Thomas' Beginnings (153:21).

NEALE, ELEANOR, bore an illegitimate ch. in   1720/1 at the house of Samuel Dorsey; was ind. for bast. in Aug. 1723; may be the Eleanor Neale who m. Edward Ristone in Feb. 1723/4 (23: 436; 25:437; 133:147).

NEAL, JOHN, Irish, age c.28, ran away from Stephen Onion at the Gunpowder Ironworks before March 1747 (307-69:205).

NEALE, MORRIS, was in Balto. Co. by 1692 as a taxable in Spesutia Hund. (138).

NEALE, PATRICK, m. Sarah (---), and had iss.: JEREMIAH,. b. 24 Nov. 1716; MARGARET, b. 7 June 1718; JAMES, b. 12 May 1721; ELEANOR, b. 16 Feb. 1723 (133:6).

NEARN/NAIRN/NERN, ROBERT, m. Ann Tarman on 29 Oct. 1724; they had iss.: ELIZABETH, b. 18 July 1726 (tried for bast. in March 1745/6 and had a dau. Priscilla b. 12 Sept. 1745), poss. the Elizabeth who m. Ambrose Leach on 5 July 1749; ANNE, b. 4 July 1729, m. William Tayman on 25 Dec. 1750; BENJAMIN, b. 22 Dec. 1732, m. Elizabeth Keys on 11 Feb. 1752; JOHN, b. 14 Nov. 173(4?) (35:806; 131).

NEIFE, ROBERT, was in Balto. Co. by Aug. 1668 when he conv.to William Pearce the tract Neife's Choice, on e. side of Fendall's Creek; Robert's w. Elizabeth also signed the deed (60:63).

NELL, RALPH (1), of Balto. Co., imm. c.1671, and had iss.: HENRY (388).

NELL, HENRY (2), orphan of Ralph (1), age 12 last 3 June, was bd. to John Arding in Aug. 1684 (18:173).

NELSON, AMBROSE (1), d. in Balto. Co. by 12 March 1722; may have been the Ambrose Nelson who was naturalized in Balto. Co. in 1712; d. leaving a will, 15 Aug. 1717 - 12 March 1728, left 50 a. Smith's Range to grandson Ambrose Johnson, res. to w. Martha, and

named granddau. Ruth Johnson, and the ch. named below; had iss.:
AMBROSE; RICHARD; JOHN; MARTHA, m. William Pinkston on 4 March
1717; SARAH, m. (---) Frizzell; SARAH (or poss. ANN) who m.
Samuel Johnson on 17 Feb. 1708 (125:112; 200-38;165; 219-2; 404).

NELSON, JOHN (2), s. of Ambrose (1), m. Frances Rhodes on 12
Jan. 1718; in Aug. 1734 purch. two-thirds of 200 a. of Burr from
Henry Rhodes, eld. s. of Henry and Catherine Rhodes; d. by 14
June 1740 when admin. bond was posted by George Hollandsworth
with Thomas Shea and Henry Rhodes; est. was admin. on 4 Dec.
1741 and 17 July 1753; Frances d. leaving a will, 9 April 1740 -
7 Aug. 1740, leaving to s. Aquila her share of 66 a. Burr; John
and Frances had iss.: HANNAH, b. 10 Aug. 1720, m. George Hollandsworth on 1 Dec. 1737; JOHN, b. 23 Dec. 1737; CATHERINE, b. 13 Dec.
1726, m. James Garrettson on 24 April 1746; PRISCILLA, b. 28 Feb.
1729; AQUILA, m. Sarah Chancey on 20 Jan. 1757; ANN, may have m.
Adam Burchfield on 2 Oct. 1753 (4:94; 5:269, 286; 12:342; 35:301;
74:94; 126:95; 129:253, 299, 342, 358, 377; 131).

NELSON, JOHN (3), s. of John (2), was b. 23 Dec. 1723; in 1750
owned 136 a. part Burr; d. by 28 May 1752 when admin. bond was
posted by George Hollandsworth with Robert Pattison (12:359; 131;
153:33).

NELSON, AQUILA (4), s. of John (2), m. Sarah Chancey on 20
Jan. 1757, and had iss.: JOHN, b. 19 Nov. 1757 (129:358).

NELSON, HANCELIP, m. Dorcas Nelson on 10 Aug. 1747 in St. Margaret's Par., A. A. Co.; may be the Hance Nelson listed in 1750
as owning 77 a. Littleworth (153:104; 219-4).

NELSON, WILLIAM, d. by 13 Feb. 1712/3 when admin. bond was
posted by Richard Colegate, admin., with Dr. Thomas Major; his
est. was inv. on 21 Jan. 1712/3 by Nicholas Haile and Jno. Merryman and val. at £ 4.1.6 (12:331; 50:361).

NELSON, WILLIAM, of Cecil Co., Md., had bros. Jarrett and
Benjamin; came to My Ladys Manor in 1753; had iss.: JOHN; HANNAH,
b. 1757, m. Thomas Hope; CATHERINE, m. Archibald Simpson; ANN, m.
John Wiley; REBECCA; and ROBERT ("Nelson, Smith, and Pocock
Records," at the Md. Hist. Soc.)

NERN. See NEARN.

NETCOMB, GEORGE, m. Sarah Gregory on 5 June 1759 (131).

NETT, JAMES, serv., was listed in the 1732 inv. of Joseph
Johnson (63:133).

NEVILL, THOMAS, was in Balto. Co. by 2 Aug. 1703 when he purch.
100 a. Spring Neck from John and Jane Taylor; d. by 24 May 1705
when admin. bond was posted by Henry Wriothesley and Enoch Spinks;
est. was inv. on 29 June 1705 by John Wells and Walter Bosley
(12:329; 48:86; 66:273).

NEWELL, JOHN, was in Balto. Co. by 1694 as a taxable in n.
side of Gunpowder Hund. (139).

NEWELL, MARY, was ind. for bast. in Nov. 1740 (32:350).

NEWES, TIMOTHY, m. Rebecca Rhodes on 11 March 1741, and had
iss.: ANN, b. 17 Jan. 1743 (131:105/r).

NEWHAM, JOSEPH, was in Balto. Co. by 1692 as a taxable in n.
side Gunpowder Hund. (138).

NEWLAND. See NOLAND.

NEWMAN, ANN, serv. to John Poteet, was ind. for bast. in Aug.
1744, and tried in Nov. 1744 (35:293, 389).

NEWMAN, CATHERINE, was ind. for bast. in Nov. 1719 (23:245).

NEWMAN, DENNIS, m. Katherine, extx. of Thomas Knightsmith on
or by 19 Sept. 1709; d. by 16 April 1718 when admin. bond was
posted by admnx. Katherine Newman, with William Anglin and Timothy Sullivan; est. was inv. on 25 May 1718 by Jo'n Gray and John
Risteau and val. at Ł 34.0.2; est. was admin. by Katherine Newman on 9 Feb. 1718 (1:278, 348; 2:104; 12:332; 48:321).

NEWMAN, JOHN, pet. the court in Aug. 1719; d. leaving a will,
19 March 1732 - 7 Nov. 1733, naming w. Rebecca and dau. Rebecca;
in May 1735 his wid. Rebecca conv. part Mount Organ to Charles
Motherly and John Sinclair; wid. Rebecca m. 2nd Charles Motherly; had iss.: REBECCA (74:216, 219; 126:56; 338-16:117).

NEWMAN, ROGER, d. in Balto. Co. leaving a will, 10 May 1704 -
14 June 1704, naming Charles Greenberry, his sis. Susanna Coatsworth, Dr. Caleb Coatsworth, Mrs. Rachel Greenberry, Heneage Robinson, Edward Hancox, Eliza Samson, and James Reade; admin. bond
was posted 30 June 1704 by Edward Hancox with Thomas Tench and
Philip Lynes; in Dec. 1704 admin. was granted to his sis. Susan,
w. of Caleb Coatsworth; est. was inv. 16 July 1704 by Thomas
Freeborne and Robert Eagle and val. at Ł 337.14.8½ plus Ł 15.17.6
from the sloop Neptune; est. was admin. 29 Nov. 1705 by Edward
Hancox (2:221; 12:330; 50:321, 331; 51:106; 122:42).

NEWMAN, ROGER, was dead by 1750 when his heirs were listed
as the owners of 380 a. Jonas' Range and 450 a. Newman's Neglect
(153:55).

NEWMAN, THOMAS, m. Ann (---), and had iss.: THOMAS, b. 16 May
1744, bd. to Abraham Jarrett in Nov. 1757 (46:88; 128:335).

NEWMAN, WILLIAM, m. Mary Gain on 25 July 1734 (133:152).

NEWPORT, GEORGE, was in Balto. Co. by May 1721 when he admin.
the est. of George Hopham; d. 8 May 1722 when admin. bond was
posted by William and Jane Hopham, with John Harryman and Thomas
Hine;; est. was inv. 7 March 1722 by Thomas Biddison and John
Hillen and val. at Ł 73.7.4; dec. left no known rel. in the Province (1:246; 12:336; 23:250; 52:27).

NEWS, TIMOTHY, m. Rebecca Rhodes on 11 March 1741 (131).

NEWSOME, THOMAS (1), was b. c.1672, and d. 5 Feb. 1720/1; m.
Catherine (---) who d. 23 March 1720; on 18 Dec. 1701 purch. 200
a. Contrivance from James Phillips; admin. bond was posted 11 April 1721 by exec. Peter Lester with John Stokes and John Durbin;
est. was inv. 19 April 1721 by Joseph Johnson and Edgar Tipper
and val. at Ł 109.7.8, and Mary Newsome (dau.-in-law) signed as
the mother of the heirs; est. admin. 8 Oct. 1723 by Peter Lester
(who m. Newsome's exec.), and legacies were paid to Eliza Emison,
Jr., Mary Newsome, the accountant, and his son; dec. left iss.:
JOHN, b. 28 Sept. 1694; and SUSANNA, b. and d. 1696 (1:120, 171;
4:170; 12:334; 52:24; 66:149; 124:59 (cont. abstract of Thomas'
will); 128:1,4, 5, 37).

NEWSOME, JOHN (2), s. of Thomas (1), was b. 28 Sept. 1694, and
d. 19 April 1720; m. Mary Stinchcomb, dau. of Nathaniel and Hannah (Randall) Stinchcomb, in Feb. 1715; she m. 2nd by 3 Aug.

1723 William Smith, s. of George; in June 1724 the orphans of
John Newsome were Thomas and Ellinor; in Nov. 1730 son Thomas
was made a ward of Peter Lester; in June 1733 William Smith was
ind. for not educating Newsom's orphans; John and Mary had iss.:
THOMAS, b. 16 Dec. 1715, d. 5 March 1733; HELEN, b. 14 Aug.
1718, m. John Bailey by 1 Sept. 1739 (17:316; 29:51; 30:2; 128:
1, 35, 36, 37, 77; Stinchcomb data comp. by the late Donnel M.
Owings and in poss. of the author).

NESTER, THOS., m. Anne Freeman on 4 Feb. 1749/50 (133:16?).

NEWTON, ANN, had iss.: JOHN, b. 26 June 1748 (131:128/r).

NEWTON, CHARLES, m. Sarah Rice on 6 Feb. 1732 (131).

NEWTON, HUGH, m. Eleanor (---), and had iss.: SHADRACK, b. 11
June 1746 (131:118/r).

NEWTON, JOHN, of Balto. Co., imm. c.1674 (388).

NICHOLAS, ANN, had iss.: PHEBE, b. 12 Sept. 1732; ALEXANDER,
b. 12 June 1735, and in June 1740 at age 4 was bd. to Richard
Deaver (32:227; 128:99).

NICHOLAS, WALTER, English, age c.36, was a runaway conv. serv.
from near Deer Creek, Nov. 1754 (385:317).

NICHOLETTS, CHARLES, minister, was conv. 150 a. at Steelpone
Creek, by John James, Gent., on 8 Nov. 1671; Nicholetts and his
w. Justice conv. the 150 a. to John James on 5 March 1671/2 (97:
126; 98:47).

NICHOLS/NICHILLS/NICHOLLS, AMOS, of Penna., in Aug. 1686 purch.
400 a. from Thomas Lightfoot; in Aug. 1690 he was in Cecil Co..,
when he sold land to Thomas Brown (59:208, 321).

NICHOLS, HUMPHREY, was in Balto. Co. by 1 March 1669/70 when
Gabriel Brown conv. him 150 a. called Homley (96).

NICHOLS, JAMES, m. Drucilla (---), and had iss.: SARAH, b. 15
Aug. 1750(?), and LUCRETIA, b. 25 Sept. 1760 (131:21/r, 64/r).

NICHOLS, JOHN, was in Balto. Co. by 1683 and d. there by 16
May 1694; m. Mary (---); bought 200 a. at Bow Creek from Michael
and Jane Judd in Aug. 1683; d. leaving a will dated 4 May 1691,
naming w. Mary and four ch. named below; est. was inv. on 16
May 1694 by Israel Skelton and John Rallings and val. at £ 42.
12.4; dec. left iss.: JOHN; THOMAS, d. 12 July 1704; MARY; and
SARAH (51:39; 106:287; 121:124; 128:18).

NICHOLS, THOMAS, m. Frances James on 21 Aug. 1740; had iss.:
THOMAS, b. 3 Dec. 1742 (131:27. 108/r).

NICHOLS, WILLIAM, d. by 7 June 1733 when admin. bond was posted by Josias Middlemore with Thomas and William Bond, the wid.
Mary having renounced (12:337).

NICHOLS, WILLIAM, came to Md. for 7 years as a transport, and
was sold to William Kelly living at the Garrison Ridge; he was
advised to apply to Charles Homewood for news of a legacy from
England (Md. Gaz., 23 April 1752).

NICHOLSON, JOHN (1), d. in A. A. Co., by June 1737; admnx.
Mary m. George Presbury of Balto. Co.; dec. left iss.: NATHAN;
JAMES; MOSES; and MARY (31:51; 32:404).

NICHOLSON, NATHAN (2), s. of John (1), m. Ruth Bond, sis. of
William Bond, on 16 March 1749; in Jan. 1756 was named as cousin
in the will of Elizabeth, wid. of Thomas Hines (131; 210-30:28;
210-37:85).

NICHOLSON, JAMES (3), s. of John (1), in Jan. 1756 was named
as cousin in the will of Elizabeth, wid. of Thomas Hines; may be
the James who m. Ducella Durbin on 24 Dec. 1757; was the James
Nicholson who earlier in June 1746 chose Nathan Nicholson as his
guardian (36:3; 131; 210-30:28).

NICHOLSON, DANIEL, of Kent Co., in 1750 owned owned 100 a. of
Nicholson's Delight (153:93).

NICHOLSON, JAMES, was in Balto. Co. by March 1725 when Edward
and Jean Cox conv. him 100 a. Cox's Prospect (70:64).

NICHOLSON, JOHN, was in Balto. Co. by July 1688 when he surv.
the tract Plaisterer's Hall; on 1 March 1698 John and w. Rebecca
now in A. A. Co. conv. 100 a. of that tract to Henry Carter (63:
410; 207).

NICHOLSON, JOHN, d. by Nov. 1693 when his extx. Mary m. 2nd
John Wallford; about 1696 his est. was inv. by Edmund Hesnley
and Thomas Heath and val. at £ 48.12.6; his est. was admin. 2
Sept. 1696 by Thomas Staley and Robert Olosse, admins. of Mary
Warfoote, the orig. admnx. of John Nicholson (20:165; 206-14:
154, 155). Cf. to William Nicholson below.

NICHOLSON, NICHOLAS, m. by 14 May 1680 Hester Larkin, admnx.
of William Gough (200-69:233, 337; 206-7A:118).

NICHOLSON, WILLIAM, d. by 22 Oct. 1698, d. by 22 Oct. 1698
when his est. was admin. by Thomas Staley and Robert Olosse, admins. of Mary Warfoot, formerly Nicholson; payments were made
to Miles Gibson and Mark Richardson (2:33). Cf. to John Nicholson above.
NICHOLSON, WILLIAM, d. by 1750 when his heirs were listed as
owning 4200 a. Nicholson's Manor (153:51).

NIEL, THOMAS, m. Mary Wagster after the banns were pub. in
April 1747 (131).

NIXON, THOMAS, m. Sarah Thompson on 23 July 1747; had iss.:
WILLIAM, b. 27 March 1748, d. 14 Oct. 1751; THOMAS, b. 29 March
1750; WILLIAM, b. 20 April 1752; MILDRED, b. 25 Sept. 1755, d.
same year; PAMELA, b. 1 Aug. 1759 (131:128/r, 139/r, 140/r, 64/r).

NOAH, RICHARD, m. Martha Meads on 9 June 1734; had iss.: MARY,
b. 10 Feb. 1733 (128:78).

NOBLE, WILLIAM (1), was in Balto. Co. by 1694 as a taxable in
n. side Gumpowder Hund.; m. 1st Elizabeth (---); m. 2nd on 21
Feb. 1731 Ann Durbin; on 28 March 1707 purch. 100 a., being one-
third of 300 a. Dennis' Choice, from Simon Pierson; on 6 March
1715 William and Elizabeth conv. 100 a. to James Preston; d. having made a will made 14 March 1731/2, proved 8 April 1732, naming
Samuel Durham, tracts Turkey Range and Noble Desire, and his own
w. Ann; admin. bond was posted 5 Feb. 1732 by exec. John Poteet
with Simon Pearson and John Powell; had iss.: WILLIAM, (prob. b.
posthumously)   (12:340; 59:543; 67:379; 125:232; 131; 139).

NOBLE, WILLIAM (2), s. of William (1), was in Augusta Co.,
Va., by 17 Aug. 1754 when as son and heir of William Noble, dec.,
he conv. parcels of Turkey Range and Noble Range to William Dallam (82:297).

NOBLE, CATHERINE, had s.: ALLEN GRAY, b. 7 Feb. 1739 (129: 340).

NODEN. See NORTON.

NOELL, LEWIS, was in Balto. Co. by 1692 as a taxable in s. side Gunpowder; m. Mary Ferrill on 25 Nov. 1704 (131:22; 138).

NOLAND/KNOWLAND/NEWLAND/NOWLAND, ANDREW, was b. c.1717; signed a lease in 1744 which named his w. Margaret, b. c.1721, and dau.: FRANCES, b. c.1741 (78:221).

NOLAND, EDWARD, d. by 7 Jan. 1747 when admin. bond was posted by Lawrence Watson, admin., with John Ensor, Jr., and Moses Rutter (12:346).

NOLAND, THOMAS, m. by 23 Sept. 1723, Mary (---) who joined him in a deed with John and Dinah Cole, Thomas and Anna Broad, and Rebecca Hawkins in conv. to Lancelot Todd the land bought by the late Matthew Hawkins from Col. Thomas Hammond, called Best Success (69:209).

NOLAND, THOMAS, m. Frances Smith on 10 Jan. 1740 (129:344).

NOLL. Dr. HENRY, was in Balto. Co. by Oct. 1753 when he mortgaged land to Edward Dorsey (82:88).

THE NORMAN FAMILY was investigated by the late Donnell M. Owings in his unpublished study of the Randall Family.

NORMAN, GEORGE (1), was b. c.1648, d. testate in A. A. Co. by 28 Aug. 1677; was transported to Md., c.1662; m. Johanna (---) who m. 2nd Christopher Randall, and 3rd John Gadsby; George Norman d. leaving a will, 13 Jan. 1675 - 28 Aug. 1677, appointing his w. as extx., and leaving all his land to his s. George; had iss.: GEORGE; AMY, m. 1st Hector McLane, and 2nd, John Townsend (120:195; 211; 388; unpub. notes on the Norman fam. by Donnell M. Owings).

NORMAN, GEORGE (2), s. of George (1), was b. c.1669; d. in Balto. Co. by 24 March 1697/8; m. Elizabeth, dau. of James Smith of Middle Neck Hund., A. A. Co.; d. leaving a will, 28 Feb. 1697 - 24 March 1697/8, naming w. Eliza, sons George and William, and mentioning an unborn ch.; est. was inv. 7 April 1698 by Richard Cromwell and James Murray, and val. at £ 74.10.0; John Gadsby later held land for Norman's orphans; George and Eliza (Smith) Norman had iss.: GEORGE; WILLIAM; SUSANNA, b. posthumously, may have m. Henry Butler (48:106; 54:22; 138; 211; 121:135; notes by Donnell M. Owings).

NORMAN, ANNA MARIA, Low Dutch, runaway conv. serv. from William Williams at the Balto. Iron Works was advert. for in Oct. 1746 (384:586).

NORMAN, MARGARET, m. William Harvey on 2 Feb. 1726 (219-1).

NORRINGTON, JOHN (1), was b. c.1664; gave his age as 60 in March 1724 when he pet. to be levy free; m. Elizabeth (---); in March 1703 John purch. 106 a. Webster's Enlargement from John and Hannah Webster; in Aug. 1714 John and Elizabeth Norrington conv. the tract to Peter Overard; had iss.: JOHN; MARY, b. in March 1711 (ind. for bast. in March 1733/4, tried in June 1734); ELIZABETH, b. 1714; FRANCIS, b. June 1718; JANE, b. 25 Dec. 1712 (27:121; 64:5; 67:302; 131).

NORRINGTON, JOHN (2), s. of John (1), m. Mary Hayes on 1 Aug.
1737, and had at least one ch.: MARY, b. 30 April 1741 (131).

NORRINGTON, FRANCIS (3), s. of John (1), was b. in June 1718;
m. Mary Everett, dau. of John Everett, on 19 Feb. 1749/50 (131;
210-30:482).

THE NORRIS FAMILY has been the subject of Thomas M. Myers'
The Norris Family of Maryland (pub. 1916), and Henry A. Davis'
unpub. typescript on the Norris Family, in the Rare Book Room
at the Library of Congress in Washington. Unfortunately, much
of the Davis multi-volume work is undocumented, and thus must
be used with care).

NORRIS, THOMAS (1), progenitor, is stated by Davis to have
been born c.1608 in Congham, Norfolk, Eng., s. of Geoffrey Norris; came to Nansemond Co., Va., c.1630/1, where (again acc. to
Davis) he m. Anne, dau. of Thomas Hynson of Nansemond, Va., and
of Kent Co., Md.; Norris came to St. Marys Co., Md., c.1637, and
may have been the father of: THOMAS, b. c.1638; EDWARD, b. Oct.
1639; GEOFFREY, b. c.164-(?), and d. young; DANIEL, b. April
1643; ALICE, b. June 1644, m. William Evans and ret. to Eng.;
CUTHBERT, b. c.1645, drowned, age 23; ROBERT, b. Dec. 1647; ANN,
b. c.1650, m. Francis Shepherd; JOHN, b. c.1652 (data from the
Davis typescript).

NORRIS, THOMAS (2), s. of Thomas (1) and Ann, was b. c.1638
in St. M. Co.; d. June 1683; m. 1st, c. 1661, Martha, dau. of
William Ironmonger, and 2nd, by 1671, Elizabeth Hosier of Kent
Co.; said (by Davis) to have had iss.: MARTHA, b. c.1662; THOM-
AS GEOFFREY, b. c.166-(?), d. young; ANN, b. c.1677, d. young; by
2nd w.: JOHN, b. c.1672; ELIZABETH, m. c.1700 John Abbott of Talbot Co.; RACHEL, b. c.1680, m. 1728 Nicholas Bowles; JOSEPH, b.
c.1683 (Davis).

NORRIS, EDWARD (3), s. of Thomas (1), and Ann, was b. Oct.
1639 in St. M. Co.; d. intestate c.1695/6; m. 1st, by 1661, Mary
(d. c.1678), dau. of William and Mary Freeman; m. 2nd, c.1689,
Sarah Wichell, wid. of John Kemp; was in Balto. Co. by 1692 as
a taxable in n. side Patapsco Hund.; d. by 15 Feb. 1696 when his
est. was inv. by John Mansfield and James Bowen, and val. at
£ 30.17.0; had iss.: WILLIAM, b. c.1661; JOHN, b. c.1663; MARY,
b. c.166-(?); THOMAS, b. c.1668; ELIZABETH, b. c.167-(?); GEOF-
FREY, b. c.1670, d. age 10; ANNE, b. 1687; SARAH, b. c.169-(?),
d. in inf.; (48:18, 34; 138; Davis).

NORRIS, DANIEL (4), s. of Thomas (1), and Anne, was b. c. April 1643; d. by 1707 in Kent Co.; m. by 1683 Elizabeth (---) who
d. 1706; left a will, 13 Jan. 1706 - 23 March 1707, naming son-in-
law William Bentley (and his ch. Mary and Patience Bentley); ch.
Daniel and Eliza (to have 120 a. left to the testator by his bro.
Thomas), the ch. of a sister who might arrive from Eng., and his
dec. w. Elizabeth; had iss.: ELIZABETH, b. c.1683, d. in inf.;
dau., b. c.1685, m. William Bentley; ELIZABETH JANE, m. after
1706 John Ball; and DANIEL, d. unm. in 1725 (122:106; Davis).

NORRIS, ROBERT (5), s. of Thomas (1), is said by Davis to
have been b. Dec. 1647 in Nansemond Co., Va.; d. c.1698; m. by
1674 Tabitha Ostley, dau. of Barbara Ostley who m. Thomas Collins; Tabitha m. 2nd Philip Davis; Robert and Tabitha had iss.
THOMAS GEOFFREY, b. c.1674, d. unm.); JAMES, b. c.1676; ELIZA-
BETH, b. c.1680, m. John Abbott; JOHN, b. c.1683; SAMUEL, b. c.
1685; DANIEL CUTHBERT, b. 1689; WILLIAM, b. 1690; ANNE TABITHA,
b. c.169-(?), m. John Carey and had iss. (Davis).

NORRIS, JOHN (6), s. of Thomas (1), was b. c.1652 in St. M.
Co.; d. 1709; m. c.1680 Susanna, dau. of John and Susanna Heard;
Susanna Heard, wid. of John Heard, in her will dated 13 May
1706 named dau. Susanna Norris, and grandch. Jno., Luke, Mark,
and Elizabeth Norris; John and Susanna (Heard) Norris had iss.:
JOHN, b. c.1680; MONICA; ELIZABETH; LUKE, b. 1689; MARY, b.
c.169-(?), m. after 1710 Stephen Gough; MARK, b. c.1695; THOMAS,
b. c.1697 (122:98; Davis).

NORRIS, JOHN (7), prob. s. of Edward (3), was b. c.1663, d. c.
1740 in A. A. Co.; m. 1st, c.1685 Elizabeth, dau. of Thomas and
Isabella Parsons; Elizabeth d. c. Nov. 1714, and John m. 2nd,
on 3 April 1716 Mary Newman; purch. 243 a. Prospect in Balto. Co.
from Peter Bond and William Hamilton in Nov. 1716; also purch.
365 a. Everly Hills from Thomas Preston in March 1718, and 150 a.
Spring Garden from William and Susan Parrish in Sept. 1726; d.
leaving a will, 1 Nov. 1737 - 5 Dec. 1740, leaving Norris' Addition to grandson Thomas, named s. John (and his s. John), sons
Thomas and Benjamin (to have parts of Everly Hills), dau. Mary
Metcalfe (to have 150 a. Spring Garden), sons Joseph and Edward
(to have The Prospect), and w. Mary to be extx.; had iss.: ELIZA-
BETH, b. 6 May 1686; SUSANNA, b. 2 Feb.1689; JOHN, b. 28 Feb.
1691; HANNAH, b. 20 Aug. 1698; BENJAMIN, b. 20 Aug. 1698; EDWARD,
b. 4 Feb. 1701; JOSEPH, b. 20 Feb. 1705/6; by 2nd w.: THOMAS, b.
26 Dec. 1716; MARY, b. 16 Feb. 1718/9 (127:110; Myers).

NORRIS, THOMAS (8), prob. s. of Edward (3), was b. c.1668
(acc. to Davis), and was in Balto. Co. by 1692 as a taxable in
n. side Gunpowder Hund.; in May 1696 took up Envell Chase on the
Bush R.; gave his age as 72 in Nov. 1724 (which would make his
year of birth 1652), stated he had been a res. of Balto. Co. for
over 30 years; gave his age as 79 in 1729; m. Elizabeth (---),
who d. Dec. 1710; had iss.: JOHN, d. c.1761 (27:37; 128:27;
138; 211; Myers).

NORRIS, JOHN (9), s. of John (7), was b. 28 Feb. 1691, d. c.
1741; said to have m. Clare Wells , dau. of Thomas and Mary (Hopkins) Wells, in 1714 in St. James Par., A. A. Co.; had iss.:
ELIZABETH, b. 15 Nov. 1715; JOHN, b. 31 Oct. 1720; SARAH, b. 27
Feb. 1723; MARTIN. b. 21 Nov. 1730 (Myers).

NORRIS, BENJAMIN (10), s. of John (7), was b. 20 Aug. 1698,
d. c.1772 in Balto. Co.; m. Sarah Whitaker on 8 Oct. 1719 in St.
John's Par. (she was a dau. of John and Catherine Whitaker, and
was b. 10 Nov. 1699); in 1750 owned part Everly Hills, 121 a.
part Bire, 100 a. Sheppard's Range, 270 a. Gibson's Ridge, and
136 a. Addition to Gibson's Ridge; d. leaving a will, 4 April
1770 - 25 Feb. 1772 mentioned tracts Boir, Gibson's Ridge, Everly Hill, The Enlargement, Sheppard's Range, and Addition to
Sheppard's Range, w. Sarah, father John, and the ch. named below;
had iss.: ELIZABETH, b. 28 Nov. 1720, m. (---) Hughes; JOHN, b.
4 March 1722; SARAH, b. 29 May 1725; HANNAH, b. 16 July 1727;
m. James Hendon; SUSANNA, b. 21 April 1730; JOSEPH, b. 14 Jan.
1730/1; BENJAMIN, b. 20 Oct. 1732; and ABRAHAM, b. 22 July 1739
(112:229; 131:15, 18, 36/r, 60/r, 81/r, 45/r, 51/r, 82/r, 92/r,
100/r, 115/r, 120/r; 153:32).

NORRIS, EDWARD (11), s. of John (7), was b. 4 Feb. 1701/2, d.
1763; m. c.1724, Hannah Scott, dau. of Daniel and Elizabeth; in
1750 owned 116 a. part Prospect, 90 a. The End; left a will, 5
Dec. 1761 - 21 March 1763; had iss.: JOSEPH, b. 5 Dec. 1725, m.
Philizanna Barton; SARAH, b. 15 Dec. 1727, m. Daniel Treadway on
2 Aug. 1724; DANIEL, b. 27 Dec. 1728, m. Sarah Beaver in 1762;
ELIZABETH, b. 23 June 1735, d. in inf.; ELIZABETH, b. 29 April
1736, m. John Taylor on 18 Oct. 1757; HANNAH, b. 7 Sept. 1738,

m. John Fulton on 4 Oct. 1754; EDWARD, b. 8 April 1741; JAMES,
b. 25 Feb. 1742; MARY, b. 1745, d. 1825 unm.; JOHN, b. 26 Jan.
1747, m. Martha Long; THOMAS; AQUILA, b. 13 June 1754; SUSAN-
NAH, m. George Garrison (112:3; 131; 153:76; Myers).

NORRIS, JOSEPH (12), s. of John (7), was b. 20 Feb. 1705, d.
c.1784; m. Mary (---); in 1750 owned 127 a. part Prospect; had
iss.: ELIZABETH, b. 30 Dec. 1735, m. Ezekiel Bosley; JOHN, b. 10
Sept. 1737; RACHEL, b. 21 July 1739, m. Gist Vaughan in 1769;
SUSANNA, m. Walter Wyle; MARY, b. 1 June 1742, m. William Sinclair;
HANNAH, b. 28 May 1743; JOSEPH, b. 18 April 1745; BENJAMIN, b. 17
Jan. 1749; EDWARD, b. 29 July 1751; WILLIMEN, m. Vincent Bosley
on 28 March 1771; TEMPERANCE, b. 2 Feb. 1753; JAMES, b. 29 March
1756 (113:31; 131:63/r, 78/r, 94/r, 109/r, 122/r, 141/r; 153:52).

NORRIS, THOMAS (13), s. of John (7), was b. 26 Dec. 1716, and
was alive in 1750; m. Avarilla Scott on 10 Oct. 1738; in 1750 he
owned 38 a. Everly Hill, 100 a. Norris' Chance, and 100 a. Choat's
Contrivance; had iss.: (1st two ch. b. in St. John's Par., 3rd
and 4th were b. in St. Thomas' Par.); WILLIAM, b. 24 Dec. 1739;
NATHANIEL, b. 16 Dec. 1741; MARY, b. 5 Feb. 1743; JOHN, b. 5 May
1746 (131:91/r; 134:7; 153:33; Myers).

NORRIS, JOHN (14), s. of Thomas (8), d. in Balto. Co. c.1761,
having m. Ann (---) in 1712; in 1750 owned 100 a. part Expectation and 50 a. Norris' Adventure; left a will, 28 March 1760 -
18 May 1761, mentioning tracts Expectation and Rebecca's Lot;
had iss.: THOMAS, b. 25 Nov. 1713; ANN, b. 7 Sept. 1717, m. (---)
Greer; JAMES, m. Elizabeth Davis on 1 Jan. 1744; SARAH, b. 22
April 1719 or 24 April 1720, m. Asael Hitchcock on 8 Oct. 1741;
REBECCA, b. 15 Sept. 1729, m. Thomas Elliott, Jr., on 30 Jan.
1753; WILLIAM, m. Elizabeth Horn on 24 Jan. 1751; MARY, m. (---)
Love (4:359; 111:328; 131:6, 12/r; 153:3; Myers).

NORRIS, JOHN (15), s. of Benjamin (10) and Sarah, was b. 4
March 1722/3, m. Sarah Bradford, dau. of William and Elizabeth,
on 3 April 1744; had iss.: BENJAMIN, b. 16 Aug. 1745; JOHN, b.
6 June 1747; WILLIAM, b. 26 March 1749; MARTHA, b. 16 Aug. 1750,
m. Vincent Richardson; JACOB, b. 10 May 1753; SUSANNAH, b. 10
May 1753, m. George Taylor; SARAH, b. 23 Jan. 1756, m. Aquila
Norris; ALEXANDER, b. 15 May 1759; MARY, b. 15 May 1759 (131:
26, 142/r, 143/r; Myers).

NORRIS, BENJAMIN (16), s. of Benjamin (10), was b. 20 Oct.
1732, m. Mary Duvall, dau. of Samuel and Elizabeth (Talbot) Duvall, on 7 March 1754; had iss.: BENJAMIN; JOHN; and ABRAHAM
(Myers).

NORRIS, JOSEPH (17), s. of Edward (11), was b. 5 Dec. 1725, m.
Philizanna Barton on 2 Aug. 1750; had iss.: WILLIAM, b. Feb. 1758;
JOSEPH, b. Feb. 1761 (131:155/r; Myers).

NORRIS, DANIEL (18), s. of Edward (11), was b. 27 Dec. 1728,
d. 1804; m. 1st, 28 Sept. 1762, Sarah Beaver, and 2nd, Catherine
(---); d. testate without issue (Myers).

NORRIS, THOMAS (19), s. of John (14), was b. 25 Nov. 1713, d.
1761; m. Elizabeth McComas on 26 Dec. 1736; in 1750 owned 100 a.
Macedon; left a will, 26 Dec. 1757 - 24 March 1761, mentioning
tracts Macedon, Turkey Range, and Hills and Dales; had iss.:
JOHN, b. 11 Dec. 1737; ELIZABETH, b. 11 July 1741; ALEXANDER, b.
9 Dec. 1744; AQUILA; THOMAS; and JAMES (131:53/r, 101/r, 109/r;
153:25; 210-31:269; Myers).

NORRIS, JAMES (20), s. of John (14), was b. c.1715, d. c.1798;
m. Elizabeth Davis, dau. of William, on 1 Jan. 1744; had iss.:

WILLIAM, b. 13 Feb. 1745; JAMES; HENRY; SARAH, m. (---) White
(112:149; 131:27, 107/r; 210-37:585; Myers).

NORRIS, (---), m. by 2 May 1758 Hannah, dau. of Elizabeth
Scott (210-30:493).

NORRIS, JOSEPH, m. Esther (---), and had iss.: EDWARD, b. 29
July 1751 (131:141/r).

NORRIS, MARY, m. Henry Millen on 5 July 1720 (129:225).

NORRIS, RACHEL, m. Nicholas Bowles on 21 Jan. 1728 (131:37).

NORRIS, SARAH, was tried for bast. in Nov. 1746 (36:245).

NORRIS, SUSANNA, m. Richard Atherton on 1 Nov. 1721 (131).

NORRIS, THOMAS, m. Mary (---), and had iss.: HENRY, b. 20
Oct. 1713 (129:222).

NORRIS, THOMAS, in 1750 owned 50 a. Turkey Cock Alley (153:77).

NORRIS, THOMAS, was named by Rebecca Potee as the father of
her child, and was tried for bast. in Nov. 1756 (41:311).

NORRIS, WILLIAM, d. 2 May 1720; left a will dated 2 May 1720,
leaving his entire est. to daus. Mary and Else, with Henry Million
as exec.; admin. bond was posted 21 May 1721 by Henry Millen with
Peter Lester and Thomas Newsom; est. was inv. on 17 Aug. 1720 by
Thomas Cord and Jo'n Clark, and val. at £ 127.0.4, plus 7104 lbs.
tob.; est. was admin. by Henry Millain on 9 May 1722. incl. a
payment for 2 suits of mourning for the daus of the dec.; by w.
Sarah left iss.: MARY, b. 31 March 1704, m. Henry Millen or Millain on 5 July 1720; ELIS, b. 16 April 1713 (3:38; 12:333; 48:
239; 124:7; 128:20, 29, 38).

THE NORTH FAMILY was discussed in great detail by W. H. Chippindall, in his History of Whittington, in the Chetham Society
Publication, new ser., vol. 99 (1938), pp. 130-147. It should be
noted that this account supercedes the one published by this
author in vol. II of The Green Spring Valley, so far as the generations in England are concerned.

NORTH, OLIVER (1), progenitor of this branch of the family,
was listed in the Subsidy Roll of 35 Henry VIII (1543) as having
goods worth £ 3, on which he paid 3 d; was bur. in Whittington
Parish on 28 April 1557; will proved 18 Nov. 1557; had iss.:
THOMAS; dau., m. William North; dau., m. (---) Heylton; and dau.
m. Richard Cheeseman (Chippindall).

NORTH, THOMAS (2), s. of Oliver(1), of Docker, was bur. at
Whittington on 26 Dec. 1585; m. Anne (poss. Laborey); she was
bur. at Whittington on 24 June 1603; Thomas left a will, 11 Dec.
1585, proved 22 Jan. 1585/6, naming w., s. Richard, and sister-
in-law Jane Laborey; had iss.: RICHARD; ISABEL, m. Robert Robinson
of Capernwray; dau., m. Thomas Curwen; JANE, bur. at Halton on
14 March 1617/8 (Chippindall).

NORTH, RICHARD (3), s. of Thomas (2), inherited the farmhold
in 1585; prob. m. a Miss Baleman of Over Kellett; was called bro.
by Richard Baleman in latter's will; in 1623 Richard signed the
bond for his dau. Jane to admin. the est. of her dec. husb.,
Thomas Widder; d. leaving a will, 8 April 1627 - 24 May 1627; est.
was inv. 21 May 1627, and val. at £ 1066.17.0; had iss.: THOMAS,
bapt. 26 Feb. 1579/80; ELIZABETH, bapt. 1 Oct. 1582, m. Thomas

Robinson on 28 July 1599; JANE, m. Thomas Widder on 8 May 1608;
RICHARD, bapt. 11 Aug. 1588, m. Margaret Widder; OLIVER, bapt.
9 Aug. 1592, m. Agnes Hirdson on 20 Aug. 1606; ANNE, bapt. 16
Feb. 1594/5, bur. 6 April 1597 (Chippindall).

NORTH, THOMAS (4), s. of Richard (3), was bapt. 26 Feb. 1579/
80 at Whittington; in 1638 he gave his age as 60; m. Agnes (---)
who was bur. 16 Sept. 1658 at Whittington; he wss bur. on 4 Oct.
1658; had iss.: Margaret, bapt. 8 May 1610; RICHARD, bapt. 28
Jan. 1612/3; JANE, bapt. 25 Sept. 1615; ALICE, bapt. 25 May
1620; ELIZABETH; FRANCIS; (Chippindall).

NORTH, RICHARD (5), s. of Thomas (4), was bapt. 28 Jan. 1612/
13, styled himself "Gent.," when he testified in the lawsuit of
Widder vs. Goddard in July 1647; m. Alice (---), who was bur. at
Whittington on 15 Nov. 1666; he died v.p., and was bur. on 31
Dec. 1655; had iss.: THOMAS, bapt. 10 March 1632/3; MILES, bapt.
7 Dec. 1634, bur. 5 Feb. 1700/1 at Newton; Margaret, bapt. 5 Aug.
1638, m. Thomas Turner on 25 Aug. 1658; OLIVER, bapt. 8 July
1640; ELIZABETH, bapt. 4 Sept. 1642, bur. 24 Oct. 1642; JANE,
bapt. 9 Nov. 1643; AGNES, b. c.1636, m. Thomas Atkinson of William on 3 June 1658 (Chippindall).

NORTH, THOMAS (6), s. of Richard (5) was bapt. 10 March 1632;
m. either at Whittington or Over Kellett, on 28 April 1655, Elizabeth Wilson; she was bur. at Whittington on 16 Dec. 1671; inher.
his grandfather's farm, and was an attorney; was Steward of Mr.
Carus' manor until he d. 1712; left a will, 16 Sept. 1705 - 17
April 1712; had iss.: RICHARD, bapt. 23 Jan. 1657/8; ALICE, bapt.
5 July 1660 at Over Kellett, m. 1st Christopher Hopkins of Holme
House; m. 2nd Thomas Townson of Kirkby Lonsdale, and 3rd, Augustine Greenwood; THOMAS, bapt. 27 Nov. 1665; MILES, had a legacy
from his uncle Miles, and was bur. 3 April 1712 (Chippindall).

NORTH, THOMAS (7), s. of Thomas (6), was bapt. 27 Nov. 1655
at Whittington, and m. Ellen, dau. of William Lonsdale; d. leaving a will, 21 April 1747 - 19 May 1750, contained a seal with a
coat of arms: On a chevron between three (fleurs-de-lis?), three
crescents; was bur. 17 Feb. 1749/50; his widow Ellen d. leaving
a will, 4 Feb. 1760 - 27 Jan. 1761; Thomas and Ellen had iss.:
THOMAS, bapt. 28 Dec. 1690; WILLIAM, bapt. 13 Nov. 1692, d. by
1766, prob. unm.; JOHN, bapt. 21 April 1695, bur. 29 Oct. 1719;
MILES, bapt. 1695, bur. 1699; ROBERT, bapt., 29 Oct. 1698; MILES,
bapt. 1700, bur. 1702; SEPTIMUS, bapt. 10 May 1703; SAMUEL, b.
and d. 1704; ELIZABETH, bapt. 7 Dec. 1705, d. c.1790; MARY, b.
and d. 1707; MARY, bapt. 6 Sept. 1708, d. 1779; RICHARD, bapt.
5 Nov. 1709; MILES, bapt. 27 Nov. 1711; BENJAMIN, bapt. 9 July
1713 (Chippindall).

NORTH ROBERT (8), s. of Thomas (7) and Ellen, was bapt. 29
Oct. 1698, and d. 21 March 1758/9 in Balto. Co.; m. 1st, on 2
July 1729, Frances, dau. of Thomas and Elizabeth Todd; she d.
25 July 1745, and he m. 2nd, Catherine (---) who surv. him; in
1750 owned 295 a. Charles' Forest; his heirs owned 200 a. Phillips' Addition, 500 a. Shawan Hunting Ground, 150 a. Hooker's
Addition, and other lands; in Aug. 1733 he was one of the Gentle-
men Justices of the county court, and was appointed by the General Assembly as one of the commissioners to lay out Jones Town
or Old Town; left a will, 20 March 1748 - 5 April 1749, mentioning
that his dau. Ellen was to have a legacy due her from her grandmother Ellen North; admin. bond was posted 25 May 1749 by Alex.
Lawson with James Wardrop and George Maxwell; est. was inv. 23
Aug. 1749, and val. at £ 3985.10.1½; an additional inv. was filed
26 March 1750; had iss. (all by 1st w.): Thomas, b. 16 Feb.
1732, d. 27 Feb. 1750/1, after he chose Alexander Lawson as his
guardian; ELLEN, b. 29 April 1740 or 1741, m. John Moale; and

FRANCES, b. 1 Nov. 1743, d. 24 Dec. 1743 (2:111; 12:348; 29:229;
30:63; 37:151; 53:320; 54:527; 110:411; 133:20, 27, 65; 153:6,
103; 259).

NORTH, THOMAS, d. leaving a will, 13 Dec. 1698 - 3 March 1699,
naming w. as extx., s. Robert, and daus. Jane, Eliza, and Avies;
est. was inv. by William Foreman and Thomas Knightsmith; had iss.:
ROBERT; JANE; ELIZA; and AVIES (50:93; 121:165).

NORTH, THOMAS, was made levy free in Nov. 1756 (41:303).

NORTON, JOHN (1), was b. c.1678, d. 24 March 1726/7, giving
his age as 37 in 1714/5, and stating he had lived in Balto. Co.
for about 17 years; was in Balto. Co. by 1694 as a taxable in
s. side Gunpowder; in May 1707 purch. Norton's Lot (being part
of a larger tract called Jones' Inheritance) from John and Mary
Boring; his will, proved 3 April 1727, named w. Elizabeth and
ch.: William, John, Richard, Ann, Elizabeth, and Mary; admin.
bond was posted 15 July 1727 by execs. Thomas and Elizabeth Harryman, with George and Samuel Harryman, John Norton having ren.
his right to admin.; est. was inv. 14 June 1728 by Benjamin Bowen
and Richard Lenox and val. at £ 12.6.0; additional inv. was
filed in 1728; est. was admin. by Eliza, w. of Thomas Harryman, on
10 April 1729; dec. left a wid. and five ch.: WILLIAM; JOHN;
RICHARD; ANN; ELIZABETH; and MARY (2:281; 12:341; 51:82, 272;
59:612; 68:18; 125:15; 133:193; 139; 203-3:110).

NORTON, WILLIAM (2), s. of John (1), was left 1 shilling by
his father's will; might be the William Norton who m. Elizabeth
Clark on 1 Feb. 1732; on 31 March 1739 William Norton and w. Ann
conv. 50 a. Jones' Addition and 40 a. Norton's Addition to William Lynch (75:218; 128:77).

NORTON, JOHN (3), s. of John (1), may be the John Norton who
m. Susanna (---) by Aug. 1719, and was conv. Cole's Adventure by
John and Dinah Cole (68:18).

NORTON, RICHARD (4), s. of John (1), was bd. to Thomas Sligh
in June 1731 (29:156).

NORTON, RICHARD, s. of Peter Norton who lately left the county
was age 11 next Oct., in June 1712 was bd. to serve Martin and Sarah Taylor to age 21 (21:314).

NORTON, SAMUEL, d. by 10 May 1722 when admin. bond was posted
by Thomas Sheredine with William Galloway and Samuel Harryman;
est. was inv. on 7 July 1722 by Thomas Sheredine, Benjamin Bowen and
John Eaglestone and val. at £ 10.5.6, and was signed by Susanna
Norden, Thos. Cockey, and Jona. Tipton; est. was admin. by Thomas
Sheredine on 15 Jan. 1722 (1:102; 12:335; 52:19).

NORVIL, JANE, d. 27 Jan. 1739 (128:110).

NORVILL, JOHN, m. Mary Bayley on 2 Feb. 1735 (she d. 9 July
1744), and had iss.: SARAH, b. 23 Dec. 1736; MARY, b.. 20 Sept.
1738; JAMES, b. 26 March 1741; HANNAH, b. 4 Aug. 1743 (128:91,
94, 101, 114; 129:335).

NORWOOD, Capt. JOHN (1), progenitor, came to A. A. Co., Md.,
from Va. in 1649, nephew of Edward Bennett, merchant; d. in A. A.
Co., c.1672, having m. Anne (---), who m. as her 2nd husb. James
Boyd; she d. 1674; Norwood was Sheriff and Chief Justice of A. A. C
Co.; had iss.: ANDREW, d. c.1701; PHILIP, d. c.1724; JOHN, d. c.
1683; SAMUEL, d. 1709; poss. JOSEPH, d. c.1684; poss. EDWARD,
d. by 1729, m. Ruth Owings (200-65:192; 388; Johnston, "Norwood
Notes," at the Md. Hist. Soc.).

NORWOOD, EDWARD (2), poss. s. of John (1), was listed as "dead; no effects," in the est. of Thomas Hedge of Balto. Co., in 1699; may be the father of: EDWARD, d. by 1729 (2:49).

NORWOOD, EDWARD (3), poss. s. of Edward (2), d. by 1729 in Balto. Co., having m. c.1718 Ruth, dau. of Richard and Rachel Owings; on 3 Nov. 1729 Richard Owings and w. Sarah conv. his sis. Ruth Norwood, wid., a parcel of land called Owings' Addition; Ruth Norwood was listed as the owner of this tract as late as 1750; in the Dorsey Family, Edward and w. are stated to have had iss.: EDWARD, d. by 1770; RACHEL, m. (Samuel?) Gott; RUTH, m. John Hurd on 8 June 1739; SAMUEL, d. c.1773, m. Sarah Bankson; SARAH; ANN, b. 1 Aug. 1729 (72:113; 133:29; 134; 153:86; Dorsey et al, The Dorsey Family; Owings et al, Owings and Allied Families, 3rd ed., p. 4).

NORWOOD, EDWARD (4), s. of Edward (3) and Ruth, d. in Balto. Co. by 1772; m. Mary Fitzsimmons, dau. of Nicholas and Martha (Morgan) Fitzsimmons, on 9 Nov. 1746; in 1750 he owned 10 a. Norwood's Chance, 22 a. Partnership, 128 a. Bachelor's Fear, and other lands; d. leaving a will, 25 March 1770 - 21 Jan. 1772; had iss.: NICHOLAS; EDWARD; SAMUEL; JOHN; ELIZABETH: RUTH; and MARY (112: 200; 133:160; 153:86).

NORWOOD, SAMUEL (5), s. of Edward (3) and Ruth, d. c.1773; m. Sarah Bankson; d. leaving a will, 10 July 1773 - 2 Aug. 1773; left iss.: RUTH, m. by 10 July 1773 Charles Ridgely (112:263).

NORWOOD, PHILIP, in Nov. 1754 admitted he was the father of Mary Odle's illegitimate child (39:448).

NOWELL, AVARILLA, m. James Preston on 17 July 1726 (131).

NOWELL, JOHN, d. by 6 Aug. 1741, when admin. bond was posted by Alexander Lawson with John Carroll and Patrick Lynch (12:344).

NOWELL, JOHN, d. by 27 Feb. 1748 when admin. bond was posted by John Paca with William Dallam (12:349).

NOWELL, LEWIS,d. by 20 Jan. 1724; on 7 March 1716 Lewis Nowell purch. 20 a. Aberly Lodge from James Isham and w. Julian; on 4 March 1723 Lewis and his w. Jane conv. that tract, part John's Interest, and 100 a. Crow Perches to Henry Wetherall; wid. Jane ren. right to admin. his est. on 20 Jan. 1724 and admin. bond was placed by James Maxwell with Luke Raven and Bloys Wright (12:338; 67:455; 69:277).

NOWLAND. See NOLAND.

NUGENT, JOHN, d. by 26 July 1746 when admin. bond was posted by John Kelly with William Daugherty (12:345).

NUSUM. See NEWSOME.

O(---), WILLIAM, d. by 18 April 1693 when his est. was admin. by Martha, now w. of Robert Gibson(206-10:332).

OAKDIN, JOHN, m. Susannah Harps on 23 Oct. 1748 (131).

OAKERSON/OKINSON, ISAIAH, d. by 13 Feb. 1749 when admin. bond was posted by John Stinchcomb with Christopher Randall and Joshua Randall; est. was admin. by Stinchcomb on 1 Feb. 1753 (5:282; 12: 406).

OAKEY, THOMAS, serv., was listed in the 1732 inv. of Thomas Hutchins (52:244).

OAKLEY, THOMAS, was b. c.1712; m. Prudence (---) who was b.
c.1715; with s. Thomas they were named in a 1742 lease of part
of My Lady's Manor; had iss.: THOMAS, b. c.1741, alive in 1742;
THOMAS, b. 16 June 1744 (77:135; 131).

OAKLEY, THOMAS, m. Susannah, and had iss.; WILLIAM, b. 16
June 1744 (131).

OAR, CHARLES, m. Margaret (---), and had iss.: JOHN, b. 26
Sept. 1721; DANIEL, b. 13 Sept. 1724 (133:11).

O'BRYAN, DANIEL, m. Mary (---), and had iss.: CHARLES, b. 5
May 1708 in Cecil Co. (128:29).

O'BRYAN, MARY, in June 1757 was tried for bast. (46:35).

O'BRYAN, TERENCE, m. Margaret (---), and had iss.: DANIEL,
b. 19 Sept. 1709 in Cecil Co. (128:28).

O'BRYAN, THOMAS, m. Amelia Wooling on 14 June 1757 (131).

OCAIN, MANNUS, m. Eliza McKenly on 26 Nov. 1750 (131).

OCHISSON, JOSEPH, m. Elizabeth (---), and had iss.: JOHANNA,
b. 25 April 1739 (128:103).

O'DANIEL, THOMAS, was in Balto. Co. by 1663 when he surv. 150
a. Daniel's Neck or Nest; d. by 5 Nov. 1684; left iss.: MARY, m.
by 5 Nov. 1684 William Horne who joined her in sale of 50 a. of
afsd. tract to John Hall; JANE, m. by 27 Feb. 1686 Thomas Thurcall who joined her in sale of 50 a. to William Westbury; and
MARGARET, m. 1st William Westbury, and 2nd, by 4 June 1695
Robert Oless (59:101, 188, 466; 211).

O'DANIEL. See also DANIEL.

ODELL, WILLIAM,, was in Balto. Co. by June 1742 when he purch.
50 a. Arnold's Chance from Anthony and Mary Arnold; d. by 24
Dec. 1748 when admin. bond was posted by admnx. Elizabeth Odell
with Edward Oursler and John Hurd; in 1750 his heirs owned 50 a.
Arnold's Chance, 50 a. Odell's Addition, and other land; his
est. was admin. by Elizabeth Odell on 30 May 1750 and 21 May
1753; had iss.: MARY, b. c.1736 (may be the Mary Odell who named
Philip Norwood as the father of her child in Nov. 1754); JOHN,
b. c.1738; WILLIAM, b. c.1740; WALTER, b. c.1742; ELIZA, b. c.
1744; RICHARD, b. c.1745; RIGNAL, b. c.1746; TALBOT, b. c.1748
(5:150, 292; 12:401; 37:163; 39:449; 77:50; 153:66).

OFFLEY, JAMES, in Nov. 1719 stated he was aged and infirm, and
pet. the court to be made levy free (23:241).

OG(---), WILLIAM, left an est. val. at £ 4.4.0 by Thomas Besson and John Garner (48:69).

OGBURN, WILLIAM, was in Balto. Co. before 1700 when he surv.
100 a. Eastland Hills on 9 June 1672; d. by 1700 without heirs
(211).

OGDEN, JOHN, m. Susanna Harps on 19 Nov. 1748 (131).

OGG, GEORGE (1), progenitor, was in A. A. Co. by 1703 when he
was involved in a lawsuit with George Peacock; was in Balto. Co.
by 1723; m. Elizabeth (---) also alive in 1723; in 1697 he acqu.
300 a. Parrishes Range from Edward Parrish, surv. 150 a. called
Bashan in 1706; purch. 100 a. Addition from Thomas Randall in

1711; and surv. 100 a. George's Beginnings in Nov. 1715; in Nov.
1713 was named father-in-law in the will of William Talbot;
in Dec. 1722 conv. all his goods and chattells to his s. George
Ogg, Jr., on cond. that the s. would provide for his mother and
bro. John, and that he would pay his sister Catherine Risteau
£ 25 in current money; in Dec. 1723 George and w. Elizabeth conv.
all their real est. to s. George, Jr., retaining a life interest
in the property; had iss.: JOHN, b. 24 Sept. 1691, alive in 1723;
GEORGE, Jr., b. 30 April 1696; CATHERINE, m. 1st William Talbot
and 2nd John Risteau (64:76; 67:176; 69:56, 232; 110:108; 207;
259; 340-15:225).

OGG, GEORGE, Jr. (2), s. of George (1), was b. 30 April 1696
in A. A. Co.; was alive in Nov. 1756; m. Mary Potee on 22 Aug.
1722; in Sept. 1723 surv. 50 a. Security; in 1750 owned 150 a.
Morgan's Tents, 30 a. Plumb Tree Bottom, and 25 a. Hobson's
Choice; was Constable of Upper Hund. of Patapsco in June 1731,
and donated 500   pounds tobacco for the building of St. Thomas' Church; in Nov. 1756 conv. personal prop. to his ch.; had
iss.: GEORGE, b. 12 April 1724; SARAH, b. 5 Sept. 1726, m. by Nov.
1756 John Whips; KATHERINE, b. 15 July 1728, m. George Shipley,
Jr., by Nov. 1756; MARY, b. 10 Oct. 1730 (may have m. Philemon
Barnes); REBECCA, b. 16 Oct. 1732, m. by Nov. 1756 William Shipley; RACHEL, b. 20 Sept. 1735; DUNCAN, alive in 1756; WILLIAM,
may have been b. before 1724 (in 1742 was granted 25 a. William's
Delight), m. Sarah, dau. of William Beasman; RUTH, alive in 1756
(22:232; 29:159; 61:310; 77:251; 78:331; 79:382; 82:377, 613;
92:202; 112:108; 133:14, 45, 48, 49; 153:4; 207; 219-1; 229;
228 ff.; 259).

OGG, GEORGE (3), s. of George (2), was b. 12 April 1724; d.
leaving a will 13 Aug. 1767 - 23 Aug. 1770; m. by 29 April 1748
Helen, dau. of William Hamilton; in 1750 he owned 200 a. Carga-
furgus; had iss.: BENJAMIN, b. 29 April 1748; GEORGE; RACHEL;
WILLIAM HAMILTON; MARY; and JAMES (111:315; 153:96; 259).

OGG. WILLIAM (4), s. of George (2), was granted 25 a. Williams
Delight in 1742; on 5 Oct. 1767 he and w. Sarah (dau. of William
Beasman) sold the land to William Lyon, Charles Graham, and James
Dick (92:202; 112:112).

OGG, BETHIA, m. William Garland on 10 June 1728 (129:245).

OGG, FRANCIS, d. in Balto. Co. on 26 Dec. 1733; m. 1st, by
June 1710, Katherine (Stockett), admnx. of Henry Rhodes; m. 2nd,
by 3 Aug. 1726, Mary, admnx. of William Beardy; d. leaving a
will, 25 Dec. ---, 18 March 1733, naming w. Mary, s. Stockett,
and mentioning 5 younger ch.; admin. bond was posted 18 March
1733 by Mary Ogg with Edward Sanders and John Ellson; est. was
admin. on 5 Nov. 1739; left iss.: four unidentified ch., and
CATURINAH, b. 31 Dec. 1721, may be the Katherine tried for bast.
in March 1743/4; STOCKETT, d. 28 Dec. 1733 (2:161, 323; 3:61,
203; 12:389; 21:156; 31:43, 103; 35:172; 52:23; 128:52, 78).

OGG, LABAN, alias Laban Hicks, with w. Ruth, conv. prop. to
James and Rebecca Yeo (82:491).

OGG, THOMAS, m. Sarah, dau. of Joseph and Rachel Beasman.

OGLE, Rev. HENRY, was inducted into St. Johns Par., Balto.
Co., on 24 July 1739; and served until he resigned on 21 July
1742 when he was inducted into Portobacco Parish, Charles Co.
(303).

OGLE, JOHN, m. by 24 June 1743 Rosanna, admnx. of Jonas Robin-

son and John Bowen; Rosanna d. by 4 June 1746 when admin. bond
was posted by Thomas Sligh with Robert Wilkinson and John Sargent; her est. was admin. in Feb. 1749 by Thomas Sligh (3:259;
3:324; 5:87; 12:390).

OGLESBY, DANIEL, m. Martha (---), and had iss.: MARY, b. 26
May 1717; ELISHA, b. 1 Sept. 1718; RUTH, b. 6 Jan. 1720/1; DANI-
EL, b. 20 June 1722; SABRID, b. 17 June 1724; MARGARET, b. 8 Ap-
ril 1726; ELISHA, b. 17 Aug. 1727; WILLIAM, b. 18 June 1729;
RICHARD, b. 13 Oct. 1731 (128:40, 74).

OGLESBY, GEORGE, m. by 5 Aug. 1684 Johanna (---); in March
1681 he purch. 64 a. Horne's Point from William and Mary Horne;
in Aug. 1684 George and Johanna conv. the tract to Thomas James;
in March 1691 George and Johanna conv. 46 a. Oglesby's Mount to
George Goldsmith (59:92; 64:84, 159).

OKINSON. See OAKERSON.

OLDHAM, WILLIAM, m. Ruth Talbott on 1 April 1754 (131).

OLDTON, JOHN, d. by 30 June 1709; m. 1st, by Sept. 1693, Anne,
dau. of Rev. John and Anne (Lovelace) Gorsuch; she was the wid.
of Capt. Thomas Todd, and Capt. David Jones; Oldton m. 2nd Mary,
mother-in-law of Francis Watkins; was captain of the Baltimore
County Rangers; d. leaving a will, 4 May 1709 - 30 June 1709,
leaving his entire est. to w. Mary; admin. bond was posted 23
Sept. 1709 by John Hayes and with John Taylor and Robert Cutchin;
est. was inv. on 5 or 11 Oct. 1709 by John Roberts and Roger
Matthews, Jr., and val. at L 105.14.6; an additional inv. was
filed 17 Jan. 1710; est. was admin. on 27 Feb. 1710 and 4 March
1712; Mary Oldton was alive on 28 July 1709 when her son-in-law
Francis Watkins conv. her livestock; she d. by 7 Oct. 1709 when
admin. bond on her est. was posted by James Crook with John
Stokes and Edward Hancock; her est. was inv. on 10 Dec. 1709 by
Luke Raven and William Holland, and val. at L 30.3.6, and was
signed by Francis Watkins (1:30; 2:126; 12:381, 383; 20:126; 48:
137, 283; 67:10; 110:34; 338:110 ff.; 398).

OLEE, JOHN, serv. to John Durbin, d. 10 Sept. 1720 (128:38).

OLESS, ROBERT, was in Balto. Co. by 1692 as a taxable in n.
side Gunpowder; in Dec. 1694 he surv. 37 a. Norram; m. by June
1695 he m. Margaret, wid. of William Westbury and dau. of Thomas
O'Daniel; on 4 June 1695 Robert and Margaret conv. 1/3 of Daniel's
Nest to E. Westbury, spinster (59:466; 138; 207).

OLIFF, MARY, had an illeg. ch. by March 1709/10, when William
Talbott paid her fine (21:94).

OLIVE, (---), m. Sarah, dau. of Samuel Hinton, by 4 April
1720 (124:33).

OLIVER, JOHN, m. Sarah, dau. of Edward Smith on 14 July 1720
(131).

OLIVER, JOHN, m. Alice Twelves on 6 July 1745 (133).

OLIVER, RICHARD, was in Balto. Co. by 1692 as a taxable in
Spesutia Hund. (138).

OLWEL, JOHN, of A. A. Co., m. by 10 April 1711 Elizabeth, wid.
of William Geff.

O'MELY or O'MALLEY, BRIANT, was in Balto. Co. by 19 June 1666

when he conv. 200 a. of Mulberry Mould to James Magriges; may
have m. Ann, former w. of Abraham Morgan, who was conv. land on
14 March 1667/8 by George Goldsmith and w. Mary (60:57; 94; 95).

O'NEAL, HENRY (1), was in Balto. Co. by 11 Jan. 1748 when admin. bond was posted by Thomas She and John Haven; in 1750 he or
his heirs were listed as owning 100 a. Murdock's Chance; his est.
was admin. 20 Jan. 1749, 1 June 1751, 23 Jan. 1752, and 20 July
1753; had iss.: prob. BENNETT; ELIZA, b. c.1743; MARY, b. c.1747;
BARNETT, b. c.1749; and SARAH (4:214; 5:208, 246, 283; 12:405;
39:18; 153:19).

O'NEAL, BENNETT (2), prob. s. of Henry (1), was designated
as son of Henry in a deed of 24 Feb. 1754 when Thomas and Johanna
Gash conv. him 50 a. Gash's Purchase, part of a larger tract
called Westwood (82:159).

O'NEAL, DANIEL, m. Susanna Lacey on 12 June 1743 (131).

O'NEAL, JAMES, was in Balto. Co. by 1694 as a taxable in n.
side Patapsco Hund. (139).

ONEIL, MARY, was pardoned for a felony in May 1738 (303).

ONION, STEPHEN (1), was in Balto. Co. by 1747; d. at his Ironworks on Gunpowder R. on 26 Aug. 1754; m. Deborah (---) who m.
as her 2nd husb. Joseph Smith on 16 May 1757; in 1750 Onion
owned 50 a. Eliza French's Lot, 260 a. Ann's Delight, and other
tracts; d. leaving a will, 24 Aug. 1754 - 5 Sept. 1754, naming
a bro. Thomas in Braywood, Staffordshire, Eng., a sis. Susanna
Barrett and her s. Zacheus Barrett who was to take the name of
Zacheus Onion, and another niece Joyce Holmes; admin. bond was
posted 18 Sept. 1754 by Deborah Onion with Nathaniel Chapman
and William Young; est. was inv. on 8 Oct. 1754 with John Hall
and John Paca and val. at £ 4830.18.0; est. was admin. by Deborah Onion on 26 July 1755 and 19 July 1757, 3 July 1759 and 10
May 1763; had iss.: ELIZABETH RUSSELL, b. 12 July 1734, prob.
d. young (4:245, 273, 287; 5:325; 12:398; 49:214; 111:62; 131;
133:53; 153:20, 98; 262).

ONION, SUSANNA (2), sis. of Stephen (1), was mentioned in her
brother's will as having m. (---) Barrett and having had one s.:
ZACHEUS (111:62).

ONION, ZACHEUS BARRETT (3), s. of Susanna (2), took the name
Onion in accordance with his uncle's will; was in Md. by Nov.
1757 when he was judges to be over 14; m. Hannah Bond on 2 Nov.
1757; d. 1781; had iss.: ELIZABETH, b. 2 Feb. 1759; STEPHEN, b.
1760, d. 1761; STEPHEN, b. 19 Nov. 1761; THOMAS BOND, b. 1 Feb.
1762; JOHN, b. 23 May 1764; ZACHEUS, b. 12 April 1765; WILLIAM
FRANCIS HEATH, b. 29 March 1769; CORBIN, b. 8 May 1770 (44; 111:
62; 131; 208-3).

ONOHOSELL, MARGARET, serv. to Thomas Sligh, was ind. for bast.
in Aug. 1724, tried in Nov. 1724, and ordered to have 15 stripes
(26:438; 27:43).

ORAM, COOPER, was in Balto. Co. by 1736; m. Hannah (---), and
in 1750 owned 225 a. part Maiden's Choice, was named as bro. in
the will of John Wright; had iss.: JOHN, b. 27 Oct. 1736; THOMAS,
b. 8 April 1739; HENRY, b. 20 Sept. 1741; ANN, b. 7 Feb. 1748;
SAMUEL, b. 3 Dec. 1745 (age 5 last 13 March, in Aug. 1754 was bd.
to Daniel McComas of William, with the consent of his mother);
COOPER, b. 13 Sept. 1750(39:346; 111:20; 133:68; 153:67).

ORAM, ELIZABETH, was fined for bast. in Nov. 1759, and named John Garrettson as the father (46:242).

ORBAN, JOHN, m. Mary (---), and had iss.: JOSEPH, b. 17 Dec. 1735 (133:48).

ORCHARD, WILLIAM, was in Balto. Co. by March 1663/4 when he sold 150 a. Orchard's Neck to James Browne; on 5 March 1667/8 he sold Walter Tucker et al 250 a. Chilberry; in March 1666/7 he and w. Susanna sold 200 a. Wandsworth to Edward Ayres; d. by 12 June 1668 when admin. bond was posted by Nathaniel Stiles, admin., with Thomas Overton; wid. Susanna m. 2nd James Phillips and 3rd Benjamin Arnold (12:384; 93; 94; 95).

ORDER, JOHN, d. by 23 Jan. 172-(?), leaving one or more sons and a dau.: MARY, m. Herbert Pritchard (69:81).

ORGAN, CATHERINE, was tried for bast. in June 1729 and again in June 1733; the second time she denied the charges and there were no witnesses (28:145; 30:14).

ORGAN, ELLINOR, had iss.: WILLIAM, b. 14 Jan. 1722 (133:13).

ORGAN, MATTHEW, m. 1st, after 11 May 1697, Catherine, extx. of John Carrington and admnx. of Michael or Turlo Michael Owen whose est. was admin. by Matthew and Katherine on 27 April 1705; in March 1724 he was named as the father-in-law in the will of James   of Balto. Co. (2:47, 166, 226, 227; 124:198).

ORGAN, MATTHEW, formerly of Balto. Co., but now of Prince William Co., Va., conv. 100 a. Organ's Fancy to several others (213-PL#8:388).

ORGAN, WILLIAM, d. by 1698 when his est. was inv. by Thomas Besson and John Garner and val. at £ 4.4.0 plus 220 lbs. tob. in debts (48:69).

ORGAN, WILLIAM, m. Esther Majors on 20 April 1752, and had iss.: CORNELIUS, b. 25 Sept. 1754; WILLIAM, b. 25 Aug. 1757, ELEANOR, b. 14 April 1760 (134:31, 32, 72).

ORMAN, SAMUEL, d. by 28 Dec. 1748 when admin. bond was posted by Isaac Risteau; est. was admin. by Risteau; dec. had m. Ann Lambeth on 19 May 1746 (4:125; 12:403; 133:159).

ORR,   m. Mary (---), and had iss.: MARTHA, b. 12 Oct. 1754; JAMES, b. 20 July 1756; MARY, b. 1 April 1758; ANN, b. 10 Aug. 1760 (129:368).

ORRELL, JOHN, being "aged and poor" was allowed 500 lbs. of tob. in Aug. 1724 (26:441).

THE ORRICK FAMILY has been discussed in Stella Pickett Hardy's Colonial Families, and in one of the articles in the column, "Maryland Heraldry," in the Baltimore Sun, 24 Feb. 1907.

ORRICK, JAMES (1), s. of Elizabeth who m. as her 2nd husb. Richard Moos or Moss, was in Md. by 1650, took up tracts Orrick and Orrick's Fancy; m. Mary, wid. of John Riggs, and poss. heir of Wm. Slade; d. leaving a will, 9 April 1690 - 11 Nov. 1690, naming sons William, John, and James, and land which came by the heirs of William Slade; had iss.: WILLIAM, b. c.1680; JOHN, b. c. 1685; JAMES, b. c.1687 (121:45; 206-7A:368; 211, where his name is given as Orwick; and 388).

ORRICK, WILLIAM (2), s. of James (1), was b. c.1680; d. by 19
Oct. 1720; m. 1st, on 22 Oct. 1700 in A. A. Co., Catherine Duvall;
m. 2nd, on 16 Oct. 1704 Hannah (poss. Greeneff) who may have m.
2nd Gideon Howard; in Nov. 1718 was made Constable of Elk Ridge
Hund. in place of Benjamin Howard; d. by 19 Oct. 1720 when admin.
bond was posted by the wid. Hannah, with John Orrick and John
Howard; est. was inv. on 2 Nov. 1720 by Thomas Hammond and John
Gardner and val. at L 138.19.9 and signed by Hannah Orrick, John
Orrick, and Mary Eagle; est. was admin. 23 Oct. 1723 by Gideon
and Hannah Howard; dec. left iss.: (by 1st w.): CHARLES, b. 1703,
d. 1708; (by 2nd w.): WILLIAM, b. 1705; JAMES GREENIFFE, b. 1709;
JOHN GRINIFFE, b. 1712 (1:116; 12:388; 23:32; 51:162).

ORRICK, JOHN (3), s. of James (1), was b. c.1685, d. 1749; m.
on 15 Dec. 1719 Susanna, dau. of Col. Thomas and Rebecca Hammond;
in 1750 his heirs owned 100 a. Rich Neck and 150 a. William's
Lot; d. leaving a will proved 20 Oct. 1749; had iss.: RACHEL, b.
Nov. 1720, m. William Hopkins of Gerard; JOHN, b. 20 Feb. 1722,
m. Caroline Hammond; NICHOLAS, b. 1 May 1725; NATHAN, b. 1727,
d. 1733; THOMAS, b. 1732, d. 1733, REBECCA, b. 14 Sept. 1733, m.
Dr. Henry Murray; CATHERINE, b. 19 Aug. 1736, m. (---) Hall;
CHARLES, b. 28 Feb. 1738, m. Rebecca Stewart; SARAH, b. 3 April
1741, m. 1st William Chilton, and 2nd (---) Douglas; SUSANNA, b.
9 Jan. 1743, m. (---) Sullivan (153:99; Hardy).

ORRICK, JOHN (4), s. of John (3) and Susanna, was b. 20 Feb.
1722, m. Caroline Hammond on 20 Feb. 1757; had iss.: ELIZABETH,
b. 1 April 1758, m. Nicholas Ruxton Moore; JOHN, b. 1760, d.
1793, s.p. (133:103, 105, 166).

ORRICK, NICHOLAS (5), s. of John (3) and Susanna, was b. 1 May
1725; d. 1 Feb. 1785; m. 1st, Hannah, dau. of Capt. John and Hannah (Rattenbury) Cromwell; m. 2nd, on 16 March 1769, Mary Bell;
served in the Rev. War; had iss.: ANN, b. 16 Dec. 1750, m. 1st
Joseph Cromwell, and 2nd, Rev. Sater Stevenson; JOHN, b. 1752,
d. 1753; JOHN, b. 1753, d. 1810; MARGARET, m. Job Smith in 1781;
SUSAN, m. Absolom Butler; NICHOLAS, b. 1759, m. Mary Pendleton;
SARAH, m. (---) Jackson; CHARLES; (by 2nd w.): WILLIAM, b. 1770,
d. 1804 unm.; SYDNEY, b. 1771, d. 1825 unm. (134:21; Hardy).

ORTIAN, MARY, orphan of Abel Ortian, age 14 last Oct., in
Nov. 1742 was bd. to William Mitchell (34:64).

OSBORNE, WILLIAM (1), progenitor, was b. c.1627, giving his
age as 76 in 1703; came to Md. c.1664; in 1664 surv. 100 a.
Clemment's Den; in 1688 with John Lee surv. 100 a.Mate's Angle;
in June 1667 surv. Mate's Neck, and in that same month surv. 450
a. Covent Garden; in July 1684 surv. 500 a. Osborne's Lot; in
Sept. 1666 he sold 350 a. Sprye's Marsh to John Lee; in Feb.
1666/7 he conv. 100 a. Clement's Den to John Bradford; on 4
March 1667/8 John Lee and William Osborne conv. 100 a. Crab Hill
to Oliver Spry; same day the two bought 175 a. Sprye's Marsh
from Sprye; on 10 March 1672/3 Lee conv. his half of Sprye's
Marsh to Osborne; on 2 June 1673 Lee and Osborne conv. 100 a. of
Mate's Angle to Anthony Brispo; William had at least one s.:
WILLIAM, Jr. (60:67; 63:110; 95; 211; 388).

OSBORNE, WILLIAM (2), s. of William (1) was of age in 8 Nov.
1688 when he apptd. James Phillips innholder his atty. to act in
all things concerning him; m. by June 1686 Margaret (---) who
joined him in selling certain lands on the river adjacent the
court house to James Phillips; William may have m. as his 2nd
w. Rebecca, dau. of John Hill, whose will dated 17 March 1691,
named a dau. Rebecca Osborne; Osborne m. as 3rd w., some time in
1693 Margaret, extx. of John Wallston; d. leaving a will, 1 Jan.
1704 - 7 March 1704/5, naming ch. James, William, Benjamin,

Thomas, and Rebecca, with w. Margaret to be extx.; admin. bond
was posted 7 March 1704/5 by extx. Margaret, with Samuel Brown
and Benjamin Smith; est. was inv. 7 May 1705 by Anthony Drew and
Roger Matthews and val. at E 30.19.10; est. was admin. on 8 March
1705/6 by extx. Margaret now w. of William Wise; dec. left iss.:
JAMES, b. 15 Nov. or Dec. 1705; WILLIAM; REBECCA; BENJAMIN, b.
17 June 1695; MARY, twin, b. 13 Aug. 1698; THOMAS, twin, b. 13
Aug. 1698 (2:243; 12:386; 48:87; 108; 122:46; 128:5, 20, 21, 22;
206-12:139).

OSBORNE, WILLIAM (3), s. of William (2), was b. c.1685, giving
his age as 48 in 1733; m. 1st, on 24 Jan. 1710, Avarilla, dau.
of William Hollis (she d. 26 March 1724); m. 2nd, on 1 March
1727/8, Catherine Rhodes; on 5 Nov. 1724 William Hollis, bro. of
William's dec. w. Avarilla, conv. 150 a. Hollis' Desire to William's s. William; on 7 Nov. 1734 Henry Rhodes, son and heir at
law of Henry Rhodes, dec., conv. 200 a. Birr to his sis. Catherine, now w. of William Osborne; in 1750 he owned 50 a. Covent
Garden, 71 a. Birr, 97 a. Osborne's Addition, 50 a. part St. Martin's Ludgate, 50 a. Scotchman's Generosity, and other lands; d.
by 14 April 1750 when admin. bond was posted by admnx. Catherine,
with Nicholas Ruxton Gay and James Matthews; est. was admin. 15
July 1750; William had iss. (by 1st w.): JAMES, b. 6 Jan. 1711;
MARY, b. 6 Oct. 1713, d. Oct. 1715; AVARILLA, b. 6 Oct. 1718, m.
Thomas Little; MARY CLARK, b. 13 Aug. 1721, d. Aug. 1723; WIL-
LIAM, b. 26 March 1724; (by 2nd w.): BENJAMIN, b. 13 June 1729;
FRANCIS, b. 10 Dec. 1731; MARY ANN, b. 9 Feb. 1733; MARTHA, b.
11 July 1737, m. 1st, John Everett, and 2nd Amos Hollis; AVARIL-
LA, b. 8 Feb. 1741 (5:102; 12:402; 70:28; 74:131; 128:5, 20, 22,
36, 40, 43, 56, 57, 65, 83, 97; 129:323; 153:27; 225:180).

OSBORNE, BENJAMIN (4), s. of William (2), was b. 17 June 1695,
was alive in 1739; may be the Benjamin who in 1750 owned 40 a.
part Padden, 50 a. Robin Hood's Forest, and 55 a. Drisdale's
Habitation; m. Sarah (---), and had iss.: SUSANNA, b. 6 Jan. 1716;
MARGARET, b. 10 March 1717, d. 15 Oct. 1719; WILLIAM, b. 17 July
1719; HANNAH, b. 14 Oct. 1721; BENJAMIN, b. 10 June 1726; MARGA-
RET, b. 15 March 1727; JAMES, b. 25 March 1730; THOMAS, b. 10
April 1732; SARAH, b. 1 Aug. 1734; JACOB, b. 3 Oct. 1736; JOHN,
b. 15 July 1730 (69:43, 91, 92, 133; 75:43; 128:47, 48, 59, 64,
82, 94, 105; 153:1; 224:188).

OSBORNE, JAMES (5), s. of William (3) and Avarilla, was b.
6 Jan. 1711, and gave his age as 42 in March 1754; m. Jane Hughes
on 17 Sept. 1743; in 1750 owned 150 a. Covent Garden and 176 a.
Parker's Lot; had iss.: JOSIAS, b. 17 Sept. 1743; JAMES, b. 16
Nov. 1744; WILLIAM, b. 15 July 1746; CYRUS, b. 17 July 1750; MARY,
b. 12 Nov. 1752; BENJAMIN, b. 10 Aug. 1755; SEMELIA, b. 10 Feb.
1756; ELIZABETH , b. 11 Jan. 1758; MARTHA, b. 10 Aug. 1758 (131:
44; 129:332, 333, 340, 358; 153:81; 224:259).

OSBORNE, WILLIAM (6), s. of William (3) and Avarilla, was b.
26 March 1724; as William Jr., in 1750 he owned 50 a. Hollis'
Nest, 50 a. Planter's Neglect, and 50 a. Hollis' Chance and Hollis' Refuse Combined; may be the William who m. Margaret Lyall
on 18 June 1745; had iss.: HANNAH, b. 13 Oct. 1746; ANN, b. 24
Nov. 1748; SARAH, b. 2 Feb. 1750; SUSANNA, b. 20 June 1753; JOHN,
b. 27 Dec. 1755; JAMES, b. 4 April 1758 (129:358; 153:81).

OSBORNE, THOMAS (7), s. of Benjamin (4), was b. 10 April 1732;
m. Elizabeth Simpson on 3 Aug. 1751, and had iss.: WILLIAM, b. 3
Sept. 1751; SARAH, b. 11 Nov. 1752; MARY, b. 29 June 1755; BENJA-
MIN, b. 15 March 1757; FRANCIS, b. 2 Feb. 1759; BENNETT, b. 8
Feb. 1761 (129:381).

OSBORNE, BENJAMIN, m. Elizabeth (---), and d. by 28 Nov. 1758 when admin. bond was posted by admnx. Elizabeth, with George Chauncy and Henry Wetherall; Elizabeth conv. prop. to her ch. Catherine and William in 1761, and mentioned her s. Samuel Groome Osborne; had iss.: CATHERINE; WILLIAM; and SAMUEL GROOME OSBORNE (12:394; 47:85, 86; 131:44).

OSBORNE, BENJAMIN,(prob. s. of Benj. and Sarah # 4 above); d. leaving a will, 1759 - 10 Jan. 1760, mentioning tract Robin Hood's Forest, and s.: JOHN (210-30:823).

OSBORNE, BENJAMIN, d. by 6 Dec. 1762 when admin. bond was posted by John Treadway with Joseph Lusby; est. was admin. 1 March 1763 by Treadway, who stated that the dec. left 3 ch. (6:37; 12: 393).

OSBORNE, JACOB (poss. s. of Benj. and Sarah # 4 above), m. Sarah Fowler on 24 Feb. 1758, and had iss.: MARY, b. 18 Dec. 1758 (129:358).

OSBORN, JOHN, m. Mary Sullivan on 24 Dec. 1732, and had iss.: DANIEL SULLIVAN OSBORNE (133:150).

OSBORNE, JOHN, with Edward and Susanna Stevenson, conv. 50 a. Friendship to James Kelly in Aug. 1746 (79:208).

OSBORNE, JOSEPH, in 1750 owned 135 a. Turkey Cock Hall (153: 95).

OTHERS, BRIDGET, had iss.: ELIZABETH DAY, b. 31 March 1707 (129:207).

OUCHTERLONY, FRANCIS, in May 1719 purch. 10 or 12 a. of Harborough from William and Hannah Orrick (63:539).

OULTON, ANN, orphan of Edward, age 6½, in Nov. 1756 was bd. to William Barney (41:303).

OULTON, JOHN, was b. in Eng., came to Md. c.1750, ran away from Charles Carroll in June 1753; ran away from the Baltimore Iron Works in April 1754: was captured by John Orrick, but he stabbed Orrick and escaped(385:237, 254, 278).

OURSLER, EDWARD, progenitor, was b. c.1705, giving his age as 59 in 1764; d. testate in Balto. Co. betw. 22 Sept. 1789 and 4 April 1795; m. Ruth Owens on 21 Nov. 1754; in 1750 owned 120 a. Long Looked For; had iss.: MARY, b.9 May 1738, m. Joseph Miller on 11 Sept. 1759; ELIZABETH, b. 28 Oct. 1739, m. Benjamin Jarvis; ELAM or ELI, b. 8 Oct. 1741; MARGARET, b. 4 Feb. 1743; EDWARD, b. 6 Feb. 1746; JACOB, b. 5 July 1748; ORMAND, twin, b. 25 April 1749; ABRAHAM, twin, b. 25 April 1749; CATHERINE, b. 1 Nov. 1751, m. (---) Ware; WILLIAM, b. 31 July 1753; CHARLES, b. 27 April 1755; JOHN, b. 5 April 1758; SARAH, b. 7 July 1761, m. James Grimes (114:244; 133:152; 134; 153:57; 310).

OVERARD, PETER, was in Balto. Co. by 1 Aug. 1714 when he purch. 106 a. Webster's Enlargement from John and Elizabeth Norrington: on 4 June 1718 Peter, desc. as a sadler, and w. Mary conv. the land to Josias Middlemore of London, surgeon(63:441; 67:302).

OVERTON, THOMAS, m. by June 1676 Jane (---); was called bro. in the will of Bernard Utie; was in Balto. Co. by March 1665/6 when he purch. 100 a. Hamstead Marsh from John Browne,; in 1661 he and William Hollis brought information about Indian activity to the Council of Maryland; on 3 April 1675 Bernard Utie made a will naming bro. Thomas Overton and cousins John, Nathani-

el and Jean Overton; Thomas d. by 15 Dec. 1677 when admin. bond
was posted by George Gunnell and John Stanesby with William Hollis; est. was admin. by Gunnell who had m. the wid. Jane; had
iss.: JANE, m. by 22 April 1700 William Loney who sold Penny Come
Quick and Natty's Island, formerly the prop. of Thomas Overton,
to Robert Gibson; (poss.) JOHN; (poss.) NATHANIEL (2:72; 12:382;
66:54, 81; 94; 101; 120:88; 200-3:414).

OWEN, OWENS. See OWINGS.

THE OWINGS FAMILY has been dealt with in this author's Hist.
of the Green Spring Valley, vol. II, and in Addison D. and Elizabeth S. Owings' Owings and Allied Families, 1685-1985 (3rd
ed. pub. 1985).

OWINGS, RICHARD (1), progenitor, was in Balto. Co. by 1703 as
a taxable in n. side of Patapsco Hund.; d. by 14 Nov. 1716; m.
Rachel Robert, dau. of Robert Pugh of Llwyn-dedwydd, and sis. of
Hugh Robert, the Quaker minister; she d. 1729; Owings was a captain of rangers along the frontier and the Potomac; on 20 Oct.
1706 was living at Herring Creek, A. A. Co., when he purch. Cole's
Chance from John and Johanna Cole; d. by 14 Nov. 1716 when admin.
bond was posted by Rachel Owings with Richard and Henry Owings;
Rachel was d. by 27 May 1729 when her s. and heir, Richard, offered the home plantation for sale; had iss.: RACHEL, b. c.1683,
d. May 1761, m. John Wilmot, Jr.; RICHARD, b. c.1688; HENRY, b.
c.1692; JOHN, b. c.1694; RUTH, b. c.1696, m. Edward Norwood; ROB-
ERT, b. 15 March 1698/9; SAMUEL, b. 1 April 1702; JOSHUA, b. 5 April 1704 (12:387; 66:183; 145; 259; Owings and Allied Fam.).

OWINGS, RICHARD (2), s. of Richard (1) and Rachel, was b. c.
1688, and d. c.1736; m. c.1710 Sarah, dau. of Stephen Hart; she
d. 1769; in Nov. 1729 Richard and Sarah conv. Owings' Addition
to his widowed sis. Ruth Norwood; Sarah inher. one-half of Scutt's
Level from her step-father, John Scutt; she inher. 310 a. Knowles
Purchase from her 2nd step-father Henry Knowles; Richard and
Sarah (Hart) Owings had iss.: RICHARD, b. c.1711, m. Anne
Stonestreet; moved to S. C.; RUTH, b. c.1713, m. c.1735 Aquila
Conaway; STEPHEN HART, b. c.1715; CATHERINE, b. c.1717, d. unm.;
JOHN, b. c.1719, d. c.1779 (72:113; 110:118; 122:114; 259).

OWINGS, HENRY (3), s. of Richard (1) and Rachel, was b. c.
1692 and d. in June 1763 in A. A. Co.; m. Helen, dau. of Capt.
Nathaniel Stinchcomb c.1718; Helen d. some time after May 1784;
in 1750 Henry owned 90 a. part Long Acres, and 150 a. The Gilead;
in the same year he pet. to be levy free; d. leaving a will
proved 23 Feb. 1764; left iss.: ELIJAH, b. c.1719, moved to N.
Carolina; BEZALEEL, b. c.1721, moved to North Carolina; MICHAEL,
b. 1723, d. unm. in 1787; LEAH, b. c.1727, m. Capt. Alexander
Wells on 12 July 1753; HENRY, b. c.1729; NATHANIEL, b. c.1731,
m. Urath, dau. of William Kelly, in 1763 (41:303; 134:71; 153:
28; 210-30:1086; 259).

OWINGS, JOHN (4), s. of Richard (1) and Rachel, was b. c.1694;
d. Oct. 1765; m. 1st, c.1726, Hannah (---); she d. on 22 Jan.
1738/9, and he m. 2nd, c.1743, Asenath (---) who d. April 1792;
in 1750 he owned 136 a. Long Acres; d. leaving a will proved in
A. A. Co., on 30 Oct. 1765; had iss.: SOPHIA, b. 12 Sept. 1727,
m. Nathan Dorsey; HANNAH, b. 2 Dec. 1729, m. (---) Petticoat;
CALEB, b. 18 March 1731/2; JOHN, b. 23 Jan. 1734/5; RACHEL, b. 11
Nov. 1737; ASENATH, b. c.1744, m. (---) Odell; LANCELOT, b. c.
1746; SARAH, b. c.1748, m. Anthony Gott; ANN, c. 1750, m. William
Marr (112:8; 133:63; 153:28; 259).

OWINGS, ROBERT (5), s. of Richard (1) and Rachel, was b. 15

March 1698/9, d. 9 Sept. 1759 in York Co., Penna.; m. Hannah,
dau. of Allen Farquhar of York Co., on 23 Dec. 1730; in 1750
owned 500 a. Bear Garden; had iss.: RACHEL, b. c.1732, m. Timothy Sullivan c.1772 ; SUSANNA, b. c.1734, d. 1784 unm.; ROBERT,
b. 9 March 1736/7; MARY, b. 1739, m. Arnold Livers in 1759; WIL-
LIAM, b. c.1741; THOMAS, b. c.1743; JOSHUA, b. c. 1745; JOHN,
b. c.1747; CHARLES, b. c.1749, d. by 26 Sept. 1797 unm.; HANNAH,
b. c.1751, m. Nicholas Grate   (133:150; 153:91; 259).

OWINGS, SAMUEL (6), s. of Richard (1) and Rachel, was b. 1 April 1702, d. 6 April 1775; m. on 1 Jan. 1730 Urath, dau. of Thomas and Hannah (Bale) Randall; she was b. 22 Jan. 1707, d. 15 Dec.
1792; in 1750 owned 286 a. Green Spring Punch, 150 a. Addition,
100 a. Severn, 350 a. Timber Level, 50 a. Come By Chance, and
other lands; had iss.: BALE, b. 19 Aug. 1731, d. 30 Dec. 1781,
unm.; ; SAMUEL, b. 17 Aug. 1733; RACHEL, b. 2 May 1736, m. Henry
Stevenson on 16 Dec. 1762; URATH, b. 26 June 1738, m. Benjamin
Lawrence on 28 Jan. 1762; THOMAS, b. 18 Oct. 1740; HANNAH, b.
17 April 1743, d. 26 Jan. 1745; CHRISTOPHER, b. 16 Jan. 1744,
m. Elizabeth Lawrence; RICHARD, b. 26 Aug. 1746, d. 1747; ; HELEN,
b. and d. 1747; RICHARD, b. 16 July 1749, m. Ruth Warfield; HAN-
NAH, b. 27 Jan. 1750/1; REBECCA, b. 21 Oct. 1756, m. Joshua A.
Howard (112:516; 114:70; 133:69; 134:1, 6, 15, 16, 17, 24, 46,
48; 153:4; 259).

OWINGS, JOSHUA (7), s. of Richard (1) and Rachel, was b. 5
April 1704, d. 11 April 1785; m. Mary, dau. of Capt. John Cockey,
on 9 March 1735/6; she d. 10 Dec. 1768; in 1750 he owned 120 a.
Owings' Choice, 150 a. Shiloh, and 100 a. Difficult; was one of
the first vestrymen of St. Thomas' Church; was later one of the
first converts to Methodism; had iss.: JOHN COCKEY, b. 11 Jan.
1736, d. Feb. 1810, m. Colegate Deye Colegate; RICHARD, b. 13
Nov. 1738, d. 1756, a noted Methodist preacher; JOSHUA, b. 22
March 1740; EDWARD, b. 1 Nov. 1743; MICHAL, b. 12 Feb. 1745, m.
Charles Wells on 27 Dec. 1764 and later moved to Ohio Co. (now
West) Va.; MARCELLA, b. 5 July 1748, m. Thomas Worthington;
GEORGE, b. 14 March 1749/50, d. after 20 Oct. 1832, unm.; REBEC-
CA, b. 27 Jan. 1751/2, m. Samuel Mummy; RACHEL, b. 22 March
1756, m. c.1764 Samuel Chew, and 2nd, in Aug. 1779 Talbot Ship-
ley; EPHRAIM, b. 1758, d. 1784 unm.; ELIZABETH, d. c.1783 (112:
523, 566; 117:471; 133:55, 61, 155; 134:5, 13, 55; 153:42; 259).

OWINGS, RICHARD (8), s. of Richard (2), was b. c.1711; m.
Anne, dau. of Edward Stonestreet of Charles Co.; in 1750 owned
250 a. Scutt's Level; later moved to S. C. with his w. and fam.;
had iss.: SARAH, b. 29 July 1738; RACHEL, b. 12 March 1741; RICH-
ARD, b. 20 March 1743; EDWARD STONESTREET, b. 15 May 1746; BUT-
LER, b. 24 Aug. 1748; ARCHIBALD, b. 2 March 1750; GREENBERRY, b.
13 April 1752 (134:6, 10, 21; 153:64; 259).

OWINGS, STEPHEN HART (9), s. of Richard (2), was b. c.1715;
d. Feb. 1801; m. Sarah, dau. of Richard Gott, in 1742; in 1750
owned 60 a. Bachelor's Hall; was a constable of Soldier's Delight
Hund. in Nov. 1739; was a churchwarden of St. Thomas' Parish in
1756 and 1744; had iss.: SARAH, b. 19 March 1742/3, d. unm.;
RICHARD GOTT, b. 18 Jan. 1744/5; CALEB or CAPELL, b. 23 Dec.
1746, d. unm.; SAMUEL, b. 12 Sept. 1748, d. 1816; STEPHEN HART,
b. 24 June 1750; CASSANDRA, b. 1752, m. (---) Wright; NICHOLAS,
b. 30 Sept. 1755; HANNAH, b. 1757, d. 1819 unm.; and BEAL, b.
1759, d. July 1828, unm. (32:77; 112:417; 116:197; 118:79; 133:
72; 134:10, 21; 153:49; 259).

OWINGS, JOHN, was in Balto. Co. by Aug. 1670 when Richard and
Mary Winley conv. him part Taylor's Mount; in Jan. 1670/1 he sold
the land to William Chapman; purch. it back from Chapman in Sept.
1671; sold the land to Thomas Marley in March 1671/2; conv. land

to Edward Phillips in June 1676 (96:231; 97:125; 98:45, 47; 101: 299).

OWINGS, RICHARD, m. Sarah (---), and had iss.: RUTH, b. 27 March 1730 (133:61).

OWINGS, SARAH, was tried for bast. in Aug. 1733 and named Thomas Burke as the father; fined for bast. in March 1736; and was tried for bast. in Aug. 1737 (30:76; 31:1, 101).

OWINGS, (TURLO) MICHAEL, d. by 27 Feb. 1702/3 when admin. bond was posted by Catherine Mitchell Owen with Thomas Stone and Matthew Hawkins; est. was inv. on 12 March 1702/3 by Thomas Stone and Matthew Hawkins, and val. at £ 63.4.6; est. was admin. by Catherine, now w. of Matthew Organ, on 27 April 1705 and 9 Feb. 1707 (2:166, 227; 12:380; 48:118).

OWINGS, ZACHARIAH, son of Sarah Owings, dec., aged 16 next March, in Nov. 1758 was bd. to Elinor Frazier (46:170).

OXLEY, MARGARET, was tried for bast. in June 1737 (31:54).

OYSTON, HENRY, in Oct. 1736 purch. 48 a. Rider's Industry from James Rider (61:266),

OYSTON. LAWRENCE, was b. c.1737, giving his age as 48 in 1785 (310).

THE PACA FAMILY was discussed in Helen E. Davis' Kindred: Davis-Stansbury Lines (hereinafter cited as 313).

PACA, ROBERT (1), progenitor, d. in A. A. Co. some time after 26 April 1681, when his will was dated; m. Mary Parker Hall, wid. of John Hall, and dau. of William Parker of Calvert Co.; Robert's w. Mary d. 24 Dec. 1699 in her 67th year; Robert's will named his w. and one s.: AQUILA (128:9; 120:9).

PACA, AQUILA (2), s. of Robert (1), d. in Balto. Co. on 10 Sept. 1721, m. Martha, dau. of James Phillips the Elder, on 11 Sept. 1699;; High Sheriff of Balto. Co.; c.1706 he helped to build the meeting house for Bush River Friends; d. leaving a will, 8 May 1720 - 10 Nov. 1721, naming w. Martha and ch. Aquila, John, James, Susanna, Mary, and Priscilla; he directed his ch. were to be brought up as Quakers; admin. bond was posted 8 Jan. 1721 by extx. Martha Paca, with John Hall, John Crockett, and John Webster; est. was inv. on 2 May 1722 by Col. John Dorsey and Daniel Scott, Jr., and val. at £ 2461.18.11, and signed by bro. John Hall, nephew Edward Hall, and sis.-in-law Mary Smithers; additional inventories were later filed; est. was admin. on 8 Nov. 1723 and 7 Aug. 1724; had iss.: AQUILA, b. 1700; JOHN; JAMES; MARY, b. 14 Sept. 1701, m. Samuel Chew; SUSANNA, b. 5 May 1705, m. Joseph Galloway in 1722; PRISCILLA, d. c.1742, m. Winston Smith; a dau. d. Sept. 1709; a s. b. 28 Oct. 1701 (1:97; 2:266, 366; 12: 444; 50:117, 373; 51:229; 124:101; 129:189; 131; 200-35:93; 313; 433:365).

PACA, AQUILA (3), s. of Aquila (2) and Martha, d. 8 Feb. 1743; m. 1st, by 14 April 1725 Frances, dau. of John Stokes; m. 2nd, by 19 July 1732, Rachel, dau. of William Blay; d. leaving a will, 23 Jan. 1743 - 13 March 1743, naming w. Rachel, ch. John and Martha, bro. John, latter's son Aquila, sis. Susanna Galloway, sis. Priscilla Smith, and son-in-law Peregrine Brown; the wid. ren. the will and claimed her thirds;; admin. bond was posted 8 July 1744 by Rachel Paca the acting extx., with Nathan Rigbie, Richard Johns, and Peregrine Frisby, John Hall having ren. as

exec.; Rachel Paca d. leaving a will, 27 Jan. 1745, naming her
s. Peregrine Brown, dau. Martha Paca, and six cousins: John Tilden, William Blay Tilden, William, Samuel, and John Weathershead;;
admin. bond on her est. was posted 23 June 1746 by Peregrine
Brown, with Winston Smith and William Smith; est. of Aquila Paca
was admin. by Peregrine Brown on 12 Dec. 1748, and 21 April 1749;
admin. the est. of Rachel Paca on 9 May 1749; est. of Aquila
Paca was inv. on 1 May 1745 by William Paca and William Dallam
and val. at £1953.1.8; various lists of debts were also filed;
dec. left iss.: (by 1st w.): JOHN, b. 14 April 1725; (by 2nd
w.): MARTHA, b. 25 Jan. 1732 (4:199; 5:72, 92; 12:478, 479; 49:
152, 154, 155; 125:232; 127:276; 128:46, 77; 129:339; 200-35:
382; 210-24:37; 313).

PACA, JOHN (4), s. of Aquila (2) and Martha, was b. c.1712,
and d. 1785 (or 1781); m. Elizabeth Smith on 2 Nov. 1732; was
Commissioned Ranger of Balto. Co. on 9 June 1743; as Capt. John
Paca in 1750 he was listed as owning 200 a. part Gibson's Park,
20 a. Paca's Chance, 670 a. part Paca's Park, 100 a. Askin's
Hope, 27 a. Security, and other tracts; had iss.: MARY, b. 3
Aug. 1733; AQUILA, b. 21 June 1738; WILLIAM, b. 31 Oct. 1740,
Governor of Maryland, and Signer of the Declaration of Inde-
pendence; ELIZABETH, b. 8 Sept. 1742; MARTHA, b. 3 Feb. 1743
(131; 153:63; 303; 313).

PACA, JAMES (5), s. of Aquila (2) and Martha, inher. 400 a.
of Gibson's Park and 329 a. Charles' Neighbor; no other record.

PACA, JOHN (6), s. of Aquila (3) and Frances, was b. 14 April
1725; d. by 1 Dec. 1757; m. Margaret Lee on 6 Feb. 1752; in Aug.
1744 he chose his uncle John Paca as his guardian; in 1750 he
owned 600 a. Delph, 120 a. Delph Neck, 630 a. Paca's Park, 50
a. Peter's Addition, and other lands; left a will, 17 Sept. 1757
1 Dec. 1757, naming w. Margaret, and ch. Aquila, James, and John;
admin. bond was posted 1 Dec. 1757 by Margaret Paca, John Paca,
and Robert Adair, admins., with John Hall of Swan Town and Walter
Tolley; est. was admin. on 4 June 1760 and 21 May 1770; left
iss.: AQUILA, b. 30 March 1753; JAMES, b. 25 Oct. 1754; JOHN
STOKES, b. 22 Sept. 1757 (4:301; 6:211; 12:483; 35:295; 129:349,
351; 153:75; 210-30:435; 313).

PACA, (---), m. Elizabeth, dau. of Thomas Sheredine, by 5 Oct.
1746 (79:185).

PACQUINET, MICHAEL. See PASQUINET, MICHAEL.

PADGET, JAMES, m. Mary (---), and had iss.: ELIZABETH, b. 6
Jan. 1721; and SUSANNA, b. 14 April 1723 (131:43/r).

PAGE, JOHN, d. by 27 May 1758 when admin. bond was posted by
John Bain, with John Grant (12:528).

PAGE, WILLIAM, m. Esther Miller on 3 Oct. 1748 (133:162).

PAIN, CONSTABELLA, was tried for bast. in June 1739 (32:407).

PAINTER, EDWARD, d. 28 April 1737; admin. bond was posted 26
Aug. 1737 by admnx. Margaret Painter, with Ford Barnes and Thomas Mitchell, Sr. (12:461; 128:98).

PAINTER, NICHOLAS, surv. 1640 a. Andover in Balto. Co. in Sept.
1677; d. in A. A. Co. leaving a will proved 27 Dec. 1684, naming
Nicholas Courtney of Thomas, and Charles, Eliza, William, Benjamin, Joseph, and Anne, ch. of Col. William Burgess (120:135; 211).

PALLEN. See PAULING.

PALMER, ANN, m. Thomas Fretwell on 22 Oct. 1727 (129:258).

PALMER, DANIEL, was in Balto. Co. by 1692 as a taxable in n.
side Patapsco Hund.; d. by 12 May 1698 when admin. bond was posted by Anthony Drew, with Mark Richardson and James Phillips;
est. was inv. by William Hollis and Henry Jackson on 9 May 1699
and val. at £ 93.16.11, plus 13,160 lbs. tob. (12:424; 48:309;
138).

PALMER, GEORGE, m. Mary Tipper on 30 Aug. 1761 (131).

PALMER, JACOB, and w. Rosina, servants each with 5 yrs. to
serve, were listed in the inv. of Stephen Onion, 8 Oct. 1754
(49:221).

PALMER, THOMAS, m. Jude Elliott on 28 Dec. 1732 (131).

PALMER, WILLIAM, was in Balto. Co.. by Sept. 1673 when he
surv. 600 a. Palmer's Forest in Spesutia Hund.; in June 1671 he
conv. John Ryler and John Webster land on the s. side of Sassafras R.; d. by 1679 leaving a wid. and admnx. Elizabeth who m.
as her 2nd husb. Peter Elliss; no heirs claimed the land (97:
125; 99:347; 100:118; 101:300, 304; 200-70:134).

PANER, NICHOLAS (/), m. by Feb. 1753 Elizabeth, extx. of Erick
Erickson of Balto. Co. (201-33:427).

PARDOE. See PERDUE.

PARIS, ELIZABETH, was ind. for bast. in Aug. 1740; had s.:
JOSHUA, b. 16 May 1740 (32:291; 129:340).

PARISH. See PARRISH.

PARK. See PARKS.

THE JOHN PARKER FAMILY

PARKER, JOHN (1), was in Balto. Co. by 1692 as a taxable in
Spesutia Hund.; m. Clemency (---) who d. 5 (---ember) 1698; d.
12 Jan. 1704/5 when admin. bond was posted 2 March 1706/7 by Thomas Preston, Sr., with Francis Dallahide and Anthony Drew; est.
was inv. by Charles Baker and William Hicks in 1707; est. was admin. by Preston and Hicks on 5 July 1708; this John may have m.
as 2nd w. Isabella Smith and had a s. Joseph; had iss.: ELIZABETH
HARTSHORNE, b. 20 Dec. 1698; JOHN; and WILLIAM (of age in 1694
when he was listed with his father in Spesutia Hund.), d. 27
Dec. 1698; SAMUEL, d. 7 March 1698/9 (2:87, 91; 12:428; 48:23;
128:6, 21; 138).

PARKER, JOHN (2), s. of John (1), was b. c.1678, and was at least
16 when he was listed as a taxable in 1694 in Spesutia Hund. with
John Parker, Sr.; m. Isabella, wid. of Thomas Smith, on 12 Sept.
1699; they admin. Thomas Smith's est. on 3 Oct. 1704; John d. by
30 March 1720 when admin. bond was posted by Joseph Johnson with
William Marshall and Richard King; est. was inv. on 8 May 1720 by
Henry Willan and Peter Lester and val. at £ 49.5.0; prob. had
iss.: JOHN; JOSEPH, b. 4 March 1700/1 (2:186; 12:448; 51:271;
79:174; 128:11; 129:189).

PARKER, JOHN (3), prob. s. of John (2), m. Elizabeth Danby on
1 Jan. 1739; on 21 Aug. 1746 John and Elizabeth conv. 176 a. of
Parker's Lot to Abraham Snelson; in June 1737 they conv. Parker's

Folly to Henry Rhodes; had iss.: MARTIN, b. 9 Jan. 1740, and d. the same month; SARAH, b. 26 Feb. 1741; JOHN, b. 2 Sept. 1744 (61:472; 79:174; 131).

PARKER, Mrs., m. Robert Roberts on 15 Oct. 1706 (129:201).

PARKER, CHARLES, was made levy free in Aug. 1755 (40:220).

PARKER, CLEMENT, d. by 1 Feb. 1704/5 when admin. bond was posted by John Parker with Cornelius Herrington and Martin Taylor; est. was inv. 16 April 1705 by Roger Matthews and Thomas Newsham and val. at £ 15.8.4; est. was admin. 5 July 1708 by John Parker who stated that the sons of the dec. had been satisfied (2:90; 12:430; 48:55).

PARKER, ELIZABETH, was b. c.1685, giving her age as 42 in 1727 (225:14).

PARKER, ELIZABETH, servant of Robert Clarke, was tried for bast. in June 1724, naming David Pearce, another servant of sd. Clarke as the father; son James, now age 17, was bd. to Robert Clark to age 21 (26:333; 27:305).

PARKER, GABRIEL, was listed in 1750 as owning 306 a. Topley Neck (153:93).

PARKER, JAMES, was b. 4 March 1723, d. 31 May 1726 (128:48).

PARKER, JOHN, Jr., m. Junio (---) who d. 20 Aug. 1703 (128: 17; 129:199).

PARKER, JOHN, sold 180 a. Gibson's Ridge to Thomas Bond on 2 March 1738 (75:193).

PARKER, JOHN, m. Elizabeth Carback on 3 Jan. 1757 (128:48).

PARKER, MARY, m. Henry Hedge after banns were pub. on Whitsunday 1700 (129:191).

PARKER, QUINTON, was in Balto. Co. by Jan. 1673 when he surv. 330 a. Parker's Range, later held by Joshua Merriken; d. leaving a will, 16 Jan. 1674 - 7 May 1675, naming Margaret Penroy, James Smith, Elizabeth Harris,Anthony Hendrick, and dau. Elizabeth to be of age at 13; had iss.: ELIZABETH (120:88; 211).

PARKER, ROBERT, was in Balto. Co. by 1692 as a taxable in n. side Patapsco; in 1695 was granted 500 a. Parker's Palace; in June 1716 conv. 50 a. Parker's Palace to Nicholas Rogers and Christopher Randall; in March 1718 was fined for taking the Lord's name in vain; had iss.: KETURAH, m. by 21 Nov. 1730 Henry Lewis who sold 250 a. Parker's Palace to George Buchanan (23:66; 67: 422; 73:50; 138; 211).

PARKER, THOMAS, m. Anne Crain on 13 Sept. 1730 (133:149).

PARKS, EDWARD (1), progenitor, was in Balto. Co. by 1705 as a taxable in Spesutia Hund.; m. Dorothy (---); on 2 March 1720 was conv. 100 a. Expectation by Thomas and Mary Morris; on 16 Nov. 1728 Edmund Parks (sic) recorded a bond to Simon Jackson whereby Parks promised to conv. to him 100 a. of a larger tract called Expectation; in 1724 Edmund Parks conv. prop. to his s. Robert; had iss.: MARY, b. 12 Aug. 1706; ROBERT, b. 12 Sept. 1707; (poss.) PHILIP; (poss.) JOHN; (poss.) WILLIAM; (poss.) SARAH, m. William Lynchfield on 26 March 1749; (poss.) ELIZABETH, m. Aquila Milhughs on 17 Dec. 1749; (poss.) EDMUND (59:678; 69: 297; 75:9; 128:19, 31; 131; 147).

PARKS, ROBERT (2), s. of Edward (1), and Dorothy, was b. 12
Sept. 1707; had a cattle mark recorded for him on 16 Oct. 1724;
on 2 June 1741 was conv. 100 a. Come By Chance, by William Jarman and w. Sarah; conv. prop. to his s. Laban on 21 Jan. 1763;
had iss.: LABAN, alive in 1763; (poss.) ROBERT, Jr., m. Mary
Fuller on 19 Nov. 1761 (69:297; 75:507; 131).

PARKS, PHILIP (3), poss. s. of Edward (1), was b. 29 Dec.
1712 (but parents not named); m. Hannah Packow on 22 Dec. 1746;
131).

PARKS, JOHN (4), poss. son of Edward (1), m. Bridget Milhughes
on 13 Sept. 1743 or 29 Oct. 1743, and may be the John who m. 2nd
Sarah Linchfield on 10 Sept. 1748; in 1750 owned 50 a. Ebenezer's
Park, 310 a. The Range, and 319 a. The Forest; Parks 1st w. was
the wid. of Bartholomew Milhouse, whose est. they admin. on 21
July 1744 (3:361; 73:297; 126:223; 131; 133:161; 153:32).

PARKS, WILLIAM (5), poss. s. of Edward (1), may have been b.
c.1714; in 1754 purch. 50 a. Turkey Cock Alley from Thomas Cockey
Deye, and in 1761 was conv. 19 a. Chenowth's Adventure by Richard Chenoweth (82:220; 85:342; Parks Notes, at the Maryland Historical Society).

PARKS, RICHARD (or NICHOLAS), was in Balto. Co. by 1701 as a
taxable in s. side Patapsco Hund. (143).

PARLETT, MARTIN, m. Mary (prob. dau. of Henry Fitch), on 16
April 1723 in P. G. Co., when he m. Mary Burrows; was in Balto.
Co. by 20 Jan. 1728 when he wit. the will of Thomas Reviss of
Balto. Co.; on 3 Feb. 1734 Henry Fitch of Balto. Co., for love
he bore his dau. Mary Parlett conv. her 200 a., one-half of
Chance; iss.: MARY, b. 6 June 1727; ELIZABETH, b. 13 Sept. 1731
(74:166; 125:92; 133:12, 26; 263).

PARLETT, WILLIAM, was in Balto. Co. by 1748 and d. there in
1780; m. by 14 Oct. 1751 Sarah, dau. of Charles Gorsuch; in 1750
owned 50 a. Parlett's Fancy and other land; d. leaving a will
proved 15 Aug. 1780; had iss.: CHARLES; JOSHUA; DAVID; WILLIAM;
POLL , m. (---) Martin; MARY, b. 12 June 1748, m. Nicholas Grimes;
SARAH, b. 12 May 1750, m. Thomas Roberts(on); RACHEL (5:197; 10:
256; 112:411; 133:89; 153:62).

THE PARRISH FAMILY is the subject of Scott Lee Boyd's The
Parrish Family (Santa Barbara: 1935).

PARRISH, EDWARD (1), progenitor, was b. c.1640, and d. c.1680
at West R., A. A. Co.; m. c.1664 Clara (---); was transp. into
Md. in 1655 by William Piper; surv. many tracts incl. 2000 a. of
Parrish's Range and 50 a. Parrish's Choice; d. by 17 April 1680
when Clara Parrish ren. right to admin. in favor of Col. Thomas
Taylor; had iss.: EDWARD, b. c.1669/70; JOHN, b. c.1672; ANN, b.
c.1674, m. Matthew Hawkins; MARY, b. c.1676, m. as 2nd w. Matthew
Hawkins; WILLIAM, b. c.1678, d. c.1771/2 (206-7A:66; 209-12:35;
211; 386; Boyd).

PARRISH, EDWARD (2), s. of Edward (1), was b. c.1669/70, and
d. c.1723 in A. A. Co.; m. Mary Roberts, dau. of Andrew and Mary
Roberts; she m. 2nd, on 16 March 1735, Stephen Warman; he gave
his age as c.48 in Nov. 1718; d. leaving a will, May 1722/3 - 14
June 1723; will of Mary Roberts Parrish Warman was made 5 April
1750; had iss.: SARAH, b. c.1691 m   Thomas Norris in 1708;
ELIZABETH, b. c.1693, m. Jacob Duhadaway in 7 mo., 1712; EDWARD,
b. c.1693,. Rachel Harwood on 10 Dec. 1722 at Tred Haven Meeting;
JOHN, b. c.1698, m. Elizabeth Roberts, in 11 mo., 1722; ANN, b.

1702, d. 1776, m. 1st William Puntany and 2nd Mayberry Helms;
MARY, b. 1704, m. Samuel McCubbin in 1727; and WILLIAM, b. Jan.
1713, d. 1731 unm. (Boyd).

PARRISH, JOHN (3), s. of Edward (1) and Clara, was b. c.1672,
m. 3 d, 11 mo., 1700/1, Sarah Franklin, wid. of William Horne,
and dau. of Robert and Sarah (Gott) Franklin; John d. by 16 June
1725 when Sarah Parrish posted admin. bond, with John Parrish;
est. was admin. 9 Aug. 1727 and 24 May 1731 by Sarah, who said
that the dec. left 9 ch.; in Aug. 1728 his orphans under age
were Clare, Susanna, and Richard; had iss.: WILLIAM, b. c.1701/2,
d. 1728; JOHN, Jr., b. c.1703/4; EDWARD, b. c.1705/6; ELIZABETH,
m. James Bosley on 26 Nov. 1730; SARAH, m. Anthony Arnold; ART-
RIDGE, m. "out of meeting in 1730;" CLARE; SUSANNA; RICHARD, m.
Rachel Owens and lived to be 104 years, in Monongalia Co. (now
W.) Va. (3:70, 95; 12:453; 28:27; 30:10; Boyd).

PARRISH, WILLIAM (4), s. of Edward (1) and Clara, was b. c.
1678 in A. A. Co., d. c.1771 in Balto. Co.; m. Susannah (---)
and had iss.: EDWARD; WILLIAM; JOHN, b. 30 June 1723, m. Mary
Price on 30 March 1744; SUSANNA, m. Aquila Carr on 26 d, 2 mo.,
1745; MARY; and JOSEPH (Boyd).

PARRISH, JOHN (5), s. of Edward (2), was b. c.1698, d. Oct.
1745; m. Elizabeth Roberts in 11 mo., 1722; admin. bond was posted 4 June 1746 by Elizabeth Parrish with Alexander Lawson and
Richard Croxall; est. was admin. by Elizabeth Parrish on 5 Sept.
1747 and by Joseph Taylor, exec. of Eliz. Parrish, on 26 April
1750; dec. left iss.: ROBERT, b. 12 Oct. 1727; JOHN, b. 20 Jan.
1729; EDWARD, b. 12 Feb. 1731; ISAAC, b. 9 Oct. 1735; MARY, b.
8 Aug. 1738; ELIZABETH, b. 16 Oct. 1740; ANN, b. 10 Jan. 1745
(4:184; 5:120; 12:477; 136; Boyd).

PARRISH, JOHN (6), s. of John (3), was b. c.1703/4, d. c.1785;
m. 1st Catherine (---), and 2nd, on 2 Jan. 1733 in St. Paul's
Par., Elizabeth Thomas; as John Parrish, Jr., in 1750 owned 100
a. part Parrish's Forest; had iss.: JOHN; WILLIAM; JONATHAN;
RICHARD, d. 1820, m. 1776 Sarah Baker; CLARA; ELIZABETH; ANNE;
RACHEL; SARAH; and MARY (133:151; 153:49; Boyd).

PARRISH, EDWARD (7), s. of John (3), was b. c.1705/6, d. testate in Balto. Co.; m. Elizabeth, dau. of Stephen and Elizabeth
(Hubbard) Gill. on 3 May 1735 in St. Paul's Par.; in 1750 owned
100 a. Parrish's Forest; d. leaving a will, 26 May 1773 - 26 July
1773; had iss.: RICHARD; EDWARD, m. Prudence (---); STEPHEN, m.
Margaret (---); WILLIAM; JOHN; BENJAMIN; JAMES: SARAH; ELIZABETH;
ARTRIDGE; and SUSAN (112:240; 153:49; Boyd).

PARRISH, RICHARD (8), s. of John (3), was under age in Aug.
1728; m. Rachel Owen; in 1750 owned 50 a. Bachelor's Fancy;
moved to Fayette Co., Penna.; had iss. (28:27; 153:57; Boyd).

PARRISH, RICHARD (9), s. of William (4), was b. c.1719, d. 5
d, 7 mo., 1788 in his 70th yr; m. on 5 Feb. 1742/3 Keturah Price,
b. c.1720, d. 22 d, 2 mo., 1789: may be the William who in 1750
owned 250 a. part Roberts Forest in 1757 was appointed an elder
of Gunpowder Meeting; had iss.: WILLIAM, b. 5 April 1744; MARY,
b. 26 Dec. 1746, m. Samuel Price; SUSANNA, b. 3 June 1749, d. 24
Jan. 1820; KETURAH, b. 23 Oct. 1753 (136; 153:8; Boyd).

JOHN (1), s. of William (4), was b. 30 June 1723, d.
2 Aug. 1796, m. on 30 March 1744 at Gunpowder Meeting, Mary
Price, b. 20 March 1726, d. 31 d, 8 mo., 1793, dau. of John Price;
his home was the site of an indulged meeting, 1760; he later became lame in both legs and a committee of Friends was appointed
to collect £ 10 to pay his doctor; had iss.: HANNAH, b. 5 July

July 1748; MORDECAI, b. 3 Feb. 1750; ANN MARIA, b. 3 June 1753; MORDECAI, b. 3 Feb. 1755, m. Rachel Malone; AQUILA, b. 15 Aug. 1737 (136; Boyd).

PARRISH, JOSEPH (11), s. of William (4), in 1755 reported himself as having married "out of meeting;" was later disowned for fighting in 1759 (136).

PARRISH, (---), m. by 8 May 1751, (---), dau. of John Harryman (5:199).

PARRISH, (---), m. by 16 Jan. 1754, Ketura, dau. of Samuel Merryman (111:55).

PARRISH, ALEXANDER, m. Jane Chatto on 1 Feb. 1737 (128:95).

PARRISH, EDWARD, m. by 30 May 1751 a dau. of John Harryman, and in 1750 owned 592 a. Parrish's Range (153:94; 201-30:78).

PARRISH, WILLIAM, d. by 10 March 1728 when admin. bond was posted by John Parrish, exec., with William and Edward Parrish (12:457).

PARSLEY, ISRAEL, m. Sarah Cheyrton on 5 Feb. 1743 (131).

PARSONS, ANN, was ind. for bast. in June 1738 (31:221).

PARSONS, MARY, was tried for bast. in Aug. 1738 (31:274).

PARSON, SIMEON. See PEARSON, SIMON.

PARSONS, THOMAS, came into the country last Christmas with Capt. James Bustell; was sold to Amos Fogg and then to Edward Day; pet. for his freedom in Nov. 1759 (46:237).

PARTRIDGE, Dr. BUCKLER (1), was in Balto. Co. by Nov. 1718 when the court ordered that he be given a certificate showing he was a freeholder and res. of the county; may be the Buckler Partridge, merch. of Bristol, who purch. 165 a. Partridge Chance (formerly called Thomas Adventure) from Thomas and Sarah Matthews; in June 1735 purch. Partridge's Forest, formerly part of Selsed, from John Boring; in Sept. 1740 purch. part Balleston from John and Eleanor Long; d. by 4 Aug. 1742 when admin. bond was posted by Jane Partridge with Thomas Sligh and Henry Morgan; est. was admin. 5 June 1747, 24 Oct. 1750, and 8 Sept. 1760; in Dec. 1749 Samuel Smith conv. 57 a. Richardson's Neglect to Jane Partridge; in 1750 Jane owned 55 a. Thomas' Adventure, 26 a. part Good Luck, 25 a. Thomas' Range, and 34 a. Richardson's Neglect; Jane d. leaving a will, 6 Sept. 1758 - 3 Nov. 1761, naming ch. William, Daubeny Buckler, Ann w. of Joshua Bond, Frances w. of Jacob Bond, and Elizabeth w. of Heigh Sollers; admin. bond on her est. was posted 7 Feb. 1763 by William Partridge with Joshua Bond; Buckler and Jane had iss.: WILLIAM, prob. d. after 1763 unm.; DAUBENY BUCKLER; ANN, m. Joshua Bond; FRANCES m. Jacob Bond on 28 Dec. 1747; ELIZABETH, m. Heighe Sollers; and FLURRE, b. 24 March 1736 (4:152, 325; 6:6, 161; 7:195; 12:469, 484; 23:38; 70:208; 74:221; 75:449; 111:339; 134:47; 153:81).

PARTRIDGE, DAUBENY BUCKLER (2), s. of Dr. Buckler (1), d. c. 1769 in Balto. Co.; m. Ann (prob. dau. of Sabrett Sollers); gave his age as 45 in 1767; in 1750 owned 2/3 Thomas Adventure, 175½ a. part Good Luck, and 50 a. Thomas Range; d. leaving a will, 2 April. 1767 - 10 Nov. 1769, named w. Anne, and these ch.: WILLIAM; DAUBENY BUCKLER; and JOHN (112:119; 153:81; 210-30:860; 310).

PASQUINET/PACQUINET, MICHAEL, m. by 27 Dec. 1726 Charity, dau. of Richard Tydings, and moved to Bath Co., N. C., where he and his w. conv. power of attorney to their "loving cousin" John Belt of Balto. Co. (71:36, 61).

PASSMORE, REBECCA, was ind. for bast. in Nov. 1738 (31:307).

PATON, JOHN, d. by 12 May 1744 when his est. was admin. by Thomas White (3:356).

PATRIDGE, JOSEPH, m. Elizabeth (---), and had iss.: SARAH, b. 9 July 1759 (133:104).

PATTERSON, ROBERT, d. in Balto. Co. by 29 Jan. 1765; m. by 17 Sept. 1756 Jane, dau. of George Little; in 1750 owned 75 a. of Whitticar's Ridge and 100 a. Miles Hill; in April 1762 bought 50 a. Pearson's Outlet and Wetherall's Addition, from Samuel and Sarah Day; d. leaving a will, 28 Dec. 1764 - 29 Jan. 1765; had iss.: SARAH, b. 12 Nov. 1739; CYNTHIA, b. 21 Jan. 1741; JOHN, b. 15 Nov. 1745 (?); GEORGE, b. 22 May 1748 (?) (86:49; 112:10; 128:109; 129:323, 342, 345; 153:60; 210-30:297).

PAULING/PALLEN/PAWLEY/PAWLING, JOHN (1), was in Balto. Co. by March 1700 when Martha Bowen conv. prop. to him, and to his bro. and sis. William and Honour Reeves; m. Sarah (---) who survived him; d. 14 April 1722; in June 1725 Sarah Pawley bd. Elizabeth Pawley (age 11 next 27 Oct.) and Benjamin Pawley (age 8 next 8 Dec.) to Patrick and Martha Lynch to ages 15 and 20 respectively; Sarah was ind. for bast. in March 1730/1; John and Sarah had iss.: ELIZABETH, b. c.1714; BENJAMIN, b. 8 Oct. 1717; WILLIAM, b. 24 May 1723; and AQUILA, b. 25 Oct. 1727 (27:243; 9:96; 66:57; 133: 3, 14, 193).

PAULING, ELIZABETH (2), dau. of John (1), age 11 next 25 Oct., in June 1725 was bd. to Patrick and Martha Lynch by Sarah Pauling; bd. to Patrick Lynch again in Nov. 1730; may be the Elizabeth Pauling who had a s.: ROBERT NEWMAN, b. 18 April 1734 (17:243; 19:57; 133:59).

PAULEY, WILLIAM, in 5 Oct. 1701 surv. 400 a. Pay My Debts (207).

PAULSON. See POULSON.

PAUMER, JOHN, m. Elizabeth (---), and had iss.: COMFORT, b. 16 Jan. 1731 (128:104).

PAYNE, WILLIAM, in Nov. 1756 was fined for bast. as the father of Mary Young's child (41:312).

PAYWELL, MARY, m. Cadwallader Jones on 30 April 1704 (129:259).

PEACOCK, JACOB (1), progenitor, d. by 30 Nov. 1713; m. by 1707 the wid. of John Kendall; Jacob d. leaving a will, 7 July 1709 - 30 Nov. 1713, leaving entire est. to w. Jane; admin. bond was posted 30 Nov. 1713 by Philip Sindall with John Norton and Robuck Lynch; est. was inv. 1 Oct. 1713 by Benjamin Bowen and John Eaglestone and val. at £ 12.10.0 and signed by Catherine Sindall and Jacob Peacock; est. was admin. by Philip Sindall (who m. a dau. of the dec.) on 17 March 1720/1 and 22 July 1721; Jane Peacock, 7 Nov. 1713 - 30 Nov. 1713, naming s. Jacob, and son-in-law Philip Sindall; had iss.: JACOB; CATHERINE, m. Philip Sindall (1:203, 239; 12:415; 50:297; 122:257).

PEACOCK, JACOB (2), s. of Jacob (1), m. 26 Feb. 1720 Honor, wid. of (---) Arden; d. by 12 May 1728 when admin. bond was posted by James and Honour Lenox with Henry Jonass and Samuel Harryman; his est. was inv. 6 July 1728 by I. Darby and Luke Raven, and val. at £ 89.0.2; James Lenox stated there were no relations in the Province (but this may have meant there were no relations of age); had iss.: RUTH, b. 25 Oct. 1723 (12:456; 51:86; 133:4, 147).

PEACOCK, LUKE (3), poss. s. of Jacob (2), was mistreated by James Lenox, who was ind. for that offense in in Aug. 1737; m. Constantlove Sicklemore, dau. of Sutton Sicklemore, on 26 July 1753, and had iss.: SAMUEL SICKLEMORE (31:97; 112:221; 131).

PEACOCK, RUTH (4), dau. of Jacob (2), was b. 25 Oct. 1723; her legacy from James Lenox was mentioned in the est. of Thomas Todd on 4 Aug. 1741 (3:375; 133:4).

PEACOCK, ELIZABETH, was charged with bast. in Nov. 1723; was summoned to answer the charge in March 1723/4 (26:212).

PEACOCK, JOHN, m. 1st Frances (---), and 2nd, on 29 Dec. 1747, Ann Wiggin or Higgins, and had iss.: (by 1st w.): JOHN, b. 14 Dec. 1734 (128:91; 131).

PEAKE, GEORGE (1), progenitor, was in Md. by 4 Nov. 1657 when he m. the relict of Robert Parr; in his will proved 23 July 1669 John Parr named his mother Mary Peake, and also Katherine and Johanna Peake; George d. leaving a will made 27 March 1671, naming w. Mary, and ch. George, Joseph, and Johanna, and poss. other ch.; will of Mary Peake, 15 May 1671 - 30 Dec. 1671, named Jane Merritt and ch.: George, Joseph, and Katherine; George and Mary had iss.: GEORGE; JOSEPH; JOHANNA, m. by 1675 James Garrett; and KATHERINE (120:47, 60, 65; 200-10:554; 206-1:140).

PEAKE, JOSEPH (2), s. of George (1), was in Balto. Co. by 1692 as a taxable in n. side of Patapsco Hund.; m. by 1698 Jane, extx. of Jane Long; in Dec. 1698 purch. 120 a. No Name from Giles and Rebecca Stevens; on 1 Aug. 1699 Joseph and w. Jane conv. 575 a. Boughton's Forest to Edward Smith; Joseph and Jane Peake admin. the est. of Jane Long on 6 March 1696/7; Joseph d. leaving a willl proved 27 Oct. 1700, naming w. Jane, 175 a. Boughton's Forest, 100 a. Peake's Purchase, and ch. George and Jane; est. was admin. by w. Jane, now m. to Charles Merryman, on 14 Jan. 1709 and 13 May 1718; in Oct. 1739 John Kemp, Mary w. of John Caggill, and Jemima w. of John Broad, grandch. of Joseph Peake, conv. 575 a. Boughton's Forest to Daniel Dulany; dec. left iss.: GEORGE; JOHN; and perhaps others (1:19; 2:34, 110; 63:320, 384; 75:336; 121:205; 121:200; 138; 206-16:208).

PEAKE, CATHERINE, d. 15 Jan. 1714 (131).

PEARCE, (---), m. by Dec. 1772 Rachel, dau. of Dennis Garrett Cole (112:252).

PEARCE, BENJAMIN, in 1750 owned part Mount Ferado (153:27).

PEARCE, ELIZABETH, was ind. for bast. in March 1710/11 (21:205).

PEARCE, GEORGE, age c.40, English, runaway conv. serv. of William Jenkins, Oct. 1754 (385:310).

PEARCE, JOHN, d. by 13 May 1680; John Pearce (Peerce), the exec., sued Thomas Hedge of Balto. Co. (200-69:204).

PEARCE, JOSEPH, d. by 28 April 1676 when admin. bond was posted by John Bird with Thomas Richardson (12:423).

PEARCE, THOMAS, m. Mary (---), and had iss.: MARY, b. 16 Feb. 1747 (133:78).

PEARCE, WILLIAM, was in Balto. Co. by Aug. 1668 when he purch. Neife's Choice on the e. side of Fendall's Creek from Robert and Elizabeth Neife; in March 1668/9 he conv. 200 a. on s. side of Charn Creek to John William; in March 1669/70 conv. 200 a. Tibballs by Philip and Mary Holleger; in Nov. 1670 he and w. Isabel conv. 150 a. at Fendall's Creek, part of Neve's Choice, to Thomas Weymouth and John Powell (95; 96).

PEARCE, WILLIAM, m. Mary Grafford or Crawford on 3 June 1725; in 1750 he owned 10 a. Molly's Industry (133:153; 153:74).

PEARLE WILLIAM (1), m. Ann (---); d. by Nov. 1693 when his wid. Ann had m. 2nd Philip Pitstow, and 3rd Stephen Bentley; had iss.: WILLIAM; MARY, b. c.1681, in Nov. 1692 was bd. to William Wilkinson (19:300, 307, 333).

PEARLE, WILLIAM (2), s. of William (1), was b. c.1677, was age 15 prev. July when in Nov. 1692 he chose John Bayes(?) to be his guardian; was a taxable in n. side Patapsco Hund. in 1695; d. by 10 June 1715 when admin. bond was posted by Edward Sweeting and Philip Washington; est. was inv. 18 June 1715 by Michael Young and S. Hinton ; a second admin. bond was posted 20 Sept. 1716 by Philip Washington with John Norton (12:416, 420; 17:333, 335; 50:214; 140).

PEARLE, RICHARD, was in Balto. Co. by 1692 as a taxable in s. side Patapsco Hund. (138).

PEARSON, ROBERT, of Chester Co., Penna., conv. 150 a. Whiteacre's Ridge to Aquila Paca on 20 Aug. 1720 (68:224).

PEARSON, SIMON, was b. c.1659/60, giving his age as 69 in 1728, 71 in 1731, and 78 in 1738; m. 1st Emma (---), who d. 7 June 1714, and 2nd, on 25 July 1715 Sarah Schaw; on 9 March 1704 he and w. Emma conv. 100 a. Keitherminster to John Roberts; in March 1707 conv. 100 a. Dennis' Choice (part of a larger tract) to William Noble; had come to Balto. Co. by 1692 as a taxable in n. side of Patapsco Hund.; w. Sarah was the wid. of Thomas Shaw and dau. of Thomas Thurston; Simon and Sarah admin. the est. of Thomas Shaw in 1715 and 1716; in 1731 he mentioned his mother-in-law Margaret Anlis (or Owless); was involved in many land transactions; last identified deed was in Feb. 1736 when Pearson conv. to Edward Hall late sheriff of Balto. Co., three parcels, Turkey Range, Noble's Desire, and Pearson's Priviliege; no record of any admin. of his est. has been found; left iss. (by 1st w.): MARY, m. by 10 Sept. 1717 George Berry; SIMON, b. 7 May 1714; (by 2nd w.): ANN, b. 15 Dec. 17--; MOSES, b. 21 May 1716; COMFORT, b. 25 Sept. 1718, m. John Everett in Aug. 1739; SAMUEL, b. 2 March 1723 (59:554; 60:189; 69:142; 72:351; 131:7, 9, 10, 12, 84/r; 133:1, 8, 10, 12, 22; 138; 163:131; 164:37; 209-22:14, 91; 210-15:545; 224:131; 225: 37; Avant, Southern Colonial Families, II).

PEARSON, THOMAS, m. Ann (---), and had iss.: ANN, b. 28 April 1759; ENOCH, b. 27 Sept. 1761 (129:376).

PEART, THOMAS, was in Balto. Co. by 3 June 1682 when Thomas Long and w. Jane conv. 100 a., part of Northwick, to him; d. by 1 May 1701 when admin. bond was posted by Susanna Robinson, admnx.; had iss.: ELIZABETH, who in July 1682 was conv. 50 a. Salisbury Plains by Robert Benger (who had orig. taken up the tract in partnership with her father) (12:418; 64:170).

PECKETT. See PICKETT.

PEDDER, JOHN, m. Christian Williams on 9 July 1738 (131).

THE PEDDICORD/PEDDICOAT/PETTICOAT FAMILY of Anne Arundel and Baltimore Counties is discussed in Dorsey et al, The Dorsey Family, pp. 28-33.

PEDDICORD, JOHN (1), m. by 1 Oct. 1702, Sarah, wid. of John Norwood, and dau. of Col. Edward Dorsey; John may have been the s. of William Petticoat transp. to Md. by 1667; in June 1729 John gave his age as c.60; by July 1737 John Peddicord was in Balto. Co. when he mortgaged prop. to Richard Gist, and had iss.: JOHN, b. c.1702, bapt. 5 Feb. 1706; WILLIAM, b. c.1703; KETURAH, bapt. 5 Feb. 1706; NATHAN, b. c.1710, m. Sarah; NICHOLAS, b. c. 1712, m. Ann Jacks; DORSEY, b. c.1714, m. Sarah (---) (61:470; The Dorsey Family).

PEDDICORD, JOHN (2), s. of John (1) and Sarah, was b. c.1702, as John Peddicord, Jr., pat. Petticoat's Wish, 180 a., in 1724, and Petticoat's Addition, 150 a., in 1720; gave bond to Zebediah Baker in June 1725; sold Petticoat's Wish to William Peddicoat on 2 Feb. 1726 (70:246, 334; The Dorsey Family).

PEDDICORD, WILLIAM (3), s. of John (1) and Sarah, was b. c. 1703, and d. 1776 in Balto. Co.; m. Sarah (---); in 1750 owned 100 a. Norwood's Delight and 303 a. Petticoat's Banter; d. leaving a will, 30 May 1770 - 26 July 1776, naming w. Sarah and these ch.: NATHAN; WILLIAM; JASPER; HUMPHREY;; NICHOLAS; CALEB; ALTHEA; ESTHER; and CASSANDRA, m. (---) Johnson (112:321; 153:9; The Dorsey Family).

PEDDICORD, NATHAN (4), s. of John (1), and Sarah, was b. c. 1710 in A. A. Co., and d. c.1763 in Frederick County; m. c.1738 Sarah (---), and had iss.: WILLIAM, b. 5 April 1739; BASIL, b. 2 July 1740; ELEANOR, b. 2 April 1744; THOMAS, b. 4 Feb. 1745 (The Dorsey Family).

PEDDICORD, NICHOLAS (5), s. of John (1) and Sarah, was b. c. 1712, and was alive in 1778; m. Ann Jacks on 23 Dec. 1735 in St. Paul's Par., Balto. Co.; surv. 60 a. Petticoat's Hope in July 1745; sold this tract to William Chamier and William Lux in Nov. 1755; no known ch. (82:178; 133; The Dorsey Family).

PEDDICORD , DORSEY (6), s. of John (1) and Sarah, was b. c. 1714; was in Balto. Co. in 1762; in Nov. 1746 was allowed 600 lbs. tob. by the court, for maintaining his mother-in-law; in March 1746/7 admitted paternity of Mary Barnes' child; in 1750 owned 140 a. Petticoat's Beginning; in March 1751 with w. Sarah sold John Randall 140 a. Friendly Purchase; in Nov. 1762 with w. Sarah conv. Morris Baker 150 a. Petticoat's Lot; had iss.: at least one s.: DORSEY (36:227, 392; 81:132; 86:488; 153:72; The Dorsey Family).

PEERCE. See PEARCE.

PEIRPOINT. See PIERPOINT.

PEMBERTON, HENRY, m. Margaret (---), had iss.: ANN, b. 1 May 1746 (134:22).

PEMBERTON, JOHN, d. leaving a wid. Margaret who m. 2nd Robert Grundy; est. was divided among the wid. and James, John, and Benjamin (1:288).

PENHALLOW, JOSEPH, mariner, d. by 6 Aug. 1741 when admin. bond was posted by Buckler Partridge with John Bayly and Thomas Taylor;

est. was admin. 4 June 1747 by Penhallow's original admnx., Jane Partridge (4:154; 12:480).

PENN, JOHN, in 1750 owned 200 a. Hope's Lot (153:52).

PENNINGTON, HENRY, of Balto. Co., claimed land for service in 1670; in Aug. 1671 purch. 400 a. Happy Harbour from Richard Leake and w. Gwilthien (98:488; 388).

PENNINGTON, JOHN, m. Mary (---) by Aug. 1744; in 1750 owned 100 a. Jackson's Chance; had iss.: ELIZABETH, b. 25 Aug. 1744; MARTHA, b. 28 Dec. 1745; URATH, b. 27 Feb. 1747; MARY, b. 20 April 1750 (133:85, 95; 153:9).

PENRICE, JOHN, d. June 1741; admin. bond was posted 3 June 1714 by Charles Simonds, exec., with John Deaver and William Peckett; dec. left a will, 15 May 1714 - 2 June 1714, naming James Demitt, s. of William and Eliza, and Charles Simonds; est. was inv. on 26 July 1714 by W. Whitehead and Jno. Taylor, and val. at £ 7.11.7; est. was admin. by Charles Simonds in July 1715 (1: 319; 12:434; 48:159; 123:15; 131:6).

PERDUE/PARDOE/PURDUE, CHRISTOPHER, was in Balto. Co. by 1692 as a taxable in s. side Patapsco (138).

PERDUE, MARY, was ind. for bast. in Nov. 1737, tried in March 1737/8; tried again for bast. in Aug. 1741; had iss.: ANN, b. 3 May 1741 (31:129, 187; 33:88; 131:100/r).

PERDUE, PRUDENCE, was ind. for bast. in June 1740, and tried in Aug. 1740 (32:226, 304).

PERDUE, SARAH, in June 1721 named Francis Arrow as the father of her child; was charged with bast. in Nov. 1723; may be the same Sarah who was later tried for bast. in Aug. 1750 and Nov. 1750 (23:15; 26:96; 37:175; 38:24).

PERDUE, WILLIAM, m. Jeane (---), was made exempt from levy in March 1739/40; had iss.: WILLIAM, b. 3 June 1716; MARY, b. 17 Jan. 1715 (32:149; 131:11).

PEREGOY, JOSEPH (1), progenitor, came to Md., c.1685; as Joseph "Peregois, a Frenchman of full age," was bound to Robert Burman, of Md., for 5 years, starting in July 1685; was in Balto. Co. by 1692 as a taxable in the household of Edward Mumford in n. side of Patapsco Hund.; m. Sarah, dau. of afsd. Mumford; came to possess 100 a. Burman's Forest, a 350 a. tract orig. surveyed 12 Feb. 1685 for Robert Burman of London, blacksmith; in 1714 Joseph gave his age as 49 (placing his birth date as c.1663), and w. Sarah gave her age as 42 and named her father Edward Mumford; d. by 10 May 1720 when admin. bond was posted by Sarah Peregoy with William Loyall and Henry Peregoy; Joseph and Sarah had iss.: EDWARD, d. by 14 Jan. 1746/7; JOSEPH, Jr., d. 1745; HENRY, may have d. 1765 in Fred. Co., Va.; FRANCES, m. John Gollohan on 16 Feb. 1723 (12:449; 133:147; 138; 203-3:104; 211; 439:64; Lee notes compiled by Harry H. Lee and graciously made available to the compiler).

PEREGOY, EDWARD (2), s. of Joseph (1) and Sarah, d. by 14 Jan. 1746/7 when admin. bond was posted by Avarilla Peregoy with Samuel Bowen and Peter Dowell; on 17 Oct. 1716 Ebenezer Blackiston and w. Sarah conv. 100 a. Goodwill, being part of a larger tract called Burman's Forest, to Edward; est. of Edward Peregoy was admin. by his wid. Avarilla on 4 June 1747, 29 May 1750, and 3 Nov. 1753; by May 1750 she m. as her 2nd husb. Thomas Sollers; left iss. two

ch., who as the heirs of Edward Peregoy were listed as owning 100
a., part Burman's Forest; had iss.: JOHN; NATHAN (4:172; 5:153,
275; 12:475; 67:412; 153:43; Peregoy notes by Lee).

PEREGOY, JOSEPH (3), s. of Joseph (1) and Sarah, d. by 5 June
1745 when admin. bond was posted by John Morgan with Thomas Sligh
and John Frashier; m. Flora Rider on 17 Feb. 1735; she m. as her
2nd husb. John Morgan; on 17 Oct. 1716 Ebenezer and Sarah Blacki-
iston conv. 97 a. Interest (part of Burman's Forest) to Joseph
Peregoy; est. admin. by John Morgan on 28 Feb. 1745 and 9 Dec.
1745; Joseph and Flora had iss.: NATHAN, b. 20 Oct. 1737; JAMES,
twin, b. 19 Dec. 1742; JOSEPH, twin, b. 19 Dec. 1742; DANIEL, b.
5 April 1744 (5:37, 38; 12:465; 35:804; 67:412-414; 133:59, 89,
90, 155; Peregoy notes by Lee).

PEREGOY, HENRY (4), s. of Joseph (1) and Sarah, may be the Henry who d. c.1765 in Frederick Co., Va.; on 17 Oct. 1716 Edward
and Sarah Blackiston conv. 100 a. Success (part of Burman's Forest)
to Henry Peregoy; on 3 April 1728 Henry and w. Amy conv. 50 a.
Green's Purchase (part of Success, which was part of Burman's
Forest) to Robert Green; on 2 Sept. 1729 Henry and Amy conv. 50
a. Success to John Miller; pat. Henry's Delight in Amy's Garden
on 1 May 1743, and sold 20 a. of this to Thomas Sligh on 18 April
1749; had iss.: ANN, b. 25 Sept. 1719, m. William Brock; HENRY,
Jr., b. 29 Dec. 1722; ANDREW, m. Alice Edwards on 21 June 1750;
JOSEPH, d. 1792; ROBERT, b. c.1728; EDWARD, b. 25 Dec. 1730; MARY,
b. 16 Aug. 1736; MARY, b. 15 Oct. 1746, m. Archibald Tracey (67:
412-414; 71:128-130; 72:174-176; 80:217-219; 131:126/r; 133:
4, 54; 207; Peregoy notes by Lee).

PEREGOY, JOSEPH, in 1750 was listed as Joseph Perrigo the
owner of 50 a. part Cradon on the Hill (153:41).

PERKINS, RICHARD (1), progenitor, was in Balto. Co by 1683 when
he surv. 100 a. Parkinton at the head of Musketo Creek in Spesutia Hund.; may be the Richard Parkins who was transp. to Md. c.
1674; m. Mary (---) who m. as her 2nd husb. John Belcher; on 28
Aug. 1697 he and William Lofton surv. 100 a. Brotherly Love which
was later held by Lofton's orphans; later Lofton conv. 180 a. of
Eightrupp to Perkins; in 1696 Perkins admin. the est. of Robert
Drisdale, and in June 1699 he was one of the appraisers of the
est. of Francis Chatham; in June 1704 Thomas Gash named Perkins
as one of his executors; Perkins d. by 16 April 1706 when admin.
bond was posted by wid. Mary Perkins with William Perkins and John
Mills; his est. was inv. on 28 May 1706 by Thomas Brown and Henry
Wright, and val. at £ 67.14.6 plus 5128 lbs. tobacco; est. was admin. by Mary w. of John Belcher on 1 July 1708 (the banns of her
2nd marr. were posted in Feb. 1706) Richard and Mary had iss.:
RICHARD, b. 9 July 1689; WILLIAM, b. 15 March 1692; MARY, b. 2
April 1695; ELISHA, b. 15 Dec. 1697; SARAH, b. 15 Dec. 1699, d.
28 Dec. 1699 (or 1700); MARTHA, b. 31 March 1701 (2:88, 90, 136;
12:422; 48:117, 164, 286; 59:62; 64:19; 122:41; 128:2, 3, 9, 12;
129:201, 214; 211; 388).

PERKINS, RICHARD (2), s. of Richard (1), was b. 9 July 1689,
gave his age as 55 in 1736; may be the Richard who m. Mary (---)
as late as 1742; in March 1721 was ind. by the court for neglecting to register the births of three children in St. George's Par.;
Richard left iss. (poss. by two different wives): RICHARD, b. 18
Dec. 1713; ch., unregistered, b. by 1721; BENJAMIN, s. of Richard
and Mary, b. 6 Jan. 1733; MARY, dau. of Richard and Mary, and
granddau. of William Sherwill, b. 1 Dec. 1739; AVENTON, b. 23
March 1742 (23:445; 128:32, 78; 129:310, 330; 224:236).

PERKINS, WILLIAM (3), s. of Richard (1), was b. 15 March 1692 and d. after 1750; m. Elizabeth, dau. of John Cottrell, by 22 Jan. 1721 when John Cottrell made a will naming his dau. Elizabeth w. of William Perkins, and a granddau. Mary Perkins; in March 1721 William was ind. for neglecting to register the birth of a child in St. Georges Parish; in 1750 he owned 121 a. part Eightrupp; William and Elizabeth had iss.: JOHN, b. 13 Feb. 1717; MARY, b. 17 June 1720; REUBEN, b. 12 Feb. 1721/2; ELIZABETH, b. 30 Sept. 1726; ISABEL, b. 30 Oct. 1728; STEPHEN JOHN, b. 9 Jan. 1730, d. 18 Feb. 1735; WILLIAM, d. Sept. 1739; RACHEL, b. 13 March 1735; MARGARET, b. 14 Dec. 1739 (23:445; 125:163; 128:36, 41, 74, 78; 129:106, 287; 153:50).

PERKINS, ELISHA (4), s. of Richard (1), was b. 9 June 1697, and m. Margaret Sherill on 1 Dec. 1718; may have m. a 2nd time for in March 1721 he was ind. for neglecting to register his marriage and the birth of a child; in June 1721 Mary Belcher pet. the court on behalf of her s. Elisha; may be the Elisha Perkins who moved to Orange Co., Va., and gave bond to Jonathan Jones he would conv. him 94 a. part Eightrupp; had iss.: ELIZABETH, b. 18 Nov. 1719; ch., b. by 1721; ELISHA, b. 31 Aug. (---) (23: 445, 505; 81:111; 128:39, 84).

PERKINS, RICHARD (5), s. of Richard (2), is prob. the Richard who was b. 18 Dec. 1713 (no parents named), m. Elizabeth Cutchin on 5 Jan. 1735, and had iss.: ROBERT BIGGIN, b. 16 March 1736 (129:214, 288, 294).

PERKINS, REUBEN (6), s. of William (2), was b. 12 Feb. 1721/2 and m. Avarilla Durbin on 5 Nov. 1748; had iss.: HANNAH, b. 6 Dec. 1749; WILLIAM, b. 10 July 1752; RACHEL, b. 26 March 1755; ELIZABETH, b. 13 April 1757; RICHARD, b. 14 Aug. 1759 (129:346, 370).

PERKINS, ADAM, m. Mary Walters on 23 May 1743 (129:332).

PERKINS, ISAAC, m. Mary Lee in May 1739, and had iss.: WILLIAM, b. 23 Oct. 1740 (129:305, 330).

PERKINS, JOSEPH, m. Mary (---), and had iss.: RACHEL, b. 6 Jan. 1725; MARY, b. 20 Dec. 1728; and HANNAH, b. 24 May 1731 (129:260).

PERKINS, WILLIAM, m. Martha Miles on 3 Feb. 1703/4, and may be the William who was bur. 8 Jan. 1703 (129:200, 203).

PERREIR, GILBERT, was bur. 25 March 1699 (129:187).

PERRIN, GILBERT, was in Balto. Co. by 1692 as a taxable in n. side of Gunpowder (138).

PERRINE, WILLIAM, was in Balto. Co. by 21 Oct. 1760 when he bought 200 a. Bond's Gift from William and Mary Few of N. C, (84: 388).

PERRY, WILLIAM (1), m. Sarah McCarty on 12 Dec. 1726, and had iss.: WILLIAM, b. 14 Sept. 1726 (128:48, 68).

PERRY, WILLIAM (2), s. of William (1), was b. 14 Sept. 1726, and m. Eliza Bellaw (Isabella?) Perkins on 4 Dec. 1751; had iss.: MARY, b. 14 Aug. 1754; JAMES, b. 2 Oct. 1756; RACHEL, b. 12 Feb. 1758 (129:361).

PERRY, JOHN, m. Sarah (---), and had iss.: JOSEPH, b. 4 Oct. 1737; ELIZABETH, b. 1 March 1740 (133:70).

PERRY, MARY, was ind. for bast. in March 1743/4 (35:154).

PERRYMAN, ROGER, formerly of Cecil Co., was in Balto. Co. on or soon after 5 Feb. 1741 when he purch. 100 a. Stony Ridge and 50 a. Addition to Stony Ridge from Richard Dawson; m. 1st (poss.) Mary (---) who d. 14 May 1742; m. 2nd, on 15 July 1742, Martha Armstrong; d. leaving a will proved 25 May 1749, naming w. Martha and Samuel John Perryman as execs., and ch.: Patience, Elizabeth, John, Samuel, Isaac, Jacob, Mary, Susan (or Sarah); admin. bond was posted 25 May 1749 by extx. Martha Perryman with Thomas Oakley and Henry Armstrong; est. was admin. 16 Oct. 1749 and 11 May 1750; dec. left iss.: PATIENCE, b. c.1726; ELIZABETH, b. c.1730; JOHN, b. c.1734; SAMUEL, b. c.1736; JACOB, b. c.1741; MARY, b. c.1745; ISAAC, b. c.1746; SUSANNA, b. c.1747 (5:164; 8: 59; 12:516; 76:80; 129:337; 210-26:101).

PERVEAL, JOHN, m. Mary (---), and had iss.: ELIZABETH, b. 13 Jan. 1744; GIDEON, b. 13 Aug. 1747; MARY, b. 15 Jan. 1749/50 (133:83, 93).

PETERS, JOHN, m. by Oct. 1701 Hester, mother of John Fuller (66:93).

PETERSON, (---), (1), was the father of at least three ch., all of whom immigrated to Md. c.1664: ANDREW; CORNELIUS; and EZER (388).

PETERSON, ANDREW (2), s. of (---) (1), from Sweden, was bro. of Cornelius and Ezer; came to Md. c.1664; with John and Ann Cock conv. 300 a. The Leney to William Ward in Nov. 1671; d. by 16 May 1692 when admin. bond was posted by Judith Dorman, spinster, with John Hayes, and Selah Dorman (12:429, 430; 97:126; 379).

PETERSON, CORNELIUS (3), s. of (---) (1), from Sweden; was bro. of Andrew (2) and Ezer; imm. c.1664; in Nov. 1669 conv. 150 a. on s. e. side of Bear Creek to John Cock, being part of the land formerly taken up by Peterson and Bartlett Hendrickson; was naturalized in 1674 (60:76; 379).

PETERSON, ANDREW, d. by 7 May 1682 when est. was inv. by John Baxter and Jno. Haiden and val. at £ 19.4.6 (206-10:484).

PETERSON, HANCE, imm. to Md. c.1665 from Holland and New York w. wife Ingebar; with James Watson bought 300 a. Indian Range from Richard Leake and w. Gwilthin (99:346).

PETETE. See POTEET.

PETIT. See POTEET.

PETTICOTE. See PEDDICORD.

PETTY, ANN, serv. to John Fuller, was ind. for bast. in June 1743 (34:185).

PETTY, FRANCIS. See POTEET, FRANCIS.

PEVERELL, DANIEL, was in Balto. Co. as early as 1688 (when he took up 454 a. Daniel's Lot); d. c.1691/2, having m. Hannah (---), who m. as her 2nd husb. George Smith (d. 1704), and 3rd, David Thomas; Peverell also acquired 300 a. Hunting Neck and 100 a. Mate's Angle; these tracts were later held by George Smith and David Thomas for the "orphans of Daniel Peveral;" d. leaving a will, 22 March 1691/2 - 2 May 1692, naming w. Hannah and dau. Sarah; est. was inv. 14 June 1692 by Laurence Taylor and William Osbourne and val. at £ 63.0.10, plus 4070 lbs. tobacco; est. was

admin. 15 May 1694 by execs. Hannah Peverell and Samuel Browne;
on 16 May 1704 George Smith made his will naming his w. Hannah
and her dau. Sarah Peverell; Daniel and Hannah had at least one
ch.: SARAH, b. 7 Aug. 1691, m. Richard Ruff. (122:37; 129:183;
206-12:129; 206-13A:51; 211).

PHELPS, THOMAS (1), in Aug. 1738 told the vestry of St. Geo.
Parish he had m. Rose (---) on 28 May 1710; his w. had formerly
eloped from one (---) Swift; on 26 Sept. 1741 Elizabeth McShaine
bd. her s. David to Thomas and Rose Phelps; in 1750 Thomas owned
50 a. Jones' Inheritance and 50 a. Arabia Petrea; d. leaving a
will dated 2 April 1758 in which he named w. Rosanna, and s. Avinton who was to be a ward of Edward Morgan; friends David and Hannah McSwain; had iss.: AVINTON (76:29; 130:292; 153:49; 210-30:
483).

PHELPS, AVINTON (2), s. of Thomas (1), in April 1762 was in
Rowan Co., N.C., when he and David McSwain conv. 50 a. Jones'
Venture to Edward Morgan (86:73).

PHELPS, AVINTON, m. Rachel Muckeldory on 23 April 1730 (128:
59).

PHELPS, THOMAS, of A. A. Co., in Oct. 1672 bought Wolf Neck
from Robert Chapman also of A. A. Co. (99:347).

PHELPS, WILLIAM, d. by 2 July 1703 when his est. was inv. by
William Hawkins and William Forman and val. at L 42.10.10 (48:
132).

PHENIX/FENIX, WILLIAM, d. 1708; m. Bridget Linsey on 31 Dec.
1702 in St. James Par., A. A. Co.; d. by 1 Dec. 1709 when admin.
bond was posted by John Hall and George Chauncey; est. was inv.
on 6 June 1710 by Jos'h Johnson and John Gallion and val. at
L 18.15.0; William had iss.: WILLIAM, b. 26 Sept. 1705, d. 6
Sept. 1707; prob. MARY, b. 2 Feb. 1708 (13:70; 48:170; 128:23,
25; 219-3:319).

PHILLIPS, ANTHONY (1), of Milwich, Staffordshire, Eng., m.
there on 8 Nov. 1590 Margerie Hill; they had at least one s.:
ANTHONY, bapt. 19 April 1595 (Par. Reg. of Milwich, pub. by the
Staffordshire Par. Reg. Society).

PHILLIPS, ANTHONY (2), s. of Anthony (1), was bapt. 19 April
1595 at Milwich; m. Joyce Parks on 26 Dec. 1636 at Sedgeley,
Staffordshire; she was b. 8 April 1607 at Wolverhampton, Staffordshire, dau. of Francis Parks innkeeper at Wolverhampton, and
his w. Johan or Joan Watton; Joyce d. 29 June 1657 at Sedgeley;
Anthony and Joyce had at least one s.: JAMES, bapt. 11 Drc. 1642
at Sedgeley (Parish Registers of Sedgeley and Wolverhampton, all
pub. by the Staffordshire Parish Register Society).

PHILLIPS, JAMES (3), s. of Anthony (2) and Joyce, was bapt. 11
Dec. 1642 at Sedgeley (the registrar entered the pious hope that
"the Lord Grant that the child be a better man than the father!")
and d. by 4 June 1689 in Balto. Co.; when in Balto. Co. was an
innkeeper; m. Susanna, wid. of William Orchard; she m. as her 3rd
husb. one Benjamin Arnold, and she d. testate c. Jan. 1708/9;
James took up a number of tracts including 2000 a. Phillips' Purchase in 1683, the tract Sedgeley, and in Nov. 1685 as James Phillips, cooper, conv. 100 a. at Leigh Neck to Christopher Tapley
and Francis Elling; d. leaving a will, 27 March 1687 - 4 June 1689,
naming his four ch.; est. was inv. 24 and 29 June 1689 by John
Hall and William Osbourne and val. at L 426.18.5; in 1696 his est.
was admin. by his s. James; will of Susanna (---) (Orchard Phillips) Arnold, 22 Sept. 1706 - 4 Jan. 1708/9, named her dau. Mary

Carvill, and the latter's dau. Avarilla, dau. Martha w. of Aquila
Paca and her dau. Mary; James and Susanna had iss.: JAMES; ANTHO-
NY, d. by 6 June 1698 leaving a will naming his mother Susanna Arnold, bro. James, and sisters Martha and Mary Carville; admin.
bond on his est. was posted 23 May 1698 by extx. Susanna Arnold
with James Phillips; est. was inv. 4 March 1698/9 by George Smith
and Samuel Browne and val. at £ 100.14.19; MARY, m. 1st John
Carville, and 2nd Richard Smithers; MARTHA, m. Aquila Paca (48:
83, 307; 110:180, 250; 206-15:25; 211).

PHILLIPS, JAMES (4), s. of James (3) and Susanna, d. 3 March
1720; m. 1st Bethia, dau. of George and Susanna (Goldsmith) Utie;
she d. 13 Dec. 1714; James m. 2nd, in 1716, Johannah (---), wid.
of (---) Kemp; she d. 1735 having m. 3rd Aquila Hall; on 8 June
1701 Mark Richardson who m. George Utie's wid. Susanna, made a
will naming his son and dau.-in-law James and Bethia Phillips;
d. leaving a will, 30 March 1720 - 30 April 1720, naming w. Johanna, daus. Susanna and Johanna, son James, sisters Mary and
Mathew (Martha); est. was inv. on 12 Jan. 1721/2 by Daniel
Scott, Jr., and Jos. Middlemore, and val. at £ 3123.3.9½ plus
43,000 lbs. tob.; James' wid. Johanna m. Aquila Hall on 17 Dec.
1720; she admin. the est. of James Phillips on 22 May (?) and
11 July 1727; her 3rd husb. admin. Phillips' est. on 19 July
1739; James had iss. (by 1st w.): BETHIA, b. 25 Aug. 1702; (by
2nd w.): JAMES, b. 13 Dec. 1716; SUSANNA, b. 5 Sept. 1718, m.
1st George Stokes, and 2nd Winston Smith, and 3rd Talbot Risteau;
JOHANNA, b. 28 March 1720, m. Jacob Giles (2:266; 3:71; 4:31;
51:179; 66:42; 122:3, 73; 128:15, 35, 36, 41; 129:214).

PHILLIPS, JAMES (5), s. of James (4) and Johanna, was b. 13
Dec. 1716, and was alive in 1755; m. Mrs. Sarah Knight on 27
Sept. 1737; in 1750 as Capt. James Phillips he owned 400 a. Ben-
jamin's Choice, 134 a. part Huntingworth, 400 a. Chilberry, 100
a. Mate's Angles, 100 a. Upper Eling, and other lands; had iss.:
SARAH, b. 22 Aug. 1738, m. 1st (---) Hall, and 2nd Daniel Magee;
JAMES, b. 9 Feb. 1740; JOHANNA, b. 11 Oct. 1742; SUSANNA, b. 8
April 1745, d. 17 May 1745; CORDELIA, b. 8 July 1746; MARY, b. 4
Nov. 1749; MARY, b. 4 Nov. 1750; SUSANNA, b. 25 Sept. 1752; RE-
BECCA KNIGHT, b. 28 July 1755 (128:101, 112; 129:297, 327, 342,
343, 347, 348, 350; 153:56).

PHILLIPS, EDWARD, was in Balto. Co. by June 1676 when he purch.
100 a. Swan Point from John Owen (101:299).

PHILLIPS, EDWARD, m. Mary Medcalf on 1 Jan. 1736 (131).

PHILLIPS, ELIZA, serv., with 3 years, 4 mos. to serve, listed
in the 1747 inv. of Edward Day (54:226).

PHILLIPS, ELIZABETH, was ind. for bast. in March 1746/7 (36:
378).

PHILLIPS, JANE, in March 1715/6 named Paul Philpott as the
father of her child (21:675).

PHILLIPS, JOHN, d. by 20 Dec. 1755 when admin. bond was posted
by John Paca with Robert Adair (12:529).

PHILLIPS, SAMUEL, m. Solvolitle Boswell on 28 Sept. 1749 (131:
34).

PHILLIPSON, THOMAS, d. by 8 April 1712 when admin. bond was
posted by John Taylor with James Read and John Newman; est. was
inv. by Charles Simmons and Oliver Harride and val. at £ 11.12.6
plus 4665 lbs. tobacco; dec. left no kindred (12:436; 50:362).

PHILPOT, BRIAN, b. c.1695 in Newbury, Co. Berks, Eng., poss. s. of Philip Philpot, gave his age as 32 in 1727; d. c.1768 in Balto. Co. leaving a wid. Mary for whose benefit the Legislature passed an Act allowing her to sell some of her husband's real estate; left iss.: JOHN, d. 1778 at Stamford, Balto. Co.; BRIAN, b. c.1749; ANN, b. c.1762 (12:522, 523; 200-61:461-463; 310; Dunlop's Md. Gaz., 9 June 1778; Balto. Md. Journal, 9 June 1778 and 27 Jan. 1792).

PHIPPER, (---), m. by 22 Sept. 1755 Sarah, dau. of Edward Richards (210-30:26).

PHIPPS, JOHN, m. Mary, wid. of John Willis of Balto. Co., on 28 Dec. 1719 (24:353; 133:148).

PHIPPS, JOHN, of A. A. Co. d. by June 1737; wid. Clare m. as her 2nd husb. William Maccubbin; in Aug. 1739 William Maccubbin gave bond for the balance of the est. (31:50; 32:5).

PHIPS, ROBERT, of Back River, m. by 6 May 1696 Ellis (---) (Md. Courts of Appeals Reports, 1:281).

PICKE, ELSA, age c.30-40, was a runaway conv. serv. from William Mattingly on Patapsco R.; was advert. for in Oct. 1740 (384: 283).

PICKETT/PECKETT, WILLIAM (1), progenitor, m. 1st, some time after 1700 the heiress of Joseph Heathcote; after his death, his wid. (poss. his 2nd w.) m. John Taylor; delegate to the Assembly from Balto. Co. in 1708; d. leaving a will, 1709 - 18 July 1710, naming dau. Mary Miles, son William (to have Foxhole and Waterton's Neglect), son Heathcote, dau. Eliza, son George (not yet 21) (to have Samuel's Delight), dau. Temperance, mentioned a ring bearing the Heathcote coat of arms; by codicil dated 10 June 1710 left 50 a. Inheritance, bought from John Morrow to s. Heathcote; admin. bond was posted 3 Aug. 1710 by extx. Elizabeth, now w. of John Taylor, with John Hayes and John Roberts; est. was inv. 17 Aug. 1710 by Matthew Greene and Moses Groome, and val. at Ł 154.15.4 plus 51,115 lbs. tobacco, and signed by William Pickett and Temperance Love as kin; est. was admin. by Elizabeth, now w. of John Taylor on 2 Aug. 1714; William left iss.: MARY, m. by 20 April 1709 (---) Miles; TEMPERANCE, m. William Lowe on 6 July 1710; WILLIAM; ELIZABETH, in Aug. 1716 bd. herself to William and Elizabeth Holland; may have m. Benjamin Jones; HEATHCOTE, b. 1706; GEORGE, in Aug. 1710 was bd. to Luke Sternborow (Stansbury) to learn trade of carpenter (1:9; 2:319; 12:419; 21:162, 163; 52:107; 122:180; 129:209; 211; 371).

PICKETT, WILLIAM (2), s. of William (1), d. by 2 April 1723 when admin. bond was posted by William Lowe and Benjamin Jones, with Edward Ward and Thomas Preston; est. was inv. on 2 July 1723 by Archibald Rollo and William Hitchcock and val. at Ł 113.10.8, and signed by Heathcote Pickett and Elizabeth Jones as kin and by William Low and William Jones as kin; additional inv. by Rollo and Hitchcock was filed 8 Sept. 1724 and val. at Ł 8.14.4; est. was admin. 8 Sept. 1724, with a notation that he m. Sarah, wid. of Gideon Skaats; had iss. by w. Sarah: SARAH, b. 16 June 1713 (3:15; 12:439; 51:216; 52:31; 131).

PICKETT, HEATHCOTE (3), s. of William (1), was b. c.1706, and acc. to an article by William B. Marye, was hanged during the Rev. War as a Tory, at Joppa Gate; m. 1st, by 26 Oct. 1728 Mary (---), and 2nd, on 26 Jan. 1742 Elizabeth (---), who m. 1st William Wright, and 2nd James Greer; in 1750 owned 100 a. Jacob's

Inheritance, 200 a. Good Hope, and 100 a. Fuller's Outlet; left
iss.: GEORGE, b. 26 Oct. 1728; WILLIAM, b. 7 Nov. 1730; ANN, b.
2 April 1735; LUCRETIA, b. 11 Oct. 1737; JOHN, b. 13 Feb. 1738;
AVARILLA, b. 11 Feb. 1739; (poss. by 2nd w.): ELIZABETH, b. 15
Nov. 1744; HEATHCOTE, b. 20 March 1746 (3:312, 358; 131; 153:42;
340:119).

PICKETT, GEORGE (4), s. of William (1), in Aug. 1710 bd. himself to Luke Stansbury for 3 years; in July 1715 purch. 50 a.
Long Point from John Boring; d. by 4 June 1717 when admin. bond
was posted by Richard Gist with Josephus Murray and William
Hamilton; his wid. Mary renounced the admin.; est. was inv. on
17 Aug. 1717 by Thomas Hooker and George Hitchcock and val. at
₤ 23.3.3 and signed by Sarah Spinks and Luke Stansbury the mother
and bro. of the dec.; m. Mary, dau. of Tobias Stansbury; no record of any children (12:450; 21:163; 48:322; 52:287; 67:383).

PICKETT, GEORGE (5), s. of Heathcote (3), was b. 26 Oct. 1728;
prob. the George who m. Barbara, dau. of Charles Gorsuch, on 16
Feb. 1751; d. by 10 March 1769; and wid. Barbara, now w. of John
Wilkinson admin. the est.; left iss.: WILLIAM, b. 31 March 1752;
ELIZABETH, b. 11 June 1755; MARY, b. 1 Dec. 1759 (5:197; 7:61;
133:96, 97, 103).

PICKETT, JOHN (6), s. of Heathcote (3), was b. 13 Feb. 1738,
m. Pamela Dukes on 3 Oct. 1756; had at least one ch.: WALTER, b.
5 Aug. 1757 (131).

PICKETT, WILLIAM (7), s. of Heathcote (3), was b. 7 Nov.1730
and m. Mary Dukes on 23 Dec. 1756 (129:214).

PICKTON, JAMES, age 16 last 18 Feb., was bd. to Edmund Talbot
in March 1724 to age 21 (39:16).

PICKTON, JOHN, d. by 15 April 1740 when admin. bond was posted
by Thomas White with John Lloyd (12:466).

PIERCE, THOMAS, m. Mary Humphreys on 28 Dec. 1747 (133:161).

PIERCEY, JOSEPH, in Sept. 1672 purch. 100 a. Taylor's Delight
from Robert Taylor (99).

THE PIERPOINT FAMILY is the subject of a chart at the Maryland Historical Society compiled by a Mr. Stickney; unfortunately
there is no documentation for the English generations, so the
pedigree must be accepted with reservations, until such time as
the chart can be verified.

PIERPOINT, GEORGE (1), m. 29 July 1543 at Benington, Herts.,
Eng., Margaret Cook, and had iss.: ROBERT, d. 1619; HENRY, d.
1623: JOANNA, m. Richard Barton on 3 Oct. 1575 at Benington;
MARGARET m. Richard Field on 3 Oct. 1586 at Benington (Stickney chart).

PIERPOINT, ROBERT (2), s. of George (1) and Margaret, d. testate on 1 June 1619; m. Joanna Thorogood on 5 Oct. 1572 at Ardley
or Yardley, Herts.; she d. 4 March 1624 at Watton-on-Stone; Robert had iss.: ROBERT; BARTHOLOMEW; RICHARD; WILLIAM, d. 10 May
1623 at Watton; ELIZABETH (Stickney chart).

PIERPOINT, HENRY (3), s. of George (1) and Margaret, d. 10
March 1623 at Benington, where he m. on 15 Jan. 1572/3 Agnes
Harvey and had iss.: MOSES; ROBERT; RICHARD, d. 1612; AMOS, d.
1638 (Stickney chart).

PIERPOINT, ROBERT (4), s. of Robert (2) and Joanna, m. 4 July 1603 at Watton Elizabeth Searll, and had: ELIZABETH, bapt. 25 April 1610 (Stickney chart).

PIERPOINT, BARTHOLOMEW (5), s. of Robert (2) and Joanna, m. 29 July 1612 at Watton, Co. Herts., Jane Snell; he must have d. by 20 Jan. 1633 when she m. as her 2nd husb. John Jordan; Bartholomew and Jane had: ALLIS, bapt. 4 June 1615; ANN, bapt. 1620/1; WILLIAM, b. and d. 1623 (Stickney chart).

PIERPOINT, ROBERT (6), s. of Henry (3) and Agnes, d. by 1641; m. Ann Brooke on 8 Oct. 1609; had iss.: JOHN, bapt. 1610; MOSES, bapt. 1612; ANN, bapt. 1619, m. Thomas Clark in 1654; ELIZA-BETH, bapt. 1622; ROBERT, bapt. 1625/6 (Stickney chart).

PIERPOINT, AMOS (7), s. of Henry (3) and Agnes, d. 20 March 1638 having made a will; had iss.: HENRY, bapt. 1629 (Stickney chart).

PIERPOINT, ROBERT (8), s. of Robert (6) and Anne, was bapt. 21 Jan. 1625/6 at Braughing, Herts.; m. 3 June 1655 Mary Thurgood, bur. 4 Jan. 1698/9 at All Hallows; had iss.: ROBERT, bapt. 1655/6; THOMAS, bapt. 1658; JOHN, bapt. 1661, came to Md.; MOSES, bapt. 1664 (Stickney chart).

PIERPOINT, HENRY (9), s. of Amos (7), was bapt. 27 May 1629 ... at Benington; imm. to Md. by 1655 with w. Elizabeth and ch. Amos, Jabez, Moses, Elizabeth, and Hannah; became a member of the Society of Friends; had iss.: AMOS, d. 1718, s.p.; JABEZ, d. 1721 s.p.; MOSES; ELIZABETH, m. 1st Thomas Simson, and 2nd Francis Day; HANNAH, b. by 1655; CHARLES, b. c.1680; FRANCIS, d. s.p. having m. Elizabeth Mitchell; MARY, m. Thomas Davis; SARAH, m. Alexander Warfield (388; Stickney chart).

PIERPOINT, JOHN (10), s. of Robert (8), was bapt. 8 May 1661 at Braughing, Herts.; came to Md., where he m. c.1703 Mehitable, wid. of Otho Holland and dau. of John Larkin; had iss.: LARKIN, bapt. 4 Feb. 1703/4 at All Hallows; m. 1st, 18 Nov. 1725 Charity Duckett, and 2nd, in 1730 Sarah Simmons (Stickney chart).

PIERPOINT, AMOS (11), s. of Henry (9), d. testate in A. A. Co., leaving a will, 1 June 1718 - 24 June 1718, naming his bro. Alexander Warfield (123:179).

PIERPOINT, JABEZ (12), s. of Henry (9), d. testate in Balto. Co., leaving a will, 1 Oct. 1720 - 24 April 1721, naming Henry, s. of bro. Charles, the extx. Ellinor Rogers dau. of testator's wife, and Ellinor's ch.: William, Catherine, Ellinor, and Sarah Rogers, his sisters Sidney, Eliza Dea, Mary Davis, and Sarah Warfield; admin. bond was posted 1 Nov. 1724 by Lloyd Harris and wife (3:1, 9; 12:441; 124:48).

PIERPOINT, CHARLES (13), s. of Henry (9), was b. c.1680 in Md.,; d. 1748; m. c.1710, Sydney, dau. of William and Sydney (Wynne) Chew; w. Sydney was b. c.1692 and d. post 1755; on 15 Nov. 1720 Sydney Chew Pierpoint posted admin. bond on the estate of her bro. William Chew; Charles and Sydney had iss.: JOHN; HENRY; FRANCIS, m. Sarah Richardson in 1737; CHARLES, d. 1785; JOSEPH; MISEAL; ABRAHAM; MARY; CHEW; CALEB, m. 28 Feb. 1750 at Elk Ridge Thomas Taylor of Fairfax Mtg., Va., and Fred. Co., Md.; SYDNEY; BATHSHEBA; MARGARET, m. Nicholas Gassaway, Jr.; ELIZABETH, m. Valentine Brown(1:109; 11:294; 26:199; 136; Emison 1962 Supplement, p. 164; McCurley, "Pierpoint Notes," at Md. His. Soc.).

PIERPOINT, CHARLES (14), s. of Charles (13), was b. c.1720, giving his age as 33 in 1753/4; d. 1785; m. Joanna (prob. Randall) in 1750 owned 200 a. Cannon's Lot; had iss. (153:102; 225:245).

PIERPOINT, FRANCIS (15), s. of Charles (13), m. Sarah Richardson, dau. of Joseph and Sarah (Thomas)Richardson, on 19 Jan. 1737/8 at West River Meeting; in Nov. 1750 was granted a certificate to Fairfax Meeting; had iss.: MARY, b. 13 d, 9, 1762 Richard Richardson; OBED, b. 3 d, 9, 1740, m. 1773 Esther Myers; FRANCIS, disowned for marrying out of unity in 1773 (136).

PIGGLAR, CHRISTIAN, in 1750 owned 50 a. part Great Meadows (153:67).

PIGGLAR, JOHN, and wife purchased 100 a. Great Meadows from Andrew Magill in 1742; on 4 Aug. 1746 John and Christian conv. Great Meadows on s. side of Codorus Creek to Peter Lemmon (77: 334; 79:121).

PIKE, (---), m. by 29 May 1742 Ann, dau. of Rebecca Potee (111:80).

PIKE, ELIZABETH, m. Francis Freeman on 17 June 1724 (129:254).

PIKE, JOHN M., m. Mary Poteet on 1 Sept. 1747 (131).

PIKE, or PYKE, MARY, m. William Crabtree on 17 Feb. 1725 (131).

PIKE, SARAH, m. Henry Morgan on 14 May 1744 (131).

PIKE, SARAH, named James Taylor as the father of her child in Nov. 1756 (41:313).

PIKE, WILLIAM, d. by 7 March 1721 when admin. bond was posted by Jarvis Gilbert with John Hall and Joseph Johnson; est. was admin. by Gilbert on 7 June 1722 (2:9; 12:442).

PIKE, WILLIAM, m. by 1741 Ann, admnx. of Abraham Whitacre; in 1750 owned 160 a. Whitacre's Lot; in Sept. 1751 purch. part of Whitacre's Ridge from James Gallion, Jr. (s. of John) and w. Ruth; may be the William Pike who m. Mary Crabtree on 9 June 1752 (4: 120; 81:219; 131; 153:8).

PILE, RALPH, of Chester Co., Penna., purch. 81 a. Isaac's Delight from Isaac and Margery Bullock; in 1750 owned the same tract (80:191; 153:72).

PILGRIM, AMOS, age 16, of Ipswich, Suffolk, Eng., in Feb. 1724 bd. himself to serve 5 years in Md.; m. Rachel McMahon on 25 June 1730; on 2 March 1743 Amos and w. Rachel leased 100 a. Pilgrim's Rest to Skipwith Coale; had iss.: MARY, twin, b. 27 April 1732; RACHEL, b. 27 April 1732; AMOS, b. 21 Aug. 1734; THOMAS, b. 10 Jan. 1736 (77:423; 128:85, 90; 440).

PILLS(?), DAVID, serv. of John Hall of Cranberry, was bur. 13 Nov. 1700 (128:10).

PILLES, THOMAS, m. Margaret Finex in Sept. 1730 (133:149).

PILLY, JOHN, m. Mary Wheely on 8 July 1736 (133:155).

PINDELL, JOHN, s. of Philip and Elizabeth (Holland) Pindell, was b. 8 Dec. 1718 in Queen Anne's Par., P. G. Co.; came to Balto. Co. by 7 Jan. 1744 when he purch. 90 a. Friendship and 77 a. Gist's Search from John Chilcoat; Pindell owned both tracts in

1750; m. 1st Eleanor, dau. of Richard and Mary Bond; she d. 17
June 1756 in her 26th year; he m. 2nd, on 6 Nov. 1757 in St.
Thomas' Parish, Eleanor, dau. of John and Mary (Rogers) Gill;
d. leaving a will, 16 Nov..1788 - 5 Sept. 1789; had iss.: (by
1st w.):ELIZABETH, b. 19 Jan. 1749; PHILIP, b. 29 March 1752;
JOHN, b. 6 Feb. 1754; (by 2nd w.): KATHERINE, b. 13 Sept. 1759;
MARY, b. 22 June 1761; THOMAS, b. 1 Aug. 1763; SARAH, b. 29 June
1765, m. Christopher Bond by lic. 13 Dec. 1787 (78:29; 134:16,
21, 27, 33, 38, 82, 295; 153:72; Queen Anne's Par., P. G. Co.).

PINDER/PINDAR, THOMAS, d. by March 1691/2; wid. and admnx.
Mary m. 2nd Thomas Gillibourn (19:164).

PINDERGRASS, MARY, serv., with 2 years to serve was listed in
the 1749 inv. of Capt. Robert North (53:373).

PINE, EASTER, m. Henry Burk on 6 Jan. 1706/7 (129:201).

PINES, CHARLES (1), m. 1st (unidentified); m. 2nd, in Aug.
1741, Eliz. Bayes; gave his age as 36 in a dep. of July 1743;
had iss.: (by 1st w.): ABRAHAM, b. 20 April 1738(?); (by 2nd w.):
PRISCILLA, b. 7 Feb. 1742 (131:100/r; 224:84).

PINES, ABRAHAM (2), s. (or orphan?) of Charles (1), "age 15"
in March 1746/7, with the consent of his father (sic) was bd.
to George Presbury; m. Phillis Beven on 11 Sept. 1754 (36:382;
131).

PINKHAM, RICHARD, m. Phillis Noble on 26 Nov. 1733; was made
levy free in June 1743; in 1750 owned 50 a. Matthews' Forest (34:
190; 133:151; 153:77).

PINKSTON, PETER, on 25 Aug. 1725 gave his age as c.58 (70:191).

PINKSTON, WILLIAM, m. Martha, dau. of Ambrose Nelson of Balto.
Co., on 4 March 1716/7 in St. Anne's Par. Reg., A. A. Co. (125:
112; 219-2:398).

PINKSTON, WILLIAM, m. Ann Inman in Oct. 1743; had iss.: JOHN,
b. 24 July 1744; NAOMI, b. 18 Dec. 1745; GREENBERRY, b. 17 April
1747 (131).

PINKTON, MARGARET, was ind. for bast. in March 1737/8 (31:168).

PISSIONS, WILLIAM, m. Ann, relict of William Pearce; d. by
Nov. 1692; Ann placed her five ch. in care of William Wilkinson
who pet. the court; she m. 3rd Stephen Bentley (19:307).

PITSTOW, PHILIP (1), d. by Nov. 1692; had iss.: PHILIP (19:
308).

PITSTOW, PHILIP (2), s. of Philip (1), gave his age as 30 in
1714; in Nov. 1692 he was bd. to William Wilkinson; d. by 22
Sept. 1723 when admin. bond was posted by Mary Pitstow with Henry Jones and Samuel Harryman; a 2nd admin. bond was posted 27
Jan. 1724 by Henry Jones with Nathaniel Darby and John Moorecock;
est. was inv. in 1724 and 1745; est. was admin. on 26 Feb. 1726
(3:59; 12:438, 452; 19:308; 51:226; 52:179; 203-3:108; 310).

PITSTOW, ROBERT LOVE, m. Anne Royston on 23 Sept. 1736 (133:
155).

PLANT, ELIZABETH, living at John Giles, was ind. for bast. in
Nov. 1724 (27:32).

PLATER, GEORGE, in 1750 owned 250 a., part Tasker's Camp
(153:103).

PLATT, BRAY, tailor, m. Elizabeth (---), and d. by 26 May
1718 when admin. bond on his est. was posted by the wid. Elizabeth with Joseph Gostwick and James Ford; est. was inv. on 28
May 17(?) by Moses Edwards and Isaac Sampson, and val. at
£ 13.2.8; had iss.: COMFORT, b. 12 April 1712; BRAY, b. 6 April
1716 (12:432; 51:55; 133:10).

PLATT, JOHN, age c.24, husbandman from Staffordshire, Eng.,
ran away from the Baltimore Ironworks in Nov. 1752 and July
1752; had been imported the prev. Fall in the Biddeford, comman-
ded by John Knell (307-69:208; 385:208).

PLOWMAN, JONATHAN (1), m. by Feb. 1713/4 Ann (---) mother of
Richard Vickory, to whom John and Ann conv. certain prop.;   d.
by 30 March 1747; had iss.: RACHEL, b. 22 Feb. 1715; JONATHAN,
b. 25 Feb. 1717; prob. JOHN (67:359; 79:386; 133:3).

PLOWMAN, JONATHAN (2), s. of Jonathan (1) and Ann, was b.
25 Feb. 1717; m. Elizabeth (---); in Aug. 1740 he and John
Plowman were conv. 50 a. Jacks Double Purchase by their cousin
Richard King Stevenson; on 30 March 1747 Jonathan Plowman (with
consent of w. Elizabeth), Ann Plowman (mother of Jonathan) and
John Plowman (Jonathan's bro.) conv. 50 a. Selsed, called Jack's
Double Purchase, to Thomas Ford; had iss.: STEVENSON, b. 27 June
1749; JAMES, b. 24 Sept. 1751; JONATHAN, b. 13 Feb. 1754; RICH-
ARD, b. 23 Dec. 1756; EDWARD, b. 12 March 1759 (75:438; 79:
386; 134:16, 21, 23, 27; 153:74).

PLOWMAN, JOHN (3), s. of Jonathan (1) and Ann, is mentioned
as half bro. of Richard Stevenson Vickory c.1735; m. Sarah Chambers on 3 May 1736; was conv. land in 1740, and helped to sell
the same tract in 1747 (but his wife Sarah is not mentioned)
(75:438; 79:386; 133:155).

PLOWMAN, MARY, had a bast. ch. bd. to Lloyd Harris in June
1729 (28:142).

PLOWRIGHT, ANN, in Aug. 1756 was ind. for bearing three bast.;
she was tried, and her three ch.: GEORGE, age 8, NERO, age 6,
and ROGER, age 4, were to be sold (41:223).

PLUMMER, ANN, m. Anthony Bob on 18 June 1717 (129:216).

THE POCOCK FAMILY is the subject of a typescript by Edward
Kinsey Voorhees, "Notes on the Pocock Family," dated May 1930,
at the Maryland Historical Society.

POCOCK, DANIEL (1), was in Balto. Co. as early as Aug. 1730
and was still there in Aug. 1752; not mentioned by Voorhees, but
his existence is established by these facts: in Aug. 1730, Salem Pocock, 2 years old, s. of Daniel, was bound to Archibald
and Marianna Rollo to age 21; on 15 Feb. 1743 Thomas Brerewood
leased part of My Lady's Manor to Daniel Pocock, the lease to
run for the lifetimes of Pocock's wife, age 53, son John, 17,
and son Abel. age 10; in Aug. 1752 Daniel Pocock, Sr., living
on the forks of Gunpowder, advert. for a runaway servant; had
iss.: DANIEL, b. c.1720; JOHN, b. c.1726; SALEM, b. c.1728;
ABEL, b. c.1733; poss. JAMES, m. Jemima Barton on 20 Sept. 1756;
poss. ELIZABETH who m. Skelton Standiford on 4 Nov. 1755; DAVID;
and poss. SUSAN who m. Ephraim Rutledge on 6 Feb. 1766 (29:5;
77:450; 131; 385:90).

POCOCK, DANIEL, Jr. (2), s. of Daniel (1), was called Daniel Pocock, Jr., when he m. Sarah Jones on 26 June 1751; acc. to Voorhees he was b. c.1720, and d. 1800; his w. was b. 1728, and d. 6 Feb. 1818; had iss.: SALEM, b. 26 March 1753, m. Mary Huim (sic); DANIEL, b. 24 March 1755; m. Fanny Hayes and moved to Wayne Co., Ohio; MARY, b. 11 April 1757, m. William Galloway on 20 Feb. 1774 (Voorhees gives her husband's name as Thomas Galloway); JAMES, b. 15 March 1759, m. Nancy Fugate and moved to Butler Co., Ohio; JESSE, b. 20 June 1760, m. Catherine and moved to Fulton Co., Ohio; ELEANOR, b. 26 May 1762, m. Charles Rockhold; SUSANNA, b. 15 Sept. 1764, m. Cornelius Garrison; DAVID, b. 11 Nov. 1766, m. Mary Smith; CHARITY, b. 13 Dec. 1768, m. James Brown; ELIJAH, b. 29 Dec. 1770, m. Catherine Hughes and moved to Wayne Co., Ohio; CHARLOTTE, b. 30 Oct. 1774, m. John Sharp (131; Voorhees).

POCOCK, JOHN (3), s. of Daniel (1), was b. c.1726, and was age 17 in 1743 when he was named in his father's lease of My Lady's Manor; m. Ruth Gott on 30 Nov. 1757; d. leaving a will, 1 March 1791 - 14 June 1791; had iss.: SUTTON; SUSANNA; GEORGE; THOMAS; JOSHUA; JOHN; ASHEL; DILEY (may be the Delilah Pocock who m. Edward Kelly on 12 Nov. 1789); ELIZABETH (113:551; 131).

POCOCK, SALEM (4), s. of Daniel (1), was b. c.1728, and in Aug. 1730 at age 2 years and 5 mos. when he was bound to Archibald Rollo; no further record (29:5).

POCOCK, ABEL (5), s. of Daniel (1), was b. c.1733, and was age 10 in 1743 when his father named him in the abovementioned lease.

POCOCK, JAMES (6), poss. s. of Daniel (1), m. Jemima Barton on 20 Sept. 1756 (131).

POCOCK, SUSANNA, was assaulted by Samuel Hendon in June 1733 (30:16).

POGUE. See POLLOCK.

POLION, ANNE, m. Joseph Rhodous in June 1725 (131).

POLLARD, WILLIAM, m. Rebecca Hays on 2 Oct. 1752 (131).

POLLARD, WILLIAM, m. Elizabeth Smith on 13 Oct. 1753 (131).

POLLARD, WILLIAM, m. Mary Hildebrand on 19 May 1755 (131).

POLLETT, WILLIAM, m. Elizabeth Hall in 1753 (131).

POLLOCK/POLOKE/POGUE, DANIEL (1), m. Jane Antil on 25 Jan. 1737; was in Balto. Co. by Jan. 1732 when he wit. the will of Mary Buchanan; on 1 Nov. 1744 Daniel Poloke and John Hampton purch. 50 a. Conquest and 50 a. Hall's Park from Francis and Blanche Bucknall; Daniel prob. d. by 19 July 1748, for on that date Jane m. James Cole; had iss.: ANN, b. 3 March 1742, may have m. William Judd; MARY, b. 30 April 1745 (77:660; 126:23; 129:300, 360).

POLLOCK, JOHN (2), no known rel. to Daniel, m. Sarah, dau. of Mary Buchanan by 17 Jan. 1732; Mary Buchanan named her grandson Joseph Poloke in her will; on 31 May 1750 John Pogue and w. Sarah conv. Brotherly Love and Johnson's Rest to Jacob Giles; had iss.: JOSEPH, b. 22 Nov. 1724; MARY, b. 7 Feb. 1725; ELIZABETH, b. 28 April 1734; ANN, b. 29 Jan. 1735, m. Zachariah Spencer on 29 Sept. 1755; GEORGE, b. 16 April 1738; WILLIAM, b. 7 April 1740 (81:3; 126:23; 128:46, 79, 82; 129:321, 373).

POLLOCK, or POGUE, JOSEPH (3), s. of John (2), was b. 22 Nov. 1724; m. Sarah Farmer on 30 July 1752; had iss.: SUSANNA, b. 1 July 1755; JOHN, b. 3 Dec. 1756; HANNAH, b. 10 April 1758; SARAH, b. 24 June 1759; ANN, b. 3 Sept. 1762 (129:375).

POLLOCK, or POGUE, GEORGE (4), s. of John (2), was b. 16 April 1738; may be the George Polock listed in the 1790 Census of Balto. Town (128:100; 1790 Census of Md., p. 18).

POLTON, WILLIAM, serv. with 6 years and 2 mos. to serve, was listed in the 1746 inv. of John Mahone (53:260).

PONTENAY. See PUNTENAY.

POOLE, JOHN, was in Balto. Co. by Nov. 1672 when he purch. 175 a. at Omelly's Creek from James Macgreegory (99:347).

POOLE or PULLEY, LANCELOT, was in Balto. Co. by 1692 as a taxable in n. side of Patapsco (138).

POOR/POWER, NICHOLAS, was in Balto. Co. by 1692 as a taxable in n. side of Patapsco Hund.; d. by 1703 when his est. was inv. by Thomas Roberts and Joseph Gostwick and val. at £ 23.19.4; his est. was admin. by James Poor on 19 May 1704 (1:345; 51:127; 138).

POPEJOY, WILLIAM, was in Balto. Co. by Aug. 1719 when John Newman and others complained that he had blocked a road (338:117).

POREY, JOSEPH, d. by Nov. 1684; left iss.: JOHN, b. c.1673, age 11 in Nov. 1684 when he was bd. to John Bird (18:213).

PORLIN, SIMON, serv. of Maj. Thomas Long, was judged to be between 15 and 18 in March 1685/6 (18:397).

PORT, ELIZABETH, was tried for bast. in Nov. 1754; named one Philip Quinlin as the father (39:461).

PORTER, AARON, m. Jane MacKenny on 19 Aug. 1740; had iss.: THOMAS, b. 9 Jan. 1742 (128:114, 119:329).

PORTER, AGNES, widow, in Aug. 1750 purch. Meadow Land from Stephen Onion; the deed mentioned her s.: ALEXANDER (80:557).

PORTER, JOHN, m. Anne (---); in 1750 he owned 100 a. Ashmole's Retirement and 100 a. Meadow Land; had iss.: JANE, b. 25 Jan. 1742 (129:331; 153:74).

PORTER, NATHANIEL, m. by 25 Jan. 1744 Sarah (---) who on that day joined him in selling 150 a. Jones' Gift to John and William Montgomery; in Sept. 1744 he purch. 100 a. Brother's Discovery from Thomas and Jane Renshaw (77:572; 78:14).

PORTER, THOMAS, was listed in the 1725 inv. of John Israel as a serv. with one year to serve; prob. the Thomas who m. by 13 July 1734 Eleanor (---) who on that day joined him in selling 100 a. Crowley's Venture to William Rogers; in 1750 owned 50 a. Porter's Hall, which he conv. in 1779 to Philip Porter; had iss.: THOMAS, b. 2 April 1736; ELIZABETH, b. 14 June 1737 (52:184; 74:107; 133:55; 134:12; 153).

POSEN, (---), a mulatto woman, bore three ch. out of wedlock; in June 1718 the ch. were bd. to serve Rebecca Day; had iss.: ANN, REBECCA; JOSEPH (22:226).

POSEY, MARY, d. by Aug. 1725; est. was admin. by Francis Posey (27:352).

POTEET/POTEE/PETEET, FRANCIS (1), progenitor, was in Balto. Co. by 3 Jan. 1667/8 and d. there by 1688; was certainly dec. by Nov. 1692; m. Mary (---) who may have m. as her 2nd husb. Michael Hastings, some time before 1688; on 3 Jan. 1667/8 purch. 80 a. of land from Richard and Mary Ball (prob. Gunworth, 81 a. orig. surv. for Walter Dixon and later held by Francis "Petite"); is stated in the Rent Roll to have died without heirs, but on another page is said to have died leaving one daughter; was the father of. SUSANNA; poss. FRANCIS, d. c.1709; poss. LEWIS; poss. JOHN, d. by 1721; poss. PETER, d. c.1740 (19:304; 95:356; 211:91-92).

POTEET, SUSANNA (2), dau. of Francis (1), formerly the ward of Benjamin Stanley; in Nov. 1692 Anthony Johnson pet. to be her guardian; she died under mysterious circumstances, and in March 1692/3 Anthony's wife was tried for Susanna's Murder; later Johnson himself was also tried (19:304, 347, 411).

POTEET, FRANCIS (3), poss. s. of Francis (1), d. in Balto. Co. by 3 Aug. 1709; m. Lucy (---) who m. as her 2nd husb. John Swinyard; d. leaving a will, 3 June 1707 - 3 Aug. 1709, in which he named his bro. John, wife Lucy, and dau. Mary; admin. bond was posted 4 Aug. 1709 by Lucy "Potee;" est. was inv. on 9 Feb. 1709/10 by John Deaver and John Webster, and val. at £ 76.12.8; his only relations were three bros. who lived at the house of the extx. and who refused to sign the inv.; est. was admin. by Lucy, now w. of John Swinyard, on 8 Oct. 1712; had iss.: MARY, not yet 16 in 1707; may be the Mary who m. George Ogg, Jr., on 22 Aug. 1722 (1:354; 12:42; 48:354; 122:145; 133:155).

POTEET, LEWIS (4), poss. s. of Francis (1), and def. bro. of Francis (3), may be the Lewis who m. Catherine Green on 12 June 1722, and had at least two ch., on 2 Nov. 1726, Lewis and w. Katherine, dau. and coheir of Matthew Green, and granddau. of Jane Boone, conv. part Levy's Tribe, Green's Chance, and Choice Tripass, to Thomas Cole; had is.: REBECCA, b. 9 Dec. 1722; and ANN, b. 5 Oct. 1727 (70:290; 131:17, 10/r).

POTEET, JOHN (5), poss. s. of Francis (1), and def. bro. of Francis (3) and Lewis (4),; was named in the 1709 will of his bro. Francis, d. by 2 May 1721 when admin. bond on his est. was posted by w. Elizabeth, with James Durham and Joseph Elledge; his wid. Elizabeth m. as her 2nd husband John Powell who joined her in admin. John's estate; in Aug. and Nov. 1723 his heirs were named in the court proceedings; had iss.: JOHN; REBECKAH, b. 9 Oct. 1712, m. John Everett; SUSANNA, b. 8 Feb. 1715; ABRA-HAM, b. 20 June 1715 (12:443; 25:427; 26:89-92; 131).

POTEET, PETER (6), poss. s. of Francis (1), and def. bro. of Francis (3), Lewis (4), and John (5), d. by 2 April 1740; m. Rebecca (poss. Bond) who d. c.1758; on 15 July 1737 John Baker conv. 200 a. Preston's Luck to Rebecca, w. of Peter Potee; Peter d. leaving a will, 5 Oct. 1733 - 2 April 1740, naming w. Rebecca, ch. Lewis, Catherine Miles, Rebecca Fovy or Foyy, Ann Whitaker, Sarah Preston, and Mary and Elizabeth; in 1750 Rebecca owned 200 a. Preston's Luck; her will, 29 May 1742 - 28 March 1755, named ch. Lewis, Catherine Miles, Rebecca Foy, Ann Pike, Sarah Preston, Mary Clark or Chalk, and Elizabeth; Peter and Rebecca had iss.: LEWIS (in 1750 owned 125 a. Bond's Last Shift and

200 a. **Burr**) CATHERINE, m. Thomas Miles by 18 Aug. 1719; REBEC-
CA, m. Thomas Foy on or by 18 Jan. 1726; ANN, m. 1st Abraham
Whitacre on 15 July 1725, and m. 2nd William Pike; SARAH m.
James Preston, Jr., in 1733; MARY, m. (---) Chalk; ELIZABETH
(61:516; 111:80; 127:75; 131; 153:8, 106).

POTEET, JOHN (7), s. of John (5), m. Ann, extx. of William
Noble; in May 1734, John Poteet, Jr., and w. Ann conv. 179 a.
Hereford to Thomas Miles; may be the John Poteet who in 1750
owned 100 a. Bear's Range and 100 a. Good Luck; on 9 March 1732
John conv. his Niece Mary, dau. of John and Rebecca Everett some
property (30:107; 73:337; 74:53; 153:39).

POTEET, FRANCIS m. Elizabeth (---), and had iss.: FRANCIS,
b. 30 Sept. 1737; BENJAMIN, b. 17 Nov. 1737(?); WILLIAM, b. 5
Jan. 1739; JOHN, b. 12 Feb. 1750 (133:59, 69, 93).

POTEET/POTTEE, JAMES, m. Elizabeth (---), and had iss.: LEWIS
b. 23 Oct. 1722; CATHERINE, b. 2 Nov. 1725; JAMES, b. 2 July
1728; MARY, b. 19 Oct. 1720 (131).

POTEET, JAMES, m. Elizabeth Crabtree on 20 Sept. 1748 (131).

POTEET, REBECCA, was tried for bast. in Nov. 1756 and named
Thomas Norris as the father (41:311).

POTEET, WILLIAM, purch. 100 a. Harris' Delight from John and
Dorothy Harris on 4 June 1735; d. by 6 May 1741 when admin. bond
was posted by Johanna Poteet with Abraham Jarrett and William
Crabtree, Jr.; William m. Jane (or Johanna)Stewart on 12 June
1733; she m. 2nd, by 1 Dec. 1744 John Ramsey, on which day they
admin. William's est.; had iss.: JOHN, b. 29 May 1734; ISABEL,
b. 22 Dec. 1736; MARY, b. 31 Aug. 1739 (5:1; 12:473; 36:209; 74:
224; 128:76, 80, 98, 105).

POTTER, JOHN, d. by 1721 when his est. was inv. (51:325).

POTTY, ANN, serv. to John Fuller, was tried for bast. in Aug.
1743 (35:13).

POULSON, CORNELIUS (1), was in Md. by Feb. 1717 when he wit.
the will of John Hitchcock; m. Ann Empson on 23 Dec. 1720, dau.
of James and Rebecca Empson; in July 1757 Cornelius and Ann,
formerly of Balto. Co., now of Fred. Co., conv. 100 a. Elberton
(which descended to Ann Poulson as a dau. of James Empson; had
iss.; ELIZABETH, b. 6 Jan. 1720/1; REBECCA, b. 5 Oct. 1724; AN-
DREW, b. 18 Feb. 1734 (sic) (83:22; 123:129; 128:41; 129:226).

POULSON, ANDREW (2), s. of Cornelius (1), was b. 18 Feb.
1734; d. 1807 in Fred. Co.; m. by 27 Nov. 1758 Prudence, dau.
of John Evans (5:237).

POULSON, ELIZABETH, was tried for bast. in June 1730 (28:421).

POULSON, ELIZABETH, was exempt from the levy in June 1737
(31:49).

POULSON, FRANCIS, in March 1757 conv. to William Dallam 83 a.
Polson's Lot and part My Lady's Manor (82:648).

POULSON, HANNAH, serv. to Edward Day, was tried for bast.
in June 1743; ind. and tried again in Nov. 1745; as a serv. to
Avarilla Day was tried for bast. in March 1746/7; had iss.:
JOSEPH (34:203; 35:734, 748; 36:417).

POULSON, JOHN, age 13, s. of Elizabeth Poulson; formerly bd. to Nicholas Day; in June 1739 was bd. to Elizabeth Day (32:403).

POULSON, JOSEPH, m. Frances Allen in 1739, and had iss.: NATHANIEL, b. 29 April 1740; JOSEPH, b. 2 Aug. 1748 (131).

POULSON, REBECCA, was ind. for bast. in Aug. 1742 and tried in Nov. 1742; ind. for bast. again in March 1750/1 (34:1, 73; 38:270).

POWELL, JOHN (1), was in A. A. Co. with James Powell by 1 April 1686 when they surv. 125 a. Powell's Inheritance on the south side of Severn River; John's w. Elizabeth later m. Thomas Jacks; John and Elizabeth had iss.. JOHN, d. by 15 Aug. 1726; JOSEPH (211; 70:276; 123:70).

POWELL, JOHN (2), d. in A. A. Co. leaving a will 7 Nov. 1715 - 6 April 1716, naming bro. Joseph and mother Eliza. Jacks (123:70).

POWELL, JOSEPH (3), s. of John (1), was alive on 15 Aug. 1726 when he conv. Powell's Inheritance to his (half-)bro. Richard Jacks (70:276).

POWELL, BENJAMIN, m. Mary Pierpoint of A. A. Co. on 24 d, 1 mo., 1755 (136).

POWELL, DANIEL, m. Mary (---) and had iss.: ELIZABETH, b. 31 Aug. 1750 (133:94).

POWELL, HOWELL, imm. to Md. by 1659; assigned a pat. to William Lewis in Aug. 1662; assigned 100 a. Powell's Neck to Philip Stevenson in Nov. 1663; in 1667 he conv. w. Elizabeth conv. 70 a. adj. to Robert Gorsuch's land to Warner Shudall (93).

POWELL, JAMES, m. Elizabeth (---) and had iss.: JAMES, b. 11 April 1720; REBECCA, b. 18 Jan. 1723; PHILIP, b. 29 June 1725, d. 2 Dec. 1728 (133:4, 9, 193).

POWELL, JAMES, m. by 20 Oct. 1724 Rebecca, wid. and extx. of Richard Colegate; had iss.: ELINOR, b. 18 May 1728 (1:322; 3:7; 133:17).

POWELL, JAMES, m. by 17 Oct. 1737 Eleanor, dau. of Richard Hewett (3:250).

POWELL, JAMES, d. by 16 Nov. 1744 when admin. bond was posted by Burridge Scott of A. A. Co. with William Mattingly and Wm. Ensor; est. was admin. by Burridge Scott on 10 Sept. 1746 (4:135; 12:471).

POWELL, JOHN, was in Balto. Co. by Nov. 1670 when William and Isabel Pearce conv. him and Thomas Weymouth 150 a. Neve's Choice; in Aug. 1672 he conv. his share of the latter tract to Weymouth (96:232; 98:47).

POWELL, JOHN, serv. with 21 mos. to serve in inv. of Aquila Paca, Aug. 1722 (50:142).

POWELL, JOHN, m. by 2 July 1722 Eliza, extx. of John Poteet; on 7 Aug. 1733 they conv. 100 a. Powell's Choice to Jacob Bull; on 15 May 1734 they quitclaimed Herriford (Hereford?) to John Poteet, Jr. (73:407; 74:55).

POWELL, JOHN, m. Philis (---) in Sept. 1725; on 29 Oct. 1725 they conv. 150 a. The Fork to Solomon Armstrong; had iss.: ELEA-

NOR, b. 3 Nov. 1726; HANNAH PENINAH WINIFRED, b. 7 March 1722 (?) (70:19; 128:49, 56; 131).

POWELL, MARY, was sentenced to death for the murder of Mrs. Clark in Feb. 1752 (385:164).

POWELL, PATIENCE, als. Connor, was ind. for bast. in March 1750/1 (38:270).

POWELL, REBECCA, in 1736 was named as testator's mother in the will of Simon Gregory of Balto. Co. (126:196).

POWELL, RICHARD, d. 16 Feb. 1715/6 (128:34).

POWELL, THOMAS, imm. by 1659; was one of the commissioners of Balto. Co. in June 1661; purch. 287½ a. Roade River from Walter Dickenson in June 1659; in March 1661/2 purch. part of 300 a. from Richard Gorsuch; by Aug. 1664 was in Talbot Co., Md. (93; 95; 200-3:424; 388).

POWELL, WILLIAM, d. by March 1737/8; left iss.: JOHN, b. c. 1727, age 10 on 31 Dec. 1737 when he was bd. to Walter Tolley; WILLIAM, b. c.1732, age 6 in Oct. 1738, bd. to John Starkey in March 1737/8 (31:169).

POWER, JAMES, m. by March 1746 Sarah, dau. of George Linager of Kent Co.; she was granddau. of John Linager who owned 200 a. John's Habitation; in 1753 James owned 200 a. of the same tract (79:537; 153:92).

POWER, NICHOLAS, m. by 1753 Eliza., extx. of Eric Errickson, and had iss.: JAMES, b. 24 Nov. 1753 (5:285; 131).

PRATT, WILLIAM, d. by 11 June 1745 when admin. bond was posted by Jacob Giles with John Paca and N. Ruxton Gay, Pratt's wid. Ann having renounced the right to admin. (12:474).

PREBLE, THOMAS (1), progenitor, was 21 and over on 20 Aug. 1684 when he bd. himself to Robert Shanks of Wapping, Mddx., to serve Shanks or his assigns for 4 years after his arrival in Md.; m. Mary (---) who m. as her 2nd husb. Archibald Buchanan; was granted 100 a. Hazard on w. side of Swan Creek; in June 1699 Nathaniel Andrews made a will naming Ann and John, ch. of Thomas Preble, and witnessed by Mary Preble; on 4 March 1703/4 James Ives made a will naming Thomas' sons John and Thomas; d. by Nov. 1704; admin. bond was posted 19 July (?) 1704 by wid. and admnx. Mary Preble with John Hall; est. was inv. on 3 Jan. 1703/4 by Thomas Greenfield and Thomas Carr, and val. at ℒ 49.17.0; est. was admin. by Archibald and Mary Buchanan on 30 Sept. 1706; Mary, former w. of Thomas Preble, and later w. of Archibald Buchanan d. leaving a will, 17 Jan. 1732 - 6 June 1733, naming grandsons Perry, James, and Samuel Brown, s. John Preble, grandch. Sarah and Thomas Preble, daus. Elizabeth Simpson, granddau. Hannah Simpson, dau. Sarah Poloke and grandson Joseph Poloke, dau. Ann Hawkins, granddau. Elizabeth Hawkins (dau of Robert), son Archibald, son John Poloke, and son-in-law William Simpson; Thomas and Mary had iss.: ANN, b. 8 Nov. 1689, m. Robert Hawkins on 15 Nov. 1709; THOMAS, b. 27 July 1691; MARY, b. 6 June 1695; JOHN, b. 21 June 1696; ELIZABETH, b. 27 Dec. 1699, m. William Simpson; SARAH, b. 12 Aug. 1702, m. John Poloke (2:233; 12:427; 18:222; 48:67; 121:178; 122:30; 126:33, 128:1, 5, 7, 13, 16; 211).

PREBLE, JOHN (2), s. of Thomas (1), was b. 21 June 1697 in St. George's Par. and was alive on 6 June 1759 when he conv. prop. to his s. Stephen; m. Ann, dau. of John Gallion; in 1750 John Preble owned 80 a. Neighbor's Goodwill and 50 a. West Favor;

in 1733 Archibald Buchanan named Sarah and Thomas Preble as his
grandch.; John and Ann had iss.: SARAH, b. 22 Dec. 1719; THOMAS,
b. 25 March 1724; MARY, b. 3 Oct. 1726, may have m. William Rigdon; SOPHIA, b. 25 March 1733; STEPHEN, b. 15 Aug. 1736; JAMES,
b. 21 Jan. 1739 (47:50; 125:200; 128:5, 44, 49, 93A, 106; 153:
62).

PREBLE, THOMAS (3), s. of John (2), was b. 5 March 1724; may
have m. Elizabeth Teegarden by whom he had: THOMAS, Jr., m. Hannah Enoch; RACHEL, m. George Teagarden in 1763; JOB; REUBEN
(128:44).

PREBLE, JOHN, m. by 12 July 1758 a dau. of James Law or Lowe
of Balto. Co. (4:321; 6:2½).

PRESBURY, JOSEPH (1), of London, married Hannah Bradford, and
according to an article by William B. Marye in the Maryland
Historical Magazine, was the father of: JAMES, b. c.1684; JOS-
EPH, d. 7 June 1724 (342:249).

PRESBURY, JAMES (2), poss. s. of Joseph (1), was b- c.1684
and d. in Balto. Co. c.1746; m. 1st, on 26 Feb. 1708, Martha
Goldsmith (coheiress with Mary w. of William Marshall); m. 2nd
Anne (Burney); James d. leaving a will, 3 Dec. 1744 - 2 Jan. 1746,
naming ch. George, Martha Garrettson, Thomas Burney alias Presbury, William, Sarah, Hannah, Elizabeth, Susanna, Mary, and John;
admin. bond was posted 24 March 1746 by Thomas Burney als. Presbury with William Bradford and James Maxwell; est. admin. 3 June
1749; dec. left 4 ch. by 1st w., and 8 by his 2nd w.: GEORGE,
b. 18 Aug. 1710; MARY, b. 22 Feb. 1712/3; JOHN, b. 18 Oct. 1716
(in March 1733/4 his father pet. he be exempt from the levy);
MARTHA, b. 27 Oct. 1718, m. 1st Bennett Garrett, 2nd (---) Todd,
and 3rd, on 1 Nov. 1744 George Garrettson; (by 2nd w.): THOMAS
BURNEY; ELIZABETH; WILLIAM, d. 1774; SUSANNA , m. Samuel Cross;;
SARAH; GEORGE BEDLE; HANNAH, b. 3 Aug. 1726; BRADFORD, b. 5 Oct.
1728 (5:90; 12:470; 30:189; 128:25; 129:207; 131; 200-38:417;
210-24:542; Kenneth W. Cameron, "Chart of the Presbury Family,"
at Md. Hist. Society).

PREBSURY, JOSEPH (3), s. of Joseph (1), d. 7 June 1724; m.
Mrs. Eleanor Carlisle, extx. of John Rallings, on 11 July 1723;
she m. as her (4th?) husband Henry Wetherall on 20 Dec. 1724; in
Aug. 1718 Presbury qualified as Clerk Assistant to the Baltimore
County Court; admin. bond was posted 3 March 1724 by Henry
Wetherall with John Crockett and Theophilus Jones; est. was inv.
18 Feb. 1725/6 by John Dorsey and Thomas Tolley and val. at £9.2.4;
est. was admin. by Henry Wetherall on 10 April 1726; Joseph and
Eleanor had iss.: JOSEPH, age 14 in Sept. 1738 (2:333; 3:46; 12:
454; 23:3; 26:254; 51:51; 131).

PRESBURY, GEORGE (4), s. of James (2) and Martha, was b. 18 ·
Aug. 1710, and d. 1786; m. 1st Mary (---), and 2nd, by 20 Sept.
1742, Isabella, admnx. of John Bond, and dau. of William Robinson; in 1750 owned 500 a. Sawyer's Mount, 46 a. Oglesby's Mount,
50 a. Small Hopes, 410 a. Elk Neck, and other lands; had iss.
(by 1st w.): GEORGE GOLDSMITH, b. 1 May 1737; (by 2nd w.):
WILLIAM ROBINSON, b. 20 Sept. 1742 (chose his father to be his
guardian in Aug. 1759); MARTHA, b. 19 May 1749, m. George Garrettson in 1768; GEORGE, b. 22 April 1754 (4:464; 35:159; 79:34;
131; 153:24; Presbury Chart by Cameron).

PRESBURY, THOMAS (5), s. of James (2) and Ann, was alive in
1759 having m. Ann Woodward in Dec. 1749; in 1750 he owned 65 a.
Oxford which he inher. from his father; had iss.: MARY, b. 1751;
JOHN, b. 1755; HANNAH, b. 1759 (131; 153:31).

PRESBURY, JOSEPH (6), s. of Joseph (3), was b. c.1724, and was alive in 1769; m. Sarah Pycraft on 11 Jan. 1749; in Nov. 1738 he pet. the court that Henry Wetherall had m. his mother and had made a will leaving a plantation to him; in March 1738/9 he chose William Bradford as his guardian; in 1750 he owned 191 a. Carlisle's Neglect; had iss.: MARY, b. 29 Oct. 1750; ELEANOR, b. 19 Nov. 1752; JOSEPH, b. 5 Sept. 1758; THOMAS PYCRAFT, b. 7 May 1761; JAMES, b. 10 Feb. 1764; WILLIAM, b. 2 Dec. 1766; HENRY, b. 18 June 1769 (31:310; 32:352; 131; 153:80).

PRESBURY, GEORGE GOLDSMITH (7), s. of George (4), was b. 1 May 1737; m. Elizabeth Tolley on 10 June 1756; had iss.: MARY GOLD-SMITH, b. 1 July 1758; GEORGE GOLDSMITH, b. 21 Feb. 1759; MARTHA GOLDSMITH, b. 7 May 1761; WALTER GOLDSMITH, b. 11 Sept. 1764; FRANCIS GOLDSMITH, b. 17 Feb. 1766; JAMES TOLLEY, b. 31 Oct. 1772 (131:47, 148/r).

PRESGROVE, BARNETT, age 8 last 1 Nov., was bd. to Robert Brierly, Sr., and Robert, Jr., in Aug. 1757 (46:58).

PRESGROVE, GEORGE, servant, was listed in the 1742 inv. of Charles Rockhold (53:413).

THE PRESTON FAMILY was the subject of John Frederick Preston's Preston Genealogical Story (Washington: 1963) hereinafter cited as Preston.

PRESTON, THOMAS (1), progenitor, was in Balto. Co. by 7 Nov. 1677 when Edward Reeves conv. him 43 a. Chance; prob. the Thomas Preston who was named as exec. of Thomas Arminger on 21 June 1667; claimed land for service in 1680; d. in Balto. Co. by 1710 having m. Mary, heiress of Joseph Hewes; in Dec. 1681 was conv. 25 a. George's Hill by Arthur Taylor and w. Frances; on 20 Feb. 1701 Thomas and w. Mary conv. Pitchcraft to Robert Shaw; on 2 March 1701 the Prestons conv. 242 a. Aberly Lodge to Charles Baker, and on 2 March 1702 they conv. 200 a. of Preston's Luck to Isaac Baker of Calvert Co.; Preston d. leaving a will, 7 Dec. 1708 - 30 Dec. 1710, leaving to his w. 43 a. of Chance and 30 a. Lodwick's Refuse; to s. Thomas he left Preston's Chance, son James to have Friendship, dau. Sarah Skats to have Broadwell Hill, and dau. Esther Raven to have one-half of Cheapside; also named granddau. Katherine Skats; est. was inv. on 5 Jan. 1710/11 by John Roberts and Jeremiah Downes and val. at £ 68.15.9; an additional inv. was filed 6 Aug. 1713 and val. at £ 123.3.4; Mary Preston admin. the est. in Aug. 1713; She d. by 29 Dec. 1714 when admin. bond was posted by James Preston with Edw. Smith and Abr. Taylor, Jr.; her est. was inv. on 31 Jan. 1715 by John Roberts and Jeremiah Downes and val. at £ 28.6.6; Thomas and Mary had iss.: THOMAS; JAMES; SARAH, m. Gideon Skats; ESTHER, m. Luke Raven (1:39, 60; 12:435; 48:90; 50:314; 66:132, 133; 101; 103; 122:185; 211; 388; Preston).

PRESTON, THOMAS (2), s. of Thomas (1), m. Elizabeth Deaver on 9 Dec. 1721; she was the dau. of John Deaver; they had iss.: JAMES, b. 2 Feb. 1721/2; ESTHER, b. 24 Dec. 1724; JOHN, b. 28 Dec. 1725; THOMAS, b. 22 May 1727; DAVID, b. 29 May 1731; LUKE, b. 7 Aug. 1733, in June 1745 with cons. of his mother was bd. to Benjamin Roads to learn trade of a weaver (35:542; 125:215; 131).

PRESTON, JAMES (3), s. of Thomas (1), d. in Balto. Co. by 5 Nov. 1729; m. c.1709 Sarah, dau. of Daniel Scott; may be the James Preston who, with Thomas Burton, bought 300 a. Land of Nod, part of James' Choice from Simon and Eme Pearson; may be the James Preston, "barber," who in Aug. 1719 was ind. and fined for refusing to repair his roads; d. leaving a will, 5 Nov. 1728

- 5 Nov. 1729, leaving 300 a. Dennis' Choice to sons James and
Daniel, 100 a. Preston's Chance to s. Bernard, named w. Sarah
and dau. Grace w. of Charles Anderson; admin. bond was posted
5 Nov. 1729 by Sarah Preston, with Michael Gilbert and Jacob
Harrington; in March 1731 his wid. Sarah had m. Thomas Pycraft
(m. on 5 Feb. 1731); had iss.: GRACE, m. Charles Anderson on 2
Nov. 1726; SARAH, b. 3 Dec. 1711; JAMES, b. 25 March 1713; DANI-
EL, b. 10 Oct. 1715; ELIZABETH, b. 19 Dec. 1720; HANNAH, b. 9
May 172-(?); ANN, b. 20 July 1725; BERNARD, b. 13 Jan. 1727/8
(3:18; 12:460; 23:218; 29:231-233; 67:52; 125:130; 129:248; 131;
Preston).

PRESTON, JAMES (4), s. of James (3), was b. 25 March 1713; d.
in 1766; m. 1st Sarah Poteet, on 15 May 1733; and 2nd Clemency
Bond on 31 March 1749; in 1750 owned 150 a. part Dennis' Choice,
100 a. Preston's Chance, 100 a. The Vineyard, and 25 a. part of
Andrew's Addition; d. leaving a will, 17 Sept. 1766 - 13 Oct.
1766; had iss.: 5 ch. by 1st w., and 3 by his 2nd w.; had iss.:
(by 1st w.): SARAH, b. 24 Feb. 1734, m. (---) McComas; JAMES, b.
25 Sept. 1735; ELIZABETH, b. 15 Oct. 1739, m. (---) Gilbert;
HANNAH, b. 4 Feb. 1741; ANN, b. 4 Sept. 1744; (by 2nd w.): MARTIN,
b. 19 Oct. 1750; MARY, b. 22 May 1754; BERNARD, b. 2 Aug. 1756
(112:48; 128:76, 79, 99; 129:323, 338, 375; 153:12).

PRESTON, DANIEL (5), s. of James (3), was b. 10 Oct. 1715,
and d. 1772; m. Ann, dau. of William Grafton on on 5 Jan. 1737;
in 1750 owned 150 a., part Dennis' Choice, and 25 a. Daniel's
Lot; d. leaving a will, 4 Oct. 1771 - 22 June 1772; had iss.:
MARGARET, b. 30 July 1739; SARAH, b. 17 Nov. 1741, d. 31 July
1745; DANIEL, b. 4 Dec. 1743, d. 21 Nov. 1746; GRAFTON, b. 26
March 1746; DANIEL, b. 3 Nov. 1748; JAMES, b. 15 April 1751;
BARNETT, b. 28 Oct. 1753; SARAH, b. 24 March 1756; WILLIAM, b.
13 May 1758; CORBIN, b. 22 Oct. 1760 (112:211; 129:104, 290, 332,
343, 345, 347, 348, 351, 352).

PRESTON, BERNARD (6), s. of James (3), was b. 13 Jan. 1727/8,
and d. 1789; m. Sarah Ruff on 28 Dec. 1749; in 1750 he owned 123
a. part Matthews Neighbor, and 150 a. part Ruff's Chance; had
iss.: SARAH, b. 23 Sept. 1751; BERNARD, b. 29 April 1754; MARY,
b. 9 March 1757, m. Robert Johnson; ANNA, b. 17 May 1760, m.
Henry Ruff, Jr.; DANIEL, b. c.1762, went to Lexington, Ky.;
JAMES, b. c.1762 (129:366; 153:96).

PRESTON, ANN, m. Isaac Miles on 28 Oct. 1742 (129:124).

PRESTON, JAMES, m. Elizabeth Pritchard in Oct. 1713; had iss.:
JAMES, b. 1716; THOMAS, b. 12 Oct. 1717; ELIZABETH, b. March
1718, d. April 1718; RICHARD, b. 28 Feb. 1713 (131).

PRESTON, JAMES, m. Avarilla Nowell on 17 July 1726; she d.
Dec. 1727; had iss.: JANE, b. 25 Aug. 1727, d. Sept. 1728 (131).

PRESTON, JAMES, m. by 9 May 1752 Mary, admnx. of Robert Mc-
Ilvain (5:234).

PRESTON, JAMES, Jr., m. 11 May 1756, Mary Bond, she d. 11 July 1759; had iss.: BENJAMIN, b. 15 Oct. 1758 (131).

PRESTON, JOHN, m. Mary Garrett or Garnett on 29 Aug. 1743;
had iss.: ANN, b. 28 Feb. 1744 (129:337).

PRESTON, SARAH, m. Michael Gilbert on 17 Dec. 1728 (129:254).

PRESTON, THOMAS, d. by 6 Nov. 1730(?) or 1739(?) when est.
was admin. by Sarah Preston (2:252).

PRESTON, THOMAS, serv., with 5 years to serve, was listed in
the 1704 inv. of Martha Bowen (51:125).

PRESTON, THOMAS, age 8 next 14 Feb., son of Elizabeth (Howard?)
was bd. to Hugh Merriken in Aug. 1716 (22:55).

PRESTWOOD, RICHARD, age c.40, runaway Eng. conv. serv. from
Nottingham Ironworks, advert. in April 1749 (385:46).

THE PRICE FAMILY has been the subject of a great deal of
research, but no one has ever published a completely documented
family history.

PRICE, THOMAS (1), alleged progenitor, is said to have been
b. c.1610, and d. c.1701; and to have come to Maryland with the
Ark and Dove expedition of 1634; m. Elizabeth Phillips; on 6 Feb.
1673 Robert Phillips and Elizabeth Price wit. the will of John
Wright of Calvert Co.; in April 1688 Robert Phillips made a will
naming Francis Price s. of Edward as exec. and residuary legatee of all Phillips' estate; on 9 April 1703 Thomas Price came
into court and made oath that Thomas Price, Sr., now dec., owed
no one any money at the time of his death; Thomas and Elizabeth
had iss.: THOMAS, b. c.1635; poss. EDWARD (120:78; 121:166; 206-
27:79).

PRICE, THOMAS (2), s. of Thomas (1), is said to have m. Eliza
Johnson, and to have been b. c.1635 and d. c.1703, leaving the
following ch.: MORDECAI, b. c.1660; poss. JOHN (Price notes by
various researchers at the Maryland Historical Society).

PRICE, EDWARD, (3), s. of Thomas (1), was mentioned in the
1686 will of Robert Phillips as being the father of Francis Price,
was alive in Nov. 1697 and m. Elizabeth, dau. of Thomas Lun; d.
by 1707; his wid. m. Samuel Maccubbin; had iss.: FRANCIS (121:
166; 211:122).

PRICE, MORDECAI (4), s. of Thomas (2), is said to have been
b. c.1660, and is known to have d. c.1715; m. Mary, dau. of Thomas and Isabella Parsons; c.1707 he held 116 a. Locust Neck in his
own right and 18 a. for the orphans of Anthony Holland; also
owned 50 a. Papa Ridge and 50 a. Greenwood; his wid. Mary d.
leaving a will, 8 May 1718 - 15 June 1718, naming ch. John, Thomas, Benjamin, Stephen, Mordecai, Rachel, Hannah, Elizabeth w. of
Thomas Carr, Leah Ford, Mary, and Sarah Price, and granddau. Mary
Carr; est. was admin. 4 Nov. 1726 by Thomas Carr and named dec."s
dau. Mary w. of Jonathan Hanson; est. was admin. 10 Nov. 1729
naming William Wheeler as the husband of Constant, wid. and admnx
of Stephen Price, and a dau. who m. Thomas Taylor; est. was
admin. 25 May 1728; Mordecai and Mary had iss.: ELIZABETH, b. c.
1685, m. Thomas Carr on 22 Oct. 1705 at West River Meeting; STE-
PHEN, b. c.1687; MARY, b. c.1688/9, m. 1st, on 29 Aug. 1718,
Jonathan Hanson, and 2nd, Dr. George Walker; JOHN, b. c.1690;
LEAH, m. 1 Jan. 1711 at All Hallows Par., in A. A. Co. to Thomas
Ford; HANNAH, m. 1st William Tipton, and 2nd John Bosley; ISA-
BELLA, m. William Wheeler; MORDECAI, b. c.1702; SARAH, b.. April
1705, m. Thomas Taylor in Oct. 1725; RACHEL, b. c.1706, m. Den-
nis Garrett Cole; BENJAMIN, b. c.1709, m. Elizabeth Hewett on 22
June 1730; THOMAS, b. 1 Jan. 1711; SAMUEL, b. c.1713 (2:303, 307,
315; 210-14:628; 211).

PRICE, STEPHEN (5), s. of Mordecai (4), was b. c.1687, d. in
Balto. Co. c.1726/7; m. in May 1716 Constant Horne, dau. of William and Sarah (Franklin) Horne; Constant m. 2nd William Wheeler;
admin. bond was posted 2 Aug. 1726 by Constant Price with George
Hitchcock and Richard Gott; est. was admin. 29 Dec. 1727 by

Constant Price, and on 20 Feb. 1729 by Constant Wheeler; William
Wheeler, Jr., posted bond in June 1730 he would pay the balance
of Stephen's est. to the latter's ch.: Elizabeth, Stephen, Sarah
and Mary; Stephen and Constant had iss.: ELIZABETH; STEPHEN, m.
Rebecca Hicks on 20 April 1749; SARAH; MARY, may have been the
Mary who m. John Gorsuch (2:247, 271, 356; 12:451; 28:23, 418,
419; 123:167).

PRICE, JOHN (6), s. of Mordecai (4), was b. c.1690/2, d. c.
1790; m. Rebecca Merryman, dau. of Samuel Merryman; d. leaving a
will, 12 Dec. 1784 - 8 May 1790; had iss.: MARY, b. 20 d, 1,
1726, m. John Parrish on 30 d, 1, 1744; JOHN, b. 28 March 1729,
d. 14 d, 4, 1809, m. 1st Mary Parrish, and 2nd Urith Cole; MOR-
DECAI, b. 27 d, 12, 1731/2; LEAH, b. 7 Oct. 1733; AQUILA, b. 27
Nov. 1735, d. 8 d, 2, 1773, m. Ann Griffith; ELIZABETH, b. 25
Feb. 1737/8; KETURA, b. 21 April 1739, m. Richard Belt; ISABELLA,
b. 4 Aug. 1742, d. 11 d, 5, 1836; AGNES, b. 28 Jan. 1745; BENJA-
MIN, b. 5 Jan. 1747; RACHEL, b. 2 April 1751, m. (---) Wooden;
ANN, m. (---) Stevenson; poss. REBECCA (113:422; 133; 136).

PRICE, MORDECAI (7), s. of Mordecai (4), was b. 1702; d. after
1734, and was prob. the Mordecai Price living in 1750 as owner
of 300 a. Price's Claim, 100 a. Price's Outlet, 150 a. Price's
Goodwill, and 100 a. Price's Delight; m. Elizabeth White on 28
April 1724; she was b. 1708, d. 1765, dau. of Guy and Elizabeth
White; had iss.: SARAH, b. 1 Sept. 1730, m. Thomas Cole on 23
d, 2, 1747; RACHEL, b. 11 June (---), m. Thomas Matthews on 25
Oct. 1751; MORDECAI, b. 28 Jan. 1734, m. Rachel Moore on 27 d,
12, 1759 at Gunpowder; BENJAMIN; LEAH; SOPHIA, b. 28 d, 12,
1736, m. Nathan Haines on 23 d, 10, 1755; SAMUEL, b. 28 d, 12,
1739, m. Anne Moore; ELIZABETH, b. 22 d, 6, 1741, m. Warwick
Miller; MARY, b. 9 d, 12, 1744, m. Daniel Haines on 25 d, 3,
1762(6:146; 136).

PRICE, BENJAMIN (8), s. of Mordecai (4) and Mary, was b. c.
1709; m. Elizabeth, wid. of Richard Hewett on 22 June 1730; on
17 Feb. 1737 Benjamin and Elizabeth admin. the est. of Richard
Hewett; on 17 June 1738 Benjamin and Elizabeth sold 150 a. The
Land in Kind to Thomas Taylor (3:252; 75:95, 98; 133).

PRICE, THOMAS (9), s. of Mordecai (4) and Mary, was b. 1 Jan.
1711 at St. James Par., A. A. Co.; d. c.1740/1, having m. on 1
July 1732, at St. Paul's Par., Balto. Co., Keturah, dau. of Samuel and Mary Merryman; Thomas b. by 5 Aug. 1741 when admin. bond
was posted by Keturah Price; she admin. his est. on 19 Nov. 1742
and m. as her 2nd husb. William Parrish on 25 Feb. 1743; in Aug.
1744 William Parrish posted bond he would pay the orphans of
Thomas Price (Benjamin, Samuel, Thomas, and Rebecca) their share
of their father's est.; in 1750 Keturah owned 200 a. part Executor's Management; had iss.: BENJAMIN, b. 8 March 1732/3; SAMUEL;
THOMAS; and REBECCA (3:280; 12:482; 35:301; 133; 153:12; 219-3).

PRICE, STEPHEN (10), s. of Stephen (5), d. 1809 in Balto. Co.,
m. Rebecca Hicks on 20 April 1749; in 1750 owned 150 a. Long
Looked For, 150 a. Long Tract, 100 a. James' Meadow, and 93 a.
Williams' Hopyard; d. leaving a will, 29 Feb. 1809 - 1809; had
iss.: WILLIAM; ABRAHAM; (---), m. (---) Howell; ARTRIDGE, m. Mordecai Cole by lic. 4 May 1778; ELIZABETH, m. John Gorsuch by lic.
22 April 1791; CONSTANT, m. (---) Rose; CHARLOTTE, m. (---) Hall;
NEHEMIAH (117:438; 131; 153:79).

PRICE, JOHN (11), s. of John (6) and Rebecca, was b. 26 March
1729; d. 14 April 1809; m. Mary Parrish on 26 Aug. 1748; m. 2nd
on 26 Jan. 1753 Urith Cole (b. 1728), dau. of Dennis and Rachel
(Price) Cole; had iss.: LEAH, b. 1 Sept. 1749; (by 2nd w.):

522   BALTIMORE COUNTY FAMILIES, 1659 - 1759

REBECCA, b. 25 Nov. 1753; RACHEL, b. 13 June 1758, d. 1761;
poss. SARAH; poss. MARY (136).

PRICE, MORDECAI (12), s. of John (6) and Rebecca, was b. 27
Feb. 1731/2; d. 5 Sept. 1807, age 76 years, 6 mos., 6 days; m.
1st on 30 d, 8, 1754, Mary Hyatt; she d, 2 d, 9, 1770; he m. 2nd,
on 1 Jan. 1772 Tabitha Tipton, b. 5 July 1747, d. 14 Sept. 1827,
dau. of William and Angelica Tipton; had iss.: (by 1st w.): EST-
HER, b. 28 Nov. 1755, m. (---) Tipton; RUTH, b. 2 Feb. 1758, d.
8 Feb. 1775; JOHN, b. 26 Feb. 1760, d. 28 June 1786; MARY, b. 2
May 1762, m. (---) Underwood; JESSE, b. 14 Feb. 1763; PHOEBE, b.
12 Oct. 1765, d. 30 July 1813; ANN, b. 27 Feb. 1768; (by 2nd w.):
ISABEL, b. 22 Oct. 1772, d. 1843; JOSHUA, b. 2 July 1774, d. 1804;
REBECCA, b. 9 Oct. 1776, d. 1785; AQUILA, b. 24 Oct. 1778, d. 27
Aug. 1797; WILLIAM, b. 22 Oct. 1780, d. 1857; RACHEL, b. 9 July
1782, d. 1800; BENJAMIN, b. 23 Aug. 1784; ELIZABETH, b. 25 Aug.
1786; JOHN, b. 23 May 1791, d. 1831; KETURA, b. 2 June 1792
(136).

PRICE, AQUILA (13), s. of John (6) and Rebecca, was b. 27 d,
9, 1735, d. 28 Feb. 1773; m. Ann Griffith (b. c.1752, dau. of
Isaac and Ann Griffith) on 27 Feb. 1772; Ann m. 2nd William Matthews; had iss.: LEAH, b. 10 Dec. 1772, m. John Matthews (136).

PRICE, MORDECAI (14), s. of Mordecai (7), was b. 28 Nov. 1733,
and d. 1796 in Balto. Co.; m. Rachel Moore on 27 d, 12, 1759;
she was b. 1741, dau. of Walter and Ann Moore; Mordecai left a
will, 1 March 1796 - 8 June 1796; had iss.: ANN, m. (---) Matthews; MORDECAI; RACHEL, m. Amos Scott by lic. 18 April 1789;
SARAH, m. Jesse Morgan by lic. 19 Aug. 1795; ELIZABETH, b. 2 Dec.
1771, m. James Benson; JOSEPH; ELIJAH (114:379; 232; Christopher
Johnston, chart of Price Family at Md. Hist. Soc.).

PRICE, BENJAMIN (15), s. of Mordecai (7), was b. 7 Feb. 1734;
d. 3 Dec. 1794; m. Temperance Bosley, b. 1735; had iss.: THOMAS,
b. 1 Dec. 1755, d. 1847; JAMES, b. 14 Jan. 1757; JOSHUA, b.15
Jan. 1759; JARRETT, b. 27 Dec. 1760; KETURAH, b. 1762; ELIZABETH,
b. 1764; REBECCA, b. 18 Nov. 1769; BEALE, b. 4 Oct. 1772(Price
data compiled by George A. Price, and graciously made available
to the compiler).

THE JOHN PRICE FAMILY

PRICE, JOHN (16), no known rel. to any of the above, was b.
c.1685, and d. c.1782 in Balto. Co.; on 9 Nov. 1721 he m. Hannah
or Honour Brian in All Hallows Par., A. A. Co.; on 1 Feb. 1724
Richard Wigg of A. A. Co. made a will, naming his kinfolk
Richard, William, and Abigail Briant, and Hannah Price; in 1750
John owned 220 a. Tom's Choice; d. leaving a will, 19 April 1781
- 28 Aug. 1782; had iss.: JANE, b. 14 Sept. 1722; JOHN, b. 14
Jan. 1724; ABSALOM, b. 22 March 1726/7; MARY, b. 4 June 1729, m.
John Cook on 29 Jan. 1748; RACHEL, b. 8 July 1732, m. (---)
Hissey; ELIZABETH, b. 5 Oct. 1734, m. (---) Knight; REBECCA, b.
19 Aug. 1739; AMON, b. 3 Jan. 1743/4 (87:197; 112:486; 133; 153:
51; 219-1).

PRICE, ABSOLOM (17), s. of John (16), was b. 22 March 1726/7;
d. by 19 April 1781, m. Martha; had iss.: JOSHUA; RICHARD, m.
Mary (---); RACHEL, m. Elijah Norwood; ANN, m. Thomas Lloyd on
13 Nov. 1793; MARY, m. Jesse Walker; HONOUR, m. Richard Brown
by lic. 8 March 1793; ROSANA; JOHN; SAMUEL (112:486; 231-WG#84:
106; 232).

PRICE, CHARLES, in Nov. 1756 pet. the court to be levy free
(41:303).

PRICE, DAVID, m. Mary Ann Elliott on 18 Nov. 1755 (131).

PRICE, GRIFFITH, m. Maria (---), and had iss.: MARY, b. 26
Sept. 1723; MARY, b. 7 July 1725: LUCRASA, age 12 last Feb., in
Aug. 1743 was bd. to John Taylor, plasterer (35:4; 128:53).

PRICE, LUCRETIA, in June 1732 was bd. to James and Mary Stamford (29:290).

PRICE, MORDECAI, in 1750 owned 300 a. Price's Claim, 100 a.
Price's Outlet, 150 a. Price's Good Will, 100 a. Price's Delight
(153:9).

PRICE, PHILIP, m. Hannah (---), and had iss.: MARY, b. 12
Sept. 1743; PHILIP, b. 18 Jan. 1744 (134:1).

PRICE, ROBERT, m. 1st, on 31 Dec. 1734, Elizabeth Shepherd
who d. 29 June 1738; m. 2nd, on 18 Sept. 1739 Elizabeth Miles,
admnx. of Evan Miles; had iss.: (by 1st w.): JOHANNAH, b. 22
June 1738, m. William Gordon on 29 Jan. 1761; (by 2nd w.): ROB-
ERT, Jr., b. 11 Nov. 1740; THOMAS, b. 6 March 1742; JAMES, b. 23
July 1745; ROBERT, b. 6 Dec. 1747; MARY, b. 24 Dec. 1749 (4:26;
131).

PRICE, THOMAS, m. Martha Spencer on 29 Jan. 1726; Martha d.
22 April 1741; had iss.: MARY, b. 9 Nov. 1728 (128:54, 115).

PRICE, THOMAS, m. Sarah Cross on 4 May 1743 (129:331).

PRICE, WILLIAM, was in Balto. Co. by June 1665 when Thomas
Edmonds conv. him 300 a. The Dividing (94).

PRIGG, WILLIAM, m. 21 Nov. 1749 Martha Morgan and had iss.:
EDWARD, b. 10 Feb. 1750/1; WILLIAM, b. 27 March 1753; MARY, b.
24 Jan. 1755; SARAH, b. 2 Nov. 1756 (129:364).

PRIOR, JOSEPH, b. Penna., age c.28, and his w., b. in Ireland, ran away from George Brown of Joppa, Md., April 1742 (384:
356).

THE OBADIAH PRITCHARD FAMILY

PRITCHARD, OBADIAH (1), progenitor, was in Balto. Co. by 1710
and d. there on 9 Oct. 1727; m. Margaret (---) who d. by 7 Nov.
1739; d. leaving a will, 1 Oct. 1727 - 9 Nov. 1727, naming w.
Margaret, and ch. Samuel, Obadiah, James, and Sarah; admin.
bond was posted by the extx. Margaret on 7 Aug. 1728 with Samuel
Hughes and Samuel Pritchard; est. was inv. on 24 Oct. 1728 by
John Durbin and John Gallion, and val. at £ 216.6.7, with debts
totalling £ 82.7.14, and signed by Samuel and Obadiah Prithcard
as kin; est. was admin. 14 June 1735 and named Richard Deaver as
the husb. of Obadiah's dau. Sarah; Margaret the wid. d. leaving
a will, 26 March 1739 - 12 May 1739, naming sons Obadiah, Samuel
and James, dau. Sarah, and son Charles Anderson; admin. bond was
posted 7 Nov. 1739 by Samuel Pritchard with Robert Courtney and
Andrew Thompson; Obadiah and Margaret had iss.: SAMUEL, prob. b.
6 March 1710; OBADIAH, prob. b. 25 March 1711; JAMES, prob. b.
17 May 1713; OBADIAH, b. 25 May 1713 (sic); SARAH, b. 12 Feb.
1715/6, m. Richard Deaver by 14 June 1735 (3:209; 11:458, 463;
51:200; 125:46; 127:36; 128:27, 31, 32, 38, 55).

PRITCHARD, SAMUEL (2), s. of Obadiah (1), was prob. the Samuel
b. 6 March 1710; m. 1st, on 13 July 1735 Isabella Cotrell, and
2nd, by 22 Aug. 1748 Elizabeth (---); in 1750 he owned 50 a. part
Mould's Success; had iss.: (by 1st w.): JOHN, b. 13 July 1736;

OBADIAH, b. 21 Sept. 1738; REUBEN, b. 7 Jan. 1740; CHARLES AN-
DERSON, b. 10 July 1743; JAMES, b. 27 Dec. 1746; (by 2nd w.):
SAMUEL, b. 22 Aug. 1748; THOMAS, b. 15 July 1750; CHARLES, b.
27 Aug. 1752 (128:27, 96, 101, 111; 129:341, 348, 349; 153:23).

PRITCHARD, JAMES (3), s. of Obadiah (1), was prob. the James
b. 17 May 1713; m. Elizabeth Durbin on 1 May 1735, and in 1750
owned 50 a. Obadiah's Venture, 50 a. Improved Venture, and 50 a.
Hughs' Enlargement; had iss.: MARGARET, b. 6 Feb. 1735; AVARIL-
LA, b. 18 Jan. 1738; DANIEL, b. 24 Nov. (---); JAMES, b. 16 Aug.
1743 (128:87, 94, 102, 111; 129:333; 153:35).

PRITCHARD, OBADIAH (4), s. of Obadiah (1), was b. 25 May 1713;
d. by 18 May 1742 when admin. bond was posted by admnx. Elizabeth
Pritchard with Samuel Hughes and Isaac Wood; m. Elizabeth, dau.
of Thomas Litton on 7 Feb. 1733; had iss.: SAMUEL, b. 2 Jan.
1735; JAMES, b. 13 Jan. 1738, d. 14 May 1740; JAMES, b. 9 Feb.
1740/1; ANN, b. 13 Dec. 1736 (12:466; 128:76, 89, 103, 107, 111;
129:335; 210-31:419).

THE WILLIAM PRITCHARD FAMILY

PRITCHARD, WILLIAM (5), no known rel. to any of the above,
was in Balto. Co. by 1692 as a taxable in Spesutia Hund.; d. by
25 Nov. 1713 when admin. bond was posted by Edgar Tipper with
Jonathan Massey and John Roberts; est. was inv. by Ellinor(?)
Petticoat and Robert Cutchin, and val. at £ 106.13.0; est. was
admin. by Edgar Tipper and w. Elizabeth on 17 Sept. 1714; William m. Elizabeth (---) who may have m. Tipper as her 2nd husb.;
William, who d. 25 Jan. 1713, and w. Elizabeth had iss.: WILLIAM,
b. 23 May 1697; MARY, b. 9 May 1701; MARYANN, b. 9 April 1702;
poss. JOSEPH (1:28; 11:433; 50:246; 128:11, 15, 19, 30).

PRITCHARD, JOSEPH (6), poss. s. of William (5), is so placed
because in his will, Joseph named a sis. Mary; Joseph d. Jan.
1733, leaving a will, 25 Jan. 1733 - 6 March 1733, leaving 60 a.
of land to Benjamin, s. of William and Catherine Osborne, and the
res. of his est. to his sis. Mary, w. of Abraham Cord; admin.
bond was posted 15 Nov. 1734 by Abraham Cord with Thomas Cord
and Thomas Brown (12:402; 126:64; 128:78).

PRITCHARD, ELIZABETH, was tried for bast. in March 1742/3, ind.
for same offense in June 1743, and tried in Aug. 1745; had iss.:
ELIZABETH, b. 28 Jan. 1743/4; SARAH, b. 17 March 1744/5 (34:
121, 135, 185; 35:620; 129:352).

PRITCHARD, HERBERT, and w. Mary, dau. of John Arden, conv.
all land lately belonging to John Arden, to Richard Gist on 23
June 1721; had iss.: WILLIAM, by 11 Dec. 1744, in Orange Co., Va.
(69:81, 78:118).

PRITCHETT, WILLIAM, serv., with 4 years to serve, was listed
in the 1742 inv. of Jonas Robertson (53:202).

PROCTOR, MARGARET, serv. of Edmund Talbott, was ind. for bast.
in June 1740 and tried in Aug. 1740 (32:266, 303).

PROCTOR, NATHANIEL, in Aug. 1659 joined George Gouldsmith in
surv. 200 a. Proctor's Hall, in Spesutia Hund. (211).

PROMET, AMBROSE. See PRUETT, AMBROSE.

PROSSER, CHARLES, serv., was listed in the 1732 inv. of Thomas Hutchins; m. Mary Jarvis on 20 Nov. 1738; had iss.: ELIZA-
BETH FRANCES, b. 5 July 1739; SARAH, b. 28 April 1741; HENRY, b.

22 Oct. 1744; SUSANNA, b. 23 Jan. 1746; JNO., b. 30 June 1748
(52:244; 131).

PROSSER, MATTHEW, was in Balto. Co. by 1692 as a taxable in
Spesutia Hund. (138).

PRUETT/PROMETT, AMBROSE, d. by 4 Jan. 1698 when admin. bond
was posted by Rossoman Pruett, admnx., with Abraham Taylor and
Robert Olies; his est. was inv. in 17(4 by Abraham Taylor and
John Boon and val. at £ 16.1.4 (12:422; 48:89).

PRYOR, THOMAS, of Balto. Co., imm. c.1665; m. by March 1671/2
Margaret (---) who joined him in selling one-half of a 200 a.
tract, Henn's Roost, to Matthew Adams (98:44; 388).

PUGH, HUGH, aged 19 or 20, was advert. for in June 1759 as a
runaway conv. serv. of John Orrick of Balto. Town (307-69:209).

PULLEY. See POOLE.

PUMPHREY, NATHAN (1), d. in Balto. Co. by 25 March 1721 when
admin. bond was posted by extx. Mary Pumphrey with Ebenezer Pumphrey and Anthony Johnson; m. Mary (---) who d. by 23 Dec. 1723;
Nathan d. leaving a will, 23 Feb. 1721 - 23 March 1720/1, naming
w. Mary and ch. Ebenezer, Joseph, Nathan, Daiburene, Walter, Silvanus, and Lazarus; est. was admin. by Mary Pumphrey on 1 June
1722; after her death a second admin. bond on his est. was posted
23 Dec. 1723 by Silvanus Pumphrey with John Miller and Edward Kitten; Silvanus admin. the est. on 27 April 1726; admin. bond on the
est. of Mary Pumphrey was posted 23 Dec. 1723 by Silvanus Pumphrey with John Miller, John Buck, and Edward Kitten; her est. was
inv. 27 Jan. 1723/4 by John Cromwell and John Gardiner and val.
at £ 219.14.2, with Alexander Mitchell and Ebenezer Pumphrey signing as kin; Walter and Mary had iss.: EBENEZER; NATHAN; WALTER;
LAZARUS; SYLVANUS; JOSEPH; and DAIBURENE (dau.) (2:11, 298; 12:
437, 445, 446; 51:216; 124:51).

PUMPHREY, NATHAN (2), s. of Walter (1), m. by March 1722/3
the wid. of William Cockey (3:34, 83; 25:219).

PUMPHREY, SYLVANUS (3), s. of Walter (1), was ind. in March
1718 for begetting a ch. on the body of Sarah Cockey (23:62).

PUMPHREY, JAMES, c.1724 conv. prop. to his ch.: GEORGE; JOHN;
MARTHA; THOMAS; and SARAH (70:34).

THE PUNTANY/PONTENY FAMILY is discussed in Boyd's The Parrish Family, pp. 47-48.

PUNTANY, WILLIAM (1), progenitor, d. by 8 Jan. 1730 having m.
Ann Parrish, dau. of Edward Parrish; she was b. 1702, and d. 1776,
marrying as her 2nd husb., Mayberry Helms, on 6 Feb. 1734; on 13
Jan. 1725 William Puntany, butcher of Annapolis, purch. Walnut
Neck in Balto. Co. from Stephen Gill, and w. Elizabeth; William
and Ann had iss.: WILLIAM, m. Sarah Wooden; MARY, may have m.
John Howard; EDWARD; and JOHN HOWARD (73:90; 213-PL#6:128).

PUNTANY, WILLIAM (2), s. of William (1), was living in Balto.
Co. as late as 1760; m. Sarah Wooden on 29 Sept. 1745, and may
have m. as a 2nd w. Rosanna (---); in 1750 he owned 75 a. Parrish's
Range; William had one s. by 1st w., and three daus. by his 2nd w.:
EDWARD, in 1760 was named as a grandson in the will of John Wood-
en; ELEANOR, b. 20 Jan. 1758, m. Conrad Hush on or about 4 Nov.
1778; MARY, b. 20 Jan. 1758; ROSANNA, b. 31 May 1760, m. Conrad
Fite (134:100, 108, 157; 153:74; 210-37:82; 232).

PUNTANY, EDWARD (3), s. of William (1) and Ann, is prob. the
Edward who d. by 18 Feb. 1778; m. Sarah (---); in 1783 she was
living in Middlesex Hundred, owning 119 a. Parrish's Range, and
with 6 whites in the household; Edward d. leaving a will, 20 June
1777 - 18 Feb. 1778, naming w. Sarah, tracts Parrish's Range and
Parrish's Fear, and the following ch.: SUSANNA; RACHEL; ANN; SAR-
AH; ELIZABETH; MARY; and ELEANOR (283; Balto. Co. Orig. Wills,
Box 16, folder 23).

PUNTANY, JOSEPH, no known rel. to any of the above, was b.c.
1728, and in 1776 was living in Harford Lower Hund., Harf. Co.;
m. Sarah (---), b. c.1736; Joseph and Sarah had iss.: AQUILA, b.
c.1729, by 15 Nov. 1783 was in Westmoreland Co., Pa.; ANN, b. c.
1761; PRISCILLA, b. c.1765; GEORGE H., b. c.1767; NELSON, b. c.
1770; SAMUEL, b. c.1772; JAMES, b. c.1774; JOHN, b. c.1776 (241-
JLG#E:427; 277:171).

PURDUE. See PERDUE.

PURTELL, THOMAS, carpenter, ran away from his bail, Jacob Giles
of Balto. Co., and was advert. for in June 1747 (384:635).

PUTON. JOHN, d. 15 Jan. 1732 (128:105).

PUTTEE. See POTEET.

PYCRAFT, THOMAS, m. 6 Feb. 1730, the wid. Sarah Preston; in
1750 owned 100 a. Edmond's Camp, and 85 a. part Emm's Delight;
was a trustee of Bush River Meeting; d. leaving a will, 24 Nov.
1766 - 13 July 1767; had iss.. SARAH, b. 25 Dec. 1731, m. Joseph
Presbury (112:5; 128:65; 153:6; 433:366).

PYKE. See PIKE.

PYLE, JOHN, of Balto. Co., in Sept. 1755 conv. 50 a. Pyle's
Addition to Ralph Pyle of Chester Co., Penna.; John's w. Sarah
gave her consent (82:454).

QUARE, JOHN, was named by Margaret Cannadah as the father of
her child in June 1719 (23:198).

QUICK, ELIZABETH, serv, to Lance Todd, was ind. for bast. in
March 1724 (27:127).

QUINCEY, SARAH, aged 3 years, was bd. to William Burney, Jr.,
s. of William, to age 16, in Aug. 1729 (28:274).

QUINE. HENRY. See JAMES, HENRY QUINE.

QUINE, WILLIAM, in 1738 was named as bro.-in-law of John Ingram of Balto. Co.; m. Elizabeth (---) and had: JANE, b. 20 June
1713, m. William Detter (127:75; 131).

QUINLIN, PHILIP, was in Balto. Co. by Nov. 1754 when he was
named as the father of Elizabeth Port's child; in Aug. 1758 he
and w. Charity sold to John Cretin land which Charity Quinlin had
inher. from her father Isaac Butterworth (39:461; 83:221).

QUINSEY, JOHN, age 28, unm., of the parish of Walsit, Co.
Linc., on 7 Feb. 1718 bd. himself as apprentice to William Bradley of London (68:91).

RACKSTONE. See RUXTON.

RAGAN, DANIEL, m. Sarah Lewis on 26 Dec. 1732; in 1750 owned
50 a. Ragan's Ambition; had iss.: EZEKIEL, b. 19 Jan. 1733;

URATH, b. 4 Nov. 1734; DANIEL, b. 4 Nov. 1736 (133:59, 150; 153: 54).

RAGAN, DARBY, d. by 5 April 1722 when admin. bond was posted by Abigail Ragan, admnx., with Matthew Organ and Henry Carrington; est. was inv. on 10 Dec. 1722 by Edward Norwood and Tobias Eminson, and est. was val. at £ 23.12.6; the children were desc. as minors, and Lance Todd and Jno. Israel signed as creditors (14:346; 52:29).

RAGAN, MICHAEL, servant to Thomas Ald, was judged to be 14 years old in Nov. 1716 (22:61).

RAILEY, WILLIAM, m. Margaret Rhodes on 17 Sept. 1759 (131).

RALLINGS. See RAWLINGS.

RALSTON, GAVIN, was in Balto. Co. by 1754; m. Elizabeth (---); d. leaving a will, 27 July 1760 - 15 Sept. 1760, naming a w. Elizabeth, dau. Elizabeth, and bro. John; wife Elizabeth could take the whole estate with her if she chose to leave the country and visit friends in Scotland; admin. bond posted 29 Sept. 1760 by extx. Elizabeth Ralston with Samuel Webb and James Brice; Gavin and Elizabeth had iss.: ELIZABETH, b. 16 Oct. 1754 (15:235; 129:375; 210-31:27).

RAMSAY/RAMSEY, WILLIAM (1), progenitor, acquired Leafe's Chance and William the Conqueror; m. Pretiotia (---); d. in A. A. Co. leaving a will, 12 May 1689 - 20 June 1689, naming w. Pretiotia, and these ch.: CHARLES (eld. s., to have land in Balto. Co.); WILLIAM; JOHN (121:44; 211).

RAMSAY, CHARLES (2), s. of William (1), was in Balto. Co. by 1692 as a taxable in Spesutia Hund.; m. by March 1691/2 Elizabeth, wid. of John Whalley and dau. of Thomas Thurston; on 2 Nov. 1692 Charles and w. Elizabeth conv. Simm's Choice to Michael Judd; in 1696 they conv. part Leafe's Chance to William Lennox, and in 1703/4 conv. part of same tract to Edward Selby; Charles and w. Elizabeth (who d. May 1710) had iss.: THOMAS, b. 4 Feb. 1692/3; MARY, b. 17 Aug. 1695; ELIZABETH, b. 17 Dec. 1697; ANN, b. 9 April 1700; CHARLES, b. 10 May 1702; WILLIAM, b. c.1703 (19:152; 21:379; 59:356; 128:3, 4, 10, 14; 129:209; 138; 341:121, 122).

RAMSAY, JOHN (3), s. of William (1), may be the John who was in Balto. Co. by 1695 as a taxable in Spesutia Hund. (140).

RAMSAY, THOMAS (4), s. of Charles (2), was b. 4 Feb. 1692/3; m. Rachel (---); on 30 June 1721 conv. Simon Pearson of Balto. Co. any lands Thomas had laid claim to on 8 Jan. 1716; had iss.: THOMAS, b. 23 Feb. 1720/1 (69:1; 131).

RAMSAY, CHARLES (5), s. of Charles (2), was b. 10 May 1702; age 12 last 10 May, in June 1713 was bd. to John and Mary Bond to age 21; in Aug. 1719 was bd. to his bro. Thomas Ramsay (21: 379; 23:213).

RAMSAY, WILLIAM (6), s. of Charles (2), was b. c.1703 (age 10 this 10 June; in June 1713 was bd. to William Bond and w. Elizabeth to age 21); m. Elizabeth Dew on 21 Dec. 1730; had iss.: CHARLES, b. 2 June 1731; SARAH, b. 4 March 1734; ELIZABETH, b. 18 July 1736; WILLIAM, b. 9 Jan. 1738; CHARLES, b. 11 Feb. 1740; MARY, b. 13 Nov. 1742; JOHN, b. 29 Oct. 1748 (21:381; 73:82; 128: 71; 129:338, 364; 153:85).

RAMSEY, JAMES,, m. Elizabeth Milam on 3 Jan. 1733 (133:151).

RAMSEY, JOHN, m. Christian (---), and had iss.: ELEANOR, b.
27 June 1741 (128:115).

RAMSEY, JOHN, Jr., m. by 1 Dec. 1744, Johanna, admnx. of William Poteet; had iss.: CHRISTIAN, b. 18 Feb. 1743; WILLIAM, b. 18
Feb. 1743 (5:4; 131:118/r).

RAMSEY, NATHANIEL, m. by 11 Sept. 1751, Sarah, extx. of John
Miller (209-35:80).

RAMSEY, THOMAS, was in Balto. Co. by Aug. 1673 when he purch.
100 a. Fareall from John George; on 3 June 1674 Ramsey sold the
tract to John West (99:347; 100:117).

THE RANDALL FAMILY is one of the families discussed in
Barnes, The Green Spring Valley, Its History and Heritage, vol.
II (259).

RANDALL, CHRISTOPHER (1), progenitor of the family, was in
Baltimore Co. by Nov. 1675; d. intestate by 25 Feb. 1684/5; m.
Johanna (---), wid. of George Norman (who had d. 1677); Johanna
m. as her 3rd husb. John Gadsby; Randall's marr. to the wid.
Johanna Norman was performed by Anthony Demondidier, one of "His
Lordship's Justices of the Peace" for Balto. Co. on 31 Jan. 1678;
Edward Lunn brought an action against the wedding on the grounds
that Demondidier had neglected to publish the banns, but Lunn
had waited too long to inform, so the case was dismissed, and the
charges were dropped; Randall had three tracts of land surv. for
him in A. A. Co. betw. July 1679 and June 1680: they were: 5½ a.
Randall's Fancy,102 a. Randall's Purchase, and 100 a. Randall's
Range; all three tracts were later held by Gadsby, who had m.
Randall's wid.; Randall d. shortly before 25 Feb. 1684/5 when letters of admin. were granted to his wid. Johanna; the inv. of
his est. was taken on 20 March 1684/5 by Francis Meade and Matthew
Howard and val. at ₤ 14.9.8; the est. was admin. by Johanna Randall on 5 Aug. 1686; Christopher and Johanna had iss.: CHRISTOPHER,
b. c.1682; HANNAH, b. c.1682, m. 1st c.1695 Nathaniel Stinchcomb,
and 2nd, in 1710 Edward Teal; THOMAS, b. c. 1684 (200-70:270-272;
206-9:11, 142, 143; 209-3:210; 211:250, 251, 252; 259).

RANDALL, CHRISTOPHER (2),. s. of Christopher (1) and Johanna;
b. c. 1682; d. 2 Feb. 1734; m. Anne, dau. of William and Sydney
(Wynne) Chew, c . 1719; Anne was b. c.1704, and m. 2nd by 7 May
1741 James Burke; Christopher Randall's will, 23 Sept. 1734 - 28
March 1735, named w. Anne and ch.: Roger, Aquila, John, Johanna,
Rachel, and Ruth; admin. bond was posted 28 March 1735 by extx.
Anne Randall with John Moale and William Fell; the est. of Christopher Randall was admin. by Ann Randall on 16 Oct. 1739 and by
Anne Burke on 7 May 1741; Christopher and Anne had iss.: ROGER,
b. 3 Jan. 1720; AQUILA, b. 9 May 1723; SUSANNA, b. 1724, m. Benjamin Browne; JOHN, b. 3 July 1726; JOHANNA, b. c. c.1729 and
chose Roger Randall as her guardian in March 1743/4; RACHEL, b.
20 June 1732, m. John Frost; RUTH, b. 20 March 1734/5 (14:330;
33:3, 71; 35:155; 111:206; 133:10, 11, 41; 259).

RANDALL, THOMAS (3), s. of Christopher (1) and Johanna, was b.
c.1684; d. by 9 March 1722; m. Hannah, sis. of Thomas and Anthony
Bale, c. 1707; she d. by 31 May 1727; admin. bond on the est. of
Thomas Randall was posted 16 April 1722; est. was inv. on 1 Aug.
1723 by Benjamin and John Howard, and val. at ₤ 19.18.6, plus
₤ 5.18.6; est,.was admin. by Mrs. Hannah Randall on 5 Oct. 1723
and 3 June 1726; Hannah Randall d. leaving a will, 23 Oct. 1726 -
31 May 1727, naming ch. Christopher and Urith, dau.-in-law Katherine; bro.-in-law Christopher Randall and his son Roger; admin.

bond on Hannah Randall's est. was posted 17 June 1727 by Christopher Randall, Jr.; her est. was inv. 20 Nov. 1728 by William Hamilton and val. at Ɫ 43.0.7; est. was admin. 9 Feb. 1732; Thomas and Hannah had iss.: CHRISTOPHER, b. c.1708; URATH, b. 1 Jan. 1713/4, m. Samuel Owings on 1 Jan. 1729/30 (1:133; 3:64, 110; 12:552; 51:82; 52:35, 96; 125:28; 134:15; 259).

RANDALL, ROGER (4), s. of Christopher (1) and Anne, was b. 3 Jan. 1720, and was alive in Nov. 1754; m. Rachel Stevens on 26 Dec. 1742; served on the Balto. Co. Grand Jury in Nov. 1742; in 1750 owned 220 a. called Stout; in Nov. 1754 he and his w. Rachel conv. 329 a. Stout to William Williams, iron founder, and his w. Mary; Roger and Rachel had iss.: BENJAMIN, b. 2 Jan. 1744; AQUILA, b. 17 Nov. 1746; BENJAMIN, b. 11 Sept. 1749 (133:75, 76, 84; 163: 19; 259).

RANDALL, AQUILA (5), s..of Christopher (2) and Ann, was b. 9 May 1723, and d. in A A. Co. in 1801, having m. Margaret, dau. of Joshua and Margaret (Chew) Browne; by April 1763 he was living in Delaware Bottom,a. a. Co.; during the Rev. War he rendered patriotic service; Aquila and Margaret had iss.: CHRISTOPHER, m. Anne Crandall in 1788; JOHN; AQUILA, Jr., m. Rebecca Cord in June 1779; DELILAH, m. on or about 22 Jan. 1785 Ichabod Davis; NATHAN, m. Ruth Davis; BRICE CHEW, b. 6 Aug. 1771; RUTH, m. Michael Cramblett; ANNE, m. Joseph Hobbs (33:8; 133:10; 232; 259; 353).

RANDALL, JOHN (6), s. of Christopher (2) and Anne, was b. 3 July 1726, chose William Fell as his guardian in March 1740/1, and and may be the John Randall whose est. was admin. in 1770 (33:3; 133:11; 201-64:187).

RANDALL, CHRISTOPHER (7), s. of Thomas (3), and Hannah, was b. c.1708, and was alive in 1761; m. Catherine Larkin c.1726; in 1750 he owned 100 a. Green Spring Punch, 133 a part George's Park, 150 a. part Jeopardy, 75 a. Randall's Meadows, and 51 a. Randall's Lot; had iss.: THOMAS, b. 11 Jan. 1726; BALE, b. 1 Aug. 1728, d. 20 Oct. 1728; CHRISTOPHER, b. 25 Sept. 1729; WILLIAM, b. 18 Aug. 1731; REBECKAH, b. 27 Dec. 1733, prob. d. by 1738; HANNAH, b. 27 Oct. 1736; REBECKAH, b. 1738, d. 1759; NICHOLAS, b. 1740, d. 1758; SUSANNA, b. 7 May 1743;BALE, b. 7 Aug. 1745; LARKIN, b. 10 June 1749 (133:53; 134:4, 5, 16; 153:30; 259).

RANDALL, CHARLES, was found dead on 6 Nov. 1763 on the road near Solomon Wooden's in Balto. Co.; he is supposed to have been killed instantly as the result of a fall from his horse the night before (262:150).

RANDALL, JOHN, shipwright, was in Balto. Co. by March 1751 when Dorsey and Sarah Peddicord conv. him 140 a., Friendly Purchase (81:132).

RANDALL, JOHN, in 1750 owned 100 a. Randall's Fancy; on 27 July 1761 John Randall and wife Catherine(?) conv. 170 a. Randall's Fancy and 140 a. Peddicord's Beginnings to Roger Boyce (85:202; 153:19).

RANDALL, Capt. JOHN, d. by 6 Dec. 1755 when his est. was admin. by Joseph Ensor (5:344).

RANDALL, WILLIAM, was in Balto. Co. by 1756 when he wrote to his uncle, Mr. James Kitely, gardener near Vaux Hall Gardens in Lambeth, and to his aunt; mentioned his bros. and sisters in Eng., and his cousins in America, John and Charles, who "do have hard places" (300-65:262).

RANGER CHARLES, in May 1687 surv. 200 a. Ranger's Lodge; d. c.1700; land was later held by children of his bro. in .A A. Co. (211).

RANKIN, WILLIAM, d. by 4 Nov. 1707 when admin. bond on his est. was posted by Roger Matthews and John Ewings (12:549).

THE RATTENBURY FAMILY was the subject of a chart by Christopher Johnston, on file at the Maryland Historical Society.

RATTENBURY, JOHN (1), was in Balto. Co. by 1701 as a taxable in s. side of Patapsco Hundred; m. Margaret Besson , sis. of Ann Besson who m. Richard Cromwell on 26 Oct. 1697, and dau.of Thomas and Marg. (Saughier) Besson; was named as extx. of John Lockett's will in Jan. 1704/5 and of Thomas Eager's will on 17 April 1708; was named as heir in the will of John Parker; wife Margaret and dau. Hannah were named in the 1717 will of Richard Cromwell; in Nov. 1712 was named as the father of Margaret Durham's child; d. by 25 March 1720 when admin. bond on his est.,was posted by Margaret Rattenbury with John Cromwell and William Slade; est. was inv. on 6 April 1720 and val. at **E** 309.18.9, and signed by Sarah Brice, Hannah Jones, and Thomas and Hannah Worthington; est admin. by Margaret Rattenbury on 6 March 1720/1, 2 Oct. 1721, and 3 Nov. 1721; the will of Margaret Rattenbury, 24 Sept. 1728 - 11 March 1742, named ch.: John, Ann Jones, and Hannah, w. of John Cromwell, and their ch. John and Margaret Cromwell; Dr John and Margaret (Besson) Rattenbury had iss.: HANNAH, b. 30 Oct. 1704, m. Philip Jones on 18 Sept. 1719; m. 2nd John Cromwell; ANN, b. 20 Oct. 1706, m. Philip Jones cn 2 Oct. 1727; JOHN, b. 12 .Sept. 1708 (1:67, 80, 352; 2:23, 152, 183, 234; 14:337; 21:335; 48:312; 122:47, 91, 110, 165; 123:112; 127:188; 143).

RATTENBURY, JOHN (2), s. of John (1) and Margaret, was b. 12 Sept. 1708, and d. 30 March 1745; m. Margaret Jones on 3 Nov. 1745; d. leaving a will, 3 March 1746 - 4 June 1746, naming w. Margaret, nephews John Cromwell, Rattenbury Jones, and Nicholas Jones, as well as Capt. Philip Jones, schoolmaster George Bramwell, and Richard Ireland; admin. bond on his est. was posted 4 June 1746 by Philip Jones, acting exec., with Thomas Harrison and Cornelius Howard (15:173; 133:58; 210-24:446).

THE RAVEN FAMILY was the subject of a chart by Christopher Johnston on file at the Maryland Historical Society.

RAVEN, LUKE (1), came to Va. in 1662 or 1664 and was in Md. by 1671; was among 22 persons transported to Virginia by John Washington between 1662 and 1664; acquired two tracts in Balto. Co. laid out for Peter Sterling: 350 a. Oldborough, and 100 a. The Triangle; in May 1687 he had surv. 317 a. called Luke's Adventure, which was later held by his descendants; prob. had at least two ch.: SARAH, m. 1st Tobias Stansbury, and 2nd Enoch Spinks; Maj. LUKE (48:270; 100:117; 211; 420:448).

RAVEN, Maj. LUKE (2), s. of Luke (1), d. in Balto. Co. c. 1735, having m. 1st Esther Preston, dau. of Thomas Preston, and 2nd Elizabeth, dau. of Thomas and Mary Hughes; on 7 Dec. 1708 Thomas Preston made his will naming his dau. Esther Raven; on 13 March 1724 Luke Raven recorded in Balto. Co. Land Records that some time ago he had married Elizabeth, dau. of Thomas and Mary Hughes, that she had deserted him, and that he would not be responsible for her debts; Raven was a Justice in Balto. Co. in 1712 and a captain and later major of militia; after his death his wid. Elizabeth m. (on 26 Aug. 1735) Col. William Hammond; by his 1st w., Luke Raven had iss.: WILLIAM, b. 1696, d. 1718; ESTHER, b. 1712, d. 1719; WILLIAM, b. 1719, d. 1720; LUKE, d.

1761; ISAAC, d. 1757; ABRAHAM, d. 1773; ELIZABETH, m. 1st, on 7 Oct. 1729, Solomon Hillen, and 2nd, Thomas Wheeler; MARY, m. Samuel Griffith; AVARILLA, m. Nathaniel Scott (70:30; 122:185; 131; 133:154; Johnston chart).

RAVEN, LUKE (3), s. of Luke (2) and Esther, d. in Balto. Co. in 1761; m. by 21 April 1729 Sarah Major who m. 2nd, on 16 March 1763 John Cottrell; Sarah was a daughter of Thomas Major or of James and Sarah (Crook) Major; on 11 June 1726 he was conv. land by his father; in 1750 he owned 100 a. Triangle, 317 a. Luke's Adventure, and 125 a. Outlet; on 7 Dec. 1737 Sarah Crooke of Annapolis. wid., made a will naming her grandchildren Sarah, Chloe, Mary, Arabella, and Luke, ch. of Luke and Sarah Raven; Luke Raven d. leaving a will made 1 Sept. 1760; ; his est. was admin. by exec. Luke Raven on 13 June 1763 and 10 March 1764; the est. of Sarah Cottrell was admin by Luke Raven on 17 Dec. 1785; Luke and Sarah had iss.: LUKE, d. 1798; SARAH CHLOE, m. George Harryman on 17 Oct. 1749; MARY, m. James Brian on 4 July 1754; AVARILLA, m. Nicholas Merryman on 1 May 1755, and RACHEL, m. (---) Harryman (2:309; 6:83; 8:172; 126:232; 131; 153: 23: 210-31:123; Johnston chart).

RAVEN, ISAAC (4), s. of Luke (2) and Esther, d. by 26 July 1757; m. Letitia Ward, dau. of Joseph Ward; on 11 June 1726 was conv. land by his father; in 1750 owned 350 a. Alborough, and 100 a. part Norwich; admin. bond was posted 26 July 1757 by Luke Raven with Christopher Duke and Luke Raven; est. was admin. by Lettice Raven on 17 July 1769; dec. had iss. by his w. Letitia: LUKE, d. 1758 unm.; MARY, m. Richardson Stansbury on 23 Feb. 1747; ELIZABETH, m. Charles Harryman on 6 Feb. 1752; LETITIA, m. Josias Reeves on 11 Jan. 1756: AVARILLA; ESTHER, m. Robert Dew on 3 Oct. 1754: KEZIAH, m. Asher; DRUSILLA, m. (---) Johnson; MILLICENT, m. (---) Parks; WILLIAM (7:22, 228; 13:189, 234; 70:270, 271; 131; 153:8).Johnston chart).

RAVEN, ABRAHAM (5), s. of Luke (2) and Esther, d. in Balto. Co. in 1773; m. Sarah (---); in June 1726 was conv. land by his father Luke; in 1750 owned 300 a. Fellowship, 100 a. Cox's Fancy, 22 a. Richardson's Neglect, 15 a. Luke's Addition, and 100 a. Philemon's Addition; est. of Abraham Raven was admin. 24 May 1775 by Sarah Raven; Sarah Raven d. leaving a will, 3 Oct. 1791 - 29 July 1795; Abraham and Sarah had iss.: ELIZABETH, m. 1st on 21 Feb. 1748 Isaac Risteau; m. 2nd William Cromwell (6:334; 78:402; 81:58; 114:296; 131; 153:85; Johnston chart).

THE AARON RAWLINGS FAMILY

RAWLINGS, AARON (1), was in A. A. Co. by April 1711 when he was named in the will of Henry Darnall of that co.; he may be the Aaron Rawlings of A. A. Co., Quaker, who gave his age as 72 in 1738; he came to possess 870 a. called Brown's Adventure and 563 a. of Bridge Hill; he also owned 350 a. Jones' Lot; d. leaving a will, 25 March 1741 - 14 April 1741, naming w. Susannah and the ch. named below; his will also disposed of tracts Brown's Adventure, Young's Lot, and 200 a. Darnall's Grove; had iss.: WILLIAM; STEPHEN; JONATHAN; AARON; and ANN, m. (---) Jones (122:198; 127: 146; 211; 217-IB#I:115).

RAWLINGS, WILLIAM (2), son of Aaron (1), may be the William who m. Elizabeth Green on 28 April 1734 or 1735 (133:151, 154).

RAWLINGS, JONATHAN (3), s. of Aaron (1), may have moved to Balto. Co. by 1750 where a William Rawlings owned 100 a. Brotherly Love (153:103).

RAWLINGS, AARON (4), s. of Aaron (1), may be the Aaron Rawlings who moved to Balto. Co. by 1750 when he was listed in the debt book as owning 100 a. Wiltshire; poss. m. Susanna Beard on 14 Dec. 1725 in All Hallows Parish; Susanna went back to A. A. Co. and left a will, 7 March 1762 - 17 May 1762, naming a son-in-law Gassaway Watkins , and these ch. (the daughters were all married): AARON (may be the Aaron who joined Gunpowder Meeting on 26 d, 11 m., 1755; MOSES; RICHARD; ANN; SUSANNA; RACHEL; ELIZABETH (136; 210-31:590; 217-IB#I:167; 219-1:101).

RAWLINGS, DANIEL, was b. c.1694/5, and was alive in 1758; gave his age as 48 in 1743; m. Mary Rumney on 12 July 1716; in April 1720 surv. 250 a. Lucky Adventure; joined Gunpowder Meeting in Sept. 1758 and left without settling his affairs in order; had at least one ch.: DANIEL, was in Balto. Co. in 1750 as Daniel, Jr., and owning 100 a. Jeopardy, and 100 a. Addition to Jeopardy (136; 153:9; 207; 217-IB#I:167; 219-1:273).

RAWLINGS, or RAWLAND, JAMES, was in Balto. Co. by 1750 when he owned 100 a. Bear Hill (153:73).

RAWLINGS, JOHN, purch., 100 a. The Narrows from Jenkin Smith of Calvert Co.; in Nov. 1686 he purch, 150 a., being one-half of Collett's Neglect from Miles Gibson; was in Balto. Co. by 1692 as a taxable in n. side Gunpowder Hund. (59:210, 222; 138).

RAWLINGS, JOHN, d. in Balto. Co. by 4 March 1722 when his est. was inventoried; m. Eleanor Ridgely on 13 Jan. 1712 in All Hallows Par., A. A. Co.; admin. bond was posted on his est. on 19 Feb. 1722 by extx. Eleanor Carlisle, with James Presbury and Thomas Hatchman; John d. leaving a will, 28 Jan. 1722/3 - 19 Feb. 1722/3 naming Eleanor Carlisle as extx., and leaving property to Joseph Presbury; when his est. was inv. on 4 March 1722 by Edmund Talbot and Charles Baker, and val. at £ 216.2.0; there was a notation that he had no relations; Eleanor Presbury, the extx., admin. the est. on 2 Sept. 1724 (2:33; 14:347; 52:20; 124:135; 219-1:272).

RAWLINGS, JOHN, was in Balto. Co. by Nov. 1718 when his w. Dorothy was mentioned in the court proceedings; in 1720 Dorothy Rawlings was mentioned in the will of her uncle John Rawlings; this John d. by March 1743/4 for in March of that year Dority Rawlings (sic) was ind. for bast. and tried in June 1744 (23:38; 35:154, 237; 124:101; 131).

RAWLINGS, MICHAEL, was in Balto. Co. by 1750 as the owner of 50 a. Chattam (153:95).

RAYMAN, WILLIAM, m. Elizabeth (--) and had iss.: SAMUEL, b. 6 March 1730; HANNAH, b. 25 Feb. 1732 (133:21, 27).

RAYNOR, PETER, m. Mary Perren on 14 Feb. 1754 (131).

REA, HUGH, m. Margaret (---) and had iss.: RACHEL, twin, b. 2 Dec. 1756; WILLIAM, twin, b. 2 Dec. 1756 (129:354).

READ/REED, ALEXANDER, blacksmith, servant, was listed in the 1743 inv. of Luke Stansbury with one year to serve (52:458).

READ, BETSY, drowned on Christmas Eve, 1752, when the ice broke while she was skating (385:212).

READ, JAMES, was in Balto. Co. by 1695 as a taxable in n. side of Patapsco; was co-exec. of the est. of Thomas Eager on 10 July 1710 and 7 Oct. 1710 (1:352; 2:157; 140).

READ, JOHN, m. Mary (---) and had iss.: ANNES, dau., b. 9 May 1744 (129:336).

READ, JOHN, m. Eliza Jackson on 12 April 1757 (129:355).

READ, LUKE, d. by 18 May 1713 when admin. bond was posted by Mary Reed with Thomas Croker and Joseph Conway; est. was inv. on 21 May 1713 by Joseph Conway and Thomas Croker and val. at £ 59 7.7; est. was admin. in 1714 by Gerrard Ward; dec. left no children (1:13; 12:557; 50:287).

REED, WILLIAM, was made exempt from the levy in June 1738 (31: 224).

REAGAN, JOHN, m. Mary Norris on 21 Jan. 1733; had iss.: JOHN, b. 29 Oct. 1734 (133:40, 151).

REASIN, MATTHEW, m. Mary Dickson on 27 Dec. 1754; had iss.: JAMES, b. 13 March 1758, d. after 1791, served in the Rev. War (129:360; 359).

REASON, RICHARD m. Alice (---), and had iss.: MARTHA, b. 18 Nov. 1744; SARAH, b. 9 April 1748; THOMAS, b. 9 Feb. 1749 (129: 356).

REASTON. See RISTON.

REDBURN, JOHN, on 6 Aug. 1684 bound himself to serve Richard Heath for 4 years after his arrival in Md. (18:258).

REDDELL, JOHN, m. Eleanor Daugherty on 23 April 1760; had iss.: SARAH, b. 10 Jan. 1761 (129:366).

REDDELL. See RIDDLE/RIDDELL.

REDMAN, CHRISTOPHER, m. Ann Bell on 3 June 1737 (128:96).

REESE, SOLOMON (1), d. in Balto. Co. leaving a will, 23 Nov. 1751 - 16 Oct. 1751; m. Jane (---) who was named extx.; admin. bond on his est. was posted 18 Oct. 1752 by Jane Reese with Thomas Scarlett abd Jno. Preble; dec. had iss.: SOLOMON; DANIEL (14:335; 111:45).

REESE, SOLOMON (2), s. of Solomon (1), may have been the Solomon who m. Mary Draper on 6 Nov. 1737; Solomon and Mary had iss.: SARAH, b. 3 March 1748; SOLOMON, b. 21 Oct. 1743 (128:98; 129:334)

REESE, DANIEL (3), s. of Solomon (1) m. Elizabeth Night (Knight?) on 28 Dec. 1743; had iss.: ABRAHAM, b. 11 June 1744 (129:339)

REESE, EDWARD, on 11 Jan. 1684, was named as bro. in the will of John Tilliard (121:10).

REESE, WILLIAM, was b. c.1717, and was living in 1776 in Broad Creek Hundred of Harford Co.; m. Ann O'Herd on 10 July 1746; she was b. c.1721, and was alive in 1776; William and Ann had iss.: MARY, b. 8 July 1747, alive 1776; WILLIAM, b. 6 Nov. 1749; ELIZABETH, b. 19 Nov. 1751; RACHEL, b. 29 Dec. 1753; ANN, b. 22 Feb. 1755; alive in 1776; HANNAH, b. 1 June 1757, alive in 1776; NELLY, b. 1760; MARGARET, b. c.1762; ALEXANDER, b. c.1764; poss. WILLIAM, b. c.1768; JESSE, b. c.1776 (129:353; 285).

REESTON. See RISTON.

REAVES. See REEVES.

REEVES/REAVES, EDWARD (1), progenitor, is prob. the Edward
who was transp. to Md. c.1667 with Ann, Francis, and John Reeves;
in July 1676 surv. 43 a. The Chance; in Nov. 1677 with w. Ann he
conv. the 43 a. to Thomas Preston; in Aug. 1679 he and Ann conv.
175 a. part The United Friendship to William Burn; in May 1681 he
purch. 110 a. Clement's Dane and 50 a. Clement from George and
Elizabeth Skipwith of A. A. Co.; by Aug. 1683 he had m. as his
2nd w. Henrietta, wid. of William Robinson; in July 1683 he posted
bond and recorded a deed of gift to Elizabeth, dau. of Edward Swanson, now the wife of John Wood; on 3 Feb. 1684/5, for "love and
affection" he conv, part Clement's Dean to Elizabeth, wife of John
Serjeant; in Sept. 1684 he and wife Henrietta admin. the est. of
Thomas Cannon; on 15 Nov. 1684 aurv. 50 a. Hog Neck; d. by 4 March
1690 when his est. was admin. by his 3rd w. Mary, now the w. of
Richard Askew; in March 1690 Askew and Mary conv. one-half of
United Friendship, formerly taken up by Lodowick Williams and
Edward Reeves, to Thomas Preston; Edward, m. 1st, by 1679 Ann
(---); m. 2nd, by Aug. 1683, Henrietta, widow of William Robinson
and Thomas Cannon; m. by 1690, Mary (---) who m. as her 2nd husb.
Richard Askew; Edward had iss.: ROGER; EDWARD; ANN, m. 1699 John
Savory; poss. ELIZABETH, m. John Serjeant (18:187; 59; 60; 64;
211:67).

REEVES, ROGER (2), poss. s. of Edward (1), m. by Oct. 1694, Ann,
wid. of (---) Pauling; she m. 3rd Jonas Bowen, and 4th, on 20 Dec.
1732 Jonas Hewling; he was at least 16 by 1692 when he was listed
as a taxable on the North side of Patapsco Hund.; in Oct. 1694 he
and Ann wit. the will of Nathaniel Henchman; in Feb. 1695 he surv.
100 a. Roger's Road (later held by John Royston); on 24 March 1700
Martha Bowen conv. John Pauling a cow, but if he died before the
age of 16 the cow was to pass to Pauling's bro., William Reeves;
on the same day Martha Bowen conv. a cow to Honour Reeves, and
if she died before the age of 16, the cow was to go to her bro.,
John Pauling; William and Ann's ch. may be tentatively identified as: WILLIAM; HONOUR (66:57; 121:111; 138; 211:83).

REEVES, EDWARD (3), s. of Edward (1), was an orphan in 1693
when he chose Richard Askew to be his guardian; was at least 16
by 1695 when he was listed as a taxable in the household of James
Maxwell(20:83; 140).

REEVES, WILLIAM (4), s. of Roger (2), was under 16 in 1700,
but was 16 or more in 1705 when he was listed as a taxable in
S. side of Patapsco Hund.; in July 1725 William purch. 50 a. of
Reeves Neck from Edward and Jane Cox; on 21 Jan. 1726/7 William
and wife Elizabeth conv. 100 a. Rogers' Road to John Wilmot;
in Dec. 1728 he was named as a son in the will of Jonas Bowen
(who m. William's mother Ann); William was listed in the 1750
Debt Book as owning 50 a. Reeves' Neck; William and wife Elizabeth had at least four children: WILLIAM, b. 27 July 1720;
ELIZABETH, b. 5 July 17-(?)(she may be the Elizabeth Reeves who
m. George Ensor on 24 Dec. 1739); ROGER, b. 21 Jan. 1725; MARGA-
RET, b. 9 Jan. 1728 (may be the Margaret Reeves who m. Emmanuel
Mallonee on 13 Feb. 1749/50 (70:144, 327; 125:93; 131; 147; 153:
9).

REEVES, WILLIAM (5), s. of William (4), was b. 27 July 1720;
was prob. the William Reeves whose marr. to Mary Gott was stopped
"for bigamy" by the vestry of St. John's Par. (131; 132).

REEVES, ROGER (6), s. of William (4), was b. 21 Jan. 1725; m.
Phoebe Progden on 12 Sept. 1756 (131).

REEVES, ANN, wit. the will of Sarah Strawbridge of Balto. Co.
on 30 March 1699 (L@L:178).

REEVES, EMMANUEL m. Mary (---) and had iss.: GEORGE, b. 16
Sept. 1746; JOHN, b. 12 July 1748; MARY, b. 10 April 1750;
MARGARET, b. 7 April 1752; ANN, b. 29 March 1754; ELEANOR, b. 15
June 1756 (129:372).

REEVES, JOSIAS, m. Letitia Raven on 11 Jan. 1756; they had at
least one dau.: ELIZABETH, b. 18 Dec. 1756 (129:356; 131:47).

REEVES/REVIS, THOMAS, d. leaving a will, 20 Jan. 1728 - 25
Jan. 1728, in which he left his pers. est. to his execs. John and
George Harryman, and a tract called Revis Lot to the execs. and
to Thomas Sheredine; the execs. posted admin. bond on 25 Jan.
1728 with Martin Parlett and Thomas Sutton; the est. was admin.
on 6 July 1731 (5:175; 14:328; 125:92).

REGAN, DARBY, d. by 5 April 1722 when admin. bond was posted
by the admnx. Abigail Regan, with Matthew Organ and Henry Carrington (14:346).

REIVES. See REEVES.

RELPH, HENRY, d. 1 Jan. 1708/9 (128:25).

RENCH, RALPH, m. Margaret Watkins, on 21 Dec. 1755 (131).

RENOLDS. See REYNOLDS.

RENSHAW, THOMAS (1), the progenitor, was in Balto. Co. by 3
Sept. 1744, when he and w. Jane sold 134 a. Brother's Discovery
to James Rigbie, and 100 a. of the same tract to Nathaniel Porter;
Thomas may be the same individual who m. Ann Charvel on 16 Dec.
1718 in St. Anne's Par., A. A. Co.; m. leaving a will, leaving
250 a. Brother's Discovery to his eld. s. John, 250 a. of the
same tract to his 2nd s. Abraham, and also naming son Thomas (to
have yet another 250 a,), and children Joseph and Jane; admin.
bond was posted in Oct., 1748 by extx. Jane Renshaw with Robert
Clark and James Brice; Thomas was the father of: JOHN; ABRAHAM;
THOMAS; JOSEPH; and JANE (15:182; 77:567, 572; 210-25:102; 219-
2:406).

RENSHAW, JOHN (2), s. of Thomas (1), d. in Balto. Co. by 8 Dec.
1752; m. Mary Litton on 27 March 1735; she m. as her 2nd husb.
Patrick Cavenagh; in 1750 he owned 250 a. Giles and Webster's
Discovery; left a will, 25 Nov. 1750 - 8 June 1751, naming his w.
Mary as extx. and his daus. Alice, Hannah, Ann, Cassandra, Mary,
Elizabeth, and a possible unborn ch.; admin. bond was posted on
5 June 1751 by extx. Mary Renshaw with Edward Wakeman and Samuel
Webb; est. was admin. by Mary Renshaw and then Mary wife of Patrick Cavenagh on 8 Dec. 1752, 18 Aug. 1753, and 5 Sept. 1760;
John and Mary had iss.: ALCE HANNAH, b. 22 March 1735; ANN, b.
19 Feb. 1741; CASSANDRA, b. 16 Dec. 1743; MARY; ELIZABETH; poss.
an unborn ch. (4:319; 5:259, 288; 15:209; 128:86, 91; 129: 327,
336; 210-28:68).

RENSHAW, ABRAHAM (3), s. of Thomas (1), was alive in 1750, and
may have been alive later; m. Ann, dau. of Robert Hawkins, on 15
June 1738; in 1750 he owned 250 a. Giles and Webster's Discovery;
by w. Ann he had: THOMAS, b. 20 Oct. 1739; JOHN, b. 17 June 1741;
JOSEPH, b. 7 June 1744; ABRAHAM, b. 14 Sept. 1746; poss. ISAAC,
b. c.1748; poss. ANN, b. c.1755 (128:92/r, 105; 129:325, 343;
153:74; 210-31:417).

RENSHAW, THOMAS (4), s. of Thomas (1) was in Balto. Co. at
least as late as 1760; m. Frances, dau. of Robert Clark on 29
Jan. 1739; m. 2nd, widow Mary Brice; in 1750 he owned part

Clark's Den, 50 a. Murray in Antrim, 200 a. Giles and Webster's
Discovery, and 82 a. Renshaw's Desire; in April 1751 Thomas and
Frances conv. 7 a. Giles and Webster's Discovery to Samuel Webb;
had iss.: JANE, b. 6 Dec. 1740; WILLIAM, b. 9 Nov. 1742, d. 1770
in Rowan Co., N.C.; THOMAS, b. 19 Feb. 1745; FRANCES, b. 16 Nov.
1749; SELINA, b. 3 April 1752; JAMES, b. 28 Aug. 1754; ROBERT, b.
18 June 1757; MARTIN, b. 30 Jan. 1760; BENNETT, b. c.1762; HOSEA,
b. c.1764 (81:205; 153:74; 128:81; 129:367, 368; 210-30:221).

RENSHAW, JOSEPH (5), s. of Thomas (1), was b. c.1723, and was
living in 1776 in Bush River Lower Hund., Harf. Co.; m. Elizabeth
Wells on 28 Oct. 1742; in 1750 he owned 300 a. Clark's Den and 19
a. Giles and Webster's Discovery; had iss.: CASSANDRA, b. 8 Sept.
1743; JANE, b. c.1750; JOSEPH, Jr., b. c. 1751; ELIZABETH, Jr.,
b. c.1753; THOMAS, b. c.1755; PHILIP, b. c.1758; SAMUEL, b. c.
1761; and SUSANNA, b. c.1765 (129:328, 336; 153:129; 285).

RENSHAW, ANN, age 5 in June 1754, was bound to Margaret Brownley and her dau. (39:185).

RENSHAW, MARY, m. Peter Carroll on 3 May 1710 (129:209).

RENSHAW or RENCHER, MARY, m. John White in 1722 (133:147).

RESTON. See RISTON.

REVISS. See REEVES.

REYCROFT, John, d. leaving a will, 20 Sept. 1675 - 11 Dec.
1675, naming Thomas Jones; sworn to by James and Elizabeth Armstrong (120:117).

REYNOLDS, THOMAS, of Calvert Co., in 1750 owned 300 a. Clarkson's Hope (153:104).

REYNOLDS, THOMAS, in 1750 owned 106 a. Smith's Forest; may
have been the Thomas Reynolds fined in Nov. 1757 for bast. as
the father of Ann Young's child (46:75; 153:28).

REYNOLDS, WILLIAM, was in Balto. Co. by 1694 as a taxable in
Spesuita Hund. (139).

REYNOLDS, WILLIAM, d. by 4 March 1729 when admin. bond was
posted by George Elliott, with Darby Henley and John Fuller
(14:324).

REYSTONE. See RISTON.

RHODES, HENRY (1), progenitor, d. in Balto. Co. by 3 Dec. 1709;
m. Katherine Stockett on 15 Jan. 1697/8 in All Hallows' Parish
A. A. Co.; Katherine m. as her 2nd husb. Francis Ogg some time
before 3 March 1710; admin. bond on his est. was posted 3 Dec.
1709 by admx. Katherine Rhodes with Charles Baker and Thomas
Preston; his est. was inv. on 16 Dec. 1709 by Matthew Green and
Thomas Bond; est. was admin. by Katherine, now w. of Francis
Ogg, on 3 March 1710; Henry and Katherine had iss.: HENRY, Jr.;
poss. FRANCES, m. John Nelson on 12 Jan. 1718; ANN, m. William
Hollis on 13 March 1720; CATHERINE, m. William Osborn on 1 March
1727/8 (2:161; 12:544; 48:31; 129:229, 245; 131:10).

RHODES, HENRY (2), s. of Henry (1) and Katherine, was b. c.
1705; was age in in 1723 when with consent of his father-in-law
Francis Ogg he was bound to Richard Legg; m. Ann (---); on 6
March 1733 Henry and Ann conv. 50 a. Gibson's Ridge to Edward
Sanders; on 7 Nov. 1733 as son and heir of Henry Rhodes, dec.,

he conv. 200 a. part Birr to his sis. Catherine, w. of William
Osborn; d. by 8 March 1748/9 when admin. bond was posted by Jacob Giles with Amos Garrett; est. was admin. 22 April 1756 by
Jacob Giles; Henry and Ann had iss.: MARY, b. 6 Sept. 1733;
CATHERINE, b. 17 Nov. 1734, d. 16 Feb. 1734/5: MARTHA, b. 1 May
1736; SARAH, b. 13 Nov. 1738, d. 5 Oct. 1739; GEORGE LESTER,
b. 2 Sept. 1740; HENRY, b. 1 Nov. 1745, age 9 in Aug. 1754 when
he was bound to Benjamin Davis (5:303; 15:236; 21:156; 26:192;
39:346; 128:74, 83, 87, 92, 104, 113; 129:331).

RHODES, RICHARD (3), no known rel. to the above, m. Magdalen
(---); on 19 Nov. 1747 Richard and Magdalen and James Amos and
wife Hannah conv. 100 a. Necessity to Robert Collins; Richard
and Magdalen had iss.: RICHARD, b. 1 Dec. 1713; MARY, b. 5 Feb.
1715, m. Joseph Elledge on 4 Sept. 1733; REBECCA, b. 6 March
1723; ANN, b. 22 April 1725; WILLIAM, b. Sept. 1726, d. Sept.
1729; BENJAMIN, b. 16 Nov. 1729, d. 22 Nov. 1729; ELIZABETH, b.
10 July 1730 (79:601; 131:6, 10, 9/r, 15/r, 44/r, 53/r).

RHODES, RICHARD (4), s. of Richard (3), was b. 1 Dec. 1713,
and d. in Balto. Co. leaving a will, 27 Feb. 1767 - 13 June 1768;
m. Sarah Whitaker on 9 Feb. 1768; in 1750 owned 50 a. Poor Man's
Purchase; in his will left Poor Man's Purchase and Rhodes' Last
Shift to his son John; the tract Necessity and 15 a. John's
Forest was to go to his son Thomas; the residue of John's Forest was to go to his sons Richard and Alexander McComas; est.
of Richard Rhodes was admin. on 3 July 1769; Richard and Sarah
had iss.: HANNAH, b. 2 May 1741; JOHN, b. 20 Dec. 1743; RICHARD,
b. 30 Nov. 1745 "the first born twin;" ALEXANDER McCOMAS, "the
second born twin," B. 30 Nov. 1745; THOMAS, b. 1 March 1747;
AQUILA; WILLIAM; SARAH; PRISCILLA; and MARTHA (7:12; 15:231;
112:90; 131:85/r, 111/r; 153:11).

RHODES, ANTHONY, d. by 29 July 1761 when admin. bond was
posted by Clare Rhodes, with William Lyon, and Thomas Sligh;
est. was admin. 29 Aug. 1763 by Clare Rhodes; dec. left no ch.,
but had some relations in Eng. (6:29).

RHODES, JAMES, age 7 "last April," in Nov. 1737 was bound to
Jonathan and Jane Hughes (31:133).

RHODES, JOHN, age c. 25, from Hampshire, Eng.; ran away from
Balto. Iron Works, before Dec. 1758(307-69:210).

RHODES/RHODOUS, JOSEPH, m. Ann Polson in June 1725; in June
1734 Ann Rhodes bound her dau. Sophia age 9 "last 26 May" to
Theophilus Jones; had iss.: SOPHIA, b. 26 May 1725, m. John Hely
on 23 Dec. 1744 (30:254; 131:27, 41/r).

RHODES, RICHARD, m. Mary (---); in Aug. 1725 he gave his consent for his s. John, age 5 years and 9 mos., to be bound to William and Elizabeth Bradford; had iss.: THOMAS, b. 15 March 1717/8,
may be the Thomas who m. Margaret Allen on 23 June 1743; JOHN, b.
28 March 1720, may be the John who m. Mary Keon on 17 Oct. 1754
(27:306; 129:330; 131).

RHODES, WILLIAM, m. Mary Matthews, prob. dau. of Henry Matthews,
on 17 Jan. 1717; on 2 Nov. 1726 he signed the inv. of said Henry
Matthews as kin; on 24 Nov. 1731 William and Mary conv. one-half
of Matthews' Double Purchase to William Smith; on 5 June 1734 he
purch. 10 a. Hughes' Choice from Thomas and Sarah Cross; William
and Mary had iss.: MARY, b. 2 March 1719; ELIZABETH, b. 30 Aug.
1721; porb. JOHN, b. 20 Sept. 1738 (51:66; 73:185; 74:67; 128:
108; 131:10, 14, 40/r).

RICE, SOLOMON, was in Balto. Co. by 1694 as a taxable in Spe-sutia Hund. (139).

RICE, WILLIAM, m. Rachel (---), and had iss.: SARAH, b. 23 Feb. 1725; ELIZABETH, b. 1 May 1728 (131:6/r).

RICE, WILLIAM, m. Elizabeth Buttram on 15 Aug. 1731; she d. 12 May 1740; William and Elizabeth had iss.: WILLIAM, b. 6 Aug. 1732, prob. d. young; WILLIAM, b. 14 April 1734; JOHN, b. 22 April 1736; MARY, b. 14 April 1738 (128:68, 71, 79, 91, 110).

RICE, WILLIAM, m. Ann (---) and had iss.: ELEANOR, b. 30 Sept. 1743 (129:334).

RICH, JOHN, m. Ann Massey on 2 Oct. 1759 (131).

RICHARD, JAMES, of Balto. Co., was b. in Rochelle, France, and was naturalized in 1744; gave his age as over 40 on 2 July 1764 (89:309; 210-42:602; 404:13).

RICHARDS, EDWARD (1), may have been in Dor. Co. with wife Mary on 5 July 1729 when they conv. 100 a. The Dawns to Francis Sher-wood of Tal. Co.; came to Balto. Co. where he patented the tract Spring Garden in 1730; in March 1740 he and w. Mary conv. that tract to John Cole; in 1750 he owned 50 a. Rattlesnake Ridge; d. leaving a will, 22 Sept. 1755 - 29 Nov. 1755, naming the ch. listed below; admin. bond was posted 15 Dec. 1755 by exec. Rich-ard Richards with Chris.Vaughan and Thomas Story; est. was admin. 12 May 1757; Edward and Mary had iss.: BENJAMIN; RICHARD; STEPH-EN, DANIEL; MATTHEW; ANNE, m. (---) Morgain; SARAH, m. (---) Phippen; ELIZABETH, m. (---) Semons; RACHEL, m. (---) Sier; PATIENCE, m. Thomas Story; LYDIA, m. William Winchester; and MARY, m. (---) VAUGHAN (5:323; 14:338; 75:472; 110:480; 153:19; 207).

RICHARDS, BENJAMIN (2), s. of Edward and Mary, m. by 3 Aug. 1739 Ann, dau. of Charles Merryman; in 1750 he owned 50 a. Spring Garden, which he sold in April 1750 to William Stiles; had iss.: EDWARD, b. 25 June 1731; RUTH, b. 27 April 1733; and CHARLES, b. 23 Feb. 1747 (4:21; 80:538; 133:26, 29, 83; 153:16).

RICHARDS, RICHARD (3), s. of Edward (1), was b. c.1725, d. c.1811; m. Sarah Hooker on 14 July 1754; gave his age as near 75 in 1800; in 1750 owned Transylvania; acquired numerous tracts in Balto. Co. by patent and by purchase, including 50 a. Chestnut Level, 25 a. Corn Hill, 50 a. Bachelor's Choice, New Market, 50 a. Frugality; m. Sarah Hooker on 14 July 1754; left a will, 27 Feb. 1808 - 29 June 1811; had iss.: NICHOLAS; RICHARD, m. Anne Brown; ARTHUR; ELIZABETH; RUTH, m. Edward Gill; SARAH, m. Edward Brown; MARY, m. (---) McComiskey; SAMUEL; JOHN; and RACHEL, m. George Null (118:142; 153:95; 207; 231-WG#67:165).

RICHARDS, DOROTHY, in March 1716/7 named John Hays as the father of her baseborn ch.; had iss.: ZACHEUS, b. 17 Oct. 1716 (in Nov. 1718 he was bound to Alice Barrett to age 21 (22:95; 23: 37; 133:20).

RICHARDS. JAMES, in 1750 owned 50 a. Jones' Farm, 950 a. North Carolina, 4 lots in Balto. Town, and 645 a. Carolina Felix (153: 78)

RICHARDS, JOHN, in Aug. 1755 was made levy free (40:220).

RICHARDS, JOHN, m. Elizabeth (---) and had iss.: MARY, b. 1 Aug. 1731 (may be the Mary Richards bound to William Johnson in Nov. 1737 at age 10, until she reached age 16 (31:133; 133:26).

RICHARDS, RICHARD, m. Elizabeth (---), and had iss.: MARY, b.
30 Aug. 1721 (133:26).

RICHARDS, WILLIAM, m. Mary (---), and had iss.: SAMUEL, b. 3
Nov. 1731; JEREMIAH, b. 25 Aug. 1734 (128:100; 129:300).

THE LAWRENCE RICHARDSON FAMILY

RICHARDSON, LAWRENCE (1), came to Md. c.1649, and d. c.1666;
settled in A. A. Co., where he surv. 200 a. Richardson's Folly on
19 Jan., 1661, and 280 a. called Upper Tauton on 15 Dec. 1662;
d. leaving a will proved 14 Oct. 1666, leaving the home plantation to his oldest son, and 280 a. Upper Tauton to his two youngest sons; had iss.: THOMAS (prob. the eldest s. as he was named
exec.): SARAH (called eldest dau.; may have m. Joshua Dorsey);
MARY; JOHN: LAWRENCE; ELIZABETH (120:38; 211; 388; Beale Howard
Richardson, "Richardson and Allied Families," typescript at Md.
Hist. Soc.).

RICHARDSON, THOMAS (2), s. of Lawrence (1), is prob. the Thomas who d. in Balto. Co. in 1702; m. 1st by 9 May 1685 Rachel,
wid. and extx. of John Towers; m. 2nd Mary (---); m. 3rd, by
18 March 1699 Susanna (---); she m. 2nd by March 1709 Thomas
Hutchins; on 19 May 1680 a band of Indians attacked his house,
but Thomas and his bro., Lawrence drove them away; on 16 Aug.
1692 he was commissioned surveyor for Baltimore County, and was
Chief Ranger for the county south of Back River; on 1 April 1681
Thomas conv. 200 a. Richardson's Level to John Rockhold; on 9
May 1685 Thomas and Rachel conv. 150 a. Hog Neck, formerly the
prop. of Rachel's first husb. John Towers, to Michael Judd; on
3 Aug. 1697 Richardson conv. Long Point and Dixon's Choice to
his s. John; on 18 March 1699 Thomas and wife Susanna conv. to
Thomas Sterling of Calvert Co., tract Sterling's Purchase, orig.
part of Richardson's Outlet; d. leaving a will, 12 June 1701 -
24 April 1702; admin. bond was posted 20 July 1702 by Susanna
Richardson with Michael Judd, John Love, John Roberts, and John
Seals; left iss.: JOHN, alive 1681; d. leaving a will, 3 Jan.
1702/3 - 7 Jan. 1703, naming wid. Susanna, bro. John, and James
Crooke, who admin. John's est. on 14 May 1707, 20 Oct. 1709 and
24 Oct. 1709; ELIZA; MARY; JAMES; poss. unborn ch. (2:105, 137,
174; 12:543; 21:120; 61:166; 64:118; 66:15; 109:215; 121:237;
122:89; Balto. Co. Orig. Inventories, Box 2, folder 6; Richardson typescript).

RICHARDSON, LAWRENCE (3), s. of Lawrence (1), d. in Balto. Co.
by 13 June 1705; m. Ann (---), who m. as her 2nd husb. Oliver
Harriott; admin. bond was posted 13 June 1705 by the wid. Ann
Richardson, who admin. the est. on 9 Oct. 1710 and 13 June 1711
(the second time by Ann, w. of Oliver Harriott); Lawrence and
Ann had at least one child:THOMAS, b. c.1692(2:2, 134; 12:556).

RICHARDSON, THOMAS (4), s. of Lawrence (3), was b. c.1692,
and was alive at least as late as 1750; m. Sarah "Standove"
(prob. Standiford) on 20 May 1720; on 7 Aug. 1723 Thomas and
Sarah conv. 75 a. part Arthur's Choice (which Thomas' father
had bought from Richard Smithers) to John Hatch; in 1750 he owned
170 a. Timber Hills, and in 1750 he had surv. Richardson's Outlet; w. Sarah d. leaving a will, 29 Dec. 1769 - 1 Feb. 1771,
leaving Timber Hill, a patent she had had before her marr., to
her sons Thomas and Vincent; Thomas and Sarah had iss.: MARY, b.
26 May 1721; JAMES, b. 5 or 17 Jan. 1723; THOMAS, b. 16 May 1726;
JOHN, b. 15 or 17 Jan. 1728/9; BENJAMIN, b. 5 Nov. 1730, m. Jemima Standiford on 5 March 1753; SAMUEL, b. 2 Nov. 1734, m. Sarah
Davis on 30 Dec. 1756; WILLIAM, b. 11 April 1737; SARAH, b. Jan.
1745; VINCENT, b. 1748, d. 1777, m. Martha Norris in 1771 (112:
199; 131; 207; Richardson typescript).

RICHARDSON, JAMES (5), s. of Thomas (4), was b. January 1723, d. by 23 Jan. 1776; m. Sophia Standiford on 3 Jan. 1744; left a will, 3 Sept. 1775 - 23 Jan. 1776; had iss.: DELILAH, b. 12 May 1746, m. (---) Pimple; JOHN: MARY, m. Skelton Standiford on 5 Nov. 1772; JAMES; ELIZABETH, m. William Chenoweth on or about 8 April 1789; DAVID: SKELTON: SAMUEL: VINCENT, m. Penelope Standiford on 8 Oct. 1795; THOMAS; BENJAMIN; SARAH, m. Zachariah Price on or about 23 Oct. 1783 (112:317; 131; 232).

RICHARDSON, SAMUEL (6), s. of Thomas (4), was b. 2 Nov. 1734, and was alive in 1761; m. Sarah Davis, dau. of William Davis on 30 Dec. 1755; had iss.: DELIA, b. 18 Dec. 1756; ELIZABETH, b. 25 July 1758; SARAH, b. 9 Sept. 1761 (112:149; 129:375; 210-37:585).

RICHARDSON, WILLIAM (7), s. of Thomas (4), was b. 11 April 1737; m. Mary Davis, dau. of William and sis. of Henry Davis, on 27 March 1759 (131; 210-37:585).

RICHARDSON, ANN, m. John Roberts on 7 Feb. 1714 (131).

RICHARDSON, BENJAMIN, d. by 12 Aug. 1745, when admin. bond was posted by Darby Lux admin., with George Buchanan and Thomas Jennings (15:181).

RICHARDSON, DANIEL, m. by 17 March 1708 Elizabeth, dau. of John Giles (67:5).

RICHARDSON, ELIZABETH, was ind. for bast. in June 1711 (21: 210).

RICHARDSON, JAMES, in Aug. 1715 was named by Margaret Gibson as the father of her bastard ch. (21:626).

RICHARDSON, JAMES, m. Rachel Stone on 16 Jan. 1759 (131).

RICHARDSON, JAMES, m. 31 Jan. 1759, Mary, wid. of Richard Ruff; had iss.; JAMES, b 30 Jan. 1761 (4:311; 129:367).

RICHARDSON, JOHN, surv. 200 a. Bushy Neck on 2 Nov. 1695 (207).

RICHARDSON, JOHN, d. by 13 June 1714 when admin. bond was posted by James Richardson with Benjamin Dorsey and William Collison (14:322).

RICHARDSON, JOHN, from Yorkshire, wheelwright and wagonmaker, ran away from the Lancashire Ironworks at Joseph Watkins' at the head of Back River (307-69:211).

RICHARDSON, LAWRENCE, in 1750 owned 50 a. Avarilla's Garden (153:15).

RICHARDSON, MARK, m. by June 1683, Susanna, wid. and extx. of George Utie; surv. 1000 a. Poplar Neck on 20 Sept. 1683; d. 19 Feb. 1704/5; left a will, 8 June 1701 - 27 Feb. 1704/5, naming w. Susanna, dau.-in-law Bethia Phillips, son-in-law James Phillips, and (dau.-in-law) Susanna Utie; admin. bond was posted 26 Aug. 1706 by extx. Susanna Richardson, now w. of Thomas Wainwright (whom she m. 21 Jan. 1705/6), with John Stokes and Henry Wright; est. was inv. on 13 Sept. 1706 by Samuel Jackson and Thomas Cord and val. at £ 440.5.7 (12:539; 18:45; 48:218; 122:13; 128:21; 129:201, 203; 206-10:170; 211:6).

RICHARDSON, MARY, surv. 218 a. Maiden's Choice in Nov. 1684; later m. Richard Lenox (207).

RICHARDSON, MARY, named Samuel Corbett as the father of her child, in Nov. 1710 (21:184).

RICHARDSON, NATHAN, m. Elizabeth Crockett, dau. of John and Mary, on 30th d, 8 m., 1735; the marr. cert. at West River identified his parents as William and Margaret; on 11 June 1742 he admin. the est. of John Crockett, who left his son-in-law the tract Colerain; Nathan owned the 602 a. tract in 1750 (3:283; 153:76; Register of West River Meeting, Soc. of Friends, 219-6).

RICHARDSON, NATHAN, m. Hannah Webster Gover, widow of Samuel Gover, and dau. of Isaac Webster on 20 April 1749, at Nottingham Monthly Meeting; his admin. bond was posted in 175-(?) by Hannah Richardson with Isaac Webster, Jr.,; his est. was admin. on 8 Oct. 1757 and again on 5 Mar 1760; he left one child; ELIZABETH (4:290; 5:317; 15:196; Register of Nottingham Meeting, Soc. of Friends, HR).

RICHARDSON, NATHAN, d. leaving a will, 7 Jan. 1756 - 5 Aug. 1756, naming his w. Elizabeth as extx., naming mother-in-law Margaret Webster and bro.-in-law Isaac Webster, and the ch. named below: ELIZABETH; MARGARET, m. (---) Hill; SARAH; WILLIAM; NATHAN: and DANIEL (111:105).

RICHARDSON, NATHANIEL, m. Elizabeth Gott on or after 10 May 1747, the banns having been pub. three times (131).

RICHARDSON, RICHARD, in 1750 owned 350 a. part Owings' Adventure, 100 a. part Owings' Addition, and 15 a. Massey's Neglect; on 28th d., 6 m., 1752 he and w. Margaret and their relatives Aquila and Jonathan Massey were granted a certificate from Gunpowder Meeting to move to Fairfax Meeting in Va. (136).

RICHARDSON, WILLIAM, s. of John, came to Md., and was a serv. to Samuel Tipton of Balto. Co. in 1754; he was advised to apply to the printer of the Md. Gazette (Annapolis, Md. Gaz., 8 Jan. 1767, in 255:49).

RICHEN, SARAH, was ind. for bast. in Nov. 1738; as a serv. to Priscilla Simkins she was tried for bast. in Aug. 1739 (31:307; 32:12).

RICKALY, THOMAS, age c. 26, was a runaway serv. from Charles Green of Balto. Co.; advert. was dated 14 July 1743 (384:414).

RICKETTS, BENJAMIN, was in Balto. Co. by 1746 when he m. 1st, on 18 Oct. 1746, Elinor Maxwell, granddau. of James Maxwell; m. 2nd, on 2 June 1759 Mary Cutchin; in 1750 he owned 361 a. part Conclusion; had iss.: ELIZABETH, b. 1 Jan. 1747; HANNAH MERITER, b. 18 Oct. 1751 (82:6; 131:51, 118/r, 123/r, 129/r; 153).

RICKETTS, NATHANIEL, m. Ann (---) and had iss.: NATHANIEL, b. Jan. 1749 (131:127/r).

RICKETTS, SAMUEL, m. Hannah, dau. of Edward Meads on 24 Dec. 1753; had iss.: ANN, b. 1 Sept. 1754, d. 20 March 1759; EDWARD, b. 6 March 1756; CATHERINE, b. 6 Nov. 1758 (131:17/r).

RICKETTS, THOMAS, m. Mary (---); in 1750 he owned 86 a. The Bird Cage, and on 17 July 1750 Thomas and Mary Ricketts conv. 50 a. of The Bird Cage to Samuel Owings; Thomas and Mary had iss.: ELIZABETH, b. 30 Nov. 1744; RUTH, b. 4 June 1746; MARY, b. 4 July 1749 (153:86; 134:11, 13).

RIDDLE, ANDREW, m. Ann Nicholas on 1 Jan. 1738, and had iss.: ELIZABETH, b. 6 Feb. 1739 (128:104, 111).

RIDDLE, MARY, was was tried for bast. in Nov. 1754 (39:452).

RIDDLE, ROBERT, d. c.1739; m. Sarah, dau. of Sarah Scribner of Stanstead, Essex; Robert's widow m. 2nd, Robert Rix and had iss.: three sons and one dau. (300-65:257).

RIDDLE. See also REDDELL.

RIDEN, SAMUEL in Dec. 1732 inher. Bouer's Purchase and Broom's Bloom from his grandfather Nicholas Waterman of Kent Co. (126:35).

RIDER, JAMES (1), was in Balto. Co. by 1701 when he was listed as a taxable in North Side Patapsco Hund.; on 21 Jan. 1709 he wit. the will of Thomas Roberts, and signed Roberts' inv. in Oct. 1709; m. Mary (---) who d. 4 April 1729; on 25 Oct. 1736 purch. 48 a. Rider's Industry from Henry Oyston; on 22 Nov. 1736 conv. prop. to his s. Francis; d. by 10 Aug. 1739 when admin. bond on his est. was posted by Francis Rider, with John Bowen, Jr., and Ab'm Eaglestone; est. was admin. by Francis on 17 Sept. 1740; had iss.: FRANCIS, of age in 1739; AVARILLA, b. 15 Sept. 1724; and RHODA, b. 5 Feb. 1726 (4:63; 14:35; 51:14; 61:266, 327; 122: 168; 133:7, 12, 194; 143).

RIDER, FRANCIS (2), s. of James (1), was so named in a 1736 deed; m. 1st, by 1738, Anne (---), and m. poss. 2nd, on 7 Aug. 1750 Frances Hopham; in 1750 owned 80 a. Goose Harbor and 65 a. The Wedge; had iss.:MARY, b. 26 June 1738; ELIZABETH, b. 4 May 1740 (77:241; 131; 133:40, 64; 153:53).

RIDER, JANE, m. Henry Yostain on 24 Jan. 1730 (133:150).

RIDER, MARY, m. Joseph Jennings on 24 April 1734 (131).

RIDER, THOMAS, was in Balto. Co. by 1701 when he purch. 100 a. Walnut Neck from Thomas and Sophia Sparrow; mentioned in the will of Richard Banks on 6 Dec. 1703 (66:77; 122:36).

RIDGE, JAMES, was in Balto. Co. by Feb. 1673/4 when he was appointed attorney by John Masters of Gunpowder River, to conv. land (100:116).

THE RIDGELY FAMILY OF HAMPTON is the subject of one of the entries in Harry Wright Newman's Anne Arundel Gentry, Revised and Enlarged, Volume Three (Annapolis: the Author, 1979).

RIDGELY, ROBERT (1), progenitor of the Ridgelys of Hampton, Balto. Co., d. by 24 Dec. 1681 at St. Inigoe's, St. Mary's Co., having come to Md. in The Assurance; served as Clerk of the Provincial Court, Chief Clerk to the Secretary of Md., and Depu- ty Secretary of Md.; d. leaving a will, 20 Dec. 1680 - 24 Dec. 1681; had iss.: ROBERT; CHARLES: WILLIAM, and MARY, m. c.1699 Lewis Duvall (120:102; 365; Newman).

RIDGELY, CHARLES (2), s. of Robert (1) and Martha, d. c. 1705 in A. A. Co,. m. Deborah, dau. of Hon. John and Pleasance (Ely) Dorsey; est. was admin. in Balto. Co. on 14 Oct. 1705 by Debo- rah Ridgely; had iss.: Col. CHARLES, d..1772; ROBERT; WILLIAM (2:222; Newman).

RIDGELY, Col. CHARLES (3), s. of Charles (2) and Deborah, was b. 1702, and d. 1772 ; m. 1st in 1721 Rachel, dau. of John Howard, Jr.; Rachel d. 1750, and he m., 2nd Elizabeth (---), and 3rd Lydia Warfield, dau. of Dr. Stringer; was exec. of Richard Hewett on 17 Oct. 1737; in April 1743 bought part of Tanyard from William Baker, Sr.; negotiated an antenuptial contract with

Lydia Stringer, wid. of Dr. Samuel Stringer of A. A. Co.; in
1750 he owned 103 a. part Rich Neck, and other lands; acquired
Northampton basis of present day Hampton estate; was Justice of
Balto. Co. Court, 1741, and 1747 - 1751; was also a Burgess from
Balto. Co.; left a will, 1 April 1772 - 8 June 1772; left iss.:
JOHN, b. 14 June 1723; PLEASANCE, b. 24 Nov. 1724, m. Lyde Good-
win; CHARLES, b. 21 April 1727, d. young; ACHSAH, b. 22 July
1729, m. three times; WILLIAM, b. 10 May 1731; CHARLES, b. 17
Sept. 1733, m. Rebecca Dorsey (he was the Builder of Hampton);
RACHEL, b. 5 Dec. 1734, m. Capt. Darby Lux; BENJAMIN, b. 22 July
1734 (3:141, 225, 250, 252; 47:126; 78:326; 112:201; 153:14;
BB3f, 26; Newman).

RIDGELY, JOHN (4), s. of Charles (3) and Rachel, was b. 4
June 1723; d. by 1 May 1771; m. Mary, dau. of Caleb Dorsey; left
a will, 19 March 1771 - 1 May 1771; had iss.: CHARLES, d. 30 Aug.
1748; ACHSAH, m. 1770, William Goodwin; CHARLES, d. 15 Dec. 1786
having m. Rebecca Lawson; WILLIAM, m. Anne (---); JOHN, m. Mary
Emmitt; EDWARD; DEBORAH, m. Capt. John Sterett; RACHEL, m. John
Tolley Worthington; ELEANOR, m. Benjamin Lamming; MARY, m. Benjamin Nicholson (112:187, 192; Newman).

RIDGELY, NICHOLAS. admin. the est. of John Harper on 5 April
1727 (3:74).

RIEN, MARY, in Nov. 1754 was tried for bast. (39:451).

RIGBY, JAMES (1), came to Md. c.1659; pat. 125 a. Rigby, and
other lands; d. c.1681, age c.50, having m. Katherine Ceely who
d. 1698, and who m. 2nd Henry Constable; James Rigby left a will,
8 Nov. 1680 - 30 April 1681, mentioning poor Quakers, lands in
Kent and Balto. Cos., w. Katherine, and these ch.: JAMES, b.
c.1662, d. c.1700; JOHN, d. c.1700; MARY; ELIZABETH (120:99;
206-7C:335; Henry C. Forman, "The Family of Col. James Rigbie,"
in 346-2:303-312).

RIGBY, JAMES (2), s. of James (1) and Katherine, was b. by 1662;
d. 1700; m. by 18 Sept. 1698 Elizabeth Smith, bapt. 1698 at age 25,
dau. of Nathan and Margaret Smith; in 1691 was named as bro. in
the will of Mary, wid. of John Ceely, of A. A. Co.; had iss.:
NATHANIEL, b. 28 April 1695; JAMES, b. 4 Jan. 1696, m. Elizabeth
(---); THOMAS (121:46; Forman).

RIGBY, JOHN (3), s. of James (1) and Katherine, m. Eliza Galloway; d. leaving a will, 26 Oct. 1700 - 23 Nov. 1700; had a dau.:
ELIZABETH (121:209; Forman).

RIGBY, NATHANIEL (4), s. of James (2) and Elizabeth, was b.
28 April 1695, d. by 29 Aug. 1752; m. 1st (---) (?); m. 2nd , in
1717, Cassandra Coale, dau. of Philip and Cassandra (Skipwith)
Coale; m. 3rd Sabina Rumsey; in 1750 owned 900 a. Phillips' Purchase, 500 a. Brown's Discovery, 275 a,. part Parker's Chance,
and 500 a. Rigbie's Hope; d. by 29 Aug. 1752 when admin. bond was
posted by Sabina Rigbie with Sidney George and William Rumsey;
est. was inv. 8 Dec. 1752 by John Hall and James Lee and was
val. at L 1362,17.and 3/4; est. was admin. 9 Aug. 1754 by Sabina; Nathaniel had iss.: JAMES, b. 1720; NATHANIEL, b. 18 June
1723; JOHN, d. 1767 in Cecil Co.; THOMAS; PHILIP; SKIPWITH, d.
1754; ELIZABETH, m. William Smith by 1748; CASSANDRA, m. (---)
Webster; ANN, b. 1 March 1735, m. Samuel Willitts; SUSAN, m.
William Rumsey (4:239; 15:197; 49:78, 102, 103; 50:53; 129:332,
349; 153:49; Forman).

RIGBY, JAMES (5), s. of Nathaniel (4), was b. 1720, and d. 6
Jan. 1790 in Harford Co.; m. 1st, in 1741, Elizabeth Harrison,

dau. of Samuel and Sarah (Hall) Harrison; she d. 22 July 1759, and James m. 2nd,.on 5 Feb. 1761, Sarah, widow of Aquila Massey; in 1750 he owned 217 a. part Bachelor's Good Luck, 134 a. part Bachelor's Good Luck, 150 a. part Paradise; had iss.: (by 1st w.): NATHAN, b. 8 Jan. 1742; SARAH, b. 1744, m. Samuel Wallace; CASSAN-DRA, b. 1746, m. John Corse; ELIZABETH, b. 1748, m. William Coale; SUSANNA, b. 1751, m. Joseph Brinton; MARY, b. 1755, d. 1756; JAMES, Jr., b. 1756; (by 2nd w.): MASSEY, b. 1762, d. 1767; ANNE, b. 1764, m. Aquila Massey; MERCY, b. 1770 (153:65; Forman).

RIGBY, NATHANIEL, Jr. (6), s. of Nathaniel (4), in 1750 owned 275 a. part Parker's Chance (153:66).

RIGBY, SKIPWITH (7), s. of Nathaniel (4), d. by 6 Aug. 1752 when admin. bond was posted by Nathan Rigby with James Rigby and Herman Husband; est. was admin. by Nathan Rigby on 4 March 1755 (5:356; 15:183).

RIGBY, JOHN COALE, d. by 11 March 1742 when Joseph Johnson admin. the est. (3:254).

RIGBY, JOANNA, was ind. for bast. in June 1742; tried for bast. in June 1743; ind. again for same in June 1744 and June 1746; tried Aug. 1746; in April 1747 was summoned by the vestry of St. John's Par. for unlawful cohabitation with James Maxwell (33:434; 34:195; 35:228; 36:1, 126; 132:82).

RIGBY, SUSANNA, was summoned by the vestry of St. John's Par. in July 1749 for unlawful cohabitation with James Maxwell (132:97).

RIGDON, GEORGE (1), progenitor, was in Balto. Co. by 1706 as a taxable in Spesutia Hund.; d. by 12 June 1756 when admin. bond was posted by Thomas Baker Rigdon and William Rigdon, with James Rigdon and Stephen Rigdon; est. was admin. by the admins. on 21 Jan. 1767; m. Elizabeth (poss. Baker since their third s. was Thomas Baker Rigdon); was ind. by the Balto. Co. Grand Jury for refusing to repair his road; in 1750 owned 100 a. Shitterminster. 100 a. Rigdon's Escape, 200 a. Rock Quarter, and 40 a. Hogyard; George and Elizabeth had iss.: CHARLES, b. 30 June 1705; ELIZA-BETH, b. 7 Feb. 1708 (may be the Elizabeth who m. Beaven Spain on 6 Jan. 1734); GEORGE, b. 5 April 1710; THOMAS BAKER, b. 18 April 1713; JOHN, b. 17 April 1716; WILLIAM, b. 17 Jan. 1719; ENOCH, b. 4 Jan. 1725/6; STEPHEN, b. 30 July 1729; ANN, b. 4 July 1731, d. 31 Dec. 1739 (4:361; 7:306; 15:309; 23:218; 129:208, 211, 253, 261, 280, 307; 148; 153:3).

RIGDON, GEORGE (2), s. of George (1), was b. 5 April 1710; m. Sarah Thompson on 12 Dec. 1734; had iss.: ANN, b. 10 June 1735; GEORGE, b. 10 March 1737; ELIZABETH, b. 17 Dec. 1740; WILLIAM, b. 15 June 1744 (129:288, 300, 319).

RIGDON, THOMAS BAKER (3), s. of George (1), was b. 18 April 1713, and d. 1787; m. Anne (---) who d. 1797; wife was prob. dau. of Margaret Leslie of Balto. Co. whose will of 9 July 1757 named dau. Ann Rigdon; had iss.: ALEXANDER, b. 12 April 1743, d. 1820; THOMAS BAKER; WILLIAM, b. 1750; STEPHEN; BENJAMIN, b. 1753; HANNAH, m. (---) Preston; MARGARET ELIZABETH, m. Robert Clark in Dec. 1770; ELIZABETH (131; 210-30:401; Gov. William Paca Chapter, N.S.D.A.R., "Bible and Family Records, Harford County," typescript at Md,. Hist. Soc., pp. 129-135).

RIGDON, JOHN (4), s. of George (1) and Elizabeth, was b. 17 April 1716; d. 1766; m. Elizabeth Oachisson on 11 March 1740; by 23 Aug. 1742 he was m. to a dau. of William Bond; Anne Bond of

Balto. Co. named a sister Elizabeth Rigdon and a niece Joanna Occhison in her 1743 will; Elizabeth Bond had m. 1st (---) Occhison or Oakerson, and 2nd John Rigdon; Rigdon d. leaving a will, 26 March 1766 - 25 Aug. 1766, naming w. Elizabeth, son Baker, step-dau. Johanna Hitchcock, and mentioning other children; est. was admin. by Elizabeth Rigdon on 29 Feb. 1768; left iss.: ELIZABETH, b. 5 Jan. 1741; JOHN, b. 18 June 1744; ANN, b. 18 Aug. 1745; MARY, b. 25 Jan. 1748; BAKER, b. 30 July 1750; MARGARET, b. 3 Jan. 1753; RUTH, b. 3 July 1755; JOHN, b. 11 Sept. 1757; WILLIAM, b. 3 Jan. 1761 (3:271; 7:327; 128:115; 129:323, 377; 210-23:56; 210-34:439).

RIGDON, WILLIAM (5), s. of George (1) and Elizabeth, was b. 17 Jan. 1719; m. Mary Preble on 10 Nov. 1748; prob. the William who owned 40 a. Friendship in 1750; d. by 5 Nov. 1764 when admin. bond was posted by Mary Rigdon and John Love; William and Mary had iss.: ANN, b. 24 Oct. 1750; GEORGE, b. 26 April 1753; MARY, b. 6 Nov. 1756; JAMES, b. 15 Sept. 1759; WILLIAM, b. 7 Sept. 1761 (15:247; 129:324; 153:74).

RIGDON, ELIZABETH (prob. wid. of George (1) above), d. by 20 Jan. 1761 when admin. bond was posted by Stephen Rigdon, who admin. her est. on 25 Feb. 1762, 17 May 1762; dec. left six children (4:372, 377; 6:138; 15:252).

RILEY, (---) (1), d. by 1 Aug. 1732; m. Elizabeth (---) who m. 2nd, by that date, Francis Russell; had iss.: JOHN (73:267).

RILEY, JOHN, son of (---) (1) and Elizabeth, age 14 on 16 Dec. 1732 when he bound himself on 1 Aug. 1732, with the cons. of his aunt Lucy and his father-in-law Francis Russell, to Joshua Wood (73:267).

RILEY, FRANCIS, orphan in Aug. 1730 when he was bound to John Bayley; m. Elizabeth England on 5 March 1738; d. by June 1756; had iss.: JOSEPH, b. 26 Dec. 1740; was age 16 in June 1756 when he was bound to Henry Stump (29:2; 41:2).

RILEY, HANNAH, was listed in the 1759 inv. of Abraham Jarrett (54:346).

RILEY, HESCOT, was an orphan in Aug. 1730 when he was bound to John Bayley to age 21 (29:2).

RILEY, JOHN, was in Balto. Co. by June 1671 when he and John Webster purch. land on Swan Creek from William Palmer; in June 1673 he and Webster divided the land (97:125; 99:347).

RILEY, JOHN, m. Ruth Ansher on 28 Jan. 1742; had iss.: FRANCIS, b. 20 Sept. 1743 (129:328, 335).

RILEY, JOHN, d. by 9 Nov. 1758 when admin. bond was posted by John Hall; est. was admin. on 9 Aug. 1759 by Col. John Hall (4:282; 15:193).

RISTEAU, Capt. JOHN (1), progenitor, was in Balto. Co. by 1730 when he took up lots in Balto. Town; d. by 12 May 1760; m. Catherine, wid. of William Talbot, and dau. of George and Elizabeth Ogg; she d. by 22 Feb. 1762; on 23 March 1742/3 was commissioned coroner of Balto. Co.; on 23 April 1745 surv. tract (St.) George's Plains; in 1750 owned 311 a. Credentia, 163 a. part Oldton's Garrison, 100 a. St. George's Plains, 200 a. Risteau's Enlargement, and 50 a. Benjamin's Prospect; his will was made 26 Dec. 1752, proved 12 May 1760; admin. bond was posted 10 Dec. 1760; will of Catherine Risteau was made 12 Nov. 1761, and

proved 22 Feb. 1762; est. of John Risteau was admin. 23 April
1761 by George Risteau; John and Catherine had iss.: TALBOT;
ISAAC; CATHERINE, m. Rev. Thomas Cradock on 31 March 1746;
GEORGE; DAVID, in Nov. 1743 surv. 50 a. Hebron which he still
owned in 1750; poss. MARY, m. Isaac Sampson on 20 April 1747
(4:348; 15:249; 111:148, 273; 153:49; 210-30:858; 259; 303:248).

RISTEAU, TALBOT (2), s. of Capt. John (1), d. 23 Nov. 1753
"of a nervous fever;" at the time of his death was clerk of
Balto. Co.; m. Mary Stokes, admnx. of Humphrey Wells Stokes on
20 June 1745; m. 2nd, by 24 sept. 1751, Susanna, admnx. of Winston Smith: on 29 Jan. 1754 admin. bond on his est. was posted by
Susannah Risteau, with John Hall (of Swan Town), and James Phillips (5:108; 15:188; 131:194; 209-35:101; 259).

RISTEAU, ISAAC (3), s. of Capt. John (1) and Catherine, was
b. 14 Nov. 1724; d. 1764; m. Elizabeth, dau. of Abraham Raven,
on 21 Feb. 1748; that same year Abraham Raven conv. to his dau.
Elizabeth Risteau 535 a. Enlarged Lott; in 1750 Isaac Risteau
owned that land and 500 a. Quinn and 10.75 a. Hutchins' Neglect;
d. leaving a will, 22 May 1764 - 29 June 1764; had iss.: SARAH,
b. 18 Feb. 1749, m. William Worthington on 2 March 1769; CATHE-
RINE, b. 20 May 1750, m. James Amos on 2 June 1773; MARY, b.
27 Oct. 1751; ABRAHAM, b. 4 March 1753, d. by 18 Sept. 1783;
JOHN TALBOTT, b. 11 Nov. 1754; DAVID, b. 18 Dec. 1756; JOSEPH,
b. 22 July 1760; GEORGE; ELIZABETH RAVEN, m. William Cromwell
on 16 June 1768; FRANCES RAVEN, m. (---) Cromwell (111:159; 131;
153; 259).

RISTEAU, GEORGE (4), s. of Capt. John (1) and Catherine, d.
in Balto. Co. in 1792; m. Francis Todd, dau. of Thomas and Eleanor Dorsey Todd, on 17 Aug. 1757; d. leaving a will, 4 April
1783 - 14 April 1792; had iss.: KATHERINE, b. 17 June 1758, m.
Robert North Carnan; ELEANOR, b. 15 Jan. 1760; THOMAS, b. 16 Jan.
1763; JOHN, b. 14 April 1765; FRANCES, b. 26 July 1767, m. Nicholas Owings; REBECCA, b. 5 Dec. 1770 (113:356; 134:31, 35, 42, 45;
259).

RISTON/RESTON, EDWARD, was in Balto. Co. by 7 Oct. 1712 when
he admin. the est. of Aquila McCarty; m. 1st, Johanna (---) who
was bur. 10 Jan. 1723; m. 2nd, in Feb. 1723, Eleanor Neal; m.
3rd Rachel (---) who m. as her 2nd husb. Rinaldo Monk; on 7 Aug.
1722 Edward and Johanna conv. 100 a. part Betty's Adventure to
John Gardner; in Nov. 1741 Edward was made exempt from the levy;
d. by 24 March 1749 when admin. bond was posted by Rachel Riston
and Edward Stevenson, with Jonathan Plowman and Edward Stevenson,
Jr.; est. was admin. by Rachel, now w. of Rinaldo Monk, on 28
July 1755; had iss.: (by 2nd w.): SARAH, b. 1 Dec. 1724; (by 2nd
w.): HENRY, b. 18 Sept. 1735; ANNE, b. 4 Sept. 1736, m. Thomas
Johnson in 1752; ZACHARIAH, b. 10 Dec. 1744; CATURAH, b. 10 Oct.
1745 (5:348; 15:215; 1:370; 33:160; 69:30; 133:7, 44, 51, 147,
193; 134:6; 153:68; 210-27:179).

RISTON, JOHN, was in Balto. Co. by 1692 as a taxable on north
side of Patapsco (138).

RISTON, MARY, m. Isaac Sampson on 17 April 1747 (131).

RIX, ROBERT, m. after 1739 Sarah, wid. of Robert Riddle, and
dau. of Sarah Scribner of Stanstead, Essex; wife Sarah was alive
in 1756 when she wrote a letter home to Eng.; had a son, unnamed,
b. c.1742 (300-65:257).

RIX, WILLIAM, in 1750 owned 50 a. James Choice (153:68).

ROACH, JOHN, m. Rozanna Dennis on 2 Feb. 1726, and had iss.: WILLIAM, b. 2 Aug. 1728 (128:53).

ROACH, MARY, serv. of Luke Raven, was found innocent of the charge of bast., March 1736 (31:39).

ROADES. See RHODES.

ROBASS, JOHN, d. by 3 Nov. 1757 when admin. bond was posted by admnx. Sarah Waters with John White (15:219).

ROBERSON/ROBESON, (---), m. by by May 1759, Sophia, widow of Thomas Demmitt (83:414).

ROBERSON, JACOB, m. Mary (---), and had iss.: JOHN, b. 2 May 1715; MARY, b. Aug. 1717 (131:39/r).

ROBERSON, JOSEPH, age 2 last 14 April, in Nov. 1730 was bd. to Josephus Murray; was s. of Mary Robeson (29:56).

ROBERSON, PETER, m. Martha (--) and had: MARTHA, b. 20 Jan. 1749/50 (133:92).

ROBERSON, RICHARD. See ROBINSON, RICHARD.

ROBERSON, WILLIAM, of Back River, made a will 24 April 1671, naming wife Henerica (Henrietta?), and an unborn child (110:67). See also ROBINSON, WILLIAM.

ROBERSON, WILLIAM, d. by 28 March 1718 when admin. bond was posted by admnx,. Eliza Roberson with Francis Whitehead, James Isham, John Ballings, and Geo. Middleton (14:320).

ROBERSON, WILLIAM, m. Elizabeth (---), and had iss.: MARY, b. 5 Feb. 1718/9 (131).

See also ROBERTSON and ROBINSON.

THE THOMAS ROBERTS FAMILY

ROBERTS, THOMAS (1), progenitor, was in Balto. Co. by 1688; d. there by 1 Feb. 1709; on 27 March 1688 he surv. 153 or 159 a. Roberts' Choice; on 17 July 1694 he surv. 200 a. Roberts' Park; by 1707 he owned 200 a. Phillips' Addition; in 1692 was a taxable in n. side Patapsco Hund; was one of the Rangers of Balto. Co., on 23 March 1693/4; he did not get along with Capt. John Oldton; testified before the Council on 3 July 1691, giving his age as c.40; d. leaving a will, 21 Jan. 1709 - 1 Feb. 1709, leaving tract Roberts' Choice or Long Mountain to his dau. Mary, dau. Eliza and son Thomas Francis were to have 200 a. Roberts' Choice, and Susan, dau. of Robert and Margaret Burkett was to have 50 a. Roberts' Forest, and another 100 a. of that tract was left to John Wilmot, and the residue of the tract went to Roberts' w. Elizabeth who was named extx; admin. bond was posted 5 Dec. 1710 by Edward Stevenson and Charles and John Merryman; his est. was inv. 22 Dec. 1710 by James Read and Jno. Merryman and val. at E 24.10.11, with Mary Roberts and James Rider signing as kin; on 17 March 1711 Elizabeth Roberts conv. to John Cross 100 a. called Hog's Norton, part of Roberts' Forest; an act of the General Assembly passed to quiet title to the land in 1725 stated that Cross later sold the tract to James Moore, and mentioned "Francis" Roberts, eld. s. of said Thomas Roberts; Thomas and Elizabeth had iss.: MARY; THOMAS FRANCIS; and ELIZABETH, m. Matthew Hawkins (12:538; 51:14; 67:179; 121:168; 138; 200-20:452; 200-38:383; 211).

ROBERTS, THOMAS FRANCIS (2), s. of Thomas (1), was living
in 1750 when he owned 50 a. Roberts' Choice; m. Comfort (---)
who consented on 11 Oct. 1745 to his conv. all his title and
interest in 83 a. Roberts' Park to his sis. Elizabeth, wife of
Matthew Hawkins; by Comfort he had iss.: WILLIAM, b.
1 April 1727; MARY, b. 7 March 1729; THOMAS, b. 15 Jan. 1731 (78:374;
133:13, 16, 23; 153:49).

THE ANDREW ROBERTS FAMILY

ROBERTS, ANDREW (3), of A. A. Co., no known rel. to any of
the above, was settled in A. A. Co. by 3 April 1663 when he surv.
100 a. Triangle, which his s. John later sold to Thomas Tench;
d. leaving a will, 4 April 1682 - 22 May 1682, naming wife Jane,
and the children listed below: JOHN, under 21 in April 1692;
HENRY, under 21 on same date; MARY; KATHERINE (120:106; 211).

ROBERTS, JOHN, (4), s. of Andrew (3), was b. after 1661 (as
he was not yet 21 in April 1682), and d. by 28 March 1713; had
iss.; JOHN (76:236, 496).

ROBERTS, HENRY (5), s. of Andrew (3), was under age 20 in
April 1682; m. Anne, dau. of Gerard Hopkins (she was left prop-
erty in the will of John Chappell, made 31 Dec. 1706); had iss.:
JOHN, mentioned in John Chappell's will of 1706 (123:17).

ROBERTS, JOHN (6), s. of John (4), was alive on 28 March
1713 when he sold Richard Taylor 464 a. Roberts' Choice, and a
plantation in A. A. Co. where Henry Roberts was then living, and
which the grantor John had from his father, John Roberts of A.
A. Co.; he may poss. be the John Roberts whose will, 4 Oct. 1735-
10 Nov. 1735, described him as living on Garrison Ridge, and
named his w. Enor and these children: JOHN; WILLIAM; EDWARD
(76:236, 496; 126:169).

ROBERTS, JOHN (7), s. of John (6) and Enor, may be the John
who m. by 1731 Anne (---) by whom he had these ch.: EDWARD, b.
20 Aug. 1731; SARAH, b. 11 June 1736; WILLIAM, b. 11 June 1739;
ELEANOR, b. 27 April 1742; BELINDA, b. 8 June 1743; ANN, b. 18
March 1744/5; RICHARD, b. 10 June 1748; GILBERT, b. 16 Jan. 1750/1
(133:60, 87, 95).

ROBERTS, (---), m. by 1695 Eliza or Mary, dau. of Nicholas
Corbin (121:126).

ROBERTS, Dr. (---) was in Balto. Co. by 1694 as a taxable in
n. side Patapsco (139).

ROBERTS, ANN, m. Archibald Buchanan on 28 April 1729.

ROBERTS, ANN, was ind. in Aug. 1744 and again in Nov. 1746
for unlawful cohabitation with Richard Marsh (35:293; 36:220).

ROBERTS, ASRAELL, m. Mary Ingram on 16 Dec. 1742 (131).

ROBERTS, BENJAMIN, m. Martha Cullison on 4 May 1754 (131).

ROBERTS, BILLINGSLEY, m. Betty Manen on 2 March 1758, and had
iss.: JOHN, b. 20 Nov. 1759; MARY ANN, b. 18 March 1760 (sic)
(131).

ROBERTS, CHARLES, in Nov. 1755 was named by Mary Wiley as
the father of her child (40:400).

ROBERTS, EDWARD, gave his age as c.59 in a deposition made

made 10 June 1732; is prob. the Edward Roberts who deeded livestock to Peter Majors, Jr., and Esther Majors in 1739, and in
Sept. 1739 was indebted to Richard Gist with Peter Majors, Sr.
(75:265, 266, 267, 284; 225:166).

ROBERTS, ELIZABETH, had a son: JAMES, b. 13 Sept. 1726 (128:
56).

ROBERTS, FRANCES, was ind. for bast. in Nov. 1738 (31:307).

ROBERTS, JEREMY, serv. of Maj. Thomas Long, was judged to be
15 years old in March 1683/4 (18:128).

ROBERTS, JOHN, of St. John's Par., Balto. Co., d. in Balto.
Co. between 9 Feb. 1728 and 6 March 1728 (dates of signing and
proving of his will); m. Mary Jackson on 11 April 1705, wid. of
Thomas Jackson; on 13 Feb. 1705/6 John and Mary conv. 200 a. of
Drysdale's Habitation (granted on 1 June 1685 to Henry Wriothesley who left it in his will to his "son" Thomas Jackson who left
it in his will to his w. Mary, now w. of Roberts); on 15 Aug.
1706 Roberts and his w. admin. the est. of Thomas Jackson;
Roberts' will, made 9 Feb. 1728 left 200 a. Wetherall's Last Addition to dau. Mary w. of William Talbott, tracts Foster's Neck
and Wolf Harbor and lots in Joppa Town to sons John and Stephen,
400 a. The Forest to daus. Ann, Frances, and Lucina; admin. bond
was posted 24 June 1729 by Mary Roberts, with John Roberts, Archibald Rollo and Archibald Buchanan; extx. Mary, now w. of David
Hughes admin. the est. of John Roberts on 19 June 1731, 15 Nov.
1733 and 19 Dec. 1733; John and Mary had iss.: JOHN, b. 1 June
1708; MARY, b. 24 Nov. 1710, m. William Talbot on 30 Jan. 1729;
ANN, b. 20 Aug. 1713, m. Archibald Buchanan; STEPHEN, b. 24 Feb.
1716; FRANCES, b. 13 April 1719; LUCINA, b. 18 Feb. 1723, d. 18
Oct. 1723; LUCINA, b. 11 March 1725 (2:239, 249; 3:99, 129, 133,
161; 14:325; 29:233, 234; 30:9, 356; 64:20; 125:93; 128:22; 131).

ROBERTS, JOHN, and Grace Roberts, wit. the will of John Kemball of Balto. Co. (122:56).

ROBERTS, JOHN, alias Campbell, was b. c.1691, and gave his
age as 41 in 1732, son-in-law of John Campbell; in June 1713
he was deeded land by his mother Eleanor Campbell (21:379; Land
Commission # 1, f. 146).

ROBERTS, JOHN, m. Ann Richardson on 7 Feb. 1714 (131).

ROBERTS, JOHN, in Nov. 1734 was made exempt from the levy
(30:354).

ROBERTS, JOHN, in 1750 owned 200 a. Goldsmith's Neck, 14 a.
Brother's Delay, 318 a. part Wolf Harbor, 2 lots in Joppa, and
other land; may be the son of John who d. 1728 (153:49).

ROBERTS, JOHN, d. by 26 Sep. 1756 when admin. bond was posted
by Daniel Chamier with John Carnan and John Howard (15:185).

ROBERTS, JONATHAN, m. Johanna Thomas on 13 Sept. 1730 (133:
149).

ROBERTS, MARREN, d. leaving a will, 15 March 1754 - 25 Nov.
1754; named dau.: ANNE (111:57).

ROBERTS, ROBERT, was ind. by the Grand Jury for breach of the
sabbath in Nov. 1719 (23:245).

ROBERTS, ROGER, m. Rebecca Crawford on 2 Nov. 1752, and had

iss.: RACHAEL, b. 14 May 1755, and ELIZABETH, b. 8 November 1753
(131:60/r).

ROBERTS, STEPHEN, d. 3 April 1723 (128:50).

ROBERTS, WILLIAM, "of Patapsco," in 1750 owned 50 a. Friendship (153:84).

ROBERTS, WILLIAM, "of Pipe Creek," in 1750 owned 125 a. Level
Glade (153:88).

ROBERTSON, (---) (1), of Scotland, had at least two sons:
ROBERT, d. in Md. in 1736; and DANIEL (82:40).

ROBERTSON, ROBERT (2), s. of (---) (1), went to Md. c.1716;
d. in Balto. Co. testate; m. Sarah, admnx. of Martin Taylor, on
9 Nov. 1721; d. leaving a will, 25 May 1736 - 14 Aug. 1736, leaving his entire est. in Balto. Co. to wife Sarah; named his step-
ch., Martin, Clemency and Mary Taylor; directed that after the
death of his wife his est. was to go to the eld. s. of his bro.
Daniel; admin. bond was posted 16 Aug. 1736 by exec. Martin
Taylor with Jonathan Hughes and John Bond, Sr.; another admin.
bond was posted 16 July 1737 by Sarah Robertson and Benj. Bond
with Matthew Beck and Joshua Starkey; est. was admin. by Sarah
Robertson on 20 July 1740 (she was joined by Benjamin Bond who
had m. Clemency Taylor); Sarah Robertson d. leaving a will, 17
Dec. 1748 - 8 Aug. 1748, naming daus. Jane, Mary, and Clemency
Bond, and granddau. Mary Bond (4:53; 14:343; 15:179; 111:450;
126:189).

ROBERTSON, DANIEL (3), s. of (---) (1), and bro. of Robert
(2), had a s.: JOHN (82:40).

ROBERTSON, JOHN (4), s. of Daniel (3), lived in Athol, Perth-
shire, Scotland, when on 31 March 1753 he sold the lands of his
uncle Robert (82:40).

ROBERTSON, ANN, serv., was listed in the 1739 inv. of Rev.
Joseph Hooper (52:327).

ROBERTSON, ANN, was ind. for bast. in March 1743/4, and was
tried for bast. in Aug. 1744 (35:228, 307).

ROBERTSON, EDWARD, m. Margaret Standiford on 21 April 1752
and had iss.: ELIZABETH, b. 23 July 1755, d. May 1760; RICHARD,
b. 9 April 1753 (131:24/r, 145/r, 175).

ROBERTSON, ELIAS, of Cecil Co., in March 1683 sold 200 a. of
Bailey to Andrew Mattson of Balto. Co. (59:87).

ROBERTSON, ELIZABETH, was tried for bast. in in March 1750/1
(38).

ROBERTSON, JAMES, was in Balto. Co. by April 1658 when he surv.
Harmer's Swan Town with Godfrey Harmer (211).

ROBERTSON, JAMES, was in Balto. Co. by 1692 as a taxable in
n. side of Patapsco Hund. (138).

ROBERTSON, JOHN, was in Balto. Co. by 1692 as a taxable in
n. side Patapsco Hund. (138).

ROBERTSON, JOHN, d. by 23 Nov. 1700 when admin. bond was
posted by Susanna Robertson with William Barker (12:545).

ROBERTSON, JOHN, m. by June 1744 the admnx. of Philip Jarvis (35:233).

ROBERTSON, RICHARD, was in Balto. Co. by Sept. 1685 when he surv. 38 a. Robertson's Addition; d. leaving orphans for whom William Mackartee held the land (211).

ROBERTSON, RICHARD, in Aug. 1744 was made guardian of Ann Robertson (35:296).

See also ROBERSON and ROBINSON.

ROBESON. See ROBERSON, ROBERTSON, and ROBINSON.

THE JAMES ROBINSON FAMILY

ROBINSON, JAMES (1), was in Balto. Co. by March 1693/4 when he asked pardon "in open court, on bended knee," for having made a false report on George Ashman and others, to the Grand Jury; m. Elizabeth, dau. of Jonas and Rebecca Bowen; d. leaving a will made 28 March 1695 naming sons James and Jonas, both under 18, wife Eliza, and Jonas Bowen, Sr., as overseer; admin. bond was posted 5 July 1695 by Jonas Bowen with John Thomas and Richard Sampson; est. was inv. on 11 June 1695 by Robert Wilmot and Roland Thornbury, and val. at Ł 39.10.0; est. was admin. Feb. 1696 by Jonas Bowen; James and Elizabeth had iss.: JAMES; and JONAS (12:554; 20:217; 121:97; 206-10:457; 206-14:150).

ROBINSON, JAMES (2), s. of James (1), was living on 26 March 1699 when he was named as a grandson in the will of Jonas Bowen (121:171).

ROBINSON, JONAS (3), s. of James (1), d. by 11 May 1742; m. Rosanna (---) who m. 2nd John Bowen, Jr., and 3rd John Ogle; was age 35 in 1732; admin. bond was posted 15 Oct. 1741 by Rosanna Bowen with Thomas Sligh and William Rogers; est. was admin. 11 May 1742 by Rosanna Bowen, on 25 June 1743 by Rosanna and her husb. John Ogle, and on 12 July 1749 by Thomas Sligh; on 13 Dec. 1742 Rosanna Bowen of St. Paul's Parish conv. for love and affection conv. two slaves to her daus. Rosanna and Rebecca; Jonas and Rosanna had iss.: TABITHA, b. 23 Feb. 1726; ROSANNA, b. 4 June 1729, chose Thomas Sligh as her guardian in Aug. 1743; ELIZABETH, b. 23 Feb. 1733/4; and JOHANNA REBECCA, b. 13 Aug. 1736(3:259, 310; 5:58½; 15:174; 35:2; 37:165; 77:72, 96; 133: 4, 12, 16, 52; 224:143).

THE RICHARD ROBINSON FAMILY

ROBINSON, RICHARD (4), no known rel. to any of the above, was in Balto. Co. by 1750 when he owned 100 a. Robinson's Venture 100 a. Tricks, and Things, and 200 a. Robinsons; on 19 Nov. 1769 he and w. Mary conv. 100 a. Clarkson's Purchase to John Taylor; d. leaving a will, 21 June 1770 - 13 Aug. 1770, naming w. Mary, tracts Robinson's Venture and Clarkson's Purchase; Richard and Mary had iss.: WILLIAM; RICHARD (his children and heirs); EDWARD; ANN, m. Thomas Elliott on 14 April 1748; HANNAH, m. Isaac Bull on 23 Jan. 1749; CHARLES; and JEMIMA, m. John Standiford on 11 Jan. 1759 (112:169; 131; 153:12; 231-AL#A:525).

ROBINSON, CHARLES (5), s. of Richard (4), d. leaving a will, 11 March 1772 - 23 March 1772, naming bros. and sisters William, Edward, Ann Elliott, Jemima Standiford, and Elizabeth Hutchins (112:233).

ROBINSON, ABRAHAM, m. Sarah Simpson on 24 Sept. 1744 (129: 337).

ROBINSON, CHARLES, was in Balto. Co. by March 1720/1 when he was tried for unlawful cohabitation with Eliza Whitehead; m. Judith Welsh by June 1733; in 1750 owned 50 a. Welch's Fancy and 100 a. Bosley's Parish; may be the Charles Robinson who d. by 12 Oct. 1766 when admin. bond was posted by Neal Haile; or may be the Charles Robinson whose est. was admin. by William Robinson; d,. intestate before 17 Oct. 1774 when his daus. sold Bosley's Palace and Robinson's Addition to Thomas Finley; had iss.: AVARILLA, b. 23 May 1726, m. (---) Boring; REBECCA, m. Matthew Hale; ELIZABETH, m. Nehemiah Hicks; SARAH, m. Neal Haile (6:277; 15:241; 23:447; 25:384; 133:22; 153:9; 231-AL#L:208).

ROBINSON, Capt. DANIEL, d. 5 Dec. 1758, having m. Susanna Brown on 18 July 1751; admin. bond was posted 7 June 1759 by Susanna Robinson, with Jacob Giles and Amos Garrett; est. was admin. on 12 Dec. 1760; Daniel and Susanna had iss.: MARY, b. 28 Jan. 1753, d. 8 Aug. 1760; ANNE, b. 22 Oct. 1754; SUSANNAH, b. 21 Feb. 1758 (4:351; 15:192; 129:366, 385).

ROBINSON, FRANCIS, was in Balto. Co. by 1692 as a taxable in n. side of Patapsco; on 4 Nov. 1694 purch. 200 a. from John Love; admin. bond was posted 8 Dec. 1698 by Joseph Peake with Thomas Richardson and Thomas Staley; est. was inv. on 11 Dec. 1698 by Josiah Bridge and John Gay, and val. at £ 59.18.6 (12:558; 48:71; 59:433; 138).

ROBINSON, JACOB, m. Mary Whitaker on 5 July 1714; on 7 March 1728/9 conv. 50 a. Ward's Adventure to John Ward, son of Joseph Ward (Jacob's wife Mary consented); had iss.: JOHN, b. 2 May 1715; MARY, b. Aug. 1717 (70:271; 131).

ROBINSON, JAMES, was in Balto. Co. by 1659 when he surv. 200 a. Relye (211).

ROBINSON, JAMES, age 14 "last 18 March," bd. himself to his bro. William in Aug. 1709 (21:49).

ROBINSON, JEMIMA, was tried for bast. in Nov. 1755 (40:399).

ROBINSON, JOHN, of Mockjack Bay, Va., bought land from Thomas Montross on 13 April 1664 and sold it to Nicholas Rackstone also of Mockjack Bay on 23 April 1664 (93).

ROBINSON, JOHN, was in Balto. Co. by 1694 as a taxable in n. side Patapsco Hund. (139).

ROBINSON, JOHN, servant with one year to serve, was listed in the 1725 inv. of John Israel (52:184).

ROBINSON, JOHN, m. Elizabeth (---), and had iss.: ELIZABETH, b. 16 July 1736; ABSOLOM, b. 6 Sept. 1745; TEMPERANCE, b. 4 Nov. 1747; RACHEL, b. 11 Jan. 1747 (133:51; 134:4, 11, 13).

ROBINSON, JOHN, m. Hannah (---), and had iss.: ANN, b. 9 June 1739 (133:63).

ROBINSON, JOHN, m. by 8 May 1744, Mary, admnx. of Philip Jarvis; had iss.: JOHN, b. 16 Aug. 1744; ROGER, b. 3 June 1750; SARAH, b. 3 Jan. 1741/2 (3:380; 133:68, 73; 134:14).

ROBINSON, JOHN, m. by 1 Dec. 1749 (---), dau. of Capt. Henry Butler (5:74).

ROBINSON, JOHN, planter, in 1750 owned 100 a. Trenton (153: 72).

ROBINSON, JOHN, carpenter, in 1750 owned 50 a. Robinson's Beginning; later sold the land to Richard King Stevenson (82: 214; 153:75).

ROBINSON, JOSEPH, tailor, b. in Scotland; runaway serv. of George Hargroves of Bush R.; advert. for in Aug. 1752 (385:192)

ROBINSON, MARY, m. William Connell on 2 April 1721 (133:146).

ROBINSON, PETER, in 1750 owned 125 a. part Parker's Palace (153:88).

ROBINSON, REBECCA, in 1750 owned 100 a. Rozinante's Range (153:82).

ROBINSON, RICHARD, was in Balto. Co. in 1692 as a taxable in s. side Patapsco Hund.; on 12 Sept. 1695 surv. 38 a. called Robertson's Addition which later held for his orphans by William Mackartee; d. by 7 Sept. 1699 when admin. bond was posted by William Macartie with John Scutt (12:542; 138; 211).

ROBINSON, RICHARD, m. Elizabeth Slade on 12 Jan. 1713 and had: ABEL, b. 11 Nov. 1715, d. May 1716; CHARLES, b. 10 March 1717/8, d. in a few mos.; ELIZABETH, b. 12 Dec. 1718; WILLIAM, b. 27 March 1729 (131).

ROBINSON, RICHARD, Jr., d. by 4 June 1752 when admin. bond was posted by admin. Nicholas Ruxton Gay with Talbot Risteau (15:207).

ROBINSON, THOMAS, age 30, was b. in Yorkshire, Eng.; runaway serv. from Balto. Co., Aug. 1752 (385:190).

ROBINSON, THOMAS, m. Catherine (---) and had iss.: WILLIAM, b. 18 March 1755 (129:359).

ROBINSON, WILLIAM, d. leaving a will dated 24 April 1671, naming w. Henerica (Henrietta), and an unborn ch.; admin. bond was posted 8 April 1672 by Edward Swanston; wid. Henrietta m. Edward Swanson; she m. 3rd Thomas Cannon, and 4th, by 1682 Edward Reeves (12:537; 110:67).

ROBINSON, WILLIAM, d. c.1719; m. Elizabeth (---); in April 1711 and Oct. 1712 he admin. the est. of William McCarty; in 1706 he purch. Leaf's Chance which he later sold to Stephen Onion; admin. bond was posted 28 June (1718?) by admnx. Elizabeth Robinson with Francis Whitehead and James Isham; est. was inv. on 13 July (1717?) by John Taylor and John Standiver (Standiford?), and val. at £ 39.10.1 plus 7308 lbs. tob., with Jos. Page signing as kin, and Mathew Hale as creditor; est. admin. 8 Nov. 1722 by Elizabeth, now w. of James Isham; Elizabeth d. 1736; the iss. of William and Elizabeth were: PROVIDENCE, m. by 24 Nov. 1730 Charles Baker, Jr.; ELIZABETH, b. 7 Feb. 1711, d. c.1730/45; MARY, b. 1 Feb. 1718/9, m. John Bosworth; ISABELLA, m. George Presbury; and HANNAH, m. Josias Hendon (1:233, 371; 2:28; 14: 320; 52:123; Robinson material in Filing Case A at the Md. Hist. Soc.).

ROBINSON, WILLIAM, m. Sarah Combest on 11 Dec. 1703 or 8 Dec. 1713; had iss.: BLANCH, b. 5 Oct, and d. 18 Dec. 1720; SARAH, b. 15 Dec. 1722 (128:38, 43; 129:213, 256).

ROBINSON, WILLIAM, in Aug. 1728 was named as the father of Elizabeth Robinson's child (28:32).

ROBINSON, WILLIAM, d. by 9 Dec. 1730 when admin. bond on his est. was posted by Stephen Body with Richard Caswell and Christopher Dukes; est. was admin. by Body on Nov. 1731 (3:101; 14:326).

ROBINSON, WILLIAM, m. Alice (---), and had iss.: ROBERT, b. 13 May 1737 (131:64/r).

ROBINSON, WILLIAM, in 1750 owned 100 a. Robin Hood's Forest and 18 a. Knavery Prevented (153:2).

ROBINSON, WILLIAM, "of Gunpowder," in 1750 owned 25 a. part Barton's Chance, 100 a. Turkey's Hills, and 49 a. Archibald's Addition (153:19).

ROBUCK/ROEBUCK, BENJAMIN, son of Ann, age 7 "last 8 April," in Nov. 1741 was bd. to John Stringer to age 21 (33:156).

ROBUCK, THOMAS, orphan of Ann Rhodes, age 7 the previous Aug., in Nov. 1756 was bd. to Aquila McComas (41:303).

ROCK, GEORGE, was a res. of Cecil Co. on 7 April 1747 when he leased 100 a. Lyon's Tent to Samuel Scarlett and his wife Ruth for their lifetimes; in 1750 owned 100 a. part Elberton, 100 a. Contrivance, 100 a. "Lin's" Tents, and 525 a. "Lin's" Addition (79:390; 153:46).

THE ROCKHOLD FAMILY is discussed by Nannie B. Nimmo, in "The Rockholds of Early Maryland," in 346-2:312-317.

ROCKHOLD, ROBERT (1), progenitor, came to Va. c.1647, settled in Md. c.1649; prob. d. by 30 July 1666; m. Sarah (---), and had iss.: ROBERT; JOHN; THOMAS; and ANN, m. 1st Stephen White, and 2nd William Hawkins (Nimmo).

ROCKHOLD, ROBERT (2), d. of Robert (1), m. and may have had at least one son: EDWARD, who m. Mary, wid. of John Nelson of Charles Co. (Nimmo).

ROCKHOLD, JOHN (3), s. of Robert (1), m. Mary (---); in April 1681 purch. 200 a. Richardson's Level from Thomas Richardson and wife; later this land was held by his orphans; d. in A. A. Co leaving a will, made 17 Feb. 1698, mentioning tracts Rockhold's Purchase and Richardson's Level and Rockhold's Search in Balto. Co., wife Mary and three sons: Thomas, Charles, and Jacob; wife Mary d. leaving a will, 2 March 1703 - 15 May 1704, named the same three sons as above; also son Lance Todd, and daus. Sebrah, Susan Crouch, and Eliz. Todd; admin. bond on Mary Rockhold's est. was posted 15 May 1704 by exec. Lancelot Todd with William Cromwell and Wm. Cocke; John and Mary had iss.: THOMAS; CHARLES; JACOB; SUSAN, m. (---) Crouch; ELIZABETH, m. Lancelot Todd; and SEBRA (12:540; 64:118; 110:14; 121:166; 211; Nimmo).

ROCKHOLD, CHARLES (4), s. of John (3), m. Elizabeth Wright; d. leaving a will, 17 Aug. 1741 - 12 Nov. 1741; admin. bond was posted 6 May 1742 by extx. Elizabeth Rockhold with Charles and John Rockhold; est. was admin. by Elizabeth Rockhold on 28 May 1744; dec. left iss.: CHARLES; WRIGHT: REASON: ASSELL; and JOHN (3:367; 15:175, 177; 127:171; Nimmo).

ROCKHOLD, JOHN, m. Elizabeth Eleanor, and had iss.: JACOB, b. 27 Aug. 1740; JOHN, b. 28 Feb. 1742; MARY, b. 1 March 1745; CHARLES, b. 17 June 1749; THOMAS, b. 12 March 1756; ELIZABETH, b. 31 Aug. 1758 (131:57/r, 111/r, 112/r).

RODES. See RHODES.

ROE, JAMES, m. Mary Boyle in March 1739 (128:106).

ROE, THOMAS, m. Mary (---) and had iss.: GEORGE, b. 22 Nov. 1751; WILLIAM, b. 18 Jan. 1745 (133:81, 96).

ROE, WILLIAM, m. Mary Jones on 15 Jan. 1730; was made exempt from the levy in March 1754; had iss.: SARAH, b. 22 Feb. 1731; ANNE, b. 2 March 1733; WILLIAM, b. 5 Sept. 1736 (39:16; 131).

ROEBUCK. See ROBUCK.

ROGERS, NICHOLAS (1), progenitor, was in Balto. Co. by 1688 when as "Nicholas Rogier" he signed a deed; d. c.1693; in 1689 was assigned part of Andrew's Conquest by Samuel Underwood; had at least one son: NICHOLAS, d. c.1720 (59:312; 313:302; Chart of the Rogers family by Christopher Johnston at the Md. Hist. Soc.).

ROGERS, NICHOLAS (2), s. of Nicholas (1), d. in Balto. Co. by 19 Oct. 1720; m. Eleanor (---), step-dau. of Jabez Pierpoint; Eleanor m. 2nd Lloyd Harris on 4 July 1721; Rogers acquired 100 a. Parker's Haven and 100 a. Kemp's Addition from Richard Kemp and John Boring in 1707, 200 a. Hab Nab at a Venture from John and Mary Eaglestone in 1710, and other lands; Eleanor Rogers and her ch. William, Catherine, Ellinor, and Sarah Rogers, were named in the will of Jabez Pierpoint on 1 Oct. 1720; Rogers d. leaving a will, 28 Feb. 1720 - 19 Oct. 1720; named his w. and ch., and a serv. named Josias Hendon; admin. bond was posted 18 Oct. 1720 by extx. Eleanor Rogers; est. was inv. 3 Jan. 1720/1 by Richard Gist and Richard Owings and val. at Ł 655.7.6¼; in March 1724/5 daus. Catherine and Elizabeth chose William Hamilton as their guardian while Eleanor, Sarah, and Mary chose their bro. William as their guardian; in 1756 James Lloyd Harris, son of Eleanor by her 2nd husb. was living in Kington, Herts., Eng., when he wrote to his half-bro. Niholas Rogers of Balto. Town; Nicholas and Eleanor had iss.: WILLIAM, of age in 1720; SARAH, m. John Merryman on 30 Dec. 1725; ELEANOR,, b. 1705, d. 1758, m. Dr. George Buchanan; MARY, b. 1712, m. John Gill; ELIZABETH; KATHERINE, d. unm. in 1799; NICHOLAS, b. 20 May 1721 (23:38; 27:128; 51:168; 115:232; 124:48; 133; 300-65:258; 313:302-303).

ROGERS, WILLIAM (3), s. of Nicholas (2), was of age in 1720; d. 11 June 1761; m. Sarah Gill, dau. of Stephen and Elizabeth Gill ; Sarah Gill Rogers d. 1792; William and Sarah were m. by 13 Aug. 1736; in 1750 William owned much land incl. 100 a. Crowley's First Venture, 100 a. Parker's Haven, 318 a. Morgan's Delight, and other lands; left a will, 5 June 1761 - 11 July 1761; had iss.: NICHOLAS TEMPEST, b. 10 May 1728; ELEANOR, b. 25 Feb. 1729, m. Clement Brooke; WILLIAM, b. 15 March 1731; BENJAMIN, b. 8 July 1734, prob. d. young; BENJAMIN, b. 28 Aug. 1740; SARAH, b. 22 March 1743/4, m. 1st John Addison Smith, and 2nd John Merryman; CHARLES, b. 28 March 1746 (3:220; 26:83; 73:183; 75:115; 111:319; 133:39, 68, 73, 78; 153:106; 262).

ROGERS, NICHOLAS (4), s. of Nicholas (2), was b. 20 May 1721; d. 7 May 1758; m. Henrietta Maria Jones on 18 Aug. 1745; she was b. 18 Aug. 1728, d. May 1790, dau. of Philip Jones; d. leaving a will, 3 May 1758 - 18 June 1758; admin. bond was posted 8 June 1758 by Thomas Jones;; had iss.: JAMES LLOYD, b. 5 July 1748;, PHILIP, b. 23 Nov. 1749; NICHOLAS, b. 7 Oct. 1753; ANN, b. 12 July 1758 (15:200; 11:64; 133:8, 27, 78, 102, 103, 156, 198; 153:68; 300-65:258; 405-3:833).

ROGERS, DOROTHY, m. John Harris in Dec. 1721 (131).

ROGERS, GRACE, had a mulatto ch., ISHMAEL, being cared for by Jacob Bull (28:30).

ROGERS, JAMES, m. by Nov. 1692 Mary (---); he got her with child and then left her (19:320).

ROGERS, JAMES, m. Sarah (---) and had iss.: ELIZABETH, b. 3 Jan. 1748; JAMES, b. 3 Feb. 1750/1 (133:95).

ROGERS, JOHN, on 3 March 1719 purch. 50 a. Michael's Beginning from Michael Byrne; on 8 July 1738 he conv. that tract and 40 a. John's Beginning; m. Jane (---) and had iss.: THOMAS, b. 27 March 1727 (68:182; 75:89; 133:13).

ROGERS, JOSEPH, on 12 May 1746 purch. 58 a. part Arabia Petrea from Joseph and Patience Jones; owned the land in 1750 (79:56; 153:79).

ROGERS, MARY, was b. 26 Sept. 1712, parents not named (129: 213).

ROGERS, ROBERT, was in Balto. Co. by 1695 as a taxable in s. side of Patapsco Hund. (140).

ROGERS, ROBERT, m. Ruth Williams on 26 DEc. 1758 (131).

ROLES. See ROWLES.

ROLLO, ARCHIBALD (1), was in Balto. Co. by 1702 as a taxable in n. side of Gunpowder Hund.; m. Rebecca (---); in Nov. 1733 was sec. for John Roberts' wid. and extx. Mary who had m. David Hughes; left a will, 28 July 1747 - 27 Aug. 1747, naming dau. Mary Ann Standiford, to have Temperance Lot, dau. Rebecca Rollo to have 100 a. Rollo's Adventure, dau. Temperance Robinson to have 100 a. Turkeys Hills and 40 a. Archibald's Addition, James Hicks (s. of Henry and Mary) was to have 52 a., res. of Rollo's Adventure; w. Rebecca was to have servant William Edwards for the rest of his term; his heirs owned 52 a. part Rollo's Adventure in 1750; had iss.: TEMPERANCE, b. 9 Aug. 1713, m. James Barton; ARCHIBALD, b. 11 Jan. 1716, d. 13 Sept. 1725; MARY ANN, m. (---) Standiford; REBECCA (3:161; 110:401; 131; 144; 153:31).

ROLLO, REBECCA (2), dau. of Archibald (1), was ind. for bast. in March 1736; tried for bast. in Aug. 1737; ind. in June 1750, and tried in Aug. 1750; in 1750 owned part Rollo's Adventure; had iss.: TEMPERANCE, b. 20 Feb. 1739 (31:1, 101; 37:2, 190; 131; 153:84).

ROLSTON. See RALSTON.

ROOTER, THOMAS, and wife Hester were in Balto. Co. by 23 Jan. 1721 when they conv. 50 a. Edward's Lot to Jonathan Hanson (59:671). See RUTTER, THOMAS.

ROPER, PHILIP, was in Balto. Co. by 1692 as a taxable in s. side of Patapsco Hund.; on 14 May 1698 conv. Roper's Rest to Sarah Teale (61:225; 138).

ROPER, SARAH, was ind. for bast. in Aug. 1717 (22:152).

ROPER, THOMAS, and Mary Roper, were transp. to Md. c.1660; Thomas was in Balto. Co. by Feb. 1669/70 when Charles Gorsuch sold him 50 a. Cold Comfort and 100 a. Rich Level; by Nov. 1675 was in A. A. Co. when he and his w. Mary sold land to Anthony Demondidier; left a will, 19 Sept. 1677 - 26 Oct. 1677, left land to his wife Mary and to his dau. Mary; had iss.: MARY, m. Cornelius Howard who later held Roper's Increase (97:126, 127; 101:300; 120:197; 211).

ROSBY, JOHN, was in Balto. Co. by 1692 as a taxable in Spesu-Hund. (138).

ROSE, BENJAMIN, d. by June 1710; had iss.: BENAJMIN, age 14 "next 10 Nov.," in June 1710 was bd. to John Roberts (21:136).

ROSE, WILLIAM, d. by 29 Nov. 1736 when admin. bond was posted by Philip Jones with John Rattenbury and Jacob Rowles; est. was admin. by Philip Jones on 10 June 1737 and 6 March 1739 (3:249; 4:35; 14:345).

ROSS, ANN, age 6 "last June," in Nov. 1743 was bd. to John Deaver (35:76).

ROSS, DAVID, d. leaving a will, 19 Feb. 1757 - 4 May 1762; left furniture for Robert Division and made Daniel Preston his exec.; admin. bond was posted by Daniel Preston, with Jacob Bond on 31 May 1762; est. admin. by Preston on 22 Aug. 1763 (6: 23; 15:206; 111:155).

ROSS, EDWARD, age c. 30, ran away from James Moore in the Forks of Gunpowder by 17 Aug. 1748 (307-69:211).

ROSS, SAMUEL, m. Rebecca (---) and had iss.: THOMAS, b. 30 Sept. 1730 (128:67).

ROSS, SAMUEL, m. Elizabeth Lee on 6 Jan. 1735 (128:95).

ROSS, THOMAS, d. by 7 June 1760 when admin. bond was posted by Zachariah Smith, with James Osborn (15:191).

ROUSE, JOHN, was in Balto. Co. by 1692 as a taxable in n. side Patapsco Hund.; d. by 3 Jan. 1710 when admin. bond was posted by admnx. Sarah Rouse with John Thomas, Sr., and John Christian; est. was inv. by John Thomas and H. Whitehead and val. at Ŀ 22.14.10; est. was admin. 13 April 1713 by Sarah Rouse (1:222; 12:551; 48:192; 138).

ROUSE, JOHN, m. Elizabeth Perryman on 8 Sept. 1744 (129:337).

ROUSE, ZACHARIAH, d by Nov. 1739; m. Ann Adkinson on 28 Sept. 1736; she d. 19 Aug. 1737; had iss.: ELIZABETH, b. 3 Oct. 1736; in Nov. 1739 was bd. to Francis Freeman to age 16 (32:76; 128: 92, 93/b, 97).

ROWE/ROW, JAMES, m. Lydia (---), and had iss.: STEPHEN, b. 13 April 1759 (128:108).

ROWE, JOHN, m. Sarah Wharton on 29 May 1751 (131).

ROWE, JOHN, m. Bridgett Moony on 22 July 1755 (131).

ROWE, WILLIAM, b. c.1704; in July 1742 leased part Lord Balti-more's Gift for his lifetime and the lives of his children: WIL-LIAM, Jr., b. c.1736, and ANN, b. c.1734 (76:218).

ROWING, JOHN, m. Comfort Brown on 14 Feb. 1751; had iss.: WILLIAM, b. 20 July 1758; JOHN, b. 30 Dec. 1753 (131:38, 132/3, 151/r).

ROWLAND, JAMES, was in Balto. Co. by 28 Jan. 1741 when he purch. 100 a. Bare Hills from Thomas and Ann Litton (76:97).

ROWLES, CHRISTOPHER (1), progenitor, was transp. to Md. c. 1649; in Dec. 1653 was conv. 60 a. by Jno. Browne and John

Clarke; in Aug. 1662 Edward Lloyd conv. 100 a. of land to Christopher Rowles; in 1701 this land was sold by Christopher's grandson Thomas Rowles to William Taylard; prob. had iss.: CHRISTO-
PHER (217-WH#4:46; 217-WT#1:224; 388).

ROWLES, CHRISTOPHER (2), s. of Christopher (1), d. c. 1691 in
A. A. Co ., having m. Elizabeth (---); she m. 2nd Joseph Hawkins;
may have been the Christopher Rowles called cousin in the May
1674 will of Thomas Meeres of A. A. Co.; in Aug. 1681 surv. 11 a.
Rowles' Chance which was later held by his orphans; had iss.:
THOMAS; prob. WILLIAM; JOHN; MARY, m. 3 Jan. 1700 Philip Jones;
MARTHA (120:83; 206-18:194; 211; 219-4:99).

ROWLES, THOMAS (3), s. of Christopher (2), d. c.1743 in A. A.
Co.; m. Sarah Fisher, who d. 1756; was conv. Burton's Hope by Joseph Hawkins, who m. his mother; in Dec. 1701 conv. to William
Taylard land conv. to his grandfather Christopher Rowles; in
Sept. 1704 he and w. Sarah conv. 40 a. Burton's Hope to Edward
Hall; by Nov. 1720 was in Balto. Co. when he and his w. conv.
to John Mills various lands in Dor. Co. which had been devised
to Sarah Rowles (formerly Fisher, by her mother's husband Phil-
ip Griffin; d. leaving a will, 20 Oct. 1738 - 18 May 1743.
naming children given below, these tracts: Gray's Luck, The
Stones, Solomon's Hills; est. admin. 8 June 1751; will of Sarah
Rowles, 17 Sept. 1754 - 13 Sept. 1756; Thomas and Sarah had iss.:
THOMAS; JOHN; ELIZABETH, m. 1st, Jacob Bell on 18 Feb. 1727,
and 2nd (---) Graham; RUTH, m. 1st (---) Witham, and 2nd (---)
Graham; MARY, m. (---) Cheney; COMFORT, m. O'Neal Robinson on
13 Nov. 1740; RACHEL, m. Edward Kitten; CONSTANT, m. Robert Yield-
hall; SARAH, m. John Smith on 3 Aug. 1736; SUSANNAH, m. (---)
Stewart (127:233; 133:149; 201-30:84; 210-30:294; 217-WT#1:201,
204; 217-WT#2:166; 219-4:106; Dor. Co. Land Records Old Liber
8:1., HR).

ROWLES, WILLIAM (4), prob. s. of Christopher (2), d. c.1750
in Balto. Co.; m. Martha Smith in 1707; m. 2nd, by Dec. 1720 Ann,
dau. of John Davis; in 1750 owned 200 a. Jones' Adventure, 100
a. William The Conqueror, 72 a. Jacob's Delight, and 25 a. Rowles'
Care; d. leaving a will, 31 Jan. 1748/9 - 12 Dec. 1750, naming w.
Ann and ch. Jacob, David, John, and William; admin. bond posted
1 Dec. 1750 by Jacob Rowles with David Rowles and Stephen Wilkinson; had iss.: CHRISTOPHER, b. 9 May 1708; WILLIAM, b. 1 Aug. 1710
1710; MARY, b. 1 Aug. 1710; JACOB,, d. c. 1768; DAVID, d. c.1780
in Balto. Co.; and JOHN (15:245; 153:35; 210-27:427; 217-CW#1:
160, 168, 293, 300; 217-RD#3: 212, 248).

ROWLES, JOHN (5), prob. s. of Christopher (2), d. by 3 Jan.
1700, having m. Mary, wid. of James Crouch and dau. of William
Hill; she m. 3rd, Philip Jones, who on 20 May 1713, with his w.
Mary (dau. of William Hill, dec.), conv. part North Crouchfield
to James Crouch and John "Rolls" (Rowles, sons of Mary Jones by
her former husbands John and Mary had iss.: JOHN (217-IB#2:93).

ROWLES, JACOB (6), s. of William (4), d. by 3 Aug. 1768; m.
1st, on 27 Jan. 1723, Ann Lynch who d. 30 April 1727; m. 2nd, 4
Jan. 1727/8 Constance Sampson, dau. of Richard and Elizabeth
Sampson; m. 3rd, on 28 Sept. 1746 Mary Scarf, with whom he admin.
the est. of James Scarf on 8 Aug. 1749 and 21 Jan. 1750; may have
m. 4th, by 7 Aug. 1750 Patience, admnx. of Nathaniel Stinchcomb;
in 1750 owned 100 a. part Triple Union, 50 a. Sampson's Addition,
45 a. Harleystone, and 40 a. part Johnson; d. leaving a will, 26
Aug. 1760 - 5 Aug. 1768; left iss.: RICHARD, b. 1728; WILLIAM;
CHRISTOPHER; RUTH (had dau. Anne) (5:54, 113, 114; 112:84;
126:212; 133:15, 146, 149, 193; 153:43; 225:219).

ROWLES, RICHARD (7), s. of Jacob (6) and Constance, was b. 25
Sept. 1728; m. Anne Gorswick on 30 Jan. 1753; had iss.: ELIZA-
BETH. b. 3 Nov. 1753; JACOB, b. 21 July 1756; RACHEL, b. 6 March
1759; ANNE, b. 6 March 1761 (133:15, 108, 109, 166).

ROWLES, RUTH (8), dau. of Jacob (6), was known to have had a
dau. Ann b. by 26 Aug. 1760; was ind. for bast. in Nov. 1757,
named Jethro Lynch Wilkinson as the father (5:54; 46:74).

ROWLES, ELIZABETH, in Jan. 1684 was called dau. in the will of
Benjamin Richand (120:140).

ROWLES, JOHN, son of William, in June 1757 chose William Murphy as his guardian (44; 46:38).

ROWLES, MARY, was ind. for bast. in March 1733/4 (30:188).

ROYON, JOHN, was being raised by John Crow as Roman Catholic
in Aug. 1754 when Royon's god-father, Isaac Wood, petitioned to
have the boy bound to him (30:306).

ROYSTON, ROBERT (1), was the father of at least one son:
JOHN (439).

ROYSTON, JOHN (2), s. of Robert (1), was bd. to Robert Burman
on 21 July 1685 for at least 5 years in Md.; by 1692 was a taxable in s. side Patapsco Hund.; name is spelled in various ways:
Restone, Riston, and Rishton; m. 1st, by 10 March 1697, Ann, wid.
and admnx. of Roland Thornborough; m. 2nd Jane (---) who posted
admin. bond on his est. in 6 Sept. 1699 with John Thomas and
William Wilkinson; Jane Royston held 100 a. Roger's Road (surv.
for Roger Reeves on 10 Feb. 1695) for the orphans of John Royston; John had iss.: JOHN; poss. ANN who m. Robert Love Pitstow
on 23 Sept. 1736; and poss. but not likely EDWARD, who was at
least 16 in 1705, and whose descendants used the spelling Riston
(q.v.) (12:83; 121:111; 133; 138; 139; 140; 206-16:25; 439).

ROYSTON, JOHN (3), s. of John (2), does not appear in the
tax lists for 1699-1706, so he was prob. b. after 1690; m. Mary
(---) who m. as her 2nd husbn. Henry Cross; was left land on
Little Run by the June 1717 will of John Barrett; on 5 Nov.
1734 John Royston, planter, conv. to Thomas Green a 125 acre
tract Barrett's Rest; John's wife Mary gave consent; on 25 Feb.
1724 Royston surv. Royston's Study; d. by 21 April 1740 when
Henry Cross posted admin. bond with William Johnson and Staley
Durham; est. was admin. on 5 Dec. 1743 and in Aug. 1743; had
iss.: JOHN, b. 5 Dec. 1722; ROBERT, b. 21 Sept. 1724; THOMAS,
b. 9 March 1726; RACHEL, b. 8 June 1732; BENJAMIN, b. 23 May
1735; ABRAHAM, b. 10 July 1737 (4:96; 12:550; 35:5-8; 74:126;
123:146; 133:2, 9, 16, 17, 30, 45, 57; 207).

ROYSTON, JOHN (4), s. of John (3), was b. 5 Dec. 1722, and
d. by 1798; m. Sarah Sinkler or Sinclair on 17 or 21 May 1747; on
6 Aug. 1747 John and Sarah sold William Bannister 50 a. Royston's
Study; in 1750 owned 50 a. Taylor's Addition; both John and Sarah
died testate; had iss.: MARGARET, m. Benjamin Thomas; MARY; SARAH,
m. Joshua Kidd; SOPHIA, m. (---) Spindler; prob. a son (unnamed)
since John had a grandson John (79:497; 115:104; 116:274; 131;
153).

ROYSTON, THOMAS (5), s. of John (3), was b. 9 March 1726, m.
Margaret Sinclair on 28 Nov. 1751 (131).

ROYSTON, BENJAMIN (6), s. of John (2), was b. 23 May 1735,
and was security for Moses Collett in Nov. 1782 (15:136).

RUARK, PATRICK (1), was in Balto. Co. by 9 Aug. 1725 when he purch. 100 a. The Agreement from Simon Pearson; on 29 Aug. 1724 purch. Hazard from William Greenfield; on 6 Jan. 1731 m. Ann Carliss; d. by 8 March 1732 when admin. bond on his est. was posted by Thomas Robinson and Jacob Giles, the wid. Ann Ruark having assigned the right of admin. to said Robinson; had iss.: ANN, b. 4 May 1731 (age 3 "next 4 May" in Nov. 1734 when she was bd. to Henry Moore and his w. Agnes); RUTH, twin, b. 30 April 1732; SARAH, twin, b. 30 April 1732; poss. an older s. PATRICK (14: 332; 30:351; 69:183; 70:161; 128:68, 74, 90; 129:266).

. RUARK, PATRICK (2), placed as s. of Patrick (1) because in 1750 he owned part The Agreement (153:92).

RUFF, RICHARD (1), progenitor, d. 28 May 1733; m. c.1707 Sarah, dau. of Daniel and Hannah (---) Peverell; Sarah was b. 7 Aug. 1691; Richard d. leaving a will, 16 May 1733 - 8 June 1733, naming tracts Come By Chance, Hunting Neck, Ruff's Chance, and ch.: Richard, Daniel, Henry, Sarah, Henry, Mary, and Sarah; admin. bond was posted 8 June 1733 by execs. Richard and Daniel Ruff, the wid. Sarah having renounced; est. was admin. on 14 June 1734 and 9 May 1750; Richard and Sarah had iss.: RICHARD, b. 28 Sept. 1710; DANIEL, b. 22 Jan. 1712; JOHN, b. 23 June 1714; MARY,   b. 12 Oct. 1717, d. 10 July 1722; SARAH, b. 6 July 1726; HENRY, b. 2 April 1729 (3:147; 5:147; 14:329; 126:21; 128:27, 33, 35, 37, 41, 50, 55, 71; 129:262; 211).

RUFF, RICHARD (2), s. of Richard (1), was b. 28 Sept. 1710, and d. by 31 Jan. 1756 when admin. bond was posted by Henry Ruff, with Richard Dallam and George Bradford; in 1750 owned 14 a. of Strawberry Hills, 350 a. Ruff's Chance, 80 a. Come By Chance, 430 a. Daniel's Lot, 95 a. part Howard's Harbor, 123 a. Bond's Adventure; est. was admin. 18 June 1760 by James and Mary Richardson; m. Mary (---) who m. 2nd James Richardson; had is.: RICHARD, in March 1757 chose John Paca as guardian (4:311; 15: 232; 44; 153:27).

RUFF, DANIEL (3), s. of Richard (1), was b. 27 Jan. 1712; m. Elizabeth Webster on 11 May 1740; d. leaving a will, 15 Oct. 1749 - 7 Nov. 1749, named w. Elizabeth, ch.: John, Daniel, and Hannah, and tract Hunting Neck; admin. bond was posted 7 Nov. 1749 by execs. Eliza Ruff and Michael Webster with John Paca and William Smith; est. admin. 17 June 1751 by Eliza, now w. of Guy Little, and admin. again on 1 March 1753; had iss.: JOHN, b. 6 May 1743; ELIZABETH, b. 26 Dec. 1744; HANNAH, b. c.1747 (age 4 in 1751 and 12 in 1753); DANIEL, b. c.1747 (age 4 in 1751); and JOHN, b. c.1749 (age 2 in 1751) (5:182, 269; 15:237; 129: 341; 131:139/r).

RUFF, HENRY (4), s. of Richard (1), was b. 2 April 1729; m. Hannah, dau. of James Preston; she d. 12 Jan. 1761; had iss.: SARAH, b. 17 Nov. 1758; HANNAH, , twin, b. 2 March 1760; HENRY, twin, b. 2 March 1760(4:344, 352; 129:369; 210-34:419).

RUFF, CHARLES, d. by 1717, having m. Jane (---) and had iss.: JOHN, in Nov. 1717 was bd. to Alexander McComas (22:199).

RUFF, CHARLES, d. by Aug. 1750, leaving an orphan: CHARLES, age 7 "last Nov.," in Aug. 1750 was bd. to Alexander McComas of Alex. to age 21 (37:152).

RUFF, JOHN, m. Mary Freeman in March 1741; had iss.: CHARLES, b. 6 May 1743 (131:109/r).

RUFF, SARAH, d. by 19 Nov. 1747, when admin. bond was posted by
John Bull with George Bradford and James Amos; est. admin. on 16
June 1749; the dec. left six ch. (5:56; 15:178).

RULEY, FRANCIS, m. Elizabeth (---), and had iss.: SARAH, b. 11
Feb. 1742 (129:328).

RUMMAGE, GEORGE, m. 15 May 1754 Mary Noble; had iss.: MARGARET,
b. 29 June 1754; DAVID, b. 7 Aug. 1755; ELIZABETH, b.. 7 March
1756 (129:353, 354).

RUMSEY. See RAMSEY.

RUNAGAN, PHILEMON, was in Balto. Co. by 1695 as a taxable in
Spesutia Hund. (140).

RUSSELL, THOMAS (1), was in Balto. Co. at least as early as
1700 as a taxable in Spesutia Hund.; m. 1st, on 27 July 1702 Mary
Cabell or Cahill; she d. 26 Aug,. 1703, and Thomas prob. m. 2nd
Mary Boreing on 7 Nov. 1714; had iss.: by 1st w.: FRANCIS, bapt.
25 Sept. 1703 (128:15, 17, 20, 33; 142).

RUSSELL, FRANCIS (2), s. of Thomas (1), was bapt. 25 Sept. 1703;
in June 1710 was bd. to George Wells to age 21; m. 1st, by 1 Aug.
1732, Elizabeth, wid. of (---) Riley; may have m. 2nd Jane (---),
by whom he had iss.: JOHN, b. Dec. 1737; MARY, b. 1 April 1741;
JANE, b. 14 Aug. 1745 (73:267; 128:20; 131:122/r).

RUSSELL, EDWARD, was in Balto. Co. by 1692 as a taxable in
n. side Patapsco Hund. (138).

RUSSELL, RICHARD, was in Balto. Co. by 1692 as a taxable in s.
side Patapsco Hund. (138).

RUSSELL, THOMAS, d. by 3 June 1682 when admin. bond was posted
by Elizabeth Russell, als. Croshaw, with William Croshaw (who had
m. the wid, of the dec.), with William Osburn (14:350).

RUSSELL, VAUGHAN, of Balto. Co., imm. from Va. c.1665 (388).

RUTH, MOSES, was b. c.1697, giving his age as 62 in 1759; in
1743 bought 200 a. Widow's Care from William Hunter and wife; in
1750 owned 200 a. Widow's Care and 125 a. part Uncle's Good Will
(77:141; 153:67).

RUTH, THOMAS, m. and had iss.: SARAH; MARGARET, age 16 last
March in a deposition made 6 Aug. 1759; mentioned her sis. Sarah
who was age 9 last 11 June; Margaret also deposed that her father's
horse had bitten her ear off (47:53).

RUTLEDGE, EDWARD (1), was transp. to Md. c.1670; may have been
the father of at least two sons, who appear as taxables in separate
households in 1692 in n. side of Patapsco Hund.; may have had:
MICHAEL; and EDWARD (138; 388).

RUTLEDGE, MICHAEL (2), poss. s. of Edward (1), was a taxable
in 1692 in n. side of Patapsco Hund.; on 8 June 1698 was conv. 60
a. of Hopewell by Robert and Deborah Benger; d. by 20 July 1709
when admin. bond was posted by Ann Rutledge with William Farfarr
and Thomas Shaw; est. was inv. on 4 Aug. 1709 by Luke Raven and
William Wright, and val. at £ 40.10.3; may have had at least one
s.: MICHAEL (12:553; 48:103; 61:235; 138; 211).

RUTLEDGE, EDWARD (3), poss. s. of Edward (1), was a taxable in
1692 and may be the Edward Rutledge whose est. was admin. by

Charles Haile or Hall, who m. Edward's widow Susanna; Edward left
as his only heir a dau.: PENELOPE (138; 237-18:257).

RUTLEDGE, MICHAEL (4), poss. s. of Michael (2), was b. c.1696,
giving his age as 34 in Feb. 1729/30; d. by 28 Sept. 1745; m.
Hannah (---) who d. by 3 June 1765; on 6 Nov. 1718 Michael and
Hannah conv. Thomas Hinds the tract Hazard; on 3 June 1734 he
was granted Rutledge's Delight; on 5 Nov. 1751 Hannah, widow,
conv. all her property to her son Abraham; Hannah d. by 2 Feb.
1765 when admin. bond was posted by John Rutledge; est. was admin. 3 June 1765; Michael and Hannah had: WILLIAM; ABRAHAM; JOHN;
and RUTH (6:163; 15:204; 63:472; 78:399; 79:53).

RUTLEDGE, WILLIAM (5),.s. of Michael (4), was so named in a
deed made 28 Sept. 1745 when he sold John Jones a tract called
Rutledge's Delight; Michael's wid. Hannah claimed her dower
rights at this time; William may have had iss.: THOMAS (78:399).

RUTLEDGE, ABRAHAM (6), s. of Michael (4), d. in Balto. Co.,
by 1807, having m. on 13 Oct. 1747 a cousin Penelope Rutledge;
in Dec. 1752 or 1754 Abraham Rutledge leased from Thomas Bladen
part of Blathnia Cambria; the lease named Abraham's w. Penelope
and s. John; d. leaving a will proved 13 Sept. 1807; had iss.:
JOHN; EDWARD; JACOB; JOSHUA; ABRAHAM; RUTH; JEAN, m. (---) Wilson; PENELOPE, m. (---) Kelso (82:361; 117:263; 131).

RUTLEDGE, JOHN (7), s. of Michael (4), d. in Balto. Co. leaving a will, 4 April 1773 - 9 June 1773; m. Elizabeth Milhouse on
10 Dec. 1742, and had iss.: JOHN; MARY; HANNAH, b. 10 June 1743,
m. William Tivis; SABRA or SOPHIA, b. 10 June 1743; m. (---)
Hughes; KEZIA, b. 16 June 1745, m. (John) Parks (7:231; 112:370;
131).

RUTLEDGE, JOHN, on 7 June 1732 purch. part Franklin's Gift
from Thomas Franklin; in Sept. 1747 he and w. Jane conv. part
of this land to John Wilmot (73:251; 79:559).

RUTLEDGE, ALEX, was living on 9 Aug. 1709
the inv. of Michael Rutledge (48:103).

RUTLEDGE, BENJAMIN, m. Mary Roe on 28 April 1748 (131).

RUTLIS, WORTEN, of Balto. Co. advert. that his wife Hannah
had eloped with Peter Hines (255:51).

RUTTER, THOMAS (1), d. in Balto. Co. by 22 Jan. 1746, having
m. Esther (---); on 9 June 1719 he admin. the est. of Henry
Thompson who may have been a relative, since Thomas named one
of his sons Henry Thompson; on 23 Jan. 1721 Thomas and wife Hester conv. 50 a. part Edwards Lot to Jonathan Hanson; Thomas d.
leaving a will, 26 Sept. 1744 - 29 Jan. 1746, naming w. Esther,
son Richard (to have Edwards' Enlargement), son Henry Thompson
(to have Salisbury Plains), son Thomas, son Solomon (to have Edwards' Enlargement), son Moses, dau. Esther, and granddau. Susannah, dau. of Ann Goodwin; on 31 July 1747 admin. bond was posted
by Esther Rutter, with Richard and Moses Rutter; Thomas and Esther had iss.: ANN, m. George Goodwin on 29 March 1730; RICHARD,
b. c.1714; HENRY THOMPSON; MOSES, b. 8 Nov. 1723 (1:162; 15:177;
59:671; 133; 210-24:547).

RUTTER, RICHARD (2), s. of Thomas (1) and Esther, was b. c.
1714; gave his age as 42 in 1756; m. 1st, by July 1735 Sophia
(---) who was alive in 1747; m. 2nd, on 3 June 1750 Mary, wid.
and extx. of William Barney; in 1750 owned 50 a. Edwards' Enlarge-

ment; d. leaving a will, 9 Oct. 1757 - 9 Nov. 1757, naming ch.
Esther, Henry, Thomas, and Moses, with William Isgrig appointed
exec., and son Moses to be bound out as a joiner; admin. bond
was posted by William Isgrig on 12 Nov. 1757 with William Nicholson and William Lux; Isgrig admin. the est. of Rutter on 10
Sept. 1761; Mary Rutter d. leaving a will, 13 Feb. 1779 - 9 April
1779; iss. of Richard and Sophia: ANN, b. 23 July 1735, may have
d. young; HENRY; ESTHER; THOMAS; and MOSES, b. 17 Nov. 1747 (4:
347; 5:216, 264; 6:9; 15:195; 112:388; 133; 153:78; 210-30:403).

RUTTER, HENRY THOMPSON (3),s. of Thomas (1) and Esther, d. by
Nov. 1762; m. Elizabeth (---) who survived him; admin. bond on
his est. was posted by Elizabeth Rutter on 4 Nov. 1762, with Josias Bowen and Thomas Rutter; est. was admin. on 12 Sept. 1763;
Henry and Elizabeth had iss.: THOMAS, b. c.1742 (on 7 March 1743
Jacob Morris "for love and affection" conv. 50 a. Jacob's Lot to
Thomas Rutter, son of Henry); JOSEPH, b. c.1752; RUTH, b. c.
1754; SARAH, b. 6 July 1757; RICHARD, b. 11 April 1761 (6:29; 15:
186; 77:428; 133).

RUTTER, MOSES (4), s. of Thomas (1), was b. 8 Nov. 1723; in
1750 was conv. lot # 28 in Balto. Town by widow Sarah Boring; on
the same day Moses conv. her lot # 29; in 1750 he owned 30 a.
part Adventure; he d. by 27 Jan. 1752 when admin. bond was posted
by Keziah Rutter, with Thomas Ward and Edmond Talbot (15:210;
78:151, 152; 153:67).

RUTTER, SOLOMON (5), s. of Thomas (1), was b. 31 Aug. 1730;
in Nov. 1756 he was fined for begetting a bast. (46:161; 133:19).

RUTTER, THOMAS (6), s. of Thomas (1), was b. 17 Dec. 1732; in
1750 he owned 100 a. part Salisbury Plains; d. by 8 Dec. 1773 when
his est. was admin. by Hannah Rutter; may be the Thomas who conv.
prop. to two of his children in Jan. 1762; had iss.: JONATHAN,
alive 1762; and ESTHER, alive in 1762 (7:262; 30:105, 107).

RUTTER, WILLIAM, m. Ann (---), and had iss.: ELIZABETH, b.
20 July 1733; and MOSES, b. 2 July 1735 (133:35, 46).

RUXTON, NICHOLAS (1), and w. Alice imm. from Va. c.1664; was
desc. as "of Mockjack Bay" when he was conv. land by John Robinson in April 1664; in May 1674 Nicholas and Alice conv. 200 a.
Nash's Rest to Thomas Jones; d. by 31 May 1681 when his est. was
admin. by John Thomas of Balto. Co.; est. was inv.and val. at
2432 lbs., tobacco; the lands he had surveyed on 12 May 1679 were
later held by Mary Ruxton for the heirs of Nathaniel Ruxton; had
iss.: NATHANIEL; poss. FRANCES (2:42; 93; 95; 100:118; 211; 388).

RUXTON, NATHANIEL (2), s. of Nicholas (1), was b. c.1675, his
age was 17 in Nov. 1692 when he pet. the court that Major John
Thomas be made his guardian; m. Mary (---) who held lands for
his orphans; d. by 30 Aug. 1701 when his wid. Mary conv. Ruxton's
Range and Howell's Point to Richard Colegate (19:316; 66:89).

RUXTON, FRANCES (3), pos. dau. of Nicholas (1), m. by 3 Sept.
1701 John Gay, when they conv. 100 a. Ruxton's Range and Howell's
Point to Richard Colegate (66:90).

RYAN, JOHN, in June 1719 was summoned for breach of peace
against Francis Sutton (23:131).

RYAN, JOHN, m. Ann, dau. of Edward Wilburne, by 10 Nov. 1747/8
(80:112).

RYAN, JOHN, age 23, tinker, Irish servant, ran away from Amos
Garrett by 14 May 1747 (384:626).

RYAN, MARGARET, in March 1721/2 was charged with bast. (24: 31).

RYDER. See RIDER.

RYE, MARY, servant of James Phillips, in Aug. 1711 named George, the slave of said Phillips as the father of her child (21:245).

RYLEY. See RILEY.

RYSTONE. See RISTONE.

SACKIELD, AGNES, in March 1716/7, named Thomas Taylor as the father of her child (32:95).

SADDLER, JOHN, was in Balto. Co. by 1750 when Peter and Susanna Bond conv. him 36 a. Buck's Park (81:141).

SALISBURY, WILLIAM, of Balto. Co. with w. Sarah, imm. c. 1671; sold land to William Morgan and William Welsh in Aug. 1673 (99:347; 388).

SALMON, THOMAS, was in Balto. Co. by July 1673 when William and Sarah Salisbury conv. him 200 a. of land (99:348).

SALTHUBER, MARGARETTA, "housewench," with 5 years to serve, was listed in the 1747 inv. of William Fell (54:204).

SAMPSON, RICHARD (1), was in Balto. Co. by 2 Nov. 1682 when John Arden conv. him 100 a. Arden's Adventure; on 25 July 1687 Thomas and Sarah James conv. him 100 a. The Forest; d. by 4 July 1709 when admin. bond was posted by exec. Isaac Sampson with William Wilkinson and Richard Colegate; est. was inv. by John Gay and Charles Merryman and val. at £ 115.9.6, signed by Isaac and Richard Sampson as kin; est. was admin. 7 Aug. 1709 and 17 Aug. 1713 by Isaac Sampson; had iss.: ISAAC, b. c.1669/73; and RICHARD, b. c.1677 (2:16, 149, 156; 13:429; 48:105; 59:14, 277; 138).

SAMPSON, ISAAC (2), s. of Richard (1), was b. c.1669/73, giving his age as 60 in 1729 and 71 in 1744; in 1692 was a taxable in n. side Patapsco Hund.; pet. to be levy free in Nov. 1718, but it was rejected; wit. the will of Joseph Gostwick in Balto. Co.; by c.1709 possesed 100 a. The Forest, 101 a. The Addition; on 11 March 1708 conv. Richard Sampson Arden's Adventure, and the Addition to it, totalling 150 a.; on 8 Feb. 1728/9 conv. 100 a. The Forest, 100 a. Sampson's Addition, and 26½ a. Sampson's Angle, to Luke Stansbury (23:33; 59:650; 71:284; 125: 71; 138; 211; 224:99; 225:104).

SAMPSON, RICHARD (3), s. of Richard (1), was b. c.1677 as he became 16 between 1692 and 1694; d. by 8 March 1714 when Elizabeth Sampson, extx., posted admin. bond with John Downes and James Bagford; m. Elizabeth (---) who m. 2nd Thomas Stone; d. leaving a will, 6 Feb. 1714 - 8 March 1714/5, naming children Richard (to have 100 a. Arden's Adventure), John (to have 50 a. Sampson's Addition), and Constance; est. was inv. on 12 March 1714/5 and val. at £ 85.0.2, and signed by his bro. Isaac; est. was admin. by Eliza, now w. of Thomas Stone on 30 May 1721; Richard had iss.: RICHARD; JOHN; and CONSTANCE, m. (---) Rowles (1:43, 225; 48:144; 123:29).

SAMPSON, RICHARD (4), poss. s. of Richard (3), married Ann

Empey on 15 May 1734; may be the Richard who in 1750 owned 25 a. Small Hopes(133:152; 153:15).

SAMPSON, JOHN (5), s. of Richard (3), was left land in the 1735 will of his mother Elizabeth Stone; he was to have one-half of Bachelor's Delight, and was to maintain Sarah Hinton Olive (126:212).

SAMPSON, (---), m. by 1713, Sarah, dau. of Thomas Freeborne of A. A. Co. (122:257).

SAMPSON, BENJAMIN, m. Jemima Standiford on 11 Feb. 1766 (131).

SAMPSON, ISAAC, m. Mary Risteau on 20 April 1747, and had iss.: RUTH, b. 24 Nov. 1748; RICHARD, b. 1 Nov. 1750 (131:31, 17/r).

SAMPSON, MARY, m. John Green in Dec. 1720 (133:147).

SAMPSON, RICHARD, m. Ann Wyle on 17 Dec. 1758 (131).

SAMPSON, THOMAS, was in Balto. Co. by Aug. 1659 when he surv. 100 a. Upper Eling in Spesutia Hund.; d. by 1662 when William Hollis took out letters of admin. (211; 341:357).

SAMPSON, THOMAS, m. Eleanor (---), and had iss.: RICHARD, b. 26 Dec. 1714; WILLIAM, b. 28 Jan. 1718; ELEANOR, b. 11 July 1721 (129:234).

SANDAGE, JOHN, m. Sarah Grover on 19 Sept. 1751 (131).

SANDEL. See SINDALL.

SANDERS, (---) (1), m. Elizabeth (---), and d. by June 1713, leaving at least one son: EDWARD (21:379).

SANDERS, EDWARD (2), s. of (---) (1) and Elizabeth, age 9 "the previous 10 Oct.," in June 1713 was bound to serve Francis and Catherine Ogg to age 21; m. Christian Beardy on 29 Oct. 1728; in March 1733 purch. 50 a. Gibson's Ridge from Henry and Ann Rhodes; in 1750 still owned that tract; prob. the Edward who d. leaving a will, 22 July 1765 - 13 March 1770, naming w. Christian, tract Gibson's Ridge, and sons Samuel, Thomas, and Daniel; had iss.: MARY, b. 11 April 1729; EDWARD, b. 23 Aug. 1731; SAMUEL; THOMAS; and DANIEL (21:379; 74:182; 112:173; 128:56; 153:1).

SANDERS, JAMES, m. Elizabeth (---), and had iss.: WILLIAM, b. 23 Sept. 1753; FRANCES, b. 20 March 1755; SARAH, b. 27 Dec. 1758 (128:359).

SANDERS, JOHN, serv. of Zachariah Maccubbin, was on trial in March 1737/8 (31:183).

SANDERS, ROBERT, of Balto. Co. was transp. by 1664 (388).

SANDERS, ROBERT, in 1750 owned 250 a. part James' Forest (153:57).

SANDERS, STEPHEN, in Nov. 1719 had his petition to be levy free rejected (23:248).

SAPPINGTON, NATHANIEL, was in Balto. Co. by 1695 as a taxable in Spesutia Hund. (140).

SARGEANT/SERGEANT, JOHN, was in Balto. Co. by 3 Feb. 1684/5, when his w. Elizabeth was conv. part Clement's Dean by Edward Reeves (59:109).

SARGEANT, JOHN, was in Balto. Co. by 4 Nov. 1730 when he purch. 100 a. Hab Nab at a Venture from James and Hannah Hendon; m. Elizabeth Gostwick on 4 Feb. 1732; they admin. the est. of Thomas Gostwick in Aug. 1737; d. leaving a will, 19 Jan. 1741 - 9 March 1748. leaving Wells Angles to son-in-law John Yoston Gostwick, naming w. Elizabeth and ch. Samuel and Benjamin, Mary Ann and Elizabeth, and dau.-in-law Ann Yoston Gostwick; admin. bond was posted 7 March 1748 by John Yoston Gostwick with Samuel Sollers and Samuel Bowen; may be the John Sargeant listed in 1750 as owning 100 a. Adventure and 238 a. Wells Angles; est. was admin. by Gostwick on 29 May 1750 and again in 1753; left iss.: SAMUEL; BENJAMIN; MARY ANN; ELIZABETH (3:229; 5:270; 15:346; 73: 30; 110:441; 133;54, 69, 150).

SARGENT, SETH, d. by c.1700, leaving no heirs (211).

SARTER, PETER, m. Jane (---) and had iss.: ELIZABETH, b. 8 Jan. 1735/6; MARY, b. 22 Feb. 1737/8 (133:59).

THE SATER FAMILY has been discussed in Isaac Walker Maclay's Henry Sater, 1690-1754 (pub. 1894), and in vol. II of The Green Spring Valley: Its History and Heritage. (259).

SATER, HENRY, progenitor, was in Balto. Co. by Jan. 1716 when he surv. 50 a. Whitehall; d. in May 1754; m. 1st, by June 1718 Mary, admnx. of Edward Stevenson; m. 2nd Dorcas, poss. a dau. of William Towson; in 1750 he owned 50 a. Whitehall, 350 a. Sater's Addition, 30 a. Egypt, and 77 a. part Chevy Chase; in Nov. 1742 for 2 shillings he sold 1 a Sater's Addition to Henry Loveall, William Towson, and William Brown, the pastor and elders of the church, congregation, or people of God called General Baptists; d. leaving a will, 16 Nov. 1753 - 30 May 1754, in which he named his w. Dorcas, ch. George, Henry, John, and an unborn ch.; admin. bond was posted 7 Jan. 1755 by Dorcas Sater with Reese Bowen and William Tipton; had iss.: GEORGE, b. 20 Oct. 1740, m. Rachel Hamilton; PRUDENCE, b. 25 Nov. 1743, m. Benjamin Howard; HENRY, b. 27 April 1745; DISCRETION, b. 3 April 1749, m. Thomas Walker; JOHN, b. 1 April 1751; JOSEPH, b. 25 Dec. 1753 (15:362; 22:316; 77:238; 111:271; 153:8; 259).

SAUNDERS. See SANDERS.

SAVAGE, HILL (1), m. by 17 May 1718 Eleanor, wid. of Peter Bond; d. by May 1753 leaving one dau.: SARAH, m. John Thomas (1: 309; 48:332; 81:548).

SAVAGE, SARAH (2), dau. of Hill (1), in March 1738/9 was ind. for bast., having borne a s. Hill; m. by May 1753 John Thomas; known iss.: HILL, b. 22 Dec. 1738 (31:351; 81:548; 133:73).

SAVAGE, JOHN, m. Ann (---), and had iss.: THOMAS, b. 13 May 1747 (131:126/r).

SAVEN, WILLIAM, m. Elizabeth (---) by 10 April 1667 when they conv. land to Rowland Williams (94).

SAVORY, JOHN (1), earliest known Savory of the name in Balto. Co., m. Ann Reeves on 27 June 1699; had iss.: JOHN, b. 12 Sept. 1701, bapt. 30 Nov. 1706; DIANA, b. 21 Jan. 1703/4 (128:12, 14, 20; 129:187, 192, 195, 203).

SAVORY, JOHN (2), s. of John (1), was b. 12 Sept. 1701, bapt. 30 Nov. 1706; m. Mary Bucknal on 29 Aug. 1734; had iss.: WILLIAM, b. 14 April 1735 (128:12, 14, 82, 88).

SAVORY, JOHN, age 5, was bd. to John Botts in Aug. 1739 (32:2).

SAVORY, WILLIAM, m. Mary (---); admin. the est. of James Maxwell on 17 Nov. 1733, 19 Dec. 1733, 29 May 1734 and 20 July 1737;
in 1750 owned 542 a. part Conclusion, 45 a. Savory's Privilege,
24 a. Gist's Inspection, 26 a. Gist's Addition, and 2 lots in
Balto. Town, as well as other land; in March 1753 was summoned
by the vestry of St. John's Parish for unlawful cohabitation with
Mary Mead; d. by 23 April 1759 when admin. bond on his est. was
posted by John Mercer, Jr., and Robert Porter, with Augustine
Boyer, Jr., John Hammond Dorsey, William Andrew, and Thomas Gilpin; est. was admin. by John Mercer and Robert Porter on 17 Feb.
1762; William and Mary had iss.: WILLIAM, b. 20 Feb. 1733 (3:
137, 143, 236; 4:362; 16:58; 131:91/r; 132; 153:25).

SCARFF, HENRY, m. Patty Hardesty on 28 Dec. 1758; had iss.:
JOHN, b. 29 Oct. 1759; SARAH, b. 24 June 1761 (131:53, 153/r,
157/r).

SCARFF, JAMES, d. by 5 Nov. 1746 when admin. bond was posted
by Jacob Rowles with John Sargent and Peter Dowell; est. was admin. by Rowles on 1 Aug. 1749 and 21 Jan. 1750; had iss.: BENJA-
MIN, b. c.1728; JAMES, b. c.1730; MARY, b. c.1736 (in March
1750/1 chose John Lynch as her guardian); REBECCA, b. c.1739;
WILLIAM, b. c.1741 (5:59, 114; 16:13; 38:272).

SCARFF, JONATHAN, was in Balto. Co. by 1750 when he was listed
as owning 419 a. Brown's Adventure (153:94).

SCARFF, NICHOLAS, d. by 12 Feb. 1753 when admin. bond was
posted on his est. by Benjamin Guyton with John Holt and Abraham
Inloes; est. was admin. by Guyton, naming as the heirs of the
dec.: dau., m. John Smith; SARAH (4:243; 15:290).

SCARLETT, HENRY, d. by Aug. 1754; est. was admin. by Bothya
Scarlett; dec. left iss.: JAMES; RACHEL; WILLIAM; RICHARD; MARY;
FORD; BETHYA (39:350).

SCARLETT, STEPHEN, m. Ruth Belsher on 7 April 1740; dec. left
iss.: THOMAS, b. 13 Feb. 1740; JAMES, b. 7 Dec. 1742; MARY, b. 20
March 1744 (128:106, 112; 129:329, 338).

SCATES. See SKATS/

SCHOLFIELD, JOHN, Jr., and wife and family were rec. on cert.
into Gunpowder Meeting, Soc. of Friends, on 23 d, 5, 1759; had
iss,: WILLIAM, b. 14 d, 12, 1752; ANN, b. 2 d, 6, 1757; JOSEPH
LEONARD, b. 12 d, 8, 1760; ANDREW, b. 11 d, 9, 1762; ISSACHER,
b. 17 d, 6, 1765; MAHLON, b. 2 d, 10, 1769 (136).

SCOTLAND, WILLIAM, m. Elizabeth Taylor on 15 July 1749 (131:
34).

SCOTT, DANIEL (1), progenitor, was in Balto. Co. by 1682 and
d. there by 9 July 1725; m. Jane, dau. of the wid. Deborah Johnson (Deborah m. as her 2nd husb., Robert Benger); Jane Johnson
Scott m. as her 2nd husb., on 12 May 1729, John Watson; she d. 23
Dec. 1732 or 1733; in March 1682/3 Robert and Katherine Benger
conv. Daniel Scott, then of A. A. Co., 150 a. Oliver's Reserve
and 30 a. Jenifer's Kindness; he surv. 500 a. Scott's Grove in
Nov. 1695, and Scott's Hopewell in Nov. 1696; betw. March 1700
and Nov. 1700 he purch. various tracts from John Chadwell of John;
d. by 4 June 1723 when admin. bond on his est. was posted by his
s. Daniel, the wid. Jane, having renounced; est. was inv. by Luke
Raven and William Galloway on 17 April 1724, and val. at Ł 411.9.
2½; the inv. was signed by John Durbin and James Preston as kin;

est. was admin. on 9 July 1725; Daniel and Jane had iss.:
DANIEL, d. 20 March 1745; ANN, m. Thomas Smithson; NATHANIEL;
JANE, m. 1st Francis Watkins, and 2nd, on 4 Nov. 1714, Samuel
Hughes; SARAH, m. James Preston; AVARILLA, m. John Durbin on 1
March 1715 (3:18; 51:209; 66:12, 95, 213; 13:434; 131; 211).

SCOTT, DANIEL (2), s. of Daniel (1) and Jane, d. 20 March
1745; c.1706 m. Elizabeth, wid. of Robert Love; she d. in May
1758; rep. Balto. Co. in the General Assembly, 1725-1727, 1728-
1731, 1732-1734, 1742-1744; also Justice of Balto. Co., 1718-
1733; on 21 July 1724 John Jones of Balto. Co., and w. Margaret,
dau. and sole heir of John Chadwell the Younger, conv. to Daniel
Scott the Younger, son of Daniel, the Elder, tracts Chestnut Neck,
Stanharket, and Harman's Hope; d. leaving a will, 13 March 1744/5-
15 April 1745, naming w. Elizabeth, and ch.: Daniel, James, Aquila,
Martha, w. of Daniel McComas, Elizabeth w. of Thomas Bond, Jr.,
Hannah w. of Edward Norris, Sarah, w. of Thomas Wheeler, Mary,
and a number of grandchildren; in 1750 Elizabeth, wid. of Daniel
Scott owned 310 a. Scott's Improvement, and 100 a. part Bin or
Birr; Elizabeth Scott, wid. of Daniel, d. leaving a will, 2 May
1758 - 31 May 1758; Daniel and Elizabeth had iss.: DANIEL, b. 23
Feb. 1712; MARTHA, b. 27 Feb. 1714, m. Daniel McComas; REBECCA,
b. 20 Jan. 1717; JAMES, b. 6 May 1720; AQUILA, b. 1722, d. 1724;
AQUILA, b. 18 Nov. 1724; MARY, b. 16 June 1727, m. (---) Amos;
ELIZABETH, m. Thomas Bond, Jr., on 13 April 1725; HANNAH, m. Ed-
ward Norris; SARAH, m. Thomas Wheeler (2:109, 180; 69:352; 111:
212; 131:109; 153:71; 210-30:493; 371).

SCOTT, NATHANIEL (3), s. of Daniel (1) and Jane, d. by June
1733; m. Avarilla, dau. of Luke Raven; was dead in June 1733
when his bro. Daniel Scott pet. the court that Nathaniel Scott
had died leaving a daughter who had been raised by her grandmother Jane Scott, later Jane Watson; now Jane was dead, and
Daniel pet. that the child be placed in his care; Nathaniel had
iss.: AVARILLA, m. Thomas Norris on 10 Oct. 1738 (30:8; Christopher Johnston, chart of Scott Family, at Md. Hist. Soc.).

SCOTT, DANIEL (4), s. of Daniel (2) and Elizabeth, was b. 23
Feb. 1712, and d. c.1752; m. Hannah Butterworth on 27 Jan. 1740;
she m. 2nd John Giles; he is listed in the 1750 Debt Book as owning 680 a., part Scott's Improvement; d. leaving a will, 19 Nov.
1751 - 16 Feb. 1752, naming his w. Hannah, s. Nathan, dau. Elizabeth, bro. James, and friend Joshua Bond; admin. bond was posted
28 March 1752 by extx. Hannah Scott with Isaac Raven and Charles
Harryman; est. was admin. on 1 June 1753 by John Giles and w.
Hannah, and admin. again on 20 Jan. 1757; in Sept. 1752 John
Giles was summoned by the vestry of St. John's Parish because he
had m. the sister of his late wife, but he refused to put his
second wife Hannah away; Daniel and Hannah had iss.: ELIZABETH,
b. 4 Sept. 1743; NATHAN, b. 14 Aug. 1749 (5:273, 319; 15:310;
111:40; 131; 132:113; 153:71).

SCOTT, JAMES (5), s. of Daniel (2) and Elizabeth, was b. 6
May 1720, and d. 1762; m. Anne Wheeler on 18 Feb. 1741; in 1750
owned 100 a. part Benjamin's Camp, 216 a. James' Forest, 340 a.
Addition to James' Forest, and 100 a. Scott's Close; d. leaving
a will, 17 Dec. 1761 - 29 March 1762; wid. Anne ren. the will on
10 May 1762; inv. was appraised by Ignatius Wheeler and val. at
£ 150.6.3½; est. was admin. on 9 July 1762 by Ann Scott; James
had iss.: DANIEL, b. c.1744; JAMES, b. c.1747; ELIZABETH, b. c.
1749; BENJAMIN, b. c.1751; AQUILA, b. c.1756; MARTHA, b. c.1758;
and ANN, b. c.1761 (6:90; 49:249, 250; 111:151; 129:322; 131;
153:58).

SCOTT, AQUILA (6), s. of Daniel (2) and Elizabeth, was b. 18

Nov. 1724; d. by 7 March 1760; m. Elizabeth Potee, who d. by 10
Nov. 1760; in 1750 owned 400 a. part Bell's Camp, 256 a. Scott's
Hopewell, 180 a. Scott's Range, 100 a. Trust, and 75 a. Addition
to Trust; Aquila d. leaving a will, 10 Oct. 1759 - 7 March 1760,
naming w. Elizabeth, and ch. Daniel, Aquila, James, Martha,
Elizabeth, Rebeckah, and Sarah; Elizabeth Scott died leaving a
will, 2 Sept. 1760 - 10 Nov. 1760, naming ch. Martha, Daniel,
Aquila, James, Elizabeth, Rebecca, and Sarah; Aquila and Elizabeth, who were married 13 Oct. 1743, had iss.: MARTHA; DANIEL,
b. 1747; AQUILA, b. 1751, m. Mary Preston in 1770; ELIZABETH;
REBECCA; JAMES, b. 1757; SARAH (131; 153:71; 210-30:824; 210-31:
29).

SCOTT, (---), m. by 11 May 1697 Katherine, extx. of Stephen
Hunt (2:47).

SCOTT, ABRAHAM, Sr., s. of John and Elizabeth (Cope) Scott,
was granted a cert. from Woodhall Meeting to Gunpowder Meeting
in 1722; m. Elizabeth Dyer of Phila. in 1726; had iss.:ABRAHAM
(Henry Chandlee Forman, Tidewater Maryland: Architecture and
Gardens, pub. 1956, p. 165).

SCOTT, ABRAHAM, Jr., s. of Abraham and Elizabeth (Dyer), owned
Pleasant Prospect and Regulation; m. Elizabeth Rossiter of Wales
in 1751; had iss.: RACHEL, m. on 2 March 1780 James Mason, s. of
George and Jane (Forman, op. cit., p. 165).

SCOTT, ANDREW, m. Anne Smith on 28 April 1737, and had iss.:
DAVID, b. 24 Dec. 1738; ANN, b. 19 July 1741; ANDREW, b. 18
July 1743 (131:51/r, 88/r, 108/r).

SCOTT, AQUILA, d. by 10 Nov. 1760 when admin. bond was posted
by James Scott, admin., with Benjamin Wheeler; est. was admin. 11
Aug. 1762 by Ignatius Wheeler, the admin. de bonis non; heirs
were: JAMES, DANIEL, and the w. of Lemuel Howard (4:375; 16:48).

SCOTT, BURGESS, in 1750 owned 100 a. Stone Ridge and 50 a.
Addition to Stone Ridge (153:92).

SCOTT, DAVID, m. Ann (---) and had iss.: SUSANNAH, b. 10 March
1736 (131:88/r).

SCOTT, EDWARD, was in Balto. Co. by 1692 as a taxable in s.
side Patapsco (138).

SCOTT, ELIZABETH, m. Thomas Bond on 13 April 1725 (131:36).

SCOTT, JOHN, merchant of Sarum, purch. 300 a. Taylor's
Choice from John and Arthur Taylor in March 1669/70 (96:230,
233).

SCOTT, JOHN, was in Balto. Co. by 1692 as a taxable in n.
side Patapsco Hund.; in March 1695 surv. 400 a. Morning Choice
(138; 207).

SCOTT, MARY, in 1750 owned 107 a. Stone Ridge (153:15).

SCOTT, RICHARD, m. Mary Kean on 28 June 1735; on 29 May 1735
purch. 60 a. Brown's Entrance from Gabriel Brown (74:268; 128:88).

SCOTT, ROBERT, was in Balto. Co. by 1730; m. 1st Ann (---)
and had 6 ch.; m. 2nd, on 29 March 1749, Mary Carlisle, and had
one dau.; in 1750 owned 31 a. Coat Hill and 60 a. part Moore-
fields; had iss.: (by 1st w.): ELIZABETH, b. Dec. 1730; JANE, b
1733; JOHN, b. 1735; MARGARET, b. 1737; DAVID, b. 14 Nov. 1741;

HUGH, b. 23 May 1744; (by 2nd w.): MARY, b. 1748/9 (131; 153:44).

SCOTT, THOMAS, of Balto. Co., gave his age as 28 in the year 1671 (388).

SCOTT, WILLIAM, m. Elizabeth Taylor after the banns were pub. three times , on 2 July 1749 (131).

SCOTT, WILLIAM, m. Jane Hughs on 4 Aug. 1754 (131:45).

SCOTT, WILLIAM, m. 19 May 1757, Mary Smith (131).

SCOTTER, BEVANS, m. Mary Perrord on 19 July 1761 (131).

SCRIBER, ANDREW. See SHRIVER, ANDREW.

SCRIVENER, WILLIAM, was in Balto. Co. by 30 March 1744 when he m. Elizabeth, coheir of John Clark, s. of Matthew Clark of Balto. Co., dec.; on that date he and his w. joined John Carr and his wife Lewsey (another coheir of said John Clark), in selling land to Samuel Gover (77:565).

SCUDAMORE, THOMAS, was in Balto. Co. by June 1682 when he and w. Abigail conv. 131 a., part of 420 a. Dickinson, formerly the plantation of John Dickson, and where Long now dwells with his wife; d. by 27 Feb. 1687/8 when admin. bond was posted by Abigail Scudamore, admnx. with Thomas Long; est. was inv. 26 Sept. 1687/8 by John Boring and Francis Watkins, and val. at 2000 lbs. tob. (13:445; 64; 206-9:509).

SCUTT, JOHN, d. by 3 Aug. 1703 when admnx. Catherine Scutt posted admin. bond with Thomas Bale and Dennis Crowley; Catherine, wid. of (---) Carrington and Stephen Hart; after Scutt's death his wid. m. as her 4th husb. Henry Knowles; will of John Scutt, 4 May 1703 - 5 Aug. 1703, named daus. Sarah Hart and Mary Scutt, Henry, Margaret, and Catherine Carrington, ch. of John Carrington; left tracts Morning's Choice and Morning Choice Addition to dau Mary; est. was inv. 12 Aug. 1703 by John Stinchcomb and Matthew Hawkins, and val. at ₤ 339.2.0; John Scutt left iss.: MARY, m. William Douglas (13:435; 48:275; 122:14; 200-39: 38).

SEABROOK, WILLIAM, m. Jemima, sis. of Christopher Gist, on 26 March 1742; in 1750 owned 100 a. Taylor's Farm and 50 a. London; was alive in 1761 when he conv. 100 a. of the former to Peter Gosnell, stating the tract had formerly been laid out for one Thomas Taylor; had iss.: JAMES, b. 4 Oct. 1738; AGNES, b. 18 March 1742/3: GEORGE, b. 25 Feb. 1747: ELIZABETH, b. 29 Dec. 1749 (85:37; 133:72; 134:8, 14; 153:79).

SEALE, WILLIAM, d. by 7 April 1757 when admin. bond was posted by exec. William Morton, with Martin and John Bacon (15:336).

SEALY, EMANUEL, d. 14 Jan. 1708 (128:25). See   also Ceely.

SEALY, SARAH, d. May 1709 (128:26).

SEAMER, ELIZABETH, in Nov. 1722 pet. the court that the child she was carrying was that of Capt. Richard Smithers; was ind. for bast. in March 1722; in Aug. 1723 was also called Elizabeth Smithers; had iss.: SOPHIA, b. 26 Sept. 1720; THOMAS, d. 1723 (15:15, 215, 436; 128:38, 58).

SEARS, JOHN, d. by 25 Jan. 1706/7 when admin. bond on his est. was posted by James Crooke, with Oliver Harriott and John Love;

est. was inv. on 13 Feb. 1706/7 by John Taylor and William Holland (13:436; 48:110).

SEAVERS, NICHOLAS, was b. c.1706; m. Elizabeth (---) who was b. c.1711; in May 1737 was commissioned coroner of Codorus Hund.; leased land in Balto. Co. in 1744; in Nov. 1746 was a schoolmaster when he was sued by Talbot Risteau, and was a planter in March 1746/7 when he was sued by Daniel Campbell; had iss.: LYDIA, b. c.1734; CHARLES, b. c.1735; PRUDENCE, b. c.1739; NICHOLAS, Jr., b. c.1743; RICHARD, b. 17 April 1746 (36:336, 493; 77:606, 610, 616; 131:114/r; 303:149).

SEDDON, JOHN, m. Margaret Evans on 3 Oct. 1745, and had iss.: JAMES, b. 20 Oct. 1745 (133:126, 158).

SEDGEHILL, ELIZABETH, servant to Samuel Stansbury, was tried for bast. in June 1757, named Robert Crosbie or Crosley (also a servant to Stansbury) as the father (46:37).

SEDGWICK, BENJAMIN, inherited 100 a. Chevy Chase , in Feb. 1731/2, from his father Joshua Sedgwicks of Calvert Co. (126:46).

SEDGWICK, RICHARD, in 1750 owned 100 a. John's Beginning (153:48).

SEDWELL, ROGER, was in Balto. Co. by June 1673 when he purch. 86 a. Prospect from Charles Gorsuch; d. by 1679 leaving a wid. who m. John Boring; also had an heir, poss. a dau., Jane who m. by July 1695 Selah Dorman; on the latter date George and Jane Chancey sold Prospect to George Chancy; iss.: (prob.) JANE, m. by July 1695 Selah Dorman (59:507; 62:212; 63:412; 206-6:423). See also SIDWELL, ROGER.

SEEDS, SAMUEL, m. Mary (---) and had iss.: SAMUEL, b. 18 Jan. 1760 (133:103).

SEELAH/SEELEY/SEELY. See CEELY.

SELY, EMANUEL, was in Balto. Co. by 1692 as a taxable in Spesutia Hund.; d. by 1709 when est. was inv. by John Cottrell and William Loney and val. at £ 4.15.4; est. was admin. 8 Aug. 1711 by John Cock (or Catishay) (1:252; 48:232; 138). See also CEELY.

SEEMONS. See SIMONS.

SEGER, WILLIAM, was in Balto. Co. by 1692 as a taxable in s. side Patapsco Hund. (138).

SEIMMONS. See SIMMONS.

SELLMAN, CHARITY, dau. of Richard Tydings of A. A. Co., in Dec. 1750 sold 375 a. part Nanjemoy to Thomas Harrison (81:107).

SELLMAN, WILLIAM, in 1750 owned 300 a. Merriton's Lot; may be the William Sellman of Thomas who bought 159 a. part Additional Progress from John Whipps of A. A. Cö. (83:533; 153:102).

SERGEANT. See SARGENT.

SERRIL, MARGARET, m. Elisha Perkins on 1 Dec. 1718 (129:227).

SERVIN, DAVID, servant with 7 years to serve was listed in the 1745 inv. of John Lloyd (54:125).

SEWELL, CHRISTOPHER, in 1750 owned 40 a. Sewell's Defense (153:65).

SEWELL, JOSHUA, in 1750 owned 84 a. Saplin Ridge and 50 a. part Arabia Petrea; on 28 June 1754 he and wife Mary conv. 77 a. Joshua's Expectation to Thomas Wainwright; d. by 22 Aug. 1763 when admin. bond on his est. was posted by Christopher Sewell, W. Sewell Young, and William Towson; est. was admin. in 1764 by Christopher Sewell; dec. left 5 ch. (unnamed), all of age (6:117; 15:203; 38:20; 69:288; 153:203).

SEWELL, PHILIP, was in Balto. Co. by 17 Aug. 1724 when he and w. Sarah conv. 100 a. Sewell's Coffer to Lawrence Todd (69:301)

SEWELL, SAMUEL in 1750 owned 20 a. part Sewell's Ruby (153: 70).

SEWELL, SARAH, in March 1736 was tried for bast. (31:20).

SHADOWS, DAVIS, m. Ann Boswell on 26 Dec. 1749 (131).

SHADWELL. See CHADWELL.

SHARD, THOMAS, was in Balto. Co. by 1692 as a taxable in n. side Gunpowder (138).

SHAREWELL, THOMAS, m. Ann (---) and had iss.: JOHN, b. 13 Oct. 1732 (133:31).

SHARP, JOHN, b. c.1713, w. Elizabeth, b. c. 1710, and Nathaniel Shepherd of William, b. c.1732, were named in 1742 lease of part of My Lady's Manor (77:130).

SHARPE, JOHN, m. Hannah Cook on 20 Nov. 1752 (131).

SHARPNER, MICHAEL, serv. to Edward Punteny, in Nov. 1755 was named as the father of Catherine Kibner's child, and was tried for bast. (40:401, 404).

SHAVERS, ABRAHAM, m. by 1 Oct. 1719 Susannah (---) who joined him on that day in conv. 38 a. Westminster to Mary Lynch (68: 171).

SHAW, CHRISTOPHER (1), was transp. to Md. by c.1668; in Aug. 1680 surv. 100 a. Shaw's Fancy; in June 1688 surv. 97 a. Shaw's Delight; he and w. Elizabeth conv. Shaw's Choice to John Asher; by 1692 was a taxable in n. side Gunpowder Hund.; d. leaving a will, 11 Feb. 1739 - 3 March 1739, leaving est. to John Ingle and w. Ruth Bayes, and also naming Elizabeth Bayes, Jr., Christopher Durbin and Mary Shaw (dau. of Thomas);admin. bond was posted 3 March 1739 by John Bayes, Jr., with Solomon Hillen and Jarvis Biddison; est. was admin. 3 Oct. 1741 and again on 22 Nov. 1742 by John Bayes, Jr.; an account was filed by Solomon Hillen naming "Thomas and Mary Durbin, ch. of the said Shaw;" dec. left iss.: THOMAS, d. by Nov. 1715; JOHN INGLE (named as orph. of deceased in June 1742); ROBERT BOYD (or BAYES) (named as orphan of dec. in June 1742) (3:279; 4:102; 15:279; 32:447; 59:211; 77:382; 127:67; 138; 211:77, 388).

SHAW, THOMAS (2), s. of Christopher (1), is placed as one of the sons of Christopher because he appears with him in the tax lists of 1702, 1703, 1704, and 1705; d. by 15 Nov. 1715 when admin. bond on his est. was posted by admins. Simon Pearson with w. Sarah, and with Thomas Cannon and John Fitzredmond; m. Sarah, dau. of Thomas Thurston; she m. 2nd, on 25 July 1715, Simon

Pearson; Shaw and w. Sarah had iss.: CHRISTOPHER DURBIN, d. by
23 Nov. 1746; MARY (13:422; 144; 145; 146, 147; 13:.).

SHAW?, JOHN INGLE (3), placed as a son of s. of Christopher
(1), who named him as a s. in his will; on 15 Oct. 1743 conv. to
George Harryman his share of the real est. of Shaw; in 1750 Harryman owned 100 a. Shaw's Fancy, 97 a. part Shaw's Delight, and 83
a. Shaw's Privilege (77:382; 153).

SHAW, CHRISTOPHER DURBIN (4), s. of Thomas (2) and Sarah, m.
by 1733 Susannah (---) and d. 24 Nov. 1746; wife married as her
2nd husb. John Kersey on 27 Feb. 1749; will of Christopher Durbin Shaw, 23 Nov. 1746, named tract Shaw's Privilege, w. Susanna,
and these ch.: THOMAS, b. 1 Oct. 1733; MARY, b. 30 Dec. 1735;
ELIZABETH, b. 29 Aug. 1738; SUSANNA; and SARAH (1:404; 131:36,
184/r; 210-25:60).

SHAW, JOHN (5), no known rel. to any of the above, d. by March
1748; in July 1746 purch. 50 a. Todd's Range from Samuel and Comfort Harryman; on 9 Feb. 1746 Johanna Impey conv. him all her
property, if he would maintain her for the rest of her life;
Shaw d. leaving a will, 9 Jan. 1748 - 12 May 1749, naming s. William to manage all his affairs; admin. bond was posted 9 March
1748 by William Shaw with Aquila Gorswick and John Bays; est. was
admin. on 8 June 1750 by the exec.; dec. left iss.: WILLIAM, b.
c.1725; NATHAN, b. c.1729; ELIZA, b. c.1736; FRANCES, b. c.1739;
JOHN, b. c.1741; PETER, b. c.1744 (5:161; 16:30; 79:274, 277;
110:472).

SHAW, WILLIAM (6), s. of John (5), was in Balto. Co. in 1750
as the owner of 50 a. part Todd's Range; prob. the William Shaw
to whom Thomas Knightsmith Shaw, s. of Thomas Shaw, was bound
(46:76; 153:75).

SHAW, (---), m. by 1700 Eliza, dau. of Deborah (---) Johnson
Benger; Elizabeth Shaw inherited Benger's Privilege and Addition
to Privilege from her mother (121:197).

SHAW, BENJAMIN, age 8 "next 28 July" and MORDECAI SHAW, aged
5 "next 5 March," in June 1739 were bound to James Billingsley
and w. Sarah, until the boys reached age 21 (32:402).

SHAW, CATHERINE, was ind. for bast. in Aug. 1728; John Moorcock paid the fine, and agreed to be responsible for bringing up
the child, in Nov. 1728; she was tried for bast. in Aug. 1733,
March 1736, and March 1737/8 (in the latter case the father was a
slave, so the child was to be sold for 31 years, and Catherine
was to be sold for 7 years); tried for bast. again in June 1737;
as a servant to William Grafton was tried for bast. in Nov. 1738;
in Aug. 1745 she admitted to having had another ch.; in Nov. 1746
was ind. for bast.; in June 1750 was tried for the same offense
and ordered to be sold for 7 years (28:22, 74; 30:69; 31:35,
173, 321; 35:645; 36:220; 37:10).

SHAW, DANIEL, was in Balto. Co. by 3 June 1737 when he admin.
the est. of Anne Hall; in Dec. 1737 leased 100 a. Blathnia
Cambria from Benjamin Tasker for the lifetimes of Shaw, his w.
Eliza, and of William Hall, s. of Thomas and Ann; d. by 5 Aug.
1739 when admin. bond was posted by Charles Green with James Thompson and James Cannidy, Anne Shaw having relinquished the right of
admin.; est. was admin. by Charles Green on 9 June 1744 (3:251;
5:7; 15:265; 75:72).

SHAW, HANNAH, in June 1739 was ind. for bast.; tried in Aug.
1739; ind. again for bast. in Nov. 1741; in March 1741/2 as serv-

ant to William Grafton admitted to having a ch. by a slave (the ch., now 1 year old was sold to Grafton to age 30); was ind. for bast. again in March 1746/7 (28:401; 33:152, 333; 36:378).

SHAW, JOHN, was in Balto. Co. by 1692 as a taxable in n. side of Patapsco; on 17 May 1699 as servant to Thomas Todd was given his freedom; on 15 Jan. 1700 was in Cecil Co. when he sold to Alexander Graves the tracts Hopewell, Salisbury Plains, and Privilege; may have m. Elizabeth, dau. of Deborah (---) Johnson Benger (63:388; 66:53; 138).

SHAW, JOHN, d. by 24 April 1722 when admin. bond was posted by admnx,. Mary Shaw, with Edward Coyle and Robert Jubb; est. was inv. 9 May 1722 by Jos. Conaway and Hugh Merriken and val. at E 105.10.6, and signed by Mary Shaw; additional inv. was filed 5 Dec. 1723, val. at E 32, and filed by the admnx. Mary, now known as Mary Allerhellick (13:440; 50:372; 52:100).

SHAW, MARY, free black, was ind. for bast. in March 1710/11 (21:205, 214).

SHAW, MARY, was tried for bast. in Nov. 1724, having been ind. c.June 1724; servant of Christopher Durbin, was ind. again in June 1730; in Nov. 1736 bd. her son Weymouth to William Wright and w. Elizabeth; had iss.: WEYMOUTH (26:309; 27:42; 28:419; 75:50).

SHAW, ROBERT, was in Balto. Co. by 1694 as a taxable in n. side Gunpowder; in Feb. 1701 purch. Pitchcraft from Thomas and Mary Preston; d. by 8 Jan. 1708/9 when admin. bond was posted by Thomas Chamberlain with John Rawlings and John Stokes; est. was inv. 19 Jan. 1708/9 by Charles Baker and Matthew Green and val. at E 24.11.0; est. was admin. 29 May 1712 by Thomas Chamberlain (1:362; 13:448; 51:40; 66:132; 138).

SHAW, RUTH, dau. of Catherine, in March 1744/5 was bd. to William Grafton (35:473).

SHAW, SUSANNAH, mulatto ch., age 4 last 28 Feb., in Aug. 1729 was bd. to Thomas Biddison; in Nov. 1745 and Nov. 1746 was ind. for bast. (28:274; 35:734; 36:220).

SHAW, THOMAS, d. by 22 Oct. 1748 when admin. bond was posted by William Bennett with John Sargent; est. was admin. 4 March 1749 by Bennett; in Nov. 1757 his s. Thomas Knightsmith Shaw was bd. to William Shaw; had iss.: THOMAS KNIGHTSMITH SHAW (5:77; 16:4; 46:76).

SHEA, THOMAS, was in Balto. Co. by Nov. 1737 when he and w. Elizabeth conv. 100 a. part Uncle's Goodwill to Hester Butterworth; m. by 14 March 1743 (poss. as 2nd w.?) Ann (---), who joined him in sale of 50 a. Thomas' Beginning to John Digges of Balto. Co.; may be the Thomas Shea who d. by 27 March 1767 when admin. bond was posted by exec. Thomas Frisby Henderson with Aquila Nelson and Joseph Punteny (15:341; 75:37; 77:465; 153:35).

SHEAY, JAMES, in June 1719 was sentenced to serve Edward Parker 340 extra days for 34 days' runaway time from his former master Thomas Harris (23:134).

SHEERLOCK, JOHN, age c. 25, a runaway servant from Alexander Lawson and Co., at White Marsh, Balto. Co.; advert. for in May 1746 (384:561).

SHELDS, JOHN. See SHIELDS, JOHN.

SHELMERDINE, REBECCA, was ind. for bast in Nov. 1757 (46:73).

SHENTONE, Widow, in 1750 owned 121 a. Temperance Lott (153:87).

THE ROWLAND SHEPPERD FAMILY

SHEPPERD, ROWLAND (1), progenitor, was in Balto. Co. by June 1709 when he surv. 147 a. Shepperd's Choice; d. 10 Feb. 1731; m. Bridget (---); d. leaving a will, 13 Jan. 1731/2 - 9 March 1731/2, naming ch. Ann, Sarah Brown, and Christopher;.admin. bond was posted 13 March 1731/2 by exec. Christopher Shepperd, with Abraham Cord and William Smith; est. was admin. on 29 May 1738 and 24 July 1738; had iss.: MARY, b. 10 March 1695/6, m. (---) Little; CHRISTOPHER, b. 10 March 1695/6 (prob. d. young); ROWLAND, b. 28 March 1698; ELIZABETH, b. 4 March 1700; GEORGE, b. 4 Jan. 1702; CHRISTOPHER, b. 19 Nov. 1710; ANN; SARAH, m. Absolom Brown on 19 Jan. 1728/9 (15:276; 125:215; 128:19, 27, 74; 129:246; 207).

SHEPPERD, ROWLAND (2), s. of Rowland (1), was b. 28 March 1698, d. 21 April 1728, having m. Jane Taylor, on 22 June 1727; left one s.: ROWLAND, b. 9 Aug. 1728 (128:51, 57).

SHEPPERD, CHRISTOPHER (3), s. of Rowland (1), was b. 19 Nov. 1710, and served as exec. of father's will; in 1750 owned 100 a. The Marsh, 100 a. Shnott Island, 147 a. Shepperd's Choice, 28 a. Sheppard's Adventure, and 122 a. Shepperd's Friendship; on 6 Nov. 1753 conv. 100 a. The Marsh and part Natty's Island to John Atkinson; m. Sarah Drew on 5 Sept. 1733, and had iss.: SUSANNA, b. 7 Aug. 1734; JAMES, b. 1 July 1738; and MARIANA, b. 8 May 1736 (82:115; 128:78, 83, 93, 93/r; 153:26).

SHEPPERD, NATHANIEL (4), no known rel. to any of the above, was b. c.1672; in Nov. 1742 leased part of My Lady's Manor, the lease to run for the lifetimes of his w. Elizabeth, b. c.1692, and ch.: JOHN, b. c.1712; TEMPERANCE; TESIA, and ELIZABETH (77:85, 265).

SHEPPERD, JOHN (5), s. of Nathaniel (4), was b. c.1712; may be the John who m. Margaret Elliott on 14 Aug. 1753 and had iss.: ELIZABETH, b. 7 April 1754; MARY, b. 21 Nov. 1756; JOHN, b. 9 Aug. 1758; MARGARET, b. 17 Nov. 1760; and NATHANIEL, b. 20 Nov. 1761 (131:42, 72/r).

SHEPPERD/SHEPHERD, NATHANIEL (6), no known rel. to any of the above, was s. of (---) and Mary who m. as her 2nd husb. by Nov. 1727 James Stanford; in Nov. 1727 he was made ward of John Fuller; d. by Aug. 1748 leaving a s.: WILLIAM (71:28; 80:63).

SHEPPERD, WILLIAM (7), s. of Nathaniel (6), on 20 Aug. 1748 conv. 100 a. Cooper's Paradice to Stephen Onion (80:63).

SHEPPERD, WILLIAM (8), no known rel. to any of the above, m. poss. Elizabeth (---); had s. NATHANIEL, b. c.1732 (77:130).

SHEPPERD, NATHANIEL (9), s. of William (8), was b. c.1732, and was age 10 in 1742 when he was named in the lease of part of My Lady's Manor, along with John Sharp, b. c.1713, and latter's w. Elizabeth, b. c.1710 (77:130).

SHEPPERD/SHEPHERD/ SHEPPARD, CHARLES, of Balto. Co. claimed land for service in 1669 (388).

SHEPPERD, CONSTANT, m. Michael James on 26 Aug. 1736, and had iss. (before marriage): JOHN, b. 29 July 1731; MARY, b. 20 May 1732; SOLOMON, b. 20 April 1735 (128:90; 131:51/r).

SHEPPERD, EDWARD, on 7 Dec. 1749 conv. 45 a,. Shepherd's
Paradice to James Morgan (80:348).

SHEPPERD, JOHN, m. Sarah (---), and had iss.: SARAH, b. 28
Aug. 1725; ELIZABETH, b. 13 Oct. 1728; RACHEL, b. 5 Sept. 1731;
ANN, d. 5 April 1729; MARY, d. 15 Aug. 1731 (128:69).

SHEPPERD, JOHN, of P. G. Co., in 1750 owned 260 a. Constant
Friendship (153:92).

SHEPPERD, JOHN, of Patapsco, in 1750 owned 36 a. part Gist's
Lime Pits; prob. the John Shepperd of Balto. Town who advert. in
Sept. 1751 he intended (to go to) for London next Spring (153:92;
Annapolis, Md. Gazette, 18 Sept. 1751, in 255:52).

SHEPPERD, MARY, servant to William Fell, was tried for bast.
in Aug. 1743, and again in June 1746 (35:14; 36:11).

SHEPPERD, PEASWICK, age 63 in June 1725, pet. to be levy free
(27:311).

SHEPPERD, THOMAS, was in Balto. Co. by 1695 as a taxable in
n. side Gunpowder (140).

SHEPPERD, THOMAS, m. Jean (---), and had iss.: THOMAS WARD,
b. 8 July 1755; MATHEW, or MARTHA, dau., b. 21 April 1758 (133:
102).

SHEPPERD, WILLIAM, m. Margaret (---), and had iss.: ANN, b. 3
Nov. 1723; JENITIA, b. 2 Oct. 1726; JEMIMA, b. 2 Aug. 1729; WIL-
LIAM, b. 24 March 1736; MARGARET, b. 7 March 1740 (131:20, 42/r,
88/r, 64/r).

SHEPPE(S?), HENRY, was in Balto. Co. by 1694 as a taxable in
s. side Patapsco (139).

THE SHEREDINE FAMILY is the subject of a chart compiled by
Christopher Johnston at the Maryland Historical Society.

SHEREDINE, THOMAS (1), progenitor, d. in Calvert Co. leaving
a will, 2 April 1676 - 19 Oct. 1677, naming w. Eliza, and these
ch.: DANIEL, d. 1700; THOMAS, may have d. 1701; JOHN; RICHARD;
JEREMIAH, d. c.1703, m. by 1687 Jane, wid. of Nicholas Buttram;
and ELIZABETH (120:197; Johnston chart).

SHEREDINE, DANIEL (2), s. of Thomas (1), d. in Calvert Co.
leaving a will, 12 April 1700 - 3 May 1700, naming w. Sarah, and
these ch.: THOMAS (to have dwelling plantation after death of
testator's w.): ELIZA (to have 120 a. Sheridan's Reserve) (121:
205).

SHEREDINE, Maj. THOMAS (3), s. of Daniel (2), was b. c.1699,
d. 28 May 1752; m. Tabitha (---), b. 1700, d. 21 Oct. 1769; in
Oct. 1746 made a deed of gift to his ch.: Daniel, Thomas, Jeremiah, Upton, Sarah Hammond, Elizabeth Paca, and Tabitha; in
1750 owned 150 a. Sheredine's Bottom, 246 a. Sheredine's Search,
141 a. Murray's Desire, 140 a. Tipton's Puzzle; d. 28 May 1752
of small pox at his house in Balto. Co., for many years a magistrate and a representative, and at the time of his death was
Sheriff of the county; admin. bond was posted 14 July 1752 by
Tabitha Sheredine with Thomas Sheredine, James Cary, and Thomas
Norris; est. was admin. 30 Aug. 1754, 15 May 1756, and 8 Oct.
1760; Thomas and Tabitha had iss.: SARAH, b. 8 Jan. 1721, m.
William Hammond on 9 March 1739; DANIEL, b. 3 Jan. 1724, d. 1749;
THOMAS, b. 27 March 1726; ELIZABETH, b. 26 May 1728; ELIZABETH,

b. 2 Aug. 1730, m. (---) Paca; WILLIAM MILLS, b. 14 Aug. 1734;
JEREMIAH; UPTON; and TABITHA (4:239, 322; 5:304; 13:452; 79:
185; 134:1, 12, 15, 43, 156; 153:18; 262:166; Johnston chart).

SHEREDINE, THOMAS (4), s. of Maj. Thomas (3), was b. 27
March 1726, d. 1769; m. Ann, dau. of Capt. John Cromwell of A.
A. Co., by 4 Jan. 1763; d. testate leaving a will, 4 Jan. 1763-
10 Nov. 1769, naming w. Ann, bros. Jeremiah and Upton, and one
s.: DANIEL, b. by 4 Jan. 1763 (112:164).

SHERLOCK, JOHN, m. Elizabeth Chesher on 30 Nov. 1737, and
had iss.: THOMAS, b. 27 Oct. 1738, d. 1739 (131:88/r).

SHERSEY, JOHN, was in Balto. Co. by 1750 as the owner of 50
a. Three Brothers (153:36).

SHEWBRIDGE/SHOWBRIDGE, JOHN, m. Mary Norris on 28 Sept. 1732;
in Nov. 1742 leased part My Lady's Manor for the lifetimes of
his ch. Elizabeth, age 7, Mary, age 5, and Jobn, age 2; had
iss.: ELIZA, b. 2 June 1733; MARY, b. 30 Jan. 1735; ISABELLA, b.
4 Nov. 1737; JOHN, b. 26 June 1739; FRANCES, b. 12 Sept. 1741;
SUSANNAH, b. 25 March 1743; CHARLES, d. May 1733 (77:106; 131:
108/r, 109/r).

SHIEF, ELIZABETH, servant, with 13 mos. to serve, was listed
in the 1722 inv. of Aquila Paca (50:142).

SHIELDS, HENRY (1), was in Balto. Co. by 28 Aug. 1704 when
he purch. 100 a. Ferry Range from John and Mary Boring; d by
24 April 1721 when admin. bond was posted by Luranna Shields;
est. was admin. by Lawranna w. of Humphrey Yates on 2 Sept.
1725; had iss.: SOLOMON (3:37; 15:273; 66:360).

SHIELDS, SOLOMON (2), s. of Henry (1), d/ by 18 March 1747
when admin. bond was posted by the admnx. Elizabeth Shields,
with John Maccomican and William Barney; est. was admin. by
Elizabeth Shields on 31 May 1749 and by Elizabeth w. of Jacob
Sindall on 19 Oct. 1751 and 1 Nov. 1752; before his death may
have given bond he would conv. Ferry Range to William Barney;
had iss.: PHILIP, b. 20 Aug. 1740; HENRY, b. 13 May 1742; JOHN,
b. 31 Oct. 1744; ABRAHAM, b. 21 Nov. 1747 (5:94, 189, 231; 16:
20; 82:10; 133:92).

SHIELDS, PHILIP (3), s. of Solomon (2), was b. 20 Aug. 1740;
conv. to Jacob Sindall 100 a. Ferry's Range, conv. in 1704 to
Henry Shields, grandfather of said Philip, by John Boring; now
Philip's w. Rachel consents (85:383).

SHIELDS, SOLOMON, son of Henry, d. by June 1730 when his est
was inv. and val. at E 13.3.6 (30:12).

SHIELDS, SOLOMON, d. by 1750 when his heirs owned 100 a.
part Ferry's Range (153:28).

SHIELDS, SOLOMON, on 20 July 1750 gave bond he would conv.
Ferry Range to William Barney (82:10).

SHILLING, JACOB, Jr., was in Balto. Co. by Aug. 1755 when he
sold part Jacob's Pasture, 14 a., to Richard Richards; was naturalized in A. A. Co. in 1757 (82:423; 404:19).

SHINDALL. See SINDALL.

SHIPLEY, ADAM in July 1724 conv. 100 a. part Andover to Lancelot Todd (69:299).

SHIPLEY, ADAM, and w. Ruth conv. 397½ a. Adam's Garden to
John Elder in Sept. 1751 (82:456).

SHIPLEY, ADAM, s. of Adam, d. by 14 Oct. 1765 when Hammutal
Shipley posted admin. bond with Robert Tivis and Thomas Bennett
(15:287).

SHIPLEY, ADAM, s. of Charles, and w. Ann, in Sept. 1767 conv.
50 a. Long Valley to Dr. John Stevenson; Margaret, the relict of
Charles Shipley also consented (92:38).

SHIPLEY, GEORGE, m. Katherine (---); in 1750 he owned 50 a.
Shipley's Choice; in Oct. 1760 he bought 100 a. Stinchcomb's
Reserve from John and Catherine Stinchcomb; had iss.: (perhaps
with others): ROSANNAH, b. 2 Feb. 1748 (84:416; 134:12; 153:96).

SHIPLEY, RICHARD, was in Balto. Co. by March 1716; m. Susanna
(---); left a will, 5 Oct. 1724 - 24 Aug. 1725, leaving tract
Adam the First to sons Adam, Richard, Samuel, and Peter, all
under 21, and 25 a. Brother's Partnership to dau. Lewis, named
w. Susanna, bro. Robert, and Benjamin Stevens; admin. bond was
posted 24 Aug,. 1725 by Susannah Shipley with Robert Shipley;
est. was inv. on 30 Nov. 1725 by Jos'h Dorsey and John Dorsey
and val. at £ 147.3.6 and signed by Susanna Shipley, extx.,
with Peter and Robert Shipley, bros. of the dec.; had iss.:
JOHN, b. 25 March 1716; ADAM; RICHARD; SAMUEL; PETER; LOIS (3:
66; 15:774; 51:46; 124:198; 131:90/r).

SHIPLEY, SAMUEL, in 1750 owned Greenbury's Grove; in Nov.
1753 he and w. Martha conv. 225 a. part Meton's Resolution and
72 a. Addition to Greenbury's Grove to Sewell Young (82:91, 206;
153:70).

SHIPTON, JOHN, in Oct. 1757 m. Mary Spear, and had iss.:
JNO., b. 13 Oct. 1758; and ROBERT, b. 17 Sept. 1761 (131:157/r).

SHLY, JOHN, in June 1759 surv. 50 a. Shly's Adventure (207).

SHOEBRIDGE. See SHEWBRIDGE.

SHOEMAKER, JAMES; d. by 15 Nov. 1751 when his est. was admin.
by Elizabeth Shoemaker (5:119, 209).

SHOEN, MARY, servant to Edward Roberts, was tried for bast.
in Nov. 1729 (28:314).

SHOWBRIDGE. See SHEWBRIDGE.

SHOWEL, THOMAS RHODES, was living in Balto. Co. in 1756; was
a grandson of Thomas Roades, without Lawford's Gate, Bristol,
when he wrote to his grandfather, mentioning his mother, uncle,
and sisters (300-65: 266).

SHOY, WILLIAM, m. Ruth (---), and had iss.: WILLIAM, b. 12
March 1758 (133:101).

SHRIDER, WILLIAM, was in Balto. Co. by April 1757 when he and
w. Susannah conv. to Thomas Johnson 100 a. part Logsdon's
Addition, and part Bedford Resurveyed (83:162).

SHRIVER, ANDREW, was in Balto. Co. by 1750 when he owned 100
a. Mistake, and 50 a. The Addition; when he purch. them from
William Mewis in 1742 he was described as Andrew Schriber of
Penna. (77:93, 634; 153:90).

SHRIVER, LODWICK, was in Balto. Co. by 1750 as the owner of
100 a. Lodwick's New Mill (153:91).

SHUDALL, WARNER, was in Balto. Co. by 1667 when Howell and
Elizabeth Powell conv. him 70 a. on the n. side of Patapsco;
in March 1667/8 Warner and his w. Ann conv. 70 a. to Nathaniel
Ruxton (95).

SHY, THOMAS, m. Eliz. Maryfield on 23 July 1706, and had iss.:
SARAH, b. 31 Dec. 1707 (128:18, 24).

SICKLEMORE, SAMUEL (1), was b. c.1659, and was in Balto. Co.
by 13 Sept. 1683 when he surv. 150 a. Samuel's Delight; on 1
Jan. 1695 surv. 262 a. Turkey Hill; also surv. 100 a. Rayman in
April 1687 and 318 a. Wolf Harbor in June 1689; by 1692 was a
taxable on n. side Gunpowder River; vestryman of St. John's Par.
in 1696 and representative from Balto. Co. in the Assembly of
1701 and 1702; in 1705 he gave his age as 46; on 5 Nov. 1703 sold
Neighbor's Affinity to William James of Calvert Co.; on 27 Oct.
1706 gave attorney to his w. Sarah to sell land; on 14 July 1711
conv. Wolf Harbor to his s. Samuel, 200 a. of land at Winter's
Run to his s. Sutton, and Sicklemore's Dock to his dau. Hannah;
all they ch. were to live together until marriage, and were to
teach Thomas Wriothesley Sicklemore to read and write; Henry
Wriothesley of Balto. Co. in his will dated 18 May 1709 conv.
200 a. of land to Thomas Wriothesley Sicklemore; iss. of Samuel
Sicklemore: SAMUEL; SUTTON; HANNAH (59:560; 66:302; 67:244; 138;
210-12:150; 211; 371).

SICKLEMORE, SAMUEL (2), s. of Samuel (1), m. 1st Ruth Cammel
on 8 Dec. 1713; she evidently d. young because he m. 2nd, on 12
Sept. 1716, Katherine Herrington; had iss. by 1st w.: RUTH SARAH,
b. 23 Dec. 1715, d. 22 Sept. 1716 (131:8, 9, 11, 20/r).

SICKLEMORE, SUTTON (2), s. of Samuel (1), d. in Balto. Co.
by 23 Aug. 1765; m. 1st Constant, dau. of John Love; she d.
after 8 March 1744 when she gave consent to a conveyance of
land; m. 2nd, on 29 July 1762 Prudence Hindon (or Hendon); d.
leaving a will, 9 July 1762 - 23 Aug. 1765, naming grandsons
Samuel Sicklemore Peacock, and Sutton Sicklemore Ward, and these
ch.: SARAH, b. 21 March 1717, m. Thomas Burke on 14 April 1737;
CONSTANT LOVE, m. Luke Peacock on 26 July 1753; ELIZABETH, b. 17
Dec. 1730, m. John Holland on 23 Dec. 1755; HANNAH, m. (---)
Ward (78:67; 112:21; 131).

SICKLEMORE, ELIZABETH, m. John Brown, s. of Thomas, on 18
Nov. 1705 (129:206).

SICKLEMORE, THOMAS WRIOTHESLEY, was named in the 1709 will
of Henry Wriothesley, and was mentioned in a 1711 deed of Samuel
Sicklemore (67:244; 210-12:150).

SIDWELL/SEDWELL, ROGER, of Balto. Co., imm. from Va., c.1667;
was granted 50 a. in 1670; in June 1673 he was conv. 86 a. Prospect by Charles Gorsuch; d. by 1677; his wid. m. John Boring;
23 Oct. 1677 admin. bond was posted by John Boring with John
Arden and John Leakins; his heir Jane m. Selah Dorman; may have
had dau. JANE, m. Selah Dorman (13:451; 59:307; 62:212; 63: 325;
206-6:423; 388). See also SEDWELL, ROGER.

SILBY, ANNA, ind. for bast. in March 1740/1 and tried in
March 1741/2 (33:2, 309). See also ROBERT COLLINS.

SILBY, JOHN, m. Ann (---), and had iss.: JAMES, b. 5 Jan.
1731; MARTHA, b. 11 June 1734; CALEB, b. 22 April 1736 (128:77,
82, 92).

SILVAINE, DANIEL, d. by 7 Nov. 1670 when admin. bond was posted by William Dunkerton and Nicholas Allan; purch. 150 a. on n.
side Worton Creek, 350 a. Buck Neck, formerly taken up by Joseph
Hopkins (15:312; 95).

SIMKIN. See SIMPKINS.

SIMM, WILLIAM, of P. G. Co., d. by 24 May 1755 when his est.
was admin. in Balto. Co. by William Lyon (5:354).

SIMMONS/SEEM(M)ONS/SEIMMONS/SYMONDS, CHARLES (1), d. in Balto Co. by 8 May 1738; m. Hannah (---); admin. the est. of Thomas
Jones and on 7 July 1715 admin. the est. of John Penrice who had
named his exec.; on 3 March 1718 he and w. Hannah sold 100 a. of
Tower Hill to Thomas Miles; in Aug. 1729 was named as a son-in-
law in the will of Edward Smith; d. leaving a will, 20 June 1736-
8 May 1738, mentioning tract Claxon's Purchase, naming w. Hannah
and ch.: George, Charles, Thomas, Josias, Kezia Taylor, and Hannah Simmons; admin. bond was posted 8 May 1738 by Hannah, George,
and Charles Simmons, with John Taylor and Richard Robinson; est.
was admin. on 30 July 1739, and bond was given to two minor orphans, John and Thomas, in Nov. 1740; had iss.: GEORGE, b. 4
July 1714; JOHN, b. 2 March 1718; THOMAS, b. 5 Sept. 1719 (prob.
d. young); JOSIAS, b. 19 March 1728; KEZIAH, m. 1st John Taylor;
m. 2nd Joshua Hardesty; CHARLES; HANNAH; JOHN (under age in 1740);
THOMAS (under age in 1740) (1:319; 2:238; 5:277; 32:355, 356; 63:
530; 125:172; 126:246; 131).

SIMMONS, GEORGE (2), s. of Charles (1), was b. 4 July 1714; m.
1st, on 7 Dec. 1736, Jemima Standiford; she d. 25 Dec. 1737, and
he m. 2nd, on 24 Oct. 1738, Eliz. Fuller; he d. by 28 May 1770
when his est. was admin. by Elizabeth Simmons; left iss.: HANNAH,
b. 9 Oct. 1739 (may be the Johanna who m. Lewis Barton on 30
June 1757); RACHAEL, b. 8 April 1751, m. Luke Pendergast on 26
Jan. 1768; ISAAC; ABRAHAM; MARGARET, m. (---) Murray; DEBORAH,
m. Luke White on 17 Jan. 1762; ABIGAIL; and MARY, m. Jonathan
Starkey on 23 June 1757 (6:188; 131:72, 52/r, 78/r, 86/r, 134/r).

SIMMONS, CHARLES (3), s. of Charles (1), m. Elizabeth Poteet
on 19 Oct. 1742; had iss.: JOHN, b. Sept. 1744; CHARLES, b. 3
Aug. 1746 (131:95/r, 113/r, 126/r).

SIMMONS, JOSIAS (4), s. of Charles (1), was b. 19 March 1728;
on 15 July 1754 sold 64 a. Clarkson's Purchase to Margaret James
(82:272).

SIMMONS, THOMAS (5), s. of Charles (1), was under age in 1740;
may be the Thomas who m. Priscilla, dau. of Alexander McComas,
on 6 Feb. 1753 (131).

SIMMONS, (---), m. by Sept. 1755, dau. of Edward Richards
(210-30:26).

SIMMONS, JOHN, m. Eliz. Powell on 30 March 1755 (131).

SIMMONS, JOSEPH, was in Balto. Co. by Aug. 1674 when he was
conv. 100 a. part Rading, by Stephen and Ann White (100:118).

SIMMONS, SAMUEL, m. Mary (---), and had iss.: ELEANOR, b. 4
Feb. 1734 (128:87).

SIMMS/SIMS, WILLIAM (1), hadat least one s.: RICHARD (120:
173).

SIMMS, RICHARD (2), s. of William (1), was named in the will,

made 22 Dec. 1675, of Roger Hill; purch. tract Swanson from Edward Swanson on 22 July 1672; on 5 April 1676 was named as son-
in-law of John Taylor; in Nov. 1673 surv. Sims Choice, 150 a.,
later held by Michael Judd; d. by 20 Dec. "in the 10th year
of the Dominion of (?);" admin. bond was posted by James Phillips with Richard Skelton; in Nov. 1684 Thomas Walley was made
guardian of Richard's children: THOMAS; and MARY (13:444; 18:
212; 120:170, 173; 211).

SIMMS, MARY (3), dau. of Richard (2), ward of Thomas Walley
had been placed with her own grandmother, who d. be Dec. 1691;
when Elizabeth Whalley, widow, pet. the court as next of kin, to
have charge of the girl (19:131).

SIMMS, WILLIAM, in 1750 owned 250 a. part Tasker's Camp; m.
Mary (---); in June 1754 he and Mary conv. William Askew Lot
80 in Balto. Town; had iss.: MARY, b. 26 Oct. 1751; ISABELL,
b. 16 Dec. 1754; GEORGE, b. 27 March 1756 (82:238; 133:96, 98;
153:103).

SIMMS, THOMAS, m. Sarah (---), and had iss.: RUTH, b. 2 July
1760 (133:107).

SIMPKINS, JOHN (1), d. in Balto. Co. by 3 April 1739; m.
Priscilla (---); was in Balto. Co. by 1701 as a taxable in n.
side Patapsco Hund.; in March 1714/5 surv. 100 a. Simpkins'
Choice; in Oct. 1732 took up 100 a. Addition to Simpkins' Re-
pose; d. leaving a will, 14 March 1738 - 3 April 1739, naming w.
Priscilla, son John, and daus. Avarilla Hammond, Rachel Simpkins,
Mary Hawkins, Hannah Briant, and Elizabeth Harryman, and a grand-
dau. Priscilla Hawkins; est. was inv. by John Risteau in Aug.
1739 and val. at ₤ 213.12.3, and filed in court by Priscilla
Simpkins in Nov. 1739; est. was admin. by Priscilla Simpkins on
10 Nov. 1739, and 10 Oct. 1741; dec. left iss.: ELIZABETH, m.
Robert Harryman on 24 Jan. Jan. 1733; MARY, b. 6 Aug. 1716, m.
John Hawkins on 12 June 1733; AVARILLA, m. 21 June 1734 Lawrence
Hammond; HANNAH, m. by 14 March 1738 (---) Bryant; RACHEL, unm.
in 1738; JOHN, b. 19 March 1722 (4:207, 109; 127:29; 133:14, 151,
152; 134:19; 143; 205-24:300; 207).

SIMPKINS, JOHN (2), s. of John (1) and Priscilla,, was b. 19
March 1722; m. Mary (---); in 1750 owned 40 a. Organ and Simpkins' Addition, and 100 a. Simpkins' Repose; on 13 Sept. 1765 he
conv. Simpkins' Repose, at the Garrison, cont. 100 a., to Richard Croxall; had iss.: JOHN, b. 25 Dec. 1746, m. 1st Mary Jenifer
and 2nd Elizabeth Lamar; was an Associate Judge in Allegany Co.;
SUSANNA, b. 2 Feb. 1748; PRISCILLA, b. 29 Dec. 1750; WILLIAM,
b. 1754/5; poss. son DICKERSON (91:26; 153:76; 134:20; Irma R.
Anderson, The Blake-Ambrose Family History, (1966), p. 14).

SIMPKINS, THOMAS, servant to Joseph Johnson, d. 5 Dec. 1729
(128:58).

SIMPSON, RICHARD (1), was in Balto. Co. by 1692 as a taxable
in Spesutia Hund.; d. by 7 June 1711 when admin. bond was posted
by Thomas Simpson, exec., with Samuel Brown and Thomas Gilbert;
in 1715 his wid. Ann, and ch. Thomas, Ann, and Elizabeth, were
mentioned in county court records; his daus. Ann and Elizabeth,
with the consent of their bro. Thomas, bound themselves to
John and Elizabeth Clarke; Richard had iss.: THOMAS, b. 1 Nov.
1691; SUSANNA, b. 5 April 1693; WILLIAM, b. 14 Feb. 1695; ELIZA-
BETH, b. 5 April 1697, bur. 30 Sept. 1698; JONATHAN, b. 12 Nov.
1699; MATTHEW, age 6 on 27 Aug. 1708; prob. ANNE, age 3 on 25
Jan. 1708; ELIZABETH, age 7 mos. on 27 Feb. 1708 (13:420; 21:626;
129:180, 186, 206; 138).

SIMPSON, THOMAS (2), s. of Richard (1), was b. 1 Nov. 1691 and was age 17 on 7 Nov. 1706; gave his age as 42 in 1732 when he made a deposition in which he stated his father Richard had been living 28 years earlier; m. 1st Eleanor (---), and 2nd, on 13 Feb. 1717, Mary, dau. of Emanuel Smith; had iss.: (by 1st w.): RICHARD, b. 26 Dec. 1714; (by 2nd w.): WILLIAM, b. 28 Jan. 1718; ELEANOR, b. 11 July 1721; GILBERT, b. 21 July 1724, d. 22 July 1725; MARY, b. 7 March 1726/7; THOMAS, b. 3 Feb. 1729; MARTHA, b. 7 Dec. 1736; JOSHUA, b. 6 Jan. 1737 (ADDENDA: on 13 June 1722 Thomas and w. Mary conv. 120 a. Sister's Discovery to Joshua Wood) (69:72; 128:3, 24, 44, 46, 49, 64, 95, 101; 224: 139).

SIMPSON, SUSANNA (3), dau. of Richard (1), was b. 5 April 1693; age 15 on 2 April 1707; ind. for bast. in March 1710/11; in June 1711 named Garrett Close as the father of her ch.; in Aug. 1716 named James Collins as the father of: SARAH COLLINS SIMPSON, b. 27 Feb. 1715 (21:205, 210; 22:56; 128:3, 35; 129: 206).

SIMPSON, WILLIAM (4), s. of Richard (1), was b.14 Feb. 1695, was age 14 on 14 Feb. 1707; age 31 in 1732; age 41 in 1736 when he made a deposition in which he named his uncle Thomas Gilbert; m. Elizabeth, dau. of Mary Buchanan; she d. 1732/3; in July 1721 surv. 100 a. Simpson's Hazard, which he conv. to John Stokes in Aug. 1726; had iss.: MARY, b. 4 Feb. 1714; WILLIAM, b. 31 March 1721; HANNAH, b. 31 Jan. 1722; SARAH, b. 16 Feb. 1729; ANN, b. 19 April 1734; JOHN, b. 29 June 1737 (70:301; 128: 3, 39, 43, 65, 79, 97; 207; 223:135, 140, 240).

SIMPSON, ANNA, m. Samuel Smith on 28 Aug. 1726 (129:241).

SIMPSON, JOHN, d. by 20 May 1742, when his est. was admin. by extx. Priscilla, now w. of Charles Motherly (3:282).

SIMPSON, MARTHA, m. William Hamby on 25 Dec. 1722 (129:231).

SIMPSON, PATRICK, admin. the est. of Thomas Cromwell on 3 Nov. 1724 (2:363; 3:17).

SIMPSON, RICHARD, d. by 30 May 1721, when Thomas Stone was m. to his extx. Eliza (1:43, 225).

SIMPSON, RICHARD, m. Elizabeth (---), and had iss.: THOMAS, b. 23 Sept. 1739; NATHANIEL, b. 11 July 1745 (128:106; 129:343).

SIMPSON, SARAH, was ind. for bast. in Aug. 1743; had s. THOM-AS, b. 11 June 1737 (35:305; 128:98).

SIMPSON, WILLIAM, m. Mary Larrissee on 12 Nov. 1739; dau. ANN, b. 2 Feb. 1739 (128: 106).

SIMPSON, WILLIAM, m. Avarilla Perkins on 18 Aug. 1742 (129: 329).

SIMS. See SIMMS.

SIMSON. See SIMPSON.

SINCLAIR, JAMES, m. Mary Lester on 25 Dec. 1742; in 1750 owned 100 a. Claxons' Forest, which he had purch. in March 1746 from Clarkson and Rosanna Bowen; d. leaving a will, 9 May 1760 5 May 1761; named eld. s. Lester and ch. James, George, William, Elizabeth, Mary, Martha, and John; est. was to be val. by Robert and Thomas Bryarly; will of Mary Sinclair, 7 May 1771 - 19

Aug. 1771, naming tract Bond's Discovery and ch.: William, John,
Mary, Martha, Lester, James, and Elizabeth Tate, and David Tate;
dec. left iss.: LESTER; ELIZABETH, m. (---) Tate; JOHN; MARY;
MARTHA; JAMES; GEORGE, prob. d. by 7 May 1771); and WILLIAM
(79:378; 111:341; 112:182; 129:332; 153:11).

SINCLAIR, WILLIAM, in 1750 owned 50 a. part Executor's Management; in 1734 purch. 50 a. Mary's Good Hope from Thomas Price;
m. Mary Hines on 26 Nov. 1730 and had iss.: WILLIAM, b. 16 Nov.
1735; poss. others (74:61; 128:92; 133:150; 153:15).

SINDALL/CHINDALL/SHINDALL/SYNDALL, PHILIP (1), was in Balto.
Co. as a servant with 4 years to serve, in the April 1704 inv.
of Martha Bowen; m. by 22 July 1721, dau. of Jacob and Jane Peacock; 1st w. may have been Catherine Peacock who signed the inv.
of Jacob Peacock on 1 Oct. 1713; 2nd w. may have been Elizabeth;
d. leaving a will, 15 May 1738 - 13 June 1738, naming w. Elizabeth as extx., ch. Jacob, Samuel, Jane, and also a William Sindall; admin. bond was posted 13 June 1738 by Elizabeth Sindall
with Thomas Green and John Gregory; est. was admin. 5 Nov. 1739
by Elizabeth, now w. of Jeremiah Cooke; had iss.: JACOB; SAMUEL;
JANE: MARY; and WILLIAM (1:203; 3:206; 15:315; 32:151, 294; 50:
297; 51:125; 74:45; 126:252).

SINDALL, JACOB (2), s. of Philip (1), d. by Dec. 1779; m.1st,
by 19 Oct. 1751, Eliza, admnx., of Solomon Shields; m. 2nd, by
6 July 1779, Temperance; d. leaving a will, 6 July 1779 - 1 Dec.
1779, naming w. "Tempey," and the ch. named below; est. was admin. on 3 March 1791; had iss.: DAVID, b. 20 July 1757; WILLIAM;
ROSANNA, m. Joseph Wells (5:189; 10:308; 112:386).

SINDALL, SAMUEL (3), s. of Philip (1), m. Elizabeth Carter, on
21 Feb. 1744; in Nov. 1754 was charged with bast. as the father
of Elizabeth Goswick's child; had iss.: PHILIP, b. 4 Dec. 1745;
SAMUEL, b. 9 July 1748; SARAH, b. 27 March 1760 (39:450;115:
266; 131; 133:94, 115).

SINDALL, JANE (4), dau. of Philip (1), was ind. for bast. in
Nov. 1734 (30:350).

SINDALL, WILLIAM (5), s. of Philip (1), m. and d. by 28 Jan.
1760 when admin. bond on his est. was posted by William Johnston
with Samuel Sindall and Richard Carter; est. was admin. 9 Sept.
1763 by Johnson; dec. left 1 ch., a dau., aged 7 (6:76; 16:45).

SING, JOHN, m. Mary (---), had iss.: BENJAMIN, b. 26 Aug.
1726 (133:17).

SING, MARY, was tried for bast. in Nov. 1729 and Nov. 1733;
had iss.: RUTH, b. 24 Aug. 1729 (28:315; 30:134; 133:20).

SING, PHILIP, d. by Aug. 1739 when est. was admin. by Philip
Sing (32:49).

SITLEMEYER, (SE)BASTIAN, innholder of Balto. Co., d. leaving
a will, 14 Oct. 1758 - 15 March 1760, naming w. Mary and ch.:
Christopher, Eve, and Catherine; admin. bond was posted 15 March
1760 by extx. Mary Sitlemeyer with Nicholas Ruxton Gay and Daniel Barnet; wid. Mary d,. leaving a will, 24 Aug. 1768 - 12 June
1769; admin. bond was posted 15 June 1769 by admin. Barbara Sitlemeyer with Andrew Stiger and Morrice Wershler; Sebastian and
Mary had iss.: CHRISTOPHER; EVE: and CATHERINE (16:1, 2; 83:263;
111:85; 112:133).

SKARABON, PETER, m. Eliz. Sharf on 13 March 1745 (131).

THE SKATS/SCATES FAMILY is the subject of research by Dr. John T. Palmer of Santa Rosa, California, who has generously shared some of his data with the author.

SKATS, REINER (1), and w. Catherine (Benson) Skats, lived in Albany, N. Y.: IN Dec. 1723 Catherine, the wid., had m. 2nd to (---) Broadhurst, when she deposed that her husb: had been k. with one of their sons, by the French and Indians about 1689 at Schenectady; had iss.: GIDEON, b. c.1682 in Albany, N.Y. (69:287).

SKATS, GIDEON (2), s. of Reiner (1) and Catherine, was b. c. 1682 at Albany, N. Y., was in Balto. Co. by 12 May 1705 when he purch. 15 a. Addition to Swanson; m. by 1708 Sarah, dau. of Thomas Preston, whose will proved 1710 named his dau. Sarah Skats and granddau. Catherine Skats; Gideon later came to possess 150 a. Symes' Choice which had been laid out for Richard Simms; Gideon d. by 27 Dec. 1705 when admin. bond was posted by Sarah Skats with Thomas Preston, Sr., and Moses Groome, Gent.; wid. Sarah m. 2nd, William Pickett; Gideon and Sarah had iss.: KATHERINE, m. by 8 Sept. 1724 Vaughan Davis (2:129; 3:15; 13:418; 21:202; 60:147; 122:185; 211).

SKELTON, ISRAEL, was b. c.1645, giving his age as 60 in 1705; was in Balto. Co. by 6 Jan. 1676 when he wit. the will of Samuel Boston of Balto. Co.; on 2 June 1691 William Standiford sold Israel Skelton land on Seneca Ridge; William's w. Mary gave her consent; d. leaving a will, 24 April 1706 - 31 Aug. 1706, leaving his entire est. to wid. Mary until she should die or remarry; grandson Skelton Standiford, dau. of testator's dau. Margaret, was to have Spring Neck; daus. Margaret Standiford and Hannah York were to have personalty; admin. bond was posted 13 Aug. 1706 by Mary Skelton with John Standiford and George York; est. was inv. on 11 Oct. 1706 by Thomas Preston and William Hicks and val. at £ 81.17.2; est. was admin. by wid. Mary Skelton on 14 Jan. 1708/9; wid. Mary m. Samuel Brown on 2 Jan. 1709/10; Israel had two daus.: MARGARET, m. 1st John Standiford, and 2nd James Hicks; HANNAH, m. George York (2:89; 13:421; 48:21; 64:77; 120: 186; 122:74; 129:208).

SKELTON, JOHN, m. by 1686 Anne, wid. of Robert Groft (206-9: 145).

SKELTON, THOMAS, was in Balto. Co. when John Collett sold him some land; Collett sold Skelton a second tract on 9 Nov. 1664 (93; 94).

SKINNER, ROBERT, d. by 6 June 1693 when admin. bond on his est., was posted by Moses Edwards with John Hayes and John Roberts (13:420).

SKIPWITH, GEORGE, m. by Oct. 1676 Eliz., dau. of Thomas Thurston who conv. all his goods in Md., to his dau. Elizabeth; on 11 May 1681 George and Elizabeth conv. 100 a. Clement's Dane and 50 a. Clement to Edward Reeves, and appointed James Phillips their atty. to acknowledge the sale in open court (101; 103).

SKY, THOMAS, m. Elizabeth Maryfield on 23 July 1706; had iss.: SARAH, b. 31 Dec. 1707 (129:201, 206).

SLAINEY, MICHAEL, Irish servant, collier and miller, ran away from John White near Joppa, in Sept. 1751 (385:147).

SLADE, WILLIAM (1), may be the William "Slayd" who was transp. to Md. c.1648/9 as a servant, and settled in A. A. Co., where he

50 a. Slade's Hope on 20 Feb. 1662 (later held by Edward Peake),
100 a. Wolf Neck on 2 June 1662 (later held by Mary Eagle), and
50 a. Slade's Addition on 3 July 1671 (also later held by Mary
Eagle); d. leaving a will, 15 May 1675 - 5 June 1675, naming s.
William (to have 200 a. on Patapsco), dau. Eliza (to have home
plantation and 100 a. Wolf Neck), dau. Anne, and Henry Lewis;
had iss.: WILLIAM; MARY, m. (---) Eagle; ELIZA; and ANN (120:88,
172; 211; 388).

SLADE, WILLIAM (2), s. of William (1), was in Balto. Co. as a
taxable in s. side Patapsco in 1692; surv. 188 a. Slade's Camp
in Feb. 1695; surv. 112 a. Slade's Addition in April 1695; in
July 1702 bought 200 a. Windley's Rest from Francis and Sarah
Dallahide; d. leaving a will, 2 April 1726 - 19 May 1731, naming
s. Josias (to have 300 a. on Curtis Creek), s. William (to have
200 a. Winlow's Range), s. Thomas (to have 238 a. Slade's Camp),
s. Ezekiel (to have £ 30), daus. Elizabeth Cockey and Mary
Buckingham; had iss.: JOHN, d. 1713; ROBERT, d. 1710; WILLIAM;
JOSIAS; THOMAS: EZEKIEL; ELIZABETH, m. (---) Cockey by 2 April
1726; MARY, m. (---) Buckingham, by 2 April 1726 (66:174; 125:
202; 138; 211).

SLADE, JOHN (3), prob. s. of William (2), d. 30 Nov. 1713; m.
Elizabeth Crouch on 9 Feb. 1709 in St. James' Par., A. A. Co,;
wid. Elizabeth may have m. David Robinson on 12 Jan. 1713/4;
John and Elizabeth had iss., b. in St. John's Parish, Balto.
Co.: WILLIAM, b. 5 Nov. 1710; ROBERT, b. 30 June 1712 (131:5,
20/r; 219-3).

SLADE, ROBERT (4), poss. s. of William (2), d. by 17 April
1710 when admin. bond was posted by William Slade, with John
Slade and Luke Reed; est. was inv. in 1710 by Luke Reed and Thomas Croker, and val. at £ 55.4.0; est. was admin. 9 July 1713 by
William Slade; Robert left an orphan: SUSAN (2:5; 13:432; 48:263;
21:571; 145; 146; 147; 148).

SLADE, WILLIAM (5), s. of William (2), as son and heir of
William Slade, dec., conv. to Besaleel Foster on 16 Jan. 1740
100 a. called Windleys; m. Elizabeth Dulany; had iss. (among
others?): MARGARET, b. 18 Sept. 1742, m. Edward Talbot on 7 April
1763; she m. 2nd (---) Hughes (75:460; 77:199; 114:48; 131).

SLADE, JOSIAS (6), s. of William (2), m. Mary Day on 16 Jan.
1738 in St. Margaret's Par.; she was b. 23 Oct. 1713, dau. of
Nicholas Day, Jr.; in 1746 Josias was licensed to keep an inn;
Josias and Mary had iss.: BETSY ANN, m. Isaac Bull on 26 May 1761;
BELINDA, m. Thomas Talbott on 21 Jan. 1766, and as a 2nd husb.
Edmund Stansbury; WILLIAM, b. c.1746, m. Elizabeth Stansbury on
16 Jan. 1770; MARY, m. Elisha Dorsey on 15 Dec. 1768; NICHOLAS,
b. c.1755/7 (129:224, 257, 259; 131).

SLADE, EZEKIEL, m. Ann Whitaker on 7 Jan. 1754, and had iss.:
JOSIAS, b. 13 Oct. 1754 (131).

SLADE, RICHARD, was in Balto. Co. by 1695 as a taxable in n.
side Patapsco (140).

SLADE, THOMAS, m. Hannah Miles on 29 Sept. 1748 (131).

SLEMAKER, JAMES, d. in Balto. Co. by 16 April 1750; m. Elizabeth (---) who m. 2nd, Joseph Bankson, by 4 Sept. 1757; d. leaving
a will, 24 March 1759 - 16 April 1750, naming mother Hannah, bro,.
John in Eng., sis. Mary, w. Elizabeth, and s. John; admin. bond
was posted on 16 April 1750 by Elizabeth Slemaker with William and
Samuel Hopkins; est. was admin. on 4 Sept. 1757 by Joseph Bankson;
had is.: JOHN, b. 13 July 1746 (5:336; 111:30; 133:112).

SLIDER, MARY, had a s. b. in July 1727 and was ind. for bast.
in June 1730; tried in Aug. 1730; may have been rel. to the
Christopher Slider who wit. the will of Albert Greening on 1
March 1721/2; m. Peter Major on 27 Oct. 1730; had iss.: CHRIS-
TOPHER, b. 18 July 1727; a child, b. June or Aug. 1730 (28:
415; 29:8; 124:110; 133:45, 148).

SLIGH, THOMAS (1), was in Balto. Co. by 12 Dec. 1728 when
he wit. the will of Jonas Bowen; d. there by 11 Aug. 1774; m.
Sophia Wilkinson on 17 April 1734; she was a dau. of William
and Tamar (Love) Wilkinson; on 10 Sept. 1737 he purch. part of
Corbin's Rest from Edward and Jane Corbin; in 1750 owned many
tracts including 100 a. Sophia's Garden, 30 a. Find Me Out, 440
a. Privilege, 50 a. Michael's Beginning and 40 a. John's Beginning; d. leaving a will, 27 July 1774 - 11 Aug. 1774, naming
a Mrs. Ann Flannigan and a granddau. Elizabeth Sligh; Thomas
and Sophia had at least one ch.: WILLIAM, b. 9 Jan. 1734/5 (75:
13; 83:447; 112:293; 133:40, 152; 153:29).

SLIGH, WILLIAM (2), s. of Thomas (1), and Sophia, was b. 9
Jan. 1734/5; d. in Annapolis in March 1757, of the small-pox;
was age 22. and served as Clerk of the City and Provincial
Court; left a widow and one ch.: had iss.: ELIZABETH (133:40;
262:168).

SMALLEY, JOHN, m. Elizabeth (---), and had iss.: JOHN, b.
Sept. 1734; NATHAN, b. Jan. 1736 (131).

SMALLWOOD, SAMUEL, m. Martha (---); was in Balto. Co. by Nov.
1716 when he pet. that the two small ch. he had entrusted to
Nicholas Fitzsimmons be taken away as the said Fitzsimmons was
mistreating them; the pet. was rejected, but in Aug. 1718 his
sons were taken away; may be the Samuel Smallwood who was named
in Nov. 1714 as the father of Elizabeth Stevenson's child; had
iss.: RICHARD, living in Aug. 1718; SAMUEL, living in 1718
(21:192, 577; 22:64; 23:2, 5).

SMALLWOOD, THOMAS, was in Balto. Co. by 1692 as a taxable in
n. side Patapsco (138).

SMART, JOHN, in June 1710 was named as the father of Grace
Brown's child (21:136).

SMISER, MATTHEW, in 1750 owned 272 a. part Providence, which
he purch. from John Henthorn in 1743 (77:690; 153:91).

THE CHARLES SMITH FAMILY

SMITH, CHARLES (1), sold land to Luke Stansbury some time
before 1749; had s.: SAMUEL (80:417).

SMITH, SAMUEL (2), s. of Charles (1), m. Elizabeth Cox on 3
Sept. 1727; on 6 Dec. 1749 Samuel and Elizabeth Smith sold 57 a.
Richardson's Neglect to Jane Partridge; on 4 Sept. 1741 Samuel
alone had sold 57 a. of same tract to Buckler Partridge; Samuel
and Elizabeth had iss.: SAMUEL, b. 30 July 1728; ELIZABETH, b.
3 June 1730; SOPHIA, b. 21 June 1732; CHARLES MERRYMAN, b. 5
Dec. 1734; ABNER, b. 19 Nov. 1737 (76:72; 80:417; 133).

THE GEORGE SMITH FAMILY

SMITH, GEORGE (3), no known rel. to any of the above, d. in
Balto. Co. 20 April 1704, and was bur,. 22 April; may be the
George Smith who, with w,. Elizabeth, on 6 Aug., 1678, conv.100
a. Crab Hill to James Phillips; may have m. as 2nd w. Hannah

(---), wid. of Daniel Peverell; she m. 3rd David Thomas and d.
intestate 12 April 1718; Smith owned 100 a. Mate's Angle, 100 a.
Chelsea, 200 a. Little Marley (which had been left to him by
John Hathaway); d. leaving a will, 16 April 1704 - 25 May 1704.
left 200 a. Mates Angle and Chelsea to s. William, 200 a. Little
Marley to dau. Selinah, and also named w. Hannah and her dau.
Sarah Peverall; admin. bond was posted 21 June 1704 by admnx.
Hannah Smith w. Samuel Brown and Nicholas Day; est. was inv. on
4 July 1704 by Henry Jackson and Samuel Bane and val. at £ 122.
9.4, and admin. 25 July 1706 by Hannah, now w. of David Thomas;
dec. had iss.: GEORGE, Jr., b. c.1675 (as he was not 16 until
1695), bur. 27 Jan. 1699; WILLIAM, b. 1 May 1695; SELINA, bapt.
14 July 1700, m. Robert Clark on 18 Feb. 1718/9 (2:232; 13:446;
51:139; 59:350; 101:303; 122:37; 128:1, 8, 10, 14, 21; 129:219;
138; 140; 211).

SMITH, WILLIAM (4), s. of George (3) and Hannah, was b. 1
May 1695, d. 27 Nov. 1738; m. by 3 Aug. 1723 Mary, wid. of John
Newsom of Thomas, and dau. of Nathaniel and Hannah (---) Stinchcomb; he and w. were subject of warrants on 3 Aug. 1723 and 21
Oct. 1723 in the case of admin. the est. of John Newsom; Smith
d. leaving a will, 26 Nov. 1738 - 2 Jan. 1738/9, naming w. Mary
and ch.: George, William, Jr., Nathaniel, and Hannah, and lands
200 a. Contrivance, 50 a. Newsom's Meadows, and 254 a. Benjamin's Choice; on 1 Sept. 1739, Mary, wid. of William Smith, conv.
254 a. Benjamin's Choice to John and Helen Bailey; admin. bond
on the est. of William Smith was posted by Mary Smith; admin.
bond on Mary Smith's est. was posted 25 June 1740 by John Bailey who admin. the est. of Smith on 8 Aug. 1747; William and
Mary had iss.: WILLIAM, b. 8 Jan. 1722/3, d. by 8 Aug. 1747;
GEORGE, b. 27 July 1725, d. by 8 Aug. 1747; NATHANIEL, b. 2 April 1728; HANNAH, b. 20 Nov. 1735 (4:170; 15:311, 355; 51:90;
75:271; 127:13; 128:1, 51, 90, 93, 115; Test. Proc., Box 29,
folder 39, HR).

SMITH, NATHANIEL (5), s. of William (4) and Mary, was b. 2
April 1728; was live in 1762; m. Elizabeth Webster on 11 March
1752; in 1750 owned 200 a. Contrivance and 50 a. Newsom's Meadows; had iss.: ELIZABETH, b. 22 Nov. 1754; MARY, b. 24 April
1756; HANNAH, b. 14 Jan. 1759; ALICEANNA, b. 4 Aug. 1721; WILLIAM,
b. 14 Aug. 1762 (128:51; 129:357, 379; 153:56).

THE THOMAS SMITH FAMILY

SMITH, THOMAS (6), no known rel. to any of the above, was in
Balto. Co. by March 1688 when he surv. 100 a. Smith's Beginning
(leter held by his orphans); on 6 June 1693 Thomas Smith and w.
Isabella sold 100 a. Smith's Beginnings to Robert Benger; on the
same day Thomas purch. 100 a. Rama from Samuel and Sarah Sicklemore (which was later held by John Parker for the orphans of sd.
Smith; d. by 27 Jan. 1699; wid. Isabella m. John Parker on 12
Sept. 1699; est. of Thomas Smith was inv. on 29 Jan. 1699/1700
by John Rollings and James Standiford, and val. at £ 166.0.3,
plus 28,218 lbs. tobacco (worth in itelf £ 117.11.4), plus another 2000 lbs. tobacco in desperate debts; est. admin. by John and
Isabella Parker on 3 Oct. 1704 and 5 July 1708 by Thomas Preston
and William Hicks, admins. de bonis non; had iss.: ZACHARIAH;
poss. others (2:186, 187; 48:199; 59:381, 382; 211:56, 69).

SMITH, ZACHARIAH (7), s. of Thomas (6), d. by Aug. 1744, having m. Margaret (---); in Aug. 1744 two of his orphans were bd.
to James Osborne; had iss.: THOMAS, b. 27 April 1725; ZACHARI-
AH, b. Oct. 1728; JOHN, b. c.1731 (in Aug. 1744 age c.13 was bd.
to Osborne; WILLIAM, b. 27 July 1732; REBECCA, b. April 1734;
THOMAS, b. 3 Oct. 1736(35:296; 131:43/r, 47/r, 64/r).

SMITH, ZACHARIAH (8), s. of Zachariah (7), was b. Oct. 1728; in Aug. 1744, age 15 "last Spring," was bd. to James Osborne; in 1750 owned 100 a. Raymor (35:296; 153:97).

THE WILLIAM SMITH FAMILY

SMITH, WILLIAM (9), no known relation to any of the above, was in Balto. Co. by Nov. 1731 when he purch. one half of Matthew's Double Purchase from William and Mary Rhodes; d. leaving a will, 21 Nov. 1739 - 9 April 1743, mentioning a wife, and naming a s. Samuel (to have Fool's Refuse and a share of Matthew's Double Purchase), s. Joseph (to have 70 a. of same tracts), and a granddau. Margaret Horton (to have part of Chance); admin. bond was posted 30 April 1743 by Samuel Smith with Eric Erickson and Benjamin Bond; est. was admin. on 1 May 177; dec. left iss.; SAMUEL; JOSEPH; and poss. a dau. (unnamed) who m. (---) Horton (3:357; 16:34; 73:185; 127:212).

SMITH, SAMUEL (10), s. of William (9), was of age in Nov. 1739; in 1750 owned 180 a. Fool's Refuse, 70 a. part Matthews' Double Purchase, and 50 a. part Chance (153:42).

SMITH, JOSEPH (11), s. of William (9), may be the Joseph Smith of Gunpowder who d. 17 Dec. 1748; admin. bond was posted 18 March 1748/9 by Samuel Smith with William Dallam and George Presbury; est. was admin. by Samuel Smith on 11 March 1749 (5:351; 131).

ANOTHER WILLIAM SMITH FAMILY

SMITH, WILLIAM (12), no known rel. to any of the above), d. 30 Jan. 1731; m. Elizabeth, wid. of Richard Dallam, by 11 April 1726, when they admin. Dallam's est.; William d. leaving a will, 11 Jan. 1731 - 4 March 1731, leaving Martin's Rest and Gash's Neglect to son Winston, left Owen's Outland Plains to dau. Elizabeth, left Broom's Bloom to his s. William; also named his mother Elizabeth Smith, nephew Richard Caswell, and son-in-law William Dallam; admin. bond was posted 8 March 1731 by Elizabeth Smith; est. admin. on 16 Sept. 1734, and 20 Oct. 1736; dec. left iss.: WILLIAM; WINSTON; and ELIZABETH, m. John Paca (2: 253; 3:49, 60, 157, 216; 15:271; 125:214; 128:75; 206-37A:114).

SMITH, WILLIAM (13), s. of William (12), was living in Balto. Co. as late as 1753; m. Elizabeth (---), on 23 Dec. 1743; in 1750 owned 100 a. Broom's Bloom, which he and w. Elizabeth sold to John Beaver on 14 Sept. 1753; had iss.: ELIZABETH, b. 12 March 1745; CASSANDRA, b. 6 April 1747, d. Sept. 1754; SARAH, b. 31 March 1749; WINSTON, b. 8 Nov. 1750; WILLIAM, b. 3 Dec. 1752; and NATHAN, b. 8 Oct. 1753 (82:76; 129:349; 153:62).

SMITH, WINSTON (14) s. of William (12), d. in Balto. Co. by 8 April 1749 when admin. bond was posted by Susannah Smith with Richard Dallam and John Hall of Swan Town; m. 1st, on 5 Feb. 1740, Priscilla Paca, who d. 17 Sept. 1742; m. 2nd, on 18 July 1743, Mrs. Susanna Stokes, extx. of George Stokes; she m. 3rd Talbot Risteau; the est. of Winston Smith was admin. by Susanna Smith on 9 Oct. 1750 and by Susanna w. of Talbot Risteau on 3 Feb. 1752; in 1750 his heirs owned 64 a. Gash's Neglect, 386 a. Martin's Rest, 200 a. Planter's Delight and other lands; Winston Smith left iss.: (by 1st w.): PRISCILLA, b. 9 Jan. 1742; (by 2nd w.): WILLIAM, b. 29 March 1747 (4:179; 5:109, 240; 15:345; 40:223; 129:337, 390; 153:39).

UNPLACED SMITHS

SMITH, AARON, orphan, age 5 "last Feb.," in June 1716 was bd. to Andrew Berry and w. Elizabeth (39:11).

SMITH, ALEXANDER, age 6 "last Jan.," in June 1743 with consent of his mother was bd. to John Sumner and w. Ann to age 21 (51:187).

SMITH, ANNE, admitted bearing a bast. in June 1737; ind. for same in Nov. 1738 and tried in March 1739/40; ind. again in June 1743 (48:62, 351; 49:154; 51:185).

SMITH, BENJAMIN, d. 5 April 1745, having m. Sarah Hollis on 25 Feb. 1704/5; admin. bond was posted 3 June 1707 by George Chauncy with Lawrence Draper and Charles Baker; est. was inv. on 3 July 1707 by Thomas Lowe and Henry Hedge and val. at E 158. 10.8; est. admin. by Chancy, who m. Smith's wid. Sarah on 22 June 1706 (2:171; 13:445; 48:47; 128:20, 22; 129:201).

SMITH, CATHERINE, was ind. for bast. in Nov. 1737 and tried in March 1737/8; ind. for bast. in Aug. 1742 and tried that Nov. (48:129, 186; 51:1, 74).

SMITH, CHARLES, was b. c.1654, was a taxable in s. side of Gunpowder in 1692; was aged 70 in 1724 (69:380; 138).

SMITH, CHARLES, conv. 200 a. Smith's Chance to Henry Fitch in June 1730 (61:310).

SMITH, CHARLES, m. Margaret, dau. of Francis Brown, by 12 July 1749 (5:58).

SMITH, CHARLES, m. Ann Connell on 28 Jan. 1747 (133:161).

SMITH, CHARLES, d. by 29 Oct. 1750 when his est. was admin. by Isaac Risteau (5:107).

SMITH, EDWARD, d. in Balto. Co. by 7 Feb. 1676/7 when admin. bond was posted by John Arden with Giles Stevens; took up 260 a. Bachelor's Delight in March 1678, with John Arden; d. intestate and without heirs (13:439; 200-51:213, 240).

SMITH, EDWARD, was in Balto. Co. by 1 Aug. 1699 when he purch. 575 a. Boughton's Forest from Joseph and Jane Peake; m. 1st, by 5 March 1700, Elizabeth (---) who joined him in selling 160 a. Gray's Lot and 45 a. Smith's Addition to Richard Banks; in March 1700 sold 212 a. Smith's Forest to Joseph Benton; m. by 1 Nov. 1709 Bridget , prob. admnx,. of Charles Jones (Edward held 200 a. Swan Harbor and 100 a. Cadwallader for the orphans of said Jones); on 1 Nov. 1709 Edward and Bridget sold 54 a. Long Aire to William Smith; on 7 March 1716 Edward and Bridget conv. 400 a. of 575 a. Boughton's Forest to Richard Burroughs; on 8 Aug. 1717 with w. Bridget conv. 60 a. Smith's Lot to Robert Smith, cordwainer; on 6 March 1723/4 Edward conv. 120 a. Smith's Range to John Crockett; on 16 July 1724 mortgaged 77 a. Smith's Discovery and Phill's Choice (later called Smith's Purchase) to Josias Middlemore and John Crockett; in 1728 Bridget Smith was named as mother in the will of Theophilus Jones (1:297; 63:384; 66:11, 49; 67:19, 428, 480; 69:243, 344; 126:169; 211: 38, 39)

SMITH, EDWARD, had iss.: SARAH, m. Edward Oliver on 14 July 1720 (131).

SMITH, EDWARD, m. by 25 June 1711, dau. of William Hawkins, Sr., of Balto. Co. (122:195).

SMITH, EDWARD, d. by Aug. 1724 when Edward Coyle admin. the est. (26:507).

SMITH, EDWARD, d. leaving a will, 13 Aug. 1729 - 6 Nov. 1730,
leaving his entire est. to son-in-law Charles Symonds, who ren.
in favor of John Crockett; admin. bond was posted 7 Nov. 1730
by John Crockett; est. admin. by Crockett on 11 May 1732
(3:119; 15:272; 125:172).

SMITH, Mrs. ELIZABETH, d. 6 Dec. 1734 (128:82).

SMITH, ELIZABETH, was ind. for bast. in Nov. 1736, ind. again
in June 1750; tried in Nov. 1750; tried for bast. in Nov. 1754
and again in Nov. 1758; had s.: AQUILA (36:220; 37:2; 38:27; 39:
449; 46:165).

SMITH, EMANUEL, was in Balto. Co. by 4 March 1699 when he
purch. 120 a. Sister's Dowry from Gideon Gamble of Calvert Co.
and w. Mary; m. Susan, wid. of (---) Teague; d. 20 April 1704
leaving a will, 19 April 1704 - 3 June 1704. naming his children-
in-law (i.e., step-children) William, Catherine, and Ann Teague;
bro. Benjamin Smith, daus. Martha and Mary not yet 16, and w.
Susan, extx.; admin. bond was posted 3 July 1704 by extx. Susanna Smith with Lawrence Draper and Thomas Cord; est. was inv. on
18 July 1704 by Thomas Browne and (---) Garrettson, and val. at
£ 78.11.4; est. was admin. by extx. Susanna on 16 Oct. 1706; dec.
left iss.: MARTHA, b. 16 Feb. 1698/9; MARY, b. 1 June 1701, m.
Thomas Simpson on 13 Feb. 1717 (2:205; 13:447; 54:23; 66:36;
122:37; 128:6, 12, 21; 129:286).

SMITH, FRANCES, was ind. for bast. in June 1730 (28:415).

SMITH, FRANCIS, was in Spesutia Hund,. as a taxable by 1692;
m. Elizabeth (---) who d. 10 Aug. 1702 and was bur. 15 Aug. 1702;
on 20 Oct. 1704 sold 500 a. Ann's Lot to Thomas Edmunds (66:189,
362; 128:13; 138).

SMITH, GEORGE, in June 1746 was ind. for bast.; in Aug. 1746
admitted the paternity of Jane Willson's child (36:2, 129).

SMITH, GEORGE, blacksmith, on 17 Nov. 1758 sold 55 a. Arabia
Petrea to Hugh Doran, tailor (83:288).

SMITH, HENRY, m. Elizabeth Duley in June 1738; had iss.:
JAMES, b. 29 Oct. 1739; ELIZABETH, b. 27 Dec. 1743 (131).

SMITH, HENRY, weaver, d. by 16 Oct. 1749 when admin. bond was
posted by Samuel Tate with Robert Brierly; est. was admin. by
Tate on 3 July 1752 (6:22; 16:33).

SMITH, HENRY, m. Catherine (---), and had iss.: WILLIAM, b. 27
March 1752 (131:130/r).

SMITH, JAMES, was in Balto. Co. by 1692 as a taxable in s.
side Patapsco (138).

SMITH, JEREMIAH, was in Balto. Co. by 1692 as a taxable in
Spesutia Hund. (138).

SMITH, JOHN, servant, of Balto. Co., was transported by 1664
(388).

SMITH, JOHN, was in Balto. Co. by 1692 as a taxable in s. side
Patapsco Hund. (138).

SMITH, John, of "Biteford," Co. Devon, Eng., bought lot # 3,
in the town of Absolute on Patapsco River, from William Wilkinson (59:414).

SMITH, JOHN, d. 21 Dec. 1713, having m. Mary, admnx. of Henry Hedge on 2 Feb. 1709; she d. 20 Dec. 1713; John and Mary admin. the est. of Henry Hedge on 25 Oct. 1711; admin. bond on his est. was posted 7 Jan. 1713/4 by John Parker and Thomas Norris, with John Thomas and Francis Whitehead; est. was inv. on 23 Jan. 1713/4 by David Thomas and Samuel Jackson, and val. at £ 72.10.6 plus 4255 lbs. tobacco; Thomas Smith signed as kin and Roger Matthews signed as creditor (1:378; 13:442; 50:243; 128:26, 31; 129:212).

SMITH, JOHN, son of Jane, now w. of Richard Treadway, was age 13 "last 9 Jan.," in June 1713 was bound to Aquila Paca, Gent., to age 21 (21:379).

SMITH, JOHN, m. by 22 Feb. 1719 Dorothy, wid. of Thomas Williamson, whose est. they admin. on that day, and also on 31 Jan. 1720 (1:52, 331; 23:626).

SMITH, JOHN, m. Mary (---) and had iss.: ANN, b. 12 Feb. 1723; ABRAHAM, b. 13 March 1727; ISAAC, b. 4 July 1729; JACOB, b. 18 Feb. 1732 (128:62, 88).

SMITH, JOHN, in 1750 owned 100 a. Coom's Adventure (153:90).

SMITH, JOHN, m. on 18 Dec. 1752 Margaret, heir of Nicholas Scarf or Scharf (3:243; 131).

SMITH, JOHN, m. Mary (---), and had iss.: JOHN, b. 20 June 1758; ADAM, b. 25 May 1762 (129:376).

SMITH, JOHN, Scottish servant, ran away from Pleasance Goodwin's in Soldier's Delight, by 17 Aug. 1752 (307-69:213).

SMITH, JOSEPH, m. Mary Morgan on 11 April 1737 (133:156).

SMITH, JOSEPH, in April 1747 was summoned by the Vestry of St. John's Par. for unlawful cohabitation with Esther Cameron (132:82).

SMITH, JOSEPH, m. Mary Shephard on 15 Oct. 1747 (131:29).

SMITH, JOSEPH, of Winter's Run, d. by 11 Aug. 1752 when admin. bond on his est. was posted by John Bond with Charles Baker; est. was admin. by John Bond on 1 Jan. 1753 (4:226; 15:360).

SMITH, JOSEPH, had iss.: ISAAC, age 9 on 1 Sept. 1758 and was bound to Samuel Tate in June 1759 (44).

SMITH, JOSEPH, m. on 16 May 1757 Deborah (---), extx. of Stephen Onion; she d. 22 Sept. 1767 (47:29; 131:16/r, 52/r; 201-41:110).

SMITH, LAWRENCE, Irish, age c. 30, ran away from Joseph Smith at Onion's Iron Works, on or by 26 July 1759 (307-69:214).

SMITH, MARK, in Nov. 1745 was ordered to be levy free (35:743).

SMITH, MARY, d. 20 Dec. 1713 (128:31).

SMITH, MARY, d. by 25 June 1740 when admin. bond was posted by John Bailey, admin., with George Ashman and John Wright (15:354).

SMITH, NATHAN, m. Blanch Dooley on 1 June 1757 and had iss.: WILLIAM, b. 3 April 1758 (129:362).

SMITH, NICHOLAS, in 1750 owned 100 a. Welch's Fancy (153:49).

SMITH, PHILEMON, was in Balto. Co. by 1695 as a taxable in s. side Patapsco Hund. (138).

SMITH, PHILIP, in 1750 was dead and his heirs owned 100 a. part Stout (153:85).

SMITH, RICHARD, m. Philizanna (---), and had iss.: JOHN, b. 3 Aug. 1704; GEORGE, b. 29 Jan. 1708;MARY, b. 15 Oct. 1710 (the only child whose mother is named) (128:25, 27).

SMITH, RICHARD, m. Elizabeth (---), and d./ by June 1733; had iss.: RICHARD, b. 15 Nov. 1721, age 12 next 15 Nov., in June 1733 was bd. to James Moore and w. Frances to learn trade of shoemaker; GEORGE, b. 25 Sept. 1724, also bound to James and Frances Moore in June 1733 (30:4, 133:6, 8).

SMITH, RISDELL, m. Hannah Chettle on 26 Nov. 1755 (133:165).

SMITH, ROBERT, was in Balto. Co. by 1694 as a taxable on s. side Gunpowder R.; prob. the Robert who d. by ,1703 when his est. was inv. by James Presbury and Edmund Talbot and val. at ₤ 114.8.5; inv. was signed by Jos'h Middlemore and Jas. Isham; dec. left no rel. in the Province (48:264; 139).

SMITH, ROBERT, cordwainer, was in Balto. Co. by 8 Aug. 1717 when he purch. 60 a. of Smith's Lot from Edmund and Bridget Smith; d. leaving a will proved 9 Sept. 1721, naming w. Mary as sole heir; admin. bond was posted 9 Nov. 1721 by extx. Mary Smith with Edward Smith and John Weasley; by 8 April 1703 his wid. had m. Eric Erickson, and on that date they sold two tracts, one called Levy's Tribe, to Thomas Coale (15:275; 67:480; 72:210; 124:74).

SMITH, SAMUEL, was in Balto. Co., by 1692, as a taxable on the s. side of Patapsco (138).

SMITH, SAMUEL, of St. George's Parish, m. Anna Simpson on 28 Aug. 1726; she d. 26 March 1734, and he may be the Samuel who m. (as his 2nd w.) Elizabeth Gallion, on 18 June 1734; he had two (or three) ch. by his 1st w., and four by his 2nd w.; he left iss.: (by 1st w.): SARAH, b. 10 Oct. 1726; NATHAN, b. 29 Jan. 1733; poss. JOSIAH, "son of Samuel," d. 15 Sept. 1734; (by 2nd w.): ELIZABETH, b. 25 June 1735; ANN, b. 10 Sept. 1738; GRACE, b. 10 Oct. 174-(?); HANNAH, b. 29 Dec. 1743 (128:49, 80, 82, 92, 100; 129:325, 333).

SMITH, SAMUEL, of St. John's Parish, m. Avarilla Beck, dau. of Matthew Beck, on 30 Aug. 1738; on 7 Aug. 1771 they admin. the est. of Charles Beck; had iss.: MARY, b. 8 Aug. 1740; WILLIAM, b. 28 Oct. 1742, d. 22 Jan. 1746; SAMUEL, b. 13 Sept. 1745, d. 12 Jan. 1746; DELIA WILLIAM (?), b. 13 June 1748; JOSIAS, b. 13 June 1754; BENJAMIN, b. 30 Aug. 1757 (5:60; 7:116; 131).

SMITH, SAMUEL, had iss.: JOSEPH, age 9 "next April," in Nov. 1737 bd. to Garvice Gilbert (31:129).

SMITH, SAMUEL, in 1750 owned 160 a., part East Humphreys (153:4).

SMITH, SAMUEL, of Swan Creek, in 1750 owned 100 a. Margaret's Mount; on 7 March 1754 he conv. 104 a. of this tract to Richard Dallam (82:183; 153:73).

SMITH, THOMAS, was in Balto. Co. by 1692 as a taxable in n. side Gunpowder Hund.; another Thomas was a taxable in n. side of Patapsco by 1695 (138; 140).

SMITH, THOMAS, m. by 8 March 1699 Elizabeth (---), with whom he purch. 50 a. Sidwell from George Chancy; d. by 6 Jan. 1698/9(?) when admin. bond was posted by Elizabeth Smith, with Thomas Preston and William Hicks; est. was admin. on 5 July 1708 by Preston and Hicks (2:86, 187; 13:417; 63:325).

SMITH, THOMAS, b. c.1670, gave his age as 45 in 1715, and deposed he had lived in this country for about 21 years (203-3:109).

SMITH, THOMAS, m. Mary (---), and d. by 24/31 Aug. 1715/6 when Mary Smith posted admin. bond with Henry Matthews and Patrick Wayland; est. was admin. by Mary Smith (1:317; 13:421; 131:8).

SMITH, THOMAS, m. Alice (---), and d. leaving a will, 23 Jan. 1717 - 17 March 1717, naming w. Alice as extx., and ch.: Thomas, then his eld. dau., and then each of "his said children;" admin. bond was posted 17 March 1717 by Alice Smith with Henry Jones and Abraham Shaver; est. was inv. on 4 April 1718 by S. Hinton and Edward Mahane, and val. at £ 55.6.6; filed by the extx. Alice Smith, his widow, who m. Robert Montgomery on 12 Aug. 1718; they admin. the est. on 27 June 1726 (3:55; 13:427; 52:129; 123:146; 133:47).

SMITH, THOMAS, m. Nancy (---) and they had iss.: EDWARD, b. 29 July 1755; DANIEL, b. 31 Dec. 1757; and THOMAS, b. 4 March 1760 (133:110).

SMITH, WILLIAM, was in Balto. Co. by 1 Nov. 1709 when he purch. 54 a. Long Aire from Edward and Bridget Smith (67:19).

SMITH, WILLIAM, m. Mary (---), and had iss.: WILLIAM, b. 12 Sept. 1733 (133:41).

SMITH, WILLIAM, d. by 12 May 1739 when admin. bond was posted by Mary Smith, with Abraham Cord and Adam Birchfield (15:311).

SMITH, WILLIAM, d. by 20 March 1742; m. Rachel (---), who d. 2U Dec. 1741, having had iss.: WILLIAM; poss. another WILLIAM, b. 28 Oct. 1722, d. 26 Oct. 1740 (131:8, 94/r, and 95/r).

SMITH, WILLIAM, of Lancaster Co., Penna., purch. Jonathan's Inheritance from Jonathan Jones of Balto. Co.; may be the William Smith who d. leaving a will, 18 March 1746 - 10 June 1746, naming w. Johanna, sons Thomas, William, and John, and daus. Esther and Christian; admin. bond was posted 10 June 1746 by Johanna Smith with Thomas Smith of Lancaster Co., Penna., as execs., with Joseph and Samuel Crockett; est. was admin. on 8 Aug. 1747; dec. had iss.: THOMAS, in Lancaster Co., Penna.; WILLIAM; JOHN; CHRISTIAN, and ESTHER (4:164; 16:10; 75:522; 110:370).

SMITH, WILLIAM, in 1750 owned 42 a. Harryman's Pasture (153:76).

SMITH, WILLIAM, m. Anne Peacock in Dec. 1751 (131).

SMITHERS, (---) (1), m. Frances (---) who m. as her 2nd husb. some time before 3 March 1683/4, Arthur Taylor, who with his w. conv. 300 a. on s. side Bird River to her s. James Smithers; dec. left iss.: JAMES; and RICHARD, d. 1731 (106:287).

SMITHERS, JAMES (2), s. of (---) (1) and Frances, was in Balto.

Co. by 1692 as a taxable in n. side Gunpowder; was exempt from paying levy in June 1731 (29:160; 138).

SMITHERS, RICHARD (3), s. of (---) (1), and bro. of James (2), d. by 18 May 1731 in Kent Co,; m. 1st, on 14 Feb. 1770/1 Blanche, dau. of Col. George Wells; she was exec. of est. of James Ives in July 1708; she d. 19 March 1708/9, and he m. 2nd Philizanna Maxwell; m. 3rd Mary, dau. of James Phillips, and extx. of John Carville of Kent Co.; in Nov. 1724 he was summoned for contempt of court in not delivering the est. of his s. John to the court; on 1 Oct. 1722 conv. prop. to his s. John, and on 24 Sept. 1723 conv. prop. to dau. Blanch; d. leaving a will, 23 Dec. 1730 - 18 May 1731, naming w. Mary, who had been wid. of John Carville, bro. James, ch. Blanch and John, also Parker Hall and Peter Lester; had iss.: BLANCH, b. 28 Feb. 1702; JOHN, b. 3 Aug. 1704, living in 1731; GEORGE, b. 29 Jan. 1708 on 25 April 1715 bound himself to Col. George Wells of Balto. Co.; MARY, b. 15 Oct. 1710 (1:54; 2:95, 266; 26:312; 27:44; 67:367; 69:37, 304; 128: 14, 25, 26; 200-38:355; 201-1:147).

SMITHERS, ELIZABETH, in Aug. 1723 bore a bast. at the house of Sarah Cockey, and named Joseph Johnson as the father (15:422).

SMITHS, JAMES, was in Balto. Co. by 1694 as a taxable in s. side of Gunpowder (139).

SMITHSON, THOMAS (1), progenitor, was in Balto. Co. at least by 1706; d. by 8 March 1732; m. Anne, dau. of Daniel Scott; left a will, 11 Aug. 1731 - 8 March 1732, leaving his entire est. to his w. Anne, and then named his four unm. ch.: Thomas, Daniel, Sarah, and Avarilla, and his four marr. daus.: Eleanor, w. of Samuel Durham, Rebecca w. of Samuel Wilson, Rachel w. of Henry Donahue, and Elizabeth w. of Robert Clark; Thomas and Anne (Scott) Smithson had iss.: ELLINOR, b. 24 May 1704, m. Samuel Durham on 15 Jan. 1722/3; RACHEL, b. 9 Oct. 1706, m. Henry Donahue; REBECCA, b. 2 April 1707, m. Samuel Wilson in 1729; ELIZABETH, b. 10 Oct. 1710. m. Robert Clarke on 5 Dec. 1729; THOMAS, b. 30 Jan. 1712; DANIEL, b. 2 Jan. 1714; SARAH, b. 12 Jan. 1718; AVARILLA, b. 28 Dec. 1720, prob. the Avarilla Smithson ind. for bast. in Aug. 1739 and tried in June 1740 (3:18; 125:253; 131).

SMITHSON, THOMAS (2), s. of Thomas (1) and Ann, was b. 30 Jan. 1712; d. by 27 Oct. 1795 in Harf. Co.; m. Mary (---), b. c.1723; in 1750 owned 100 a. part Bells Camp; in 1776 lived with his fam. in Bush River Lower Hund.; in Dec. 1785, at age 72, deposed that he first saw his grandfather, Daniel Scott, when he was 7 or 8, and that his uncle Daniel Scott, Jr., was a member of the House of Delegates; Thomas d. leaving a will, 14 June 1795 - 27 Oct. 1795; Thomas left iss.: THOMAS, d. v.p. leaving three ch.; ANN, m. (---) Durham; ELIZABETH, m. John Durbin on 2 Jan. 1759; WILLIAM; SARAH, m. David Durham on 14 Nov. 1765; DANIEL; NATHANIEL, b. c. 1755; MARY, Jr., b. c.1758, not in father's will; MARGARET, b. c. 1760, m. James Barton; CASSANDRA, b. c.1763, m. (---) Green; ARCHIBALD, b. c.1765 (131; 153:2; 241-JLG#F:361; 244-AJ#R:98; 285).

SMITHSON, DANIEL (3), s. of Thomas (1) and Ann, was b. 2 Jan. 1714, and d. 22 Feb. 1798 in Harf. Co.; m. and had iss. (345: 662).

SMYSER, MATTHIAS, was in Balto. Co. by 3 May 1745 when he purch. 272 a. part Providence from John and Margaret Henthorn (77:690).

SNELSON, ABRAHAM (1), was in Balto. Co. by 1709; d. 6 Jan. 1722/3; m. Rachel (---), who after his death had a right of dower in 176 a. Parker's Lot; had iss.; WILLIAM, b. June 1709 (26:318; 128:51).

SNELSON, WILLIAM (2), s. of Abraham (1), was b. in June 1709; d. 7 March 1739; m. Margaret Hogg on 4 Feb. 1732; on 7 June 1734 purch. 176 a. Parker's Lot from Edgar Tipper and w. Mary; William d. leaving a will, 12 Feb. 1739 - 22 May 1741, leaving above land to his s. Abraham at age 21, named dau. Rachel; made William Hollis exec.; admin. bond was posted 26 May 1741 by exec. Wm. Hollis with William Garland and George Chancey; est. was admin. by Hollis on 7 Aug. 1747 and showed payment to William Hunter for registering the deaths of Snelson on 7 Feb. 1739 and his w. Margaret who d. 1 Feb. 1739; dec. left iss.: RACHEL, b. 14 Jan. 1733; ABRAHAM, b. 14 June 1737 (4:147; 13:459; 74:72; 127:139; 128:56, 70, 83, 97, 112).

SNELSON, ABRAHAM (3), s. of William (2), was b. 14 June 1737; as "son of William and grandson of Abraham Snelson" he purch. 176 a. Parker's Lot from John Parker (s, of John, dec.) and w. Elizabeth); d. leaving a will, 4 May 1760 - 17 June 1760, leaving Parker's Lot to George Chancy, Sr., and also named George Chancy, Jr., Amos Hollis, James Chaney, Catherine Robertson, the dau. of William Hollis, Keziah Hollingsworth, James Garland, and John Rhodes of Henry (79:124; 210-30:859).

SOCKWELL, LANCELOT, was in Balto. Co. by Jan. 1665/6 when he conv. 300 a. East Humphreys to Richard Ball (94).

THE SOLLERS FAMILY is discussed more fully in Taney and Allied Families (New York: American Historical Society, 1935).

SOLLERS, JOHN (1), progenitor, was in Md. by March 1668; d. in Calvert Co. in 1699; m. Anne (---) who m. as her 2nd husb. William Dalrymple; in 1668 was named as kinsman in the will of Anthony Salway of A. A. Co.; member of the Board of Commissioners for London Town, and in 1679, 1680, and 1685 was a Justice for A. A. Co.; later moved to Calvert Co.; as John "Sallers" d. leaving a will, 15 Feb. 1699 - (date of probate not given); leaving land in A. A. Co. to s. Robert, 50 a. to s.-in-law Samuel Lyle, and res. of plantation to w. Anne; named these ch.: ROBERT; ANNE, m. Samuel Lyle; VERLINDA (transcribed in Md. Cal. Wils as "Belinda"), m. John Clagett on 14 Sept. 1714; ELIZABETH; MARY; and SABRETT (121:94; 210-27:222; Taney).

SOLLERS, ROBERT (2), s. of John (1), d. by 18 March 1749/50 when his will was filed in Calvert Co., naming w. Dorothy, and these ch.: BENNETT; ALETHEA, poss. other ch. (210-27:222).

SOLLERS, SABRETT (3), s. of John (1), was b. after 1671, since he was not yet 18 when his father made his will in 1699; moved to Balto. Co., where he d. in 1760; m. Mary, dau. of James and Anne Heighe, some time before 26 July 1725 when James Heighe of All Saints Par., Calvert Co., made his will naming his dau. Mary and s.-in-law Sabrett Soller; Sabrett was in Balto. Co. by 1750 when he was listed as owning 200 a. part Kinderton, 900 a. Timber Neck, 60 a. Gardner's Addition, 20 a. Jones' Chance, and 208 a. Gunworth Resurveyed; d. leaving a will made 6 Feb. 1760, naming w. Mary, ch. Sabrett, Heighe (and his s. William), Thomas, John, Eleanor, Ann Partridge, and Mary Bowen, as well as John Bowen of Nathan; admin. bond was posted on 1 June 1760 by execs. Mary, Heighe, and Thomas Sollers, with William Baxter; wid. Mary d. leaving a will, 24 Dec. 1760 - 4 Jan. 1773; Sabrett and Mary d. leaving iss.: MARY, m. Nathan Bowen; SABRETT, d. July 1786; HEIGHE, m. Elizabeth Partridge; THOMAS, m. Ariana Dorsey; JOHN, m. Mary Bowen; ELEANOR; ANN, m. (---) Partridge (16:59; 112: 242, 342; 124:203; 153:6; 210-30:860; Taney).

SOLLERS, HEIGHE (4), s. of Sabrett (3), d. in Balto. Co. by

15 April 1777; m. 1st Rosanne (---); m. 2nd Elizabeth, dau. of
Buckler Partridge; in 1750 owned 150 a. The Hope, and 70 a. Cuckoldmaker's Hall; on 24 Oct. 1750 Jane Partridge admin. the est.
of Buckler Partridge naming a dau. as w. of Heighe Sollers; d. by
1777 when Sabrett Sollers advert. he would settle the est.; est.
was admin. 13 Feb. 1788 by Jehu Bowen and Jeremiah Johnson who
had m. the admnx. Eleanor Sollers; Heighe Sollers left iss. (by
1st w.): WILLIAM, b. 31 Dec. 1746; (by 2nd w.): ELEANOR, m. Jeremiah Johnson; ANN, m. Hickman Johnson; MARY; ELISHA, b. c.1770
(6:6; 7:177; 9:157; 133:96; 153:44; Taney).

SOLLERS, ABRAHAM, m. Ann (---), and had iss.: ISAAC, b. 17 Feb.
1749 (133:94).

SOLLERS, ELEANOR, d. leaving her est. to be admin. by William
Lux (6:53).

SOLLERS, JOSEPH, and Eleanor Sollers were summoned by the vestry of St. Thomas' Par. on 2 Sept. 1746 for unlawful cohabitation
(135:101).

SOMNER, EDWARD, m. Anne (---), and had iss.: LIGHTWOOD, b. 23
Jan. 1737 (131:69/r).

SORTER, PETER, m. Jane (---), and had iss.: HANNAH, b. 12 May
1732 (133:27).

SOUCH/SOUTH/LOUGH, JOHN, son of William, was age 12 "last 15
March," in June 1739 was bound to Walter Bosley (21:40).

SOUTHARD/SOUCHARD, JAMES, and w. Welthen, in Oct. 1665 conv.
300 a. on the west side of Fishing Creek to George Scisco (94).

SOUTLER, MARY, serv. to Claxon Bowen, in Nov. 1740 was tried
for bast. (32:366).

SPAIN, BEAVEN, m. Elizabeth Rigdon on 6 Jan. 1734; in 1750
owned 148 a. Turkey Range, Noble Desire, and Pearson's Privilege;
had iss.: THOMAS, b. 23 Oct. 1735; JOSHUA, b. 20 April 1737 (128:
85, 90, 97; 153:49).

SPAIN, CONSTABELLA, in March 1738/9 was ind. for bast. (31:351).

THE SPARKS FAMILY has been the subject of considerable research
by James B. McCurley, Jr., who has graciously made some of his material available to the author.

SPARKS, THOMAS (1), was b. prob. by 1691, d. c.1727 in A. A.
Co.; had iss.: THOMAS, d. after 1777; MATTHEW, b. 1714/5; JOSIAH
(data from McCurley).

SPARKS, THOMAS (2), s. of Thomas (1), b. c.1710/11, d. after
1777; m. by 1749 Elizabeth (---), b. c.1718, d. after 1777; may
have moved to Pittsylvania Co., Va. (data from McCurley).

SPARKS, MATTHEW (3), s. of Thomas (1), was b. c.1714/5; m.
Eleanor (---); in 1777 moved to Pittsylvania Co., Va., and by
1790 may have been on the Pacolet River in South Carolina; may
have had iss.: MATTHEW, b. c.1744; SARAH, b. 1753; SAMUEL, b.
1759; JOSIAH, b. 1761; TRUELOVE, b. 1763; JANE (query in Genealogical Helper, Dec. 1965, p. 308).

SPARKS, JOSIAH (4), s. of Thomas, was prob. b. in A. A. Co.
by 1729; d. in Balto. Co. by 10 Oct. 1764 when admin. bond on
his est. was posted by admnx. Penelope Sparks, with Charles Cole

and Richard Sampson, Jr.; m. at St. Anne's in Annapolis Penelope
Brown; she m. 2nd, on 10 April 1770, Aquila Wyle; Josiah and
Penelope had iss.: FRANCIS, b. c.1750; JOSIAH, b. c.1752; ELI-
JAH, b. 1754; THOMAS, b. 23 May 1758; MATTHEW, b. c.1760 (16:
22; 131; 219-2; data from McCurley).

SPARKS, HUGH, orphan, in March 1740/1 was bound to John Mac-
Kenley (33:4).

SPARROW, WILLIAM, with 1 year, 11 mos., to serve, was listed
in the Aug. 1721 inv. of John Bradshaw (51:316).

SPEARS, SARAH, was ind. for bast. in March 1733 (15:215).

SPEGLE, JOHN COLE, m. Deborah Cottrall on 19 May 1735 (129:
283). See also COLESPEGLE.

SPENCER, ZACHARIAH (1), m. 2 Feb. 1728 Christiana Cobb, dau.
of James Cobb; they had iss.: ELIZABETH, b. 16 May 1730; RACHEL,
b. 31 Jan. 1731 (dau. of Zachariah and "Charity"); ZACHARIAH, b.
13 March 1732 (3:155, 247; 128:64, 74, 91).

SPENCER, ZACHARIAH (2), prob. s. of Zachariah (1), was b. 13
March 1732; m. Ann Pogue on 29 Sept. 1755; had iss.: ELIZABETH,
b. 17 Nov. 1757; SARAH, b. 27 Feb. 1758; ANN, b. 10 Oct. 1759;
ZACHARIAH, b. 28 Feb. 1761 (129:373).

SPENCER, ALEXANDER, m. Elizabeth Lee on 17 April 1737 (128:96).

SPENCER, CHARITY, had iss.: CHARITY, b. 19 Feb. 1744; JOHN, b.
28 Dec. 1747; MARGARET, b. 2 Jan. 1751; WILLIAM, b. 8 April 1755
(129:373).

SPENCER, CHRISTIANA, m. Daniel Veal on 15 Aug. 1726 (129:245).

SPENCER, JAMES, m. Beatrix Dorney on 17 Aug. 1758, and had
iss.: ANN, b. 6 April 1750, d. the following 23 Aug.; NICHOLAS,
b. 30 Sept. 1761 (131).

SPENCER, MARTHA, was ind. for bast. in March 1723/4, and tried
in June 1724; had iss.: MARTHA, b. 28 Feb. 1723 (26:201, 331; 128:
54).

SPENCLY, JOHN, b. c.1720, m. Jane (---), b. c.1720; had iss.:
a dau. Elizabeth, named in a 1744 lease; had iss.: ELIZABETH,
b. c.1739 (77:509).

SPICER, EDWARD (1), was bur. in St. James Par., A. A. Co., on
27 Dec. 1711; may have had the following ch.: ANN, m. John Holland on 11 Dec. 1701; ELEANOR, m. John Davis on 6 June 1703; ELIZA-
BETH, m. John Owens on 4 Feb. 1705; JOHN; WILLIAM, m. Anne Disney
on 28 Jan. 1724 (219-1; 219-3).

SPICER, JOHN (2), poss. s. of Edward (1), m. Juliatha Hawkins
on 10 Nov. 1709; placed as a s. of Edward because he was in the
same par. as Edward (1), and because he had a s. named Edward;
on 23 Jan. 1716 leased 50 a. on the n. side of Patapsco from John
Talbott; on 11 March 1724 bought 50 a. The Fancy from James Boring;
in 1727 took up Spicer's Inheritance; d. leaving a will, 6 Jan.
1738 - 7 March 1739, naming w. Juliatha, ch. Thomas, Edward, Elizabeth, Juliatha, Ann, Susanna, Sarah, and Dinah; on 11 July
1742 the wid. Juliatha sold 50 a. The Fancy to Charles Ridgely;
in 1750 the wid. of John "Spier" (sic) owned 100 a. Spicer's Inheritance; John and Juliatha had iss.: SARAH, b. 30 Nov. 1710, m.
Jonathan Hanson on 12 June 1733; MARY, b. 9 Nov. 1712; THOMAS, b.

26 Aug. 1714; EDWARD, living on 6 Jan. 1738; JULIATHA, may have
m. Henry Worrell on 30 Jan. 1745; DINAH, m. Joshua Hall; ANN,
may have m. James Cain on 15 April 1746; may have m.
2nd Joshua Hall; ELIZABETH, b. 4 July 1731 (67:483; 77:63; 79:169; 70:49;
127:67; 133; 153:11; 207; 219-3:338).

SPICER, THOMAS (3), s. of John (2) and Juliatha, was b. 26
Aug. 1714, d. by 9 March 1748 in Balto. Co.; m. Rebecca Merryman
on 1 Jan. 1735; she was a dau. of John and Martha (Bowen) Merryman, and was living in 1783 in Middlesex Hund.; d. leaving a
will proved 9 March 1748, naming ch. John, Valentine, Eleanor,
Austin, Sarah, Temperance, Edward, and Thomas; Thomas and Rebecca had iss.: JOHN, b. 15 Sept. 1736; d. by 15 Jan. 1788; VALEN-
TINE; ELEANOR, m. Richard Taylor on 9 Jan. 1785; AUSTIN, alive
on 27 Oct. 1758; SARAH; TEMPERANCE; EDWARD; and THOMAS (133;
210-25:546; 210-31:670; 219-3).

SPINK, ROGER (1), progenitor, was in Md. by 11 June 1688 when
he surv. 27 a. Speedwell; this land was later held by Enoch
Spinks; in Nov. 1692 he bound his s. to serve Thomas Staley; may
have m. a dau. of Eliza Hemstead; Enoch and Sarah, ch. of Roger,
were named in the Dec. 1690 will of Eliza Hemstead; Roger had
iss.: ENOCH; SARAH, pet. the court in Sept. 1694; in 1695 was
left 50 a. by Robert Gates, and may be the Sarah Spink who m.
Robert West on 10 Nov. 1695 (19:333; 20:301; 121:51, 97; 129:
236; 211:70).

SPINK, ENOCH (2), s. of Roger (1), was age 16 in 1694 as a
taxable in n. side Gunpowder; in Nov. 1692 was bound to serve
Thomas Staley; on 5 Aug. 1702 named Eliza Hemstead "our grandmother by consanguinity;" in Nov. 1703 surv. 1000 a. Bachelor's Good
Luck, and in Sept. 1709 surv. 200 a. Bachelor's Chance; by Oct.
1710 Sarah (Raven), admnx. of Tobias Starnborough; in Aug. 1714
Sarah Spinks pet. the court that her husb. had run away from her
and not left her any substance (19:333; 21:543; 66:159; 139; 207;
209-21:281).

SPRIGG, EDWARD, III, did not live in Balto. Co. but in 1750
owned 500 a. Gassaway's Ridge (153:69).

SPRIGG, THOMAS, in 1750 owned 45 a. Sparrow's Addition, 23 a.
Prevention, and 300 a. Hood alias Bowe (153:102).

SPRIGS, ELIZABETH, was in Balto. Co. by 1756 living at Richard
Cross's; was dau. of John Sprigs, whitesmith, in White Cross St.,
near Cripplegate St., London (300-65:257).

SPRING, JAMES, servant, with 2 years, 10 mos., to serve in
the 1739 inv. of Joseph Hooper (52:327).

SPRY, OLIVER, was in Va., by Sept. 1636 when he was granted
50 a. in Isle of Wight Co., Va., for his personal adventure;
in Sept. 1646 was Justice of Nansemond Co.; came to Md., and in
1658 his son Godfried was mentioned in a letter; in June 1663
conv. land to his dau. Mary w. of Godfrey Harmer; d. by 1675 leaving a wid. Johanna, whose will, 6 Oct. 1674 - 1675, naming the w.
of Thomas Howell of Cecil Co., the two ch. of James Denton, John
Waterton, Richard Randsey, her dau. Mary, ·who m. 1st Godfrey
Harmer, and 2nd John Stansby, and her grandch. Sarah, Elizabeth, and Mary Harmer; had iss.: MARY, m. 1st Godfrey Harmer, and
2nd, by 6 Oct. 1674, John Stansby (93; 206-4:463; 388; 434:184,
654; Balto. Co. Original Wills, Box 1, folder 7).

SQUIRES, JOHN, was in Balto. Co. by 1692 as a taxable in n.
side of Gunpowder Hund. (138).

STACEY, RICHARD, was in Balto. Co. by 1694 as a taxable in s. side Patapsco (139).

STACKEY. See STARKEY.

STAINES, THOMAS, was in Balto. Co. by 31 March 1739 when he purch. 50 a. Merryman's Adventure from Levin Bufking; on 22 March 1745 purch. 50 a. Turkey Cock Alley from Thomas and Mary Wright; in April 1752 he and w. Sarah conv. 50 a. Turkey Cock Alley to Thomas Cockey Deye; in Feb. 1754 he and w. Sarah conv. 40 a. Warlerick and Tommy and Sally's Delight, to John Wilmot; in Nov. 1756 was made levy free (75:203; 79:80; 81:355; 82:155).

STALEY, THOMAS, was in Balto. Co. by 1692 as a taxable in n. side Gunpowder; may be the Thomas Staley who m. by April 1701 Mary, wid. of Thomas Jones; his est. was admin. by James Durham (66:105; 138; 206-23:79).

STAMBURGH, TOBIAS. See STANSBURY, TOBIAS.

STAMFORD, JAMES, m. by 15 Nov. 1727 Mary, mother of John Fuller (71:28).

STAND, JOHN, m. by 14 Feb. 1732, Rosanna, dau. of Jacob Grove (3:108).

STANDAR, ISAAC, in June 1734 was bound to Peter Sarter to age 21 (30:254).

STANDAR, MARY, in June 1734 was bound to Peter Sarter to age 16 (30:254).

STANDERLINE, JOHN. d. 1749 (131).

STANDIFORD, WILLIAM (1), was in Md. by 13 Dec. 1661, when as William Stanfort he wit. the will of Forker Frissell of St. Marys Co.; m. Mary (---); moved to Balto. Co.; in June 1687 surv. 204 a. Hopewell; in June 1691 he and w. Mary conv. land on Seneca Ridge to Israel Skelton; in 1692 was a taxable in n. side Gunpowder Hund.; in 1694 he was joined by William, Jr., and Samuel; in 1695 Jno. Standiford was in the household; prob. had iss.: WILLIAM, Jr., b. c.1676/8; SAMUEL, b. c.1676/8; JOHN, b. c.1679; JAMES, b. c.1680 ; EPHRAIM, d. 15 Dec. 1742; MARY; JEMIMA (64:77; 120:20 78; 138; 139; 140; 211; data compiled by Lulu Reed Boss).

STANDIFORD, WILLIAM (2), s. of William (1), was b. c.1676/8; in 1694 was a taxable in n. side Gunpowder Hund.; may have had one s.: WILLIAM, d. 1776 (139).

STANDIFORD, SAMUEL (3), s. of William (1), was b. c.1676/8, and in 1694 was a taxable in n. side Gunpowder Hund.; d. by 22 July 1708 when his wid. and extx. Mary posted admin. bond on his est. with George York and Robert Smith; d. leaving a will, 9 June 1708 - 22 July 1708, empowering his w. Mary to sell Timber Hill to Archibald Rollo; est. was inv. on 22 July 1709 by Jno. Rallings and Matt. Green, and val. at £ 108.16.9 plus 6043 lbs. tobacco; wid. Mary m. John Bond by 26 Aug. 1711 when she admin. Samuel's est., and on 26 Feb. 1712/3; may have had iss.: SAMUEL (1:370; 2:172; 13:437; 50:344; 122:110).

STANDIFORD, JOHN (4), s. of William (1), was b. c.1679, and in ;695 was a taxable in n. side Gunpowder Hund.; d. 12 April 1720; m. Margaret, dau. of Israel Skelton, by 24 April 1706; admin. the est. of Cornelius Boyce c.1704, and with John Taylor admin. the est. of William Robinson on 13 July 1717; on 24 April 1706 Israel Skelton made a will directing that Spring Neck was to go

to his wid. Mary and then to his grandson Skelton Standiford;
on 11 March 1720 the est. of John Standiford was inv. by Nicholas
Day and John Taylor and val. at Ł 90.5.3, signed by Edmund Standifer and John Crockett, and filed by the admnx. Mrs. Margaret
Standiford; John and Margaret had iss.: SKELTON; JOHN, m. Esther
Fuller; ISRAEL, b. 4 Sept. 1720 (2:131; 51:293; 52:123; 122:74;
131).

STANDIFORD, JAMES (5), s. of William (1) was b. c.1680; may
be the James "Standifor" who with John Rallings inv. the est. of
Thomas Smith on 27 Jan. 1699; may be the James who on 2 April
1728 was conv. 50 a. part The Chance by Thomas and Sarah Cross;
may have had iss.: JAMES, m. Martha (---) on 6 Oct. 1737 (48:
199; 71:77).

STANDIFORD, EPHRAIM (6), poss. s. of William (1), d. in St.
John's Parish on 15 Dec. 1742, having m. Sarah (---), and had
iss.: FRANCES, b. 22 March 1740; JEMIMA, b. 10 Sept. 1743 (131).

STANDIFORD, WILLIAM (7), poss. s. of William (2), d. in Balto Co. in 1776; m. three times; 1st, on 28 May 1731, Ann Hutchins, who d. July 1738; 2nd, on Nov. 1739 or 8 Dec. 1740 Christiana Enloes Wright, wid. of Thomas Wright; and 3rd, on 16 July
1750, Elizabeth (?) Carlisle; she m. as her 3rd husb. James Amos;
on 16 Aug. 1734 William admin. the est. of James Hicks; on 19
July 1740, 16 April 1742, and 8 Jan. 1743 he and w. Christiana
admin. the est. of Thomas Wright; in 1750 owned 100 a. part
Hutchins' Addition; d. leaving a will, 30 Oct. 1775 - 29 May
1776, naming w. Elizabeth, and ch.: James, Anne w. of Francis
Moore, David, Hutchings, James, David, John, Benjamin, Sarah,
Delah, Susanna, Elizabeth, and Ellinor; the ch. of his two first
wives were to have one shilling each; William had three ch. by
his 1st w., four by his 2nd., and ten by his 3rd; his ch. were:
HUTCHINGS, b. 3 Sept. 1733; PRISCILLA, b. 17 Dec. 1735; ANNE, m.
Francis Moore (by 2nd w.): AQUILA, b. 24 Aug. 1741; WILLIAM, b.
Nov. 1742; AVARILLA, b. 24 Aug. 1741, m. John James on 14 April
1761; ABRAHAM, b. 18 May 1745; (by 3rd w.): JAMES; JOHN;
BENJAMIN, m. Rachel Amos c. 9 Jan. 1798; DAVID, b. 23 Sept. 1758;
MARY, m. 5 June 1774 Jacob Marshall; DELAH, m. John Bull; SARAH,
m. David Johnson; SUSANNA, m. James Amos of William; ELIZABETH,
m. Edmund Talbott; ELEANOR, m. (---) Allsworth (3:176, 308, 333;
4:66, 129; 112:330; 131; 153:40; 232; 242).

STANDIFORD, SAMUEL (8), poss. s. of Samuel (3), was living
in 1745; m. Ann Rollo on 30 Nov. 1732; had iss.: RICHARD, b. 11
May 1733; BETHIA, b. 20 Dec. 1735; JEMIMA, b. 20 Feb. 1737; KEZIAH,
b. 20 Feb. 1737; SAMUEL, b. 20 Oct. 1740; JOHN, b. 26 May 1743;
NANCY, b. 16 Aug. 1745 (131).

STANDIFORD, SKELTON (9), poss. s. of John (4) and Margaret,
d. by 29 Sept. 1752 having m. Esther Fuller on 1 Jan. 1726; on
10 Nov. 1743 leased land from Charles Carroll for the lifetimes
of John, Skelton, and William Standiford; in 1750 he owned 120 a.
Franklin's Beginning and Nancy's Ending; admin. bond was posted
29 Sept. 1752 by Esther Standiford with Michael Duskin and Abraham Ditto; she admin. the est. and stated he left nine ch.; in
March 1755 she posted an additonal bond she would pay orphans
their share of their father's estate; John and Esther had iss.:
SKELTON, b. 31 Aug. 1734; JOHN, b. 4 Nov. 1734; WILLIAM, b. 13
Feb. 1736; ISAIAH; PHILISANNA; BENJAMIN; VINCENT: JACOB; and
SARAH (4:242; 13:453; 40:17; 77:457; 131; 153:41).

STANDIFORD, ISRAEL (10), poss. s. of John (4) and Margaret, was
b. 4 Sept. 1720, and d. 1794 in Orange Co., N. C.; m. Cassandra
Anderson on 6 Jan. 1743; on 16 Feb. 1743 leased land for his

lifetime, that of his wife, age 17, and of Benjamin Anderson,
aged 11; ch. of Israel and Cassandra Standiford may tentatively
be identified as: EPHRAIM; JOSHUA; ISRAEL; BENJAMIN; SARAH, m.
(---) Rhodes; ROSANNA, m. (---) Rhodes; CASSANDRA, m. (---)
Hendon; MARY; ELIZABETH; RUTH, m. William Turner (77:453; 131).

STANDIFORD, JAMES (11), poss. s. of James (5), was living in
1747; m. Martha Watkins on 6 Oct. 1737; they had iss.: CLORINDA,
b. 23 April 1737; JAMES, b. 3 June 1739; ISRAEL, b. 13 Nov. 1740;
JAMES, b. 29 March 1742 (mother's name is given as Mary); HANNAH,
b. 6 June 1743; LUKE, b. 25 Jan. 1745; ALIZANTHIANAH, b. 5 March
1747 (131).

STANDIFORD, ARCHIBALD, m. Elizabeth Armstrong on 25 June 1754;
she was admnx. of William Armstrong; in 1763 admin. bond on the
est. of Archibald Standiford was posted by James Yeo with Thomas
Gittings and William Bell; Yeo admin. the est. in Feb. 1767 (5:
339, 345; 7:285; 15:301; 131).

STANDISH, JAMES, orphan of Thomas, age 5 "last 20 April," in
June 1732 was bound to John Jones (29:293).

STANDISH, MARY, servant of John Norrington, was ind. and tried
for bast. in Aug. 1740 (32:289, 365).

STANDOVE, SARAH, m. Thomas Richardson on 20 May 1720 (131).

STANFORD, JOHN, d. by 17 April 1679 when admin. bond was
posted by James Phillips with William Osborn and John Walston
(13:438).

STANLEY, RICHARD, m. Ann (---), and had iss.: JOHN, b. 1 Jan.
1724 (128:75).

STANLEY, WILLIAM, soap boiler, in Jan. 1663/4 conv. 300 a.
Oxelle Neck back to Axel Stills; in Nov. 1666 bought 175 a.
Bluntville from Nathaniel Stiles; by Nov. 1668 was in Talbot
Co., when he sold the latter tract to Richard Fixum (94).

STANNY, ANN, living at Thomas Heath's, was reported to have
borne an illeg. ch., March 1683/4 (18:132).

THE STANSBURY FAMILY is discussed by Christopher Johnston in
the Maryland Historical Magazine, IX (1914), 72-88, and X (1915),
62-63, and reprinted in 346-2:398-415.

STANSBURY/ STERNBERG, DETMAR (1), progenitor, came to Md.
in 1658 with w. Renske and s. Tobias, and was living in 1678
when the Balto. Co. Court allowed him 4o lbs,. tobacco out of
the levy; no record of any probate of his est. has been found;
his name has been the occasion of discussion for the names of
the immigrant and his wife are of Low German or Dutch origin,
yet there is no record of any naturalization; had one known s.:
TOBIAS, d. 1709 (388; Johnston article).

STANSBURY/STARNBOROUGH, TOBIAS (2), s. of Detmar (1), was b.
by 1658 and d. by 23 April 1709; m. Sarah, sister of Luke Raven;
she m. 2nd Enoch Spinks, and was alive in 1714; in Jan. 1670/1
Tobias surv. 100 a. Poplar Neck and in June 1688 surv. 135 a.
Huntington; in 1695 was one of the Baltimore County Rangers under
Capt. John Oldton; d. by 23 April 1709 when admin. bond was posted by admnx. Sarah Starnborough with William Farfarr and John
Barrett; est. was inv. on 3 Aug. 1709 by John Gay and John Merryman and val at £ 246.11.6 and signed by Luke Raven, bro. of the
admnx.; in Oct. 1710 Sarah and her 2nd husb. gave security for

the admin. of his est.; Tobias and Sarah had iss.: DANIEL, twin,
b. 1678; THOMAS, twin, b. 1678; LUKE, b. 1689; TOBIAS, b. 1691;
SAMUEL, d. 1783; TABITHA, a minor in 1714 (13:443; 48:270; 206-
29:408; 209-21:281; 211:90, 108).

STANSBURY, DANIEL (3), s. of Tobias (2) and Sarah, was b.
1678, d. April 1763 in Balto. Co.; m. Elizabeth (poss. Richardson
since Daniel and Elizabeth had a s. named Richardson); in Nov.
1713 conv. Daniel's Gift, part of a larger tract called Strife,
to his bro. Thomas; Thomas and Daniel were later granted a cert.
to resurvey Strife; the cert. stated Strife had formerly been
owned by their father Tobias; in 1750 Daniel owned 80 a. Prospect, 100 a. Poplar Neck, 960 a. Strife, and 50 a. Force Pitt;
Daniel's obituary in the Md. Gazette of 7 April 1763 stated
that he died "last week having eaten a hearty supper the night
before he died," leaving a twin brother, and that he was in his
85th year; had iss.: WILLIAM, b. 20 Jan. 1716; RICHARDSON, b. 20
May 1723; RICHARD, b. 22 May 1725; DANIEL, b. 23 July 1727; ELI-
ZABETH, b. 21 Oct. 1730, m. Aquila Gostwick on 14 Jan. 1749/50;
ANNE, b. 26 Dec. 1735, may have m. Thomas Harryman on 1 March
1756 (67:252; 133:1, 10, 21, 51; 153:5; 207; 262; Johnston
article).

STANSBURY, THOMAS (4), s. of Tobias (2) and Sarah, was b.
1678, and d. 4 May 1766; m. Jane Hayes, dau. of John and Abigail (Dixon) Hayes (Johnston erroneously stated Jane's name was
Dixon; her descent is given in a case argued before the Provincial Court concerning ownership of the tract Dixon's Neck);
in 1713 Thomas was conv. Daniel's Gift by his bro. Daniel; in
1724 he surv. 268 a. Stansbury; in 1750 he owned 200 a. Gorsuch Chance, 120 a. Selah's Point, 100 a. Inloes, 284 a. part
Dickenston, 268 a. Stansbury's Chance, 112 a. Stansbury's Venture, 682 a. Stansbury's Plains, and other lands; d. leaving a
will, 21 Feb. 1748 - 4 June 1766, naming the ch. listed below;
had iss.: JOHN, b. 1710; THOMAS, b. 24 April 1714; DANIEL, b. c.
1716/8; DIXON, b. 6 Dec. 1720; EDMUND, b. 13 Jan. 1724; JEMIMA,
b. 19 July 1727, m. Robuck Lynch on 16 Aug. 1747 (112:46; 133:
8, 20; 153:22; 214-EI#10:743-ff.; Johnston article).

STANSBURY, LUKE (5), s. of Tobias (2) and Sarah, was b. 1689;
d. 1742; m. Jane (---), who d. 6 April 1759; in Dec. 1709 was
assigned by his mother Sarah all her right to 105 a. The Lot;
d. leaving a will, 25 March 1742 - 7 May 1742, naming w. Jane,
dau. Elizabeth Bond, dau. Bethia, s. Luke, and grands. William
Bond; admin. bond was posted 11 May 1742 by Tobias Stansbury
with Robert North and William Fell; est. admin. on 8 May 1744;
his wife Jane d. leaving a will, 16 April 1759 - 9 May 1759,
naming ch. Tobias, Elizabeth Bond, Bethia w. of John Hall, and
Luke Bond; Luke and Jane had iss.: Capt. TOBIAS, b. c.1718/9;
BETHIA, b. 1726, d. 10 July 1780, m. Capt. John Hall of Cranberry on 9 Aug. 1743;RUTH, b. 10 Jan. 1728/9, may have m. Nathan
Nichols; LUKE, b. and d. 26 Dec. 1715; ELIZABETH, m. William
Bond; LUKE BOND, alive in 1759 (3:317; 5:1; 15:353; 111:304;
127:169; 133:15, 99; letter dated April 1979 from Mrs. J. Nolan
Callahan of Baltimore, to the author).

STANSBURY, TOBIAS (6), s. of Tobias (2) and Sarah, was b. in
1691; d. 1764; m. Honour Bowen, dau. of Jonas and Martha Bowen;
on 8 June 1737 Thomas Stansbury conv,. to Luke and Tobias Stansbury part of Mount Hayes; on 30 Oct. 1745 Merryman and Honour
Cox conv. 40 a. East Humphreys to Tobias; in 1750 owned 125 a.
Stansbury's Chance, 166 a. Stansbury's Purchase, 31 a. Stansbury's
Puzzle, 19 a. Stansbury's Neglect, and 80 (sic) a. East Humphreys;
no proof of exact date of death has been found; Honour may be the

"H. Stansbury, aged 98, bur. 23 Sept. 1799, near Towson's Tavern,"
Tobias and Honour had iss.: SOPHIA, m. 1st, on 26 Dec. 1734 Thom-
as Demmitt, and 2nd (Peter?) Robinson; AVARILLA, b. 9 Oct. 1723;
TOBIAS, b. 11 Feb. 1726/7; GEORGE, b. 3 July 1732; BOWEN; HON-
OUR, m. (---) Gambrill; HELEN, m. Jonathan Eaglestone (7:321;
61:442; 79:229; 133:6, 13, 22; 153:9; Stansbury Notes in the
F. S. Hayward Gen. Collection at the Md. Hist. Soc.; letter to
the author from Mrs. J. Nolan Callahan).

STANSBURY, SAMUEL (7), s. of Tobias (2) and Sarah, was a
minor in 1714, and d. 1783; m. 1st (poss.) Miss Porter, said to
be from London; m. 2nd, on 24 May 1777, the wid. Mary Ann Cullison (who m. as her 3rd husb. James Hughes); in 1714 Sarah, then
w. of Enoch Spinks, gave bond she would pay Samuel and Tabitha
orphans of Tobias their share of their father's est.; in 1720
Samuel surv. 100 a. Long Island; in 1750 he owned that tract,
142 a. Addition, and 150 a. Venture Not; in April 1780 he conv.
to his dau. Bethia and her husb., Aquila Galloway the tracts Venture Not, Resurvey on Fellowship, and Gay's Inspection; d. leaving a will, 19 April 1783 - 9 May 1783, naming grandch. William
Welsh, s. Solomon, John Ensor Stansbury s. of William, s. Jasper Stansbury Cullison or Colston, daus. Ruth Stansbury Colston
and Tabitha Cross, Polly Stansbury Colston, and also Zebedee
Hicks, Luke Stansbury, Matthias Golly, and Ruth Hicks; had iss.:
TABITHA, m. 1st, on 24 Dec. 1737 William Hicks, and 2nd, on 1
Jan. 1761, Richard Cross; BETHIA, m. Aquila Galloway on 6 Jan.
1761; SAMUEL, d. c.1799 in Caswell Co., N. C.; AVARILLA, m.
William Welch; SOLOMON (112:547; 131; 133:173; 153:60; 231-WG#E:
336; E. C. Welsh, "Stansbury Data," unpub. notes at the Md. Hist.
Soc.).

STANSBURY, WILLIAM (8), s. of Daniel (3) and Elizabeth, was
b. 20 Jan. 1716, d. 3 Nov. 1788; m. Elizabeth, dau. of John
Ensor, on 14 Feb. 1739/40; she was b. 12 July 1721, d. 10 Sept.
1799; as heir at law he made provision for his brothers after
the death of their father; on 25 April 1763 conv. 100 a. Poplar
Neck on Bear Creek to Richard Stansbury s. of Daniel; on same
day conv. 80 a. Prospect to Daniel Stansbury of Daniel; on 10
April 1771, John Ensor made a will naming his grandson John Ensor Stansbury, s. of his dau. Elizabeth Stansbury; William and
Elizabeth had iss.: RUTH, b., 28 April 1744, m. James Edwards
on 9 March 1775; WILLIAM, b. 4 April 1746; ABRAHAM, d. 1811;
ISAAC, b. 2 July 1752, d. Oct. 1792 s.p.; JACOB, b. 14 March
1755, d. s.p.; ELIJAH, b. c.1756; JOHN ENSOR, b. c.1760;
ELIZABETH, m. James Brown on 19 Dec. 1782 (87:350-353; 112:257;
133:88, 171; 264; Johnston article).

STANSBURY,RICHARDSON (9), s. of Daniel (3) and Elizabeth, was
b. 20 May 1723; d. 30 Jan. 1797; m. Mary Raven, dau. of Isaac
and Letitia Raven, on 23 Feb. 1747; in 1750 owned 114 a. part
Addition to Poor Jamaica Man's Plague; d. leaving a will, 30
Jan,. 1797 - 22 April 1797, naming grands. William Boswell and
the ch. listed below; in 1798 his est. was admin.; dec. left
iss.: JOSEPH WARD, b. 24 Jan. 1749; ISAAC; RICHARDSON; DRUSILLA,
m. Charles Pearce on 3 Sept. 1793; SARAH, m. Thomas Knightsmith
Shaw on 6 Jan. 1778; DEBORAH: CASSANDRA, b. 13 April 1761, m.
John Bonfield on 23 Dec. 1783 (114:507; 133:1, 91; 153:76; 264;
Johnston article).

STANSBURY, RICHARD (10), s. of Daniel (3) and Elizabeth, was b.
22 May 1725; d. 1791; m. Sarah (---); three of their children,
Solomon, Sarah, and Elizabeth, drowned in June 1782 when their
canoe overturned; d. leaving a will, 28 May 1791 - 6 Oct. 1791;
had iss.: DANIEL; THOMAS, b. 2 Sept. 1770; JOSIAS, d. 26 April
1825; JOSHUA; KEZIAH; TABITHA; PRISCILLA; SOLOMON, drowned 1782;

SARAH, drowned 1782; ELIZABETH, drowned 1782 (114:11; 262;
Johnston article).

STANSBURY, DANIEL (11), s. of Daniel (3), was b. 23 July
1727; d. in Oct. or Nov. 1803; m. but wife's name has not been
determined; in 1763 was conv. 80 a. Prospect by his bro. William;
in 1786 was conv. 100 a. The Adventure by Aquila Gostwick; d.
leaving a will, 26 Oct. 1803 - 26 Nov. 1803, naming ch. listed
below; est. admin. 18 Feb. 1804; had iss.: DANIEL: WILLIAM;
REBECCA, m. Edward Bowen on 29 Nov. 1792; ELIZABETH, m. Austin
Phipps on 1 March 1798 (87:353; 116:7; 231-AL#A:39; 237-15:496;
Johnston article).

STANSBURY, JOHN (12), s. of Thomas (4) and Jane, was b. c.
1710; d. 1785; m. Anne Ensor, dau. of John and Jane Ensor, on
12 Feb. 1734; gave his age as 75 in 1785 and named his father
Thomas; in 1750 owned 90 a. Carr's Lot, which Thomas Carr had
conv. to him in 1742; he inher. 132 a. Dickinson's Relief,
Needs Must, 127 a. Daniel's Gift, and 112 a. Stansbury's Adventure from his father; had iss.: (order of birth uncertain):
JANE , b. 26 June 1736, m. Henry Stevenson; JOHN, b. 23 Jan.
1737/8; ELIZABETH, b. 25 Feb. 1739, m. Richard Daugherty;
WILLIAM, d. 1800; ANNE, m. John Long; RICHARD, d. s.p. 1787,
having m. Elizabeth (---) who m. 2nd James Stansbury; JAMES,
d. s.p.; THOMAS, b. 1741; JOSEPH, d. 1798; CALEB, m. 1st Rebecca
Cook, and 2nd, Elizabeth Shilling; JOSHUA, d. 18 Sept. 1767
(77:336; 112:46; 133:153; 153:50; F. S. Hayward, "Stansbury
Notes," in his gen. coll. at the Md. Hist. Soc.; Johnston article).

STANSBURY, THOMAS (13), s. of Thomas (4) and Jane, was b. 24
April 1714; d. 1798; m. Hannah, dau. of Charles and Sarah (Cole)
Gorsuch, on 2 March 1735; in 1742 was conv. 450 a. Dixon's Neck
by John Long, and by 1750 he also owned 90 a. Stansbury's Good
Luck, 100 a. Father's Care, 700 a. Jerrico, 111 a. Luke's Good-
will; 685 a. Franklin's Purchase; had iss.: CHARLES, b. 24 Jan.
1736, m. Elizabeth Buck on 25 April 1763; SARAH, b. 7 March 1739;
HANNAH, b. 20 April 1743, m. Henry Sater; LUKE, b. 24 April 1747;
JANE, b. 14 April 1750, m. William Wilson on 14 July 1774; BEN-
JAMIN, b. 28 June 1752; JOHN DIXON, b. 19 Dec. 1754, m. 1st Ruth
(---), and 2nd Wlizabeth Johnson; DAVID, b. 27 Jan. 1757, m.
Henrietta Maria Fowler on 11 April 1786; DANIEL, b. 8 May 1759,
m. Elizabeth (---), wid. of James Stansbury; WILLIAM, b. 11
Sept. 1764, m. 1st, Ruth Welsh, and 2nd, Susanna (---); THOMAS,
m. Ruth Lemmon; RACHEL, m. (---) Lemmon (77:341; 133:50, 60, 69,
89, 96, 99, 103; 153:21, 98; Johnston article).

STANSBURY, DANIEL (14), s. of Thomas (4) and Jane, was b. c.
1716/8; d. in A. A. Co.; m. c.1740 Elizabeth Ashman, b. 24 Dec.
1718, dau. of John and Constant; Elizabeth d. by 7 Dec. 1795
when her est. was dist. among her heirs; Daniel and Elizabeth
moved to A. A. Co., and the births of their ch. were recorded
in St. Margaret's Parish; Daniel d. leaving a will, 22 Dec.
1769 - 29 Jan. 1770; had iss.: EZEKIEL, b. 13 March 1740; EMANU-
EL, b. 21 Feb. 1743/4; JOSEPH, b. 19 Feb. 1745/6, m. Ruth Chenoweth; CHARITY, b. 31 Jan. 1748, m. George Presstman; ELIZABETH,
b. 9 April 1750, m. Charles Boone on 11 Sept. 1773; BENJAMIN,
b. 9 Dec. 1754; PATIENCE, b. 14 July 1757, m. (---) Hall (210-
37:487; 219-4; A. A. Dist. Book, JG # 1, f. 61; Johnston article).

STANSBURY, DIXON (15), s. of Thomas (4) and Jane, was b. 6
Dec. 1720; d. 1805; m. Penelope Body on 4 Jan. 1740/1; she was
b. 27 Nov. 1724, dau. of Stephen Body; in 1750 he owned 100 a.
Dublin; took the Oath of Fidelity to the State of Maryland in

1778 before the worshipful Jesse Dorsey; d. leaving a will, 19
March 1805 - 4 Dec. 1805; had iss.: BENJAMIN, b. 1 Oct. 1741;
DIXON, b. 22 July 1744; EDMUND, b. 6 Oct. 1746; ELIZABETH, b. 7
June 1749, m. 1st William Slade on 16 Jan. 1770, and m. 2nd Ben-
nett Bussey; JAMES, b. 7 Nov. 1751, m. Jemima Gorsuch on 7 Feb.
1789; ELIJAH (117:10; 131; 153:68; 417-6:63; Johnston article).

STANSBURY, EDMOND (16), s. of Thomas (4) and Jane, was b. 13
Jan. 1724/5; d. 22 April 1780; m. c.1775 Kezia Gostwick, b. 1753,
d. 7 July 1809; after Edmond's death she m. Joseph Cromwell;
Edmond and Kezia had iss.: JANE, b. 3 Oct. 1776; MARY, b. 30
Oct. 1778; KEZIA, b. 22 Feb. 1780 (Johnston article).

STANSBURY, Capt. TOBIAS (17), s. of Luke (5) and Jane, b. 23
March 1718/9; d. in Balto. Co. by Oct. 1757; on 27 April 1746
he m. Mary Hammond, dau. of Thomas and Catherine (Emerson) Hammond; on 6 Aug. 1754 sold 97 a. Addition to Joshua's Lot to
Josephus Murray; d. leaving a will, 6 Oct. 1757 - 3 March 1758,
naming w. Mary, tracts Long's Addition, Timber Swamp, Paradise
Regained, and Water Course, and mentioning his ch.; admin. bond
was posted 31 March 1758 by Mary Stansbury admnx.; she admin. the
est. on 18 June 1759, 7 Aug. 1759, 20 July 1761, and 2 Sept. 1767;
Capt. Tobias and Mary had iss.: HENRIETTA MARIA, b. 26 Feb.
1747/8; CATHERINE, b. 28 March 1749, m. Aquila Stinchcomb;
REBECCA, b. 22 April 1751, m. Thomas Bond; JANE, b. 9 June 1753,
d. unm.; MARY, twin, b. 12 Sept. 1755, m. Buckler Bond; SARAH,
twin, b. 12 Sept. 1755; TOBIAS EMERSON, b. 1757 (4:270, 287,
358; 7:307; 16:18; 82:275; 133:77, 99; 210-30:481; Johnston article).

STANSBURY, TOBIAS (18), s. of Tobias (6) and Honour, was b.
11 Feb. 1726/7; d. 1799; m. 1st Blanche (---), and 2nd Catherine; prob. the Tobias who in 1750 owned 200 a. Westwood, 100 a.
Addition to Westwood, 36 a. Luke's Privilege, 200 a. Stansbury's
Privilege, and 200 a. Addition to Privilege, as well as other
lands; Tobias and Blanche had iss.: CATHERINE, b. 4 July 1754,
m. John Partridge; SARAH, b. 20 Oct. 1756, m. 1st Josias Bowen
and 2nd John M. Gorsuch; NATHANIEL, b. 10 March 1759, d. c.1808
unm.; ELLEN; TOBIAS, d. c.1811 (153:28; Johnston article).

STANSBURY, GEORGE (19), s. of Tobias (6), and Honour, was b.
3 July 1732; d. 1789; m. Mary Eaglestone, dau. of Abraham Eaglestone; est. was admin. 18 Aug. 1790 and 19 Feb. 1791; had iss.:
RUTH, b. 19 Nov. 1760, m. William Lynch on 10 Feb. 1781; REBECCA,
b. 19 Feb. 1766, m. Rev. Nathaniel Watts on 24 Dec. 1789; GEORGE,
b. 18 April 1771; WILLIAM; CATHERINE, m. Joseph Green on 26 March
1789; ELLEN, m. John Battee on 1 May 1787; SARAH; DARIUS;
ELIJAH; MARY (10:186, 296, 299; 133:108, 125; Johnston article).

STANSBURY, SAMUEL (20), s. of Samuel (7), d. in Caswell Co.,
N. C.; may be the Samuel who m. Mary Harrod on 1 April 1771,
poss. as a 2nd w.; had iss.: SOLOMON, b. 26 Sept. 1755; LUKE,
d. 1848 (131; Johnston article).

STANSBURY, (---), and (---) Cromwell, in 1750 were joint
owners of 500 a. Joshua's Lot and 83 a. Milford (153:85).

STANSBURY, AVARILLA, was fined for bast. in Nov. 1756 (41:313).

STANSBURY, SOLOMON, d. by 12 Aug. 1748 when admin. bond was
posted 12 Aug. 1748 by Richard Coop with Henry Hughes and William
Whitely; may be the Solomon who m. Hannah Hicks on 27 Oct. 1743
(16:8; 131).

STANSBY, JOHN, was transp. to Md. c.1658; m. 1st, by 22 June

1667, Ann, dau. of Richard Wells of A. A. Co.; m. 2nd Mary, wid. of Godfrey Harmer, and dau. of Oliver and Johanna Spry; was called John Stansby, chirurgeon, when he was sued by Edward Inglish in 1678; represented Balto. Co. in the Lower House of the Assembly from 1676 to 1678, and was sheriff of Balto. Co. 1679 - 1682, and Justice of the County Court, 1675/6 - 1679; d. by 30 May 1684 when admin. bond was posted by admnx. Mary Stansby with Benjamin Gundry and John Hall; by Dec. 1691 his wid. Mary m. Richard Adams; in 1692 admin. was granted to his bro. William Stanesby (sic) (13:419; 19:146; 120:40; 206-4:463, 563; 209-13: 5; 210-67:271; 298; 388).

STANTON, ISAAC, age 13, was bound to William Rogers in March 1739/40, to age 21 (32).

STANTON, SARAH, was ind. for bast. in Nov. 1742 and Aug. 1746 and tried in March 1746/7 (34:59; 36:116, 394).

STANWIDGE, CHRISTOPHER, servant, with 3 years, 10 mos., to serve in the 1742 inv. of Jonas Robinson (53:201).

STAPLETON, EDWARD, was in Balto. Co. between 1736 abd 1765; m. Rachel (---); on 21 March 1736 he purch. 150 a. Paradise from John Lowe and w. Elizabeth; owned that land in 1750; had iss.: ALCE, b. 10 June 1737; JOSEPH, b. 5 Feb. 1742; HANNAH, b. 14 May 1744; JOSHUA, b. 22 June 1746; EDWARD, b. 1 Aug. 1749 (61:405; 128:92/b; 129:372; 153:15).

STAPLETON, JOHN, d. by 27 Aug. 1764 when his est. was admin. by Edward Stapleton; also admin. on 20 May 1765 (6:108, 161).

STAPLETON, THOMAS, m. Sarah Crook on 15 Jan. 1756; they had iss.: MARGARET, b. 20 March 1756; ALICE, b. 15 Sept. 1758; SARAH, b. 22 April 1760 (129:373).

STARKE, HANER, servant, was listed in the 1727 inv. of Joshua Merriken (51:263).

STARKEY, JOHN (1), d. in St. John's Par. on 28 Nov. 1737; m. Elizabeth Boyle on 1 Jan. 1707 in All Hallow's Par., A. A. Co.; admin. bond was posted 6 June 1733 by Joshua Starkey with John Scott and Richard Caswell (the wid. Eliz. renounced right to admin. on the grounds she was too old, and ren. in favor of her s. Joshua); est. was admin. by Joshua Starkey on 15 Jan. 1734 and 15 Jan. 1735; John and Elizabeth had iss.: JOSHUA; JONATHAN; JOSEPH; JACOB; and JOHN (3:179, 198; 15:269; 131; 219-1:76).

STARKEY, JOSHUA (2), s. of John (1), d. in Balto. Co. leaving a will, 2 March 1743 - 6 June 1744; m. Hannah Meads on 29 Sept. 1743; admin. his father's est. in 1734 and 1735; will mentioned his w. and bros. Jonathan, Jacob, Joseph, and John; admin. bond was posted 21 July 1744 by Jonathan Starkey with Heathcote Pickett and John Starkey (16:6; 127:277; 131).

STARKEY, JONATHAN (3), s. of John (1), admin. his brother's est. in 1744; in March 1753 was summoned by the vestry of St. John's Parish for unlawful cohabitation with Hannah, wid. of his bro. Joshua; m. Mary, dau. of George Simmons on 23 June 1757; in 1750 owned 200 a. Collingbourne; had iss.: ELIZABETH, b. 19 May 1758; WILLIAM, b. 21 Nov. 1759; JONATHAN, b. 12 March 1761; MARY, b. 14 Aug. 1762 (6:188; 131:49, 152/r; 132:117; 153:25).

STARKEY, JOHN (4), s. of John (1), m. Ann Greer on 10 July 1738; in 1750 owned 100 a. Green Park and 58 a. Green's Improvement; had iss.: MARY, b. 10 Sept. 1739; JOHN, b. 12 Feb. 1741;

ELIZABETH, b. 8 May 1744; JOSHUA, b. Dec. 1744 (sic) (131:74/r, 108/r, 116/r; 153:22).

STEADMAN, JOHN, m. Mary Minson on 10 Oct. 1747 (131).

STEELE, JOHN, m. Mary Clarke on 11 Nov. 1709; in Nov. 1718 Honour Donahue claimed that Steele had threatened her life; John and Mary had iss.: MARY, age 3 on 30 June 1715 was bound to Henry and Honour Donahue in Nov. 1715 (21:662; 23:32; 128:26).

STEELE, JOHN, was in Balto. Co. by 19 Feb. 1721 when he purch. 100 a. from Archibald and Jane Edmondston of P. G. Co.; m. Sarah (---); d. leaving a will, 21 Dec. 1730 - 3 March 1730/1, leaving entire est. to w. Sarah; in 1750 his wid. owned 60 a. Johnson's Island (69:14; 125:180; 153:94).

STEELE, JOS., m. Eliz. Tomley on 29 Jan. 1744 or 3 Feb. 1743/4 (in one place wife is named as Tomlin) (131).

STEELE, MARY, servant to Edward Wakeman, was ind. for bast. in Aug. 1739 and tried in June 1740 (32:1, 237).

STEERE, RICHARD, was in Balto. Co. by 1692 as a taxable in s. side Patapsco Hund. (138).

STEIRS, SARAH, spinster, was in Balto. Co. on 4 Nov. 1701 when she purch. 224 a. Steir's Progress from John Francis Holland and w. Jane (66:96).

STEPHENS. See STEVENS.

STERLING, MARY RICHARDS, in Nov. 1738 was ind. for bast. (31: 307).

STERLING, THOMAS, of Calvert Co., purch.Sterling's Purchase, part of Richardson's Outlet, from Thomas and Susanna Richardson (66:15).

STEUART. See STEWART.

STEVENS, GILES (1), progenitor, immigrated to Md. by 1670 and d. by 1679; m. Sarah (---) who posted admin. bond on his est. on 22 April 1679, with John Arden and Jacob Jenifer; surv. 300 a. (prob. called Paradice) on Back River, on 5 May 1673; sold 300 a. Paradice to Richard Bennett on 27 Feb. 1673/4; on 11 Nov. 1674 he surv. 200 a. St. Giles later held by his s. Giles, Jr.; wid. Sarah m. Thomas James by 1682; as Sarah James she admin. Stevens' est. on 20 Feb. 1682; had iss.: GILES, Jr. (2:35; 13:450; 100; 388).

STEVENS, GILES (2), s. of Giles (1), was a taxable on s. side of Gunpowder in 1694; d. by 13 July 1713; m. Rebecca (---); on 20 June 1696 was conv. 64 a. Hain's Point by his father-in-law Thomas James at that time living in Chester Co., Penna.; on 30 Dec. 1698 he and w. Rebecca conv. 120 a. No Name to Joseph Peake; admin. bond posted 13 July 1713 by admnx. Rebecca Stevens with John Ensor and William Holland; wid. Rebecca m. John Rogers on 25 April 1714; dec. was prob. the father of: GILES; THOMAS, m. Mary Wright by 28 April 1731; poss. JOHN, d. 1734; SAMUEL (13: 426; 59:529; 63:320; 131; Stevens notes in William N. Wilkins Gen. Collection).

STEVENS, GILES (3), s. of Giles (2), m. Alice Gudgeon in 1722; on 4 Nov. 1742 he and w. Alice conv. 28 a. Haphazard and 64 a. Horn Point to Joseph Thomas; had iss.: WILLIAM, b. 13 Aug. 1721,

m. Sarah Duke on 25 Dec. 1750; GILES; JAMES, m. Eliza Cadle on
2 Nov. 1752 (77:50; 131; Stevens notes in William N. Wilkins
Gen. Coll. at the MHS).

STEVENS, THOMAS (4), s. of Giles (2), m. Mary Wright on 28
April 1737; they had iss.: SARAH, b. 10 June 1738 (131).

STEVENS, SAMUEL (5), poss. s. of Giles (2), was in Balto.
Co. by 8 Aug. 1726 when he and his w. Martha conv. 200 a.St.
Giles to James Durham; on 5 March 1741 Samuel and Martha sold
50 a. James' Forest to Joseph Thomas (tract was orig. surv. for
Thomas James); on 16 April 1742 he and w. Martha conv. 150 a.
Stevens' Hope to Andrew MacGill (70:283; 76:146, 148).

STEVENS, GILES (6), s. of Giles (3), m. Avarilla Pickett on
13 Jan. 1757 and had iss.: DAVID, b. 21 Nov. 1756; WILLIAM, b.
27 June 1758; and JOHN, b. 13 Oct. 1760 (131; Wilkins notes on
the Stevens Family).

STEVENS, JOHN, servant of John Boring, was judged to be 14
in March 1683/4; had 9 mos. to serve when listed in the 1690 inv.
of said Boring (18:128; 51:6).

STEVENS, JOHN, was in Balto. Co. by 1692 as a taxable with
William Stevens (138).

STEVENS, JOHN, d. Feb. 1734 (128:86).

STEVENS, MARY, was ind. for bast. in Nov. 1733 (30:135).

STEVENS, RICHARD, was made levy free in Nov. 1750 (38:20).

STEVENS, THOMAS, was living at the widow Spencer's on Patapsco when an advert. in May 1752 urged him to contact the printer
(of the Md. Gazette) for news of a legacy from an uncle (255:56).

STEVENS, WILLIAM, was in Balto. Co. by 1692 as ataxable in s.
side Patapsco; on 10 March 1704 purch. 100 a. Expectation,
now called Morris' Folly, from Thomas and Elizabeth Morris (60:
146; 138).

THE EDWARD STEVENSON FAMILY has been more fully discussed
in the author's Descendants of Edward and Mary Stevenson of
Baltimore County (Baltimore: the Author, 1966).

STEVENSON, EDWARD (1), progenitor, d. in Balto. Co. by 17 April 1716; m. Mary (---) who m. 2nd Henry Sater; may have been the
Edward Stevenson transp. to Md. in c.1671 by Thomas Todd; by
1694 was a taxable in s. side of Back River; was styled Edward
Stevenson, Gent., in March 1709/10; represented Balto. Co. in
the Assembly, 1712; the election was contested, but Edward was
reelected in Oct. 1713; lands owned included Fellowship, Addition to Fellowship, Enlargement, and Edward's and Wills' Valley
and Hills; d. leaving a will, 25 Jan. 1715/6 - 17 April 1716;
admin. bond was posted 11 Nov. 1717 by extx. Mary Stevenson with
John Israel and William Barney; est. was inv. on 14 Jan. 1717/8
and val. at £ 493.18.7½, and signed by John Merryman as the
nearest relation; Mary and her 2nd husb. were summoned for not
administering the est. promptly; Edward and Mary had iss.:
EDWARD; HENRY; RICHARD KING: JOHN; MARY: ELIZABETH, ind. for
bast. in June 1714, in Nov. 1714 named Samuel Smallwood as the
father (1:182; 2:342; 3:79; 13:429; 21:505, 572; 123:79; 139;
210-29:128, 136, 270; 388; Test. Proc., Box 3, folder 77, at
Hall of Records).

STEVENSON, EDWARD (2), s. of Edward (1) and Mary, d. in Balto. Co. in June 1760; m. prior to 1724 Susan (poss. Tracey); on 2 March 1735 conv. 202 a. Addition to Fellowship to his bro. Henry; same day sold 290 a. part Edward and Will's Valleys and Hills to bro. Richard King Stevenson, and 290 a. of the latter tract to his bro. John; in 1750 owned 200 a. Fellowship and 150 a. Canaan; d. leaving a will, 9 June 176 0 30 June 1760, naming w. Susanna, father Edward, bros. Richard King and John Stevenson and sis. Mary w. of George Brown, and his own ch. Edward, Henry, John, Joshua, and Mary; had iss.: EDWARD, b. 6 Nov. 1725; WILLIAM, b. 1 Feb. 1731; FRANCIS: SARAH, b. 23 April 1733; MARY, b. 17 March 1734; MARY SUSAN, b. 11 March 1735, d. 25 July 1820; HENRY, b. 27 June 1737; JOHN, b. Feb. 1739, d. 3 July 1804; JOSHUA, b. 13 Nov. 1742 (74:384, 386, 388; 111:64; 133:35, 42, 58; 153:27; Stevenson Gen. by Barnes).

STEVENSON, HENRY (3), s. of Edward (1) and Mary, was living in 1775; m. Jemima, dau. of Charles and Jane (Long) Merryman, on 19 June 1735; in 1750 owned 202 a. Addition to Fellowship and 100 a. The Dairy; conv. parts of his lands in Frederick Co. to sons Henry, Jr., Charles, and again Henry, Jr., in 1769, 1770, and 1775; list of children has been compiled from St. Paul's Parish Reg., and the will of his dau. Jemima; Henry and w. Jemima had iss.: RUTH, b. 15 Sept. 1735, prob. d. young; JEMIMA, b. 7 Jan. 1736; HENRY, b. 2 March 1739; CHARLES, b. 14 Dec. 1740; MARY, m. Thomas Maguire on 15 April 1779; ANNE, m. Richard Taylor; JOSIAS; RUTH, b. 20 Jan. 1748; WILLIAM, b. 1 Jan. 1750/1; poss. a dau. who m. (---) Welch (133:47, 55, 60, 83, 95; 153: 32; Fred. Co. Deeds, Libers H:139; M:370; N:520; BD#2:66; Stevenson Gen. by Barnes).

STEVENSON, RICHARD KING (4), s. of Edward (1) and Mary, was b. c.1705; d. c.1777; m. Rachel (---); was named in the will, made 5 Nov. 1711, of John Vickory of Balto. Co.; on 30 Oct. 1737 Richard and w. Rachel conv. 120 a. Selset, also known as Jack's Double Purchase, which descended to Richard King Stevenson by the death of Richard Stevenson Vickory; on 3 Aug. 1740 for love he bore his cousins John and Jonathan Plowman he conv. them 50 a. Jack's Double Purchase; d. leaving a will, 7 Aug. 1773 - 9 Dec. 1777, naming w. Rachel, granddaus. Elizabeth and Sarah Gott, and these ch.: EDWARD, b. 22 May 1739; ELIZABETH, b. 2 Dec. 1731; RICHARD, b. 7 Dec. 1733; MORDECAI; SATER, b. 2 Nov. 1740; DANIEL; MARY, m. John Smith; RACHEL, b. 1 Jan. 1745, d. 1804, m. Nicodemus Bond (74:386; 75:32, 438; 112:337; 133:33; 153:4; Stevenson Gen. by Barnes).

STEVENSON, JOHN (5), s. of Edward (1) and Mary, d. 1786; m. 1st Mary Tipton, b. 18 Feb. 1717, dau. of Thomas and Sarah Tipton; m. 2nd Susanna (---); in 1750 owned 290 a. Edward and Will's Valleys and Hills, and 100 a. part Molly's and Sally's Delight (the latter tract conv. to him by Jonathan and Juliatha Tipton on 22 June 1747; d. leaving a will, 26 Oct. 1785 - 22 June 1786, naming ch. William, John, Edward, Joshua, (Elizabeth?) Todd, and Mary and Susanna Stevenson; inv. of est. totalled ₤ 274.9.0, and est. was admin. 19 July 1786, 16 April 1788, and 9 Feb. 1791; John had iss.: JOHN, b. 1757; WILLIAM, b. c.1763; GEORGE, b. 1768; EDWARD; JOSHUA, b. poss. 1776; ELIZA(BETH), m. (---) Todd; MARY, m. William Johnson; and SARAH, m. Stephen Gambrill on 3 May 1798 (74:383; 79:461; 113:147; 153:28; 235-1; Stevenson Gen. by Barnes).

STEVENSON, MAPLE, m. Richard Treadwell on 7 June 1752; had s. JAMES SHEREDINE STEVENSON, b. 23 Aug. 1749 (131:40, 128/r).

STEVENSON, PHILIP, was transp. to Md. from Va. c.1665, with

Sarah, Katherine, and Elizabeth Stevenson; in Nov. 1663 was assigned 100 a. Powell's Neck by Howell Powell; in July 1664 conv.
his interest in patent land to Richard Hensworth (93; 388).

STEVERT, ALEXANDER, m. Mary M'Kinley on 11 Dec. (1754?) (131).

STEWART/ STEUART/STEWARD/STUART, DAVID (1), was in Md. at
least by 15 Feb. 1670 when he wit. the will of Abram Delap; d.
in A. A. Co. 11 Oct. 1696 - 21 May 1697, naming w. Margaret
and ch.: David, Robert, Charles, and James; believed to have
been the father of: DAVID, d. 1703; CHARLES; ROBERT,b. c.1675,
d. 1740 having m. Susanna Watts; JAMES, bapt. 28 Jan. 1699;
ELIZABETH, m. John Frizzell; MARY, m. (---) Davis (120:60; 121:
123; 122:25).

STEWART, JAMES (2), s. of David (1), was bapt. "as a young man,"
on 28 Jan. 1699 in All Hallow's Parish, A. A. Co.; m. Rachel Wych-
oll on 21 July 1710; may have d. c.1752 in A. A. Co.; had iss.:
DAVID, bapt. 8 Oct. 1717; MARGARET, bapt. 18 Oct. 1717; JAMES,
bapt. 18 Aug. 1723 (219-1:55, 280, 322).

STEWART, JAMES (3), s. of James (2), was bapt. 18 Aug. 1723
in A. A. Co., and d. 1767 in Balto. Co.; m. Mary Wood on 10 Feb.
1741; in 1750 owned 49 a. Greenfield's Double Purchase, 33 a.
Wood's Chance, and 34 a. Wood's Choice; gave his age as 50 in
1759; d. leaving a will, 13 Feb. 1767 - 5 March 1767; had iss.:
MARGARET, b. 8 Jan. 1742/3; ANN, b. 4 May 1745; JAMES, b. 23 Feb.
1746/7; MARY, b. 9 Dec. 1749; MITCHELL, b. 16 Dec. 1751 (112:76;
129:324, 365; 153:88; 219-1:322).

STEWART, ALEXANDER, m. Sarah (---) and had iss.: ANN, b. 24
July 1758 (133:102).

STEWART, ASWELL, orphan of Elizabeth, in Nov. 1741 was bound
to John and Ann Norris (33:157).

STEWART, CHARLES, m. Mary (---), and had: JANE, b. 8 June
1742; JAMES, b. 2 June 1744 (129:336, 337).

STEWART, CICELY, in Aug. 1720 named John Wilde as the father
of her child (23:365).

STEWART, CORNELIUS, m. Mary Low on 25 Nov. 1747 (131).

STEWART, ELIZABETH, mulatto ch. of Elizabeth Stewart (who had
run away), was bound to John and Ann Norris in Nov. 1716 to age
31 (22:61).

STEWART, ELIZABETH, was ind. for bast. in March 1733/4, tried
in Nov. 1744, ind. in March 1745/6, and tried in June 1746 (35:
154, 389, 800; 36:7).

STEWART, ISABELLA, in Aug. 1715 was ind. for bast. (21:624).

STEWART, JOAN, dau. of Eliza Lewis, in Feb. 1720 was named as
a legatee of Anthony Drew (1:151).

STEWART, MARGARET, was ind. for bast. in Nov. 1719 (23:245).

STIGAR, ANDREW, was naturalized in 1759; m. Mary (---), and
had iss.: LOUISA, b. 26 Oct. 1756; ELIZABETH, b. 1 March 1760
(133:105; 404).

STIGINGS, WILLIAM, m. Mary Masters on 13 July 1721 (128:40).

STILES, NATHANIEL, imm. to Md. by c.1651; was added to the Commission of Balto. Co. in Oct. 1664; was sheriff in May 1669; purch. 300 a. Bayley from Godfrey Bayley in June 1661; in Aug. 1666 conv. 500 a. Yapp to Joseph Gundry; moved to Cecil Co. where he d. leaving a will, 19 Sept. 1676 - 2 Jan. 1676/7, naming Katherine, w. of Henry Stockett, father Nathaniel, sisters Mary and Frances, John Hill and Frances Trippas, with William Scrimshire as exec., and Henry Stockett and John Stanley as overseers (93; 94; 96:232; 97:125; 98:45, 46; 120:179; 200-3:503; 200-51:328).

STILES, ROBERT, was in Balto. Co. by 1692 as a taxable in n. side Patapsco Hund. (138).

STILES, WILLIAM, purch. Spring Garden from Benjamin Richards in April 1750; left a will, 3 Jan. 1764, leaving that tract and Styles Delitable to w. Ann (80:538; 210-31:1087).

STILL, AXELL, imm. to Md. c.1650, was living in 1662; in Jan. 1663/4 claimed 300 a. Oxelle Neck from William Stanley, soapboiler, as Stanley had not paid for the tract; in Feb. 1663/4 conv. the land to William Fisher (94;388).

STIMSON, ELIZABETH, in Nov. 1695 was fined for bast., naming Christopher Bembridge as the father (20:503).

THE STINCHCOMB FAMILY has been the subject of unpublished research by the late Donnell M. Owings, and the subject of an article by Frank W. Gardner in the National Genealogical Society Quarterly, 28:8-13. There are discrepancies in the two accounts, and so the compiler of this work has included only data he has verified from primary sources.

STINCHCOMB, NATHANIEL (1), was b. c.1671 in A. A. Co., prob. the Nathaniel who came to Balto. Co. by 1694 as a taxable in s. side Patapsco Hund.; m. c.1697 Hannah, dau. of Christopher Randall; d. by May 1710 when admin. bond on his est. was posted by Hannah Stinchcomb with Christopher and Thomas Randall; his wid. m. 2nd Edward Teal; his est. was inv. 13 June 1710 by Jno. Israel and Jno. Whips and val. at ₤ 75.17.8, and signed by Thomas Randall and Chris. Randall; est. was admin. 2 March 1712/3 by Edmund and Hannah Teal (sic); left iss.: MARY, b. c.1698, m. 1st, on 16 Feb. 1714/5 John Newsom of Thomas, and 2nd, by 1723, William Smith of George; JOHN, b. c.1700; HELEN, b. c.1702, m. Henry Owings; poss. NATHANIEL, b. c.1704, d. by 1746/7; HANNAH, b. c. 1706, m. John Owings c.1726; poss. ANNA, b. c.1706, m. (---) Galloway; poss. REBECCA, b. c.1708 (1:368; 13:431; 48:237; data from D. M. Owings).

STINCHCOMB, JOHN (2), s. of Nathaniel (1) and Hannah, b. c. 1700; m. Catherine, dau. of Hector McLean on 23 July 1733; in April 1721 surv. 50 a. Addition to Bachelor's Hope; in Dec. 1737 conv. Bachelor's Hope and Addition to Bachelor's Hope to Nathaniel Stinchcomb; in 1750 owned 100 a. Stinchcomb's Reserve, 300 a. Hector's Chance. 75 a. part Pistole, and 150 a. Overlooked; d. 1779; had iss.: REBECCA, b. 4 March 1733/4; NORMAN, b. 26 Sept. 1735; SARAH, b. 23 April 1737; JOHN, b. 6 July 1739; HANNAH, b. 10 Jan. 1740; NATHANIEL, b. 22 March 1742; ANNA, b. 2 Sept. 1745; WILLIAM, b. 11 Nov. 1746; AQUILA, b. 7 May 1749; McLANE; ENOCH; CHRISTOPHER; GEORGE (75:41; 84:416; 111:44; 112: 382; 124:33; 133:37, 47, 84, 85, 151; 153:37; 207).

STINCHCOMB, NATHANIEL (3), poss. s. of Nathaniel (1) and Hannah, d. by 8 July 1748, having m. Patience Rowles on 15 Jan. 1733; she was the wid. of (---) Rowles and her maiden name was Burle; in Dec. 1737 purch. Bachelor's Hope and Addition to Bache-

lor's Hope from John Stinchcomb; in 1750 his heirs owned 100 a.
Bachelor's Hope, 50 a. Bachelor's Addition, 75 a. Pistole, and
75 a. Addition to Pistole; admin. bond was posted 8 July 1748 by
Patience Stinchcomb with John Stinchcomb and Christopher Randall;
est., admin. by Patience, now w. of Jacob Rowles on 16 June 1750,
4 Aug. 1750, and 7 Aug. 1750; Nathaniel had iss.: NATHANIEL, b.
7 Nov. 1734; JOHN, b. 25 Jan. 1738/9;PATIENCE, b. 22 Sept. 1736;
SARAH, b. 24 Sept. 1741; MARY, b. 5 Sept. 1743; and THOMAS (4:
185; 5:113, 115, 154; 16:11; 37:6, 172; 38:3; 75:41; 133:64, 72,
151; 153:46).

STINCHCOMB, JOHN, m. Mary Davis on 6 Nov. 1740; had iss.:
RACHEL, b. 6 Feb. 1745; JOHN, b. 21 Dec. 1748 (219-4:53, 64, 108).

STINCHCOMB, PATIENCE, in June 1757 had borne a bast.; Nathaniel Stinchcomb said he would be financially responsible (46:30).

THE STOCKETT FAMILY is discussed in the 1642 Visitation of
Kent (Harleian Society Publications, 42:184), and in Frank H.
Stockett, Genealogy of the Family of Stockett, 1558-1892 (Balto.:
Wm. K. Boyle and Son, n.d.).

STOCKETT, LOUIS (1), was b. 1558, and d. 1603, was listed as
progenitor in the Vis. of Kent; res. in St. Stephen's Parish,
Kent, Eng., and had iss.: THOMAS, of Gray's Inn; JOANNA, m. Walter Aylworth, son of John and Elizabeth (Ashton) Aylworth (Walter and Joanna had at least one dau., Frances, who m. her cousin
Thomas Stockett) (Vis. of Kent, 1642).

STOCKETT, THOMAS (2), s. of Louis (1), m. Joanna, dau. of (---)
Biggs of Kent; he is listed as armiger in the 1642 Visitation, and
he and his wife had iss.: FRANCES, d. unm.; THOMAS, of St. Steph-
en's; and LUCIA, m. Capt. Michael Wood (Vis. of Kent, 1642).

STOCKETT, THOMAS (3), s. of Thomas (2) and Joanna, m. his 1st
cousin, Frances Aylworth, dau. of Walter and Joanna (Stockett)
Aylworth; he had one s. listed in the Vis., but Frank H. Stockett
states he had other ch.: JOHN, listed in the Vis. of "ob. Incuna-
bilis;" FRANCIS, b. c.1634; HENRY; THOMAS; Col. LEWIS; and AYL-
WORTH (1642 Vis.; and Stockett Gen.)

STOCKETT, FRANCIS (4), s. of Thomas (3), said to have been b.
c.1634, d. 1687; imm. to Md. c.1658 with his bros. Henry and Thomas; res. on Balto. and A. A. Cos.; physician; represented Balto.
Co. in the Lower House in 1659/60; d. by 14 Aug. 1687 in A. A. Co.
(371:779; 388).

STOCKETT, HENRY (5), s. of Thomas(3) and Frances, came to Md.
c.1658 with bros. Francis and Thomas; m. Katherine (---) by Oct.
1669 when they conv. 115 a. Delph Island to Thomas Thurston; in
Dec. 1670 was in A. A. Co. when he and w. Katherine conv. 300 a.
Repulta to Thomas Ford; on 22 Feb. 1672 Matthew Harding of A. A.
Co. made a will naming Henry's w. Katherine and their dau. Katherine as his sole legatee; Henry d. leaving a will, 21 June 1682 -
23 Oct. 1682, naming w. Katherine and these ch.: LEWIS (not yet
21); (dau.) HENRICO; PENELOPE; and KATHERINE (later m. Henry
Rhodes) (95; 98:44; 120:72, 140).

STOCKETT, THOMAS (6), s. of Thomas (3) and Frances, came to
Md. with bros. Francis and Henry c.1658; m. by 1667 Mary, dau. of
Richard Wells; rep. Balto. Co. in the Lower House, 1661, 1662, and
1663-1664; Justice of Balto. Co. 1661-1664, Sheriff of A. A. Co.
1669-1670; d. leaving a will, 23 April 1671 - 4 May 1671, naming
w. Mary, ch. Thomas and unnamed daus., cousin Henry White, bros.
Francis and Henry, and Richard Wells; wid. Mary m. 2nd George

Yate; had iss.: THOMAS, m. 1st c.1689 Mary, sis. of Thomas Sprigg, and 2nd, by March 1708, Damaris, dau. of John Welch; FRANCES, m. Mareen Duvall; poss. other daus.(67:5; 120:60; 371:779-780).

STOCKETT, LEWIS (7), poss. s. of Thomas (3), claimed land for transporting himself in 1666; was in Md. by 20 April 1665 when he wit. the will of Thomas Griffith (120:35; 388).

STOCKSDALE, EDWARD, d. in Balto. Co. in 1779; m. Catherine (---) who was living in 1786; was in Balto. Co. by 16 April 1728 when he wit. the will of William Parrish; in 1729 acquired 50 a. Gosnell's Range from Morris and Susanna Gosnell; by 1750 owned 50 a. Gosnell's Camp, 100 a. Stocksdale's Hills, 50 a. Stocksdale's Forest, 75 a. Addition to Stocksdale's Forest, and 50 a. Buckingham's Purchase; d. leaving a will, 16 Aug,. 1779 - 13 Oct. 1779; est. admin. 9 Oct. 1786; dec. left iss.:   SOLOMON, b. 30 Oct. 1731; MARGARET, b. 6 Oct. 1734, m. (---) Davis; HANNAH, m. (---) Hooker; JOHN; THOMAS; CATHERINE, m. Jacob Brown; RACHEL, m. (---) Griffith or Griffee; ELEANOR, m. David Sutherland on 10 Sept. 1776: EDWARD (8:324; 61:220; 80:303; 82:142; 84:184; 86:278, 281; 90:461; 112:376; 123:45; 125:89, 225; 133:28, 42; 137:12; 153:10).

STOCKSDALE, JOHN, was in Balto. Co. by Aug. 1728 when he was tried for bast.; in 1750 owned 83 a. Brotherly Love; d. leaving a will, 10 March 1757 - 3 Sept. 1757, naming Nathaniel Brothers, and these ch.: THOMAS; JOHN; ELIZABETH; PRUDENCE; and PATIENCE (28:37; 153:41; 210-30:372).

STOCKSDALE, ROBERT, was in Balto. Co. by 1692 as ataxable in n. side Patapsco; in Nov. 1711 was made levy free on the grounds of his being ancient and feeble, and having a great charge of children (21:269; 138).

STOCKSDALE, THOMAS, age 8 in March 1723/4 when he was bound to George Ogg, Jr.; in May 1741 Joseph and Elizabeth Cornelius conv. him one-half of Curgafurgus, orig. surv. for William Hammond; in 1750 owned 50 a. Stocksdale's Abode; in Jan. 1756 he and w. Sarah conv. that tract to John Rudge; in Oct. 1767 he and unnamed w. conv. 50 a. Gorsuch Retirement to Dr. John Stevenson (26:193; 77:539; 82:492; 92:64; 153:53).

STODDART, (---), with (---) Holliday in 1750 owned 417 a. part Trueman's Acquaintance (153:94).

STOKES, JOHN (1), progenitor, was in Balto. Co. by 1705 and d. there by 5 Sept. 1732; m. Susanna Maria Wells, dau. of George Wells; she d. by 26 March 1746; in Aug. 1718 Stokes qualified as Clerk of the Court; in Aug. 1719 he asked permission to be absent from his duties as Clerk as he had to go to England to claim an estate he had inherited from his mother; d. leaving a will, 2 March 1727 - 5 Sept. 1732, naming ch. George, John, Humphrey, Frances, w. of Aquila Paca, and kinsman Philip Key; admin. bond was posted 6 Sept. 1732 by extx Susanna Stokes with Humphrey Wells Stokes and Peregrine Frisby; est. was admin. on 4 Dec. 1741 by Susanna Stokes; Susanna d. leaving a will, 25 Aug. 1745 - 26 March 1746, naming s. John, grandchildren Robert, Cordelia, and Frances Stokes, and John Paca; Peregrine Frisby posted admin. bond on 1 May 1746; he died, and Mary Frisby posted a second admin. bond on 25 March 1747; she must have d. as a third admin. bond was posted 15 June 1748 by Mary Henderson of A. A. Co,. with John Hall of Swan Town, and Jno. Paca; Mary Frisby admin. the est. on 5 March 1747, and Mary Henderson admin. the est. on 14 Nov. 1749; John and Susanna Maria (Wells) Stokes had iss.: FRANCES, b. 4 Jan. ,1705, m. Aquila Paca; JOHN, b. 4 Jan. 1707;

HUMPHREY WELLS, b. 27 March 1709; MARY, b. 9 June 1712; GEORGE (4:99, 212; 5:80; 15:268; 16:7, 12, 32; 23:3, 136, 210; 110: 375; 125:232).

STOKES, JOHN (2), s. of John (1) and Susanna Maria, was b. 4 Jan. 1707; d. by 1763; on 10 June 1733, Susanna, wid. of John Stokes (1), conv. to her s. John land she had inher. from her father, called The Old Plantation; in June 1750 John Stokes was named as the father of Elizabeth Tolson's child; he was tried in Aug. 1750; in 1750 he owned 100 a. Planter's Delight, 266 a. Goldsmith's Hall, 67½ a. Timber Proof, and 27 a. Walltown Habitation, and part Matthews' Neglect; est. was admin. by admnx. Rebecca Stokes, with one-third of the est. going to the acct., one-third to the wife of Dr. Alexander Stenhouse, and one-third to the w. of Dr. Henry stevenson; dec. had iss.: CORDELIA, m. 1st, on 21 July 1754 Charles Christie, and 2nd, on 21 June 1761 Dr. Alexander Stenhouse; poss. dau. who m. Dr. Henry Stevenson (6:39; 37:23, 182; 73:418; 129:320; 131; 153:50).

STOKES, HUMPHREY WELLS (3), s. of John (1) and Susanna Maria, was b. 27 March 1709, and. d. by 4 July 1741; m. Mary, dau. of Stephen and Mary Knight, on 31 Dec. 1730; his wid. m. 2nd Talbot Risteau, on 20 June 1745; admin. bond was posted on his est. on 4 July 1741 by Mary Stokes, with Edward Wakeman and James Phillips; est. was admin. 15 May 1746, and by Mary w. of Talbot Risteau, on 1 June 1750; in 1750 he or his heirs were listed in the Debt Book as owning 200 a. part Westwood, 618 a. Germantown Resurveyed, 100 a. Frisby's Connection, and 200 a. Ebenezer's Lot; Humphrey Wells and Mary had iss.: ROBERT, b. 8 Dec. 1731 (4:130; 5:108; 16:3; 131; 153:59).

STOKES, GEORGE (4), s. of John (1) and Susanna Maria, d. by 13 June 1741 when admin. bond was posted by extx. Susanna Stokes, Jr., with Peregrine Frisby and James Phillips; m. Susanna (---) who later m. 2nd, Winston Smith, and 3rd, Col. James Phillips; d. leaving a will, 8 April 1741 - 13 June 1741, naming w. Susanna, daus. Cordelia, and Frances, his father John, and his grandfather Col. George Wells; in Nov. 1750 Susanna Smith gave bond to Cordelia and Frances Stokes she would pay them their share of their father's est.; his est. was admin. by Susanna w. of Winston Smith on 13 Dec. 1743, and on 24 Nov. 1747; had iss.: CORDELIA, b. 4 March 1734; FRANCES (3:331; 4:31, 179; 13:460; 38:14; 127:139; 128:91; 131:49).

STOKES, ROBERT (5), s. of Humphrey Wells (3) and Mary, was b. 8 Dec. 1731; d. in Balto. Co. leaving a will, 30 Oct. 1756 - 29 Nov. 1756, naming w. Rebecca, unborn ch., Mrs. Cordelia Christie, Miss Frances Stokes, father-in-law Col. William Young, and friend Samuel Young; admin. bond was posted 9 Dec. 1756 by Rebecca Stokes, who admin. the est. on 11 Jan. 1758 and 2 April 1760; Robert m. Rebecca, dau. of William Young, on 15 Aug. 1756 and had iss.: ROBERT YOUNG, b. 13 July 1757 (4:266; 6:18; 15:359; 111:110; 129:363; 131:47, 213, 215).

STOKES, ELIZABETH, had iss.: ELIZABETH, b. 23 Dec. 1735 (128: 90).

STONE, HENRY, m. Constance James on 2 July 1740 (128:110).

STONE, JOHN, was in Balto. Co. by 12 March 1742 when he purch. 50 a. The Adventure from his father-in-law Charles Yates; in July 1743 John and his w. Mary sold the tract to Moses Rutter (77:269).

STONE, THOMAS, was in Balto. Co. by 2 March 1685 when Edward Mumford conv. 100 a. Long Island Point to Stone and to Dennis

Garrett; in 1692 was a taxable in n. side Patapsco Hund.; on
1 March 1691 conv. Long Island Point to the children of Dennis
Garrett and w. Barbara; in 1750 conv. 50 a. of same tract to
Richard Owen; Stone's w. Christiana gave consent; on 26 Nov.
1709 Thomas and Christiana conv. 174 a. Stone's Range to George
Cole; in Aug. 1715 pet. to be levy free; on 14 Feb. 1725/6 conv.
property to his son-in-law James Bagford, and on same day conv.
Arden's Adventure to his son-in-law Richard Simpson; in Nov.
1733 the county decided he was past his labours and ordered him
to be exempt from the levy; on 12 June 1733 Thomas Stone and w.
Elizabeth conv. 100 a. The Olive Yard to Philip Jones, Jr.; m.
by 1712 Elizabeth, widow and admnx. of Richard Sampson or Simpson,
extx of Samuel Hinton, and widow of (---) Bagford; her will, 28
Jan. 1736 - 13 June 1737 named her s. John Sampson (to have one-
half of Bachelor's Delight), said son to maintain Sarah Hinton
Olive, son James Bagford (to have other half of tract), William
Rogers, and dau. Constant Rowles also mentioned (1:43, 255; 17:
623; 30:125; 51:63; 59:341; 60:119; 67:25; 70:387, 388; 73:399;
108; 126:212; 138; 211).

STORY, CHARLES, m. Ann Brittain on 15 May 1733 (129:265).

STORY, CHARLES, white servant, with 2 years, 8 mos. to serve
was listed in the June 1734 inv. of Aquila Hall (49:320).

STORY, ELIZABETH, was ind. for bast. in March 1750/1 (38:270).

STORY, ELIZABETH, had iss.: EZEKIEL, b. 16 March 1757, twin;
JOSHUA, twin, b. 16 March 1757 (133:110).

STORY, JANE, was ind. for bast. in June 1744, in Aug. 1744
named John Watts as the father; ind. for bast. again in March
1746/7 (35:227, 323; 36:378).

STORY, JOSHUA, m. Margaret Briscoe on 14 Oct. 1762 (129:379).

STORY, WILLIAM, was in Balto. Co. by 1692 as a taxable in
n. side Patapsco Hund. (138).

STOTTS, ABRAHAM, m. Margaret Johnson on 26 June 1760 (131).

STOUT, ELIZABETH, m. Thomas Walters on 13 July 1713 (131).

STRANGE, ANN, and Charles Motherby were ind. for unlawful cohabitation in Aug. 1750 and tried in Nov. 1750 (37:150).

STRANGEWAYS, CHRISTOPHER, deeded a lot in Balto. Town to
John Ensor, Jr., on 15 Dec. 1751 (81:337).

STRAWBRIDGE, JOSEPH, was in Balto. Co. by 1692 as a taxable
in n. side Patapsco; m. by Aug. 1694 Sarah, admnx. of John Arden
of Balto. Co.; his est. was inv. 7 July 1699, with that of his
w. Sarah, and val. at ₤ 27.14.0, appraised by William Wilkinson
and Robuck Lynch; Sarah Strawbridge d. leaving a will,30 March
1699 - 10 April 1699, naming daus. Susanna Strawbridge, Mary
Harding (i.e., Arden), and Samuel Harding (Arden); also Ann
Reeves and Sarah's former husb. John Arden, with Nicholas Haile
as exec.; admin. bond was posted 7 July 1699 by said Haile with
William Wilkinson and Robuck Lynch; est. was admin. 28 Sept.
1705 and again in 1714; dec. left dau.: SUSANNA (1:7; 2:213; 13:
424; 20:285; 48:134; 138).

STREET, FRANCIS, was in Balto. Co. by June 1707 when he surv.
100 a. Street's Adventure; d. by 29 Oct. 1719 when admin. bond
was posted by Richard Gist with Luke Stansbury and Joseph Murray;

est. inv. 16 Jan. 1719/20 by George Ogg, Jr., and Edward Roberts and val. at E 45.18.10; est. admin. 3 March 1719 and 17 Sept. 1720 (13:428; 398:428).

STREET, THOMAS, m. Sarah Feeler in 1733; had is.: THOMAS, b. 20 Aug. 1737 (128:82, 97).

STREET, THOMAS, m. Mary Fox on 16 Dec. 1755 (131).

STRINGALL, JOSEPH, was in Balto. Co. by 1695 as a taxable on n. side Patapsco (140).

STRINGER, Dr.; in 1750 his heirs owned 235 a, Chestnut Ridge (153:99).

STRINGER, JOHN, of A. A. Co.; m. Ann (---) who m. 2nd John Collier; 3rd, by March 1673, William York; had iss.: MARY, m. Lodowick Williams (209-6:42).

STRINGER, JOHN, m. Mary Collier on 2 July 1733; prob. the John Stringer who purch. 100 a. St. Albans from John Swinyard on 6 March 1738 (75:186; 128:75).

STRINGER, Dr. SAMUEL, d. by 24 June 1755 when his est. was admin. by his extx. Lydia, now w. of Charles Ridgely (whom she m. by Aug. 1750); est. also admin. 1 Sept. 1757; dec. left ch. LUCEY, SAMUEL, ANN, and RICHARD (5:334, 347; 37:159; 38:275).

STRONG, GEORGE, was in Balto. Co. by Oct. 1665 when he purch. 300 a. on the west side of Fishing Creek (94).

STROUP, JACOB, was in Balto. Co. by 1750 when he owned 20 a. Jacob's Lot and 140 a. Major's Choice (153:92).

STRUTT, ELIZA, was tried for bearing a negro bast. in Nov. 1743 (35:82).

STUART. See STEWART.

STULTS, PETER, was in Balto. Co. by 1750 when he owned 209 a. part Diggs' Choice (153:97).

STURMAY, MARGARET, was ind. for bast. in Nov. 1758; had child: JEREMIAH (46:163).

SULLIVAN, DANIEL (or DAVID), was convicted c. May 1751 for murdering Donald McKennie, overseer for Mr. Digges, in Balto. Co. (385:126).

SULLIVAN, DANIEL, and w. Winifred were in Balto. Co. on 13 Oct. 1752 when they conv. 115 a. part Eightrupp to Robert Brierly, Jr. (81:434).

SULLIVAN, ELIZABETH, was tried for bast. in March 1754; she refused to name the father, but John Watson was tried as the father (39:29, 30).

SULLIVAN, JOHN, his pet. to be levy free was granted in June 1731 (29:160).

SULLIVAN (?), JULIAN, was ind. for bast. in Nov. 1712 (21:334).

SULLIVAN, OWEN, was in Balto. Co. by 1699 as a taxable in Spesutia Hund.; m. on 27 Sept. 1701, Dorothy, wid. of (---)

Taylor; appraised the est. of Jo's Gouly in March 1703 and the
est. of Hugh Brannahan in Oct. 1709; with Ann Sullivan wit. the
will of John Murphy of Balto. Co. in March 1729 (48:135; 51:27;
125:131; 129:193; 141). See also SWILLIVAN.

SUMMERS, WILLIAM, was in Balto. Co. by Aug. 1714 when he complained to the county court about William Popejoy; d. by 7 Aug.
1717 when admin. bond was posted by Francis Street with Josephus
Murray and John Simkins, the wid. Violette Summers having ren.
the right to admin. in favor of her bro.-in-law said Street;
est. was inv. 28 Oct. 1717 and val. at £ 21.11.7, and signed by
Villata Summers, Francis Street, Edward Roberts, and Henry Butler (1:289; 13:430; 52:298; 338:117).

SUMNER, JOHN, was in Balto. Co. by 1750 as the owner of 100
a. Sumner's Deer Park, 100 a. Franklin Choice, and 500 a. part
Hill's Camp; d. leaving a will, 1 Dec. 1757 - 23 Jan. 1758, naming Phebe Jackson and her dau. Hannah Jackson, Samuel Foster (or
Porter), Richard Williams, David Carlisle, and Richard Williams;
est. was admin. 7 May 1759 and 3 Nov. 1760, dec. was said to have
left "no heirs in the Province" (4:267, 313; 16:57; 111:70; 153:
27).

SUMNER, JOSEPH, was in Balto. Co. by Aug. 1672 when he and
Robert Garrett purch. 450 a. Dixon's Neck from John Dixon; later
stated to have left the Province (48:46; 211).

SUTHARD, JAMES, and w. Welthen were in Balto. Co. by Oct. 1665
when they sold 300 a. to George Strong; James d. by Aug. 1668
leaving his wid. "poor and homeless," when Richard Leake conv.to
her life tenure in a chamber and houseroom in his plantation,
and 100 a. adjacent Fenn Island Creek (94; 95)

SUTTON, THOMAS (1), of Balto. Co., d. 2 July 1729; m. Dorcas
(---), who m,. 2nd Joseph Thomas; admin. bond was posted 17 Nov.
1729 by admnx. Dorcas Sutton with Christopher Duke and Walter
James; est. was inv. in 1729, and est. was twice admin., the 2nd
time in 1733 by Dorcas, now w. of Joseph Thomas, whom she m. on
4 Feb. 1732; court records in Nov. 1734 state he d. leaving four
ch., but he seems to have had five ch.: CHRISTOPHER, b. c.1720;
THOMAS, b. 17 April 1722; JOSEPH, b. 9 July 1724; RUTH, b. 18
June 1726, m. Adam Hance on 25 Oct. 1744; BENJAMIN, b. 24 Sept.
1728 (3:142; 5:177; 15:266; 30:356; 52:163; 131:27; 133:10, 11,
194).

SUTTON, CHRISTOPHER (2), prob. s. of Thomas (1), so placed
because he had a dau. Dorcas; m. Sarah League on 12 Oct. 1746;
in 1750 owned 50 a. Bachelor's Delight; d. by 30 April 1763
when admin. bond was posted by Benjamin Buck, with John Buck and
Luke Raven; est. admin. 27 Feb. 1764; left iss.: DORCAS, m. Benjamin Buck on 10 Feb. 1763 (6:93; 15:305; 131:60, 62; 153:97).

SUTTON, JOSEPH (3), s. of Thomas (1), was b. 9 July 1724; m.
Ruth Adams on 1 May 1748; he and w. Ruth were named in the will
of Walter James; in 1750 owned 100 a. part Fell's Forest; on 13
Sept. 1762 Charles Bond conv. to him 113 a. Teague's Revenge;
admin. the est. of Henry Adams on 4 Aug. 1766; Joseph and Ruth
had iss.: SARAH, b. 28 July 1749, m. Vincent Wiley on 2 Jan.
1769; CATHERINE, b. c.1753, m. John Dunnock on 1 Dec. 1771; HENRY
ADAMS, b. c.1756; THOMAS; JOSEPH, Jr. (7:177; 86:464; 131; 133:
89; 153:97; 210-28:98).

SUTTON, ABRAHAM, m. Martha Arrowsmith on 3 July 1745 (133:
157).

SUTTON, FRANCIS, summoned John Ryan to court for breach of peace, in June 1719 (23:131).

SUTTON, JEREMIAH, m. Anne (---); on 26 Nov. 1730 he and w. Anne conv. land in Joppa to Mary Hollandsworth; had iss.: JOHN, b. 16 Aug. 1728; JOSEPH, b. 11 Dec. 1734; JEREMIAH, b. 24 June 1732 (73:36; 128:80, 84; 129:273).

SUTTON, ROBERT, m. Mary (---), and had iss.: SAMUEL, b. 18 June 1733 (128:78).

SUTTON, SAMUEL, m. Ruth Cantwell on 25 Aug. 1757, and had iss.: MARY, b. 4 Oct. 1757 (129:355).

SUTTON, SAMUEL, m. Ann Woodcock on 20 Nov. 1760 (131).

SWAN, BURCH (1), m. Margaret (---), and had iss.: SAMUEL, b. LL Jan. 1740; Muriel, b. 22 Sept. 1742, m. Henry Gooding on 15 June 1766; DOROTHY, b. 19 Aug. 1744, m. William Demmitt; BASIL, b. 31 March 1746; PENCEAS EALAH, b. 16 May 1748; AQUILA, b. 28 Jan. 1751; THOMAS BURCH, b. 7 Aug. 1753; JOSEPH, b. 24 Sept. 1756 (131:70, 132/r, 133/r).

SWAN, SAMUEL (2), s. of Burch (1) and Margaret, was b. 11 Jan. 1740, m. Eliza Demmitt on 25 Oct. 1763, and had iss.: ANN, b. 3 Aug. 1764 (131:64, 132/r, 156/r).

SWAN, EDWARD, m. Eliz. Griffith on 24 Jan. 1703/4; may have m. 2nd Frances (---), who d. 8 Dec. 1711; he d. leaving a will, 16 Dec. 1709 - 1 April 1712, naming w. Frances, tract Stepney, Aquila Hall s. of his late master John Hall, and in a codicil a servant named Elizabeth Durham; admin. bond posted 4 April 1712 by John Hall with Nicholas Haile and Thomas Stone; same day his est. was inv. by Garrett Gilbert and John Gallion and val. at £ 28.4.3, plus 15, 202 lbs. tobacco, signed by Elizabeth Durham as kin; est. admin. 3 June 1713 (1:31; 13:441; 50:357; 122:220; 128:22, 28).

SWANSON, EDWARD, m. by 22 Nov. 1675 Henrietta, wid. of William Robinson; she later m. as her 3rd husb. Thomas Cannon, and 4th (---) Reeves; d. by 1683; had iss.: ELIZABETH, who was given 100 a. Phillis' Choice by Edward Reeves on 29 July 1683, and m. by 5 Sept. 1688 John Wood (64:67; 206-1:474).

SWEENY, JAMES, in Feb. 1708 surv. 100 a. Martin's Favor (207).

SWEETING, EDWARD (1), was in Balto. Co. by 1701 as a taxable in n. side Patapsco Hund.; on 17 April 1708 he wit. the will of Thomas Eager; was left entire est. in the Dec. 1713 will of Ralph Winter, whose est. was admin. by Sweeting on 30 Dec. 1714; d. by 13 Nov. 1716 when his est. was inv. by Hinton and Henry Jones and val. at £ 18.7.3; earlier, on 8 Oct. 1716 Francis Whitehead posted admin. bond with John Thomas and George Walker; Sweeting prob. had iss.: ROBERT, alive 1731; EDWARD, alive in 1732; MARY, b. c.1707, age 11 in Nov. 1718 when she was bound to serve Sarah Spink to age 16; may be the Mary Sweeting who m. Richard Merchant on 28 July 1723 (1:19; 13:423; 48:213; 122: 110, 225; 133:146; 143).

SWEETING, ROBERT (2), poss. s. of Edward (1), m. Sarah Lane on 5 Dec. 1731; not listed in the 1750 Debt Book of Balto. Co. as owning any land; might be the Robert Sweeting of Carolina who on 25 March 1777 sold William Wilkinson 150 a. Upper Spring Neck; iss. of Robert and Sarah: EDWARD, b. 23 Oct. 1732; ELIZABETH, b. 25 Aug. 1734   (133:46, 150; 231-AL#O:288).

SWEETING, EDWARD (3), s. of Edward (1), m. Mary Watts on 21
Dec. 1732; in Nov. 1734 Mary Sweeting was ind. by the county court
for having two husbands: Edward Watts and Edward Sweeting, both
still living (Edward and Mary Watts had a s. Robert b. 24 July
1732); Edward and Mary had at least one ch.: WILLIAM, b. 8 Nov.
1736 (30:350; 133:22, 54, 150).

SWEETING, EDWARD (4), s. of Robert (2) and Sarah, was b. 23
Oct. 1732; m. Ruth Trotten on 6 June 1756, and had iss.: ELIZA,
b. 28 Feb. 1757 (133:110, 166).

SWEETING, MARY, wid., conv. Upper Spring Neck to Philip Washington and mentioned property due her by inheritance, on 24 June
1716 (this deed strengthens the supposition that Robert Sweeting
(2) was a s. of Edward (1).) (67:408).

SWEETING, REBECCA, had iss.: MARY, b. 8 July 1759 (131:25/r).

SWEETING, ROBERT, was fined for bast. in Nov. 1759 (46:241).

SWETNAM, EDWARD, was transp. to Md. by 1671, and was in Balto.
Co. by 1673 when he claimed land for service (388).

SWIFT, MARK (1), was in Balto. Co. by 1695 as a taxable in
n. side Gunpowder Hund.; in Feb. 1696 was described in the will
of Thomas Staley as having m. the latter's niece Elizabeth; in
Nov. 1698 was given p/a by John Sheffield of London; in Aug.
1699 purch, 150 a. Hathaway's Trust from William and Oliver
York; in March 1702 he and w. Elizabeth conv. 24 a. Addition to
Privilege to Abraham Taylor; d. by 22 April 1708 when admin.
bond was posted by Elizabeth Swift with Abraham Taylor, Edw. Carter, Jr., and H. Wriothesley; Elizabeth Swift d. by 13 June 1708
when Abr. Taylor posted admin. bond ; Mark Swift left iss.: MARK,
Jr.; and LYDIA, m. John Downey in March 1716 (13:436, 448; 63:
316, 388; 66:128; 69:205; 131; 140; 207).

SWIFT, MARK (2), s. of Mark (1), d. by 6 July 1723, leaving
a s.: MARK, not yet of age, made ward of Abraham Taylor (69:
205).

SWIFT, FLOWER, m. Elizabeth Whitaker on 13 May 1725, and had
iss.: THOMAS, b. 19 Jan. 1725/6; MARGARET, b. 19 Feb. 1728 (128:
45, 59).

SWIFT, LUKE, m. Lydia Thrift on 28 Oct. 1758 (131).

SWILLIVAN, OWEN, m. Ann Millener on 30 Nov. 1723; on 9 March
1726/7 Owen and w. Ann conv. 100 a. Cavan to Thomas Price; Owen
and Ann had iss.: MARY, b. 13 Dec. 1724; JOHN, b. 13 Dec. 1724
(70:315; 128:60). See also SULLIVAN.

SWINDELL, DANIEL, was in Balto. Co. by 1694 as a taxable in
n. side Patapsco Hund.; m. Elizabeth (---); he d. by 1 July 1701
when admin. bond was posted by admnx. Elizabeth Swindell with
Selah Dorman and William Wright; est. admin. by Elizabeth Swindell on 2 June 1702; on 6 Aug. 1702 Elizabeth Swindell conv. half
her est. to her granddau. Sarah Dorman; Elizabeth d. leaving a
will, 23 Feb. 1704/5 - 18 May 1705, naming s. Sealah Dorman and
dau. Judith Garmaton; admin. bond posted 18 May 1705 by Selah
Dorman with John Oldton, and Thomas Long; her est. was inv. by
Oldton and Long on 19 May 1708 and val. at £ 23.5.4; est. was
admin. Aug. 1708(?) by Dorman (2:238; 6:129; 13:426, 441; 48:111;
66:151; 110:45; 139).

SWINYARD, JOHN, m. by 8 Oct. 1712 Lucy, extx. of Francis Po-

tee; stated he was b. under the Dominions of the King of France
when he was naturalizaed in 1724; ind. for bast. in June 1731;
ind. for bast. with Sarah Harris in Aug. 1725; on 6 March 1738
sold 100 a. St. Alban's to John Stringer (1:354; 27:306; 29:
156; 75:186; 200-38:346).

SWINYARD, JOHN, m. Sarah Wilson on 30 April 1747; in 1750 he
owned 222 a. Bond's Discovery, 300 a. Swinyard's Delight, 70 a.
part Colegate's Forest, and 30 a. part Preston's Luck (131; 153:
31).

SYBELL, LODOWICK, d/ by June 1756, leaving iss.: LODOWICK,
age 10 in 1756 when he was bound to Valentine Larsch (41:3).

SYER, JOHN, was in Balto. Co. by Nov. 1754 when he was made
levy free (39:442).

SYER, SARAH, m. Benjamin Corbin on 9 Dec. 1755 (131).

SYMMONDS/SYMONDS. See SIMMONS.

SYMORE, ELIZA, bore a bast. and Richard Smithers was charged
as the father in June 172-(?) (23:550).

SYMPSON. See SIMPSON.

SYMS. See SIMMS.

SYNDALL. See SINDALL.

SYNG. See SING.

SYORDALL, SAMUEL, in 1750 owned 125 a. part Dear Bitt (153:
61).

TALBEE/TOLBY/TALBY, EDWARD (1), d. by 14 Sept. 1709 when admin. bond was posted by Mary Talbee with Moses Groom and William
Jenkinson; m. Mary (---), who d. by 4 June 1712 when admin. bond
was posted by Archibald Rollo with John Fuller and William
Hitchcock; est. was inv. by John Taylor and William Hitchcock
and val. at Ⱡ 1.1.9; dec. left one s.: SAMUEL, b. c.1709 (14:
227, 232; 50:313).

TALBEE, SAMUEL (2), s. of Edward (1) and Mary, age 3 on last
1 Nov.; in June 1712 was bound to Archibald and Rebecca Rollo to
age 21; m. Elizabeth Hitchcock on 1 Dec. 1736; in 1745 Samuel,
age c.1710, Elizabeth, b. c.1722, and their s. Zephania, age c.
3, were named in a lease; Samuel had iss.: ANN, b. 6 Oct. 1737,
m. William Huggins on 19 Dec. 1754; ASAEL, b. 10 Feb. 1739;
ZEPHANIAH, b. 29 Dec. 1741, m. Mary Wolling on 21 July 1763;
EMILIE, b. 26 Aug. 1744; SAMUEL, b. 12 Nov. 1758; ISAAC, b. 10
June 1761 (21:314; 78:217; 131).

TALBOT, EDMUND (1), progenitor, d. in Balto. Co. in June
1731; m. Mary (---); d. leaving a will, 3 Nov. 1731 - 24 Nov.
1731, naming sons Edmund, William, and John, and dau. Elizabeth
Ellinor; admin. bond was posted 26 Nov. 1731 with William and
Edmund Talbott (the wid. Mary having renounced her right to ad-
min.), with John Powell and John Roberts; est. was admin. 25
June 1733; dec. left a wid. Mary and four ch.:on 9 March 1732/3
John Taylor conv. to William Talbot tracts Bond's Gift and
Ogg King of Bashan for the lifetime of Mary Taylor, relict of
Edmund Talbot; Edmund and Mary had iss.: EDMUND; WILLIAM; JOHN;
and ELIZABETH ELLINOR, b. 30 Oct. 1721 (3:127; 30:194, 195; 73:
392; 125:200; 131).

TALBOT, EDMUND (2), s. of Edmund (1) was definitely alive in 1739; may have been the Edmund who in 1750 owned 400 a. Thomas Bond's Gift; may have been the Edmund of Harford Co. who d. leaving a will, 16 May 1794 - Dec. 1794; m. Mary (---), and had iss.: CHARLES, b. 1 Dec. 1730; RUTH, b. 16 Nov. 1733, may have m. William Oldham on 1 April 1754; THOMAS, b. 8 Dec. 1735, may have been the Thomas who m. Belinda Slade on 21 Jan. 1766; MARY, b. 28 Nov. 1737; EDMUND, b. 3 Nov. 1739 (131; 153:10; 244-AJ#R:134).

TALBOT, WILLIAM (3), s. of Edmund (1), d. in Balto. Co. in 1752; m. Mary Roberts on 30 Jan. 1723; in 1750 owned 300 a. incl. Ogg King of Bashan, Pearson's Outlet, and Wetherall's Addition; d. leaving a will, 25 Feb. 1752 - 24 April 1752, naming s. James, sons William, Edmund, and Matthew, and daus. Sarah w. of Samuel Day. Mary, and Ann; admin. bond was posted 27 April 1752 by Mary Talbot with Edmund Talbot and Samuel Day; William and Mary had iss.: JAMES, b. 20 Aug. 1731; SARAH, b. 7 July 1733, m. Samuel Day; WILLIAM, b. 10 Feb. 1735; EDMUND, b. 20 April 1738, d. 10 Dec. 1739; LUCINA, b. 17 June 1743; MATTHEW; MARY, may have m. Thomas Ensor in 1770 (14:266; 111:38; 131; 153:44).

TALBOT, CHARLES (4), s. of Edmund (2), was b. 1 Dec. 1730; may be the Charles who m. Elizabeth Young on 15 July 1754 (131).

TALBOT, JAMES (5), s. of William (3), was b. 20 Aug. 1731; on 4 Aug. 1757 conv. 50 a. part Pearson's Outlet and Wetherall's Last Addition to Samuel Day (83:45; 131).

TALBOT, CHARLES, m. Elizabeth Wood on 4 June 1713 (128:30).

TALBOT, CHARLES, of Balto. Co., d. leaving a will, 21 Nov. 1755 - 29 Dec. 1755, naming sisters Nancy and Honour, and bros. Edward and Henry; admin. bond was posted 26 Jan. 1756 with John Everett and Samuel Day; est. admin. 25 May 1757 by Edmund Talbot (5:331; 14:249; ; 111:232).

TALBOT, EDMUND, M. Darcas Hall on 26 Oct. 1749; had iss.: BENJAMIN, b. 18 Aug. 1753 (133:95, 165).

TALBOT, EDMUND, m. Rebecca Robinson on 18 June 1752; had iss.: BENJAMIN ROBINSON, b. 1 Oct. 1754; SUSANNA, b. 3 Sept. 1756 (133:97, 165).

TALBOT, EDWARD, d. by 2 Sept. 1721 when admin. bond was posted by James Powell with John Gardner and Henry Ridgely (14:241).

TALBOT, EDWARD, having been married in a church was excluded from Gunpowder Meeting, 5 d, June 1745 (136).

TALBOT, JOHN, m. by Jan. 1726/7 dau. of Col. Richard Colegate (1:322).

TALBOT, WILLIAM, was in Balto. Co. by 1692 as a tacable in n. side Patapsco Hund.; d. by 16 Nov. 1713; m. Catherine, dau. of George Ogg, Sr; she m. 2nd John Risteau; on 11 June 1700 surv. 300 a. Credentia; in Nov. 1708 gave bond he would be responsible for the raising of Mary Freeland's bast., and in March 1709/10 paid the fine of Mary Oliff who had been found guilty of bast.; was elected to represent Balto. Co. in the Lower House of the Maryland Assembly in 1712-1714, was reelected to the 2nd session which he attended until he became "very sick;" d. leaving a will, 8 Nov. 1713 - 16 Nov. 1713, naming his w., bro.-in-law George Ogg, Jr., dau. Margaret, and the children of his bro. Thomas in Lancashire, Eng.; admin. bond was posted 10 May 1714 by execs. Edward Stevenson and George Ogg; est was val. at Ł 199.15.1; est.

was admin. by George Ogg on 5 July 1717, 31 Aug. 1719, and 20
Feb. 1721; dec. left iss.: MARGARET, m. Benjamin Hammond (1:50,
193; 2:20; 14:229; 21:17; 61:377; 110:108; 122:180; 138; 207;
371:798).

TANNER, MARTHA, servant to Richard Deaver, was tried for bast.
in June 1746, having been ind. in March 1745/6 (35:800; 36:6).

TANSEY, ALEXANDER, m. Rebecca (---), and had iss.: REBECCA,
bapt. 12 July 1702 (128:14).

TANSEY, ALEXANDER, m. Katherine (---); granted a cert. to
Monacacy   Meeting on 24 March 1741/2; had iss.: ANN, b. 18
Jan. 1729; MARY, b. 25 Jan. 1731; ABRAHAM, b. 18 Jan. 1733/4
(133:32, 33; 136).

TAPLEY, CHRISTOPHER, boatwright, was in Balto. Co.by Nov.
1665 when he and Francis Elling bought 100 a. at Leigh Neck
from James Phillips; d. leaving a will proved Oct. 1682, naming
w. Jane and ch.: EDWARD; SAMUEL; and JOAN (95; Balto. Co. Orig.
Wills, Box 1, folder 30).

TARKINTON, JOHN, was in Balto. Co. by 28 Feb. 1669/70 when
Samuel Collett conv. him 250 a. Woodland Neck; on 3 Aug. 1674
he and w. Prudence conv. that and other tracts to William Palmer (96:229; 100:118).

TASKER, BENJAMIN, in 1750 owned 200 a. part Parker's Palace,
100 a. White Hall, and 200 a. Crawley's Contrivance (153:103).

TAYLARD, JOHN, was in Balto. Co. by March 1667/8 when John
Collett conv. to him 200 a. Beaver Neck; on 11 Nov. 1670 he conv.
the land to John Mascord, and his w. Sarah gave power of atty.
to James Ives to ackn. sale of the land (61:62, 99).

THE ABRAHAM TAYLOR FAMILY

TAYLOR, ABRAHAM (1), was in Balto. Co. by 1695 as a taxable
in s. side Gunpowder Hund.; d. in Balto. Co. on 10 July 1719;
m. Jane (---) who on 9 June 1699 joined him in posting admin.
bond on the est. of John Armstrong, with Thomas Preston and
Thomas Staley; may be the Abraham Taylor who conv. 50 a. Privilege to his s.-in-law John Courkin on 9 Dec. 1701; d. leaving a
will made 1717, proved 6 Aug. 1719, leaving Ayres' Addition to
s. John, and naming s. Abraham and dau. Lettice Doddridge; admin.
bond was posted 11 Aug. 1719 by John Taylor with Francis Dallahide and Matthew Hale; est. admin. on 10 May 1721, 1 Aug. 1721,
and 4 Nov. 1729; Jane, or Jean, Taylor, poss. the widow m. Benjamin Lego on 4 Nov. or 11 Dec. 1723; Abraham had iss.: JOHN;
ABRAHAM; and LETTICE, m. William Doddridge (1:226, 285, 305; 11:
29; 14:223; 66:114, 128; 123:213; 131; 140).

TAYLOR, JOHN (2), s. of Abraham (1), was alive in 1758; prob.
the John Taylor who m. 1st Judith (---) who d. Jan. 1723, and
2nd in April 1726 Rachel, wid. of James York; John Taylor admin.
the est. of James York; on 7 March 1732 Taylor, the devisee of
Abraham Taylor conv. 100 a. Ayres' Addition to Mary Tolley, extx.
of Thomas Tolley; Taylor had two ch. by Judith and two by Rachel:
REBECCA, b. and d. Aug. 1719; ABRAHAM, b. Aug. 1720; JOHN, b.
19 Aug. 1727; HENRY, b. and d. March 1729 (2:324; 75:351; 131).

TAYLOR, ABRAHAM (3), s. of Abraham (1), m. Dinah White (date
not given); in 1728 Abraham and Dinah conv. 100 a. of land to
William Barney; Abraham and Dinah had iss.: ROBERT, b. 13 Oct.
1709; ANN, b. 29 March 1712; JACOB, b. 5 or 6 Oct. 1714; RACHEL,

b. 9 Oct. 1717; JOSEPH, b. 19 or 20 Aug. 1720; ABRAHAM, b. 20
Oct. 1723; ISAAC, b. 25 Nov. 1725 (71:100; 131).

TAYLOR, JOHN (4), s. of John (2) and Rachel, was b. 19 Jan.
1702; may be the John Taylor who m. Sarah Ward on 15 June
1742, by whom he had: JOSEPH, b. 6 Oct. 1744; JOHN, b. 22 June
1747; ELIZABETH, b. 13 Oct. 1758 (131).

LINE OF FRANCIS TAYLOR

TAYLOR, FRANCIS (5), no known rel. to any of the above, was
b. in Yorkshire, m. Mary Brian, and had iss.: FRANCIS, d. 6 Ap-
ril 1762 at Fort St. George in the E. Indies; FREEMAN, d. 11
June 1766 in London; EVERARD, b. 1708; and BRIAN, d. in Balto.
Co. (Md. Gen. Records Committee, vol. 1, p. 95, typescript at
NSDAR Library in Washington, D.C.).

TAYLOR, EVERARD (6), s. of Francis (5), was b. 1708, and d.
27 Sept. 1747 in Calvert Co., having m. Sarah Johnson; in 1736
he renounced right to admin. the est. of Brian Taylor and asked
that letters of admin. be granted to Richard Caswell; on 17 Aug.
1743 Everard conv. part Wolf Harbor and part Howard's Addition
to Stephen Onion; Everard and w. Sarah had iss.: BRIAN, b. 11
May 1742, d. 1793, m. Mary Dawkins; MARY, b. 1 Jan. 1744; SARAH,
b. 22 March 1746 (11:275; 77:318; Md. Gen. Records Committee,
1:95, cited above).

TAYLOR, BRIAN (7), s. of Francis (5), d. in Balto. Co. leaving a will proved 4 Dec. 1736, mentioning a will written in
Eng., naming bro. Everard, cousin Elizabeth Smith, Cousin Margaret Rogers, and serv. William Patridge, who was to go to Eng.
adn who was to have his freedom; admin. bond was posted 10 Dec.
1736 by Richard Caswell (Brian's bro. Everard having ren.);
as he was a bachelor formerly of St. Stephen's, Coleman St.,
London, admin. was granted in Eng., to May 1737 to his bro.
Freeman Taylor, his mother Mary Taylor, wid., having ren. and
the exec. Philip Smith having died (4:7, 38; 14:198; 126:196;
299).

THE JOHN TAYLOR FAMILY

TAYLOR, JOHN (8), progenitor, no known rel. to any of the
above, was in Balto. Co. by c.1659; d. c.1675 leaving a nuncupative will; m. Margaret (---); on 28 July 1661 surv. 100 a. known
as Taylor's Mount; on 15 March 1669/70 he and Arthur Taylor conv.
to Arthur Scott 300 a. Taylor's Choice; left a will, 5 April
1676 - 16 May 1676, naming sons Arthur, James, and Robert, and
dau. Eliza, as well as two grandchildren by Richard Sims, and
one by Richard Winley; est. admin. 1677; had iss.: ARTHUR,
ROBERT (not living in 1677; could he be the Robert Taylor who
conv. 100 a. Taylor's Delight to Joseph Piercey, carpenter);
JAMES; MARY, m. Richard Winley, and poss. 2nd Richard Sims;
ELIZABETH, stated by Marye to have m. Richard Sims, but she was
under age in 1677 (96; 99:345; 120:170; 206-4:336; 211; 388).

TAYLOR, ARTHUR (9), s. of John (8), was b. by 1659 when he
was brought into the Province by his father; m. 1st Margaret
(---) who d. by 7 Jan. 1678/9; m. 2nd Frances, wid. of (---)
Smithers; surv. 100 a. Fall Hill on 22 Aug. 1669, and 300 a.
Arthur's Choice on 20 Aug. 1683; with w. Margaret sold Fall
Hill and one-half of Taylor's Mount ("which John Taylor had
bought from Benjamin Reid"); bought 150 a. at Foster's Neck from
James and Martha Ives; on 7 Jan. 1678/9 with w. Frances sold
315 a. Spring Neck to Thomas Cooke; in Dec. 1681 Arthur and w.
Frances sold 25 a. George's Hill to Thomas Preston; in March

1683/4 he and Frances conv. 150 a. out of 300 a. taken up by Arthur, to James Smithers, s. of said w. Frances; Arthur had at least two ch.: JOHN, b. c.1671; ANNE, m. 1st James Greer, and 2nd Lawrence Richardson (96:230; 101:302; 102; 103; 106:28; 211; William B. Marye, article on Taylor Family of Taylor's Mount, in Hayes' Maryland Genealogical Bulletin, 9:16-19, and 12:7-9).

TAYLOR, JOHN (10), s. of Arthur (9) and prob. Margaret, was b. c.1671, giving his age as 21 in 1692; m. 1st, Jane (---), and wnd, by June 1711, Elizabeth, extx. of William Peckett; on 2 Aug. 1703 he and w. Jane conv. s. Spring Neck to Thomas Nevill; other deeds incl. sale on 5 June 1695 by John Taylor, s. of Arthur, of 200 a. Winley's Rest to John Fuller, and sale on 12 June 1701 of one-half of Samuel's Delight to Michael Judd, Jr.; John Taylor was mentioned in a deposition made by his nephew John Greer in 1732 as having been Deputy Surveyor; John and his w. had iss.: ARTHUR, d. Nov. 1728 at Edward Day's, and AVARILLA, m. 1st Edward Day, and 2nd, Patrick Lynch (1:9; 19:185; 21:213, 216; 59:461; 66:108, 223; 131; 340:118; Marye article).

THE JOHN AND KEZIAH (SIMMONS) TAYLOR FAMILY

TAYLOR, JOHN (11), no known rel. to any of the above, m. Keziah, dau. of Charles and Hannah (---) Simmons or Symonds; on 4 March 1741 Taylor was conv. 180 a. part Clarkson's Purchase by George, John, and Thomas Symonds, three of the sons and devisees of Charles Symonds, dec. (Hannah relict of Charles, for love and affection for her son-in-law, released her right of dower); om 9 Oct. 1742 Charles Symonds, another s. and devisee of said Charles, conv. part of Clarkson's Purchase to Taylor; John Taylore d. leaving a will, 19 March 1745 - 20 April 1745, naming s. Charles (to have part of Clarkson's Purchase where his uncle George Simmons lived), s. John (to have another part of same tract), s. Thomas (to have tract Taylor's Good Luck and land bought from William Deal, daus. Elizabeth and Hannah; admin. bond was posted 5 June 1745 by extx. Kezia Taylor with Richard Roberson and Wm. Dallam; est. admin. by Keziah Taylor on 10 May 1746, and by Keziah now w. of Joshua Hardesty on 2 Jan. 1747, 30 Dec. 1749, and 8 DEc. 1750; John and Keziah had iss.: CHARLES, b. 4 Feb. 1730; HANNAH, b. 19 Jan. 1733/4; JOHN, b. 24 Sept. 1736; THOMAS, b. 30 April 1739; and ELIZABETH (4:141, 176; 5:89, 100; 14:286; 76:105; 77:178; 111:211; 131).

TAYLOR, CHARLES (12), s. of John (11) and Keziah, was b. 4 Feb. 1730; m. Elizabeth Standiford on 25 Dec. 1750; on 20 June 1752 conv. to Joshua Hardesty all that 63 a. of Clarkson's Purchase, and 32 a. Timber Swamp; Charles' w. Elizabeth consented; had iss.: ANN, b. 3 Oct. 1752; JOHN, b. Oct. 1754; JAMES, b. 17 Feb. 1756; and JOSEPH, b. July 1758 (81:366; 131).

TAYLOR, THOMAS (13), s. of John (11) and Keziah, was b. 30 April 1739; may be the Thomas Taylor who d. by 29 March 1762 when admin. bond was posted by Charles Taylor with Edw. Robertson (14:275; 131).

THE LAWRENCE TAYLOR FAMILY

TAYLOR, LAWRENCE (14), no known rel. to any of the above, was in Balto. Co. by 1692 as a taxable in Spesutia Hund.; was bur. 23 July 1699 having m. Dorothy (---) who m. 2nd, on 27 Sept. 1700, Owen Sullivan; Lawrence Taylor surv. God Speed on 21 Sept. 1685 and in 1696 was on the vestry of St. George's Parish; left a will, 19 July 1699 - 25 Nov. 1701, naming w. Dorothy and s.: LAWRENCE (121:233; 138).

TAYLOR, LAWRENCE (15), s. of Lawrence (14) and Dorothy, d. in St. George's Parish on 11 Nov. 1727; m. 1st Mary Miles on 5 Feb. 1699/1700; and 2nd, on 7 Feb. 1703/4 Agnes Montague; d. leaving a will, 6 Nov. 1727 - 5 March 1727/8, leaving 200 a. God Speed to his sons James and Abraham, and also naming dau. Sarah; admin. bond on his est. was posted 6 March 1727 by extx. Agnes Taylor with Richard Deaver and Adam Burchfield; wid. Agnes m. 2nd Henry Moore (q.v.); est. of Lawrence Taylor was inv. on 22 May 1728 by Bennett Garrett and John Clark, and val. at E 112.10.5; Lawrence and Agnes had iss.: MARY, b. 1 Feb. 1706, bur. 19 June 1708;LAWRENCE, b. and d. in June (---); JAMES, b. 11 Jan. 1713; SARAH, b. 3 June 1719; and ABRAHAM (14:214; 51:76; 128:18, 19, 24, 29, 33, 39, 57; 129:190, 202, 207).

TAYLOR, JAMES (16), s. of Lawrence (15) and Agnes, was b. 11 Jan. 1713, and m. 1st, on 26 Nov. 1731, Mary Foster; she d. 13 July 1744 and he m. 2nd, on 9 May 1747, Sarah, dau. of Rowland Kimball; James and Sarah had signed an antenuptial contract on 4 May 1747; on 19 Oct. 1734 James and Mary Taylor sold Rowland Kimball 300 a. Jackson's Outlet; on 15 July 1738 James and Mary bound her s. Moses Thomas, age 13, s. of John Thomas, to William Daugherty to age 18; in 1750 James owned 90 a. Crabtree's Rest 70 a. part Jackson's Outlet, and part Goodspeed; James had five ch. by 1st w., and 9 by his 2nd: LAWRENCE, b. 1 Feb. 1731, d. 15 June 1735; LURENE, b. 17 Feb. 1733; JAMES, b. 2 July 1736; AGNES MOUNTAGUE, b. 20 April 1738, m. Richard Monk; MARY, b. 30 March 174-(?), m. Robert Elder; STEPHEN, b. 27 July 1748; ABRAHAM, b. 9 Jan. 1749; ROBERT, b. 16 Aug. 1751; HENRIETTA, b. 28 Jan. 1753, m. (---) Miers; ASA, b. 11 Sept. 1754; AMASA, b. 27 May 1756; JEREMIAH, b. 4 March 1758; SARAH, b. 7 Dec. 1759; LAAMA, b. 5 Nov. 1761; and JESSE (31:230; 74:155; 79:380; 111:45; 128:64, 78, 87, 95; 129:290, 322, 357. 359; 153:23).

TAYLOR, ABRAHAM (17), s. of Lawrence (15), d. in Balto. Co. on 1 May 1755; m. Hannah (---) who m. as her 2nd husb. (---) Munday; on 23 Feb. 1748 Joshua Wood, s. of Joshua conv. 250 a. Benjamin's Choice, 100 a. Wood's Choice, and 50 a. Hobson's Choice, to Abraham Taylor; in 1750 he owned 67 a. part Goodspeed, 169 a. part Benjamin's Choice, 68 a. part Wood's Choice, and 34 a. Hobson's Choice; will of Abraham Taylor made 13 April 1753. proved 31 May 1755, naming ch.: Michael, Thomas, Aquila, Frances, and Sarah, as well as w. Hannah; admin. bond posted 28 June 1755 by extx. Hannah Taylor, with James Taylor and Amos Garrett; will of Hannah Munday, 9 Aug. 1757 - 26 Oct. 1757, named former husb. Abraham Taylor and her ch.; Abraham had iss.: MICHAEL, b. 17 Sept. 1738; THOMAS, b. 23 Jan. 1740; LAWRENCE, b. 9 Feb. 1742; AQUILA, d. under age; FRANCES, alive 14 Feb. 1764; SARAH, d. by 14 Feb. 1764 (5:311; 14:210; 80:157; 83:7; 110:489; 128:101, 114; 129:329, 357; 153:13).

TAYLOR, MICHAEL (18), s. of Abraham (17), was b. 17 Sept. 1738 and was alive in 1762; m. Mary Mitchell on 24 May 1759; prob. not the Michael who in 1750 owned 342 a. part Bin; on 15 Jan. 1760 Michael sold 100 a. Goodspeed, formerly owned by Abraham Taylor to Rev. Andrew Lendrum; in the deed Michael stated that he believed he was born before 14 Nov. 1738; in March 1760 he and w. Mary sold 216 a. Combine's Choice to Garrett Garrettson; in this deed Taylor stated he was the eldest s. of Abraham Taylor who left 66 a. of the land to him, 150 a. to s. Thomas, and 66 a. to s. Aquila, who had since died under age, leaving his share to Michael; Michael and Mary had iss.: ELIZABETH, b. 27 March 1761; and AQUILA, b. 15 Aug. 1762 (84:71; 129:370; 153:94).

TAYLOR, THOMAS (19), s. of Abraham (17), in March 1757 chose Henry Munday as his guardian; prob. the Thomas who m. Jane Hamby

on 4 June 1758; on 9 Feb. 1762 Thomas and Jane conv. to Jacob
Giles 150 a. Come By Chance, and 59 a. of same tract to Freeborn
Garrettson; had iss.: HANNAH, b. 19 Sept. 1759; MARY, b. 29 March
1761; ABRAHAM, b. 5 April 1763 (44; 85:500, 508; 129:370, 386).

THE RICHARD TAYLOR FAMILY

TAYLOR, RICHARD (20), no known rel. to any of the above, was
b. c.1667; d. by 18 May 1729; m. Ann Trasey on 7 d., 6, 1687; on
5 Sept. 1699 Richard and Ann, then living in P. G. Co., sold 600
a. called Denton to William Bladen; in Dec. 1713 Richard purch.
Friendship, part of Darley Hall, from John Ensor; in March 1713
he purch. 464 a. Roberts Choice from John Roberts; d. leaving a
will, 1726 - 18 May 1729, naming dau. Frances (to have 275 a.
Taylor's Discovery), s. Thomas (to have 300 a. Taylor's String,
125 a. Addition to Taylor's String, and 80 a. Taylor's Discovery),
s. Joseph (to have 860 a. Taylor's Range, and 99 a. Addition to
Shoemaker's Hall), s. Richard (to have shillings), and granddau.
Margaret Sing (to have 150 a. Taylor's Discovery) w. Ann; the
1 acre bought of John Ensor was left to s. Joseph to be used as
a meeting house and burial place for the people called Friends;
Richard and Ann had iss.: RICHARD, b. c.1688; EDWARD (may be the
Edward who m. by Aug. 1750 Ann, admnx. of John Hankey); SAMUEL:
THOMAS, b. c.1704; JOSEPH, b. c.1705; JOHN; FRANCES, m. (---)
Simms; KATHERINE, m. (---) Daughaday; dau., m. (---) Floyd, and
poss. another dau. m. (---) Daughaday (37:245; 66:236, 277, 496;
125:130; Reg. of West River Meeting, Soc. of Friends in 219-6).

TAYLOR, RICHARD (21), s. of Richard (20), was b. c.1688, and
was alive in 1739 when he gave his age as 51; m. by 16 April
1723 Mary (---) when he was in Stafford Co., Va., and sold Stone's
Delight; on 8 Sept. 1739 he was in Goochland Co., Va., when he
gave his age as 51, and stated that his father Richard was dec.
(69:400; 75:279).

TAYLOR, THOMAS (22), s. of Richard (20), was b. c.1704, and
d. 20 April 1788; m. Sarah Price, b. April 1705, dau. of Mordecai
and Mary (Parsons) Price; on 5 Nov. 1736 purch. 390 a. Friend's
Discovery from Nathaniel and John Giles; on 14 June 1737 Thomas
Taylor and w. Sarah conv. 400 a. Bachelor's Fancy, being part of
Friend's Discovery, to Henry Morgan; in June 1738 purch. 150 a.
Land In Kind from Benjamin and Elizabeth Price; in March 1744
Thomas sold 80 a. Taylor's Discovery and 50 a. Smallwood to Nicho-
las Haile; in Feb. 1749 Thomas Taylor and s. John (now living
in Penna.) sold 125 a. Addition to Taylor's String; Thomas and
Sarah had iss.: RACHEL, m. Solomon Wheeler; JEMIMA, m. Samuel
Meredith on 2 Feb. 1748; JOSEPH NEAL, d. 1762 unm.; JOHN, m.
Susanna (---), and by 1749 was living in Penna.; RICHARD, b. in
1738; MARY, m. Moses Lawson; SAMUEL, b. 1740; SARAH, m. John Head
(61:424; 75:20, 95, 570; 78:63, 246, 286; 79:445; 80:374; Carroll
Taylor Sinclair, "The Taylor Family of Maryland," 6 vols., typescript, at MHS).

TAYLOR, JOSEPH (23), s. of Richard (21), was b. c.1705, and
d. by March 1789; in 1740 purch. part The Forest from Benjamin
Long; in 1750 he owned 888 a. Continuance, 70 a. Addition to Taylor's Range, 150 a. Addition to Shoemaker's Hall, 1 a. Friendship,
139 a. The Forest, and 200 a. Bought Dear; d. leaving a will,
19 April 1788 - 9 March 1789, naming his cousins (i.e., nephews),
Richard and Samuel the sons of Thomas Taylor, Joseph Daughaday,
cousins Joseph, Abraham, John, and Thomas Daughaday, sons of
Catherine, cousins John and Joseph Floyd, John Taylor of Sarah,
cousins Richard Daughaday, Jemima Meredith, Mary Lawson; nephew
Samuel Taylor (now dec.) and his ch.: Joseph, Samuel, Isaac,
Jacob, Elijah, Richard, Mary, Sarah, Hannah, and Ann Taylor (79:
4;0; 113:346, 347; 153:44).

TAYLOR, (---), m. by 12 April 1714, Elizabeth, wid. of Edward Welch (1:1).

TAYLOR, (---), d. by 1744; m. Margaret, dau. of Ulick Burke; she m. 2nd, on 11 Oct. 1744 Thomas Miles, Jr. (q.v.).

TAYLOR, AQUILA, d. Sept. 1757 (129:357).

TAYLOR, BENJAMIN, m. Ann Hawkins on 24 June 1737 and had iss.: JOHN, b. 16 April 1738 (128:97, 100).

TAYLOR, BENJAMIN, in 1750 owned 50 a. Narrow Bottom (153:92).

TAYLOR, BRAYPLATT, in Feb. 1709 surv. 50½ a. Sampson's Favor; he conv. that tract to Thomas Sligh in April 1739; had iss.: JOHN, b. c.1745; in Aug. 1755 was bound to Salathiel Galloway (40:220; 75:213; 207).

TAYLOR, COMFORT, m. Samuel Harryman on 3 June 1728 (133:149).

TAYLOR, EDWARD, m. by Aug. 1750 Ann, admnx. of John Hankey (37:245).

TAYLOR, ELIZABETH, m. Robert Chapman on 30 June 1736 (131).

TAYLOR, FRANCES, was ind. for bast. in June 1731 (29:155).

TAYLOR, FRANCIS, m. Elizabeth Whitaker on 6 Oct. 1729; on 6 May 1732 he and w. Elizabeth admin. the est. of Mark Whitaker; on 24 Nov. 1735 he and Elizabeth conv. part Elburton; on 23 July 1746 he and w. Elizabeth conv. 50 a. Taylor's Delight to John Risteau; had iss.: GRACE, b. 5 Aug. 1730; RACHEL, b. 16 Nov. 1732 (3:117; 74:339; 79:131; 128:62, 76).

TAYLOR, GEORGE, m. Ann (---) and had iss.: ROBERT, b. 15 Oct. 1740 (129:313).

TAYLOR, HENRY, m. Sarah Armstrong on 3 Oct. 1745; had iss.: RACHEL, b. 3 Dec. 1745 (131:28, 114/r).

TAYLOR, JAMES, in Nov. 1756 was fined for fathering a child on the body of Sarah Pike (41:313).

TAYLOR, JANE, m. Rowland Shepherd on 22 June 1727 (129:244).

TAYLOR, JANE, m. Robert Ellsom on 15 Dec. 1735 (133).

TAYLOR, JEMIMA, m. Samuel Meredith on 2 Feb. 1748 (133).

TAYLOR, JOHN, purch. 150 a. Discovery from James and Anne Thompson on 29 Feb. 1691/2 (59:341).

TAYLOR, JOHN, was in Balto. Co. by 1692 as a taxable in n. side Gunpowder; another John was a taxable in s. side Gunpowder (138).

TAYLOR, JOHN, on 7 Jan. 1694 purch. 53½ a. George's Hill from Samuel and Sarah Sickelmore; on 27 Jan. 1694 he conv. this land to John Evins of Balto. Co., boatwright (59:447, 450).

TAYLOR, JOHN, surv. 15 a. Weepit in April 1704 (207).

TAYLOR, JOHN, d. by 28 July 1705 when admin. bond was posted by Samuel Taylor of Back River, admin., with John Harryman and William Wilkinson; est. was inv. on 4 Sept. 1705 by Thomas Smith and Robuck Lynch and val. at ₤ 26.1.0 (14:226; 48:60).

TAYLOR, JOHN, d. by 4 Oct. 1714; Susanna Taylor, age c.30, deposed she heard him leave prop. to Tabitha Stansbury, and gave
instructions to his bro. Samuel Taylor (67:322).

TAYLOR, JOHN, in Aug. 1725 was ind. for incontinency with Mary
Gilbert (27:306).

TAYLOR, JOHN, about 1730 purch. 100 a. Better Hopes from Joseph and Elizabeth Elledge (73:59).

TAYLOR, JOHN, m. Anne (---), and had iss.: SARAH, b. 10 May
1730 (131:90/r).

TAYLOR, JOHN, purch. Jack's Peacock from Thomas Jack and w.
Mary (70:7).

TAYLOR, JOHN, m. by 9 March 1732/3 Mary, relict of Edward
Talbot (actually Edmund Talbot); on that date they conv. to William Talbot 200 a. Bond's Gift and Ogg, King of Bashan (73:392).

TAYLOR, JOHN, m. Margaret (---), and had iss.: ELIZABETH, b.
20 July 1740 (133).

TAYLOR, JOHN, d. by 18 May 1741 when admin. bond was posted
by Peter Johnson with Alexander McComas; est. was admin. by Johnson on 12 March 1742 (3:257; 14:281).

TAYLOR, JOHN, d. by 1750 when his heirs owned 500 a. Belt's
Park (153:103).

TAYLOR, JOHN, in 1750 owned 200 a. Roper's Increase and 50 a.
Howard's Addition (153:96).

TAYLOR, JOHN, m. Elizabeth Norris on 18 Oct. 1757; had iss.:
SUSANNA, b. 23 March 1758; JOHN, b. 4 Oct. 1759 (131:50, 141/r,
143/r).

TAYLOR, MARGARET, m. John Macklane on 14 Jan. 1733 (133).

TAYLOR, MARGARET, d. 4 May 1737 (131:68/r).

TAYLOR, MARTIN, was in Balto. Co. by 1692 as a taxable in n.
side Patapsco Hund.; m. Sarah (---) who m. 2nd Robert Robertson;
on 25 Aug. 1698 purch. 86 a. part Wittly from Thomas Preston;
on 21 May 1711 as landlord of John Mark was made exec. of the
latter's will; d. on Good Friday, 7 April 1721; admin. bond was
posted 7 June 1721 by admnx. Sarah Taylor, with Isaac Butterworth and John Somner; est. admin. on 2 July 1723 by Robert
Robertson and w. Sarah; will of Sarah Robertson, 17 Dec. 1748 - 8
March 1748/9, naming daus. Jane, Mary, and Clemency Bond, and
granddau. Mary Bond; Martin and Sarah had iss.: CLEMENCY, b. 14
April 1714, m. Benjamin Bond on 28 May 1737; MARY, b. 9 Oct. 1716;
JANE, m. by 4 Nov. 1742 Jonathan Hughes (1:110; 11:450; 14:211;
63:286; 77:164; 123:202; 131; 138).

TAYLOR, MARY, d. by 13 Sept. 1709 when admin. bond was posted
by Abraham Taylor with Daniel Mackentosh and John Bayly (14:233).

TAYLOR, MICHAEL, b. c.1701, m. by 1st, by Nov. 1722 wid. Ann
Bale; she d. 7 May 1726, and he m. 2nd Margaret (---); in May
1736 Johanna Hall pet. on behalf of her s. Richard Kemp, John
Kemp, pet. that Ann Taylor, late of Balto. Co., dec., late w. of
Michael Taylor held several tracts which she devised to the peti-
tioners; they accused Taylor, who had moved to P. G. Co., of pre-
tending that his w. had made another will; in May 1727 Michael
Taylor refused to serve as churchwarden of St. George's Par.,

was fined 1000 lbs. tobacco; had iss.: (by 1st w.): dau., b. 20
Aug. 1725; (by 2nd w.): THOMAS, b. 27 May 1728 (25:195; 128:52;
130; 209-30:135).

TAYLOR, MICHAEL, in 1750 owned 342 a. part Bin (153:94).

TAYLOR, ROBERT, in Sept. 1672 conv. 100 a. Taylor's Delight
to Joseph Piercey (99).

TAYLOR, ROBERT, was in Balto. Co. by 1692 as a taxable in n.
side Patapsco (138).

TAYLOR, ROBERT, m. Jane (---), and had iss.: ANN, b. 21 Nov.
1741 (129:325).

TAYLOR, SAMUEL, d. by 28 Jan. 1714/5 when admin. bond was
posted by Thomas Knighton with Thomas Cannon and John Fitzredmond; est. was admin. by the two securities and by John Leakings
and was inv. on 25 Sept. 1716 by Knighton and val. at Ŀ 19.8.3
(1:197; 14:237; 50:213).

TAYLOR, SARAH, in Nov. 1757 named John Daugherty as the father
of her child; fined for bast. in Nov. 1758 (46:75, 161).

TAYLOR, THOMAS, of A. A. Co., in Dec. 1688 conv. to Anthony
Demondidier 300 a. Timber Neck (105).

TAYLOR, THOMAS, conv. 100 a. Taylor's Palace (now called Bosley's Palace) to Walter Bosley on 1 April 1712 (67:183).

TAYLOR, THOMAS, m. by June 1714 Elizabeth, extx. of Edward
Welch; d. by 8 Aug. 1722 when admin. bond was posted by admnx.
Elizabeth Taylor, with Thomas Sheredine and Christopher Shaw;
est. was inv. in 1722 (14:212; 21:513; 52:47).

TAYLOR, THOMAS, on 14 Oct. 1715 purch. 50 a. Cold Comfort
from Margaret Gray, wid. of George Gray of Calvert Co. (67:357).

TAYLOR, THOMAS, on 14 Jan. 1717 conv. 120 a. Turkey Cock Hall
to Samuel Merryman; his w. Elizabeth consented; on 19 May 1724
he and w. Elizabeth conv. 50 a. Cold Comfort, 100 a, Rich Level,
and 100 a. Fox Hall to Philip Smith (63:430; 69:318).

TAYLOR, THOMAS, gave his age as 54 in 1733 (163:174).

TAYLOR, THOMAS, native of Md., broke out of Balto. Co. jail,
some time before 23 Oct. 1746 (384:586).

TAYLOR, THOMAS, of Fairfax Meeting, and of Frederick Co., Md.,
m. 28 Feb. 1750 at Elk Ridge, Caleb Pierpoint, dau. of Charles
and Sydney Pierpoint (136).

TAYLOR, WILLIAM, was in Balto. Co. by 1694 as a taxable on n.
side of Patapsco; bur. 27 Nov. 1707 (129:207; 139).

TAYLOR, WILLIAM, barber, was ordered to serve three mos.,
without freedom dues, listed in the 1741/2 inv. of Richard Gist
(53:169).

TAYMAN, BENJAMIN, m. Sarah wid. of (---) Hanson; d. in Balto.
Co. leaving a will, 6 June 1731 - 2 Nov. 1731, which named
'Quiller" and William, sons of Phyllis Cammel, John Tayman,
Elizabeth Davis, and Phyllis Cammell was named extx.; she d.
and on 3 Nov. 1731 admin. bond was posted by his widow Sarah
Tayman with Robert Robinson and Jacob Hanson; Sarah Tayman, age

65 in 1736; she admin. the est. of Benjamin Tayman in 1736 and
1737; she d. leaving a will, 14 Feb. 1739 - 9 Nov. 1745, naming
grandch. Jacob Hanson, Sybil Hanson, Sarah Mariarte, Benjamin
Hanson, Hollis Hanson and Avarilla Hanson, Thomas and Jacob Hanson, dau.-in-law Sarah Hanson, son Jacob Hanson and the ch. he
begat of his first w. Rebecca, also Christopher Redman and James
Osborne; admin. bond was posted 18 Nov. 1746 by Jacob Hanson with
Hudson Davidge and James Osborn; her est. was admin. 30 Sept. 1749
and 11 Oct. 1751 by Jacob Hanson, who named as her heirs the w.
of Patrick Brannon, Thomas Hanson, Avarilla Hanson and Sarah Mariarte (3:221; 5:65, 192; 14:204; 287; 31:53; 110:284; 111:217;
125:100).

TAYMAN, SABRET, m. Jemima Hitchcock on 16 Jan. 1742/3 (131).

TAYMAN, WILLIAM, m. Ann Nearn on 25 Dec. 1750; had iss.: ELIZA-
BETH, b. 19 Feb. 1747; BENJAMIN, b. 14 March 1750; JEMIMA, b. 13
March 1753 (131).

TAYMAN, WILLIAM CAMMELL, m. Ann Williams on 25 Dec. 1750 (131).

TEAGUE, (---), d. by 19 April 1704 when his wid. Susan m.
Emanuel Smith, and had iss.: WILLIAM; CATHERINE; ANNE (122:37).

TEAL, EDWARD (1), d. by Dec. 1693 when his wid. Sarah was conv.
1 mare colt by Thomas Corne; admin. bond was posted 24 May 1694
by the wid. Sarah Teal with Philip Roper; his est. was inv. on
24 May 1694 by Philip Roper and William Slade, and val. at
£ 7.15.0; on 14 March 1698/9 Sarah Teal, wid., purch. 150 a. of
Phillips' or Roper's Rest from Philip Roper; on 30 March 1699
John Copus conv. 100 a. Roper's Rest to his dau.-in-law Ales
Teale; his w. Sarah Copus is mentioned in the deed, but she
signed the deed as Sarah Teal; Edward and Sarah had iss.: def.
ALICE; poss. EDWARD; poss. JOHN; poss. WILLIAM (14:235; 51:24;
61:225; 63:343, 538).

TEAL, EDWARD (2), poss. s. of Edward (1), d. in Balto. Co.
by 14 Jan. 1720/1, having m. by Nov. 1711 Hannah, wid. and admnx.
of Nathaniel Stinchcomb, and dau. of Christopher and Johanna
Randall; Edward Teal and _w._ signed the inv. of Capt. Nathaniel
Stinchcomb; on 1 April 1710 Edward Teal gave bond for the faithful execution of duties as Chief Ranger of Balto. Co.; he d. leaving a will, 5 May 1720 - 14 Jan. 1720/1, naming his ch. Emanuel
and Ruth, son-in-law (i.e., stepson) John Stinchcomb; his est.
was inv. on 27 Jan. 1720/1 by Benjamin and John Howard and filed
11 March 1720/1 by Hannah Teal, val. at £ 224.9.3, and signed by
John and William Teal as bros. of the dec.; Hannah Randall Stinchcomb Teal was living on 30 June 1740 when she signed the inv. of
her dau. Mary Stinchcomb Newsham Smith; Edward and Hannah had
iss.: RUTH, b. c.1711, m. 1st, on 27 Feb. 1728/9 Edmond Howard,
s. of Joshua; m. 2nd, by 30 May 1747 William Lewis; EMANUEL, b.
c. 1713 (1:368; 21:274, 297; 68:209; 110:158; 214-21:371; Balto.
Co. Orig. Inventories, Box 3, folder 28, and Box 9, folder 23).

TEAL, JOHN (3), poss. s. of Edward (1), d. by 31 March 1722,
having m. Jane (---), who m. as her 2nd husb. (---) Long; John
signed the inv. of his bro. Edward on 27 Jan. 1720/1; he d. leaving a will, 12 March 1721 - 31 March 1722, naming w. Jane, sons
Edward and John, and tracts Bowden's Adventure and Teal's Adventure; admin. bond was posted by extx. Jane Teal on 31 March 1722,
with Thomas Cromwell and George Bailey; est. was admin. by Jane,
now w. of (---) Long on 6 July 1723 and 4 April 1724; John and
Jane had iss.: EDWARD; JOHN, in 1750 owned 50 a. Teal's Choice
(1:92; 2:341; 14:242; 110:188; 153:95).

TEAL, WILLIAM (4), prob. s. of Edward (1), was living in Balto. Co. by April 1726; in March 1723/4 and again in Nov. 1724 was charged with incontinency with Christian, w. of Thomas Evans; m. Christian (---) (poss. the same one) by April 1726 when they had iss.: EDWARD, b. 17 April 1726 (26:212; 27:45; 133:13).

TEAL, EMANUEL (5), s. of Edward (2), and Hannah, was b. c.1713, giving his age as 40 in 1753; d. after 1790 in Pitt Co., N.C., having m. Katherine, dau. of Anthony Johnson, on 24 Dec. 1734; in 1750 owned 293 a. part Tanyard, 100 a. Robin's Camp, and 100 a. Johnson's Range; on 24 Feb. 1763 Emanuel Teal conv. 51 a. of Teal's Search to John Ford; Emanuel and Hannah had iss.: CAROLINE, b. 13 March 1735/6; EDMUND, b. 24 March 1737/8, m. Sarah Stinchcomb; BELINDA, b. 25 March 1740, later drowned; RACHEL, b. 16 Feb. 1742; GEORGE, b. 27 Feb. 1743; JOHN, b. 10 March 1746; LLOYD, b. 25 Oct., 1750; BELINDA, b. 25 July 1754; CHARLES, b. 24 Oct. 1756; poss. HANNAH, who m. Nicholas Jessop (70:285; 92: 374; 133:48, 63, 71, 75, 94, 106, 153; 153:29; Henry Griswold Jesup, Edward Jesup of West Farms, West Chester Co., New York, and His Descendants (Cambridge: 1887), pp. 369-371).

TEDDER, HENRY, age c.38, b. in Essex, Eng., raised up as a gardener and had been in the king's service; ran away from John Hall and Jacob Giles, Oct. 1753 (385:258).

TEIRST, MARTIN, in Dec. 1755 sold land to Thomas Sligh; his w., unnamed, consented (82:487).

TELL. See TEAL.

TEMPLE, THOMAS (1), was in Balto. Co. by 1695 as a taxable in Spesutia Hund.; m. Eleanor Loreson on 17 April 1699; she d. in April 1709, and he m,. 2nd Elizabeth (---); d. leaving a will, 4 May 1710 - 8 June 1710, naming daus. Ellinor, Johanna, and Susannah; admin. bond was posted 1 Jan. 1710 by John Webster with Simon Person, and Richard Ruff; est. was inv. on 3 Oct. 1718 by Jno. Deaver and William Howard, and val. at E 19.10.8; it was inv. again on 3 Oct. 1719 and val. at E 14.0.8, and signed by David Thomas and Aquila Paca;; est. was admin. by John Webster on 9 Aug. 1711; Thomas had iss.: SUSANNA; PHILISANNA: JOHANNA; and ELINOR (1:375; 14:247; 50:228; 52:117; 123:170; 129:185, 186, 209; 140).

TEMPLE, SUSANNA (2), dau. of Thomas (1) and Eleanor, was b. 21 Aug. 1699; in June 1710 was bound to John Webster to age 16; in Aug. 1724 was ind. for bast., and tried in Nov. 1724 where she was described as a servant of Daniel Scott, named Abraham Whitaker as the father, and was sentenced to 15 stripes with the lash; she m. Henry Munday on 25 Nov. 1725; she had a s.: MICHAEL, b. 11 July 1724 (21:137; 26:438; 27:42; 128:8, 68; 129:259).

TEMPLE, PHILISANNA (3), dau. of Thomas (1), was not named in her father's will, but in June 1710 she was bound to John Webster; on 9 May 1710 she was left personalty by the will of Edward Wildy, and she m. John Powell in Sept. 1725 (21:137; 123:167; 131).

TEMPLE, JOHANNA (4), dau. of Thomas (1), was b. 31 Aug. 1707, age 3 in June 1710 when she was bound to Mary w. of Christopher Cox and to Mary's dau. Elizabeth w. of Nicholas Day (21:137).

TEMPLE, ELINOR (5), dau. of Thomas (1) and Elizabeth, was b. 1 Oct. 1709; in June 1712 was bound to John Webster to age 16; m. Sherwood Lee on 3 Nov. 1729 (21:315; 129:254).

TEMPLE, MILES, d. in Balto. Co. by 24 April 1705; m. (wife

not identified); on 4 March 1704/5 bought Temple's Claim from
John Watts of Patapsco River; d. leaving a will, 5 April 1705 -
24 April 1705, leaving his entire est. to his w.; admin. bond
was posted 9 May 1705 by Richard Colegate with John Wallis and
John Eaglestone; est. was inv. on 11 June 1705 by Charles Merryman and John Barrett and val. at £ 27.14.0; est. was admin. on
12 April 1707 by Capt. Richard Colegate; no record of any children found (2:80; 14:238; 48:136; 60:135; 123:152).

TENCH, HANNAH, of Balto. Co., spinster, on 26 March 1740 conv.
all her personal est. to Rhoda, w. of Nathaniel Ayres, except
£ 100 out of £ 200 left Hannah by her aunt, Maria Boserys in Amsterdam, Holland; in the same deed Hannah mentioned her son Samuel Tench, gunstock maker in London (75:365).

TENO, SIMON, servant, was mentioned in the April 1688 inv. of
Thomas Lightfoot (51:6).

TERRAS, ROBERT, servant, of Balto. Co., was transported c.
1664 (388).

TERRY, JOHN, d. by 25 May 1668 when admin. bond was posted by
Nathaniel Utie, with Hans de Ringh (14:221).

TESSELL, EDWARD, was in Balto. Co. by 1692 as a taxable in s.
side of Patapsco Hund. (138).

TEVIS, ROBERT, and w. Margaret sold 100 a. Tevis' Adventure
to Nathan Hammond in Sept. 1740; in 1750 he owned 80 a. Treadway's Quarter; on 7 Aug. 1758 Robert and Margaret Tevis and Anthony and Mary Musgrove sold 135 a. Addition to Treadway's Quarter
to Abel Browne (75:448; 83:207; 153:87).

TEWKES, FRANCIS, d. by 20 Oct. 175-(?) when his est. was admin. by James Walker (5:138).

TEY, JOHN, in 1750 owned 200 a. Broad Meadow and 100 a. James'
Meadow (153:89).

THACKER, RICHARD, m. by 1725 Hannah, dau. of Christopher Gardner; on 10 April 1727 they conv. 100 a. Gardner's Mill, 367 a.
Long Discovery, and 320 a. Thacker's Chance, to Thomas Cockey
(70:358; 124:208).

THACKER, WILLIAM, m. Hannah Cox on 14 Feb. 1750/1 (133:165).

THACKHAM, WILLIAM, m. Hannah (--), and had iss.: MARY, b. 2
June 1751 (133:110).

THAYER, GEORGE, m. Katherine Graves in Nov. 1748 (131).

THERRELL, RICHARD, was in Balto. Co. by March 1670/1 when he
was named as kinsman by Joseph Hawkins, Gent.; d. leaving a will,
22 Sept. 1675 - 23 March 1675/6, leaving entire est. to w. Margaret after paying debts to Capt. Thomas Long; Therrell could not
sign the will because he had lost the use of his hands; wid.
Margaret d. by 1677 leaving a will naming daus. Sarah and Elizabeth Hawkins, sons-in-law John Lokins and Robert Benger, and
grandchild John Lorkins (110:3; Balto. Co. Orig. Wills, Box 1,
folder 58).

THE DAVID THOMAS FAMILY

THOMAS, DAVID (1), d. by 28 May 1720; m. by 8 April 1708
Hannah (---), wid. of Daniel Peverell and George Smith (latter

d. 1704); David Thomas surv. 62 a. Landilo in Oct. 1705; David
d. leaving a will made 13 May 1720 (date of probate not given),
naming sons David and Henry (to have tracts Landillo and Hunting North), sis. Priscilla Freeborn, dau.-in-law Sarah Ruff, also David and John Ruff, and Samuel Brown; admin. bond posted
28 May 1720 by exec. Richard Ruff, with Peter Lester and Antel
Deaver; est. of David Thomas was inv. 30 May 1720 by Thomas Newsom and Edgar Tipper, and signed by William Smith and Robert
Clare as kin; although David's wife Hannah (who d. 12 April
1718) is mentioned in several documents, Thomas may have also
been married to Ann, sister of Richard Freeborne; David and Hannah had iss.: DAVID, twin, b. 8 April 1708; HENRY, twin, b. 8
April 1708; HANNAH, dau. of "Daniel" and Hannah, b. 30 April
1710 (2:232; 14:224; 51:311; 124:6; 128:23, 25, 27; 129:220;
207).

THOMAS, DAVID (2), s. of David (1), was b. 8 April 1708; d.
in Balto. Co. by 20 Sept. 1746; m. by Elizabeth, dau. of Benjamin Wheeler, in Feb. 1732; d. leaving a will, 15 June 1746 - 20
Sept. 1746, naming w. Elizabeth, children David, Elizabeth, Hannah, and Mary, and possible unborn child; admin. bond was posted
20 Sept. 1746 by Elizabeth Thomas with Thomas Wheeler and Benjamin Wheeler; in Nov. 1750 the extx. Elizabeth m. Henry Green;
David and Elizabeth had iss.: DAVID, d. c.1769; ELIZABETH, b.
14 Sept. 1736, m. Benjamin Green by 6 Feb. 1769; HANNAH; MARY,
b. 24 Dec. 1743 (14:250; 38:12; 110:363; 112:309; 129:268).

THOMAS, HENRY (3), s. of David (1), was b. 8 April 1708, in
1750 owned 50 a. part Rachel's Delight, 50 a. The Addition,
56 a. Henry's Plains, and 40 a. Henry's Hope; m. Jane Poteet on
22 Jan. 1737 (129:303; 153:40).

THE COLONEL JOHN THOMAS FAMILY

THOMAS, Col. JOHN (4), noknown rel. to any of the above, came
to Balto. Co. c.1676 as an indentured servant; d. by 3 Jan. 1717
when admin. bond was posted by extx. Sarah Thomas, with Benjamin Bowen and James Rider; m. 1st. Jane, wid. or dau. of William
Clapham of Lancaster Co,, Va.; m. 2nd, Sarah (---) who survived
him; in March 1693/4 conv. 50 a. Gardeson to James Wells in con-
sideration that Thomas be excused from teaching Wells to read or
write; on 11 Aug. 1684 surv. 200 a. Good Luck (on 1 Sept. 1702
as Col. John Thomas deeded 123.3/4 a. called The Glebe, being
part of Good Luck, to the vestry of St. Paul's Parish; Jane
Thomas gave power of atty. to Richard Colegate to conv. her int.
in the land);other tracts owned by Col. John Thomas incl.:
140 a. Major's Choice, surv. 19 July 1694; 400 a. Chevy Chase
granted to him on 10 Aug. 1695; Bristol Folly, which John and
w. Sarah conv. to Buckler Partridge of Bristol, surgeon; on 11
Sept. 1717 Col. John Thomas conv. livestock to his s. John (no
wife signed the deed); admin. bond posted as above on 3 Jan.
1717/8; est. inv. 31 March 1718 and val. at £ 50.12.0 and signed
by Charles Whitehead as kin; left iss.: JOHN; PHOEBE (48:19; 66:
171, 225, 227; 67:445, 454; 211; 371:808).

THOMAS, JOHN (5), s. of Col. John (4), was conv. prop. by his
father on 11 Sept. 1717; on 29 Nov. 1737 he conv. 239 a. Gardeson (except for 50 a. conv. to James Wells by John Thomas) to
William Tweedy; no wife signed (75:40)

THE JOHN AND MARY THOMAS FAMILY

THOMAS, JOHN (6), no known rel. to any of the above, m. Mary,
poss. dau. of Samuel Jackson; she m. 2nd (---) Foster, and 3rd,
on 26 Nov . 1731 James Taylor; d. by 12 Nov. 1722 when admin.

bond was posted by Francis Holland with Roger Matthews, and Bennett Garrett; est. was inv. on 27 Nov. 172-(?) by Peter Lester and John Clark, val. at Ł 126.12.9½, signed by Hannah Kimble and Mary Thomas as kin, and filed by Francis Holland; est. was admin. by Francis Holland in Aug. 1729 and March 1733/4; dec. left orphan Moses; John and Mary had iss.: MOSES, b. 26 June 1721 (14:208; 28:275; 30:195; 69:e33; 128:40).

THOMAS, MOSES (7), s. of John (6) and Mary, was b. 26 June 1721; on 15 July 1738 James Taylor and his w. Mary bound Moses Thomas, age c.18, son of said Mary Taylor by her (former) husb. John Thomas, to William Daugherty (75:230; 128:55).

THOMAS, (---), m. by 1713 Jane, dau. of Thomas Freeborne; had dau.: FREENATER (122:257).

THOMAS, ARTHUR, was in Balto. Co. by 1695 as a taxable in n. side Patapsco (140).

THOMAS, CHARLES, was in Cecil Co. by 1 April 1734 when he purch. 130 a. Scudamore's Last from Philip and Elizabeth Sindall; on 7 March 1734 he and w. Ann sold 130 a. to Thomas Sligh; had iss.: WILLIAM, b. 6 June 1729 (74:45, 213; 129:352).

THOMAS, DOROTHY, and her s. ASHIA, formerly bound to John Barrett, in Nov. 1724 were to kept and maintained by Thomas Weeks (27:32).

THOMAS, EDWARD, was in Balto. Co. by March 1754 when he sold livestock to John Ridgely (82:191).

THOMAS, HENRY (See 3 above), m. Jane Poteet on 22 Jan. 1737; in Nov. 1748 he and w. Jane conv. 50 a. Henry's Pleasure to Samuel Forwood; had iss.: JOHN, b. 26 Jan. 1740 (82:348; 128: 101, 115).

THOMAS, JAMES, par. not named, was bapt. 13 April 17-(?), aged 25 years and 11 mos. (133:41).

THOMAS, JOHN, admin. the est. of Nicholas Ruxton on 31 May 1681 (2:42).

THOMAS, JOHN, surv. 150 a. Thomas' Range on 5 Sept. 1683; may be the same John Thomas who surv. 165 a. Thomas' Adventure on 2 Sept. 1688 (211).

THOMAS, JOHN, m. Mary, and had iss.: JOSEPH, b. 8 Oct. 1723; and JOHN, b. 1 Nov. 1733 (128:50, 83).

THOMAS, JOHN, m. Sarah (---), and had iss.: JOHN, b. 1 April 1721; JOSEPH, b. 29 Aug. 1723; NATHAN, b. 1 April 1726 (128:79).

THOMAS, JOHN, purch. 50 a., part Murphy's Hazard from John Murphy on 12 Jan. 1732 (73:320).

THOMAS, JOHN, m. Sarah (---); on 19 Nov. 1742 they conv. White Oak Bottom to Thomas Matthews; had iss.: ELEANOR, b. 8 Oct. 1742; SARAH, b. 23 March 1744 (77:70; 134:1).

THOMAS, JOHN, in 1750 owned 50 a. Thomas' Choice (153:77).

THOMAS, JOHN, m. by 14 May 1753 Sarah, dau. and heir of Hill Savage; on previous date they conv. 150 Rich Level, being part of Spring Garden to John Metcalfe (81:548).

THOMAS, JOSEPH, m. Dorcas, admnx. of Thomas Sutton; on 8 March 1731 purch. 100 a. being one-half of Pickett's Venture, from Heathcote and Mary Pickett; on 30 Aug. 1740 sold 200 a. Turner Hall to William Mattingly; on 22 Oct. 1740 purch. Felks' Forest from John and Eliz. Young of Va.; on 5 March 1741 purch. 50 a. James' Forest from Samuel and Martha Stevens; d. leaving a will, 4 July 1748 - 7 Sept. 1748, naming dau. Ruth Sing, and w. Dorcas; admin. bond posted 25 Oct. 1748 by extx. Dorcas Thomas with Chris. Sutton and Adam Hendrickson; est. admin. on 4 June 1750, 23 May 1752, and 30 June 1752; in 1750 his heirs owned 50 a. of Thomas' Purchase Resurveyed and 250 a. Joseph's Privilege; had iss.: RUTH, m. (---) Sing (3:142; 5:162, 235, 236; 14:285; 73: 199; 75:441, 458; 76:146; 110:392; 153:81).

THOMAS, MARTHA, was ind. for bast. in June 1744, and named Abraham Brucebanks as the father; ind. for bast. again in March 1745/6, and tried in June 1746; had iss.: JOHN, b. Feb. 1747 (35:228, 243, 800; 36:7; 131:132/r).

THOMAS, PHILIP, in 1750 owned 1307 a. part Clagett's Forest (153:100).

THOMAS, SUSANNA, m. Philip Brannican; banns were pub. in Feb. 1699/1700 (129:190).

THOMPSON, ANDREW (1), progenitor, d. in Balto. Co. on 20 Feb. 1739; on 12 March 1714 Simon Pearson conv. him 100 a. Pearson's Lodge; d. leaving a will, 20 May 1738 - 6 March 1739, naming ch. Andrew, Thomas, John, Alexander, and heirs of his dec. s. James; also 100 a. Pearson's Lodge; admin. bond posted 7 March 1739 by Andrew Thompson with Daniel Scott, Jr., and William Garland; est. admin. 19 Sept. 1741, by Andrew Thompson; dec. left a wid. and these ch.: ANDREW; THOMAS; JOHN; ALEXANDER; and JAMES (4:124; 14:205; 67:218; 127:67; 128:107).

THOMPSON, ANDREW (2), s. of Andrew (1), d. by 8 June 1761, having m. Elizabeth Shaw on 13 May 1731; d. leaving a will, 19 Dec. 1760 - 8 June 1761; est. admin. 5 Oct. 1761 and 29 Oct. 1764; dec. had iss.: SARAH, b. 7 Oct. 1733, m. Joshua Durham; ELIZABETH, b. 11 June 1736, m. Isaac Bush; HANNAH, b. 1 Dec. 1738; ALEXANDER; MARTHA; and PRISCILLA (4:347; 6:109; 111: 329; 128:75, 79, 93/b, 103; 129:335).

THOMPSON, THOMAS (3), s. of Andrew (1), d. by 9 May 1758; m. Sarah Durham on 15 Jan. 1744; in 1750 owned 40 a. Pearson's Lodge, and 25 a. part Andrew's Addition; admin. bond was posted by Sarah Thompson on 9 May 1758 with Samuel Durham and Samuel Durham, Jr.; est. admin. 7 Sept. 1760 by Sarah Thompson; dec. left 6 ch., names unknown (4:320; 13:257; 131; 153:84).

THOMPSON, JOHN (4), s. of Andrew (1), may be the John b. 2 April 1705, no parents named; in 1750 owned 60 a. part Pearson's Lodge (128:31; 153:84).

THOMPSON, ALEXANDER (5), s. of Andrew (1), m. Sarah Smithson on 30 April 1734. and in 1750 owned 50 a. part Wilson's Choice; had iss.: THOMAS, b. 6 Feb. 1736; MATTHEW, b. 29 March 1738 (128:90, 91, 103; 153:58).

THOMPSON, JAMES (6), s. of Andrew (1), d. by 20 May 1738; m. Elizabeth Gilbert on 30 Oct. 1727; had iss.: AQUILA, b. 28 March 1728; MARGARET, b. 28 March 1730; JAMES (posthumous s.) b. 11 Nov. 1732 (128:61, 71).

THOMPSON, ANNA, m. Christopher Bellroes on 25 Sept. 1719 (129:223).

THOMPSON, AQUILA, m. Catherine Whitaker on 20 Feb. 1753; in 1757 was received in membership in Gunpowder Meeting (136).

THOMPSON, DANIEL, m. Margaret Clark on 24 Oct. 1758 (131).

THOMPSON, EDWARD, in Nov. 1759 was fined for bast. (46:240).

THOMPSON, HENRY, d. by 27. Nov. 1717 when admin. bond was posted by Thomas Rutter, with Richard Lenox and John Standiford; est. was inv. in 1718 by Moses Edwards and Richard Gist and val. at ₤ 16.8.5 with Nicholas Haile and John Hurst signing; est. was admin. by Thomas Rutter (1:162; 14:240; 51:119).

THOMPSON, JAMES, in March 1683 owned Taylor's Choice which later desc. to his wid. Ann who m. Edward Felkes; on 4 Jan. 1693 James Thompson, Gent., and w. Ann conv. 200 a. Thompson's Choice to Gabriel Parrott; it was on the wid. Ann Felks' land that Joppa was laid out; in 1692 James was a taxable in n. side Gunpowder (59:364; 138; 340:111).

THOMPSON, JAMES, m. Sarah Miller on 28 June 1730 (133:149).

THOMPSON, JOHN, was in Balto. Co. by 1692 as a taxable in Spesutia Hund. (138).

THOMPSON, JOHN, d. 11 March 1733 (128:77).

THOMPSON, JOHN, m. 1st on 14 Nov. 1740 Mary Potee;she d. 16 July 1754 and John m. 2nd, on 18 July 1755 Margaret Gilbert; John had iss.: JAMES, b. 14 Sept. 1741; JOHN, b. 8 Nov. 1743; HANNAH, b. 22 Dec. 1745; ELIZABETH, b. 6 Dec. 1747; SARAH, b. 17 June 1748; (by 2nd w.): JARVIS, b. 1 Jan. 1758; ANN, b. 13 DEc. 1759; MARGARET, b. 2 Sept. 1762 (129:313, 315, 321, 375).

THOMPSON, JOHN, m. Sarah Blackwell on 25 Dec. 1743, and had iss.: ELIZABETH, b. March 1741; MARGARET, b. 15 April 1747 (131).

THOMPSON, JOHN, m. Anne Petty in July or Aug. 1748 (131).

THOMPSON, MARY, in June 1685 bound herself to serve Nicholas Darnall for 4 years after her arrival in Md. (18:354).

THOMPSON, MARY, formerly Chalk, was reported for marrying out of unity; was a member of the Gunpowder Meeting, May 1760 (136).

THOMPSON, PETER, imm. c.1667 from Northumberland Co., Va., to Marrow Creek, Balto. Co. (388).

THOMPSON, RICHARD, d. by 30 June 1696; was in Balto. Co. by 1692 as a taxable in n. side Patapsco Hund.; in 1693 purch. 50 a. part Bachelor's Delight and Halberston from John and Sarah Arden; admin. bond was posted 30 June 1696 by John Rous with Joseph Strawbridge and John Coale; est. of Richard and Anne Thompson was inv. on 30 June 1698 by John Cole and Joseph Strawbridge and val. at ₤ 50.19.2 (14:234; 51:30; 59:437; 138).

THOMPSON, SABRA, was ind. for bast. in Aug. 1746 and tried in Nov. 1746 (46:116).

THOMPSON, SIMON, and Savory Lett, blacks, were m. 10 Nov. 1734 (133:152).

THOMPSON, THOMAS, m. Ellinor Egon on 4 Dec. 1752 and had

iss.: JOHN, b. 28 Sept. 1753; THOMAS, b. 16 March 1755; RACHAEL,
b. 18 Jan. 1758; JAMES, b. 10 Jan. 1759 (129:362).

THOMPSON, WILLIAM, d. by 11 Dec. 1668 when admin. bond was
posted by Lodwick Williams and William Osborne (14:239).

THOMPSON, WILLIAM, d. by March 1675 when George Wells and
Thomas Long were ordered to inquire what lands Thompson owned
at his death, "by the oaths of twelve men" (200-51:170).

THORN, JANE, was ind. for bast. in Nov. 1755 (40:402).

THORN, SAMUEL, d. by 19 May 1761 when admin. bond was posted
by James Taylor with John Taylor and John Biddison; est. was admin. by James Taylor on 17 May 1762 (6:138).

THORN, SARAH, was tried for bast. in Nov. 1755, naming Lemuel
Hardesty as the father; was tried again in March 1755/6 (40:22,
403).

THE THORNBOROUGH FAMILY was the subject of a typescript by
Delmar Leon Thornbury, "Original Source Records Relating to the
Thornbury Family," 1931, a copy of which is at the Library of
Congress.

THORNBOROUGH, ROLAND (1), progenitor of the family in Balto.
Co., is stated by Delmar Leon Thornbury to have been a s. of
Thomas and Alice (---) Thornborough of Va. and Md., and a grandson of Nicholas and Janet (Brookbank) Thornborough; Roland was
in Md. by 1662 when he and others were ordered to be kept in the
sheriff's hands until they found sufficient security to appear
at the next Provincial Court; in July 1694 he was in Balto. Co.
when he took up 900 a. Selsed; also surv. Goose Harbor, later
held by Joseph Wells for Roland's orphans; d. leaving a will, 25
July 1695 - 23 June 1696, naming w. Anne, sons John, Roland, and
Francis, and daus. Catherine, Jane, and Anne, and directing that
if his sons should die without heirs the tract Selsed was to pass
to his next of kin, the Thornboroughs of Hampsfield, Lancashire,
England; his est. was inv. on 24 June 1696 by Joseph Strawbridge
and William Wilkinson, and val. at £ 81.8.0; est. was admin. on
10 March 1697 by wid. Ann and her 2nd husb. John Royston; dec.
left iss.: JOHN; FRANCIS; ROLAND; JANE; CATHERINE, may have m.
Joseph Wells, and ANNE, may have m. James Wells (121:111; 200-
3:449; 206-14:30; 206-16:25; 211).

THORNBOROUGH, JOHN (2), s. of Roland (1), d. by 21 Nov. 1733
when Luke Stansbury posted admin. bond, John's wid. Elizabeth
having ren., with Thomas Harris and John Gregory; John went to
Va., where he m. by 10 Dec. 1726 Elizabeth Tayloe, dau. of Joseph and Barbara (Billington) Tayloe of Lancaster Co.; was in
Va. by 1711 when (by Thomas Biddison, his atty.) he conv. part
of Selsed to John Boring; was back in Balto. Co. by 1733 when
he and w. Elizabeth made a deed of gift to Charles Yates; his
est. was admin. by Luke Stansbury on 27 Dec. 1735; left a wid.
and three ch.: ANN, m. William Yates; ELIZABETH, b. 1 July
1728, m. by 9 Oct. 1764 Thomas Elledge; and JOHN (3:235; 14:
220; 31:175, 176; 67:152; 73:433; 90:97, 121; 133:45; George H.
S. King, Marriages of Richmond County, Virginia, 1668-1853
(1964), p. 209).

THORNBOROUGH, FRANCIS (3), s. of Roland (1), was living in
1732; in Sept. 1716 joined his bro. John in conv. 200 a. part
Selsed to John Boring; in March 1732 conv. part of Selsed to
Thomas Tipton (63:499; 73:263).

THORNBOROUGH, ROLAND (4), s. of Roland (1), was b. c.1684; d. by 1734; moved to Richmond Co., Va.. where he m., c. March 1715/6, Marcy Baylis, dau. of Thomas and Catherine (Samford) Baylis; on 15 Dec. 1733 Nicholas Haile and Roland Thornborough conv. pt. Buck's Purchase to Henry Sater; d. by 15 May 1734 when admin. bond was posted by Edward Evans with Walter Dallas and Thomas Sligh, Frances Thornborough having ren. the right of admin.; had iss.: BALY (dau.), age 13 in March 1733/4 when she was bound to Thomas Todd; FRANCIS, in June 1734 was bd. to Daniel Stansbury to age 21; THOMAS, age 9 in March 1733/4 when he was bd. to Edward Evans to age 21, and was age 12 in March 1736 when he was bd. to Thomas Gist to age 21 to learn the trade of blacksmith (14:201; 30:245, 246, 255; 31:2).

THORNBOROUGH, JOHN (5), s. of John (2), was age 2 "last March 22" when in March 1733/4 he was bd. to William and Susannah Kemp to age 21; in June 1734 was bd. to Luke Trotten (30:245, 255).

THORNBOROUGH, FRANCIS (6), s. of Roland (4), was b. 23 Sept. 1717 in North Farnham Par., Richmond Co., Va.; m. by 26 March 1763 Mary (---); on that day as "son and heir of Roland Thornbury, dec.," he and w. Mary conv. pt. Selsed to Thomas Cockey; in Feb. 1765 conv. pt. Selsed to Samuel Norwood; had at least one s.: THOMAS, m. Sarah Shepherd (87:118; 90:55; Nat. Cyclopedia of Amer. Biog., 38:142).

THORNBOROUGH, ANN, was ind. for bast. in June 1742; was tried in June 1743 (33:309; 35:84).

THORNBOROUGH, CHARLES, was in Balto. Co. by 1694 as a taxable in n. side of Patapsco Hund. (139).

THORNBOROUGH, ELIZ'TH, had iss.:BETHIA, b. 8 Feb. 1734 (128: 88).

THORNBOROUGH, JOHN, in June 1704 was sued by John Mortimer of A. A. Co. (Anne Arundel Court Proc., Liber G, f. 432 at Hall of Records).

THORNBOROUGH, JOHN, m. Elizabeth Stone on 7 Aug. 1733 (133: 151).

THORNBURNE, ROBERT,in June 1704 sued John Frizzell in A. A. Co. (Anne Arundel Court Proc., Liber G, f. 435, HR).

THORNHILL, SAMUEL, m. Mary Clybourn on 4 Feb. 1747/8 (131).

THORNTON, ANN, in March 1759 had iss.: ELIZABETH, age 6½ next 20 Aug.; JOHN, age 2 next 20 Aug. (46:198).

THORNTON, CONSTANT, was tried for bast. in Nov. 1757 (46:74).

THORP, EDWARD, m. Catherine Cullings on 6 Jan. 1731; he and w. Catherine adm. the est. of Thomas Cullins on 1 July 1737; in Nov. 1743 purch. 329 a. Charles' Neighbors from John and Aquila Paca; still owned this land in 1750 (3:226; 77:389; 129:259; 153:13).

THORP, EDWARD, m. Mary Green on 31 May 1760 (131).

THORTON, JANE, was ind. for bast. in March 1731 (29:225).

THRAP, ROBERT, m. Eliz. Hilton on 28 Feb. 1760 (131).

THRIFT, RICHARD (1), m. Mary (---), and d. by 3 March 1725; on 31 Dec. 1722 he purch. 126 a. Thompson's Neglect from William

and Sarah Groves; admin. bond on his est. was posted 3 March
1725 by Mary Thrift with John Crockett and Richard Caswell;
est. was inv. 9 June 1726 by James Presbury and Richard Caswell
and val. at **L** 39.2.6, and was approved by Sutton, John, and
Mary Thrift; est. was admin. on 4 April 1727; dec. left iss.:
SUTTON, b. 6 Oct. 1705; WILLIAM, b. 14 June 1714; SARAH, b. 20
Oct. 1717; MARY, b. 8 Jan. 1720; RICHARD, b. 20 Jan. 1722; and
PRUDENCE, b. 1 Jan. 1727 or 1729; also JOHN, date of birth not
known; may have been eldest son (2:294; 14:210; 48:210; 69:125;
131:6, 16, 18, 6/r).

THRIFT, JOHN (2), prob. eld. s. of Richard (1), m. 1st, in
May 1728 Rebecca Blackledge, and 2nd, in 1732 Sarah Dorney; in
1751 he dep. he was s. of Richard; in 1750 he owned 126 a. Thomas
Neglect and 38 a. Addition to Thomas Neglect; d. 13 Dec. 1751;
admin. bond was posted 11 April 1752 by admnx. Sarah Thrift with
John and William York; est. admin. on 20 Dec. 1752 by Sarah
Thrift; in Aug. 1754 she gave bonds to John's orphans James,
Charlotte, Ichabod, Richard, and John; had iss. (by 1st w.):
JOHN, b. Oct. 1729; (by 2nd w.): LYDA, b. June 1738, m. Luke
Swift on 28 Oct. 1758; PRUDENCE, b. 7 April 1743 (sic); ICHABOD
(or MICHABOD, dau.), b. 6 May 1743 (sic), m. William Thomas
on 6 April 1765; CHARLOTTE, b. 5 April 1746, m. John Thomas;
JAMES, b. 14 Nov. 1748; RICHARD, b. 25 March 1751 (5:248; 14:
267; 40:347, 348; 131:40, 52, 67, 6/r, 129/r; 153:31; 224:192).

THRUSTON, THOMAS, in Nov. 1745 was bd. to John Caudrick to
age 21 (35:743).

THURCALL, THOMAS, m. by Aug. 1684 Jane O'Daniel, dau. of
Thomas O'Daniel, and step-dau. of James Denton; in Feb. 1686
Thomas and Jane Thurcall conv. 50 a. Daniel's Neck to William
Westbury (18:164; 59:188).

THURMAN, JOSEPH, was in Balto. Co. by 10 March 1737 when
he conv. 75 a. Egypt to Henry Austin (75:56).

THURRELL, RICHARD, planter, was in Balto. Co. by June 1669
when Thomas Todd, Gent., conv. him 50 a. on s. side of Back
River orig. laid out for Thomas Thomas and William Batten; in
March 1671/2 was named as kinsman by Joseph Hopkins (95; 98:46).

THURSTON, THOMAS (1), was b. c.1622, prob. in Gloucestershire,
Eng.; d. 1693 in Balto. Co.; imm. c.1658 from Va.; in July 1658
was brought before the Council of Maryland by the sheriff because
he had been in the province for over a month without informing
the Governor or the Secretary and without taking the Oath of
Fidelity, had persuaded others not to do so or not to abide
by the laws or any of the Proclamations; later that month Thurston was given a safe conduct to leave the Province; in Aug.
1659 he still had not done so, and was ordered to leave within
7 days or be given 30 lashes, and be "whipped from constable
to constable;" anyone harboring him or helping him was to be
fined 500 lbs. tobacco; ret. to Md. in 1663 with his w. and
two daus.; rep. Balto. Co.in the Lower House from 1686 to 1688,
and was at the Associators' Convention 1689-1692; between 1690
and 1692 was a colonel;in Aug. 1683 surv. 1000 a. Elberton; in
May 1684 surv. 200 a. Strawberry Hill and 600 a. Littleton and
200 a. Come By Chance; in 1690 he and his dau. Eliz. "Waly"
were named in the will of Eliza Hemsted; d. leaving a will,
21 Dec. 1692 - 13 April 1693; left Strawberry Hill to his s.
Thomas (under age), also part Come By Chance and 618 a. Thornberry; dau. Eliza w. of Charles Ramsey was to have pers.; dau.
Sarah was to have Littleton and res. of Come By Chance; w. Mary
was to have dower rights; if his three ch. by his last w. Mary

died under age or without iss., his entire est. was to pass
to the ch. of his bro. Samuel in Thornberry, Gloucestershire,
Eng.; est. was inv. 25 May 1695 and val. at Ł 176.4.7; a 2nd
inv. was taken c.1696; est. was admin. on 9 March 1695 and again
in 1696; had iss.: ELIZABETH, m. 1st, by 1676 George Skipwith
and 2nd, William Coale, and 3rd Samuel Chew; ANN, m. c.1676
Miles Gibson; and (a 2nd dau.) ELIZABETH, m. 1st John Walley
and 2nd, Charles Ramsey; SARAH, m. c.1693 Robert Love (2:52,
178; 19:152; 101; 121:51, 60; 200-3:348, 353, 364; 200-67:279;
206-10:282; 206-13/A:314; 206-13/B;86; 211; 371; 388).

THURSTON, THOMAS (2), s. of Thomas (1), was under age when
his father made his will; inher. Strawberry Hill, Thornberry,
and part Come By Chance; on 2 Nov. 1702 sold 200 a. Strawberry
Hill to John Mortimer of A. A. Co.; d. 11 Jan. 1715 (66:207;
121:60; 129:218).

THURSTON, DAVID, was in Balto. Co. by 1694 as a taxable in
n. side Patapsco Hund. (139).

THURSTON, GEORGE, m. Frances (---), and had iss.: JOHN, b.
25 May 1749 (131:126/r).

THURSTON, MARTHA, d. by 20 May 1710 when Mathias Gray posted
admin. bond, with Joseph Peregoy and John Thomas; est. was inv.
26 May 1709 (sic) by James Read and Thomas Smith and val. at
Ł 15.9.10; est. was admin. by Mathias Gray on 14 May 1711 (1:
214; 14:228; 48:33).

THURSTON, WILLIAM, was in Balto. Co. by 1692 as a taxable
in n. side of Patapsco (138).

THWAITE, MARY, and her ch. William and Thomas, were named
in the Aug. 1671 will of William Boulding of Bohemia River,
Balto. Co. (120:70).

THYLER, GEORGE, m. Catherine Graves on 1 Jan. 1748 (131).

TIBBETT, JAMES, servant, with 2 yrs, 5 mos. to serve was
listed in the April 1706 inv. of Col. Edward Dorsey (48:43).

TIBBETT, JAMES, m. Rebecca Wordsworth on 19 Feb. 1760 (131).

TIBBS, WILLIAM, Rector of St. Paul's Par., d. leaving a will
25 Sept. 1732 - 13 Oct. 1732, naming sis. Ann who was to have
his dwelling plant.; est. was inv. at over 1000 lbs.; admin.
bond was posted 15 Feb. 1732 by extx. Ann Tibbs, with Buckler
Partridge, and Richard Caswell (14:216; 125:233; Joseph Towne
Wheeler, "Reading Interests of...the Clergy," MHM, 36:187-188).

TIFFEN, WILLIAM, mariner, d. by 13 Feb. 1748 when his est.
was admin. by Lyde Goodwin with W. Hammond and Brian Philpot,
Jr.; est. was admin. by Lyde Goodwin on 6 Oct. 1751 and 19 June
1753 (5:194, 291; 14:284).

TIGH, JOHN, gave his age as c.36 in Aug. 1723 (25:442).

TILBURY, SARAH, alias DEHAY, was ind. for bast. in March
1736; as serv. to William Petticoat was tried in June 1737;
David Dahee agreed to pay charges (31:1, 55).

TILLIARD, JOHN (1), imm. from Va. c.1665; settled in Balto.
Co. by 4 March 1667/8 when John Collett conv. him 100 a., being
one-half of Beaver Neck; on 11 Nov. 1670 Tilliard sold the same
land to John Mascord; his w. Sarah gave p/a to James Ives to

ackn. sale of land; in March 1670/1 John Tilliard purch. 200 a.
at Bohemia River from Rowland Williams; in July 1676 surv. 40 a.
Sarah's Delight and 200 a. God's Providence; John d. by 11 Dec.
1686 (or 1696; records not clear); when his est. was inv. by John
Taylor and Robert L(-?-). and val. at Ŀ 55.14.6; had iss.: RICH-
ARD; poss. JOHN (60:62, 99; 98:47; 206-9:228; 211; 388).

TILLIARD, RICHARD (2), s. of John (1), was of age to be a taxable in Balto. Co. by 1695; on 6 Nov. 1699 conv. one-half of Sarah's Delight and one-half of his goods and chattells to his good
friend John Hopkins; d. by 13 Oct. 1725 leaving iss.: JOHN (63:
409; 70:192; 140).

TILLIARD, JOHN (3), poss. s. of John (1), may be the John who
was a taxable in Balto. Co. by 1692 as a taxable on n. side Gunpowder Hund.; no other record (138).

TILLIARD, JOHN (4), s. of Richard (2), was in Kent Co., Md.,
by 13 Oct. 1725 when he sold 80 a. Sarah's Delight to George Debruler, stating that the tract had formerly been granted to John
Tilliard, who left it to his son Richard, who was the father of
the present grantor (70:192).

TILLY, MARY, was ind. for bast. in Nov. 1737 and tried some
time after that (31:129, 189).

TIMMONS, JOHN, m. Sarah Copeland on 18 April 1745; on 19 Oct.
1749 purch. 400 a. Friendship from William and Jane Copeland;
in 1750 owned 150 a. of that land (77:285; 131; 153:33).

TIMS, WILLIAM, was in Balto. Co. by 1694 as a taxable in n.
side Patapsco Hund. (139).

TINMORE, JOS'H, tailor, servant with 4½ years to serve, was
listed in the 1759 inv. of Richard Winn (54:309).

TIPER, or TYLER, EDGAR, m. Elizabeth, admnx. of William Pritchett, on 30 Oct. 1713; on 7 June 1734 Edgar and w. Mary (2nd
w.?) conv. 176 a. Perkins Lot to William Snelson (1:28; 74: 72;
128:30).

TIPPER, ELIZABETH, d. 17 Jan. 1724/5 (128:51).

TIPPINS, THOMAS, d. 8 May 1739 (128:102).

THE TIPTON FAMILY has been the subject of a typescript by
Charles Brunk Heinemann, "Tipton Family of Maryland, Virginia,
Tennessee, Kentucky, Ohio, Indiana, Illinois, and Indiana," at
the Maryland Historical Society, compiled in 1942. More recent-
ly Ervin Charles Tipton published We Tiptons and Our Kin (San
Rafael, CA, c.r. 1975).

TIPTON, EDWARD (1), probable progenitor of the family, may
have settled in Jamaica c.1639 where his son Jonathan was born;
was transported to Md. c.1668; claimed land for his service in
1674; may have then moved to Northumberland Co., Va., where it
is possible he m. Margaret Downing, wid. of Capt. William Downing; may have been the father of: JONATHAN, b. c.1639 in Jamaica;
and JOSEPH, b. c.1650, was living in Northumberland Co. in 1716
when he wit. the will of John Downing; in 1717 a lawsuit mentioned
deed from his mother Elizabeth (sic) (Heinemann; see also William
and Mary Quarterly, 1st ser., 24:89, and 25:46-47).

TIPTON, JONATHAN (2), poss. s. of Edward (1), is the first
definitely proven Maryland progenitor; believed to have been b.

in Jamaica c.1639; d. in Balto. Co. on 21 Jan. 1757 when his
newspaper obituary stated that he died "at the beginning of this
month, in Baltimore County, aged 118 years;" was b. in Kingston,
Jamaica, which he left while very young, and has lived almost
ever since in this province; he had his perfect senses to the
last, and his youngest sons are reckoned to be the oldest men in
the county; was def. in Md. by 23 Nov. 1700 when he wit. the will
of Robert Goldsborough of A. A. Co.; was in Balto. Co. by Aug.
1714 when he surv. 350 a. Port Royal; in March 1716/7 he surv.
929 a. Poor Jamaica Man's Plague; in Aug. 1730 gave bond he would
educate two orphans William and Richard Cross; in June 1731 he
pet. the court that he had been in the province almost 60 years
and was over 70 years, and was made exempt from the levy; gave his
age as 90 in May 1747 and 105 in June 1754; his wife's name is not
definitely known; may have m. 1st Sarah (poss. Pearce), and 2nd,
on 15 Dec. 1709 Mary Chilcoat; on 12 Sept. 1719 Thomas and William
Tipton were named as nephews in the will of William Pearce of
A. A. Co.; had iss.: THOMAS, b. 8 April 1693, bapt. 25 April 1699;
WILLIAM, b. 27 July 1696, bapt. 25 April 1699; JONATHAN, b. 25
March 1699, bapt. 25 April 1699; JOHN (may have m. Mary Kemp)
(29:9, 161, 294; 55:119; 71:231; 74:102, 107; 123:215; 207;
219-3; 225; 262; Heinemann).

TIPTON, THOMAS (3), s. of Jonathan (2), was b. 8 April 1693
in St. James Parish, A. A. Co.; may have d. c.1734; on 8 March
1732 purch. part Selsed from Francis Thornborough; m. Sarah
(---), and had iss.: MARY, b. 18 Feb. 1717, m. John Stevenson;
WILLIAM, b. 27 Feb. 1719; THOMAS, b. 8 March 1721; JONATHAN, b.
2 Sept. 1723; JOHN, b. 6 July 1726; LUKE, b. 24 Jan. 1728 (in
April 1759 purch. 50 a. Hog Island from Richard Richards); SOLO-
MON , b. 17 March 1732; SARAH, b. 17 July 1734 (73:263; 133:49;
Heinemann).

TIPTON, WILLIAM (4), s. of Jonathan (2), was b. 27 July 1696
in St. James Par., A. A. Co.; d. 1726, having m. in 1719/20, Hannah, dau. of Mordecai and Mary (Parsons) Price; d. leaving a will,
5 April 1726 - 2 Aug. 1726, named ch.: Samuel, Mordecai, and
Sarah; admin. bond was posted 30 Sept. 1726 by Jonathan Tipton,
with Thomas Ford and Thomas Tipson, the widow Hannah having ren.
her right to admin. her husband's est.; est. was admin. on 21
June 1727; William and Hannah had iss.: SAMUEL, b. 13 May 1721;
SARAH, b. 3 Oct. 1722 (may have m. Christopher Cole); and MORDE-
CAI, b. 1724, d. 1795 (2:359; 14:209; 124:233; 133:52).

TIPTON, JONATHAN, Jr. (5), s. of Jonathan (2), was b. 25 March
1699 in St. James Par., A. A. Co.; may have m. twice; 1st, to
Elizabeth Edwards, c.1727; and m. 2nd, c.1735 Mary Chilcoat;
Worth S. Ray, in Tennessee Cousins, p. 67, states that Jonathan
Tipson, Jr., settled in the Shenandoah Valley of Virginia, and
that he had iss.: EDWARD, b. 27 Oct. 1728; Col. JOHN, b. 15 Aug.
1730, d. 1813; JONATHAN, b. 1732, settled in Washington Dist.,
Tenn.; JAMES; SARAH, b. 12 Aug. 1734; WILLIAM, b. 30 Aug. 1736;
and JOSEPH, went to Washington Dist., Tenn. (133:52; Ray, Tennessee Cousins, repr. Baltimore: Gen. Pub. Co., 1980, p. 67).

TIPTON, JOHN (6), s. of Jonathan (2), was livin on 26 Nov.
1725 when he and his bro. Jonathan wit. the will of Richard Kemp;
in that will Mary Kemp was placed in charge of Mary Tipton until
the younger girl came of age; on 24 Aug. 1730 Tipton purch. 100 a.
Benjamin's Beginning from Richard Wheeler; d. by 13 Nov. 1775
when his dau. Rachel, wife of Benjamin Ford, sold her share of
Benjamin's Beginning to her sis. Mary, now w. of James Chambers;
John had iss.: MARY (prob. the Mary who rec'd one-half of Molly
and Sally Delight from her grandfather Jonathan Tipton on 10 Dec.
1735; m. James Chambers; RACHEL, m. Benjamin Ford (73:18; 74:360;
231-AL#N:513).

TIPTON, EDWARD, in Oct. 1758 conv. James Mecamis (McComas?) 25 a. Tipton's Lot; in March 1765 he and w. Jemima conv. John Foster 50 a. Tipton's Fancy (83:239; 90:147).

TIPTON, JOHN, in 1750 owned 100 a. Bachelor's (sic) Beginning (153:50).

TIPTON, SAMUEL, m. c.1742 Mary, dau. of Richard Herett (or Hewitt); in 1750 owned 100 a. Painter's Level; in Sept. 1757 purch. Cromwell's Park from John and Elizabeth Cromwell of A.A. Co.; had iss.: HANNAH, m. Samuel Cole; and PATIENCE, m. Samuel Taylor (83:44; 153:79; 231-WG#65:161).

TIPTON, SARAH, in Nov. 1757 was fined for bast. in Nov. 1757 (46:73).

TIPTON, THOMAS, Jr., was b. 1721 d. 1754; m. Mary (---); in 1750 owned 50 a. William's Beginnings (153:40).

TIPTON, WILLIAM, d. 14 d, 3 mo., 1797, m. Angelica (---), and was rec'd in membership in Gunpowder Meeting, 28 d, 5, 1755; had iss.: TABITHA, b. 5 d, 5, 1747; ISABELLA, d. 1817; LUKE, d. 1788; NICHOLAS, b. 1753; ANN; REBECCA, and JOSHUA (136).

TIPTON, WILLIAM, in 1750 owned 50 a. Tipton's Puzzle; in Oct. 1760 purch. 40 a. part Bond's Industry from John and Keturah Bond (84:424; 153:75).

TIVIS. See TEVIS.

THE TODD FAMILY

There are two published accounts of separate Todd families in Maryland. One, by J. Hall Pleasants, dealt with the Todds of North Point, Balto. Co., and of Va., and was published as part of his lengthy articles on the Gorsuch and allied families in the Virginia Magazine of History and Biography, starting in vol. 25. The other family was located primarily in A. A. Co. (although some family members appear in Balto. Co. records), and was the subject of an article by Christopher Johnston in the Maryland Historical Magazine, IX, 298-305.

TODD, GEOFFREY (1), of Denton, Co. Durham, Eng., d. 1637; his will was dated 8 Feb. 1637, and his est. was inv. on 9 March 1637; had iss.: MARGARET, b. c.1610, m. George Runthwaite on 10 June 1625 at Denton; CHRISTOPHER, prob. b. by 1615; JOHN, b. 16 May 1613 at Denton; and THOMAS, b. 12 Sept. 1619 (Pleasants, in Va. Mag., 26:99).

TODD, CHRISTOPHER (2), s. of Geoffrey (1), was prob. b. by 1615, and d. in 1680; m. Jane Burden on 24 Nov. 1636, at Denton; had iss.: WILLIAM, b. 22 Oct. 1637; CHRISTOPHER, b. 31 May 1640; GEOFFREY, b. 9 July 1643 (had iss.: MARY, b. by 1679); LANCELOT, b. 14 Oct. 1647; THOMAS, b. 25 April 1654; JOHN, b. 28 Feb. 1659; ANN, prob. b. after 1660 (Pleasants, Va. Mag., 26:100-102).

TODD, THOMAS (3), s. of Geoffrey (1), was b. 12 Sept. 1619 at Denton, Co. Durham; came to Md., where he d., having m. Anne Gorsuch, dau. of Rev. John and Anne (Lovelace) Gorsuch; after Todd's death she m. 2nd David Jones, and 3rd Capt. John Oldton; in Aug. 1664 Todd was in Gloucester Co., Va., when he purch. three tracts from Thomas Powell of Talbot Co.: 287½ a. Road River, half of Dickson, 100 a. with houses, and 300 a. Richardson; Thomas conv. these three tracts to Robert and John Todd on the same day; rep. Balto. Co. in the Lower House of the Assembly 1674-75; d. leaving a will, 26 Feb. 1675 - 30 May 1677, naming w. Anne,

daus. Anne, Johanna, Frances, and Avarilla, bro. Christopher, and
s. Thomas; on 18 Jan. 1676/7 Anna Todd conv. all her prop. to her
ch. if they allowed her maintenance, and she named her bro.
Charles Gorsuch; on 16 Jan. 1678 the est. of Thomas Todd was inv.
by Matthew Hawkins and John Arden, one-third of the prop. was to
go to David Jones who m. the widow; Thomas and Anne (Gorsuch)
Todd left iss.: THOMAS, of Va., m. Elizabeth Bernard; JOHN; ROB-
ERT: poss. JAMES: ANNE, m. Miles Gibson; JOHANNA; FRANCES, and
AVARILLA (48:284; 95; 110:190; 371:835-836; Pleasants, in Va.
Mag., 25:85-86).

TODD, THOMAS (4), s. of Thomas (3), was b. c.1660, and d. 16
Jan. 1724/5 in Gloucester Co., Va., having m. Elizabeth, dau. of
Col. William Bernard; had iss.: THOMAS, b. c.1681; RICHARD, b. c.
1681-88; WILLIAM, b. betw. 1681 and 1688, d. betw. 1736-45, m.
Martha Vicaris; PHILIP, b. betw. 1681-88, d. by 1761; CHRISTOPHER,
b. 2 April 1690, d. 18 July 1720; ANNE, b. 9 Nov. 1692, d. 18
July 1720, m. John Cooke; LUCY, m. 1st (---) O'Brien; and 2nd,
in 1698, John Baylor; ELIZABETH, m. 1st, Henry Seaton, and 2nd,
Augustine Moore; FRANCES, b. 12 April 1692 or 1693, d. 5 Nov.
1703; dau., m. Jonathan Hyde; FRANCES, b. 1709, d. 25 July 1745,
m. Robert North (Pleasants, in Va. Mag., 25:87-91).

TODD, ROBERT (5), s. of Thomas (3), and his bro. John, were
living on 17 Aug. 1664 when their father Thomas, of Gloucester
Co., Va., conv. them three tracts on Patapsco, which the elder
Todd had purch. from Thomas Powee (95).

TODD, JOHN (6), s. of Thomas (3), was alive in 1664 (95).

TODD, JAMES (7), s. of Thomas (3), was b. c.1670, and drowned
9 May 1709; m,. 1st, Elizabeth (---), and 2nd, Penelope, dau. of
Thomas Scudamore; was in Balto. Co. by 1694 as a taxable in n.
side Patapsco Hund.; in June 1703 assigned a serv. named John
Ashburn to William Wilkinson; admin. bond was posted 17 May 1709
by Anthony Bale with Thomas Chamberlaine and Roger Matthews; est.
was inv. 24 March (or May) 1709 by Lawrence Draper and Roger
Matthews and val. at £ 27.9.9, and James had iss.: (by 1st w.):
ANNE, b. c.1697, d. by 1745, m. Joseph Johnson on 5 July 1713
(14:231; 48:33; 66:283; 139; Pleasants, in Va. Mag., 25:91).

TODD, THOMAS (8), s. of Thomas (4), was b. c.1680, and d. by
3 June 1715; m. Elizabeth (---), who m. as her 2nd husb., Rev.
Hugh Conn; Todd d. leaving a will, 11 Jan. 1714/5 - 3 June 1715,
naming ch. Thomas and Robert, bros. William, Philip, and Christopher, bro. William's w. Martha, and appointed Richard Colegate
and James Phillips as execs. in Md., and bros. William Todd and
Jonathan Hyde as execs. in Va.; admin. bond was posted on 9 July
1716 by extx. Eliza Conn, with Hugh Conn, Patrick Hepburn, and
John Rattenbury; a second admin. bond was posted 12 Oct. 1719 by
William Todd of Va. with James Phillips and John Cromwell; est.
was inv. 25 Aug. 1716 by John Rattenbury and Lance Todd and val.
at £ 641.5.1, and a second inv. was made 30 Aug. 1717, and val.
at £ 94.0.0; Thomas left iss.: THOMAS, b. 1706; ROBERT; and
FRANCES, b. 1710 (14:222; 52:7, 312; 123:51; Pleasants, in Va.
Mag., 25:212-217).

TODD, THOMAS (9), s. of Thomas (8), d. 1738/9 in Balto. Co.;
m. 1st, Lettice Thacker, by June 1730; and 2nd, Eleanor, dau. of
Caleb Dorsey; she m. 2nd, on 6 Sept. 1740, William Lynch; Thomas
d. leaving a will, 9 Dec. 1738 - 2 April 1739, naming w. Eleanor,
and ch.: Elizabeth, Eleanor, Frances, Mary, and Thomas; admin.
bond was posted 2 April 1739 by Eleanor Todd, Basil Dorsey and
Caleb Dorsey; est. was admin. on 4 Aug. 1741, and mentioned a
legacy from James Lenox to Ruth Peacock; in 1750 the heirs of

Thomas Todd owned 190 a. Denton, 300 a. North Point, 546 a. Old Road, and 100 a. Shawan Hunting Ground; these tracts were held jointly with Basil and Caleb Dorsey; Thomas had iss.: (by 1st w,): LETTICE, b. 4 June 1730; (by 2nd w.): ELIZABETH, b. 13 Dec. 1732, m. John Cromwell; ELEANOR, m. John Ensor, Jr., on 6 March 1753; THOMAS, b. 27 Nov. 1738, in Aug. 1757 chose Robert Wilkinson as his guardian, d. 1 Sept. 1798, m. by 13 Aug. 1759, Sarah, dau. of Robert Wilkinson; FRANCES, m. George Risteau on 17 Aug. 1757; MARY, m. John Worthington (3:375; 14:199; 127:19; 133:17, 26, 91; 153:105; 44; 210-30:823).

TODD, DAVID, m. Catherine Porter on 21 April 1753 (131).

TODD, LANCE, was in Balto. Co. by 25 March 1706 when he admin. the est. of Mary Rockhold; also admin. the est. on 24 June 1707 (2:102, 235).

TODD, LANCELOT, was in Balto. Co. by July 1724 when Adam Shipley sold him 100 a. part Andover; on 17 Aug. 1724 purch. 100 a. Sewell's Coffer from Philip and Sarah Sewell; admin. the est. of John Lockett on 12 Sept. 1721 and 15 Nov. 1722, and admin. the est. of Col. Richard Colegate on 12 April 1727 and 10 June 1731 (1:169, 202; 2:291, 397; 69:299, 301).

TODD, LANCELOT, in 1750 owned 50 a. part Todd's Forest (153: 104).

TODD, LANCELOT, Sr., m. Rachel (---), and had iss.: RACHEL, b. 17 Jan. 1752; LYDIA, b. 11 March 1755; NICHOLAS, b. 7 June 1757 (133:128).

TODD, MARTHA, admin. the est. of Bennett Garrett on 23 Dec. 1742 (3:274).

TOLE, HENRY, of Balto. Co., immm. c.1671 (388).

THE TOLLEY FAMILY has been the subject of a great deal of study by Margaret Smith Keigler of Monkton, Md.; she has graciously shared the results of that research with the author.

TOLLEY, WALTER (1), progenitor, d. in Kent Co., Md., by 29 June 1699; m. Eliza (---);on 3 April 1685 Robert Chapman made a will leaving 220 a. Hinchingham to Thomas and William, sons of Walter and Eliza Tolley at age 21; if the boys should die the land was to go to their bro. Walter, Jr.; Walter Tolley, Sr., was made exec. of the will; Walter Tolley of Kent Co. d. leaving a will, 23 April 1699 - 29 June 1699 leaving part of Hinchingham Haven to daus. Mary and Eliza, and the res. of his est. to his two daus. aforesaid and to son Thomas; Walter and Eliza had iss.: THOMAS, d. 1732; WILLIAM, alive in 1685, d. young; WALTER, alive in 1685 died young; JOHN, alive in 1685, d. young; GEORGE, alive in 1685, d. young; dau. MARY, who inherited one-half of Hinchingham; ELIZABETH (120:151; 121:187).

TOLLEY, THOMAS (2), s. of Walter (1), was b. b. 1685, prob. in Kent Co.; d. in Balto. Co. by 9 Oct. 1732; m. (just before the birth of their fourth ch.) Mary Freeborne, dau. of Thomas Freeborne of A. A. Co.; a suit in Kent Co. Court attempted to stop him from cohabiting with the said Mary Freeborne; Tolley sold his land in Kent Co., and moved to Balto. Co.; on 5 Nov. 1716 purch. 100 a. of Walter's Hope from John and Susannah Morrow; was a major, and also served as Burgess and Justice of Balto. Co. and Commissioner to lay out town of Joppa; d. leaving a will, 12 Sept. 1732 - 9 Oct. 1732, leaving house to w. Mary, after her death any profits from land to be divided among his three sons and when Michael Miller, son of Michael and Elizabeth (Tolley) Miller came of age, the land was to go to him; Thomas' sons Walter, James, and Thomas were left portions of various tracts, the rector of St. John's Par. was left personalty, and Garrett Garrettson and John Scott were also mentioned; an admin. bond, prob. a 2nd one, was posted 16 Nov. 1735 by Walter Tolley with Darby Henley, John Holloway, H. Wells Stokes, and John Stokes; wid. Mary Tolley d. leaving a will proved 15 Jan. 1733, naming sons Thomas, Walter, and James, and dau. Elizabeth w. of Michael Miller; admin. bond on Mary Tolley's est. was posted 15 Jan. 1734 by exec. JohnScott and Thomas Giddings and Richard Caswell entered a petition; Thomas and Mary had iss.: THOMAS, d. by 10 Aug. 1734; WALTER; JAMES, d. on 17 Oct,. 1744; ELIZABETH, m. Michael Miller (14:203, 213; 67:467; 125:233; 126:74; 209-30:4; 313:119-125, 234).

TOLLEY, THOMAS (3), s. of Thomas (2), and Mary, d. leaving a will, 17 Jan. 1733 - 10 Aug. 1734, naming bro. James, son and heir of Thomas Tolley, bro. Walter and sis. Elizabeth w. of Michael Miller; admin. bond was posted 21 Feb. 1734/5 by Walter Tolley with Bryan Taylor and Humphrey Wells Stokes; a second admin. bond was posted 16 Nov. 1735 by Walter Tolley; est. was admin. 13 Dec. 1739; no known issue (3:230; 14:207, 214; 126: 104).

TOLLEY, WALTER (4), s. of Thomas (2) and Mary, d. in March or April 1783; m. 1st, on 20 Dec. 1735, Mary Garrettson; she d. 19 July 1749; and Walter m. 2nd, on 22 Dec. 1751, Martha Hall; in Aug. 1739 he was ind. for assault; by 1750 owned 200 a. Tracey's Level, 107 a. Taylor's Mount, Dicon's Chance and Long Point, 192 a. Pimlico, and 125 a. Nothingworth, as well as other lands; was a delegate to the General Assembly, a member of the Convention of 1774, and was a colonel of the Gunpowder Battalion of Militia; his obit. stated he d. aged 67; left a will, 26 July 1781 - 6 June 1783; left iss.: (by 1st w.): ELIZABETH, b. 16 Nov. 1736, d. 27 May 1785, m. George Goldsmith Presbury on 10 June 1756; THOMAS, b. 15 Oct. 1738, d. 15 April 1743; MARY, b. 21 March 1740, d. 4 Jan. 1777, m. Samuel Worthington on 17 Jan. 1759; SOPHIA, b. 1742, m. William Allender; WALTER, b. 10 May 1744, d. 21 Sept. 1776 having been a delegate to the General Assembly, and was a member of the conventions and a colonel in the militia; JAMES, b. 20 June 1746 (prob. the James Tolley, student at law in Balto. Town who d. Nov. 1768); THOMAS GARRETTSON; (by 2nd w.): MARTHA, b. 1752, d. 2 June 1755; ANN, b. 7 July 1756, m. Aquila Hall; MARTHA, b. 17 Sept. 1758(32:1; 112;507; 129:349; 131; 153:64; 313:234).

TOLLEY, JAMES (5), s. of Thomas (2), and Mary, d. 17 Oct. 1744; m. Mary Hammond who d. 9 Nov. 1744; admin. bond was posted 6 Nov. 1744 by Walter Tolley, exec., with Thomas Gittings and James Maxwell, Geo. Brown and John Lawson; his est. was admin. 6 Jan. 1745 and named as heirs, wid. Mary, nephew Walter, Jr., niece Eliza Tolley, nieces Mary and Sophia Tolley, and bro. Walter and sis. Mary; the will of Mary Hammond Tolley, 20 Oct. 1744 - 9 Nov. 1744, named sis. Frances Hammond Dorsey, bro.-in-law John Hammond Dorsey, and the sis. of her dec. husb., Elizabeth Miller; admin. bond was posted 17 Nov. 1744 by exec. John Hammond Dorsey, with Vincent Dorsey and John Day of Edward (5:41; 14:260, 288; 111: 21; 36:235).

TOLLEY, EDWARD. See TULLY, EDWARD.

TOLSON, ELIZABETH, in June 1750 named John Stokes as the father of her child (37:23, 182).

TOLSON, JOSEPH, was in Balto. Co. by 1692 as a taxable in s. side Patapsco Hund. (138).

TOMS, EVAN, servant with 2 years to serve, was listed in the 1709 inv. of Henry Wriothesley (50:227).

TONGUE, THOMAS, late of Cal. Co., had his est. in Balto. Co. admin. 19 July 1750 by his wid. Mary; she m. 2nd Maj. Sabrett Sollers (6:8).

TOPHAM, CHRIS., in 1750 owned 168 a. New Rochester (153:86).

TOPPING, GARRETT, was in Balto. Co. by 1692 as a taxable in Spesutia Hund. (138).

TOUCHSTONE, RICHARD (1), was in Balto. Co. by 25 Feb. 1717 when he m. Sarah, dau. of Daniel Johnson; on 16 Feb. 1724 he purch. 50 a. Freeland's Mount from George Freeland, and on the same day conv. 50 a. of this tract to Alexander Urqhart; on 27 Oct. 1731, with Thomas Cresap, William Cannon, and Edward Evans and Robert Cannon also he conv. 60 a. Johnson's Island to Stephen Onion of Cecil Co.; by 1734 was moving to Frederick Co. where he leased partof Carrollton from Charles Carroll of Annapolis; on 6 March 1739 he surv. Anchor and Hope in the Catoctin Valley; he and his w. had iss.: RICHARD; CALEB; DANIEL; HENRY; and STEPHEN (3:124; 70:51; 73:214; 129:256; Tracey and Dern, Pioneers of Old Monacacy, Baltimore: Gen. Pub. Co., 1987, 28, 222).

TOUCHSTONE, HENRY (2), s. of Richard (1), m. Margaret Mahen in Cecil Co., on 12 Nov. 1749 (263:181).

TOULSON, or TOLSON, WILLIAM, of Balto. Co., Gent., surv. the tract Tolchester in 1673, and in March 1667 purch. 100 a. Tombeye from Abraham Coffin (95; 207).

TOWARD, JOHN, m. Dorcas (---), and had iss.: WARNER, b. Feb. 1731 (133:79).

TOWERS, JOHN, d. by 14 March 1675 when admin. bond on his est. was posted by his widow and admnx.. Rachel, with Arthur Taylor and John Owen; in May 1685 Rachel was now w. of Thomas Richardson and conv. 150 a. Hogg Neck to Michael Judd (14:209; 59:216).

TOWGOOD, JOSIAS, m. by 17 March 1708, Mary, dau. of John Welch (67:5).

TOWNSEND, JOHN, m. Amy, wid. of Hector McLane, and dau. of George and Johanna Norman; had iss.: DOROTHY, b. 1 Feb. 1727; MARGARET, b. 30 Sept. 1728 (3:12, 126; 133:14, 16).

TOWNSEND, DOROTHY, poss. dau. of John above, had iss.: MARGARET, b. 5 Aug. 1749 (133:94).

TOWRY. See LOWRY.

THE TOWSON FAMILY is the subject of Winifred Levering Holman Dodge's ms. "Towson Family of Maryland," MHS.

TOWSON, (---), (1), unnamed progenitor, is stated by Dodge to have had three sons: CHARLES, b. c.1680; WILLIAM, b. c. 1685; and THOMAS, b. c.1688 (Dodge).

TOWSON, CHARLES, (2), s. of (---) (1), was b. c.1680, and gave his age as 39 in 1718 (Chancery Record PL # 3, p. 582, at Hall of Records).

TOWSON, WILLIAM (3), s. of (---) (1), is stated by Dodge to
have d. after 1715, to have m. Catherine Allen, and to have had
at least two ch.: DARIUS, b. c.1710; DORCAS, b. c.1715, m. Henry
Sater (Dodge, offers no documentation).

TOWSON, THOMAS (4), s. of (---) (1), was b. c.1688, and d.
by 11 Nov. 1728; m. c.1710 Sarah (---) who m. as her 2nd husb.
one Duncan Coleman; admin. bond on his est. was posted 27 July
1728 by admnx. Sarah Towson with Thomas Ford, Charles Robinson,
Thomas Sheredine, and Richard Caswell; his est. was inv. on 11
Nov. 1728 by Luke Stansbury and Thomas Matthews and val. at
£ 184.9.2; John and Mary Tipton signed as kin; Sarah Towson was
admnx.; est. was admin. 16 April 1731 by Sarah and her 2nd husb.
Duncan Coleman; in March 1733/4 Coleman posted bond, with Thomas
Matthews and Nicholas Haile, that he would pay the orphans of
Thomas Towson their share of their father's est.; on 7 Nov. 1734
Coleman posted a notice he would not be responsible for the debts
of his wife Sarah; Thomas and Sarah had iss.: ABRAHAM; THOMAS;
WILLIAM; DARIUS; JOSEPH; also pos. RICHARD who m. Tabitha Rut-
ledge on 26 Dec. 1758 (3:85; 14:215; 30:191, 192;;51:79; 74:
135; Dodge).

TOWSON, DARIUS (5), s. of William (3), is stated by Dodge to
have been b. c.1710; may be the Darius who had iss.: WILLIAM,
b. 23 Jan. 1735 (133:50).

TOWSON, ABRAHAM (6), s. of Thomas (4) and Sarah, d. by 9
June 1752 when admin. bond was posted by James Carey with Thomas
Norris; m. Elizabeth Mahone on 1 Jan. 1745; his est. was admin.
by James Carey on 18 Sept. and 21 Nov. 1754; the first admin.
acct. contained an entry for expenses for "burying the wife of
the deceased;" Abraham and Elizabeth had two children who chose
their uncle William as their guardian; left iss.: MARY; DORCAS
(4:224, 240; 14:276; 40:19, 220; 133:158).

TOWSON, THOMAS (7), s. of Thomas (4) and Sarah, was b. c.1725;
m. Elizabeth (---) and had iss.: (b. in St. Thomas Parish):
THOMAS, b. 25 April 1752; SARAH, b. 18 Jan. 1754; JOSHUA, b. 18
Jan. 1756; HANNAH, b. 23 Oct. 1758; JAMES, b. 21 Sept. 1760;
SHADRACH, b. 3 Sept. 1762 (134:36, 37).

TOWSON, WILLIAM (8), s. of Thomas (4) and Sarah, was b. c.1712;
d. in Balto. Co. in 1772; m. 1st, on 24 Feb. 1735, Ruth Gott;
m. 2nd, c.1740, Dinah Wilmot; in Nov. 1730 as orphan of Thomas
Towson he chose Walter James as his guardian; in March 1743/4 was
tried on a charge of fathering an illeg. ch.; in 1750 he was
listed as owning 200 a. Vulcania; in April 1752 he bought part of
Gunner's Range from Samuel Gott, and in June 1761 he and w. Dinah
sold 18 a. part Towson's Chance, to Isaac Risteau; d. leaving a
will, 8 April 1772 - 1 Aug. 1772, naming w. Dinah and ch. Ezekiel,
Abraham, Rachel w. of Thomas Bailey, John Thomas, Ruth w. of one
Green, and Charles, also naming Ezekiel's dau. Ann, granddau.
Rachel Bailey of Rachel, Catherine w. of John Avery and her ch.
William Towson Allen and Isaac Towson Avery; est. was admin. on
11 Feb. 1792 by exec. Thomas Bailey; he paid legacies to William
Towson Allen,Rachel Bailey, Ann Towson, Charles Towson; Abraham
Towson had "not been home in ten years," so his share was paid
to Ezekiel, Charles and John; the wife of the exec. was pd. a
share, and Isaac Towson was paid for the support of the ch. of
Catherine Avery; William had two ch. by his 1st w.: EZEKIEL, b.
28 Dec. 1736; RACHEL, m. Thomas Bailey on 26 Dec. 1750; (by 2nd
w..): CATHERINE, b. c.1740, m. 1st (---) Allen, and 2nd John
Avery; ABRAHAM, b. c.1742; WILLIAM, Jr., b. c.1743, d. 1767, m.
Frances (---); JOHN, b. c.1745; THOMAS, b. c.1747; RUTH, b. c.
1749, m. George Green; CHARLES, m. Betsy Ann Trapnell (10:527;

29:55; 35:172; 85:132; 112:96; 133:53, 155; 153:37; 210-38:690; Dodge).

TOWSON, JOSEPH (9), s. of Thomas (3) and Sarah, may be the Joseph whose will was made 17 Jan. 1745, proved 5 March 1745, naming his w. Elizabeth, and directing that his unborn ch. was to be named Joseph if a boy and Elizabeth if a girl (111:218).

THE TRACEY FAMILY has been the subject of a great deal of research by Mrs. J. W. T. Armacost of Hampstead, Md.; she has graciously shared her work with the author.

TRACEY, THADY or TEAGUE (1), was in Md. by 1694 when he m. Mary James on 3 Nov. of that year in St. James Parish, A. A. Co.; d. in Balto. Co. by 18 June 1712; when his est. was inv.; on 30 March 1699 he and his w. sold land called Cuckold Point in Chas. Co.; may be the "Thady" Tracey who pat. 200 a. in Balto. Co. in Jan. 1706 and called it James Meadows; on 10 June 1706 he pat. 100 a. Tracey's Park; on 9 Sept. 1709 sold 100 a. part of James Meadows to Mordecai Price of A. A. Co.; admin. bond on his est. was posted by Mary Tracey, with Dutton Lane and Jonathan Hanson, on 16 June 1712; his est. was admin. by the wid. Mary, now w. of George Hitchcock on 22 July 1713 and 31 Aug. 1714; had four ch. b. in St. James' Par., A. A. Co., and poss. one other s. Basil, identified bv Mrs. Armacost; Teague and Mary (James) Tracey had iss.: DINAH, b. 18 Dec. 1695; SARAH, b. 7 April 1698; JAMES, b. 18 April 1700; TEAGUE, b. 18 April 1703; poss. BASIL (1:4, 7; 12:379; 50:364; 67:146; 207; 219-3).

TRACEY, JAMES (2), s. of Teague (1) and Mary, was b. 18 April 1700 in St. James' Par.; on 4 Nov. 1724 he sold Tracey's Park, adj. James Meadows, to his step-father George Hitchcock; by March 1745/6 had moved to Craven Co., N. C., when he appointed John Ensor his atty. to conv. James Meadows and Teague's Park to John Cole; may have been the father of James and Nathaniel, two Revolutionary soldiers from N. C., but this has not been proved (69:397; 79:248; 219-3).

TRACEY, TEAGUE (3), s. of Teague (1) and Mary, was b. 18 April 1703 in St. James Par., A. A. Co.; m. Katherine (---); on 26 Feb. 1732 patented 50 a. Bought Dear in Balto. Co.; on 10 June 1734 he pat. 50 a. Round About; on 12 Sept. 1741 bought from Charles and Sarah Gorsuch part Cole's Contrivance, and in May 1745 he purch. 16 a. Coale's Chance from John Gorsuch; in Nov. 1745 sold parts of these tracts to William Fell, and no w. signed the deed, so Katherine may have died; may be the Teago Tracey who surv. 34 a. called Hard Scuffle in 1752; he and his w. had at least four ch.,. b. in St. Pauls' Par.: TEAGUE, b. 25 Oct. 1728; BENJAMIN, b. 14 April 1730; JOHN, b. 26 May 1733; SARAH, b. 14 April 1735; (and poss.) WARNEL (76:19; 78:110, 353; 133:40, 45; 207; 219-3).

TRACEY, BASIL (4), s. of Teague (1), and Mary, is so placed by Mrs. Armacost; may be the Basil who pat. 30½ a. Basil's Profit; may have m. 1st Rachel or Kezia Tipton, and 2nd Melinda Boring; BASIL, m. Mary Cammell by lic. dated 4 Aug. 1781; JOSHUA, m. Nancy, dau. of Jacob Stiffler; JAMES, m. Mary, dau. of Absolom Barney; JOHN, m. Felty (Unpublished research by Mrs. Armacost and hypothetical placement by the author; this line needs a great deal more work).

TRACEY, SAMUEL, of Balto. Co. imm. c.1670; d. by 23 March 1675/6 when admin. bond was posted by Giles Stevens, with Thomas Long; on 9 March 1670 had surv. 200 a. Tracey's Level; dau. ANN m. Richard Taylor in 1687 (14:197; 97:124, 125; 98:46; 99: 347; 211; 263).

TRACY, SUSANNAH, was ind. for bast. in June 1731 (29:156).

TRAPNALL, HANNAH, was ind. for bast. in June 1729 (28:41).

TRAPNALL, PHILIP, pet. the Balto. Co. Court to b levy free in Nov. 1719, but his pet. was rejected (23:248).

TRAPNALL, PHILIP, Jr., on 25 June1726 purch. 50 a., being one-half of Richardson's Prospect, from Mary Bosley, widow; on 9 March 1732 with cons. of his w. Elizabeth he sold the land to Richard Caswell (70:253; 71:349).

TRAVIS, JOHN, m. Anne Kelsey in Nov. 1743; in Aug. 1757 conv. 400 a. Friendship to John Sligh (83:27; 131).

THE TREADWAY FAMILY was the subject of a book by William T. Treadway, History of the Treadway Family, (Pittsburgh; 1930). This author has found no confirmation of the statements made by some researchers that Richard and Thomas Treadway, the earliest settlers of the name in Baltimore County, were sons of Josiah and Sarah (Sweetman) Treadway, and grandsons of Nathaniel and Suffrany (Haynes) Treadway of Sudbury and Watertown, Mass.

TREADWAY, RICHARD (1), may have been b. c.1677; was in Balto. Co. by 1701 as a taxable in n. side of Gunpowder Hund.; m. (Jane?) Parker on 17 Dec. 1705; in 1713 his wife was referred to as Jane, mother of John Smith; in June 1714 he pet. the court that he was a poor man with three small children; he d. by 13 May 1720 when his wid. Jane was paid one year's wages from the est. of George Wells; Jane Treadway d. on 15 Jan. 1720/1, and her est. was inv. on 22 April 1721 by Isaac Butterworth and J. Moulton and val. at Ł 14.0.11, and signed by Timothy Keen as one of the creditors; Richard and Jane had iss.: RICHARD, b. 8 Dec. 1706; MARY, b. 12 Jan. 1709 (in March 1720/1 was bd. to Antil Deaver and w. Sarah to age 21); and THOMAS, b. 6 March 1711 (1:164; 21:379, 510; 25:146; 128:22, 23, 30; 143; 205-5:100).

TREADWAY, RICHARD (2), s. of Richard (1) and Jane, was b. 8 Dec. 1706; m. Martha (---) ; may have moved to Pittsylvania Co. Va. by 1746, and m. 2nd Elizabeth (---); may be the Richard R. Treadway who d. testate in Cumberland Co., N. C., in 1777; had three ch. b. in St. George's Par., Balto. Co., and may have had two more after he left Md.: JANE, b. 26 March 1729; THOMAS, b. 15 Aug. 1732; RICHARD, b. 25 Feb. 1735; other ch. (undocumented): ANN; JOHN, b. 1741; by 2nd w.: MOSES, poss. b. c. 1747; DEDIMAUH; HANNAH; SARAH; and DANIEL, b. c.1752 (128:23, 86, 93/b; an undocumented chart of the Treadway family in possession of the author).

TREADWAY, THOMAS (3), s. of Richard (1) and Jane, was b. 6 March 1711; in March 1720/1, at age 10 he was bd. to Antil Deaver and w. Sarah; may have m. three times: 1st, on 27 Dec. 1734, Mary Ball; 2nd, by 1744, Elizabeth, dau. of William McComas; Elizabeth was b. c.1718; m. 3rd, Mary (---); on 10 June 1757 William and Elizabeth Smith conv. Thomas Treadway, innholder, (160?) a. Turkey Hills and Strawberry Hills; on 4 May 1759 Thomas and w. Elizabeth conv. to John Goodwin 40 a. White Oak Bottom and 70 a. Strawberry Hills; on 25 April 1769 Thomas and w. Mary conv. 50 a. Turkey Hills and Strawberry Hills to Joseph Stiles; d. testate in Harford Co., leaving a will, 22 May 1783 - 13 Aug. 1783; naming s. Daniel and grandchildren Thomas, George, James, Daniel, and Crispin Cunningham; had iss.: 5 ch. by Mary Ball, and 3 by Elizabeth McComas (by 1st w.): JOHN, b. 25 Jan. 1724; WILLIAM, b. 23 Oct. 1738; CRISPIN, b. 19 June 1736; DANIEL, b. 1737 : MARTIN, b. 7 Oct. 1741 (by 2nd w.): AARON, b. 2 Nov.

1744; MOSES, b. 22 Feb. 1746; and MARY, b. 1748, may have m. (---) Cunningham (5:75, 135; 23:436; 83:47; 84:161; 128:30, 86, 94, 92/b; 129:321, 348; 231-AL#A:197; 244-AJ#R:117).

TREADWAY, DANIEL, m. Sarah Norris on 2 Aug. 1744; she was a dau. of Edward and Hannah (Scott) Norris (Myers, The Norris Family).

TREADWAY, DANIEL, unconnected for some time, was received in membership by Gunpowder Meeting, Society of Friends, on 23 d, 4, 1755 (136).

TREADWAY, THOMAS, m. Anne (---), and had iss.: DANIEL, b. 22 Nov. 1724; MARY, b. 8 Nov. 1726; THOMAS, b. 20 May 1730 (131).

TREADWAY, THOMAS, d. Balto. Co., leaving a will, 21 July 1749 - 2 Aug. 1749, naming cousin Thomas Brown, friend Thomas Treadway, and Mary Cunningham; admin. bond was posted 2 Aug. 1749 by exec. Thomas Tredway, with Amos Garrett and Abr. Taylor (14:206; 110:469).

TREAGE, SUSAN, m. John Cowing on 25 Sept. 1712 (129:216).

TREAGLE, CHRISTOPHER, m. Mary Rowles on 27 May 1734 (133:152).

TREAGLE, MARY, was ind. for bast. in March 1745/6; William Arnold admitted paternity of her ch. (32:805; 36:5).

TREDWELL, RICHARD, m. Maple Stevenson on 7 June 1752; had iss.: DANIEL, b. 30 April 1754; MARY, b. 10 Nov. 1759 (131:40, 23/r, 137/r).

TREEL, MARY, was ind. for bast. in Aug. 1742 (34:8).

TREEL, SAMUEL, s. of Mary Combest, was b. 3 March 1688, and was bur. 5 Jan. 1700 (128:1, 10).

TRELL, BETHENA, no parents named, was b. 10 July 1690 (128:1).

TRENCH, EDWARD, d. by 6 Nov. 1705 when admin. bond was posted by Edward Hancox and George Valentine of A. A. Co. (14:236).

TRIBLE, THOMAS, d. 4 May 1709 (128:25).

TRIERLE, MARY, was ind. for bast. in June 1747 (33:434).

TRIGGER, ZEBEDIAH, had iss.: SUSANNAH, b. 1 July 1755 (131:137/r).

TRINSON, JAMES, was in Balto. Co. by 1694 as a taxable in n. side Gunpowder Hund. (139).

TRIPPAS, FRANCIS, and w. Anna imm. c.1650; purch. 200 a. Foster's Neck from Richard Windley and James Phillips in Nov. 1666; in March 1670 they conv. to William York 15 a. on east s. of Bush River; he d. by 11 Dec. 1672 when admin. bond was posted by Thomas Arminger with James Phillips and Lodowick Williams (14:218; 94; 96:230; 388).

TROOT, ELIZABETH, was ind. for bast. in June 1734 and tried in Aug. 1734 (30:253, 309).

TROTT, ELIZABETH, servant to Dr. Josias Middlemore, was tried for bast. in Aug. 1728 and ind. again for bast. in March 1729/30 (28:32, 362).

TROTTEN, LUKE (1), progenitor, was here by 1719 when he served as coexec. of the est. of John Downes and admin. of Samuel Heathcote; m. 1st, by June 1725, Ruth, dau. of Joseph Heathcote; 2nd, on 3 Oct. 1735, Elizabeth Lenox, and 3rd, on 14 Jan. 1744 Elizabeth (--) Owens Body, wid. of (---) Owens and of Stephen Body; in 1750 owned 15 a. Hopewell, 50 a. part North Canton, 156 a. Wall Town, 137 a. part Triple Union, 170 a. Ballistone, and 52 a. of Sure Inheritance; d. leaving a will, 15 Jan. 1739 - 17 Jan. 1752, naming s. Luke (s. by his 1st w. Elizabeth), who was to have Salter Mumford, daus. Martha, Ruth (to have Triple Union), and Elizabeth (to have tracts near Hunting Ridge called Parkston Place); admin. bond was posted 29 May 1752 by Luke Trotten with Thomas Sligh and Dixon Browne; the will of Elizabeth Trotten, 29 Oct. 1765 - 5 May 1765, named grandchildren Stephen and Joshua Body, Ruth Murray, Jean and John Long, and Elizabeth and Edmond Stansbury (the latter two by Elizabeth's dau. Penelope w. of Dixon Stansbury(and dau. Eleanor McConikin, w. of John McConikin; Luke Trotten left iss., all by his 1st w.: MARTHA, b. 7 June 1725; ELIZABETH, b. 6 March 1728, m. Dixon Brown on 17 June 1746; LUKE, b. 30 Jan. 1729; and RUTH, b. 16 June 1733, m. Edward Sweeting on 6 June 1756 (1:190; 2:17; 3:10, 39; 14:277; 112:44; 131:192; 133:10, 14, 19, 29, 159, 166; 153:30; 210-28: 237).

TROTTEN, LUKE (2), s. of Luke (1) and Ruth, was b. 30 Jan. 1729; d. by 8 Oct. 1792; m. Susannah Long, dau. of John and Eleanor (Owings) Long, on 10 Feb. 1754; had iss.: RUTH, b. 14 Nov. 1754; LUKE, b. 14 July 1756; RACHEL, b. 18 March 1758; SUSANNAH, b. 31 May 1761; ELEANOR, b. 14 May 1767; JOHN, b. 26 Sept. 1771 (8:96; 133:109, 120, 134, 166).

TRUSH, MARTIN, d. by 19 March 1764, when his est. was admin. by his w. Elizabeth, now w. of Philip Emmice; had iss.: JACOB, b. c.1722; EVE, b. c.1727; CATHERINE, b. c.1740; VALENTINE, b. c. 1750; ELIZABETH, b. c.1752; MARY, b. c.1755 (6:96).

TUCKER, SEABORN (1), was bapt. (as an adult), 25 Sept. 1698 in St. James Par., A. A. Co.; m. Dorothy, amdnx. of Charles Harrington of Cal. Co.; had iss.: ANNE, b. 12 Feb. 1695, bur. 17 Aug. 1699; JOHN, twin, b. 17 Aug. 1698; JACOB, twin, b. 17 Aug. 1698; ROBERT, twin, b. 4 Dec. 1700; MARY, twin, b. 4 Dec. 1700; SEABORN, b. 2 Oct. 1704; ANNE, m. Samuel Birckhead (206-10:447; 206-17:74; 210-28:434; 219-3:294, 303, 314, 325).

TUCKER, SEABORN (2), s. of Seaborn (1), was b. 2 Oct. 1704 in St. James Par., A. A. Co.; m. Margaret, dau. of James Cobb, on 2 April 1730; d. in Balto. Co. by 8 Aug. 1740 when admin. bond was posted by Margaret Tucker with Francis Jenkins and Thomas Bradley; Margaret m. 2nd Thomas Litton, Jr.; iss. of Seaborn and Margaret: JACOB, b. 22 May 1731; SUSANNA, b. 15 April 1734, m. Mordecai Crawford on 16 Sept. 1750; and MARGARET, b. 28 Aug. 1736 (3:294; 128:66, 88, 96; 131:36).

TUCKER, JOHN, age 45, ship carpenter, broke out of the county jail at Joppa, Balto. Co. c. Feb. 1755 (385:324).

TUCKER, LEWIS, m. Katherine Partridge ; d. by 5 May 1744 when admin. bond was posted by Parker Hall with Mich. Gilbert; had iss.: LEWIS, b. 21 Jan. 1738; poss. s. WILLIAM, in Aug. 1745 bd. to Daniel Deaver to age 21 (14:289; 35:614; 128:93).

TUCKER, WILLIAM, and w. Welthy were in Balto. Co. by 4 Dec. 1725 when they conv. 100 a. Tucker's Delight and 150 a. Add'n to Tucker's Delight to Thomas Cockey (70:216).

TUCKER, WILLIAM, m. Ann Palmer on 26 Dec. 1759 (131).

TUDOR, HUMPHREY, m. by 1733, Dorcas, dau. of John Ingram who
d. in that year; on 21 Feb. 1738 John Ingram named his sis. Dorcas
Tudor and bro.-in-law Humphrey Tudor in his will; Dorcas Tudor
was ind. for bast. in March 1742/3 and tried in March 1743/4,
indicating that Humphrey had prob. d. by the earlier date; Dorcas
m. Abraham Wright on 23 May 1745 (34:121; 35:166; 126:23; 127:
75; 131:28).

TUCKER, JOS'H, m. Elizabeth Everett on 20 June 1756, and had
iss.: JOHN, b. 15 Sept. 1756; MARY, b. 22 July 1759; ELIZABETH,
b. 10 June 1761; WILLIAM, b. 11 Aug. 1763; by a 2nd w. Mary
(---),. Jos'h had iss.: MARY, d. March 1764; WILLIAM, d. March
1764 (131:47, 64/r, 154/r; it may be that the clerk of the
parish incorrectly entered Mary as the mother of the last two
children).

TUDOR, KEZIA, m. Soll Davice on 20 Nov. 1760 (131:57).

TUDOR, THOMAS, m. Mary Edwards on 15 Feb. 1758 (131:51).

TULLY, EDWARD, d. by 11 Jan. 1710 when his est,. was admin.
by Mary Tully (or Tolley) (2:153).

TULLY, EDWARD, was b. c.1687, giving his age as 62 in a 1749
dep.; may be the Edward who wit. the will of Pierce Welch of
Balto. Co. on 9 Jan. 1722 (124:126; 224:167).

TULLY, EDWARD, and his bro. Michael were bequeathed the tract
Hopyard by the will of James Carroll of A. A. Co. on 12 Feb.
1728 ; on 14 June 1742 Edward and Michael Tully, sons of Michael
Tully, dec., sold 100 a. part Hopyard, which they had from James
Carroll, to Jacob Young; in 1750 Edward owned 100 a. Hunter's
Hopyard, 200 a. Littleworth, and 14 a. Tully's Beginnings (76:
184; 125:133; 153:17).

TULLY, MICHAEL, was in Balto. Co. by 8 June 1721 when he wit.
the will of James Barlow ; d. by 17 April 1732 when admin. bond
was posted by wid. Elizabeth Tulley (or Tolley) with Jonathan
Tipton, John Israel, Edw. Dorsey, and John Chambers; wid. Elizabeth may be the Elizabeth Hogan of Cecil Co., whose will, 8 March
1743 - 20 March 1743, named sons Michael and William, and daus.
Elinor and Mary and refererd to Edward, the heir at law (14:213;
124:74; 127:251).

TULLY, MICHAEL, prob. s. of above, and his bro. Edward were
left Hopyard by their cousin James Carroll, on 12 Feb.1728; on
14 June 1742 he and Edward decided to sell the land to Jacob
Young (125:133; 127:251; 76:184).

TUNEKS, ANN, servant, with 3 years to serve, was listed in
the May 1725 inv. of Joseph Presbury (52:172).

TUNIS, JOHN, m. Martha, dau. of William Hill, on 21 Aug. 1755;
d. in Dec. 1760, and Martha m. 2nd, on 29 Aug. 1768, Benjamin
Van Horne; iss. of John and Martha: MARY, b. 22 July 1757;
MARTHA, b. 22 May 1760 (112:24; 131:46, 74, 23/r, 24/r, 141/r).

TUNIS, JOHN, m. Phebe (---), and had iss.: LEVINER, b. 5
March 1760 (131:23/r).

TURBELL, EDWARD, d. 12 April 1727; m. Sarah Gay on 10 April
1723; Sarah was ind. for bast. in June 1731; iss. of Edward and
Sarah: MARY, b. 24 April 1727 (29:156; 133:12, 148, 193).

TURBETT, ISAAC, was ind. for bast. in Aug. 1738 (31:267).

TURNBULL, GEORGE, carpenter, in July 1749 conv. Richard Jacks 40 a. part Fountain of Friendship; George's w. Grace consented (80:248).

TURNER, MATTHEW (1), m. 1st Rachel (---), and prob. m. 2nd Sarah (---); d. by 20 June 1756 when admin. bond on his est. was posted by Sarah Turner, with Edward Bowen and Lawrence Yanston; est. was admin. 14 Oct. 1757; dec. left iss.: FRANCIS, of age; JOSEPH, b. 8 June 1742; RACHEL, b. 16 Jan. 1744; JACOB, b. 14 Nov. 1757; MATTHEW, b. 11 April 1750 (5:334; 14:293; 133: 88).

TURNER, FRANCIS (2), s. of Matthew (1), was of age in 1757; m. Anne (---), and had iss.: SARAH, b. 28 d, (no month) 1758; ELIZABETH, b. 20 April 1761 (133:107).

TURNER, ANN, was ind. for bast. in June 1741, and admitted her guilt in Nov. 1741 (33:56, 173).

TWINE, RICHARD, d. by 18 Jan. 1710/11 when admin. bond was posted by admnx. Ann Twine with Philip Washington and Samuel Harden ; est. was inv. 31 Jan. 1711 by Samuel Hinton and Philip Washington, and val. at £ 45.4.2; Ann Twine was ind. for bast. in June 1711 and again in Nov. 1712; she m. 2nd Samuel Greening on 1 March 1714 (14:217; 21:210, 334; 48:234; 131).

TWITT, CATHERINE, was ind. for bast, in Nov. 1730 (29:49).

TYE, JOHN (1), m. Eleanor (---), and was in Balto. Co. by Aug. 1729 when they sold John Cockey tract Tye's Delight; d. leaving a will, 21 Nov. 1739 - 5 March 1739/40, naming s. John, dau. Susanna Bell, and grandsons John, Francis, and Arthur Bell; left iss.: JOHN; SUSANNAH, m. by Nov. 1739 (---) Bell (72:61; 127: 67).

TYE, JOHN (2), prob. s. of John (1), in 1750 owned 200 a. Broad Meadow and 100 a. James Meadow; may have d. by July 1754 leaving a wid. Presiosa who conv. to Thomas Cockey Deye land left by George Hitchcock to his grandson George Tye; had iss.: GEORGE (82:259; 153:89).

TYLER, ELIZABETH, was ind. for bast. in Aug. 1723 (15:438).

UANY, EDWARD, m. by 27 July 1713, Lydia, admnx. of Zachariah Brown (1:26).

ULDEREY, STEPHEN, of Balto. Co., was a native of High Germany; was naturalized on 4 June 1738 with his ch.: STEPHEN, GEORGE; DANIEL; JOHN; ELIZABETH; and SUSANNA (303:57).

UNDERHILL, ANN, was b. 1 d, 10, 1687; d. 15 d, 8, 1760; brought a cert. from East Nottingham to Gunpowder Meeting; cert. was delivered after her death, but was entered in records so the Friends could make a record of death and burial (136).

UNDERWOOD, THOMAS (1), of A. A. Co., was there by Oct. 1683 when he surv. 100 a. The Landing on n. side of Severn; on 9 Feb. 1662 surv. 50 a. Middle Neck; d. leaving at least one s.: SAMUEL (77:17; 211:201, 236).

UNDERWOOD, SAMUEL (2), s. of Thomas (1), d. by Oct. 1742; on 29 Sept. 1682 surv. 22½ a. Addition; in May 1688 purch. almost all of the land of Samuel Matson; on 10 June 1689 he and w. Mary conv. 300 a. purch. from Andrew Mattson to Nicholas Rogers; may be the same Samuel Underwood of Newcastle Co., Penna., who on 24 July 1719 conv. part Andrew's Conquest to Edward Hall; had iss.: SAMUEL (59:267, 312; 68:73; 77:17; 211:256).

UNDERWOOD, SAMUEL (3), s. of Samuel (2), and grandson of Thomas (1), on 1 Oct. 1742 sold 700 a. The Landing, Middle Neck, and (Mattson's Lot?) to his kinsman Thomas Cockey; some of this land had been taken up by the grantor's grandfather Thomas; Samuel d. leaving a will, 27 d, 11, 1745/6 - 7 Aug. 1746, naming w. Mary, and these ch.: SAMUEL; ELIZABETH, m. Edward Choat (77:17; 110: 375).

UNDERWOOD, SAMUEL (4), s. of Samuel (3), was living in Balto. Co. in 1750 when he was listed as the owner of 100 a. part of Friendship (153:53).

UNDERWOOD, JOHN, was in Balto. Co. by 1692 as a taxable in the household of James Roberson (138).

UNDERWOOD, THOMAS, m. Ann Petty on 1 Aug. 1743 (131).

UNGEFARE, JOHN MARTIN, planter of Balto. Co., and a native of High Germany, was naturalized on 4 June 1738 with his children: GEORGE; FRANCIS; and CATHERINE (303:57).

URIEL, Capt. GEORGE, m. Eleanor Welch on 24 July 1734; d. by 30 Nov. 1753 when his est. was admin. by "Helena," (sic), now w. of Robert Gilchrest (5:296; 133:152).

URQUHART, ALEXANDER (1), m. 1st Elizabeth (---) who d. 4 Feb. 1734; m. 2nd, in April 1735, Mary Reese; on 16 Feb. 1724 he purch. 50 a. Freeland's Mount from Richard Touchstone; had iss.: (by 1st w.): MARY, b. 30 Nov. 1719; ANN, b. 1 Sept. 1721; JOHN, b. 21 March 1724; HANNAH, b. 30 Jan. 1725; ELIZABETH, b. 27 Sept. 1727; SARAH, b. 28 July 1729; RACHEL, b. 5 Dec. 1731; WILLIAM, b. 31 Aug. 1733 (70:51; 128:72, 85, 87).

URQUHART, WILLIAM (2), s. of Alexander (1), conv. 50 a. Freeland's Mount to Thomas Allender, hammerman, on 5 March 1760 (84: 114).

THE UTIE FAMILY was the subject of an article, "Captain John Utie of Utiemara, Esq.," reprinted in Genealogies of Virginia Families from the William and Mary Quarterly Historical Magazine (Baltimore: Genealogical Publishing Company, 1982), V, 298-304. The author is also grateful to Peter S. Craig of Washington, D. C., who has made suggestions for material that might be included.

UTIE, Capt. JOHN (1), was on Hogg Island with w. Mary Ann and s. John, Jr., in 1625; served as ensign, captain, burgess, and Member of the Council of Va., between 1631-1635; wid. Mary Ann may have m. Richard Bennett; had iss.: JOHN, Jr.; poss. NATHANIEL; and GEORGE (370; 426).

UTIE, JOHN (2), s. of Capt. John (1) and Mary, disappears from Va. records after c.1645 (426).

UTIE, NATHANIEL (3), s. of John (1) and (Mary) Ann, was in Md. by 1658/9 when he was granted Utiesly on Sassafras R., 800 a. Oakington in Feb. 1659, and 2300 a. Spesutia Island in Aug. 1661; he was a graduate of Harvard University in 1635; d. 1675, having m. in 1663 Mary, wid. of Lawrence Ward, and dau. of Rev. Joshua and Susan (Collett) Mapletoft of Lincolnshire, Eng.; Mary was b. c.1629 and d. 30 Sept. 1665 of a wound given her by a slave;

Nathaniel m. 2nd, after Jan. 1667, Elizabeth, dau. of John Carter;
Nathaniel was a delegate to the Upper House of the Maryland Assembly in 1658; he rep. Balto. Co. in the Lower House in 1662, 1666,
and 1669; he d. by 22 Jan. 1675 when admin. bond was posted by
the admns. Elizabeth Utie, with Samuel Boston, and Henry Haslewood; the est. of Nathaniel Utie was inv. and val. at 105,013
lbs. of tobacco; his est. was admin. on 7 Sept. 1686 by Elizabeth
now w. of Henry Johnson; the est. was admin. on 11 June 1694 by
Edward Boothby who had m. Johnson's relict; the heirs were: a
niece who had m. Anthony Drew, nephew George, and niece Sophia
Utie (101:30, 301; 200-41:326; 200-49:92; 206-12:143, 145; 209-
7:206; 209-13:273; 211).

UTIE, GEORGE (4), s. of John (1) came to Md. c.1658; d. by 24
Oct. 1676; m. Susanna, dau. of Samuel and Joanna Goldsmith; she
m. 2nd Mark Richardson; the will of George Utie, 11 Sept. 1674 -
24 Oct. 1678, named w. Susanna and ch.: George, Mary Ann and
Bethia, bro. Nathaniel, and friend Thomas Long; George and Susanna had iss.: GEORGE, Jr.; MARY ANN, m. Anthony Drew; and
BETHIA m. James Phillips (110:59; 370; and 388).

UTIE, GEORGE (5), s. of George (4) and Susanna, d. by 1695
in Balto. Co.; m. Mary, dau. of Edward Beedle; she was bur. 30
April 1697; in June 1683 George Utie, Jr., pet. to have a guarda-
an appointed and he was made a ward of his step-father Mark
Richardson; in May 1687 he surv. 45 a. Utie's Addition; in Aug.
1694 he sold 300 a. half of Planter's Delight (orig. surv.
for John Hawkins and Thomas Goldsmith, and which came to George
Utie "by descent"), in exchange for 400 a. Benjamin's Choice;
he was bur. on 16 Oct. 1695; admin. bond was posted by wid. Mary
on 17 Jan. 1695/6; the est. of George Utie was inv. in 1696 by
Lodowick Martin and Daniel Palmer and val. at £ 200.4.2 plus
36834 lbs. tob.; the will of Mary Utie named dau. Susanna,
sis. Martha Hall, bro. John Hall, Daniel Palmer, and mother of
the testatrix Susanna Richardson; George and Mary had iss.:
SUSANNA, b. 24 Sept. 1695, m. Francis Holland, and in Nov. 1710
John Hall surrendered care of her real est. (14:194; 18:44; 45;
21:183; 59:407; 121:118; 128:4, 5; 206-15:20; 206-16:120; 209-
16:120; 211).

UTIE, BERNARD, no proven rel. to any of the above, was in
Balto. Co. by 1668 and d. 1675; in Aug. 1673 John Mascord and
John Knivington conv. him 300 a. Beaver Neck; he d. leaving a
will, 3 April 1675 - 20 April 1677, naming cousins Jean and
Nathaniel Overton, brother Thomas Overton, and friend Henry
Haslewood; in April 1677 Overton admin. the est. of his bro. Ber-
nard Utie(63:126; 120:88; 209-9:66).

VANCE, PATRICK, was in Balto. Co. by 3 March 1741 when he
purch. 100 a. Rachel's Delight from Abraham Jarrett and w. Ellinor
and from Francis Freeman; may have d. by by July 1747 leaving as
heir his son or bro. ANDREW (76:113).

VANCE, ANDREW (2), heir of Patrick (1), m. Sarah Low on 4 Jan.
1745; on 23 July 1747 conv. 100 a. part Rachel's Delight to
Robert Brierly (79:140; 131).

VAN DEAVER, JACOB, m. by 26 Nov. 1718 Jane, wid. and admnx. of
John Gill; she d. leaving a will, 2 July 1730 - 25 July 1730, naming kinswoman Sarah Gambrell; admin. bond was posted 12 Sept. 1730
by Sarah Gambrell with Thomas Todd and John Parrish (1:338; 2:
142; 14:181; 125:163).

VAN HACK, JOHN, came to Md., prob. fom Va., with his mother
Katherine and her 2nd husb., George Mee, c.1651; was in Balto.
(later Cecil) Co. by 1669/70 when he conv. to Thomas Hawker 300

a. at Fendall's Creek; rep. Balto. Co. in the Lower House in 1669; also held office in St. Mary's and Cecil Counties (96; 371; 388).

VAN SANT, ISAIAH,, m. Mary (---) and had iss.: JAMES, b. 27 July 1756; SUSANNAH, b. 23 Oct. 1758 (137:89).

VANSBEEF (or VOSS BEECH), ELIZABETH, in Aug. 1720 named Edmond Wiseman as the father of her ch.; had iss.: HENRY WISEMAN, b. 26 Aug. 1719 (23:367; 128:44).

THE VAUGHN FAMILY was discussed at some length in Dorsey et al, Christopher Gist of Maryland, p. 79.

VAUGHN, ABRAHAM (1), was in Balto. Co. by 1692 as a taxable in n. side Patapsco Hund.; in Jan. 1716 surv. 50 a. Bachelor's Neck; on 5 Sept. 1738 purch. 150 a. part of World's End from John and Elizabeth Holloway; in March 1742 conv. 150 a. of this land to Skelton Standiford, with consent of his w. Caty (or Laty); in March 1746 he and (2nd?) w. Edith sold 140 a. Addition to Bachelor's Neck to William Rogers; d. by 27 June 1763 when Edith Vaughn posted admin. bond, with Abraham and Gist Vaughn; second admin. bond was posted on 2 Sept. 1765 by Gist Vaughn; m. 1st Caty (---) by March 1742; m. 2nd, by March 1746 Edith, dau. of Richard Gist; left iss.: GIST, b. c.1732; THOMAS; CHRISTOPHER; MILICENT, m. (---) Price; ABRAHAM; dau. m. Reuben Boring; dau. m. Zebediah Cox; and RICHARD (14:189, 191; 75:100; 77:193; 79:430; 138; 207; Dorsey et al, Christopher Gist).

VAUGHN, GIST (2), s. of Abraham (1), was b. c.1732, d. 1800, age 68; m. 2 March 1769 Rachel Gist; had at least one s.: GIST, b. c.1780 (131; 222).

VAUGHN, THOMAS (3), s. of Abraham (1), was fined for bast. in Nov. 1759; m. Mary Poteet on 15 Dec. 1763 (46:241; 131).

VAUGHN, CHRISTOPHER (4), s. of Abraham (1), in April 1759 purch. 140 a. Spring Garden from Jacob Schilling, Jr.; m. by 12 May 1757 Mary, dau. of Edward Richards; in April 1760 sold 50 a. Vaughn's Delight to Richard Richards (83:361; 84:168).

VAUGHN, ABRAHAM (5), s. of Abraham (1), in Oct. 1754 assigned to Joseph Bosley a lease for Dean's Ridge (82:324).

VAUGHN, RICHARD (6), s. of Abraham (1), m. a dau. of Edward Richards; had iss.: MILICENT, m. Roger Parks; REBECCA, m. Jacob Shaw; RUTH, m. Andrew Carr (204:no. 142, HR).

VAUGHN, JOHN,, no known rel. to any of the above, was in Balto. Co. by 1674 when he surv. 100 a. London, later held by his orphans (211).

VEALE, CHRISTOPHER, of Shoreditch, Middlesex, Eng., woolcomber, on 12 Aug. 1718, had James Cowley of Westminster, St. James, Middlesex, bind himself to Veal for 4 years' service in Md. (69:25).

VEAL, DANIEL, m. Christian Spencer on 15 Aug. 1726, and had iss.: ELIZABETH, b. 7 Nov. 1726; HANNAH, b. 17 Jan,. 1728/9; ANN, b. 15 Nov. 1731; ANN, b. 10 Nov. 1733; MARY, b. 25 Feb. 1734; RACHEL, b. 17 Nov. 1736 (128:52, 75, 99).

VEARE, ANN, m. Daniel Bryan on 28 Nov. 1703 (129:200).

VEARES, MARY, was ind. for bast. in Aug. 1717 (22:152).

VEASEY, THOMAS, in 1750 owned 200 a. part Arabia Petrea; in June 1754 he and w. Henrietta conv. part of this to Edward Mitchell (82:266; 153:17).

VERNON/VERNUM, John, m. Susannah Skipton on 17 March 1757 (131).

VERNON, OLIVER, m. Mary Brown on 4 March 1738; had iss.: JOHN, b. 8 June 1739; OLIVER, b. May 1740; ABRAHAM, b. 3 May 1741 (128: 95, 104, 116; 129:335).

VESTERMAN, THOMAS, m. Mary (---), and had iss.: SARAH, b. 26 June 1750 (133:89).

VICKORY, RICHARD STEVENSON, was in Balto. Co. by Feb. 1713/4 when his parents, Jonathan and Ann Plowman conv. him certain property; d. by 2 March 1735 when admin. bond was posted by Geo. Buchanan with Thomas Sligh and Robert Chapman, since John Plowman, Vickory's brother of the half blood and heir at law, ren. the right to admin.; est. was admin. by George Buchanan on 11 Nov. 1736 (4:17; 14:195; 67:359).

VIGOE, FRANCIS, Dutch shoemaker, was a runaway serv. from John Metcalfe at Patapsco, May 1752 (385:178).

VINBELL, THOMAS, was in Balto. Co. by 1695 as a taxable in s. side Gunpowder Hund. (138).

VINE, ROLAND (1), d. by 27 Feb. 1746/7 when admin. bond was posted by Sarah Vine with John Chocke and William Amos, Jr.; m. 1st, by July 1728, Elizabeth (---); m. 2nd, by Nov. 1730, Sarah (---); on 27 March 1735 he purch. 100 a. Brown's Lot from Nathaniel and Rhoda Ayres; d. leaving a will, 29 Dec. 1746 - proved 27 Feb. 1746/7, leaving Brown's Lot to his s. Thomas after the dec. of Thomas' mother; named his four ch. Thomas, Mary, Sarah, and Richard; wife Sarah was to be extx.; est. was admin. 18 Aug. 1747 by Sarah Vine; Roland left iss.: (by 1st w.): THOMAS, b. 11 July 1728; (by 2nd w.): MARY, b. 8 Nov. 1730, d. that yr.; JOHN, b. 22 May 1733, d. same yr.; SARAH, b. 11 June 1734; JOHN, b. 1735 (may have d. young); MARY, b. 19 March 1732, m. James Graham on 25 Dec. 1753; RICHARD, alive in 1746 (4:182; 14: 183; 74:271; 110:373; 131:54/r).

VINE, THOMAS (2), s. of Roland (1) by 1st w. Elizabeth, was b. 11 July 1728; d. by 1750 leaving heirs who owned 100 a. of Brown's Lot (131:43/4; 153:11).

VINE, GODFREY, m. Sarah Beddoes on 14 May 1733 in St. Paul's Par., Q. A. Co.; had iss.: GODFREY, b. 5 July 1733; SARAH, b. 6 Sept. 1736; JOHN, b. 7 March 1738 (128:91, 108; 130:284).

VINER, ELIZABETH, serv. of William Osborne, d. 28 March 1703 (128:17).

VINER, JANE, had iss.: HENRY, b. 20 Feb. 1743 (129:345).

VINES, WILLIAM (1), was in Balto. Co. by 20 March 1697 when he pat. 60 a. Vine's Fancy, which he sold on 9 Nov. 1719 to John Hatherly; in Aug. 1706 he surv. 200 a. Vine's Chance; prob. had s. WILLIAM (68:128; 207).

VINES, WILLIAM (2), prob. s. of William (1), was of Stafford Co., Va., and Balto. Co., Md., when he sold Vine's Chance in Balto. Co. to John Todd of Stafford Co., Va.; William's wife Christian consented (213-PL#6:56).

VINES, JOHN, of A. A. Co., in Aug. 1725 sold 25 a. Bachelor's Hope in Balto. Co. to John Brown; Vines' w. Elizabeth consented (213-PL#6:87).

VISSAGE, JOHN, m. Hannah (---) and had iss.: JAMES, b. 31 March 1753; JANE, b. 1 Oct. 1755; JACOB, b. 1 April 1755 (sic). (129:353).

VOIS HENNESSEE, ELIZABETH, had iss.: ELIZABETH, b. 1 March 1725 (128:88).

VOMABLE, JAMES, Irish weaver, was a runaway serv. from Alexander Lawson's at White Marsh, May 1746 (384:561).

VOSS BEECH, ELIZABETH. See VANSBEEF, ELIZABETH.

WAALER, GEORGE, m. Mary (---); had iss.: WILLIAM,.b. April 1742 (131:101/r).

WABLINGTON, WILLIAM, d. 19 Oct. 1705 (128:22).

WAINWRIGHT, THOMAS, m. Ann (or Susanna) Richardson, on 21 Jan. 1705/6 (129:201, 203).

WAINWRIGHT, THOMAS, m. Pleasance Dorsey on 30 Nov. 1722; on 29 June 1724 purch. 77 a. Joshua's Expectation from Joshua Sewell (69:288; 133:146).

WAIT, SAMUEL, m. Mary (---); had iss.: SAMUEL, b. 25 July 1736; JAMES, b. 23 Feb. 1737/8 (128:98, 99).

WAKEFIELD, JOHN, age 35 or 40, and belonging to the Widow Buchanan, imported this fall in the Biddeford, was a runaway conv. serv. in Nov. 1752 (385:208).

WAKEMAN, EDWARD, surgeon, was in Balto. Co. by 8 Aug. 1730 when he purch. 200 a. The Addition from Roger and Elizabeth Matthews; in 1750 owned that tract and 125 a. Hall's Plains; d. leaving a will, 9 Dec. 1753 - 27 Dec. 1753, leaving Hall's Plains to dau. Elizabeth, Addition to dau. Sarah, E 30 to dau. Mary, and also naming son-in-law James Prichard, Avarilla Hall, Thomas Treadway, John Atkinson, John Hall of Cranberry; admin. bond was posted on 27 Dec. 1753 by exec. John Hall of Cranberry with Andrew Lendrum and Aquila Hall; est. was inv. on 10 Sept. 1758 by William Dallam and Nat'l Matthews, and val. at E 534.19.8; est. was admin. 3 March 1769 by John Hall; dec. left iss.: ELIZABETH (may be the Elizabeth Wakeman or Prichard who m. William Morton on 21 March 1759); SARAH; and MARY (7:59; 14:173; 48:335; 73:411; 111:251; 129:367; 153:1).

WALDEN, LAWRENCE, was in Balto. Co. by 1692 as a taxable in n. side Patapsco Hund.; came to poss. 100 a. Gooseberry Neck which was later held by Thomas Biddison; as Lawrence "Wolden" was named as son of testator;s w. Martha in the will, made 26 March 1699, of Jonas Bowen (121:171; 138; 211:87).

WALFORD. See WALLFORD.

THE WALKER FAMILY was the subject of a chart by the late William B. Marye at the Maryland Historical Society. The Scottish ancestry of the family, based on Mr. Marye's chart, was published in this author's History of the Green Spring Valley, 259.

WALKER, JAMES (1), s. of John, of Patrick, of James of Peterhead, Aberdeen, Scotland, was living in 1708; m. Mary Thom

on 28 Feb. 1704 at Peterhead, and had iss.: JAMES, M.D., b. 11
May 1705; GEORGE, M.D., d. 1743 (Marye chart of Walker Family,
pub. in 259).

WALKER, JAMES (2), s. of James (1) and Mary (Thom), was b. 11
May 1705 at Peterhead, Scotland, and d. 14 Jan. 1759 in A. A.
Co., Md.; on 26 Aug. 1731, m. Susannah (b. 12 March 1713, d. 4
March 1795), dau. of John and Elizabeth Gardiner; James and Susan-
nah (Gardiner) Walker had iss.: MARY, b. 16 June 1732, d. 3 Nov.
1733; JOHN, b. 26 Feb. 1734, d. 12 Feb. 1794; GEORGE, b. 3 April
1736, went back to Scotland where he died; SUSANNAH, b. 6 Feb.
1738, d. July 1787, m. Rev. William West, Rector of St. Paul's
Par., on 28 April 1768; JAMES, b. 29 July 1740, d. March 1810;
MARGARET, b. 19 July 1742, d. 23 Sept. 1801 unm.; CHARLES, b.
b./ 9 Nov. 1744, , d. 1825, m. Ann Cradock in 1772; AGNES, b. 25
July 1746, d. by 1783, m. John Young Day; MARY, b. 22 Nov. 1748,
d. 1824; CATHERINE, b. 16 Feb. 1754, d. Dec. 1787 (127:192; 257:
63; 259:108).

WALKER, GEORGE (3), s. of James (1) and Mary (Thom), d. in
Balto. Co. in 1743; m. Mary Price on 14 Nov. 1728; she was a
dau. of Mordecai and Mary (Parsons) Price, and had been the wid.
of Jonathan Hanson before she m. Dr. Walker; built the est. known
as Chatsworth; d. leaving a will, 5 April 1743 - 15 July 1743,
naming his "dau.-in-law," Mary Hanson, and his dau. Agnes, also
George, John, and James Walker, sons of his bro. James, wife
Mary was co-extx.; admin. bond on his est. was posted 15 Jily
1743 by extx. Mary Walker with Thomas Harrison and James Walker;
est. was admin. by Mary Walker in 1745; in 1750 his heirs owned
100 a. Gill's Fancy, 625 a. Mary's Plains, 222 a. Walker's Wilder-
ness, and 110 a. Walker's Wild Camp; George andMary had iss.: AG-
NES, b. 1 March 1733, m. William Lux on 16 July 1752, and d. at
Chatsworth in her 52nd year (5:33; 14:25; 112:496; 127:224; 153:
18; 256:30; 259:108-109).

WALKER, ELIZABETH, had iss.: WILLIAM, b. 28 Oct. 1755; JANE,
b. 17 Feb. 1745 (128:92; 129:373).

WALKER, EZEKIEL, m. Sarah (---), and had iss.: SARAH, b. 25
Sept. 1738 (133:62).

WALKER, JOHN, m. the wid. Mary Cox on 12 June 1714 (131).

WALKER, JOHN, d. by 10 Dec. 1723, when admin. bond was posted
by Moses Groome with George Buchanan and Robert Love (14:43).

WALKER, JOHN, m. Rachel Bottom on 23 Jan. 1742/3 and had
iss.: DINAH, b. 18 Feb. 1743/4; JOHN, b. 5 Oct. 1745; MARY, b.
30 July 1747; GEORGE, b. 30 March 1750; JONATHAN, b. c.1751 (133:
74, 86, 164; 44).

WALKER, JOHN, par. not given, was b. Shrove Tues., Feb. 1731
(128:84).

WALKER, MAPLE, serv. to Maurice Baker, was ind. for bast. in
Aug. 1739 and tried in Nov. 1739 (32:2, 88).

WALKER, MARY, was tried for bast. in June 1737; ind. for bast.
in Aug. 1739, and tried again in Nov. 1739 (31:54; 32:2, 87).

WALKER, MARY, had iss.: THOMAS, b. 19 April 1742; and ELEANOR,
b. 24 May 1754 (129:329, 371).

WALKER, ROBERT, was in Balto. Co. by 1695 as a taxable in n.
side Gunpowder Hund. (140).

WALKER, WILLIAM, d. 14 Jan. 1731; m. Elizabeth.(---), and had iss.: ELIZABETH, b. 20 May 1723; JOHN, b. 6 March 1725; WILLIAM, b. 20 June 1727; MARY, b. 1 Aug. 1730 (128:63).

WALLER, WILLIAM, on 26 Jan. 1748 purch. 50 a. Triple Union from Abigail Copley, wid. of Thomas Copley; d. leaving a will, 27 Jan. 1748 - 18 April 1749, naming w. Elizabeth and s. John; admin. bond was posted 8 April 1749 by extx. Elizabeth with John Heaven and John Waller (14:122; 80:212; 110:464).

WALLEY, JOHN, d. by March 1691/2 having m. Elizabeth, dau. of Thomas Thurston; she m. 2nd Charles Ramsey (19:152; 59:356).

WALLFORD, JOHN, was in Balto. Co. by 1692 as a taxable in n. side Gunpowder Hund.; m. Mary, wid. of John Nichols; she d. by 12 June 1694 when admin. bond on her est. was posted by Thomas Staley and Robert Owlas with James Maxwell and Richard Adams (14:74; 20:165; 138).

WALLIS, HENRY (1), of Kent, Eng., is alleged to have purch. Boothby's Fortune in Talbot Co., and to have been the father of: SAMUEL (Parran, II, 330).

WALLIS, SAMUEL (2), poss. s. of Henry (1), d. 1724; m. by 29 May 1711, Frances, dau. of Arthur Young of Calvert Co.; came from A. A. Co. to Bush River c.1700; had iss.: HENRY; SAMUEL, Jr.; RUTH; JOHN; HUGH; MARGARET; and WILLIAM (122:201; 433:366).

WALLIS, SAMUEL (3), s. of Samuel (2), d. March.1754; m. on 23 d, 2, 1730, Cassandra, dau. of John Talbot; m. 2nd, on 21 d, 4, 1744, Grace Jacob, dau. of Thomas and Mary; in 1750 owned 100 a. Cobb's Delight and 417 a. part Arabia Petrea; d. leaving a will, 8 Dec. 1753 - 6 March 1754; admin. bond was posted in March 1754 by Grace Wallis, with James Rigbie and Joseph Hopkins; in Nov. 1754 his orphans Edward and John chose Samuel Wallis as their guardian; est. was admin. 30 June 1760 by Grace Wallis who stated the dec. left iss.: (by 1st w.): JOHN, b. 12 May 1732; MARY, b. 24 Nov. 1734; SAMUEL, b. 21 April 1736; EDWARD; JOHN; poss. others (4:304; 14:158; 39:442; 111:60; 128:102; 153: 35; 263:185, 186; 433:366).

WALLIS, ABRAHAM, d. by 11 June 1747 when admin. bond was posted by Richard Dallam and Richard Ruff (14:136).

WALLIS, DIANA, orphan of Elizabeth, age 5 "last month," in Aug. 1743 was bd. to James Caine (35:8).

WALLIS, ELIZABETH, was ind. for bast. in June 1738 (31:221).

WALLIS, EXPERIENCE, serv. to Col. Hall, was ind. for bast. in Aug. 1740 and tried in Nov. 1740 (32:290, 361).

WALLIS (or WALLICE), JOHN, m. Elizabeth.(---) and had iss.: HANNAH, b. 31 July 1744; JANE, b. 28 Nov. 1742 (131).

WALLOX, JOHN, m. Elizabeth (poss. admnx. of Jacob Jones) on 5 Aug. 1731; she d. 2 Dec. 1740; he m. 2nd,.on 16 Dec. 1741, Elizabeth Yates who d. by 4 Sept. 1742 (3:291; 128:71, 72; 129: 322, 323).

WALLSTON, JOHN, imm. to Md. c.1675; by 1692 was a taxable in Spesutia Hund.; m. Margaret (---) who m. 2nd, William Osborne; on 4 June 1686.purch. 200 a. Proctor's Hall from George and Martha Goldsmith; on 16 Oct. 1686 he leased 100 a. from Peter Fucatt; d. by March 1693/4; had iss.: JOHN, b. 12 March 169-(?), d. 7 Dec.

1704; ARABELLA, b. 2 June 1690, m. William Love on 27 April 1706; m. 2nd Bennett Garrett who on 2 April 1736 joined her in sale of Proctor's Hall; SARAH, b. 4 Sept. 1694, m. Jonathan Ward on 28 Sept. 1712 (20:205; 59:208, 212; 74:424; 128:8, 21; 129: 1891 201, 222; 388).

WALONG, HENRY, was ind. for bast. in June 1750 (37:2).

WALTER, ROBERT, was in Balto. Co. by 1692 as a taxable in n. side Gunpowder Hund. (138).

WALTERS, EDWARD, m. Mary (---), and had iss.: SARAH, b. 30 Dec. 1726; THOMAS, b. 10 Jan. 1728 (131:11/r, 19/r).

WALTERS, JAMES, in 1750 owned 50 a. Kingsale (153:77).

WALTERS, THOMAS, m. Elizabeth Stout on 13 July 1713 (131).

WALTERS, "alias VATOS." WILLIAM, m. Mary Jones on 25 July 1736; had iss.: MARGARET, b. 28 Aug. 1736 (128:92, 96).

WALTERS, WILLIAM, d. by 1750 leaving heirs who owned 50 a. Triple Union (153:77).

WALTHAM, JOHN, age 3 in June 1742 when he was bound to Richard Minson and w. Mary to age 21 (33:437).

WALTHAM THOMAS, m. by 7 June 1753 Elizabeth, granddau. of James Maxwell; had iss.: ELIZABETH, b. 24 June 1759; MARY, b. 16 Nov. 1762; THOMAS, b. 29 March 1768; PHILIZANNA, b. 21 Aug. 1771(82:6; 131:68/r, 160/r).

WALTON, JOHN, in April 1669 conv. 120 a. Wallton to John Arhorne (Arden?) and Thomas Green (96).

WALTON, JOSEPH, m. Sarah Matheny on 23 March 1746 (131).

WALTON, JOSEPH, m. Mary Gibbins on 31 Dec. 1753 (131).

WALTON, THOMAS, b. c.1726, d. by 1773; m. on 26 Oct. 1747 Elizabeth Williams who m. 2nd (---) Cresswell; in Oct. 1752 he purch. 50 a. Barnes' Level from William and Elizabeth Gosnell; had iss.: WILLIAM; JOHN, m. c.1775 Ann Jones (81:448; 133:160).

WALTON, THOMAS, m. Eliz. Maxwell on 21 June 1750 (131).

WANN. See WONN.

WARD, JOSEPH (1), was in Balto. Co. by 1707; d. by 7 March 1754; m. Bridget (---); in June 1733 he purch. from John Long 100 a. part of Ballstone which he still owned in 1750; d. leaving a will, 7 Feb. 1748/9 - 7 March 1754, naming granddau. w. of Richardson Stansbury and dau. of Isaac and Letitia Raven as heiress of Ballstone, named other grandch. Elizabeth, Letitia, and Luke Raven, and Hester, Keziah, Avarilla, Drusilla and Nancy Harryman, daus. of Prudence Harryman; admin. bond was posted 6 June 1754 by Richardson Stansbury with Thomas Sligh and Christopher Duke; est. was admin. 28 July 1755 by Richardson Stansbury, heirs named were: wife of Robert Drew, dau. of Isaac Raven, Lettice Raven, wife of Charles Harryman or Merryman, Ann Harryman and Luke Raven; dec. left iss.: ELIZABETH, b. 1 May 1707; JOHN, b. 22 Nov. 1711; RICHARD, b. 15 March 1713 or 1 March 1714; JOSEPH, b. and d. last of June 1717; MARY, b. 1 July 1717 (sic); MARY, b. July 1719; JOSEPH, b. 22 Jan. 1720/1; JOSEPH, b. 1 April 1722; SARAH, b. Sept. 1724; LETITIA, m. Isaac Raven (5:351; 14: 178;   73:378; 111:50; 131:7, 9, 11, 36/r, 43/r; 153:61).

WARD, JOHN (2), s. of Joseph (1) and Bridget, was b. 22 Nov.
1711; m. Sarah Burrough on 17 Dec. 1737; on 7 March 1728/9 purch.
50 a. Ward's Adventure from Jacob Robinson and w. Mary; had iss.:
WILLIAM, b. 10 March 1738; ELIZABETH, b. 21 June 1741;
JOHN, b. Nov. 1742; SARAH, b. 1745 (70:271; 131:11, 78/r, 86/r,
117/r).

WARD, RICHARD (3), s. of Joseph (1) and Bridget, was b. 15
March 1713 or 1 March 1714; m. Mary Gross on 15 Aug. 1739; had
iss.: JOHN, b. 1 Aug. 1740; MARY GROSS, b. 17 May 1742; RICHARD,
b. 28 March 1742; BRIDGET, b. 18 Dec. 1746 (113:117/r).

WARD, JOSEPH (4),s. of Joseph (1) and Bridget, was b. 22 Jan.
1720/1 or 1 April 1722; may be the Joseph Ward, Jr., who in March
1736 was tried for fathering an illeg. ch. on the body of Prudence Harryman (but he would have been only 14 or 16 at the time);
m. 1st, on 24 Aug. 1743, Hannah Lee; may have m. 2nd, on 13 Feb.
1748, Mary Perkinson; had iss.: (by 1st w.): RACHAEL, b. 6 Nov.
1745; (by 2nd w.): SARAH, twin, b. 8 Oct. 1761; ELIZABETH,
twin, b. 8 Oct. 1761; JOSEPH, b. 8 April 1764; STEPHEN, b. 17
March 1766 (31:38; 131:33, 97/r, 111/r, 152/r, 153/r, 156/r).

WARD, EDWARD (5), no known rel. to any of the above, d. by 5
Nov. 1730; m. Anne (---) who m. 2nd, on 11 Jan. 1730/1 Lemuel
Howard; d. leaving a will, 21 April 1730 - 5 Nov. 1730, naming w.
Ann and dau. Camilla; admin. bond was posted 3 June 1731 by
Lemuel Howard with John and Gideon Howard; est. was admin. 8
June 1733 by Lemuel and Anne Howard; acct. stated that the dec.
left a wid. and one ch.; had iss.: CAMILLA; poss. a s. EDWARD
(14:33; 30:357; 92:246; 125:80; 131:68/r).

WARD, EDWARD (6), poss. s. of Edward (5), in 1750 owned 284
a. part Arabia Petrea; m. Mary Griffith on 5 April 1761; on 22
Dec. 1763 sold to William Wilkinson land formerly belonging to
Edward Ward, Sr. (88:379; 129:370; 153:51).

WARD, (---), had iss.: MARY, b. 11 Jan. 1711; STEPHEN, b. 5
Nov. 1713 (128:32).

WARD, CATHERINE, was ind. for bast. in Aug. 1738 (31:267).

WARD, DANIEL, m. Ann Boyd on 27 May 1733 (133:151).

WARD, ELIZABETH, d. 13 Dec. 1716 (131:9).

WARD, ELIZABETH, was ind. for bast. in Nov. 1730 (29:49).

WARD, GARRARD, admin. the est. of Luke Raven in 1714 (1:13).

WARD, HENRY, mariner, purch. land on s. side Elk River from
William Fisher, chirurgeon, of Va., on 4 March 1666/7; on 4 Nov.
1662 he surv. 550 a. Mount Surredoe; on 10 Feb. 1669/70 he was
allowed out of the public levy 189 lbs. tobacco for the accomo-
dation of Jerome White, Esq., at Barrones, 231 lbs. tob. for his
expenses at Amickim, and other sums; on 17 Dec. 1670 he was sworn
in as Deputy Surveyor of Balto. Co.; d. by 1700 when his heirs
owned 550 a. Mount Surredoe (94; 200-57:116, 723; 211).

WARD, ISAAC, m. Ann Fields in 1753 (131).

WARD, JANE, was ind. for bast. in March 1738/9; her dau.:
ELEANOR, b. May 1738 (31:351; 128:108).

WARD, JOHN, m. Susannah Goby on 26 Dec. 1721; had iss.: MARY,
b. 21 May 1723 (128:42).

WARD, JOHN, d. in Jan. 1746; admin. bond was posted on 20 Feb. 1746 by William Dallam with Talbot Risteau, Walter Tolley and N. Ruxton Gay (14:137; 131:117/r).

WARD, JOHN, m. Elizabeth Potter on 26 Dec. 1757 (131:50).

WARD, JONATHAN, m. 1st, on 28 Sept. 1712, Sarah Walston who d. 3 March 1715/6; he m. 2nd, on 8 Jan. 1717/8 Ann Hall; iss. by 1st w.: GEORGE, b. 3 March 1715/6 (128:36).

WARD, JOSEPH, d. in Jan. 1746 (131:117/r).

WARD, LAWRENCE, imm. to Md. c.1651; d. by 1663 leaving a wid. Mary who m. 2nd Nathaniel Utie; in Sept. 1663 she surrendered certain land patents (200-49:92; 388).

WARD, MARY, was ind. for bast. in March 1740/1, and tried in June 1741; tried again in March 1745/6; had iss.: ROSANNA, b. 27 Jan. 1740; WILLIAM, b. 9 Oct. 1745 (33:2, 78; 35:809; 131:86/r, 109/r).

WARD, SAMUEL, d. in St. John's Par., leaving a will, 1 Sept. 1731 - 5 Nov. 1731, naming grandsons Simeon Collins and Samuel Collins, granddaus. Amey Collins and Hanner Ashbrook, two grandch. of Mary Ann Ward; daus. Mary Ann Ward, Hannah, and Rosanna, extx. and Ephraim Tomlinson and Joseph Tomlinson of Gloucester Co., N.J. ; had iss.: MARY ANN; HANNAH, and ROSANNA; poss. a dau. who m. (---) Collins (125:217).

WARD, SIMON, m. Margaret, wid. of Joseph Lobb, on 3 Sept. 1723; in Nov. 1724 the court authorized him to provide sufficient clothing for Richard Gardner (27:34; 133:148).

WARD, THOMAS, and w. Elizabeth conv. Lot # 33 to Dr. John Stansbury in May 1754 (82:255).

WARFOOTE, JOHN, m. by 1696 the wid. of John Nichols (or Nicholson) of Balto. Co.; Mary Warfoot d. by 22 Oct. 1698 when her admins. Thomas Staley and Robert (---) admin. the est. of William Nicholson(2:33;206-14:155).

WARRANT, JOS., m. Jane James on 15 Dec. 1760 (131).

WARRELL, SAMUEL, m. Mary White on 1 May 1742; she d. 21 Dec. 1748; had iss.: SAMUEL HATFIELD, b. 24 Sept. 1745, d. 13 Oct. 1746; MARTIN, b. 13 March 1741 (131:89/r, 112/r, 122/r).

WARREN, JOHN, m. Eliz. Keen or Caine on 16 Feb. 1751 (131).

WARREN, THOMAS, m. Mary, wid. of (---) Jones and mother of Thomas, Lewis, and Jonathan Jones; d. 4 May 1736 near Susquehanna R.; admin. bond posted 21 June 1736 by wid. Mary Warren with Thomas Shea and Thomas Jones; est. admin. 9 Oct. 1736 by Mary Warren (4:13; 14:28; 31:53; 75:69, 70, 71; 128:92).

WARRICK WILLIAM, m. Jannet Thaker on 17 Oct. 1756 (131).

WARRILL, HENRY, m. Juliatha Spicer in 1746 (133:159).

WARRINGTON, HENRY, m. Mary (---) and had iss.: JOHN, b. 20 Aug. 1741 (131:146/r).

WARRINGTON, JOHN, m. Mary (---) and had iss.: ELIZABETH, b. Sept. 1745; MARY, b. Sept. 1747; WILLIAM, b. 18 July 1752; HENRY, b. 8 March 1754; SUSANNAH, b. 17 April 1756; ANN, b. 1 Dec. 1743 (131:146/r).

WARTERS, HANNAH, was tried for bast. in Nov. 1755 and named Abraham Isaac Whitaker as the father (40:401).

WARTON, JOHN,; est. was admin. (date not given) by James Collier and William York (2:57).

WASHINGTON, PHILIP, b. c.1665, was age 50 in 1715; was a serv. in the 1699 inv. of Capt. John Ferry; m. by May 1707 Alice, wid. and extx. of Peter Bond; in Aug. 1708 they agreed to live apart and Peter Bond, Jr., agreed to support his mother; his est. was inv. (date not given) by Charles Merryman and Benjamin Bowen and val. at £ 87.17.0 (2:82; 48:124; 51:138; 67:359; 310 cites PL, p. 109).

WASKELL, ISAAC, d. by 19 Nov. 1698 when his est. was inv. by William Harper and Daniel (Swindell?), and val. at £ 17.9.0 (48:69).

WASON, THOMAS, in April 1716 surv. 150 a. Wason's Farm (207).

WASSON, WILLIAM, d. by March 1736 when Stephen Onion admin the est. (31:42).

WATERS, GODFREY (1), d. 15 May 1754; m. Sarah White on 3 Nov. 1726 in St. Margaret's Par., A. A. Co.; on 3 June 1726 signed the inv. of Thomas Gwins as kin; d. leaving a will, 7 April 1754 - 5 June 1754, naming w. Sarah as sole extx., and the ch. named below; admin. bond was posted 7 Nov. 1754 by admnx. Sarah Waters with William Kitely and John Waters; had iss.: JOHN; HENRY; MARY, m. Francis Deves on 21 Nov. 1753; GODFREY; NICHOLAS; ANN; STEPHEN, b. 15 March 1747; WALTER, b. 8 Feb. 1749; WILLIAM, b. 18 Oct. 1751 (5:355; 14:153; 51:45; 111:51; 131:43, 133/r; 219-4: 103).
    WATERS, JOHN (2), s. of Godfrey (1) and Sarah, m. Providence Baker on 5 Feb. 1756; she d. 4 Jan. 1763 and he m. 2nd, on 22 Feb. 1767 Mary Horner; had iss. (by 1st w.): GODFREY, b. 21 March 1759; CHARLES, b. 17 June 1761; (by 2nd w,): SARAH, b. 29 Dec. 1767 (131:47, 133/r, 135/r, 145/r).

WATERS, HENRY (3), s. of Godfrey (1), d. by 27 March 1749 when admin. bond was posted by Godfrey Waters of A. A. Co., with Charles Carroll; m. on 14 July 1748 Ann, (---), wid. of Nicholas Horner and Matthew Beck; est. was admin. by Godfrey Waters on 11 Aug. 1749, naming heirs: Nathan, s. of Nicholas Horner, Sarah Horner, Susanna Hance, and Mary Horner; est. admin. on 1 Nov. 1749 naming heirs: Samuel Beck, Matthew Beck, Elijah Beck, and the w. of Samuel Smith (all ch. of Matthew Beck) (5:52, 60; 14:122, 123; 131:32).

WATERS, EDWARD, was in Balto. Co. by 1692 as a taxable in Spesutia Hund..(138)

WATERS, HENRY, m. Mary Ruff on 13 Dec. 1757 and had iss.: GODFREY, b. 5 Nov. 1758; HENRY, b. 24 June 1762 (129:374; 131: 50).

WATERS, JAMES, m. Lydia Guyton on 13 March 1750 (131).

WATERS, ROBERT, m. Anne Allen on 13 Dec. 1701 (128:15).

WATERTON, JOHN, d. by 1682; may have been b. in Hampshire or Isle of Wight, Eng.; imm. c.1670 and came to Balto. Co. where he served as a delegate to the Assembly, 1671-1675, and 1676-1682; d..leaving a will, 1 June 1682 - 20 July 1682, naming Edward York, John York's sons in Hampshire and their mother Mary York, Ellenor Copeling and James Mesord, leaving all lands in Isle of

Wight, Hampshire, and in Md. to his nephews, and naming Thomas
Reed and Thomas Ridge as execs.; admin. bond was posted 21 July
1682 by admins. James Collier and William York with John Tilliard
and James Thompson; est. was admin. 7 May 1686 with an inv. val.
at £94.9.11, and legacies were paid to Edward York, John York,
William York and his w., and to James Mussard and Ellinor Cop-
lin, the heirs were his nephews in the Isle of Wight (14:72; 120:
142; 206-9:8; 371:868-869; 388).

WATKINS, FRANCIS (1), imm. to Balto. Co. by 1680 and d. there
by 11 April 1696; m. 1st, by 7 June 1681 Christiana Waites or
Wright, dau. of Thomas Long's wife Jane; m. 2nd Mary (---) who
survived him and married 2nd, by 1698 William Barker, and 3rd Capt.
John Oldton; on 7 June 1681 Thomas Long conv. 185 a. Hopewell to
Francis Watkins who m. Christiana, dau. of Long's w. Jane; in Feb.
1685 Watkins surv. 74 a. Bettor's Hope; in 1693 he was a member
of the first vestry of St. Paul's Parish; rep. Balto. Co. in the
Lower House in 1692-1694 and 1694-1697; d. leaving a nuncupative
will, proved 11 April 1696, naming w. Mary, sons Francis and Samuel and daus. Margaret and Christiana; admin. bond was posted 27
June 1696 by Mary Watkins and William Barker with John Hayes and
Nicholas Fitzsimmons; est. was inv. on 12 May 1696 by John Hayes
and Nicholas Fitzsimmons and val. at £ 169.11.4 plus 6782 lbs. tob.
in debts; est. was admin. by William and Mary Barker in 1698;
Mary (---) Watkins Barker Oldton d. by 10 Dec. 1709 when her inv.
was signed by her son-in-law Francis Watkins; Francis Watkins left
iss., the first two def. by 1st w.: CHRISTIANA, d. leaving a will,
22 April 1703 - 12 Nov. 1703, naming Mary Oldton and Francis and
Samuel Watkins; est. admin. 6 Aug. 1707 by extx. Mary Oldton;
FRANCIS, d. by 21 May 1713; SAMUEL, d. 1743; MARGARET (2:86;
14:69; 48:283; 64:123; 121:110, 230; 122:35; 206-14:25; 206-17:
298; 211; 371:869; 388).

WATKINS, FRANCIS (2), s. of Francis (1), d. by 11 May 1713;
m. Jane, dau. of Daniel Scott; she d. c.1765 having m. as her 2nd
husb., some time before Nov. 1713, Samuel Hughes; Watkins was
alive on 10 Dec. 1709 when he signed the inv. of his mother-in-
law (i.e., step-mother), and dead by 11 May 1713 when admin. bond
was posted by Jane Watkins with Daniel Scott, Jr., and Thomas
Biddison; his est. was inv. 21 May 1713 by William Wright and
John Hilton and val. at £ 21.18; and signed by his bro. Samuel
Watkins; est. was admin. by Jane Watkins on 29 March 1714; on 4
Nov. 1714 she m. Samuel Hughes; when Jane Scott Watkins Hughes d,.
leaving a will, 14 April 1762 - 31 Oct. 1765 she named the ch. of
her s. Francis Watkins (i.e,,Daniel Scott, Francis, Jane, Elizabeth and Nathaniel Watkins); Francis and Jane had one s.:
FRANCIS, d. by 17 May 1757 (1:3; 14:47; 48:283; 50:285; 64:9;
67:10; 112:27; 129:215).

WATKINS, SAMUEL(3), s. of Francis (1), d. 1743; m. Mary
(prob. dau. of William Wright whose will of 25 Feb. 1723/4 named
a dau. Mary Watkins); Samuel d. leaving a will, 2 April 1743 -
22 Aug. 1743, naming s. Samuel, dau. Mary Anne, and "other children;" admin. bond was posted 27 Aug. 1743 by exec. Samuel Watkins
with Abraham Ditto and William Demmitt; est. was inv. on 27 July
and his est,. was admin. 13 Oct. 1744 by Samuel Watkins; had iss.
(his ch. were named in a court proc. of Aug. 1746): MARTHA, b.
15 Jan. 1715, m. James Standiford on 6 Oct. 1737; SAMUEL, b. 15
Nov. 1717; WILLIAM, b. 10 Dec. 1720, m. Ann Barkabee on 9 Dec.
1741, and d. leaving a will 26 Aug. 1753 - 10 June 1754, naming
w. Anne and his bros. and sisters; JOHN; MARY; and SOLOMON (3:
369; 36:208; 111:61; 127:225; 131:40, 39/r, 77/r).

WATKINS, FRANCIS (4), s. of Francis (2) and Jane, d. by 17
May 1757, m. Elizabeth Mead on 19 Jan. 1738/9; in 1750 owned part

Bosley's Expectation and 50 a. Arthur's Choice; admin. bond was posted 25 March 1754 by admnx. Eliza Watkins with Moses Galloway and John Parks; est. was admin. 17 May 1757, naming ch. listed below (with exception of Benjamin); dec. left iss.: DANIEL SCOTT, b. 5 Dec. 1739; FRANCIS, b. 27 Sept. 1741; JANE, b. 17 Nov. 1743; BENJAMIN, b. 10 Aug. 1745, d. 18 Oct. 1745; ELIZABETH, b. c.1748; NATHANIEL, b. c.1749; and MARY, b. c.1752 (5: 322; 14:157; 131:70, 100/r, 110/r; 153:58).

WATKINS, SAMUEL (5), s. of Francis (2) and Jane, was b. 15 Nov. 1717; d. in Balto. Co. betw. July and Nov. 1795; m. Frances Hardesty on 2 June 1757, but may have m. Margaret (---) as his 1st w.; had iss.: MARY, dau. of Samuel and Margaret, was b. April 1753; JOHN; SAMUEL; MARTHA; and SARAH (114:336; 131:49, 130/r).

WATKINS, JOHN (6), s. of Francis (2) and Jane, m. 1st, Elizabeth Jones on 10 Feb. 1747, and 2nd, on 25 June 1750 Elizabeth James (131:29, 36).

WATKINS, JAMES, m. Mary (---), and had iss.: BENJAMIN, b. 11 Jan. 1745 (131:114/r).

WATKINS, JAMES, m. Unity Green on 4 May 1758 (131:52).

WATKINS, JOHN, m. Margaret, dau. of Benjamin Loney; d. by 9 Nov. 1742 when his est. was admin. by his father-in-law Benjamin Loney; Margaret, wid. of John Watkins, d. by 6 Aug. 1740 when admin. bond on her est. was posted by Benjamin Loney with William Greenfield and Abraham Taylor; her est. was admin. by Benjamin Loney on 1 Feb. 1742/3; John and Margaret had iss.: THOMAS, b. 18 March 1728; JOHN, b. 15 March 1731; WILLIAM, b. 22 Oct. 1737 (3:263, 264; 14:107; 128:90, 93).

WATKINS, JOHN, poss. s. of above John and Margaret, was bd. to William Dougherty in March 1743/4, age was "12 next April;" m. Purify Greenfield on 9 Oct. 1754; they had iss.: MARGARET, b. 14 Oct. 1754; ELIZABETH, b. 24 Jan. 1756; SUSANNA, b. 23 Feb. 1758; JOHN, b. 14 Jan. 1760; WILLIAM, b. 22 Nov. 1762 (35:156; 129:355, 379).

WATKINS, MARY, was ind. for bast. in March 1738/9; tried for bast. and named Uriah Davis as the father (31:351; 32:305).

WATKINS, RICHARD; d. by unspecified date; est. was admin. by Sarah Watkins (2:231).

WATKINSON, FRANCIS, b. Darbyshire, age c.21 in Sept. 1754, was listed as a runaway serv. from Baltimore Ironworks (385:305).

WATSON, (---) (1), m. Mary (--7), who m. as her 2nd husb., by 19 July 1738, Martin Bacon; she was the mother of a son by her 1st husb.: WILLIAM, b. c.1737 (33:303).

WATSON, WILLIAM (2), s. of (---) (1) and Mary, was b. c.1737; in March 1741/2 Edward Mortimer testified he had the child in his care but the ch. was taken from him by Martin and Mary Bacon; in Oct. 1742, age 5, William was named in a lease for three lifetimes , as s. of Mary Bacon, age 22, w. of Martin Bacon, age 26; may be the William who m. Bethia Thornbury on 5 May 1757 (33: 303; 77:55; 131:215, 102/r).

WATSON, ABRAHAM, m. Margaret Ginkins (or Jenkins) on 4 Feb. 1705/6 (128:18).

WATKINS, HUGH, tinker, was listed in May 1739 as a runaway serv. of Nathan Rigbie of Balto. Co. (384:224).

WATSON, JOHN, m. Jean Scott on 12 May 1729 (131:26).

WATSON, JOHN, m. Mary Chenoweth on 24 May 1733; her father, John Chenoweth, named John and Mary's s.: JOHN, b. by 1746 (131:40).

WATSON, JOHN, in March 1754 was named as the father of Elizabeth Sulavan's ch. (39:30).

WATSON, MARY, bore an illeg. ch. in Aug. 1740 and Ulick Burke submitted a bill for the child's care (32:295).

WATSON, THOMAS, was listed in the 1750 Debt Book as owning 50 a. Watson's Trust; on 5 Nov. 1753 he and w. Mary conv. 50 a. of this land to Benjamin Wayger of A. A. Co. (82:95; 153:95).

WATSON, WILLIAM, was in Balto. Co. by 29 April 1678 when he surv. 76 a. Watson's Chance; he died without heirs (211).

WATSON, WILLIAM, m. Elizabeth (---); in 1743 John Claussey conv. him 50 a. Matthew's Forest, which he still owned in 1750; had iss.: SARAH, b. 8 Jan. 1742; ELIZABETH, b. 18 Sept. 1744 (77:422; 131:3; 153:70).

WATTS, JOHN (1), d. in Balto. Co. by 25 July 1714 when John Watts ren. right of admin. in favor of John Jones; Watts was in Balto. Co. by 1 March 1688/9 when he purch. 50 a. Peter's Forest from John Arden; on 4 March 1704/5 sold Temple's Claim to Miles Temple; admin. bond on Watts' est. was posted 3 Aug. 1714 by John Jones with John Gill; est. was inv. 11 Oct. 1714 by John Dorsey, Sr., and Richard Shipley, and val. at ₤ 4.1.10½; est. was admin. 3 Oct. 1714; had one and poss. two sons: JOHN; and poss. EDWARD (1:21; 14:52; 48:191; 59:295; 60:135).

WATTS, JOHN (2), s. of John (1), is prob. the same John who m. Sarah (---), and d. by Nov. 1738 leaving iss.: ELINOR, b. 16 Nov. 1724; MARY, b. 15 Oct. 1727; JOHN, b. 3 July 1730; and WILLIAM, b. 8 Dec. 1735 (31:309; 133:21, 52).

WATTS, EDWARD (3), poss. s. of John (1), m. Mrs. Mary Morgan, wid., and d. by 1750 leaving his wid. who was listed in the 1750 Debt Book as owning 200 a. Merriton's Lot; had iss.: JOHN, b. 5 Dec. 1722; MARY, b. 23 May 1725; FRANCES HOLLAND, b. 19 Oct. 1728, m. William Barney on 26 Jan. 1743; EDWARD, b. 26 Oct. 1730; ROBERT, b. 24 July 1732 (133:3, 11, 15, 18, 22, 146, 167; 153:99).

WATTS, JOHN (4), s. of John (2) and Sarah, was b. 3 July 1730, and in Nov. 1738 was bd. to Edmund and Mary Baxter (31:309; 133:3).

WATTS, JOHN (5), s. of Edward (3) and Mary, was b. 5 Dec. 1722, m. Ann Body on 15 July 1743; m, 2nd, on 20 April 1756 Sarah Eaglestone; in 1750 owned 50 a. part Waterford; had iss.: (by 1st w.): JOHN, b. 21 Jan. 1746/7; EDWARD ALLISON, b. 24 March 1749; PENELOPE, b. 5 April 1751; (by 2nd w.): JOSIAS, b. 3 Jan. 1757; DICKINSON, b. 17 March 1758; BEALE, b. 21 Feb. 1760; THOMAS; a dau. who m. Jacob Young; NATHANIEL; SARAH; and BENJAMIN JOHN, b. c.1767 (9:62, 63; 35:323; 133:62, 63, 108, 166; 153).

WATTS, FRANCIS, servant to Richard Deaver, ran away for 150 days in Nov. 1719 (23:247).

WATTS, JOHN, was tried for fathering Jane Story's ch. in Aug. 1744 (35:323).

WAYLAND. See WHAYLAND.

WAYTS, GERRITT, of Cloucester Co., Va., in Aug. 1662 agreed
to mortgage his land in Balto. Co. to Thomas Powell and to deliver one servant; in Nov. 1662 agreed to pay Powell 500 lbs.
tob. (93).

WEALS, JOHN; d. by 1721 when his est. was inv. (51:331).

WEATHERSHEAD, JOHN: SAMUEL; and WILLIAM, in 1745 were named
as cousins in the will of Rachel Paca, wid. of Aquila Paca
(210-24:37).

WEBB, EDMUND, was Md. by 1672 when he claimed land for service;
was in Balto. Co. by 8 Jan. 1668/9 when he named Thomas Howell
his atty. to give Thomas King possession of None So Good in Finland; on 3 March John Cock conv. Webb 200 a. of this tract (95).

WEBB, SAMUEL, tanner, was in Balto. Co. by 1741; on 2 Nov.
1743 he purch. 79 a. Bond's Wharf from Jacob Giles and Isaac
Webster; on 28 June 1744 advert. for the ret. of a runaway serv.,
one John Castelo; in 1750 owned 200 a. St. Anne's Lot, 500 a.
Spittlecraft, 69 a. Bond's Hope, and 36 a. Balch's Abode; on 29
April 1751 purch. 7 a. Giles and Webster's Discovery from Thomas
and Frances Renshaw; on 10 Oct. 1753 he and w. Jane conv. 69 a.
Bond's Hope to John Allen; had iss.: JANE, b. 9 March 1741;
FAITHFUL, b. 19 Sept. 1743; SAMUEL, b. 8 April 1746; MARGARET,
b. 19 Oct. 1752; SARAH, b. 2 Oct. 1755 (77:347; 81:205; 82:140;
129:325, 336, 368; 153:55; 384:450).

WEBB, WILLIAM, was listed in the inv. of Capt. Robert North as
a servant with 6 years to serve (53:375).

WEBB, WILLIAM, was in Balto. Co. by 1750 when he owned 300 a.
Webb's Discovery; may be the same William who m. Elizabeth Lee on
12 July 1758; had iss.: MARGARET, b. 30 May 1761 (129:368; 153:
53).

THE WEBSTER FAMILY is discussed in Walter V. Ball's Gen. of
the Butterworth Family (553).

WEBSTER, JOHN (1), progenitor, was b. c.1662 on Kent Island
and d. April 1753 in Balto. Co.; m. 1st, Hannah Butterworth; m.
2nd, on 17 April 1735 Mary Talbott; was in Balto. Co. by 1694 as
a taxable ; on 9 March 1703 John and Hannah sold part of Webster's
Enlargement to John Norrington; in 1700 was called bro. in the
will of Thomas Letton, and admin. the est. of Thomas Temple on 9
Aug. 1711 and the est. of John Clark on on 15 Aug. 1712; on 22
Nov. 1704 John and his w. Hannah joined William Howard and his w.
Martha in selling Cow Pasture to Christopher Cox; by 1750 owned
200 a. Sedgely, 1000 a. Best Endeavors, 170 a. Webster's Forest,
20 a. Webster's Desire, and 170 a. Webster's Enlargement; d.
"Friday last,"in Balto. Co. aged 91 years, a native of Kent Co.;
lived all his days in the Province; among other virtues he en-
joyed temperance, which "doubtless contributed greatly to his
longevity;" he lived to see 108 of his posterity, 22 of whom died
before him; left a will, 3 Sept. 1751 - 18 April 1753, naming
the heirs of his dec. s. John, and grandchildren Sarah Rigbie,
Martha Gilbert, and w. Mary, as well as the last five ch. listed
below; had iss.: JOHN, Jr.; JAMES, d. 16 March 1719; MICHAEL;
ISAAC; SAMUEL, b. c.1700; SARAH, m. (---) Deaver, and ALICEANNA,
b. 21 Feb. 1715, m. (---) Bond (1:224, 375; 64:3, 6; 97:125; 99:
347; 128:33, 37; 153:212; 210-29:374' 262:196; 433:368; 553:12 ff.).

WEBSTER, JOHN (2), s. of John (1), d. 6 April 1720; m. Mary
McDaniel on 28 Feb. 1714; she m. 2nd William Hunter; admin. bond
was posted 11 April 1721 by extx. Mary Webster with Benjamin Wheeler

and William Hunter; est. was inv. in 1721, and admin. 20 April
1722 by William Hunter and w. Mary; had iss.: JOHN, b. 24 June
1717; MARTHA, b. 15 Aug. 1714, m. Samuel Gilbert; MICHAEL, b. 7
Feb. 1719, d. 17 Feb. 1719 (1:66; 14:41; 51:332; 128:32, 35, 40,
42).

WEBSTER, MICHAEL (3), s. of John (1) and Hannah, d. Balto. Co.
by 30 April 1764; m. Elizabeth, dau. of Nathaniel Giles of Balto.
Co.; his will, 10 May 1761 - 30 April 1764, left Endeavor to sons
John and Michael, named granddau. Hannah Ruff, nephews Isaac and
John L. Webster, mentioned Webster's Enlargement and Webster's
Desire, and the following ch.: ELIZABETH, b. 1 Nov. 1723, m. 1st,
on 11 M,ay 1740, Daniel Ruff, and 2nd, (---) Little; HANNAH, b.
8 or 24 March 1724; JOHN, b. 5 May 1727; MICHAEL, b. 12 July
1729; MARY, b. 12 Aug. 1731; JAMES, b. 20 Jan. 1733; MARY, b. 22
Aug. 1738; MARGARET, b. 7 Nov. 1741; and FRANCES (125:172; 128:
43, 44, 71, 93; 129:291, 315, 332; 210-32:96).

WEBSTER, ISAAC (4), s. of John (1), d. in Balto. Co. by 23
May 1759; m. Margaret, dau. of James Lee of Balto. Co.; on 9 Nov.
1732 purch. all the lands to which Simon Person had any right,
title or interest; in 1750 owned lany tracts incl. 300 a. part
Friendship, 20 a. Friendship Addition, 4 a. Littleworth, 100 a.
Wilson's Range, 500 a. Ranger's Lodge; d. leaving a will, 9
March 1755 - 23 May 1759, naming w. Margaret and ch. listed
below; his est. was inv. 15 d, 11, 1760 by William Cox and Wil-
liam Wilson and val. at £ 1253.1.7, and signed by Margaret Webster
and Hannah Richardson; est. admin. 18 Dec. 1760; dec. left iss.:
HANNAH, b. 28 March 1724, m. Daniel Richardson; MARGARET, b. 21
Jan. 1725/6, m. John Talbot; MARY, b. 6 April 1728, m. Robert
Pleasant; ISAAC, b. 23 Dec. 1730; JOHN LEE, b. 6 March 1732;
SUSANNA, b. 13 April 1735; CASSANDRA, m. Jonathan Woodland;
ELIZABETH, m. Dr. Thaddeus Jewett; SARAH, m. William Cole in
1761; ANN; SAMUEL (4:306, 317; 50:25; 73:319, 320; 125:253; 128:
43, 52, 59, 76, 89; 129:232, 245, 251, 268, 284; 153:2, 98; 210-
30:574, 753).

WEBSTER, SAMUEL (5), s. of John (1) and Hannah, was alive in
1742; m. Elizabeth Dallam on 2 Feb. 1726; in 1710 he was named
in the will of William Howard; on 16 April 1736 as "one of the
People called Quakers," he admin. the est. of James Cave; had
iss.: ELIZABETH, b. 25 Nov. 1727, d. 10 Nov. 1729; ALICEANNA, b.
15 Jan. 1729; ELIZABETH, b. 10 March 1731, m. Nathaniel Smith
on 11 March 1752; JOHN, b. 19 June 1734, m. Hannah Wood; SAMUEL,
b. 9 June 1736, d. 28 April 1740; RICHARD DALLAM, b. and d. 15
April 1738; RICHARD, b. 7 April 1740; MICHAEL, b. 25 Feb. 1742;
(3:215; 123:146; 129:339).

WEBSTER, JACOB, had iss.: HANNAH, m. Samuel Gover of Balto.
Co., who d. 1744/5 (127:253).

WEBSTER, JOHN, m. Hannah Gilbert on 26 June 1739 (128:111).

WEBSTER, JOHN, m. Mary Lynch on 1 Jan. 1755 (131).

WEBSTER, JOHN, age 13 last 1 Feb.,. son of John Webster of
Roan Oak, in June 1758 was bd. to Michael Webster (46:122).

WEBSTER, MICHAEL, age 13 next 15 Jan., son of John Webster
of Roan Oak, in Aug..1759 was bd. to Daniel Anderson (46:222).

WEBSTER, SAMUEL, s. of Samuel, m. Margaret Stewart on 19 July
1759 (129:368).

WEEKS. See WICKS.

WEEN, JOHN, m, Eliz. Godard in 1760 (131).

WEGLEY. See WIGLEY.

WEIMER, BERNARD, b. in Germany, in May 1736 as a planter of Balto. Co., was naturalized (303:43).

WEIR, THOMAS, m. Sarah Puttee in 7 Dec. 1756 (131).

WELBOURNE. See WILBOURN.

THE PIERCE WELCH FAMILY

WELCH/WELSH, PIERCE (1), d. in Balto. Co. by June 1722; m. Catherine (---) who m. as her 2nd husb. Ambrose Geoghegan; in Jan. 1703/4 surv. 200 a. Welch's Adventure, and in April 1706 surv. 200 a. Tramore; Edward Welch in his will of 12 May 1713 named Helen, Katherine, and James, children of Pierce Welch; Pierce Welch d. leaving a will, 9 Jan. 1722 - 1 Sept. 1722, leaving his two tracts to his seven children equally at their majority; wife Catherine was to have 1/3 of the personal est.; admin. bond was posted 18 June 1722 by extx. Catherine Welch with Tobias Eminson, Thomas Taylor, John Giles, and John Israel; est. was admin. 8 Sept. 1724 by Catherine, now w. of Ambrose Geoghegan; Pierce and Catherine had iss.: PIERCE, Jr.; HELEN, m. 1st, Capt. George Uriel, and 2nd, Robert Gilchrest; CATHERINE, alive in May 1713; JAMES; JOHN; MARY, m. John Cook; poss. ANN, m. John Bayley; poss. EDWARD, d. 1795 (2:369; 14:36; 122:248; k24: 126; 207; 259:110-111).

WELCH, JAMES (2), s. of Pierce (1) and Catherine, was b. c. 1711 and d. c.1787 in Balto. Co.; inherited 200 a. Tramore from his father; still owned the prop. in 1750; in March 1752 he surv. 115 a. Angel's Fortune; signed the pet. in favor of removing the county seat from Joppa Town to Baltimore Town in 1768; left iss.: JOHN, d. c.1804; HELENA; CATHERINE; MARGARET; MARY (78:185; 153: 68; 200-61:535; 231-AL#E:314; 259:110-111; 398:53).

WELCH, JOHN (3), s. of Pierce (1), d. 1786 in Balto. Co.; d. leaving a will, 5 July 1786 - 21 Aug. 1786, naming ch. of his bro. James Welch (John, Catherine, Margaret, and Mary), Helena Welch, John Geoghegam son of Ambrose Geoghegan; had one s.: JOHN, m. Betsy, dau. of Thomas Davis (113:165; 259:111).

THE WILLIAM WELCH FAMILY has been the subject of study by Edwin Welch of Santa Barbara, California; Mr. Welch's notes (or some of them) are at the Maryland Historical Society in Baltimore.

WELCH, WILLIAM (4), no known rel. to any of the above was in Balto. Co. by 1692 as a taxable in Spesutia Hund.; may be the William Welch who d. by 1 April 1721 when admin. bond was posted by Judith Welch with Thomas Carr and Thomas Ford; in 1712 purch. 100 a. Welch's Hopeful Palace from Thomas Taylor, and in same year agreed to buy certain property from William Bausley or Bosley; c.1720 pat. 50 a. called Welch's Fancy which was later held by Thomas Welch; left iss.: WILLIAM; THOMAS (14:38; 67:163; 82: 488; 138; notes by Edwin C. Welch, described more fully in the Bibliography under Welch).

WELCH, WILLIAM (5), s. of William (4) may be the William Welch, Jr., who in 1752 sold 100 a. Welch's Hopeful Palace to Thomas Findley; he is the William listed in 1750 as owning 100 a. Taylor's Palace

WELCH, (---), m. by 12 Nov. 1723 Katherine, dau. of James
Lewis of A. A. Co. (124:234).

WELCH, ANN, was ind. and tried for bast. in Nov. 1734 (30:
350, 365).

WELCH, DANIEL, was named by Capt. John Oldton to be a Ranger
on 23 March 1693/4; was in Balto. Co. by June 1688 when he surv.
102 a. Welch's Addition, which was later held by his orphans; in
1692 was a taxable in n. side Patapsco Hund. (138; 211; 338:111).

WELCH, EDWARD, d. leaving a will, 12 May 1713 - 4 July 1713,
naming Helen, Katherine, and James (children of Pierce Welch),
Richard Progden, Pierce Welch, and his own w. Eliza who was to
be extx. and hold the dwelling plantation for her life after
which it was to pass to the aforesaid James Welch; admin. bond
was posted 13 July 1713 by Elizabeth Welch with Henry Knowles
and Thomas Randall; est. was inv. on 13 Nov. 1713 by Henry
Knowles and Thomas Randall and val. at £ 81.18.0; est. was admin.
12 April 1714 by wid. now w. of (---) Taylor; she stated that
the dec. had no children or relations (1:1; 14:48; 50:308; 122:
248).

WELCH, JOHN, age 6 in June 1714, son-in-law of Daniel Banbury,
was bd. to Charles Merryman in Nov. 1714 (21:576).

WELCH, JOHN, m. Ann Hollandworth on 4 July 1724; had iss.:
JOHN, b. 14 Aug. 1725 (128:51).

WELCH, JOHN, d. 19 Jan. 1738 (128:92/b).

WELCH, JOHN, in 1750 owned 100 a. Welch's Delight (153:65).

WELCH, LABAN, s. of Ann West (q.v.), was b. 22 Aug. 1734 in
St. Paul's Par.; prob. the Laban who m. Leah Corbin on 3 Sept.
1761 (131:222; 133:41).

WELCHER, JOHN, m. Unity Coffee on 7 Aug. 1750 (131). (See
also WILTSHIRE).

WELDON, HENRY, d. by 9 March 1695/6 when admin. bond was
posted by John Underwood with Isaac Jackson and Joseph Tolson;
est. was inv. on 9 March 1695/6 by James Jackson and William
Slater and val. at £ 9.18.6(14:64; 50:267).

WELDY. See WILDEY.

THE JAMES WELLS FAMILY · has been the subject of extensive
study by Mrs. Florence Montgomery, whose typescripts are at the
Maryland Historical Society, and are fully cited in the Bibliography; also unpub. material of Mr. and Mrs. H. H. Arnold.

WELLS, JAMES (1), progenitor of this branch, was transp. to Md.
in 1669 in the Nightingale of York; on 1 July 1671 was conv. 100
a. of Mascall's Haven in A. A. Co. by Richard Mascall; by 1673
had moved to Balto. Co. when he and Thomas Richardson purch. 350
a. Taylor's Mount from Samuel Tracey; d. by 22 Feb. 1681/2
when his est. was inv. by Christopher Gist and John Thomas; was
prob. the father of: JOHN; JOSEPH; STEPHEN; and JAMES (63:114;
206-7C:44; 388).

WELLS, JOHN (2), s. of James (1), is so placed because on 1
Nov. 1697 he conv. 100 a. Mascall's Haven to Jonathan Neale;
in 1692 was a taxable in n. side Patapsco Hund.; may have owned
50 a. Thurrell's Neck (later held for his orphans by Joseph

Wells); m. Eleanor (---), and d. by 24 April 1699 when she posted admin. bond with Tobias Starnborough; his est. was admin. by Eleanor on 6 Sept. 1699; inv. had been val. at L 13.13.6 plus 1500 lbs. in tobacco; by 1700 Eleanor Wells had died and Joseph Wells admin. the est.; had iss., but names are not known (2:60; 14:73; 63:289, 303; 211:78).

WELLS, JOSEPH (3), s. of James (1), in Nov. 1682 was bound to Thomas Long to age 21; in 1692 was a taxable at the Widow Long's in n. side Patapsco Hund.; in Aug. 1698 was assigned 30 a. by his bro. John; he included this with other land when he surv. 178 a. Wells Angles; in 1702 he admin. the est. of his bro. John's wid., Eleanor Wells; on 22 April 1702 he and w. Katherine conv. 100 a. Wells Angles to Robert Longland; on 28 Oct. 1703 he sold 178 a. of Wells Angles to Richard Miller; in 1702 was guardian of the orphans of Roland Thornborough, and he may have gone with them to Va. (66:142, 330; 138; Pat. Liber D.D. # 5, p. 118, HR; Testamentary Papers, Box 6, folder 28, HR; Wells notes by Mr. and Mrs. H. H. Arnold in poss. of this author).

WELLS, STEPHEN (4), s. of James (1), was a taxable in Balto. Co. in 1694 (household of John Rowse) and in 1695 (household of James Todd) (139; 140).

WELLS, JAMES(5), s. of James (1), d. in Balto. Co. by Nov. 1771; in 1694 John Thomas gave James 50 a. Wells Lot since Wells released Thomas from the obligation to teach the said Wells to read and write; James may have gone to Va., to visit his bro. Joseph, and some desc. believe he m. Ann Thornborough; in 1717 he is called servant in the will of John Barrett; in 171; in 1750 owned 100 a. Rogue's Ridge; d. by 14 Nov. 1771 when his est. was admin. by Alexander Wells; James and Ann had iss.: THOMAS; PATIENCE, m. (---) McGuire; JAMES, b. 27 Jan. 1716; PRUDENCE, b. 16 March 1720; RICHARD, b. 15 March 1722; HONOUR, b. Oct. 1724, m. 1st William Holmes and 2nd, Col. Richard Brown; ALEXANDER, b. 12 March 1727; ANN, b. 17 Feb. 1729 (7:109; 133:56; 153:37; 216-TC#1:169).

WELLS, THOMAS (6), s. of James (5) and Ann, was b. c.1709 and d. 1804 age 95; m. 16 Sept. 1736 Elizabeth, dau. of Joshua and Joanna Howard; in 1748 was conv. 100 a. Rogue's Ridge by James Wells; in 1750 Alexander Wells conv. him Wells Prospect; Thomas and Elizabeth had iss.: FRANCIS, b. 26 June 1737; JOSEPH, b. 29 May 1739; JOHN, b. 25 March 1743; JAMES, b. 5 Nov. 1747; THOMAS, b. 9 Aug. 1750; RICHARD, b. 30 June 1753; ANN, b. 11 March 1756 (134:44; notes by Mr. and Mrs. Arnold).

WELLS, JAMES (7), s. of James (5) and Ann, was b. 1716 and d. 1804 in Balto. Co.; m. Honora (---); may be the James Wells, Jr. listed in the 1750 Debt Book as owning James Fancy and 50 a. Hickory Bottom; had issue: RICHARD, b. 1742, m. Edith Cole, (Montgomery, "Little Wells Family," p. 120, at MHS; 153:64).

WELLS, RICHARD (8), s. of James (1) and Ann, was b. 15 March 1722, d. 1808 in Ross Co., Ohio; m. 1st, Nancy, dau. of George and Mary (Stevenson) Brown; m. 2nd, (---), poss. Stevenson; had iss.: GEORGE, b. 1745; ALEXANDER, m. Rachel (---); MARY, b. 1748, m. Rev. John Doddridge; JAMES, b. 1751, d. 1814 in Fairfield Co. Ohio; dau., m. (---) Barton; dau., m. (---) Carr; THOMAS, b. 10 Jan. 1758; PATIENCE, b. 1759, m. Rev. James Kerr; HUGH; RICHARD; (by 2nd w.): JOSEPH; NICHOLAS; AARON; JOSHUA; JOHN; RUTH, poss. others (Montgomery, "Little Wells," pp. 122-128).

WELLS, ALEXANDER (9), s. of James (5) and Ann, was b. 12 March 1727, d. 9 Dec. 1813 in Washington Co., Penna.; m. 12 July

1753 Leah Owings, d. 20 Jan. 1815 aged 86; had iss.: HENRY, b.
7 Sept. 1754; ALEXANDER, b. 6 March 1756; ANNE, b. 12 Jan. 1758;
MICHAL (dau.), b. 12 March 1759; NATHANIEL, b. 1 April 1761; and
BEZALEEL, b. 28 Jan. 1763 (134:28, 30, 38, 71).

THE RICHARD WELLS FAMILY

WELLS, RICHARD(10), no known rel. to any of the above; came
from Va. c.1652 with w. Frances, dau. of Richard and Lady Cathe-
rine (Weston) White, and sis. of Jerome White; had settled in
Charles City Co., Va., c.1637; was elected to the Va. House of
Burgess from Upper Norfolk Co., in 1645; after coming to Md. was
made a member of the Parliamentary Commission by Gov. Stone, was
Commissioner of A. A. Co., 1657-1661; was styled chirurgeon of
A. A. Co. when he was conv. land by John Langford of Middlesex,
Eng.; d. leaving a will, 22 June 1667 - 31 Aug. 1667, naming
tracts 600 a. Wells, 100 a. Little Wells, 420 a. Wells Hills, 300
a. Planters' Delight in Balto. Co., as well as other lands;
his will named these ch.: RICHARD; WILLIAM; Col. GEORGE; JOHN;
ROBERT; BENJAMIN, d. 1672; MARTHA, m. 1st William Ayres, 2nd
Anthony Salway; MARY, m. 1st Thomas Stockett, and 2nd (---)
Yates; ANN, m. Dr. John Stansby; ELIZABETH; FRANCES (120:40;
200-57:139, 184; 355:611; 388).

WELLS, RICHARD(11), s. of Richard(10), d. 1671, s.p., having
m. Sophia, dau. of Maj. Richard Ewen; she m. 2nd Henry Beedle
(355:611-612).

WELLS, GEORGE (12), s. of Richard (10), d. c.1696; m. on or
after 7 Oct. 1667 Blanch, dau. of Samuel Goldsmith; rep. Balto.
Co. in the Assembly, 1674/5, and was Justice of the Balto. Co.
Court, 1672 - 1689; in 1672 the sheriff of Balto. Co.was ordered
to bring George Wells to the Court of Chancery to answer certain
complaints at the suit of Henry and Sophia Beedle; was bur. 19
July 1696 at his plantation at the Bay Side; d. leaving a will,
made 20 Feb. 1695; est. was inv. 27 July 1696 by James Phillips
and Daniel Palmer and val. at £ 1422.5.0; Mrs. Blanch Wells, wid.
of George, d. 21 April 1704; her will, proved 12 June 1704;
admin. bond posted 22 June 1704 by George Wells with James Phillips and James Maxwell; est. inv. by Henry Jackson and Samuel
Cowen; est. was admin. 6 July 1708 by George Wells; George and
Blanch had iss.: GEORGE, d. 1716; BENJAMIN, d. 1702; BLANCH, m.
Richard Smithers; SUSANNA MARIA, m. John Stokes, and FRANCES,
m. William Frisby (2:94; 14:13;.54:2; 97:124; 98:45; 121:110;
122:37; 128:5; 24:345; 128:5; 200-51:94; 206-15:8; 371:876-877).

WELLS, GEORGE (14), s. of Richard (10), inher. 1500 a. Lank-
ford's Neck in Talbot Co. from his father; may be rel. to the
John Wells of Kent Island whose will of 10 March 1713/4 ment.
land at Langford's Bay (120:40; 123:20).

WELLS, GEORGE (15), s. of George (12), d. 28 Dec. 1716, having
m. Mary, wid. of Robert Gibson; she m. 3rd William Marshall; admon. bond was posted 29 April 1717 by Mary Wells with John Hall
and Aquila Paca; 7 May 1717 his est. was inv. by Daniel Scott,
Jr., and William Howard, and val. at £ 842.4.6½ plus 21104 lbs.
tob.; an additional inv. was filed in 1717 by Scott and Howard
and val. at £ 923.6.7 plus 39567 lbs. tob. in debts, and signed
by Richard Smithers; est. admin. 4 Aug. 1719 by William Marshall
and w. Mary; est. admin. again on 13 May 1720; payment was
made to Jane, relict of Richard Tredway who was due one year's
wages (1:54, 164; 2:121; 14:54; 48:244, 323; 52:291; 128:36).

WELLS, BENJAMIN (16), s. of George (12), was in Balto. Co.
by 1692 as a taxable in Spesutia Hund.; d. by June 1702 when

admin. bond was posted by his mother Blanch Wells, with Mark Richardson, Aquila Paca, and Samuel Brown; est. was inv. in June 1702 by Robert Gibson and Henry Jackson and was val. at £ 495.2.1 (14:27; 51:115; 128:13; 138).

WELLS, BENJAMIN, m. Temperance Butler, and had iss.: CHARLES, b. 6 April 1745; ABSOLOM; NICHOLAS; JOHN; AMON; WILLIAM; and CALEB (data compiled by Mr. H. H. Arnold).

WELLS, CHARLES, m. Sarah (---) who on 3 June 1726 joined him in admin. the est. of Jno. Wright and of Anthony Arnold; Charles d. leaving a will, 16 Dec. 1738 - 5 Nov. 1741, naming sons Benjamin (to have 100 a. Lurgan), Charles (to have 50 a. Macclan's Friendship), and wife (to have Timber Neck, and Airy Hills and Pleasant Springs), and bro.-in-law William Arnold; in 1750 the wid. of Charles Wells owned 50 a. Markland's Friendship, 100 a. Linegan, 100 a. Timber Neck, and 100 a. Airy Hills and Pleasant Springs ; had iss.: CHARLES, b. 7 Sept. 172-(?); BENJAMIN (3: 60, 62; 127:152; 133:118; 153:34)..

WELLS, JOHN, d. by 22 April 1695 when his est. was inv. by Richard Adams and Michael Innes, and val. at £ 122.15.0 (48:37).

WELLS, JOHN, d. by 10 May 1721 when Margaret Wells posted admin. bond with Thomas Taylor, Robert Parker, John Israel, and John (?Snow) (14:39).

WELLS, MARY, was ind. for bast. in Aug. 1728 (28:33).

WELLS, NATHAN, d. leaving a will, 6 Jan. 1756 - 14 Feb. 1756, naming Nathan, s. of Amos Gates, and mentioning his own mother and father and bros. and sis. (111:113).

WELLS, RICHARD, m. Elizabeth (---); in Aug. 1737 Isaac and Margaret Webster and Jacob Giles conv. Richard 300 a. Arabia Petrea; still owned this land in 1750; still owned this land in 1750; had iss.: FRANCES, b. 20 Dec. 1720; ELIZABETH, b. 10 May 1722; MARY, b. 23 April 1724; CASSANDRA, b. 14 Jan. 1725/6; SARAH, b. 4 Nov. 1729; SUSANNA, b. 17 Nov. 1731; JAMES, b. 6 June 1736; WILLIAM, b. 18 Dec. (1740?) (75:1; 128:47, 72, 95, 114; 153:50).

WELLS, RICHARD, m. by 7 Aug. 1754 Jane, dau. of Jane Renshaw; had iss.: CASSANDRA; LURANA; ELIZABETH; (229:250).

WELLS, SAMUEL, d. by 9 June 1757 when admin. bond was posted by Richard Wells, who admin. the est. on 9 Aug. 1759 (4:277; 14: 166).

WELLS, THOMAS, Jr., in 1750 owned 50 a. Thomas' Adventure, 50 a. Wells Meadow, 100 a. Hollow Rock, and 50 a. Jacob's Well (153:42).

WELLS, WILLIAM, d. by 1717 when an additional inv. on his est. was filed by Wm. Stokes and Richard Smithers (48:252).

WELLS, WILLIAM, in 1750 owned 100 a. part Bond's Pleasant Hills (153:61).

WELLS, WILLIAM, m. Ann (---), and had iss.: JOSEPH, b. 21 March 1733 (133:31).

WELLS, WILLIAM, Sr., on 13 Sept. 1763 conv. prop. to his ch.: CHARLES; PLEASANCE; ELINOR; and SUSANNAH (47:216).

WELSH. See WELCH.

WELTY, PETER, in 1750 owned 86 a. part Digges' Choice (153:97).

WEND, MARY, par. not named; b. 20 Dec. 1695 (128:5).

WENHAM, DINAH, in June 1714 was ind. for bast.; in Aug. 1714
named Mingo, the slave of Solomon Sparrow, as the father; ind.
for bast. in Aug. 1718 (21:505, 537; 23:4).

WESLEY, JOHN, m. by 8 June 1722, Mary, extx. of John Bond
(1:229).

WEST, ROBERT (1), progenitor, was in Balto. Co. by 1692 as a
taxable in n. side of Gunpowder Hund.; d. by 6 Jan. 1764; m.
Sarah Spinks on 10 Nov. 1695; prob. the Sarah,dau. of Roger, who
pet. the court in Sept. 1694; in 1750 owned 37½ a. Long Acre;
in Nov. 1740 had been made exempt from the levy; his est. was
admin. by Col. John Hall on 6 Sept. 1764; Robert and Sarah had
iss.: SARAH, b. 24 Oct. 1701; CONSTANTIA, b. 24 April 1703, m.
Job Barnes on 11 Oct. 1722; ROBERT, Jr., b. 6 Nov. 1706; PRISCIL-
LA, b. 28 March 1709; JOHN, b. 29 Dec. 1711; JONATHAN, b. 28 June
1714; MARY, b. 28 April 1716; SUSANNA, b. 6 March 1717; ENOCH, b.
17 May 1721 (6:113; 20:301; 32:363; 128:32, 33, 34, 38, 39, 46;
138; 153:70).

WEST, SARAH (2), dau. of Robert (1), was b. 24 Oct. 1701; in
June 1721 named her father's serv. as the father of her child; in
March 1723/4 named John Gay as the father of her child; prob.
the Sarah West who m. John Cook on 30 Dec. 1736; had iss.: MOSES,
b. 28 March 1721; DANIEL, b. 17 Dec. 1723 (as Daniel West alias
Daniel Gay he was made levy free in Nov. 1745) (23:49; 26:213;
35:743; 128:20, 39, 42; 129:226, 231, 243).

WEST, ROBERT (3), s. of Robert (1), was b. 6 Nov. 1706; m.
1st, on 22 Jan, 1730 Johanna (---); m. 2nd, on 22 Jan. 1732
Johanna Gash; had iss.: THOMAS, b. 13 June 1732; ROBERT, b. 5
March 1734; SARAH, b. 23 March 1736, d. 15 Oct. 1738; JONATHAN,
b. 14 July 1740; JOHANNA, b. 10 March 1741; SARAH, b. 5 April
1743, d. 10 Nov. 1744; JOHN, b. 18 Feb. 1746; MICHAEL, b. 1 May
1749 (128:68, 74, 85; 129:347).

WEST, JONATHAN (4), s. of Robert (1), was b. 28 June 1714;
prob. the Jonathan who owned 170 a. Maiden's Mount in 1750 and
who was made levy free in Aug. 1750 (37:153; 128:33; 153:64).

WEST, ENOCH (5), s. of Robert (1), was b. 17 May 1721; was
conv. 75 a. Daniel's Neglect by his father in 1742, and owned
37½ a, of this land in 1750 (77:93; 129:391; 153:61).

WEST, ANN, had s.: LABAN WELCH, b. 22 Aug. 1734 (133:41).

WEST, BENJAMIN, m. Hannah Parks on 29 April 1756 (131).

WEST, EASTER, was ind. for bast. in March 1730/1 (29:96).

WEST, JOHN, m. Susanna Osbourn on 26 Jan. 1735 (129:287).

WEST, JOHN, m. by 12 Aug. 1738, Elizabeth, dau. of Samuel
Maccubbin (4:208).

WEST, JONATHAN, m. Sophia (---), and had iss.: RUTH, b. 13
Dec. 1749 (129:353).

WEST, JONATHAN, Jr., m. Sophia Kimball on 31 March 1758;
had iss.: ROBERT, b. 3 Dec. 1759 (129:359).

WEST, MARTHA, was tried for bast. in Nov. 1755 and named James Clark as the father of her child (30:398).

WEST, MARY, m. Daniel Gordon on 23 Nov. 1729 (129:258).

WEST, ROBERT (prob. Robert # 1 above), made a will, 29 April 1747, proved 7 Sept. 1748, leaving everything to his w. Sarah (110:408).

WEST, THOMAS, in 1750 owned 150 a. Good Luck (153:12).

WEST, THOMAS, was made levy free in Nov. 1756 (30:303).

WEST, THOMAS, m. Ann Pritchard on 8 Sept. 1757, and had iss.: ELIZABETH, b. 2 March 1758 (129:363).

WEST, WILLIAM, living at William Bond's, d. 17 March (year not given) (131).

WESTALL, GEORGE (1), was in A. A. Co. by 1680; m. Sarah (---) and had iss.: SARAH, b. 31 Aug. 1680, m. Thomas Cheney on 19 Aug. 1697; JANE, b. 8 Sept. 1682; RICHARD, b. 24 April 1689; GEORGE, b. 1 March 1690; ALICE, b. 21 Sept. 1693; RACHEL, b. 20 Jan. 1695; JOHN, b. 14 June 1699 (all ch. born in All Hallow's Par., A. A. Co.) (219-2).

WESTALL, GEORGE (2-1), s. of George (1), was b. 1 March 1690; m. Anne Jacob on 23 Oct. 1711; she m. Hugh Merriken; was in Balto. Co. by June 1718; d. leaving a will, 23 June 1718 - 6 Oct. 1718, naming w. Ann, bro. John, cousin Thomas Bayley, and sons George, and Richard; admin. bond was posted on 18 Dec. 1718 by extx. Ann Westall with Richard Duckett and Benjamin Jacobs of P. G. Co.; est. was inv. 23 March 1718/9 by William Slade and val. at £ 81.11.9, and signed by Richard Duckett and Benjamin Jacob as kin; est. was admin. 23 Dec. 1719 by the execs. Ann and Hugh Merriken; dec. left iss.: GEORGE; RICHARD; and SARAH (1:46, 47;14:50; 23:400; 51:99; 123:185).

WESTBURY, WILLIAM, orig. of A. A. Co., was transp. c.1667; on 4 May 1678 surv. 150 a. Chestnut Neck on s. side of Gunpowder R. (later held by his orphans and still later by Simon Pierson); was in Balto. Co. by 5 April 1676 when he wit. the will of John Taylor; on 27 Feb. 1686 Thomas Thurcall and w. Jane conv. him 50 a. Daniel's Neck; d by 3 March 1690/1 when wid. and admnx. Margaret posted admin. bond with Robert Olass, Thomas Staley and Mich. Judd; est. was inv. 16 March 1690 by John Hall and James Newell, and val. at 8227 lbs. tob., plus £ 44.19.6; on 4 June 1695 wid. Margaret, now w. of Robert Oless conv. 1/3 of Daniel's Neck to her dau. E. Westbury, spinster; in March 1710 John Butteram and w. Elizabeth, and William Bond and w. Mary conv. to Simon Pierson their interest in any lands belonging to Thomas, Daniel, and William Westbury; deeds suggest Margaret, wid. of William Westbury, may have been a dau. of Thomas O'Daniel; iss. of William and Margaret: WILLIAM, of age 1702; DANIEL, d. by 1710; THOMAS, d. by 1710; ELIZABETH, unm. in 1703, m. by 1710 Thomas Butteram; MARY, m. by 1710 William Bond; poss. EMMA, m. as 1st w. Simon Pierson (14:68; 48:166; 59:188, 466; 66:274; 67:63; 120:170; 144; 211:36; 388).

WESTCOMBE, SAMUEL, m. Sarah Thomas on 19 Jan. 1732; had iss.: HANNAH, b. 6 April 1732; SARAH, b. 31 March 1735, d. 3 March 1738; TRYAL, b. 28 Aug. 1738; SARAH, b. 6 July 1742 (128:79, 86, 93, 100; 129:325).

WESTCOMBE, SAMUEL WINTRAP, d. by 20 Dec. 1743 when admin.

bond was posted by Thomas Clayton with Jacob Giles and William Boulding; Sarah Wintrap Westcombe ren. right of admin. (14:142).

WESTERLY, SYBIL, d. 19 Feb. 1713 (128:32).

WESTERMAN, THOMAS, m. 14 July 1750 Mary Tongue (131).

WESTRELL, WILLIAM, was in Balto. Co. by 1692 as a taxable in n. side Gunpowder Hund. (138).

WESTRY, MICHAEL, m. Jean Solemon on 10 Dec. 1705 and had iss.: SOLOMON, b. 26 Nov. 1706 (128:12, 19).

WESTWOOD, ELIJAH, d. by Aug. 1740; m. Mary (---) and had iss.: JOHN, b. 13 April 1726; SUSANNA, b. 10 July 1729; WILLIAM, b. 29 Nov. 1735, was age 5 in Aug. 1740 when he was bound to George Elliott and w. to age 21 (32:291; 128:92; 131).

WETHERALL, HENRY (1), d. c.1738 in Balto. Co.; m. 1st, on 20 Dec. 1722, Mrs. Mary Chamberlaine; she d. 6 Nov. 1723, and he m. 2nd, on 20 Dec. 1724, Mrs. Eleanor Presbury; in Aug. 1718 he qualified as under-sheriff of Balto. Co.; admin. the est. of Jos'h Presbury; on 4 March 1723 purch. Aberly Lodge, part John's Interest and 100 a. Crow Perches(?) from Lewis and Jane Nowell; on 8 June 1723 purch. 311 a. Happy Choice from James Frizzell, s. of James Frizzell, dec.; in March 1731 purch. 140 a., being one-half of Matthews' Double Purchase (alias Heath Purchase) from Thomas Cross and w. Sarah; d. leaving a will, 23 March 1737/8 - 8 May 1738, naming William Bradford as exec., and ch. Henry, James, , Elizabeth, Lettis, and Elizabeth, son-in-law Joseph Presbury, kinswoman Isabella Lumbert, and tracts: 100 a. Locust Neck, 60 a. Hanson's Neglect, 160 a. Johnson's Interest, 47 a. Sam's Hills, 100 a. Lewis Double Purchase, 70 a. Matthews' Double Purchase and other tracts; admin. bond was posted 8 May 1738 by William Bradford with John Paca and George Presbury; inv. filed 12 April 1740 and val. at £ 180.12.9, approved by William Savory and William Dallam and signed by Dominic Lombard and Isabella James; est. admin. 1 July 1741 and 9 May 1753 by Wm. Bradford, last acct. named Henry's daus. Elizabeth and Lettice and John Jamison and w. Isabella, formerly Isabella Lumberland; in 1750 the heirs of Henry Wetherall owned 100 a. Locust Neck, 45 a. part of Samuel's Hills, 50 a. Johnson's Interest, and 100 a. part Lewis Purchase; Henry had iss.: (By 1st w.): HENRY, b. 5 Oct. 1723, d. 12 Nov. 1723; (by 2nd w.): ELIZABETH, b. 20 Nov. 1725; JAMES; HENRY; LETTIS, m. Edmond Hernly on 17 Sept. 1759 (3:46; 4:104; 5:294; 14:23; 40:1; 50:178; 69:191, 277; 73:198; 126:246; 131: 54, 2/r, 3/r; 153:59).

WETHERALL, HENRY (2), s. of Henry (1) and Eleanor, was b. c. 1729; age 30 in 1759; m. Mary Ann Osborn on 25 Sept. 1753; had iss.: SARAH, b. 31 Dec. 1754; MARY, b. 5 Dec. 1756; JAMES, b. 15 Feb. 1759; HENRY, b. 4 Jan. 1761; and WILLIAM, b. 1 June 1768 (131:21/r).

WETHERALL, ELIZABETH, serv. of Thomas Hooker, judged to be age 12 (20:41).

WEYATT, HENRY. See WYATT, HENRY.

WHALTON, DARBY, servant, with three years to serve, was listed in the May 1699 inv. of Capt. John Ferry (48:124).

WHAYLAND, PATRICK (1), m. by 2 Nov. 1726 Katherine, dau. of Henry Matthews, whose inv. Patrick signed on that date; d. by Nov. 1737; had iss.: HENRY, b. 6 Aug. 1712; MARGARET, b. 17 Nov.

1715; WILLIAM, b. 10 May 1717; SARAH, b. 13 Feb. 1720; PATRICK, b. 29 April 1722 (51:66; 131).

WHAYLAND, HENRY (2), s. of Patrick (1), m. Rebecca Lego on 27 Jan. 1746; on 28 May 1748, Henry Whayland, w. Rebecca, and his mother Catherine, wid., conv. 100 a. Plumb Point to Edward Brusbanks (80:25; 131).

WHAYLAND, PATRICK (3), s. of Patrick (1), was b. 29 April 1722; in 1737 was bound to Aquila Massey to age 21; m. Mary Cowdrey on 26 Jan. 1749 (31:134; 131).

WHAYLAND, ANN, in Nov. 1750 bore a son; Stephen White was tried as the father of her ch. born out of wedlock (38:40).

THE WILLIAM WHEELER FAMILY

WHEELER, WILLIAM (1), progenitor of this line, was b. c.1658 and d. in Balto. Co., c.1738; m. 1st, Susanna (---) who d. 22 April 1703 in All Hallow's Par., A. A. Co.; m. 2nd, on 14 Nov. 1706, also in All Hallow's Par., Martha West; in 1706 pat. Hooker's Prosperity; on 16 Aug. 1722 conv. his s. Thomas a brown mare; in 1729 pat. Hannah's Lot; in March 1728/9 he pet. the Balto. Co. Court to be levy free as he was 70 years old and "unable to get his living;" in 1737 was listed as levy free living in Back River Upper Hund.; d. leaving a will, 19 April 1732 - 6 June 1738, naming ch.: John, William, Richard, Thomas, Samuel, Weeston, William, Jr., Moses, Solomon, Isaac, Mary Murray, Martha, and Ann, and w. Martha; admin. bond was posted 7 Jan. 1738 by Martha Wheeler with Richard Gott and Edw. Stevenson; est. was inv. 24 Aug. 1738 by Thomas Carr and Joseph Taylor and val. at Ł 96.16.2, and signed by Thomas and Wason Wheeler as kin, and Jabez Morray and Thomas Taylor as creditors; the inv. was filed 5 Sept. 1738 by wid. Martha; an additional inv. was taken 26 Oct. 1738, val. at Ł 0.4.0 and filed 15 June 1739; in Aug. 1739 Martha Wheeler gave bond to Solomon and Isaac Wheeler she would pay them their share of their father's est.; in 1750 the wid. still owned 51 a. Hooker's Prosperity; William had iss.: (by 1st w.): JOHN; WILLIAM, b. 8 d, 1, 1693/4; RICHARD, b. 2 Jan. 1697/8; SAMUEL, and WASON (by 2nd w.): THOMAS, bapt. 29 March 1711 in All Hallow's Par.; MARY, bapt. 29 March 1711, m. Jabez Murray; MARTHA, b. 28 Feb. 1718 in St. Paul's Par., m. James Boring on 25 Dec. 1736; ANNE, b. 25 May 1721, m. Thomas Cook on 3 Oct. 1739; MOSES, b. 2 Sept. 1723; SOLOMON, b. 10 March 1724/5; ISAAC, b. 1 Oct. 1728 (14: 22; 28:95; 32:8; 51:387; 69:36; 126:252; 133; 149; 153; 207; 219-1).

WHEELER, WILLIAM (2), s. of William (1) by 1st w., was b. 8 d, 1 mo. (March) 1693/4; d. 3 d, 1, 1766/7; m. 1st, Isabel sis. of John Price, and m. 2nd, Constant Horne, wid. of Stephen Price; on 9 June 1726 conv. to Elizabeth and Benjamin (his ch. by his 1st w.) property and stated that his wife's bro. was to be their guardian; on 15 Dec. 1733 he and w. Constant conv. Hannah's Lot to Thomas Wheeler; in 1750 he owned 50 a. Bachelor's Neck, 24 a. Addition, 70 a. Tipton's, and 100 a. Hooker's Ridge; d. leaving a will, 2 June 1764 - 12 Jan. 1764, naming w. Constant and ch. Elizabeth Peregoy, William, Benjamin, and Nathan, and son-in-law Abraham Vaughan; admin. bond was posted 12 Jan. 1767 by Nathan Wheeler with Alexius Lemmon and Geo. Harryman; est. was inv. on 20 April 1767 by Nicholas Merryman and Abraham Ensor with Benjamin and William Wheeler signing as kin, est. val. at Ł308.15.5; left iss.: (by 1st w.): ELIZABETH, m. Joseph Peregoy; BENJAMIN: (by 2nd w.): NATHAN; WILLIAM; poss. a dau. who m. Abraham Vaughan (2:247; 14:126; 57:256; 70:240; 74:24; 112:75; 153:13).

WHEELER, RICHARD (3), s. of William (1) and Susanna, was b. 2 Jan. 1697/8 in All Hallow's Par.; d. by 26 March 1751 in Fairfax Co., Va.; m. 1st (---) (poss. Drummond); m. 2nd Rebecca (---), wid. of (---) Davis; in 1720 purch. Benjamin's Beginnings from Benjamin Martin; in 1730 sold 100 a. of the tract to John Tipton; d. leaving a will, 5 June 1750 - 26 March 1751, naming w. Rebecca, sons Drummond and George Simpson and dau. Susanna Simpson; will of Rebecca Wheeler, 15 April 1758 - 19 April 1763, named daus. Susanna Williams and Susanna Simpson and Edward Davis; left iss.; DRUMMOND; and SUSANNA, m. (---) Simpson (59:667; 73:18; 442:8, 14).

WHEELER, SAMUEL (4), s. of William (1) and Susanna, d. c.1771 in Balto. Co.; m. Avarilla (---); in 1747 purch. Samuel's Industry and 50 a. part Morgan's Delight from Jabez Murray; in 1750 owned Morgan's Delight; d. leaving a will, 4 Dec. 1770 - 14 Oct. 1771, leaving latter tract to his s. John, and naming the ch. listed below; admin. bond was posted by John Wheeler with John and Sater Stevenson; had iss.: RICHARD; KEZIAH, m. (---) Allender; JOHN; AVARILLA; MARY; RACHEL; MARTHA, and ANN (14:98; 79:663; 112:179; 153:87).

WHEELER, WASON (5), s. of William (1), was alive in 1763; in 1741 surv. 50 a. Wheeler's Lot; on 13 Feb. 1746 conv. 56½ a. of Hooker's Prosperity to Charles Ridgely; in 1750 owned 50 a. of Wheeler's Lot; conv. that tract to James Brian in 1763; may have had one s.: NATHAN (79:298; 87:128; 153:58).

WHEELER, THOMAS (6), s. of William (1) and Martha, was bapt. 29 March 1711; m. Ann Hawkins on 20 Oct. 1736; on 16 Jan. 1747 conv. Hannah's Lot to Charles Ridgely, with cons. of his (Thomas') w. Ann; known iss.: BENJAMIN, b. 9 Oct. 1738; MARTHA, b. 28 May 1741 (79:660; 133).

WHEELER, WILLIAM, Jr. (7), s. of William (1) and Martha, was b. 2 Sept. 1723; m. Catherine (---); had iss.: MARY, b. 24 May 1750 (133:37, 90).

WHEELER, SOLOMON (8), s. of William (1) and Martha, was b. 10 March 1724/5; d. 1785; m. Rachel Taylor in Feb. 1746; had iss.: AGNES, b. 5 Jan. 1746/7, m. (---) Crage; SARAH ANNA, b. 11 Nov. 1748, m. (---) Hart; RACHEL, b. 19 March 1749, m. (---) Pearce; JOSEPH; THOMAS TAYLOR; SUSANNA; ELIZABETH; JEMIMA, m. James Perigo; HANNAH, m. John Wilmot, and BENJAMIN R. (113:204; 133; 134).

THE JOHN WHEELER FAMILY

WHEELER, JOHN (9), no known rel. to any of the above, d. by 6 July 1725 when admin. bond was posted by admnx. Dinah Wheeler with John Wheeler, George Hitchcock, and William Wheeler, Jr.; est. was inv. 17 Sept. 1726 by Luke Stansbury and Samuel Stouker and val. at £ 72.4.17, signed by Dinah Cross as admnx. and by William and Thomas Wheeler as kin; est. was admin. on 3 Oct. 1731 by John Cross and w. Dinah; 1/3 was paid to the wid., and 1/3 to each of the two ch.; in Nov. 1733 John Cross, George Hitchcock and Richard Land gave bond they would pay to the orphans of John Wheeler, the sum of £ 33.10.2½; John Wheeler m. Dinah (---) (who m. 2nd John Cross) and had iss.: JOHN; SUSANNA (3:120; 14: 24; 30:133; 51:74). (There is a possibility that this John was the eldest s. of William Wheeler no. 1 above).

WHEELER, JOHN (1), s. of John (9), m. by 19 Aug. 1752 Elizabeth (---) who on that date joined him, and John and Dinah Cross in conv. 50 a. Wheeler's Beginnings and 50 a. Cross's

Chance to Abraham Raven; d. by 20 March 1769 when admin. bond
was posted by Elizabeth Wheeler with John Foster and Thomas Cullins; est. was inv. on 23 March 1769 by Nicholas Merryman and
Samuel Tipton and val. at Ł 104.16.7 and signed by Dinah Cross and
Solomon Cross, and filed by Elizabeth Wheeler; est. was admin.
by Elizabeth Wheeler; dec. left iss.: GEORGE; RUTH; ELIZABETH;
MARY; poss. JOHN, and poss. others (7:56; 14:161; 56:162; 81:
408).

WHEELER, JOHN (11), prob. s. of John (10) and Elizabeth, d.
in Balto. Co. by 20 March 1769 when admin. bond was posted by
Delila Wheeler with George Merryman and John Price; est. was
inv. 31 March 1769 by Jacob Cox and Christopher Vaughan and val.
at Ł 31.13.0½, and mentioned land judged to be the prop. of John
Wheeler the Elder; the relations refused to sign the inv. as pt.
of the property had been appraised in the inv. of John Wheeler
the elder; est. was admin. by Delia (sic) Wheeler on 13 July
1771 and 31 July 1771 (6:77; 7:132; 14:103; 56:164).

THE WHEELER FAMILY OF CHARLES AND BALTIMORE COUNTIES has been
thoroughly discussed in Walter V. Ball's John Wheeler, 1630-
1693 of Charles County and Some of His Descendants. For that
reason only the generations that settled in Baltimore County
are touched upon here.

WHEELER, BENJAMIN (12), descendant of John Wheeler of Charles
Co., was in P. G. Co. on 24 Jan. 1714 when he purch. Pearson's
Range from Simon Pearson; m. Elizabeth (---); d. leaving a will,
16 Sept. 1741 - 26 Nov. 1741, naming w. Elizabeth, and ch. Thom-
as, Benjamin, Ignatius, Leonard, Anna, Mary, Jane Butterworth,
Elizabeth Thomas, and Charity Colegate; d. 12 Oct. 1741; wife
Elizabeth d. 21 June 1742; had iss.: THOMAS, b. 1698; BENJAMIN;
IGNATIUS; LEONARD; ANNA; MARY; JANE, m. (---) Butterworth;
ELIZABETH, m. (---) Thomas; and Charity, m. (---) Colegate (127:
160; 128:60, 115; 129:325; Ball, Wheeler Gen.).

WHEELER, THOMAS (13), s. of Benjamin, was b. 1698, d. 1770;
m. 1st Sarah Scott; m. 2nd Elizabeth (Raven), admnx. of Solomon Hillen of Balto. Co.; in 1750 owned 155 a. Wheeler's Enlargement, 150 a. Roughborough, 370 a. The Beginning, and 50 a. of
Wheeler's Search; had iss.: (by 1st w.): ELIZABETH, b. 8 Dec.
1729, m. (---) Amos; BENJAMIN, b. 29 Oct. 1731; SARAH, b. 6 July
1733, m. Edward Green; THOMAS, b. 10 Feb. 1734; MARTHA, b. 12
May 1737; MARY, b. 31 May 1739; HANNAH, b. 16 Feb. 1740; JOSIAS;
CHARITY, m. Michael Jenkins (128:60, 76, 87, 97, 105, 372;
129:377 states that Thomas and Elizabeth had: JOSIAS, b. 13
Sept. 1751; ELIZABETH, b. 16 Feb. 1754; SUSANNA, b. 19 Jan. 1757
(128:60, 76, 87, 97, 107; 129:377; 153:106; 201-33:155; Ball,
Wheeler Gen.; Raskob, The Raskob-Green Record Book).

WHEELER, BENJAMIN (14), s. of Benjamin (12), was b. 1699, d.
1770; in 1750 owned 500 a. part Three Sisters, part Austins and
Deal's Chance, 100 a.; m. Rebecca Miles Bevan, and had iss.:
BENEDICT; JACOB; ELIZABETH ; JANE; THOMAS; MARY, m. Leonard
Green; LEONARD, m. Theresa Green; SARAH, m. Basil Cooper; and
ANNE, m. (---) Dyer(153:17; Ball, Wheeler Gen.).

WHEELER, IGNATIUS (15), s. of Benjamin (12), in 1750 owned
316 a. part Wheeler and Clark's Contrivance, and Pearson's
Range, 67½ a. Benjamin's Camp, 55 a. part Brother's Care (153:
58; Ball, Wheeler Gen.).

WHEELER, LEONARD (16), s. of Benjamin (12), was b. 18 Sept.
1722; d. by 30 Jan. 1747; m. Ann Bond on 16 Feb. 1741; d. leaving a will, 1 Sept. 1747 - 30 Jan. 1747/8, naming w. Ann, dau.

Elizabeth and unborn ch.; admin. bond was posted 30 Jan. 1747 by
execs. Thomas Wheeler and Ann Wheeler with Thomas Bond, Jr., and
Nich. Ruxton Gay; est. admin. by Thomas Wheeler and Ann now w.
of William Clemens on 12 Feb. 1749, 10 April 1749, 12 Aug. 1751,
and 1 Sept. 1752; in 1750 his heirs owned 315 a. Wheelers and
Clark's Range, 67½ a. Benjamin's Camp, and 55 a. part Brotherly
Love; had iss.: THOMAS, b. 25 Jan. 1743, prob. d. young; ELIZA-
BETH, b. c.1745; LEONARD, b. c.1747 (5:68, 84, 185, 266; 14:128;
37:168; 110:405; 129:322, 339; 153:17; Ball, Wheeler Gen.).

    WHEELER, JOHN, in 1734 he and w. Margaret conv. 110 a. unnamed,
71 a. Thomas' Lot, and 229 a. James' Park to Abraham Burkholder
of Conestoga, Lancs. Co., Penna. (74:59).

    WHEELER, ROBERT, of P. G. Co., had his est. admin. in Balto.
Co. by the ests. Ann w. of Matthew Robertson on 11 April 1753
(5:278).

    WHEELOCK, EDWARD, was named as a s. of the testator's w. Mary
in the will of Thomas Bucknall of A. A. Co.; d. by 8 March 1698
when admin. bond was posted by extx. Ann Wheelock with Edward
Wheelock; est. inv. 23 March 1698/9 by James Hammond and John
Peasley and val. at £ 46.14.0 plus 1500 lbs. tob.; est. was later
admin. by Ann Wheelock (2:78; 14:58; 48:209; 120:125).

    WHETCOMB. See WHITECOMB.

    WHINERY, THOMAS, d. 24 Nov. 1736 (128:94).

    THE WHIPPS FAMILY: its origins are deduced from a transcrip-
tion of Whips Family Bibles, pub. in the Bulletin of the Maryland Gen. Society,17:165, and from the Parish Registers of
Thirsk, Yorkshire, vol. 42 of the Yorkshire Parish Register
series (see 443).

    WHIPPS, JOHN (1), res. in the par. of Thirsk, Yorkshire, and
had iss.: FRAUNCES, bapt. 28 July 1592; JOHN, bapt. 5 Feb. 1594;
WILLIAM, bapt. 13 April 1596; ROBERT, bapt. 13 April 1600; JANE,
bapt. 10 Jan. 1601/2; THOMAS, bapt. 22 Feb. 1605/6 (443:102,
104, 105, 106, 107, 110).

    WHIPPS, THOMAS (2), s. of John (1), was bapt. at Thirsk on 22
Feb. 1605/6, and m. Sybil Hodge on 3 Aug. 1627; she was bur. at
Thirsk on 8 June 1640; Thomas and Sybil hadat least four ch.;
the last five listed may be a child of a 2nd marr., or else were
not baptized until some years after their birth: JANE, bapt. 26
July 1629; JOHN, bapt. 18 Dec. 1631; FRANCIS, bapt. 6 March
1635/6; CHRISTOPHER, bapt. 7 Nov. 1637, bur. 16 Dec. 1638; (poss.
by an unidentified 2nd w.): ANNE, bapt. 1 May 1642; ROGER,
bapt. 6 Oct. 1643; CICELIE, bapt. 15 July 1645; ELLEN, bapt. 11
Dec. 1646; ELIZABETH, bapt. 21 March 1648/9 (443:38, 86, 110,
129, 132, 136, 138, 141, 143, 144, 146, 148; 85).

    WHIPPS, JOHN (3), s. of Thomas (2), was bapt. 18 Dec. 1631;
is placed as the immigrant to Md. although the Whips Family
Bibles, printed in 1816, states that "John Whips of Calvert Co.,
was born in the year of Our Lord 1622 within 16 miles of York
City in a town commonly called Thursk;" aged at this time 98
years of age; the par. reg. of Thirsk lists no John, b. 1622;
the most likely one is John bapt. in 1631; is prob. the father
of: JOHN, poss. b. c.1650 (Whips Bible; 443).

    WHIPPS, JOHN (4), s. of John (3), wass prob. b. c.1650; m.
Elizabeth (poss. Metcalfe); in 1701 conv. land to his granddau.
Philothea Stanforth; d. leaving a will in Calvert Co., 10 Dec.

1716 - 26 Dec. 1716, naming w. Elizabeth and ch. Abigail Evans,
Jane Jones, Sarah Busey, Susanna Stanford, and John Whips, Jr.;
est. was inv. 9 Dec. 1718 by the exec. John Whipps now living in
Balto. Co., and was val. at Ł 196.5.3.⅓; Elizabeth Whipps was
paid Ł 215 as her thirds, and the balance was retained by the
accountant; Elizabeth d. leaving a will, 11 Nov. 1729 - 5 Dec.
1729 leaving her entire est. to her ygr. bro. and sis. William
and Jane "Madcaff" living near Askrigg, Yorkshire, except for
legacies to Thomas Vernon, Rachel Griffith, and Elizabeth Foudry;
Elizabeth may not have been the mother of John's children; her
inv. taken 15 March 1729, was val. at Ł 81.11.9, with a notation
that the dec. had no kin in the Province; John was the father of:
JANE, b. 1 Feb. 1670, m. by 10 Dec. 1716 (---) Jones; SUSANNA,
b. 29 May 1677, m. (---) Stanford (his name is given as Morgan
Stanford in one place, but John Stanford is named as the father
of Joseph Whips Standford, Elizabeth Stanford, and Philothea
Stanford); JOHN, Jr., b. 30 April 1680; ABIGAIL, b. 28 July 1687,
m. (---) Evans; SARAH, m. (---) Busey; ELIZA (123:56, 127; 125:
142; 205-15:471; 206-39C:113; 217-IH#3:28; 231-1:297; Whips
Bible).

WHIPPS, JOHN (5), s. of John (4), was b. 30 April 1680, was
alive in Jan. 1733; m. Margaret Theerston on 14 Nov. 1702 in St.
James' Par., A. A. Co.; she d. by 4 April 1764 in Balto. Co.;
was conv. 200 Stout out of 529 a. taken up by Thomas Bale; in
July 1724 John Whipps and w. Margaret mortgaged this tract to
Philip Smith of London; 19 Jan. 1733 John conv. 200 a. Stout to
Richard Gist; d. by 10 June 1736 when Adam Shipley filed an inv.
val. at Ł 43.16.2; Margaret d. leaving a will, 4 May 1760 - 4
April 1764, naming dau. Susanna and son-in-law Adam Shipley;
John and Margaret had iss.: URATH, b. 15 Oct. 1713; SUSANNA, b.
17 Nov. 1711; JOHN, b. 9 July 1719; SAMUEL, b. 21 July 1721;
BENJAMIN, b. 3 Oct. 1723; MARY, b. 27 March 1726 (60:137; 69:
348; 74:125; 111:233; 133; 210-32:99; 231-14:254; Whips Bibles).

WHIPPS, JOHN (6), s. of John (5) and Margaret, was b. 9 July
1719; d. by Dec. 1783 in A. A. Co.; m. Sarah Lucrese Ogg, b. 5
Sept. 1726, d. c.1782 in A. A. Co., dau. of George Ogg; on 2 Nov.
1754 John Whipps of A. A. Co. conv. to Edward Dorsey the Progress;
in 1750 he owned 20 a. Molly's Habitation; on 2 Nov. 1754 George
Ogg, Sr., conv. various chattels to his ch. and grandch., incl.
his dau. Sarah w. of John Whips; Sarah Lucrese Whipps d. leaving
a will, 1 Jan. 1781 - 6 July 1782; John and Sarah had iss.:
USLEY, b. 9 April 1746; RACHEL, b. 15 or 25 June 1747; RUTH, b.
13 Feb. 1749, m. Peter Poole; KATHERINE, b. 31 July 1751; VALITE
(?), b. 13 July 1751 (sic); SAMUEL, b. 20 Jan. 1753; SARAH LU-
CRETIA, b. 2 July 1754; BENJAMIN, b. 5 Aug. 1750; GEORGE, b. 15
Jan. 1761 (82:334; 83:256, 257; 134; 153:77; 229:228; Whips
Bibles).

WHIPPS, SAMUEL (7), s. of John (5) and Margaret, was b. 21
July 1721; m. Mary McComas on 22 Jan. 1742 in St. John's Par.; on
1 Aug. 1745 conv. to Benjamin Whipps 125 a. Whipps Purchase, w.
cons. of his w. Mary; on 3 March 1747 Samuel and Mary conv. Long
Valley to William Gosnell (78:255; 79:670; 131).

WHIPPS, BENJAMIN (8), s. of John (5) and Margaret, was b. 3
Oct. 1723; in 1750 owned 125 a. Whipps Purchase; d. by 1757 when
his will named his mother Margaret, widow, and his sister
Susanna (111:233; 153:73).

WHISTLER, ULRICK, was in Balto. Co. by 1750 when he owned 50
a. Plymouth; d. 1761; m. Esther (---) who d. by March 1763; his
will, 5 May 1761 - 7 Aug. 1761, mentioned w. and ch., but did
not name them; 1st admin. bond was posted 7 Sept. 1761 by extx.

Esther Whistler, with John Price of John (at Garrison) and Henry
Feather; 2nd admin. bond was posted 31 Oct. 1763 by John Rorer,
admin. de bonis non, with Andrew Stigar; est. of Ulrick Whistler
was admin. 1 Jan. 1763; admin. bond on the est. of Esther Whistler was posted 8 March 1763 by John Rorer, with Jeremiah Johnson;
a 2nd admin. bond was posted 16 June 1767 by Catherine Rorer, w.
Adam Brunt and George Lavely; her est. was admin. 13 June 1769 by
Catherine now w. of George Lavely; Ulrick and Esther had iss.:
a son, unnamed in 1761 will; CHRISTIAN, m. Abraham Rinsinger;
dau., m. Jacob Myre; dau. m. Michael Bear; JUDITH, m. Jacob She-
gay (6:63; 7:30; 14:44, 132, 148, 162; 111:346; 153:95).

THE WHITAKER FAMILY is the subject of ab article by Beaumont
W. Whitaker, "The Whitaker Family of Baltimore County, Maryland,
1677 - 1767," Maryland Historical Magazine 79 (2) 165-182.

WHITAKER, JOHN (1), progenitor, was in Balto. Co. by March
1694 when he surv. 74 a. Whitaker's Purchase; in Oct. 1696 he
pat. Whitaker's Chance, and in Dec. 1697 he bought 150 a. Whitaker's Ridge from Robert and Sarah Love; m. 1st, Catherine (---);
m. 2nd Mary (---); d. 30 Nov. 1713; left a will, 9 Nov. 1713 -
26 Dec. 1713, leaving 250 a. Whitaker's Ridge to sons John and
Charles, rights to Enlargement to sons Peter and Abraham, 150 a.
Whitaker's Ridge to s. Isaac and unborn ch.,; named w. Elizabeth
and daus. Elizabeth, Sarah, and Hannah; admin. bond was posted
14 Jan. 1713/4 by John Whitaker with Thomas Preston and William
Bond; est. was inv. by Thomas Bond and William Howard on 26 Jan.
1713, and val. at £ 99.3.3., with Daniel and Elizabeth Scott as
kin; est. was admin. on 16 March 1713; dec. left iss.: ELIZABETH,
b. 12 Jan. 1687; RUTH, b. 27 March 1690, prob. d. young;
JOHN, b. 23 April 1691; CHARLES, b. 12 Oct. 1693; PETER, b.
27 April 1696; SARAH, b. 10 Nov. 1699, m. Benjamin Norris on 8
Oct. 1719; ABRAHAM, b. 19 Sept. 1702; ISAAC; HANNAH, m. 1st Alexander McComas, and 2nd, by 1762 Thomas Miles (1:22; 14:53; 50:
249; 61:182; 123:3; 128:15, 39).

WHITAKER, JOHN (2), s. of John (1), was b. 23 April 1691, and
d. 26 April 1720; m. Ann Dadd or Dodd on 26 April 1714; had iss.:
PETER, b. 6 May 1716; JOHN, b. 14 Sept. 1718, d. 4 Oct. 1719
(128:15; 129:226; 131).

WHITAKER, CHARLES (3), s. of John (1), was b. 12 Oct. 1693
and d. 3 Oct. 1739; m. Mary, wid. of William Kemball, on 30 Jan.
1717/8; admin. bond was posted 5 March 1739/40 by John Whitaker
with Samuel and Obadiah Pritchard; est. was admin. 20 Nov. 1744
by John Whitaker; Charles' w. Mary d. 30 Aug. 1739; Charles and
Mary had iss.: LURANA, b. 27 March 1720; JOHN, b. 2 July
1722; CHARLES, b. 11 Jan. 1723/4 (in Nov. 1741 chose Parker Hall
as his guardian); JAMES, b. 22 Dec. 1726; MARY, b. 3 Aug. 1728,
m. Daniel Butler; CATHERINE, b. 10 Dec. 1733, m. Aquila Thompson;
ISAAC, b. 5 May 1735; ABRAHAM, b. 1 Aug. 1737 (3:15; 5:15; 14:31;
128:36, 38, 42, 48, 56, 75, 87, 98, 104, 110; 129:221).

WHITAKER, PETER (4), s. of John (1), was b. 27 April 1696; m.
Frances Brown on 10 Jan. 1722; on 6 March 1722 Peter and Frances
conv. 64 a., being one-half of Enlargement, to William Bradford;
known iss.: BLANCH, b. 10 April 1728, m. John Long on 31 Jan.
1748; PETER, b. 1 Dec. 1729; FRANCES, b. 9 March 1734; DANIEL
(69:120; 128:42, 47, 56, 68, 86; 6:84).

WHITAKER, ABRAHAM (5), s. of John (1), was b. 19 Sept. 1702
and d. 31 Dec. 1739; m. Ann Poteet on 15 July 1725; she m. 2nd,
by 7 Sept. 1741, William Pike; in Nov. 1724 Abraham was ind. for
begetting a baseborn ch. on Susanna Temple; he d. by 31 Dec.
1739 when admin. bond was posted by Ann Whitaker with Benjamin

Norris and John Chocke; est. was admin. 7 Sept. 1741 by William
Pike and w. Ann; in Aug. 1743 his ch. were listed as Abraham,
Isaac, Peter, Hannah, and Ann; had iss.: PETER, b. 7 July 1726;
ABRAHAM, b. 11 Aug. 1727; HANNAH, b. 26 March 1729, m. William
Crabtree on 29 May 1746; ISAAC; and ANN (14:37; 27:32; 35:8, 9;
131).

WHITAKER, ISAAC (6), s. of John (1), d. c.1765; was left 150 a
Whitaker's Ridge by his father; m. Sarah (---).

WHITAKER, PETER (7), s. of John (1), was b. 6 May 1716; d. c.
1760; m. Emele Hitchcock on 10 Feb. 1745; she was b. c.1724, and
m. 2nd, Thomas Fisher on 18 Feb. 1761; Fisher admin. Peter's est.
on 5 Dec. 1763; Peter and Emele had iss.: JOHN, b. 21 May 1753;
HEZEKIAH, b. c.1754; ISAAC, b. c.1757; two other ch. (6:34; 131).

WHITAKER, JOHN (8), s. of Charles (3), was b. 2 July 1722; d.
c.1798; m. Mary McComas c.1741; they had iss.: CHARLES, b. 11
Dec. 1742; JOHN, b. c.1746; ABRAHAM, b. c.1751; ISAAC; JESSE;
AQUILA, b. 25 Aug. 1755; HANNAH; and ELIJAH (129:331; Whitaker
article).

WHITAKER , ISAAC, was tried in Nov..1755 for fathering a ch.
by Hannah Warters; m. Elizabeth Hill on 13 Dec. 1759 (40:402;
131).

WHITAKER, JAMES, in 1750 owned 50 a. Whitaker's Chance (153:
50).

WHITAKER, JAMES, in 1750 owned 50 a. Stony Baker (153:65).

WHITAKER, MARK, d. 1 May 1729; m. 1st, on 13 May 1705, Katherine Teague who d. 15 Nov. 1717; m. 2nd, on 13 Feb. 1717/8, Elizabeth Emson; d. by 4 June 1729 when admin. bond was posted by
Elizabeth Whitaker with John White and Gregory Farmer; est. was
admin. 6 May 1732 by Elizabeth now w. of Francis Taylor; in
June 1733 Francis Taylor was ind. for not taking care of Whitaker's orphans; Mark was the father of: ELIZABETH, b. 25 Feb.
(1704?), m. Flower Swift on 13 May 1725; THOMAS, b. 13 June 1712
(in June 1729, at age 17 pet., the court that he had left his
mother-in-law, i.e., step-mother, and would like to live with his
uncle Thomas Mitchell); MARK, b. 15 Feb. 1715/6; (by 2nd w.):
CHARITY, b. 8 dec. 1718; JAMES, b. 8 Feb. 1720/1; EMPSON, b. 30
Sept. 1724; ELIZABETH, b. 28 Aug. 1726 (3:117; 14:45; 28:151;
30:2; 128:22, 35, 36, 38, 44, 62; 129:215, 234, 254).

WHITCOMB. See WHITECOMB.

THE FRANCES AND JEROME WHITE FAMILY has a clue to its origins
in Alfred Rudulph Justice, "Genealogical Research in England:
Addendum: The Weston Family," English Origins of New England
Families (Baltimore: 1984), I, 587.

WHITE, RICHARD (1), m. Mary Plowden, dau. of Edmund Plowden of Shropshire, and had iss.: RICHARD, b. c.1580 (Justice).

WHITE, RICHARD (2), s. of Richard (1) and Mary, was b. c.
1580; inherited Hutton, Essex; d. at Rome; m. 1st Anne Gray;
m. 2nd, Catherine, bapt. at Roxwell, Essex, 8 June 1607, d.
in Rome on 22 Oct. 1645; she was a dau. of Sir Richard Weston,
1st Earl of Portland; Richard and Catherine had iss.: FRANCES,
b. c.1622 at Hutton Hall, Co. Essex, came to Va., c.1637; m.
Richard Wells; JEROME, Surveyor General of Md. (in 1667 was
granted 2000 a. Portland Manor in A. A. Co.; d. s.p. and Portland Manor was inher. by his bro.): GEORGE (inher. Portland
Manor (371:882; 388; Justice).

THE STEPHEN WHITE was the subject of research by Christopher Johnston, whose notes on the White Family are at the Maryland Historical Society, Baltimore.

WHITE, STEPHEN (3), no known rel. to any of the above, was brought to Md. c.1659 acc. to a claim made in 1663 by James Southard; in Oct. 1674 he pat. White's Addition on s. side of Patapsco; later owned Radnage, surv. for George Yates; m. Ann, sis. of John Rockhold who d. 1698 (she m. 2nd William Hawkins); Stephen White d. leaving a will, Sept. 1676 - 19 March 1676/7. naming w. Ann and s. Stephen; est. was inv. 24 April 1677; est. was admin. 13 Aug. 1679 by Anne, now w. of William Hawkins who in his nuncupative will named three grandsons John, Stephen, and William White; iss. of Stephen and Ann: STEPHEN (100:118; 122:195; 206-4:13; 206-6:441; Johnston notes on White Family).

WHITE, STEPHEN (4), s. of Stephen (4), and Ann, was named in the 1698 will of his uncle John Rockhold; d. in Balto. Co. by 1717; m. Sarah (---) who m. 2nd, c.1718 John Cornelius; in June 1710 Christopher Cox and w. Mary conv. him their share of Radnage; by 1692 was a taxable in s. side Patapsco Hund.; admin. bond was posted 17 Feb. 1717/8 by John Cornelius and w. Sarah with William Jones and Richard Hampton; est. was inv. 6 March 1717 by John Buckingham and Wm, Anderson and val. at ₤ 73.9.0, and signed by William Hawkins and John Gray as kin; est. was admin. 13 July 1719 and 31 Aug. 1721; Stephen had iss.: JOHN; STEPHEN; WILLIAM, mentioned 1711 but not in 1719; HANNAH; ANNE; SARAH; and JOSHUA (1:279; 5:360; 14:51; 48:242; 67:75; 138; Johnston notes on White Family).

WHITE, JOHN (5), s. of Stephen (4), was alive in 1735; m. Mary Rencher in 1722 as 1st w.; m. 2nd Mary Wood in Jan. 1726; in 1731 John and Mary sold Radnage, 160 a., and 180 a. White's Addition to Thomas Cockey; by 1739 were living in St. John's Par.; had iss.: (by 1st w.): ANNE, b. 23 March 1722/3; STEPHEN, b. 23 March 1723/4 (both b. in St. Margaret's Par., A. A. Co.); (by 2nd w.): MARY, b. 16 Jan. 1726/7, m. Samuel Warrell; JOHN, b. 25 Dec. 1727; COMFORT, b. 31 March 1729, m. John Brown on 21 Feb. 1747; SARAH, b. 31 March 1731, m. Francis Ingram on 8 Jan. 1756; JOSHUA, b. 4 Nov. 1735 (131; 133; 219-4; Johnston notes on White Family).

WHITE, JOSHUA (6), s. of Stephen (4), m. Mary Ashley in 1740 and had iss.: MILCAH, b. 1742; SAMUEL, b. 1744; THOMAS, b. 1751 (Johnston notes).

WHITE, STEPHEN (7), s. of John (5), was b. 23 March 1723/4 in St. Margaret's Par., A. A. Co.; moved to St. John's Par.; in 1750 was named as the father of Ann Whayland's child; m. on 1 Jan. 1751 Hannah, dau. of Morris Baker; Hannah m. 2nd by 1755 Samuel Everett; Stephen d. by 4 Dec. 1754 when admin. bond was posted by Hannah White with Morris Baker and William Grafton; est. was admin. in Jan. 1756 by Hannah, now w. of Samuel Everett; dec. left iss.: GRAFTON, b. c.1752; STEPHEN, b. c.1753 (5:315; 14:L75; 38: 40; 131; Johnston notes on White Family).

THE THOMAS WHITE FAMILY is the subject of a lengthy pedigree pub. in William White Bronson, Account of the Meeting of Descendants of Col. Thomas White (no date).

WHITE, JOHN (8), progenitor of this line, no known rel. to any of the above, was of Hulcote, Co. Bedford, Eng.; d. leaving a will, 6 Oct. 1501 - 20 Dec. 1501; m. Agnes, and had iss., among others: THOMAS; JOHN, and two daus. (Bronson).

WHITE, JOHN (9), s. of John (8), was under age in 1501; bought the manor of Caldicot in Newport-Bagnell, 1539/40; d. 25 Aug. 1572; bur. at Newport-Bagnell; had iss.: THOMAS; GEORGE; JOHN; and ROGER (Bronson).

WHITE THOMAS (10), s. of John (9), was age 56 and upwards in 1573; inherited Caldicot, which he conv. to s. Lawrence in 1586; bur. at Newport-Bagnell on 30 Aug. 1603; m. Agnes, dau. of Lawrence Manley; she was bur. at Newport-Bagnell on 6 April 1594; had iss.: LAWRENCE; THOMAS; WILLIAM; CATHERINE; ELIZABETH, m. William Simpkin; JOANE, m. Henry Tyce (Bronson).

WHITE, LAWRENCE (11), s. of Thomas (10); of Caldicot; b. by 1557; d. 29 Dec. 1600; bur. at Newport-Bagnell; m. Margaret (---) who was living 19 Jan. 1600/1; had iss.: THOMAS: HENRY; and JOHN (Bronson).

WHITE, THOMAS (12), s. of Lawrence (11); of Caldicot; was bapt. 20 Nov. 1583 at Newport Bagnell, and was bur. there on 1 June 1661; m. Elizabeth, dau. of William Fisher of Carlton, Co. Bedford; she was bur. 7 Aug. 1627; had iss., among others: WILLIAM (Bronson).

WHITE, WILLIAM (13), s. of Thomas (12), Citizen and Haberdasher of London; will dated 24 Nov. 1676 - 18 Dec. 1676; m. 1st Catherine Best on 21 Dec. 1637 at St. Benet Grace-Church, London; m. 2nd, on 13 Feb. 1654/5 at St. Stephen's, Walbrook, London; iss.; by 1st w., among others: WILLIAM (Bronson).

WHITE, WILLIAM (14), s. of William (13) and Catherine, was bur. at St. Martin's Ludgate, London, 12 Sept. 1709; by his unidentified wife he was the father of WILLIAM (Bronson).

WHITE, WILLIAM (15), s. of William (14), was bur. at St. Martin's Ludgate on 7 Feb. 1708/9; m. Elizabeth Leigh, only dau. of John and Susanna (Downes) Leigh; marr. settlement was dated 2 Feb. 1696/7; she was bur. at Leighton Buzzard 4 Sept. 1742, aged 66; iss.: WILLIAM; THOMAS; JOHN; ELIZABETH, d. unm., bur. at Twickenham, Co. Middlesex on 20 Sept. 1776; SARAH, m. Daniel Midwinter; CHARLOTTE, m. Charles Weekes; MARY, (Bronson).

WHITE, THOMAS (16), s. of William (15) and Elizabeth, came to Balto. (later Harf. Co.) where he d. 29 Sept. 1779; m. Sophia, dau. of John Hall; on 4 March 1743 was comm'd Deputy Surveyor of Balto. Co.; in 1750 owned 673 a. Sophia's Dairy, 168 a. Dairy Enlarged, 114 a. Simmond's Neglect, 200 a. Hall's Plains, and other lands; on 2 Aug. 1762 was living in Philadelphia when he sold 92 a. Littleton to James McComas; m. 2nd Esther Hewlings; iss. (by 1st w.): SOPHIA, b. 8 May 1731, m. Aquila Hall; ELIZABETH, b. 28 Jan. 1733; SARAH CHARLOTTE, b. 21 Oct. 1736; (by 2nd w.): WILLIAM, b. 4 April 1748 in Phila., Bishop of Penna. (86: 271; 128:70, 78, 101; 129:325; 153:38; 303:249; 402:576; Bronson).

WHITE, ANN, in Aug. 1728 was tried for bast., and named Michael Taylor as the father (28:38).

WHITE, CORNELIUS, d. by 23 Feb. 1713/4 when his est. was inv. by William Smith and Jos'a Holdsworth and val. at ₤ 91.2.3, and signed by Thomas Cooper, and by Daniel Dulany on behalf of the two creditors, Charles Carroll and Amos Garrett (50:206, 207).

WHITE, CORNELIUS, d. by 25 May 1714 when his est. was inv. by Jno. Thomas and Jno. Andrews and val. at ₤ 4.15.0 (48:294; 50: 40).

WHITE, DINAH, m. (date not given) Abraham Taylor (131).

WHITE, ERIC, s. of Mary White who m. Samuel Warrell on 1 May 1742; in 6 June 1745 bound himself as an apprentice; may be the same Eric White who m. Rachel Bevans on 19 April 1756 (78:112; 131).

WHITE, FRANCIS, m. Ann Wilkinson on 1 Jan. 1732; had iss.: THOMAS, b. 12 Oct. 1733 (131:75, 80).

WHITE, JANE, was ind. for bast. in March 1741/2 (33:294).

WHITE, JOHN, m. Priscilla Cobb on 18 May 1726; on 4 June 1734 sold 50 a. Paradice to Nathan Rigbie; had iss.: JOHN, b. 2 Sept. 1728; JAMES, b. 7 Dec. 1730 (74:76; 128:66).

WHITE, JOHN, m. Mary (---), and had iss.: FRENETTA ERICKSON, b. 30 Aug. 1739 (131).

WHITE, JOHN, m. Sarah Lego on 4 Oct. 1744, and had iss.; WILLIAM, b. 20 Aug. 1745 (131).

WHITE, JOHN, m. Jane (---), and had iss.: ELIZABETH, b. 3 Nov. 1745 (131).

WHITE, JOHN, in 1750 owned 1000 a. Prospect (153:51).

WHITE, Capt. JOHN, in 1750 owned 167 a. White's Level (153: 90).

WHITE, JOHN, m. Mary Horton after banns were pub. three times betw. 26 March and 14 May 1749 (131).

WHITE, JOHN, m. Elizabeth Gott on 29 Jan. 1751 (131:38).

WHITE, JOHN, Jr., m. Henn. Yeates on 12 May 1751 (131).

WHITE, JOSEPH, and ELIZA WHITE, were named in the will of Thomas Troute of Balto. Co. on 6 July 1680, as son and dau. of Joseph White of Balto. Co. (120:93).

WHITE, MARY, was fined for bast. in March 1718/9; bore a ch. in March 1721/2 (23:63; 24:33).

WHITE, WILLIAM, m. Anne, wid. of Samuel Baker on 12 Aug. 1699 (129:189; 206-19½B:108).

WHITE, WILLIAM, had iss.: THOMAS, d. 19 Oct. 1746 (131).

WHITECOMB, SARAH, d. by 19 Jan. 1757; d. leaving a will, 30 Nov. 1756 - 19 Jan. 1757, naming Mrs. Sarah Phillips, Mrs. Hannah Hall, Mrs. Sarah Hall, Mrs. Mary Hall w. of Col. John Hall, Mrs. Jōhannah Phillips, Cordelia Phillips, Rebecca Matthews, Mary Phillips, exec. James Matthews, Edward Hall and Absolom Brown; admin. bond was posted 19 Jan. 1757 by James Matthews with Edward Hall and Absolom Brown (14:171; 210-30:223).

WHITEFORD, MICHAEL, d. leaving a will, 3 Jan. 1759 - 25 May 1762, naming w. Margaret, bros. James Read and Hugh Whiteford, and the ch. listed below; admin. bond was posted 25 May 1762 by Margaret and Hugh Whiteford the Younger, with Hugh Whiteford and John Balch; had iss.: MARY; HUGH; WILLIAM; JEAN; ANN; MARGARET; and AGNES (6:94; 14:127; 111:133).

WHITEHEAD, (---), m. by 10 Sept. 1750 Susan, dau. of William Wood (5:137).

WHITEHEAD, CHARLES, of A. A. Co., on 2 Aug. 1699 purch. 45 a. Hopewell, part of Arthur's Choice, from Walter and Mary Bosley (63:378).

WHITEHEAD, ELIZA, was charged with bast. in March 1723/4 and again in June 1724 (26:201, 309).

WHITEHEAD, FRANCIS, was in Balto. Co. by Oct. 1694 when he surv. 79 a. Billingate; in Sept. 1698 purch. 100 a. Emanuel's Rest from Emanuel and Sarah Ceely; in 1696 had purch. 200 a. of Oglesby's Chance from Thomas and Mary Jones; in Aug. 1718 he and w. Elizabeth were lic. to keep an ordinary; in March 1718/9 was fined for profanity; d. leaving a will, 4 April 1722 - 9 May 1722, warning all persons from having any dealings with his "undutiful son" Robert who was not yet 21, leaving Billins and Golden Mine to daus. Frances and Phebe; wid. Elizabeth m. 2nd (---) Fincham, and d. leaving a will, 5 Nov. 1738 - 5 Feb. 1738/9, naming William Grover, Sarah Burket, Francis Whitehead, and ch.: Phebe Ingram, Elizabeth and Robert Whitehead; had iss.: ABIEZER FRANCIS, b. 20 March 1689; DANNELANA, b. 25 Jan. 1696/7; dau. FRANCES (poss. the Frances who was ind. for bast. in Nov. 1728); ROBERT, not yet 21 in 1722; PHEBE, m. William Ingram on 6 Nov. 1731; ELIZABETH (in Aug. 1743 was named as admnx. of William Ingram whose wife had d. the previous week (3:343; 23:6, 66, 214; 28:65; 59:524; 63:292; 124:105; 127:14; 128:3, 4; 131; 211).

WHITEHEAD, ROBERT, s. of Francis, was b. c.1700; m. Elizabeth (---); on 5 Aug,. 1735 purch. 50 a. Low's Range, now Whitehead's Folly, from James and Mary Low; in 1744 with w. Elizabeth (b. c. 1704), and s.: THOMAS, b. c.1740 (74:278; 28:180).

WHITEHEAD, THOMAS, in March 1733 was ind. for begetting an illegitimate ch. on the body of Johanna Lemmon (30:199).

WHITEHEAD, WILLIAM BOND, m. Susanna, dau. of William Bond on 26 Feb. 1749/50 (5:137; 131).

WHITLATCH, CHARLES, m. Elizabeth (---), and had iss.: CHARLES, b. 22 Sept. 1749; SARAH, b. 7 March 1751; RACHEL, b. 6 July 1753; JOHN, b. 4 Aug. 1755; MARY, b. 20 March 1759; WILLIAM, b. 22 April 1761 (129:362).

WHOLESTOCKS, HANNAH, was ind. for bast. in Aug. 1724; in Nov. 1724 was called serv. to Michael Gormacon when she was sentenced to 15 stripes for bast. (26:438; 27:43).

WIATH, ELIZABETH, was ind. for bast. (25:231).

WICKINS, ROBERT, m. Jemima Holloway on 3 June 1745 (133:157).

WICKS/WEEKS, JOHN , was in Balto. Co. by 1729 when he purch. 50 a. Rutledge's Venture from Michael Rutledge; owned the land in 1750 (72:186; 153:93).

WICKS, THOMAS, was in Balto. Co. by Nov. 1718 when he was fined for profanity; in Nov. 1724 obliged by "keeping and maintaining" Dorothy Thoman (formerly bound to John Barrett) and her s. Ashia (23:36; 27:32).

WICKS, THOMAS, m. Eliza Enloes on 15 Dec. 1742; had iss.: JOHN, b. 15 May 1743; THOMAS, b. 27 Dec. 1744; MARY, b. 11 Feb. 1746, m. John Holland on 4 March 1766 (131).

WIGLEY, EDWARD, was in Balto. Co. by 2 Jan. 1749/50 when he m. Jane Fisher; in Jan. 1762 bought part Chevy Chase from John Ensor; had iss.: EDWARD, Jr. (11:481; 12:156; 86:445; 133).

WILBOURN, EDWARD (1), d 24 June 1731 leaving a will, 23 Jan.
1730/1 - 3 March 1730/1, naming w. Elizabeth and ch. Anne, William, Thomas, and Elizabeth Wood; admin. bond was posted 8 Sept.
1731 by Thomas Wilbourne with Thomas Mitchell, the wid. Elizabeth having ren. admin. in favor of her s. Thomas Mitchell; dec.
left iss.: THOMAS; WILLIAM; ANNE; ELIZABETH, m. (poss. Isaac)
Wood (14:35; 125:180).

WILBOURN, THOMAS (2), s. of Edward (1) and Elizabeth, was b.
c.1701, giving his age 31 in 1732 in a dep. in which he named
his dec. father Edward; m. Margaret (---); had iss.: THOMAS, b.
18 Jan. 1730; MARTHA, b. 16 Dec. 1733 (128:73, 78; 163:151).

WILBOURN, WILLIAM (3), s. of Edward (1), was b. c.1708, giving
his age as 24 in 1732; m. Ann Crabtree on 21 Jan. 1731, and by
26 Sept. 1753 was in Fred. Co. when he conv. to Isaac Wood land
he (William) had inher. from his father Edward; had iss.: JANE,
b. 28 Jan. 1732; WILLIAM, b. 25 Oct. 1734; JAMES, b. 18 Aug.
1736 (82:70; 128:78, 82, 93b; 129:231; 163:151).

WILBOURN, MARGARET, dau. of Margaret, age 9 next "12 tide," in
Aug. 1730 was bound to Bethia Calvert to age 16 (29:3).

WILD, JONATHAN, m. Sarah Preble on 30 Nov. 1738 (129:303).

WILD, SARAH, was fined for bast. in Nov. 1759 (46:240).

WILDEY/WILD/WELDY, EDWARD, was in Balto. Co. by 1692 as a
taxable in Spesutia Hund.; on 23 March 1699 purch. 150 a. The
Fork from James and Bethia Phillips; d. 17 May (year not given)
(61:258; 128:27; 138).

WILES, JONATHAN, m. Sarah Preble on 30 Nov. 1734 and had iss.:
MARY, b. 15 Nov. 1739 (128:102, 106).

WILES, STEPHEN, was in Balto. Co. by 1692 as a taxable in n.
side Patapsco Hund. (138).

WILEY, MARGARET, in Oct. 1745 gave consent for John Daugherty,
age 15, to be bound to Samuel Collier to learn the trade of
blacksmith (78:331).

WILEY, MARY, serv. of John Bosley, in Nov. 1755 was tried for
bast. in Aug. 1738; named Charles Roberts as the father (40:400).

WILEY. See also WYLEY.

WILFORD, ELINOR, serv. to Nathaniel Sheppard, was ind. for
bast. in Aug. 1738 (31:267).

WILKINS, RICHARD, serv. with 1 year, 10 mos. to serve, was
listed in the March 1676/7 inv. of Capt. Samuel Boston (51:110).

WILKINS, ROBERT, shoemaker, was listed in the 1747 inv. of
William Fell (55:204).

THE WILLIAM WILKINSON FAMILY

WILKINSON, WILLIAM (1), was in Balto. Co. by 5 March 1681
when he surv. 50 a. Wilkinson's Spring; in Nov. 1684 was made an
allowance for accommodating the jury for the laying out of (an
early) Baltimore Town; on 7 March 1693 conv. to John Smith of
Biteford (Biddiford?), Co. Devon,. lot # 3 in the Town of Absolute on the Patapsco River; m. by Sept. 1694 Elizabeth, heir of
Abraham and Sarah Clark; in March 1693 had been named by Martha

Cage as the father of her ch.; on 11 June 1694 William Hollis and
w. Mary dau. of Abraham and Sarah Clarke, conv. Landisell (which
formerly belonged to Mary) to William Wilkinson; in 1708 John Love
made a will naming William Wilkinson as his bro.-in-law: on 16
June 1705 William and w. Tamar conv. 89 a. Wilkinson's Folly to
Moses Edwards; d. leaving a will, 21 April 1718 - 16 June 1718,
leaving dwelling plantation to s. Robert, Cumberland to daus.
Jane Corbin, Ann, Philisanna, and Sophia , and naming w. Tamar as
extx.; est. of Wilkinson was inv. on 28 June 1718 by John Norton
and S. Hinton, and val. at E 162.3.9; est. was admin. on 4 June
1725 and 4 July 1725 by Tamar, now w. of Richard Lenox; William
was twice m.; 1st. by Sept. 1694 to Elizabeth, heir of Abraham
and Sarah Clark; 2nd, by 1705 to Tamar, dau. of Robert Love;
Tamar m. 2nd Richard Lenox; had iss.: ROBERT; JANE, m. by 27
March 1722 Edward Corbin; ANNE, m. George Harryman by 30 March
1725; SOPHIA, m. Thomas Sligh on 17 April 1734; PHILISANNA
(2:330, 360; 14:56; 18:199, 202; 20:175, 176; 59:401, 414;
67:284; 122:131; 123:162; 131; 133; Christopher Johnston, chart
of Love Family, MHS).

WILKINSON, ROBERT (2), s. of William (1), d. in Balto. Co.
in 1760; m. Rachel Lenox on 8 June 1736; in June 1733 chose his
mother, Tamar Lenox as guardian; in 1750 owned 425 a. Land Is
All, 34 a. Wilkinson's Chance, and 50 a. Wilkinson's Spring; on
22 May 1758 Edward and Jane Corbin conv. to Robert Wilkinson the
land they had earlier conv. to his mother, Tamar; in Aug. 1759
conv. prop. to s. William; d. leaving a will, 13 Aug. 1759 - 6
March 1760, naming dau. Sarah Todd,s. William, and grandson Thomas Todd, and w. Rachel Richardson Wilkinson (sic); had iss.:
SARAH, m. Thomas Todd; WILLIAM, b. 10 Aug. 1736 (30:4; 47:58; 83:
157; 133:57, 154, 155; 153:31; 210-30:823).

WILKINSON, PHILISANNA (3), dau. of Tamar, was fined for
bast. in June 1733 and again in June 1738; on 7 July 1740 for
love and affection conv. to her s. Jethro Lynch Wilkinson 100
a. Cumberland; had iss.: JETHRO LYNCH, b. c.1733, m. Elizabeth
Harryman on 29 Jan. 1761, earlier in Nov. 1755 he was fined for
bast. as the father of Ruth Rolls' child (30:14; 31:237; 46:74;
75:398;131; 133:36).

WILKINSON, JOHN, was in Balto. Co. by 1694 as a taxable in
n. side of Patapsco Hund.; d. by 13 April 1722 when his est. was
admin. by Eliza Wilkinson (7:157; 139).

WILKINSON, PHILIP, in Sept. 1747 with cons. of w. Rebecca conv.
250 a. part Sewell's Fancy to Alexander Lawson (79:686).

WILKINSON, ROBERT, of Bear Creek, Patapsco River, in Sept.
1756 write to his cousin Japhet Wilkinson at the King's Arms near
Hatton Garden, Holbourn, stating that Japhet's cousin Moore had
d. in 1755; referred to a cousin Thomas, and to a neighbor who
was a bro. to Thomas Henshaw at the White Horse in the Mincrel
(300-65:261).

WILKINSON, SAMUEL, m. Mary Asher on 14 April 1748 (131).

WILKINSON, SAMUEL, m. Mary Wood on 12 Feb. 1759 (131).

WILKINSON, SARAH, was ind. for bast. in March 1729/30 (28:
362).

WILKINSON, Rev. STEPHEN, d. 10 March 1743; m. Ruth (---)
and had: THOMAS, b. 4 March 1731; JOHN, b. 13 Aug. 1733; ANN:
ISABELLA, b. 1 Dec. 1736 (128:77, 87, 97).

WILKINSON, STEPHEN, d. by 3 Nov. 1744 when admin. bond was posted by admnx, Rachel Paca with Parker Hall and John Hall (14: 119).

WILKINSON, STEPHEN, in 1750 owned 100 a. Northampton (153:57).

WILKINSON, THOMAS, in June 1759 with cons. of w. Hannah sold 25 a. Margaret's Purchase on Swan Creek to Benjamin Culver (83: 468).

THE JOHN WILLIAMS FAMILY

WILLIAMS, JOHN (1), was in Balto. Co. by 6 Dec. 1706 when he m. Mary Wheeler in St. Geo. Par.; d. 12 Feb. 1733, leaving iss.: MARY, b. 11 Jan. 1707; JOHN, b. 10 Aug. 1709; ELIZABETH, b. 11 Sept. 1711; ANN, b. 18 April 1713; MORRIS, b. 10 Oct. 1716; WILLIAM, b. 12 Oct. 1720; THOMAS, b. 12 Sept. 1725, d. 4 May 1726 (128:73, 84).

WILLIAMS, JOHN (2), s. of John (1), was b. 10 Aug. 1709, was prob. the John who d. by 30 April 1748 when admin. bond was posted by Margaret Williams and Ford Barnes, with Thomas Mitchell and Jonathan Jones; m. Margaret Clark on 2 Dec. 1736; est. was admin. by Margaret, now w. of William James, on 1 June 1750; John and Margaret had iss.: PETER, b. 21 Jan. 1737; JOHN, b. 25 July 1740: MARGARET, b. 26 Dec. 1742 (5:172, 210; 14:168; 128:92b; 129: 324, 334).

WILLIAMS, MORRIS (3), s. of John (1), was b. 10 Oct. 1716; may be the Morris Williams who m. Ann Du on 28 June 1748; had iss.: EDWARD, b. 28 Dec. 1751; MARTHA, b. 17 Jan. 1754; MARTHA, b. 8 Jan. 1757; and JOHN, b. 29 Aug. 1761 (129:382).

WILLIAMS, WILLIAM (4), s. of John (1), was b. 12 Oct. 1720; may be the William who d. 12 Sept. 1737 having m. Lucy Ann Bayley on 22 May 1735, and had iss.: MOSES, b. 14 Jan. 1735 (128:87, 91, 99).

THE JOSEPH WILLIAMS FAMILY

WILLIAMS, JOSEPH (5), no known rel. to any of the above, was in Balto. Co. by 1692 as a taxable in s. side Patapsco Hund.; d. by 24 May 1693 when admin. bond on his est. was posted by John and Edith Beecher; m. (1st w. unknown); m. 2nd Edith Cromwell, wid. of of Richard Gist; she m. 3rd John Beecher; d. leaving a will, 24 Sept. 1692 - 11 March 1692/3, naming w. Edith as extx. and ch. James, Joseph, and Richard, and Mary (prob. by 1st w.); also named Benjamin Williams of Benjamin, and John Robertson and mentioned tracts: Esington, Bell Meade, Heathcote's Cottage, and Hickory Hills; est. was inv. at various times by Leonard Wayman and John Powell, showing £ 124.13.0 at the Cecil Co. plantation, £ 147.15.11 in A. A. Co., and £ 12.11.0 in Calvert Co., totalling £ 357.6.7; est. was admin. by Benjamin Williams of A. A. Co., on 27 July 1708 and 27 Aug. 1708; by 1st w. had iss.: JAMES; JOSEPH; RICHARD; and MARY (2:122, 123; 14:62; 48:41, 57; 121:60; 138; 206-13A:283; see also Christopher Johnston, "Gist Family," in Md. Hist. Mag. 8 (1913), 372-373).

WILLIAMS, JAMES (6), s. of Joseph (5), inher. Esington on the farther side of the Patuxent; no other record (111:60).

WILLIAMS, JOSEPH (7), s. of Joseph (5), inher. 100 a. Bell Meade; no other record (111:60).

WILLIAMS, RICHARD (8), s. of Joseph (5), inher. 100 a. of Hickory Hills; no other record (111:60).

WILLIAMS, BENJAMIN, in Nov. 1758 purch. Long Valley from William Gosnell, Jr., and w. Sarah (83:280).

WILLIAMS, CHARLES, m. Judith Jones on 13 July 1739 (129:109).

WILLIAMS, CHARLES, was listed in the 1759 inv. of David Bissett (52:230).

WILLIAMS, GEORGE, in 1750 owned 50 a. Jenkins' Delight; as George Jenkins of Cecil Co., d. by 21 June 1758 when admin. bond was posted by admin. Jesse Bussey with Edward Bussey; est. was admin. on 5 Nov. 1759 and 1 Sept. 1760 (4:258, 324).

WILLIAMS, GERMON, d. by 15 Oct. 1748 when admin. bond was posted by Edward Martin with Stephen Onion (14:57, 82).

WILLIAMS, HENRY, m. Rachel Williams on 16 Jan. 1755 (131).

WILLIAMS, ISAAC, m. 1st Lydia (---), and 2nd, on 2 d, 10, 1783 Rebecca Hayward (poss. wid. of Joseph Hayward and dau. of Jacob and Hannah Scott); had is. (births recorded in Records of Gunpowder Meeting: ENNION, b. 9 d, 10 1745, d. 12 d, 7 1747; HANNAH, b. 21 d, 2 1747; WILLIAM, b. 28 d, 6, 1749, d. 28 d, 7, 1767, age 16; LYDIA, b. 28 d, 2, 1752; ISAAC, b. 26 d, 6, 1754, m. Mary, dau. of William Hayward; ENNION, b. 2 d, 8, 1756, m. Hannah, dau. of Joseph Hayward; RACHEL, b. 6 d, 10, 1758; and MARY, b. 7 d, 3, 1761 (136).

WILLIAMS, JOHN, age c.30, b. in Herefordshire and "bred a farmer," was a runaway conv., serv. of Charles Carroll in June 1753 (385:237).

WILLIAMS, JONAS, was in Balto. Co. by 1692 as a taxable in s. side Patapsco Hund. (138).

WILLIAMS, JONATHAN, had two sons who were conv. a cow by Richard Cromwell in April 1699; had: JOHN; JONAS (63:343).

WILLIAMS, LODOWICK, was in Balto. Co. by 19 Aug. 1670 when he surv. 150 a. Williams' Fortune; on 7 Sept. 1699 conv. 400 a. of Bachelor's Hope on the west side of Hunting Creek and 50 a. at the mouth of Hunting Creek to Walter Tucker and company; m. by 13 Nov. 1674, Mary, dau. of James Stringer of A. A. Co.; had iss.: EDWARD, conv. Williams Fortune to Richard Colegate (73:311; 95; 98:47; 101:304; 200-51:135).

WILLIAMS, MARY, was ind. for bast. in Nov. 1730; as serv. to William Connell was tried for bast. in March 1731; had iss.: MARTHA, b. 31 June 1731 (29:49, 236; 133:20).

WILLIAMS, MARY, late of Stafford Co., Va., was in Balto. Co. by Oct. 1743 when she conv. 200 a. in Prince William Co., Va., Hamilton Parish to John Hunt; it was the same land she had inher. from her father John Toward (79:592).

WILLIAMS, MARY, serv. to Nicholas Britton, was fined for bast. in Nov. 1757 (46:73).

WILLIAMS, OWEN, d. by 28 June 1679/80 when admin. bond was posted by admin. Lawrence Taylor with Edward Bedell and John Wallston; est. was admin. 5 March 1686 by Taylor who stated the est. had been inv. at a value of 3796 lbs. tob. (14:64; 206-9: 223).

WILLIAMS, PAUL, m. Mary (---), and had iss.: JANE, b. 13 May 1725; DAVID, b. 13 Oct. 1727; DANIEL, b. 13 Aug. 1730 (128:61).

WILLIAMS, RALPH, merch. of Bristol, Eng., in April 1668/9
conv. 300 a. Notch Point to Thomas Todd, merch. of Patapsco
(60:71).

WILLIAMS, RICHARD, m. Anne Nearn on 12 June 1746 (131).

WILLIAMS, ROBERT, serv., was listed in the 1759 inv. of
Charles Christie (54:298).

WILLIAMS, ROWLAND, of Balto. Co., imm. c.1667; in April 1667
William and Elizabeth Saven conv. him 200 a. on branch of the
Bohemia River (94; 97:124, 126; 98:47; 100:117; 398).

WILLIAMS, ROWLAND, M. Alice (---); on 28 Aug. 1741 Rowland and
w. Elsie (sic) conv. Shipley's Well to Luke Mercer; had iss.:
HANNAH, b. 19 Jan. 1731; ELIZABETH, b. 19 Aug. 1735; THOMAS, b.
26 July 1736; ROWLAND, b. 21 Oct. 1740 (76:12; 133:44, 64).

WILLIAMS, SARAH, was tried in March 1746/7 for bearing three
illeg. children (36:410).

WILLIAMS, THOMAS, was in Balto. Co. by 1692 as a taxable in
Spesutia Hund. (138).

WILLIAMS, THOMAS, was b. c.1694, giving his age as c.42 in
1736; Lucy Williams, was b. c.1698, giving her age as c.38 in
the same year (223:240).

WILLIAMS, THOMAS, m. Susannah Higgs on 10 June 1759 (131).

WILLIAMS, WILLIAM, m. Jean Asshe on 26 May 1716 (131).

WILLIAMS, WILLIAM, son of William, was age 13 in June 1739
when he was bound to William James (32:401).

WILLIAMS, WILLIAM, m. Sarah Ellwood on 8 Dec. 1746 (131).

WILLIAMS, WILLIAM, m. by 17 Oct. 1754 Mary, extx. of William
Matthau (4:232).

WILLIAMS, WILLIAM, iron founder, and w. Mary, in Nov. 1754
were conv. 329 a. part Stout by Roger and Rachel Randall (82:
336).

WILLIAMSON, GEORGE, m. Keturah Durbin on 15 June 1758 (131).

WILLIAMSON, MARY, m. Matthew Talbot on 5 July 1722 (133:146).

WILLIAMSON, THOMAS, d. by 20 May 1719 when admin. bond was
posted by wid. and admnx. Dorothy Williamson with William Barnett and Edward Lenthall; on 4 Aug. 1719 est. was inv. by Thomas
Randall and Walter Pumphrey and val. at £ 94.8.6 and signed by
Dorothy Williamson; est. was admin. on 22 Feb. 1719 by Dorothy,
now w. of John Smith, with bal. to the widow and two daus.;
on 31 Jan. 1720 est. was admin. and dist. to widow and the daus.;
in Aug. 1721 Mary Lintall and Elizabeth Williamson pet. that
they had not rec. their share of their father's plantations, that
their mother was willing to divide the land but being married
she could do nothing; in Nov. 1721 Lance Todd was appointed to
divide the land between John Smith and wife, and her two daus.
now Mary Hewett and Elizabeth Williamson; iss. of Thomas and Dorothy: MARY, m. 1st (---) Lintall, and 2nd, by Nov. 1721 (---)
Hewett; ELIZABETH, unm. in Nov. 1721 (1:52, 331; 14:53; 23:556,
626; 51:153).

WILLIAMSON, THOMAS, m. Mary (---) who in Nov. 1721 pet. the court concerning the treatment of her son, who had been bound to Edward Meeds (23:621).

WILLIAMSON, THOMAS, was b. c.1693, giving his age as 50 in 1743; m. 1st, Sarah (---) who d. 15 Oct. 1738; m. 2nd, on 14 Aug. 1739 Elizabeth Bois; on 30 Aug. 1732 Thomas and w. Sarah conv. 11 a. George's Hall to Bennett Garrett; had iss.; (by 1st w.): HANNAH, b. 15 Sept. 1725 (73:323; 128:49, 101, 105; 224:94).

WILLING, MARY, m. William Cannon on 18 Feb. 1695 (129:177).

WILLING, SAMUEL, d. by 16 May 1712 when admin. bond was posted by Simon Pierson with Francis Dallahide (14:49).

WILLIS, JOHN, on 2 March 1709 purch. 200 a. James Park from John Ewings (59:646).

WILLS, HENRY, tailor, from Balto. Co., escaped from gaol in Philadelphia Co.; May 1751; had been charged with passing counterfeit money (385:131).

WILLS, JOHN, d. by 10 May 1721 when admin. bond was posted by Margaret Wells (or Wills) with Thomas Taylor and Thomas Parker (14:39).

WILLSON. See WILSON.

WILMOT, JOHN (1), was in Balto. Co. by 1692 either as the John who was in n. side Patapsco Hund. as head of a household, or the John who was in the county with Robert Wilmot; m. Jane (---); d. leaving a will, 15 Sept. 1719 - 5 Nov. 1719, naming w. Jane, grandsons John and Richard Wilmot, son John, son-in-law John Ashman; admin. bond was posted 13 Nov. 1719 by John Wilmot with John Ashman and John Cromwell; est. was inv. 18 Oct. 1719 by John Israel and Lance Todd, and val. at £ 403.2.10; on 24 Oct. 1719 his wid. renounced the will; est. was admin. by John Wilmot on 4 May 1722 who named the wid. and a dau. who m. John Ashman; had iss.: JOHN; and (CONSTANT) m. John Ashman (1: 253; 14:55; 48:253; 50:184; 123:216; 138).

WILMOT, JOHN (2), of John (1), was prob. the John Wilmot b. c.1682 who gave his age as 48 in 1730; d. by 16 March 1748 when admin. bond was posted by acting exec. Robert Wilmot with James Moore, Jr., and Richard Wilmot; m. c.1710 Rachel, dau. of Richard and Rachel Owings; admin. the est. of David Gay or Guy on 7 Aug. 1729; on 21 Jan. 1726/7 purch. 100 a. Rogers Road from William and Elizabeth Reeves; on 9 Sept. 1747 purch. 100 a. Franklin's Gift from John and Jane Rutledge; est. was admin. on 4 April 1750 by Robert Wilmot, naming heirs: his wife Rachel and ch. Richard, Anne Jones, Hannah w. of James Moore, John, Constant w. of William Cromwell and Dinah w. of William Towson; in 1750 his heirs owned 61 a. Jeopardy Tertus and 325 a. part Rachel's Prospect; Rachel d. leaving a will, 11 June 1758 - 8 June 1761; iss. of John and Rachel: JOHN; RICHARD; RUTH, m. Thomas Franklin on 26 Oct. 1729; CONSTANT, m. William Cromwell; ROBERT; RACHEL; HANNAH, m. James (or Joseph) Moore; DINAH, m. William Towson; and ANNE, m. (---) Jones (2:304; 5:146, 214; 14:141; 70:327; 79:560; 133:149; 153:6; 163:99; 210-31:319).

WILMOT, JOHN (3), s. of John (2), d. in Balto. Co. by 8 April 1783; m. by 1 May 1758 Avarilla, dau. of Thomas Carr; in Nov. 1746 was ind. for bast,. and admitted paternity of Ellinor Copes' child; in 1750 owned 100 a. Franklin's Gift, 192 a. Litchfield City, and 60 a. part Rachel's Prospect; on 11 Feb. 1754 purch.

40 a. of Walerich from Thomas and Sarah Stevens; d. leaving a
will, 6 Dec. 1782 - 8 April 1783, naming w. Avarilla, and these
ch.: JOHN; RACHEL, m. (---) Bosley; HANNAH; ELIZABETH, m. (---)
Thompson; MARY; and SARAH (36:220, 248; 82:185; 112:550; 153:
83; 210-30:501).

WILMOT, RICHARD (4), s. of John (2) and Rachel, m. Mary Gittings on 22 Dec. 1741; on 22 Sept. 1753 he purch. 50 a. Baker's
Chance from Indimeon Baker; had iss.: THOMAS, b. 22 Dec. 1742;
RACHAEL, b. 15 Nov. 1744; JOHN, b. 1 Feb. 1746; ELIZABETH,
b. 20 Jan. 1748; RICHARD, b. 24 Dec. 1750; MARY, b. 28 Jan.
1753 (82:135; 83:72; 131).

WILMOT, ROBERT (5), s. of John (2) and Rachel, d. c.1773 in
Balto. Co.; m. Sarah, dau. of John and Sarah (Rogers) Merryman,
on 15 Dec. 1748; d. leaving a will,8 Oct. 1773 - 4 Nov. 1773,
naming these ch.: JOHN; WILLIAM, b. c.1752; ROBERT, b. 25 Dec.
1757, d. 5 Aug. 1839, m. Priscilla Ridgely Dorsey; RICHARD;
BENJAMIN; SARAH, m. Benjamin Talbot; ELEANOR, m. (---) Bowen;
RUTH, m. (---) Bowen; MARY (112:265; 133:162; Francis B. Culver,
"Last Bloodshed of the Revolution," Md. Hist. Mag. 5 (1910),
329-334).

WILMOT, JOHN, was transp. to Md. c.1676 (388).

WILMOT, ROBERT, was in Balto. Co. by 5 July 1689 when he and
Jane Wilmot conv. land to Charles Gorsuch; d. leaving a will, 9
May 1696 - 29 June 1696, leaving personalty to Jone (or John)
Burgin, appointing his w. Jane as extx., naming her son (by a
previous marr.?) John Cooper or Copper; and cousin John Wilmot;
his est. was inv. 5 May 1696 (sic) by Jonas Bowen and John
Mountfield and val. at Ł 50.4.9 (59:303; 121:110; 206-14:28).

WILMOT, SAMUEL, age 7, orphan of Thomas, was bound to Joseph
Parrish in June 1754 (39:185).

WILSHIRE. See WILTSHIRE.

THE JOHN WILSON FAMILY

WILSON, JOHN (1), was b. c.1630, d. c.1690 in A. A. Co.; came
to Md. c.1656 with John Burrage and Gerard Hopkins; in 1688
conv. to his only s. John Wilson, Jr., the tract Burrage and
1000 a. in Balto. Co. called Friendship, and a lot in Herrington; Friendship was orig. surv. for Robert Lockwood, later held
by John Wilson, and still later by the heirs of John Wilson of
A. A. Co.; had iss.: JOHN (211; 388; Mrs. William Bain of Seattle, Washington has generously shared her Wilson research with
the author).

WILSON, JOHN (2), s. of John (1), was b. c.1665 and d. 1702;
may have m. Margaret, dau. of William Kidde of Calvert Co., whose
will, 20 March 1692 - 20 April 1693, named dau. Margaret Wilson;
about 1707 James Lee is listed in the Anne Arundel County Rent
Rolls as holding several tracts for the orphans of John Wilson:
parts of Burrage, Burrage Blossom, Burrage's End, Trent, and Spencer's Search; John and Margaret had iss.: JOHN; JOSEPH; and
WILLIAM (59:242; 63:511; 69:176; 121:64; 211; data from Mrs.
Bain).

WILSON, JOHN (3), s. of John (2), m. Ruth Child by 1714;
d. s.p. by 20 June 1731 when his wid. Ruth had m. 2nd (---)
Robins; Henry Child of A. A. Co. made a will on that date naming
a dau. Ruth Robins (127:83; data from Mrs. Bain).

WILSON, JOSEPH (4), s. of John (2), d. in Harf. Co. leaving
a will dated 7 Feb. 1785; m. Hannah Farmer on 4 Feb. 1729; in
1737 bought Neighborhood from Michael and Elizabeth Webster; in
1750 he owned 84 a. Daugherty's Chance, 37½ a. Wilson's Chance,
and part Neighborhood; his will mentioned tracts Cobb's Knavely,
Wilson's Choice, Neighborhood and Daugherty's Chance; had iss.:
JOHN, b. 12 Feb. 1730; JOSEPH, b. 20 April 1731; SAMUEL, b. c.
1736, age 40 in 1776, d. by 7 Feb. 1785; HANNAH, b. 4 April 1736,
m. Stephen Jay; MARTHA, b. 10 Nov. 1739; MARY, b. 24 May 1743, m.
John Dallam; SARAH, b. c.1748; ELIZABETH (75:3; 128:64, 95, 109;
129:330; 153:40; 244-AJ#C:232; 277:167; data from Mrs. Bain).

WILSON, WILLIAM (5), s. of John (2), said to have m. Rachel,
poss. dau. of Henry Child of A. A. Co.; on 9 May 1716 conv. 300
a. Friendship to James Lee; w. Rachel consented; on 23 Jan. 1722
as guardian and heir at law to John Wilson of A. A. Co., conv.
Friendship (except for 300 a. already sold to Lee) to William
Holland; in 1750 owned 200 a. part Thomas Bond's Gift, 100 a.
Elizabeth's Purchase, and 30 a. Cox's Hope; d. by 22 July 1753
when will was proved, leaving Amnor to s. John Wilson as well as
Cox's Freehold and part Elizabeth's Purchase, sons Benkid (not
to marry Mary Smith), Henry, and William; also named w. Rachel;
had iss.: JOHN; BENKID; WILLIAM; HENRY (63:511; 69:176; 127:
83; 153:81; 210-28:504).

WILSON, (---), m. by 1709 Elizabeth, dau. of William Gosnell
of A. A. Co. (122:168).

WILSON, ANNE, was ind. for bast. in June 1730 (28:415).

WILSON, ELIZABETH, serv. of John Cook, was tried for bast.
in June 1734 (30:265).

WILSON, GARRETT, m. Rosanna Smith on 21 Jan. 1745; in March
1746/7 he was ind. on charge of bast.; had iss.: WILLIAM, b.
17 Oct. 1745; THOMAS, b. 15 April 1747; EDWARD, b. 21 Aug. 1748;
GARRETT, b. 16 Jan. 1749 (33:379; 133:86, 158).

WILSON, GEORGE, of Balto. Co., was "in Virginia" on 29 July
1669 when he purch. 1000 a. Verina from Thomas and Penelope
Cornwallis of Stanhow, Co. Norfolk, Eng.; on 7 Sept. 1669 conv.
to Thomas Bostock the land where the latter was living; on 1
June 1674 conv. Richard Lee 125 a. part of Verina; prob. the
George who d, leaving a will, 24 May 1675 - 1 March 1676, naming
w. Winifred and these ch.: PETER; JAMES; ELIZA; and JOHN (95:
260; 96:229; 100:118; 110:168).

WILSON, HENRY, and w. Priscilla (Gover) were rec'd into membership in Gunpowder Mtg. 27 d, 6, 1753, by a cert. from Nottingham Mtg. dated 19 d, 5, 1753; m. in A. A. Co. on 7 d., 11 m. (Jan.)
1743 at West River, Priscilla Gover; Henry was later approved
elder for Little Falls Mtg.; iss. of Henry and Priscilla:
HENRY, b. 19 June 1747; PRISCILLA, b. 29 Oct. 1749; RACHEL, b.
9 Nov. 1751; and ELIZABETH, b. 13 March 1754 (136).

WILSON, HENRY, in 1750 owned 230 a. part Rush Grove (153:81).

WILSON, JANE, was charged with bast. in March 1723/4; tried in
June 1724; tried for bast. in Aug. 1730; ind. again in Nov. 1730;
ind. in June 1746 (George Smith admitted paternity in this case);
had iss.: HEZEKIAH, b. 18 Nov. 1723; SARAH, b. 12 May 1725 (26:
201, 332; 29:7, 49; 33:49, 129; 128:50).

WILSON, JOHN, of Balto. Co. imm. by c.1678 (388).

WILSON, JOHN, was in Balto. Co. by 1692 as a taxable   in n. side Patapsco Hund. (138).

WILSON, JOHN, d. by 10 July 1709 when admin. bond was posted by Edward Smith with Matthew Green and Henry Matthews; est. was admin. by said Green and Matthews on 6 Aug. 1709 and val. at B 3.14.0 (14:61; 51:25).

WILSON, JOHN, in 1750 owned 63½ a. Arabia Petrea (153:3).

WILSON, JOHN, m. Mary (---) who on 24 Jan. 1744 conv. 100 a. Wilson's Range to Isaac Webster; had iss.: MARGARET, b. 26 March 1733; SARAH, b. 19 Nov. 1734; BENJAMIN, b. 4 April 1739; MOSES, b. Whitsunday, 1738, prob. d. young; MOSES, b. 27 April 1740 (78:8; 128:73, 83, 100, 110, 116).

WILSON, JOHN, in Nov. 1746 was made levy free (35:384).

WILSON, JOHN, was b. c.1726; d. 21 March 1807, m. Susanna Gittings on 8 Sept. 1747, and had iss.: JOHN; HENRY; GITTINGS, b. 1750; SAMUEL; AZRAEL; MARY, m. Ezekiel Williams; WILLIAM; JAMES; ELIZABETH, m. (---) Pearce (345:769).

WILSON, MARY, m. Thomas Burchfield on the last of June 1709 (129:208).

WILSON, MARY, was ind. for bast. in June 1724 (26:127).

WILSON, MARY, m. Joseph Foresight on 28 Dec. 1724 (131).

WILSON, ROBERT, on 29 Dec. 1670 surv. 320 a. Utopia on s. side Patapsco; prob. the Robert who d. by 21 Nov. 1678 when admin. bond was posted by George Yate with John Larkin and Rowland Nance; Yate sued William Cromwell in 1679/80 (14:78; 200-69:205; 211).

WILSON, SAMUEL, m. Rebecca, dau. of Samuel Smithson, and had iss.: SARAH, b. 14 April 1728; SAMUEL, b. 13 April 1731 (128: 76).

WILSON, SOPHIA, alias Jane Smith, was ind. for bast. in March 1754; her ch. Elizabeth and Aquila, mulattoes, were sold to William Rogers (39:15, 20, 26).

WILSON, WILLIAM, Jr., m. Cassandra Gover on 19 d, 7, 1740 at West River; evidently moved to Nottingham Meeting; had a cert. from Nottingham dated 19 d, 5, 1753 which they brought to Gunpwder, where they were rec'd into membership on 27 d, 6, 1753; William, Jr., was a bro. of Henry Wilson who m. Priscilla Gover (see above); William and Cassandra had iss.: RACHEL, b. 19 June 1741; WILLIAM, b. 14 Nov. 1747; GOVER, b. 3 March 1749/50; SAMUEL, b. 11 Feb. 1752 (136).

WILSON, WILLIAM, "of Pipe Creek," in 1750 owned 100 a. Long Valley (153:53).

WILSON, WILLIAM, "of Soldier's Delight," in 1750 owned 50 a. Wilson's Adventure (153:69).

WILSON, WILLIAM, Jr., in 1750 owned 230 a. Rush Grove (153: 81).

WILSON, WILLIAM, m. Sarah (---) and had iss.: ANN, b. 29 May 1736; WILLIAM, b. 1 July 1738 (131).

WILSTON, JOHN, age c.30, was a runaway conv. serv. from the Gunpowder Ironworks; Irish birth; April 1747 (384:613).

WILTSHIRE, JOHN, m. (as John Welcher) Unity Coffee on 7 Aug. 1750; d. by 12 July 1762 when admin. bond was posted by Unity Wiltshire with John Skinner; est. admin. by Unity on 16 May 1763 and 10 Sept. 1764 (6:43, 101; 14:143; 131).

WINCHESTER, WILLIAM, was b. 22 Dec. 1710 in London, Eng., and d. 2 Sept. 1790 in Westminster (now Carroll Co.), Md.; m. on 22 July 1747 Lydia Richards, b. 4 Aug. 1727, d. 19 Feb. 1809, dau. of Edward and Mary Richards; in 1750 owned 50 a. Collenton and 50 a. Winchester's Lot; had iss.: KATHERINE, b. 22 Nov. 1748, d. 1815, m. Edward Hotchkiss; WILLIAM, b. 1750, d. 1812, m. Mary Parks; JAMES, b. 1752, d. 1826, m. Susan Black; MARY, b. 1755, d. 1799, m. (---) Roberts; GEORGE, b. 1757, d. 1794; RICHARD, b. 1759, d. 1822, m. Rebecca Lawrence; STEPHEN, b. 1761, d. 1815, m. Sally Howard; ELIZABETH, b. 1763, d. 1847; LYDIA, b. 1766, d. 1849; DAVID, b. 1769, d. 1835 (134:14; 153:17; Ferdinand B. Focke, "Winchester-Owens,-Owings-Price, and Allied Families," Md. Hist. Mag. 25 (1930), 385-405).

WINDLEY. See WINLEY.

WINE, DANIEL, d. by 9 July 1686 when admin. bond was posted by Thomas Jones with William Osborn and John White; est. was inv. 9 July 1686 by William York and Thomas Preston and val. at £8.19.8; est. was admin. by Thomas Jones on 22 Sept. 1687 (14:46; 206-9:194, 435).

WINFIELD, THOMAS, d. by 11 Dec. 1675 by William Hollis and James Phillips and Miles Gibson; est. was admin. on 9 Oct. 1677, the acct. mentioned 6050 lbs. tob. (2:209; 14:75).

WINIER, JANE, was ind. for bast. in March 1743/5 and tried in June 1744 (35:154, 237).

WINKS, JOS., m. Mary Palmer on 27 Nov. 1763 (131).

WINLEY/WINDLEY, RICHARD, was in Balto. Co. by Nov. 1666 when he and James Phillips sold 200 a. to Francis Trippas; m. by 3 Nov. 1688 Mary, sis. of Arthur Taylor; on that day Richard and Mary sold 100 a. Windley's Forest to Oliver Sprye; he d. by 6 April 16(78?) when admin. bond was posted by John Owen with William Westbury and Thomas Richardson (14:69; 20:220; 94; 95; 98:46).

WINN, MARY, in Aug. 1717 named Benjamin Hanson as the father of her child (22:124).

WINN, RICHARD, d. leaving a nuncupative will made 23 Sept. 1758, proved 2 Oct. 1758 by John and Hannah Moore, Anne Douglas and Peter Bond, leaving his est. to William Askew; admin. bond was posted 2 Oct. 1758 by William Askew with John Moore and Thomas Rutter (14:177 ; 111:86).

WINTER, RALPH, d. leaving a will, 8 Dec. 1713 - 15 Dec. 1713, leaving est. to Edward Sweeting; admin. bond was posted by Edward Sweeting with George Hitchcock and Henry Stone; est. was inv. on 18 Dec. 1713 by said Hitchcock and William Wheeler and val. at £ 9.6.6; est. was admin. by Sweeting on 30 Dec. 1714 (1:19; 14:76; 50:355; 110:108).

WINWRIGHT, JOHN, m. Mrs. Ann Richardson in 1705 (128:18).

WISE, EDWARD, d. by Nov. 1759 leaving an orphan: EDWARD, age 12 on 7 Dec. following when he was bound to George Goldsmith Presbury in Nov. 1759 (26:246).

WISE, HENRY, d. by 1 March 1748 when admin. bond was posted by Dr. Charles Carroll of Annapolis, surgeon (14:121).

WISE, WILLIAM, m. Margaret, admnx. of William Osborne on 15 Oct. 1705; d. by 10 Nov. 1710 when admin. bond was posted by Margaret Wise with William Loney and William Pritchard; est. was inv. 21 Dec. 1710 by Pritchard and David Thomas and val. at a total of £ 90.15.10; an additional inv. worth 4471 lbs. tob. was filed 3 Aug. 1711; est. admin. 8 Oct. 1712 (1:365; 2:243; 14:63; 48:178; 52:122; 128:22).

WISLEY, JOHN, m. 20 Oct. 1721 Mary Bond, admnx. of John Bond (24:12; 131).

WISEMAN, HENRY, s. of Elizabeth Voss Beech, was b. 26 Aug. 1719; as Henry Wiseman alias Henry Beech, m. Jane Garvin on 29 April 1740 (128:111; 129:233).

WISHER, JOHN, m. Unity (---) and had iss.: JOHN, b. 27 Dec. 1757 (133:99) (See WILTSHIRE, JOHN).

WITH, GEORGE, m. Elizabeth (---); d. leaving a will, 16 Dec. 1745 - 6 Aug. 1751, naming w. Elizabeth and daus. Lucready and Elizabeth; in 1750 his heirs owned 50 a. part Burman's Forest (purch. by With from John Miller and mortgaged in 1737 to John Bowen); had iss.: MARY, b. 20 Aug. 1714; MARTHA, b. 16 Jan. 1715; DANCEYBELL, b. 26 Feb. 1718; LUCINDA (or LUCREDA), b. 18 Aug. 1721; ELIZABETH, b. 13 Jan. 172-(?) (75:17; 112:416; 133:11, 12; 153:12).

WITH, ELIZABETH, was ind. for bast. in June 1746 and tried in Aug. 1746; ind. again in Nov. 1750 and tried in March 1751 (36:1, 126; 38:1, 283).

WITTAM, JOHN, m. Anne (---), and had iss.: PETER, b. 6 May 1715 (131).

WITTIS, MARY, wid., m. John Phipps on 28 Dec. 1719 (133:148).

WOFORD, WILLIAM , in Aug. 1744 was ind. for unlawful cohabitation with Abigail D(?) (35:293).

WOLDEN, LAWRENCE, was named as s. of testator's w. Martha in the will of Jonas Bowen (121:171).

WOLFF, MARIN, was made levy free in Nov. 1718 (23:33).

WOLLEY, JOHN, inher. part Sim's Choice from Nicholas Hemsted; d. by 2 Nov. 1692 when wid. Eliz. (dau. of Thomas Thurston) m. Charles Ramsey (59:356).

WOLLOX. See WALLOX.

WONN/WANN/WOONE, EDWARD, was in Balto. Co. by 23 July 1747 when he m. Prudence Marsh; in 1750 he owned 50 a. Wonn's Chance; in March 1753 he conv. 50 a. of this land to Benjamin Wells, with cons. of his w. Prudence (82:11; 133:160; 153:78).

THE JOSHUA WOOD FAMILY

WOOD, JOSHUA (1), of Delph, Balto. Co., was in Balto. Co. by 1692 as a taxable in n. side Gunpowder Hund.; m. 1st Mary (---);

m. 2nd, on 15 Dec. 1704, Elizabeth Pittock; d. by 8 March
1709/10 when admin. bond was posted by Elizabeth Wood with Anthony Drew and William Wise; had iss.: (by 1st w.): JOSHUA, b.
1 Oct. 1694; ISAAC, b. 2 June (or 8 July) 1700; (by 2nd w.):
SARAH, b. 21 Oct. 1706 (14:77; 128:9, 10, 22; 129:192, 195, 204;
138).

WOOD, JOSHUA (2), s. of Joshua (1), was b. 1 Oct. 1694; was
age 15 when he pet. the court in March 1709 that his bro. Isaac
be taken from Thomas Collins to serve the petitioner; m. 1st
(Martha (---) who d. 20 April 1728; m. 2nd, on 15 April 1729,
Priscilla West who d. 22 Sept. 1739; m. 3rd, in Sept. 1732, Mary
Garrett; in June 1722 purch. 170 a. Sister's Dowry from Thomas
and Mary Simpson; in March 1725 he and w. Martha conv. 90 a. of
Chestnut Ridge to Isaac Wood; in June 1725 with w. Martha sold
100 a. Wood's Venture, 145 a. part Drisdale's Habitation, and
40 a. The Division to Michael Jenkins; d. by 15 Aug. 1740 when
admin. bond was posted by Mary Wood with Isaac Wood and Michael
Gilbert; est. was admin. 27 May 1742 by Mary, now w. of James
Stewart; had iss.; (by 1st w.): MARY, b. 23 Sept. 1720, m. (---)
Hawkins; ISAAC, b. 18 Jan. 1722; MARTHA, b. 14 Feb. 1724, m.
(---) Baker; JOSHUA, b. 18 Dec. 1727; (by 2nd w.): STEPHEN, b.
13 Jan. 1733, d. 10 Dec. 1739; HANNAH, b. 30 Oct. 1735; JOHN, b.
14 Feb. 1736/7 (in March 1750/1 chose John Stewart as his guardian); SARAH, b. 2 Feb. 1738 (5:125, 168; 14:32; 21:94; 22:12; 35:
302; 38:272; 69:72; 70:105, 113; 128:40, 42, 54, 57, 60, 77,
78, 92, 97, 112).

WOOD, ISAAC (3), s. of Joshua (1), was b. 2 June 1700; m.
Elizabeth (---); in Aug. 1711 was bound to Thomas Cullins or
Collins; in 1750 owned 90 a. Chestnut Ridge, 25 a. Isaac's Lot;
100 a. Woods Meadow; and 100 a. Wilburn's Venture; in Sept. 1753
William Wilburn of Fred. Co. sold to Isaac Wood 100 a. Wilburn's
Venture; had iss.: JOSHUA, b. 17 April 1722, d. 26 Aug. 1741;
ISAAC, b. 28 May 1725; ELIZABETH, b. 5 March 1726; HANNAH, b. 15
Nov. 1731; SOPHIA, b. 24 Sept. 1732; JAMES, b. 1 Dec. 1734; WIL-
LIAM, b. 18 Nov. 1736; BENJAMIN, b. 18 March 1738; MOSES, b. 20
Aug. 1741; HANNAH, b. 20 Nov. 1743 (17:249; 82:70; 128:43, 44,
50, 60, 79, 85, 94, 102; 129:115, 134; 153:37).

WOOD, JOSHUA (4), s. of Joshua (2), was b. 18 Dec. 1727, d.
leaving a will, 21 March 1749 - 17 May 1749, leaving 148 a. of
Greenfield's Double Purchase, and naming sis. Hannah, Sarah,
Mary Hawkins and Martha Baker;; admin. bond was posted 17 May
1749 by Jno. Matthews with Abraham Taylor and Thomas Cord (14:
139; 210-26:99).

THE WILLIAM WOOD FAMILY

WOOD, WILLIAM (5), no known rel. to any of the above, d. in
Balto. Co. by 4 April 1736; m. Jane (---); on 20 Sept. 1721 William and Jane conv. 50 a. Division to Simeon Jackson; on 18 May
1723 William and Jane conv. 100 a. of same tract to Thomas
Mitchel; d. leaving a will, 8 April 1732 - 4 April 1736, naming
w. Jane, sons William and Samuel, and a dau.; admin. bond was
posted 30 March 1736 by Jane Wood with Samuel Wood and John Watson; dec. left iss.: WILLIAM; SAMUEL; and an unnamed dau. (14:
30; 69:61, 275; 126:7).

WOOD, WILLIAM (6), s. of William (5), d. by 26 Aug. 1748 when
admin. bond was posted by Ann Wood with Richard Jones and John
Denton; in 1750 his heirs owned 125 a. part Arthur's Choice;
est. was admin. 10 Sept. 1750; William had iss.: JAMES, b. c.
1731; SUSAN, b. c.1732, m. William Bond Whitehead on 26 Feb. 1749;
ANN, b. c.1736; WILLIAM, b. c.1740; MARY, b. c. 1742; SAMUEL, b.
c.1745 (5:90, 137; 14:413; 131; 153:32).

WOOD, (---), m. by Jan. 1730/1, Elizabeth, dau. of Edward Wilbourne (125:180).

WOOD, ANN, orphan of Matthew, in March 1685/6 bound herself to George and Elizabeth Coningham (18:404).

WOOD, CHARLES, on 7 Jan. 1675 was named as son-in-law in the will of John Lee (120:178).

WOOD, EADY, was ind. for bast. in March 1730/1 (29:96).

WOOD, ELIZABETH, was ind. for bast. in June 1711 (21:210).

WOOD, JAMES, m. Mary (---) and had iss.: MORDECAI, b. 5 May 1729; WARNAL, b. 14 Feb. 1732; JAMES, b. 2 Feb. 1734 (133:42).

WOOD, JAMES, was fined for bast. in Nov. 1759 (46:240).

WOOD, JOHN, m. by 5 Sept. 1688 Elizabeth, dau. of Edward Swanson (64:67).

WOOD, JOHN, d. by 15 April 1693 when admin. vond was posted by William York who had m. the wid., with Robert Owlas and William Lenox; est. was inv. on 6 Aug. 1692/3(?) by Thomas Jones and val. at £ 34.1.0, plus £ 52.19.10, plus 640 lbs. tob. (14:66; 19:186, 187; 48:177).

WOOD, JOHN, m. Elizabeth Bradford in Nov. 1739; had iss.: ALCE, b. 2 Feb. 1741 (129:323).

WOOD, JOHN, m. Sarah (---) and had iss.: REBECCA, b. 18 Oct. 1759; MARY, b. 13 Jan. 1762; SUSANNA, b. 18 April 1764; SARAH, b. 3 April 1766; ELIZABETH, b. 9 March 1768; JOSHUA, b. 16 March 1733; JOHN, b. 19 Aug. 1776 (129:385, 386, 388, 391).

WOOD, JOHN (or JOSEPH), serv., b. in the Jerseys, wheelwright, and millwright, runaway servant from William Worthington, Jr., of Newfoundland, Balto. Co., was adevrtised in Jan. 1745 (384: 478).

WOOD, JOSHUA, s. of Moses and Aaron (sic), was b. 29 March 1704 (128:20).

WOOD, MARY, m. Robert Kinsby on 1 Aug. 1710 (129:209).

WOOD, MARY, was ind. for bast. in Aug. 1719; she was sentenced to receive nine lashes and to serve Lawrence Taylor and extra 5 months (23:219).

WOOD, MATTHEW, d. by Nov. 1685 when his wid. m. John Copas; had two daus.: ANN, and MARY (18:356, 404, 405).

WOOD, REBECCA, m. Samuel Ross on 30 Nov. 1727; she had iss.: JOHN (Wood), b. 25 Dec. 1727, and THOMAS, b. 3 Sept. 1730 (128:66; 129:257).

WOOD, WILLIAM, s. of Isaac, age 20, was ordered to be levy free in Nov. 1756 (41:302).

WOOD, WILLIAM, m. Ann Watkins on 3 Oct. 1754 (131).

WOOD, WILLIAM, d. by 11 April 1759, leaving iss.: WILLIAM; MARY, m/ Samuel Wilson (47-BB#F:89-90).

WOODALL, RALPH, of Balto. Co. on 10 March 1731 purch. Ebene-zer's Park from John Jones and w. Margaret; d. leaving a will,

24 March 1733/4 - 15 May 1734, naming w. Ann, dau. Jane, and
w. Ann's s. Joseph Brooks (73:288; 126:86).

WOODCOCK, LAWRENCE, servant, was listed in the 1725 inv. of
the est. of Samuel Dorsey (52:138).

WOODCOCK, WILLIAM, m. Mary Amboy on 24 Dec. 1713 (129:213).

WOODEN, JOHN (1), progenitor, was b. by 1680, and d. in A. A.
Co. c.1747; m. Elizabeth, dau. of Solomon Sparrow; on 26 June
1700 Edward and Mary Parish conv. him 2000 a. Parrish's Range;
on 17 Alril 1718 Solomon Sparrow of A. A. Co. made a will naming
Elizabeth w. of John Wooden; Wooden d. leaving a will, 22 July
1741 - 12 Dec. 1747, leaving 270 a. in Balto. Co. to s. John,
50 a. Mary's Mount and the dwelling plant. to s. Solomon, and
naming dau. Elizabeth Battee; had iss.: JOHN, b. c.1698; ELIZA-
BETH, b. c.1702, m. Ferdinando Battee on 11 Dec. 1718 in All
Hallow's Par., A. A. Co.; SOLOMON, b. c.1708 (123:183; 210-25:
313; 213-TL#2:325; 219-1:288).

WOODEN, JOHN (2), s. of John (1), was b. c.1698, d. in Balto.
Co. in 1769; m. Mary Gill on 27 Jan. 1716; in 1750 owned 570 a.
Parrishes Range; in March 1754 he and w. Mary conv. 120 a.of this
tract to s. Solomon, and 150 a. to s. William; d. leaving a will,
29 Aug. 1760 - 17 April 1769, naming w. Mary and ch. John, Steph-
en, Mary, Eleanor wid. of John Frazier, Sophia w. of Luke Chapman, Kezia, Jemima, and Sarah mother of Edward Puntany; had iss.:
ELIZABETH, b. 11 dec. 1717; MARY, b. 9 July 1719, may be the Mary
who m. Richard Croswell on 28 May 1746; JOHN, b. 10 Sept. 1721;
ELEANOR, b. 20 Oct. 1723, m. 1st on 30 Jan. 1745 Francis Cutler,
and 2nd John Frazier; SARAH, b. 24 Sept. 1725, m. William Puntany
on 29 Sept. 1745; SOPHIA, b. 29 Sept. 1727, m. 1st on 17 Dec.
1747 Charles Conaway, m. 2nd Luke Chapman; SOLOMON, b. 7 Dec.
1729; KEZIAH, b. 12 Oct. 1731; WILLIAM, b. 13 Dec. 1733, d. unm.
leaving a will, made 14 June 1761, naming his f. John, and bros.
and sis. Solomon, Stephen, John, Eleanor Frazier, Mary Wooden,
Sophia Chapman, Kezia, and Jemima; RUTH, b. 13 Jan. 1736;
STEPHEN, b. 11 March 1737/8; JEMIMA, b. 11 Aug. 1740 (82:171;
133:11, 16, 22, 36, 51, 58, 73, 148, 157, 158, 159, 160; 153;
210-31:357; 210-37:82).

WOODEN, SOLOMON (3), s. of John (1), was b. c.1708, d. in
A. A. Co. in 1749; m. Sarah Greshamon 17 Aug. 1726, b. c.1710
in Kent Co., dau. of John and Sarah Gresham and she d. c.1752 in
A. A. Co.; he d. leaving a will made 25 Jan. 1749, naming w. Sarah, and daus. Sarah, Elizabeth, and Priscilla; Sarah Gresham
Wooden d. leaving a will, 10 Jan. 1751/2 - 26 March 1752, naming
daus. Elizabeth and Priscilla (to have 100 a. Brewerton), and s.-
in-law Charles Connant; had iss.: SARAH, m. Charles Connant;
ELIZABETH, m. Joseph Hill; PRISCILLA, m. Morgan Jones on 20 Jan.
1757 (72:31; 133:24; 210-27:269; 210-28:253; 219-3:396).

WOODEN, JOHN (4), s. of John (2) and Mary, was b. 10 July
1721; d. 1790; m. 1st, by 5 Dec. 1743, Susanna (---) and 2nd, by
24 Sept. 1754 Rachel, admnx. of John Gassaway; d. leaving a will,
3 May 1790 - 2 June 1790; wid. Rachel d. leaving a will, 20 Aug.
1793 - 27 May 1797; had iss.: ELIZABETH, b. 1742, m. Jacob Cromwell; STEPHEN GILL, b. 5 Dec. 1743; POLLY, m. (---) Slade; SOPHIA,
m. Robert White; RUTH, m. Absolom Johnson; SOLOMON; JOHN; THOMAS,
CHARLES; ELEANOR (113:425; 114:537; Fred. Co. Admin. Accts., 1:
57; HR; Durham, Wooden, p. 17).

WOODEN, SOLOMON (5), s. of John (2) and Mary, was b. 7 Dec.
1729 and d. 1794; m. Ann Hood, dau. of John Hood; she m. 2nd
Christian Alter on 13 May 1796; Solomon d. leaving a will, 16
May 1794 - 4 June 1794, leaving all his prop. to his wife Anne;

had iss.: SOLOMON, Jr., on 11 June 1791 was named as an heir to
the est. of John Hood (114:161; Durham, Wooden, p. 12; Anne Arundel Co. Admin. Accts., JG#1:381, HR).

WOODEN, STEPHEN (6), s. of John (2), was b. 11 March 1737/8,
d. by 22 Nov. 1798; m. Sarah, dau. of Dixon Brown; she m. 2nd
(---) Smith; his est. was admin. 17 Oct. 1795; heirs (named in
various deeds): WILLIAM; MARY, m. Charles Peck; REBECCA, m. 1st
Samuel Hagsman, and 2nd Joseph McDonough; JOHN; RICHARD; THOMAS;
FRANCIS (92:223; 112:251; 118:177; 237-12:336; 241-WG#RR:537;
241-WG#54:174).

WOODEN, KEZIAH, was ind. for bast. in Nov. 1760 (44).

WOODEN, MARY, was ind. for bast. in Aug. 1746 (36:117).

WOODEN, SOLOMON, of Balto. Co., and w. Sarah, conv. part of
Gresham College to William McComas in June 1729 (72:31).

WOODEY, JOHN, m. Mary Lynsey on 27 Dec. 1738; in 1750 he
owned 49 a. part Neighborhood, and 11 a. Arabia Petrea; had iss.:
ELEANOR, b. 23 May 1739; HANNAH, b. 23 Oct. 1740; ROBERT, b. 8
Nov. 1742 (128:108; 129:330; 153:69).

WOODFORD, ROBERT, d. by 3 Feb. 1747 when admin. bond was posted by Nathan Rigbie with Nicholas Ruxton Gay; est. was admin. on
5 July 1748 (4:198; 14:116).

WOODLAND, BLACKLEDGE, m. Eliz. Jackson on 20 April 1760 (131).

WOODLAND, CHRISTIAN, d. by 3 March 1760 when admin. bond was
posted by James Danney with John Dover and James Spencer (14:173).

WOOD, MOSES, m. Arianna (---), and had iss.: JOSHUA, b. 29
March 1704 (129:203). (See Joshua Wood above).

WOODVINE, JOHN, was in Balto. Co. by Oct. 1672 when he surv.
Alderwood; d. without issue (211).

WOODWARD, THOMAS (1), cooper of Balto. Town, d. by 25 Sept.
1744; m. Mary (---) who surv. him; owned Hog's Norton and Shoemaker's Lot; d. leaving a will, 2 June 1736 - 25 Sept. 1744,
leaving two tracts to his s. John, now in Eng., naming w. Mary,
daus. Anne and Mary, and a possible unborn ch.; admin. bond was
posted 6 June 1744 by Mary Woodward with John Ensor and John
Hunt; in 1750 his heirs owned 11 a. Shoemaker's Hall and 188 a.
Frogmorton (Hog's Norton?); had iss.: JOHN; ANN, may be the Ann
who m. Thomas Presbury on 29 Dec. 1748; MARY; ELIZABETH, b. 7
June 1736 (14:20; 111:17; 133:57; 162; 153:41).

WOODWARD, JOHN (2), s. of Thomas and Mary, d. in Balto. Co.
leaving a will, 30 Oct. 1780 - 22 Jan. 1782; m. Jemima; est. was
admin. 4 May 1782 and 23 June 1786; had iss.: THOMAS; CHARLES;
SARAH, m. Daniel Weatherly or Weatherby on 23 March 1778; MARY;
ELIZABETH JEMIMA, m. John Coffee on 17 May 1798 (8:97, 280;
112:468; 261:65; 264:242).

WOODWARD, AMOS, of Annap., d. by 22 July 1741 when his est.
was admin. by Achsah w.of Edward Fottrell (4:86).

WOODWARD, THOMAS, chose his father to be his guardian in Nov.
1740 (32:351).

WOODY, JOHN, in 1750 owned 49 a. part Neighborhood, and 11 a.
part Arabia Petrea (153:69).

WOOFORD, WILLIAM, was ind. for unlawful cohabitation with Abigail Draper in Nov. 1746 (36:221).

WOOLEY, JOHN, m. Ann (---); on 14 Aug. 1736 theu sold 100 a. Wooley's Range to John Jones; on 5 Jan. 1739 he purch. 60 a. Arabia Petrea from Henry and Eleanor Jones; d. by 19 Aug. 1747 when admin. bond was posted by John Jones and John   Logsdon, the wid. Ann having ren. her right to admin. the est. in favor of her two sons-in-law; est. admin. 30 Nov. 1747; John and Ann had iss.: dau., m. John Jones; dau., m. John Logsdon (4:151; 14: 117; 61:329; 75:345).

WOOLING, MAJOR, m. Frances Johnson on 5 Nov. 1756 (131).

WOOLSHER, (---), m. Daniel Mackarte on 23 Jan. 1703/4 (129: 200).

WOONE, EDWARD. See WONN, EDWARD.

WORGIN, WILLIAM, was in Balto. Co. by 1695 as a taxable in Spesutia Hund. (138).

WORRELL, HENRY, m. Juliatha (---); in 1750 owned 250 a. Timber Grove; had iss.: HENRY, b. 19 Jan. 1747; THOMAS, b. 15 Dec. 1748; JOHN, b. 13 March 1752; JULIATHA, b. 22 Sept. 1754; ELIZABETH, b. 21 May 1756; MARY, b. 25 Nov. 1757; AMON, b. 5 Dec. 1759; and HANNAH, b. 9 July 1762 (134:34, 35; 153:97).

WORRELL, MARTIN, orphan of Samuel Worrell, age 13 in Aug. 1755 when he was bound to Alexander McComas of Alex (40:220).

WORRINGTON, JOHN, in Nov. 1756 was made levy free by the county court (41:303).

WORTHINGTON, CHARLES, m. Sarah (---), and in 1750 owned 352 a. part Stone Hills, and 500 a. part Phillips; had iss.: JOHN, b. 5 Oct. 1732; ELIZABETH, b. 22 July 1735; CHARLES, b. 6 July 1736; ANN, b. 10 June 1738 (128:107; 153:16).

WORTHINGTON, JOHN, in 1750 owned 600 a. Nathaniel's Park and 2000 a. Welch's Cradle (153:99).

WORTHINGTON, SAMUEL, m. Mary Tolley on 17 Jan. 1759 (131).

WORTHINGTON, THOMAS, in 1750 owned 180 a. part Petticoat's Benefit, 100 a. Norwood's Discovery, 100 a. Ruth's Lot, and 130 a. Petticoat's Addition (153:98).

WORTHINGTON, VACHEL, m. Priscilla, sis. of William Bond on 17 Nov. 1757; had iss.: ELIZABETH, b. 25 Nov. 1759 (112; 104; 131; 134).

WORTHINGTON, WILLIAM, m. Hannah Cromwell on 30 June 1734; may be the William Worthington who d. by 3 Sept. 1750 when admin. bond was posted by Jno. Hood of A. A. Co. with Joseph Hobbs and James Barnes; est. was admin. on 24 May 1750 and 17 July 1752 (5:200, 242; 14:115; 134:152).

WRATH, JAMES, servant, of Balto. Co., was transp. c.1664; m. Elizabeth (---) (97:125; 98:48; 99:349; 388).

THE WRIGHT FAMILY has been the subject of much study by Mrs. Robert Hughes of Boulder, Colorado, and Mr. Allender Sybert of Worcester, Mass., both of whom have shared their research with the author; see also Mary Catherine Downing, The Heath Family of

Wicomico County, Maryland. Milford: 1953; also Charles W. Wright,
The Wright Ancestry of Caroline, Dorchester, Somerset, and Wicomico Counties. Baltimore: 1907.

WRIGHT, WILLIAM (1), was an inhabitant of Somerset Co., Md.,
where m. Frances, dau. of Thomas and Frances Bloyse, on 7 Dec.
1669; they were the parents of: ELIZABETH, . b. 12 May 1672;
TEMPERANCE, b. 12 Aug. 1674; JUDITH, b. 12 July (?); BLOYCE, b.
5 March 1681, m. Sarah (---); FRANCES, b. 2 Feb. 1683; MATHEW, b
13 March 1685; WILLIAM, b. 1 May 1687; poss. ALOS; SOLOMON;
and poss. THOMAS (Wright, Wright Ancestry).

WRIGHT, BLOYSE (2), s. of William (1) and Frances, was b. 5
March 1681 in Somerset Co.; d. by 31 Jan. 1737 in Balto. Co.;
m. Sarah (---) who d. after 1737; in Nov. 1722 he stated he
would not pay the debts of his w. Sarah who had deserted him; on
24 Sept. 1730 he conv. pers. prop. to his sons Thomas and William
Wright; d. leaving a will, 20 June 1733 - 31 Jan. 1737 naming
wid. Sarah and sons Thomas and William; admin. bond was posted
31 Jan. 1737 by exec. Thomas Wright with Charles Rockhold and
John League; a second admin. bond was posted 15 Sept. 1740 by
William Standiford who admin. the est. on 25 May 1740; Bloyse
and Sarah had iss.: THOMAS, b. 29 July 1703; SARAH, b. 5 July
1706; WILLIAM, m. 1738, Sarah Day (4:66; 14:26, 40; 69:49; 72:
304, 305; 126:232).

WRIGHT, THOMAS (3), s. of Bloyse (2) and Sarah, was b. 29
July 1703 at Little Mony, Somerset Co., Md.; d. 1739 in Balto.
Co.; m. on 5 May 1735 Christiana Enloes, b. c.1710, dau. of Abraham and Elizabeth Enloes; Christiana m. 2nd William Standiford; Thomas inher. 150,a. Swallow Fork and other lands from
his father; d. by 6 June 1739 when admin. bond was posted by
admnx. Christiana Wright with William Wright of Bloyse and Abraham Enloes; est. was admin. 19 July 1740, 16 April 1742, and 8
Jan. 1743; in March 1746/7 Standiford gave bond to Bloyse and
Elizabeth, orphans of Thomas; in 1750 the heirs of Thomas owned
100 a. Swallow Fork, 150 a. The Island, 45 a. Chadwell's Outlet,
and 50 a. Cuckoldmaker's Hall; iss. of Thomas and Christiana:
BLOYCE, b. 17 Nov. 1735; ELIZABETH, b. c.1737, m. Nathan John-
son(3:308, 333; 4:129; 14:29; 36:386; 126:232; 153:16).

WRIGHT, WILLIAM (4), s. of Bloyse (2) and Sarah, m. Sarah
Day, dau. of Nicholas and Sarah Day, on 26 Feb. 1738; d. by 24
Dec. 1750 when admin. bond was posted by Sarah Wright; est. was
admin. by Sarah, now w. of Philip Lackey Elliott (5:286; 14:130;
131).

WRIGHT, BLOYSE (5), s. of Thomas (3) and Christiana, was b.
17 Nov. 1735; d. 1 Jan. 1788; m. Mary Talbott on 26 Nov. 1757;
had iss.: THOMAS, b. c.1759; PRUDENCE, b. c.1762; CASSANDRA,
b. c.1765; ELIZABETH, b. c.1768; BLOYCE, b. c.1772; JOHN T., b.
1774; WILLIAM, b. 1778 (data from Mrs. Hughes).

THE WILLIAM WRIGHT FAMILY

WRIGHT, WILLIAM (6), no known rel. to any of the above, was
in Balto. Co. by 6 Nov. 1691 when he purch. 100 a. Fuller's Outlet
from Robert and Deborah Benger; was a taxable in s. side Gunpowder Hund. in 1692; m. Juliana Benbow on 5 Sept. 1714, prob. as
his 2nd w.; on 6 Nov. 1704 purch. 200 a. Edmond's Camp from Edmond Hansley; on 25 June 1723 William and w. Gillion sold this
to Samuel Durham; on 8 Aug. 1723 William and Julian sold the
remaining 100 a. to Edmond Hays; on 10 May 1722 William conv.
100 a. Jacob's Inheritance to s. William; d. leaving a will, 25
Feb. 1723/4 - 9 March 1723/4, naming sons William, Jacob (to have

Wright's Forest , Solomon (to have the manor plantation), and
daus. Elizabeth, Christiana, and Mary Watkins; admin. bond was
posted 27 April 1724 by Juliana Wright, with Thomas Baley and
Samuel Stephens; est. was admin. on 28 Feb. 1725/6; dec. left
iss.: WILLIAM; JACOB; SOLOMON; ELIZABETH; CHRISTIANA: MARY, m.
(---) Watkins (14:29; 59:333; 64:1; 69:28, 177, 240; 110:207;
138; 209-27:246).

WRIGHT, WILLIAM (7), s. of William (6), m. Elizabeth Barton
on 7 May 1727; on 27 Nov. 1731 was given a receipt by Selah Barton for ₤80.18.6 for his full share of his father's est.; on 20
Nov. 1736 Mary Shaw bound her son Weymouth Shaw to William and
Elizabeth Wright; on 9 June 1738 Solomon Wright conv. him 100 a.
Fuller's Outlet; d. leaving a will, 23 Aug. 1740 - 20 Sept. 1740,
leaving Jacob's Inheritance to s. William, 100 a. Fuller's Outlet and 200 a. Fell's Forest to sons Abraham and Jacob, leaving
1/3 of his est. to his w. Elizabeth, and ordering the tract 150
a. Dugg Hills to be sold; admin. bond was posted 20 Sept. 1740
by extx. Elizabeth Wright; on 16 May 1741 Elizabeth Wright made
the sum of ₤ 35 over to her s. Jacob when he would become 21;
Elizabeth admin. her husband's est., and m. 2nd James Greer,
and 3rd Heathcote Pickett; William and Elizabeth had iss.:
WILLIAM, b. 3 Dec. 1735; ABRAHAM, b. 16 Feb. 1735; ISAAC, b. 16
July 1738; JACOB, b. c.1740/1 (3:312, 358; 5:45; 14:27; 73:220;
75:50, 81, 500; 127:103, 225; 131).

WRIGHT, JACOB (7), s. of William (6), was b. c.1701, giving
his age as 37 in 1738; inher. Wright's Forest from his father;
in 1745 leased 157 a. Gunpowder Manor for the lifetimes of
Solomon Watkins Wright, b. c.1727, and Ezekiel Wright, b. c.1728;
in Aug. 1755 pet. the court to be levy free; prob. the Jacob who
d. leaving a will, 11 July 1763 - 15 Aug. 1770, naming w. Sarah,
and ch. Absolom, Mary, Ann, William, John, Elizabeth, and Sarah:
had iss.: ABSOLOM; MARY; ANN; WILLIAM; JOHN; ELIZABETH, m. William Allen on 5 Oct. 1756; SARAH, m. (---) Jarvis; poss. SOLOMON
WATKINS, b. c.1728; and EZEKIEL, b. c.1728 (40:255; 112:170; 131;
164:46; 389:10).

WRIGHT, SOLOMON (8), s. of William (6), inher. the manor
plantation from his father; on 9 June 1738 sold 100 a. Fuller's
Outlet to his bro. William (75:81).

WRIGHT, ABRAHAM, m. Darkes Tudor on 23 May 1745 and had iss.:
SOLOMON, b. 7 March 1747 (131:28, 130/r).

WRIGHT, FRANCIS, was elected a Burgess for Balto. Co. in 1663,
but when the Council met in Sept. 1664 he had gone on a special
service to the Susquehannock Fort to bring back accurate information to the Assembly; Col. Nathaniel Utie presented a pet. asking that Wright be excused; d. leaving a will, 25 July 1666 - 25
March 1667, naming Jacob Clawson de Young, Lewis and Francis
Stockett, Edmund Cantwell, and William Gyles; also named bro.
Thomas Wright and younger bro. Raphael Wright of Boville, Wales;
admin. bond was posted Oct. 1671 by admnx. Margaret Penry with
Jacob Young and George Harris (14:70; 120:41; 200-1:511; 200-5:
13).

WRIGHT, HENRY, purch. 200 a. Clarkson's Purchase from John
and Milcah Bowen; prob. the Henry Wright who admin. the est. of
William York on 18 Jan. 1706 (2:233; 67:136).

WRIGHT, JOHN, was in Balto. Co. by Nov. 1684 when he sued
Emanuel Ceely for killing a horse earlier in June 1682; on 16
May 1685 executed an antenuptial agreement with the wid. Jane
Claridge; prob. the John Wright who d. by 4 Aug. 1702 when his
est. was admin. by John Gallow (2:217; 59:136; 341:363).

WRIGHT, JOHN, was the name of two individuals in Balto. Co. in 1692 as taxable in n. side Patapsco Hund., and in n. side Gunpowder Hund. (138).

WRIGHT, JOHN, d. by 11 Feb. 1722 when admin. bond was posted by Sarah Arnold with Matthew Organ and Henry Carrington; est. was inv. 29 Oct. 1723 by Edward Norwood and Thomas Eminson and val. at £ 12.19.2, signed by Mary Arnall; inv. was filed by the admnx. Sarah Arnold; by 3 June 1726 she and her new husb. Charles Wells admin. the est. (3:60; 14:42; 51:64).

WRIGHT, JOHN, d. leaving a will, 29 Nov. 1744 - 3 Jan. 1744/5, leaving 225 a. Maiden's Choice to cousin Cooper Oram, elsewhere named Cooper Oram as brother; admin. bond was posted 22 April 1745 by Cooper Oram with John Highter and Henry Oram (14:129; 111:20).

WRIGHT, JOSEPH, pet. to be levy free in Nov. 1740 (32:363).

WRIGHT, JOSEPH, m. Margaret James in 1750 (131).

WRIGHT, MARTIN, was in Balto. Co. by 1737 as a taxable in Back River Upper Hund. (149:21).

WRIGHT, PHILBURD, PHILBURD, had two sons, both of whom went to North Carolina where they served in the Rev. War; had iss.: PHILBURD, Jr., moved to Orange Co., N.C.; RICHARD, d. c. 1786 in Rowan Co., N. C. (400:153).

WRIGHT, RICHARD, d. by 2 April 1664, leaving a wid. Ann who m. as her 2nd husb., some time before 16 July 1664 David Fox (200-49:189, 254).

WRIGHT, THOMAS, was listed as a servant in the 1737/8 inv. of Charles Daniel (53:87).

WRIGHT, THOMAS, m. Mary (---); in Nov. 1738 purch. 50 a.of Turkey Cock Alley from Charles Harryman; had iss.: ELIZABETH, b. 28 June 1733; KATHERINE, b. 6 Aug. 1736 (75:130; 133:52).

WRIGHT, WILLIAM, Jr., m. Ann Rowles on 4 Sept. 1721; she d. 12 Sept. 1722 (131).

WRIGHT, WILLIAM, "of Patapsco," in 1750 owned 50 a. Carter's Choice (153:84).

WRIOTHESLEY, HENRY, was in Balto. Co. by Aug. 1699 when he surv. 500 a. Southampton; in July 1700 surv. 200 a. Ann's Delight; on 4 March 1702 purch. 200 a. Pearson's Park from Simon and Emma Pearson; in 1705 purch. 200 a. Drysdale's Habitation from John and Mary Roberts; d. leaving a will, 18 May 1709 - 20 July 1709, naming w. Ann as extx., and leaving Drisdale's Habitation to Thomas Wriothesley Sickelmore; admin. bond was posted 20 July 1709 by wid. Ann with John Rattenbury and John Stokes; est. was inv. 12 Feb. 1709 and val. at £ 111.11.2; est. was admin. by Ann on 4 April 1710, and 22 June 1711 (2:3, 199; 14:59; 50:223; 64:20; 66:120; 122:146; 207).

WYATT, HENRY, was in Balto. Co. by 1692 as a taxable in s. side of Patapsco Hund. (138).

WYATT, JOHN, was in Balto. Co. by April 1754 when John and Elizabeth Haven sold him Knight's Increase (82:203).

WYATT, THOMAS, d. by 2 July 1756 when admin. bond was posted by Thomas Jay with Jacob Giles and Richard Johns; est. was admin.

on 13 March 1759 by Jacob Giles who had posted a second admin.
bond with John Giles and Amos Garrett on 2 Oct. 1756 (4:261; 5:
332; 14:150, 159).

WYLE, JOHN (1), m. Hannah (---), and in 1750 owned 60 a. part
Sign of the Painter (Panther?); in 1744 leased land for the lifetimes of his sons John, b. c.1728, William, b. c.1736, and Abel,
b. c.1738; by wife Hannah had iss.: poss. JOHN, b. c.1728; SARAH,
b. 31 May 1733; BENJAMIN, b. 25 Nov. 1734; poss. WILLIAM, b. c.
1735/6; ABEL, b. 15 May 1736; JOHN, b. 22 March 1737; ANN, b.
Sept. 1738; MARGARET, b. April 1742 (77:201; 131; 153:43).

WYLE, BENJAMIN (2), s. of John (1), was b. 25 Nov. 1734; m.
Elinor Samson on 30 Oct. 1755 (131).

WYLE, ABEL (3), s. of John (1), was b. 15 May 1736, m. Sarah
Samson on 25 Jan. 1759 (131).

WYLE, ANN, m. Richard Samson on 17 Dec. 1758 (131).

WYLE, ELIZABETH, m. Moses Collett on 12 Jan. 1743 (131).

WYLE, LUKE, was b. c.1706, was age 36 in July 1742 when he
leased part of My Lady's Manor from Thomas Brerewood, the lease
to run for his own lifetime, and those of his sons Luke, Jr.,
age 3 years and Walter, age 3 months; m. Kesiah (---), and had
iss.: MATHEW, b. 16 Nov. 1730; WILLIAM, b. 31 Jan. 1731; MARY,
b. 20 Dec. 1735; ATHEA, b. 31 Dec. 1737; LUKE, b. 29 March 1740;
WALTER, b. 8 May 1742 (77:24; 131).

WYLE, MARY, m. Abraham Bull on 1 June 1749 (131).

WYLE, MARY, m. Edward Norris of Joseph on 19 Sept. 1754 (131).

WYLE, WILLIAM, m. Margaret Ling or Sing on 23 Dec. 1734 (133:
152).

WYLE, WILLIAM, d. by 1750 when his wid. owned 150 a. part of
Discovery (153:15).

WYLE, WILLIAM, m. Elizabeth Little on 1 Jan. 1753 (131).

WYLE. See also WILEY.

WYNN, ANN, d. by 7 March 1759 when admin. bond was posted by
William Wynn of Va., with Joseph Sutton and Benja. Ingram (14:
155).

YANSTON/YOSTON, LAWRENCE (1), was in Balto. Co. by 1692 as a
taxable in n. side Patapsco Hund.; d. by 18 Nov. 1713 when admin. bond was posted by Thomas Todd, Jr., with Luke Stansbury
and Richard Colegate; est. was inv. on 14 Dec. 1713 by Robuck
Lynch and Samuel Merryman and val. at £ 32.11.1, and signed by
Richard Samson; est. was admin. 1 April 1715; had iss.: HENRY;
and WILLIAM (1:210; 14:10; 50:305; 138).

YANSTON, HENRY (2), s. of Lawrence (1), was so named in Aug.
1718 when he was bound to James and Elizabeth Bagford to age 21;
his age was given as 15 as of Oct. 1718; m. Jane (---), and was
prob. alive in 1750 when Henry Yanston owned 75 a. part Robert's
Choice; had iss.: MARY, b. 1 Dec. 1731; LAWRENCE, b. 16 Oct.
1734; ANN, b. 17 Oct. 1737; JOHN, b. 1 Jan. 1739/40 (23:4; 133:
23, 41, 90; 153:28).

YANSTON, WILLIAM (3), s. of Lawrence (1), was made a ward of
John Eager in Aug. 1718 (23:4).

THE YATE/YATES/YEATS FAMILY has been discussed by John G.
Hunt, in "English Ancestry of George Yate (ca. 1640-1691) of
Maryland," National Genealogical Society Quarterly 64 (1976),
176-179; and by Harry Wright Newman, Anne Arundel Gentry, Revised, vol. II, 517 ff.

YATE, THOMAS (1), s. of Francis Yate of Lyfford, and desc. of
the Yates of Lyford and Charney, d. at Lyford between 1654 and
1658; m. 1st Mary Tregian, dau. of Francis Tregian of Golden,
Cornwall; m. 2nd Dorothy, dau. of Nicholas Stephens of Bould-
thorpe, Wiltshire; by his 2nd w. Thomas had several children
alive in 1623: JOHN, b. c.1613; THOMAS, b. c.1615; WILLIAM, m.
Katherine Ayleworth at West Hannay, Berkshire; and DOROTHY
(Hunt, p. 178).

YATE, JOHN (2), s. of Thomas (1) and Dorothy, was b. c.1613,
may have d. by 1654; m. Mary (or Elizabeth), dau. of George Tat-
tershall of Ufton Court; had iss.: JOHN, b. c.1634; GEORGE, b.
c.1640; ELIZABETH, a minor in 1656 (Hunt, pp. 178-179).

YATE, GEORGE (3), son of John (2), was b. c.1640, is placed
by Hunt as the settler in Maryland, because he surveyed several
plantations in Md. (Lyford in Talbot Co., Ufton Court and Denchworth in Baltimore County, and other tracts: Radnage, Charney,
and Sway) after the homes of his ancestors in England; came to
Md., where he was Deputy Surveyor of the Prov.; was called cousin
of Jerome White; m. c.1672 Mary, wid. of Capt. Thomas Stockett
and dau. of Richard Wells; d. leaving a will, 6 June 1691 - 11
Nov. (year of probate not stated; erroneously called Joseph
Yates in Baldwin's Md. Cal. of Wills), naming w. Mary, tracts
Yate's Forbearance, Padworth Farm, Charney, Rich Level, and others, and these ch.: GEORGE, d. 1717; JOHN, d. c.1722; ANN, m.
William Plummer (121:48; 207; 211; 357:517 ff.; Hunt, pp. 176-
177).

YATE, GEORGE (4), s. of George (3), was b. c.1674, d. leaving
a will, 13 Nov. 1717 - 18 Nov. 1717; m. 1st Rachel Warfield, a
dau. of Capt. Richard and Eleanor Warfield, and 2nd Ruth (---)
who surv. him and m. 2nd Joseph Ary (or more probably Joseph
Earp); his will, made 13 Nov. 1717, named bro. John and John's
w. Elizabeth, Jno. and Richard Warfield, John Teall, and these
ch.: George, Joshua, Samuel, Benjamin, Eleanor, Mary, and Rachel;
admin. bond was posted 17 March 1717 by execs. Ruth Yates and
Edward Teale with Nicholas Rogers and John Wooley; est. was inv.
on 10 June 1718 by Christopher Randall and William Hamilton, val.
at £ 55.11.9 and signed by his bro. John; had iss.: GEORGE;
JOSHUA; SAMUEL, d. 1779 having settled in Loudoun Co., Va.;
BENJAMIN; ELEANOR; MARY; and RACHEL, m. (---) Deaver (14:4; 48:
304; 123:145; 357).

YATE, JOHN (5), s. of George (3), d. by 19 March 1721 when
admin. bond was posted by admnx. Elizabeth Yate with Benjamin
Hood and William Tucker (14:11).

YATE, GEORGE (6), s. of George (4), d. 1743 having moved to
King William Co., and later Caroline Co.; in 1726 sold part Yates'
Contrivance and part Yates Forbearance to Col. Thomas Cockey
(357).

YATES, CHARLES, about 1733 was conv. a deed of gift by John
and Elizabeth Thornbury; in Sept. 1740 John and Elizabeth Ensor
conv. him 50 a. Adventure (73:433; 75:463).

YATES, HUMPHREY, m. by 2 Sept. 1725 Lawranna, admnx. of Henry
Shields (3:37).

YATES, JOSEPH, m. Mary Cowdrey on 5 Nov. 1712; she d. 12 July 1734; had iss.; SUSANNA, b. 4 Feb. 1714/5, d. May 1735; ROBERT, b. 2 Feb. 1718; WILLIAM, b. 1 May 1720; JOSEPH, b. 4 May 1725; MARY, b. 4 May 1735 (128:51, 79, 88).

YATES, JOSEPH, m. Mary Evans, who d. 12 July 1734; they had: JOHN, b. 19 Aug. 1729 (128:58).

YATES, JOSEPH, m. 15 Sept. 1735 (acc. to St. George's Par. Reg.) or 14 Sept. 1736 (acc. to St. John's Par. Reg.) Catherine Herrett or Turret, and had iss.: GEORGE GILBERT, b. 21 April 1738, prob. d. 9 Nov. 1740 (129:284; 131:89/r, 123/r).

YATES, JOSEPH, d. Oct. 1748; prob. the same Joseph who was made exempt from the levy in Nov. 1737 (31:133; 131:123/r).

YATES, THOMAS, m. Elizabeth (---), and had iss.: ELIZABETH, b. 18 Aug. 1720; THOMAS, b. 26 Aug. 1723; JOHN, b. 26 March 1728; WILLIAM, b. 29 Oct. 1728 (sic); JOHN, b. 26 March 1728/9 (128: 53).

YATES, THOMAS, m. Eliz. Martin on 21 June 1741 (131).

YATES, WILLIAM, m. Ann Thornbury on 8 Sept. 1744; by 1 Aug. 1764 William and Ann had moved to Bedford Co., Va., when they leased part of Selsed to Thomas Cockey; the deed stated that Ann was a dau. of John, son of Roland Thornbury (90:121; 131).

YATES, WILLIAM, m. Ann Dorney or Downey on 28 April 1748; d. 6 Dec. 1748; admin. bond was posted 6 Jan. 1748/9 by Ann Yates with Daniel Downey; dec. left one dau.: SUSANNA (5:69; 14:12; 37:166; 38:8; 131).

YATES, WILLIAM, m. by 9 May 1757 Sarah, extx. of Joseph Chew (5:335).

YEAKLEY, JOHN, was in Balto. Co. by May 1701 when Thomas and Sarah Hooker conv. him Maiden's Dairy (66:66).

YEARLY, JOHN, m. Margaret Phillips on 4 March 1754 (133:168).

YEO, JAMES, m. on 25 May 1755 Rachel Rollo, dau. of Archibald Rollo; on 2 Dec. 1755 James and his w. conv. prop. to Laban Ogg alias Hicks (82:490; 88:137; 131).

YEO, Rev. JOHN , was the first Anglican clergyman known to have settled in Maryland; in 1676 wrote a letter to the Archbishop of Canterbury; m. by 2 Oct. 1686 Semelia, wid. and admnx. of Ruthen Garrettson; d. by 2 Nov. 1686 when admin. bond was posted by Miles Gibson with James Phillips and Thomas Richardson; est. was inv. by Thomas Hedge and James Phillips and val. at a total of £ 35.6.6; in 1702 the heirs of John Yeo of Eng. (Arthur Lamprey of Biddiford, Co. Devon, who m. Elizabeth, wid. of Joseph Yeo who was a bro. of John Yeo, clerk of Md., and Joseph Yeo s. of the aforesaid Joseph Yeo) appointed William Pauley their atty. to sell any prop. formerly belonging to John Yeo; may have left a s. John and a married dau., but if so, they would have been his heirs (48:129; 66:242; 200-5:130).

YESTWOOD, MICHAEL, d. 26 May 1739; m. Elizabeth (---) on 30 June 1729; had iss.: JAMES, b. 7 June 1730; HANNAH, b. 3 Feb. 1732; MARY, b. 12 June 1734, d. 1 Oct. 1738; ELIZABETH, b. 2 Dec. 1736, d. 12 Sept. 1738; MICHAEL, b. 18 Jan. 1738, d. 18 Sept. 1738 (128:84, 102, 111).

YESTWOOD. See also EASTWOOD.

YOAKLEY, Capt. STEPHEN, in Aug. 1719 was named as the father Elizabeth Hitchins' child (23:131, 136, 138).

YORK, WILLIAM (1), was in Md. by 1658 when he and Samuel Keister were summoned to testify in the case of Nathaniel Utie vs. Peter Sharpe; surv. various lands in Balto. Co. incl. 200 a. York's Hope, 125 a. York's Chance, 300 a. Edwards' Lot, purch. 150 a. Bridewell Dock from Francis and Ann Trippas; m. 1st, by 1669, Elizabeth, who joined him selling land; m. 2nd, by 9 March 1673 Ann, wid. of John Collier, and extx. of James Stringer; m. 3rd Mary (---) who surv. him and m. as her 2nd husb. by Nov. 1692 James Frizzell; William d. leaving a will, 23 Nov. 1690 - 5 Feb. 1690/1 naming w. Mary, and five sons listed below; none of them were yet 16; on 10 July 1699 James and Mary Frizzell rel. her right of dower in Edwards' Lot and Hathaway's Trust to William and Oliver York, sons of William; James and Mary Frizzell admin. William York's est. on 23 May 1696; Mary York Frizzell d. by 10 April 1726 when George York signed her admin. bond; William was the father of: WILLIAM; OLIVER; JOHN; GEORGE; JAMES (16:92; 59: 331; 60:73; 63:391; 96:230; 200-41:185; 209-16:71; 209-27:294; 211).

YORK WILLIAM (2), s. of William (1), d. by 18 Sept. 1704; m. by 1695 Elizabeth, wid. of Jacob Looten; she d. 24 Nov. 1703; in 1695 was granted lic. to keep an ordinary on s. side of Susque-hannah, and to keep a ferry; d. by 18 Sept. 1704 when admin. bond was posted by Henry Wright, John Hall, and Thomas Cord; est. was inv. 1 July 1704 by Thomas Cord and Samuel Jackson and val. at E 24.14.0; est. of William and Elizabeth York was admin. 18 Jan. 1706 by Henry Wright; had iss.: ELIZABETH, by June 1723 was liv-ing in Cecil Co. when she conv. her share of Bridewell Dock and York's Chance to her uncle George York (2:233; 14:16; 20:391, 540; 54:26; 69:204; 128:21).

YORK, OLIVER (3), s. of William (1), was not yet 16 in 1690; in 1695 was a taxable in n. side Gunpowder Hund.; on 8 Aug. 1699 joined his bro. William York in conv. 150 a. Hathaway's Trust to Mark Swift (63:388, 391; 140).

YORK, GEORGE (4), s. of William(1), m. 1st, by April 1706, Hannah or Susannah (---); m. 2nd on 7 May 1721 Lettice Dawdridge; on 24 April 1706 Israel Skelton made a will naming dau. Hannah York; on 2 Sept. 1724 George York admin. the est. of William Dottridge; in 1750 owned 50 a. part Bridewell Dock and 125 a. York's Chance; d. by 20 Feb. 1754 when admin. bond was posted by William York with Godfrey Waters and John Armstrong; had iss.: (by Susannah): GEORGE, b. 1712; (by Hannah): ANNE, b. 2 April 1717; (by Lettice): EDWARD, b. 24 May 1721 (2:336; 14:9; 81: 122, 124; 131; 153:7).

YORK, JAMES (5), s. of William, d. Dec. 1724; m. Rachel (---) who m. as her 2nd husb. in April 1726 John Taylor; amdin. bond was posted 10 April 1726 by John Taylor with George York and John Armstrong; 27 May 1726 est. was inv. by James Presbury and William Burney, val. at E 38.11.3½ and signed by George York and James Frizzell; est. admin. by John Taylor; George and Rachel had iss.: RACHEL, b. 12 Jan. 1713; MARY, b. 28 Nov. 1716; JAMES, b. 11 Aug. 1718; ABRAHAM, bapt. 14 Sept. 1718; WILLIAM, b. 8 Aug. 1720; MARY JANE, b. 25 April 1723; REBECCA, b. 1 Aug. 1724, m. Jonathan Ady on 27 March 1742/3 (or on 4 April 1731 (2:324; 14:9; 51:50; 131).

YORK, GEORGE (6), s. of George (4), was b. c.1712; was prob. the George who m. by 19 June 1751 Eleanor. coheir of Edward Selby, Sr., who joined his dau. and his s. Edward Selby, Jr., in conv. Selby's Hope to Robert Adair (81:168).

YORK, EDWARD (7), s. of George (4), was b. 24 May 1721, and
d. by 13 Aug. 1770; m. Ann Dorney or Downey on 21 Oct. 1742;
left a will, 19 Oct. 1765 - 13 Aug. 1770, naming w. Anne, s.
George, and mentioning other ch.; est. was admin 10 Aug. 1772
by Ann York, who stated that the dec. left 10 ch., of whom 2
have been identified: GEORGE, b. Aug. 1750; and ELIZABETH, b.
30 April 1753 (7:136; 112:176; 131).

YORK, GEORGE, m. Eliner Meads in Feb. 1738 (131).

YORK, JOHN, m. Sarah Horner on 16 Oct. 1752; d. by 11 May
1758 when admin. bond was posted by Sarah York with John Roberts
and Nathan Horner; est. was admin. by Sarah York on 9 April 1759
and 6 Feb. 1760 (4:283, 323; 14:6; 131).

YORK, MARY, al's MINSON, was ind. for bast. in June 1740
(32:226).

YORK, WILLIAM, m. by June 1692 the rel. of John Wood (19:186,
187).

YORK, WILLIAM, m. 1 Jan. 1733 Elizabeth, dau. of George Debruler; d. by 12 June 1764 when admin. bond was posted by Eliza
York with Edward York and Benj. Debruler; his est. was admin.
by Eliza York on 6 Feb. (date not clear); had two ch. (6:20;
14:3; 126:142).

THE SAMUEL YOUNG FAMILY

YOUNG, SAMUEL (1), was bv. c.1662, prob. in Eng., d. c.1736
in A. A. Co.; m. 14 July 1687 Mary (d. c.1723), wid. of Maj.
Thomas Francis, and dau. of Robert and Milcah Clarkson; rep.
A. A. Co. in the Legislature, at various sessions between 1697
and 1725; on 19 May 1725 conv. 500 a. New Stadt and 400 a. of
Holland's Lot to s. Joseph Young; on 8 Aug. 1735 purch. 159 a.
Double Trouble from Robert and Sarah Robertson; on 12 Nov. 1731
conv. 1200 a. Young's Escape to s. Samuel, Jr., of Calvert Co.;
d. leaving a will, 22 Jan. 1732/3 - 7 July 1736, naming ch.
Richard, Joseph, Samuel, Sarah Budd (and her s. Samuel Budd
and her husb. George Budd), John (and his daus. Mary and Elizabeth), son Joseph's daus. Mary and Milcah, and his own bro.
Richard; had iss.: JOHN, d. c.1731/2; RICHARD, d. 1748; JOSEPH,
d. c.1737; SAMUEL, d. young; HENRY, d. young; SAMUEL, d. 1743;
SARAH, m. 1st George Budd, and 2nd in 1737 Edward Fottrell
(59:308; 66:122; 72:330; 126:198; 371:931-932).

YOUNG, JOHN (2), s. of Samuel (1), d. c.1731/2 in St. Marys
Co.; m. prb. Mary, d. by 1737, poss. dau. of John Leech; rep.
St. Marys Co. in the Legislature, 1728 - 1731; his two daus.
Mary and Elizabeth were mentioned in the will of their grandfather
Samuel as inheriting Good Neighborhood Enlarged in Balto. Co.;
had iss.: MARY; ELIZABETH (126:198; 371:931).

YOUNG, JOSEPH (3), s. of Samuel (1), d. in Cecil Co., leaving
a will, 9 Feb. 1736/7 - 7 May 1737, leaving Holland's Lot to
dau. Milcah, and New Stadt to youngest dau., and dau. Mary; had
iss.: MILCAH; MARY; and unnamed dau. (126:207).

YOUNG, SAMUEL (4), s. of Samuel (1), d. in Calvert Co.,
leaving a will, 6 Oct. 1742 - 18 Oct. 1743, naming uncle
Richard, dau.-in-law Ann Cockshutt, sis.-in-law Mary Young, and
two sons Samuel and Joseph who were to have Young's Escape in
Balto. Co.; had iss.: SAMUEL; JOSEPH; MARY, m. Pollard Keene;
and ELIZABETH, m. John Keene (81:142; 127:229; 153:57).

YOUNG, JOSEPH (5), s. of Samuel (4), in Oct. 1742 inher.
part of Young's Escape from his father; may be the Joseph Young,
orphan of Samuel Young, who chose his bro. Samuel as his guardian in March 1757 (44; 127:229).

YOUNG, ALEXANDER, in 1750 owned 150 a. part Southampton
(153:35).

YOUNG, ANN, was fined for bast. in Nov. 1757; she named Thomas
Reynolds as the father (46:75).

YOUNG, GEORGE, OF Cal. Co., on 17 June 1703 purch. 550 a. of
Parker's Chance from George Buxton; on 2 March 1705 Young and his
w. Mary conv. 550 a. of the tract to Thomas Gray, also of Cal.
Co. (64:26, 30).

YOUNG, HENRY, and RICHARD, were named as grandsons in the
will of Richard Acton of Balto. Co., in 1740/1 (127:123).

YOUNG, HENRY, m. by 18 June 1752 the wid. of John Evans (5:
237).

YOUNG, JACOB, on 14 June 1742 purch. Hopyard from Edward Tully; on 9 March 1746 Young sold   19 a. The Hopyard to John Bosley;
Young's w. Elinor consented; in 1750 Jacob owned   81 a. part of
Hector's Hopyard, and 50 a. Young's Delight (67:184; 79:532; 153:
21).

YOUNG, JOHN, d. leaving a will, 10 Aug. 1758 - 7 June 1762,
appointing his w. as extx. and naming his bro. William, as well
as the six ch. listed below; admin. bond was posted 1 July 1762
by extx. Rebecca Young with Edward Bussey and Michael Jenkins;
had: WILLIAM, GEORGE, REBECCA, MARY, SARAH, and ELIZABETH (4:5;
111:145).
YOUNG, HENRY, m. Urith (---), and had iss.: PLEASANT, b. 4
March 1759; REBECCA, b. 8 Dec. 1760; poss. HENRY who d. 1784
naming his mother Urith w. of John Young (112:565; 133:106).

YOUNG, MARY, alias Enloes, was ind. for bast. in March
March 1719/20; in June 1721 her husb. appeared in court (23:
279, 435, 514).

YOUNG, MARY, was tried for bast. in Nov. 1756 and named William Payne as the father (41:312).

YOUNG, MICHAEL, was in Balto. Co. by 1692 as a taxable in n.
side Patapsco Hund.; gave his age as 50 in 1714; on 7 July 1702
purch. 50 a. John's Interest (part of Todd's Range) from John
and Elinor Harryman; d. by 25 May 1716 when admin. bond was posted by Henry Jones with Thomas Biddison and Samuel Hinton; est.
was admin. 5 June 1717 and 16 June 1718 (1:263, 264; 14:15; 66:
155; 138).

YOUNG, NATHANIEL, m. Ann Butler on 25 Dec. 1733; had iss.:
JOHN, b. 4 Aug. 1741; ANN, b. 29 Aug. 1744; RUTH, b. 29 Aug.
1744; THOMAS, b. 6 May 1747; WILLIAM, b. 31 Aug. 1749; MARY, b.
18 Nov. 1754; HENRY, b. 16 March 1758 (133:87, 107, 151).

YOUNG, PAUL, m. Rosanna Marsh on 30 May 1733; m. Mary David
on 24 April 1743; made levy free in Nov. 1756; had iss.: ROSANNA,
b. 15 June 1733 (41:302; 133:42, 151, 156).

YOUNG, ROBERT, m. Jane Mortimer on 27 Jan. 1757 (131).

YOUNG, SEWELL, m. Margaret, dau. of Richard Acton, on 13 Jan.

1736; had iss.: HENRY, b. by 1740/1; RICHARD, b. by 1740/1 (127: 123; 133:156).

YOUNG, WILLIAM, of Calvert Co., on 1 Aug. 1737 sold 1000 a. Sewell's Fancy to Roger Boyce; Young's w. Clare (formerly Clare Tasker) consented; on the same day Boyce conv. the same 1000 a. to Young; on 8 March 1744/5 Sutton sickelmore and w. Susanna conv. 107 a. part Jamaica to William Young; in 1750 William owned 750 a. Sewell's Fancy, 52 a. Jamaica, and 108 a. Tipperare (61: 481, 482; 81:67; 153:55).

YOUNGBLOOD, THOMAS (1), m. Mary (---), and had iss.: JOHN MILES, b. 31 Oct. 1708 (128:33).

YOUNGBLOOD, JOHN MILES (2), s. of Thomas (1), was b. 31 Oct. 1708; m. Mary Coal on 21 Jan. 1729; on 1 April 1732 was called s. by John Miles in a deed; on 3 Nov. 1736 he and w. Mary conv. 100 a. Miles' Improvement to Jacob Giles; had iss.: HENRY MILES, b. 17 Jan. 1730; MARY, b. 7 Sept. 1732; JOHN, b. 17 Oct. 1734 (61:297; 69:136; 128:63, 73, 86).

YOUNGBLOOD, PETER, m. Mary Wheals on 26 Nov. 1750 (131).

ADDENDA

As is inevitable with a work of this size, information on a number of families came to light after the text was typed. This additional information is offered here to make the records of Baltimore County families more complete.

ALLEN, FRANCIS, servant, arrived as a convict 5 Sept. 1723 on the ship _Alexander_; on 7 Dec. 1726 Alexander Parrish gave him a certificate of freedome (70:317).

ASHER, ANTHONY, was conv. Cross's Outlet on 3 June 1734 by John League, "for love and affection;" on 26 March 1741 John and Mary League conv. 100 a. (unnamed) to Anthony Asher; Anthony prob. d. by 26 Oct. 1765 leaving a s.: ANTHONY (74:60; 75:489; 213-DD#4:1).

ASHER, ANTHONY, s. of Anthony of Balto. Co., dec., on 26 Oct. 1765 conv. 110 A. Asher's Purchase to Charles Carroll of Annapolis (213-DD#4:1).

ATHERTON, RICHARD, advertised his w. Susanna had deserted him on 5 June 1723 (69:143).

AUSTIN, HENRY, was in Balto. Co. by 10 March 1737 when Joseph Thurman conv. him 75 a. Egypt (75:56).

BANNEKER, ROBERT, and his s. BENJAMIN, were conv. 100 a. by Richard Gist being one-half of 200 a. that John Whips bought from Thomas Bale, and that Whips had sold to Gist (75:58).

BOYCE, CORNELIUS, s. and heir of Cornelius Boyce, dec., conv.
100 a. Gallion's Bay to Michael Judd on 2 Sept. 1696 (61:129).

BROWN, ELINOR, servant, was listed in the inv. of Anthony Demondidier (48:127).

BURNEY, WILLIAM, executed a deed on 4 July 1723 making all his
property over to his sons SIMON and WILLIAM, after his death (69:
192).

BOURDILLON, Rev. ALEXANDER, clerk of Balto. Co., d. leaving
a wid. Jane and a son Andrew Theodore Bourdillon, both of whom
were living in London on 1 Dec. 1767 (213-DD#4:362).

BOWDEN, ROBERT, and w. Mary were in Balto. Co. in Aug. 1739
when they were ind. for a felony; the charge was dropped (32;1).

CAMP, THOMAS, servant man, was recorded in 1722 by Mary Crouch
for her s. William Linch (69:36).

CASTEPHENS, THOMAS, servant with 15 months to serve was in
the Oct. 1690 inv. of John Boring (51:2).

CHADWELL/SHADWELL, JOHN, d. by 15 April 1677/8 when his est.
was admin. by his relict Katherine now w. of (Robert) Benjor;
the acct. mentioned an inv. of 14735 lbs. tob.; payments were
made to Edward William (2:41).

CHAPMAN, JOHN, and w. Ann conv. 100 a. Friendship to George
Buchanan on 13 March 1723 (69:280).

CHOAT, EDWARD, in June 1725 advert. he would not be responsible for his w. Constant who had left him (70:133).

COLLIER, JOHN, d. by 9 March 1673; m. Ann, extx. of James
Stringer; she m. 3rd William York; iss. of John and Ann (all
under age) were: JOHN, PHILIP; WILLIAM; SARA; ELIZABETH; and
JANE (209-6:42).

COLLYER, JAMES, was conv. Hunting Worth by Abraham Hollman
(who had been granted it by Lord Baltimore on 15 Feb. 1659);
Collyer died by 1687 and the land descended to Edward Collyer
feltmaker of Philadelphia, who on 13 Feb. 1687 conv. the land to
Samuel Browne (59:263).

CONAWAY, ANNE, servamt, was named in the 1679 inv. of James
Ives (51:103).

COPUS, JOHN (1), was in Balto. Co. by 6 Sept. 1683 when he
surv. 100 a. Copus Harbor; m. Sarah, wid. of Edward Teale, by
30 March 1699 when he conv. 100 a. Roper's Rest to his dau.-in-
law Ales Teal; his w. signed the deed as Sarah Teal; d. by 2 Aug.
1699 when admin. bond was posted by Sarah Copus, with Alexander
Lumley, Philip Roper, John Hall, and Richard Thrift; left iss.
(prob. by an unidentified 1st w.): THOMAS (11:311; 63:338; 211:
84).

COPUS, THOMAS (2), s. of Thomas (1), was in Balto. Co. by
1 May 1703 when as s. and heir of John, he and w. Jane conv.
100 a. Copus Harbor to Thomas Hedge (60:135).

COWLEY, JAMES, age c.22, unm., of St. James, Westminster,
Middlesex, coachman, on 12 Aug. 1718 bound himself to Christopher Veale of Shoreditch, Middlesex, woolcomber, to serve four
years in Md. (69:25).

DALLAHIDE, FRANCIS, of Balto. Co., d. by 8 June 1723, leaving
a s. and heir Francis, who on that day conv. 100 a. part Wansworth, 50 a. Daniel's Neck, and 30(?) a. Hornisham and 117 a.
Watterstown to James Maxwell (69:160).

DAVES, NIC'D, servant man with three years to serve, listed
in the 1703 inv. of Robert Hopkins (51:38).

DEBINE, LEWIS, servant boy in 1679 inv. of James Ives (51:
103).

DELMEYOSSA, ALEXANDER, was conv. 200 a. Brown's Survey by
Richard Kirkland on 25 May 1714 (66:342).

DERUMPLE, JOHN, and w. Sarah conv. 50 a. Come By Chance to
Samuel Owings in 1744 (77:683).

DEVOSS, MATTHIAS, late of Balto. Co. was named as a bro. of
Matthias Mattson of Penna., and of Andrew Mattson (69:58).

DOWNES, JOHN, servant, was listed in the April 1688 inv. of
Thomas Lightfoot (51:6).

DUDMAN, THOMAS, servant with four years to serve was listed
in the May 1699 inv. of Capt. John Ferry (48:121).

EARP, JOHN, and JOSEPH, of A. A. Co., conv. 100 a. Lurgan
and 100 a. McLain's Friendhsip to Charles Wells in 1728 (71:254.
258).

ENGLISH, DENNIS, d. by 27 Feb. 1715, leaving a s. and heir:
JOHN, who on that date deeded 40 a. Hazle Park to Aquila Paca
(59:555).

THE ENLOES FAMILY data presented here was made available to
the author by Mrs. Robert Hughes of Boulder, Colorado, and was
the result of work done by Mrs. Hughes, Mary C. Wright, Mr. G.
L. Brier, Evelyne McCracken and Mrs. John S. Slattery.

ENLOES, HENDRICK (1), was b. c.1632 in Holland, and d. by 18
May 1708 in Balto. Co., Md.; res. Delaware, and Kent Co.; m.
Christiana (---); pat. 100 a. Swallow Fork in Balto. Co. in 1683;
d. leaving a will, 10 Dec. 1707 - 18 May 1708, leaving 100 a. of
Triangle, 100 a. Dutch Neck, and 30 a. Enloes' Meadow to s. Abra-
ham, 1 shilling each to ch. John, Hester, and Margaret, and dower
rights to w. Christiana; had iss.: HENRY, b. c.1675, d. 1703;
JOHN, b. c.1668, d. c.1703, m. Elizabeth (---) who m. 2nd John
Leakins; HESTER, m. after 1711 William Wright; MARGARET, m. (---)
Durham; ABRAHAM, d. 1709 (122:116; data from Mrs. Hughes).

ENLOES, JOHN (2), s. of Hendrick (1) and Christiana, was b.
c.1668, d. by 1703; m. Elizabeth (---) who m. 2nd John Leakins;
had iss.: HENRY, in Kent Co., Md., c.1738; three daus., b. betw.
1696 to 1703; ABRAHAM, b. 20 March 1701 (data from Mrs. Hughes).

ENLOES, ABRAHAM (3), s. of Hendrick (1) and Christiana, was
b. c.1678; d. 1707; m. Elizabeth (---) who later m. John Ensor;
Abraham d. leaving a will, 24 April 1709 - 20 July 1709, leaving
100 a. Triangle Neck to sons Anthony and John; 50 a. Duck Neck
to s. William, 50 a. to s. Abraham, dau. Margaret Enloes, w.
Eliza, and an unborn ch.; also mentioned 30,a. Enloes' Meadow;
had iss.: JOHN, b. c.1703, alive in 1768; MARGARET, b. c.1704;
ABRAHAM, b. c.1705, d. 1758, m. Mary Deason; WILLIAM, b. c.1706
and moved to Beaufort Co., N. C.; ANTHONY, b. c.1708, m. Elinor
Cheney; poss. CHRISTIANA, b. c.17109 (m. Thomas Wright), or poss.
ELIZABETH, b. 1709/10 (122:145; data from Mrs. Hughes).

ENLOES, HENRY (4), s. of John (2) and Elizabeth, m. Mary
(---) and was in Kent Co., Md., by 1738; in 1724 conv. 100 a.
Swallow Fork to Bloyce Wright (data from Mrs. Hughes).

ENLOES, ABRAHAM (5), s. of Abraham (3) and Elizabeth, was b.
c.1705, d. 1758 in Balto. Co.; m. Mary Deason, b. c.1711, d. in
York Co., S. C., in 1774; had iss.: THOMAS, b. 1729, m. Sarah
James on 2 June 1754; ENOCH, b. betw. 1730 and 1741, d. in York
Co., S. C.,; m. 1st (---) Sprucebank, and 2nd Jane McCord; AN-
THONY, b. Aug. 1731; ABRAHAM, b. c.1732/3 in Balto. Co., m. Je-
mima Elliott on 28 Nov. 1754; AVARILLA, b. 5 May 1735, m. Robert
Gardner or Garner; BENJAMIN, b. 19 Jan. 1738; SARAH, b. 16 Feb.
1740; ISAAC, b. 13 Feb. 1743, d. 10 June 1819 in York Co., S.
C., m. Violet Porter; DEASON, b. c.1747; MARY, CHRISTEN; poss.
HENRY, b. c.1740/1, m. Mary Elliott on 26 May 1763; poss. POTTER,
b. c.1749; JOHN, b. c.1751 (data from Mrs. Hughes).

FENTON, AMY, widow, conv. 100 a. Ardington to Thomas Stans-
borough on 9 Nov. 1724 (70:85).

FOX, JOHN, servant, was listed in the April 1688 inv. of
Thomas Lightfoot (51:6).

GIBBONS, JOHN, servant, with 4 years to serve, was listed in
the Oct. 1690 inv. of John Boring (51:2).

GOYNE, WILLIAM, servant with 3 years to serve, was listed in
the May 1699 inv. of Capt. John Ferry (48:121).

JEFFERY, RICHARD, servant with 4 years to serve, was listed
in the Oct. 1690 inv. of John Boring (51:2).

THORNBOROUGH, ROLAND (1), according to data compiled by Cynthia Snider of Oakland, California, may have been a grandson of
Rowland and Jane (Dalton) Thornborough of Hampsfel. Mrs. Snider's theory is based in part on the facts that Rowland the
settler of Baltimore County used names for his children that
were used in the family of Rowland and Jane, and partly on the
fact that the Settler left his property in Maryland to his kins-
men at Hampsfell.

THE TREADWAY FAMILY has been the subject of extensive
research by Mrs. Bruce Baher of Richmond, Virginia. She feels
there were two distinct families in Baltimore County and Harford
Counties. She makes the following distinctons:

TREADWAY, THOMAS (3), s. of Richard (1) and Jane, was b. 6
March 1711; in March 1720/1 at age 10 he was bound to Antil Dea-
ver and w. Sarah; and is the Thomas Treadway who d. in Balto.
Co. leaving a will, 21 July 1749 - 2 Aug. 1749 (See page 651).

TREADWAY, THOMAS (4), no known rel. to any of the above,
is the one who died in Harford County leaving a will, 22 May
1783 - 13 Aug. 1783, having been married four times, and had
iss. (among others): DANIEL, b. 1724; MARY, m. (---) Cunningham;
THOMAS; JOHN, d. 1756; MOSES; and AARON.

TREADWAY, DANIEL (5), s. of Thomas (4), was b. 22 Nov. 1724,
and m. Sarah Norris on 2 Aug. 1744, dau. of Edward and Hannah
(Scott) Norris; they had iss.: ELIZABETH, m. as 2nd w. Thomas
Miles of Harford Co.

TULLY, MICHAEL (1), was in Balto. Co. by 8 June 1721 when he
wit. the will of James Barlow; m. Elizabeth (---) who m. as her
2nd husb., by Nov. 1723, John Hogan; d. by 17 April 1722 when

the 1st admin. bond on his est. was posted by Elizabeth Tully
with Jonathan Tipton and Thomas Tipton; in 1723 Jonathan and
Thomas Tipton pet. the court that they had been bondsmen for the
est. of Michael Tully, dec., and that John Hogan, new husb, of
Tully's wife, had extravagantly indebted himself to divers merchants and hadthen run away taking a horse and a mare; a 2nd admin. bond was posted 17 April 1732 by admnx. Elizabeth Tully
(sic) with Jonathan Tipton, John Israel, Edw. Dorsey and John
Chambers; Elizabeth Hogan, spinster, of Frederick Town, Cecil Co.,
d. leaving a will, 8 March 1743 - 20 March 1743, naming sons
Michael and William Tully, and daus. Elinor Tully and Mary (Tully?); the will was proved in the presence of Edward Tully, the
heir at law; Michael and Elizabeth had iss.: EDWARD; MICHAEL;
poss. WILLIAM; ELINOR; and poss. MARY (14:123, 213; 26:93; 124:
74; 127:251).

TULLY, EDWARD (2), prob. bro. of Michael (1), was b. c.1687,
giving his age as c.62 in a dep. in 1749; on 9 Jan. 1722 he wit.
the will of Pierce Welch of Balto. Co.; on 12 Feb. 1728 James
Carroll left Hopyard to his cousin Edward Tully and the two sons
of Michael Tully (124:126; 125:133; 224:167).

TULLY, EDWARD (3), s. of Michael (1), was named as the heir at
law in the probate of the will of Elizabeth Hogan; in 12 Feb.
1728 was one of two sons of Michael who were left part of Hopyard
by James Carroll; on 14 June 1732 he and bro. Michael sold 100 a.
of this land, "inher. from James Carroll," to Jacob Young; in
1750 owned 100 a. "Hunter's" Hopyard, 200 a. Littleworth, and 14
a. Tully's Beginnings (76:184; 127:251; 153:47).

TULLY, MICHAEL (4), s. of Michael (1), was a legatee in the
1728 will of James Carroll, snd the 1743 will of Elizabeth Hogan,
and joined Edward Tully in the 1742 deed cited above (76:184;
125:133; 127:251).

WALLIS, SAMUEL, d. c.1724; imm. to Md., c.1702; m. Anne (---);
wid. of (---) Beck; he rep. Kent Co., in the Lower House of the
Assembly in 1708 and 1722; had iss.: HENRY, b. c.1702/3; SAMUEL,
b. 1703, d. 1766, m. Elizabeth (---); JOHN, b. 1709, d. 1761;
HUGH, b. 1711, d. 1766; WILLIAM, b. 1714/5, d. 1757; RUTH, b.
1706/7, m. John McDaniel; MARGARET, b. 1712, m. John Hurt (371:
957-858).

WORRELL/WARRELL, HENRY, was in Balto. Co. by 30 July 1746
when he m. his 1st w., Juliatha Spicer; she d. and he m. 2nd, by
22 Sept. 1754 Rachel (---); in 1750 he owned 250 a. Timber Grove;
iss. (by 1st w.): HENRY, b. 19 Jan. 1747; THOMAS, b. 15 Dec. 1749;
JOHN, b. 13 March 1752; (by 2nd w.): JULIATHA, b. 22 Sept. 1754;
ELIZABETH, b. 21 May 1756; MARY, b. 25 Nov. 1757; AMON, b. 5 Dec.
1759; HANNAH, b. 19 July 1762; CALEB, b. 9 July 1765; JESSE, b.
15 Nov. 1770   (133:159; 134:34, 35; 153:97).

BIBLIOGRAPHY

This Bibliography is in four parts. Part I consists of items numbered 1 through 165 and which relate to Baltimore County records found either at the Hall of Records in Annapolis or at the Maryland Historical Society in Baltimore. Part II contains items numbered 200 through 441 which pertain to various records located at either of the two above named repositories and to some basic published sources. Part III lists items numbered 500 through 575 which refer to individual families. Part IV contains items which have not been numbered but which are referred to in the text, either by author's name alone, or by author's name and an abbreviated form of the title.

In some sources, where the data is arranged alphabetically, or where the particular item is already indexed, page numbers have been omitted.

Some numbers have not been assigned. These are designated "Unassigned" in the list of sources.

Abbreviations used in the Bibliography

BMGS	- Bulletin of the Maryland Genealogical Society.
CH	- court house.
HR	- Hall of Records, Annapolis.
MDG	- Maryland and Delaware Genealogist.
MHM	- Maryland Historical Magazine.
MHS	- Maryland Historical Society, Baltimore.
MMG	- Maryland Magazine of Genealogy.
MS	- manuscript.
NEHGR	- New England Historic Genealogical Register.
NGSQ	- National Genealogical Society Quarterly.
TAG	- The American Genealogist.
transc.	- transcribed.

I. BALTIMORE COUNTY RECORDS

Administration Accounts, HR.

1 - Liber 1	6 - Liber 6
2 - Liber 2	7 - Liber 7
3 - Liber 3	8 - Liber 8
4 - Liber 4	9 - Liber 9
5 - Liber 5	10 - Liber 10

Administration Bonds, HR.

11 - Liber 1	15 - Liber 5
12 - Liber 2	16 - Liber 6
13 - Liber 3	17 - Liber 7
14 - Liber 4	

Court Proceedings, HR.

18 - Liber D	23 - Liber IS#C
19 - Liber F#1	24 - Liber IS#TW#1
20 - Liber G#1	25 - Liber IS#TW#2
21 - Liber IS#B	26 - Liber IS#TW#3
22 - Liber IS#IA	27 - Liber IS#TW#4

Court Proceedings (cont'd).

28 - Liber HWS#6	38 - Liber TR#6
29 - Liber HS#7	39 - Liber BB#A
30 - Liber HWS#9	40 - Liber BB#B
31 - Liber HWS#1A	41 - Liber BB#C
32 - Liber HWS#TR	42 - Liber BB#D
33 - Liber TB#TR	43 - Liber BB#E
34 - Liber TB#D	44 - Rough Minutes, 1755-63
35 - Liber for 1743-1745/6	45 - Rough Minutes, 1765
36 - Liber TB#TR#1	46 - Criminal Proc.,1757-59
37 - Liber TR#5	47 - Court Proceedings, ms.
	at MHS.

Inventories, HR.

48 - Liber 1	54 - Liber 7
49 - Liber 2	55 - Liber 8
50 - Liber 3	56 - Liber 9
51 - Liber 4	57 - Liber 10
52 - Liber 5	58 - Liber 11
53 - Liber 6	

Land Records, HR.

59 - Liber RM#HS	76 - Liber TB#A
60 - Liber IR#PP	77 - Liber TB#C
61 - Liber IS#IK	78 - Liber TB#D
62 - Liber G#J	79 - Liber TB#E
63 - Liber TR#RA	80 - Liber TR#C
64 - Liber IR#AM	81 - Liber TR#D
65 - Liber HW#3	82 - Liber BB#I
66 - Liber HW#2	83 - Liber B#G
67 - Liber TR#A	84 - Liber B#H
68 - Liber TR#DS	85 - Liber B#I
69 - Liber IS#G	86 - Liber B#K
70 - Liber IS#H	87 - Liber B#L
71 - Liber IS#I	88 - Liber B#M
72 - Liber IS#K	89 - Liber B#N
73 - Liber IS#L	90 - Liber B#O
74 - Liber HWS#M	91 - Liber B#P
75 - Liber HWS # 1-A	92 - Liber B#Q

93 -   Sisco, Louis Dow. "Earliest Records of Baltimore Coun-
       ty." MHM 24 (1929), 151-156.
94 -   ————. "Baltimore County Land Records, 1665-1667."
       MHM 24 (1929), 342-348.
95 -   ————. "Baltimore County Records of 1668 and 1669."
       MHM 25 (1930), 255-262.
96 -   ————. "Baltimore County Land Records of 1670."
       MHM 26 (1931), 228-233.
97 -   ————. "Baltimore County Land Records of 1671."
       MHM 27 (1932), 123-127.
98 -   ————. "Baltimore County Land Records of 1672."
       MHM 28 (1933), 44-48.
99 -   ————. "Baltimore County Land Records of 1673."
       MHM 28 (1933), 345-350.
100 - ————. "Baltimore County Land Records, 1674 and 1675."
       MHM 29 (1934), 116-120.
101 - ————. "Land Records of Baltimore County, 1676 to
       1678." MHM 29 (1934), 299-304.
102 - ————. "Land Records of Baltimore County, 1679 and
       1680." MHM 30 (1935), 271-277.
103 - ————. "Baltimore County Land Records of 1681."
       MHM 31 (1936), 36-39.
104 - ————. Baltimore County Land Records of 1682."
       MHM 31 (1936), 242-247.
105 - ————. "Baltimore County Land Records of 1683."
       MHM 32 (1937), 30-34

106 - ————. "Baltimore County Land Records of 1684."
    MHM 32 (1937), 286-290.
107 - ————. "Baltimore County Land Records of 1685."
    MHM 33 (1938), 176-182.
108 - ————. "Baltimore County Land Records of 1686."
    MHM 34 (1939), 284-290.
109 - ————. "Baltimore County Land Records of 1687."
    MHM 36 (1941), 215-219.

Wills, HR.
110 - Liber 1   115 - Liber 6
111 - Liber 2   116 - Liber 7
112 - Liber 3   117 - Liber 8
113 - Liber 4   118 - Liber 9
114 - Liber 5   119 - Liber 10

Published Wills.
    Cotton, Jane Baldwin. Maryland Calendar of Wills. 8 vols.
        Baltimore:1904-1928.
120 - Volume I.   124 - Volume V.
121 - Volume II.   125 - Volume VI.
122 - Volume III.   126 - Volume VII.
123 - Volume IV.   127 - Volume VIII.

Church Records, MHS and HR.
    Except where otherwise noted, transcriptions of Church Records
    at the Maryland Historical Society were made by Lucy H. Harri-
    son.
128 - Register of St, George's Protestant Episcopal Church.
        Original Register, HR.
129 - Register of St. George's Protestant Episcopal Church.
        Transcription, MHS.
130 - Vestry Proceedings of St. George's Protestant Episcopal
        Church. Transcription, MHS.
131 - Register of St. John's Protestant Episcopal Church
        Church. Index to Register made by Helen W. Brown.
        Typescript, MHS.
132 - Vestry Proceedings of St. John's Protestant Episcopal
        Church. Transcription, MHS.
133 - Register of St. Paul's Protestant Episcopal Church.
        Transcription, MHS.
134 - Register of St. Thomas' Protestant Episcopal Church.
        Transcription, MHS.
135 - Vestry Proceedings of St. Thomas' Protestant Episcopal
        Church. Transcription, MHS.
136 - Records of Gunpowder Meeting, society of Friends.
        Transcription prepared for William Wade Hinshaw but
        never published, MHS.
137 - Register of First Presbyterian Church, Baltimore.
        Transcription, MHS,

Tax Lists, Petitions, and Other Lists.
    William N. Wilkins. "Baltimore County Tax Lists..." Type-
    script, MHS.
138 - "...for 1692."   144 - "...for 1702."
139 - "...for 1694."   145 - "...for 1703."
140 - "...for 1695."   146 - "...for 1704."
141 - "...for 1699."   147 - "...for 1705."
142 - "...for 1700."   148 - "...for 1706."
143 - "...for 1701."   149 - "...for 1737."

150 - Petition, 1738, included in article in MHM 15 (1920),
        220.
151 - List of Levy Papers, 1739, in Calendar of Maryland
        State Papers: No. 1 The Black Books. 1943. Repr.
        Baltimore:1967. Item 391, pp. 59-60.

152 - Petition, 1739, included in article in MHM 15 (1920), 221
153 - Baltimore County Debt Book for 1750. ms. in Calvert Papers, MHS.
154 - Petition, post 1750, Calendar of Maryland State Papers: No. 1 The Black Books. 1943. Repr. Baltimore:1967. Item 633, p. 95.
155 - Petition,c.1753-1769. Ibid. Item 751, p. 109.
156 - Petition to repair St. Paul's Church, 1755. Ibid. Item 825, pp. 119-120.
157 - Tax List of St. Thomas Parish, 1763. Harford County Historical Society Papers, MHS.
158 - Petition to repair organ in St. Paul's Church, post 1763. Cal. of Md. State Papers, Black Books, op. cit., Item 1307, p. 189.
159 - Assessment Books of Sheriff Aquila Hall, c.1764/5. MS.1565, MHS.
160 - Petitions for and against removal of county seat from Joppa Town to Baltimore Town, 1768, in Archives of Maryland, 61:520-580.
161 - William N. Wilkins. "Baltimore County Tax List for 1773." Typescript, MHS.
162 - List of Taxables in St. Paul's Parish, 1774 - 1787 in Ethan Allen. "History of St. Paul's Parish." Ms., MHS, 274-302.
163 - Unassigned.
164 - Baltimore County Original Wills, HR.
165 - Register of St. James' Protestant Episcopal Church. Transcription, MHS.
166 through 199 - Unassigned.

II. OTHER COUNTY RECORDS AND PUBLISHED SOURCES.

In the case of multi-volume series of records, the first number is the series designation. Following a hyphen the volume number is given, followed by a colon, and then in the case of un-indexed works, the specific page number. For example, 200-1:18 would refer to the Archives of Maryland (series 200), vol. 1, p. 18.

200 - Archives of Maryland. v.1-   . Baltimore:1883-
201 - Maryland Administration Accounts, HR.
202 - Maryland Balance of Final Distribution Books, HR.
203 - Maryland Chancery Cases (bound volumes), HR.
204 - Maryland Chancery Papers, HR.
205 - Maryland Inventories, HR.
206 - Maryland Inventories and Accounts, HR.
207 - Card Index to Maryland Grants, HR.
208 - Calendar of Maryland State Papers. Annapolis:1943-1958.

    208-1. The Black Books.
    208-2. The Red Books, part 1.
    208-3. The Red Books, part 2.
    208-4. The Red Books, part 3.
    208-5. The Brown Books.

209 - Maryland Testamentary Proceedings, HR.
210 - Maryland Will Books, HR.
211 - Maryland Rent Rolls: Baltimore and Anne Arundel Counties, 1700-1707, 1705-1724. Baltimore:1976.
212 - Maryland Historical Magazine (used for articles not otherwise specifically identified).
213 - Provincial Court Deeds, HR.

214 - Provincial Court Judgments, HR.
215 - Unassigned.
216 - Anne Arundel County Court Judgments, HR.
217.- Anne Arundel County Land Records, HR.
218 - Anne Arundel County Marriage Licenses, HR.
219 - Anne Arundel County Parish Registers.
    219-1 - All Hallows Parish Register. Transcription by
       Lucy H. Harrison, MHS.
    219-2 - St. Anne's Parish Register. Transcription by
       Lucy H. Harrison, MHS.
    219-3 - St. James' Parish Register. Transcription by
       Lucy H. Harrison, MHS.
    219-4 - St. Margaret's Parish Register. Transcription by
       Lucy H. Harrison, MHS.
    219-5 - Register of Cliffs Monthly Meeting, Society of
       Friends, HR.
    219-6 - Register of West River Monthly Meeting, Society
       of Friends. Transcribed by John J. Brinkley.
       BMGS 14 (1973) no. 2, 1-4; no. 3, 5-8; no. 4,
       1-4; 15 (1974) 98-103, 119-122, 229-233.
220 - Unassigned.
221 - Unassigned.
222 - See no. 165 above.
223 - Baltimore County Land Commissions, Liber HWS#1, HR.
224 - Miller, Richard B. "Abstracts of Baltimore County Land
    Commissions, Liber HWS#3, Ms. in possession of the
    author.
225 - Miller, Richard B., Abstracts of Baltimore County Land
    Commissions, Liber HWS#BB#4, Ms. in possession of the
    author..
226 through 228 - Unassigned.
229 - Baltimore County Chattel Records, Liber TB#E, HR.
230 - Baltimore County Chattel Records, Liber B#G, HR.
231 - Baltimore County Land Records following Liber B#Q, HR.
232 - Card Index of Baltimore County Marriage Licenses, HR.
233 - Baltimore County Survey Book, c.1771-1776. MS.71, MHS.
234 - Baltimore County Tax Lists later than 1759.
235 - Baltimore County Register of Administrations, HR.
236 - Baltimore County Will Books following Will Book 10, HR.
237 - Baltimore County Administration Accounts following
    Liber 10, HR.
238 - Unassigned.
239 - Unassigned.
240 - Baltimore County Orphans Court Proceedings, HR.
241 - Harford County Land Records, CH.
242 - Harford County Marriage Licenses, CH.
243 - Harford County Tax Lists.
244 - Harford County Wills, CH..
245 - Harford County Directory. Baltimore:1955.
246 - Preston, Walter W. History of Harford County, Maryland.
    Baltimore:1901.
247 through 250 - Unassigned.
251 - Allen, Ethan. The Garrison Church. New York:1898.
252 - Allen Ethan. "Historical Sketches of St. Paul's Parish in
    Baltimore County, Maryland." Baltimore:155. ms., MHS.
253 - Ardery, Mrs. William Breckenridge. Kentucky Records.
    (1928). Repr. Baltimore:1981.
254 - Barnes, Robert W. "The Em(er)son-Cobb-Hawkins Connection."
    MMG 4 (1981), 67-73.
255 - ————. Gleanings from Maryland Newspapers, 1727-1775.
    Lutherville:1976.
256 - ————. Gleanings from Maryland Newspapers, 1776-1785.
    Lutherville:1975.
257 - ————. Gleanings from Maryland Newspapers, 1786-1790.
    Lutherville:1975.

258 - ————. Gleanings from Maryland Newspapers, 1791-1795. Lutherville:1976.
259 - ————. The Green Spring Valley-Its History and Heritage; Volume II: Genealogies. Baltimore:1978.
260 - ————. "Heirs to Baltimore County Estates." MDG 7 (1966) 9-10, 28-29, 52-53, 76-77; 8(1967) 6-7, 32-33, 56-57, 78-79.
261 - ————. Marriages and Deaths from Baltimore Newspapers, 1796ᴜ- 1816. Baltimore:1978.
262 - ————. Marriages and Deaths from the (Annapolis) Maryland Gazette, 1727-1839. Baltimore:1973.
263 - ————. Maryland Marriages, 1634-1777. Baltimore:1975.
264 - ————. Maryland Marriages, 1778-1800. Baltimore:1979.
265 - ————. "Maryland Pioneers to the Frontier." MDG 18 (1977) 6-7, 32-33, 67-57.
266 - ————. "Heirs of Baltimore County Estates, 1755-1765." NGSQ 53 (1965) 290-298.
267 through 270 - Unassigned.
271 - Barnes, Walter Denny. The Barnes-Bailey Genealogy. Baltimore:1939.
272 - Bevan, Edith Rossuter. "Druid Hill, Country Seat of the Rogers and Buchanan Families." MHM 44 (1949), 190-199.
273 - ————. "Perry Hall: Country Seat of the Gough and Carroll Families." MHM 45 (1950), 33-46.
274 - Bristol and America: A Record of the First settlers in North America, 1654-1685. (1929). Repr. Baltimore: 1967.
275 - See no. 131 above.
276 - Brumbaugh, Gaius Marcus. Maryland Records: Colonial, Revolutionary, County and Church, From Original Sources. Volume I. (1915). Repr. Baltimore:1967.
277 - ————. ————. Volume II (1918). Repr. Baltimore: 1967.
278 - Burke's American Families with British Ancestry. (1939). Repr.: Baltimore:1977.
279 through 281 - Unassigned.
282 - Burns, Annie Walker. Abstracts of Pension Papers: Soldiers of the Revolution, 1812, and Indian Wars who Resided in ... No p., no date.
    282-1 - Morgan County, Kentucky.
    282-2 - Oldham County Kentucky.
    282-3 - Shelby County, Kentucky.
283 - Carothers, Bettie Stirling. 1783 Tax List of Baltimore County, Maryland. Lutherville:1978.
284 - ————. "Record of Burials Attended by William Nevins, Pastor of the First Presbyterian Congregation of Baltimore, Maryland." MMG 3 (1980) 86-90.
285 - ————. 1776 Census of Maryland. Chesterfield:1972.
286 - ————. Maryland Source Records, Volume I. Lutherville: 1975.
287 - ————. ————. Volume II. Lutherville:1979.
288 - Unassigned.
289 - Cary, Wilson Miles, Genealogical Collection. MS.G-5010, M MHS.
290 - Chalkley, Lyman. Chronicles of the Scotch-Irish Settlement in Virginia. 3 vols. (1912). Repr. Baltimore:1974.
291 - Clark, Raymond B., Jr., and Sara Seth Clark. Baltimore County Tax Lists, 1699-1706. Washington, D.C.:1964.
292 - Unassigned.
293 - Unassigned.
294 - Clement, Maud Carter. The History of Pittsylvania County, Virginia. (1929). Repr. Baltimore:1981.
295 - Cochrane, William C. Memoirs of the Dead and the Tomb's Remembrancer. Baltimore:1806.
296 - Coldham, Peter Wilson. English Convicts in Colonial

America, Volume I: Middlesex, 1617-1775. New Orleans: 1974.
297 - ————. ————. Volume II, London. New Orleans, 1976.
298 - ————. English Estates of American Colonists: American Wills and Administrations in the Prerogative Court of Canterbury, 1610-1699. Baltimore:1980.
299 - ————. ————.1700-1799. Baltimore:1980.
300 - ————. "Genealogical Gleanings in England." pub. in NGSQ in the volumes and on the pages indicated in individual citations.
301 - ————. Bonded Passengers to America. 3 vols. Baltimore:1983.
302 - Unassigned.
303 - "Commission Book 82." MHM 26 (1931) 139-158, 244-263, 342-361; 27 (1932) 29-37.
304 - Cordell, Eugene Fauntleroy. The Medical Annals of Maryland, 1799-1899. Baltimore:1903.
305 - The County Court Notebook, Volumes I-X, and Ancestral Proofs and Probabilities, Numbers 1-4. Edited by Milnor Ljungstedt (1921-1931, 1935-1936). Repr. Baltimore:1972.
306 - Cox, Richard J. "Eighteenth Century Baltimoreans." MDG 21 (1980) 114-138, 220-236.
307 - ————. "Maryland Runaway Convict Servants, 1745-1780." NGSQ 68 (1980) 105-114, 232-233, 299-304; 69 (1981) 51-58, 125-132, 205-214, 293-300.
308 - ————. "More Eighteenth Century Baltimoreans." BMGS 22 (1981) 170-185.
309 - ————. "Servants at Northampton Forge, Baltimore County, Maryland, 1772-1774." NGSQ 63 (1975) 110-117.
310 - Cregar, William Francis, and Dr. Christopher Johnston. "Index to Chancery Depositions, 1668-1789." MHM 23 (1928), 101-154, 197-242, 293-343.
311 - Cunz, Dieter. "German Settlers in Early Colonial Maryland." MHM 42 (1947) 101-108.
312 - ————. The Maryland Germans: A History. Princeton: 1948.
313 - Davis, Helen E. Kindred:Davis-Stansbury Lines. Philadelphia:1977.
314 - Dielman-Hayward Clipping File, MHS.
315 - Unassigned.
316 - Flavell, Carol Willsey. "Maryland Grantees, Steubenville, Ohio, Federal Land Office." MMG 2 (1979) 22-29.
317 - ————. "Maryland Pioneers in Cincicnnati, Ohio." MMG 1 (1978) 33.
318 - Focke, Ferdinand B.,Genealogical Collection. MS.G-5019, MHS.
319 - Focke, Ferdinand B. "Winchester-Owens-Owings-Price and Allied Families." MHM 25 (1930) 479-486.
320 - Gardner, John H., Jr. The First Presbyterian Church of Baltimore: A Two Century Chronicle. Baltimore:1962.
321 - Genealogy and Biography of the Leading Families of the City of Baltimore and Baltimore County. New York:1897.
322 - Hayward, Francis Sidney, Genealogical Collection. MS. 5024, MHS.
323 - Hocker, Edward W. Genealogical Data Relating to the German Settlers of Pennsylvania and Adjacent Territory, From Advertisements Published in German Newspapers Published in Philadelphia and Germantown, 1743-1800. Baltimore:1981.
324 - Howard, McHenry, Genealogical Collection. MS.G-5087, MHS.
325 - Howard, McHenry. "Some Abstracts of Old Baltimore County Records." MHM 18 (1923) 1-22.
326 - Hughes, Joseph L., Genealogical Collection. MS.G-5048, MHS.

327 - Irish, Donna R. <u>Pennsylvania German Marriages</u>. Balti-
      more:1982.
328 - Johnston, Christopher, Genealogical Collection. MS.
      G-5029, MHS.
329 - Johnston, Christopher. Genealogical Notes on Various
      Families (not in no. 328 above), MHS.
330 - Kates, Frederick Ward. <u>Bridge Across Four Centuries:</u>
      <u>The Clargy of St. Paul's Parish, Baltimore County,</u>
      <u>1692 - 1957</u>. Baltimore:1957.
331 - <u>Kentucky Ancestors</u>. v.1- , 1965- .
332 - Loeschke, Mrs. Donald B. "Taylor's Chapel." <u>MDG</u> 12
      (1971) 27-28.
333 - Marine, William M. <u>The British Invasion of Maryland,</u>
      <u>1812-1815</u>. (1913). Repr. Hatboro:1965.
334 - Marks, Lillian Bayly. "Doctor Weisenthal's Patients."
      <u>BMGS</u> 21 (1980), 180-215.
335 - ————. Reister's Desire. Baltimore:1975.
336 - Marye, William B. "Baltimore City Place Names: Stony
      Run: Its Plantations, Farms, Country Seats, and
      Mills." <u>MHM</u> 58 (1963) 211-232, 344-377.
337 - ————. "Baltimore City Place Names: Part 4." <u>MHM</u> 59
      (1964) 52-93.
338 - ————. "The Baltimore County 'Garrison' and the Old
      Garrison Road." <u>MHM</u> 16 (1921) 105-149, 207-259.
339 - ————. "The Great Maryland Barrens." <u>MHM</u> 50 (1955)
      11-23, 120-142, 234-253.
340 - ————. "The Old Indian Road." <u>MHM</u> 15 (1920) 107-124,
      208-229, 345-394.
341 - ————. "The Place Names of Baltimore and Harford
      Counties." <u>MHM</u> 25 (1930) 321-364.
342 - ————. "Place Names of Baltimore and Harford Coun-
      ties." <u>MHM</u> 53 (1958) 34-57, 238-252.
343 - ————. "Some Baltimore City Place Names." <u>MHM</u> 54
      (1959) 15-35, 353-364.
344 - Marye, William B., Genealogical Collection. ms, MHS.
345 - Maryland State Society DAR. <u>Directory of Maryland State</u>
      <u>Society Daughters of the American Revolution and</u>
      <u>Their Revolutionary Ancestors, 1892-1965</u>. Bel Air:
      1966.
346 - <u>Maryland Genealogies: A Consolidation of Articles from</u>
      <u>the Maryland Historical Magazine</u>. 2 vols. Baltimore:
      1980.
347 - Unassigned.
348 - Unassigned.
349 - McAdams, Mrs. Harry Kennett. <u>Kentucky Pioneers and</u>
      <u>Court Records</u>. (1929). Repr. Baltimore:1980.
350 - McGhee, Lucy K. <u>Maryland Pension Abstracts</u>. Washing-
      ton, D.C.:1966.
351 - ————. <u>Maryland Revolutionary War Pensioners, War of</u>
      <u>1812, and Indian Wars</u>. Washington, D.C.:1952.
352 - Meyer, Mary K. <u>Divorces and Names Changed in Maryland</u>
      <u>By Act of the Legislature, 1634-1854</u>. Pasadena:1970.
353 - National Society of the Daughters of the American Revolu-
      tion. <u>Patriot Index</u>. Volume I. Washington, D.C.:
      1966.
354 - ————. <u>Patriot Index</u>. Volume II. Washington, D.C.:
      1979.
355 - Newman, Harry Wright. <u>Anne Arundel Gentry</u>. Washing-
      ton,D. C.:1933.
356 - ————. <u>Anne Arundel Gentry: Revised and Enlarged</u>.
      Vol. I.
357 - ————. ————. Vol. II.
358 - ————. ————. Vol. III.
359 - ————. <u>The Flowering of the Maryland Palatinate</u>.
      Washington: 1961.

360 - Nimmo, Nannie Ball, Genealogical Collection. MS.G-5042, MHS.
361 - O'Byrne, Estella A. Roster of Soldiers and Patriots of the American Revolution Buried in Indiana. Volume I. Brookeville:1938.
362 - ————. ————. Volume II. Brookeville:1966.
363 - ————. ————. Volume III. Brookeville: 1980.
364 - Oficial Roster of the Soldiers of the American Revolution Buried in the State of Ohio. Columbus:1929.
365 - Owings, Donnell M. His Lordship's Patronage: Offices of Profit in Colonial Maryland. Baltimore:1953.
366 - ————. "Private Manors: An Edited List." MHM 33 (1938) 307-333.
367 through 369 - Unassigned.
370 - Papenfuse, Edward C., Alan F. Day, David W. Jordan, and Gregory A. Stiverson. A Biographical Dictionary of the Maryland Legislature, 1635-1789. Volume 1:A-H. Baltimore and London:1979.
371 - ————. ————. Volume 2:I-Z. Baltimore and London: 1985.
372 - Parks, Gary W. "Deer Creek Society of Friends, Vital Records, 1767-1823, Harford County, Maryland." BMGS 22 (1981) 195-207.
373 -Price, Elbridge C., Genealogical Collection. MS.G-5046, MHS.
374 - Quinan, John R. Medical Annals of Baltimore, 1608-1880. Baltimore:1884.
375 - Radoff, Morris L. "Notes on Baltimore County Land Records." MHM 33 (1938) 183-186.
376 - Ray, Worth Stickley. Tennessee Cousins: A History of Tennessee People. (1950. Repr. Baltimore:1984.
377 - Ridgely, Helen W. Historic Graves of Maryland and the District of Columbia. (1908). Repr.: Baltimore:1967.
378 - Rogers, Charles B., Genealogical Collection. MS.G-5057, MHS.
379 - Russell, George Ely. "The Swedish Settlement in Maryland, 1654." TAG 54 (1978) 203-210.
380 - Scharf, John Thomas. The Chronicles of Baltimore: Being a Complete History of "Baltimore Town" and Baltimore City from the Earliest Period to the Present Time. Baltimore:1874.
381 - ————. History of Baltimore City and County. (1881). Repr. Baltimore:1971.
382 - ————. History of Western Maryland: Including Biographical Sketches of Their Western Maryland. (1882). Repr. in Two vols. Baltimore:1968.
383 - Unassigned.
384 - Scott, Kenneth. Abstracts from Ben Franklin's Pennsylvania Gazette, 1728-1748. Baltimore:1975.
385 - ———— and Janet R. Clarke. Abstracts from the Pennsylvania Gazette, 1748-1755. Baltimore:1977.
386 - Scisco, Louis Dow. "Colonial Records of Baltimore County." MHM 22 (1927) 245-259.
387 - Silverson, Katherine T. Taney and Allied Families. New York:1935.
388 - Skordas, Gust. The Early Settlers of Maryland: An Index of Names of Immigrants Compiled from Records of Land Patents, 1633-1680, in the Hall of Records, Annapolis, Maryland. (1968). Repr.: Baltimore:1986.
389 - Slattery, Bradleigh V. Gunpowder Manor: Individual Plats. Baltimore:1976.
390 - Smith, Dorothy H. "Orphans in Anne Arundel County, Maryland, 1704-1709." MMG 3 (1980) 34-42.
391 - Unassigned.
392 - Society of Colonial Wars in the State of Maryland. Genealogies of the Members and Records of Services of

Ancestors. Volume I. Compiled by Christopher Johnston. Baltimore:1905.
393 - ————. ————. Volume II. Compiled by Francis B.
Culver. Baltimore:1940.
394 - Spencer, Edward. "Soldiers Delight Hundred in Baltimore County." MHM 1 (1906), 150-154.
395 - Steuart, Rieman. The Maryland Line: A History of the
Maryland Line in the Revolutionary War, 1775-1783.
Baltimore:1969.
396 - Unassigned.
397 - Tepper, Michael. New World Immigrants: A COnsolidation
of Ship Passenger lists and Associated data from Peri-
odical Literature. 2 vols. Baltimore:1980.
398 - Thomas, Dawn F. The Green Spring Valley-Its History
and Heritage: Volume One - A History and Historic
Houses. Baltimore:1978.
399 - Walker, Mrs. Harriet J. Revolutionary Soldiers Buried
in Illinois. Baltimore:1967.
400 - Waters, Margaret R. Revolutionary Soldiers Buried in
Indiana. 2 vols. in 1. (1949, 1954). Repr. Baltimore:
1970.
401 - Waters, Mary E., Genealogical Collection. MS.G-5070,
MHS.
402 - Who Was Who in America: Historical Volume, 1607-1896.
Chicago:1963.
403 - see no. 161 above.
404 - Wyand, Jeffrey A. and Florence Leone Wyand. Maryland
Colonial Naturalizations. Baltimore:1975.
405 - Baltimore:Its History and People. Clayton Colman Hall,
ed. 3 vols. New York:1912.
406 - Bowie, Effie Gwynn. Across the Years in Prince George's
County. (1947). Repr. Baltimore:1975.
407 - Register of Christ Evangelical Lutheran Church, York
County, Pennsylvania. Trancription, York County
Historical Society, York, Pennsylvania.
408 - Crozier, William Armstrong. Virginia Colonial Militia,
1651-1776. (1905). Repr. Baltimore:1982.
409 - Dyer, Albion Morris. First Ownership of Ohio Lands.
(1911). Repr. Baltimore:1982.
410 - Emison, James Wade. Supplement (1962) to the Emison
Families, Revised (1954). Vincennes:1962.
411 - Genealogies of Pennsylvania Families from the Pennsylvania Genealogical Magazine. 3 vols. Baltimore:1982.
412 - Genealogies of Pennsylvania Families from the Pennsylvania Magazine of History and Biography. Baltimore:
1981.
413 - Genealogies of Virginia Families from Tyler's Quarterly
Historical and Genealogical Magazine. 4 vols. Balti-
more:1981.
414 - Genealogies of Virginia Families from the Virginia Magazine of History and Biography. 5 vols. Baltimore:
1982.
415 - Genealogies of Virginia Families from the William and
Mary Quarterly. 5 vols. Baltimore: 1981.
416 - Genealogy and History. Washington, D. C.:1940-1964.
(The number following 416 is the number of a specific
query.)
417 - Hodges, Margaret Roberts. "Unpublished Revolutionary
Records of Maryland." 1939-1941. Typescript, MHS.
418 - Howard, Louise Ogier, and Mildred McKenney Trice. Guar-
dianships Involving Orphans As Abstracted from the
Orphans Court of Baltimore County. 2 vols. No p.:
1975-1976. (Volume I covers Liber WB#1, 1778-1787;
Volume II covers Liber WB#2, 1787-1792).
419 - McIntire, Robert. Annapolis, Maryland, Families. Bal-
timore:1979.

420 - Nugent, Nell Marion. <u>Cavaliers and Pioneers: Abstracts of Virginia Land Patents and Grants, 1623-1666</u>. (1934). Repr.: Baltimore:1983.
421 - Quisenberry, Anderson Chenault. <u>Revolutionary Soldiers in Kentucky</u>. (1896). Repr. Baltimore:1982.
422 - Rupp, Israel Daniel. <u>A Collection of Upwards of Thirty Thousand Names of German, Swiss, Dutch, French and Other Immigrants in Pennsylvania from 1727 to 1776</u>. (1876, 1931). Repr.: Baltimore:1985.
423 - see no. 165 above.
424 - Strassburger, Ralph B., and William J. Hinke. <u>Pennsylvania German Pioneers</u>. (3 vols., 1934). Repr. vols. 1 and 3 only Baltimore:1966.
425 - Andrews, Matthew Page. <u>Tercentenary History of Maryland</u>. 4 vols. Baltimore:1925.
426 - Jester, Annie L., with Martha W. Hiden. <u>Adventurers of Purse and Person, Virginia, 1607-1625</u>. 2nd ed. Richmond:1964.
427 - Moss, Bibbie Gilmer. <u>Roster of South Carolina Patriots in the American Revolution</u>. Baltimore:1983.
428 - Weis, Frederick Lewis. <u>The Colonial Clergy of Maryland, Delaware, and Georgia</u>. Lancaster:1950.
429 - Goldsborough, Henry Hollyday. "List of Civil Officers of Maryland." 3 vols. <u>Ms.</u>, MHS
430 - Unassigned.
431 - Ford, Henry A., and Kate B. Ford. <u>History of Hamilton County, Ohio</u>. (1881). Repr. 1974).
432 - Gibson, John. <u>History of York County, Pennsylvania</u>. (1886). Repr. Evansville:1973.
433 - Sutherland, Henry C. "A Brief History of the Bush River Friends Meeting of Harford County, Maryland." <u>MHM</u> 77 (1982) 365-369.
434 - <u>Virginia Land Records</u>. Baltimore:1982.
435 - Weis, Frederick Lewis. <u>Ancestral Roots of Sixty Colonists Who Came to New England Between 1623 and 1650</u>. 5th ed. (1976). Repr. Baltimore:1985.
436 - Weis, Frederick Lewis, and Arthur Adams. <u>The Magna Charta Sureties, 1215</u>. (With Additions and Corrections by Walter Lee Sheppard, Jr.). (1979). Repr. Baltimore:1982.
437 - Unassigned.
438 - The Woodlawn History Committee. <u>Woodlawn, Franklintown, and Hebbville</u>. No p.:1977.
439 - Ghirelli, Michael. <u>A List of Emigrants from England to America, 1682-1692</u>. Baltimore:1968.
440 - Kaminkow, Jack, and Marion J. Kaminkow. <u>A List of Emigrants from England to America, 1718-1759</u>. Baltimore:1964.
441 - Hastings, Mrs. Russell. "Calvert and Darnall: Gleanings from English Wills." <u>MHM</u> 21 (1926) 303-324; 22 (1927) 1-22, 115-138, 211-245, 307-349
442-499 - Unassigned.

III. NUMBERED ITEMS REFERRING TO INDIVIDUAL FAMILIES.

500 - Ady family papers made available to the author by Ella Rowe of Baltimore, Maryland.
501 - Ady Family Bibles. <u>BMGS</u> 20 (1979) 237-240.
502 - Ady query published in the <u>Hartford Times</u>, 21 December 1957.
503 - Amos family notes in 322 above.

504 - Archer Family. Magazine of American Genealogy. No. 7
      (Feb. 1930) Section IV, pp. 71-72.
505 - Burrage, Will. "John Archer." Dictionary of American
      Biography. I, 340.
506 - Unassigned.
507 - Mr. and Mrs. H. H. Arnold. Unpublished Arnold Notes.
      Typescript in poss. of the author.
508 - Lantz,Emily Emerson. "Ashman, Cromwell, Jacob, Taylor,
      Trehearne, Wilmot, Towson and Other Families."
      Baltimore Sun, 11 August 1907.
509 - Baynes, John W., Jr. Bayne Family Newsletter. No. 1
      (Nov. 1971).
510 - Balch, Thomas Willing. Balch Genealogica. Philadel-
      phia:1907.
511 through 515 - Unassigned.
516 - "Ball Family." Tyler's Quarterly Historical and Genea-
      logical Magazine 29 (July 1947), 43-49.
517 - Gossett, Josie. "My Connection with the Ball Family."
      Repr. in 413-1:61-ff.
518 - Johnston, Christopher. "A Forgotten Member of the
      Ball Family." Repr. in 414-1:23-27.
519 - Sweeny, Mrs. William Montgomery. "Colonel William
      Ball of Balleston, Maryland, and Millenbeck, Virginia;
      Great-Grandfather of George Washington." Repr. in
      413-1:74-80.
520 - Walne, Peter. "The English Ancestry of Colonel William
      Ball of Millenbeck." Repr. in 414-1:16-22.
521 - Baker, Henry E. "Benjamin Banneker, the Negro Mathema-
      tician and Astronomer." Journal of Negro History
      3 (April 1918) 99-118.
522 - Bedini, Silvio. The Life of Benjamin Banneker.
      New York:1971.
523 - Adams, William Frederick. Commodore Joshua Barney.
      Springfield:1912.
524 through 526 - Unassigned.
527 - Humphreys, Allan Sparrow. Some Maryland Baxters and
      Their Descendants. St. Louis:1948.
528 through 530 - Unassigned.
531 - Bennett, Archibald. "Bennett." Repr. in 415-1:285-
      287.
532 - Boddie, John Bennett. "Edward Bennett of London and
      415-1:270-284.
533 - Davis, Harry Alexander. The Billinglsey Family.
      Washington:1936.
534 through 537 - Unassigned.
538 - Bond Family Notes in 322 (see above).
539 - Bond, Henry. "Descendants of Peter Bond." Typescript,
      MHS.
540 - Hecklinger, Edwin G., and Edwin C. Boring. The Descen-
      dants of John Boreing, Maryland Planter. Cambridge:
      1950.
541 - Keith, A. L. "Bosley Notes." Typescript, MHS.
542 - Miller, Richard B. "James Bosley - Three of Them (The
      Case of Mistaken Identity)." BMGS 19 (1978) 17-19.
543 - Miller, Richard B. "The Three Hannahs." BMGS 20 (1979)
      188-191.
544 - Barnes, Robert W. "The Bowen Family of Baltimore Coun-
      ty, Maryland." MMG 3 (Spring 1980) 28-33.
545 - Barnes, Robert W. "The Bowen Family Reconsidered."
      MMG 4 (Spring 1981) 38-39.
546 - History of Strathendrick, pp. 330-334, cited in:
      Francis Joseph Baldwin. "Ancestral Records: Ellen
      Douglas Baldwin, nee Jamison." Typescript, MHS.
547 - Unassigned.
548 - Unassigned.

550 - Little Millie Albert. Chronicles of the Little-Lee and
       Albert-Buckingham Families. Westminster:1938.
       (also Little, Millie Albert. "The Buckingham Family."
       1938. Typescript, MHS).
551 - Unassigned.
552 - Unassigned.
553 - Walter V. Ball. The Butterworth Family of Maryland and
       Virginia. Silver Spring:1960.
554 through 557 - Unassigned.
558 - Same as no. 553 above.
559 - The Registers of the Parish of St. Mary, Reading,
       Berks., 1538-1812. Transcribed by Gibbs Payne Craw-
       furd. 2 vols. Reading:1891-1892.
560 - Carnan Family Notes. Wilson M. Cary Genealogical Col-
       lection. Folder F.17, MHS.
561 through 569 - Unassigned.
570 - Earp, Charles Albert. The Levi Chalk Family. Baltimore:
       1965.
571 - Evans, Regina. Carville Tudor Chalk and His Descen-
       dants, 1784-1970. n.p.;1970.
572 - Hyman, Minna Chalk. The Chalk Family of England and
       America, 1066-1942. Hyman:1942.
573 - Chapman family data compiled by Robert T. Nave and
       in this compiler's possession.
574 - Chapman family data compiled by Mrs. Kenneth Warren and
       in this compiler's possession,
575 - Beirne, Rosamond R. "The Reverend Thomas Chase: Pugna-
       cious Parson." MHM 59 (1964) 1-14.
576 - Hiatt, Cora Viola. History of the Chenoweth Family Be-
       ginning 449 A. D. Winchester:1925.
577 - Keith, Arthur L. "The Chenoweth Family." Repr. in
       413-1:348-355.
578 - Chenoweth, Alex. Crawford. Genealogy and Chart of the
       Chenoweth and Cromwell Families of Maryland and Vir-
       ginia. New York:1894.
579 - Unassigned.
580 - "Christie of Durie." in Sir Bernard Burke and Ashworth
       P. Burke. A Genealogical and Heraldic History of
       the Landed Gentry of Great Britain. London:1906.
       p. 318.
581 - Cameron, K. W. "Chart Four - The Early Colegate Line
       of Maryland." MHS.
582 - Abbe, Truman, and Herbert Abbe Howson. Robert Colgate
       the Immigrant. New Haven:1941.
583 - Collett, John D. Genealogy of the Descendants of John
       Collett. Indianapolis:1929.
584 - Mayor, J. E. B. "Ferrar Pedigree by John Farrar,
       1590-1657." Repr. in 414-2:777.

IV. UNNUMBERED ITEMS

The items in this section of the Bibliography are either
sources mentioned in the text pertaining to individual families,
or they are recent publications which have appeared in the last
few years. These are included because they may shed additional
light on the families of Baltimore County. Items in this section
of the Bibliography are arranged alphabetically by the family
discussed.

Schmitz, Maureen Collins. The AMOS Family. Dubuque:1964.
Johnston, Christopher. ASHMAN Chart. MHS.
BAIN Bible Record. NGSQ 59 (1971) 32.

(BAKER Family). Keech, Mabel L. A Partial History of the
DeWitt and Other Families. Chicago:1956.
"BAKER Bible Record." Maryland DAR Genealogical Records Com-
mittee Report. 32:78. Typescript, DAR Library in Washing-
ton, D. C.
BAKER Family data compiled by Mrs. Richard Turley and made
available to this compiler.
BALCH Queries. Genealogy and History. Queries 4821 and 4359.
BARNES Family. See under Dorsey Family: Dorsey et al, The
Family
Hiatt, Catherine C. A Partial View of the BEASMAN-BASEMAN
Family of Maryland. Baltimore:1986.
Barnes, Robert W. "Beasman Family of Baltimore County, Mary-
land." MDG 9 (1968) 16-17.
Bell, Edward J. Edward Johnzey BELL: His Ancestors and Descen-
dants. Bozeman:1970.
"BELT-Wells Bible Record." NEHGR. 110 (1956) 310-311.
Johnston, Christopher. "BELT Family." Repr. in 346-1:28-35.
Coldham, Peter W. "Major David BISSETT of Baltimore County,
Maryland, 1756." NGSQ 65 (1977) 259.
Johnston, Christopher. "BLADEN Famiuly." Repr. in 346-1:
43-45.
Barnes, Robert W. "BOSLEY Family Lineage." MDG 7 (1966)
16-18.
BOSLEY Family. Keith, Arthur Leslie. "Notes on Hardwick,...
and Related Families." Repr. in 415-3:623 ff.
BOYCE Family. Abercrombie, Ronald. "Sweet Air or Quinn, Bal-
timore County." MHM 38 (1943) 19-36.
Wirgman, Stewart Lux. "The BOWLY and Wirgman Families in
America." 1966. Typescript, MHS.
BRADFORD, Samuel Webster, Genealogical Collection. MS.1870,
MHS.
Hutton, Amy. "BUCHANAN Family Reminiscences." MHM 35 (1940)
262-269.
CARNAN Family. Musgrave, William. Obituary Prior to 1800.
The Harleian Society, vols. 44-49. London:1899-1901.
CARNAN Family. Page, William, ed. Vistoria History of the
Counties of England: A History of Berkshire, Volume I.
Haymarket:1905.
Barnes, Robert W. "Carnan Family." 259:6-10.
CHAPMAN Family. O'Dell,, Walter G. Letter to Editor.
The [Baltimore] Sun. 3 June 1906.
"Robert CHAPMAN of Baltimore County, Maryland, and His
Descendants." DAR Library, Washington, D. C.
Culver, Francis B. "CHEW Family." Repr. in 346-1:254-272.
Hopkins, Joseph Carroll. "Colonel Henry CHEW of Maryland
and North Carolina." MMG 5 (1982) 51-65.
CHILCOTT Family data compiled by Fred. M. Chilcott, and made
available to this compiler.
CHILCOTT Family. Jordan, John W. The Juniata Valley, 3 vols.
1913. 3:1157.
COCKEY Family. Keech, Mabel Louise. A Partial History of
the DeWitt, Boss, Chamberlain, Cromwell, D'Arcy, Cockey
and Allied Families. Chicago:1956.
Lantz, Emily Emerson. "Maryland Heraldry: COCKEY Lineage and
Arms." The [Baltimore] Sun. 24 June and 1 July 1906.
Rogers, Charles B. "The Progenitors and Descendants of Charles
Thomas COCKEY and of Susannah Delilah (Brown) Cockey, His
Wife." Ms., MHS.
Russell, George Ely. "Mr. William Vanheesdunk Riddleson,
Alias William CORNWALLIS: A 'Person of Matchless Charac-
ter.'" MMG 4 (1981) 57-60.
Elder, William Voss. "Bloomsbury, A CRADOCK House in the
Worthington Valley." MHM 53 (1958) 371-379.
Skaggs, David Curtis. "Thomas CRADOCK and the Chesapeake

Golden Age." William and Mary Quarterly, 3rd Series. 30
(1970). 95-99.
Thomas, Dawn F. "The Reverend Thomas CRADOCK: A Study of His
Life and Contributions." 1966. Paper submitted for Semi-
nar in Maryland History at Towson State College. copy, MHS.
CRESAP Family. High, James. "The Origins of Maryland's Mid-
dle Class in the Colonial Aristocratic Pattern." MHM 57
(1962) 341 ff.
Culver, Francis B. "CROMWELL Family: A Possible Clue."
Repr. in 346-1:339-356.
Johnston, Christopher. CROMWELL Family Chart. ms, MHS.
Barnes, Robert W. "CROXALL Family." 259:28-30.
Dallam, David E. The DALLAM Family. Philadelphia:1929.
"Nathaniel DAVIS." 398:33.
DEAN Family. Marks, Lillian Bayly. Reister's Desire: The
Origin of Reisterstown, Maryland. Baltimore:1975.
DEAVER Family. Hinshaw, William Wade. Encyclopedia of Ameri-
can Genealogy, Vol. VI. 1950. Repr. Baltimore:1973.
DEAVER Family. Pension Application. NGSQ 23 (1933) 52-53.
DIXON Family. See Pleasants, J. Hall. "Gorsuch and Love-
lace Families." Repr. in 414.
DORSEY Bible Record. NGSQ 5:46.
Bulkeley, Caroline Kemper. "Identity of Edward DORSEY I: A
New Approach to an Old Problem." Repr. in 346-1:377-406.
Culver, Francis B. "Priscilla of the DORSEYS: A Century Old
Mystery." Repr. in 346-1:406-409.
Dorsey, Maxwell J., Jean Muir Dorsey, and Nannie Ball Nimmo.
The DORSEY Family. n.p.:1947.
DOWNEY Family. 382-1:609.
Lord, Mrs. Jere Williams. "Genealogy of the Dukehart Family."
1954. Typescript.
DURBIN FAMILY. Heinemann, Charles B. First Census of Kentuc-
ky, 1790. 1940. Repr. Baltimore:1981.
Bate, Kerry W. "Thomas DURBIN of Baltimore County, Maryland."
MDG 15 (1974) 56-57, 80-82.
Welch, Edwin C. "DURBIN Family," MDG, 3:67-68.
ENLOE, Thomas A., Genealogical Collection. MS.5099, MHS.
"Diary of John EVANS." Transcript, Lovely Lane United Methodist
Church Museum, Baltimore.
FLOYD Family records of Laurence Hall, made available to this
compiler.
Nimmo, Nannie Ball. "Ford Notes," MHS.
FORD Family. Focke, Ferdinand B. "The Linthicum Family of
Anne Arundel County, Maryland, and Branches." Repr. in
346-2:155-168.
FORD Family data compiled by Mark B. Ford and made available
to this compiler.
FORD Family notes compiled by Robert T. Nave and made available
to this compiler.
FOTTRELL Family. Johnston, Christopher. "Lloyd Family."
Repr. 346-2:169-179.
Culver, Francis B. "Frisby Family." Repr. in 346-1:451-467.
GARRETT Family. Crowe, Maud . Descendants of First Families
of Virginia and Maryland. Washington: the Author, 1978.
Garréttson, Earl Aquila. "The GARRETTSON Family." Typescript,
MHS.
Axford, Elizabeth. GARRETTSON Family Chart, in possession of
this compiler.
Peden, Henry C., Jr. GILBERT Records in Harford County,
Maryland. Bel Air:1986.
Major, Nettie Leach. "Gilbert Family." MDG 19 (1978) 18-21.
GILBERT Family. See under Horner Family, gen. by Hinds.
Gill, James D. The GILL Family of Maryland 1642, 1659, and
and 1950. n.p.:1970.
Dorsey, Jean Muir, and Maxwell J. Dorsey. Christopher GIST
of Maryland and Some of His Descendants, Chicago:1958.

Johnston, Christopher. "GIST Family of Baltimore County."
    Repr. in 346-1:504-512
Goodwin, John S. "GOODWIN Families of America." Repr. in
    415-2:417 ff.
Overman, Michael. A GORSUCH Pedigree. n.p.:1982.
Pleasants, J. Hall. "GORSUCH and Lovelace Families." Repr.
    414-3:232-546.
Johnston, Christopher. GOTT Family Chart. MHS.
Gott, John K. "GOTT Family of Maryland and Fairfax County,
    Virginia." MDG 7 (1966) 38-40, 64-65.
Uhrbrock, Richard S, "GOTT Family." MDG 7 (1966) 65-66, 84-85.
GRAPE Family Bible Record. BMGS 13 (1972) 277-278.
Raskob, John Jacob, and Helena   Green Raskob. Raskob-
    GREEN Record Book. Claymont:1921.
GREER Family data of Mrs. James Mero of Hampton, Virginia,
    and graciously made available to the compiler.
Revolutionary Pension Application of Aaron GUYTON. NGSQ
    21 (1931) 48-50.
(HAILE Family). "Heale Family." Repr. in 415-3:1-6.
Cameron, K. W. "Chart One: The HALL Family." MHS.
"HANSON Family Bible Record." BMGS 3 (1962) 26-29.
(HARROTT/HARRIOTT Family). Keith, Arthur L. "Notes on Hard-
    wick (Hardridge), Kincheloe, McCarty, McConathy, Crook,
    Dawson, Lawson, and Related Families." Repr. in 415-3:
    609-629.
Barnes, Robert W. "HARRYMAN Family." MDG 7 (1966) 36-37.
(HAWKINS Family). Nimmo, Nannie Ball. "The Rockholds of
    Early Maryland." Repr. in 346-2:312-317.
HAY Family Bible Record. MDG 9 (1968) 79.
"Jacob HOOK Bible." BMGS 20 (1979) 344.
(HOOPER Family). See 330:13.
Hinds, Virginia Horner. Our HORNER Ancestors. Chicago:1974.
Howard, Cary. "John Eager Howard: Patriot and Public Ser-
    vant." MHM 62 (1967) 300-317.
Howard, McHenry.   "Family of John Eager Howard." Repr. in
    415-3:71-73.
(HOWARD Family). "Recreation of Grey Rock, Baltimore County."
    MHM 50 (1955) 82-92.
Ogburn, Fielding. "Benjamin HOWARD, 1742-1828, of Maryland
    and North Carolina." NGSQ 64 (1976) 13-14.
Howard, Charles. "HOWARD Family." Ms., MHS.
(HOWARD Family). 259:38-45; 398:242-244, 290-295, 332-335,
    337-338.
Barnes, Robert W. "HUNT Family." 259:45-48.
Crowther, Rodney G., III. "JOHNS Family Tree." MDG 4 (1963)
    58-59, 75-77.
"JONES Bible Records." Repr. in 346-2:106-109.
Kendall, (?). "LANE Notes." ms, MHS.
Slagle, A. Russell. "Major Samuel LANE (1628-1681): His
    Ancestry and Some American Descendants." Repr. in 346-2:
    128-141.
(LAWSON Family). See article by Arthur L. Keith cited under
    Harrott/Harriott Family above.
Focke, Ferdinand B. "LINTHICUM Family of Anne Arundel Coun-
    ty and Branches." Repr. in 346-2:155-164.
Bate, Kerry William. "LITTON and Jones Families of Baltimore
    County, Maryland." TAG 53 (1977) 23.
Johnston, Christopher. "LLOYD Family." Repr. in 346-3:
    169-179.
Welch, Edwin C. "The Maryland LOGSDON Family." 1947. Type-
    script, MHS.
Johnston, Christopher. LYON Family Chart. MHS.
LYON Genealogical Collection. G.5034, MHS.
Cameron, K. W. "Chart Five: Our Early LYTLE or Little An-
    cestors." MHS.

Dorman, John Frederick. "MAYNARD Family of Frederick County, Maryland." NGSQ 48 (1960) 187-195.

McComas, Henry Clay, and Mary Winona McComas. The McCOMAS Saga: A Family History Down to the Year 1950. Baltimore: 1950.

Culver, Francis B. "MERRYMAN Family." Repr. in 346-2:208-232.

Martin, Mrs. John N. "MERRYMAN Notes." Repr. in 415-4: 625-627.

(MITCHELL Family). See Horner Gen. by Hinds under Horner Family above.

(MOALE Family). See 414:3:356-359.

"MUMFORD and Munford Families." Repr. in 413-2:736-745.

Lee, Harry H. "Mumford Family." MDG 3 (1962) 65-67.

Barnes, Robert W. Descendants of James MURRAY and Jemima Morgan of Baltimore County. Baltimore:1964.

Thorne, Zelda Norman. NORMANS of Maryland. n.p.:1972.

Josserand, Gertrude Cleghorn. Kentucky Descendants of Thomas NORRIS of Maryland, 1630-1953. Ann Arbor:1953.

Myers, Thomas M. NORRIS Family of Maryland. New York:1916.

(NORTH Family). Chippindall, [Col.] W. W. A History of Whittington. Vol. 99, new series. Chetham Society. Manchester: 1938.

(NORTH Family). See 414-3:351-355.

"ODELL Family Cemetery Inscriptions." NGSQ 25 (1937) 61.

Focke, Ferdinand B. "Owen-Owens-OWINGS and Allied Families." ms, MHS.

Focke, Ferdinand B. "Thomas Deye OWINGS of Maryland: Soldier and Pioneer of the West; A Record of His Life." MHM 30 (1935) 39-41.

(OWINGS Family). "Old Maryland Bibles." Repr. in 346-2: 270-278.

Owings, Addison D., and Elizabeth S. Owings. OWINGS and Allied Families. New Orleans:1976.

Owings, Rev. H. Duane. "OWINGS Burial ground." BMGS 22 (1981) 148-149.

Silverman, Albert. "William PACA, Signer, Governor, Jurist." MHM 37 (1942) 1-25.

(PARTRIDGE Family). See 387.

Pearce, Marvin J. PEARCE Pioneers in Kentucky. El Ceritto: 1969.

Lee, Harry H. "PEREGOY-Perrigo Family Marriage Records of Baltimore County." MDG 5 (1964) 35, 55, 75.

Brannan, Pauline Mae. The POE Family Line. Bel Air:1974.

Culver, Francis B. "Lineage of Edgar Allan POE." MHM 37 (1942) 420-422.

Cameron, K. W. "Chart Three: The Early PRESBURY LINES." MHS.

————, "Chart Six: Children of George PRESBURY of William." MHS.

(PRESTON Family). See Horner Gen. by Hinds, under Horner Family above.

Preston, John Frederick. The PRESTON Genealogical Story. Washington:1963.

Buxton, Mrs. Robert J. "The PRIBBLES of Kentucky." Kentucky Ancestors 12 (1976) 19-23.

"RICHARDSON Family of Baltimore County, Maryland." BMGS 17 (1976) 21-22.

Johnston, Christopher. RIDDELL Family Chart. MHS.

(RIDGELY Family). Scarff, John H. "'Hampton,' Baltimore County, Maryland." MHM 43 (1948) 96-107.

Forman, Henry Chandlee. "The Family of Colonel James RIGBIE." Repr. in 346-2:303-312.

Levin, Alexandra Lee. "Colonel Nicholas ROGERS and His Country Seat, 'Druid Hill.'" MHM 72 (1977) 78-82.

(ROGERS Family). See 272.

Johnston, Christopher. ROGERS Family Chart. MHS.
Lantz, Emily Emerson. "Maryland Heraldry: The SATER Lineage
   and Arms." The [Baltimore] Sun. 14 Jan, and 21 Jan. 1906.
Maclay, Isaac Walker. "Henry SATER, 1690-1754." 1897.
   Typescript, MHS.
Barnett, Mrs. G. L. "SHIPLEY-Barnett Bible Records." BMGS
   15 (1974) 22-27.
Nelker, Mrs. Marshall H. "James SLEMAKER Family." BMGS 19
   (1978) 145-147.
Johnston, Christopher. "SMITH Family of Calvert County."
   Repr. in 346-2:373-386.
(SOLLERS Family). See 387.
Johnston, Christopher. "STANSBURY Family." Repr. in 346-2:
   398-415.
Scheffell, Iva. Genealogy of the STANSBURY Family, 1658-1938;
   Supplement and Index. Mountain View:1942.
STINCHCOMB Cemetery Inscriptions. NGSQ 20 (1930) 69.
Swope, Gilbert Ernest. History of the SWOPE Family. Lancas-
   ter:1896.
Saul, Edith Ray. "Descendants of Richard TAYLOR, Quaker Emi-
   grant." MDG 13 (1974) 68-69, 90-91.
Sinclair, Carroll Taylor. "The TAYLOR Family of Maryland."
   6 vols. 1964. Typescript, MHS.
"Giles THOMAS Family Record." NGSQ 66 (1978) 64.
(TIBBS Family). See 330:9-13.
Heinemann, Charles B. "TIPTON Family of Maryland." Type-
   script, MHS.
Tipton, Ervin Charles. We TIPTONS and Our Kin. San Rafael:
   1975.
(TODD Family). See 414-3:265 ff.
Tolley, Oscar Kemp. "TOLLEY Family Records." 1940. Type-
   script, MHS.
Wheeler, Towson Ames. "TOWSON Genealogy." c.1966. Type-
   script, MHS.
Dodge, Mrs. Frank Riley. "TOWSON Family of Maryland."
   Typescript, MHS.
Treadway, Oswell Garland. Edward TREADWAY and His Descen-
   dants. Chicago:1931.
Tredway, William Thomas. History of the TREDWAY Family.
   Pittsburgh:1930.
Treadway, William E. TREADWAY and Burkett Families. n.p.:
   1951.
Walker, Henry M. "Biographical Notes of the Walker Family."
   MHS.
"Captain John UTIE of Utimara, Esq." Repr. in 413-5:298-304.
High, Paul A. "Millard Fillmore WATKINS Family Bible."
   BMGS 11 (1970) 15-17.
Watkins Family nites. See 360.
Watkins Family data compiled by Bradleugh V. Slattery who
   has graciously made it available to this author.
Welch, Edwin C. "Evidences of the WELCH-WELSH-WALSH Families
   in Baltimore County Maryland During the 17th and 18th
   Centuries." 1960. Typescript, MHS.
"WELLS (Dupuis) Bible Records." Annotated by Mary Keysor
   Meyer. MMG 1 (1978) 9-11.
(WELLS Family). Justice, Alfred Rudulph. "Genealogical
   Research in England: Addendum: The Weston Family." English
   Origins of New England Families. Baltimore. 1 (1984)
   582-588.
Ball, Walter V. John WHEELER, 1630-1683, of Charles County
   and Some of His descnedants. Chevy Chase:1966.
Dexter, M. L. "WHIPS Bible Records." BMGS 17 (1976) 165-168.
Cameron, K. W. "Chart Two: Relationships Between the WHITE,
   Hall, and Presbury Families." MHS.
Wilbank, William White. "Colonel Thomas WHITE of Maryland."
   Pennsylvania Magazine of History and Biography 1 (1877)
   420-438.

Bronson, William White. Account of the Meeting of the Descendants of Colonel Thomas WHITE of Maryland, Held at Sophia's Dairy, on the Bush River, Maryland, June 7, 1877. Philadelphia:1879.

(WILMOT Family). See 578.

(WILMOT Family). Culver, Francis B. "Last Bloodshed of the Revolution." MHM 5 (1910) 329-334.

Durham, Helen Davis Gibson. WOODEN, Wooding, Woodin and Allied Families. n.p.:n.d.

Hopkins, Joseph Carroll. "Charles WORTHINGTON, Planter." BMGS 23 (1982) 71-82.

Batchelder, Wm. G. "William WRIGHT Family of Maryland." MDG 6 (1965) 91-92.

Hunt, John G. "English Ancestry of George YATE (c.1640-1691) of Maryland." NGSQ 64 (1976) 176-180.

This index includes names of individuals
and names of tracts of land.

BAYARD, Nicholas 323
BAYES, Eliz. 509
  Elizabeth 572
  John 33, 41
  John, Jr. 572
  Ruth 572
  Bayley 611
BAYL(E)Y, Ann
  (WELCH) 671
  Elizabeth (GILL)
  255
  Godfrey 33, 611
  John 92, 498, 545,
  628, 671
  Lucy Ann 92, 692
  Mary 281, 476
  Thomas 677
  William 255
BAYLEY - See BAILEY
BAYLIS, Catherine
  (SAMFORD) 638
  Marcy 638
  Thomas 638
BAYLOR, John 644
  Lucy (TODD) 644
  Bayly 430
BAYLY - See BAILEY
BAYNE, Ann 19
  Catherine 19
  John 19
  Mary 19
  Mary (WEBER) 19
  William 19
BAYNE - See BAIN
BAYNES, Christopher
  33
  John 497
BAYS, Allinor
  (HARRYMAN) 306
  Eleanor (HARRYMAN)
  33
  John 33, 41, 306,
  573
BAYSPOLE, John 18,
  33
BAZE, (?) 275
  Ann (GRAY) 275
BEACH, Elizabeth 35
  Henry 35
  Jane (GARVIN) 35
  Thomas 35
BEACH - See BEECH
BEAL, Samuel 33
  Thomas 33
Beal's Camp 135
BEALE, Edward 212
BEALL, Sarah
  (GIBSON) 250
BEALLY, (?) 220
  Eleanor (FLANAGAN)
  220
  Nelly (FLANAGAN)
  220
BEAMSLEY, Mary 33,
  382
  Thomas 33

BEANS, Christopher
  33
BEAR, Michael 684
Bear Garden 487
Bear Hill 532
Bear Neck 64
Bear's Range 514
Bear's Thicket 356
BEARD, Cas. 198
  James 441
  John 441
  Susanna 532
  William 34
BEARDY, Christian
  565
  Christiana 34
  William 479
BEASLEY, Elizabeth
  34, 404
BEASMAN, Anne 34
  Elizabeth 34
  Elizabeth (HAWKINS)
  311
  Helen 34
  John 34
  Joseph 34, 311, 479
  Katherine 34
  Mary 34
  Mary (PERSIAS) 34
  Rachel 34, 479
  Ruth 34
  Ruth (HAMILTON) 34
  Sarah 34, 479
  Sarah (GORSUCH) 34,
  268
  Sarah (OGG) 479
  Thomas 34, 268
  William 34, 479
BEASON, Diana 34
  Nicholas 34, 390,
  391
BEATTY, Archibalds
  321
BEATY, John 34
Beautiful Island
  346
BEAVAN, John 39
  Sarah 39
Beavan's Adventure
  9
BEAVEN, John, Sr. 34
BEAVENS, John 34
BEAVENS - See BEVAN,
  BEVINS
BEAVER, Blanche 34
  Francis 34
  Henry 34
  John 15, 34, 312,
  588
  Mary 34
  Michael 34
  Sarah 472, 473
  Sarah (HAWKINS) 34,
  312
  Thomas 436
  William 34

Beaver Neck 201,
  292, 354, 389,
  426, 464, 622,
  640, 656
BECHLEY, Frances,
  Mrs. 34
BECK, Ann 35, 665
  Ann (HORNER) 340
  Anne 719
  Avarilla 35, 592
  Charles 35, 592
  Clemency 35
  Elijah 35, 665
  Elisha 35
  Martha (GREENLEAF)
  35
  Mary 35
  Mary (GROVES) 35
  Matthew 35, 340,
  341, 550, 592, 665
  Samuel 35, 665
  Sarah (BAKER) 35
BECKETT, Symon 35
BECKHAM, Jno. 35
BECKLEY, Frances 447
BEDDOE, John 35, 405
  Sarah (LITTEN) 35
  Sarah (LITTON) 405
BEDDOES, Sarah 658
BEDELL, Edward 74,
  215, 243, 244,
  365, 693
  Martha 74
  Mary Ann 74
Bedford 15, 338,
  407
BEDFORD, John 35
  Sarah 35, 253
Bedford Resurveyed
  49, 138, 578
Bedlam 201, 300
BEDLE, Edward 261
BEECH, Elizabeth 35
  Elizabeth Voss 700
  Henry 35, 700
  Jane (GARVIN) 35
  Thomas 35
BEECHAM, Ann
  (BURTON) 35
  John 35
BEECHER, Edith
  (CROMWELL) 35,
  146, 257, 692
  John 35, 146, 257,
  692
BEEDLE, Edward 35,
  99, 186, 243, 292,
  656
  Henry 674
  Martha 35, 292, 424
  Mary 35, 292, 656
  Mary (GARRETT) 243
  Mary Ann 292
  Sophia (EWEN) 674
Beedle's Reserve 35
Beef Hall 392

BOSTON, Samuel,
Capt. 64, 690
Sarah 60
BOS(S)WELL, Ann 60,
572
James 60
John 60
John Irvine 112
Margaret (CHRISTIE)
112
Mary (CHANLEY) 60
Mary (JENNINGS) 60
Ruth 60
Solvolitte 60, 504
Thomas 60
William 603
BOSWITH, John 60
BOSWORTH, Daniel 60
John 553
Mary (ROBINSON) 553
BOTT, Ketura (PRICE)
60
Richard 60
BOTTOM, Rachel 660
BOTTS, Abraham 60
Avarilla 60
George 60
Isaac 60
John 60, 567
Mary 60
Sarah 60
Sarah (WOOD) 60
BOUCHELLE, Mary 207
BOUCHER, Richard 60
Susannah 60
Bouer's Purchase
542
Bought Dear   626,
649
Bought Well   440
Boughton Ashley   272
Boughton's Forest
71, 187, 496, 589
BOULDIN, William 60
BOULDING, William
640, 678
BOULIN, Eliza 97
John 97
BOULSON, Elizab.
(STEWART) 60
John 60
BOULTON, Ann
(HIGGINSON) 60
Charles 60
BOURDILLON,
Alexander, Rev.
716
Andrew Theodore 716
Benedict, Rev. 60
David 61
Jacob 61
Jane 716
Janette Jansen 61
Johanna Gertrude
(JANSSEN) 61
Thomas 61

BOURDILLON, William
Benedict 61
BOURN, Barbara
(BURKE) 61
John 61
Bourne   254
BOURNE, Jasper 38
Mary 38
BOURTON, Denes
(GOODWIN) 263
John 263
Bow Creek   379, 468
Bow's Lot   251
BOWDEN, (?) 416
Elizabeth (LUX) 416
John 61
Mary 716
Robert 716
Bowden's Adventure
630
Bowden's Liberty   61
BOWEN, (?) 696
Ann 61, 63, 323
Ann (PAULING) 534
Ann (REEVES) 61
Anne 63
Aquila 62
Basil 63
Bejamin 495
Benjamin 10, 61,
62, 63, 96, 142,
199, 221, 248,
319, 330, 332,
337, 364, 384,
386, 411, 418,
432, 445, 476,
633, 665
Catherine 63
Charles 63
Chloe 63
Clarkson 582
Claxson 63
Claxton 596
Edward 16, 62, 63,
604, 654
Elam 63
Eleanor 63
Eleanor (WILMOT)
696
Eli 63
Elijah 62, 63
Eliza 62, 69
Elizabeth 61, 62,
63, 551
Elizabeth
(HETHERINGTON) 62
Elizabeth
(HUMPHREYS) 63
Hannah 63
Honor 61
Honour 63, 602
Jacob 63
James 63, 471
Jehu 63, 596
Jemima (EVANS) 62

BOWEN, Jemima
(MERRYMAN) 62, 445
John 61, 62, 63,
134, 330, 480,
595, 700, 707
John, Jr. 116, 542,
551
Jonas 10, 61, 62,
63, 69, 84, 134,
196, 266, 270,
275, 319, 417,
444, 458, 534,
551, 586, 602,
659, 696, 700
Joseph 63
Joshua 62, 63
Josiah 62
Josias 62, 63, 563,
605
Katherine 63
Lydia 63
Margaret (ROBINSON)
63
Martha 61, 62, 110,
197, 417, 444,
453, 495, 520,
534, 583, 598, 602
Martha (HENCHMAN)
61
Mary 61, 62, 63,
276, 595
Mary (CARR) 62, 96
Mary (RUXTON) 61
Mary (SOLLERS) 62,
63
Milcah 707
Milcha (CLARKSON)
116
Naomi 62
Nathan 62, 354,
418, 595
Prudence
(STANSBURY) 63
Rebecca 61
Rebecca 275, 319,
551
Rebecca (STANSBURY)
604
Reese 63, 566
Rosanna 62, 582
Rosanna (ROBINSON)
551
Ruth 62
Ruth (WILMOT) 696
Sabrett 63
Samuel 62, 63, 499,
566
Sarah 61, 62, 63,
418
Sarah (STANSBURY)
605
Solomon 62, 207
Tabitha 62, 64
Temperance 62, 63
Temperance (ENSOR)
62, 207

DORSEY, John Hammond
115, 180, 181,
199, 247, 298,
431, 567, 646
John Hammond, Jr.
181
John, Col. 179,
180, 181, 488
John, Hon. 178, 180
John, Sr. 668
Jos'h 394, 578
Joshua 178, 179,
180, 181, 220, 539
Ketura 181
Kezia 179
Lacon 178, 179
Larkin 179
Lucretia 180
Lucy 179
Lydia 180
Margaret 179
Margaret (LACON/
LARKIN) 178, 353
Martha (GAITHER)
180
Mary 181, 543
Mary (BELT) 37, 180
Mary (CROCKETT) 145
Mary (SLADE) 180,
585
Mary Hammond 181
Maxwell J. 178
Nancy Dorsey
(ELDER) 180
Nathan 486
Nicholas 178, 179,
180, 181, 187, 464
Nicholas, Col. 180
Orlando 180
Patrick 182
Peregrine 180
Phebe 178
Pleasance 178, 396,
659
Pleasance (ELY) 542
Priscilla 95, 179,
180, 463
Priscilla Ridgely
696
Providence 180
Rachel 180
Rachel (EWING) 181
Rebecca 181, 543
Ruth 178, 180
Samuel 32, 178,
179, 465, 703
Sarah 48, 148, 178,
179, 180, 298, 498
Sarah (BOND) 48
Sarah (DAY) 162,
180, 181
Sarah (FELL) 180
Sarah (GRIFFITH)
179, 180
Sarah (RICHARDSON)
178

DORSEY, Sarah
(RICHARSON) 539
Sarah (WYATT) 178
Sophia 179, 180
Sophia (OWINGS)
181, 486
Stephen 181
Sylvia (HEATHCOTE)
181, 317
Thomas 179
Thomas Bond 48
Thomas Edward 214
Vachel 21, 22, 180
Venesha 298
Venetia 179, 180
Vincent 162, 180,
181, 298, 438, 646
Dorsey's Addition
179, 463
Dorsey's Goodwill
22
Dorsey's Plains 187
Dorsey's Prospect
181
DORTRIDGE - See
DOTTRIDGE
DORUMPLE - See
DERUMPLE
DOTTRIDGE, Leah 182
Lettice 182
Lettice (TAYLOR)
182
Margaret (MURPHY)
182
Rachel 182
Sarah 182
William 182, 712
Zelpha 182
Double Diligence
141
Double Trouble 713
DOUBTY, Luraner
(POULSON) 182
Thomas 182
DOUCE, Edward 459
DOUGH, Bridget 182
Elizabeth 182
DOUGHERTY, William
182, 667
DOUGHTERY, Nathaniel
212
DOUGHTERY - See
DAUGHERTY
DOUGLAS, (?) 483
Alen's 182
Anne 699
Mary 182
Mary (SCUTT) 570
Sarah (ORRICK) 483
William 570
DOUGLASS, Mary
(KNOWLES) 390
DOUSE, Edward 305
DOUSE - See DOWSE
DOVER, John 704
DOWCRA, Thomas 434

DOWELL, Ann Wilson
182
Charity 182
Edward 304
Elizabeth 182
John 182
Luke 182
Mary Breshiers 182
Peter 62, 182, 275,
499, 567
Philip 182, 337
Richard 182
DOWLAS, Robert 164
DOWLEY - See DOOLEY
DOWLING, Daniel 182
DOWNES, Denny 76
Jere. 324
Jeremiah 168, 322,
518
John 40, 139, 189,
564, 652, 717
Margaret 139
Mary (DELAP) 168
Susanna 687
DOWNES - See DOWNS
DOWNEY, Ann 182,
183, 713
Ann (COUDREY) 183
Ann (COWDREY) 139
Beatrix 183
Daniel 183, 711
Frances 183
Hannah 183
James 182, 183
John 182, 183, 619
Joseph 183
Lydia (SWIFT) 182,
619
Mary 182, 183
Mary (YATES) 183
Ruhama (STOCKSDALE)
183
Sarah 182, 408
Thomas 139, 183
William 183
DOWNIE, Christian
(CHRISTIE) 111
Michael 111
DOWNING, John 641
Margaret 641
William, Capt. 641
DOWNMAN, Priscilla
289
DOWNS, Ann 183
Bridget 183
Darby 183
Denny 183
Elizabeth 183
Elizabeth
(COLEGATE) 125
Gulielmus (GOODEN)
183
Jere. 362
Jeremiah 183
John 92, 183, 189
Kedemoth 183

GARRET(T), Francis
243
Garrett 243
Hannah 242
Henry 50, 88, 242,
427
Isaac 242
James 243, 496
Jno. 243
Joanna 70
Johanna 120, 206,
243
Johanna (PEAKE)
243, 496
John 21, 242
Margaret (BAKER)
21, 243
Martha 242
Martha (PRESBURY)
244, 517
Mary 242, 243, 519,
701
Mary (BAKER) 21
Mary (BUTTERWORTH)
88, 242
Richard 85, 242
Rutgerston 204
Ruth 28, 242
Rutten 243
Sarah 131, 242
Stephen 257
Urath (GILL) 257
GARRETTS, Garrett
243
Rutgertson 308
Rutten 243
Somelia 243
GARRETTSON, (?) 301,
590
Aquila 245
Avarilla (HANSON)
245
Benjamin 245
Bennett 244, 245
Bridget 124
Catherine (NELSON)
244, 466
Cordelia 244, 245
Edward 244, 245
Eliza 244, 245
Elizabeth 244, 245
Elizabeth
(CANTWELL) 124
Elizabeth
(FREEBORN) 229,
244, 245
Frances 244, 245
Freeborn 244, 245,
626
Freenata 244
Garrett 75, 99,
169, 184, 229,
244, 245, 308,
360, 413, 625, 646
Garrett 'foter' 35

GARRETTSON, George
244, 424, 517
Goldsmith 244
Henry 124
James 244, 245, 466
Job 174, 207
John 244, 245, 482
Martha 245, 424,
447
Martha (PRESBURY)
244, 517
Mary 244, 646
Mary Goldsmith 244
Priscilla (NELSON)
245
Richard 244, 245
Ruthen/Rutten 244,
711
Sarah 244, 245
Sarah (HANSON) 244,
301
Semelia 711
Somelia 244, 301
Sophia 244, 245
Susanna (HIGGINSON)
75
Susannah (ROBINSON)
245
Thomas 244
GARRISON, Cornelius
511
Elizabeth 245
Elizabeth (FRAZIER)
245
Elizabeth Ady 420
Garrett 245
George 473
Harriett 245
Job 245, 420
Mary 245
Paul 245
Rebecca 245
Shadrack 245
Susanna (POCOCK)
511
Susanna Lavinia 24
Susannah (NORRIS)
473
William 245
Garrison Ridge 47
GARROD, Elizabeth
245
Hustice 245
Leonard 245
Mary 245
GARVIN, Jane 35, 700
GARVISE, Ann 245
GARY, (?) 210
Edward 210
Everett 210
Laurence 210
Sarah 210
GASCON, Robert 246
GASEMAN, Mary 246
GASH, Blanch 246
Eliza 246

GASH, Elizabeth
(PRESTON) 251
Hannah (GILBERT)
246, 252
Hannah (GILBERT)
246
Johanna 246, 481,
676
Johannah (GILBERT)
246
Mary 246
Michael 246, 251
Nicholas 247
Sarah 84, 246
Thomas 34, 246,
252, 481, 500
Gash's Discovery
247
Gash's Neglect 588
Gash's Purchase
246, 481
GASKIN - See GASCON
GASON, Robert 246
GASQUOINE - See
GASCON
GASSAWAY, Anne 329
Hester (BESSON) 40
John 703
Margaret
(PIERPOINT) 246,
507
Nicholas 40, 246,
394, 411
Nicholas, Jr. 246,
507
Rachel 246
Thomas 246
Gassaway's Addition
246
Gassaway's Ridge
598
GATCH, Ann 247
Benjamin 247
Catherine 247
Conduce 247
Conduel 247
Conjuist 247
Conrad 247
Cornrow 247
Elizabeth 247
Frederick 221, 247
Godfrey 246, 247
Hannah (SHAW) 247
Maria 246
Mary 247
Nicholas 247
Philip 247
Presocia (BURGAN)
247
Rachel (DAUGHADAY)
221
Sarah 247
Thomas 247
William 247
GATES, Amos 675
Nathan 675

GILBERT, Mary
(FOWLER 253
Mary (TAYLOR) 251
Mich. 652
Michael 189, 246,
250, 251, 252,
253, 519, 701
Michael, Jr. 250
Nem 252
Preston 251
Rachel 251, 252,
253, 419, 437
Rebecca 252, 344
Rebecca (HOW) 342
Robert 250
Ruth 44, 252, 253
Samuel 176, 251,
437, 460, 465, 670
Sarah 251, 252,
342, 458
Sarah (BEDFORD) 35,
253
Sarah (PRESTON)
251, 519
Solomon 251
Susanna 251, 253
Thomas 35, 250,
252, 253, 324,
581, 582
Thomas, Jr. 252,
253
William 251, 253
Gilbert's Addition
251, 451
Gilbert's Adventure
253
Gilbert's Chance
251
Gilbert's Outlet
183, 251, 451
GILBOURNE, Mary
(PINDER) 253
Thomas 253
GILCHREST, Eleanor
(WELCH) 655
Helen 253
Helena (WELCH) 655,
671
Robert 655, 671
GILCHRIST, Helen 253
James 253
Robert 253
William 253
GILCOAT, Alexander
253
Mary 253
Robert 253
GILCREST, Robert 179
Gile's Addition 254
Gilead 486
GILES, (?) 50
Ann (BOND) 50, 214
Anna 254
Anna Maria 148
Aquila 255
Artridge 253

GILES, Betty 254,
402
Cassandra 339
Cassandra (SMITH)
254
Edward 255
Eliza 255
Elizabeth 253, 254,
255, 540, 770
Elizabeth (ARNOLD)
254
Hannah 254
Hannah
(BUTTERWORTH) 568
Hannah (WEBSTER)
254
Hannah Kitty 106
Hester 254
Jacob 27, 34, 39,
66, 166, 169, 230,
253, 254, 255,
273, 296, 318,
331, 333, 342,
362, 377, 396,
406, 418, 504,
511, 516, 526,
537, 552, 560,
631, 669, 675,
678, 708, 709, 715
James 214, 255
Johannah 255
Johannah (PHILLIPS)
254, 504
John 14, 96, 148,
220, 253, 254,
255, 288, 313,
339, 393, 402,
464, 509, 540,
568, 626, 671, 709
Margaret 311
Mary 121, 253, 254,
255
Nathaniel 253, 254,
626, 770
Rachel 255
Rebecca 255
Richard 311
Samuel 255
Sarah 254, 255,
339, 464
Sarah (BUTTERWORTH)
88, 254
Sarah (WELSH) 148,
254
Sophia 254, 464
Thomas 255
Thomas John 88
Giles and Webster's
Discovery 199,
200, 366, 368,
431, 535, 536, 669
GILHAMPTON - See
GALHAMPTON
GILL, Alice 47, 255
Benjamin 257

GILL, Cassandra
(COLE) 121
Charles 223
Edward 256, 538
Eleanor 256, 509
Elizabeth 133, 224,
255, 256, 493
Elizabeth (HUBBERT)
256
Elizabeth Rogers
256
Jane 255, 256, 393,
656
Jane (GUINN) 255
Jemima (MURRAY) 257
John 29, 71, 100,
132, 224, 255,
256, 268, 509,
555, 668
Joshua 256
Leah (BARNEY) 29
Mary 255, 257, 703
Mary (ROGERS) 132,
256, 509, 555
Nicholas 256, 257
Priscilla (FORD)
223
Prudence 119, 256,
257
Rachel 256
Rachel (GILL) 256
Ruth 257
Ruth (CROMWELL) 147
Ruth (RICHARDS)
256, 538
Sarah 132, 256, 555
Sarah (GORSUCH)
224, 268
Stephen 47, 87,
119, 121, 255,
256, 257, 349,
396, 434, 493, 525
Stephen, Jr. 256
Steven, Jr. 256
Susanna 257
Thomas 256
Urath 257
Urath (BUTLER) 256
Urith (BUTLER) 87
William 147, 256,
555
Gill's Fancy 255,
256, 660
Gill's Outlet 255
Gill's Range 256
GILLESPIE, Elizabeth
(MAXWELL) 257, 431
Robert 257, 431
GILLETT, Ambrose
230, 257, 343
Jane 257, 343
Thomas 257
GILLHAM, Ralph 257
Sarah 257
GILLIAN - See
GILLHAM

818

HARPER, John 303,
443, 543
Mary (SHIELDS) 303
Samuel 303
Sarah 303
Sarah (MACCRAREE)
303
Thomas 303
William 665
HARPLE, Edward 303
HARPS, Susanna 478
Susannah 477
Harr's Park 511
HARRAPP, Thomas 303
HARRARD, Mary 8
HARRIDE, Oliver 504
HARRINGTON, Charles
652
Cornelius 333, 447
Jacob 519
HARRINGTON - See
HERRINGTON
HARRIOT, Oliver 184
Unity 184
HARRIOTT, Ambrose
304
Ann (RICHARDSON)
304, 539
Ann (TAYLOR) 280
Elizabeth 304
Mary 8, 304
Oliver 8, 280, 304,
327, 459, 539, 570
Oliver, Jr. 304
Richard 304
Susanna 304
Susanna (MORROW)
304, 459
Unity 304
William 304
Harriott's Hope 304
HARRIS, (?) 304
Agnes 200
Ann 304, 305
Bathsheba (BARLOW)
27, 304
Benjamin 305
Catharine 10
Charles 305
Darcas 305
Dorothy 514
Dorothy (ROGERS)
305, 555
Edward 304
Eleanor 155, 305
Eleanor (ROGERS)
555
Elizabeth 124, 149,
305, 450, 491
Elizabeth (HOLLIS)
334
Elizabeth (RUSSELL)
143, 305
Elizabeth Walters
304

HARRIS, Frances
(JOHNSON) 304
George 304, 707
Isaiah 89
James 304
James Lloyd 305,
555
Jane (BUTTERWORTH)
89
John 514, 555
John III 414
Katherine 305
Lloyd 111, 155,
240, 305, 387,
507, 510, 555
Margaret 305, 426
Martha
(BUTTERWORTH) 89
Mary 304, 305
Mary (GINN) 305
Mary Ann (JOHNSON)
304
Rhoda 118
Robert, Capt. 3
Sarah 39, 305, 620
Susannah 305
Thomas 38, 305,
315, 370, 574, 637
William 89, 143,
149, 305, 334
Harris' Delight
305, 514
Harris' Trust 48,
54, 98, 216, 305,
330
HARRISON, (?) 184,
305, 358
Elizabeth 543
James 145
Johanna (MORRIS)
306
John 306, 439
Margaret
(MACKINTOSH) 306
Mary 145, 184, 305,
306, 372
Mary (DOWSE) 184,
358
Richard 392
Samuel 544
Sarah 392
Sarah (HALL) 544
Thomas 298, 306,
373, 530, 571, 660
William 392
Harrison's Dock 306
Harrison's Meadows
306
HARROD, Mary 605
HARRYMAN, (?) 494,
531
Alice 306
Allinor 306
Ann 307, 662
Ann (STANSBURY) 306

HARRYMAN, Ann
(WILKINSON) 116,
307, 691
Anne (STANSBURY)
602
Avarilla 307, 662
Charles 306, 307,
531, 568, 662, 708
Comfort 573
Comfort Platt
(TAYLOR) 306, 627
Drusilla 662
Eleanor 33, 212,
306, 307
Elinor 714
Elizabeth 306, 307,
328, 476, 691
Elizabeth (RAVEN)
531
Elizabeth (SIMKINS)
307
Elizabeth
(SIMPKINS) 581
George 49, 50, 116,
306, 307, 351,
476, 531, 535,
573, 679, 691
Hester 662
Jane (SMITH) 306
Jemima 306
John 93, 212, 306,
307, 370, 451,
467, 494, 535,
627, 714
Keziah 662
Mary 93, 306
Nancy 662
Patience 307, 357
Priscilla 307
Prudence 306, 307,
662, 663
Rachel 307
Rachel (BOND) 49,
50
Rachel (RAVEN) 531
Robert 306, 307,
328, 581
Ruth 306
Samuel 174, 188,
212, 306, 379,
422, 476, 496,
509, 573, 627
Sarah 306, 307
Sarah Chloe (RAVEN)
531
Sophia 116, 307
Tamar 307
Temperance 307
Thomas 171, 306,
476, 602
William 307
Harryman's Delight
307
Harryman's Hope 307
Harryman's Outlet
307

HUGHES, Sarah 48,
151, 212, 231,
346, 347, 404
Sophia (RUTLEDGE)
562
Susannah 346
Thomas 179, 267,
346, 347, 377,
425, 530
William 26, 255,
347
Hughes' Chance 151,
373
Hughes' Choice 189
Hughes' Enlargement
189, 190
Hughes' Fortune 347
Hughes' Hogyard 347
Hughes' Island 316
HUGHS, Jane 570
Rebecca (LUX) 416
Hughs' Enlargement
524
Hughs' Island 429
HUIM, Mary 511
HULL, David 347
Joseph 347
HUMBLES, Thomas 347
HUMPHREY, Elizabeth
(JONES) 375
Richard 375
Humphrey's Creek
309
HUMPHREYS, Ann 428
Eliza 348
Elizabeth 63
Frances 348
John 348
Margaret Roberts
186
Mary 25, 348, 388,
506
Richard 348
Thomas 25, 348
HUNN, Francis 348,
359
Margaret (JAMES)
348, 359
Mary 348
HUNT, (?) 272
Christina
Eberhardine 348
Elizabeth 348
Epictetus 348
James 348
Job 339
John 348, 377, 693,
704
Margaret (HOPKINS)
339
Mary (MURRIN) 348
Onesiphorus 348
Phineas 50
Priscilla 348
Sarah 166, 348
Seneca 348

HUNT, Stephen 569
Susan (BOND) 50
Susanna (GOTT) 272
Temperance 16, 348
William 348
HUNTER, Ann (CHANCE)
103
Bradbury 348
Esther 348
James 348
John 348
Jonathan 103
Joseph 348
Margarett 348
Mary 348
Mary (MC DANIEL)
669, 670
Owen 348
William 34, 176,
348, 561, 595,
669, 670
Hunter's Forest 464
Hunter's Hopyard
653, 719
Hunter's Park 454
Hunting Creek 693
Hunting Neck 101,
334, 502, 560
Hunting North 633
Hunting Quarter
128, 148, 304
Hunting Worth 716
Huntington 601
Huntingworth 73,
504
HURD, Andrew 348
Elizabeth 348
Jacob 348
John 15, 179, 349,
477, 478
Joshua 349
Ruth (NORWOOD) 349,
477
Sarah 349
Hurd's Camp 343
HURLEY, Katherine
(GAYER) 349
Timothy 349
HURST, Ann(e) (GORE)
265, 349
Bennett 349
Jno. 47
John 266, 349, 422,
636
Jonathan 265, 349
Timothy 349
Hurst's Marsh 349
HURT, John 719
Margaret (WALLIS)
719
HUSBAND, Herman 349,
544
Thomas 144
HUSBANDS, William
154
HUSE, William 384

HUSH, Conrad 525
Eleanor (PUNTANY)
525
HUSON, Mary 349
HUST, Anne 349
John 349
Jonathan 349
Ruth 349
Hutchin's Addition
234
HUTCHINS - See
HUTCHIN(G)S
Hutchings' Neglect
64
HUTCHIN(G)S, Ann
350, 383, 600
Anne 349, 350
Catherine 138, 350
Elizabeth 349, 350
Elizabeth (BURRAGE)
391
Elizabeth
(ROBINSON) 551
Elizabeth (WRIGHT)
349
Francis 391, 392
Hannah (SEEMONS)
350
Jacob 350
James 350
Jemima (JOHNSON)
366
John 349
Joshua 350
Keziah 350
Nicholas 130, 138,
349, 350
Richard 350
Sarah 366
Susanna 349, 350
Susanna
(RICHARDSON) 539
Thomas 8, 177, 226,
319, 349, 350,
366, 396, 459,
477, 524, 539
William 338, 350
Hutchins' Addition
349, 366, 600
Hutchins' Beginnings
349
Hutchins' Lot 64,
350
Hutchins' Neglect
349, 350, 546
HUTCHINSON, Margaret
350
Martha 350
Richard 350
Will 210
HUTSON, Joshua 338
Susanna (HOOKER)
338
HUTTON, Jane 350
HUTTS, John 350

JONES, David 101,
123, 266, 284,
373, 375, 395,
480, 643, 644
Deborah 374
Diana 374
Diana (DAY) 443
Dorothy 375
Edward 205, 309,
370
Eleanor 371, 375,
705
Elisha 371
Eliza 376
Elizabeth 4, 47,
340, 370, 371,
372, 373, 375,
376, 378, 379,
394, 667
Elizabeth (BRICE)
373
Elizabeth (CHALK)
102
Elizabeth (JAMES)
370
Elizabeth (JONES)
372
Elizabeth (LINLEY)
375
Elizabeth (PICKETT)
370, 505
Elizabeth
(WILLIAMS) 379
Ellinor 372
Esther 371
Evan 178
Evana 375
Eveula 373
Ezekiel 133
Frances 286, 322,
373
Frances (COBB) 117,
373
Francis 375
Gay 377
George 117, 375
Gilbert 379
Hannah 343, 346,
371, 372, 405, 530
Hannah (RATTENBURY)
372, 530
Hannah (WOOLEY) 371
Hannah/Johannah 372
Henrietta 346, 375
Henrietta Maria
372, 555
Henry 40, 288, 344,
348, 375, 509,
593, 618, 705, 714
Hinton 618
Hugh 60, 206, 317,
364, 376, 432, 434
Humphrey 73, 309,
376
Immanuel 376, 390
Isaac 379

JONES, Jacob 302,
373, 374, 376,
379, 399, 400, 661
James 376
Jane (WHIPPS) 683
Jemima (EAGER) 195
Jemima (MURRAY)
372, 463
Johanna 376
John 102, 238, 248,
370, 371, 372,
375, 376, 377,
413, 437, 562,
568, 601, 668,
702, 705
Jonathan 27, 371,
377, 406, 501,
593, 664, 692
Joseph 377, 556
Joshua 308, 371
Judith 693
Katherine 372
Lewis 371, 664
Lydia 4
Magdalen 379
Margaret 371, 372,
374, 377, 427,
530, 568, 702
Margaret (CHADWELL)
102, 376
Martha 371
Martha (FARMER) 371
Martha (LOVELL) 413
Mary 9, 240, 247,
248, 371, 372,
373, 376, 394,
555, 599, 662,
664, 689
Mary (BAKER) 19
Mary (DOOLEY) 371
Mary (ELLIS) 202,
373
Mary (HARRISON) 372
Mary (HARVEY) 308
Mary (HILL) 558
Mary (HINTON) 328,
370
Mary (PAYWELL) 177,
373, 495
Mary (ROWLES) 372,
558
Mary (SIMMONS) 378
Mary (WARREN) 371
Morgan 703
Moses 377
Nathan 378
Nicholas 372, 530
Patience 377, 556
Peckett 370
Peter 260, 378
Philip 158, 195,
372, 378, 401,
463, 530, 555,
557, 558
Philip, Capt. 530

JONES, Philip, Jr.
148, 454, 615
Philip, Maj. 372
Priscilla 371
Priscilla (WOODEN)
703
Rachel 102, 322,
372, 373, 378
Rachel (COTTRELL)
374, 399
Randall 378
Rathvael 372
Rathvale 373
Rattenbury 372, 530
Rebecca 373
Richard 24, 329,
372, 378, 397, 701
Richard, Jr. 77
Robert 42, 243,
356, 378, 401,
Samuel 377
Sarah 370, 371,
372, 376, 377,
378, 399, 400,
437, 511
Sarah (LAKE) 390
Sarah (LEEK) 376
Silvestine 328
Solomon 372, 377,
394
Sophia 371
Sophia (SIMMONS)
212
Stephen 376, 379
Sylvanus 370
Sylvester 370
Theophiilus 589
Theophilus 373,
406, 517, 537
Thomas 177, 322,
335, 371, 372,
373, 378, 406,
439, 536, 555,
563, 580, 599,
664, 689, 699, 702
Thomas, Maj. 30
Timothy 381
William 240, 372,
373, 374, 376,
378, 379, 394,
505, 686
Wills 379
Winifred 379
Jones' Addition
376, 378, 398, 476
Jones' Adventure
359, 558
Jones' Chance 195,
238, 275, 302,
376, 377, 595
Jones' Contrivance
372
Jones' Farm 377,
538
Jones' Gift 431,
453, 512

LONG, Ann 289, 410
Anne (STANSBURY)
604
Benjamin 158, 410,
626
Blanch (WHITAKER)
410, 684
Eleanor 410, 436,
494
Eleanor (OWINGS)
410, 652
Galvilla 386, 409
George 409
Jane 230, 250, 386,
410, 444, 496,
497, 609, 666
Jane (DIXON) 409
Jane (TEAL) 630
Jean 652
Jeane 410
John 47, 187, 409,
410, 494, 604,
652, 662, 684
Joshua 410
Josias 410
Margaret Grace
(WORBELTON) 410
Martha 473
Mary 410
Moses 410
Robert 409
Ruth 410
Susanna 47, 148,
410
Susanna (MEAD) 409,
410, 441
Susannah 652
Tabitha 409
Thomas 56, 114,
120, 148, 187,
205, 230, 248,
250, 314, 319,
361, 379, 409,
410, 424, 426,
441, 497, 570,
619, 637, 649,
656, 666, 673
Thomas, Capt. 632
Thomas, Maj. 175,
257, 282, 444,
512, 549
William 410
Long Acre 676
Long Acres 486
Long Aire 589
Long Crandon 228
Long Discovery 240,
632
Long Island 603
Long Island Point
71, 214, 243, 289,
317, 460, 614, 615
Long Looked For
325, 485, 521
Long Men 296
Long Mountain 547

Long Point 506,
539, 646
Long Port 409
Long Tract 521
Long Valley 269,
578, 683, 693, 698
Long's Addition 605
LONGLAND, Richard
315, 411
Robert 673
Longland's Purchase
315, 352, 411
LONGMAN, John 411
Mary 84, 411
Longworth 76
LONSDALE, Ellen 475
William 475
LOOTEN, Elizabeth
712
Jacob 712
LORAH, Henry 411
Lord Baltimore's
Gift 68, 557
LORESON, Eleanor 631
LORKET - See LOCKETT
LORKETT, John 406
LORKINGS, Elizab 411
Elizabeth (ENLOES)
204
John 204, 411
LORKINS, John 632
LORKINS - See LOKINS
LORKITT - See
LOCKETT
LORRESON, Eleanor
411
Lot, The 602
LOTON - See LOTTEN
LOTTEN, Elizabeth
411
Jacob 411
LOUCHLY, Elizabeth
411
Selina 411
LOUGH - See LOWE
LOUGH - See SOUCH
Lough's Lot 413
LOVE, (?) 473
Alice 67
Alice (BRASHAR)
411, 412
Ann 412
Anne 411
Arabella
(WAL(L)STON) 412,
662
Constant 411, 579
Elizabeth 120, 412
Jean Land 412
John 43, 67, 252,
411, 412, 539,
545, 552, 570,
579, 691
John, Capt. 83
Julian 434
Juliana 412

LOVE, Mary 325, 411,
412
Mary (NORRIS) 473
Miles 129, 412
Rachel 412
Robert 21, 43, 48,
319, 366, 411,
412, 568, 640,
660, 684, 691
Ruth 43, 412
Sarah 83, 412, 684
Sarah (BOND) 43,
48, 412
Sarah (THURSTON)
412, 640
Tamar 43, 411, 412,
586, 691
Temperance 505
Thamar 414
William 390, 411,
412, 662
Love's Addition 43
LOVEALL, Henry 413,
566
Martha 413
Zebulon 413
LOVELACE, Anne 266,
375, 480, 643
Anne (BARNE) 266
Francis 250
William, Sir 266
Loveless' Addition
267
LOVELL, John 413
Martha 413
Lovely Hill 412
LOVEPITSTOW, Ann 413
Mary 413
Robert 413
LOVETT, Richard 413
LOVINGTON, Martha
(WARREN) 413
Richard 413
LOW(E), Abraham 414
Alexander 414
Alice 382
Ann 281, 413, 414
Ann (DAVIS) 160,
414
Ann Haynes 281
Archibald 154
Charles 414
Daniel Johnson 413
Eliz. 279
Elizabeth 169, 359,
413, 414, 606
Elizabeth (JOHNSON)
367
Flora (DORSEY) 414
Hannah 414
Henry 39
Hugh 31, 230, 414
Isaac 414
Isabella 414
James 413, 414,
517, 689

ROBINSON, William 8,
47, 51, 91, 98,
105, 126, 127,
300, 341, 353,
369, 400, 405,
434, 448, 517,
534, 551, 552,
553, 554, 599, 618
Wm. 8
ROBINSON - See also
ROBERSON,
ROBERTSON
Robinson's Addition
552
Robinson's Beginning
553
Robinson's Chance
52
Robinson's Outlet
367
Robinson's Park 419
Robinson's Venture
551
Robinsons 551
Roborarum 463
ROBOSSON, Comfort
147
ROBSON, Mary 380
ROBUCK, Benjamin 554
Thomas 554
Rochford 371
ROCK, George 554
Rock Quarter 544
Rockford 222, 223
ROCKHOLD, Ann 554,
686
Assell 544
Charles 71, 232,
511, 518, 554, 706
Chas. 406
Edward 554
Eleanor (POCOCK)
511
Eliz. 554
Elizabeth (ELEANOR)
554
Elizabeth (WRIGHT)
554
Jacob 554
John 231, 313, 539,
554
Lance Todd 554
Mary 231, 554, 645
Mary (NELSON) 554
Reason 554
Robert 554
Sabra 231
Sarah 554
Sebrah 554
Susan 554
Thomas 554
Wright 554
Rockhold's Purchase
554
Rockhold's Range 55

Rockhold's Search
554
Rockwell's Range
406
Rocky Point 410
RODES - See RHODES
RODGERS, Alexander
112
Elizabeth 24
Martha (CHRISTIE)
112
Mary 509
RODGET, Barton 429
ROE, Anne 555
George 555
James 555
Mary 555, 562
Mary (BOYLE) 555
Mary (JONES) 555
Sarah 555
Thomas 555
William 379, 555
ROEBUCK - See ROBUCK
Roger's Road 534,
559
ROGERS, Ann 555
Benjamin 555
Catherine 507, 555
Charles 555
Constant 615
Dorothy 305, 555
Eleanor 79, 256,
555
Eleanor (BUCHANAN)
79
Elizabeth 555, 556
Ellinor 507, 555
Grace 555
Henrietta Maria
(JONES) 555
Ishmael 555
James 556
James Lloyd 555
Jane 556
John 171, 249, 400,
556, 607
Joseph 556
Katherine 555
Margaret 623
Mary 132, 256, 555,
556
Nicholas 26, 60,
71, 79, 202, 256,
266, 305, 319,
328, 383, 396,
422, 445, 459,
491, 555, 655, 710
Nicholas Tempest
555
Philip 555
Rebecca (STEVENS)
607
Robert 556
Ruth (WILLIAMS) 556

ROGERS, Sarah 141,
268, 445, 507,
555, 556, 696
Sarah (GILL) 256,
555
Thomas 556
William 124, 141,
148, 256, 257,
276, 295, 328,
349, 402, 507,
512, 551, 555,
606, 615, 657, 698
William, Capt. 393
William, Jr. 283
Rogers Road 695
ROGIER, Nicholas 555
Rogue's Ridge 673
ROLES, William 429
ROLES - See ROWLES
ROLLINGS, John 587
ROLLINS, John 161
ROLLO, Ann 600
Archibald 31, 65,
70, 193, 505, 510,
511, 549, 556,
599, 620, 711
Marianna 510
Mary Ann 556
Rachel 711
Rebecca 70, 556,
620
Temperance 31, 556
Rollo's Adventure
556
ROLLS, John 558
Ruth 691
Rolls' Adventure
324
ROLSTON - See
RALSTON
ROOTER, Hester 556
Thomas 556
ROPER, (?) 298
Mary 298, 556
Philip 556, 630,
716
Sarah 556
Thomas 556
Roper's Increase
556, 628
Roper's Rest 556,
630, 716
RORER, Catherine 684
John 684
ROSBY, John 557
ROSE, (?) 521
Benjamin 557
Constant (PRICE)
521
Edward 454
Mary (CHILCOTT) 108
Paulus 108
William 557
Rosemary Ridge 307
Roses Green 88
Rosindale 322

918

WHITLATCH, Charles
689
Elizabeth 689
John 689
Mary 689
Rachel 689
Sarah 689
William 689
WHITTICAR, John 114,
412
Whitticar's Ridge
412, 495
WHITTON, Richard 427
WHOLESTOCKS, Hannah
689
WIATH, Elizabeth 689
WICHELL, Sarah 383,
471
WICKINS, Jemima
(HOLLOWAY) 689
Robert 689
WICKS, Eliza
(ENLOES) 689
John 689
Mary 689
Thomas 381, 689
WIDDER, Jane (NORTH)
474, 475
Margaret 475
Thomas 474, 475
Widow's Care 561
WIGG, Richard 522
WIGGIN, Ann 496
WIGGLEFIELD, Jane
341
WIGHT, Mary 37
WIGLEY, Edward 689
Jane (FISHER) 689
Wignall's Rest 181
WILBORN - See
WILBO(U)RN(E)
WILBO(U)RN(E), Ann
563
Ann (CRABTREE) 143,
690
Anne 690
Edward 563, 690,
702
Elizabeth 690, 702
James 690
Jane 690
Margaret 690
Martha 690
Thomas 690
William 143, 690,
701
WILBOURNE - See
WILBO(U)RN(E)
WILBURN - See
WILBO(U)RN(E)
Wilburn's Venture
701
WILBURNE - See
WILBO(U)RN(E)
WILD, Abraham 252
Jonathan 690

WILD, Mary 321
Sarah 690
Sarah (PREBLE) 690
WILD - See WILDEY
WILDE, John 610
WILDEY, Edward 690
WILDY, Edward 631
WILES, Jonathan 690
Mary 690
Sarah (PREBLE) 690
Stephen 690
WILEY, Ann (NELSON)
466
John 96, 466
Luke 7
Margaret 158, 690
Martha M. 7
Mary 690
Marya 548
Sarah (SUTTON) 617
Vincent 617
WILEY - See WYLEY
WILFORD, Elinor 690
WILHIDE, Francis 225
WILKERSON, John 353
WILKINS, Richard 690
Robert 690
WILKINSON, (?) 267
Ann 307, 688, 691
Barbara (GORSUCH)
267, 506
Eliza 691
Elizabeth 103, 690,
691
Elizabethe (CLARKE)
691
Elizabeth (CLARK)
114
Elizabeth
(HARRYMAN) 691
Hannah 154, 692
Isabella 691
Jane 134, 691
Japhet 691
Jethro Lynch 559,
691
John 409, 506, 691
Mary (ASHER) 13,
691
Mary (WOOD) 691
Moore 691
Philip 691
Philisanna 691
Rachel (LENOX) 691
Rachel (RICHARDSON)
691
Rebecca 691
Robert 134, 321,
480, 645, 691
Ruth 691
Samuel 13, 691
Sarah 645, 691
Sophia 586, 691
Stephen 558, 692
Stephen, Rev. 691

WILKINSON, Tamar
134, 197, 307, 384
Tamar (LOVE) 411,
586, 691
Thamar 384
Thomas 154, 691,
692
William 13, 61, 90,
114, 134, 152,
172, 189, 195,
197, 275, 285,
316, 334, 400,
411, 433, 497,
509, 559, 564,
586, 590, 615,
618, 627, 637,
644, 663, 690, 691
Wilkinson's Chance
691
Wilkinson's Folly
691
Wilkinson's Spring
134, 690, 691
WILLABEE, Sarah 332
WILLAN, Henry 490
Willen 417
William 337
WILLIAM, Alice 694
Edward 716
John 497
William & Sarah's
Inheritance 300
William and
Elizabeth's Fancy
44
William and Mary
340
William Forest 393
William Resurveyed
393
William The
Conqueror 161,
163, 269, 320,
400, 527, 558
William's Beginnings
643
William's Chance
341
William's Defense
34
William's Delight
479
William's Fancy 269
William's Folly 269
William's Fortune
347
William's Hope 282
William's Lot 34,
43, 483
William's Lot
Enlarged 34
William's Ridge 341
WILLIAMS, (?) 144
Ann 630, 692
Ann (DU) 692
Anne (NEARN) 694